APPROACHES TO ETHICS

New York St. Louis San Francisco London Sydney

Toronto Mexico Panama

SECOND EDITION

APPROACHES TO ETHICS

Representative Selections from Classical Times to the Present

EDITED BY

W. T. Jones

Frederick Sontag

Morton O. Beckner

DEPARTMENT OF PHILOSOPHY
POMONA COLLEGE

Robert J. Fogelin

DEPARTMENT OF PHILOSOPHY
YALE UNIVERSITY

McGraw-Hill Book Company

APPROACHES TO ETHICS

Library of Congress Catalog Card Number 69-18729
ISBN 07-033004-2

7890 MAMM 7654

PREFACE

The chief innovation in this revised edition is the inclusion of a wholly new section, Part 6, Recent Developments. It provides materials for still another "approach" to the teaching of ethics—for a course that is focused on contemporary issues among ethical theorists. In subsequent revisions we hope to keep this part up-to-date.

We have also included selections from a number of earlier writers who do not appear at all in the first edition—Ockham, Luther, and Marx—and rounded out the selections from others. Among the more important of these additions are the following: To the Aristotle selections we have added a passage from Book VI of the *Nicomachaean Ethics,* in order to present his account of the intellectual virtues. We have supplemented the passages already included from *The City of God* with others that illustrate some characteristic Augustinian theses, such as his contention that peace is the goal of human life. In the chapter on Kant we have retained substantial parts of the *Lectures on Ethics,* which make a relatively easy introduction to Kant's ethical theories, but we have added passages from the *Critique of Practical Reason* which represent the formulations of the mature Kant and are more appropriate for advanced students. Since we were not content with our selections from Hegel's *Philosophy of History,* we have replaced these with passages from his *Early Theological Writings,* in which some characteristically Hegelian concepts are discussed in a pretechnical vocabulary. To the Kierkegaard selections we have added a note from his *Journals* and the statement on the teleological suspension of the ethical. And we have augmented the Sartre selections with passages from *Existentialism Is a Humanism.*

These extensive additions have been made possible by a considerable increase in the size of the book, but they have also necessitated a number of deletions. Readers of the first edition will at once notice that several authors have disappeared altogether. In making decisions about what to include and exclude, we were guided by a desire to achieve balance and completeness. We have also saved space by a number of smaller deletions in some of the existing selections; these we believe we have managed in such a way that they will be noticeable only to a very careful reader.

Despite these changes, the main features of the book—above all, the variety of approaches to the study of ethics which it permits—remain unaltered. Most anthologies prove a Procrustean bed for prospective users: Since each editor has chosen selections in accordance with his own notion of what constitutes a good course, the teacher who orders the book for use in his class discovers that, instead of being able to shape his course in terms of his own conception, he has to make it fit into someone else's predilections. We believe that we have escaped this rigidity, and we offer a number of sample Syllabi to illustrate this. The Syllabi suggest the variety of ways in which these readings may be exploited in different courses by showing how the selections may be arranged and rearranged so as to bring out whatever themes the individual teacher wishes to emphasize and the special issues which he holds to be of first importance. The teacher may use one or another of these prepared Syllabi, or develop his own within the variety of selections we have provided. It is for this reason that the selections are printed in the order determined by the birth of their authors—except in Part 6, where, since the authors are all contemporaries, the articles are reprinted in the order of their publication. This is the most neutral arrangement possible, and permits each teacher to organize the readings in his own way.

We have not only included selections from all major historical figures; for some thinkers whose views changed significantly through time, we have provided a cross section of this developmental process. We have also included selections of different degrees of difficulty in the hope that all readers will find matter that is both interesting and stimulating. We have provided more readings than any but the most able and ambitious will undertake, in the hope that the additional material will be an invitation to the student to go beyond assigned readings when he encounters problems that particularly interest him.

In this regard we call attention especially to the Index. All major ethical concepts and problems appear as main entries with citation of the various selections in which they are discussed. All the leading topics in each selection have also been indexed (as subentries under the author of the selection) so as to give the reader a quick summary of the subjects covered. Finally, all discussions of one philosopher's theories by other philosophers are also cited. By using the Index and the Syllabi together, students will find many topics for term papers—and also clues to the materials necessary for writing them.

In addition to the general Introduction, there are historical introductions, which can be read with profit by the student even if his instructor does not employ an historical approach, since they provide a summary account of the philosophical context of the various selections.

We have used, in all cases, the best available translations. In seventeenth- and eighteenth-century English texts we have sometimes modernized spelling and punctuation and corrected obvious typographical errors.

We have occasionally so condensed a long argument that noting all deletions in the text would be a distraction to the reader. In these cases the customary ellipses are omitted; the reader is warned in a note at the beginning of each such selection. Otherwise, all deletions except trivial ones are clearly noted.

We wish to thank a number of teachers who have commented—most of them anonymously—on the first edition. We are particularly grateful to Professor Jerome B. Schneewind for his thoughtful and detailed advice, which we have usually followed. To Brother Mannes Beissel, O.P., we are obliged for calling our attention to an editorial slip, as a result of which we attributed to St. Thomas a view which he expressly rejected.

In addition to repeating our thanks to Florence Fogelin and Diane Kelly, we wish to thank Judith Strombotne for editorial assistance with this edition.

W. T. Jones

Frederick Sontag

Morton O. Beckner

Robert J. Fogelin

SYLLABI

These five Syllabi are offered as guides for the use of this volume. They are neither complete nor definitive; they merely make suggestions for the construction of courses from five possible perspectives. It is hoped that these Syllabi, together with the Index and the Table of Contents (which supply a ready reference for the construction of additional syllabi), will exhibit the range of possible uses of this volume.

Syllabus I. The History of Ethical Theory

The Contents constitutes a detailed syllabus for the history of ethics from classical times to the present.

Syllabus II. Main Types of Ethical Theory

Syllabus III. Problems of Ethics

III. WHAT IS THE NATURE OF ETHICS WHEN IT IS TREATED AS AN EMPIRICAL SCIENCE?

Epicurus, *Letter to Herodotus*, 82
Letter to Menoeceus, 85
Principal Doctrines, 87
Machiavelli, *The Prince*, 198
The Discourses, 200
Freud, *Civilization and Its Discontents*, 439
Dewey, *Reconstruction in Philosophy*, 451
The Quest for Certainty, 456
Theory of Valuation, 462
Reconstruction in Philosophy, 451
Perry, *General Theory of Value*, 492

IV. WHAT IS THE SOURCE OF MORAL OBLIGATION?

Plato, *The Republic*, 26
Glaucon on Justice, 26
Epictetus, *The Encheiridion*, 91
Hobbes, *Leviathan*, 210
Of the First and Second Natural Laws, and of Contracts, 221
Kant, *Lectures on Ethics*, 280
Critique of Practical Reason, 296
Bentham, *An Introduction to the Principles of Morals and Legislation*, 307
Of the Four Sanctions or Sources of Pain and Pleasure, 314
Hegel, *Early Theological Writings*, 327
Mill, *Utilitarianism*, 347
Of the Ultimate Sanction of the Principle of Utility, 354
Bradley, *Ethical Studies*, 418
My Station and Its Duties, 425
Prichard, *Does Moral Philosophy Rest on a Mistake?*, 469
Rawls, *Two Concepts of Rules*, 609
Singer, *Generalization in Ethics*, 634
Searle, *How to Derive "Ought" from "Is"*, 643

V. WHAT IS THE SIGNIFICANCE OF CONSIENCE AND THE SENSE OF GUILT FOR MORALITY?

St. Anselm, *Cur Deus Homo*, 142
Butler, *Dissertation on the Nature of Virtue*, 246
Nietzsche, *Sounding Out Idols*, 402
The Genealogy of Morals, 404
Freud, *Civilization and Its Discontents*, 439
Aggression, Guilt, and Conscience, 444
The Cultural Super-ego, 448

Syllabus IV. Polarities in Ethical Theory

Syllabus V. Ways of Life

CONTENTS

Part 3 The Early Modern Period

Part 6 Recent Developments

INTRODUCTION

I. An Ethical Problem

What is ethics? It is easily defined as the attempt to state and evaluate principles by which ethical problems may be solved. But this description is incomplete without a characterization of the main features of an ethical problem; it will therefore be useful to examine in some detail a problem that everyone will agree is ethical in nature. The great variety of approaches to ethics exhibited in the writings of ethical theorists reflects the extreme complexity of the typical ethical problem; accordingly, a complete description of ethics requires a formulation of the kinds of circumstances that give rise to ethical problems and, as a consequence, initiate ethical inquiry. Let us take as our example a problem presented in James Gould Cozzens's novel *By Love Possessed*.

What ought a lawyer do when he discovers that one of his partners has embezzled from a fund entrusted to the firm's administration? If Arthur Winner reports Noah Tuttle's theft, his own law practice will be wrecked and, since he is legally responsible for the embezzlement, he will be ruined financially. Nevertheless Winner believes this is what he ought to do: every citizen, but especially a lawyer, who is an officer of the court, is obligated to report any crime that comes to his attention.

The third partner of the firm, Julius Penrose, has a very different view: he argues that he and Winner should protect Tuttle and give him a chance to repay the embezzled funds. Penrose has long known of the embezzlements, but is not legally responsible for them, since he entered the firm only after they were committed.*

"So how long have I known? Well, let's say, twelve years, give or take a month or two."

"And you said nothing? Julius, I think that's indefensible."

"Do you? To be able to know and still say nothing often seems to me the most creditable of human accomplishments. . . . What purpose but mischief, and what result but more mischief, could my saying something have? From my standpoint, the business was strictly Noah's; and he was, I soon come to see, handling it ably. I confess that before adopting this disinterested view, I made a careful check of my own legal position. You'll recognize it. Incoming partner. How, then, could saying something be my business?"

"When you know this and say nothing, you're an accessory after the fact. Julius, how could you? . . . What I can't believe is that you'd knowingly stand by—"

"But I fear you're going to have to," Julius Penrose said. . . . "My eye was on the certain results, the fruits. True, that had been done which ought not to be done. I saw that conversion, embezzlement, must have been practiced for some time—and, I confess, the 'some time' seemed to me not unimportant. . . . I've seldom applied myself with such intensity of attention to the statutes and to the reported cases. However, as I say, I was soon relieved. There weren't two opinions. The time of the original conversion, which subsequent conversions had been to cover, was what counted. If I had not been a partner when that took place, no action to recover from me personally could lie. . . . Yes; I scare easy; but recovering from my scare, I found myself rational, able to look at this from all sides. I was free to dismiss self-interest, to do right and fear no man. Whether I'm morally obligated to be my brother's keeper always seemed to me moot. However, my brother's ruiner and destroyer, and for no earthly reason, and for no personal necessity or profit—*that* I surely have no moral obligation to be. . . . Seeing myself, in your word, safe, I, no longer scared, naturally did not so much as consider such a dastardly act. . . ."

* From *By Love Possessed*, © 1957, by James Gould Cozzens. Reprinted by permission of Harcourt, Brace & World, Inc., New York, and Longmans, Green & Co., Ltd., London.

Arthur Winner said: "Julius, what you seem to be suggesting just isn't possible. There's an honest course; and a course that isn't honest. If you take the course that isn't honest, you're in trouble immediately—"

"Affirmed as stated," Julius Penrose said. "Honesty's always the easiest policy. Could that be why men so often call it the best? Weaving tangled webs is really work, very demanding."

"No, Julius. It's no good. I cannot be party to doing what's dishonest."

"But you *could* be party to causing to be laid before our Mr. Brophy such evidence of embezzlement as would require him to prosecute Noah? Hm! Specific acts must number hundreds. I see no practicable defense. . . . And you could also be not only party to, but principal in, taking immediate steps to assign all your property toward restituting and restoring the corpus of the Orcutt bequests? I've a fair idea of your current commitments. I imagine you're doing something for your mother. I know you're helping Lawrence. . . . The expense of maintaining a place at Roylan is well known to me. You have a daughter to educate! you have a wife who—again, incidentally —has, I suspect, the indefatigable hope of providing you with more children. You'd be sorry, I'm sure, to see either without proper provision. Yet, by the time you'd made your partner's stealings good, I don't think there'd be a great deal left.". . .

"The cost needn't worry you," Arthur Winner said. "I agree with your view that you can't be held liable."

"The law is clear. There is no other view," Julius Penrose said. "But I, also, am human, am not without human weaknesses of vanity and self-regard. I have an—er—honor—" he grimaced—"of my own to pet. I wouldn't, I warn you, feel able to dissociate myself, legally liable or not. If you persist in this quixotism, if you're resolved to ruin yourself, I'll have to join you. Yes; I think I can arrange that. . . ."

"Julius, that's ridiculous—"

"I think so, too. . . . I am a cripple; I am getting old. Were I neither, it might be different, of course. The easier way, the easiest policy, could then be a calculated risk—possibly worth taking. Given more life expectancy, I might chance it. Honesty, integrity, honor so well advertised, could pay off. Like Job's my patience might prove worthwhile. I might end up with more flocks, more herds—and even, were I at that age or stage, more sons and daughters—than I had to start with. But such expectancy isn't mine. I'm on the downgrade. Therefore, I ask you not to do this thing to me, Arthur."

"Julius, after what you said earlier, you can't seriously—"

"Some want of principle, yes," Julius Penrose said. "But I am not joking."

Julius Penrose's look was compassionate. He said: "Yes, yes; think of an octogenarian cast in prison; think of your unfeeling disservice to those near and dear—hard to kick against the pricks, isn't it? So stop! Or, as a wise old man once said to me: Boy, never try to piss up the wind. Principle must sometimes be shelved. Let us face the fact. In this life we cannot do everything we might like to do, nor have for ourselves everything we might like to have. We must recognize what the law calls factual situations. The paradox is that once fact's assented to, accepted, and we stop directing our effort where effort is wasted, we usually *can* do quite a number of things, to a faint heart, impossible.". . .

Arthur Winner said: "What, exactly, do you propose?"

"Ah, old friend," Julius Penrose said, "That's better! I propose that we let matters proceed as far as possible as they've been proceeding. I propose we concert our efforts and our wits on managing this—"

"Julius, the risks are terrible—"

"Agreed, agreed," Julius Penrose said. "But we are not children, nor unable, nor without resource. I think I am a man of judgment. I know you are. Let us put this judgment to use—"

"I don't think you realize just how great some of the risks are."

"If you mean there are some I don't happen to know about, you may be right. But I'm confident I'll be sufficiently sharp to see them as they appear; and I'm not unconfident that, as I see them, I'll see what to do about them. . . . What else alarms you?"

"Julius, it's everything—" Where, indeed, to begin? Numberless, the general dangers, the uncertainties, the unchartable chances, of this—this wrongdoing, this frantic dice-throwing on which he must wildly stake his—yes, honor; his career; his reputation. . . . "To let things just go on, as if we didn't know—there couldn't be a moment's peace of mind. No, Julius; if we do this thing at all, Noah's going to have to be told that we know, that we intend to do what we can to get the money paid back, and that we'll have to take charge of his accounts."

Julius Penrose said: "That, in the end, may be necessary; but I don't think we ought so to determine out of hand. Shun immediate evils is the wise, or at least the smart, man's maxim. Never do today what doesn't have to be done until tomorrow. It is, I imagine, important to Noah to think nobody knows. Told, he'd not impossibly go all to pieces. That would be no service to us; and clearly no kindness to him. . . ."

He looked seriously at Arthur Winner. "No," he said, "I think we should try for a while telling Noah nothing. . . ."

"Meanwhile, what we don't and can't escape is a whole life of lies," Arthur Winner said.

II. Ethical Deliberations

In these passages Cozzens reviews a serious ethical dilemma. Let us now use his history of Winner's deliberations in order to formulate the main features of an ethical problem.

There are four main questions that Winner is compelled to face. First of all, what are the facts of the case? Some are easily ascertained, indeed are all too clear: a felony has been committed; Winner will be ruined and Tuttle will go to prison if it becomes known; Penrose is not legally implicated, but he chooses to stand or fall with Winner; and Penrose spells out in detail the probable financial consequences for himself, for Tuttle, and for Winner's wife and children. But Penrose also points out a number of other facts that may not be so obvious: no one has been damaged by the embezzlement; no one will be benefited by a denunciation of Tuttle, who is himself an aged and respected citizen. Now notice an important point: when we use such terms as "damaged," "benefited," and "respected," it is by no means true that we are dealing only with the facts of the case: these terms already involve an element of ethical evaluation. This illustrates the point that, even as we try to find out "the facts" of the case, which ought to be the least problematical factors in ethical deliberation, we are led gradually into the area of values. Nor is this all. Sometimes the answers to questions that are clearly factual are not available; this is especially true when we try to assess the probable consequences of a decision. We know that after we make our choice and act, events pass in large degree out of our control and into the melee of a larger social context. Cozzens epitomizes this larger arena in the impersonal workings of the law: it is likely that exposure will be followed by indictment, trial, and judgment.

Second, since there is conflict among the principles which Winner lives by, he must decide which are authoritative in this case. Imbued from childhood with respect for the law, he accepts the principle that the law should be obeyed, even to one's own disadvantage. Merely discussing the question of what to do makes Winner and Penrose guilty of conspiracy to conceal a crime. And there are the still more general principles that one should be honest, that one ought to do what he believes to be right. All these are violated if he protects Tuttle. On the other hand, Penrose formulates for him other principles which he would violate if he were to denounce Tuttle—principles which Winner also accepts: his obligation to his family, indeed, to his law partners; to exercise compassion; to "shun immediate evils." These principles, and others, overlap and include each other in a tangle of conflicting demands. They must be sorted out and duly weighed, one against the other.

This is at once a more difficult and a more important task than is commonly realized. It will be helpful if we stop for a moment to consider the nature of moral principles, or demands. To begin with, they are not merely personal convictions: they are among the rules—usages, customs, norms, mores, as they are often called—that *are* the institutions in which not only Winner but his entire society live, and on which their common life depends. How they are to be evaluated is the central problem of ethics. Cozzens does not spell out the whole system, or, more accurately, the many systems, of rules that are implicit in the positions stated by Winner and Penrose; he relies on the reader's intimate acquaintance with the everyday facts of social life. But these detailed systems are in the background of every actual ethical deliberation; in a problem such as Winner's, circumstances bring segments of them into question. These systems include the body of written codes and customary practices that constitute our legal system; the rules of such special groups as professional societies, unions, business associations, and lodges; the ethical systems of the churches; and a vast system of partially articulated beliefs about the proper way of dealing with our fellow men. Many of these rules bear heavy sanctions. The legal system defines the area in which the power of the police is applicable; various associations institute their own methods of reward and punishment—for example, the disbarring of lawyers who violate professional standards. The churches claim divine authority for many ethical rules, and some of them threaten infernal punishment for transgressors. Another and extremely important sanction is public opinion, which operates both directly, in the individual's deliberation, and indirectly, by upholding the application of police and other overt powers.

From the point of view of the individual, these rules are forces to be reckoned with. Although he may undertake to change them in minor ways, for the most part he must accept them and build his own life within the limits they prescribe. Though Penrose is, relatively, an independent man, even he normally accepts the rules of the legal profession and all that this entails. Even one who considers himself in rebellion against society as a whole drives a car, shops at a market, attends concerts, and reads books—activities that are possible only through the existence of a highly complex institutional organization, which in turn is possible only on the basis of the rules which he denounces.

Of course, most of the rules of a society are not explicitly formulated: we learn them by observing how people act; by listening to teachers and ministers, even politicians; and by submitting in some measure to the discipline of recognized authorities—not by reading written codes. Consequently, in order to see clearly the exact location of the ethical problem we are confronting, it is necessary for each of us to formulate the principles that we feel are at issue. To do so is not always easy; although most people are sensitive to the existence of an ethical problem, they may lack the articulateness of a Julius Penrose in bringing the issues into focus.

And even our written codes—constitutions and statutes, judicial precedents and procedures—are not so precisely formulated that their application is always clear and unambiguous. This brings us to the third kind of question that arises in ethical deliberation: do the principles as formulated apply to the particular case in hand? Legal terms such as "conspiracy," "liability," "accessory after the fact" are defined in the law, but their definitions have to remain vague because it is impossible to specify in advance the details of all conceivable circumstances in which they must be applied. Thus not only the implicit but also the explicit rules of society must be subjected to constant interpretation. In the law, this function is exercised by all courts and is the chief duty of the Supreme Court; but interpretation plays a role in everyone's ethical deliberations. Winner, for example, accepts the principle that he ought not to inflict unnecessary suffering; but does the principle apply in the case of Noah Tuttle? Is the suffering consequent upon just punishment for an illegal act "unnecessary"? "My brother's ruiner and destroyer, and for no earthly reason, and for no personal necessity or profit—*that* I surely have no moral obligation to be." We all, Winner as well as Penrose, believe this; but would Tuttle's ruin really be "for no earthly reason"? The answers to these questions are dictated neither by the relevant facts nor by the form of the principles themselves. How, then, in the face of these difficulties, can Winner make the decision forced upon him?

This brings us to the final aspect of ethical deliberation.

After ascertaining the facts, after sorting and weighing the conflicting principles, and applying partially indeterminate principles to the particular circumstances, Winner must bring himself to a decision. Much of ethical deliberation consists in coming to know one's own mind; it is a further step to make up one's mind and act upon the decision. This aspect of deliberation is heavily emphasized by contemporary existentialism; indeed, in popular usage, a moral problem just consists in bringing oneself to do what one believes to be right. However, most ethical philosophers hold that ethics is not primarily concerned with getting people to do what they believe to be right, but rather with helping them to decide what *is* right.

III. Ethical Theory

With this characterization of the nature of ethical problems and ethical deliberation, we may return to our original question, What is ethics? We have described it as the attempt to state and evaluate principles by which ethical problems may be solved. This means that the ethical theorist does *not* ask such questions as "What would I do in Winner's position?" or "What decision would society (or the district attorney, or the church, or any other group) approve?" Ethics seeks the principles that will tell us what is the *right* thing to do, or what things are *worth* doing, no matter what people in fact approve or disapprove and no matter what people will be damaged by the decision. It is not concerned at all with what public opinion on moral matters actually happens to be, but with what public opinion ought to be, just as the scientist is not concerned with what people believe about the shape of the earth but with its actual shape. To be sure, some ethical theorists deny that ethics can validate its principles in the way that the scientist can; but the analogy is useful in characterizing the central question of traditional ethics.

How does ethical philosophy proceed in formulating its principles? The best answer to this question can be found by actually reading the selections in this volume. Like any intellectual discipline, ethics is difficult to characterize meaningfully to one who is unfamiliar with it. A definition of mathematics, for example, as the study of types of order is unintelligible to anyone who does not already have a thorough grounding in mathematics. The function of this volume of readings is to exhibit examples of ethical theories rather than to arrive at a definition of its subject matter and methods. By studying the finest works written in the field and thinking critically about them, the reader will come to understand the nature of ethics in a way far surpassing the understanding gained by memorizing an aphorism.

There are, however, some things which can be said if they are not taken as definitions but as suggestions as to what to look for. There are some features which ethics shares with other branches of intellectual inquiry. First, and most obviously, it attempts to reduce complexity by introducing general principles that apply to a great variety of cases. Spinoza and Kant, for example, in very different ways, try to deduce principles for evaluating alternative standards from a few axioms, just as the mathematician tries to deduce theorems from a few basic assumptions. Kant's axiom, the Categorical Imperative, is itself an ethical principle; Spinoza's axioms are very general metaphysical statements about the nature of God and man. Other philosophers, Bentham and Dewey, for example, introduce order into the tangle of ethical rules by trying to show that there is a single procedure that can be applied uniformly to all ethical problems. The attempt to subsume diverse cases under a few laws is a fundamental feature of all intellectual organization; up to the twentieth century few would have thought of questioning the legitimacy of at least making the attempt. Nowadays, however, the existentialists maintain that the quest for generality is based upon a misconception of the nature of man; they thus challenge a large and essential proportion of the historical tradition of ethical theorizing. Whether or not the existentialists are correct, it remains a fact that the search for general standards of value and of conduct is the central task of ethics as conceived by the majority of writers.

But the philosopher is not content merely to formulate ethical principles. He wants to justify them—to prove them, or at least to demonstrate that they are reasonable and effective. A necessary step in justification of an ethical theory—a system of ethical principles—is to establish its internal consistency, since inconsistency means that the theory as a whole cannot be accepted. And in a complex theory, inconsistency may not be easy to detect; the principles must be formulated with care and exactitude, and their consequences spelled out for critical examination. It must be admitted that philosophers sometimes fail to do this, in which case the student should conduct the investigation for himself.

Since, however, bare internal consistency is merely a minimal requirement for an ethical theory, what else is required in a justification? Though this is itself a controversial point among philosophers, we can note two points. The philosopher tries to develop his theory in the light of the leading intellectual movements of his day. This does not mean that he lets the contemporary views of the nature of man, society, and the world—which after all have changed radically in the past and will no doubt continue to change—dictate his views on ethics, but rather that he rightly tries to avoid flagrant conflicts with current opinion. It follows that today the ethical philosopher must come to grips with the natural and social sciences, even if he is not particularly interested in science, or indeed even if he is critical of its claims and results. Moreover, the philosopher tries to make his theory as true as possible to the moral experience of his culture. One of the most damaging (although not necessarily fatal) criticisms that can be directed against an ethical theory consists in showing that its principles require actions that every sane person would admit to be wrong; and we would certainly regard any theory as at least incomplete if it had nothing to say about such fundamental ethical beliefs as, for instance, the conviction that it is wrong to inflict unnecessary pain. A standard criticism of such widely divergent theorists as Bentham and Nietzsche is that their theories are *immoral.* This point should not be misunderstood. In trying to do justice to the moral convictions of his culture, the philosopher of course interprets them in his own way, and there is plenty of room for difference of opinion as to what these convictions are. Again, the philosopher may be concerned precisely to *criticize* large segments of these convictions. But in any case he cannot afford to ignore them.

Further, the ethical philosopher wants not only to justify his proposed principles but to explore their relations to other fields of inquiry. And on examination, it often turns out that ethical principles are involved in the principles of other disciplines. Consider, for example, Karl Marx's version of the labor theory of economic value. It was presented by him, and is widely accepted today, as a straightforwardly scientific analysis of economic institutions, devoid of any element of ethical evaluation. But its fundamental thesis—that the value of a commodity is measured by the amount of labor required to produce it—is an uncritically accepted ethical principle. Since it has the immediate consequence that workers cannot possibly be paid full value for their labor in a capitalist system, Marx was able to make of his theory an instrument of political revolution. In effect, the Marxist argues that he has shown scientifically that capitalism is unjust, but the imputed injustice is already assumed in the "scientific" premises of this claim.

However we decide the merits of Marx's argument, if scientists with their incalculable power both in technology and in public opinion are in fact working with concealed ethical principles, it is clearly of the greatest importance to discover what they are and subject them to critical scrutiny. One important aspect of the relations of ethics to other fields consists in just this: on the one hand philosophers try to uncover the values that underlie various disciplines; and on the other hand they seek the ethical principles that may be implicit in other theories. One important movement, stemming from the researches of Karl Mannheim, holds indeed that ethical evaluations are embodied in *all* opinions, much as an evaluation is embodied in Marx's economic theory.

It is characteristic of all inquiry that as questions are formulated more and more clearly, their answers must be sought in unexpected directions. For example, Galileo saw that the explanation of the motions of pendulums and projectiles depended upon the mathematical analysis of acceleration; before the question was raised in this form, no one would have suspected that the key to understanding motions on earth would be provided by an examination of the motions of the moon and planets. The history of science is, indeed, the history of such unexpected relevancies.

Similarly, as the philosopher raises questions, particularly about the justification of ethical principles, he is likely to find that the quest for an answer leads him far afield from ethics proper. In his essay *On Liberty* John Stuart Mill raises the question of whether censorship of ideas is ever justified. He argues that anyone who supports such censorship claims infallibility for himself. But since he rejects the underlying claim, the major argument in favor of censorship collapses. Mill justifies his position on this question by drawing a principle from another branch of philosophy, in this case, from the theory of knowledge —viz., that all judgments of matters of fact are subject to error. Thus a complete defense of liberty of thought and expression can involve the philosopher in an examination of *this* principle; and so on. This point is merely a restatement of the familiar fact that an answer to a question always raises further questions.

Thus far most philosophers would agree with our description of ethical theory. But many would go further, holding that ethics includes other activities than the formulation of ethical principles and the examination of their relations to other fields. And certainly the student will find other activities represented in this volume. We shall divide them into two categories—moral persuasion and methodology of ethics. Moral persuasion is the attempt to affect someone's attitude toward particular ethical principles; it includes moralizing and exhortation in all its forms. Because the moralist often employs propagandist methods, sometimes with spectacular results, he has fallen nowadays into intellectual disrepute. And at its worst, moral persuasion certainly deserves its sinister reputation, since it sometimes is no more than special pleading for an uncritically accepted moral—or immoral—position. But at its best, moral persuasion is legitimate and socially valuable, for it helps to sharpen our perception of the issues involved in an ethical question. The effective moralist does not merely tell us what principles he favors; indeed, he need not assume an explicit moral position at all. He shows us what we might well call the possibilities of human life, by exhibiting through drama, satire, and criticism the concrete forms that values may take. In his examination of bad faith, Jean-Paul Sartre, in effect, tells us to take it or leave it, but first understand clearly what it is. James Gould Cozzens is certainly a moralist—the reader of *By Love Possessed* cannot escape the conclusion that Cozzens is supporting the values of a realistic humanism, as they are exhibited in the person of Julius Penrose. Much of the world's literature is moralistic in this sense, not only the frankly didactic, but all literature that explores the human situation.

Although the philosopher sometimes employs the novelist's or poet's techniques—consider, for instance, the writings of Nietzsche and Kierkegaard—for expressing his convictions, he more commonly proceeds by asking, and answering, pointed questions where popular prejudice would prefer discreet silence. In so far as the philosopher tries to convince his readers of the truth of the ethical principles he formulates, he enters the territory of the moralist; and evidently the techniques of moral persuasion can be an important factor in the justification of his principles. Accordingly there is no sharp border line between ethics and moral persuasion in the writings of most philosophers.

The reader will have recognized that ethics is indeed a complex field. It is not surprising, therefore, that philosophers have devoted much attention to questions of the exact nature of ethical principles. In any field, at the outset of inquiry, it is common for a person to think he knows what kind of question he is asking, without in fact having a clear idea of what would count as an answer, or even of what facts would be relevant. The methodology of ethics—or "meta-ethics," as it is often called—seeks to clarify the nature of ethical inquiry itself, by examining the logical functions of ethical language and the meaning of ethical terms. Although it has always played a role in ethical philosophizing, methodology has assumed critical importance in the twentieth century. G. E. Moore argues persuasively, for example, that the key ethical term "good" cannot be defined at all, and that accordingly those ethical theories that are based on an alleged definition, e.g., Aristotle's or Bentham's, rest on an error. Others, non-cognitivists such as A. J. Ayer, maintain that though it is possible to analyze the meaning of such terms as "good" and "right," or the meaning of the sentences in which they occur, their analysis reveals that they are not employed to make assertions; accordingly such statements as "Stealing is wrong" and "Nazism is evil" cannot properly be said to be true (or false). These two controversial positions have stimulated so much methodological writing that, in the opinion of some philosophers, substantive ethical questions now tend to be neglected or ignored altogether.

Although methodology is not directly concerned with the question of what ethical principles one ought to adopt, it may have important bearings on ethics proper: any specification of the meaning of the questions "What is the good life?" and "What is duty?" may evidently influence profoundly one's views on what the good life is and what one's duties are. Like moral persuasion, methodology is not sharply separated from ethics proper in the writings of most philosophers. In its typical form, an ethical treatise consists of moralizing with the help of an ethical theory defended on methodological grounds.

IV. Postscript

What can the student expect to learn from the study of ethics? He must not expect to absorb a conception of the good life, or a ready-made code of conduct, in the manner that the student of physics can absorb a knowledge of Newtonian mechanics and the differential calculus. One who seeks merely to be told what he ought to do had best *not* read widely in the world's ethical literature—he will be more content if he picks his authority and stands by it. The point of reading any philosopher, and especially an ethical philosopher, is not to find out what he has to say, and certainly not to find an acceptable path to discipleship, but to be able to philosophize for oneself in the light of what he has said. A sure mark of an unphilosophical attitude is the attaching of undue weight to anyone's written word.

Although ethics does not provide a recipe for becoming a better person, it can provide aid for anyone who wishes to accomplish this end, by making him intelligently aware of what is involved in holding an ethical belief and by cultivating a critical style of thought. It is a great gain even if one does no more than realize clearly the great complexity of ethical problems, and the many problematical aspects of the ethical principles we habitually employ. It is a further gain to recognize the pitfalls of ethical naïveté and to achieve a grasp of what factors are relevant in the evaluation and application of ethical principles. For these purposes a first-hand knowledge of the best thought on the subject is indispensable.

Finally, the student may gain from a wide acquaintance with ethical writings all the values of any humanistic study. Just as one's understanding of an ethical treatise is aided by knowledge of the historical context in which it was written, so the ethical philosophy of a given period can shed light on the attitudes and beliefs of the men who lived at that time, and thus help in the delicate job of interpreting history. Consider, for example, the importance of St. Augustine's ethical writings for understanding the history of the medieval church, or of Machiavelli's *Prince* for the Renaissance.

In ethical philosophy one becomes acquainted with the most diverse personalities and sees in them the reciprocal influence of attitude and thought. One can compare, for example, the equanimity and balance of a Mill with the rhetoric and passion of a Nietzsche; or the absorption in God of St. Augustine with the naturalistic humanism of Dewey. There is available in ethical philosophy, as in every significant literature, a fund of knowledge about the almost infinitely diverse possibilities of human existence.

part 1

THE CLASSICAL PERIOD

From the perspective of many centuries temporal differences tend to dissolve. It is important, therefore, to remind ourselves of the time span covered by the selections in this section. Plato, the first of the philosophers dealt with, was born about 427 B.C.; Plotinus, the last, did not die until A.D. 270. Thus these selections cover a period of 700 years—almost four times as long as the history of the United States since its foundation.

In 427 B.C. The Peloponnesian War had only just begun; Athens was still at its height; Rome was but an obscure village in Italy, remote from the centers of culture and with its whole destiny ahead of it. By A.D. 270 the Roman imperium had just about run its course, decline had set in, and Christianity was on the eve of its triumph under Constantine. Is it possible to make any significant generalizations about a period of such immense change? More specifically, is it possible to point to any aspects of the social and cultural milieu which affected the character and development of ethical theory during those six centuries?

Let us at the outset put down a purely negative characteristic—there was no science at all in the modern sense. This absence of a science of nature makes more difference to ethical theory than one might at first sight believe. In the first place, ethical theorists in the classical period did not have to worry about the relation between ethics and scientific naturalism, as later thinkers were forced to do; they were quite untroubled by the question whether *evidence* in the field of ethics can meet the standards set for evidence in the field of physics and the other sciences; and whether, if it cannot, it is somehow deficient.

In the second place, without a developed physical science there could be no complex technology. This meant that the classical period was a period of scarcity; though there were here and there men of immense wealth, society as a whole was certainly not affluent. So far from having to struggle with the problems of affluence, it must have seemed almost self-evident in classical times that the existence of any sort of society was possible only because of an immense substructure of slaves who produced the goods not created by machines, and whose poverty and total lack of leisure made possible the luxury and the leisure of a small elite.

Classical ethical theory reflects in many ways these economic facts of life in a non-technological society; it assumes the existence of an elite and it is addressed to this elite. The question asked by classical ethical theory is essentially: How can this elite get the most out of life? How can it use the leisure that has been created for it to maximize the various potentialities for enrichment?

Of course, classical ethical theorists realized that, unfortunately, the hereditary upper class which actually enjoyed leisure and power in these societies was not necessarily identical with those who had the capacity and the knowledge to utilize leisure well. As Aristotle uneasily observed, some actual slaves are natural masters; some actual masters are natural slaves. Accordingly, there was a kind of tension, not wholly resolved by classical ethical theorists, between the formulation of the values of this society and the recognition of the possibility of criticizing these values. Thus, for instance, Plato believed that one of the main political and social problems was the selection of really superior men and the transference of political power to them.

So far we have mentioned some of the consequences for ethical theory of the fact that this was a period in which science and technology were virtually unknown. But to say that the classical period was unscientific is to say nothing distinctive about it. This is equally true of the Middle Ages and, indeed, of *all* societies down to quite recent times. We can distinguish the classical period from these other non-technological societies by saying that classical society needed only scientific method to be essentially modern society. We shall not stop to ask why the Greeks did not invent scientific method when they invented practically everything else; but we can say with confidence that had they known about it, they would have delighted in it. And the Romans, for their part, would have delighted in technology and gadgetry as much as twentieth-century America. Thus the classical period had the sort of mind (unlike many other periods) which is in sympathy with the scientific outlook on the world.

What qualities of mind are these? First, a concern with this world and its affairs: an interest in nature and in the natural man. Second, a thoroughgoing rationalism—a respect for evidence, as evidence was understood in those times. Third, and most important of all, curiosity. Perhaps "humanism" is as good a term as any to sum up these qualities of mind. Let us now see how they affected the character of classical ethical theory.

In the first place, these qualities of mind appear as highly regarded values in the ethical system, as attitudes which it is recommended that men cultivate and develop. For all the theorists of this period, almost without exception, the free exercise of intelligence in the pursuit of truth is the highest value. In varying degrees these thinkers attribute value to pleasure, to comfort, to security; but the principal element in "happiness" (which is the term these thinkers used to designate the highest good) is contemplation. This is especially obvious in Plato, as, for instance, the myth of the cave and the discussion in the *Philebus* show (see pp. 41 ff. and pp. 50 ff.), but it is also true of Aristotle in his account of the "intellectual virtues." All of his so-called active virtues—that is, the virtues of the active life—involve knowing as well as doing.

Again, classical humanism appears in the concentration of attention in ethical theory on a this-worldly, natural ideal. While there are certainly differences from theorist to theorist, and also a significant difference between earlier and later theorists, in this regard Aristotle's position is representative. Here we see a striking concentration of attention on natural goods, especially if we contrast his position with that of St. Thomas Aquinas (pp. 153 ff.), whose theory, as far as *form* goes, is thoroughly Aristotelian. Not only does Aristotle set up a natural end for men to aim at (happiness) in contrast to the supernal goal (union with God) set up by St. Thomas; Aristotle also regards man as capable of achieving the highest good by his own natural talents—not all men, of course, but superior ones—while St. Thomas regards the supreme good as beyond our powers. We are dependent on an act of grace from outside, and it is attainable only in an afterlife.

Moreover, if we consider Aristotle's list of virtues, we find (as we would expect in a thinker whose ideal so closely reflects the ethos of his own times and society) that all of the virtues are concerned with life in a city-state. To Aristotle it was unthinkable that a man, even a superior man, could live well or be happy in isolation from his fellows. This is what he meant when he said that man is a political, i.e., a city-dwelling, animal. Contrast this with the Christian ideal of the hermit who reaches God best in solitude. And where in a religiously oriented ethics we hear a great deal about the virtues of piety, reverence, faith, and hope, in Aristotle's naturalistically oriented ethics we hear instead about courage (and the best courage, we are told, is that of the citizen-soldier) and about justice, understood exclusively in terms of the distribution of awards and punishments in the state. And where Christian theorists discuss "love" conceived in transcendental terms, Aristotle discusses friendship, conceived as a partnership of equals directed to their mutual advantage and improvement.

We have made a very sweeping generalization in characterizing classical ethical theory as humanistic, naturalistic, and rational. We must now introduce some qualifications. First, in some respects Plato's views reflect exactly the same sorts of biases and the same sort of city-state ethos that we have found in Aristotle. After all, they were both Athenian citizens and both city-state men. And though they actually lived after the decline of city-state culture had set in, neither of them seems to have been aware of this fact.

Still, even though Plato devotes a great deal of attention to the good life of the citizen and to happiness defined in terms of the development of the talents of the superior man, his major emphasis lies elsewhere. The highest good of all turns out to be not just contemplation, but contemplation of an almost mystical "Form of the Good." And the general tone is far less optimistic than Aristotle's. It is true that, like Aristotle, Plato could not really conceive of life except in a city-state, but it is also true that he regarded life in the state as a hindrance to the achievement of the highest good. Hence, sometimes at least, Plato writes as if the political life and the cultivation of the virtues were a *duty* to be pursued against real desire, rather than as a matter of self-realization and fulfillment. This appears particularly in the myth of the cave (pp. 41 ff.), where the man who has seen the beauties of the sun and enjoyed communion with the form of the good, nevertheless feels constrained to return to the cave to try to help his fellows—even though he accomplishes nothing by this sacrifice and only gets himself killed for his pains.

The reasons for this difference in tone between Plato and Aristotle are many. In the first place, Plato seems to have been rather ascetic in outlook; though he allowed pleasure to be an element in the good (p. 44), he seems, at least some of the time, to have thought that we would all be much better off without bodies at all, whose sensuous and sensual desires only distract us from what ought to be our main concern. In this respect Plato was much closer than Aristotle to what was to become a major motif of Christian ethics. Again, Plato was on the whole pessimistic about the possibility of good government. It must be allowed that in his time, as in ours, there was unfortunately much evidence to support a pessimistic outlook. Plato belonged to an old, aristocratic Athenian family. In the immediately preceding generation the aristocracy had gradually lost power to what the Athenians called "democracy" (although we should remember it was nowhere nearly so broadly based as modern democracy); and in his own lifetime this democracy had fought and lost a disastrous war with Sparta. Moreover, political changes and military defeat were accompanied by a marked dissolution of the old values and attitudes which had been replaced by a callousness, egoism, and skepticism ("cynicism," some, including Plato, would call it), a situation not unlike that found by some critics in our own society. These changes disturbed Plato, and one of the main drives of his ethical theory was to reassert the old values—not merely to reaffirm them, of course (that would be the role of the preacher), but to *prove* them. This consuming interest of Plato's comes out very clearly in all of the selections we have presented here, but especially perhaps in *The Republic,* in the opening discussion with Glaucon, who summarizes the skepticism and egoism that Plato detested.

Thus here again we have an example of a very characteristic relation between ethical theory and the social and cultural context in which it appears. The virtue of justice which is so elaborately analyzed in *The Republic* is nothing but the immemorial lore expressed by the Delphic oracle and in other myths —Nothing in excess; and similarly, for Aristotle's definition of virtue as a mean (p. 64). Both philosophers are reinterpreting the traditional culture, restating it and reorganizing it in a systematic way; attempting, as it were, to find the common, "higher," principle imbedded in the rules of behavior that had been handed down for generations.

When we pass from Plato and Aristotle to Epictetus and Plotinus, we immediately notice a marked change. Much had occurred in the centuries that separate them: city-state society had been replaced by an enormous world-empire, in which, though men were still called "citizens," they could perforce have virtually no share in an active political life. Government had passed into the hands of bureaucrats who executed policy formulated by the emperor; hence even those who possessed political power were merely civil servants, not free citizens. It was quite impossible by the time of Epictetus for men, even for superior men, to realize the life of active virtue as Plato or Aristotle had conceived it.

Various schools of philosophy and various ethical systems sprang up which reflected these political and cultural changes. On the one hand, there were the Epicureans, who recommended a life of pleasure. Epicurus himself, so far from advocating the eat-drink-and-be-merry attitude now associated with his name, recommended mild and temperate enjoyments. In terms of the Platonic myth we may say that he advocated neither lingering on the heights of transcendent contemplation of the sun nor descending into the cave of the workaday world. Rather, he proposed getting such pleasures as one could by a careful and prudential calculus, and certainly not allowing oneself to become involved in the competitive and stressful life of ambition and achievement. Epicurus's hedonism was certainly not licentiousness, but it did entail a thorough social irresponsibility. It is as if he felt the state to be too large, too complex, and too formidable for men to intervene effectively.

The Stoics, of whom the Roman slave Epictetus is an example, took an opposite line: *because* the state was large, complex, and formidable, it was one's duty, they felt, to develop and to live by a stern sense of responsibility. The task is difficult, and men must do their duty even though a successful outcome is less than certain. The Stoics were even less optimistic than Plato: for them, men remain in the cave, rather than descend back into it. But the cave, it is important to observe, is a universal community, including all men, and not merely a city-state comprising a few superior people. Here we touch the most significant difference between Plato and Aristotle on the one hand and the Stoics on the other. And here again we see a point at which ethical theorizing has been affected by cultural change. After city-state culture had been replaced by the world-wide Roman Empire, there was a natural tendency for men to broaden their thinking about ethics. While the Greek moralists had drawn what seems to most of us a provincial distinction between the Greeks and all others, whom they thought of contemptuously as lesser breeds (the Greek word for foreigner is "barbarian"), the Roman Stoics developed the idea of a world community and of a universal equality of all men under law—thus preparing the way for the Christian insight that all men, regardless of race, creed, or economic status, are equally children of one God.

The Stoics might be said to have seen the tremendous importance of staffing the world-state with competent civil servants—not merely, or chiefly, technically competent bureaucrats but men with an ethos and an outlook, a sense of responsibility and of respect for law, which fitted them to direct a world government. Such interests on the part of the Stoics ought to strike a sympathetic chord in twentieth-century Americans, who have a similar responsibility.

With Epictetus, and even more with Plotinus, we have thinkers whose ethical theories are transitions to the next period. Late classical times were marked by what some writers have called a failure of nerve; by what other thinkers with a different orientation would call a turning of attention at long last to the really important concerns—that is, man's relation to the infinite and transcendent. In any case, however we assess the new outlook, it is certainly other-worldly rather than this-worldly, supernaturalistic rather than naturalistic. In terms of the Platonic myth, these thinkers stay and recommend that we join them outside the cave on the heights. For them the good life consists not in maximizing the enjoyments nor in realizing through the active life the potentialities of the superior man—it does not consist even in doing one's duties here below. Rather, it consists in getting into a right relation with a superhuman power and in losing one's self-identity and individuality in it.

Thus, as we come to the close of this period, we find the generalizations which applied so well to the earlier thinkers no longer apply; the natural contrast between the classical and medieval periods has broken down. While the student will find the transition from Aristotle to St. Augustine a movement from one world to another, he will find it hard to separate the writings of Plotinus from the medieval tradition.

PLATO

Plato's life (428/7–348/7 B.C.) virtually spans the period of political turbulence between the death of Pericles and the rise to power of Philip of Macedon. If the traditional accounts are true, in his youth he was torn between two vocations: as a member of an aristocratic family he could naturally have entered the politics of Athens; but he was repelled by the corruption in government and at the same time attracted to philosophy by Socrates.

From Socrates he learned to question the uncritical presuppositions of his age, and just as important, in the personality of Socrates he found exemplified a way of life untouched by the immorality he found about him. The trial and subsequent execution of Socrates on the specious charges of impiety and corrupting the young decided the matter; he now saw the impossibility of accomplishing anything through active participation within the existing political framework.

With the death of Socrates, Plato left Athens with the resolve to follow the philosophic vocation and vindicate the life of Socrates. He wrote a series of dialogues which at the same time examined philosophic problems and, by using Socrates as the main speaker, exhibited his true character. Having returned to Athens, Plato established a school in the groves of Academe: the Academy. Here he offered instruction on a variety of topics and brought together a number of able men drawn from all parts of the ancient world.

As his own thoughts developed, he speculated upon the full range of philosophic topics, but he never lost interest in the problem of the just society. In The Republic *he set forth his conception of justice in the individual and in the state. Nor was he content merely to speculate on these matters; in his fortieth year he traveled to Syracuse to seize what he took to be an opportunity to implement his ideas. Though the details of this adventure are obscure, we know that it ended in disheartening failure.*

With his return to Athens he continued his philosophic writing. The dialogues of this later period are more abstract and technical and represent his most mature reflections on philosophic topics. Philebus, *written in this period, is of central importance for the understanding of his ethical theory. It concerns the respective roles of wisdom and pleasure in the nature of the good.*

*The Republic**

Book II
Glaucon on Justice

PERSONS OF THE DIALOGUE
SOCRATES, GLAUCON, ADEIMANTUS

I[†] want to know how you classify the things we call good. Are there not some which we should wish to have, not for their consequences, but just for their own sake, such as harmless pleasures and enjoyments that have no further result beyond the satisfaction of the moment?

Yes, I think there are good things of that description.

And also some that we value both for their own sake and for their consequences—things like knowledge and health and the use of our eyes?

Yes.

And a third class which would include physical training, medical treatment, earning one's bread as a doctor or otherwise—useful, but burdensome things, which we want only for the sake of the profit or other benefit they bring?

Yes, there is that third class. What then?

* By permission. From Francis M. Cornford, *The Republic of Plato*, Clarendon Press, Oxford, 1941. Deletions are not noted in the text. Section headings have been added by the editors.

† The dialogue is narrated by Socrates and begins with Glaucon's statement and elaboration of the fundamental problem of *The Republic*.

In which class do you place justice?

I should say, in the highest, as a thing which anyone who is to gain happiness must value both for itself and for its results.

Well, that is not the common opinion. Most people would say it was one of those things, tiresome and disagreeable in themselves, which we cannot avoid practising for the sake of reward or a good reputation.

I know, said I.

Listen to me, then, and see if you agree. Nothing so far said about justice and injustice has been established to my satisfaction. I want to be told what each of them really is, and what effect each has, in itself, on the soul that harbours it, when all rewards and consequences are left out of account. So here is my plan, if you approve. First, I will state what is commonly held about the nature of justice and its origin; secondly, I shall maintain that it is always practised with reluctance, not as good in itself, but as a thing one cannot do without; and thirdly, that this reluctance is reasonable, because the life of injustice is much the better life of the two—so people say. That is not what I think myself, Socrates; only I am bewildered by all that so many others have dinned into my ears; and I have never yet heard the case for justice stated as I wish to hear it. You, I believe, if anyone, can tell me what is to be said in praise of justice in and for itself; that is what I want. Accordingly, I shall set you an example by glorifying the life of injustice with all the energy that I hope you will show later in denouncing it and exalting justice in its stead. Will that plan suit you?

Nothing could be better, I replied. Of all subjects this is one on which a sensible man must always be glad to exchange ideas.

Good, said Glaucon. Listen then, and I will begin with my first point: the nature and origin of justice.

What people say is that to do wrong is, in itself, a desirable thing; on the other hand, it is not at all desirable to suffer wrong, and the harm to the sufferer outweighs the advantage to the doer. Consequently, when men have had a taste of both, those who have not the power to seize the advantage and escape the harm decide that they would be better off if they made a compact neither to do wrong nor to suffer it. Hence they began to make laws and covenants with one another; and whatever the law prescribed they called lawful and right. That is what right or justice is and how it came into existence; it stands half-way between the best thing of all—to do wrong with impunity—and the worst, which is to suffer wrong without the power to retaliate. So justice is accepted as a compromise, and valued, not as good in itself, but for lack of power to do wrong; no man worthy of the name, who had that power, would ever enter into such a compact with anyone; he would be mad if he did. That, Socrates, is the nature of justice according to this account, and such the circumstances in which it arose.

The next point is that men practise it against the grain, for lack of power to do wrong. How true that is, we shall best see if we imagine two men, one just, the other unjust, given full license to do whatever they like, and then follow them to observe where each will be led by his desires. We shall catch the just man taking the same road as the unjust; he will be moved by self-interest, the end which it is natural to every creature to pursue as good, until forcibly turned aside by law and custom to respect the principle of equality.

Now, the easiest way to give them that complete liberty of action would be to imagine them possessed of the talisman found by Gyges, the ancestor of the famous Lydian. The story tells how he was a shepherd in the King's service. One day there was a great storm, and the ground where his flock was feeding was rent by an earthquake. Astonished at the sight, he went down into the chasm and saw, among other wonders of which the story tells, a brazen horse, hollow, with windows in its sides. Peering in, he saw a dead body, which seemed to be of more than human size. It was naked save for a gold ring, which he took from the finger and made his way out. When the shepherds met, as they did every month, to send an account to the King of the state of his flocks, Gyges came wearing the ring. As he was sitting with the others, he happened to turn the bezel of the ring inside his hand. At once he became invisible, and his companions, to his surprise, began to speak of him as if he had left them. Then, as he was fingering the ring, he turned the bezel outwards and became visible again. With that, he set about testing the ring to see if it really had this power, and always with the same result: according as he turned the bezel inside or out he vanished and reappeared. After this discovery he contrived to be one of the messengers sent to the court. There he seduced the Queen, and with her help murdered the King and seized the throne.

Now suppose there were two such magic rings, and one were given to the just man, the other to the unjust. No one, it is commonly believed, would have such iron strength of mind as to stand fast in doing right or keep his hands off other men's goods, when he could go to the market-place and fearlessly help himself to anything he wanted, enter houses and sleep with any woman he chose, set prisoners free and kill men at his pleasure, and in a word go about among men with the powers of a god. He would behave no better than the other; both would take the same course. Surely this would be strong proof that men do right only under compulsion; no individual thinks of it as good for him personally, since he does wrong whenever he finds he has the power. Every man believes that wrongdoing pays him personally much better, and, according to this theory, that is the truth. Granted full licence to do as he liked, people would think him a miserable fool if they found him refusing to wrong his neighbours or to touch their belongings, though in public they would keep up a pretence of praising his conduct, for fear of being wronged themselves. So much for that.

Finally, if we are really to judge between the two lives, the only way is to contrast the extremes of justice and injustice. We can best do that by imagining our two men to be perfect types, and crediting both to the full with the qualities they need for their respective ways of life. To begin with the unjust man: he must be like any consummate master of a craft, a physician or a captain, who, knowing just what his art can do, never tries to do more, and can always retrieve a false step. The unjust man, if he is to reach perfection, must be equally discreet in his criminal attempts, and he must not be found out, or we shall think him a bungler; for the highest pitch of injustice is to seem just when you are not. So we must endow our man with the full complement of injustice; we must allow him to have secured a spotless reputation for virtue while committing the blackest crimes; he must be able to retrieve any mistake, to defend himself with convincing eloquence if his misdeeds are denounced, and, when force is required, to bear down all opposition by his courage and strength and by his command of friends and money.

Now set beside this paragon the just man in his simplicity and nobleness, one who, in Aeschylus' words, "would be, not seem, the best." There must, indeed, be no such seeming; for if his character were apparent, his reputation would bring him honours and rewards, and then we should not know whether it was for their sake that he was just or for justice's sake alone. He must be stripped of everything but justice, and denied every advantage the other enjoyed. Doing no wrong, he must have the worst reputation for wrongdoing, to test whether his virtue is proof against all that comes of having a bad name; and under this lifelong imputation of wickedness, let him hold on his course of justice unwavering to the point of death. And so, when the two men have carried their justice and injustice to the last extreme, we may judge which is the happier.

My dear Glaucon, I exclaimed, how vigorously you scour these two characters clean for inspection, as if you were burnishing a couple of statues!

I am doing my best, he answered. Well, given two such characters, it is not hard, I fancy, to describe the sort of life that each of them may expect; and if the description sounds rather coarse, take it as coming from those who cry up the merits of injustice rather than from me. They will tell you that our just man will be thrown into prison, scourged and racked, will have his eyes burnt out, and, after every kind of torment, be impaled. That will teach him how much better it is to seem virtuous than to be so. In fact those lines of Aeschylus I quoted are more fitly applied to the unjust man, who, they say, is a realist and does not live for appearances: "he would be, not seem" unjust,

. . . reaping the harvest sown
In those deep furrows of the thoughtful heart
Whence wisdom springs.

With his reputation for virtue, he will hold offices of state, ally himself by marriage to any family he may choose, become a partner in any business, and, having no scruples about being dishonest, turn all these advantages to profit. If he is involved in a lawsuit, public or private, he will get the better of his opponents, grow rich on the proceeds, and be able to help his friends and harm his enemies. Finally, he can make sacrifices to the gods and dedicate offerings with due magnificence, and, being in a much better position than the just man to serve the gods as well as his chosen friends, he may reasonably hope to stand higher in the favour of heaven. So much better, they say, Socrates, is the life prepared for the unjust by gods and men.

Glaucon and the others begged me to step into the breach and carry through our inquiry into the real nature of justice and injustice, and the truth about their respective advantages. So I told them what I thought. This is a very obscure question, I said, and we shall need keen sight to see our way. Now, as we are not remarkably clever, I will make a suggestion as to how we should proceed. Imagine a rather short-sighted person told to read an inscription in small letters from some way off. He would think it a godsend if someone pointed out that the same inscription was written up elsewhere on a bigger scale, so that he could first read the larger characters and then make out whether the smaller ones were the same.

No doubt, said Adeimantus; but what analogy do you see in that to our inquiry?

I will tell you. We think of justice as a quality that may exist in a whole community as well as in an individual, and the community is the bigger of the two. Possibly, then, we may find justice there in larger proportions, easier to make out. So I suggest that we should begin by inquiring what justice means in a state. Then we can go on to look for its counterpart on a smaller scale in the individual.

That seems a good plan, he agreed.

Well then, I continued, suppose we imagine a state coming into being before our eyes. We might then be able to watch the growth of justice or of injustice within it. When that is done, we may hope it will be easier to find what we are looking for. My notion is that a state comes into existence because no individual is self-sufficing; we all have many needs. But perhaps you can suggest some different origin for the foundation of a community?

No, I agree with you.

So, having all these needs, we call in one another's help to satisfy our various requirements; and when we have collected a number of helpers and associates to live together in one place, we call that settlement a state. So if one man gives another what he has to give in exchange for what he can get, it is because each finds that to do so is for his own advantage.

Certainly.

Very well, said I. Now let us build up our imaginary state from the beginning. Apparently, it will owe its existence to our needs, the first and greatest need being the provision of food to keep us alive. Next we shall want a house; and thirdly, such things as clothing. How will our state be able to supply all these demands? We shall need at least one man to be a farmer, another a builder, and a third a weaver. Will that do, or shall we add a shoemaker and one or two more to provide for our personal wants?

By all means.

The minimum state, then, will consist of four or five men. Now here is a further point. Is each one of them to bring the product of his work into a common stock? Should our one farmer, for example, provide food enough for four people and spend the whole of his working time in producing corn, so as to share with the rest; or should he take no notice of them and spend only a quarter of his time on growing just enough corn for himself, and divide the other three-quarters between building his house, weaving his clothes, and making his shoes, so as to save the trouble of sharing with others and attend himself to all his own concerns?

The first plan might be the easier, replied Adeimantus.

That may very well be so, said I; for, as you spoke, it occurred to me, for one thing, that no two people are born exactly alike. There are innate differences which fit them for different occupations.

I agree.

And will a man do better working at many trades, or keeping to one only?

Keeping to one.

And there is another point: obviously work may be ruined, if you let the right time go by. The workman must wait upon the work; it will not wait upon his leisure and allow itself to be done in a spare moment. So the conclusion is that more things will be produced and the work be more easily and better done, when every man is set free from all other occupations to do, at the right time, the one thing for which he is naturally fitted.

That is certainly true.

EDITORS' NOTE: *At this point Socrates proceeds "to construct in discourse," as he puts it, "the pattern of the ideal state." Following the principle of keeping to one trade only, he divides society into three classes, according to the function that each man performs in the life of the Republic. These classes are the workers—craftsmen, farmers, shopkeepers, etc.—who provide sustenance for the state and carry out its daily domestic chores; the auxiliaries, warriors who defend the state and support its policies; and the guardians, the rulers who formulate policy. Socrates holds that each man belongs by nature to one or another of these classes, although provision is made for some class mobility. Much of Books II, III, and IV is devoted to the details of the education, life, duties, etc., of the various classes. Socrates now continues his strategy of finding the image of the just man in the social patterns of the Republic.*

Book IV
Definition of the Four Virtues

I take it that our state, having been founded and built up on the right lines, is good in the complete sense of the word.

It must be.

Obviously, then, it is wise, brave, temperate, and just.

Obviously.

Then if we find some of these qualities in it, the remainder will be the one we have not found. It is as if we were looking somewhere for one of any four things: if we detected that one immediately, we should be satisfied; whereas if we recognized the other three first, that would be enough to indicate the thing we wanted; it could only be the remaining one. So here we have four qualities. Had we not better follow that method in looking for the one we want?

Surely.

To begin then: the first quality to come into view in our state seems to be its wisdom; and there appears to be something odd about this quality.

What is there odd about it?

I think the state we have described really has wisdom; for it will be prudent in counsel, won't it?

Yes.

And prudence in counsel is clearly a form of knowledge; good counsel cannot be due to ignorance and stupidity.

Clearly.

But there are many and various kinds of knowledge in our commonwealth. There is the knowledge possessed by the carpenters or the smiths, and the knowledge how to raise crops. Are we to call the state wise and prudent on the strength of these forms of skill?

No; they would only make it good at furniture-making or working in copper or agriculture.

Well then, is there any form of knowledge, possessed by some among the citizens of our new-founded commonwealth, which will enable it to take thought, not for some particular interest, but for the best possible conduct of the state as a whole in its internal and external relations?

Yes, there is.

What is it, and where does it reside?

It is precisely that art of guardianship which resides in those Rulers whom we just now called Guardians in the full sense.

And what would you call the state on the strength of that knowledge?

Prudent and truly wise.

And do you think there will be more or fewer of these genuine Guardians in our state than there will be smiths?

Far fewer.

Fewer, in fact, than any of those other groups who are called after the kind of skill they possess?

Much fewer.

So, if a state is constituted on natural principles, the wisdom it possesses as a whole will be due to the knowledge residing in the smallest part, the one which takes the lead and governs the rest. Such knowledge is the only kind that deserves the name of wisdom, and it appears to be ordained by nature that the class privileged to possess it should be the smallest of all.

Quite true.

Here then we have more or less made out one of our four qualities and its seat in the structure of the commonwealth.

To my satisfaction, at any rate.

Next there is courage. It is not hard to discern that quality or the part of the community in which it resides so as to entitle the whole to be called brave.

Why do you say so?

Because anyone who speaks of a state as either brave or cowardly can only be thinking of that part of it which takes the field and fights in its defence; the reason being, I imagine, that the character of the state is not determined by the bravery or cowardice of the other parts.

No.

Courage, then, is another quality which a community owes to a certain part of itself. And its being brave will mean that, in this part, it possesses the power of preserving, in all circumstances, a conviction about the sort of things that it is right to be afraid of—the conviction implanted by the education which the law-giver has established. Is not that what you mean by courage?

I do not quite understand. Will you say it again?

I am saying that courage means preserving something.

Yes, but what?

The conviction, inculcated by lawfully established education, about the sort of things which may rightly be feared. When I added "in all circumstances," I meant preserving it always and never abandoning it, whether under the influence of pain or of pleasure, of desire or of fear. If you like, I will give an illustration.

Please do.

You know how dyers who want wool to take a purple dye, first select the white wool from among all the other colours, next treat it very carefully to make it take the dye in its full brilliance, and only then dip it in the vat. Dyed in that way, wool gets a fast colour, which no washing, even with soap, will rob of its brilliance; whereas if they choose wool of any colour but white, or if they neglect to prepare it, you know what happens.

Yes, it looks washed-out and ridiculous.

That illustrates the result we were doing our best to achieve when we were choosing our fighting men and training their minds and bodies. Our only purpose was to contrive influences whereby they might take the colour of our institutions like a dye, so that, in virtue of having both the right temperament and the right education, their convictions about what ought to be feared and on all other subjects might be indelibly fixed, never to be washed out by pleasure and pain, desire and fear, solvents more terribly effective than all the soap and fuller's earth in the world. Such a power of constantly preserving, in accordance with our institutions, the right conviction about the things which ought, or ought not, to be feared, is what I call courage. That is my position, unless you have some objection to make.

None at all, he replied; if the belief were such as might be found in a slave or an animal—correct, but not produced by education—you would hardly describe it as in accordance with our institutions, and you would give it some other name than courage.

Quite true.

Then I accept your account of courage.

You will do well to accept it, at any rate as applying to the courage of the ordinary citizen; if you like we will go into it more fully some other time. At present we are in search of justice, rather than of courage; and for that purpose we have said enough.

I quite agree.

Two qualities, I went on, still remain to be made out in our state, temperance and the object of our whole inquiry, justice. Can we discover justice without troubling ourselves further about temperance?

I do not know, and I would rather not have justice come to light first, if that means that we should not go on to consider temperance. So if you want to please me, take temperance first.

I will. At first sight, temperance seems more like some sort of concord or harmony than the other qualities did.

How so?

Temperance surely means a kind of orderliness, a control of certain pleasures and appetites. People use the expression, "master of oneself," whatever that means, and various other phrases that point the same way.

Quite true.

Is not "master of oneself" an absurd expression? A man who was master of himself would presumably be also subject to himself, and the subject would be master; for all these terms apply to the same person.

No doubt.

I think, however, the phrase means that within the man himself, in his soul, there is a better part and a worse; and that he is his own master when the part which is better by nature has the worse under its control. It is certainly a term of praise; whereas it is considered a disgrace, when, through bad breeding or bad company, the better part is overwhelmed by the worse, like a small force outnumbered by a multitude. A man in that condition is called a slave to himself and intemperate.

Probably that is what is meant.

Then now look at our newly founded state and you will find one of these two conditions realized there. You will agree that it deserves to be called master of itself, if temperance and self-mastery exist where the better part rules the worse.

Yes, I can see that is true.

It is also true that the great mass of multifarious appetites and pleasures and pains will be found to occur chiefly in children and women and slaves, and, among free men so called, in the inferior multitude; whereas the simple and moderate desires which, with the aid of reason and right belief, are guided by reflection, you will find only in a few, and those with the best inborn dispositions and the best educated.

Yes, certainly.

Do you see that this state of things will exist in your commonwealth, where the desires of the inferior multitude will be controlled by the desires and wisdom of the superior few? Hence, if any society can be called master of itself and in control of pleasures and desires, it will be ours.

Quite so.

On all these grounds, then, we may

describe it as temperate. Furthermore, in our state, if anywhere, the governors and the governed will share the same conviction on the question who ought to rule. Don't you think so?

I am quite sure of it.

Then, if that is their state of mind, in which of the two classes of citizens will temperance reside—in the governors or in the governed?

In both, I suppose.

So we were not wrong in divining a resemblance between temperance and some kind of harmony. Temperance is not like courage and wisdom, which made the state wise and brave by residing each in one particular part. Temperance works in a different way; it extends throughout the whole gamut of the state, producing a consonance of all its elements from the weakest to the strongest as measured by any standard you like to take—wisdom, bodily strength, numbers, or wealth. So we are entirely justified in identifying with temperance this unanimity or harmonious agreement between the naturally superior and inferior elements on the question which of the two should govern, whether in the state or in the individual.

I fully agree.

Good, said I. We have discovered in our commonwealth three out of our four qualities, to the best of our present judgment. What is the remaining one, required to make up its full complement of goodness? For clearly this will be justice.

Clearly.

Really, I said, we have been extremely stupid. All this time the thing has been under our very noses from the start, and we never saw it. We have been as absurd as a person who hunts for something he has all the time got in his hand. Instead of looking at the thing, we have been staring into the distance. No doubt that is why it escaped us.

What do you mean?

I believe we have been talking about the thing all this while without ever understanding that we were giving some sort of account of it.

Do come to the point. I am all ears.

Listen, then, and judge whether I am right. You remember how, when we first began to establish our commonwealth and several times since, we have laid down, as a universal principle, that everyone ought to perform the one function in the community for which his nature best suited him. Well, I believe that that principle, or some form of it, is justice.

We certainly laid that down.

Yes, and surely we have often heard people say that justice means minding one's own business and not meddling with other men's concerns; and we have often said so ourselves.

We have.

Well, my friend, it may be that this minding of one's own business, when it takes a certain form, is actually the same thing as justice. Do you know what makes me think so?

No, tell me.

I think that this quality which makes it possible for the three we have already considered, wisdom, courage, and temperance, to take their place in the commonwealth, and so long as it remains present secures their continuance, must be the remaining one. And we said that, when three of the four were found, the one left over would be justice.

It must be so.

Well now, if we had to decide which of these qualities will contribute most to the excellence of our commonwealth, it would be hard to say whether it was the unanimity of rulers and subjects, or the soldier's fidelity to the established conviction about what is, or is not, to be feared, or the watchful intelligence of the Rulers; or whether its excellence were not above all due to the observance by everyone, child or woman, slave or freeman or artisan, ruler or ruled, of this principle that each one should do his own proper work without interfering with others.

It would be hard to decide, no doubt.

It seems, then, that this principle can at any rate claim to rival wisdom, temperance, and courage as conducing to the excellence of a state. And would you not say that the only possible competitor of these qualities must be justice?

Yes, undoubtedly.

Here is another thing which points to the same conclusion. Do you agree with me that no great harm would be done to the community by a general interchange of most forms of work, the carpenter and the cobbler exchanging their positions and their tools and taking on each other's jobs, or even the same man undertaking both?

Yes, there would not be much harm in that.

But I think you will also agree that another kind of interchange would be disastrous. Suppose, for instance, someone whom nature designed to be an artisan or tradesman should be emboldened by some advantage, such as wealth or command of votes or bodily strength, to try to enter the order of fighting men; or some member of that order should aspire, beyond his merits, to a seat in the council-chamber of the Guardians. Such interference and exchange of social positions and tools, or the attempt to combine all these forms of work in the same person, would be fatal to the commonwealth.

Most certainly.

Where there are three orders, then, any plurality of functions or shifting from one order to another is not merely utterly harmful to the community, but one might fairly call it the extreme of wrongdoing. And you will agree that to do the greatest of wrongs to one's own community is injustice.

Surely.

This, then, is injustice. And, conversely, let us repeat that when each order —tradesman, Auxiliary, Guardian—keeps to its own proper business in the commonwealth and does its own work, that is justice and what makes a just society.

I entirely agree.

We must not be too positive yet, said I. If we find that this same quality when it exists in the individual can equally be identified with justice, then we can at once give our assent; there will be no more to be said; otherwise, we shall have to look further. For the moment, we had better finish the inquiry which we began with the idea that it would be easier to make out the nature of justice in the individual if we first tried to study it in something on a larger scale. That larger thing we took to be a state, and so we set about constructing the best one we could, being sure of finding justice in a state that was good. The discovery we made there must now be applied to the individual. If it is confirmed, all will be well; but if we find that justice in the individual is something different, we must go back to the state and test our new result. Perhaps if we brought the two cases into contact like flint and steel, we might strike out between them the spark of justice, and in its light confirm the conception in our own minds.

A good method. Let us follow it.

Now, I continued, if two things, one large, the other small, are called by the same name, they will be alike in that respect to which the common name applies. Accordingly, in so far as the quality of justice is concerned, there will be no difference between a just man and a just society.

No.

Well, but we decided that a society was just when each of the three types of human character it contained performed its own function; and again, it was temperate and brave and wise by virtue of certain other affections and states of mind of those same types.

True.

Accordingly, my friend, if we are to be justified in attributing those same virtues to the individual, we shall expect to find that the individual soul contains the same three elements and that they are affected in the same way as are the corresponding types in society.

That follows.

Here, then, we have stumbled upon another little problem: Does the soul contain these three elements or not?

Not such a very little one, I think. It may be a true saying, Socrates, that what is worthwhile is seldom easy.

Surely, I began, we must admit that the same elements and characters that appear in the state must exist in every one of us; where else could they have come from? It would be absurd to imagine that among peoples with a reputation for a high-spirited character, like the Thracians and Scythians and northerners generally, the states have not derived that character from their individual members; or that it is otherwise with the love of knowledge, which would be ascribed chiefly to our own part of the world, or with the love of money, which one would specially connect with Phoenicia and Egypt. So far, then, we have a fact which is easily recognized. But here the difficulty begins. Are we using the same part of ourselves in all these three experiences, or a different part in each? Do we gain knowledge with one part, feel anger with another, and with yet a third desire the pleasures of food, sex, and so on? Or is the whole soul at work in every impulse and in all these forms of behaviour? The difficulty is to answer that question satisfactorily.

I quite agree.

Let us approach the problem whether these elements are distinct or identical in this way. It is clear that the same thing cannot act in two opposite ways or be in two opposite states at the same time, with respect to the same part of itself, and in relation to the same object. So if we find such contradictory actions or states among the elements concerned, we shall know that more than one must have been involved.

Now, would you class such things as assent and dissent, striving after something and refusing it, attraction and repulsion, as pairs of opposite actions or states of mind —no matter which?

Yes, they are opposites.

And would you not class all appetites such as hunger and thirst, and again willing and wishing, with the affirmative members of those pairs I have just mentioned? For instance, you would say that the soul of a man who desires something is striving after it, or trying to draw to itself the thing it wishes to possess, or again, in so far as it is willing to have its want satisfied, it is giving its assent to its own longing, as if to an inward question.

Yes.

And, on the other hand, disinclination, unwillingness, and dislike, we should class on the negative side with acts of rejection or repulsion. That being so, shall we say that appetites form one class, the most conspicuous being those we call thirst and hunger?

Yes.

Thirst being desire for drink, hunger for food?

Yes.

Now if there is ever something which at the same time pulls it the opposite way, that something must be an element in the soul other than the one which is thirsting and driving it like a beast to drink; in accordance with our principle that the same thing cannot behave in two opposite ways at the same time and towards the same object with the same part of itself. It is like an archer drawing the bow: it is not accurate to say that his hands are at the same time both pushing and pulling it. One hand does the pushing, the other the pulling.

Exactly.

Now, is it sometimes true that people are thirsty and yet unwilling to drink?

Yes, often.

What, then, can one say to them, if not that their soul contains something which urges them to drink and something which holds them back, and that this latter is a distinct thing and overpowers the other?

I agree.

And is it not true that the intervention of this inhibiting principle in such cases always has its origin in reflection; whereas the impulses driving and dragging the soul are engendered by external influences and abnormal conditions?

Evidently.

We shall have good reason, then, to assert that they are two distinct principles. We may call that part of the soul whereby it reflects, rational; and the other, with which it feels hunger and thirst and is distracted by sexual passion and all the other desires, we will call irrational appetite, associated with pleasure in the replenishment of certain wants.

Yes, there is good ground for that view.

Let us take it, then, that we have now distinguished two elements in the soul. What of that passionate element which makes us feel angry and indignant? Is that a third, or identical in nature with one of those two?

It might perhaps be identified with appetite.

I am more inclined to put my faith in a story I once heard about Leontius, son of Aglaion. On his way up from the Piraeus outside the north wall, he noticed the bodies of some criminals lying on the ground, with the executioner standing by them. He wanted to go and look at them, but at the same time he was disgusted and tried to turn away. He struggled for some time and covered his eyes, but at last the desire was too much for him. Opening his eyes wide, he ran up to the bodies and cried, "There you are, curse you; feast yourselves on this lovely sight!"

Yes, I have heard that story too.

The point of it surely is that anger is sometimes in conflict with appetite, as if they were two distinct principles. Do we not often find a man whose desires would force him to go against his reason, reviling himself and indignant with this part of his nature which is trying to put constraint on him? It is like a struggle between two factions, in which indignation takes the side of reason. But I believe you have never observed, in yourself or anyone else, indignation make common cause with appetite in behaviour which reason decides to be wrong.

No, I am sure I have not.

Again, take a man who feels he is in the wrong. The more generous his nature, the less can he be indignant at any suffering, such as hunger and cold, inflicted by the man he has injured. He recognizes such treatment as just, and, as I say, his spirit refuses to be roused against it.

That is true.

But now contrast one who thinks it is he that is being wronged. His spirit boils with resentment and sides with the right as he conceives it. Persevering all the more for the hunger and cold and other pains he suffers, it triumphs and will not give in until its gallant struggle has ended in success or death; or until the restraining voice of reason, like a shepherd calling off his dog, makes it relent.

An apt comparison, he said; and in fact it fits the relation of our Auxiliaries to the Rulers: they were to be like watch-dogs obeying the shepherds of the commonwealth.

Yes, you understand very well what I have in mind. But do you see how we have changed our view? A moment ago we were supposing this spirited element to be something of the nature of appetite; but now it appears that, when the soul is divided into factions, it is far more ready to be up in arms on the side of reason.

Quite true.

Is it, then, distinct from the rational

element or only a particular form of it, so that the soul will contain no more than two elements, reason and appetite? Or is the soul like the state, which had three orders to hold it together, traders, Auxiliaries, and counsellors? Does the spirited element make a third, the natural auxiliary of reason, when not corrupted by bad upbringing?

It must be a third.

Yes, I said, provided it can be shown to be distinct from reason, as we saw it was from appetite.

That is easily proved. You can see that much in children: they are full of passionate feelings from their very birth; but some, I should say, never become rational, and most of them only late in life.

And so, after a stormy passage, we have reached the land. We are fairly agreed that the same three elements exist alike in the state and in the individual soul.

That is so.

Does it not follow at once that state and individual will be wise or brave by virtue of the same element in each and in the same way? Both will possess in the same manner any quality that makes for excellence.

That must be true.

Then it applies to justice: we shall conclude that a man is just in the same way that a state was just. And we have surely not forgotten that justice in the state meant that each of the three orders in it was doing its own proper work. So we may henceforth bear in mind that each one of us likewise will be a just person, fulfilling his proper function, only if the several parts of our nature fulfil theirs. And it will be the business of reason to rule with wisdom and forethought on behalf of the entire soul; while the spirited element ought to act as its subordinate and ally. The two will be brought into accord, as we said earlier, by that combination of mental and bodily training which will tune up one string of the instrument and relax the other, nourishing the reasoning part on the study of noble literature and allaying the other's wildness by harmony and rhythm. When both have been thus nurtured and trained to know their own true functions, they must be set in command over the appetites, which form the greater part of each man's soul and are by nature insatiably covetous. They must keep watch lest this part, by battening on the pleasures that are called bodily, should grow so great and powerful that it will no longer keep to its own work, but will try to enslave the others and usurp a dominion to which it has no right, thus turning the whole of life upside down. At the same time, those two together will be the best of guardians for the entire soul and for the body against all enemies from without: the one will take counsel, while the other will do battle, following its ruler's commands and by its own bravery giving effect to the ruler's designs. And so we call an individual brave in virtue of this spirited part of his nature, when, in spite of pain or pleasure, it holds fast to the injunctions of reason about what he ought or ought not to be afraid of. And wise in virtue of that small part which rules and issues these injunctions, possessing as it does the knowledge of what is good for each of the three elements and for all of them in common. And, again, temperate by reason of the unanimity and concord of all three, when there is no internal conflict between the ruling element and its two subjects, but all are agreed that reason should be ruler.

Yes, that is an exact account of temperance whether in the state or in the individual.

Finally, a man will be just by observing the principle we have so often stated.

Necessarily.

And the reason for all this is that each part of his nature is exercising its proper function, of ruling or of being ruled.

Yes, exactly.

Are you satisfied, then, that justice is

the power which produces states or individuals of whom that is true, or must we look further?

There is no need; I am quite satisfied.

And so our dream has come true—I mean the inkling we had that, by some happy chance, we had lighted upon a rudimentary form of justice from the very moment when we set about founding our commonwealth. Our principle that the born shoemaker or carpenter had better stick to his trade turns out to have been an adumbration of justice; and that is why it has helped us. But in reality justice, though evidently analogous to this principle, is not a matter of external behaviour, but of the inward self and of attending to all that is, in the fullest sense, a man's proper concern. The just man does not allow the several elements in his soul to usurp one another's functions; he is indeed one who sets his house in order, by self-mastery and discipline coming to be at peace with himself, and bringing into tune those three parts, like the terms in the proportion of a musical scale, the highest and lowest notes and the mean between them, with all the intermediate intervals. Only when he has linked these parts together in well-tempered harmony and has made himself one man instead of many, will he be ready to go about whatever he may have to do, whether it be making money and satisfying bodily wants, or business transactions, or the affairs of state. In all these fields when he speaks of just and honourable conduct, he will mean the behaviour that helps to produce and to preserve this habit of mind; and by wisdom he will mean the knowledge which presides over such conduct. Any action which tends to break down this habit will be for him unjust; and the notions governing it he will call ignorance and folly.

That is perfectly true, Socrates.

Good, said I. I believe we should not be thought altogether mistaken, if we claimed to have discovered the just man and the just state, and wherein their justice consists.

Indeed we should not.

Shall we make that claim, then?

Yes, we will.

Book V

Can the Ideal State Exist?

But really, Socrates, Glaucon continued, if you are allowed to go on like this, I am afraid you will forget all about the question you thrust aside some time ago: whether a society so constituted can ever come into existence, and if so, how.

Well, said I, let me begin by reminding you that what brought us to this point was our inquiry into the nature of justice and injustice.

True; but what of that?

Merely this: suppose we do find out what justice is, are we going to demand that a man who is just shall have a character which exactly corresponds in every respect to the ideal of justice? Or shall we be satisfied if he comes as near to the ideal as possible and has in him a larger measure of that quality than the rest of the world?

That will satisfy me.

If so, when we set out to discover the essential nature of justice and injustice and what a perfectly just and a perfectly unjust man would be like, supposing them to exist, our purpose was to use them as ideal patterns: we were to observe the degree of happiness or unhappiness that each exhibited, and to draw the necessary inference that our own destiny would be like that of the one we most resembled. We did not set out to show that these ideals could exist in fact.

That is true.

Then suppose a painter had drawn an ideally beautiful figure complete to the last touch, would you think any the worse of him, if he could not show that a person as beautiful as that could exist?

No, I should not.

Well, we have been constructing in discourse the pattern of an ideal state. Is our theory any the worse, if we cannot prove it possible that a state so organized should be actually founded?

Surely not.

That, then, is the truth of the matter. But if, for your satisfaction, I am to do my best to show under what conditions our ideal would have the best chance of being realized, I must ask you once more to admit that the same principle applies here. Can theory ever be fully realized in practice? Is it not in the nature of things that action should come less close to truth than thought? People may not think so; but do you agree or not?

I do.

Then you must not insist upon my showing that this construction we have traced in thought could be reproduced in fact down to the last detail. You must admit that we shall have found a way to meet your demand for realization, if we can discover how a state might be constituted in the closest accordance with our description. Will not that content you? It would be enough for me.

And for me too.

Then our next attempt, it seems, must be to point out what defect in the working of existing states prevents them from being so organized, and what is the least change that would effect a transformation into this type of government—a single change if possible, or perhaps two; at any rate let us make the changes as few and insignificant as may be. There is one change which, as I believe we can show, would bring about this revolution—not a small change, certainly, nor an easy one, but possible.

What is it?

Unless either philosophers become kings in their countries or those who are now called kings and rulers come to be sufficiently inspired with a genuine desire for wisdom; unless, that is to say, political power and philosophy meet together, while the many natures who now go their several ways in the one or the other direction are forcibly debarred from doing so, there can be no rest from troubles, my dear Glaucon, for states, nor yet, as I believe, for all mankind; nor can this commonwealth which we have imagined ever till then see the light of day and grow to its full stature. This it was that I have so long hung back from saying; I knew what a paradox it would be, because it is hard to see that there is no other way of happiness either for the state or for the individual. Now we must, I think, define whom we mean by these lovers of wisdom who, we have dared to assert, ought to be our rulers. Once we have a clear view of their character, we shall be able to defend our position by pointing to some who are naturally fitted to combine philosophic study with political leadership, while the rest of the world should accept their guidance and let philosophy alone.

Yes, this is the moment for a definition.

Book VI
The Divided Line

First we must come to an understanding. Let me remind you of the distinction we drew earlier and have often drawn on other occasions, between the multiplicity of things that we call good or beautiful or whatever it may be and, on the other hand, Goodness itself or Beauty itself and so on. Corresponding to each of these sets of many things, we postulate a single Form or real essence, as we call it.

Further, the many things, we say, can be seen, but are not objects of rational thought; whereas the Forms are objects of thought, but invisible. You have these two orders of things clearly before your mind: the visible and the intelligible?

I have.

Now take a line divided into two unequal parts, one to represent the visible order, the other the intelligible; and divide each part again in the same proportion, symbolizing degrees of comparative clearness or obscurity. Then (A) one of the two sections in the visible world will stand for images. By images I mean first shadows, and then reflections in water or in close-grained, polished surfaces, and everything of that kind, if you understand. Let the second section (B) stand for the actual things of which the first are likenesses, the living creatures about us and all the works of nature or of human hands.

So be it.

Will you also take the proportion in which the visible world has been divided as corresponding to degrees of reality and truth, so that the likeness shall stand to the original in the same ratio as the sphere of appearances and belief to the sphere of knowledge?

Certainly.

Now consider how we are to divide the part which stands for the intelligible world. There are two sections. In the first (C) the mind uses as images those actual things which themselves had images in the visible world; and it is compelled to pursue its inquiry by starting from assumptions and travelling, not up to a principle, but down to a conclusion. In the second (D) the mind moves in the other direction, from an assumption up towards a principle which is not hypothetical; and it makes no use of the images employed in the other section, but only of Forms, and conducts its inquiry solely by their means.

I don't quite understand what you mean.

Then we will try again; what I have just said will help you to understand. (C) You know, of course, how students of subjects like geometry and arithmetic begin by postulating odd and even numbers, or the various figures and the three kinds of angle, and other such data in each subject. These data they take as known; and, having adopted them as assumptions, they do not feel called upon to give any account of them to themselves or to anyone else, but treat them as self-evident. Then, starting from these assumptions, they go on until they arrive, by a series of consistent steps, at all the conclusions they set out to investigate.

Yes, I know that.

You also know how they make use of visible figures and discourse about them, though what they really have in mind is the originals of which these figures are images: they are not reasoning, for instance, about this particular square and diagonal which they have drawn, but about *the* Square and *the* Diagonal; and so in all cases. The diagrams they draw and the models they make are actual things, which may have their shadows or images in water; but now they serve in their turn as images, while the student is seeking to behold those realities which only thought can apprehend.

True.

This, then, is the class of things that I spoke of as intelligible, but with two qualifications: first, that the mind, in studying them, is compelled to employ assumptions, and, because it cannot rise above these, does not travel upwards to a first principle; and second, that it uses as images those actual things which have images of their own in the section below them and which, in comparison with those shadows and reflections, are reputed to be more palpable and valued accordingly.

I understand: you mean the subject-matter of geometry and of the kindred arts.

(D) Then by the second section of the intelligible world you may understand me to mean all that unaided reasoning apprehends by the power of dialectic, when it treats its assumptions, not as first principles, but as *hypotheses* in the literal sense, things "laid down" like a flight of steps up which it may mount all the way to something that is not hypothetical, the first principle of all; and having grasped this, may turn back and, holding on to the consequences which depend upon it, descend at last to a conclusion, never making use of any sensible object, but only of Forms, moving through Forms from one to another, and ending with Forms.

I understand, he said, though not perfectly; for the procedure you describe sounds like an enormous undertaking. But I see that you mean to distinguish the field of intelligible reality studied by dialectic as having a greater certainty and truth than the subject-matter of the "arts," as they are called, which treat their assumptions as first principles. The students of these arts are, it is true, compelled to exercise thought in contemplating objects which the senses cannot perceive; but because they start from assumptions without going back to a first principle, you do not regard them as gaining true understanding about those objects, although the objects themselves, when connected with a first principle, are intelligible. And I think you would call the state of mind of the students of geometry and other such arts, not intelligence, but thinking, as being something between intelligence and mere acceptance of appearances.

You have understood me quite well enough, I replied. And now you may take, as corresponding to the four sections, these four states of mind: *intelligence* for the highest, *thinking* for the second, *belief* for the third, and for the last *imagining*. These you may arrange as the terms in a proportion, assigning to each a degree of clearness and certainty corresponding to the measure in which their objects possess truth and reality.

I understand and agree with you. I will arrange them as you say.

Book VIII
The Myth of the Cave

Next, said I, here is a parable to illustrate the degrees in which our nature may be enlightened or unenlightened. Imagine the condition of men living in a sort of cavernous chamber underground, with an entrance open to the light and a long passage all down the cave. Here they have been from childhood, chained by the leg and also by the neck, so that they cannot move and can see only what is in front of them, because the chains will not let them turn their heads. At some distance higher up is the light of a fire burning behind them; and between the prisoners and the fire is a track with a parapet built along it, like the screen at a puppet-show, which hides the performers while they show their puppets over the top. Now behind this parapet imagine persons carrying along various artificial objects, including figures of men and animals in wood or stone or other materials, which project above the parapet. Naturally, some of these persons will be talking, others silent.

It is a strange picture, he said, and a strange sort of prisoners.

Like ourselves, I replied; for in the first place prisoners so confined would have seen nothing of themselves or of one another, except the shadows thrown by the fire-light on the wall of the Cave facing them, would they?

Not if all their lives they had been prevented from moving their heads.

And they would have seen as little of the objects carried past.

Of course.

Now, if they could talk to one another, would they not suppose that their words referred only to those passing shadows which they saw?

Necessarily.

And suppose their prison had an echo from the wall facing them? When one of the people crossing behind them spoke, they could only suppose that the sound came from the shadow passing before their eyes.

No doubt.

In every way, then, such prisoners would recognize as reality nothing but the shadows of those artificial objects.

Inevitably.

Now consider what would happen if

their release from the chains and the healing of their unwisdom should come about in this way. Suppose one of them set free and forced suddenly to stand up, turn his head, and walk with eyes lifted to the light; all these movements would be painful, and he would be too dazzled to make out the objects whose shadows he had been used to see. What do you think he would say, if someone told him that what he had formerly seen was meaningless illusion, but now, being somewhat nearer to reality and turned towards more real objects, he was getting a truer view? Suppose further that he were shown the various objects being carried by and were made to say, in reply to questions, what each of them was. Would he not be perplexed and believe the objects now shown him to be not so real as what he formerly saw?

Yes, not nearly so real.

And if he were forced to look at the fire-light itself, would not his eyes ache, so that he would try to escape and turn back to the things which he could see distinctly, convinced that they really were clearer than these other objects now being shown to him?

Yes.

And suppose someone were to drag him away forcibly up the steep and rugged ascent and not let him go until he had hauled him out into the sunlight, would he not suffer pain and vexation at such treatment, and, when he had come out into the light, find his eyes so full of its radiance that he could not see a single one of the things that he was now told were real?

Certainly he would not see them all at once.

He would need, then, to grow accustomed before he could see things in that upper world. At first it would be easiest to make out shadows, and then the images of men and things reflected in water, and later on the things themselves. After that, it would be easier to watch the heavenly bodies and the sky itself by night, looking at the light of the moon and stars rather than the Sun and the Sun's light in the day-time. Last of all, he would be able to look at the Sun and contemplate its nature, not as it appears when reflected in water or any alien medium, but as it is in itself in its own domain.

And now he would begin to draw the conclusion that it is the Sun that produces the seasons and the course of the year and controls everything in the visible world, and moreover is in a way the cause of all that he and his companions used to see. Then if he called to mind his fellow prisoners and what passed for wisdom in his former dwelling-place, he would surely think himself happy in the change and be sorry for them. They may have had a practice of honouring and commending one another, with prizes for the man who had the keenest eye for the passing shadows and the best memory for the order in which they followed or accompanied one another, so that he could make a good guess as to which was going to come next. Would our released prisoner be likely to covet those prizes or to envy the men exalted to honour and power in the Cave? Would he not feel like Homer's Achilles, that he would far sooner "be on earth as a hired servant in the house of a landless man" or endure anything rather than go back to his old beliefs and live in the old way?

Yes, he would prefer any fate to such a life.

Now imagine what would happen if he went down again to take his former seat in the Cave. Coming suddenly out of the sunlight, his eyes would be filled with darkness. He might be required once more to deliver his opinion on those shadows, in competition with the prisoners who had never been released, while his eyesight was still dim and unsteady; and it might take some time to become used to the darkness. They would laugh at him and say that he had gone up only to come back with his sight ruined; it was worth no one's while even to attempt the ascent. If they could lay hands on the man who was trying to set them free and lead them up, they would kill him.

Yes, they would.

Every feature in this parable, my dear Glaucon, is meant to fit our earlier analysis. The prison dwelling corresponds to the region revealed to us through the sense of sight, and the fire-light within it to the power of the Sun. The ascent to see the things in the upper world you may take as standing for the upward journey of the soul into the region of the intelligible; then you will be in possession of what I surmise, since that is what you wish to be told. Heaven knows whether it is true; but this, at any rate, is how it appears to me. In the world of knowledge, the last thing to be perceived and only with great difficulty is the essential Form of Goodness. Once it is perceived, the conclusion must follow that, for all things, this is the cause of whatever is right and good; in the visible world it gives birth to light and to the lord of light, while it is itself sovereign in the intelligible world and the parent of intelligence and truth. Without having had a vision of this Form no one can act with wisdom, either in his own life or in matters of state.

*Philebus**

Pleasure and Wisdom

PERSONS OF THE DIALOGUE
SOCRATES, PROTARCHUS, PHILEBUS

SOC.: Observe, then, Protarchus, what the doctrine is which you are now to accept from Philebus, and what our doctrine is, against which you are to argue, if you do not agree with it. Shall we make a brief statement of each of them?

PRO.: By all means.

SOC.: Very well: Philebus says that to all living beings enjoyment and pleasure and gaiety and whatever accords with that sort of thing are a good; whereas our contention is that not these, but wisdom and thought and memory and their kindred, right opinion and true reasonings, are better and more excellent than pleasure for all who are capable of taking part in them, and that for all those now existing or to come who can partake of them they are the most advantageous of all things. Those are pretty nearly the two doctrines we maintain, are they not, Philebus?

PHI.: Yes, Socrates, exactly. . . .

SOC.: Then let us further agree to this:

PRO.: To what?

SOC.: That each of us will next try to prove clearly that it is a condition and disposition of the soul which can make life happy for all human beings. Is not that what we are going to do?

PRO.: It is.

SOC.: Then you will show that it is the condition of pleasure, and I that it is that of wisdom?

PRO.: True.

SOC.: What if some other life be found superior to these two? Then if that life is found to be more akin to pleasure, both of us are defeated, are we not, by the life which has firm possession of this superiority, but the life of pleasure is victor over the life of wisdom. . . .

Let us, then, look at the life of pleasure and the life of wisdom separately and consider and judge them.

PRO.: How do you mean?

SOC.: Let there be no wisdom in the life of pleasure and no pleasure in the life of wisdom. For if either of them is the good, it cannot have need of anything else, and if either be found to need anything, we can no longer regard it as our true good.

PRO.: No, of course not.

* Reprinted by permission of the publishers from the Loeb Classical Library edition translated by H. N. Fowler, *Plato: Philebus*, Cambridge, Mass.: Harvard University Press.

SOC.: Shall we then undertake to test them through you?

PRO.: By all means.

SOC.: Then answer.

PRO.: Ask.

SOC.: Would you, Protarchus, be willing to live your whole life in the enjoyment of the greatest pleasures?

PRO.: Of course I should.

SOC.: Would you think you needed anything further, if you were in complete possession of that enjoyment?

PRO.: Certainly not.

SOC.: But consider whether you would not have some need of wisdom and intelligence and power of calculating your wants and the like.

PRO.: Why should I? If I have enjoyment, I have everything.

SOC.: Then living thus you would enjoy the greatest pleasures all your life?

PRO.: Yes; why not?

SOC.: But if you did not possess mind or memory or knowledge or true opinion, in the first place, you would not know whether you were enjoying your pleasures or not. That must be true, since you are utterly devoid of intellect, must it not?

PRO.: Yes, it must.

SOC.: And likewise, if you had no memory you could not even remember that you ever did enjoy pleasure, and no recollection whatever of present pleasure could remain with you; if you had no true opinion you could not think you were enjoying pleasure at the time when you were enjoying it, and if you were without power of calculation you would not be able to calculate that you would enjoy it in the future; your life would not be that of a man, but of a mollusc or some other shell-fish like the oyster. Is that true, or can we imagine any other result?

PRO.: We certainly cannot.

SOC.: And can we choose such a life?

PRO.: This argument, Socrates, has made me utterly speechless for the present.

SOC.: Well, let us not give in yet. Let us take up the life of mind and scrutinize that in turn.

PRO.: What sort of life do you mean?

SOC.: I ask whether anyone would be willing to live possessing wisdom and mind and knowledge and perfect memory of all things, but having no share, great or small, in pleasure, or in pain, for that matter, but being utterly unaffected by everything of that sort.

PRO.: Neither of the two lives can ever appear desirable to me, Socrates, or, I think, to anyone else.

SOC.: How about the combined life, Protarchus, made up by a union of the two?

PRO.: You mean a union of pleasure with mind or wisdom?

SOC.: Yes, I mean a union of such elements.

PRO.: Every one will prefer this life to either of the two others—yes, every single person without exception.

SOC.: . . . Each of us might perhaps put forward a claim, one that mind is the cause of this combined life, the other that pleasure is the cause; and thus neither of these two would be the good, but one or the other of them might be regarded as the cause of the good. . . . Then let us try to be careful in making our beginning.

PRO.: What kind of a beginning do you mean?

SOC.: Let us divide all things that now exist in the universe into two, or rather, if you please, three classes.

PRO.: Please tell us on what principle you would divide them.

SOC.: Let us take some of the subjects of our present discussion.

PRO.: What subjects?

SOC.: We said that God revealed in the universe two elements, the infinite and the finite, did we not?

PRO.: Certainly.

SOC.: Let us, then, assume these as two of our classes, and a third, made by combining these two. But I cut a ridiculous figure, it seems when I attempt a division into classes and an enumeration.

PRO.: What do you mean, my friend?

SOC.: I think we need a fourth class besides.

PRO.: Tell us what it is.

SOC.: Note the cause of the combination of those two and assume that as the fourth in addition to the previous three. . . .

PRO.: Of course.

SOC.: First, then, let us take three of the four and, as we see that two of these are split up and scattered each one into many, let us try, by collecting each of them again into one, to learn how each of them was both one and many.

PRO.: If you could tell me more clearly about them, I might be able to follow you.

SOC.: I mean, then, that the two which I select are the same which I mentioned before, the infinite and the finite. I will try to show that the infinite is, in a certain sense, many; the finite can wait.

PRO.: Yes.

SOC.: Consider then. What I ask you to consider is difficult and debatable; but consider it all the same. In the first place, take hotter and colder and see whether you can conceive any limit of them, or whether the more and less which dwell in their very nature do not, so long as they continue to dwell therein, preclude the possibility of any end; for if there were any end of them, the more and less would themselves be ended.

PRO.: Very true.

SOC.: But always, we affirm, in the hotter and colder there is the more and less.

PRO.: Certainly.

SOC.: Always, then, the argument shows that these two have no end; and being endless, they are of course infinite.

PRO.: Most emphatically, Socrates. . . .

SOC.: To avoid waste of time in discussing all the individual examples, see if we can accept this as a designation of the infinite.

PRO.: Accept what?

SOC.: All things which appear to us to become more or less, or to admit of emphatic and gentle and excessive and the like, are to be put in the class of the infinite as their unity, in accordance with what we said a while ago, if you remember, that we ought to collect all things that are scattered and split up and impress upon them to the best of our ability the seal of some single nature.

PRO.: I remember.

SOC.: And the things which do not admit of more and less and the like, but do admit of all that is opposed to them—first equality and the equal, then the double, and anything which is a definite number or measure in relation to such a number or measure—all these might properly be assigned to the class of the finite. What do you say to that?

PRO.: Excellent, Socrates.

SOC.: We spoke just now of hotter and colder, did we not? Add to them drier and wetter, more and less, quicker and slower, greater and smaller, and all that we assigned before to the class which unites more and less.

PRO.: You mean the class of the infinite?

SOC.: Yes. Mix with that the second class, the offspring of the limit.

PRO.: What class do you mean?

SOC.: The class of the finite, which we ought just now to have reduced to unity, as we did that of the infinite. We have not done that, but perhaps we shall even now accomplish the same end, if these two are both unified and then the third class is revealed.

PRO.: What third class, and what do you mean?

SOC.: The class of the equal and double and everything which puts an end to the differences between opposites and makes them commensurable and harmonious by the introduction of number.

PRO.: I understand. I think you mean that by mixture of these elements certain results are produced in each instance.

SOC.: Yes, you are right.

PRO.: Go on.

SOC.: In cases of illness, does not the proper combination of these elements produce health?

PRO.: Certainly.

SOC.: And in the acute and the grave, the quick and the slow, which are unlimited, the addition of these same elements creates a limit and establishes the whole art of music in all its perfection, does it not?

PRO.: Excellent.

SOC.: And again in the case of cold and hot weather, the introduction of these elements removes the excess and indefiniteness and creates moderation and harmony.

PRO.: Assuredly.

SOC.: And thence arises the seasons and all the beauties of our world, by mixture of the infinite with the finite?

PRO.: Of course.

SOC.: There are countless other things which I pass over, such as health, beauty, and strength of the body and the many glorious beauties of the soul. For this goddess, my fair Philebus, beholding the violence and universal wickedness which prevailed, since there was no limit of pleasures or of indulgence in them, establish law and order, which contain a limit. You say she did harm; I say, on the contrary, she brought salvation. What do you think, Protarchus?

PRO.: What you say, Socrates, pleases me greatly. . . .

SOC.: The first [class], then, I call infinite, the second limit or finite, and the third something generated by a mixture of these two. And should I be making any mistake if I called the cause of this mixture and creation the fourth?

PRO.: Certainly not.

SOC.: Now what is the next step in our argument, and what was our purpose in coming to the point we have reached? Was it not this? We were trying to find out whether the second place belonged to pleasure or to wisdom, were we not?

PRO.: Yes, we were.

SOC.: And may we not, perhaps, now that we have finished with these points, be better able to come to a decision about the first and second places, which was the original subject of our discussion?

PRO.: Perhaps.

SOC.: Well then; we decided that the mixed life of pleasure and wisdom was the victor, did we not?

PRO.: Yes.

SOC.: And do we not see what kind of life this is, and to what class it belongs?

PRO.: Of course we do.

SOC.: We shall say that it belongs to the third class; for that class is not formed by mixture of any two things, but of all the things which belong to the infinite, bound by the finite; and therefore this victorious life would rightly be considered a part of this class.

. . . There is in the universe a plentiful infinite and a sufficient limit, and in addition a by no means feeble cause which orders and arranges years and seasons and months, and may most justly be called wisdom and mind. . . . Now please pay very close attention.

PRO.: I will. Say on.

SOC.: I say, then, that when, in us living beings, harmony is broken up, a disruption of nature and a generation of pain also take place at the same moment.

PRO.: What you say is very likely.

SOC.: But if harmony is recomposed and returns to its own nature, then I say that pleasure is generated, if I may speak in the fewest and briefest words about matters of the highest import.

PRO.: I think you are right, Socrates; but let us try to be more explicit.

SOC.: It is easiest to understand common and obvious examples, is it not?

PRO.: What examples?

SOC.: Is hunger a kind of breaking up and a pain?

PRO.: Yes.

SOC.: And eating, which is a filling up again, is a pleasure?

PRO.: Yes.

SOC.: Thirst again is a destruction and a pain, but the filling with moisture of that which was dried up is a pleasure. Then, too, the unnatural dissolution and disintegration we experience through heat are a pain, but the natural restoration and cooling are a pleasure.

PRO.: Certainly.

SOC.: And the unnatural hardening of the moisture in an animal through cold is pain; but the natural course of the elements returning to their place and separating is a pleasure. See, in short, if you think it is a reasonable statement that whenever in the class of living beings, which, as I said before, arises out of the natural union of the infinite and the finite, that union is destroyed, the destruction is pain, and the passage and return of all things to their own nature is pleasure.

PRO.: Let us accept that; for it seems to me to be true in its general lines.

SOC.: Then we may assume this as one kind of pain and pleasure arising severally under the conditions I have described?

PRO.: Let that be assumed.

SOC.: Now assume within the soul itself the anticipation of these conditions, the sweet and cheering hope of pleasant things to come, the fearful and woeful expectation of painful things to come.

PRO.: Yes, indeed, this is another kind of pleasure and pain, which belongs to the soul itself, apart from the body, and arises through expectation.

SOC.: You are right. I think that in these two kinds, both of which are, in my opinion, pure, and not formed by mixture of pain and pleasure, the truth about pleasure will be made manifest, whether the entire class is to be desired or such desirability is rather to be attributed to some other class among those we have mentioned, whereas pleasure and pain, like heat, cold, and other such things, are sometimes desirable and sometimes undesirable, because they are not good in themselves, though some of them sometimes admit on occasion the nature of the good.

PRO.: You are quite right in saying that we must track our quarry on this trail. . . .

SOC.: Shall we say that pleasures and pains are true or false, or that some are true and others not so?

PRO.: But, Socrates, how can there be false pleasures or pains?

SOC.: But, Protarchus, how can there be true and false fears, or true and false expectations, or true and false opinions?

PRO.: Opinions I would grant you, but not the rest. . . .

SOC.: Then let us analyse still more clearly what we were just now saying about pleasure and opinion. There is a faculty of having an opinion, is there not?

PRO.: Yes.

SOC.: And of feeling pleasure?

PRO.: Yes.

SOC.: And there is an object of opinion?

PRO.: Of course.

SOC.: And something by which that which feels pleasure is pleased?

PRO.: Certainly.

SOC.: And that which has opinion, whether right or wrong, never loses its function of really having opinion?

PRO.: Of course not.

SOC.: And that which feels pleasure, whether rightly or wrongly, will clearly never lose its function of really feeling pleasure?

PRO.: Yes, that is true, too.

SOC.: Then we must consider how it is that opinion is both true and false and pleasure only true, though the holding of opinion and the feeling of pleasure are equally real.

PRO.: Yes, so we must. . . .

SOC.: What if we see a pain or a pleasure making a mistake in respect of that by which the pain or pleasure is caused? Shall we give it the attribute of right or good or any of the words which denote excellence?

PRO.: That is impossible if the pleasure is mistaken.

SOC.: And certainly pleasure often seems to come to us in connexion with false, not true, opinion.

PRO.: Of course it does; and in such a case, Socrates, we call the opinion false; but nobody would ever call the actual pleasure false.

SOC.: You are an eager advocate of the case of pleasure just now, Protarchus.

PRO.: Oh no, I merely say what I hear.

SOC.: Is there no difference, my friend, between the pleasure which is connected with right opinion and knowledge and that which often comes to each of us with falsehood and ignorance?

PRO.: There is likely to be a great difference. . . .

SOC.: According to our present view, then, there are false pleasures in the souls of men, imitations or caricatures of the true pleasures; and pains likewise.

PRO.: There are.

SOC.: We saw, you remember, that he who had an opinion at all always really had an opinion, but it was sometimes not based upon realities, whether present, past, or future.

PRO.: Certainly.

SOC.: And this it was, I believe, which created false opinion and the holding of false opinions, was it not?

PRO.: Yes.

SOC.: Very well, must we not also grant that pleasure and pain stand in the same relation to realities?

PRO.: What do you mean?

SOC.: I mean that he who feels pleasure at all in any way or manner always really feels pleasure, but it is sometimes not based upon realities, whether present or past, and often, perhaps most frequently, upon things which will never even be realities in the future.

PRO.: This also, Socrates, must inevitably be the case.

SOC.: And the same may be said of fear and anger and all that sort of thing—that they are all sometimes false?

PRO.: Certainly.

SOC.: Well, can we say that opinions become bad or good except as they become false?

PRO.: No.

SOC.: And we understand, I believe, that pleasures also are not bad except by being false. . . .

PRO.: But what pleasures, Socrates, may rightly be considered true?

SOC.: Those arising from what are called beautiful colours, or from forms, most of those that arise from odours and sounds, in short all those the want of which is unfelt and painless, whereas the satisfaction furnished by them is felt by the senses, pleasant, and unmixed with pain.

PRO.: Once more, Socrates, what do you mean by this?

SOC.: My meaning is certainly not clear at the first glance, and I must try to make it so. For when I say beauty of form, I am trying to express, not what most people would understand by the words, such as the beauty of animals or of paintings, but I mean, says the argument, the straight line and the circle and the plane and solid figures formed from these by turning-lathes and rulers and patterns of angles; perhaps you understand. For I assert that the beauty of these is not relative, like that of other things, but they are always absolutely beautiful by nature and have peculiar pleasures in no way subject to comparison with the pleasures of scratching; and there are colours which possess beauty and pleasures of this character. . . . And further let us add to these the pleasures of knowledge, if they appear to us not to have hunger for knowledge or pangs of such hunger as their source.

PRO.: I agree to that. . . .

SOC.: And now that we have fairly well separated the pure pleasures and those which may be pretty correctly called impure, let us add the further statement that the intense pleasures are without measure and those of the opposite sort have measure; those which admit of greatness and intensity and are often or seldom great or intense we shall assign to the class of the infinite, which circulates more or less freely through the body and soul alike, and the others we shall assign to the class of the limited.

PRO.: Quite right, Socrates.

SOC.: There is still another question about them to be considered.

PRO.: What is it?

SOC.: What kind of thing is most closely related to truth? The pure and unadulterated, or the violent, the widespread, the great, the sufficient?

PRO.: What is your object, Socrates, in asking that question?

SOC.: My object, Protarchus, is to leave no gap in my test of pleasure and knowledge, if some part of each of them is pure and some part impure, in order that each of them may offer itself for judgement in a condition of purity, and thus make the judgement easier for you and me and all our audience.

PRO.: Quite right.

SOC.: Very well, let us adopt that point of view towards all the classes which we call pure. First let us select one of them and examine it.

PRO.: Which shall we select?

SOC.: Let us first, if agreeable to you, consider whiteness.

PRO.: By all means.

SOC.: How can we have purity in whiteness, and what purity? Is it the greatest and most widespread, or the most unmixed, that in which there is no trace of any other colour?

PRO.: Clearly it is the most unadulterated.

SOC.: Right. Shall we not, then, Protarchus, declare that this, and not the most numerous or the greatest, is both the truest and the most beautiful of all whitenesses?

PRO.: Quite right.

SOC.: Then we shall be perfectly right in saying that a little pure white is whiter and more beautiful and truer than a great deal of mixed white.

PRO.: Perfectly right.

SOC.: Well then, we shall have no need of many such examples in our discussion of pleasure; we see well enough from this one that any pleasure, however small or infrequent, if uncontaminated with pain, is pleasanter and more beautiful than a great or often repeated pleasure without purity.

PRO.: Most certainly; and the example is sufficient.

SOC.: Here is another point. Have we not often heard it said of pleasure that it is always a process or generation and that there is no state or existence of pleasure? There are some clever people who try to prove this theory to us, and we ought to be grateful to them.

PRO.: Well, what then? . . .

SOC.: Then pleasure, if it is a form of generation, would be generated for the sake of some form of being.

PRO.: Of course.

SOC.: Now surely that for the sake of which anything is generated is in the class of the good, and that which is generated for the sake of something else, my friend, must be placed in another class.

PRO.: Most undeniably.

SOC.: Then if pleasure is a form of generation, we shall be right in placing it in a class other than that of the good, shall we not?

PRO.: Quite right.

SOC.: Then, as I said when we began to discuss this point, we ought to be grateful to him who pointed out that there is only a generation, but no existence, of pleasure; for he is clearly making a laughing-stock of those who assert that pleasure is a good.

PRO.: Yes, most emphatically. . . .

SOC.: This discussion of ours is now, I think, no less than when we began it, seeking a counterpart of pleasure, and therefore it . . . is considering whether there is one kind of knowledge purer than another, as one pleasure is purer than another.

PRO.: That is very clear; it was evidently introduced with that object. . . .

SOC.: Fixed and pure and true and what we call unalloyed knowledge has to do with the things which are eternally the same without change or mixture, or with that which is most akin to them; and all other things are to be regarded as secondary and inferior.

PRO.: Very true.

SOC.: And of the names applied to such matters, it would be fairest to give the finest names to the finest things, would it not?

PRO.: That is reasonable.

SOC.: Are not mind, then, and wisdom the names which we should honour most?

PRO.: Yes.

SOC.: Then these names are applied most accurately and correctly to cases of contemplation of true being.

PRO.: Certainly.

SOC.: And these are precisely the names which I brought forward in the first place as parties to our suit.

PRO.: Yes, of course they are, Socrates.

SOC.: Very well. As to the mixture of wisdom and pleasure, if anyone were to say that we are like artisans, with the materials before us from which to create our work, the simile would be a good one.

PRO.: Certainly.

SOC.: And is it, then, our next task to try to make the mixture?

PRO.: Surely.

SOC.: Would it not be better first to repeat certain things and recall them to our minds?

PRO.: What things? . . .

SOC.: Philebus says that pleasure is the true goal of every living being and that all ought to aim at it, and that therefore this is also the good for all, and the two designations "good" and "pleasant" are properly and essentially one; Socrates, however, says that they are not one but two in fact as in name, that the good and the pleasant differ from one another in nature, and that wisdom's share in the good is greater than pleasure's. Is not and was not that what was said, Protarchus?

PRO.: Yes, certainly. . . .

SOC.: And if we made any mistake at that time, let anyone now take up the question again. Assuming that memory, wisdom, knowledge, and true opinion belong to the same class, let him ask whether anyone would wish to have or acquire anything whatsoever without these not to speak of pleasure, be it never so abundant or intense, if he could have no true opinion that he is pleased, no knowledge whatsoever of what he has felt, and not even the slightest memory of the feeling. And let him ask in the same way about wisdom, whether anyone would wish to have wisdom without any, even the slightest, pleasure rather than with some pleasures, or all pleasures without wisdom rather with some wisdom.

PRO.: That is impossible, Socrates; it is useless to ask the same question over and over again.

SOC.: Then the perfect, that which is to be desired by all and is altogether good, is neither of these?

PRO.: Certainly not.

SOC.: We must, then, gain a clear conception of the good, or at least an outline of it, that we may, as we said, know to what the second place is to be assigned.

PRO.: Quite right.

SOC.: And have we not found a road which leads to the good?

PRO.: What road?

SOC.: If you were looking for a particular man and first found out correctly where he lived, you would have made great progress towards finding him whom you sought.

PRO.: Yes, certainly.

SOC.: And just now we received an indication, as we did in the beginning, that we must seek the good, not in the unmixed, but in the mixed life.

PRO.: Certainly.

SOC.: Surely there is greater hope that the object of our search will be clearly present in the well mixed life than in the life which is not well mixed?

PRO.: Far greater.

SOC.: Let us make the mixture, Protarchus, with a prayer to the gods, to Dionysus or Hephaestus, or whoever he be who presides over the mixing.

PRO.: By all means.

SOC.: We are like wine-pourers, and beside us are fountains—that of pleasure may be likened to a fount of honey, and the sober, wineless fount of wisdom to one of pure, health-giving water—of which we must do our best to mix as well as possible.

PRO.: Certainly we must.

SOC.: Before we make the mixture, tell me: should we be most likely to succeed by mixing all pleasure with all wisdom?

PRO.: Perhaps.

SOC.: But that is not safe; and I think I can offer a plan by which we can make our mixture with less risk.

PRO.: What is it?

SOC.: We found, I believe, that one pleasure was greater than another and one art more exact than another?

PRO.: Certainly.

SOC.: And knowledge was of two kinds, one turning its eyes towards transitory things, the other towards things which neither come into being nor pass away, but are the same and immutable forever. Considering them with a view to truth, we judged that the latter was truer than the former.

PRO.: That is quite right.

SOC.: Then what if we first mix the truest sections of each and see whether, when mixed together, they are capable of giving us the most adorable life, or whether we still need something more and different?

PRO.: I think that is what we should do.

SOC.: . . . But what next? If there are any necessary pleasures, as there were kinds of knowledge, must we not mix them with the true?

PRO.: Of course; the necessary pleasures must certainly be added. . . .

SOC.: But another addition is surely necessary, without which nothing whatsoever can ever come into being.

PRO.: What is it?

SOC.: That in which there is no admixture of truth can never truly come into being or exist.

PRO.: No, of course not.

SOC.: No. But if anything is still wanting in our mixture, you and Philebus must speak of it. For to me it seems that our argument is now completed, as it were an incorporeal order which shall rule nobly a living body.

PRO.: And you may say, Socrates, that I am of the same opinion.

SOC.: And if we were to say that we are now in the vestibule of the good and of the dwelling of the good, should we not be speaking the truth after a fashion?

PRO.: I certainly think so.

SOC.: What element, then, of the mixture would appear to us to be the most precious and also the chief cause why such a state is beloved of all? When we have discovered this, we will then consider whether it is more closely attached and more akin to pleasure or to mind in the universe.

PRO.: Right; for that is most serviceable to us in forming our judgement.

SOC.: And it is quite easy to see the cause which makes any mixture whatsoever either of the highest value or of none at all.

PRO.: What do you mean?

SOC.: Why, everybody knows that.

PRO.: Knows what?

SOC.: That any compound, however made, which lacks measure and proportion, must necessarily destroy its components and first of all itself; for it is in truth no compound, but an uncompounded jumble, and is always a misfortune to those who possess it.

PRO.: Perfectly true.

SOC.: So now the power of the good has taken refuge in the nature of the beautiful; for measure and proportion are everywhere identified with beauty and virtue.

PRO.: Certainly.

SOC.: We said that truth also was mingled with them in the compound.

PRO.: Certainly.

SOC.: Then if we cannot catch the good with the aid of one idea, let us run it down with three—beauty, proportion, and truth, and let us say that these, considered as one, may more properly than all other components of the mixture be regarded as the cause, and that through the goodness of these the mixture itself has been made good.

PRO.: Quite right. . . .

SOC.: Let us, then, judge each of the three separately in its relation to pleasure and mind; for it is our duty to see to which of the two we shall assign each of them as more akin.

PRO.: You refer to beauty, truth, and measure?

SOC.: Yes. Take truth first, Protarchus; take it and look at the three—mind, truth, and pleasure; take plenty of time, and answer to yourself whether pleasure or mind is more akin to truth.

PRO.: Why take time? For the difference, to my mind, is great. For pleasure is the greatest of impostors, and the story goes that in the pleasures of love, which are said to be the greatest, perjury is even pardoned by the gods, as if the pleasures were like children, utterly devoid of all sense. But mind is either identical with truth or of all things most like it and truest.

SOC.: Next, then, consider measure in the same way, and see whether pleasure possesses more of it than wisdom, or wisdom than pleasure.

PRO.: That also is an easy thing to consider. For I think nothing in the world could be found more immoderate than pleasure and its transports, and nothing more in harmony with measure than mind and knowledge.

SOC.: However, go on and tell about the third. Has mind or pleasure the greater share in beauty?

PRO.: But Socrates, no one, either asleep or awake, ever saw or knew wisdom or mind to be or become unseemly at any time or in any way whatsoever.

SOC.: Right.

PRO.: But pleasures, and the greatest pleasures at that, when we see any one enjoying them and observe the ridiculous or utterly disgraceful element which accompanies them, fill us with a sense of shame; we put them out of sight and hide them, so far as possible; we confine everything of that sort to the night time, as unfit for the sight of day.

SOC.: Then you will proclaim everywhere, Protarchus, by messengers to the absent and by speech to those present, that pleasure is not the first of possessions, nor even the second, but first the eternal nature has chosen measure, moderation, fitness, and all which is to be considered similar to these.

PRO.: That appears to result from what has now been said.

SOC.: Second, then, comes proportion, beauty, perfection, sufficiency, and all that belongs to that class.

PRO.: Yes, so it appears.

SOC.: And if you count mind and wisdom as the third, you will, I prophesy, not wander far from the truth.

PRO.: That may be.

SOC.: And will you not put those properties fourth which we said belonged especially to the soul—sciences, arts, and true opinions they are called—and say that these come after the first three, and are fourth, since they are more akin than pleasure to the good?

PRO.: Perhaps.

SOC.: And fifth, those pleasures which we separated and classed as painless, which we called pure pleasures of the soul itself, those which accompany knowledge and, sometimes, perceptions?

PRO.: May be. . . .

SOC.: Yes; but let us hear what follows. For I, perceiving the truths which I have now been detailing, and annoyed by the theory held not only by Philebus but by many thousands of others, said that mind was a far better and more excellent thing for human life than pleasure.

PRO.: True.

SOC.: But suspecting that there were many other things to be considered, I said that if anything should be found better than these two, I should support mind against pleasure in the struggle for the second place, and even the second place would be lost by pleasure.

PRO.: Yes, that is what you said.

SOC.: And next it was most sufficiently proved that each of these two was insufficient.

PRO.: Very true.

SOC.: In this argument, then, both mind and pleasure were set aside; neither of them is the absolute good, since they are devoid of self-sufficiency, adequacy, and perfection?

PRO.: Quite right.

SOC.: And on the appearance of a third competitor, better than either of these, mind is now found to be ten thousand times more akin than pleasure to the victor.

PRO.: Certainly.

SOC.: Then, according to the judgement which has now been given by our discussion, the power of pleasure would be fifth.

PRO.: So it seems.

SOC.: But not first, even if all the cattle and horses and other beasts in the world, in their pursuit of enjoyment, so assert. Trusting in them, as augurs trust in birds, the many judge that pleasures are the greatest blessing in life, and they imagine that the lusts of beasts are better witnesses than are the aspirations and thoughts inspired by the philosophic muse.

ARISTOTLE

Aristotle (384–323 B.C.), the son of a physician at the court of Macedon, was born in the small city of Stagira in Thrace. As a youth he was probably trained in medicine by his father and in his eighteenth year was sent to Athens to complete his education. He entered Plato's Academy and remained twenty years, leaving at the death of Plato in 348. For better than a decade Aristotle was absent from Athens. During this period he traveled extensively, perhaps carrying on biological research. For three years he acted as the tutor to Alexander, the son of Philip of Macedon. In 335/4 he returned to Athens and established his own school, the Lyceum, which like the Academy offered instruction but also served as an institute for advanced study. Aristotle left Athens in 323, when the Athenians, then in revolt against Macedon, attacked him because of his association with the Macedonian court. Although Aristotle's philosophy is dependent in many ways upon Plato's, his own work shows the influence of his scientific interest. He applied his techniques of observation and careful analysis to an astonishingly wide range of subjects, including logic, physics, political science, astronomy, biology, psychology, and aesthetics. In the Nicomachean Ethics *he brings to bear the full power of his critical mind and the results of many other investigations upon the problems of human conduct.*

*Nicomachean Ethics**

Book I
The Good for Man

CHAPTER 1

Every art and every inquiry, and similarly every action and pursuit, is thought to aim at some good; and for this reason the good has rightly been declared to be that at which all things aim. But a certain difference is found among ends; some are activities, others are products apart from the activities that produce them. Where there are ends apart from the actions, it is the nature of the products to be better than the activities. Now, as there are many actions, arts, and sciences, their ends also are many; the end of the medical art is health, that of shipbuilding a vessel, that

* By permission. From W. D. Ross, *Aristotle: Ethica Nicomachea,* Clarendon Press, Oxford, 1915.

of strategy victory, that of economics, wealth. But where such arts fall under a single capacity—as bridle-making and the other arts concerned with the equipment of horses fall under the art of riding, and this and every military action under strategy, in the same way other arts fall under yet others—in all of these the ends of the master arts are to be preferred to all the subordinate ends; for it is for the sake of the former that the latter are pursued. It makes no difference whether the activities themselves are the ends of the actions, or something else apart from the activities, as in the case of the sciences just mentioned.

CHAPTER 2

If, then, there is some end of the things we do, which we desire for its own sake (everything else being desired for the sake of this), and if we do not choose everything for the sake of something else (for at that rate the process would go on to infinity, so that our desire would be empty and vain), clearly this must be the good and the chief good. Will not the knowledge of it, then, have a great influence on life? Shall we not, like archers who have a mark to aim at, be more likely to hit upon what is right? If so, we must try, in outline at least, to determine what it is, and of which of the sciences or capacities it is the object. It would seem to belong to the most authoritative art and that which is most truly the master art. And politics appears to be of this nature; for it is this that ordains which of the sciences should be studied in a state, and which each class of citizens should learn and up to what point they should learn them; and we see even the most highly esteemed of capacities to fall under this, e.g. strategy, economics, rhetoric; now, since politics uses the rest of the sciences, and since, again, it legislates as to what we are to do and what we are to abstain from, the end of this science must include those of the others, so that this end must be the good for man. For even if the end is the same for a single man and for a state, that of the state seems at all events something greater and more complete whether to attain or to preserve; though it is worth while to attain the end merely for one man, it is finer and more godlike to attain it for a nation or for city-states. These, then, are the ends at which our inquiry aims, since it is political science, in one sense of that term.

CHAPTER 3

Our discussion will be adequate if it has as much clearness as the subject-matter admits of, for precision is not to be sought for alike in all discussions, any more than in all the products of the crafts. Now fine and just actions, which political science investigates, admit of much variety and fluctuation of opinion, so that they may be thought to exist only by convention, and not by nature. And goods also give rise to a similar fluctuation because they bring harm to many people; for before now men have been undone by reason of their wealth, and others by reason of their courage. We must be content, then, in speaking of such subjects and with such premises to indicate the truth roughly and in outline, and in speaking about things which are only for the most part true and with premises of the same kind to reach conclusions that are no better. In the same spirit, therefore, should each type of statement be *received;* for it is the mark of an educated man to look for precision in each class of things just so far as the nature of the subject admits; it is evidently equally foolish to accept probable reasoning from a mathematician and to demand from a rhetorician scientific proofs. . . .

CHAPTER 4

Let us resume our inquiry and state, in view of the fact that all knowledge and every pursuit aims at some good, what it is that we say political science aims at and what is the highest of all goods achievable by action. Verbally there is very general agreement; for both the general run of men and people of superior refinement say that it is happiness, and identify living well and doing well with being happy; but with regard to what happiness is they differ, and the many do not give the same account as the wise. For the former think it is some plain and obvious thing, like pleasure, wealth, or honour; they differ, however, from one another—and often even the same man identifies it with different things, with health when he is ill, with wealth when he is poor; but, conscious of their ignorance, they admire those who proclaim some great ideal that is above their comprehension. Now some[1] thought that apart from these many goods there is another which is self-subsistent and causes the goodness of all these as well. To examine all the opinions that have been held were perhaps somewhat fruitless; enough to examine those that are most prevalent or that seem to be arguable.

Let us not fail to notice, however, that there is a difference between arguments from and those to the first principles. For Plato, too, was right in raising this question and asking, as he used to do, "are we on the way from or to the first principles?"[2] There is a difference, as there is in a race-course between the course from the judges to the turning-point and the way back. For, while we must begin with what is known, things are objects of knowledge in two senses—some to us, some without qualification. Presumably, then, we must begin with things known to *us*. Hence any one who is to listen intelligently to lectures about what is noble and just and, generally, about the subjects of political science must have been brought up in good habits. For the fact is the starting-point, and if this is sufficiently plain to him, he will not at the start need the reason as well; and the man who has been well brought up has or can easily get starting points. . . .

[1] The Platonic School; cf. ch. 6.

[2] Cf. *Rep.* 511 B.

CHAPTER 5

Let us, however, resume our discussion from the point at which we digressed. To judge from the lives that men lead, most men, and men of the most vulgar type, seem (not without some ground) to identify the good, or happiness, with pleasure; which is the reason why they love the life of enjoyment. For there are, we may say, three prominent types of life—that just mentioned, the political, and thirdly the contemplative life. Now the mass of mankind are evidently quite slavish in their tastes, preferring a life suitable to beasts, but they get some ground for their view from the fact that many of those in high places share the tastes of Sardanapallus. A consideration of the prominent types of life shows that people of superior refinement and of active disposition identify happiness with honour; for this is, roughly speaking, the end of the political life. But it seems too superficial to be what we are looking for, since it is thought to depend on those who bestow honour rather than on him who receives it, but the good we divine to be something proper to a man and not easily taken from him. Further, men seem to pursue honour in order that they may be assured of their goodness; at least it is by men of practical wisdom that they seek to be honoured, and among those who know them, and on the ground of their virtue; clearly, then, according to them, at any rate, virtue is better. And perhaps one might even suppose this to be, rather than honour, the end of the political life. But even this appears somewhat incomplete; for possession of virtue seems actually compatible with being asleep, or with lifelong inactivity, and, further, with the greatest sufferings and misfortunes; but a man who was living so no one would call happy, unless he were maintaining a thesis at all costs. But enough of this; for the subject has been sufficiently treated even in the current discussions. Third comes the contemplative life, which we shall consider later.[3]

The life of money-making is one undertaken under compulsion, and wealth is evidently not the good we are seeking; for it is merely useful and for the sake of something else. And so one might rather take the aforenamed objects to be ends; for they are loved for themselves. But it is evident that not even these are ends; yet many arguments have been thrown away in support of them. Let us leave this subject, then.

CHAPTER 6

We had perhaps better consider the universal good and discuss thoroughly what is meant by it, although such an inquiry is made an uphill one by the fact that the Forms have been introduced by friends of our own. Yet it would perhaps be thought to be better, indeed to be our duty, for the sake of maintaining the truth even to destroy what touches us closely, especially as we are philosophers or lovers of wisdom; for, while both are dear, piety requires us to honour truth above our friends.

The men who introduced this doctrine did not posit Ideas of classes within which they recognized priority and posteriority (which is the reason why they did not maintain the existence of an Idea embracing all numbers); but the term "good" is used both in the category of substance and in that of quality and in that of relation, and that which is *per se,* i.e. substance, is prior in nature to the relative (for the latter is like an offshoot and accident of being); so that there could not be a common Idea set over all these goods. Further, since "good" has as many senses as "being" (for it is predicated both in the category of substance, as of God and reason, and in quality, i.e. of the virtues, and in quantity, i.e. of that which is moderate, and in relation, i.e. of the useful, and in time, i.e. of the right opportunity, and in place, i.e. of the right locality and the like), clearly it cannot be something universally present in all cases and single; for then it could not have been predicated in all the categories but in one only. Further, since of the things answering to one Idea there is one science, there would have been one science of all the goods; but as it is there are many sciences even of the things that fall under one category, e.g. of opportunity, for opportunity in war is studied by strategics and in disease by medicine, and the moderate in food is studied by medicine and in exercise by the science of gymnastics. And one might ask the question, what in the world they *mean* by "a thing itself", if (as is the case) in "man himself" and in a particular man the account of man is one and the same. For in so far as they are man, they will in no respect differ; and if this is so, neither will "good itself" and particular goods, in so far as they are good. But again it will not be good any the more for being eternal, since that which lasts long is no whiter than that which perishes in a day. . . .

Clearly, then, goods must be spoken of in two ways, and some must be good in themselves, the others by reason of these. Let us separate, then, things good in themselves from things useful, and consider whether the former are called good by reference to a single Idea. What sort of goods would one call good in themselves? Is it those that are pursued even when isolated from others, such as intelligence, sight, and certain pleasures and honours? Certainly, if we pursue these also for the sake of something else, yet one would place them among things good in themselves. Or is nothing other than the Idea of good good in

[3] See Book X, Chapters 7 and 8.

itself? In that case the Form will be empty. But if the things we have named are also things good in themselves, the account of the good will have to appear as something identical in them all, as that of whiteness is identical in snow and in white lead. But of honour, wisdom, and pleasure, just in respect of their goodness, the accounts are distinct and diverse. The good, therefore, is not some common element answering to one Idea. . . .

CHAPTER 7

Let us again return to the good we are seeking, and ask what it can be. It seems different in different actions and arts; it is different in medicine, in strategy, and in the other arts likewise. What then is the good of each? Surely that for whose sake everything else is done. In medicine this is health, in strategy victory, in architecture a house, in any other sphere something else, and in every action and pursuit the end; for it is for the sake of this that all men do whatever else they do. Therefore, if there is an end for all that we do, this will be the good achievable by action, and if there are more than one, these will will be the goods achievable by action.

So the argument has by a different course reached the same point; but we must try to state this even more clearly. Since there are evidently more than one end, and we choose some of these (e.g. wealth, flutes, and in general instruments) for the sake of something else, clearly not all ends are final ends; but the chief good is evidently something final. Therefore, if there is only one final end, this will be what we are seeking, and if there are more than one, the most final of these will be what we are seeking. Now we call that which is in itself worthy of pursuit more final than that which is worthy of pursuit for the sake of something else, and that which is never desirable for the sake of something else more final than the things that are desirable both in themselves and for the sake of that other thing, and therefore we call final without qualification that which is always desirable in itself and never for the sake of something else.

Now such a thing happiness, above all else, is held to be; for this we choose always for itself and never for the sake of something else, but honour, pleasure, reason, and every virtue we choose indeed for themselves (for if nothing resulted from them we should still choose each of them), but we choose them also for the sake of happiness, judging that by means of them we shall be happy. Happiness, on the other hand, no one chooses for the sake of these, nor, in general, for anything other than itself.

From the point of view of self-sufficiency the same result seems to follow; for the final good is thought to be self-sufficient. Now by self-sufficient we do not mean that which is sufficient for a man by himself, for one who lives a solitary life, but also for parents, children, wife, and in general for his friends and fellow citizens, since man is born for citizenship. But some limit must be set to this; for if we extend our requirement to ancestors and descendants and friends' friends we are in for an infinite series. Let us examine this question, however, on another occasion;[4] the self-sufficient we now define as that which when isolated makes life desirable and lacking in nothing; and such we think happiness to be; and further we think it most desirable of all things, without being counted as one good thing among others—if it were so counted it would clearly be made more desirable by the addition of even the least of goods; for that which is added becomes an excess of goods, and of goods the greater is always more desirable. Happiness, then, is something final and self-sufficient, and is the end of action.

Presumably, however, to say that happiness is the chief good seems a plati-

[4] Book I, Chapters 10 and 11; Book IX, Chapter 10.

tude, and a clearer account of what it is is still desired. This might perhaps be given, if we could first ascertain the function of man. For just as for a flute-player, a sculptor, or any artist, and, in general, for all things that have a function or activity, the good and the "well" is thought to reside in the function, so would it seem to be for man, if he has a function. Have the carpenter, then, and the tanner certain functions or activities, and has man none? Is he born without a function? Or as eye, hand, foot, and in general each of the parts evidently has a function, may one lay it down that man similarly has a function apart from all these? What then can this be? Life seems to be common even to plants, but we are seeking what is peculiar to man. Let us exclude, therefore, the life of nutrition and growth. Next there would be a life of perception, but *it* also seems to be common even to the horse, the ox, and every animal. There remains, then, an active life of the element that has a rational principle; of this, one part has such a principle in the sense of being obedient to one, the other in the sense of possessing one and exercising thought. And, as "life of the rational element" also has two meanings, we must state that life in the sense of activity is what we mean; for this seems to be the more proper sense of the term. Now if the function of man is an activity of soul which follows or implies a rational principle, and if we say "a so-and-so" and "a good so-and-so" have a function which is the same in kind, e.g. a lyre-player and a good lyre-player, and so without qualification in all cases, eminence in respect of goodness being added to the name of the function (for the function of a lyre-player is to play the lyre, and that of a good lyre-player is to do so well): if this is the case [and we state the function of man to be a certain kind of life, and this to be an activity or actions of the soul implying a rational principle, and the function of a good man to be the good and noble performance of these, and if any action is well performed when it is performed in accordance with the appropriate excellence: if this is the case], human good turns out to be activity of soul in accordance with virtue, and if there are more than one virtue, in accordance with the best and most complete.

But we must add "in a complete life". For one swallow does not make a summer, nor does one day; and so too one day, or a short time, does not make a man blessed and happy. . . .

CHAPTER 8

[Yet] it needs the external goods as well; for it is impossible, or not easy, to do noble acts without the proper equipment. In many actions we use friends and riches and political power as instruments; and there are some things the lack of which takes the lustre from happiness, as good birth, goodly children, beauty; for the man who is very ugly in appearance or ill-born or solitary and childless is not very likely to be happy, and perhaps a man would be still less likely if he had thoroughly bad children or friends or had lost good children or friends by death. As we said, then, happiness seems to need this sort of prosperity in addition; for which reason some identify happiness with good fortune, though others identify it with virtue.

CHAPTER 9

For this reason also the question is asked, whether happiness is to be acquired by learning or by habituation or some other sort of training, or comes in virtue of some divine providence or again by chance. Now if there is *any* gift of the gods to men, it is reasonable that happiness should be god-given, and most surely god-given of all human things inasmuch as it is the best. But this question would perhaps be more appropriate to another inquiry; happiness seems, however, even if it is not god-sent but comes as a result of virtue and some process of learning or training, to be among the most god-like things; for that which is the prize and end of virtue seems to be the best thing in the world, and something godlike and blessed.

It will also on this view be very generally shared; for all who are not maimed as regards their potentiality for virtue may win it by a certain kind of study and care. But if it is better to be happy thus than by chance, it is reasonable that the facts should be so, since everything that depends on the action of nature is by nature as good as it can be, and similarly everything that depends on art or any rational cause, and especially if it depends on the best of all causes. To entrust to chance what is greatest and most noble would be a very defective arrangement.

The answer to the question we are asking is plain also from the definition of happiness; for it has been said to be a virtuous activity of soul, of a certain kind. . . .

It is natural, then, that we call neither ox nor horse nor any other of the animals happy; for none of them is capable of sharing in such activity. For this reason also a boy is not happy; for he is not yet capable of such acts, owing to his age; and boys who are called happy are being congratulated by reason of the hopes we have for them. For there is required, as we said, not only complete virtue but also a complete life, since many changes occur in life, and all manner of chances, and the most prosperous may fall into great misfortunes in old age, as is told of Priam in the Trojan Cycle; and one who has experienced such chances and has ended wretchedly no one calls happy. . . .

CHAPTER 13

Since happiness is an activity of soul in accordance with perfect virtue, we must consider the nature of virtue; for perhaps we shall thus see better the nature of happiness. . . . But clearly the virtue we must study is human virtue; for the good we were seeking was human good and the happiness human happiness. By human virtue we mean not that of the body but that of the soul; and happiness also we call an activity of soul. But if this is so, clearly the student of politics must know somehow the facts about soul, as the man who is to heal the eyes or the body as a whole must know about the eyes or the body; and all the more since politics is more prized and better than medicine; but even among doctors the best educated spend much labour on acquiring knowledge of the body. The student of politics, then, must study the soul, and must study it with these objects in view, and do so just to the extent which is sufficient for the questions we are discussing; for further precision is perhaps something more laborious than our purposes require.

Some things are said about it, adequately enough, even in the discussions outside our school, and we must use these; e.g. that one element in the soul is irrational and one has a rational principle. Whether these are separated as the parts of the body or of anything divisible are, or are distinct by definition but by nature inseparable, like convex and concave in the circumference of a circle, does not affect the present question.

Of the irrational element one division seems to be widely distributed, and vegetative in its nature, I mean that which causes nutrition and growth; for it is this kind of power of the soul that one must assign to all nurslings and to embryos, and this same power to full-grown creatures; this is more reasonable than to assign some different power to them. Now the excellence of this seems to be common to all species and not specifically human; for this part or faculty seems to function most in sleep, while goodness and badness are least manifest in sleep (whence comes the saying that the happy are no better off than the wretched for half their lives; and this happens naturally enough, since sleep is an inactivity of the soul in that respect in which it is called good or bad), unless perhaps to a small extent some of the movements actually penetrate to the soul, and in this respect the dreams of good men are better than those of ordinary people. Enough of this subject, however; let us leave the nutritive faculty alone, since it has by its nature no share in human excellence.

There seems to be also another irrational element in the soul—one which in a sense, however, shares in a rational principle. For we praise the rational principle of the continent man and of the incontinent, and the part of their soul that has such a principle, since it urges them aright and towards the best objects; but there is found in them also another element naturally opposed to the rational principle, which fights against and resists that principle. For exactly as paralysed limbs when we intend to move them to the right turn on the contrary to the left, so is it with the soul; the impulses of incontinent people move in contrary directions. But while in the body we see that which moves astray, in the soul we do not. No doubt, however, we must none the less suppose that in the soul too there is something contrary to the rational principle, resisting and opposing it. In what sense it is distinct from the other elements does not concern us. Now even this seems to have a share in a rational principle, as we said;[5] at any rate in the continent man it obeys the rational principle—and presumably in the temperate and grave man it is still more obedient; for in him it speaks, on all matters, with the same voice as the rational principle.

Therefore the irrational element also appears to be twofold. For the vegetative element in no way shares in a rational principle, but the appetitive, and in general the desiring element in a sense shares in it, in so far as it listens to and obeys it; this is the sense in which we speak of "taking account" of one's father or one's friends, not that in which we speak of "accounting" for a mathematical property. That the irrational element is in some sense persuaded by a rational principle is indicated also by the giving of advice and by all reproof and exhortation. And if this element also must be said to have a rational principle, that which has a rational principle (as well as that which has not) will be twofold, one subdivision having it in the strict sense and in itself, and the other having a tendency to obey as one does one's father.

Virtue too is distinguished into kinds in accordance with this difference; for we say that some of the virtues are intellectual and others moral, philosophic wisdom and understanding and practical wisdom being intellectual, liberality and temperance moral. For in speaking about a man's character we do not say that he is wise or has understanding but that he is good-tempered or temperate; yet we praise the wise man also with respect to his state of mind; and of states of mind we call those which merit praise virtues.

Book II
Moral Virtue

CHAPTER 1

Virtue, then, being of two kinds, intellectual and moral, intellectual virtue in the main owes both its birth and its growth to teaching (for which reason it requires experience and time), while moral virtue comes about as a result of habit, whence also its name *ethike* is one that is formed by a slight variation from the word *ethos* (habit). From this it is also plain that none of the moral virtues arises in us by nature;

[5] See above.

for nothing that exists by nature can form a habit contrary to its nature. For instance the stone which by nature moves downwards cannot be habituated to move upwards, not even if one tries to train it by throwing it up ten thousand times; nor can fire be habituated to move downwards, nor can anything else that by nature behaves in one way be trained to behave in another. Neither by nature, then, nor contrary to nature do the virtures arise in us; rather we are adapted by nature to receive them, and are made perfect by habit. . . .

The virtues we get by first exercising them, as also happens in the case of the arts as well. For the things we have to learn before we can do them, we learn by doing them, e.g. men become builders by building and lyre-players by playing the lyre; so too we become just by doing just acts, temperate by doing temperate acts, brave by doing brave acts.

This is confirmed by what happens in states; for legislators make the citizens good by forming habits in them, and this is the wish of every legislator, and those who do not effect it miss their mark, and it is in this that a good constitution differs from a bad one. . . .

It makes no small difference, then, whether we form habits of one kind or of another from our very youth; it makes a very great difference, or rather *all* the difference. . . .

CHAPTER 2

But not only are the sources and causes of their origination and growth the same as those of their destruction, but also the sphere of their actualization will be the same; for this is also true of the things which are more evident to sense, e.g. of strength; it is produced by taking much food and undergoing much exertion, and it is the strong man that will be most able to do these things. So too is it with the virtues; by abstaining from pleasures we become temperate, and it is when we have become so that we are most able to abstain from them; and similarly too in the case of courage; for by being habituated to despise things that are terrible and to stand our ground against them we become brave, and it is when we have become so that we shall be most able to stand our ground against them.

CHAPTER 3

We must take as a sign of states of character the pleasure or pain that ensues on acts; for the man who abstains from bodily pleasures and delights in this very fact is temperate, while the man who is annoyed at it is self-indulgent, and he who stands his ground against things that are terrible and delights in this or at least is not pained is brave, while the man who is pained is a coward. For moral excellence is concerned with pleasures and pains; it is on account of the pleasure that we do bad things, and on account of the pain that we abstain from noble ones. Hence we ought to have been brought up in a particular way from our very youth, as Plato says,[6] so as both to delight in and to be pained by the things that we ought; for this is the right education.

Again, if the virtues are concerned with actions and passions, and every passion and every action is accompanied by pleasure and pain, for this reason also virtue will be concerned with pleasures and pains. . . .

The following facts also may show us that virtue and vice are concerned with these same things. There being three objects of choice and three of avoidance, the noble, the advantageous, the pleasant, and their contraries, the base, the injurious, the painful, about all of these the good man tends to go right and the bad man to go wrong, and especially about pleasure; for

[6] *Laws*, 653A ff., *Rep.* 401E–402A.

this is common to the animals and also it accompanies all objects of choice; for even the noble and the advantageous appear pleasant.

Again, it has grown up with us all from our infancy; this is why it is difficult to rub off this passion, engrained as it is in our life. And we measure even our actions, some of us more and others less, by the rule of pleasure and pain. For this reason, then, . . . the whole concern both of virtue and of political science is with pleasures and pains; for the man who uses these well will be good, he who uses them badly bad.

That virtue, then, is concerned with pleasures and pains, and that by the acts from which it arises it is both increased and, if they are done differently, destroyed, and that the acts from which it arose are those in which it actualizes itself—let this be taken as said.

CHAPTER 4

The question might be asked, what we mean by saying[7] that we must become just by doing just acts, and temperate by doing temperate acts; for if men do just and temperate acts, they are already just and temperate, exactly as, if they do what is in accordance with the laws of grammar and music, they are grammarians and musicians.

Or is this not true even of the arts? It is possible to do something that is in accordance with the laws of grammar, either by chance or at the suggestion of another. A man will be a grammarian, then, only when he has both done something grammatical and done it grammatically; and this means doing it in accordance with the grammatical knowledge in himself.

Again, the case of the arts and that of the virtues are not similar; for the products of the arts have their goodness in themselves, so that it is enough that they should have a certain character, but if the acts that are in accordance with the virtues have themselves a certain character it does not follow that they are done justly or temperately. The agent also must be in a certain condition when he does them; in the first place he must have knowledge, secondly he must choose the acts, and choose them for their own sakes, and thirdly his action must proceed from a firm and unchangeable character. These are not reckoned in as conditions of the possession of the arts, except the bare knowledge; but as a condition of the possession of the virtues knowledge has little or no weight, while the other conditions count not for a little but for everything, i.e. the very conditions which result from often doing just and temperate acts.

Actions, then, are called just and temperate when they are such as the just or the temperate man would do; but it is not the man who does these that is just and temperate, but the man who also does them *as* just and temperate men do them. It is well said, then, that it is by doing just acts that the just man is produced, and by doing temperate acts the temperate man; without doing these no one would have even a prospect of becoming good.

But most people do not do these, but take refuge in theory and think they are being philosophers and will become good in this way, behaving somewhat like patients who listen attentively to their doctors, but do none of the things they are ordered to do. As the latter will not be made well in body by such a course of treatment, the former will not be made well in soul by such a course of philosophy.

CHAPTER 5

Next we must consider what virtue is. Since things that are found in the soul are of three kinds—passions, faculties,

[7] See Book II, Chapter 1, second, third, and fourth paragraphs.

states of character, virtue must be one of these. By passions I mean appetite, anger, fear, confidence, envy, joy, friendly feeling, hatred, longing, emulation, pity, and in general the feelings that are accompanied by pleasure or pain; by faculties the things in virtue of which we are said to be capable of feeling these, e.g. of becoming angry or being pained or feeling pity; by states of character the things in virtue of which we stand well or badly with reference to the passions, e.g. with reference to anger we stand badly if we feel it violently or too weakly, and well if we feel it moderately; and similarly with reference to the other passions.

Now neither the virtues nor the vices are *passions,* because we are not called good or bad on the ground of our passions, but are so called on the ground of our virtues and our vices, and because we are neither praised nor blamed for our passions (for the man who feels fear or anger is not praised, nor is the man who simply feels anger blamed, but the man who feels it in a certain way), but for our virtues and our vices we *are* praised or blamed.

Again, we feel anger and fear without choice, but the virtues are modes of choice or involve choice. Further, in respect of the passions we are said to be moved, but in respect of the virtues and the vices we are said not to be moved but to be disposed in a particular way.

For these reasons also they are not *faculties;* for we are neither called good nor bad, nor praised nor blamed, for the simple capacity of feeling the passions; again, we have the faculties by nature, but we are not made good or bad by nature; we have spoken of this before.[8]

If, then, the virtues are neither passions nor faculties, all that remains is that they should be *states of character.*

Thus we have stated what virtue is in respect of its genus.

[8] See Book II, Chapter 1, first two paragraphs.

CHAPTER 6

We must, however, not only describe virtue as a state of character, but also say what sort of state it is. We may remark, then, that every virtue or excellence both brings into good condition the thing of which it is the excellence and makes the work of that thing be done well; e.g. the excellence of the eye makes both the eye and its work good; for it is by the excellence of the eye that we see well. Similarly the excellence of the horse makes a horse both good in itself and good at running and at carrying its rider and at awaiting the attack of the enemy. Therefore, if this is true in every case, the virtue of man also will be the state of character which makes a man good and which makes him do his own work well.

How this is to happen . . . will be made plain also by the following consideration of the specific nature of virtue. In everything that is continuous and divisible it is possible to take more, less, or an equal amount, and that either in terms of the thing itself or relatively to us; and the equal is an intermediate between excess and defect. By the intermediate in the object I mean that which is equidistant from each of the extremes, which is one and the same for all men; by the intermediate relatively to us that which is neither too much nor too little—and this is not one, nor the same for all. For instance, if ten is many and two is few, six is the intermediate, taken in terms of the object; for it exceeds and is exceeded by an equal amount; this is intermediate according to arithmetical proportion. But the intermediate relatively to us is not to be taken so; if ten pounds are too much for a particular person to eat and two too little, it does not follow that the trainer will order six pounds; for this also is perhaps too much for the person who is to take it, or too little—too little for Milo,[9] too much for the beginner in athletic

[9] A famous wrestler.

exercises. The same is true of running and wrestling. Thus a master of any art avoids excess and defect, but seeks the intermediate and chooses this—the intermediate not in the object but relatively to us.

If it is thus, then, that every art does its work well—by looking to the intermediate and judging its works by this standard (so that we often say of good works of art that it is not possible either to take away or to add anything, implying that excess and defect destroy the goodness of works of art, while the mean preserves it; and good artists, as we say, look to this in their work), and if, further, virtue is more exact and better than any art, as nature also is, then virtue must have the quality of aiming at the intermediate. I mean moral virtue; for it is this that is concerned with passions and actions, and in these there is excess, defect, and the intermediate. For instance, both fear and confidence and appetite and anger and pity and in general pleasure and pain may be felt both too much and too little, and in both cases not well; but to feel them at the right times, with reference to the right objects, towards the right people, with the right motive, and in the right way, is what is both intermediate and best, and this is characteristic of virtue. Similarly with regard to actions also there is excess, defect, and the intermediate. Now virtue is concerned with passions and actions, in which excess is a form of failure, and so is defect, while the intermediate is praised and is a form of success; and being praised and being successful are both characteristics of virtue. Therefore virtue is a kind of mean, since, as we have seen, it aims at what is intermediate.

Again, it is possible to fail in many ways (for evil belongs to the class of the unlimited, as the Pythagoreans conjectured, and good to that of the limited), while to succeed is possible only in one way (for which reason also one is easy and the other difficult—to miss the mark easy, to hit it difficult); for these reasons also, then, excess and defect are characteristic of vice, and the mean of virtue;

> *For men are good in but one way, but bad in many.*

Virtue, then, is a state of character concerned with choice, lying in a mean, i.e. the mean relative to us, this being determined by a rational principle, and by that principle by which the man of practical wisdom would determine it. . . .

But not every action nor every passion admits of a mean; for some have names that already imply badness, e.g. spite, shamelessness, envy, and in the case of actions adultery, theft, murder; for all of these and suchlike things imply by their names that they are themselves bad, and not the excesses or deficiencies of them. It is not possible, then, ever to be right with regard to them; one must always be wrong. Nor does goodness or badness with regard to such things depend on committing adultery with the right woman, at the right time, and in the right way, but simply to do any of them is to go wrong. It would be equally absurd, then, to expect that in unjust, cowardly, and voluptuous action there should be a mean, an excess, and a deficiency; for at that rate there would be a mean of excess and of deficiency, an excess of excess, and a deficiency of deficiency. But as there is no excess and deficiency of temperance and courage because what is intermediate is in a sense an extreme, so too of the actions we have mentioned there is no mean nor any excess and deficiency, but however they are done they are wrong; for in general there is neither a mean of excess and deficiency, nor excess and deficiency of a mean.

CHAPTER 7

We must, however, not only make this general statement, but also apply it to the individual facts. For among statements about conduct those which are general apply more widely, but those which are particular are more genuine, since conduct has to do with individual cases, and our statements must harmonize with the facts in these cases. . . . With regard to feelings of fear and confidence courage is the mean; of the people who exceed, he who exceeds in fearlessness has no name (many of the states have no name), while the man who exceeds in confidence is rash, and he who exceeds in fear and falls short in confidence is a coward. With regard to pleasures and pains—not all of them, and not so much with regard to the pains—the mean is temperance, the excess self-indulgence. Persons deficient with regard to the pleasures are not often found; hence such persons also have received no name. But let us call them "insensible."

With regard to giving and taking of money the mean is liberality, the excess and the defect prodigality and meanness. In these actions people exceed and fall short in contrary ways; the prodigal exceeds in spending and falls short in taking, while the mean man exceeds in taking and falls short in spending. (At present we are giving a mere outline or summary, and are satisfied with this; later these states will be more exactly determined.[10]) With regard to money there are also other dispositions—a mean, magnificence (for the magnificent man differs from the liberal man; the former deals with large sums, the latter with small ones), and excess, tastelessness and vulgarity, and a deficiency, niggardliness; these differ from the states opposed to liberality, and the mode of their difference will be stated later.

With regard to honour and dishonour the mean is proper pride, the excess is known as a sort of "empty vanity", and the deficiency is undue humility; and as we said[11] liberality was related to magnificence, differing from it by dealing with small sums, so there is a state similarly related to proper pride, being concerned with small honours while that is concerned with great. For it is possible to desire honour as one ought, and more than one ought, and less, and the man who exceeds in his desires is called ambitious, the man who falls short unambitious, while the intermediate person has no name. The dispositions also are nameless, except that that of the ambitious man is called ambition. . . . Now let us speak of the remaining states according to the method which has been indicated.

With regard to anger also there is an excess, a deficiency, and a mean. Although they can scarcely be said to have names, yet since we call the intermediate person good-tempered let us call the mean good temper; of the persons at the extremes let the one who exceeds be called irascible, and his vice irascibility, and the man who falls short an inirascible sort of person, and the deficiency inirascibility.

There are also three other means, which have a certain likeness to one another, but differ from one another: for they are all concerned with intercourse in words and actions, but differ in that one is concerned with truth in this sphere, the other two with pleasantness; and of this one kind is exhibited in giving amusement, the other in all the circumstances of life. We must therefore speak of these too, that we may the better see that in all things the mean is praiseworthy, and the extremes neither praiseworthy, nor right, but worthy of blame. Now most of these states also have no names, but we must try, as in the other cases, to invent names ourselves so that we may be clear and easy to follow. With regard to truth, then, the intermediate is a truthful sort of person and the mean may be called truthfulness, while the pretence

[10] See Book IV, Chapter 1 (not included in this selection).

[11] See preceding paragraph.

which exaggerates is boastfulness and the person characterized by it a boaster, and that which understates is mock modesty and the person characterized by it mock-modest. With regard to pleasantness in the giving of amusement the intermediate person is ready-witted and the disposition ready wit, the excess is buffoonery and the person characterized by it a buffoon, while the man who falls short is a sort of boor and his state is boorishness. With regard to the remaining kind of pleasantness, that which is exhibited in life in general, the man who is pleasant in the right way is friendly and the mean is friendliness, while the man who exceeds is an obsequious person if he has no end in view, a flatterer if he is aiming at his own advantage, and the man who falls short and is unpleasant in all circumstances is a quarrelsome and surly sort of person.

There are also means in the passions and concerned with the passions; since shame is not a virtue, and yet praise is extended to the modest man. For even in these matters one man is said to be intermediate, and another to exceed, as for instance the bashful man who is ashamed of everything; while he who falls short or is not ashamed of anything at all is shameless, and the intermediate person is modest. Righteous indignation is a mean between envy and spite, and these states are concerned with the pain and pleasures that are felt at the fortunes of our neighbours; the man who is characterized by righteous indignation is pained at undeserved good fortune, the envious man, going beyond him, is pained at all good fortune, and the spiteful man falls so far short of being pained that he even rejoices. . . .

CHAPTER 9

That moral virtue is a mean, then, and in what sense it is so, and that it is a mean between two vices, the one involving excess, the other deficiency, and that it is such because its character is to aim at what is intermediate in passions and in actions, has been sufficiently stated. Hence also it is no easy task to be good. For in everything it is no easy task to find the middle, e.g. to find the middle of a circle is not for every one but for him who knows; so, too, any one can get angry—that is easy—or give or spend money; but to do this to the right person, to the right extent, at the right time, with the right motive, and in the right way, *that* is not for every one, nor is it easy; wherefore goodness is both rare and laudable and noble. . . .

But we must consider the things towards which we ourselves also are easily carried away; for some of us tend to one thing, some to another; and this will be recognizable from the pleasure and the pain we feel. We must drag ourselves away to the contrary extreme; for we shall get into the intermediate state by drawing well away from error, as people do in straightening sticks that are bent. . . .

But this is no doubt difficult, and especially in individual cases; for it is not easy to determine both how and with whom and on what provocation and how long one should be angry; for we too sometimes praise those who fall short and call them good-tempered, but sometimes we praise those who get angry and call them manly. The man, however, who deviates little from goodness is not blamed, whether he do so in the direction of the more or of the less, but only the man who deviates more widely; for *he* does not fail to be noticed. But up to what point and to what extent a man must deviate before he becomes blameworthy it is not easy to determine by reasoning, any more than anything else that is perceived by the senses; such things depend on particular facts, and the decision rests with perception. So much, then, is plain, that the intermediate state is in all things to be praised, but that we must incline sometimes towards the excess, sometimes towards the deficiency; for so shall we most easily hit the mean and what is right.

Book III
Voluntary Action and Responsibility

CHAPTER 1

Since virtue is concerned with passions and actions, and on voluntary passions and actions praise and blame are bestowed, on those that are involuntary pardon, and sometimes also pity, to distinguish the voluntary and the involuntary is presumably necessary for those who are studying the nature of virtue, and useful also for legislators with a view to the assigning both of honours and of punishments.

Those things, then, are thought involuntary, which take place under compulsion or owing to ignorance; and that is compulsory of which the moving principle is outside, being a principle in which nothing is contributed by the person who is acting or is feeling the passion, e.g. if he were to be carried somewhere by a wind, or by men who had him in their power.

But with regard to the things that are done from fear of greater evils or for some noble object (e.g. if a tyrant were to order one to do something base, having one's parents and children in his power, and if one did the action they were to be saved, but otherwise would be put to death), it may be debated whether such actions are involuntary or voluntary. Something of the sort happens also with regard to the throwing of goods overboard in a storm; for in the abstract no one throws goods away voluntarily, but on condition of its securing the safety of himself and his crew any sensible man does so. Such actions, then, are mixed, but are more like voluntary actions; for they are worthy of choice at the time when they are done, and the end of an action is relative to the occasion. Both the terms, then, "voluntary" and "involuntary", must be used with reference to the moment of action. Now the man acts voluntarily; for the principle that moves the instrumental parts of the body in such actions is in him, and the things of which the moving principle is in a man himself are in his power to do or not to do. Such actions, therefore, are voluntary, but in the abstract perhaps involuntary; for no one would choose any such act in itself.

For such actions men are sometimes even praised, when they endure something base or painful in return for great and noble objects gained; in the opposite case they are blamed, since to endure the greatest indignities for no noble end or for a trifling end is the mark of an inferior person. On some actions praise indeed is not bestowed, but pardon is, when one does what he ought not under pressure which overstrains human nature and which no one could withstand. But some acts, perhaps, we cannot be forced to do, but ought rather to face death after the most fearful sufferings; for the things that "forced" Euripides' Alcmaeon to slay his mother seem absurd. It is difficult sometimes to determine what should be chosen at what cost, and what should be endured in return for what gain, and yet more difficult to abide by our decisions; for as a rule what is expected is painful, and what we are forced to do is base, whence praise and blame are bestowed on those who have been compelled or have not.

What sort of acts, then, should be called compulsory? We answer that without qualification actions are so when the cause is in the external circumstances and the agent contributes nothing. But the things that in themselves are involuntary, but now and in return for these gains are worthy of choice, and whose moving principle is in the agent, are in themselves involuntary, but now and in return for these gains voluntary. They are more like voluntary acts; for actions are in the class of particulars, and the particular acts here are voluntary. What sort of things are to be chosen, and in return for what, it is not easy to state; for there are many differences in the particular cases.

But if someone were to say that pleasant and noble objects have a compelling power, forcing us from without, all acts would be for him compulsory; for it is for these objects that all men do everything they do. And those who act under compulsion and unwillingly act with pain, but those who do acts for their pleasantness and nobility do them with pleasure; it is absurd to make external circumstances responsible, and not oneself, as being easily caught by such attractions, and to make oneself responsible for noble acts but the pleasant objects responsible for base acts. The compulsory, then, seems to be that whose moving principle is outside, the person compelled contributing nothing.

Everything that is done by reason of ignorance is *not* voluntary; it is only what produces pain and repentance that is *involuntary*. For the man who has done something owing to ignorance, and feels not the least vexation at his action, has not acted voluntarily, since he did not know what he was doing, nor yet involuntarily, since he is not pained. Of people, then, who act by reason of ignorance he who repents is thought an involuntary agent, and the man who does not repent may, since he is different, be called a not voluntary agent; for, since he differs from the other, it is better that he should have a name of his own.

Acting by reason of ignorance seems also to be different from acting *in* ignorance; for the man who is drunk or in a rage is thought to act as a result not of ignorance but of one of the causes mentioned, yet not knowingly but in ignorance.

Now every wicked man is ignorant of what he ought to do and what he ought to abstain from, and it is by reason of error of this kind that men become unjust and in general bad; but the term "involuntary" tends to be used not if a man is ignorant of what is to his advantage—for it is not mistaken purpose that causes involuntary action (it leads rather to wickedness), nor ignorance of the universal (for *that* men are *blamed*), but ignorance of particulars, i.e. of the circumstances of the action and the objects with which it is concerned. For it is on these that both pity and pardon depend, since the person who is ignorant of any of these acts involuntarily.

Perhaps it is just as well, therefore, to determine their nature and number. A man may be ignorant, then, of who he is, what he is doing, what or whom he is acting on, and sometimes also what (e.g. what instrument) he is doing it with, and to what end (e.g. he may think his act will conduce to some one's safety), and how he is doing it (e.g. whether gently or violently). Now of all of these no one could be ignorant unless he were mad, and evidently also he could not be ignorant of the agent; for how could he not know himself? But of what he is doing a man might be ignorant, as for instance people say "it slipped out of their mouths as they were speaking", or "they did not know it was a secret", as Aeschylus said of the mysteries, or a man might say he "let it go off when he merely wanted to show its working", as the man did with the catapult. Again, one might think one's son was an enemy, as Merope did, or that a pointed spear had a button on it, or that a stone was pumice-stone; or one might give a man a draught to save him, and really kill him; or one might want to touch a man, as people do in sparring, and really wound him. The ignorance may relate, then, to any of these things, i.e. of the circumstances of the action, and the man who was ignorant of any of these is thought to have acted involuntarily, and especially if he was ignorant on the most important points; and these are thought to be the circumstances of the action and its end. Further, the doing of an act that is called involuntary in virtue of ignorance of this sort must be painful and involve repentance.

Since that which is done under compulsion or by reason of ignorance is involuntary, the voluntary would seem to be that of which the moving principle is in the agent himself, he being aware of the particular circumstances of the action. Presumably acts done by reason of anger or appetite are not rightly called involuntary.[12] For in the first place, on that showing none of the other animals will act voluntarily, nor will children; and secondly, is it meant that we do not do voluntarily *any* of the acts that are due to appetite or anger, or that we do the noble acts voluntarily and the base acts involuntarily? Is not this absurd, when one and the same thing is the cause? But it would surely be odd to describe as involuntary the things one ought to desire; and we ought both to be angry at certain things and to have an appetite for certain things, e.g. for health and for learning. Also what is involuntary is thought to be painful, but what is in accordance with appetite is thought to be pleasant. Again, what is the difference in respect of involuntariness between errors committed upon calculation and those committed in anger? Both are to be avoided, but the irrational passions are thought not less human than reason is, and therefore also the actions which proceed from anger or appetite are the man's actions. It would be odd, then, to treat them as involuntary.

CHAPTER 2

Both the voluntary and the involuntary having been delimited, we must next discuss choice; for it is thought to be most closely bound up with virtue and to discriminate characters better than actions do.

Choice, then, seems to be voluntary, but not the same thing as the voluntary; the latter extends more widely. For both children and the lower animals share in voluntary action, but not in choice, and acts done on the spur of the moment we describe as voluntary, but not as chosen. . . .

What, then, or what kind of thing is [choice]? . . . It seems to be voluntary, but not all that is voluntary to be an object of choice. Is it, then, what has been decided on by previous deliberation?

At any rate choice involves a rational principle and thought. Even the name seems to suggest that it is what is chosen before other things.

CHAPTER 3

Do we deliberate about everything, and is everything a possible subject of deliberation, or is deliberation impossible about some things? We ought presumably to call not what a fool or a madman would deliberate about, but what a sensible man would deliberate about, a subject of deliberation. Now about eternal things no one deliberates, e.g. about the material universe or the incommensurability of the diagonal and the side of a square. But no more do we deliberate about the things that involve movement but always happen in the same way, whether of necessity or by nature or from any other cause, e.g. the solstices and the risings of the stars; nor about things that happen now in one way, now in another, e.g. droughts and rains; nor about chance events, like the finding of treasure. But we do not deliberate even about all human affairs; for instance, no Spartan deliberates about the best constitution for the Scythians. For none of these things can be brought about by our own efforts. . . .

Now every class of men deliberates about the things that can be done by their own efforts. And in the case of exact and self-contained sciences there is no deliberation, e.g. about the letters of the alphabet (for we have no doubt how they should be written); but the things that are brought

[12] A reference to Pl. *Laws* 863Bff., where anger and appetite are coupled with ignorance as sources of wrong action.

about by our own efforts, but not always in the same way, are the things about which we deliberate, e.g. questions of medical treatment or of money-making. And we do so more in the case of the art of navigation than in that of gymnastics, inasmuch as it has been less exactly worked out, and again about other things in the same ratio, and more also in the case of the arts than in that of the sciences; for we have more doubt about the former. Deliberation is concerned with things that happen in a certain way for the most part, but in which the event is obscure, and with things in which it is indeterminate. We call in others to aid us in deliberation on important questions, distrusting ourselves as not being equal to deciding.

We deliberate not about ends but about means. For a doctor does not deliberate whether he shall heal, nor an orator whether he shall persuade, nor a statesman whether he shall produce law and order, nor does any one else deliberate about his end. They assume the end and consider how and by what means it is to be attained; and if it seems to be produced by several means they consider by which it is most easily and best produced, while if it is achieved by one only they consider how it will be achieved by this and by what means *this* will be achieved, till they come to the first cause, which in the order of discovery is last. . . . And if we come on an impossibility, we give up the search, e.g. if we need money and this cannot be got; but if a thing appears possible we try to do it. By "possible" things I mean things that might be brought about by our own efforts, and these in a sense include things that can be brought about by the efforts of our friends, since the moving principle is in ourselves. The subject of investigation is sometimes the instruments, sometimes the use of them; and similarly in the other cases—sometimes the means, sometimes the mode of using it or the means of bringing it about. It seems, then, as has been said, that man is a moving principle of actions; now deliberation is about the things to be done by the agent himself, and actions are for the sake of things other than themselves. For the end cannot be a subject of deliberation, but only the means; nor indeed can the particular facts be a subject of it, as whether this is bread or has been baked as it should; for these are matters of perception. If we are to be always deliberating, we shall have to go on to infinity.

The same thing is deliberated upon and is chosen, except that the object of choice is already determinate, since it is that which has been decided upon as a result of deliberation that is the object of choice. For every one ceases to inquire how he is to act when he has brought the moving principle back to himself and to the ruling part of himself; for this is what chooses. . . . The object of choice being one of the things in our own power which is desired after deliberation, choice will be deliberate desire of things in our own power; for when we have decided as a result of deliberation, we desire in accordance with our deliberation.

We may take it, then, that we have described choice in outline, and stated the nature of its objects and the fact that it is concerned with means. . . .

CHAPTER 5

The end, then, being what we wish for, the means what we deliberate about and choose, actions concerning means must be according to choice and voluntary. Now the exercise of the virtues is concerned with means. Therefore virtue also is in our own power, and so too vice. For where it is in our power to act it is also in our power not to act, and *vice versa;* so that, if to act, where this is noble, is in our power, not to act, which will be base, will also be in our power, and if not to act, where this is noble, is in our power, to act, which will be base, will also be in our power. Now if it is in our power to do noble or base acts, and likewise in our power not to do them, and this was what being good or bad meant, then it is in our power to be virtuous or vicious.

The saying that "no one is voluntarily wicked nor involuntarily happy" seems to be partly false and partly true; for no one is involuntarily happy, but wickedness *is* voluntary. . . .

If, then, as is asserted, the virtues are voluntary (for we are ourselves somehow partly responsible for our states of character, and it is by being persons of a certain kind that we assume the end to be so and so), the vices also will be voluntary; for the same is true of them.

With regard to the virtues in *general* we have stated their genus in outline, viz. that they are means and that they are states of character, and that they tend, and by their own nature, to the doing of the acts by which they are produced, and that they are in our power and voluntary, and act as the right rule prescribes. But actions and states of character are not voluntary in the same way; for we are masters of our actions from the beginning right to the end, if we know the particular facts, but though we control the beginning of our states of character the gradual progress is not obvious, any more than it is in illnesses; because it was in our power, however, to act in this way or not in this way, therefore the states are voluntary. . . .

Book VI
Intellectual Virtue

CHAPTER 1

We divided the virtues of the soul and said that some are virtues of character and others of intellect. Now we have discussed in detail the moral virtues, with regard to the others let us express our view as follows, beginning with some remarks about the soul. We said before that there are two parts of the soul—that which grasps a rule or rational principle, and the irrational; let us now draw a similar distinction within the part which grasps a rational principle. And let it be assumed that there are two parts which grasp a rational principle—one by which we contemplate the kind of things whose originative causes are invariable, and one by which we contemplate variable things; for where objects differ in kind the part of the soul answering to each of the two is different in kind, since it is in virtue of a certain likeness and kinship with their objects that they have the knowledge they have. Let one of these parts be called the scientific and the other the calculative; for to deliberate and to calculate are the same thing, but no one deliberates about the invariable. Therefore the calculative is one part of the faculty which grasps a rational principle. We must, then, learn what is the best state of each of these two parts; for this is the virtue of each.

CHAPTER 2

The virtue of a thing is relative to its proper work. Now there are three things in the soul which control action and truth—sensation, reason, desire.

Of these sensation originates no action; this is plain from the fact that the lower animals have sensation but no share in action.

What affirmation and negation are in thinking, pursuit and avoidance are in desire; so that since moral virtue is a state of character concerned with choice, and choice is deliberate desire, therefore both the reasoning must be true and the desire right, if the choice is to be good, and the latter must pursue just what the former asserts. Now this kind of intellect and of truth is practical; of the intellect which is contemplative, not practical nor productive, the good and the bad state are truth and falsity respectively (for this is the work of everything intellectual); while of the part which is practical and intellectual the good state is truth in agreement with right desire.

The origin of action—its efficient, not its final cause—is choice, and that of choice is desire and reasoning with a view to an end. This is why choice cannot exist either without reason and intellect or without a moral state; for good action and its opposite cannot exist without a combination of intellect and character. Intellect itself, however, moves nothing, but only the intellect which aims at an end and is practical; for this rules the productive intellect as well, since every one who makes makes for an end, and that which is made is not an end in the unqualified sense (but only an end in a particular relation, and the end of a particular operation)—only that which is *done* is that; for good action is an end, and desire aims at this. Hence choice is either desiderative reason or ratiocinative desire, and such an origin of action is a man. (It is to be noted that nothing that is past is an object of choice, e.g. no one chooses to have sacked Troy; for no one *deliberates* about the past, but about what is future and capable of being otherwise, while what is past is not capable of not having taken place; hence Agathon is right in saying

> *For this alone is lacking even to God,*
> *To make undone things that have once*
> *been done.*

The work of both the intellectual parts, then, is truth. Therefore the states that are most strictly those in respect of which each of these parts will reach truth are the virtues of the two parts.

CHAPTER 3

Let us begin, then, from the beginning, and discuss these states once more. Let it be assumed that the states by virtue of which the soul possesses truth by way of affirmation or denial are five in number, i.e. art, scientific knowledge, practical wisdom, philosophic wisdom, intuitive reason; we do not include judgement and opinion because in these we may be mistaken.

Now what *scientific knowledge* is, if we are to speak exactly and not follow mere similarities, is plain from what follows. We all suppose that what we know is not even capable of being otherwise; of things capable of being otherwise we do not know, when they have passed outside our observation, whether they exist or not. Therefore the object of scientific knowledge is of necessity. Therefore it is eternal; for things that are of necessity in the unqualified sense are all eternal; and things that are eternal are ungenerated and imperishable. . . .

CHAPTER 4

. . . All art is concerned with coming into being, i.e. with contriving and considering how something may come into being which is capable of either being or not being, and whose origin is in the maker and not in the thing made; for art is concerned neither with things that are, or come into being, by necessity, nor with things that do so in accordance with nature (since these have their origin in themselves). Making and acting being different, art must be a matter of making, not of acting.

CHAPTER 5

Regarding *practical wisdom* we shall get at the truth by considering who are the persons we credit with it. Now it is thought to be the mark of a man of practical wisdom to be able to deliberate well about what is good and expedient for himself, not in some particular respect, e.g. about what sorts of thing conduce to health or to strength, but about what sorts of thing conduce to the good life in general. This is shown by the fact that we credit men with practical wisdom in some particular respect when they have calculated well with a view to some good end which is one of those that are not the object of any art. It follows that in the general sense also the man who is capable of deliberating has practical wisdom. Now no one deliberates about things that are invariable, nor about things that it is impossible for him to do. Therefore, since scientific knowledge involves demonstration, but there is no demonstration of things whose first principles are variable (for all such things might actually be otherwise), and since it is impossible to deliberate about things that are of necessity, practical wisdom cannot be scientific knowledge nor art; not science because that which can be done is capable of being otherwise, not art because action and making are different kinds of thing. The remaining alternative, then, is that it is a true and reasoned state of capacity to act with regard to the things that are good or bad for man. For while making has an end other than itself, action cannot; for good action itself is its end. It is for this reason that we think Pericles and men like him have practical wisdom, viz. because they can see what is good for themselves and what is good for men in general; we consider that those can do this who are good at managing households or states. . . .

Practical wisdom, then, must be a reasoned and true state of capacity to act with regard to human goods. But further, while there is such a thing as excellence in art, there is no such thing as excellence in practical wisdom; and in art he who errs willingly is preferable, but in practical wisdom, as in the virtues, he is the reverse. Plainly, then, practical wisdom is a virtue and not an art. There being two parts of the soul that can follow a course of reasoning, it must be the virtue of one of the two, i.e. of that part which forms opinions; for opinion is about the variable and so is practical wisdom. But yet it is not only a reasoned state; this is shown by the fact that a state of that sort may be forgotten but practical wisdom cannot.

CHAPTER 6

Scientific knowledge is judgement about things that are universal and necessary, and the conclusions of demonstration, and all scientific knowledge, follow from first principles (for scientific knowledge involves apprehension of a rational ground). This being so, the first principle from which what is scientifically known follows cannot be an object of scientific knowledge, of art, or of practical wisdom; for that which can be scientifically known can be demonstrated, and art and practical wisdom deal with things that are variable. Nor are these first principles the objects of philosophic wisdom, for it is a mark of the philosopher to have *demonstration* about some things. If, then, the states of mind by which we have truth and are never deceived about things invariable or even variable are scientific knowledge, practical wisdom, philosophic wisdom, and intuitive reason, and it cannot be any of the three (i.e. practical wisdom, scientific knowledge, or philosophic wisdom), the remaining alternative is that it is *intuitive reason* that grasps the first principles.

CHAPTER 7

Wisdom . . . Wisdom must plainly be the most finished of the forms of knowledge. It follows that the wise man must not only know what follows from the first principles, but must also possess truth about the first principles. Therefore wisdom must be intuitive reason combined with scientific knowledge—scientific knowledge of the highest objects which has received as it were its proper completion. . . .

Practical wisdom on the other hand is concerned with things human and things about which it is possible to deliberate; for we say this is above all the work of the man of practical wisdom, to deliberate well, but no one deliberates about things invariable, nor about things which have not an end, and that a good that can be brought about by action. The man who is without qualification good at deliberating is the man who is capable of aiming in accordance with calculation at the best for man of things attainable by action. Nor is practical wisdom concerned with universals only—it must also recognize the particulars; for it is practical, and practice is concerned with particulars. This is why some who do not know, and especially those who have experience, are more practical than others who know; for if a man knew that light meats are digestible and wholesome, but did not know which sorts of meat are light, he would not produce health, but the man who knows that chicken is wholesome is more likely to produce health.

Now practical wisdom is concerned with action; therefore one should have both forms of it, or the latter in preference to the former. But of practical as of philosophic wisdom there must be a controlling kind. . . .

CHAPTER 13

We must go a little further. For it is not merely the state in accordance with the right rule, but the state that implies the *presence* of the right rule, that is virtue; and practical wisdom is a right rule about such matters. Socrates, then, thought the virtues were rules or rational principles (for he thought they were, all of them, forms of scientific knowledge), while we think they *involve* a rational principle.

It is clear, then, from what has been said, that it is not possible to be good in the strict sense without practical wisdom, nor practically wise without moral virtue. But in this way we may also refute the dialectical argument whereby it might be contended that the virtues exist in separation from each other; the same man, it might be said, is not best equipped by nature for all the virtues, so that he will have already acquired one when he has not yet acquired another. This is possible in respect of the natural virtues, but not in respect of those in respect of which a man is called without qualification good; for with the presence of the one quality, practical wisdom, will be given all the virtues. And it is plain that, even if it were of no practical value, we should have needed it because it is the virtue of the part of us in question; plain too that the choice will not be right without practical wisdom any more than without virtue; for the one determines the end and the other makes us do the things that lead to the end. . . .

Book X
Pleasure and Happiness

CHAPTER 1

After these matters we ought perhaps next to discuss pleasure. For it is thought to be most intimately connected with our human nature, which is the reason why in educating the young we steer them by the rudders of pleasure and pain; it is thought, too, that to enjoy the things we ought and to hate the things we ought has the greatest bearing on virtue of character. For these things extend right through life, with a weight and power of their own in respect both to virtue and to the happy life, since men choose what is pleasant and avoid what is painful; and such things, it will be thought, we should least of all omit to discuss, especially since they admit of much dispute.

CHAPTER 4

Since every sense is active in relation to its object, and a sense which is in good condition acts perfectly in relation to the most beautiful of its objects (for perfect activity seems to be ideally of this nature;

whether we say that *it* is active, or the organ in which it resides, may be assumed to be immaterial), it follows that in the case of each sense the best activity is that of the best-conditioned organ in relation to the finest of its objects. And this activity will be the most complete and pleasant. For, while there is pleasure in respect of any sense, and in respect of thought and contemplation no less, the most complete is pleasantest, and that of a well-conditioned organ in relation to the worthiest of its objects is the most complete; and the pleasure completes the activity. But the pleasure does not complete it in the same way as the combination of object and sense, both good, just as health and the doctor are not in the same way the cause of a man's being healthy. (That pleasure is produced in respect to each sense is plain; for we speak of sights and sounds as pleasant. It is also plain that it arises most of all when both the sense is at its best and it is active in reference to an object which corresponds; when both object and perceiver are of the best there will always be pleasure, since the requisite agent and patient are both present.) Pleasure completes the activity not as the corresponding permanent state does, by its immanence, but as an end which supervenes as the bloom of youth does on those in the flower of their age. So long, then, as both the intelligible or sensible object and the discriminating or contemplative faculty are as they should be, the pleasure will be involved in the activity; for when both the passive and the active factor are unchanged and are related to each other in the same way, the same result naturally follows.

How, then, is it that no one is continuously pleased? Is it that we grow weary? Certainly all human things are incapable of continuous activity. Therefore pleasure also is not continuous; for it accompanies activity. Some things delight us when they are new, but later do so less, for the same reason; for at first the mind is in a state of stimulation and intensely active about them, as people are with respect to their vision when they look hard at a thing, but afterwards our activity is not of this kind, but has grown relaxed; for which reason the pleasure also is dulled.

One might think that all men desire pleasure because they all aim at life; life is an activity, and each man is active about those things and with those faculties that he loves most; e.g. the musician is active with his hearing in reference to tunes, the student with his mind in reference to theoretical questions, and so on in each case; now pleasure completes the activities, and therefore life, which they desire. It is with good reason, then, that they aim at pleasure too, since for everyone it completes life, which is desirable. But whether we choose life for the sake of pleasure or pleasure for the sake of life is a question we may dismiss for the present. For they seem to be bound up together and not to admit of separation, since without activity pleasure does not arise, and every activity is completed by the attendant pleasure.

CHAPTER 5

For this reason pleasures seem, too, to differ in kind. For things different in kind are, we think, completed by different things (we see this to be true both of natural objects and of things produced by art, e.g. animals, trees, a painting, a sculpture, a house, an implement); and, similarly, we think that activities differing in kind are completed by things differing in kind. Now the activities of thought differ from those of the senses, and both differ among themselves, in kind; so, therefore, do the pleasures that complete them.

This may be seen, too, from the fact that each of the pleasures is bound up with the activity it completes. For an activity is intensified by its proper pleasure, since each class of things is better judged of and brought to precision by those who engage in the activity with pleasure; e.g. it is those who enjoy geometrical thinking that become geometers and grasp the various propositions better, and, similarly, those who are fond of music or of building, and so on, make progress in their proper function by enjoying it; so the pleasures intensify the activities, and what intensifies a thing is proper to it, but things different in kind have properties different in kind. . . .

Now since activities are made precise and more enduring and better by their proper pleasure, and injured by alien pleasures, evidently the two kinds of pleasure are far apart. For alien pleasures do pretty much what proper pains do, since activities are destroyed by their proper pains; e.g. if a man finds writing or doing sums unpleasant and painful, he does not write, or does not do sums, because the activity is painful. So an activity suffers contrary effects from its proper pleasures and pains, i.e. from those that supervene on it in virtue of its own nature. And alien pleasures have been stated to do much the same as pain; they destroy the activity, only not to the same degree.

Now since activities differ in respect of goodness and badness, and some are worthy to be chosen, others to be avoided, and others neutral, so, too, are the pleasures; for to each activity there is a proper pleasure. The pleasure proper to a worthy activity is good and that proper to an unworthy activity bad; just as the appetites for noble objects are laudable, those for base objects culpable. But the pleasures involved in activities are more proper to them than the desires; for the latter are separated both in time and in nature, while the former are close to the activities, and so hard to distinguish from them that it admits of dispute whether the activity is not the same as the pleasure. (Still, pleasure does not seem to *be* thought or perception—that would be strange; but because they are not found apart they appear to some people the same.) As activities are different, then, so are the corresponding pleasures. Now sight is superior to touch in purity, and hearing and smell to taste; the pleasures, therefore, are similarly superior, and those of thought superior to these, and within each of the two kinds some are superior to others.

Each animal is thought to have a proper pleasure, as it has a proper function; viz. that which corresponds to its activity. If we survey them species by species, too, this will be evident; horse, dog, and man have different pleasures, as Heraclitus says "asses would prefer sweepings to gold"; for food is pleasanter than gold to asses. So the pleasures of creatures different in kind differ in kind, and it is plausible to suppose that those of a single species do not differ. But they vary to no small extent, in the case of men at least; the same things delight some people and pain others, and are painful and odious to some, and pleasant to and liked by others. This happens, too, in the case of sweet things; the same things do not seem sweet to a man in a fever and a healthy man—nor hot to a weak man and one in good condition. The same happens in other cases. But in all such matters that which appears to the good man is thought to be really so. If this is correct, as it seems to be, and virtue and the good man as such are the measure of each thing, those also will be pleasures which appear so to him, and those things pleasant which he enjoys. If the things he finds tiresome seem pleasant to some one, that is nothing surprising; for men may be ruined and spoilt in many ways; but the things are not pleasant, but only pleasant to these people and to people in this condition. Those which are admittedly disgraceful plainly should not be said to be pleasures, except to a perverted taste; but of those that are thought to be good what kind of pleasure or what pleasure should be said to be that proper to man? Is it not plain from the corresponding activities? The pleasures follow these.

Whether, then, the perfect and supremely happy man has one or more activities, the pleasures that perfect these will be said in the strict sense to be pleasures proper to man, and the rest will be so in a secondary and fractional way, as are the activities.

CHAPTER 6

Now that we have spoken of the virtues and the varieties of pleasure, what remains is to discuss in outline the nature of happiness, since this is what we state the end of human nature to be. Our discussion will be the more concise if we first sum up what we have said already. We said, then, that it is not a disposition; for if it were it might belong to some one who was asleep throughout his life, living the life of a plant, or, again, to some one who was suffering the greatest misfortunes. If these implications are unacceptable, and we must rather class happiness as an activity, as we have said before, and if some activities are necessary, and desirable for the sake of something else, while others are so in themselves, evidently happiness must be placed among those desirable in themselves, not among those desirable for the sake of something else; for happiness does not lack anything, but is self-sufficient. Now those activities are desirable in themselves from which nothing is sought beyond the activity. And of this nature virtuous actions are thought to be; for to do noble and good deeds is a thing desirable for its own sake.

Pleasant amusements also are thought to be of this nature; we choose them not for the sake of other things; for we are injured rather than benefited by them, since we are led to neglect our bodies and our property. But most of the people who are deemed happy take refuge in such pastimes, which is the reason why those who are ready-witted at them are highly esteemed at the courts of tyrants; they make themselves pleasant companions in the tyrants' favourite pursuits, and that is the sort of man they want. Now these things are thought to be of the nature of happiness because people in despotic positions spend their leisure in them, but perhaps such people prove nothing; for virtue and reason, from which good activities flow, do not depend on despotic position; nor, if these people, who have never tasted pure and generous pleasure, take refuge in the bodily pleasures, should these for that reason be thought more desirable; for boys, too, think the things that are valued among themselves are the best. It is to be expected, then, that, as different things seem valuable to boys and to men, so they should to bad men and to good. Now, as we have often maintained, those things are both valuable and pleasant which are such to the good man; and to each man the activity in accordance with his own disposition is most desirable, and, therefore, to the good man that which is in accordance with virtue. Happiness, therefore, does not lie in amusement; it would, indeed, be strange if the end were amusement, and one were to take trouble and suffer hardship all one's life in order to amuse oneself. For, in a word, everything that we choose we choose for the sake of something else—except happiness, which is an end. Now to exert oneself and work for the sake of amusement seems silly and utterly childish. But to amuse oneself in order that one may exert oneself, as Anacharsis puts it, seems right; for amusement is a sort of relaxation, and we need relaxation because we cannot work continuously. Relaxation, then, is not an end; for it is taken for the sake of activity.

The happy life is thought to be virtuous; now a virtuous life requires exertion, and does not consist in amusement. And we say that serious things are better than laughable things and those connected with amusement, and that the activity of the better of any two things—whether it be two elements of our being or two men—is the more serious; but the activity of the better is *ipso facto* superior and more of the nature of happiness. And any chance person—even a slave—can enjoy the bodily pleasures no less than the best man; but no one assigns to a slave a share in happiness—unless he assigns to him also a share in human life. For happiness does not lie in such occupations, but, as we have said before, in virtuous activities.

CHAPTER 7

If happiness is activity in accordance with virtue, it is reasonable that it should be in accordance with the highest virtue; and this will be that of the best thing in us. Whether it be reason or something else that is this element which is thought to be our natural ruler and guide and to take thought of things noble and divine, whether it be itself also divine or only the most divine element in us, the activity of this in accordance with its proper virtue will be perfect happiness. That this activity is contemplative we have already said.

Now this would seem to be in agreement both with what we said before and with the truth. For, firstly, this activity is the best (since not only is reason the best thing in us, but the objects of reason are the best of knowable objects); and, secondly, it is the most continuous, since we can contemplate truth more continuously than we can *do* anything. And we think happiness has pleasure mingled with it, but the activity of philosophic wisdom is admittedly the pleasantest of virtuous activities; at all events the pursuit of it is thought to offer pleasures marvellous for their purity and their enduringness, and it is to be expected that those who know will pass their time more pleasantly than those who inquire. And the self-sufficiency that is spoken of must belong most to the contemplative activity. For while a philosopher, as well as a just man or one possessing any other virtue, needs the necessaries of life, when they are sufficiently equipped with things of that sort the just man needs people towards whom and with whom he shall act justly, and the temperate man, the brave man, and each of the others is in the same case, but the philosopher, even when by himself, can contemplate truth, and the better the wiser he is; he can perhaps do so better if he has fellow-workers, but still he is the most self-sufficient. And this activity alone would seem to be loved for its own sake; for nothing arises from it apart from the contemplating, while from practical activities we gain more or less apart from the action. And happiness is thought to depend on leisure; for we are busy that we may have leisure, and make war that we may live in peace. Now the activity of the practical virtues is exhibited in political or military affairs, but the actions concerned with these seem to be unleisurely. Warlike actions are completely so (for no one chooses to be at war, or provokes war, for the sake of being at war; any one would seem absolutely murderous if he were to make enemies of his friends in order to bring about battle and slaughter); but the action of the statesman is also unleisurely, and—apart from the political action itself—aims at despotic power and honours, or at all events happiness, for him and his fellow citizens—a happiness different from political action, and evidently sought as being different. So if among virtuous actions political and military actions are distinguished by nobility and greatness, and these are unleisurely and aim at an end and are not desirable for their own sake, but the activity of reason, which is contemplative, seems both to be superior in serious worth and to aim at no end beyond itself, and to have its pleasure proper to itself (and this augments the activity), and the self-sufficiency, leisureliness, unweariedness (so far as this is possible for man), and all the other attributes ascribed to the supremely happy man are evidently those connected with this activity, it follows that this will be the complete happiness of man, if it be allowed a complete term of life, for none of the attributes of happiness is *in*complete).

But such a life would be too high for man; for it is not in so far as he is man that he will live so, but in so far as something divine is present in him; and by so much as this is superior to our composite nature is its activity superior to that which is the exercise of the other kind of virtue. If reason is divine, then, in comparison with man, the life according to it is divine in comparison with human life. But we must not follow those who advise us, being men, to think of human things, and being mortal, of mortal things, but must, so far as we can, make ourselves immortal, and strain every nerve to live in accordance with the best thing in us; for even if it be small in bulk, much more does it in power and worth surpass everything. This would seem, too, to be each man himself, since it is the authoritative and better part of him. It would be strange, then, if he were to choose not the life of his self but that of something else. And what we said before will apply now; that which is proper to each thing is by nature best and most pleasant for each thing; for man, therefore, the life according to reason is best and pleasantest, since reason more than anything else *is* man. This life therefore is also the happiest.

CHAPTER 8

But in a secondary degree the life in accordance with the other kind of virtue is happy; for the activities in accordance with this befit our human estate. Just and brave acts, and other virtuous acts, we do in relation to each other, observing our respective duties with regard to contracts and services and all manner of actions and with regard to passions; and all of these seem to be typically human. Some of them seem even to arise from the body, and virtue of character to be in many ways bound up with the passions. Practical wisdom, too, is linked to virtue of character, and this to practical wisdom, since the principles of practical wisdom are in accordance with the moral virtues and rightness in morals is in accordance with practical wisdom. Being connected with the passions also, the moral virtues must belong to our composite nature; and the virtues of our composite nature are human; so, therefore, are the life and the happiness which correspond to these. The excellence of the reason is a thing apart; we must be content to say this much about it, for to describe it precisely is a task greater than our purpose requires. It would seem, however, also to need external equipment but little, or less than moral virtue does. Grant that both need the necessaries, and do so equally, even if the statesman's work is the more concerned with the body and things of that sort; for there will be little difference there; but in what they need for the exercise of their activities there will be much difference. The liberal man will need money for the doing of his liberal deeds, and the just man too will need it for the returning of services (for wishes are hard to discern, and even people who are not just pretend to wish to act justly); and the brave man will need power if he is to accomplish any of the acts that correspond to his virtue, and the temperate man will need opportunity; for how else is either he or any of the others to be recognized? It is debated, too, whether the will or the deed is more essential to virtue, which is assumed to involve both; it is surely clear that its perfection involves both; but for deeds many things are needed, and more, the greater and nobler the deeds are. But the man who is contemplating the truth needs no such thing, at least with a view to the exercise of his activity; indeed they are, one may say, even hindrances, at all events to his contemplation; but in so far as he is a man and lives with a number of people, he chooses to do virtuous acts; he will therefore need such aids to living a human life.

But that perfect happiness is a contemplative activity will appear from the following consideration as well. We assume the gods to be above all other things blessed and happy; but what sort of actions must we assign to them? Acts of justice?

Will not the gods seem absurd if they make contracts and return deposits, and so on? Acts of a brave man, then, confronting dangers and running risks because it is noble to do so? Or liberal acts? To whom will they give? It will be strange if they are really to have money or anything of the kind. And what would their temperate acts be? Is not such praise tasteless, since they have no bad appetites? If we were to run through them all, the circumstances of action would be found trivial and unworthy of gods. Still, everyone supposes that they *live* and therefore that they are active; we cannot suppose them to sleep like Endymion. Now if you take away from a living being action, and still more production, what is left but contemplation? Therefore the activity of God, which surpasses all others in blessedness, must be contemplative; and of human activities, therefore, that which is most akin to this must be most of the nature of happiness.

This is indicated, too, by the fact that the other animals have no share in happiness, being completely deprived of such activity. For while the whole life of the gods is blessed, and that of men too in so far as some likeness of such activity belongs to them, none of the other animals is happy, since they in no way share in contemplation. Happiness extends, then, just so far as contemplation does, and those to whom contemplation more fully belongs are more truly happy, not as a mere concomitant but in virtue of the contemplation; for this is in itself precious. Happiness, therefore, must be some form of contemplation.

But, being a man, one will also need external prosperity; for our nature is not self-sufficient for the purpose of contemplation, but our body also must be healthy and must have food and other attention. Still, we must not think that the man who is to be happy will need many things or great things, merely because he cannot be supremely happy without external goods; for self-sufficiency and action do not involve excess, and we can do noble acts without ruling earth and sea; for even with moderate advantages one can act virtuously (this is manifest enough; for private persons are thought to do worthy acts no less than despots—indeed even more) and it is enough that we should have so much as that; for the life of the man who is active in accordance with virtue will be happy. Solon, too, was perhaps sketching well the happy man when he described him as moderately furnished with externals but as having done (as Solon thought) the noblest acts, and lived temperately; for one can with but moderate possessions do what one ought. Anaxagoras also seems to have supposed the happy man not to be rich nor a despot, when he said that he would not be surprised if the happy man were to seem to most people a strange person; for they judge by externals, since these are all they perceive. The opinions of the wise seem, then, to harmonize with our arguments. But while even such things carry some conviction, the truth in practical matters is discerned from the facts of life; for these are the decisive factor. We must therefore survey what we have already said, bringing it to the test of the facts of life, and if it harmonizes with the facts we must accept it, but if it clashes with them we must suppose it to be mere theory. Now he who exercises his reason and cultivates it seems to be both in the best state of mind and most dear to the gods. For if the gods have any care for human affairs, as they are thought to have, it would be reasonable both that they should delight in that which was best and most akin to them (i.e. reason) and that they should reward those who love and honour this most, as caring for the things that are dear to them and acting both rightly and nobly. And that all these attributes belong most of all to the philosopher is manifest. He, therefore, is the dearest to the gods. And he who is that will presumably be also the happiest; so that in this way too the philosopher will more than any other be happy.

EPICURUS

The traditional beliefs about the life of Epicurus (342/1–270 B.C.*) are based largely upon a biography written four centuries after his death by Diogenes Laërtius. The factual content of this biography is scant, and even the author is not entirely confident of its authenticity. This account runs as follows: The son of an Athenian citizen, Epicurus was raised on the island of Samos, at that time a colony of Athens. In his eighteenth year he went to Athens. There, though he claimed to be self-educated, he probably received instruction in the systems of Democritus and Plato. At about the age of forty-eight he founded a school on the outskirts of Athens, where he both taught his philosophy and lived a life exemplifying it.*

There is little originality in the basic tenets of his position; its distinctive feature is his grounding of hedonism, a traditional theory, in the atomistic metaphysics of Democritus. The main tenets of his atomism are presented in the selections from his Letter to Herodotus. *His* Letter to Menoeceus *and* Principal Doctrines, *here given in their entirety, state the main points of his ethical position.*

Letter to Herodotus*

. . . Nothing is created out of that which does not exist: for if it were, everything would be created out of everything with no need of seeds. And again, if that which disappears were destroyed into that which did not exist, all things would have perished, since that into which they were dissolved would not exist. Furthermore, the universe always was such as it is now, and always will be the same. For there is nothing into which it changes: for outside the universe there is nothing which could come into it and bring about the change.

Moreover, the universe is bodies and space: for that bodies exist, sense itself witnesses in the experience of all men, and in accordance with the evidence of sense we must of necessity judge of the imperceptible by reasoning, as I have already said. And if there were not that which we term void and place and intangible existence, bodies would have nowhere to exist and nothing through which to move, as they are seen to move. And besides these two nothing can even be thought of either

* By permission. From C. Bailey, *Epicurus: The Extant Remains*, Clarendon Press, Oxford, 1926.

by conception or on the analogy of things conceivable such as could be grasped as whole existences and not spoken of as the accidents or properties of such existences. Furthermore, among bodies some are compounds, and others those of which compounds are formed. And these latter are indivisible and unalterable (if, that is, all things are not to be destroyed into the non-existent, but something permanent is to remain behind at the dissolution of compounds): they are completely solid in nature, and can by no means be dissolved in any part. So it must needs be that the first-beginnings are indivisible corporeal existences.

Moreover, the universe is boundless. For that which is bounded has an extreme point: and the extreme point is seen against something else. So that as it has no extreme point, it has no limit; and as it has no limit, it must be boundless and not bounded. Furthermore, the infinite is boundless both in the number of the bodies and in the extent of the void. For if on the one hand the void were boundless, and the bodies limited in number, the bodies could not stay anywhere, but would be carried about and scattered through the infinite void, not having other bodies to support them and keep them in place by means of collisions. But if, on the other hand, the void were limited, the infinite bodies would not have room wherein to take their place.

Besides this the indivisible and solid bodies, out of which too the compounds are created and into which they are dissolved, have an incomprehensible number of varieties in shape: for it is not possible that such great varieties of things should arise from the same atomic shapes, if they are limited in number. And so in each shape the atoms are quite infinite in number, but their differences of shape are not quite infinite, but only incomprehensible in number.

And the atoms move continuously for all time, some of them falling straight down, others swerving, and others recoiling from their collisions. And of the latter, some are borne on, separating to a long distance from one another, while others again recoil and recoil, whenever they chance to be checked by the interlacing with others, or else shut in by atoms interlaced around them. For on the one hand the nature of the void which separates each atom by itself brings this about, as it is not able to afford resistance, and on the other hand the hardness which belongs to the atoms makes them recoil after collision to as great a distance as the interlacing permits separation after the collision. And these motions have no beginning, since the atoms and the void are the cause.

These brief sayings, if all these points are borne in mind, afford a sufficient outline for our understanding of the nature of existing things. . . .

Next, referring always to the sensations and the feelings, for in this way you will obtain the most trustworthy ground of belief, you must consider that the soul is a body of fine particles distributed throughout the whole structure, and most resembling wind with a certain admixture of heat, and in some respects like to one of these and in some to the other. There is also the part which is many degrees more advanced even than these in fineness of composition, and for this reason is more capable of feeling in harmony with the rest of the structure as well. Now all this is made manifest by the activities of the soul and the feelings and the readiness of its movements and its processes of thought and by what we lose at the moment of death. Further, you must grasp that the soul possesses the chief cause of sensation: yet it could not have acquired sensation, unless it were in some way enclosed by the rest of the structure. And this in its turn having afforded the soul this cause of sensation acquires itself too a share in this contingent capacity from the soul. Yet it does not acquire all the capacities which the soul possesses: and therefore when the soul is released from the body, the body no longer has sensation. For it never possessed this power in itself, but used to afford opportunity for it to another existence, brought into being at the same time with itself: and this existence, owing to the power now consummated within itself as a result of motion, used spontaneously to produce for itself the capacity of sensation and then to communicate it to the body as well, in virtue of its contact and correspondence of movement, as I have already said. Therefore, so long as the soul remains in the body, even though some other part of the body be lost, it will never lose sensation; nay more, whatever portions of the soul may perish too, when that which enclosed it is removed either in whole or in part, if the soul continues to exist at all, it will retain sensation. On the other hand the rest of the structure, though it continues to exist either as a whole or in part, does not retain sensation, if it has once lost that sum of atoms, however small it be, which together goes to produce the nature of the soul. Moreover, if the whole structure is dissolved, the soul is dispersed and no longer has the same powers nor performs its movements, so that it does not possess sensation either. For it is impossible to imagine it with sensation, if it is not in this organism and cannot effect these movements, when what encloses and surrounds it is no longer the same as the surroundings in which it now exists and performs these movements. Furthermore, we must clearly comprehend as well, that the incorporeal in the general acceptation of the term is applied to that which could be thought of as such as an independent existence. Now it is impossible to conceive the incorporeal as a separate existence, except the void: and the void can neither act nor be acted upon, but only provides opportunity of motion through itself to bodies. So that those who say that the soul is incorporeal are talking idly. For it would not be able to act or be acted on in any respect, if it were of this nature. But as it is, both these occurrences are clearly distinguished in respect of the soul. Now if one refers all these reasonings about the soul to the standards of feeling and sensation and remembers what was said at the outset, he will see that they are sufficiently embraced in these general formulae to enable him to work out with certainty on this basis the details of the system as well. . . .

And besides all these matters in general we must grasp this point, that the principal disturbance in the minds of men arises because they think that celestial bodies are blessed and immortal, and yet have wills and actions and motives inconsistent with these attributes; and because they are always expecting or imagining some everlasting misery, such as is depicted in legends, or even fear the loss of feeling in death as though it would concern them themselves; and, again, because they are brought to this pass not by reasoned opinion, but rather by some irrational presentiment, and therefore, as they do not know the limits of pain, they suffer a disturbance equally great or even more extensive than if they had reached this belief by opinion. But peace of mind is being delivered from all this, and having a constant memory of the general and most essential principles.

Wherefore we must pay attention to internal feelings and to external sensations in general and in particular, according as the subject is general or particular, and to every immediate intuition in accordance with each of the standards of judgement. For if we pay attention to these, we shall rightly trace the causes whence arose our mental disturbance and fear, and, by learning the true causes of celestial phenomena and all other occurrences that come to pass from time to time, we shall free ourselves from all which produces the utmost fear in other men. . . .

*Letter to Menoeceus**

Let no one when young delay to study philosophy, nor when he is old grow weary of his study. For no one can come too early or too late to secure the health of his soul. And the man who says that the age for philosophy has either not yet come or has gone by is like the man who says that the age for happiness is not yet come to him, or has passed away. Wherefore both when young and old a man must study philosophy, that as he grows old he may be young in blessings through the grateful recollection of what has been, and that in youth he may be old as well, since he will know no fear of what is to come. We must then meditate on the things that make our happiness, seeing that when that is with us we have all, but when it is absent we do all to win it.

The things which I used unceasingly to commend to you, these do and practise, considering them to be the first principles of the good life. First of all believe that god is a being immortal and blessed, even as the common idea of a god is engraved on men's minds, and do not assign to him anything alien to his immortality or ill-suited to his blessedness: but believe about him everything that can uphold his blessedness and immortality. For gods there are, since the knowledge of them is by clear vision. But they are not such as the many believe them to be: for indeed they do not consistently represent them as they believe them to be. And the impious man is not he who denies the gods of the many, but he who attaches to the gods the beliefs of the many. For the statements of the many about the gods are not conceptions derived from sensation, but false suppositions, according to which the greatest misfortunes befall the wicked and the greatest blessings the good by the gift of the gods. For men being accustomed always to their own virtues welcome those like themselves, but regard all that is not of their nature as alien.

Become accustomed to the belief that death is nothing to us. For all good and evil consists in sensation, but death is deprivation of sensation. And therefore a right understanding that death is nothing to us makes the mortality of life enjoyable, not because it adds to it an infinite span of time, but because it takes away the craving for immortality. For there is nothing terrible in life for the man who has truly comprehended that there is nothing terrible in not living. So that the man speaks but idly who says that he fears death not because it will be painful when it comes, but because it is painful in anticipation. For that which gives no trouble when it comes, is but an empty pain in anticipation. So death, the most terrifying of ills, is nothing to us, since so long as we exist death is not with us; but when death comes, then we do not exist. It does not then concern either the living or the dead, since for the former it is not, and the latter are no more.

But the many at one moment shun death as the greatest of evils, at another yearn for it as a respite from the evils in life. But the wise man neither seeks to escape life nor fears the cessation of life, for neither does life offend him nor does the absence of life seem to be any evil. And just as with food he does not seek simply the larger share and nothing else, but rather the most pleasant, so he seeks to enjoy not the longest period of time, but the most pleasant.

And he who counsels the young man to live well, but the old man to make a good end, is foolish, not merely because

* *Supra*, p. 82.

of the desirability of life, but also because it is the same training which teaches to live well and to die well. Yet much worse still is the man who says it is good not to be born, but

> *once born make haste to pass the gates of Death.*
>
> *(Theognis, 427)*

For if he says this from conviction why does he not pass away out of life? For it is open to him to do so, if he had firmly made up his mind to this. But if he speaks in jest, his words are idle among men who cannot receive them.

We must then bear in mind that the future is neither ours, nor yet wholly not ours, so that we may not altogether expect it as sure to come, nor abandon hope of it, as if it will certainly not come.

We must consider that of desires some are natural, others vain, and of the natural some are necessary and others merely natural; and of the necessary some are necessary for happiness, others for the repose of the body, and others for very life. The right understanding of these facts enables us to refer all choice and avoidance to the health of the body and the soul's freedom from disturbance, since this is the aim of the life of blessedness. For it is to obtain this end that we always act, namely, to avoid pain and fear. And when this is once secured for us, all the tempest of the soul is dispersed, since the living creature has not to wander as though in search of something that is missing, and to look for some other thing by which he can fulfil the good of the soul and the good of the body. For it is then that we have need of pleasure, when we feel pain owing to the absence of pleasure; but when we do not feel pain, we no longer need pleasure. And for this cause we call pleasure the beginning and end of the blessed life. For we recognize pleasure as the first good innate in us, and from pleasure we begin every act of choice and avoidance, and to pleasure we return again, using the feeling as the standard by which we judge every good.

And since pleasure is the first good and natural to us, for this very reason we do not choose every pleasure, but sometimes we pass over many pleasures, when greater discomfort accrues to us as the result of them: and similarly we think many pains better than pleasures, since a greater pleasure comes to us when we have endured pains for a long time. Every pleasure then because of its natural kinship to us is good, yet not every pleasure is to be chosen: even as every pain also is an evil, yet not all are always of a nature to be avoided. Yet by a scale of comparison and by the consideration of advantages and disadvantages we must form our judgement on all these matters. For the good on certain occasions we treat as bad, and conversely the bad as good.

And again independence of desire we think a great good—not that we may at all times enjoy but a few things, but that, if we do not possess many, we may enjoy the few in the genuine persuasion that those have the sweetest pleasure in luxury who least need it, and that all that is natural is easy to be obtained, but that which is superfluous is hard. And so plain savours bring us a pleasure equal to a luxurious diet, when all the pain due to want is removed; and bread and water produce the highest pleasure, when one who needs them puts them to his lips. To grow accustomed therefore to simple and not luxurious diet gives us health to the full, and makes a man alert for the needful employments of life, and when after long intervals we approach luxuries, disposes us better towards them, and fits us to be fearless of fortune.

When, therefore, we maintain that pleasure is the end, we do not mean the pleasures of profligates and those that consist in sensuality, as is supposed by some who are either ignorant or disagree with us or do not understand, but freedom from pain in the body and from trouble in the mind. For it is not continuous drinkings and revellings, nor the satisfaction of lusts, nor the enjoyment of fish and other luxuries of the wealthy table, which produce a pleasant life, but sober reasoning, searching out the motives for all choice and avoidance, and banishing mere opinions, to which are due the greatest disturbance of the spirit.

Of all this the beginning and the greatest good is prudence. Wherefore prudence is a more precious thing even than philosophy: for from prudence are sprung all the other virtues, and it teaches us that it is not possible to live pleasantly without living prudently and honourably and justly, nor, again, to live a life of prudence, honour, and justice without living pleasantly. For the virtues are by nature bound up with the pleasant life, and the pleasant life is inseparable from them. For indeed who, think you, is a better man than he who holds reverent opinions concerning the gods, and is at all times free from fear of death, and has reasoned out the end ordained by nature? He understands that the limit of good things is easy to fulfil and easy to attain, whereas the course of ills is either short in time or slight in pain: he laughs at destiny, whom some have introduced as the mistress of all things. He thinks that with us lies the chief power in determining events, some of which happen by necessity and some by chance, and some are within our control; for while necessity cannot be called to account, he sees that chance is inconstant, but that which is in our control is subject to no master, and to it are naturally attached praise and blame. For, indeed, it were better to follow the myths about the gods than to become a slave to the destiny of the natural philosophers: for the former suggests a hope of placating the gods by worship, whereas the latter involves a necessity which knows no placation. As to chance, he does not regard it as a god as most men do (for in god's acts there is no disorder), nor as an uncertain cause of all things: for he does not believe that good and evil are given by chance to man for the framing of a blessed life, but that opportunities for great good and great evil are afforded by it. He therefore thinks it better to be unfortunate in reasonable action than to prosper in unreason. For it is better in a man's actions that what is well chosen should fail, rather than that what is ill chosen should be successful owing to chance.

Meditate therefore on these things and things akin to them night and day by yourself, and with a companion like to yourself, and never shall you be disturbed waking or asleep, but you shall live like a god among men. For a man who lives among immortal blessings is not like to a mortal being.

*Principal Doctrines**

I. The blessed and immortal nature knows no trouble itself nor causes trouble to any other, so that it is never constrained by anger or favour. For all such things exist only in the weak.

II. Death is nothing to us: for that which is dissolved is without sensation; and that which lacks sensation is nothing to us.

III. The limit of quantity in pleasures is the removal of all that is painful. Wherever pleasure is present, as long as it is there, there is neither pain of body nor of mind, nor of both at once.

IV. Pain does not last continuously in the flesh, but the acutest pain is there for a very short time, and even that which just exceeds the pleasure in the flesh does not continue for many days at once. But chronic illnesses permit a predominance of pleasure over pain in the flesh.

* *Supra*, p. 82.

V. It is not possible to live pleasantly without living prudently and honourably and justly, nor again to live a life of prudence, honour, and justice without living pleasantly. And the man who does not possess the pleasant life, is not living prudently and honourably and justly, and the man who does not possess the virtuous life, cannot possibly live pleasantly.

VI. To secure protection from men anything is a natural good, by which you may be able to attain this end.

VII. Some men wished to become famous and conspicuous, thinking that they would thus win for themselves safety from other men. Wherefore if the life of such men is safe, they have obtained the good which nature craves; but if it is not safe, they do not possess that for which they strove at first by the instinct of nature.

VIII. No pleasure is a bad thing in itself: but the means which produce some pleasures bring with them disturbances many times greater than the pleasures.

IX. If every pleasure could be intensified so that it lasted and influenced the whole organism or the most essential parts of our nature, pleasures would never differ from one another.

X. If the things that produce the pleasures of profligates could dispel the fears of the mind about the phenomena of the sky and death and its pains, and also teach the limits of desires and of pains, we should never have cause to blame them: for they would be filling themselves full with pleasures from every source and never have pain of body or mind, which is the evil of life.

XI. If we were not troubled by our suspicions of the phenomena of the sky and about death, fearing that it concerns us, and also by our failure to grasp the limits of pains and desires, we should have no need of natural science.

XII. A man cannot dispel his fear about the most important matters if he does not know what is the nature of the universe but suspects the truth of some mythical story. So that without natural science it is not possible to attain our pleasures unalloyed.

XIII. There is no profit in securing protection in relation to men, if things above and things beneath the earth and indeed all in the boundless universe remain matters of suspicion.

XIV. The most unalloyed source of protection from men, which is secured to some extent by a certain force of expulsion, is in fact the immunity which results from a quiet life and the retirement from the world.

XV. The wealth demanded by nature is both limited and easily procured; that demanded by idle imaginings stretches on to infinity.

XVI. In but few things chance hinders a wise man, but the greatest and most important matters reason has ordained and throughout the whole period of life does and will ordain.

XVII. The just man is most free from trouble, the unjust most full of trouble.

XVIII. The pleasure in the flesh is not increased, when once the pain due to want is removed, but is only varied: and the limit as regards pleasure in the mind is begotten by the reasoned understanding of these very pleasures and of the emotions akin to them, which used to cause the greatest fear to the mind.

XIX. Infinite time contains no greater pleasure than limited time, if one measures by reason the limits of pleasure.

XX. The flesh perceives the limits of pleasure as unlimited and unlimited time is required to supply it. But the mind, having attained a reasoned understanding of the ultimate good of the flesh and its limits and having dissipated the fears concerning the time to come, supplies us with the complete life, and we have no further need of infinite time: but neither does the mind shun pleasure, nor, when circumstances begin to bring about the departure from life, does it approach its end as though if fell short in any way of the best life.

XXI. He who has learned the limits of life knows that that which removes the pain due to want and makes the whole of life complete is easy to obtain; so that there is no need of actions which involve competition.

XXII. We must consider both the real purpose and all the evidence of direct perception, to which we always refer the conclusions of opinion; otherwise, all will be full of doubt and confusion.

XXIII. If you fight against all sensations, you will have no standard by which to judge even those of them which you say are false.

XXIV. If you reject any single sensation and fail to distinguish between the conclusion of opinion as to the appearance awaiting confirmation and that which is actually given by the sensation or feeling, or each intuitive apprehension of the mind, you will confound all other sensations as well with the same groundless opinion, so that you will reject every standard of judgement. And if among the mental images created by your opinion you affirm both that which awaits confirmation and that which does not, you will not escape error, since you will have preserved the whole cause of doubt in every judgement between what is right and what is wrong.

XXV. If on each occasion instead of referring your actions to the end of nature, you turn to some other nearer standard when you are making a choice or an avoidance, your actions will not be consistent with your principles.

XXVI. Of desires, all that do not lead to a sense of pain, if they are not satisfied, are not necessary, but involve a craving which is easily dispelled, when the object is hard to procure or they seem likely to produce harm.

XXVII. Of all the things which wisdom acquires to produce the blessedness of the complete life, far the greatest is the possession of friendship.

XXVIII. The same conviction which has given us confidence that there is nothing terrible that lasts for ever or even for long, has also seen the protection of friendship most fully completed in the limited evils of this life.

XXIX. Among desires some are natural and necessary, some natural but not necessary, and others neither natural nor necessary, but due to idle imagination.

XXX. Wherever in the case of desires which are physical, but do not lead to a sense of pain, if they are not fulfilled, the effort is intense, such pleasures are due to idle imagination, and it is not owing to their own nature that they fail to be dispelled, but owing to the empty imaginings of the man.

XXXI. The justice which arises from nature is a pledge of mutual advantage to restrain men from harming one another and save them from being harmed.

XXXII. For all living things which have not been able to make compacts not to harm one another or be harmed, nothing ever is either just or unjust; and likewise too for all tribes of men which have been unable or unwilling to make compacts not to harm or be harmed.

XXXIII. Justice never is anything in itself, but in the dealings of men with one another in any place whatever and at any time it is a kind of compact not to harm or be harmed.

XXXIV. Injustice is not an evil in itself, but only in consequence of the fear which attaches to the apprehension of being unable to escape those appointed to punish such actions.

XXXV. It is not possible for one who acts in secret contravention of the terms of the compact not to harm or be harmed, to be confident that he will escape detection, even if at present he escapes a thousand times. For up to the time of death it cannot be certain that he will indeed escape.

XXXVI. In its general aspect justice is the same for all, for it is a kind of mutual advantage in the dealings of men with one another: but with reference to the individual peculiarities of a country or any other circumstances the same thing does not turn out to be just for all.

XXXVII. Among actions which are sanctioned as just by law, that which is proved on examination to be of advantage in the requirements of men's dealings with one another, has the guarantee of justice, whether it is the same for all or not. But if a man makes a law and it does not turn out to lead to advantage in men's dealings with each other, then it no longer has the essential nature of justice. And even if the advantage in the matter of justice shifts from one side to the other, but for a while accords with the general concept, it is none the less just for that period in the eyes of those who do not confound themselves with empty sounds but look to the actual facts.

XXXVIII. Where, provided the circumstances have not been altered, actions which were considered just, have been shown not to accord with the general concept in actual practice, then they are not just. But where, when circumstances have changed, the same actions which were sanctioned as just no longer lead to advantage, there they were just at the time when they were of advantage for the dealings of fellow-citizens with one another; but subsequently they are no longer just, when no longer of advantage.

XXXIX. The man who has best ordered the element of disquiet arising from external circumstances has made those things that he could akin to himself and the rest at least no alien: but with all to which he could not do even this, he has refrained from mixing, and has expelled from his life all which it was of advantage to treat thus.

XL. As many as possess the power to procure complete immunity from their neighbours, these also live most pleasantly with one another, since they have the most certain pledge of security, and after they have enjoyed the fullest intimacy, they do not lament the previous departure of a dead friend, as though he were to be pitied.

EPICTETUS

Epictetus (ca. A.D. *50–138) was born in Hierapolis in Asia Minor. He spent his youth as a slave in Nero's guard, where he studied Stoic philosophy. After attaining freedom, he left Rome in* A.D. *90, when the Emperor Domitian expelled the Stoics for their politically unorthodox opinions, and founded a school of philosophy at Nicopolis, a town in the Roman province of Macedon.*

Our knowledge of Epictetus's views is derived from the writings of his pupil, the historian Flavius Arrianus, who wrote the Discourses of Epictetus *and a short handbook summarizing the* Discourses. *This handbook, which is here reprinted in full, was intended to be memorized by devotees of the Stoic philosophy.*

*The Encheridion, or Manual**

I. Of things some are in our power, and others are not. In our power are opinion, movement toward a thing, desire, aversion (turning from a thing); and in a word, whatever are our own acts: not in our power are the body, property, reputation, offices (magisterial power), and in a word, whatever are not our own acts. And the things in our power are by nature free, not subject to restraint nor hindrance: but the things not in our power are weak, slavish, subject to restraint, in the power of others. Remember then that if you think the things which are by nature slavish to be free, and the things which are in the power of others to be your own, you will be hindered, you will lament, you will be disturbed, you will blame both gods and men: but if you think that only which is your own to be your own, and if you think that what is another's, as it really is, belongs to another, no man will ever compel you, no man will hinder you, you will never blame any man, you will accuse no man, you will do nothing involuntarily (against your will), no man will harm you, you will have no enemy, for you will not suffer any harm.

If then you desire (aim at) such great things, remember that you must not (attempt to) lay hold of them with a small effort; but you must leave alone some things entirely, and postpone others for the present. But if you wish for these things also (such great things), and power (office) and wealth, perhaps you will not gain even these very things (power and wealth) because you aim also at those former things (such great things): certainly you will fail in those things through which alone happiness and freedom are secured. Straightway then practice saying to every harsh appearance, You are an appearance, and in no manner what you appear to be. Then examine it by the rules which you possess,

* Translation by G. Long, London, 1887.

and by this first and chiefly, whether it relates to the things which are in our power or to the things which are not in our power: and if it relates to anything which is not in our power, be ready to say, that it does not concern you.

II. Remember that desire contains in it the profession (hope) of obtaining that which you desire; and the profession (hope) in aversion (turning from a thing) is that you will not fall into that which you attempt to avoid: and he who fails in his desire is unfortunate; and he who falls into that which he would avoid, is unhappy. If then you attempt to avoid only the things contrary to nature which are within your power, you will not be involved in any of the things which you would avoid. But if you attempt to avoid disease or death or poverty, you will be unhappy. Take away then aversion from all things which are not in our power, and transfer it to the things contrary to nature which are in our power. But destroy desire completely for the present. For if you desire anything which is not in our power, you must be unfortunate: but of the things in our power, and which it would be good to desire, nothing yet is before you. But employ only the power of moving toward an object and retiring from it; and these powers indeed only slightly and with exceptions and with remission.

III. In everything which pleases the soul, or supplies a want, or is loved, remember to add this to the (description, notion); what is the nature of each thing, beginning from the smallest? If you love an earthen vessel, say it is an earthen vessel which you love; for when it has been broken, you will not be disturbed. If you are kissing your child or wife, say that it is a human being whom you are kissing, for when the wife or child dies, you will not be disturbed.

IV. When you are going to take in hand any act, remind yourself what kind of an act it is. If you are going to bathe, place before yourself what happens in the bath: some splashing the water, others pushing against one another, others abusing one another, and some stealing; and thus with more safety you will undertake the matter, if you say to yourself, I now intend to bathe, and to maintain my will in a manner conformable to nature. And so you will do in every act: for thus if any hindrance to bathing shall happen, let this thought be ready; it was not this only that I intended, but I intended also to maintain my will in a way conformable to nature; but I shall not maintain it so, if I am vexed at what happens.

V. Men are disturbed not by the things which happen, but by the opinions about the things: for example, death is nothing terrible, for if it were, it would have seemed so to Socrates; for the opinion about death, that it is terrible, is the terrible thing. When then we are impeded or disturbed or grieved, let us never blame others, but ourselves, that is, our opinions. It is the act of an ill-instructed man to blame others for his own bad condition; it is the act of one who has begun to be instructed, to lay the blame on himself; and of one whose instruction is completed, neither to blame another, nor himself.

VI. Be not elated at any advantage (excellence), which belongs to another. If a horse when he is elated should say, I am beautiful, one might endure it. But when you are elated, and say, I have a beautiful horse, you must know that you are elated at having a good horse. What then is your own? The use of appearances. Consequently when in the use of appearances you are conformable to nature, then be elated, for then you will be elated at something good which is your own.

VII. As on a voyage when the vessel has reached a port, if you go out to get water, it is an amusement by the way to pick up a shell-fish or some bulb, but your thoughts ought to be directed to the ship, and you ought to be constantly watching if the captain should call, and then you must throw away all those things, that you may not be bound and pitched into the ship like sheep: so in life also, if there be given to you instead of a little bulb and a shell a wife and child, there will be nothing to prevent (you from taking them). But if the captain should call, run to the ship, and leave all those things without regard to them. But if you are old, do not even go far from the ship, lest when you are called you make default.

VIII. Seek not that the things which happen should happen as you wish; but wish the things which happen to be as they are, and you will have a tranquil flow of life.

IX. Disease is an impediment to the body, but not to the will, unless the will itself chooses. Lameness is an impediment to the leg, but not to the will. And add this reflection on the occasion of everything that happens; for you will find it an impediment to something else, but not to yourself.

X. On the occasion of every accident (event) that befalls you, remember to turn to yourself and inquire what power you have for turning it to use. If you see a fair man or a fair woman, you will find that the power to resist is temperance (continence). If labor (pain) be presented to you, you will find that it is endurance. If it be abusive words, you will find it to be patience. And if you have been thus formed to the (proper) habit, the appearances will not carry you along with them.

XI. Never say about anything, I have lost it, but say I have restored it. Is your child dead? It has been restored. Is your wife dead? She has been restored. Has your estate been taken from you? Has not then this also been restored? But he who has taken it from me is a bad man. But what is it to you, by whose hands the giver demanded it back? So long as he may allow you, take care of it as a thing which belongs to another, as travelers do with their inn.

XII. If you intend to improve, throw away such thoughts as these: if I neglect my affairs, I shall not have the means of living: unless I chastise my slave, he will be bad. For it is better to die of hunger and so be released from grief and fear than to live in abundance with perturbation; and it is better for your slave to be bad than for you to be unhappy. Begin then from little things. Is the oil spilled? Is a little wine stolen? Say on the occasion, at such price is sold freedom from perturbation; at such price is sold tranquillity, but nothing is got for nothing. And when you call your slave, consider that it is possible that he does not hear; and if he does hear, that he will do nothing which you wish. But matters are not so well with him, but altogether well with you, that it should be in his power for you to be not disturbed.

XIII. If you would improve, submit to be considered without sense and foolish with respect to externals. Wish to be considered to know nothing: and if you shall seem to some to be a person of importance, distrust yourself. For you should know that it is not easy both to keep your will in a condition conformable to nature and (to secure) external things: but if a man is careful about the one, it is an absolute necessity that he will neglect the other.

XIV. If you would have your children and your wife and your friends to live forever, you are silly; for you would have the things which are not in your power to be in your power, and the things which belong to others to be yours. So if you would have your slave to be free from faults, you are a fool; for you would have badness not to be badness, but something else. But if you wish not to fail in your desires, you are able to do that. Practice then this which you are able to do. He is the master of every man who has the power over the things, which another person wishes or does not wish, the power to confer them on him or to take them away. Whoever then wishes to be free, let him neither wish for anything nor avoid anything which depends on others: if he does not observe this rule, he must be a slave.

XV. Remember that in life you ought to behave as at a banquet. Suppose that something is carried round and is opposite to you. Stretch out your hand and take a portion with decency. Suppose that it passes by you. Do not detain it. Suppose that it is not yet come to you. Do not send your desire forward to it, but wait till it is opposite to you. Do so with respect to children, so with respect to a wife, so with respect to magisterial offices, so with respect to wealth, and you will be some time a worthy partner of the banquets of the gods. But if you take none of the things which are set before you, and even despise them, then you will be not only a fellow-banqueter with the gods, but also a partner with them in power. For by acting thus Diogenes and Heracleitus and those like them were deservedly divine, and were so called.

XVI. When you see a person weeping in sorrow either when a child goes abroad or when he is dead, or when the man has lost his property, take care that the appearance does not hurry you away with it, as if he were suffering in external things. But straightway make a distinction in your own mind, and be in readiness to say, it is not that which has happened that afflicts this man, for it does not afflict another, but it is the opinion about this thing which afflicts the man. So far as words then do not be unwilling to show him sympathy, and even if it happens so, to lament with him. But take care that you do not lament internally also.

XVII. Remember that thou art an actor in a play of such a kind as the teacher (author) may choose; if short, of a short one; if long, of a long one: if he wishes you to act the part of a poor man, see that you act the part naturally; if the part of a lame man, of a magistrate, of a private person, (do the same). For this is your duty, to act well the part that is given to you; but to select the part, belongs to another.

XVIII. When a raven has croaked inauspiciously, let not the appearance hurry you away with it; but straightway make a distinction in your mind and say, None of these things is signified to me, but either to my poor body, or to my small property, or to my reputation, or to my children or to my wife: but to me all significations are auspicious if I choose. For whatever of these things results, it is in my power to derive benefit from it.

XIX. You can be invincible, if you enter into no contest in which it is not in your power to conquer. Take care then when you observe a man honored before others or possessed of great power or highly esteemed for any reason, not to suppose him happy, and be not carried away by the appearance. For if the nature of the good is in our power, neither envy nor jealousy will have a place in us. But you yourself will not wish to be a general or senator or consul, but a free man: and there is only one way to this, to despise (care not for) the things which are not in our power.

XX. Remember that it is not he who reviles you or strikes you, who insults you, but it is your opinion about these things as being insulting. When then a man irritates you, you must know that it is your own opinion which has irritated you. Therefore especially try not to be carried away by the appearance. For if you once gain time and delay, you will more easily master yourself.

XXI. Let death and exile and every other thing which appears dreadful be daily before your eyes; but most of all death: and you will never think of anything mean nor will you desire anything extravagantly.

XXII. If you desire philosophy, prepare yourself from the beginning to be ridiculed, to expect that many will sneer at you, and say, He has all at once returned to us as a philosopher; and whence does he get this supercilious look for us? Do you not show a supercilious look; but hold on to the things which seem to you best as one appointed by God to this station. And remember that if you abide in the same principles, these men who first ridiculed will afterward admire you: but if you shall have been overpowered by them, you will bring on yourself double ridicule.

XXIII. If it should ever happen to you to be turned to externals in order to please some person, you must know that you have lost your purpose in life. Be satisfied then in everything with being a philosopher; and if you wish to seem also to any person to be a philosopher, appear so to yourself, and you will be able to do this.

XXIV. Let not these thoughts afflict you, I shall live unhonored and be nobody nowhere. For if want of honor (ἀτιμία) is an evil, you cannot be in evil through the means (fault) of another any more than you can be involved in anything base. Is it then your business to obtain the rank of magistrate, or to be received at a banquet? By no means. How then can this be want of honor (dishonor)? And how will you be nobody nowhere, when you ought to be somebody in those things only which are in your power, in which indeed it is permitted to you to be a man of the greatest worth? But your friends will be without assistance! What do you mean by being without assistance? They will not receive money from you, nor will you make them Roman citizens. Who then told you that these are among the things which are in our power, and not in the power of others? And who can give to another what he has not himself? Acquire money then, your friends say, that we also may have something. If I can acquire money and also keep myself modest, and faithful and magnanimous, point out the way, and I will acquire it. But if you ask me to lose the things which are good and my own, in order that you may gain the things which are not good, see how unfair and silly you are. Besides, which would you rather have, money or a faithful and modest friend? For this end then rather help me to be such a man, and do not ask me to do this by which I shall lose that character. But my country, you say, as far as it depends on me, will be without my help. I ask again, what help do you mean? It will not have porticoes or baths through you. And what does this mean? For it is not furnished with shoes by means of a smith, nor with arms by means of a shoemaker. But it is enough if every man fully discharges the work that is his own: and if you provided it with another citizen faithful and modest, would you not be useful to it? Yes. Then you also cannot be useless to it. What place then, you say, shall I hold in the city? Whatever you can, if you maintain at the same time your fidelity and modesty. But if when you wish to be useful to the state, you shall lose these qualities, what profit could you be to it, if you were made shameless and faithless?

XXV. Has any man been preferred before you at a banquet, or in being saluted, or in being invited to a consultation? If these things are good, you ought to rejoice that he has obtained them: but if bad, be not grieved because you have not obtained them; and remember that you cannot, if you do not the same things in order to obtain what is not in our power, be considered worthy of the same (equal) things. For how can a man obtain an equal share with another when he does not visit a man's doors as that other man does, when he does not attend him when he goes abroad, as the other man does; when he does not praise (flatter) him as another does? You will be unjust then and insatiable, if you do not part with the price, in return for which those things are sold, and if you wish to obtain them for nothing.

Well, what is the price of lettuces? An obolus perhaps. If then a man gives up the obolus, and receives the lettuces, and if you do not give up the obolus and do not obtain the lettuces, do not suppose that you receive less than he who has got the lettuces; for as he has the lettuces, so you have the obolus which you did not give. In the same way then in the other matter also you have not been invited to a man's feast, for you did not give to the host the price at which the supper is sold; but he sells it for praise (flattery), he sells it for personal attention. Give then the price, if it is for your interest, for which it is sold. But if you wish both not to give the price and to obtain the things, you are insatiable and silly. Have you nothing then in place of the supper? You have indeed, you have the not flattering of him, whom you did not choose to flatter; you have the not enduring of the man when he enters the room.

XXVI. We may learn the wish (will) of nature from the things in which we do not differ from one another; for instance, when your neighbor's slave has broken his cup, or anything else, we are ready to say forthwith, that it one of the things which happen. You must know then that when your cup also is broken, you ought to think as you did when your neighbor's cup was broken. Transfer this reflection to greater things also. Is another man's child or wife dead? There is no one who would not say, this is an event incident to man. But when a man's own child or wife is dead, forthwith he calls out, Wo to me, how wretched I am. But we ought to remember how we feel when we hear that it has happened to others.

XXVII. As a mark is not set up for the purpose of missing the aim, so neither does the nature of evil exist in the world.

XXVIII. If any person was intending to put your body in the power of any man whom you fell in with on the way, you would be vexed: but that you put your understanding in the power of any man whom you meet, so that if he should revile you, it is disturbed and troubled, are you not ashamed at this?

XXIX. In every act observe the things which come first, and those which follow it; and so proceed to the act. If you do not, at first you will approach it with alacrity, without having thought of the things which will follow; but afterward, when certain base (ugly) things have shown themselves, you will be ashamed. A man wishes to conquer at the Olympic games. I also wish indeed, for it is a fine thing. But observe both the things which come first, and the things which follow; and then begin the act. You must do everything according to rule, eat according to strict orders, abstain from delicacies, exercise yourself as you are bid at appointed times, in heat, in cold, you must not drink cold water, nor wine as you choose; in a word, you must deliver yourself up to the exercise master as you do to the physician, and then proceed to the contest. And sometimes you will strain the hand, put the ankle out of joint, swallow much dust, sometimes be flogged, and after all this be defeated. When you have considered all this, if you still choose, go to the contest: if you do not, you will behave like children, who at one time play as wrestlers, another time as flute players, again as gladiators, then as trumpeters, then as tragic actors: so you also will be at one time an athlete, at another a gladiator, then a rhetorician, then a philosopher, but with your whole soul you will be nothing at all; but like an ape you imitate everything that you see, and one thing after another pleases you. For you have not undertaken anything with consideration, nor have you surveyed it well; but carelessly and with cold desire. Thus some who have seen a philosopher and having heard one speak, as Euphrates speaks,—and who can speak as he does?—they wish to be philosophers themselves also. My man, first of all consider what kind of thing it is: and then examine your own nature, if you are able to sustain the character. Do you wish to be a pentathlete or a wrestler? Look at your arms, your thighs, examine your loins. For different men are formed by nature for different things. Do you think that if you do these things, you can eat in the same manner, drink in the same manner, and in the same manner loathe certain things? You must pass sleepless nights, endure toil, go away from your kinsmen, be despised by a slave, in every thing have the inferior part, in honor, in office, in the courts of justice, in every little matter. Consider these things, if you would exchange for them, freedom from passions, liberty, tranquillity. If not, take care that, like little children, you be not now a philosopher, then a servant of the publicani, then a rhetorician, then a procurator (manager) for Cæsar. These things are not consistent. You must be one man, either good or bad. You must either cultivate your own ruling faculty, or external things; you must either exercise your skill on internal things or on external things; that is you must either maintain the position of a philosopher or that of a common person.

XXX. Duties are universally measured by relations. Is a man a father? The precept is to take care of him, to yield to him in all things, to submit when he is reproachful, when he inflicts blows. But suppose that he is a bad father. Were you then by nature made akin to a good father? No; but to a father. Does a brother wrong you? Maintain then your own position toward him, and do not examine what he is doing, but what you must do that your will shall be conformable to nature. For another will not damage you, unless you choose: but you will be damaged then when you shall think that you are damaged. In this way then you will discover your duty from the relation of a neighbor, from that of a citizen, from that of a general, if you are accustomed to contemplate the relations.

XXXI. As to piety toward the Gods you must know that this is the chief thing, to have right opinions about them, to think that they exist, and that they administer the All well and justly; and you must fix yourself in this principle (duty), to obey them, and yield to them in everything which happens, and voluntarily to follow it as being accomplished by the wisest intelligence. For if you do so, you will never either blame the Gods, nor will you accuse them of neglecting you. And it is not possible for this to be done in any other way than by withdrawing from the things which are not in our power, and by placing the good and the evil only in those things which are in our power. For if you think that any of the things which are not in our power is good or bad, it is absolutely necessary that, when you do not obtain what you wish, and when you fall into those things which you do not wish, you will find fault and hate those who are the cause of them; for every animal is formed by nature to this, to fly from and to turn from the things which appear harmful and the things which are the cause of the harm, but to follow and admire the things which are useful and the causes of the useful. It is impossible then for a person who thinks that he is harmed to be delighted with that which he thinks to be the cause of the harm, as it is also impossible to be pleased with the harm itself. For this reason also a father is reviled by his son, when he gives no part to his son of the things which are considered to be good: and it was this which made Polynices and Eteocles enemies, the opinion that royal power was a good. It is for this reason that the cultivator of the earth reviles the Gods, for this reason the sailor does, and the merchant, and for this reason those who lose their wives and their children. For where the useful (your interest) is, there also piety is. Consequently he who takes care to desire as he ought and to avoid as he ought, at the same time also cares after piety. But to make libations and to sacrifice and to offer first fruits according to the custom of our fathers, purely and not meanly nor carelessly nor scantily nor above our ability, is a thing which belongs to all to do.

XXXII. When you have recourse to divination, remember that you do not know how it will turn out, but that you are come to inquire from the diviner. But of what kind it is, you know when you come, if indeed you are a philosopher. For if it is any of the things which are not in our power, it is absolutely necessary that it must be neither good nor bad. Do not then bring to the diviner desire or aversion (ἔκκλισιν): if you do, you will approach him with fear. But having determined in your mind that everything which shall turn out (result) is indifferent, and does not concern you, and whatever it may be, for it will be in your power to use it well, and no man will hinder this, come then with confidence to the Gods as your advisers. And then when any advice shall have been given, remember whom you have taken as advisers, and whom you will have neglected, if you do not obey them. And go to divination, as Socrates said that you ought, about those matters in which all the inquiry has reference to the result, and in which means are not given either by reason nor by any other art for knowing the thing which is the subject of the inquiry. Wherefor when we ought to share a friend's danger or that of our country, you must not consult the diviner whether you ought to share it. For even if the diviner shall tell you that the signs of the victims are unlucky, it is plain that this is a token of death or mutilation of part of the body or of exile. But reason prevails that even with these risks we should share the dangers of our friend and of our country. Therefore attend to the greater diviner, the Pythian God, who ejected from the temple him who did not assist his friend when he was being murdered.

XXXIII. Immediately prescribe some character and some form to yourself, which you shall observe both when you are alone and when you meet with men.

And let silence be the general rule, or let only what is necessary be said, and in few words. And rarely and when the occasion calls we shall say something; but about none of the common subjects, nor about gladiators, nor horse-races, nor about athletes, nor about eating or drinking, which are the usual subjects; and especially not about men, as blaming them or praising them, or comparing them. If then you are able, bring over by your conversation the conversation of your associates to that which is proper; but if you should happen to be confined to the company of strangers, be silent.

Let not your laughter be much, nor on many occasions, nor excessive.

Refuse altogether to take an oath, if it is possible: if it is not, refuse as far as you are able.

Avoid banquets which are given by strangers and by ignorant persons. But if ever there is occasion to join in them, let your attention be carefully fixed, that you slip not into the manners of the vulgar (the uninstructed). For you must know, that if your companion be impure, he also who keeps company with him must become impure, though he should happen to be pure.

Take (apply) the things which relate to the body as far as the bare use, as food, drink, clothing, house, and slaves: but exclude everything which is for show or luxury.

As to pleasure with women, abstain as far as you can before marriage: but if you do indulge in it, do it in the way which is conformable to custom. Do not however be disagreeable to those who indulge in these pleasures, or reprove them; and do not often boast that you do not indulge in them yourself.

If a man has reported to you, that a certain person speaks ill of you, do not make any defense (answer) to what has been told you: but reply, The man did not know the rest of my faults, for he would not have mentioned these only.

It is not necessary to go to the theaters often: but if there is ever a proper occasion for going, do not show yourself as being a partisan of any man except yourself, that is, desire only that to be done which is done, and for him only to gain the prize who gains the prize; for in this way you will meet with no hindrance. But abstain entirely from shouts and laughter at any (thing or person), or violent emotions. And when you are come away, do not talk much about what has passed on the stage, except about that which may lead to your own improvement. For it is plain, if you do talk much that you admired the spectacle (more than you ought).

Do not go to the hearing of certain persons' recitations nor visit them readily. But if you do attend, observe gravity and sedateness, and also avoid making yourself disagreeable.

When you are going to meet with any person, and particularly one of those who are considered to be in a superior condition, place before yourself what Socrates or Zeno would have done in such circumstances, and you will have no difficulty in making a proper use of the occasion.

When you are going to any of those who are in great power, place before yourself that you will not find the man at home, that you will be excluded, that the door will not be opened to you, that the man will not care about you. And if with all this it is your duty to visit him, bear what happens, and never say to yourself that it was not worth the trouble. For this is silly, and marks the character of a man who is offended by externals.

In company take care not to speak much and excessively about your own acts or dangers: for as it is pleasant to you to make mention of your dangers, it is not so pleasant to others to hear what has happened to you. Take care also not to provoke laughter; for this is a slippery way toward vulgar habits, and is also adapted to diminish the respect of your neighbors. It is a dangerous habit also to approach obscene talk. When then anything of this kind happens, if there is a good opportunity, rebuke the man who has proceeded to this talk: but if there is not an opportunity, by your silence at least, and blushing and expression of dissatisfaction by your countenance, show plainly that you are displeased at such talk.

XXXIV. If you have received the impression of any pleasure, guard yourself against being carried away by it; but let the thing wait for you, and allow yourself a certain delay on your own part. Then think of both times, of the time when you will enjoy the pleasure, and of the time after the enjoyment of the pleasure when you will repent and will reproach yourself. And set against these things how you will rejoice if you have abstained from the pleasure, and how you will commend yourself. But if it seem to you seasonable to undertake (do) the thing, take care that the charm of it, and the pleasure, and the attraction of it shall not conquer you: but set on the other side the consideration how much better it is to be conscious that you have gained this victory.

XXXV. When you have decided that a thing ought to be done and are doing it, never avoid being seen doing it, though the many shall form an unfavorable opinion about it. For if it is not right to do it, avoid doing the thing; but if it is right, why are you afraid of those who shall find fault wrongly?

XXXVI. As the proposition it is either day or it is night is of great importance for the disjunctive argument, but for the conjunctive is of no value, so in a symposium (entertainment) to select the larger share is of great value for the body, but for the maintenance of the social feeling is worth nothing. When then you are eating with another, remember to look not only to the value for the body of the things set before you, but also to the value of the behavior toward the host which ought to be observed.

XXXVII. If you have assumed a character above your strength, you have both acted in this matter in an unbecoming way, and you have neglected that which you might have fulfilled.

XXXVIII. In walking about as you take care not to step on a nail or to sprain your foot, so take care not to damage your own ruling faculty: and if we observe this rule in every act, we shall undertake the act with more security.

XXXIX. The measure of possession (property) is to every man the body, as the foot is of the shoe. If then you stand on this rule (the demands of the body), you will maintain the measure: but if you pass beyond it, you must then of necessity be hurried as it were down a precipice. As also in the matter of the shoe, if you go beyond the (necessities of the) foot, the shoe is gilded, then of a purple color, then embroidered: for there is no limit to that which has once passed the true measure.

XL. Women forthwith from the age of fourteen are called by the men mistresses (dominae). Therefore since they see that there is nothing else that they can obtain, but only the power of lying with men, they begin to decorate themselves, and to place all their hopes in this. It is worth our while then to take care that they may know that they are valued (by men) for nothing else than appearing (being) decent and modest and discreet.

XLI. It is a mark of a mean capacity to spend much time on the things which concern the body, such as much exercise, much eating, much drinking, much easing of the body, much copulation. But these things should be done as subordinate things: and let all your care be directed to the mind.

XLII. When any person treats you ill or speaks ill of you, remember that he does this or says this because he thinks that it is his duty. It is not possible then for him to follow that which seems right to you, but that which seems right to himself. Accordingly if he is wrong in his opinion, he is the person who is hurt, for he is the person who has been deceived; for if a man shall suppose the true conjunction to be false, it is not the conjunction which is hindered, but the man who has been deceived about it. If you proceed then from these opinions, you will be mild in temper to him who reviles you: for say on each occasion, It seemed so to him.

XLIII. Everything has two handles, the one by which it may be borne, the other by which it may not. If your brother acts unjustly, do not lay hold of the act by that handle wherein he acts unjustly, for this is the handle which cannot be borne; but lay hold of the other, that he is your brother, that he was nurtured with you, and you will lay hold of the thing by that handle by which it can be borne.

XLIV. These reasons do not cohere: I am richer than you, therefore I am better than you; I am more eloquent than you, therefore I am better than you. On the contrary these rather cohere, I am richer than you, therefore my possessions are greater than yours: I am more eloquent than you, therefore my speech is superior to yours. But you are neither possession nor speech.

XLV. Does a man bathe quickly (early)? do not say that he bathes badly, but that he bathes quickly. Does a man drink much wine? do not say that he does this badly, but say that he drinks much. For before you shall have determined the opinion, how do you know whether he is acting wrong? Thus it will not happen to you to comprehend some appearances which are capable of being comprehended, but to assent to others.

XLVI. On no occasion call yourself a philosopher, and do not speak much among the uninstructed about theorems (philosophical rules, precepts): but do that which follows from them. For example at a banquet do not say how a man ought to eat, but eat as you ought to eat. For remember that in this way Socrates also altogether avoided ostentation: persons used to come to him and ask to be recommended by him to philosophers, and he used to take them to philosophers: so easily did he submit to being overlooked. Accordingly if any conversation should arise among uninstructed persons about any theorem, generally be silent; for there is great danger that you will immediately vomit up what you have not digested. And when a man shall say to you, that you know nothing, and you are not vexed, then be sure that you have begun the work (of philosophy). For even sheep do not vomit up their grass and show to the shepherds how much they have eaten; but when they have internally digested the pasture, they produce externally wool and milk. Do you also show not your theorems to the uninstructed, but show the acts which come from their digestion.

XLVII. When at a small cost you are supplied with everything for the body, do not be proud of this; nor, if you drink water, say on every occasion, I drink water. But consider first how much more frugal the poor are than we, and how much more enduring of labor. And if you ever wish to exercise yourself in labor and endurance, do it for yourself, and not for others: do not embrace statues. But if you are ever very thirsty, take a draught of cold water, and spit it out, and tell no man.

XLVIII. The condition and characteristic of an uninstructed person is this: he never expects from himself profit (advantage) nor harm, but from externals. The condition and characteristic of a philosopher is this: he expects all advantage and all harm from himself. The signs (marks) of one who is making progress are these: he censures no man, he praises no man, he blames no man, he accuses no man, he says nothing about himself as if he were somebody or knew something; when he is impeded at all or hindered, he blames himself: if a man praises him, he ridicules the praiser to himself: if a man censures him, he makes no defense: he goes about like weak persons, being careful not to move any of the things which are placed, before they are firmly fixed: he removes all desire from himself, and he transfers aversion to those things only of the things within our power which are contrary to nature: he employs a moderate movement toward everything: whether he is considered foolish or ignorant, he cares not: and in a word he watches himself as if he were an enemy and lying in ambush.

XLIX. When a man is proud because he can understand and explain the writings of Chrysippus, say to yourself, If Chrysippus had not written obscurely, this man would have had nothing to be proud of. But what is it that I wish? To understand Nature and to follow it. I inquire therefore who is the interpreter: and when I have heard that it is Chrysippus, I come to him (the interpreter). But I do not understand what is written, and therefore I seek the interpreter. And so far there is yet nothing to be proud of. But when I shall have found the interpreter, the thing that remains is to use the precepts (the lessons). This itself is the only thing to be proud of. But if I shall admire the exposition, what else have I been made unless a grammarian instead of a philosopher? except in one thing, that I am explaining Chrysippus instead of Homer. When then any man says to me, Read Chrysippus to me, I rather blush, when I cannot show my acts like to and consistent with his words.

L. Whatever things (rules) are proposed to you (for the conduct of life) abide by them, as if they were laws, as if you would be guilty of impiety if you transgressed any of them. And whatever any man shall say about you, do not attend to it: for this is no affair of yours. How long will you then still defer thinking yourself worthy of the best things, and in no matter transgressing the distinctive reason? Have you accepted the theorems (rules), which it was your duty to agree to, and have you agreed to them? what teacher then do you still expect that you defer to him the correction of yourself? You are no longer a youth, but already a full grown man. If then you are negligent and slothful, and are continually making procrastination after procrastination, and proposal (intention) after proposal, and fixing day after day, after which you will attend to yourself, you will not know that you are not making improvement, but you will continue ignorant (uninstructed) both while you live and till you die. Immediately then think it right to live as a full-grown man, and one who is making proficiency, and let everything which appears to you to be the best be to you a law which must not be transgressed. And if anything laborious, or pleasant or glorious or inglorious be presented to you, remember that now is the contest, now are the Olympic games, and they cannot be deferred; and that it depends on one defeat and one giving way that progress is either lost or maintained. Socrates in this way became perfect, in all things improving himself, attending to nothing except to reason. But you, though you are not yet a Socrates, ought to live as one who wishes to be a Socrates.

LI. The first and most necessary place (part) in philosophy is the use of theorems (precepts), for instance, that we must not lie: the second part is that of demonstrations, for instance, How is it proved that we ought not to lie: the third is that which is confirmatory of these two and explanatory, for example, How is this a demonstration? For what is demonstration, what is consequence, what is contradiction, what is truth, what is falsehood? The third part (topic) is necessary on account of the second, and the second on account of the first; but the most necessary and that on which we ought to rest is the first. But we do the contrary. For we spend our time on the third topic, and all our earnestness is about it: but we entirely neglect the first. Therefore we lie; but the demonstration that we ought not to lie we have ready to hand.

LII. In every thing (circumstance) we should hold these maxims ready to hand:

> *Lead me, O Zeus, and thou O Destiny,*
> *The way that I am bid by you to go:*
> *To follow I am ready. If I choose not,*
> *I make myself a wretch, and still must follow.*
> *But whoso nobly yields unto necessity,*
> *We hold him wise, and skill'd in things divine.*

And the third also: O Crito, if so it pleases the Gods, so let it be; Anytus and Meletus are able indeed to kill me, but they cannot harm me.

PLOTINUS

Plotinus (ca. A.D. *204–270) was born in Egypt; he studied philosophy, notably a current version of Platonism, at the university in Alexandria. After a successful career in Rome as a teacher and spiritual counselor, he retired to a country house in Campania, where he spent the rest of his life.*

The Enneads *are the standard "collected papers" of Plotinus, arranged and edited by his pupil Porphyry into six "enneads," so called since each contained nine "tractates,"* or *treatises.*

*The Enneads**

The First Ennead

SECOND TRACTATE. ON VIRTUE

Since Evil is here, "haunting this world by necessary law," and it is the Soul's design to escape from Evil, we must escape hence.

But what is this escape?

"In attaining Likeness to God," we read. And this is explained as "becoming just and holy, living by wisdom," the entire nature grounded in Virtue.

But does not Likeness by way of Virtue imply Likeness to some being that has Virtue? To what Divine Being, then, would our Likeness be? To the Being—must we not think?—in Which, above all, such excellence seems to inhere, that is to the Soul of the Kosmos and to the Principle ruling within it, the Principle endowed with a wisdom most wonderful. What could be more fitting than that we, living in this world, should become Like to its ruler?

[Plato] declares all the virtues without exception to be purifications.

But in what sense can we call the virtues purifications, and how does purification issue in Likeness?

As the Soul is evil by being interfused with the body, and by coming to share the body's states and to think the body's thoughts, so it would be good, it would be possessed of virtue, if it threw off the body's moods and devoted itself to its own Act—the state of Intellection and Wisdom—never allowed the passions of the body to affect it—the virtue of Sophrosyny† —knew no fear at the parting from the body—the virtue of Fortitude—and if reason and the Intellectual-Principle ruled—in which state is Righteousness. Such a disposition in the Soul, become thus intellective and immune to passion, it would not be wrong to call Likeness to God; for the Divine, too, is pure and the Divine-Act is such that Likeness to it is Wisdom.

The Soul's true Good is in devotion

* By permission. From Stephen MacKenna, *Plotinus: The Enneads*, Faber & Faber, Ltd., London, and Pantheon Books, Inc., New York, 1956. Deletions are not noted in the text.

† Temperance [Eds.].

to the Intellectual-Principle, its kin; evil to the Soul lies in frequenting strangers.

The question is substantially this: how far does purification dispel the two orders of passion—anger, desire and the like, with grief and its kin—and in what degree the disengagement from the body is possible.

Disengagement means simply that the soul withdraws to its own place.

It will hold itself above all passions and affections. Necessary pleasures and all the activity of the senses it will employ only for medicament and assuagement lest its work be impeded. Pain it may combat, but, failing the cure, it will bear meekly and ease it by refusing assent to it. All passionate action it will check.

In all this there is no sin—there is only matter of discipline—but our concern is not merely to be sinless but to be God.

As long as there is any such involuntary action, the nature is twofold, God and Demi-God, or rather God in association with a nature of a lower power: when all the involuntary is suppressed, there is God unmingled, a Divine Being of those that follow upon The First.

For, at this height, the man is the very being that came from the Supreme. The primal excellence restored, the essential man is There: entering this sphere, he has associated himself with the reasoning phase of his nature and this he will lead up into likeness with his highest self, as far as earthly mind is capable, so that if possible it shall never be inclined to, and at the least never adopt, any course displeasing to its over-lord.

What form, then, does virtue take in one so lofty?

It appears as Wisdom, which consists in the contemplation of all that exists in the Intellectual-Principle, and as the immediate presence of the Intellectual-Principle itself.

And each of these has two modes or aspects: there is Wisdom as it is in the Intellectual-Principle and as in the Soul; and there is the Intellectual-Principle as it is present to itself and as it is present to the Soul: this gives what in the Soul is Virtue, in the Supreme not Virtue.

And what happens when the virtues in their very nature differ in scope and province?

The solution is in understanding the virtues and what each has to give; thus the man will learn to work with this or that as every several need demands. And as he reaches to loftier principles and other standards these in turn will define his conduct: for example, Restraint in its earlier form will no longer satisfy him; he will work for the final Disengagement; he will live, no longer, the human life of the good man—such as Civic Virtue commends—but, leaving this beneath him, will take up instead another life, that of the Gods.

For it is to the Gods, not to the Good, that our Likeness must look: to model ourselves upon good men is to produce an image of an image: we have to fix our gaze above the image and attain Likeness to the Supreme Exemplar.

FOURTH TRACTATE. ON TRUE HAPPINESS

It has been said more than once that the perfect life and the true life, the essential life, is in the Intellectual Nature beyond this sphere, and that all other forms of life are incomplete, are phantoms of life, imperfect, not pure, not more truly life than they are its contrary: here let it be said succinctly that since all living things proceed from the one principle but possess life in different degrees, this principle must be the first life and the most complete.

If, then, the perfect life is within human reach, the man attaining it attains happiness: if not, happiness must be made over to the gods, for the perfect life is for them alone.

But since we hold that happiness is for human beings too, we must consider what this perfect life is. The matter may be stated thus:—

It has been shown elsewhere that man when he commands not merely the life of sensation but also Reason and Authentic Intellection, has realised the perfect life.

But are we to picture this kind of life as something foreign imported into his nature?

No: there exists no single human being that does not either potentially or effectively possess this thing which we hold to constitute happiness.

But are we to think of man as including this form of life, the perfect, after the manner of a partial constituent of his entire nature?

We say, rather, that while in some men it is present as a mere portion of their total being—in those, namely, that have it potentially—there is, too, the man, already in possession of true felicity, who is this perfection realised, who has passed over into actual identification with it. All else is now mere clothing about the man, not to be called part of him since it lies about him unsought, not his because not appropriated to himself by any act of the will.

To the man in this state, what is the Good?

He himself by what he has and is.

And the author and principle of what he is and holds is the Supreme, which within Itself is the Good but manifests Itself within the human being after this other mode.

The sign that this state has been achieved is that the man seeks nothing else.

For man, and especially the Sage, is not the Couplement of soul and body: the proof is that man can be disengaged from the body and disdain its nominal goods.

It would be absurd to think that happiness begins and ends with the living-body: happiness is the possession of the good of life: it is centred therefore in Soul, is an Act of the Soul—and not of all the Soul at that: for it certainly is not characteristic of the vegetative soul, the soul of growth; that would at once connect it with the body.

A powerful frame, a healthy constitution, even a happy balance of temperament, these surely do not make felicity; in the excess of these advantages there is, even, the danger that the man be crushed down and forced more and more within their power. There must be a sort of counter-pressure in the other direction, towards the noblest: the body must be lessened, reduced, that the veritable man may show forth, the man behind the appearances.

Those that refuse to place the Sage aloft in the Intellectual Realm but drag him down to the accidental, dreading accident for him, have substituted for the Sage we have in mind another person altogether; they offer us a tolerable sort of man and they assign to him a life of mingled good and ill, a case, after all, not easy to conceive. But admitting the possibility of such a mixed state, it could not be deserved to be called a life of happiness; it misses the Great, both in the dignity of Wisdom and in the integrity of Good. The life of true happiness is not a thing of mixture. And Plato rightly taught that he who is to be wise and to possess happiness draws his good from the Supreme, fixing his gaze on That, becoming like to That, living by That.

FIFTH TRACTATE. HAPPINESS AND EXTENSION OF TIME

True happiness is not vague and fluid: it is an unchanging state.

If there is in this matter any increase besides that of mere time, it is in the sense that a greater happiness is the reward of a higher virtue: this is not counting up to the credit of happiness the years of its continuance; it is simply noting the high-water mark once for all attained.

But if we are to consider only the present and may not call in the past to make the total, why do we not reckon so in the case of time itself, where, in fact, we do not hesitate to add the past to the present and call the total greater? Why not suppose a quantity of happiness equivalent to a quantity of time? This would be no more than taking it lap by lap to correspond with time-laps instead of choosing to consider it as an indivisible, measurable only by the content of a given instant.

There is no absurdity in taking count of time which has ceased to be: we are merely counting what is past and finished, as we might count the dead: but to treat past happiness as actually existent and as outweighing present happiness, that is an absurdity. For Happiness must be an achieved and existent state, whereas any time over and apart from the present is non-existent: all progress of time means the extinction of all the time that has been.

Hence time is aptly described as a mimic of eternity that seeks to break up in its fragmentary flight the permanence of its exemplar. Thus whatever time seizes and seals to itself of what stands permanent in eternity is annihilated—saved only in so far as in some degree it still belongs to eternity, but wholly destroyed if it be unreservedly absorbed into time.

If Happiness demands the possession of the good of life, it clearly has to do with the life of Authentic-Existence, for that life is the Best. Now the life of Authentic-Existence is measurable not by time but by eternity; and eternity is not a more or a less or a thing of any magnitude but is the unchangeable, the indivisible, is timeless Being.

We must not muddle together Being and Non-Being, time and eternity, not even everlasting time with the eternal; we cannot make laps and stages of an absolute unity; all must be taken together, wheresoever and howsoever we handle it; and it must be taken at that, not even as an undivided block of time but as the Life of Eternity, a stretch not made up of periods but completely rounded, outside of all notion of time.

The good does not derive from the act itself but from the inner disposition which prompts the noble conduct: the wise and good man in his very action harvests the good not by what he does but by what he is.

A wicked man no less than a Sage may save the country, and the good of the act is for all alike, no matter whose was the saving hand. The contentment of the Sage does not hang upon such actions and events: it is his own inner habit that creates at once his felicity and whatever pleasure may accompany it.

To put Happiness in actions is to put it in things that are outside virtue and outside the Soul; for the Soul's expression is not in action but in wisdom, in a contemplative operation within itself; and this, this alone, is Happiness.

SIXTH TRACTATE. BEAUTY

Beauty addresses itself chiefly to sight; but there is a beauty for the hearing too, as in certain combinations of words and in all kinds of music, for melodies and cadences are beautiful; and minds that lift themselves above the realm of sense to a higher order are aware of beauty in the conduct of life, in actions, in character, in the pursuits of the intellect; and there is the beauty of the virtues. What loftier beauty there may be, yet, our argument will bring to light.

What, then, is it that gives comeliness to material forms and draws the ear to the sweetness perceived in sounds, and what is the secret of the beauty there is in all that derives from Soul?

Is there some One Principle from which all take their grace, or is there a beauty peculiar to the embodied and another for the bodiless? Finally, one or many, what would such a Principle be?

Consider that some things, material shapes for instance, are gracious not by anything inherent but by something communicated, while others are lovely of themselves, as, for example, Virtue.

The same bodies appear sometimes beautiful, sometimes not; so that there is a good deal between being body and being beautiful.

What, then, is this something that shows itself in certain material forms?

Let us, then, go back to the source, and indicate at once the Principle that bestows beauty on material things.

Undoubtedly this Principle exists; it is something that is perceived at the first glance, something which the soul names as from an ancient knowledge and, recognising, welcomes it, enters into unison with it.

But let the soul fall in with the Ugly and at once it shrinks within itself, denies the thing, turns away from it, not accordant, resenting it.

Our interpretation is that the soul—by the very truth of its nature, by its affiliation to the noblest Existents in the hierarchy of Being—when it sees anything of that kin, or any trace of that kinship, thrills with an immediate delight, takes its own to itself, and thus stirs anew to the sense of its nature and of all its affinity.

But, is there any such likeness between the loveliness of this world and the splendours in the Supreme? Such a likeness in the particulars would make the two orders alike: but what is there in common between beauty here and beauty There?

We hold that all the loveliness of this world comes by communion in Ideal-Form.

All shapelessness whose kind admits of pattern and form, as long as it remains outside of Reason and Idea, is ugly by that very isolation from the Divine-Thought. And this is the Absolute Ugly: an ugly thing is something that has not been entirely mastered by pattern, that is by Reason, the Matter not yielding at all points and in all respects to Ideal-Form.

But where the Ideal-Form has entered, it has grouped and co-ordinated what from a diversity of parts was to become a unity: it has rallied confusion into co-operation: it has made the sum one harmonious coherence: for the Idea is a unity and what it moulds must come to unity as far as multiplicity may.

And on what has thus been compacted to unity, Beauty enthrones itself, giving itself to the parts as to the sum: when it lights on some natural unity, a thing of like parts, then it gives itself to that whole. Thus, for an illustration, there is the beauty, conferred by craftsmanship, of all a house with all its parts, and the beauty which some natural quality may give to a single stone.

This, then, is how the material thing becomes beautiful—by communicating in the thought that flows from the Divine.

Let us take the contrary, the ugliness of the Soul, and set that against its beauty: to understand, at once, what this ugliness is and how it comes to appear in the Soul will certainly open our way before us.

Let us then suppose an ugly Soul, dissolute, unrighteous: teeming with all the lusts; torn by internal discord; beset by the fears of its cowardice and the envies of its pettiness; thinking, in the little thought it has, only of the perishable and the base; perverse in all its impulses; the friend of unclean pleasures; living the life of abandonment to bodily sensation and delighting in its deformity.

What must we think but that all this shame is something that has gathered about the Soul, some foreign bane outraging it, soiling it, so that, encumbered with all manner of turpitude, it has no longer a clean activity or a clean sensation, but commands only a life smouldering dully under the crust of evil; that, sunk in manifold death, it no longer sees what a Soul should see, may no longer rest in its own being, dragged ever as it is towards the outer, the lower, the dark?

An unclean thing, I dare to say; flickering hither and thither at the call of objects of sense, deeply infected with the taint of body, occupied always in Matter, and absorbing Matter into itself; in its commerce with the Ignoble it has trafficked away for an alien nature its own essential Idea.

If a man has been immersed in filth or daubed with mud his native comeliness disappears and all that is seen is the foul stuff besmearing him: his ugly condition is due to alien matter that has encrusted him, and if he is to win back his grace it must be his business to scour and purify himself and make himself what he was.

So, we may justly say, a Soul becomes ugly—by something foisted upon it, by sinking itself into the alien, by a fall, a descent into body, into Matter. The dishonour of the Soul is in its ceasing to be clean and apart. Gold is degraded when it is mixed with earthy particles; if these be worked out, the gold is left and is beautiful, isolated from all that is foreign, gold with gold alone. And so the Soul; let it be but cleared of the desires that come by its too intimate converse with the body, emancipated from all the passions, purged of all that embodiment has thrust upon it, withdrawn, a solitary, to itself again—in that moment the ugliness that came only from the alien is stripped away.

The Soul thus cleansed is all Idea and Reason, wholly free of body, intellective, entirely of that divine order from which the wellspring of Beauty rises and all the race of Beauty.

Hence the Soul heightened to the Intellectual-Principle is beautiful to all its power. For Intellection and all that proceeds from Intellection are the Soul's beauty, a graciousness native to it and not foreign, for only with these is it truly Soul. And it is just to say that in the Soul's becoming a good and beautiful thing is its becoming like to God, for from the Divine comes all the Beauty and all the Good in beings.

We may even say that Beauty *is* the Authentic-Existence and Ugliness is the Principle contrary to Existence: and the Ugly is also the primal evil; therefore its contrary is at once good and beautiful, or is Good and Beauty: and hence the one method will discover to us the Beauty-Good and the Ugliness-Evil.

And Beauty, this Beauty which is also The Good, must be posed as The First: directly deriving from this First is the Intellectual-Principle which is pre-eminently the manifestation of Beauty; through the Intellectual-Principle Soul is beautiful. The beauty in things of a lower order—actions and pursuits for instance—comes by operation of the shaping Soul which is also the author of the beauty found in the world of sense. For the Soul, a divine thing, a fragment as it were of the Primal Beauty, makes beautiful to the fulness of their capacity all things whatsoever that it grasps and moulds.

Therefore we must ascend again towards the Good, the desired of every Soul. Anyone that has seen This, knows what I intend when I say that it is beautiful. Even the desire of it is to be desired as a Good. To attain it is for those that will take the upward path, who will set all their forces towards it, who will divest themselves of all that we have put on in our descent:—so, to those that approach the Holy Celebrations of the Mysteries, there are appointed purifications and the laying aside of the garments worn before, and the entry in nakedness—until, passing, on the upward way, all that is other than the God, each in the solitude of himself shall behold that solitary-dwelling Existence, the Apart, the

Unmingled, the Pure, that from Which all things depend, for Which all look and live and act and know, the Source of Life and of Intellection and of Being.

And one that shall know this vision—with what passion of love shall he not be seized, with what pang of desire, what longing to be molten into one with This, what wondering delight! If he that has never seen this Being must hunger for It as for all his welfare, he that has known must love and reverence It as the very Beauty; he will be flooded with awe and gladness, stricken by a salutary terror; he loves with a veritable love, with sharp desire; all other loves than this he must despise, and disdain all that once seemed fair.

But what must we do? How lies the path? How come to vision of the inaccessible Beauty, dwelling as if in consecrated precincts, apart from the common ways where all may see, even the profane?

He that has the strength, let him arise and withdraw into himself, foregoing all that is known by the eyes, turning away for ever from the material beauty that once made his joy. When he perceives those shapes of grace that show in body, let him not pursue: he must know them for copies, vestiges, shadows, and hasten away towards That they tell of. For if anyone follow what is like a beautiful shape playing over water—is there not a myth telling in symbol of such a dupe, how he sank into the depths of the current and was swept away to nothingness? So too, one that is held by material beauty and will not break free shall be precipitated, not in body but in Soul, down to the dark depths loathed of the Intellective-Being, where, blind even in the Lower-World, he shall have commerce only with shadows, there as here.

"Let us flee then to the beloved Fatherland": this is the soundest counsel. But what is this flight? How are we to gain the open sea? For Odysseus is surely a parable to us when he commands the flight from the sorceries of Circe or Calypso—not content to linger for all the pleasure offered to his eyes and all the delight of sense filling his days.

The Fatherland to us is There whence we have come, and There is The Father.

What then is our course, what the manner of our flight? This is not a journey for the feet; the feet bring us only from land to land; nor need you think of coach or ship to carry you away; all this order of things you must set aside and refuse to see: you must close the eyes and call instead upon another vision which is to be waked within you, a vision, the birth-right of all, which few turn to use.

And this inner vision, what is its operation?

Newly awakened it is all too feeble to bear the ultimate splendour. Therefore the Soul must be trained—to the habit of remarking, first, all noble pursuits, then the works of beauty produced not by the labour of the arts but by the virtue of men known for their goodness: lastly, you must search the souls of those that have shaped these beautiful forms.

But how are you to see into a virtuous soul and know its loveliness?

Withdraw into yourself and look. And if you do not find yourself beautiful yet, act as does the creator of a statue that is to be made beautiful: he cuts away here, he smoothes there, he makes this line lighter, this other purer, until a lovely face has grown upon his work. So do you also: cut away all that is excessive, straighten all that is crooked, bring light to all that is overcast, labour to make all one glow of beauty and never cease chiselling your statue, until there shall shine out on you from it the godlike splendour of virtue, until you shall see the perfect goodness surely established in the stainless shrine.

When you know that you have become this perfect work, when you are self-gathered in the purity of your being, nothing now remaining that can shatter that inner unity, nothing from without clinging to the authentic man, when you find yourself wholly true to your essential nature, wholly that only veritable Light which is not measured by space, not narrowed to any circumscribed form nor again diffused as a thing void of term, but ever unmeasurable as something greater than all measure and more than all quantity—when you perceive that you have grown to this, you are now become very vision: now call up all your confidence, strike forward yet a step—you need a guide no longer—strain, and see.

This is the only eye that sees the mighty Beauty. If the eye that adventures the vision be dimmed by vice, impure, or weak, and unable in its cowardly blenching to see the uttermost brightness, then it sees nothing even though another point to what lies plain to sight before it. To any vision must be brought an eye adapted to what is to be seen, and having some likeness to it. Never did eye see the sun unless it had first become sunlike, and never can the soul have vision of the First Beauty unless itself be beautiful.

Therefore, first let each become godlike and each beautiful who cares to see God and Beauty. So, mounting, the Soul will come first to the Intellectual-Principle and survey all the beautiful Ideas in the Supreme and will avow that this is Beauty, that the Ideas are Beauty. For by their efficacy comes all Beauty else, by the offspring and essence of the Intellectual-Being. What is beyond the Intellectual-Principle we affirm to be the nature of Good radiating Beauty before it. So that, treating the Intellectual-Kosmos as one, the first is the Beautiful: if we make distinction there, the Realm of Ideas constitutes the Beauty of the Intellectual Sphere; and The Good, which lies beyond, is the Fountain at once and Principle of Beauty: the Primal Good and the Primal Beauty have the one dwelling-place and, thus, always, Beauty's seat is There.

EIGHTH TRACTATE. ON THE NATURE AND SOURCE OF EVIL

For the moment let us define the Nature of the Good as far as the immediate purpose demands.

The Good is that on which all else depends, towards which all Existences aspire as to their source and their need, while Itself is without need, sufficient to Itself, aspiring to no other, the measure and Term of all, giving out from itself the Intellectual-Principle and Existence and Soul and Life and all Intellective-Act.

All until The Good is reached is beautiful; The Good is beyond-beautiful, beyond the Highest, holding kingly state in the Intellectual-Kosmos, that sphere constituted by a Principle wholly unlike what is known as Intelligence in us.

If such be the Nature of Beings and of That which transcends all the realm of Being, Evil cannot have place among Beings or in the Beyond-Being; these are good.

There remains, only, if Evil exist at all, that it be situate in the realm of Non-Being, that it be some mode, as it were, of the Non-Being, that it have its seat in something in touch with Non-Being or to a certain degree communicate in Non-Being.

By this Non-Being, of course, we are not to understand something that simply does not exist, but only something of an utterly different order from Authentic-Being: there is no question here of movement or position with regard to Being; the Non-Being we are thinking of is, rather, an image of Being or perhaps something still further removed than even an image.

Now this (the required faint image of Being) might be the sensible universe with all the impressions it engenders, or it might be something of even later derivation, accidental to the realm of sense, or again, it might be the source of the sense-world or something of the same order entering into it to complete it.

Some conception of it would be reached by thinking of measurelessness as opposed to measure, of the unbounded against bound, the unshaped against a principle of shape, the ever-needy against the self-sufficing: think of the ever-undefined, the never at rest, the all-accepting but never sated, utter dearth; and make all this character not mere accident in it but its equivalent for essential-being, so that, whatsoever fragment of it be taken, that part is all lawless void, while whatever participates in it and resembles it becomes evil, though not of course to the point of being, as itself is, Evil-Absolute.

The bodily Kind, in that it partakes of Matter, is an evil thing. What form is in bodies is an untrue form: they are without life: by their own natural disorderly movement they make away with each other; they are hindrances to the soul in its proper Act; in their ceaseless flux they are always slipping away from Being.

Soul, on the contrary, since not every Soul is evil, is not an evil Kind.

The Soul wrought to perfection, addressed towards the Intellectual-Principle is steadfastly pure: it has turned away from Matter; all that is undetermined, that is outside of measure, that is evil, it neither sees nor draws near; it endures in its purity, only, and wholly, determined by the Intellectual-Principle.

The Soul that breaks away from this source of its reality to the non-perfect and non-primal is, as it were, a secondary, an image, to the loyal Soul. By its falling-away—and to the extent of the fall—it is stripped of Determination, becomes wholly indeterminate, sees darkness. Looking to what repels vision, as we look when we are said to see darkness, it has taken Matter into itself.

If all this be true, we cannot be, ourselves, the source of Evil, we are not evil in ourselves; Evil was before we came to be; the Evil which holds men down binds them against their will; and for those that have the strength—not found in all men, it is true—there is a deliverance from the evils that have found lodgement in the soul.

In a word since Matter belongs only to the sensible world, vice in men is not the Absolute Evil; not all men are vicious; some overcome vice, some, the better sort, are never attacked by it; and those who master it win by means of that in them which is not material.

Matter exists; Soul exists; and they occupy, so to speak, one place. There is not one place for Matter and another for Soul,—Matter, for instance, kept to earth, Soul in the air: the soul's "separate place" is simply its not being in Matter; that is, its not being united with it; that is that there be no compound unit consisting of Soul and Matter; that is that Soul be not moulded in Matter as in a matrix; this is the Soul's apartness.

But the faculties of the Soul are many, and it has its beginning, its intermediate phases, its final fringe. Matter appears, importunes, raises disorders, seeks to force its way within; but all the ground is holy, nothing there without part in Soul. Matter therefore submits, and takes light: but the source of its illumination it cannot attain to, for the Soul cannot lift up this foreign thing close by, since the evil of it makes it invisible. On the contrary the illumination, the light streaming from the Soul, is dulled, is weakened, as it mixes with Matter which offers Birth to the Soul, providing the means by which it enters into generation, impossible to it if no recipient were at hand.

This is the fall of the Soul, this entry into Matter: thence its weakness: not all the faculties of its being retain free play, for Matter hinders their manifestation; it encroaches upon the Soul's territory and, as it were, crushes the Soul back; and it turns to evil all that it has stolen, until the Soul finds strength to advance again.

Thus the cause, at once, the weakness of Soul and of all its evil is Matter.

The evil of Matter precedes the weakness, the vice; it is Primal Evil. Even though the Soul itself submits to Matter and engenders to it; if it becomes evil within itself by its commerce with Matter, the cause is still the presence of Matter: the Soul would never have approached Matter but that the presence of Matter is the occasion of its earth-life.

The Third Ennead

SECOND TRACTATE. PROVIDENCE

Nor would it be sound to condemn this Kosmos as less than beautiful, as less than the noblest possible in the corporeal; and neither can any charge be laid against its source.

The world, we must reflect, is a product of Necessity, not of deliberate purpose: it is due to a higher Kind engendering in its own likeness by a natural process.

The conflict and destruction that reign among living beings are inevitable, since things here are derived, brought into existence because the Divine Reason which contains all of them in the upper Heavens —how could they come here unless they were There?—must outflow over the whole extent of Matter.

Similarly, the very wronging of man by man may be derived from an effort towards the Good; foiled, in their weakness, of their true desire, they turn against each other: still, when they do wrong, they pay the penalty—that of having hurt their Souls by their evil conduct and of degradation to a lower place—for nothing can ever escape what stands decreed in the law of the Universe.

This is not to accept the idea, sometimes urged, that order is an outcome of disorder and law of lawlessness, as if evil were a necessary preliminary to their existence or their manifestation: on the contrary order is the original and enters this sphere as imposed from without: it is because order, law and reason exist that there can be disorder; breach of law and unreason exist because Reason exists—not that these better things are directly the causes of the bad but simply that what ought to absorb the Best is prevented by its own nature, or by some accident, or by foreign interference. An entity which must look outside itself for a law, may be foiled of its purpose by either an internal or an external cause; there will be some flaw in its own nature, or it will be hurt by some alien influence, for often harm follows, unintended, upon the action of others in the pursuit of quite unrelated aims. Such living beings, on the other hand, as have freedom of motion under their own will sometimes take the right turn, sometimes the wrong.

Why the wrong course is followed is scarcely worth enquiring: a slight deviation at the beginning develops with every advance into continuously wider and graver error—especially since there is the attached body with its inevitable concomitant of desire—and the first step, the hasty movement not previously considered and not immediately corrected, ends by establishing a set habit where there was at first only a fall.

Punishment naturally follows: there is no injustice in a man suffering what belongs to the condition in which he is; nor can we ask to be happy when our actions have not earned us happiness; the good, only, are happy; divine beings are happy only because they are good.

Now, once Happiness is possible at all to Souls in this Universe, if some fail of it, the blame must fall not upon the place but upon the feebleness insufficient to the staunch combat in the one arena where the rewards of excellence are offered. Men are not born divine; what wonder that they do not enjoy a divine life. And poverty and sickness mean nothing to the good—only to the evil are they disastrous—and where there is body there must be ill-health.

Besides, these accidents are not without their service in the co-ordination and completion of the Universal system.

The principle is that evil by definition is a falling short in good, and good cannot be at full strength in this Sphere where it is lodged in the alien: the good here is in something else, in something distinct from the Good, and this something else constitutes the falling short for it is not good. And this is why evil is ineradicable: there is, first, the fact that in relation to this principle of Good, thing will always stand less than thing, and, besides, all things come into being through it, and are what they are by standing away from it.

Humanity, in reality, is poised midway between gods and beasts, and inclines now to the one order, now to the other; some men grow like to the divine, others to the brute, the greater number stand neutral. But those that are corrupted to the point of approximating to irrational animals and wild beasts pull the mid-folk about and inflict wrong upon them; the victims are no doubt better than the wrong-doers, but are at the mercy of their inferiors in the field in which they themselves are inferior, where, that is, they cannot be classed among the good since they have not trained themselves in self-defence.

In sum: Man has come into existence, a living being but not a member of the noblest order; he occupies by choice an intermediate rank; still, in that place in which he exists, Providence does not allow him to be reduced to nothing; on the contrary he is ever being led upwards by all those varied devices which the Divine employs in its labour to increase the dominance of moral value. The human race, therefore, is not deprived by Providence of its rational being; it retains its share, though necessarily limited, in wisdom, intelligence, executive power and right doing, the right doing, at least, of individuals to each other—and even in wronging others people think they are doing right and only paying what is due.

Man is, therefore, a noble creation, as perfect as the scheme allows; a part, no doubt, in the fabric of the All, he yet holds a lot higher than that of all the other living things of earth.

part 2

THE MIDDLE AGES

Perhaps no period is more foreign to us, or requires more explanation for its understanding, than the medieval. No doubt this is largely due to the fact that at this time ethical theory was intimately involved with religion. And more than with religion; the ethical thought of this long era was also interwoven with metaphysics and theology. It should be made clear that ethical theory varies as widely among the thinkers of this age as among the philosophers of any other time. Yet despite important individual differences, medieval ethical thinkers agreed that ethics is part of a general theological and metaphysical understanding of man, of the world, and of God, and that it stands at many points in some relation to the issues of religion.

This is not strange, since philosophy and religion have always been united at least by a common ethical interest. Thus, the theologians of such an era as this are bound to discuss ethics, and such discussion is almost equally bound to spring from their general theological and religious concerns. Accordingly, the central question is: How shall such theory be treated and interpreted in an age like ours, which seems in many respects almost diametrically opposed to the Middle Ages with its religious orientation? Can we understand their ethical theory without sharing their theological interest? Must a contemporary reader share the religious views of a medieval author in order to find his ethics valid?

For many modern readers the most foreign medieval authors will be those numerous writers to whom ethics meant no more nor less than the theory and practice of the religious life. Bernard of Clairvaux is a member of this group. Other medieval theorists —among them Augustine—placed ethics in the more general setting of a study of God's nature and of the problem of evil in the world. For still another group of theorists, ethics is a more nearly autonomous inquiry. Here ethical theory can be seen as continuous with its classical setting. Thomas Aquinas, for example, picks up, elaborates, and changes Aristotle and the Stoics.

Ethical theory in the Middle Ages, then, is a study in continuity and discontinuity. On the one hand, because of its specifically Christian sources we witness attempts to reorient radically the ethical life of man, e.g., Jerome's scolding a monk for abandoning the life of a hermit. The Christian religious ideal obviously has ethical implications, and some Christian theorists sought to develop an ethical theory radical enough to express them. So far, then, there is discontinuity. On the other hand, almost all early major writers were either pagans by origin or were themselves familiar with classical theories. Because there was no radical break between Greece and Rome, or between Rome and Christendom, much medieval ethical theory was a transference of earlier theories merely incorporated into a new setting. So far there is continuity.

Ethical theory in the Middle Ages had a grand sweep. It was concerned with issues larger than man himself or his desires. The egocentricity or radical individualism which appears in other eras was ruled out in advance, because of the writers' generalized theological concern. God is sometimes as much the author's subject in ethical discussion as man. Nor did this effect disappear with the ending of the Middle Ages. Even after Renaissance philosophers declared their independence from theology, Locke, Leibniz, and Spinoza went on to construct their ethical theories in a general theological setting.

Although the medieval period stretches from Augustine and the Church Fathers to the Renaissance, it would be wrong to treat this enormous span of time (some twelve or thirteen centuries) as if it were itself uniform. Christianity began not in a secure Christian setting but as an ignored and even persecuted minority sect within the pagan culture of Rome. Hence even an Augustine was as much concerned with non-Christian philosophy as with Church doctrine. It is not really until the eleventh century that we have anything like a Christian era which felt itself at any intellectual distance from the classical world. In the transitional period monasteries served as islands of isolated Christian culture, and yet they preserved pagan concerns as much as they promoted Christian thought.

Faced with such variety and complexity, how can the ethical theory of this era be depicted? No one could or should attempt to present selections from medieval ethical theory without at least a word about the special difficulties involved. While it is true that more medieval philosophy is now available in translation than anyone would have thought possible a decade ago, it is still true that there are gaps. The reader must constantly bear in mind that much material is unavailable to us. Some is not in translation and some is imperfect even in the original. While we can begin to get a feeling for the actual multiplicity which characterizes medieval philosophy, the selections presented here hardly give an accurate picture of the full variety of the time.

What can even this brief study of medieval ethics hope to accomplish? For many the chief value may be that a consideration of ethical theory so different from the contemporary fashion will help us avoid the trap of taking some particular context for ethical theory as the obvious one. Beneath certain common characteristics, we can hope to discover the variety which is always there. If it has been hard to see that there actually is any pure philosophy in the Middle Ages, study might reveal that philosophical ethics has certain similarities no matter what its setting. Philosophy appears in every age in various guises. If one era is unable to correct its own bias internally, perhaps the study of another and contrasting era can provide the needed corrective.

ST. JEROME AND BOETHIUS

The following brief selections are representative of the period that saw the decline of classical culture and the Roman imperium, and the rise of Christianity both as a political force and as the central theme of intellectual activities.
St. Jerome (354–420), who was a contemporary of St. Augustine, the great formulator of Christian doctrine, and Boethius (480–524) were witnesses of the collapse of the Western Empire and shared the inevitable mixture of nostalgia after the old and drive toward the new that accompanies such convulsions. The ties of these thinkers with classical civilization are well illustrated in Boethius's Consolation of Philosophy, *a treatise composed in prison shortly before his execution for treason. Boethius was a classical scholar and a fountainhead for later medieval scholasticism, through his translations and commentaries on Aristotle's logical works. Roman Stoicism, even though by now it had taken a religious turn, is evident in the* Consolation. *At the same time, both writers sound a note that is profoundly non-Greek, but of central importance for medieval thought, namely, an antipathy that verges on contempt for the common duties and pleasures of everyday life. Jerome castigates a young man for availing himself of the comforts of civilized life; Boethius consoles himself with the thought that one's fortunes on earth are after all of little account. Both men have their thoughts on something higher—the achievement of salvation, at the expense, if necessary, of everything the this-worldly man holds dear.*

*St. Jerome: Scolding a Monk for Having Abandoned the Desert**

The Desert of Chalcis A.D 374

My friend Heliodorus,

Your own heart, conscious of the brotherly Christian love we share, knows how much solicitous attention and affection I exerted in trying to keep us together here in the desert. Even this letter, half blotted by tears, bears witness to the profound sorrow with which I followed your departure.

With tender soothing words, much like a child's, you smoothed over that contemptible refusal of yours to remain, so that, caught off guard, I hardly knew what to do. Should I have said nothing? A show of indifference could hardly have disguised my fervent desire to prevent you from leaving. Or should my petitions have been more vehement? But you would not have listened. You did not love me as I loved you. So now my despised affection for you has taken the only remaining recourse: unable to restrain your departure while you were still here, my love now goes searching after you. That I should send a letter of invitation, once I had settled here in the wilderness, was your final request. This I promised, so now I invite you: come, come quickly. Forget old obligations—the desert adores a man stripped of everything. Hardships of past travels must not frighten you from coming. You believe in Christ, believe also when He preaches, "Seek first the kingdom of God, and all these other things shall be given to you." Here in the desert neither financial receipts nor walking sticks are needed. That man is abundantly wealthy who is poor along with Christ.

But what am I doing? Why attempt to persuade you a second time? Away with these petitions, away with enticing rhetoric! Love should be full of anger. Since you have already spurned my request, perhaps you will listen to admonishment.

What business have you in your father's house, O you effeminate soldier? Where are your ramparts and trenches, where is the winter spent at the front lines? Listen! the battle trumpet blares from heaven, and see how our General marches fully armed, coming amid the clouds to conquer the whole world. Out of the mouth of our King emerges a double-edged sword that cuts down everything in the way. Arising finally from your nap, do you come now to the battlefield? Abandon the shade and seek the sun. But, of course, flesh accustomed to a tunic can hardly bear a coarse leather breastplate, and a head that has worn a fine silk hat refuses a helmet, while hands softened by idleness are irritated by the sword's handle. Hear, then, the proclamation of your King: "That man who is not with Me is against Me, whoever does not gather with Me scatters." Heliodorus, remember the day you enlisted when, buried with Christ in baptism, you pledged allegiance to Him, swearing that for His sake you would not even refuse to hurt your father and mother. See how the enemy is trying to assassinate Christ in your own heart; the enemy camp sighs for the bonus you received when you entered Christ's service. Although your little nephew, Nepotian, entwines his arms around your neck, and your mother, hair dishevelled and dress torn, shows you the very breasts that suckled you, and even though your father prostrates himself across the doorstep, walk right over your father and continue on your way, flying with dry eyes to the battle standard of the cross. In this case, cruelty is the only real filial love. . . .

All this is well and good, you reply, if one happens to be a martyr. What a terrible mistake, my brother, if you imagine there is ever a time when the Christian does not suffer persecution. One is attacked most powerfully when he fails to

* By permission. From St. Jerome, *The Satirical Letters of St. Jerome*, trans. by Paul Carroll, Henry Regnery Company, Chicago, 1956.

realize he is being attacked at all. Our adversary, like a roaring lion, prowls about seeking someone to devour. . . .

Then why are you such a half-hearted Christian? Recall how Peter abandoned his father and fishingnets, and how the Publican, standing up from the desk where he collected taxes, became an apostle on the spot. "The Son of Man has no place to lay His head." Are you drawing plans for spacious porticos and ample well-constructed rooms? To expect an inheritance in this world indicates that you are not a joint-heir with Christ. Always remember what "monk" signifies; it is your name. What are you doing surrounded by crowds of people? You are a monk, a solitary. . . .

Heliodorus, you have already promised to be perfect. When you deserted the army and emasculated yourself for the sake of the kingdom of heaven, what other purpose did you entertain but to achieve an immaculate way of life? An impeccable servant of Christ owns nothing beside Christ. Possessing anything beside Christ makes him imperfect, and if he is that then he was a liar when he stipulated to God to achieve perfection. Moreover, "the mouth that lies murders the soul." To conclude, then: if you really desire to be perfect, why do you covet your father's possessions? and if you are still imperfect, you have deceived the Lord. . . . All of this can be summarized by noting that a monk simply cannot be perfect in his own native country. And not to desire perfection is a sin.

*Boethius: The Consolation of Philosophy**

[*Boethius complains to Philosophy of his sufferings after his just life.*]

"You and God Himself, who has grafted you in the minds of philosophers, are my witnesses that never have I applied myself to any office of state except that I might work for the common welfare of all good men. Thence followed bitter quarrels with evil men which could not be appeased, and, for the sake of preserving justice, contempt of the enmity of those in power, for this is the result of a free and fearless conscience.

"However, I leave it to your judgment and that of philosophers to decide how the justice of this may be; but I have committed to writing for history the true course of events, that posterity may not be ignorant thereof.

"But what avails it? No liberty is left to hope for. Would there were any! I would answer in the words of Canius, who was accused by Gaius Caesar, Germanicus's son, of being cognisant of a plot against himself: 'If I had known of it, you would not have.'

"And in this matter grief has not so blunted my powers that I should complain of wicked men making impious attacks upon virtue: but at this I do wonder, that they should hope to succeed. Evil desires are, it may be, due to our natural failings, but that the conceptions of any wicked mind should prevail against innocence while God watches over us, seems to me unnatural. Wherefore not without cause has one of your own followers asked, 'If God is, whence come evil things? If He is not, whence come good?' "

"Now," said she, "I know the cause, or the chief cause, of your sickness. You have forgotten what you are. Now therefore I have found out to the full the manner of your sickness, and how to attempt the restoring of your health. You are overwhelmed by this forgetfulness of yourself: hence you have been thus sorrowing that you are exiled and robbed of all your possessions. You do not know the aim and end of all things; hence you think that if men are worthless and wicked, they are powerful and fortunate. You have forgotten by what methods the universe is guided;

* By permission. From Boethius, *The Consolation of Philosophy*, trans. by W. V. Cooper, Random House, Inc., New York, 1943.

hence you think that the chances of good and bad fortune are tossed about with no ruling hand. These things may lead not to disease only, but even to death as well. But let us thank the Giver of all health, that your nature has not altogether left you. We have yet the chief spark for your health's fire, for you have a true knowledge of the hand that guides the universe: you do believe that its government is not subject to random chance, but to divine reason. Therefore have no fear. From this tiny spark the fire of life shall forthwith shine upon you. But it is not time to use severer remedies, and since we know that it is the way of all minds to clothe themselves ever in false opinions as they throw off the true, and these false ones breed a dark distraction which confuses the true insight, therefore will I try to lessen this darkness for a while with gentle applications of easy remedies, that so the shadows of deceiving passions may be dissipated, and you may have power to perceive the brightness of true light.

"When the stars are hidden by black clouds, no light can they afford. When the boisterous south wind rolls along the sea and stirs the surge, the water, but now as clear as glass, bright as the fair sun's light, is dark, impenetrable to sight, with stirred and scattered sand. The stream, that wanders down the mountain's side, must often find a stumbling-block, a stone within its path torn from the hill's own rock. So too shalt thou: if thou wouldst see the truth in undimmed light, choose the straight road, the beaten path; away with passing joys! away with fear! put vain hopes to flight! and grant no place to grief! Where these distractions reign, the mind is clouded o'er, the soul is bound in chains.

"How many are they, think you, who would think themselves raised to heaven if the smallest part of the remnants of your good fortune fell to them? This very place, which you call a place of exile, is home to those who live herein. Thus there is nothing wretched unless you think it to be so: and in like manner he who bears all with a calm mind finds his lot wholly blessed. Who is so happy but would wish to change his estate, if he yields to impatience of his lot? With how much bitterness is the sweetness of man's life mingled! For even though its enjoyment seem pleasant, yet it may not be surely kept from departing when it will. It is plain then how wretched is the happiness of mortal life which neither endures for ever with men of calm mind, nor ever wholly delights the care-ridden. Wherefore, then, O mortal men, seek ye that happiness without, which lies within yourselves? Ye are confounded by error and ignorance. I will shew you as shortly as I may, the pole on which turns the highest happiness. Is there aught that you value more highly than your own self? You will answer that there is nothing. If then you are master of yourself, you will be in possession of that which you will never wish to lose, and which Fortune will never be able to take from you. Yet consider this further, that you may be assured that happiness cannot be fixed in matters of chance: if happiness is the highest good of a man who lives his life by reason, and if that which can by any means be snatched away, is not the highest good (since that which is best cannot be snatched away), it is plain that Fortune by its own uncertainty can never come near to reaching happiness. Further, the man who is borne along by a happiness which may stumble, either knows that it may change, or knows it not: if he knows it not, what happiness can there be in the blindness of ignorance? If he knows it, he must needs live in fear of losing that which he cannot doubt that he may lose; wherefore an ever-present fear allows not such an one to be happy. Or at any rate, if he lose it without unhappiness, does he not think it worthless? For that, whose loss can be calmly borne, is indeed a small good. You, I know well, are firmly persuaded that men's understandings can never die; this truth is planted deep in you by many proofs: since then it is plain that the happiness of fortune is bounded by the death of the body, you cannot doubt that, if death can carry away happiness, the whole race of mortals is sinking into wretchedness to be found upon the border of death. But we know that many have sought the enjoyment of happiness not only by death, but even by sorrow and sufferings: how then can the presence of this life make us happy, when its end cannot make us unhappy?

"He that would build on a lasting restingplace; who would be firm to resist the blasts of the storming wind; who seeks, too, safety where he may contemn the surge and threatening of the sea; must leave the lofty mountain's top, and leave the thirsting sands. The hill is swept by all the might of the headstrong gale: the sands dissolve, and will not bear the load upon them. Let him fly the danger in a lot which is pleasant rest unto the eye: let him be mindful to set his house surely upon the lowly rock. Then let the wind bellow, confounding wreckage in the sea, and thou wilt still be founded upon unmoving peace, wilt be blessed in the strength of thy defence: thy life will be spent in calmness, and thou mayest mock the raging passions of the air.

"The man who would true power gain, must needs subdue his own wild thoughts: never must he let his passions triumph and yoke his neck by their foul bonds. For though the earth, as far as India's shore, tremble before the laws you give, though Thule bow to your service on earth's farthest bounds, yet if thou canst not drive away black cares, if thou canst not put to flight complaints, then is no true power thine."

ST. AUGUSTINE

Aurelius Augustine (354–430), Bishop of Hippo, read Cicero during his student days, became interested in philosophy, and accepted the teachings of the Manichaeans and later those of the Neoplatonists, until his dramatic conversion to Christianity. This teacher of Latin literature and rhetoric is without question the most influential figure of the early medieval period. His writings are extensive and hard to distill, but his influence on the Church as an institution and his polemical writings against its enemies continued without intermission until his death, which occurred during a siege of Hippo by the Vandals. The dramatic time of his demise marks the beginning of the medieval and the end of the Roman era.

The selections presented here will give some indication of the progress of Augustine's thought from his apologetical writings to his more systematic and finally confessional works. His Roman training, his attraction to Neoplatonism, and his increased attention to Biblical literature and specifically Christian doctrine—all should be evident in the following selections.

*The Enchiridion**

The Problem of Evil

WHAT IS CALLED EVIL IN THE UNIVERSE IS BUT THE ABSENCE OF GOOD

In the universe, even that which is called evil, when it is regulated and put in its own place, only enhances our admiration of the good; for we enjoy and value the good more when we compare it with the evil. For the Almighty God, who, as even the heathen acknowledge, has supreme power over all things, being Himself supremely Good, would never permit the existence of anything evil among His works, if He were not so omnipotent and good that He can bring good even out of evil. For what is that which we call evil but the absence of good?

ALL BEINGS WERE MADE GOOD, BUT NOT BEING MADE PERFECTLY GOOD, ARE LIABLE TO CORRUPTION

All things that exist, therefore, seeing that the Creator of them all is supremely good, are themselves good. But because

* By permission. From St. Augustine, *The Enchiridion*, trans. by Henry Paolucci, Henry Regnery Company, Chicago, 1961. Deletions are not noted in the text.

they are not, like their Creator, supremely and unchangeably good, their good may be diminished and increased. But for good to be diminished is an evil, although, however much it may be diminished, it is necessary, if the being is to continue, that some good should remain to constitute the being. For however small or of whatever kind the being may be, the good which makes it a being cannot be destroyed without destroying the being itself. An uncorrupted nature is justly held in esteem. But if, still further, it be incorruptible, it is undoubtedly considered of still higher value. When it is corrupted, however, its corruption is an evil, because it is deprived of some sort of good. For if it be deprived of no good, it receives no injury; but it does receive injury, therefore it is deprived of good. Therefore, so long as a being is in process of corruption, there is in it some good of which it is being deprived; and if a part of the being should remain which cannot be corrupted, this will certainly be an incorruptible being, and accordingly the process of corruption will result in the manifestation of this great good. But if it do not cease to be corrupted, neither can it cease to possess good of which corruption may deprive it. But if it should be thoroughly and completely consumed by corruption, there will then be no good left, because there will be no being. Wherefore corruption can consume the good only by consuming the being. Every being, therefore, is a good; a great good, if it cannot be corrupted; a little good, if it can: but in any case, only the foolish or ignorant will deny that it is a good. And if it be wholly consumed by corruption, then the corruption itself must cease to exist, as there is no being left in which it can dwell.

THERE CAN BE NO EVIL WHERE THERE IS NO GOOD; AND AN EVIL MAN IS AN EVIL GOOD

Accordingly, there is nothing of what we call evil, if there be nothing good. But a good which is wholly without evil is a perfect good. A good, on the other hand, which contains evil is a faulty or imperfect good; and there can be no evil where there is no good. From all this we arrive at the curious result: that since every being, so far as it is a being, is good, when we say that a faulty being is an evil being, we just seem to say that what is good is evil, and that nothing but what is good can be evil, seeing that every being is good, and that no evil can exist except in a being. Nothing, then, can be evil except something which is good. Therefore every being, even if it be a defective one, in so far as it is a being is good, and in so far as it is defective is evil.

GOOD AND EVIL ARE AN EXCEPTION TO THE RULE THAT CONTRARY ATTRIBUTES CANNOT BE PREDICTED OF THE SAME SUBJECT. EVIL SPRINGS UP IN WHAT IS GOOD, AND CANNOT EXIST EXCEPT IN WHAT IS GOOD

Accordingly, in the case of these contraries which we call good and evil, the rule of the logicians, that two contraries cannot be predicated at the same time of the same thing, does not hold. No weather is at the same time dark and bright: no food or drink is at the same time sweet and bitter: no body is at the same time and in the same place black and white: none is at the same time and in the same place deformed and beautiful. And this rule is found to hold in regard to many, indeed nearly all, contraries, that they cannot exist at the same time in any one thing. But although no one can doubt that good and evil are contraries, not only can they exist at the same time, but evil cannot exist without good, or in anything that is not good. Good, however can exist without evil. For a man or an angel can exist without being wicked; but nothing can be wicked except a man or an angel: and so far as he is a man or an angel, he is good; so far as he is wicked, he is an evil. And these two contraries are so far co-existent, that if good did not exist in what is evil, neither could evil exist; because corruption could not have either a place to dwell in, or a source to spring from, if there were nothing that could be corrupted; and nothing can be corrupted except what is good, for corruption is nothing else but the destruction of good. From what is good, then, evils arose, and except in what is good they do not exist; nor was there any other source from which any evil nature could arise. For if there were, then, in so far as this was a being, it was certainly a good: and a being which was incorruptible would be a great good; and even one which was corruptible must be to some extent a good, for only by corrupting what was good in it could corruption do it harm.

IT IS NOT ESSENTIAL TO MAN'S HAPPINESS THAT HE SHOULD KNOW THE CAUSES OF PHYSICAL CONVULSIONS; BUT IT IS, THAT HE SHOULD KNOW THE CAUSES OF GOOD AND EVIL

Now, in view of these considerations, when we are pleased with that line of Maro, "Happy the man who has attained to the knowledge of the causes of things," we should not suppose that it is necessary to happiness to know the causes of the great physical convulsions, causes which lie hid in the most secret recesses of nature's kingdom, "whence comes the earthquake whose force makes the deep seas to swell and burst their barriers, and again to return upon themselves and settle down." But we ought to know the causes of good and evil as far as man may in this life know them, in order to avoid the mistakes and troubles of which this life is so full. For our aim must always be to reach that state of happiness in which no trouble shall distress us, and no error mislead us. If we must know the causes of physical convulsions, there are none which it concerns us more to know than those which affect our own health. But seeing that, in our ignorance of these, we are fain to resort to physicians, it would seem that we might bear with considerable patience our ignorance of the secrets that lie hid in the earth and heavens.

THE NATURE OF ERROR. ALL ERROR IS NOT HURTFUL, THOUGH IT IS MAN'S DUTY AS FAR AS POSSIBLE TO AVOID IT

For although we ought with the greatest possible care to avoid error, not only in great but even in little things, and although we cannot err except through ignorance, it does not follow that, if a man is ignorant of a thing, he must forthwith fall into error. That is rather the fate of the man who thinks he knows what he does not know. For he accepts what is false as if it were true, and that is the essence of error. But it is a point of very great importance what the subject is in regard to which a man makes a mistake. For on one and the same subject we rightly prefer an instructed man to an ignorant one, and a man who is not in error to one who is. In the case of different subjects, however—that is, when one man knows one thing, and another a different thing, and when what the former knows is useful, and what the latter knows is not so useful, or is actually hurtful—who would not, in regard to the things the latter knows, prefer the ignorance of the former to the knowledge of the latter? To err is just to take the false for the true, and the true for the false, or to hold what is certain as uncertain, and what is uncertain as certain, and that error in the soul is hideous and repulsive just in proportion as it appears fair and plausible when we utter it, or assent to it, saying, "Yea, yea; Nay, nay"—surely this life that we live is wretched indeed, if only on this account, that sometimes, in order to preserve it, it is necessary to fall into error. God forbid that such should be that other life, where truth itself is the life of the soul, where no one deceives, and no one is deceived. But here men deceive and are deceived, and they are more to be pitied when they lead others astray than when they are themselves led astray by putting trust in liars. Yet so much does a rational soul shrink from what is false, and so earnestly does it struggle against error, that even those who love to deceive are most unwilling to be deceived. For the liar does not think that he errs, but that he leads another who trusts him into error. And certainly he does not err in regard to the matter about which he lies, if he himself knows the truth; but he is deceived in this, that he thinks his lie does him no harm, whereas every sin is more hurtful to the sinner than to the sinned against.

*The City of God**

Book XI
Whether Positive Evil Exists

CHAPTER 22

The explanation of the goodness of creation is the goodness of God. It is a reasonable and sufficient explanation whether considered in the light of philosophy or of faith. It puts an end to all controversies concerning the origin of the world. Nevertheless, certain heretics remain unconvinced, on the ground that many things in creation are unsuitable and even harmful to that poor and fragile mortality of the flesh which, of course, is no more than the just penalty of sin. The heretics mention, for example, fire, cold, wild beasts, and things like that, without considering how wonderful such things are in themselves and in their proper place and how beautifully they fit into the total pattern of the universe making, as it were, their particular contributions to the commonweal of cosmic beauty. Nor have they observed how valuable they are even to us if only we use them well and wisely. Consider, for instance, poison. It is deadly when improperly used, but when properly applied it turns out to be a health-giving medicine, while, on the contrary, some of those things we like, such as food, drink, and sunlight, when immoderately and unwisely used are seen to be harmful.

Thus does Divine Providence teach us not to be foolish in finding fault with things but, rather, to be diligent in finding our their usefulness or, if our mind and will should fail us in the search, then to believe that there is some hidden use still to be discovered, as in so many other cases, only with great difficulty. This effort needed to discover hidden usefulness either helps our humility or hits our pride, since absolutely no natural reality is evil and the only meaning of the word "evil" is the privation of good.

What, however, is true is that there is a hierarchy of created realities, from earthly to heavenly, from visible to invisible, some being better than others, and that the very reason of their inequality is to make possible an existence for them all. For, God is the kind of artist whose greatness in His masterpieces is not lessened in His minor works—which, of course, are not significant by reason of any sublimity in themselves, since they have none, but only by reason of the wisdom of their Designer. Take the case of the beauty of the human form. Shave off one eyebrow and the loss to the mere mass of the body is insignificant. But what blow to beauty! For, beauty is not a matter of bulk but of the symmetry and proportion of the members.

It is no wonder that heretics, who hold that some positive evil has sprung and sprouted from an evil principle radically opposed to God, refuse to accept this explanation of creation—that a God who is

* By permission. From St. Augustine, *The City of God*, trans. Demetrius B. Zema and Gerald G. Walsh, in *Fathers of the Church*, vol. 8, The Catholic University of America Press, New York, 1950. Deletions are not noted in the text.

good should create things that are good. They prefer to believe that God was driven, by the sheer necessity of quelling the Evil One in rebellion against Him, to build the bulwarks of a material universe, and thus mingle the goodness of His nature with evil in order to coerce and conquer evil; so that the divine nature, prostituted and oppressed, is now in shameful and cruel captivity and can be purified and emancipated only with very great difficulty. Even then, one part will remain impervious to purification, and this is to be the prison and the chains to hold the conquered enemy in subjection.

The only way for the Manichaeans to cease from such folly—not to say insanity—is to acknowledge the nature of God to be, as it is in truth, unchangeable and absolutely incorruptible and, therefore, invulnerable; and to get in line with Christian orthodoxy, by believing that the soul—which is liable to a change for the worse by its own will and to corruption by sin and, therefore, to a loss of the light of unchangeable Truth—is a part neither of God nor of the divine nature, but merely a creature and, therefore, far from equality with God

Book XII
Evil Will Has No Efficient Cause

CHAPTER 6

If one seeks for the efficient cause of an evil will, none is to be found. For, what can make the will bad when it is the will itself which makes an action bad? Thus, an evil will is the efficient cause of a bad action, but there is no efficient cause of an evil will. If there is such a cause, it either has or has not a will. If it has, then that will is either good or bad. If good, one would have to be foolish enough to conclude that a good will makes a bad will. In that case, a good will becomes the cause of sin—which is utterly absurd. On the other hand, if the hypothetical cause of a bad will has itself a bad will, I would have to ask what made this will bad, and, to put an end to the inquiry: What made the first bad will bad? Now, the fact is that there was no first bad will that was made bad by any other bad will—it was made bad by itself. For, if it were preceded by a cause that made it evil, that cause came first. But, if I am told that nothing made the will evil but that it always was so, then I ask whether or not it existed in some nature.

If this evil will existed in no nature, then it did not exist at all. If it existed in some nature, then it vitiated, corrupted, injured that nature and, therefore, deprived it of some good. An evil will could not exist in an evil nature but only in a good one, mutable enough to suffer harm from this deprivation. For, if no harm were done, then there was no deprivation and, consequently, no right to call the will evil. But, if harm was done, it was done by destroying or diminishing what was good. Thus, an evil will could not have existed from all eternity in a nature in which a previously existing good had to be eliminated before the evil will could harm the nature. But, if it did not exist from all eternity, who, then, caused this evil will?

The only remaining suggestion is that the cause of the evil will was something which had no will. My next question is whether this "something" was superior, inferior, or equal to the will. If superior, then it was better. So, then, how can it have had no will and not rather a good will? If equal, the case is the same: for, as long as two wills are equally good, one cannot produce an evil will in the other. The supposition remains, then, that it was an inferior thing without a will which produced the evil will of the angelic nature which first sinned.

But that thing itself, whatever it was, even though it was low to the lowest point of earthliness, was, without doubt good since it was a nature and a being having its own character and species in its own genus and order. How, then, can a good thing be the efficient cause of an evil will? How, I ask, can good be the cause of evil? For, when the will, abandoning what is above it, turns itself to something lower, it becomes evil because the very turning itself and not the thing to which it turns is evil. Therefore, an inferior being does not make the will evil but the will itself, because it is a created will, wickedly and inordinately seeks the inferior being.

Take the case of two men whose physical and mental make-up is exactly the same. They are both attracted by the exterior beauty of the same person. While gazing at this loveliness, the will of one man is moved with an illicit desire; the will of the other remains firm in its purity. Why did the will become evil in one case and not in the other? What produced the evil will in the man in whom it began to be evil? The physical beauty of the person could not have been the cause, since that was seen by both in exactly the same way and yet both wills did not become evil. Was the cause the flesh of one of those who looked? Then why not the flesh of the other, also? Or was the cause the mind of one of them? Again, why not the mind of both? For the supposition is that both are equally constituted in mind and body. Must we say, then, that one was tempted by a secret suggestion of the Devil, as if it were not rather by his own will that he consented to this suggestion or enticement or whatever it was?

If so, then what was it in him that was the cause of his consent, of the evil will to follow the evil suggestion? To settle this difficulty, let us suppose that the two men are tempted equally, that one yields and consents to the temptation, that the other remains as he was before. The obvious conclusion is that one was unwilling, the other willing, to fail in chastity. And what else could be the cause of their attitudes but their own wills, since both men have the same constitution and temperament? The beauty which attracted the eyes of both was the same; the secret suggestion by which both were tempted was the same. However carefully they examine the situation, eager to learn what it was that made one of the two evil, no cause is apparent.

For, suppose we say that the man himself made his will evil. Very well, but what was the man himself before he made his will evil? He was a good nature, created by God, the immutable God.

Take a person who says that the one who consents to the temptation and enticement made his own will evil although previously he had been entirely good. Recall the facts. The one consents, while the other does not, to a sinful desire concerning a beautiful person; the beauty was seen by both equally, and before the temptation both men were absolutely alike in mind and body. Now, the person who talks of a man making his own will evil must ask why the man made his will evil, whether because he is a nature or because he is nature made out of nothing? He will learn that the evil arises not from the fact that the man is a nature, but from the fact that the nature was made out of nothing.

For, if a nature is the cause of an evil will, then we are compelled to say that evil springs from good and that good is the cause of evil—since a bad will comes from a good nature. But how can it come about that a good, though mutable, nature, even before its will is evil, can produce something evil, namely, this evil will itself?

CHAPTER 7

No one, therefore, need seek for an efficient cause of an evil will. Since the "effect" is, in fact, a deficiency, the cause should be called "deficient." The fault of an evil will begins when one falls from Supreme Being to some being which is less than absolute. Trying to discover causes of such deficiencies—causes which, as I have said, are not efficient but deficient—is like trying to see darkness or hear silence. True, we have some knowledge of both darkness and silence: of the former only by the eyes; of the latter only by the ears. Nevertheless, we have no sensation but only the privation of sensation.

So there is no point in anyone trying to learn from me what I know I do not know—unless, perhaps, he wants to know how not to know what, as he ought to know, no one can know. For, things we know, not by sensation, but by the absence of sensation, are known—if the word says or means anything—by some kind of "unknowing," so that they are both known and not known at the same time. For example, when the vision of the eye passes from sensation to sensation, it sees darkness only when it begins not to see. So, too, no other sense but the ear can perceive silence, yet silence can only be heard by not being heard.

So, too, it is only the vision of the mind that discerns the *species intellegibilis* when it understands intelligible realities. But, when the realities are no longer intelligible, the mind, too, knows by "unknowing." For "who can understand sins?"

CHAPTER 8

This I know, that the nature of God can never and nowhere be deficient in anything, while things made out of nothing can be deficient. In regard to these latter, the more they have of being and the more good things they do or make—for then they are doing or making something positive—the more their causes are efficient; but in so far as they fail or are defective and, in that sense, "do evil"—if a "defect" can be "done"—then their causes are "deficient." I know, further, that when a will "is made" evil, what happens would not have happened if the will had not wanted it to happen. That is why the punishment which follows is just, since the defection was not necessary but voluntary. The will does not fall "into sin"; it falls "sinfully." Defects are not mere relations to natures that are evil; they are evil in themselves because, contrary to the order of natures, there is a defection from Being that is supreme to some lesser being.

Thus, greed is not a defect in the gold that is desired but in the man who loves it perversely by falling from justice which he ought to esteem as incomparably superior to gold; nor is lust a defect in bodies which are beautiful and pleasing: it is a sin in the soul of the one who loves corporeal pleasures perversely, that is, by abandoning that temperance which joins us in spiritual and unblemishable union with realities far more beautiful and pleasing; nor is boastfulness a blemish in words of praise: it is a failing in the soul of one who is so perversely in love with other peoples' applause that he despises the voice of his own conscience; nor is pride a vice in the one who delegates power, still less a flaw in the power itself: it is a passion in the soul of the one who loves his own power so perversely as to condemn the authority of one who is still more powerful.

In a word, anyone who loves perversely the good of any nature whatsoever and even, perhaps, acquires this good makes himself bad by gaining something good and sad by losing something better.

Book V
Providence, Foreknowledge, and Free Will

CHAPTER 1

The cause of the greatness of the Roman Empire was neither fortune nor fate. (I am using these words in the sense of those who say or think that fortune, or chance, is what happens without cause or rational explanation, and that fate is what is bound to happen, in spite even of the will of God or of men.) On the contrary,

Divine Providence alone explains the establishment of kingdoms among men. As for those who speak of fate, but mean by fate the will and power of God, they should keep their conception but change their expression. Surely, though, it is best to say at once what one will have to say as soon as one is asked what is meant by fate.

CHAPTER 9

Cicero makes every effort to prove that there can be no foreknowledge, whether in God or in man, and, therefore, no possibility of prediction. Thus, he denies the foreknowledge of God and seeks to get rid even of the clearest cases of prophecy by baseless arguments and by limiting himself to such oracles as are easy to refute. The fact is that he does not confute even these. However, he makes a masterly refutation of the conjectures of the astrologers —for the simple reason that their mutual contradictions are their best refutation.

Nevertheless, for all their sidereal fates, the astrologers are nearer the truth than Cicero with his denial of all knowledge of the future, for it is plain nonsense for a man to admit that God exists and then to deny that He can know the future.

It is true, he seems to do this only to save free will and to reject the necessity of fate. His point is that, once any knowledge of the future is admitted, it is logically impossible to deny fate.

But, be these tortuous strifes and disputations of the philosophers what they will, we who profess belief in the supreme and true God confess, likewise, His will, His supreme power, His foreknowledge. Nor are we dismayed by the difficulty that what we choose to do freely is done of necessity, because He whose foreknowledge cannot be deceived foreknew that we would choose to do it. This was the fear that made Cicero oppose foreknowledge. It was this fear, too, that led the Stoics to admit that not everything happened of necessity, even though they held that everything happens by fate.

Let us examine, then, this fear of foreknowledge which led Cicero to attempt to deny it in his detestable disputation. He argues thus. If all that is future is foreknown, each event will occur in the order in which it is foreknown that it will occur. But, if things happen in this order, the order of things is known for certain in the mind of God who foreknows them. But, if the order of events is known for certain, then the order of causes is known for certain—since nothing can happen without a preceding efficient cause. If, however, the order of causes, by which all that happens is known for certain, then, he says, all that happens happens by fate. But, if this is so, nothing is left to our own power and, therefore, there is no choice in our will. But, he goes on, once we admit this, all human life becomes topsy-turvy; laws are made in vain; there is no point in reproaches or in praise, in scolding or in exhortation; there is no ground in justice for rewarding the good or punishing the wicked.

Thus, his motive for rejecting foreknowledge of the future was to avoid unworthy, absurd and dangerous implications for human society. He narrows down the choices of a devout mind to one or other of these alternatives: *either* the power of choice *or* foreknowledge. It seemed to him impossible that both could exist. If one stands, the other falls. If we choose foreknowledge, we lose free choice; if we choose free choice, we must lose knowledge of the future.

Magnanimous and learned as he was, and with no thought but to save human nature as best he could, Cicero made his choice. He chose free choice. To make it certain, he denied foreknowledge. Thus, to make men free, he made them give up God.

A man of faith wants both. He professes both and with a devout faith he holds both firmly. But how, one asks? For, if there is foreknowledge of the future, logical step follows logical step until we reach a point where nothing is left in the will. On the other hand, if we start from power in the will, the steps lead in the opposite direction until we come to the conclusion that foreknowledge is nonexistent. This is how the reverse argument runs. If there is free choice, not all is fixed by fate. If not all is fixed by fate, there is no certain order of all causes. If there is no certain order of causes, there is no certain order of events known in the mind of God, since events cannot happen without preceding and efficient causes. If the order of events is not certain in the foreknowledge of God, not all things happen as He foresaw they would happen. But, if all does not happen as He foresaw it would happen, then, Cicero argues, in God there is no foreknowledge of all that is to happen.

Our stand against such bold and impious attacks on God is to say that God knows all things before they happen; yet, we act by choice in all those things where we feel and know that we cannot act otherwise than willingly. And yet, so far from saying that everything happens by fate, we say that nothing happens by fate—for the simple reason that the word "fate" means nothing. The word means nothing, since the only reality in the mind of those who use the word—namely, the arrangement of the stars at the moment of conception or birth—is, as we show, pure illusion.

However, our main point is that, from the fact that to God the order of all causes is certain, there is no logical deduction that there is no power in the choice of our will. The fact is that our choices fall within the order of the causes which is known for certain to God and is contained in His foreknowledge—for, human choices are the causes of human acts. It follows that He who foreknew the causes of all things could not be unaware that our choices were among those causes which were foreknown as the causes of our acts.

In this matter it is easy enough to refute Cicero by his own admission, namely, that nothing happens without a preceding efficient cause. It does not help him to admit that nothing happens without a cause and then to argue that not every cause is fated, since some causes are either fortuitous or natural or voluntary. He admits that nothing happens without a preceding cause; that is enough to refute him.

Thus, God is the Cause of all things —a cause that makes but is not made. Other causes make, but they are themselves made—for example, all created spirits and, especially, rational spirits. Material causes which are rather passive than active are not to be included among efficient causes, for their power is limited to what the wills of spirits work through them.

It does not follow, therefore, that the order of causes, known for certain though it is in the foreknowing mind of God, brings it about that there is no power in our will, since our choices themselves have an important place in the order of causes.

Our conclusion is that our wills have power to do all that God wanted them to do and foresaw they could do. Their power, such as it is, is a real power. What they are to do they themselves will most certainly do, because God foresaw both that they could do it and that they would do it and His knowledge cannot be mistaken. Thus, if I wanted to use the word "fate" for anything at all, I should prefer to say that "fate" is the action of a weak person, while "choice" is the act of the stronger man who holds the weak man in his power, rather than to admit that the choice of our will is taken away by that order of causes which the Stoics arbitrarily call fate.

CHAPTER 10

It follows that we need not be afraid of that necessity which frightened the Stoics into distinguishing various kinds of causes. They sought to free certain causes from necessity while others were subject to it. Among the causes which they wanted free from necessity they reckoned our wills. Obviously, wills could not be free if subject to necessity.

Now, if by necessity we mean one that is in no way in our power, but which has its way even when our will is opposed to it, as is the case with the necessity to die, then, our choices of living well or ill obviously are not subject to this kind of necessity. The fact is that we do many things which we would most certainly not do if we did not choose to do them. The most obvious case is our willing itself. For, if we will, there is an act of willing; there is none if we do not want one. We would certainly not make a choice if we did not choose to make it. On the other hand, if we take necessity to mean that in virtue of which something must be so and so or must happen in such and such a way, I do not see that we should be afraid of such necessity taking away our freedom of will. We do not put the life of God and the foreknowledge of God under any necessity when we say that God *must* live an eternal life and *must* know all things. Neither do we lessen His power when we say He cannot die or be deceived. This is the kind of inability which, if removed, would make God less powerful than He is. God is rightly called omnipotent, even though He is unable to die and be deceived. We call Him omnipotent because He does whatever He wills to do and suffers nothing that He does not will to suffer. He would not, of course, be omnipotent, if He had to suffer anything against His will. It is precisely because He is omnipotent that for Him some things are impossible.

So with us, when we say we *must* choose freely when we choose at all, what we say is true; yet, we do not subject free choice to any necessity which destroys our liberty. Our choices, therefore, are our own, and they effect, whenever we choose to act, something that would not happen if we had not chosen. Even when a person suffers against his will from the will of others, there is a voluntary act—not, indeed, of the person who suffers. However, a human will prevails—although the power which permits this is God's. (For, wherever there is a mere will without power to carry out what it chooses, it would be impeded by a stronger will. Even so, there would be no will in such a condition unless there were a will, and not merely the will of another but the will of the one choosing, even though he is unable to carry out his choice.) Therefore, whatever a man has to suffer against his will is not to be attributed to the choices of man or of angels or of any created spirit, but to His choice who gives to wills whatever power they have.

The conclusion is that we are by no means under compulsion to abandon free choice in favor of divine foreknowledge, nor need we deny—God forbid!—that God knows the future, as a condition for holding free choice. We accept both. As Christians and philosophers, we profess both—foreknowledge, as a part of our faith; free choice, as a condition of responsible living. It is hard to live right if one's faith in God is wrong.

It follows, too, that laws are not in vain, nor scoldings and encouragements, nor praise and blame. He foresaw that such things should be. Such things have as much value as He foresaw they would have. So, too, prayers are useful in obtaining these favors which He foresaw He would bestow on those who should pray for them. There was justice in instituting rewards and punishments for good and wicked deeds. For, no one sins because God foreknew that he would sin. In fact, the very reason why a man is undoubtedly responsible for his own sin, when he sins, is because He whose foreknowledge cannot be deceived foresaw, not the man's fate or fortune or what not, but that the man himself would be responsible for his own sin. No man sins unless it is his choice to sin; and his choice not to sin, that, too, God foresaw.

Book XIV
Foreknowledge and the Fall of Man

CHAPTER 3

Should anyone say that the cause of vices and evil habits lies in the flesh because it is only when the soul is influenced by the flesh that it lives then in such a manner, he cannot have sufficiently considered the entire nature of man. It is true that "the corruptible body is a load upon the soul." But notice that the Apostle who, in discussing the corruptible body, had used the words, "Even though our outer man is decaying," goes on, a little further, to declare: "For we know that if the earthly house in which we dwell be destroyed, we have a building from God, a house not made by human hands, eternal in the heavens. And indeed, in this present state we groan, yearning to be clothed over with that dwelling of ours which is from heaven; if indeed we shall be found clothed, and not naked. For we who are in this tent sigh under our burden, because we do not wish to be unclothed, but rather clothed over, that what is mortal may be swallowed up by life."

On the one hand, our corruptible body may be a burden on our soul; on the other hand, the cause of this encumbrance is not in the nature and substance of the body, and, therefore, aware as we are of its corruption, we do not desire to be divested of the body but rather to be clothed with its immortality. In immortal life we shall have a body, but it will no longer be a burden since it will no longer be corruptible. Now, however, "the corruptible body is a load upon the soul, and the earthly habitation presseth down the mind that museth upon many things." Yet, it is an error to suppose that all the evils of the soul proceed from the body.

Our faith teaches [that] the corruption of the body, which is a burden on the soul, is not the cause but the punishment of Adam's first sin. Moreover, it was not the corruptible flesh that made the soul sinful; on the contrary, it was the sinful soul that made the flesh corruptible.

CHAPTER 11

Since God foresaw all things and, hence, that man would sin, our conception of the supernatural City of God must be based on what God foreknew and forewilled, and not on human fancies that could never come true, because it was not in God's plan that they should. Not even by his sin could man change the counsels of God, in the sense of compelling Him to alter what He had once decided. The truth is that, by His omniscience, God could foresee two future realities: how bad man whom God had created good was to become, and how much good God was to make out of this very evil.

Though we sometimes hear the expression, "God changed His mind," or even read in the figurative language of Scripture that "God repented," we interpret these sayings not in reference to the decisions determined on by Almighty God but in reference to the expectations of man or to the order of natural causes. So, we believe, as Scripture tells us, that God created man right and, therefore, endowed with a good will, for without a good will he would not have been "right."

The good will, then, is a work of God, since man was created by God with a good will. On the contrary, the first bad will, which was present in man before any of his bad deeds, was rather a falling away from the work of God into man's own works than a positive work itself; in fact, a fall into bad works, since they were "according to man" and not "according to God." Thus, this bad will or, what is the same, man in so far as his will is bad is like a bad tree which brings forth these bad works like bad fruit.

A bad will, however, contrary as it is to nature and not according to nature, since it is a defect in nature, still belongs to the nature of which it is a defect, since it has no existence apart from this nature. This nature, of course, is one that God has created out of nothing, and not out of Himself, as was the case when He begot the Word through whom all things have been made. Though God has fashioned man from the dust of the earth, that same dust, like all earthly matter, has been made out of nothing. And it was a soul made out of nothing which God united to the body when man was created.

In the long run, however, the good triumphs over the evil. It is true, of course, that the Creator permits evil, to prove to what good purpose His providence and justice can use even evil. Nevertheless, while good can exist without any defect, as in the true and supreme God Himself, and even in the whole of that visible and invisible creation, high in the heavens above this gloomy atmosphere, evil cannot exist without good, since the natures to which the defects belong, in as much as they are natures, are good. Moreover, we cannot remove evil by the destruction of the nature or any part of it, to which the damage has been done. We can only cure a disease or repair the damage by restoring the nature to health or wholeness.

Take the case of the will. Its choice is truly free only when it is not a slave to sin and vice. God created man with such a free will, but, once that kind of freedom was lost by man's fall from freedom, it could be given back only by Him who had the power to give it. Thus, Truth tells us: "If therefore the Son makes you free, you will be free indeed." He might equally have said: "If, therefore, the Son saves you, you will be saved indeed." For the same reason that God's Son is our Saviour He is also our Liberator.

CHAPTER 12

Some one may be puzzled by the fact that other sins do not change human nature in the way that the transgression of our first parents not merely damaged theirs but had the consequence that human nature, ever since, has been subject to death, to the great corruption which we can see and experience, and to so many and such opposing passions which disturb and disorder it, which was not the case in Eden before there was sin, even though the human body was animal then as now. However, no one has a right to be puzzled, on the assumption that our first parents' sin must have been a small, venial sin, since it involved merely a matter of food—a thing good and harmless in itself apart from being forbidden, as everything else was good which God had created and planted in that place of perfect happiness.

However, what is really involved in God's prohibition is obedience, the virtue which is, so to speak, the mother and guardian of all the virtues of a rational creature. The fact is that a rational creature is so constituted that submission is good for it while yielding to its own rather than its Creator's will is, on the contrary, disastrous.

CHAPTER 13

Moreover, our first parents only fell openly into the sin of disobedience because, secretly, they had begun to be guilty. Actually, their bad deed could not have been done had not bad will preceded it; what is more, the root of their bad will was nothing else than pride. For, "pride is the beginning of all sin." And what is pride but an appetite for inordinate exaltation? Now, exaltation is inordinate when the soul cuts itself off from the very Source to which it should keep close and somehow makes itself and becomes an end to itself. This takes place when the soul becomes inordinately pleased with itself, and such self-pleasing occurs when the soul falls away from the unchangeable Good which ought to please the soul far more than the soul can please itself. Now, this falling away is the soul's own doing, for, if the will had merely remained firm in the love of that higher immutable Good which lighted its mind into knowledge and warmed its will into love, it would not have turned away in search of satisfaction in itself and, by so doing, have lost that light and warmth. And thus Eve would not have believed that the serpent's lie was true, nor would Adam have preferred the will of his wife to the will of God nor have supposed that his transgression of God's command was venial when he refused to abandon the partner of his life even in a partnership of sin.

Our first parents, then, must already have fallen before they could do the evil deed, before they could commit the sin of eating the forbidden fruit. For such "bad fruit" could come only from a "bad tree." That the tree became bad was contrary to its nature, because such a condition could come about only by a defection of the will, which is contrary to nature. Notice, however, that such worsening by reason of a defect is possible only in a nature that has been created out of nothing. In a word, a nature is a nature because it is something made by God, but a nature falls away from That which Is because the nature was made out of nothing.

Yet, man did not so fall away from Being as to be absolutely nothing, but, in so far as he turned himself toward himself, he became less than he was when he was adhering to Him who is supreme Being. Thus, no longer to be in God but to be in oneself in the sense of to please oneself is not to be wholly nothing but to be approaching nothingness. For this reason, Holy Scripture gives another name to the proud. They are called "rash" and "self willed." Certainly, it is good for the heart to be lifted up, not to oneself, for this is the mark of pride, but to God, for this is a sign of obedience which is precisely the virtue of the humble.

There is, then, a kind of lowliness which in some wonderful way causes the heart to be lifted up, and there is a kind of loftiness which makes the heart sink lower. This seems to be a sort of paradox, that loftiness should make something lower and lowliness lift something up. The reason for this is that holy lowliness makes us bow to what is above us and, since there is nothing above God, the kind of lowliness that makes us close to God exalts us. On the other hand, the kind of loftiness which is a defection by this very defection refuses this subjection to God and so falls down from Him who is supreme, and by falling comes to be lower. Thus it comes to pass, as Scripture says, that "when they were lifting themselves up thou hast cast them down." Here, the Psalmist does not say: "When they had been lifted up," as though they first lifted themselves up and afterwards were cast down, but "when they are lifting themselves up, at that moment they were cast down," which means that their very lifting themselves up was itself a fall.

Hence it is that just because humility is the virtue especially esteemed in the City of God and so recommended to its citizens in their present pilgrimage on earth and because it is one that was particularly outstanding in Christ, its King, so it is that pride, the vice contrary to this virtue, is, as Holy Scripture tells us, especially dominant in Christ's adversary, the Devil. In fact, this is the main difference which distinguishes the two cities of which we are speaking. The humble City is the society of holy men and good angels; the proud city is the society of wicked men and evil angels. The one City began with the love of God; the other had its beginnings in the love of self.

Book XIX
Peace: Man's End

CHAPTER 11

Thus, we may say of peace what we have said of eternal life—that it is our highest good; more particularly because the holy Psalmist was addressing the City of God (the nature of which I am trying, with so much difficulty, to make clear) when he said: "Praise the Lord, O Jerusalem; praise thy God, O Sion. Because he hath strengthened the bolts of thy gates, he hath blessed thy children within thee. He hath placed peace in thy borders." For, when the bolts of that city's gates will have been strengthened, none will enter in and none will issue forth. Hence, its borders [*fines*] must be taken to mean that peace which I am trying to show is our final good. Note, too, that Jerusalem, the mystical name which symbolizes this City, means, as I have already mentioned, "the vision of peace."

However, the word "peace" is so often applied to conditions here on earth, where life is not eternal, that it is better, I think, to speak of "eternal life" rather than of "peace" as the end or supreme good of the City of God. It is in this sense that St. Paul says: "But now being made free from sin, and become servants of God, you have your fruit unto sanctification, and the end life everlasting."

CHAPTER 12

Any man who has examined history and human nature will agree with me that there is no such thing as a human heart that does not crave for joy and peace. One has only to think of men who are bent on war. What they want is to win, that is to say, their battles are but bridges to glory and to peace. The whole point of victory is to bring opponents to their knees—this done, peace ensues. Peace, then, is the purpose of waging war; and this is true even of men who have a passion for the exercise of military prowess as rulers and commanders.

What, then, men want in war is that it should end in peace. Even while waging a war every man wants peace, whereas no one wants war while he is making peace. And even when men are plotting to disturb the peace, it is merely to fashion a new peace nearer to the heart's desire; it is not because they dislike peace as such. It is not that they love peace less, but that they love their kind of peace more. And even when a secession is successful, its purpose is not achieved unless some sort of peace remains among those who plotted and planned the rebellion. Take even a band of highwaymen. The more violence and impunity they want in disturbing the peace of other men, the more they demand peace among themselves. Take even the case of a robber so powerful that he dispenses with partnership, plans alone, and single-handed robs and kills his victims. Even he maintains some kind of peace, however shadowy, with those he cannot kill and whom he wants to keep in the dark with respect to his crimes. Certainly in his own home he wants to be at peace with his wife and children and any other members of his household.

CHAPTER 13

The peace of the body lies in the ordered equilibrium of all its parts; the peace of the irrational soul, in the balanced adjustment of its appetites; the peace of the reasoning soul, in the harmonious correspondence of conduct and conviction; the peace of body and soul taken together, in the well-ordered life and health of the living whole. Peace between a mortal man and his Maker consists in ordered obedience, guided by faith, under God's eternal law;

peace between man and man consists in regulated fellowship. The peace of a home lies in the ordered harmony of authority and obedience between the members of a family living together. The peace of the political community is an ordered harmony of authority and obedience between citizens. The peace of the heavenly City lies in a perfectly ordered and harmonious communion of those who find their joy in God and in one another in God. Peace, in its final sense, is the calm that comes of order. Order is an arrangement of like and unlike things whereby each of them is disposed in its proper place.

This being so, those who are unhappy, in so far as they are unhappy, are not in peace, since they lack the calm of that Order which is beyond every storm; nevertheless, even in their misery they cannot escape from order, since their very misery is related to responsibility and to justice. They do not share with the blessed in their tranquility, but this very separation is the result of the law of order. Moreover, even the miserable can be momentarily free from anxiety and can reach some measure of adjustment to their surroundings and, hence, some tranquility of order and, therefore, some slender peace. However, the reason why they remain unhappy is that, although they *may* be momentarily free from worry and from pain, they are not in a condition where they *must* be free both from worry and pain. Their condition of misery is worse when such peace as they have is not in harmony with that law which governs the order of nature. Their peace can also be disturbed by pain and in proportion to their pain; yet, some peace will remain, so long as the pain is not too acute and their organism as a whole does not distintegrate.

Notice that there can be life without pain, but no pain without some kind of life. In the same way, there can be peace without any kind of war, but no war that does not suppose some kind of peace. This does not mean that war as war involves peace; but war, in so far as those who wage it or have it waged upon them are beings with organic natures, involves peace—for the simple reason that to be organic means to be ordered and, therefore, to be, in some sense, at peace.

Similarly, there can be a nature without any defect and, even, a nature in which there can be no kind of evil whatever, but there can be no nature completely devoid of good. Even the nature of the Devil, in so far as it is a nature, is not evil; it was perversity—not being true to itself—that made it bad.

CHAPTER 17

While the homes of unbelieving men are intent upon acquiring temporal peace out of the possessions and comforts of this temporal life, the families which live according to faith look ahead to the good things of heaven promised as imperishable, and use material and temporal goods in the spirit of pilgrims, not as snares or obstructions to block their way to God, but simply as helps to ease and never to increase the burdens of this corruptible body which weighs down the soul. Both types of homes and their masters have this in common, that they must use things essential to this mortal life. But the respective purposes to which they put them are characteristic and very different.

So, too, the earthly city which does not live by faith seeks only an earthly peace, and limits the goal of its peace, of its harmony of authority and obedience among its citizens, to the voluntary and collective attainment of objectives necessary to mortal existence. The heavenly City, meanwhile—or, rather, that part that is on pilgrimage in mortal life and lives by faith—must use this earthly peace until such time as our mortality which needs such peace has passed away. As a consequence, so long as her life in the earthly city is that of a captive and an alien (although she has the promise of ultimate delivery and the gift of the Spirit as a pledge), she has no hesitation about keeping in step with the civil law which governs matters pertaining to our existence here below. For, as mortal life is the same for all, there ought to be common cause between the two cities in what concerns our purely human living.

Now comes the difficulty. The city of this world, to begin with, has had certain "wise men" of its own mold, whom true religion must reject, because either out of their own daydreaming or out of demonic deception these wise men came to believe that a multiplicity of divinities was allied with human life, with different duties, in some strange arrangement, and different assignments: this one over the body, that one over the mind; in the body itself, one over the head, another over the neck, still others, one for each bodily part; in the mind, one over the intelligence, another over learning, another over temper, another over desire; in the realities, related to life, that lie about us, one over flocks and one over wheat, one over wine, one over oil, and another over forests, one over currency, another over navigation, and still another over warfare and victory, one over marriage, a different one over fecundity and childbirth, so on and so on.

The heavenly City, on the contrary, knows and, by religious faith, believes that it must adore one God alone and serve Him with that complete dedication which the Greeks call *latreía* and which belongs to Him alone. As a result, she has been unable to share with the earthly city a common religious legislation, and has had no choice but to dissent on this score and so to become a nuisance to those who think otherwise. Hence, she has had to feel the weight of their anger, hatred, and violence, save in those instances when, by sheer numbers and God's help, which never fails, she has been able to scare off her opponents.

So long, then, as the heavenly City is wayfaring on earth, she invites citizens from all nations and all tongues, and unites them into a single pilgrim band. She takes no issue with that diversity of customs, laws, and traditions whereby human peace is sought and maintained. Instead of nullifying or tearing down, she preserves and appropriates whatever in the diversities of divers races is aimed at one and the same objective of human peace, provided only that they do not stand in the way of the faith and worship of the one supreme and true God.

Thus, the heavenly City, so long as it is wayfaring on earth, not only makes use of earthly peace but fosters and actively pursues along with other human beings a common platform in regard to all that concerns our purely human life and does not interfere with faith and worship. Of course, though, the City of God subordinates this earthly peace to that of heaven. For this is not merely true peace, but, strictly speaking, for any rational creature, the only real peace, since it is, as I said, "the perfectly ordered and harmonious communion of those who find their joy in God and in one another in God."

When this peace is reached, man will be no longer haunted by death, but plainly and perpetually endowed with life, nor will his body, which now wastes away and weighs down the soul, be any longer animal, but spiritual, in need of nothing, and completely under the control of our will.

ST. ANSELM

St. Anselm (1033–1109), Archbishop of Canterbury, was born in Piedmont and entered the Benedictine Order, in which he became Prior and then Abbot. In general, the thought of Anselm is said to belong to the Augustinian tradition, from which he borrowed the form of his famous "ontological" argument for God's existence. Anselm's theology and philosophy are not separated in formulation or distinguished from one another systematically; his philosophy has a constant theological setting. Nevertheless, his essential rationalism is clear both in the ontological argument and in his conviction that the Trinity is a subject for demonstration by "necessary reasons," a view shared by few other medieval thinkers.

The selections presented here indicate the famous "valuational" approach to God, a view which sees the world as ordered in hierarchies, the progression through which leads to God as the archetype of all goods. There is no positive evil; all apparent evil is merely lesser good. The Cur Deus Homo, *which explains why it was necessary for God to become man, is one of the few attempts to explain the Christian doctrine of the incarnation rationally and gives a good indication of the Christian's view of man's ethical situation.*

*Monologium. On the Being of God**

THERE IS A BEING WHICH IS BEST, AND GREATEST, AND HIGHEST OF ALL EXISTING BEINGS

If any man, either from ignorance or unbelief, has no knowledge of the existence of one Nature which is the highest of all existing beings, which is also sufficient to itself in its eternal blessedness, and which confers upon and effects in all other beings, through its omnipotent goodness, the very fact of their existence, and the fact that in any way their existence is good; and if he has no knowledge of many other things, which we necessarily believe regarding God and his creatures, he still believes that he can at least convince himself of these truths in great part, even if his mental powers are very ordinary, by the force of reason alone.

And, although he could do this in many ways, I shall adopt one which I consider easiest for such a man. For, since all desire to enjoy only those things which they suppose to be good, it is natural that this man should, at some time, turn his

* By permission. From *St. Anselm,* trans. by Sidney Morton Deane, The Open Court Publishing Company, La Salle, Ill., 1958.

mind's eye to the examination of that cause by which these things are good, which he does not desire, except as he judges them to be good. So that, as reason leads the way and follows up these considerations, he advances rationally to those truths of which, without reason, he has no knowledge. And if, in this discussion, I use any argument which no greater authority adduces, I wish it to be received in this way: although, on the grounds that I shall see fit to adopt, the conclusion is reached as if necessarily, yet it is not, for this reason, said to be absolutely necessary, but merely that it can appear so for the time being.

It is easy, then, for one to say to himself: Since there are goods so innumerable, whose great diversity we experience by the bodily senses, and discern by our mental faculties, must we not believe that there is some one thing, through which all goods whatever are good? Or are they good, one through one thing, and another through another? To be sure, it is most certain and clear, for all who are willing to see, that whatsoever things are said to possess any attribute in such a way that in mutual comparison they may be said to possess it in greater, or less, or equal degree, are said to possess it by virtue of some fact, which is not understood to be one thing in one case and another in another, but to be the same in different cases, whether it is regarded as existing in these cases in equal or unequal degree. For, whatsoever things are said to be *just*, when compared one with another, whether equally, or more, or less, cannot be understood as just, except through the quality of *justness*, which is not one thing in one instance, and another in another.

Since it is certain, then, that all goods, if mutually compared, would prove either equally or unequally good, necessarily they are all good by virtue of something which is conceived of as the same in different goods, although sometimes they seem to be called good, the one by virtue of one thing, the other by virtue of another. For, apparently it is by virtue of one quality, that a horse is called *good*, because he is strong, and by virtue of another, that he is called *good*, because he is swift. For, though he seems to be called good by virtue of his strength, and good by virtue of his swiftness, yet swiftness and strength do not appear to be the same thing.

But if a horse, because he is strong and swift, is therefore good, how is it that a strong, swift robber is bad? Rather, then, just as a strong, swift robber is bad, because he is harmful, so a strong, swift horse is good, because he is useful. And, indeed, nothing is ordinarily regarded as good, except either for some utility—as, for instance, safety is called good, and those things which promote safety—or for some honorable character—as, for instance, beauty is reckoned to be good and what promotes beauty.

But, since the reasoning which we have observed is in no wise refutable, necessarily, again, all things, whether useful or honorable, if they are truly good, are good through that same being through which all goods exist, whatever that being is. But who can doubt this very being, through which all goods exist, to be a great good? This must be, then, a good through itself, since every other good is through it.

It follows, therefore, that all other goods are good through another being than that which they themselves are, and this being alone is good through itself. Hence, this alone is supremely good, which is alone good through itself. For it is supreme, in that it so surpasses other beings, that it is neither equalled nor excelled. But that which is supremely good is also supremely great. There is, therefore, some one being which is supremely good, and supremely great, that is, the highest of all existing beings.

But, just as it has been proved that there is a being that is supremely good, since all goods are good through a single being, which is good through itself; so it is necessarily inferred that there is something supremely great, which is great through itself. But I do not mean physically great, as a material object is great, but that which, the greater it is, is the better or the more worthy,—wisdom, for instance. And since there can be nothing supremely great except what is supremely good, there must be a being that is greatest and best, i.e., the highest of all existing beings.

Furthermore, if one observes the nature of things, he perceives, whether he will or no, that not all are embraced in a single degree of dignity; but that certain among them are distinguished by inequality of degree. For, he who doubts that the horse is superior in its nature to wood, and man more excellent than the horse, assuredly does not deserve the name of man. Therefore, although it cannot be denied that some natures are superior to others, nevertheless reason convinces us that some nature is so preëminent among these, that it has no superior. For, if the distinction of degrees is infinite, so that there is among them no degree, than which no higher can be found, our course of reasoning reaches this conclusion: that the multitude of natures themselves is not limited by any bounds. But only an absurdly foolish man can fail to regard such a conclusion as absurdly foolish. There is, then, necessarily some nature which is so superior to some nature or natures, that there is none in comparison with which it is ranked as inferior.

*Cur Deus Homo**

Book First
Sin and Satisfaction for Sin

WHAT IT IS TO SIN, AND TO MAKE SATISFACTION FOR SIN

ANSELM: We must needs inquire in what manner God puts away men's sins; and, in order to do this more plainly, let us first consider what it is to sin, and what it is to make satisfaction for sin.

BOSO: It is yours to explain and mine to listen.

ANSELM: If man or angel always rendered to God his due, he would never sin.

BOSO: I cannot deny that.

ANSELM: Therefore to sin is nothing else than not to render to God his due.

BOSO: What is the debt which we owe to God?

ANSELM: Every wish of a rational creature should be subject to the will of God.

BOSO: Nothing is more true.

ANSELM: This is the debt which man and angel owe to God, and no one who pays this debt commits sin; but every one who does not pay it sins. This is justice, or uprightness of will, which makes a being just or upright in heart, that is, in will; and this is the sole and complete debt of honor which we owe to God, and which God requires of us. For it is such a will only, when it can be exercised, that does works pleasing to God; and when this will cannot be exercised, it is pleasing of itself alone, since without it no work is acceptable. He who does not render this honor which is due to God, robs God of his own and dishonors him; and this is sin. Moreover, so long as he does not restore what he has taken away, he remains in fault; and it will not suffice merely to restore what has been taken away, but, considering the contempt offered, he ought to restore more than he took away. For as one who imperils another's safety does not enough by merely restoring his safety, without making some compensation for the anguish incurred; so he who violates another's honor does not enough by merely rendering honor again, but must, according to the extent of the injury done, make restoration in some way satisfactory to the person whom he has dishonored. We must also observe that when any one pays what he has unjustly

* *Supra*, p. 140.

taken away, he ought to give something which could not have been demanded of him, had he not stolen what belonged to another. So then, every one who sins ought to pay back the honor of which he has robbed God; and this is the satisfaction which every sinner owes to God.

BOSO: Since we have determined to follow reason in all these things, I am unable to bring any objection against them, although you somewhat startle me.

HOW MAN CANNOT BE SAVED WITHOUT SATISFACTION FOR SIN

ANSELM: It was fitting for God to fill the places of the fallen angels from among men.

BOSO: That is certain.

ANSELM: Therefore there ought to be in the heavenly empire as many men taken as substitutes for the angels as would correspond with the number whose place they shall take, that is, as many as there are good angels now; otherwise they who fell will not be restored, and it will follow that God either could not accomplish the good which he began, or he will repent of having undertaken it; either of which is absurd.

BOSO: Truly it is fitting that men should be equal with good angels.

ANSELM: Have good angels ever sinned?

BOSO: No.

ANSELM: Can you think that man, who has sinned, and never made satisfaction to God for his sin, but only been suffered to go unpunished, may become the equal of an angel who has never sinned?

BOSO: These words I can both think of and utter, but can no more perceive their meaning than I can make truth out of falsehood.

ANSELM: Therefore it is not fitting that God should take sinful man without an atonement, in substitution for lost angels; for truth will not suffer man thus to be raised to an equality with holy beings.

BOSO: Reason shows this.

ANSELM: Therefore, consider it settled that, without satisfaction, that is, without voluntary payment of the debt, God can neither pass by the sin unpunished, nor can the sinner attain that happiness, or happiness like that, which he had before he sinned; for man cannot in this way be restored, or become such as he was before he sinned.

BOSO: Your reply with regard to this matter suffices me for the present. And, moreover, you have so clearly shown that no man can attain happiness in sin, or be freed from sin without satisfaction for the trespass that, even were I so disposed, I could not doubt it.

WHAT MAN TOOK FROM GOD BY HIS SIN, WHICH HE HAS NO POWER TO REPAY

ANSELM: What did man take from God, when he allowed himself to be overcome by the devil?

BOSO: Go on to mention, as you have begun, the evil things which can be added to those already shown, for I am ignorant of them.

ANSELM: Did not man take from God whatever He had purposed to do for human nature?

BOSO: There is no denying that.

ANSELM: Listen to the voice of strict justice; and judge according to that whether man makes to God a real satisfaction for his sin, unless, by overcoming the devil, man restore to God what he took from God in allowing himself to be conquered by the devil; so that, as by this conquest over man the devil took what belonged to God, and God was the loser, so in man's victory the devil may be despoiled, and God recover his right.

BOSO: Surely nothing can be more exactly or justly conceived.

ANSELM: Think you that supreme justice can violate *this* justice?

BOSO: I dare not think it.

ANSELM: Therefore man cannot and ought not by any means to receive from God what God designed to give him, unless he return to God everything which he took from him; so that, as by man God suffered loss, by man, also, He might recover His loss. But this cannot be effected except in this way: that, as in the fall of man all human nature was corrupted, and, as it were, tainted with sin, and God will not choose one of such a race to fill up the number in his heavenly kingdom; so, by man's victory, as many men may be justified from sin as are needed to complete the number which man was made to fill. But a sinful man can by no means do this, for a sinner cannot justify a sinner.

BOSO: There is nothing more just or necessary; but, from all these things, the compassion of God and the hope of man seems to fail, as far as regards that happiness for which man was made.

HOW MAN WAS MADE HOLY BY GOD, SO AS TO BE HAPPY IN THE ENJOYMENT OF GOD

ANSELM: It ought not to be disputed that rational nature was made holy by God, in order to be happy in enjoying Him. For to this end is it rational, in order to discern justice and injustice, good and evil, and between the greater and the lesser good. Otherwise it was made rational in vain. But God made it not rational in vain. Wherefore, doubtless, it was made rational for this end. In like manner is it proved that the intelligent creature received the power of discernment for this purpose, that he might hate and shun evil, and love and choose good, and especially the greater good. For else in vain would God have given him that power of discernment, since man's discretion would be useless unless he loved and avoided according to it. But it does not befit God to give such power in vain. It is, therefore, established that rational nature was created for this end, viz., to love and choose the highest good supremely, for its own sake and nothing else; for if the highest good were chosen for any other reason, then something else and not itself would be the thing loved. But intelligent nature cannot fulfil this purpose without being holy. Therefore that it might not in vain be made rational, it was made, in order to fulfil this purpose, both rational and holy. Now, if it was made holy in order to choose and love the highest good, then it was made such in order to follow sometimes what it loved and chose, or else it was not. But if it were not made holy for this end, that it might follow what it loves and chooses, then in vain was it made to love and choose holiness; and there can be no reason why it should be ever bound to follow holiness. Therefore, as long as it will be holy in loving and choosing the supreme good, for which it was made, it will be miserable; because it will be impotent despite of its will, inasmuch as it does not have what it desires. But this is utterly absurd. Wherefore rational nature was made holy, in order to be happy in enjoying the supreme good, which is God. Therefore man, whose nature is rational, was made holy for this end, that he might be happy in enjoying God.

HOW MAN WOULD NEVER HAVE DIED, UNLESS HE HAD SINNED

ANSELM: Moreover, it is easily proved that man was so made as not to be necessarily subject to death; for, as we have already said, it is inconsistent with God's wisdom and justice to compel man to suffer death without fault, when he made him holy to enjoy eternal blessedness. It therefore follows that had man never sinned he never would have died.

HOW GOD WILL COMPLETE, IN RESPECT TO HUMAN NATURE, WHAT HE HAS BEGUN

ANSELM: From these things, we can easily see that God will either complete what he has begun with regard to human nature, or else he has made to no end so lofty a nature, capable of so great good. Now if it be understood that God has made nothing more valuable than rational existence capable of enjoying him, it is altogether foreign from his character to suppose that he will suffer that rational existence utterly to perish.

BOSO: No reasonable being can think otherwise.

ANSELM: Therefore is it necessary for him to perfect in human nature what he has begun. But this, as we have already said, cannot be accomplished save by a complete expiation of sin, which no sinner can effect for himself.

BOSO: I now understand it to be necessary for God to complete what he has begun, lest there be an unseemly falling off from his design.

HOW NO BEING, EXCEPT THE GOD-MAN, CAN MAKE THE ATONEMENT BY WHICH MAN IS SAVED

ANSELM: But this cannot be effected, except the price paid to God for the sin of man be something greater than all the universe besides God.

BOSO: So it appears.

ANSELM: Moreover, it is necessary that he who can give God anything of his own which is more valuable than all things in the possession of God, must be greater than all else but God himself.

BOSO: I cannot deny it.

ANSELM: Therefore none but God can make this satisfaction.

BOSO: So it appears.

ANSELM: But none but a man ought to do this, otherwise man does not make the satisfaction.

BOSO: Nothing seems more just.

ANSELM: If it be necessary, therefore, as it appears, that the heavenly kingdom be made up of men, and this cannot be effected unless the aforesaid satisfaction be made, which none but God can make and none but man ought to make, it is necessary for the God-man to make it.

BOSO: Now blessed be God! We have made a great discovery with regard to our question. Go on, therefore, as you have begun. For I hope that God will assist you.

HOW GREAT AND HOW JUST IS GOD'S COMPASSION

Now we have found the compassion of God which appeared lost to you when we were considering God's holiness and man's sin; we have found it, I say, so great and so consistent with his holiness, as to be incomparably above anything that can be conceived. For what compassion can excel these words of the Father, addressed to the sinner doomed to eternal torments and having no way of escape: "Take my only begotten Son and make him an offering for yourself;" or these words of the Son: "Take me, and ransom your souls." For these are the voices they utter, when inviting and leading us to faith in the Gospel. Or can anything be more just than for him to remit all debt since he has earned a reward greater than all debt, if given with the love which he deserves.

ST. BERNARD OF CLAIRVAUX

St. Bernard (1090–1153), Abbot of Clairvaux, was a leader in the reform of the Cistercian Order. Though he was a Burgundian nobleman, called by birth to a life of chivalry and by his talents to a career of scholarship, he rejected all in order to lead a group to revive the failing monastery of Cîteaux. At the age of twenty-five, and after only three years there, he was named abbot of the monastery at Clairvaux. His eloquence and fervor not only revived the monastic ideal; they brought him political power which he could not refuse. He was a prophet and a mystic, it is true. Yet his long record of instigating heresy proceedings sheds a somewhat different light on his character.

The selection from The Steps of Humility, *perhaps his most famous work, illustrates the monastic ethical and religious ideals. The scale of values indicated is typical of the Middle Ages.*

*The Steps of Humility**

AUTHOR'S PREFACE

You have asked me, Brother Godfrey, to set forth for you in more extended form that which I said to the brethren about the steps of humility. While my eagerness to grant your wish urged me on, the meagerness of my ability held me back, and, mindful of our Lord's warning, I did not dare begin until I had sat down and counted the cost, whether I had sufficient to finish it. But when love had cast out the fear of being mocked on account of an unfinished work, there arose another fear, that the fame of success might be more perilous than the shame of failure. Being thus placed in a dilemma between this fear and love, I hesitated a long time, wondering which path would be safe to follow, and fearing that a useful discourse would violate what humility I have, while humble silence would nullify what utility I have. Since I saw neither was safe, yet one or the other must be chosen, I have decided to share the fruit of my discourse with you, so far as possible, rather than seek my own

* Reprinted by permission of the publishers from the translation by George Bosworth Burch of *The Steps of Humility*, by Bernard, Abbot of Clairvaux, Cambridge, Mass.: Harvard University Press, Copyright, 1940, by The President and Fellows of Harvard College.

safety in the haven of silence. And I am confident that, if by chance I say anything which you approve, I shall be able to keep from being proud by the help of your prayers; while if, as is more likely, I do not accomplish anything worthy of your consideration, I shall then have nothing to be proud of.

HUMILITY, THE WAY TO TRUTH

I am going to speak, therefore, about the steps of humility, which St. Benedict proposes, not to count but to mount; first I will show, if possible, whither they lead, so that knowledge of the goal may make the toil of the ascent seem less wearisome. So let the Lord tell us of the toil of the way and of the reward of that toil. He says, *I am the way, the truth, and the life.* He calls humility the way which leads to truth. The former is the toil; the latter, the fruit of the toil. How am I to know, you ask, that he was speaking of humility when he said simply, *I am the way*? But hear this, which is clearer: *Learn of me, for I am meek and lowly in heart.* He offers himself as an example of humility, as the type of gentleness. If you follow him, you shall not walk in darkness, but shall have the light of life. What is the light of life but truth, which lighteth every man that cometh into the world and showeth where true life is? Likewise when he said, *I am the way and the truth,* he added, *and the life;* as if to say, I am the way, leading to truth; I am the truth, promising life; I am the life, and give it. *And this,* he says, *is life eternal, that they might know thee the only true God, and Jesus Christ, whom thou hast sent.* Or it is as if you should say: I know the way, humility; I want the reward, truth. But what if the toil of the way is so great that I cannot attain the desired goal? He answers, *I am the life,* that is, the means of support on the way. Thus he cries to wanderers, who have lost the way, *I am the way;* to sceptics and unbelievers, *I am the truth;* to those already mounting, but growing weary, *I am the life.* It is clear enough, I think, from the verse cited that knowledge of the truth is the fruit of humility. But hear also another: *I thank thee, O Father, Lord of heaven and earth, because thou hast hid these things,* no doubt the secrets of truth, *from the wise and prudent,* that is, from the proud, *and hast revealed them unto babes,* that is, to the humble. Here too it appears that the truth is concealed from the proud and revealed to the humble.

Humility may be defined thus: Humility is that thorough self-examination which makes a man contemptible in his own sight. It is acquired by those who set up a ladder in their hearts whereby to ascend from virtue to virtue, that is, from step to step, until they attain the summit of humility, from where, as from the Zion of speculation, they can see the truth. *For the lawgiver,* it is said, *shall give a blessing,* because he who has given the law will give a blessing too, that is, he who has commanded humility will lead to truth. Now who is this lawgiver but the gracious and righteous Lord, who teaches the abandoned in the way? For they are surely abandoned who have abandoned truth. But are they thus abandoned by the gracious Lord? Nay, for they are the very ones whom the gracious and righteous Lord commands to follow the way of humility by which they may return to knowledge of the truth. He gives an opportunity to recover salvation, because he is gracious; yet not without due discipline, because he is righteous. Gracious, because he does not allow to perish; righteous, because he does not neglect to punish.

THE FIRST STEP OF TRUTH, KNOWING YOURSELF

If he made himself wretched who was not wretched before, in order to learn what he already knew; how much more should you, I do not say make yourself what you are not, but observe what you are, that you are wretched indeed, and so learn to be merciful, a thing you cannot know in any other way. For if you regard your neighbor's faults but do not observe your own, you are likely to be moved not to ruth but to wrath, not to condole but to condemn, not to restore in the spirit of meekness but to destroy in the spirit of anger. *Ye which are spiritual,* says the apostle, *restore such an one in the spirit of meekness.* The apostle's counsel or rather command is to assist the weak brother in a gentle spirit, the spirit in which you wish to be assisted when you are weak. And that you may know how to act gently toward a trespasser, he adds, *Considering thyself, lest thou also be tempted.*

Let us see how well the disciple of Truth follows the Master's order. In the Beatitudes, which I referred to above, just as the merciful are mentioned before the pure in heart, so are the meek before the merciful. And when the apostle exhorted the spiritual to restore the carnal, he added, *In the spirit of meekness.* Restoring your brethren is the work of the merciful; the spirit is that of the meek; as if he had said, none can be considered merciful who is not meek in himself. See how the apostle clearly shows what I promised to show above, that truth is to be sought in ourselves before we seek it in our neighbors; *considering thyself,* he says, that is, how easily tempted, how liable to sin. For by considering yourself you grow meek, and thus you come to succour others in the spirit of meekness. But if you will not observe what the disciple commends, heed what the Master commands: *Thou hypocrite, first cast out the beam out of thine own eye; and then shalt thou see clearly to cast out the mote out of thy brother's eye.* The great thick beam in the eye is pride in the mind. By its great size, although empty, not sound, swollen, not solid, it dims the mind's eye and overshadows truth in such a way that, when pride fills your mind, you can no longer see yourself, you can no longer feel yourself such as you are actually or potentially; but you either fancy that you are or hope you will become such as you would love to be. For what is pride but love of your own excellence, as some saint has defined it? We may say likewise, on the other hand, that humility is contempt of your own excellence. Love, like hate, is a stranger to true judgment. Will you hear a true judgment? *As I hear, I judge;* not as I hate, not as I love, not as I fear. There is a judgment of hate, for example, *We have a law, and by our law he ought to die.* Also of fear, for example, *If we let him thus alone, the Romans shall come and take away both our place and nation.* And there is a judgment of love, as David's command concerning his parricide son, *Deal gently with the young man, even with Absalom.* And I know it is a rule in human law observed in both ecclesiastical and secular cases that personal friends of the litigants cannot be admitted as judges, lest they either defraud or be defrauded by their love for their friends. Now if your love for a friend either lessens or completely conceals his guilt in your judgment, how much more will the love of yourself deceive you in judging yourself!

He, therefore, who wants to know truth in himself fully must first get rid of the beam of pride, which prevents him from seeing the light, and then erect a way of ascent in his heart by which to seek himself in himself; and thus after the twelfth step of humility he will come to the first step of truth. When he has found truth in himself, or rather has found himself in truth, and is able to say, *I believed, and therefore have I spoken; but I was greatly humbled;* let him ascend to the heights of his heart, that truth may be exalted, and passing to the second step let him say in his passage, *All men are false.* Pray, did not David follow this order? Pray, did not the prophet feel this which the Lord felt, and the apostle, and even we feel after them and through them? *I believed,* he says, in the Truth which declares, *He that followeth me shall not walk in darkness. I believed,* following; *and therefore have I spoken,* confessing. Confessing what? The truth which I have learned in believing. But after I both believed unto righteousness and spoke unto salvation, *I was greatly,* that is perfectly, *humbled.* As if he had said: Because I was not ashamed to confess against myself truth found in myself, I attained to perfect humility. For *greatly* can be understood to mean "perfectly," as in the phrase, *That delighteth greatly in his commandments.* If anyone should contend that *greatly* here means "extremely" rather than "perfectly," because the commentators seem to say so, that is also consistent with the prophet's meaning, and we may consider him to have said as follows: When I did not yet know truth, I thought myself to be something, whereas I was nothing; but after I learned the truth by believing in Christ, that is, imitating his humility, it was itself exalted in me by my confession; *but I was greatly humbled,* that is, I became in my own sight extremely contemptible as a result of my self-examination.

THE SECOND STEP OF TRUTH, KNOWING YOUR NEIGHBOR

And so the prophet is humbled in this first step of truth, as he says in another psalm, *And in thy truth thou hast humbled me.* Let him observe himself and judge the common wretchedness from his own. And thus proceeding to the second step, let him say in his passage, *All men are false.* In what passage? In that doubtless in which, passing outside himself and cleaving to truth, he judges himself. Let him say, then, in that passage, not angrily or insolently, but pitifully and sympathetically, *All men are false.* What does this mean, *All men are false?* All men are weak, all men are wretched and impotent who can save neither themselves nor others. Just as it is said, *An horse is a vain thing for safety,* not because a horse deceives anyone, but because he deceives himself who trusts in its strength; so all men are called false, that is, frail and fickle, who can hope to achieve neither their own nor another's salvation. Rather does he incur a curse that trusteth in man. And so the prophet humbly advances under the leadership of truth, seeing in others what he deplores in himself; *and he that increaseth knowledge increaseth sorrow,* so as to say, broadly but truthfully, *All men are false.*

See how differently the proud Pharisee felt about himself. What did he exclaim in his passage? *God, I thank thee that I am not as other men are.* He exults in himself exceedingly; he insults all others arrogantly. David is otherwise. For he says, *All men are false.* He excludes none, and so deludes none, knowing that all have sinned and come short of the glory of God. The Pharisee deludes only himself when he excludes only himself and condemns all others. The prophet does not exclude himself from the common passion, lest he be excluded from the compassion; the Pharisee disdains mercy when he disclaims misery. The prophet maintains of all, as of himself, *All men are false;* the Pharisee complains of all, except himself, saying, *I am not as other men are.* And he gives thanks, not that he is good, but that he is different; not so much because of his own virtues as because of the vices which he sees in others. He has not yet cast out the beam out of his own eye, yet he points out the motes in his brothers' eyes. For he adds, *Unjust, extortioners.* This digressing passage is not in vain, I think, if you have learned to distinguish the different kinds of passage.

Now to return to the thesis. Those whom truth has caused to know, and so contemn, themselves must now find distasteful those things they used to love, even their own selves. Standing before themselves, they are forced to see that they are such as they blush to appear, even to themselves. Displeased with what they are, they aspire to what they are not and have no hope of becoming through themselves. Loudly mourning their lot, they find only this comfort, that, severe judges of themselves, who love truth and hunger and thirst after justice, contemptuous even of themselves, they require of themselves the strictest expiation and, what is more, emendation. But when they see that they are not sufficient for this (for when they have done all those things which are commanded them, they say, We are unprofitable servants), they flee from justice to mercy. In order to obtain this they follow the precept of Truth: *Blessed are the merciful, for they shall obtain mercy.* And this is the second step of truth, when they seek it in their neighbors, when they learn others' wants from their own, when they know from their own miseries how to commiserate with others who are miserable.

THE THIRD STEP OF TRUTH, KNOWING GOD

Those who persevere, therefore, in these three things, the remorse of repentance, desire of justice, and works of mercy, may then pass through contemplation to the third step, having purged the spiritual vision of the three obstacles arising from ignorance and weakness and willfulness. For these are the ways which seem good to men, to those at least *who rejoice to do evil and delight in the frowardness of the wicked,* and cover themselves with weakness or ignorance to plead as excuses in sinning. But they plead weakness or ignorance without avail who choose to be ignorant or weak in order to sin more freely. Do you suppose it availed the first man, or was it allowed that he did not sin willingly, because he pleaded his wife, that is, the weakness of the flesh, in defence? or will the stoners of the first martyr, because they stopped their ears, be excusable through ignorance? Those who feel themselves alienated from truth by delight and gladness in sinning and ovecome by weakness and ignorance, must change their delight to despite, their gladness to sadness, conquer the weakness of the flesh with the zeal of justice, and resist ignorance with philanthropy. Otherwise, if they do not know truth needy, naked, and weak as it is now; they may shamefacedly recognize it too late when it comes with great power and strength, terrifying and accusing, and may in vain answer tremblingly, *When saw we thee in need and did not minister unto thee? The Lord shall be known when he executeth judgments,* if he is not known now when he seeketh mercy. Then *they shall look on him whom they pierced,* and likewise the avaricious on him whom they despised. From every blemish, therefore, arising from weakness or ignorance or willfulness the eye of the heart is purified by weeping, hungering for justice, and devotion to works of mercy. To such a heart Truth promises to appear in his splendor: *Blessed are the pure in heart: for they shall see God.* Since there are therefore three steps or states of truth, we ascend to the first by the toil of humility, to the second by the emotion of compassion, to the third by the ecstasy of contemplation. In the first, truth is found harsh; in the second, loving; in the third, pure. Reason, by which we examine ourselves, leads us to the first; love, by which we sympathize with others, entices us to the second; purity, by which we are lifted to invisible heights, snatches us up to the third. . . .

THE STEPS OF HUMILITY

There is a way down and a way up, a way to the good and a way to evil. Shun the evil one, choose the good one. If you cannot do so of yourself, pray with the prophet and say, *Remove from me the way of lying.* How? *And grant me thy law gra-*

ciously; that law namely which thou hast given to the abandoned in the way, who have abandoned truth, and one of whom am I, surely fallen from truth. But shall not he who falls endeavor to rise again? This is why *I have chosen the way of truth,* by which I shall go up in humility thither whence I came down in pride. I shall go up, I say, singing, *It is good for me, O Lord, that I have been humbled. The law of thy mouth is better unto me than thousands of gold and silver.* David seems to have offered you two ways, but you know there is only one. Yet it is distinguished from itself and is called by different names, either *the way of lying* for those going down, or *the way of truth* for those going up. The same steps lead up to the throne and down; the same road leads to the city and from it; one door is the entrance of the house and the exit; Jacob saw the angels ascending and descending on the same ladder. What does all this mean? Simply that if you desire to return to truth, you do not have to seek a new way which you know not, but the known way by which you descended. Retracing your own path, you may ascend in humility by the same steps which you descended in pride, so that what was the twelfth step of pride going down is the first step of humility going up; the eleventh is found second; the tenth, third; the ninth, fourth; the eighth, fifth; the seventh, sixth; the sixth, seventh; the fifth, eighth; the fourth, ninth; the third, tenth; the second, eleventh; and the first, twelfth. When these steps of pride are discovered or rather remembered in yourself, there is no difficulty in finding the way of humility.

THE FIRST STEP OF PRIDE, CURIOSITY

The first step of pride, then, is curiosity, and you may recognize it by these marks. If you shall see a monk, whom you formerly trusted confidently, beginning to roam with his eyes, hold his head erect, prick up his ears, wherever he is standing, walking, sitting; you may know the changed inner man from the movements of the outer. For a wicked man *winketh with his eyes, speaketh with his feet, teacheth with his fingers;* and the strange movement of the body reveals a new disease in the soul, which has tired of introspection and which neglect of self makes curious toward others. For, as it knows not itself, it is sent forth to feed its kids. I shall rightly have called the eyes and ears kids, which signify sin; for just as death enters into the world by sin, so by these windows it enters into the mind. The curious man, therefore, occupies himself with feeding these, no longer curious to know how he has left himself within. And it would be strange indeed, O man, if while watchfully attending thyself thou shouldst likewise be extending thyself to aught else. Hearken to Solomon, thou curious fellow; hearken to the wise man, thou fool. *Keep thy heart,* he says, *with all diligence;* let all they senses be alert for keeping that out of which *are the issues of life.* For whither wilt thou withdraw from thyself, thou curious fellow? To whom wilt thou commit thyself meanwhile? How dost thou dare lift thy eyes to heaven, when thou hast sinned against heaven? Look at the earth in order to know thyself. Only it will show thee an image of thyself, *for dust thou art, and unto dust shalt thou return.*

There are two reasons, however, for which you may lift up your eyes without reproach, namely, to seek help or to offer it. David lifted up his eyes unto the hills, to seek it; and the Lord lifted up his over the multitude, to offer it. The one pitiably, the other pitifully, both blamelessly. If you also, considering the time, place, and cause, lift up your eyes because of your own or your brother's necessity, not only I do not condemn but I highly approve. For affliction excuses the one, while affection commends the other. But if for any other reason, then I will call you an imitator not of the prophet or the Lord but of Dinah or Eve or even Satan. For when Dinah goes out to feed her kids, her father loses his maid and she her maidenhood. O Dinah, why must thou go out to see the daughters of the land? What is the need? What is the use? Mere curiosity? Though thou seest them idly, thou are not idly seen. Thou lookest curiously, but are looked at more curiously. Who would then suppose that this curious idleness or idle curiosity would prove to be not idle but suicidal for thee, thy friends, and thy foes

[*At this point Bernard lists and discusses, in addition to curiosity, the following as the steps of pride:*

The second step of pride, frivolity.

The third step of pride, foolish mirth.

The fourth step of pride, boastfulness.

The fifth step of pride, singularity (i.e., thinking that "I am not as other men are").

The sixth step of pride, conceit.

The seventh step of pride, audacity.

The eighth step of pride, excusing sins.

The ninth step of pride, hypocritical confession.

The tenth step of pride, defiance.

The eleventh step of pride, freedom to sin (i.e., "allured into satisfying [one's] own desires with the confidence of freedom").

The twelfth step of pride, habitual sinning.]

CONCLUSION

You may say, Brother Godfrey, that I have set forth something other than what you requested and I promised, as I seem to have described the steps of pride instead of the steps of humility. I reply, I could only teach what I had learned. I who know more about going down than going up did not think it would be proper for me to describe the way up. Let St. Benedict tell you about the steps of humility, which he first set up in his own heart; I have nothing to tell you about except the order of my own descent. Yet if this is carefully examined, the way up may be found in it. For if when going to Rome you should meet a man coming from there and ask him the way, what way could he tell better than that which he had come? In naming the castles, towns and cities, rivers and mountains, along which he has passed, he describes his own road and prescribes yours, so that you may recognize the same places in going which he has passed along in coming. Similarly in this descent of mine you will find, perhaps, the steps leading up, and ascending will read them in your own heart better than in my book.

ST. THOMAS AQUINAS

St. Thomas Aquinas (1224–1274) is usually thought of as the great representative of the Middle Ages. At the beginning of his career, his brothers kidnaped him in a futile effort to keep him from joining the Dominican Order. Later he accompanied Albert the Great to Cologne to found a house of studies, and as Albert's pupil he followed his master in an attempt to use the available writings of Aristotle in working out a summation of all philosophy and theology. At Paris, Thomas engaged in controversy with the Averroists over their interpretation of Aristotle, but on the whole his life was one of little external excitement or activity.

The Summa Contra Gentiles *has a much simpler structure and has less scholastic paraphernalia than the* Summa Theologica, *a later and more famous work. Since Thomas made a more formal distinction between philosophy and theology than did many medieval philosophers, the selections here will indicate the scope and detail of his philosophical ethics as contrasted with his specifically theological doctrines.*

*Summa Contra Gentiles**

Prologue

There is one First Being, possessing the full perfection of the whole of being, and we call Him God. From the abundance of His perfection, He endows all existing things with being, so that He is fully established not only as the First Being but also as the original source of all existing things. Moreover, He has granted being to other things, not by a necessity of His nature but according to the choice of His will, as has been made clear in our earlier explanations. From this it follows that He is the Lord of the things that He has made, for we are masters of the things that are subject to our will. In fact, He holds perfect dominion over things produced by Himself, since to produce them He is in need neither of the assistance of an external agent nor of the

* From *Summa Contra Gentiles* by St. Thomas Aquinas. Translated and with an introduction by Vernon J. Bourke, Copyright © 1956 by Doubleday & Company, Inc., Garden City, N.Y. Reprinted by permission of the publisher. Deletions are not noted in the text. Some section headings have been added by the editors.

underlying presence of matter, for He is the universal maker of the whole of being.

Now, each of the things produced through the will of an agent is directed to an end by the agent. For the proper object of the will is the good and the end. As a result, things which proceed from will must be directed to some end. Moreover, each thing achieves its ultimate end through its own action which must be directed to the end by Him Who gives things the principles through which they act.

So, it must be that God, Who is in all ways perfect in Himself, and Who endows all things with being from His own power, exists as the Ruler of all beings, and is ruled by none other. Nor is there anything that escapes His rule, just as there is nothing that does not receive its being from Him. As He is perfect in being and causing, so also is He perfect in ruling.

Of course, the result of this rule is manifested differently in different beings, depending on the diversity of their natures. For some beings so exist as God's products that, possessing understanding, they bear His likeness and reflect His image. Consequently, they are not only ruled but are also rulers of themselves, inasmuch as their own actions are directed to a fitting end. If these beings submit to the divine rule in their own ruling, then by virtue of the divine rule they are admitted to the achievement of their ultimate end; but, if they proceed otherwise in their own ruling, they are rejected.

Good and Evil

HOW EVERY AGENT ACTS FOR AN END

The first thing that we must show, then, is that in acting every agent intends an end.

In the case of things which obviously act for an end, we call that toward which the inclination of the agent tends the end. For, if it attain this, it is said to attain its end; but, if it fail in regard to this, it fails in regard to the end intended, as is evident in the case of the physician working for the sake of health, and of the man who is running toward a set objective. As far as this point is concerned, it makes no difference whether the being tending to an end is a knowing being or not. For, just as the target is the end for the archer, so is it the end for the motion of the arrow. Now, every inclination of an agent tends toward something definite. A given action does not stem from merely any power, but heating comes from heat, cooling from cold. Thus it is that actions are specifically distinguished by virtue of a diversity of active powers. In fact, an action may sometimes terminate in something which is made, as building does in a house, and as healing does in health. Sometimes, however, it does not, as in the cases of understanding and sensing. Now, if an action does in fact terminate in something that is made, the inclination of the agent tends through the action toward the thing that is produced. But, if it does not terminate in a product, then the inclination of the agent tends toward the action itself. So, it must be that every agent in acting intends an end, sometimes the action itself, sometimes a thing produced by the action.

Again, with reference to all things that act for an end, we say that the ultimate end is that beyond which the agent seeks nothing else; thus, the action of a physician goes as far as health, but when it is attained there is no desire for anything further. Now, in the action of all agents, one may find something beyond which the agent seeks nothing further. Otherwise, actions would tend to infinity, which is impossible. Since "it is impossible to proceed to infinity," the agent could not begin to act, because nothing is moved toward what cannot be reached. Therefore, every agent acts for an end.

Furthermore, for every agent the principle of its action is either its nature or its intellect. Now, there is no question that intellectual agents act for the sake of an end, because they think ahead of time in their intellects of the things which they achieve through action; and their action stems from such preconception. This is what it means for intellect to be the principle of action. Just as the entire likeness of the result achieved by the actions of an intelligent agent exists in the intellect that preconceives it, so, too, does the likeness of a natural resultant pre-exist in the natural agent; and as a consequence of this, the action is determined to a definite result. For fire gives rise to fire, and an olive to an olive. Therefore, the agent that acts with nature as its principle is just as much directed to a definite end, in its action, as is the agent that acts through intellect as its principle. Therefore, every agent acts for an end.

THAT EVERY AGENT ACTS FOR A GOOD

Next after this we must show that every agent acts for a good.

That every agent acts for an end has been made clear from the fact that every agent tends toward something definite. Now, that toward which an agent tends in a definite way must be appropriate to it, because the agent would not be inclined to it except by virtue of some agreement with it. But, what is appropriate to something is good for it. So, every agent acts for a good.

Again, the end is that in which the appetitive inclination of an agent or mover, and of the thing moved, finds its rest. Now, the essential meaning of the good is that it provides a terminus for appetite, since "the good is that which all desire." Therefore, every action and motion are for the sake of a good.

Furthermore, every agent acts in so far as it is in act, and in acting it tends to produce something like itself. So, it tends toward some act. But every act has something of good in its essential character, for there is no evil thing that is not in a condition of potency falling short of its act. Therefore, every action is for the sake of a good.

Again, an intelligent agent acts for the sake of an end, in the sense that it determines the end for itself. On the other hand, an agent that acts from a natural impulse, though acting for an end, as we showed in the preceding chapter, does not determine the end for itself, since it does not know the meaning of an end, but, rather, is moved toward an end determined for it by another being. Now, the intelligent agent does not determine the end for itself, unless it do so by considering the rational character of the good, for an object of the intellect is only motivating by virtue of the rational meaning of the good, which is the object of the will. Therefore, even the natural agent is neither moved, nor does it move, for the sake of an end, except in so far as the end is a good; for the end is determined for the natural agent by some appetite. Therefore, every agent acts for the sake of a good.

THAT EVIL IN THINGS IS NOT INTENDED

From this it is clear that evil occurs in things apart from the intention of the agents.

For that which follows from an action, as a different result from that intended by the agent, clearly happens apart from intention. Now, evil is different from the good which every agent intends. Therefore, evil is a result apart from intention.

Again, a defect in an effect and in an action results from some defect in the principles of the action; for instance, the birth of a monstrosity results from some corruption of the semen, and lameness results from a bending of the leg bone. Now, an agent acts in keeping with the active power that it has, not in accord with the defect of power to which it is subject. According as it acts, so does it intend the end. Therefore, it intends an end corresponding to its power. So, that which results as an effect of the defect of power will be apart from the intention of the agent. Now, this is evil. Hence, evil occurs apart from intention.

Moreover, in the case of beings that act as a result of understanding or of some sort of sense judgment, intention is a consequence of apprehension, for the intention tends to what is apprehended as an end. If it actually attains something which does not possess the specific nature of what was apprehended, then this will be apart from the intention. For example, if someone intends to eat honey, but he eats poison, in the belief that it is honey, then this will be apart from the intention. But every intelligent agent tends toward something in so far as he considers the object under the rational character of a good, as was evident in the preceding chapter. So, if this object is not good but bad, this will be apart from his intention. Therefore, an intelligent agent does not produce an evil result, unless it be apart from his intention. Since to tend to the good is common to the intelligent agent and to the agent that acts by natural instinct, evil does not result from the intention of any agent, except apart from the intention.

THAT GOOD IS THE CAUSE OF EVIL

The foregoing arguments enable us to conclude that evil is caused only by the good.

For, if an evil thing were the cause of a certain evil, then the evil thing would not act, except by virtue of the good, as has been proved. So, this good must be the primary cause of the evil.

Again, what does not exist is not the cause of anything. So, every cause must be a definite thing. But evil is not a definite being, as has been proved. Therefore, evil cannot be the cause of anything. If, then, evil be caused by anything, this cause must be the good.

Besides, whatever is properly and of itself the cause of something tends toward a proper effect. So, if evil were of itself the cause of anything, it would tend toward an effect proper to it; namely, evil. But this is false, for it has been shown that every agent tends toward the good. Therefore, evil is not the cause of anything through evil itself, but only accidentally. Now, every accidental cause reduces to a cause that works through itself. And only the good can be a cause through itself, for evil cannot be a cause through itself. Therefore, evil is caused by the good.

Moreover, every cause is either matter, or form, or agent, or end. Now, evil cannot be either matter or form, for it has been shown that both being in act and being in potency are good. Similarly, evil cannot be the agent, since anything that acts does so according as it is in act and has form. Nor, indeed, can it be an end, for it is apart from intention, as we have proved. So, evil cannot be the cause of anything. Therefore, if anything is the cause of evil, it must be caused by the good.

However, in the moral order, the situation seems to be different. It does not appear that moral vice results from a defect of power, since weakness either completely removes moral fault, or at least diminishes it. Indeed, weakness does not merit moral punishment that is proper to guilt, but, rather, mercy and forgiveness. A moral fault must be voluntary, not necessitated. Yet, if we consider the matter carefully, we shall find the two orders similar from one point of view, and dissimilar from another. There is dissimilarity on this point: moral fault is noticed in action only, and not in any effect that is produced; for the moral virtues are not concerned with making but with doing. The arts are concerned with making, and so it has been said that in their sphere a bad result happens just as it does in nature. Therefore moral evil is not considered in relation to the matter or form of the effect, but only as a resultant from the agent.

Now, in moral actions we find four principles arranged in a definite order. One of these is the *executive power*, the moving force, whereby the parts of the body are moved to carry out the command of the will. Then this power is moved by the *will*, which is a second principle. Next, the will is moved by the *judgment* of the apprehensive power which judges that this object is good or bad, for the objects of the will are such that one moves toward attainment, another moves toward avoidance. This apprehensive power is moved, in turn, by the *thing apprehended*. So, the first active principle in moral actions is the thing that is cognitively apprehended, the second is the apprehensive power, the third is the will, and the fourth is the motive power which carries out the command of reason.

Now, the act of the power that carries out the action already presupposes the distinction of moral good or evil. For external acts of this kind do not belong in the moral area, unless they are voluntary. Hence, if the act of the will be good, then the external act is also deemed good, but if it be bad, the external act is bad. It would have nothing to do with moral evil if the external act were defective by virtue of a defect having no reference to the will. Lameness, for instance, is not a fault in the moral order, but in the natural order. Therefore, a defect of this type in the executive power either completely excludes moral fault, or diminishes it. So, too, the act whereby a thing moves the apprehensive power is free from moral fault, for the visible thing moves the power of sight in the natural order, and so, also, does any object move a passive potency. Then, too, this act of the apprehensive power, considered in itself, is without moral fault, for a defect in it either removes or diminishes moral fault, as is the case in a defect of the executive power. Likewise, weakness and ignorance excuse wrongdoing, or diminish it. The conclusion follows, then, that moral fault is found primarily and principally in the act of the will only, and so it is quite reasonable to say, as a result, that an act is moral because it is voluntary. Therefore, the root and source of moral wrongdoing is to be sought in the act of will.

Since reason is able to apprehend many goods and a multiplicity of ends, and since for each thing there is a proper end, there will be, then, for the will an end and a first motivating object which is not merely any good, but some determinate good. Hence, when the will inclines to act as moved by the apprehension of reason, presenting a proper good to it, the result is a fitting action. But when the will breaks forth into action, at the apprehension of sense cognition, or of reason itself presenting some other good at variance with its proper good, the result in the action of the will is a moral fault.

Hence, a defect of ordering to reason and to a proper end precedes a fault of action in the will: in regard to reason, in the case of the will inclining, on the occasion of a sudden sense apprehension, toward a good that is on the level of sensory pleasure; and in regard to a proper end, in the case when reason encounters in its deliberation some good which is not, at this time or under these conditions, really good, and yet the will inclines toward it, as if it were a proper good. Now, this defect in ordering is voluntary, for to will and not to will lie within the power of the will itself. And it is also within its power for reason to make an actual consideration, or to abstain from such a consideration, or further to consider this or that alternative. Yet, such a defect of ordering is not a moral evil, for, if reason considers nothing or considers any good whatever, that is still not a sin until the will inclines to an unsuitable end. At this point, the act of will occurs.

Thus, it is clear, both in the natural order and in the moral order, that evil is only caused by good accidentally.

THAT EVIL DOES NOT WHOLLY DESTROY GOOD

It is evident from the foregoing explanation that, no matter how much evil be multiplied, it can never destroy the good wholly.

In fact, there must always continue to be a subject for evil, if evil is to endure. Of course, the subject of evil is the good, and so the good will always endure.

THAT ALL THINGS ARE ORDERED TO ONE END WHO IS GOD

It is, consequently, apparent that all things are ordered to one good, as to their ultimate end.

If, in fact, nothing tends toward a thing as an end, unless this thing is a good, it is therefore necessary that the good, as good, be the end. Therefore, that which is the highest good is, from the highest point of view, the end of all things. But there is only one highest good, and this is God. So, all things are ordered to one good, as their end, and this is God.

Besides, in any kind of causes, the first cause is more a cause than is the secondary cause, for a secondary cause is only a cause through the primary cause. Therefore, that which is the first cause in the order of final causes must be more the final cause of anything than is its proximate final cause. But God is the first cause in the order of final causes, since He is the highest in the order of goods. Therefore, He is more the end of everything than is any proximate end.

HOW THINGS IMITATE DIVINE GOODNESS

From what has been said, then, it is clear that to become like God is the ultimate end of all. Now, that which possesses the formal character of an end, in the proper sense, is the good. Therefore, things tend toward this objective, of becoming like God, inasmuch as He is good.

Creatures do not attain goodness in the same measure that it is in God, though each thing imitates divine goodness according to its measure. For, divine goodness is simple, entirely gathered together, as it were, into one being. Indeed, this divine existing being includes the entire fullness of perfection. As a result, since anything is perfect to the extent that it is good, this divine being is His perfect goodness. In fact, for God it is the same thing to be, to live, to be wise, to be blessed, and to be whatever else seems to belong to perfection and goodness; the whole divine goodness is, as it were, His divine existing being. Again, this divine being is the substance of the existing God. Now, this cannot obtain in the case of other things. No created substance is its own act of being. Hence, if anything is good by virtue of the fact that it exists, none of them is its own act of being; none of them is its own goodness. Rather, each of them is good by participation in goodness, just as it is being by participation in existing being itself.

Again, not all creatures are established on one level of goodness. For some of them, substance is their form and their act: this is so for the creature to whom, because of what it is essentially, it is appropriate to be, and to be good. For others, indeed, substance is composed of matter and form: to such a being it is appropriate to be, and to be good—but by virtue of some part of it, that is to say, by virtue of its form. Therefore, divine substance is its own goodness, but a simple substance participates goodness by virtue of what it is essentially, while composite substance does so by virtue of something that belongs to it as a part.

There is still another way in which the goodness of a creature is defective in comparison with divine goodness. For, as we said, God in His very act of being holds the highest perfection of goodness. On the other hand, a created thing does not possess its perfection in unity, but in many items, for what is unified in the highest instance is found to be manifold in the lowest things. Consequently, God is said to be virtuous, wise, and operative with reference to the same thing, but creatures are so described with reference to a diversity of things. And so, the more multiplicity the perfect goodness of any creature requires, the more removed is it from the first goodness. If it cannot attain perfect goodness, it will keep imperfect goodness in a few items. Hence it is that, though the first and highest good is altogether simple, and the substances that are nearer to it in goodness are likewise close to it in regard to simplicity, we find some among the lowest substances to be simpler than some of their superiors, as is the case with elements in relation to animals and men; yet these lower simple beings cannot achieve the perfection of knowledge and understanding which animals and men do attain.

So, it is evident from what has been said that, though God has His own perfect and complete goodness, in accord with His simple existing being, creatures do not attain the perfection of their goodness through their being alone, but through many things. Hence, although any one of them is good in so far as it exists, it cannot be called good, without qualification, if it lack any other things required for its goodness. Thus, a man who is destitute of virtue and host to vices is indeed called good, relatively speaking; that is, to the extent that he is a being, and a man. However, in the absolute sense, he is not good, but evil. So, it is not the same thing for any creature to be and to be good without qualification, although each of them is good in so far as it exists. In God, however, to be and to be good are simply the same thing.

Felicity

WHETHER FELICITY CONSISTS IN A WILL ACT

Since happiness is the proper good of an intellectual nature, happiness must pertain to an intellectual nature by reason of what is proper to that nature. Now, appetite is not peculiar to intellectual nature; instead, it is present in all things, though it is in different things in different ways. And this diversity arises from the fact that things are differently related to knowledge. For things lacking knowledge entirely have natural appetite only. And things endowed with sensory knowledge have, in addition, sense appetite, under which irascible and concupiscible powers are included. But things possessed of intellectual knowledge also have an appetite proportionate to this knowledge, that is, will. So, the will is not peculiar to intellectual nature by virtue of being an appetite, but only in so far as it depends on intellect. However, the intellect, in itself, is peculiar to an intellectual nature. Therefore, happiness, or felicity, consists substantially and principally in an act of the intellect rather than in an act of the will.

THAT HUMAN FELICITY DOES NOT CONSIST IN PLEASURES OF THE FLESH

Now, it is clear from what we have said that it is impossible for human felicity to consist in bodily pleasures, the chief of which are those of food and sex.

In fact, in the order of nature pleasure depends on operation, and not the converse. So, if operations are not the ultimate end, the pleasures that result from them are not the ultimate end, either; nor are they concomitant with the ultimate end. It stands to reason that the operations which accompany the above-mentioned pleasures are not the ultimate end, for they are ordered to certain ends that are quite obvious: eating, for instance, to the preservation of the body, and sexual intercourse to the generation of offspring. Therefore, the aforementioned pleasures are not the ultimate end, nor are they concomitants of the ultimate end. So, felicity is not to be located in these pleasures.

Moreover, the ultimate end is the noblest appurtenance of a thing; in fact, the term means the best. But these pleasures are not aggreeable to man by virtue of what is noblest in him, namely, his understanding, but by virtue of his sense capacity. So, felicity should not be located in pleasures of this kind.

Furthermore, the highest perfection of man cannot lie in a union with things inferior to himself, but, rather, in a union with some reality of a higher character, for the end is better than that which is for the sake of the end. Now, the aforementioned pleasures consist in this fact: that man is, through his senses, united with some things that are his inferiors, that is, with certain sensible objects. So, felicity is not to be located in pleasures of this sort.

THAT FELICITY DOES NOT CONSIST IN WORLDLY POWER

Similarly, neither can worldly power be man's highest good, since in its attainment, also, fortune can play a most important part. It is also unstable; nor is it subject to man's will; oftentimes it comes to bad men—and these characteristics are incompatible with the highest good, as was evident in the foregoing arguments.

Again, man is deemed good chiefly in terms of his attainment of the highest good. Now, he is not called good, or bad, simply because he has power, for not everyone who can do good things is a good man, nor is a person bad because he is able to do evil things. Therefore, the highest good does not consist in the fact of being powerful.

THAT FELICITY DOES NOT CONSIST IN GOODS OF THE BODY

Moreover, that man's highest good does not lie in goods of the body, such as health, beauty, and strength, is clearly evident from similar considerations. For these things are possessed in common by both good and bad men; they are also unstable; moreover, they are not subject to the will.

Again, the soul is better than the body, which is not alive, and which does not possess the aforementioned goods except by means of the soul. So, a good of the soul, like understanding and that sort of thing, is better than a good of the body. Therefore, the good of the body is not man's highest good.

Moreover, many animals are better endowed than men, as far as the goods of the body go; for some are faster than man, some are stronger, and so on. If, then, man's highest good lay in these things, man would not be the most excellent of animals; which is obviously false. Therefore, human felicity does not consist in goods of the body.

THAT MAN'S ULTIMATE FELICITY DOES NOT LIE IN ACTS OF THE MORAL VIRTUES

It is clear, too, that the ultimate felicity of man does not consist in moral actions.

In fact, human felicity is incapable of being ordered to a further end, if it is ultimate. But all moral operations can be ordered to something else. This is evident from the most important instances of these actions. The operations of fortitude, which are concerned with warlike activities, are ordered to victory and to peace. Indeed, it would be foolish to make war merely for its own sake. Likewise, the operations of justice are ordered to the preservation of peace among men, by means of each man having his own possessions undisturbed. And the same thing is evident for all the other virtues. Therefore, man's ultimate felicity does not lie in moral operations.

Again, the moral virtues have this purpose: through them the mean is preserved in the internal passions and in regard to external things. Now, it is not possible for such a measuring of passions, or of external things, to be the ultimate end of human life, since these passions and exterior things are capable of being ordered to something else. Therefore, it is not possible for man's ultimate felicity to lie in acts of the moral virtues.

THAT THE ULTIMATE FELICITY OF MAN CONSISTS IN THE CONTEMPLATION OF GOD

So, if the ultimate felicity of man does not consist in external things which are called the goods of fortune, nor in the goods of the body, nor in the goods of the soul according to its sensitive part, nor as regards the intellective part according to the activity of the moral virtues, nor according to the intellectual virtues that are concerned with action, that is, art and prudence—we are left with the conclusion that the ultimate felicity of man lies in the contemplation of truth.

Indeed, this is the only operation of man which is proper to him, and in it he shares nothing in common with the other animals.

So, too, this is ordered to nothing else as an end, for the contemplation of truth is sought for its own sake.

Also, for this operation man is rather sufficient unto himself, in the sense that for it he needs little help from external things.

In fact, all other human operations seem to be ordered to this one, as to an end. For, there is needed for the perfection of contemplation a soundness of body, to which all the products of art that are necessary for life are directed. Also required are freedom from the disturbances of the passions—this is achieved through the moral virtues and prudence—and freedom from external disorders, to which the whole program of government in civil life is directed. And so, if they are rightly considered, all human functions may be seen to subserve the contemplation of truth.

However, it is not possible for man's ultimate felicity to consist in the contemplation which depends on the understanding of principles, for that is very imperfect, being most universal, including the potential cognition of things. Also, it is the beginning, not the end, of human enquiry, coming to us from nature and not because of our search for truth. Nor, indeed, does it lie in the area of the sciences which deal with lower things, because felicity should lie in the working of the intellect in relation to the noblest objects of understanding. So, the conclusion remains that man's ultimate felicity consists in the contemplation of wisdom, based on the considering of divine matters.

THAT MAN'S ULTIMATE FELICITY DOES NOT COME IN THIS LIFE

If ultimate human felicity does not consist in the knowledge of God, whereby He is known in general by all, or most, men, by a sort of confused appraisal, and again, if it does not consist in the knowledge of God which is known by way of demonstration in the speculative sciences, nor in the cognition of God whereby He is known through faith; and if it is not possible in this life to reach a higher knowledge of God so as to know Him through His essence, or even in such a way that, when the other separate substances are known, God might be known through the knowledge of them, as if from a closer vantage point; and if it is necessary to identify ultimate felicity with some sort of knowledge of God, as we proved above, then it is not possible for man's ultimate felicity to come in this life.

Again, the ultimate end of man brings to a termination man's natural appetite, in the sense that, once the end is acquired, nothing else will be sought. For, if he is still moved onward to something else, he does not yet have the end in which he may rest. Now, this termination cannot occur in this life. For, the more a person understands, the more is the desire to understand increased in him, and this is natural to man, unless, perchance, there be someone who understands all things. But in this life this does not happen to anyone who is a mere man.

Providence and Free Will

THAT GOD GOVERNS THINGS BY HIS PROVIDENCE

From the points that have been set forth we have adequately established that God is the end of all things. The next possible conclusion from this is that He governs, or rules, the whole of things by His providence.

Whenever certain things are ordered to a definite end they all come under the control of the one to whom the end primarily belongs. This is evident in an army: all divisions of an army and their functions are ordered to the commander's good as an ultimate end, and this is victory. And for this reason it is the function of the commander to govern the whole army. Likewise, an art which is concerned with the end commands and makes the laws for an art concerned with means to the end. Thus, the art of civil government commands that of the military; the military commands the equestrian; and the art of navigation commands that of shipbuilding. So, since all things are ordered to divine goodness as an end, as we showed, it follows that God, to Whom this goodness primarily belongs, as something substantially possessed and known and loved, must be the governor of all things.

THAT GOD IS THE CAUSE OF OPERATION FOR ALL THINGS THAT OPERATE

It is evident, next, that God is the cause enabling all operating agents to operate. In fact, every operating agent is a cause of being in some way, either of substantial or of accidental being. Now, nothing is a cause of being unless by virtue of its acting through the power of God, as we showed. Therefore, every operating agent acts through God's power.

HOW THE SAME EFFECT IS FROM GOD AND FROM A NATURAL AGENT

Now, it seems difficult for some people to understand how natural effects are attributed to God and to a natural agent.

For it does not seem possible for one action to proceed from two agents. So, if the action whereby a natural effect is produced proceeds from a natural body, it does not proceed from God.

Again, when a thing can be done adequately by one agent, it is superfluous for it to be done by many; in fact, we see that nature does not do with two instruments what it can do with one. So, since the divine power is sufficient to produce natural effects, it is superfluous to use natural powers, too, for the production of the same effects. Or, if the natural power adequately produces the proper effect, it is superfluous for the divine power to act for the same effect.

Besides, if God produces the entire natural effect, then nothing is left of the effect for the natural agent to produce. So, it does not seem to be possible to say that God produces the same effects that natural agents produce.

However, these points present no difficulty, provided the things previously established be considered. In every agent, in fact, there are two things to consider: namely, the thing itself that acts, and the power by which it acts. Fire, for instance, heats by means of heat. But the power of a lower agent depends on the power of the superior agent, according as the superior agent gives this power to the lower agent whereby it may act; or preserves it; or even applies it to the action, as the artisan applies an instrument to its proper effect, though he neither gives the form whereby the instrument works, nor preserves it, but simply gives it motion. So, it is necessary for the action of a lower agent to result not only from the agent by its own power, but also from the power of all higher agents; it acts, then, through the power of all. And just as the lowest agent is found immediately active, so also is the power of the primary agent found immediate in the production of the effect. For the power of the lower agent is not adequate to produce this effect of itself, but from the power of the next higher agent; and the power of the next one gets this ability from the power of the next higher one; and thus the power of the highest agent is discovered to be of itself productive of the effect, as an immediate cause. This is evident in the case of the principles of demonstration, the first of which is immediate. So, just as it is not unfitting for one action to be produced by an agent and its power, so it is not inappropriate for the same effect to be produced by a lower agent and God: by both immediately, though in different ways.

It is also evident that, though a natural thing produces its proper effect, it is not superfluous for God to produce it, since the natural thing does not produce it except by divine power.

Nor is it superfluous, even if God can by Himself produce all natural effects, for them to be produced by certain other causes. For this is not a result of the inadequacy of divine power, but of the immensity of His goodness, whereby He has willed to communicate His likeness to things, not only so that they might exist, but also that they might be causes for other things. Indeed, all creatures generally attain the divine likeness in these two ways, as we showed above. By this, in fact, the beauty of order in created things is evident.

It is also apparent that the same effect is not attributed to a natural cause and to divine power in such a way that it is partly done by God, and partly by the natural agent; rather, it is wholly done by both, according to a different way, just as the same effect is wholly attributed to the instrument and also wholly to the principal agent.

THAT MAN NEEDS THE HELP OF GRACE TO PERSEVERE IN THE GOOD

Man also needs the help of divine grace so that he may persevere in the good.

Indeed, everything that is variable in itself needs the help of an immovable mover so that it may be fixed on one objective. But man is subject to variation, both from evil to good and from good to evil. So, in order that he may immovably continue in the good, which is *to persevere,* he needs divine help.

Again, for that which surpasses the powers of free choice, man needs the help of divine grace. But the power of free choice does not extend to the effect of final perseverance in the good. This is evident as follows. In fact, the power of free choice applies to those things which fall within the scope of election. Now, what is chosen is some particular operation that can be performed. But such a particular operation is what is here and now present. Hence, that which falls under the power of free choice is something that is to be done now. But to persevere does not mean something as now operable, but the continuation of an operation throughout time. Now, this effect, of persevering in the good, is beyond the power of free choice. Therefore, man needs the help of divine grace to persevere in the good.

Besides, though man is the master of his action through will and free choice, he is not the master of his natural powers. So, while he is free to will or not to will something, he cannot by willing produce such a result that his will, by the very fact of willing, would be immovably fixed on what he wills or chooses. But this is what is required for perseverance; that is, the will must endure immovably in the good. So, perseverance is not within the scope of free choice. Therefore, the help of divine grace must be available to man so that he may persevere.

Moreover, suppose that there are several agents in succession, such that one of them acts after the action of another: the continuation of the action of these agents cannot be caused by any one of them, for no one of them acts forever; nor can it be caused by all of them, since they do not act together. Consequently, the continuity must be caused by some higher agent that always acts, just as the Philosopher proves, in *Physics* VIII, that the continuity of the generative process in animals is caused by some higher, external agent. Now, let us suppose the case of someone who is persevering in the good. There are, then, in his case many movements of free choice tending toward the good, successively following each other up to the end. So, for this continuation in the good, which is perseverance, no one of these movements can be the cause, since none of them lasts forever. Nor can all of them together, for they are not together, and so they cannot cause something together. It remains, then, that this continuation is caused by some higher being. Therefore, man needs the help of higher grace to persevere in the good.

Furthermore, if many things are ordered to one end, their entire order until they reach the end comes from the first agent directing them to the end. Now, in the case of a man who perseveres in the good there are many movements and many actions reaching to the end. So, the entire order of the movements and actions must be caused by the first agent directing them to the end. But they are directed by the divine grace to the ultimate end. Therefore, the entire order and continuity of good works, in him who perseveres in the good, is due to the help of divine grace.

However, we should note that even he who possesses grace asks God that he may persevere in the good. Just as free choice is not sufficient without the external help of God, for this effect of persevering in the good, so neither is a habit infused in us enough for this purpose. For habits that are divinely infused in us during the present state of life do not take away entirely from free choice the possibility of being moved toward evil, even though free choice is somewhat fixed in the good by means of them. And so, when we say that man needs the help of grace to persevere unto the end, we do not understand that, in addition to habitual grace previously infused to assure good operation, another must further be infused for persevering; what we do understand is that, once possessed of all the gratuitous habits, a man still needs the help of Divine Providence externally governing him.

*Summa Theologica**

Treatise on Habits
Question 55
Of the Virtues, as to Their Essence

FOURTH ARTICLE. WHETHER VIRTUE IS SUITABLY DEFINED?

Objection 1. It would seem that the definition, usually given, of virtue, is not suitable, to wit: *Virtue is a good quality of the mind, by which we live righteously, of which no one can make bad use, which God works in us, without us.* For virtue is man's goodness, since virtue it is that makes its subject good. But goodness does not seem to be good, as neither is whiteness white. It is therefore unsuitable to describe virtue as a *good quality.*

On the contrary, We have the authority of Augustine from whose words this definition is gathered, and principally in *De Libero Arbitrio* ii. 19.

I answer that, This definition comprises perfectly the whole essential notion of virtue. For the perfect essential notion of anything is gathered from all its causes. Now the above definition comprises all the causes of virtue. For the formal cause of virtue, as of everything, is gathered from its genus and difference, when it is defined as *a good quality:* for *quality* is the genus of virtue, and the difference, *good.* But the definition would be more suitable if for *quality* we substitute *habit,* which is the proximate genus.

Now virtue has no matter *out of which* it is formed, as neither has any other accident; but it has matter *about which* it is concerned, and matter *in which* it exists, namely, the subject. The matter about which virtue is concerned is its object, and this could not be included in the above definition, because the object fixes the virtue to a certain species, and here we are giving the definition of virtue in general. And so for material cause we have the subject, which is mentioned when we say that virtue is a good quality *of the mind.*

The end of virtue, since it is an operative habit, is operation. But it must be observed, that some operative habits are always referred to evil as vicious habits: others are sometimes referred to good, sometimes to evil; for instance, opinion is referred both to the true and to the untrue: whereas virtue is a habit which is always referred to good: and so the distinction of virtue from those habits which are always referred to evil, is expressed in the words *by which we live righteously:* and its distinction from those habits which are sometimes directed unto good, sometimes unto evil, in the words, *of which no one makes bad use.*

Lastly, God is the efficient cause of infused virtue, to which this definition applies; and this is expressed in the words *which God works in us without us.* If we omit this phrase, the remainder of the definition will apply to all virtues in general, whether acquired or infused.

Reply Obj. 1. That which is first seized by the intellect is being: wherefore everything that we apprehended we consider as being, and consequently as one, and as good, which are convertible with being. Wherefore we say that essence is being and is one and is good; and that one-ness is being and one and good: and in like manner goodness. But this is not the case with specific forms, as whiteness and health; for everything that we apprehend, is not apprehended with the notion of white and healthy. We must, however, observe that, as accidents and non-subsistent forms are called beings, not as if they them-

* By permission. From St. Thomas Aquinas, *Summa Theologica,* trans. by Fathers of the English Dominican Province, Benziger Bros., New York, and Burns, Oates, & Washbourne, Ltd., London, 1947. Deletions are not noted in the text.

selves had being, but because things are by them; so also are they called good or one, not by some distinct goodness or one-ness, but because by them something is good or one. So also is virtue called good, because by it something is good.

Question 62
Of the Theological Virtues

FIRST ARTICLE. WHETHER THERE ARE ANY THEOLOGICAL VIRTUES?

Objection 1. It would seem that there are not any theological virtues. For according to *Phys.* vii., text. 17, *virtue is the disposition of a perfect thing to that which is best: and by perfect, I mean that which is disposed according to nature.* But that which is Divine is above man's nature. Therefore the theological virtues are not virtues of a man.

On the contrary, The precepts of the Law are about acts of virtue. Now the Divine Law contains precepts about the acts of faith, hope, and charity: for it is written (*Ecclus.* ii. 8, *seqq.*): *Ye that fear the Lord believe Him,* and again, *hope in Him,* and again, *love Him.* Therefore faith, hope, and charity are virtues directing us to God. Therefore they are theological virtues.

I answer that, Man is perfected by virtue, for those actions whereby he is directed to happiness. Now man's happiness is twofold. One is proportionate to human nature, a happiness, to wit, which man can obtain by means of his natural principles. The other is a happiness surpassing man's nature, and which man can obtain by the power of God alone, by a kind of participation of the Godhead, about which it is written (2 Pet. i. 4) that by Christ we are made *partakers of the Divine nature.* And because such happiness surpasses the capacity of human nature, man's natural principles which enable him to act well according to his capacity, do not suffice to direct man to this same happiness. Hence it is necessary for man to receive from God some additional principles, whereby he may be directed to supernatural happiness, even as he is directed to his connatural end, by means of his natural principles, albeit not without the Divine assistance. Such like principles are called *theological virtues:* first, because their object is God, inasmuch as they direct us aright to God: secondly, because they are infused in us by God alone: thirdly, because these virtues are not made known to us, save by Divine revelation, contained in Holy Writ.

Reply Obj. 1. A certain nature may be ascribed to a certain thing in two ways. First, essentially: and thus these theological virtues surpass the nature of man. Secondly, by participation, as kindled wood partakes of the nature of fire: and thus, after a fashion, man becomes a partaker of the Divine Nature, as stated above: so that these virtues are proportionate to man in respect of the Nature of which he is made a partaker.

THIRD ARTICLE. WHETHER FAITH, HOPE, AND CHARITY ARE FITTINGLY RECKONED AS THEOLOGICAL VIRTUES?

Objection 1. It would seem that faith, hope, and charity are not fittingly reckoned as three theological virtues. For the theological virtues are, in relation to Divine happiness, what the natural inclination is in relation to the connatural end. Now among the virtues directed to the connatural end there is but one natural virtue, viz., the understanding of principles. Therefore there should be but one theological virtue.

On the contrary, The Apostle says (1 Cor. xiii. 13): *Now there remain faith, hope, charity, these three.*

I answer that, As stated above (A. 1), the theological virtues direct man to supernatural happiness in the same way as by the natural inclination man is directed to his connatural end. Now the latter happens in respect of two things. First, in respect of the reason or intellect, in so far as it contains the first universal principles which are known to us by the natural light of the intellect, and which are reason's starting-point, both in speculative and in practical matters. Secondly, through the rectitude of the will which tends naturally to good as defined by reason.

But these two fall short of the order of supernatural happiness, according to 1 Cor. ii. 9: *The eye hath not seen, nor ear heard, neither hath it entered into the heart of man, what things God hath prepared for them that love Him.* Consequently in respect of both the above things man needed to receive in addition something supernatural to direct him to a supernatural end. First, as regards the intellect, man receives certain supernatural principles, which are held by means of a Divine light: these are the articles of faith, about which is faith.—Secondly, the will is directed to this end, both as to the movement of intention, which tends to that end as something attainable,—and this pertains to hope,—and as to a certain spiritual union, whereby the will is, so to speak, transformed into that end,—and this belongs to charity. For the appetite of a thing is moved and tends towards its connatural end naturally; and this movement is due to a certain conformity of the thing with its end.

Reply Obj. 1. The intellect requires intelligible species whereby to understand: consequently there is need of a natural habit in addition to the power. But the very nature of the will suffices for it to be directed naturally to the end, both as to the intention of the end and as to its conformity with the end. But the nature of the power is insufficient in either of these respects, for the will to be directed to things that are above its nature. Consequently there was need for an additional supernatural habit in both respects.

Question 64
Of the Mean of Virtue

We must now consider the properties of virtues: and (1) the mean of virtue, (2) the connection between virtues, (3) the equality of virtues, (4) the duration of virtues. Under the first head there are four points of inquiry: (1) Whether moral virtue observes the mean? (2) Whether the mean of moral virtue is the real mean or the rational mean? (3) Whether the intellectual virtues observe the mean? (4) Whether the theological virtues do?

FIRST ARTICLE. WHETHER MORAL VIRTUES OBSERVE THE MEAN?

Objection 1. It would seem that moral virtue does not observe the mean. For the nature of a mean is incompatible with that which is extreme. Now the nature of virtue is to be something extreme; for it is stated in *De Cælo* i. that *virtue is the limit of power*. Therefore moral virtue does not observe the mean.

On the contrary, The Philosopher says (*Ethic.* ii. 6) that *moral virtue is a habit of choosing the mean.*

I answer that, The nature of virtue is that it should direct man to good. Now moral virtue is properly a perfection of the appetitive part of the soul in regard to some determinate matter: and the measure or rule of the appetitive movement in respect of appetible objects is the reason. But the good of that which is measured or ruled consists in its conformity with its rule: thus the good of things made by art is that they follow the rule of art. Consequently, in things of this sort, evil consists in discordance from their rule or measure. Now this may happen either by their exceeding the measure or by their falling short of it; as is clearly the case in all things ruled or measured. Hence it is evident that the good of moral virtue consists in conformity with the rule of reason.—Now it is clear that between excess and deficiency the mean is equality or conformity. Therefore it is evident that moral virtue observes the mean.

Reply Obj. 1. Moral virtue derives goodness from the rule of reason, while its matter consists in passions or operations. If therefore we compare moral virtue to reason, then, if we look at that which it has of reason, it holds the position of one extreme, viz., conformity; while excess and defect take the position of the other extreme, viz., deformity. But if we consider moral virtue in respect of its matter, then it holds the position of mean, in so far as it makes the passion conform to the rule of reason. Hence the Philosopher says *(Ethic.* ii. 6) that *virtue, as to its essence, is a mean state,* in so far as the rule of virtue is imposed on its proper matter: *but it is an extreme in reference to the "best" and "the excellent,"* viz., as to its conformity with reason.

FOURTH ARTICLE. WHETHER THE THEOLOGICAL VIRTUES OBSERVE THE MEAN?

Objection 1. It would seem that theological virtue observes the mean. For the good of other virtues consists in their observing the mean. Now the theological virtues surpass the others in goodness. Therefore much more does theological virtue observe the mean.

On the contrary, Wherever virtue observes the mean it is possible to sin by excess as well as by deficiency. But there is no sinning by excess against God, Who is the object of theological virtue: for it is written (*Ecclus.* xliii. 33): *Blessing the Lord, exalt Him as much as you can: for He is above all praise.* Therefore theological virtue does not observe the mean.

I answer that, As stated above (A. 1), the mean of virtue depends on conformity with virtue's rule or measure, in so far as one may exceed or fall short of that rule. Now the measure of theological virtue may be twofold. One is taken from the very nature of virtue, and thus the measure and rule of theological virtue is God Himself: because our faith is ruled according to Divine truth; charity, according to His goodness; hope, according to the immensity of His omnipotence and loving kindness. This measure surpasses all human power: so that never can we love God as much as He ought to be loved, nor believe and hope in Him as much as we should. Much less therefore can there be excess in such things. Accordingly the good of such virtues does not consist in a mean, but increases the more we approach to the summit.

The other rule or measure of theological virtue is by comparison with us: for although we cannot be borne towards God as much as we ought, yet we should approach to Him by believing, hoping and loving, according to the measure of our condition. Consequently it is possible to find a mean and extremes in theological virtue, accidentally and in reference to us.

Reply Obj. 1. The good of intellectual and moral virtues consists in a mean by reason of conformity with a measure that may be exceeded: whereas this is not so in the case of theological virtue, considered in itself, as stated above.

Question 65
Of the Connection of Virtues

FIRST ARTICLE. WHETHER THE MORAL VIRTUES ARE CONNECTED WITH ONE ANOTHER?

Objection 1. It would seem that the moral virtues are not connected with one another. Because moral virtues are sometimes caused by the exercise of acts, as is proved in *Ethic.* ii. 1, 2. But man can exercise himself in the acts of one virtue, without exercising himself in the acts of some other virtue. Therefore it is possible to have one moral virtue without another.

On the contrary, Ambrose says on Luke vi. 20: *The virtues are connected and linked together, so that whoever has one, is seen to have several:* and Augustine says (*De Trin.* vi. 4) that *the virtues that reside in the human mind are quite inseparable from one another:* and Gregory says (*Moral.* xxii. 1) that *one virtue without the other is either of no account whatever, or very imperfect:* and Cicero says (*Quæst. Tusc.* ii): *If you confess to not having one particular virtue, it must needs be that you have none at all.*

I answer that, Moral virtue may be considered either as perfect or as imperfect. An imperfect moral virtue, temperance for instance, or fortitude, is nothing but an inclination in us to do some kind of good deed, whether such inclination be in us by nature or by habituation. If we take the moral virtues in this way, they are not connected: since we find men who, by natural temperament or by being accustomed, are prompt in doing deeds of liberality, but are not prompt in doing deeds of chastity.

But the perfect moral virtue is a habit that inclines us to do a good deed well; and if we take moral virtues in this way, we must say that they are connected, as nearly all are agreed in saying. For this two reasons are given, corresponding to the different ways of assigning the distinction of the cardinal virtues. For some distinguish them according to certain general properties of the virtues: for instance, by saying that discretion belongs to prudence, rectitude to justice, moderation to temperance, and strength of mind to fortitude, in whatever matter we consider these properties to be. In this way the reason for the connection is evident: for strength of mind is not commended as virtuous, if it be without moderation or rectitude or discretion: and so forth. This, too, is the reason assigned for the connection by Gregory, who says (*Moral.* xxii. 1) that *a virtue cannot be perfect* as a virtue, *if isolated from the others:* for *there can be no true prudence without temperance, justice and fortitude:* and he continues to speak in like manner of the other virtues. Augustine also gives the same reason (*De Trin.* vi. 4).

Others, however, differentiate these virtues in respect of their matters, and it is in this way that Aristotle assigns the reason for their connection (*Ethic.* vi. 13). Because no moral virtue can be without prudence; since it is proper to moral virtue to make a right choice, for it is an elective habit. Now right choice requires not only the inclination to a due end, which inclination is the direct outcome of moral virtue, but also correct choice of things conducive to the end, which choice is made by prudence, that counsels, judges, and commands in those things that are directed to the end. In like manner one cannot have prudence unless one has the moral virtues: since prudence is *right reason about things to be done,* and the starting-point of reason is the end of the thing to be done, to which end man is rightly disposed by moral virtue. Hence, just as we cannot have speculative science unless we have the understanding of the principles, so neither can we have prudence without the moral virtues: and from this it follows clearly that the moral virtues are connected with one another.

Reply Obj. 1. Some moral virtues perfect man as regards his general state, in other words, with regard to those things which have to be done in every kind of human life. Hence man needs to exercise himself at the same time in the matters of all moral virtues. And if he exercise himself, by good deeds, in all such matters, he will acquire the habits of all the moral virtues. But if he exercise himself by good deeds in regard to one matter, but not in regard to another, for instance, by behaving well in matters of anger, but not in matters of concupiscence; he will indeed acquire a certain habit of restraining his anger; but this habit will lack the nature of virtue, through the absence of prudence, which is wanting in matters of concupiscence. In the same way, natural inclinations fail to have the complete character of virtue, if prudence be lacking.

But there are some moral virtues which perfect man with regard to some eminent state, such as magnificence and magnanimity; and since it does not happen to all in common to be exercised in the matter of such virtues, it is possible for a man to have the other moral virtues, without actually having the habits of these virtues, —provided we speak of acquired virtue. Nevertheless, when once a man has acquired those other virtues he possesses these in proximate potentiality. Because when, by practice, a man has acquired liberality in small gifts and expenditure, if he were to come in for a large sum of money, he would acquire the habit of magnificence with but little practice: even as a geometrician, by dint of little study, acquires scientific knowledge about some conclusion which had never been presented to his mind before. Now we speak of having a thing when we are on the point of having it, according to the saying of the Philosopher (*Phys.* ii, text, 56): *That which is scarcely lacking is not lacking at all.*

SECOND ARTICLE. WHETHER MORAL VIRTUES CAN BE WITHOUT CHARITY?

Objection 1. It would seem that moral virtue can be without charity. For it is stated in the *Liber Sentent. Prosperi* vii, that *every virtue save charity may be common to the good and bad.* But *charity can be in none except the good,* as stated in the same book. Therefore the other virtues can be had without charity.

Obj. 2. Further, moral virtues can be acquired by means of human acts, as stated in *Ethic.* ii. 1, 2, whereas charity cannot be had otherwise than by infusion, according to Rom. v. 5: *The charity of God is poured forth in our hearts by the Holy Ghost Who is given to us.* Therefore it is possible to have the other virtues without charity.

Obj. 3. Further, the moral virtues are connected together, through depending on prudence. But charity does not depend on prudence; indeed, it surpasses prudence, according to Eph. iii. 19: *The charity of Christ, which surpasseth all knowledge.* Therefore the moral virtues are not connected with charity, and can be without it.

On the contrary, It is written (1 Jo. iii. 14): *He that loveth not, abideth in death.* Now the spiritual life is perfected by the virtues, since it is *by them* that *we lead a good life,* as Augustine states (*De Lib. Arb.* ii. 17, 19). Therefore they cannot be without the love of charity.

I answer that, It is possible by means of human works to acquire moral virtues, in so far as they produce good works that are directed to an end not surpassing the natural power of man: and when they are acquired thus, they can be without charity, even as they were in many of the Gentiles. —But in so far as they produce good works in proportion to a supernatural last end, thus they have the character of virtue, truly and perfectly; and cannot be acquired by human acts, but are infused by God. Such like moral virtues cannot be without charity. For the other moral virtues cannot be without prudence; and that prudence cannot be without the moral virtues, because these latter make man well disposed to certain ends, which are the starting-point of the procedure of prudence. Now for prudence to proceed aright, it is much more necessary that man be well disposed towards his ultimate end, which is the effect of charity, than that he be well disposed in respect of other ends, which is the effect of moral virtue: just as in speculative matters right reason has greatest need of the first indemonstrable principle, that *contradictories cannot both be true at the same time.* It is therefore evident that neither can infused prudence be without charity; nor, consequently, the other moral virtues, since they cannot be without prudence.

It is therefore clear from what has

been said that only the infused virtues are perfect, and deserve to be called virtues simply: since they direct man well to the ultimate end. But the other virtues, those, namely, that are acquired, are virtues in a restricted sense, but not simply: for they direct man well in respect of the last end in some particular genus of action, but not in respect of the last end simply. Hence a gloss of Augustine on the words, *All that is not of faith is sin* (Rom. xiv. 23), says: *He that fails to acknowledge the truth, has no true virtue, even if his conduct be good.*

Reply Obj. 1. Virtue, in the words quoted, denotes imperfect virtue. Else if we take moral virtue in its perfect state, *it makes its possessor good,* and consequently cannot be in the wicked.

Reply Obj. 2. This argument holds good of virtue in the sense of acquired virtue.

Reply Obj. 3. Though charity surpasses science and prudence, yet prudence depends on charity, as stated: and consequently so do all the infused moral virtues.

FIFTH ARTICLE. WHETHER CHARITY CAN BE WITHOUT FAITH AND HOPE?

Objection 1. It would seem that charity can be without faith and hope. For charity is the love of God. But it is possible for us to love God naturally, without already having faith, or hope in future bliss. Therefore charity can be without faith and hope.

Obj. 2. Further, charity is the root of all the virtues, according to Ephes. iii. 17: *Rooted and founded in charity.* Now the root is sometimes without branches. Therefore charity can sometimes be without faith and hope, and the other virtues.

On the contrary, The Apostle says (Heb. xi. 6): *Without faith it is impossible to please God;* and this evidently belongs most to charity, according to Prov. viii. 17: *I love them that love me.* Again, it is by hope that we are brought to charity. Therefore it is not possible to have charity without faith and hope.

I answer that, Charity signifies not only the love of God, but also a certain friendship with Him; which implies, besides love, a certain mutual return of love, together with mutual communion, as stated in *Ethic.* viii. 2. That this belongs to charity is evident from 1 Jo. iv. 16: *He that abideth in charity, abideth in God, and God in him,* and from 1 Cor. 1, 9, where it is written: *God is faithful, by Whom you are called unto the fellowship of His Son.* Now this fellowship of man with God, which consists in a certain familiar colloquy with Him, is begun here, in this life, by grace, but will be perfected in the future life, by glory; each of which things we hold by faith and hope. Wherefore just as friendship with a person would be impossible, if one disbelieved in, or despaired of, the possibility of their fellowship or familiar colloquy; so to, friendship with God, which is charity, is impossible without faith, so as to believe in this fellowship and colloquy with God, and to hope to attain to this fellowship. Therefore charity is quite impossible without faith and hope.

Reply Obj. 1. Charity is not any kind of love of God, but that love of God, by which He is loved as the object of bliss, to which object we are directed by faith and hope.

Reply Obj. 2. Charity is the root of faith and hope, in so far as it gives them the perfection of virtue. But faith and hope as such are the precursors of charity, and so charity is impossible without them.

Question 66
Of Equality among the Virtues

SIXTH ARTICLE. WHETHER CHARITY IS THE GREATEST OF THE THEOLOGICAL VIRTUES?

Objection 1. It would seem that charity is not the greatest of the theological virtues. Because, since faith is in the intellect, while hope and charity are in the appetitive power, it seems that faith is compared to hope and charity, as intellectual to moral virtue. Now intellectual virtue is greater than moral virtue. Therefore faith is greater than hope and charity.

On the contrary, The Apostle says (1 Cor. xiii. 13): *Now there remain faith, hope, charity, these three; but the greatest of these is charity.*

I answer that, The greatness of a virtue, as to its species, is taken from its object.—Now, since the three theological virtues look at God as their proper object, it cannot be said that any one of them is greater than another by reason of its having a greater object, but only from the fact that it approaches nearer than another to that object; and in this way charity is greater than the others. Because the others, in their very nature, imply a certain distance from the object: since faith is of what is not seen, and hope is of what is not possessed. But the love of charity is of that which is already possessed: since the beloved is, in a manner, in the lover, and, again, the lover is drawn by desire to union with the beloved; hence it is written (1 Jo. iv. 16): *He that abideth in charity, abideth in God, and God in him.*

Reply Obj. 1. Faith and hope are not related to charity in the same way as prudence to moral virtue; and for two reasons. First, because the theological virtues have an object surpassing the human soul: whereas prudence and the moral virtues are about things beneath man. Now in things that are above man, to love them is more excellent than to know them. Because knowledge is perfected by the known being in the knower: whereas love is perfected by the lover being drawn to the beloved. Now that which is above man is more excellent in itself than in man: since a thing is contained according to the mode of the container. But it is the other way about in things beneath man. Secondly, because prudence moderates the appetitive movements pertaining to the moral virtues, whereas faith does not moderate the appetitive movement tending to God, which movement belongs to the theological virtues: it only shows the object. And this appetitive movement towards its object surpasses human knowledge, according to Ephes. iii. 19: *The charity of Christ which surpasseth all knowledge.*

Question 67
Of the Duration of Virtues after This Life

FIRST ARTICLE. WHETHER THE MORAL VIRTUES REMAIN AFTER THIS LIFE?

Objection 1. It would seem that the moral virtues do not remain after this life. For in the future state of glory men will be like angels, according to Matth. xxii. 30. But it is absurd to put moral virtues in the angels, as stated in *Ethic.* x. 8. Therefore neither in man will there be moral virtues after this life.

On the contrary, It is written (Wis. i. 15) that *justice is perpetual and immortal.*

I answer that, As Augustine says (*De Trin.* xiv. 9), Cicero held that the cardinal virtues do not remain after this life; and that, as Augustine says (*ibid.*), *in the other life men are made happy by the mere knowledge of that nature, than which nothing is better or more lovable, that Nature, to wit, which created all others.* Afterwards he concludes that these four virtues remain in the future life, but after a different manner.

In order to make this evident, we must note that in these virtues there is a formal element, and a quasi-material element. The material element in these virtues is a certain inclination of the appetitive part to the passions and operations according to a certain mode:—and since this mode is fixed by reason, the formal element is precisely this order of reason.

Accordingly we must say that these

moral virtues do not remain in the future life, as regards their material element. For in the future life there will be no concupiscences and pleasures in matters of food and sex; nor fear and daring about dangers of death; nor distributions and commutations of things employed in this present life. But, as regards the formal element, they will remain most perfect, after this life, in the Blessed, in as much as each one's reason will have most perfect rectitude in regard to things concerning him in respect of that state of life: and his appetitive power will be moved entirely according to the order of reason, in things pertaining to that same state. Hence Augustine says (*ibid.*) that *prudence will be there without any danger of error; fortitude, without the anxiety of bearing with evil; temperance, without the rebellion of the desires: so that prudence will neither prefer nor equal any good to God; fortitude will adhere to Him most steadfastly; and temperance will delight in Him Who knows no imperfection.* As to justice, it is yet more evident what will be its act in that life, viz., *to be subject to God:* because even in this life subjection to a superior is part of justice.

Reply Obj. 1. The Philosopher is speaking there of these moral virtues, as to their material element; thus he speaks of justice, as regards *commutations and distributions;* of fortitude, as to *matters of terror and danger;* of temperance, in respect of *lewd desires.*

Treatise on Law
Question 90
Of the Essence of Law

FIRST ARTICLE. WHETHER LAW IS SOMETHING PERTAINING TO REASON?

Objection 1. It would seem that law is not something pertaining to reason. For the Apostle says (Rom. vii. 23): *I see another law in my members,* etc. But nothing pertaining to reason is in the members; since the reason does not make use of a bodily organ. Therefore law is not something pertaining to reason.

On the contrary, It belongs to the law to command and to forbid. But it belongs to reason to command. Therefore law is something pertaining to reason.

I answer that, Law is a rule and measure of acts, whereby man is induced to act or is restrained from acting: for *lex* (law) is derived from *ligare* (to bind), because it binds one to act. Now the rule and measure of human acts is the reason, which is the first principle of human acts; since it belongs to the reason to direct to the end, which is the first principle in all matters of action, according to the Philosopher (*Phys.* ii). Now that which is the principle in any genus, is the rule and measure of that genus: for instance, unity in the genus of numbers, and the first movement in the genus of movements. Consequently it follows that law is something pertaining to reason.

Reply Obj. 1. Since law is a kind of rule and measure, it may be in something in two ways. First, as in that which measures and rules: and since this is proper to reason, it follows that, in this way, law is in the reason alone.—Secondly, as in that which is measured and ruled. In this way, law is in all those things that are inclined to something by reason of some law: so that any inclination arising from a law, may be called a law, not essentially but by participation as it were. And thus the inclination of the members to concupiscence is called *the law of the members.*

THIRD ARTICLE. WHETHER THE REASON OF ANY MAN IS COMPETENT TO MAKE LAWS?

Objection 1. It would seem that the reason of any man is competent to make laws. For the Apostle says (Rom. ii. 14) that *when the Gentiles, who have not the law, do by nature those things that are of the law, . . . they are a law to themselves.* Now he says this of all in general. Therefore anyone can make a law for himself.

On the contrary, Isidore says (*Etym.* v. 10): *A law is an ordinance of the people, whereby something is sanctioned by the Elders together with the Commonalty.*

I answer that, A law, properly speaking, regards first and foremost the order to the common good. Now to order anything to the common good, belongs either to the whole people, or to someone who is the viceregent of the whole people. And therefore the making of a law belongs either to the whole people or to a public personage who has care of the whole people: since in all other matters the directing of anything to the end concerns him to whom the end belongs.

Reply Obj. 1. A law is in a person not only as in one that rules, but also by participation as in one that is ruled. In the latter way each one is a law to himself, in so far as he shares the direction that he receives from one who rules him. Hence the same text goes on: *Who show the work of the law written in their hearts.*

FOURTH ARTICLE. WHETHER PROMULGATION IS ESSENTIAL TO A LAW?

Objection 1. It would seem that promulgation is not essential to a law. For the natural law above all has the character of law. But the natural law needs no promulgation. Therefore it is not essential to a law that it be promulgated.

On the contrary, It is laid down in the *Decretals,* dist. 4, that *laws are established when they are promulgated.*

I answer that, As stated above, a law is imposed on others by way of a rule and measure. Now a rule or measure is imposed by being applied to those who are to be ruled and measured by it. Wherefore, in order that a law obtain the binding force which is proper to a law, it must needs be applied to the men who have to be ruled by it. Such application is made by its being notified to them by promulgation. Wherefore promulgation is necessary for the law to obtain its force.

Thus from the four preceding articles, the definition of law may be gathered; and it is nothing else than an ordinance of reason for the common good, made by him who has care of the community, and promulgated.

Reply Obj. 1. The natural law is promulgated by the very fact that God instilled it into man's mind so as to be known by him naturally.

Question 91
Of the Various Kinds of Law

FIRST ARTICLE. WHETHER THERE IS AN ETERNAL LAW?

Objection 1. It would seem that there is no eternal law. Because every law is imposed on someone. But there was not someone from eternity on whom a law could be imposed: since God alone was from eternity. Therefore no law is eternal.

On the contrary, Augustine says (*De Lib. Arb.* i. 6): *That Law which is the Supreme Reason cannot be understood to be otherwise than unchangeable and eternal.*

I answer that, A law is nothing else but a dictate of practical reason emanating from the ruler who governs a perfect community. Now it is evident, granted that the world is ruled by Divine Providence, that the whole community of the universe is governed by Divine Reason. Wherefore the very Idea of the government of things in God the Ruler of the universe, has the nature of a law. And since the Divine Reason's conception of things is not subject to time but is eternal, according to Prov. viii. 23, therefore it is that this kind of law must be called eternal.

Reply Obj. 1. Those things that are not in themselves, exist with God, inasmuch as they are foreknown and preordained by Him, according to Rom. iv. 17: *Who calls those things that are not, as those that are.* Accordingly the eternal concept of the Divine law bears the character of an eternal law, in so far as it is ordained by God to the government of things foreknown by Him.

SECOND ARTICLE. WHETHER THERE IS IN US A NATURAL LAW?

Obj. 3. The more a man is free, the less is he under the law. But man is freer than all the animals, on account of his free-will, with which he is endowed above all other animals. Since therefore other animals are not subject to a natural law, neither is man subject to a natural law.

On the contrary, A gloss on Rom. ii. 14: *When the Gentiles, who have not the law, do by nature those things that are of the law,* comments as follows: *Although they have no written law, yet they have the natural law, whereby each one knows, and is conscious of, what is good and what is evil.*

I answer that, As stated above, law, being a rule and measure, can be in a person in two ways: in one way, as in him that rules and measures; in another way, as in that which is ruled and measured, since a thing is ruled and measured in so far as it partakes of the rule or measure. Wherefore, since all things subject to Divine providence are ruled and measured by the eternal law, it is evident that all things partake somewhat of the eternal law, in so far as, namely, from its being imprinted on them, they derive their respective inclinations to their proper acts and ends. Now among all others, the rational creature is subject to Divine providence in the most excellent way, in so far as it partakes of a share of providence, by being provident both for itself and for others. Wherefore it has a share of the Eternal Reason, whereby it has a natural inclination to its proper act and end: and this participation of the eternal law in the rational creature is called the natural law. Hence the Psalmist after saying (Ps. iv. 6): *Offer up the sacrifice of justice,* as though someone asked what the works of justice are, adds: *Many say, Who showeth us good things?* in answer to which question he says: *The light of Thy countenance, O Lord, is signed upon us:* thus implying that the light of natural reason, whereby we discern what is good and what is evil, which is the function of the natural law, is nothing else than an imprint on us of the Divine light. It is therefore evident that the natural law is nothing else than the rational creature's participation of the eternal law.

Reply Obj. 3. Even irrational animals partake in their own way of the Eternal Reason, just as the rational creature does. But because the rational creature partakes thereof in an intellectual and rational manner, therefore the participation of the eternal law in the rational creature is properly called a law, since a law is something pertaining to reason. Irrational creatures, however, do not partake thereof in a rational manner, wherefore there is no participation of the eternal law in them, except by way of similitude.

THIRD ARTICLE. WHETHER THERE IS A HUMAN LAW?

Objection 1. It would seem that there is not a human law. For the natural law is a participation of the eternal law. Now through the eternal law *all things are most orderly,* as Augustine states (*De Lib. Arb.* i. 6). Therefore the natural law suffices for the ordering of all human affairs. Consequently there is no need for a human law.

On the contrary, Augustine (*De Lib. Arb.* i. 6) distinguishes two kinds of law, the one eternal, the other temporal, which he calls human.

I answer that, A law is a dictate of the practical reason. Now it is to be observed that the same procedure takes place in the practical and in the speculative reason: for each proceeds from principles to conclusions. Accordingly we conclude that just as, in the speculative reason, from naturally known indemonstrable principles, we draw the conclusions of the various sciences, the knowledge of which is not imparted to us by nature, but acquired by the efforts of reason, so too it is from the precepts of the natural law, as from general and indemonstrable principles, that the human reason needs to proceed to the more particular determination of certain matters. These particular determinations, devised by human reason, are called human laws, provided the other essential conditions of law be observed. Wherefore Tully says in his *Rhetoric* (*De Invent. Rhet.* ii) that *justice has its source in nature; thence certain things came into custom by reason of their utility; afterwards these things which emanated from nature and were approved by custom, were sanctioned by fear and reverence for the law.*

Reply Obj. 1. The human reason cannot have a full participation of the dictate of the Divine Reason, but according to its own mode, and imperfectly. Consequently, as on the part of the speculative reason, by a natural participation of Divine Wisdom, there is in us the knowledge of certain general principles, but not proper knowledge of each single truth, such as that contained in the Divine Wisdom; so too, on the part of the practical reason, man has a natural participation of the eternal law, according to certain general principles, but not as regards the particular determinations of individual cases, which are, however, contained in the eternal law. Hence the need for human reason to proceed further to sanction them by law.

FOURTH ARTICLE. WHETHER THERE WAS ANY NEED FOR A DIVINE LAW?

Objection 1. It would seem that there was no need for a Divine law. Because, as stated above, the natural law is a participation in us of the eternal law. But the eternal law is a Divine law, as stated above. Therefore there is no need for a Divine law in addition to the natural law, and human laws derived therefrom.

On the contrary, David prayed God to set His law before him, saying (Ps. cxviii. 33): *Set before me for a law the way of Thy justifications, O Lord.*

I answer that, Besides the natural and the human law it was necessary for the directing of human conduct to have a Divine law. And this for four reasons. First, because it is by law that man is directed how to perform his proper acts in view of his last end. And indeed if man were ordained to no other end than that which is proportionate to his natural faculty, there would be no need for man to have any further direction on the part of his reason, besides the natural law and human law which is derived from it. But since man is ordained to an end of eternal happiness which is inproportionate to man's natural faculty, therefore it was necessary that, besides the natural and the human law, man should be directed to his end by a law given by God.

Secondly, because, on account of the uncertainty of human judgment, especially on contingent and particular matters, different people form different judgments on human acts; whence also different and contrary laws result. In order, therefore, that man may know without any doubt what he ought to do and what he ought to avoid, it was necessary for man to be directed in his proper acts by a law given by God, for it is certain that such a law cannot err.

Thirdly, because man can make laws in those matters of which he is competent to judge. But man is not competent to judge of interior movements, that are hidden, but only of exterior acts which appear: and yet for the perfection of virtue it is necessary for man to conduct himself aright in both kinds of acts. Consequently human law could not sufficiently curb and direct interior acts; and it was necessary for this purpose that a Divine law should supervene.

Fourthly, because, as Augustine says (*De Lib. Arb.* i. 5, 6), human law cannot punish or forbid all evil deeds: since while aiming at doing away with all evils, it would do away with many good things, and would hinder the advance of the common good, which is necessary for human intercourse. In order, therefore, that no evil might remain unforbidden and unpunished, it was necessary for the Divine law to supervene, whereby all sins are forbidden.

And these four causes are touched upon in Ps. cxviii. 8, where it is said: *The law of the Lord is unspotted, i.e.,* allowing no foulness of sin; *converting souls,* because it directs not only exterior, but also interior acts; *the testimony of the Lord is faithful,* because of the certainty of what is true and right; *giving wisdom to little ones,* by directing man to an end supernatural and Divine.

Reply Obj. 1. By the natural law the eternal law is participated proportionately to the capacity of human nature. But to his supernatural end man needs to be directed in a yet higher way. Hence the additional law given by God, whereby man shares more perfectly in the eternal law.

MEISTER ECKHART

Meister Eckhart (1260–1327) was a Dominican who studied at Paris and later became Vicar-General of his Order. After his move to Cologne, the Archbishop of that city instituted an inquiry into his doctrine. Eckhart appealed to the Holy See, but two years after his death eight propositions taken from his writings were condemned by Pope John XXII. Eckhart is an unconventional thinker whose ideas exerted an important influence on modern and contemporary German thought.

The following selections illustrate both the radical and the mystical elements in the doctrine for which he is famous. There is a novelty here that has made Eckhart seem to some to be more a modern than a medieval. His theological orientation is traditional, but his ethical recommendations are not.

*These Are the Talks of Instruction that the Vicar of Thuringen, the Prior of Erfurt, Brother Eckhart of the Preaching Order Held with Some of His Spiritual Children, Who Asked Him about Many Things as They Sat Together at Collation**

OF TRUE OBEDIENCE

True and perfect obedience is a virtue above all virtues. No great work can be accomplished without it; nor can there be any task, however small or insignificant, which will not be done to better purpose in obedience, whether it be hearing or reading the Mass, or prayer, or contemplation, or whatever. Take any project you please, however trifling; it is improved and exalted by obedience. Obedience brings out the best of everything; it never fails or errs in any matter; and no matter what you do, if you do it in true obedience, it will not miss being good.

Obedience has no cares; it lacks no blessing. Being obedient, if a man purifies himself, God will come into him in course; for when he has no will of his own, then God will command for him what God would command for himself. When I give my will up to the care of my prelate, and

* By permission. From *Meister Eckhart*, trans. by Raymond B. Blakney, Harper & Row, Publishers, Incorporated, New York, 1957. Deletions are not noted in the text.

have no will of my own, God must will for me; for if he were to neglect me, he would be neglecting himself. So it is with everything: where I do not choose for myself, God chooses for me.

What will He choose for me? That I shall not choose for myself. When I deny myself, his will for me is identical with his will for himself, just as if it were for him alone; and if he did not so behave, then by the truth that God is, he would not be just, nor would he be what it is his nature to be. You will never hear an obedient person saying: "I want it so and so; I must have this or that." You will hear only of utter denial of self.

OF UNDEVOTED PEOPLE WHO ARE FULL OF SELF-WILL

People say: "Alas, sir, but I would prefer to stand well with God, to have the devotion and divine calm of some people," or "I wish I could be like this or as poor as that." Or they say: "It will never do if I cannot be here or there and do thus and so. I must get away—or go into a cloister or a cell."

The truth is that you yourself are at fault in all this and no one else. It is pure self-will. Whether you realize it or not, there can be no restlessness unless it come from self-will, although not every person understands this. This is what I mean: people fly from this to seek that—these places, these people, these manners, those purposes, that activity—but they should not blame ways or things for thwarting them. When you are thwarted, it is your own attitude that is out of order.

Begin, therefore, first with self and forget yourself! If you do not first get away from self, then whatever else you get away from you will still find obstacles and restlessness. People look in vain for peace, who seek it in the world outside, in places, people, ways, activities, or in world-flight, poverty and humiliation, whatever the avenue or degree; for there is no peace this way. They are looking in the wrong direction, and the longer they look the less they find what they are looking for. They go along like someone who has missed his road; the farther they go the more they are astray.

What, then, is to be done?

Let everyone begin by denying self and in so doing he will have denied all else. Indeed, if a man gave up a kingdom, or even the whole world and still was selfish, he would have given up nothing. If, however, he denies himself, then whatever he keeps, be it wealth, honor, or anything else, he is free from it all.

HOW THE INCLINATION TO SIN IS ALWAYS BENEFICIAL

Know that the impulse to wrong is never without use and benefit to the just person. Let us notice that there are two sorts of people involved. One is so constituted that he has little or no impulse to do wrong, whereas the other is often strongly tempted. His outward self is easily swayed by whatever is at hand—swayed to anger, pride, sensuality or whatever, but his better nature, his higher self, remains unmoved and will not do wrong, or be angry, or sin in any way. He therefore fights hard against whichever vice is most natural to him, as people must who are by nature choleric, proud, or otherwise weak and who will not commit the sin to which they are liable. These people are more to be praised than the first kind. Their reward is also greater and their virtue of much higher rank. For the perfection of virtue comes of struggle, or, as St. Paul says, "Virtue is made perfect in weakness."

The impulse to sin is not sin but to consent to sin, to give way to anger, is indeed sin. Surely, if a just person could wish such a thing, he would not wish to be rid of the impulse to sin, for without it he would be uncertain of everything he did, doubtful about what to do, and he would miss the honor and reward of struggle and victory. Because of the impulse to evil and the excitement of it, both virtue and its rewards are in travail born. The impulse to wrong makes us the more diligent in the exercise of virtue, driving us to it with a strong hand, like a hard taskmaster, forcing us to take shelter in doing well. The weaker one is, the more he is warned to strength and self-conquest; for virtue, like vice, is a matter of the will.

HOW THE WILL IS CAPABLE OF ANYTHING AND VIRTUE LIES IN THE WILL, IF IT IS JUST

A man has little reason to be afraid of anything if he knows his will to be good and he should not be disturbed if he cannot realize it in deeds. Nor should he despise his virtue, knowing that virtue and every other good depend on good will. If you have good will, you shall lack for nothing, neither love, humility, nor any other virtue; what you will with all your strength you shall have, and neither God nor any creature can deprive you—if, again, your will is sound, divine and wrapt in God. Therefore, do not say "I would"—for that refers to the future; but say "I will"—that it may now be so. For notice this: if I set my heart on something a thousand miles away, it is more really mine than something I hold in my bosom but which I do not want.

Good will is not less powerful for good than bad will is for evil. Be sure of it, that even if I never do evil and yet, if I hold bad will, I shall have sinned just as much as if I had done the deed. With a will that is purely bad, I commit as great sin as if I were to murder all the people in the world, even though I did not lift a finger toward the crime. Why should not the same power reside in good will? It does—and much, incomparably more!

In fact, I may do anything at all with my will. I may bear the burdens of mankind, feed the poor, do the world's work and anything else I please. If I lack the power but not the will to do, then before God I have done it and no one may deny or dispute it for a moment. To will to do something as soon as I may, and to have done it, are the same in God's sight. Furthermore, if I choose that my will shall be a match for the total will of the world, and if my desire is perfect and great, then it shall be so; for what I will have I have. And so, if I really want to love as much as the world has ever loved, and thereby I mean to love God, or what you please, then it is so, when my will is perfect.

At this point we must observe two things about love. The first is the nature of it and the second is the action which expresses the nature of love. The seat of love is in the will alone. To have more will is to have more love; but no one can tell whether another person has more love—for that is hidden in the soul, just as God lies hidden in the soul's core. Thus love depends altogether on the will; to have more will is to have more love.

About Disinterest

I have read much of what has been written, both by heathen philosophers and sages and in the Old and New Testaments. I have sought earnestly and with great diligence that good and high virtue by which man may draw closest to God and through which one may best approximate the idea God had of him before he was created, when there was no separation between man and God; and having delved into all this writing, as far as my intelligence would permit, I find that [high virtue] to be pure disinterest, that is, detachment from creatures. Our Lord said to Martha: "*Unum est necessarium,*" which is to say: to be untroubled and pure, one thing is necessary and that is disinterest.

The teachers praise love, and highly too, as St. Paul did, when he said: "No matter what I do, if I have not love, I am nothing." Nevertheless, I put disinterest higher than love. My first reason is as follows. The best thing about love is that it makes me love God. Now, it is much more advantageous for me to move God toward myself than for me to move toward him, for my blessing in eternity depends on my being identified with God. He is more able to deal with me and join me than I am to join him. Disinterest brings God to me and I can demonstrate it this way: Everything likes its own habitat best; God's habitat is purity and unity, which are due to disinterest. Therefore God necessarily gives himself to the disinterested heart.

In the second place, I put disinterest above love because love compels me to suffer for God's sake, whereas disinterest makes me sensitive only to God. This ranks far above suffering for God or in God; for, when he suffers, man pays some attention to the creature from which his suffering comes, but being disinterested, he is quite detached from the creature. I demonstrate that, being disinterested, a man is sensitive only to God, in this way: Experience must always be an experience of something, but disinterest comes so close to zero that nothing but God is rarefied enough to get into it, to enter the disinterested heart. That is why a disinterested person is sensitive to nothing but God. Each person experiences things in his own way and thus every distinguishable thing is seen and understood according to the approach of the beholder and not, as it might be, from its own point of view.

The authorities also praise humility above other virtues, but I put disinterest above humility for the following reasons. There can be humility without disinterest but disinterest cannot be perfect without humility; perfect humility depends on self-denial; disinterest comes so near to zero that nothing may intervene. Thus, there cannot be disinterest without humility and, anyway, two virtues are better than one!

The second reason I put disinterest above humility is that in humility man abases himself before creatures, and in doing so pays some attention to the creatures themselves. Disinterest, however, stays within itself. No transference of attention [such as humility] can ever rank so high that being self-contained will not go higher. As the prophet puts it: "*Omnis gloria filiae regis ab intus,*" which means, "the glory of the king's daughter comes from within her." Perfectly disinterested, a man has no regard for anything, no inclination to be above this or below that, no desire to be over or under; he remains what he is, neither loving nor hating, and desiring neither likeness to this or unlikeness to that. He desires only to be one and the same; for to want to be this or that is to want something; and the disinterested person wants nothing. Thus everything remains unaffected as far as he is concerned.

I also put disinterest above mercy, for mercy is nothing but a man's going out to the want of a fellow and the heart is disturbed by it. Disinterest, however, is exempt from this, being self-contained and allowing nothing to disturb. To speak briefly: When I survey the virtues, I find none as flawless, as conducive to God as disinterest.

A philosopher named Avicenna said: "The rank of a disinterested mind is so high that what it sees is true, what it desires comes to pass, what it commands must be done." You may take this for the truth, that when a free mind is really disinterested, God is compelled to come into it; and if it could get along without contingent forms, it would then have all the properties of God himself. Of course, God cannot give his properties away and so he can do nothing for the disinterested mind except to give himself to it and it is then caught up into eternity, where transitory things no longer affect it. Then the man has no experiences of the physical order and is said to be dead to the world, since he has no appetite for any earthly thing.

That is what St. Paul meant by saying: "I live; yet not I, but Christ liveth in me."

You may ask: "What is this disinterest, that it is so noble a matter?" Know, then, that a mind unmoved by any contingent affection or sorrow, or honor, or slander, or vice, is really disinterested—like a broad mountain that is not shaken by a gentle wind. Unmovable disinterest brings man into his closest resemblance to God. It gives God his status as God. His purity is derived from it, and then his simplicity and unchangeable character. If man is to be like God, to the extent that any creature may resemble him, the likeness will come through disinterest, and man proceeds from purity to simplicity and from simplicity to unchangeableness, and thus the likeness of God and man comes about. It is an achievement of the grace that allures man away from temporal things and purges him of the transitory. Keep this in mind: to be full of things is to be empty of God, while to be empty of things is to be full of God.

Now I ask what the object of pure disinterest is. I reply that it is neither this nor that. Pure disinterest is empty nothingness, for it is on that high plane on which God gives effect to his will. It is not possible for God to do his will in every heart, for even though he is almighty, he cannot act except where he finds preparations made or he makes them himself. I say "or makes them" on account of St. Paul, for God did not find him ready; he prepared St. Paul by an infusion of grace. Otherwise, I say that God acts where he finds that preparations have been made.

God's activity is not the same in a man as in a stone; and there is a simile for that, too, in nature. If a bake oven is heated and lumps of dough are put into it, some of oatmeal, some of barley, some of rye, and some of wheat, then, even though there is only one heat for all in the oven, it will not act the same way on the various doughs; for one turns into a pretty loaf, another to a rough loaf, and others still rougher. That is not due to the heat but to the material, which differs. Similarly God does not work in all hearts alike but according to the preparation and sensitivity he finds in each. In a given heart, containing this or that, there may be an item which prevents God's highest activity. Therefore if a heart is to be ready for him, it must be emptied out to nothingness, the condition of its maximum capacity. So, too, a disinterested heart, reduced to nothingness, is the optimum, the condition of maximum sensitivity.

Take an illustration from nature. If I wish to write on a white tablet, then no matter how fine the matter already written on it, it will confuse me and prevent me from writing down [my thoughts]; so that, if I still wish to use the tablet, I must first erase all that is written on it, but it will never serve me as well for writing as when it is clean. Similarly, if God is to write his message about the highest matters on my heart, everything to be referred to as "this or that" must first come out and I must be disinterested. God is free to do his will on his own level when my heart, being disinterested, is bent on neither this nor that.

Then I ask: What is the prayer of the disinterested heart? I answer by saying that a disinterested man, pure in heart, has no prayer, for to pray is to want something from God, something added that one desires, or something that God is to take away. The disinterested person, however, wants nothing, and neither has he anything of which he would be rid. Therefore he has no prayer, or he prays only to be uniform with God. In this sense we may understand the comment of St. Dionysius on a text of St. Paul—"they which run in a race run all, but one receiveth the prize"—that is, all the soul's agents race for the prize but only the soul's essence receives it. Thus, Dionysius says: "This race is precisely the flight from creatures to union with the uncreated." When the soul achieves this, it loses its identity, it absorbs God and is reduced to nothing, as the dawn at the rising of the sun. Nothing helps toward this end like disinterest.

Listen to this, man of intelligence: If the pleasure we take in the physical form of Christ diminishes our sensitivity to the Holy Spirit, how much more will the pleasure we take in the comfort of transitory things be a barrier against God? Disinterest is best of all, for by it the soul is unified, Knowledge is made pure, the heart is kindled, the spirit wakened, the desires quickened, the virtues enhanced. Disinterest brings knowledge of God; cut off from the creature, the soul unites with God; for love apart from God is like water to a fire, while love with God is the honeycomb in the honey.

WILLIAM OF OCKHAM

The writings of William of Ockham (ca. 1280–1349) reflect both Middle Ages and the increasing interest in man and nature which characterizes a growing humanism. Medieval philosophy had been characterized by a controversy over the status of universals, and most philosophers had accepted at least a modified doctrine of the reality of universals. Ockham's stress on nominalism (i.e., the primary reality of individuals) was a break with theological dominance and an assertion of philosophical independence.

Our selections are concerned with the problem of free will. Ockham opposes any necessity which binds the will because he wants to make man more responsible for his own contingent decisions. Earlier theologians had tended to deny man's freedom in order to preserve God's omnipotence. In Ockham's writing can be seen the start of a modern theory of man's freedom that has wide ethical implications.

*The Nature of the Will**

The Causality of the Will

. . . The potentialities of the soul, that is, the intellect and the will, leaving the sensitive potentialities unmentioned, are really identical in relation to each other and with the essence of the soul. The intellect is no more distinguished from the will than from itself, no more than God from God, no more than a strong man from a strong man. It is not distinguished from the will either in reality or by reason. But now the manner in which the substance of the soul can have acts distinguished by reason with their respective words having different connotations is this, in so far as it elicits or may elicit acts of understanding, it is called intellect, and in so far as it elicits acts of volition, it is called will.

If we take will for the actual thing which is designated by the word or concept

* By permission. From Ockham: *Studies and Selections*, trans. Stephen C. Tornay, The Open Court Publishing Company, LaSalle, Ill., 1938.

as meaning the principle which elicits the acts of volition and cognition, the will is not more superior to the intellect than the intellect is superior to the will, both being altogether the same. Taking both, however, with reference to what their names signify, the will may be called superior to the intellect, because the act of loving, designated by the word will, is superior to the act of understanding, designated by the word intellect. . . .

The will with respect to a simple object or a complex object, such as "to be happy" or "to want to be," is called love. Not to will the same, may be called hatred or detestation. As the ultimate end, we may accept either the possible created happiness of the will or the object of this happiness. With reference to this happiness, be it shown in general or in particular, along the earthly trail or in the heavenly home; I say that the will, absolutely speaking, may want it or not want it.

The will is not necessarily attracted by the ultimate end shown in general. Natural necessity does not stand together with freedom. Freedom is opposed to necessity in the same way as necessity is opposed to contingency. Thus, freedom is some kind of indifference and contingency and is distinguished against the natural active principle. Nature and will are two active principles with opposed modes of origination. Because the mode as nature originates cannot stand with the mode as the will originates, which intends the end freely, it follows that it cannot intend the end with natural necessity. The assumption that the will intends the end freely can be proven thus. It is one and the same potentiality which intends the end and that which is in behalf of this end. Therefore, it has the same mode of acting because different modes would indicate different potentialities. But we see it operating freely in matters which promote the end. Consequently, it acts in the same manner to attain the end. It is to be denied, then, that everything by nature's necessity has an inclination, in strict sense of the word, toward its own perfection. This is true only if the thing to be perfected is active by natural necessity, which cannot be said about the will.

The will is attracted by the ultimate end shown in general in a contingent and free manner, as we explained it. This is to say that the will may like happiness and may not like it; may desire happiness and may not. This is evident from the fact that many believers, with faith in the future life, just as well as unbelievers, without faith in any future life, have killed themselves with the full use of their reason; have thrown themselves into the arms of death; these alike have not wanted to exist. And it is true, in the same way, that some may not desire happiness in specific instances. Whoever wants something efficaciously, wants everything also without which in his opinion the desired object cannot be obtained at all. Yet some of the faithful are convinced that they cannot attain happiness without a good life, and still they do not cultivate a good and saintly life. Therefore, they do not desire happiness efficiently and, consequently, with the same reason, they may not want it.

It may be said, then, that the will is free with regard to any act elicited by the same, if we consider the matter absolutely. It is to be noted, however, that by considering some act, inasmuch as it is caused by a habit, and is antecedent in the will, the will is not free with reference to that act.

It is the will of God just as much as the essence of God that is the immediate cause of everything that happens, although with natural reason we cannot demonstrate this. This view may be recommended, however, in the following manner.

God is the first and immediate cause of everything that is produced by secondary causes. An immediate cause is, obviously, one by the presence of which the effect can follow and by the absence of which the effect cannot follow. Now God is such a cause with respect to any created thing. Properly speaking any cause, in the proper sense of the word, that is, a phenomenon in the presence of which the effect follows and in the absence of which the effect does not follow, may be called immediate cause. When, therefore, God concurs with a second cause, both are immediate causes. God is the immediate cause of any effect because He is the first cause by virtue of the priority of perfection but not by virtue of the priority of duration. For in the same moment that He acts the second cause acts also with the consequence that He is partial cause of any effect produced by the secondary cause. God by concurring in the second cause, although He would be able to produce the effect without the second cause and, consequently, would be the total cause, does, however, as a matter of fact, produce it with the second cause. Consequently, God is not, in fact, the total cause. It is manifest, then, that God is immediately the first and direct cause of any effect produced by secondary causes.

Although God acts through the mediacy of secondary causes, or, more strictly, with them, we should not say that He acts mediately or that secondary causes are superfluous. In the case of man, he is a voluntary, not a necessitated agent; and even if he were necessitated, God would still act immediately. God acts in such a way that though He could be the total cause of the effect without anything else, nevertheless, in His administration, things have their own movements, as Saint Augustine teaches. God does not want to produce the whole effect alone but as a partial cause to be a co-agent with the secondary causes, although He is superior. Therefore, He is the immediate cause of everything both when He acts with other causes and when He acts without them. The secondary causes, meanwhile, cannot be called superfluous, because God reveals His power through them in a different manner.

If it could be proven that God intends something which is not Himself, it might be proven that the divine will is always realized. However, it cannot be proven that whatever is intended by God is done by God, nor that whatever is intended by God is done by somebody else. It cannot be proven by natural reason that God is the immediate cause of everything, nor that he is not the immediate cause of everything. There is no proof whatever in the light of natural reason that God is the total cause of anything. There is no proof, therefore, from natural reason that whatever God intends is done by God, nor that whatever is intended by God is done by somebody else. Since, then, it cannot be demonstrated by natural reason that God is the immediate cause of everything, it cannot be established whether or not the divine will is always realized by Himself or by somebody else.

In the same manner, it is a matter of belief that God is a free cause with regard to everything. It cannot be so demonstrated by natural reason that the unbelievers may not gainsay it. Nevertheless, it may be recommended in this way. Every cause which cannot be impeded may face everything, in fact, infinity itself in an equal manner. If at a given moment it actualizes one of the many possibilities, no other reason than its being a free agent can be given for its producing one effect rather than another. But God is such a cause with respect to all things produced by Him from eternity. Therefore, it is to be accepted as a fact that God is a cause which acts contingently. He may do otherwise than He does because any agent acting contingently may act otherwise. In the same way, God can produce souls in infinite number, because He does not have to stop at a given number. Nevertheless, He does not produce souls in an infinite, but only in a given, quantity.

God cannot be obligated to any act. It would not constitute sin even though God were to commit as a total cause the acts which He now performs with the sinner as a partial cause. Sin is nothing else than an act of commission or omission when there is an obligation for man. Only obligation constitutes one a sinner or not a sinner. But God cannot be obligated to any act. With Him a thing becomes right solely for the reason that He wants it to be so. If God as a total cause were to instigate hatred toward Himself in the will of somebody—just as He now causes it as a partial cause—such a person would not be guilty of sin and neither would God, because He is not obligated to anything. In this case the person would not be obligated either, because his act would not be in his control.

Hatred of God, stealing, adultery, and the like, of course, have sinful circumstances connected with them according to the generally accepted law, inasmuch as the person who performs them is obligated by divine precept to the contrary. As far as the absolute being of those acts is concerned, however, they may be performed by God without any sinful circumstance attached to them. They may even be meritoriously performed by man if they fall under divine precept, just as now their opposites, as a matter of fact, fall under the divine precept.

Moral goodness and malice involve the obligation of an agent to a certain act or to its opposite. Sin does not exist except in an act of will. In the same way, merit cannot be assumed except for the will at least in part.

Nothing occurring in a man living in mortal sin is the effect of predestination. To the contrary, good deeds performed in the state of mortal sin are in some way the cause why God grants His grace. The ground, moreover, why God predestines some for that reason and others without any reason is merely God's will to do so. The reason why Saint Paul was struck by God and converted without any previous merits of his own while others were not, is nothing else than the will of God.

*Whether Only an Act of Will Is Necessarily Virtuous or Vicious?**

No: For every act of will can be elicited with a bad intention; hence every act of will can be bad.

On the contrary: To love God is an act that is only virtuous and nothing but virtuous; hence this act is only virtuous.

I reply to this question: The exclusive proposition found in the formulation of this question is exponible as a pair of propositions. One is negative, viz. "No act different from the act of will is necessarily virtuous." The other is affirmative, viz. "Some act of the will is necessarily virtuous."

Concerning the negative part of the explanation, I maintain that this proposition is simply true. For every act other than an act of will which is in the power of the will is good only in such a manner that it can be bad because it can be performed for a bad end and with a bad intention. Furthermore, any other act can be performed naturally and not freely; and no such act is necessarily good. Again, every act other than an act of will can be brought about by God's sole action; consequently it is not necessarily virtuous for a rational creature.

Furthermore, every act, remaining identically the same, can be indifferently laudable or blameworthy; and it can be first laudable and afterwards blameworthy inasmuch as it can be successively in accordance with a righteous and with a vi-

* By permission. William of Ockham: *Philosophical Writings*, trans. P. Boehner, O.P.M. The Bobbs-Merrill Company, Inc., Indianapolis, 1964.

cious will. This becomes clear if we consider the act of going to church, first with a good intention, and then with a bad intention.

Furthermore, no act is virtuous or vicious unless it is voluntary and in the power of the will, because a sin is a sin only because it is voluntary; but another act can be in the power of the will at first and then afterwards beyond the power of the will. For instance, in the case where someone voluntarily jumps off a precipice, and then repents and has an act of not willing his fall, and that meritoriously for God's sake; but the fall itself is not any more in the power of the will; hence this fall is not necessarily vicious.

Concerning the affirmative part of the explanation I maintain: First, literally speaking, no act is necessarily virtuous. Proof: No act exists necessarily; and consequently, no act is necessarily virtuous. Again, every act can be performed by God's sole action; consequently it is not necessarily virtuous, since such an act [caused by God] is not in the power of the will.

However, another meaning can be attached to saying that an act is virtuous, viz. that it cannot be vicious while God's commandment stands; or, again, that such an act cannot be caused by a created will without being virtuous. If we understand "virtuous act" in this sense, then I maintain that an act may be necessarily virtuous. Proof: It is impossible that any contingently virtuous act, that is an act which can be called indifferently virtuous or vicious, can be determined to be a virtuous act, except by reason of another necessarily virtuous act. This is proved as follows: A contingently virtuous act, let us say an act of walking, is determined to be a virtuous act by its conformity with another act. About this second act I ask: Is it necessarily virtuous in the sense explained?—and then we have our intended thesis—or is it contingently virtuous and determined to be a virtuous act by some other virtuous act? About this third act we have to ask as before. Thus, either we go on *ad infinitum*, or we stop at some necessarily virtuous act.

Thirdly I maintain that a necessarily virtuous act, in the sense explained above, is an act of will, since the act by which God is loved above all and for His own sake is such an act. For this act is virtuous in such a way that it cannot be vicious, nor can this act be caused by a created will without being virtuous. First, because everyone is bound (according to time and place) to love God above all, and consequently this act cannot be vicious; secondly, because this act is the first of all good acts. Furthermore, only an act of will is essentially laudable or blameworthy. Again, according to the saints, every act is laudable or blameworthy only because of its good or bad intention; but an intention is an act of the will; therefore, etc. Again, according to St. Anselm, only the will is punished, because only the will sins; therefore, etc.

The objection may be made: God can command that He be not loved for a certain time, because He can command that the intellect be occupied with study and the will likewise, so that at this time it cannot think anything about God. I now assume that the will then performs an act of loving God; then this act is either virtuous—but that cannot be said, since it is performed against the divine command—or it is not virtuous, and then we have our intended thesis that an act of loving God above all is not virtuous.

I answer: If God could command this—and it seems that He can do it without contradiction—then I maintain that the will in this situation cannot perform such an act, because merely by performing such an act the will would love God above all and consequently would fulfil the divine precept. For to love God above all means to love whatever God wills to be loved. But by the mere fact of loving God in this way one would not (according to our assumption) fulfil the divine command. Consequently by loving God in this manner one would love God and not love God; one would fulfil the precept of God and not fulfil it. However, one could have an act of a simple and natural love, which is not the same as the love of God above all; just as, if someone did not believe in God, he could not love Him, since nothing can be loved unless it exists or can exist.

Fourthly I maintain that only a habit of the will is essentially and necessarily virtuous, since every other habit indifferently inclines to laudable and blameworthy acts.

In regard to the main argument I deny the premise, for there is an act of the will which, as it is clear from the aforesaid, cannot be performed with a bad intention.

part 3

THE EARLY MODERN PERIOD

The selections in this section begin with some passages from Machiavelli. It is impossible to read more than a sentence or two without realizing that one is in a world wholly different from the Middle Ages, that one is confronted with a wholly different mentality. Where, for instance, St. Thomas Aquinas oriented ethics toward a supernal happiness (pp. 161), Machiavelli's conception of the highest good is completely secular and natural (pp. 198). It is power: not merely power as a means to the attainment of other ends, but power for its own sake, for the freedom from external restraint and for the capacity for dominance over others which it gives us. Accordingly, for Machiavelli the religious beliefs of the masses, instead of being important indications of those transcendental dimensions of reality which define and limit the goals of human conduct, become merely instrumentalities which an essentially irreligious prince can play upon as a means to the realization of his private ambitions. Indeed, Machiavelli considers religion in purely sociological and psychological terms p. 201); it is simply one drive among others, albeit a very powerful one, of which we must take account if we want to understand and control men's behavior.

We have not heard this particular note since Glaucon's account in *The Republic* (pp. 26–30) of the nature of the good. There is thus some justice, as far as ethical theory goes, in speaking of the period with which we are now dealing as a "renaissance," as a revival of classical attitudes toward the world and toward man. But if there are close similarities, it is also important to see that this is a revival with a difference. Classical naturalism, egoism, and individualism were essentially the expression of minority opinion, whereas during the whole of the modern period they become increasingly dominant. It is symbolic of the difference to which we are pointing that whereas Plato states the naturalistic position only to disprove it (Glaucon, indeed, begs Socrates to show him where he has gone wrong—p. 29), Machiavelli affirms this position as self-evidently correct. *The Prince* is not a dialogue: there is no Socrates here to reestablish an organic and transcendental metaphysics.

A second major difference between the classical period and this early modern period is due simply to the intervening centuries of Christianity. The long dominance of Christian attitudes, beliefs, and values—to say nothing of the Church's social, political, and institutional position—could not be wiped out by a single stroke of the pen. In the first place, thinkers like Machiavelli and Hobbes, who were essentially irreligious and secular in outlook, had perforce to render lip service to religious ideals and attitudes. They feared the established churches, even if they did not respect the Christian God. But much more important than such considerations, of course, was the fact that almost all of the theorists we are considering in this section were sincerely, and indeed often deeply, pious men; they felt an internal need, as well as an external compulsion, to accommodate their views on human conduct to religious considerations—as they understood these. This is clearly the case with Butler and Kant, for instance; it is also true of Spinoza, even though in his case the religion with which his naturalistic ethics had to be reconciled was not Protestant Christianity but a unique, non-Christian kind of pantheism. Accordingly, we can say that in this period one of the main problems of ethical theory was that of working out a satisfactory compromise between naturalism and a supernaturalistic transcendentalism.

A third major difference to bear in mind is the effect of the rise of modern science, and especially of physics, on the kind of naturalism that developed in this period. Classical science had been teleological and qualitative in character; the objects it dealt with and sought to understand were ordinary objects of ordinary experience. The great shift that occurred at the beginning of the modern period was the shift of attention to unordinary objects—to objects as perceived through a microscope, telescope, or some other instrument; to objects as the result of some measuring process. "Measure everything that is measurable," was Galileo's dictum; and the history of science since the seventeenth century has been largely the patient and ingenious execution of this order. The result was a conception of nature radically different from that envisaged by the classical naturalists. Nature, according to the early modern physicists, was a vast array of masses in motion—nature was neutral: colorless, soundless, tasteless, and passionless. Yet this enormous set of particles in complex motion was held to behave in ways completely predictable from relatively simple physical laws. Though this scheme was not worked out in detail until the end of the seventeenth century, men like Hobbes had already caught the vision and formulated it; and it was increasingly and powerfully to affect ethical theorizing throughout the coming centuries.

As a result new problems came to the fore: Where, for instance, in this great machine, which, as it was believed, nature had now been shown to be, was there a place for man as a free agent, choosing the better in preference to the worse? So far as man's body was a part of the machine (and who could deny that it was?), and so far as this body influenced his will, it would seem that a man's acts must be completely determined by antecedent events in time and so wholly predictable. What then happened to the concepts of human responsibility and duty, concepts which seemed to depend on the possibility of there being a free choice? Thus, the problem of freedom, as it is called, became a major concern of ethical theorists: either they flatly denied that freedom is possible (as with Hobbes), or they identified freedom with a knowledge of necessity (as with Spinoza), or they devised more or less elaborate metaphysical formulas designed to reconcile freedom and determinism (as with Kant). In any case, the question of the nature and possibility of free will became and remained a central ethical issue.

And beyond this, there was the larger and even more formidable question of the nature of man and of the values to which he gives his allegiance—those values which the ethical theorist believes himself to be analyzing and formulating. What is the *ontological* status of values in the world that the new science was disclosing? As long as nature was regarded as teleological in character, it was easy to regard man as a purposive being and to hold that his purposes are metaphysically real. But in the new view of nature and of man which physicists began to put forward in the seventeenth century, it would seem that men's purposes were, at best, the goals of physiological drives and, at worst, simply subjective illusions. In either event, ethics would no longer be an autonomous science in its own right, but simply a branch of empirical psychology. This conclusion, already adumbrated by Machiavelli, was first stated explicitly and formally by Hobbes (pp. 223 ff.). In one way or another, all subsequent theorists of this period were affected by it, either by flatly opposing it or else by seeking to work out some compromise with it.

We can put all of this another way by saying that during the early modern period ethical theory came to be more empirically oriented, came, that is, to devote more attention to what it was believed men actually aim at, in distinction from what it might be held they ought to aim at. Indeed, the "ought" came increasingly to be derived from the "is." Kant, it is true, is an outstanding exception to this movement. But the vigor of his reaffirmation of the independence of the "ought" is itself evidence of intense pressure in the other direction; and all the other writers of the period, including both the moral-sense theorists and the early utilitarians, in varying degrees felt this pressure and were influenced by it.

As a fourth factor affecting the character of ethical theory in this period, we can put the great social and political changes that occurred during the seventeenth and eighteenth centuries. First among these was the emergence of the national territorial state as the primary political unit. This change meant, among other things, that ethical theorists had to reevaluate man's political duties and in particular to work out their own balance between the growing value set on individualism and autonomy and the massive accumulation of power which it seemed necessary to assign to the sovereign, whether monarch, king-in-parliament, or the democratic electorate itself. Thus political responsibilities came into prominence again, as they had not done since the classical period; but they now looked very different, were very different, from what they had been when the small city-state or the universal empire was the major political unit.

Other momentous changes affecting ethical theory were the increasing democratization of society and the industrial revolution. Though these movements only got under way extensively toward the close of this period, and though, therefore, their primary impact on ethical theory occurred during the nineteenth century, they had a visible influence on writers like Hume and Kant. Thus, for instance, Kant's emphasis on the fact that we are to treat all men as ends and never merely as means (pp. 294) is in effect a philosophical anticipation of the underlying insights of the French and American Revolutions and of the equalitarian societies that were to begin to emerge in the next century. We may summarize a complicated matter shortly by saying that as the equalitarian ideal was coupled with the increasing production of consumer goods made possible by the industrial revolution, welfare became an increasingly important concept to the ethical theories. As Europe changed from a society based on scarcity to a society in which plenty was for the first time possible, ethical theory began to reflect this shift: we see the first signs of it in the early utilitarians like Hume, to whom distribution instead of selection is a primary concern.

Finally, we may say that, as society grew more complex and as the unity of Christendom (a unity that was doubtless only an ideal, but nevertheless an operative ideal) was fragmented into diverse religious sects and independent states, ethical theorists were presented anew with the old problem of diversity. It was harder now, much harder than ever before, to find the uniform, universal moral principles that were supposed to hold for, and with respect to, the diversity of actual codes and practices. Kant is a good example of attempts to fight rearguard actions in this area of ethical theory. In his own way he represents a last attempt of the traditional rationalism to formulate a demonstrable, and therefore universally valid, ethics, based on the old conception of man as an essentially rational creature. In this respect, however much he may differ from Plato and Aristotle and St. Thomas in detail, Kant is united with them and so stands opposed to the tendencies that were coming to the fore in the later years of his life.

NICCOLÒ MACHIAVELLI

Niccolò Machiavelli (1469–1527) was a Florentine politician. He grew up during the regime of Lorenzo the Magnificent; and when Lorenzo died and the Medici government was overthrown, he joined the new administration, serving the Republic in various important capacities. When the Medici were restored to power in 1512, he went into retirement. He spent his remaining years in writing (The Prince, *the* Discourses on Livy, *a* History of Florence) *and in seeking, unsuccessfully, to gain the favor of the new rulers of the city.*

Machiavelli was primarily interested in formulating generalizations, derived from his reading of history and his own practical experience, about the nature and dynamics of power. The reason for including him in this volume is that, though he is not an ethical theorist in the formal sense, his political generalizations are all rooted in an implicit naturalistic ethic—an ethic which has been widely held, though seldom so frankly expressed.

*Aphorisms on the Nature of Man**

All men are bad and ever ready to display their vicious nature, whenever they may find occasion for it. (*Discourses,* I,3)

Men act right only under compulsion. (*Discourses,* I,3)

The great majority of mankind are satisfied with appearances, as though they were realities, and are often even more influenced by the things that seem than by those that are. (*Discourses,* I,25)

Ambition [is a] passion so powerful in the hearts of men that it never leaves them. (*Discourses,* I,37)

The fear to lose stirs the same passions in men as the desire to gain, as men do not believe themselves sure of what they possess, except by acquiring still more; and, moreover, these new acquisitions are so many means of strength and power for abuses. (*Discourses,* I,5)

The character of the people is not to

* By permission. From Niccolò Machiavelli, *The Prince and the Discourses,* trans. by Luigi Ricci and C. E. Detmold, Random House, Inc., New York, and Oxford University Press, Fair Lawn, N.J., 1940.

be blamed any more than that of princes, for both alike are liable to err when they are without any control. (*Discourses,* I,58)

Hatred is gained as much by good works as by evil. (*Prince,* 19)

Humility is not only of no service, but is actually hurtful. (*Discourses,* II,14)

Men change masters willingly, hoping to better themselves; and this belief makes them take arms against their rulers in which they are deceived, as experience later proves that they have gone from bad to worse. (*Prince,* 3)

Whoever is the cause of another becoming powerful is ruined himself, for that power is produced by him either through craft or force; and both of these are suspected by the one who has been raised to power. (*Prince,* 3)

It is necessary for a prince, who wishes to maintain himself, to learn how not to be good, and to use this knowledge and not use it, according to the necessities of the case. . . . Some things which seem virtues would, if followed, lead to one's ruin, and some others which appear vices result in one's great security and wellbeing. (*Prince,* 15)

Goodness does not suffice, . . . benefits will not placate malignity. (*Discourses,* III,30)

Government consists mainly in so keeping your subjects that they shall be neither able nor disposed to injure you. (*Discourses,* II,23)

One never tries to avoid one difficulty without running into another, but prudence consists in being able to know the nature of the difficulties, and taking the least harmful as good. (*Prince,* 21)

Whoever is unwilling to adopt [a] humane course must, if he wishes to maintain his power, follow [an] evil course. But men generally decide upon a middle course, which is most hazardous. (*Discourses,* I,26)

All armed prophets have conquered and unarmed ones failed. (*Prince,* 6)

*The Prince**

IT IS BETTER TO BE FEARED THAN LOVED

A prince must not mind incurring the charge of cruelty for the purpose of keeping his subjects united and faithful; for, with a very few examples, he will be more merciful than those who, from excess of tenderness, allow disorders to arise, from whence spring bloodshed and rapine; for these as a rule injure the whole community, while the executions carried out by the prince injure only individuals. And of all princes, it is impossible for a new prince to escape the reputation of cruelty, new states being always full of dangers. . . .

From this arises the question whether it is better to be loved more than feared, or feared more than loved. The reply is, that one ought to be both feared and loved, but as it is difficult for the two to go together, it is much safer to be feared than loved, if one of the two has to be wanting. For it may be said of men in general that they are ungrateful, voluble, dissemblers, anxious to avoid danger, and covetous of gain; as long as you benefit them, they are entirely yours; they offer you their blood, their goods, their life, and their children, as I have before said, when the necessity is remote; but when it approaches, they revolt. And the prince who has relied solely on their words, without making other preparations, is ruined; for the friendship which is gained by purchase and not through grandeur and nobility of spirit is bought but not secured, and at a pinch is not to be expended in your service. And men have less scruple in offending one who makes himself loved than one who makes himself feared; for love is held by a chain of obligation which, men being selfish, is broken whenever it serves their purpose; but fear

* *Supra,* p. 197.

is maintained by a dread of punishment which never fails.

Still, a prince should make himself feared in such a way that if he does not gain love, he at any rate avoids hatred; for fear and the absence of hatred may well go together, and will be always attained by one who abstains from interfering with the property of his citizens and subjects or with their women. . . . But above all he must abstain from taking the property of others, for men forget more easily the death of their father than the loss of their patrimony. . . .

I conclude, therefore, with regard to being feared and loved, that men love at their own free will, but fear at the will of the prince, and that a wise prince must rely on what is in his power and not on what is in the power of others, and he must only contrive to avoid incurring hatred, as has been explained.

THE DISADVANTAGES OF KEEPING PROMISES

You must know that there are two methods of fighting, the one by law, the other by force: the first method is that of men, the second of beasts; but as the first method is often insufficient, one must have recourse to the second. It is therefore necessary for a prince to know well how to use both the beast and the man. . . .

A prince being thus obliged to know well how to act as a beast must imitate the fox and the lion, for the lion cannot protect himself from traps, and the fox cannot defend himself from wolves. One must therefore be a fox to recognise traps, and a lion to frighten wolves. Those that wish to be only lions do not understand this. Therefore, a prudent ruler ought not to keep faith when by so doing it would be against his interest, and when the reasons which made him bind himself no longer exist. If men were all good, this precept would not be a good one; but as they are bad, and would not observe their faith with you, so you are not bound to keep faith with them. Nor have legitimate grounds ever failed a prince who wished to show colourable excuse for the non-fulfilment of his promise. Of this one could furnish an infinite number of modern examples, and show how many times peace has been broken, and how many promises rendered worthless, by the faithlessness of princes, and those that have been best able to imitate the fox have succeeded best. But it is necessary to be able to disguise this character well, and to be a great feigner and dissembler; and men are so simple and so ready to obey present necessities, that one who deceives will always find those who allow themselves to be deceived.

I will only mention one modern instance. Alexander VI did nothing else but deceive men, he thought of nothing else, and found the occasion for it; no man was ever more able to give assurances, or affirmed things with stronger oaths, and no man observed them less; however, he always succeeded in his deceptions, as he well knew this aspect of things.

It is not, therefore, necessary for a prince to have all the above-named qualities, but it is very necessary to seem to have them. I would even be bold to say that to possess them and always to observe them is dangerous, but to appear to possess them is useful. Thus it is well to seem merciful, faithful, humane, sincere, religious, and also to be so; but you must have the mind so disposed that when it is needful to be otherwise you may be able to change to the opposite qualities. And it must be understood that a prince, and especially a new prince, cannot observe all those things which are considered good in men, being often obliged, in order to maintain the state, to act against faith, against charity, against humanity, and against religion. And, therefore, he must have a mind disposed to adapt itself according to the wind, and as the variations of fortune dictate, and, as I said before, not deviate from what is good, if possible, but be able to do evil if constrained. . . .

In the actions of men, and especially of princes, from which there is no appeal, the end justifies the means. Let a prince therefore aim at conquering and maintaining the state, and the means will always be judged honourable and praised by every one, for the vulgar is always taken by appearances and the issue of the event; and the world consists only of the vulgar, and the few who are not vulgar are isolated when the many have a rallying point in the prince.

NIGGARDLINESS IS SUPERIOR TO LIBERALITY

It would be well to be considered liberal; nevertheless liberality such as the world understands it will injure you, because if used virtuously and in the proper way, it will not be known, and you will incur the disgrace of the contrary vice. But one who wishes to obtain the reputation of liberality among men, must not omit every kind of sumptuous display, and to such an extent that a prince of this character will consume by such means all his resources, and will be at last compelled, if he wishes to maintain his name for liberality, to impose heavy taxes on his people, become extortionate, and do everything possible to obtain money. This will make his subjects begin to hate him, and he will be little esteemed being poor, so that having by this liberality injured many and benefited but few, he will feel the first little disturbance and be endangered by every peril. If he recognises this and wishes to change his system, he incurs at once the charge of niggardliness.

A prince, therefore, . . . must not, if he be prudent, object to be called miserly. In course of time he will be thought more liberal, when it is seen that by his parsimony his revenue is sufficient, that he can defend himself against those who make war on him, and undertake enterprises without burdening his people, so that he is really liberal to all those from whom he does not take, who are infinite in number, and niggardly to all to whom he does not give, who are few. In our times we have seen nothing great done except by those who have been esteemed niggardly; the others have all been ruined. . . .

You may be very generous indeed with what is not the property of yourself or your subjects, as were Cyrus, Cæsar, and Alexander; for spending the wealth of others will not diminish your reputation, but increase it, only spending your own resources will injure you. There is nothing which destroys itself so much as liberality, for by using it you lose the power of using it, and become either poor and despicable, or, to escape poverty, rapacious and hated. And of all things that a prince must guard against, the most important are being despicable or hated, and liberality will lead you to one or other of these conditions. It is, therefore, wiser to have the name of a miser, which produces disgrace without hatred, than to incur of necessity the name of being rapacious, which produces both disgrace and hatred.

*The Discourses**

CUNNING AND DECEIT ARE SUPERIOR TO FORCE

I believe it to be most true that it seldom happens that men rise from low condition to high rank without employing either force or fraud, unless that rank should be attained either by gift or inheritance. Nor do I believe that force alone will ever be found to suffice, whilst it will often be the case that cunning alone serves the

* *Supra*, p. 197.

purpose; as is clearly seen by whoever reads the life of Philip of Macedon, or that of Agathocles the Sicilian, and many others, who from the lowest or most moderate condition have achieved thrones and great empires. Xenophon shows in his Life of Cyrus the necessity of deception to success: the first expedition of Cyrus against the king of Armenia is replete with fraud, and it was deceit alone, and not force, that enabled him to seize that kingdom. And Xenophon draws no other conclusion from it than that a prince who wishes to achieve great things must learn to deceive. Cyrus also practised a variety of deceptions upon Cyaxares, king of the Medes, his maternal uncle; and Xenophon shows that without these frauds Cyrus would never have achieved the greatness which he did attain. Nor do I believe that there was ever a man who from obscure condition arrived at great power by merely employing open force; but there are many who have succeeded by fraud alone, as, for instance, Giovanni Galeazzo Visconti in taking the state and sovereignty of Lombardy from his uncle, Messer Bernabo.

CHRISTIANITY ENFEEBLES POLICY

Reflecting now as to whence it came that in ancient times the people were more devoted to liberty than in the present, I believe that it resulted from this, that men were stronger in those days, which I believe to be attributable to the difference of education, founded upon the difference of their religion and ours. For, as our religion teaches us the truth and the true way of life, it causes us to attach less value to the honors and possessions of this world; whilst the Pagans, esteeming those things as the highest good, were more energetic and ferocious in their actions. We may observe this also in most of their institutions, beginning with the magnificence of their sacrifices as compared with the humility of ours, which are gentle solemnities rather than magnificent ones, and have nothing of energy or ferocity in them, whilst in theirs there was no lack of pomp and show, to which was superadded the ferocious and bloody nature of the sacrifice by the slaughter of many animals, and the familiarity with this terrible sight assimilated the nature of men to their sacrificial ceremonies. Besides this, the Pagan religion deified only men who had achieved great glory, such as commanders of armies and chiefs of republics, whilst ours glorifies more the humble and contemplative men than the men of action. Our religion, moreover, places the supreme happiness in humility, lowliness, and a contempt for worldly objects, whilst the other, on the contrary, places the supreme good in grandeur of soul, strength of body, and all such other qualities as render men formidable; and if our religion claims of us fortitude of soul, it is more to enable us to suffer than to achieve great deeds.

These principles seem to me to have made men feeble, and caused them to become an easy prey to evil-minded men, who can control them more securely, seeing that the great body of men, for the sake of gaining Paradise, are more disposed to endure injuries than to avenge them. And although it would seem that the world has become effeminate and Heaven disarmed, yet this arises unquestionably from the baseness of men, who have interpreted our religion according to the promptings of indolence rather than those of virtue. For if we were to reflect that our religion permits us to exalt and defend our country, we should see that according to it we ought also to love and honor our country, and prepare ourselves so as to be capable of defending her. It is this education, then, and this false interpretation of our religion, that is the cause of there not being so many republics nowadays as there were anciently; and that there is no longer the same love of liberty amongst the people now as there was then.

THE ROLE OF CHANCE IN HUMAN AFFAIRS

It is not unknown to me how many have been and are of opinion that worldly events are so governed by fortune and by God, that men cannot by their prudence change them, and that on the contrary there is no remedy whatever, and for this they may judge it to be useless to toil much about them, but let things be ruled by chance. This opinion has been more held in our day, from the great changes that have been seen, and are daily seen, beyond every human conjecture. When I think about them, at times I am partly inclined to share this opinion. Nevertheless, that our free will may not be altogether extinguished, I think it may be true that fortune is the ruler of half our actions, but that she allows the other half or thereabouts to be governed by us. I would compare her to an impetuous river that, when turbulent, inundates the plains, casts down trees and buildings, removes earth from this side and places it on the other; every one flees before it, and everything yields to its fury without being able to oppose it; and yet though it is of such a kind, still when it is quiet, men can make provision against it by dykes and banks, so that when it rises it will either go into a canal or its rush will not be so wild and dangerous. So it is with fortune, which shows her power where no measures have been taken to resist her, and directs her fury where she knows that no dykes or barriers have been made to hold her. . . .

He is happy whose mode of procedure accords with the needs of the times, and similarly he is unfortunate whose mode of procedure is opposed to the times. For one sees that men in those things which lead them to the aim that each one has in view, namely, glory and riches, proceed in various ways; one with circumspection, another with impetuosity, one by violence, another by cunning, one with patience, another with the reverse; and each by these diverse ways may arrive at his aim. One sees also two cautious men, one of whom succeeds in his designs, and the other not, and in the same way two men succeed equally by different methods, one being cautious, the other impetuous, which arises only from the nature of the times, which does or does not conform to their method of procedure. From this it results, as I have said, that two men, acting differently, attain the same effect, and of two others acting in the same way, one attains his goal and not the other. On this depend also the changes in prosperity, for if it happens that time and circumstances are favourable to one who acts with caution and prudence he will be successful, but if time and circumstances change he will be ruined, because he does not change his mode of procedure. No man is found so prudent as to be able to adapt himself to this, either because he cannot deviate from that to which his nature disposes him, or else because having always prospered by walking in one path, he cannot persuade himself that it is well to leave it; and therefore the cautious man, when it is time to act suddenly, does not know how to do so and is consequently ruined; for if one could change one's nature with time and circumstances, fortune would never change. . . .

I conclude then that fortune varying and men remaining fixed in their ways, they are successful so long as these ways conform to circumstances, but when they are opposed then they are unsuccessful. I certainly think that it is better to be impetuous than cautious, for fortune is a woman, and it is necessary if you wish to master her, to conquer her by force; and it can be seen that she lets herself be overcome by the bold rather than by those who proceed coldly. And therefore, like a woman, she is always a friend to the young, because they are less cautious, fiercer, and master her with greater audacity. . . .

I might cite some modern examples in confirmation of the views I have advanced, but do not deem it necessary, as that of the Romans suffices. I repeat, then, as an incontrovertible truth, proved by all history, that men may second Fortune, but cannot oppose her; they may develop her designs, but cannot defeat them. But men should never despair on that account; for, not knowing the aims of Fortune, which she pursues by dark and devious ways, men should always be hopeful, and never yield to despair, whatever troubles or ill fortune may befall them. . . .

I have often reflected that the causes of the success or failure of men depend upon their manner of suiting their conduct to the times. . . . He errs least and will be most favored by fortune who suits his proceedings to the times, and always follows the impulses of his nature. Every one knows how Fabius Maximus conducted the war against Hannibal with extreme caution and circumspection, and with an utter absence of all impetuosity or Roman audacity. It was his good fortune that this mode of proceeding accorded perfectly with the times and circumstances. For Hannibal had arrived in Rome whilst still young and with his fortunes fresh; he had already twice routed the Romans, so that the republic was as it were deprived of her best troops, and greatly discouraged by her reverses. Rome could not therefore have been more favored by fortune, than to have a commander who by his extreme caution and the slowness of his movements kept the enemy at bay. At the same time, Fabius could not have found circumstances more favorable for his character and genius, to which fact he was indebted for his success and glory. And that this mode of proceeding was the result of his character and nature, and not a matter of choice, was shown on the occasion when Scipio wanted to take the same troops to Africa for the purpose of promptly terminating the war. Fabius most earnestly opposed this, like a man incapable of breaking from his accustomed ways and habits; so that, if he had been master, Hannibal would have remained in Italy, because Fabius failed to perceive that the times were changed. . . . For any man accustomed to a certain mode of proceeding will never change it, as we have said, and consequently when time and circumstances change, so that his ways are no longer in harmony with them, he must of necessity succumb. Pietro Soderini, whom we have mentioned several times already, was in all his actions governed by humanity and patience. He and his country prospered so long as the times favored this mode of proceeding; but when afterwards circumstances arose that demanded a course of conduct the opposite to that of patience and humanity, he was unfit for the occasion, and his own and his country's ruin were the consequence. Pope Julius II acted throughout the whole period of his pontificate with the impetuosity and passion natural to his character; and as the times and circumstances well accorded with this, he was successful in all his undertakings. But if the times had changed so that different counsels would have been required, he would unquestionably have been ruined, for he could not have changed his character or mode of action.

That we cannot thus change at will is due to two causes; the one is the impossibility of resisting the natural bent of our characters; and the other is the difficulty of persuading ourselves, after having ben accustomed to success by a certain mode of proceeding, that any other can succeed as well. It is this that causes the varying success of a man; for the times change, but he does not change his mode of proceeding. The ruin of states is caused in like manner, as we have fully shown above, because they do not modify their institutions to suit the changes of the times. And such changes are more difficult and tardy in republics; for necessarily circumstances will occur that will unsettle the whole state, and when the change of proceeding of one man will not suffice for the occasion.

MARTIN LUTHER

Martin Luther (1483–1546) devoted much of his writing to protesting the corruption of Catholic doctrine by the prevailing scholastic philosophy; his works therefore abound with antiphilosophical polemic. He was far more concerned with theological and religious reform than with philosophical subtlety.

Yet Luther had a great deal to do with changing the course of philosophy in this period. Descartes is credited with responsibility for separating philosophy from theology, but Luther assisted, for his break with the Church set theology on a course independent from philosophy. Thus, from this time on philosophical ethics began to lose its theological setting and became an independent study.

Our selections are from some of Luther's best-known and politically influential writings. The Bondage of the Will *indicates both his strong opposition to Erasmus and an increasing stress on contingency. The treatise on* Secular Authority *illustrates the interesting contrast between Luther's personal discovery of theological and spiritual freedom and his continued stress, nevertheless, on the citizen's duty to obey civil authority. Both essays help set the course of debate in Christian ethics down to modern times.*

*The Bondage of the Will**

OF THE NECESSITATING FOREKNOWLEDGE OF GOD

It is fundamentally necessary and wholesome for Christians to know that God foreknows nothing contingently, but that He foresees, purposes, and does all things according to His own immutable, eternal and infallible will. This bombshell knocks "free-will" flat, and utterly shatters it; so that those who want to assert it must either deny my bombshell, or pretend not to notice it, or find some other way of dodging it. . . .

If He wills what He foreknows, His will is eternal and changeless, because His nature is so. From which it follows, by

* By permission. Martin Luther: *The Bondage of the Will*, translated by J. I. Packer and A. R. Johnston, London: James Clarke and Co., Ltd., 1957; Westwood, N.J.: Fleming H. Revell Company, 1957.

resistless logic, that all we do, however it may appear to us to be done mutably and contingently, is in reality done necessarily and immutably in respect of God's will. For the will of God is effective and cannot be impeded, since power belongs to God's nature; and His wisdom is such that He cannot be deceived. Since, then His will is not impeded, what is done cannot but be done where, when, how, as far as, and by whom, He foresees and wills. If the will of God were such that, when the work had been done and while it yet remained in being, the will ceased (as is the case with the will of a man, who, when he has built, say, the house he wants, ceases to will just as really as he does in death), then it could truly be said that things happen contingently and mutably. But the contrary is in fact true: the work ceases to be and the will remains in being—so far beyond the bounds of possibility is it that the production and continued existence of anything can be contingent. Lest we be deceived over our terms, let me explain that *being done contingently* does not, in Latin, signify that the thing done is itself contingent, but that it is done by a contingent and mutable will—such as is *not* to be found in God! And a deed cannot be called *contingent* unless we do it "contingently," i.e. by chance (as it were) and without premeditation; that is, when our will or hand fastens on something presented to us as if by chance without our having previously thought or planned anything about it.

I could wish, indeed, that a better term was available for our discussion than the accepted one, *necessity,* which cannot accurately be used of either man's will or God's. Its meaning is too harsh, and foreign to the subject; for it suggests some sort of compulsion, and something that is against one's will, which is no part of the view under debate. The will, whether it be God's or man's, does what it does, good or bad, under no compulsion, but just as it wants or pleases, as if totally free. Yet the will of God, which rules over our mutable will, is changeless and sure—as Boetius sings, "Immovable Thyself, Thou movement giv'st to all"; and our will, principally because of its corruption, can do no good of itself. The reader's understanding, therefore, must supply what the word itself fails to convey, from his knowledge of the intended significance—the immutable will of God on the one hand, and the impotence of our corrupt will on the other. . . .

OF THE COMFORT OF KNOWING THAT SALVATION DOES NOT DEPEND ON "FREE-WILL"

I frankly confess that, for myself, even if it could be, I should not want "free-will" to be given me, nor anything to be left in my own hands to enable me to endeavour after salvation; not merely because in face of so many dangers, and adversities, and assaults of devils, I could not stand my ground and hold fast my "free-will" (for one devil is stronger than all men, and on these terms no man could be saved); but because, even were there no dangers, adversities, or devils, I should still be forced to labour with no guarantee of success, and to beat my fists at the air. If I lived and worked to all eternity, my conscience would never reach comfortable certainty as to how much it must do to satisfy God. Whatever work I had done, there would still be a nagging doubt as to whether it pleased God, or whether He required something more. The experience of all who seek righteousness by works proves that; and I learned it well enough myself over a period of many years, to my own great hurt. But now that God has taken my salvation out of the control of my own will, and put it under the control of His, and promised to save me, not according to my working or running, but according to His own grace and mercy, I have the comfortable certainty that He is faithful and will not lie to me, and that He is also great and powerful, so that no devils or opposition can break Him or pluck me from Him. "No one," He says, "shall pluck them out of my hand, because my Father which gave them me is greater than all" [John 10:28–29]. Thus it is that, if not all, yet some, indeed many, are saved; whereas, by the power of "free-will" none at all could be saved, but every one of us would perish. . . .

*Secular Authority: To What Extent It Should Be Obeyed**

All who are not Christians belong to the kingdom of the world and are under the law. Since few believe and still fewer live a Christian life, do not resist the evil, and themselves do no evil, God has provided for non-Christians a different government outside the Christian estate and God's kingdom, and has subjected them to the sword, so that, even though they would do so, they cannot practice their wickedness, and that, if they do, they may not do it without fear nor in peace and prosperity. Even so a wild, savage beast is fastened with chains and bands, so that it cannot bite and tear as is its wont, although it gladly would do so; whereas a tame and gentle beast does not require this, but without any chains and bands is nevertheless harmless. If it were not so, seeing that the whole world is evil and that among thousands there is scarcely one true Christian, men would devour one another, and no one could preserve wife and child, support himself and serve God; and thus the world would be reduced to chaos. For this reason God has ordained the two governments; the spiritual, which by the Holy Spirit under Christ makes Christians and pious people, and the secular, which restrains the unchristian and wicked so that they must needs keep the peace outwardly, even against their will. . . .

If any one attempted to rule the world by the Gospel, and put aside all secular law and the secular sword, on the plea that all are baptised and Christian, and that according to the Gospel, there is to be among them neither law nor sword, nor necessity for either, pray, what would happen? He would loose the bands and chains of the wild and savage beasts, and let them tear and mangle every one, and at the same time say they were quite tame and gentle creatures; but I would have the proof in my wounds. Just so would the wicked under the name of Christian abuse this freedom of the Gospel, carry on their knavery, and say that they were Christians subject neither to law nor sword, as some are already raving and ranting.

To such an one we must say, It is indeed true that Christians, so far as they themselves are concerned, are subject to neither law nor sword and need neither; but first take heed and fill the world with real Christians before ruling it in a Christian and evangelical manner. This you will never accomplish; for the world and the masses are and always will be unchristian, although they are all baptized and are nominally Christian. Christians, however, are few and far between, as the saying is. Therefore it is out of the question that there should be a common Christian government over the whole world, nay even over one land or company of people, since the wicked always outnumber the good. Hence a man who would venture to govern an entire country or the world with the Gospel would be like a shepherd who should place in one fold wolves, lions, eagles, and sheep together and let them freely mingle with one another and say, Help yourselves, and be good and peaceful among yourselves; the fold is open, there is plenty of food; have no fear of dogs and clubs. The sheep, forsooth, would keep the peace and would allow themselves to be fed and governed in peace, but they would not live long; nor would any beast keep from molesting another.

For this reason these two kingdoms

* By permission. From *The Works of Martin Luther,* vol. III, trans. J. J. Schindel, Board of Publication, United Lutheran Church in America, Philadelphia, 1930.

must be sharply distinguished, and both be permitted to remain; the one to produce piety, the other to bring about external peace and prevent evil deeds; neither is sufficient in the world without the other. For no one can become pious before God by means of the secular government, without Christ's spiritual rule. Hence Christ's rule does not extend over all, but Christians are always in the minority and are in the midst of non-Christians. Where there is only secular rule or law, there, of necessity, is sheer hypocrisy, though the commandments be God's very own. Without the Holy Spirit in the heart no one becomes really pious, he may do as fine works as he will. Where, on the other hand, the spiritual government rules alone over land and people, there evil is given free rein and the door is opened for every kind of knavery; for the natural world cannot receive or comprehend spiritual things. . . .

You ask whether a Christian, also, may bear the secular sword and punish the wicked, since Christ's words, "Thou shalt not resist the evil," are so clear and definite that the sophists have had to make a counsel of them. I answer, You have now heard two propositions. The one is, that the sword can have no place among Christians, therefore you cannot bear it among and against Christians, who do not need it. The question, therefore, must be directed to the other side, to the non-Christians, whether as a Christian you may there bear it. Here the other proposition applies, that you are under obligation to serve and further the sword by whatever means you can, with body, soul, honor or goods. For it is nothing that you need, but something quite useful and profitable for the whole world and for your neighbor. Therefore, should you see that there is a lack of hangmen, beadles, judges, lords, or princes, and find that you are qualified, you should offer your services and seek the place, that necessary government may by no means be despised and become inefficient or perish. For the world cannot and dare not dispense with it.

The reason you should do this is, that in this case you would enter entirely into the service and work of others, which benefited neither yourself nor your property nor your character, but only your neighbor and others; and you would do it not to avenge yourself or to recompense evil for evil, but for the good of your neighbor and for the maintenance of the safety and peace of others. As concerns yourself, you would abide by the Gospel and govern yourself according to Christ's word, gladly turning the other cheek and letting the mantle go with the coat, when the matter concerned you and your cause [Matt. 5:39, 40]. In this way, then, things are well balanced and you satisfy at the same time God's kingdom inwardly and the kingdom of the world outwardly, at the same time suffer evil and injustice and yet punish evil and injustice, at the same time do not resist evil and yet resist it. For in the one case you consider yourself and what is yours, in the other you consider your neighbor and what is his. In what concerns you and yours, you govern yourself by the Gospel and suffer injustice for yourself as a true Christian; in what concerns others and belongs to them, you govern yourself according to love and suffer no injustice for your neighbor's sake; this the Gospel does not forbid, but rather commands in another place. . . .

*The Freedom of a Christian**

To make the way smoother for the unlearned—for only them do I serve—I shall set down the following two propositions concerning the freedom and the bondage of the spirit.

A Christian is a perfectly free lord of all, subject to none.

* By permission. *Luther's Works*, volume 31, *Career of the Reformer:* I, edited by Harold T. Grimm, Philadelphia: Muhlenberg Press, 1957, trans. by W. A. Lambert; revised by Harold T. Grimm.

A Christian is a perfectly dutiful servant of all, subject to all.

These two theses seem to contradict each other. If, however, they should be found to fit together they would serve our purpose beautifully. Both are Paul's own statements, who says in I Cor. 9 [:19], "For though I am free from all men, I have made myself a slave to all," and in Rom. 13 [:8], "Owe no one anything, except to love one another." Love by its very nature is ready to serve and be subject to him who is loved. . . .

Man has a twofold nature, a spiritual and a bodily one. According to the spiritual nature, which men refer to as the soul, he is called a spiritual, inner, or new man. According to the bodily nature, which men refer to as flesh, he is called a carnal, outward, or old man, of whom the Apostle writes in II Cor. 4 [:16], "Though our outer nature is wasting away, our inner nature is being renewed every day." Because of this diversity of nature the Scriptures assert contradictory things concerning the same man, since these two men in the same man contradict each other, "for the desires of the flesh are against the Spirit, and the desires of the Spirit are against the flesh," according to Gal. 5 [:17].

First, let us consider the inner man to see how a righteous, free, and pious Christian, that is, a spiritual, new, and inner man, becomes what he is. It is evident that no external thing has any influence in producing Christian righteousness or freedom, or in producing unrighteousness or servitude. A simple argument will furnish the proof of this statement. What can it profit the soul if the body is well, free, and active, and eats, drinks, and does as it pleases? For in these respects even the most godless slaves of vice may prosper. On the other hand, how will poor health or imprisonment or hunger or thirst or any other external misfortune harm the soul? Even the most godly men, and those who are free because of clear consciences, are afflicted with these things. None of these things touch either the freedom or the servitude of the soul. It does not help the soul if the body is adorned with the sacred robes of priests or dwells in sacred places or is occupied with sacred duties or prays, fasts, abstains from certain kinds of food, or does any work that can be done by the body and in the body. The righteousness and the freedom of the soul require something far different since the things which have been mentioned could be done by any wicked person. Such works produce nothing but hypocrites. On the other hand, it will not harm the soul if the body is clothed in secular dress, dwells in unconsecrated places, eats and drinks as others do, does not pray aloud, and neglects to do all the above-mentioned things which hypocrites can do. . . .

Since, therefore, this faith can rule only in the inner man, as Rom. 10 [:10] says, "For man believes with his heart and so is justified," and since faith alone justifies, it is clear that the inner man cannot be justified, freed, or saved by any outer work or action at all, and that these works, whatever their character, have nothing to do with this inner man. On the other hand, only ungodliness and unbelief of heart, and no outer work, make him guilty and a damnable servant of sin. Wherefore it ought to be the first concern of every Christian to lay aside all confidence in works and increasingly to strengthen faith alone and through faith to grow in the knowledge, not of works, but of Christ Jesus, who suffered and rose for him, as Peter teaches in the last chapter of his first Epistle, I Pet. [5:10]. No other work makes a Christian. . . .

Let this suffice concerning the inner man, his liberty, and the source of his liberty, the righteousness of faith. He needs neither laws nor good works but, on the contrary, is injured by them if he believes that he is justified by them.

Now let us turn to the second part,

the outer man. Here we shall answer all those who, offended by the word "faith" and by all that has been said, now ask, "If faith does all things and is alone sufficient unto righteousness, why then are good works commanded? We will take our ease and do no works and be content with faith." I answer: not so, you wicked men, not so. That would indeed be proper if we were wholly inner and perfectly spiritual men. But such we shall be only at the last day, the day of the resurrection of the dead. As long as we live in the flesh we only begin to make some progress in that which shall be perfected in the future life. For this reason the Apostle in Rom. 8 [:23] calls all that we attain in this life "the first fruits of the Spirit" because we shall indeed receive the greater portion, even the fulness of the Spirit, in the future. This is the place to assert that which was said above, namely, that a Christian is the servant of all and made subject to all. Insofar as he is free he does no works, but insofar as he is a servant he does all kinds of works. How this is possible we shall see.

Although, as I have said, a man is abundantly and sufficiently justified by faith inwardly, in his spirit, and so has all that he needs, except insofar as this faith and these riches must grow from day to day even to the future life; yet he remains in this mortal life on earth. In this life he must control his own body and have dealings with men. Here the works begin; here a man cannot enjoy leisure; here he must indeed take care to discipline his body by fastings, watchings, labors, and other reasonable discipline and to subject it to the Spirit so that it will obey and conform to the inner man and faith and not revolt against faith and hinder the inner man, as it is the nature of the body to do if it is not held in check. The inner man, who by faith is created in the image of God, is both joyful and happy because of Christ in whom so many benefits are conferred upon him; and therefore it is his one occupation to serve God joyfully and without thought of gain, in love that is not constrained. . . .

Our faith in Christ does not free us from works but from false opinions concerning works, that is, from the foolish presumption that justification is acquired by works. Faith redeems, corrects, and preserves our consciences so that we know that righteousness does not consist in works, although works neither can nor ought to be wanting; just as we cannot be without food and drink and all the works of this mortal body, yet our righteousness is not in them, but in faith; and yet those works of the body are not to be despised or neglected on that account. In this world we are bound by the needs of our bodily life, but we are not righteous because of them. . . .

For this reason, although we should boldly resist those teachers of traditions and sharply censure the laws of the popes by means of which they plunder the people of God, yet we must spare the timid multitude whom those impious tyrants hold captive by means of these laws until they are set free. Therefore fight strenuously against the wolves, but for the sheep and not also against the sheep. This you will do if you inveigh against the laws and the lawgivers and at the same time observe the laws with the weak so that they will not be offended, until they also recognize tyranny and understand their freedom. If you wish to use your freedom, do so in secret, as Paul says, Rom. 14 [:22], "The faith that you have, keep between yourself and God"; but take care not to use your freedom in the sight of the weak. On the other hand, use your freedom constantly and consistently in the sight of and despite the tyrants and the stubborn so that they also may learn that they are impious, that their laws are of no avail for righteousness, and that they had no right to set them up. . . .

THOMAS HOBBES

Thomas Hobbes (1588–1679) was born in Malmesbury, England, the year of the Armada. He lived through four reigns, a long and bitter civil war, and Cromwell's Protectorate, and finally died, at the age of 91, after the restoration of the Stuart monarchy. His views, especially in ethics and politics, were largely influenced by the civil and religious conflicts that he witnessed. He concluded that men are essentially egocentric and shortsighted, and that this combination of qualities dooms them to destroy themselves unless there is a strong central authority with the power to impose order and obedience. In his cynical estimate of human nature, Hobbes will remind the reader of Machiavelli. But Hobbes was deeply influenced by the new physical theories which were being developed by Galileo and others, and he attempted to formulate a whole metaphysics based on the proposition that only matter and motion exist. Hence, instead of a mere series of aphorisms on power and Realpolitik, *Hobbes's* Leviathan *(1651) is a complete philosophy of naturalism.*

*Leviathan**

OF THE INTERIOR BEGINNINGS OF VOLUNTARY MOTIONS COMMONLY CALLED THE PASSIONS, AND THE SPEECHES BY WHICH THEY ARE EXPRESSED

There be in animals two sorts of *motions* peculiar to them: one called *vital,* begun in generation and continued without interruption through their whole life—such as are the *course* of the *blood,* the *pulse,* the *breathing,* the *concoction, nutrition, excretion,* etc.—to which motions there needs no help of imagination; the other is *animal motion,* otherwise called *voluntary motion* —as to *go,* to *speak,* to *move* any of our limbs in such manner as is first fancied in our minds. That sense is motion in the organs and interior parts of man's body caused by the action of the things we see, hear, etc., and that fancy is but the relics of the same motion remaining after sense, has been already said. And because

* Thomas Hobbes, *Leviathan,* based on the Molesworth edition, London, 1841. Deletions are not noted in the text.

going, speaking, and the like voluntary motions depend always upon a precedent thought of *whither, which way,* and *what,* it is evident that the imagination is the first internal beginning of all voluntary motion. And although unstudied men do not conceive any motion at all to be there where the thing moved is invisible or the space it is moved in is, for the shortness of it, insensible, yet that does not hinder but that such motions are. For let a space be never so little, that which is moved over a greater space, whereof that little one is part, must first be moved over that. These small beginnings of motion within the body of man, before they appear in walking, speaking, striking, and other visible actions, are commonly called ENDEAVOR.

This endeavor, when it is toward something which causes it, is called APPETITE or DESIRE, the latter being the general name and the other oftentimes restrained to signify the desire of food, namely *hunger* and *thirst.* And when the endeavor is fromward something, it is generally called AVERSION. These words, *appetite* and *aversion,* we have from the Latins; and they both of them signify the motions, one of approaching, the other of retiring. For nature itself does often press upon men those truths which afterwards, when they look for somewhat beyond nature, they stumble at. For the Schools find in mere appetite to go or move no actual motion at all; but because some motion they must acknowledge, they call it metaphorical motion, which is but an absurd speech, for though words may be called metaphorical, bodies and motions cannot.

That which men desire they are also said to LOVE, and to HATE those things for which they have aversion. So that desire and love are the same thing, save that by desire we always signify the absence of the object, by love most commonly the presence of the same. So also by aversion we signify the absence, and by hate the presence of the object.

Of appetites and aversions, some are born with men, as appetite of food, appetite of excretion, and exoneration, which may also and more properly be called aversions from somewhat they feel in their bodies; and some other appetites, not many. The rest, which are appetites of particular things, proceed from experience and trial of their effects upon themselves or other men. For of things we know not at all, or believe not to be, we can have no further desire than to taste and try. But aversion we have for things, not only which we know have hurt us, but also that we do not know whether they will hurt us or not.

Those things which we neither desire nor hate we are said to *contemn,* CONTEMPT being nothing else but an immobility or contumacy of the heart in resisting the action of certain things; and proceeding from that the heart is already moved otherwise by other more potent objects or from want of experience of them.

And because the constitution of a man's body is in continual mutation, it is impossible that all the same things should always cause in him the same appetites and aversions; much less can all men consent in the desire of almost any one and the same object.

But whatsoever is the object of any man's appetite or desire, that is it which he for his part calls *good;* and the object of his hate and aversion, *evil;* and of his contempt, *vile* and *inconsiderable.* For these words of good, evil, and contemptible are ever used with relation to the person that uses them, there being nothing simply and absolutely so, nor any common rule of good and evil to be taken from the nature of the objects themselves—but from the person of the man, where there is no commonwealth, or, in a commonwealth, from the person that represents it, or from an arbitrator or judge whom men disagreeing shall by consent set up and make his sentence the rule thereof.

As in sense that which is really within us is only motion caused by the action of external objects, but in appearance to the sight light and color, to the ear sound, to the nostril odor, etc., so when the action of the same object is continued from the eyes, ears, and other organs to the heart, the real effect there is nothing but motion or endeavor, which consists in appetite or aversion to or from the object moving. But the appearance or sense of that motion is that we either call *delight* or *trouble of mind.*

This motion, which is called appetite, and for the appearance of it *delight* and *pleasure,* seems to be a corroboration of vital motion and a help thereunto.

Pleasure, therefore, or *delight* is the appearance or sense of good; and *molestation* or *displeasure* the appearance or sense of evil. And consequently all appetite, desire, and love is accompanied with some delight more or less, and all hatred and aversion with more or less displeasure and offense.

Of pleasures or delights, some arise from the sense of an object present, and those may be called *pleasures of sense*—the word *sensual,* as it is used by those only that condemn them, having no place till there be laws. Of this kind are all onerations and exonerations of the body, as also all that is pleasant in the *sight, hearing, smell, taste,* or *touch.* Others arise from the expectation that proceeds from foresight of the end or consequence of things, whether those things in the sense please or displease. And these are *pleasures of the mind* of him that draws those consequences, and are generally called JOY. In the like manner, displeasures are some in the sense, and called PAIN; others in the expectation of consequences, and are called GRIEF.

These simple passions called *appetite, desire, love, aversion, hate, joy,* and *grief* have their names for divers considerations diversified. As first, when they one succeed another, they are diversely called from the opinion men have of the likelihood of attaining what they desire. Secondly, from the object loved or hated. Thirdly, from the consideration of many of them together. Fourthly, from the alteration or succession itself.

For *appetite* with an opinion of attaining is called HOPE. The same without such opinion, DESPAIR. *Aversion* with opinion of HURT from the object, FEAR.

The same with hope of avoiding that hurt by resistance, COURAGE.

Sudden *courage,* ANGER.

Constant *hope,* CONFIDENCE of ourselves.

Constant *despair,* DIFFIDENCE of ourselves.

Anger for great hurt done to another when we conceive the same to be done by injury, INDIGNATION.

Desire of good to another, BENEVOLENCE, GOOD WILL, CHARITY. If to man generally, GOOD NATURE.

Desire of riches, COVETOUSNESS, a name used always in signification of blame because men contending for them are displeased with one another attaining them, though the desire in itself be to be blamed or allowed according to the means by which these riches are sought.

Desire of office of precedence, AMBITION, a name used also in the worse sense for the reason before mentioned.

Desire to know why and how, CURIOSITY, such as is in no living creature but *man;* so that man is distinguished, not only by his reason, but also by this singular passion from other *animals,* in whom the appetite of food and other pleasures of sense, by predominance, take away the care of knowing causes, which is a lust of the mind that, by a perseverence of delight in the continual and indefatigable generation of knowledge, exceeds the short vehemence of any carnal pleasure.

Fear of power invisible, feigned by the mind or imagined from tales publicly allowed, RELIGION; not allowed, SUPERSTI-

TION. And when the power imagined is truly such as we imagine, TRUE RELIGION.

When in the mind of man appetites and aversions, hopes and fears concerning one and the same thing arise alternately, and divers good and evil consequences of the doing or omitting the thing propounded come successively into our thoughts, so that sometimes we have an appetite to it, sometimes an aversion from it, sometimes hope to be able to do it, sometimes despair or fear to attempt it—the whole sum of desires, aversions, hopes, and fears continued till the thing be either done or thought impossible is that we call DELIBERATION.

Therefore of things past there is no *deliberation,* because manifestly impossible to be changed; nor of things known to be impossible, or thought so, because men know or think such deliberation vain. But of things impossible which we think possible, we may deliberate, not knowing it is in vain. And it is called *deliberation* because it is a putting an end to the *liberty* we had of doing or omitting according to our own appetite or aversion.

This alternate succession of appetites, aversions, hopes, and fears is no less in other living creatures than in man, and therefore beasts also deliberate.

Every *deliberation* is then said to *end* when that whereof they deliberate is either done or thought impossible, because till then we retain the liberty of doing or omitting according to our appetite or aversion.

In *deliberation,* the last appetite or aversion immediately adhering to the action or to the omission thereof is that we call the WILL—the act, not the faculty, of *willing.* And beasts that have *deliberation* must necessarily also have *will.* The definition of the *will* given commonly by the Schools, that it is a *rational appetite,* is not good. For if it were, then could there be no voluntary act against reason. For a *voluntary act* is that which proceeds from the *will,* and no other. But if instead of a rational appetite we shall say an appetite resulting from a precedent deliberation, then the definition is the same that I have given here. *Will,* therefore, *is the last appetite in deliberating.* And though we say in common discourse a man had a will once to do a thing that nevertheless he forbore to do, yet that is properly but an inclination which makes no action voluntary, because the action depends not of it but of the last inclination or appetite. For if the intervenient appetites make any action voluntary, then by the same reason all intervenient aversions should make the same action involuntary; and so one and the same action should be both voluntary and involuntary.

By this it is manifest that not only actions that have their beginning from covetousness, ambition, lust, or other appetites to the thing propounded, but also those that have their beginning from aversion or fear of those consequences that follow the omission, are *voluntary actions*

Continual success in obtaining those things which a man from time to time desires—that is to say, continual prospering —is that men call FELICITY; I mean the felicity of this life. For there is no such thing as perpetual tranquility of mind while we live here, because life itself is but motion and can never be without desire, nor without fear, no more than without sense. What kind of felicity God has ordained to them that devoutly honor him, a man shall no sooner know than enjoy, being joys that now are as incomprehensible as the word of Schoolmen, *beatifical vision,* is unintelligible.

OF THE VIRTUES COMMONLY CALLED INTELLECTUAL AND THEIR CONTRARY DEFECTS

Virtue generally, in all sorts of subjects, is somewhat that is valued for eminence, and consists in comparison. For if all things were equal in all men, nothing would be prized.

OF POWER, WORTH, DIGNITY, HONOR, AND WORTHINESS

The POWER of a man, to take it universally, is his present means to obtain some future apparent good, and is either *original* or *instrumental.*

Natural power is the eminence of the faculties of body or mind, as extraordinary strength, form, prudence, arts, eloquence, liberality, nobility. *Instrumental* are those powers which, acquired by these or by fortune, are means and instruments to acquire more, as riches, reputation, friends, and the secret working of God, which men call good luck. For the nature of power is in this point like to fame, increasing as it proceeds; or like the motion of heavy bodies, which, the further they go, make still the more haste.

The greatest of human powers is that which is componded of the powers of most men united by consent in one person, natural or civil, that has the use of all their powers depending on his will, such as is the power of a commonwealth; or depending on the wills of each particular, such as is the power of a faction or of divers factions leagued. Therefore to have servants is power; to have friends is power: for they are strengths united.

Also riches joined with liberality is power, because it procures friends and servants; without liberality, not so, because in this case they defend not, but expose men to envy, as a prey.

Reputation of power is power, because it draws with it the adherence of those that need protection.

So is reputation of love of a man's country, called popularity, for the same reason.

Also, what quality soever makes a man beloved or feared of many, or the reputation of such quality, is power, because it is a means to have the assistance and service of many.

Good success is power, because it makes reputation of wisdom or good fortune, which makes men either fear him or rely on him.

Affability of men already in power is increase of power, because it gains love.

Reputation of prudence in the conduct of peace or war is power, because to prudent men we commit the government of ourselves more willingly than to others.

Nobility is power, not in all places, but only in those commonwealths where it has privileges, for in such privileges consists their power.

Eloquence is power, because it is seeming prudence.

Form is power, because, being a promise of good, it recommends men to the favor of women and strangers.

The *value* or WORTH of a man is, as of all other things, his price—that is to say, so much as would be given for the use of his power—and therefore is not absolute but a thing dependent on the need and judgment of another. An able conductor of soldiers is of great price in time of war present or imminent, but in peace not so. A learned and uncorrupt judge is much worth in time of peace, but not so much in war. And as in other things so in men, not the seller but the buyer determines the price. For let a man, as most men do, rate themselves at the highest value they can, yet their true value is no more than it is esteemed by others.

The manifestation of the value we set on one another is that which is commonly called honoring and dishonoring. To value a man at a high rate is to *honor* him, at a low rate is to *dishonor* him. But high and low, in this case, is to be understood by comparison to the rate that each man sets on himself.

The public worth of a man, which is the value set on him by the commonwealth, is that which men commonly call DIGNITY. And this value of him by the commonwealth is understood by offices of command, judicature, public employment, or by names and titles introduced for distinction of such value.

To pray to another for aid of any kind is to HONOR, because a sign we have an opinion he has power to help; and the more difficult the aid is, the more is the honor.

To obey is to honor, because no man obeys them whom they think have no power to help or hurt them. And consequently to disobey is to *dishonor*.

WORTHINESS is a thing different from the worth or value of a man, and also from his merit or desert, and consists in a particular power or ability for that whereof he is said to be worthy; which particular ability is usually named FITNESS or *aptitude*.

For he is worthiest to be a commander, to be a judge, or to have any other charge that is best fitted with the qualities required to the well discharging of it; and worthiest of riches that has the qualities most requisite for the well using of them—any of which qualities being absent, one may nevertheless be a worthy man, and valuable for something else.

OF THE DIFFERENCE OF MANNERS

By MANNERS I mean not here decency of behavior—as how one should salute another, or how a man should wash his mouth or pick his teeth before company, and such other points of the *small morals*—but those qualities of mankind that concern their living together in peace and unity. To which end we are to consider that the felicity of this life consists not in the repose of a mind satisfied. For there is no such *finis ultimus*, utmost aim, nor *summum bonum*, greatest good, as is spoken of in the books of the old moral philosophers. Nor can a man any more live whose desires are at an end than he whose senses and imaginations are at a stand. Felicity is a continual progress of the desire from one object to another, the attaining of the former being still but the way to the latter. The cause whereof is that the object of man's desire is not to enjoy once only and for one instant of time, but to assure forever the way of his future desire. And therefore the voluntary actions and inclinations of all men tend, not only to the procuring, but also to the assuring of a contented life; and differ only in the way, which arises partly from the diversity of passions in divers men, and partly from the difference of the knowledge or opinion each one has of the causes which produce the effect desired. So that, in the first place, I put for a general inclination of all mankind a perpetual and restless desire of power after power that ceases only in death. And the cause of this is not always that a man hopes for a more intensive delight than he has already attained to, or that he cannot be content with a moderate power, but because he cannot assure the power and means to live well which he has present without the acquisition of more. And from hence it is that kings, whose power is greatest, turn their endeavors to the assuring it at home by laws or abroad by wars; and when that is done, there succeeds a new desire—in some, of fame from new conquest; in others, of ease and sensual pleasure; in others, of admiration or being flattered for excellence in some art or other ability of the mind.

Competition of riches, honor, command, or other power inclines to contention, enmity, and war, because the way of one competitor to the attaining of his desire is to kill, subdue, supplant, or repel the other. Particularly, competition of praise inclines to a reverence of antiquity. For men contend with the living, not with the dead—to these ascribing more than due, that they may obscure the glory of the other.

Desire of ease and sensual delight disposes men to obey a common power, because by such desires a man does abandon the protection that might be hoped for from his own industry and labor. Fear of death and wounds disposes to the same, and for the same reason. On the contrary, needy men and hardy, not contented with their present condition, as also all men that are ambitious of military command, are inclined to continue the causes of war, and to stir up trouble and sedition; for there is no honor military but by war, nor any such hope to mend an ill game as by causing a new shuffle.

Desire of knowledge and arts of peace inclines men to obey a common power, for such desire contains a desire of leisure, and consequently protection from some other power than their own.

Desire of praise disposes to laudable actions, such as please them whose judgment they value; for of those men whom we contemn, we contemn also the praises. Desire of fame after death does the same. And though after death there be no sense of the praise given us on earth, as being joys that are either swallowed up in the unspeakable joys of heaven or extinguished in the extreme torments of hell, yet is not such fame vain; because men have a present delight therein from the foresight of it and of the benefit that may redound thereby to their posterity, which, though they now see not, yet they imagine; and anything that is pleasure to the sense, the same also is pleasure in the imagination.

Want of science—that is, ignorance, of causes—disposes, or rather constrains, a man to rely on the advice and authority of others. For all men whom the truth concerns, if they rely not on their own, must rely on the opinion of some other whom they think wiser than themselves, and see not why he should deceive them.

Ignorance of the signification of words, which is want of understanding, disposes men to take on trust, not only the truth they know not, but also the errors and, which is more, the nonsense of them they trust; for neither error nor nonsense can, without a perfect understanding of words, be detected.

From the same it proceeds that men give different names to one and the same thing from the difference of their own passions: as they that approve a private opinion call it opinion, but they that mislike it, heresy; and yet heresy signifies no more than private opinion, but has only a greater tincture of choler.

Ignorance of natural causes disposes a man to credulity, so as to believe many times impossibilities; for such know nothing to the contrary but that they may be true, being unable to detect the impossibility. And credulity, because men like to be hearkened unto in company, disposes them to lying, so that ignorance itself without malice is able to make a man both to believe lies and tell them—and sometimes also to invent them.

Anxiety for the future time disposes men to inquire into the causes of things, because the knowledge of them makes men the better able to order the present to their best advantage.

And they that make little or no inquiry into the natural causes of things, yet from the fear that proceeds from the ignorance itself of what it is that has the power to do them much good or harm, are inclined to suppose, and feign unto themselves, several kinds of powers invisible; and to stand in awe of their own imaginations; and in time of distress to invoke them; as also in the time of an expected good success to give them thanks; making the creatures of their own fancy their gods. By which means it has come to pass that, from the innumerable variety of fancy, men have created in the world innumerable sorts of gods. And this fear of things invisible is the natural seed of that which everyone in himself calls religion, and in them that worship, or fear that power otherwise than they do, superstition.

And this seed of religion having been

observed by many, some of those that have observed it have been inclined thereby to nourish, dress, and form it into laws; and to add to it of their own invention any opinion of the causes of future events by which they thought they should be best able to govern others and make unto themselves the greatest use of their powers.

OF RELIGION

Seeing there are no signs nor fruit of *religion* but in man only, there is no cause to doubt but that the seed of *religion* is also only in man, and consists in some peculiar quality, or at least in some eminent degree thereof, not to be found in any other living creatures.

And first, it is peculiar to the nature of man to be inquisitive into the causes of the events they see—some more, some less, but all men so much as to be curious in the search of the causes of their own good and evil fortune.

Secondly, upon the sight of anything that has a beginning, to think also it had a cause which determined the same to begin then when it did rather than sooner or later.

Thirdly, whereas there is no other felicity of beasts but the enjoying of their quotidian food, ease, and lusts—as having little or no foresight of the time to come for want of observation and memory of the order, consequence, and dependence of the things they see—man observes how one event has been produced by another, and remembers in them antecedence and consequence; and when he cannot assure himself of the true causes of things (for the causes of good and evil fortune for the most part are invisible), he supposes causes of them, either such as his own fancy suggests, or trusts the authority of other men such as he thinks to be his friends and wiser than himself.

The two first make anxiety. For being assured that there be causes of all things that have arrived hitherto or shall arrive hereafter, it is impossible for a man who continually endeavors to secure himself against the evil he fears and procure the good he desires not to be in a perpetual solicitude of the time to come, so that every man, especially those that are over provident, are in a state like to that of Prometheus. For as Prometheus—which interpreted is *the prudent man*—was bound to the hill Caucasus, a place of large prospect, where an eagle feeding on his liver devoured in the day as much as was repaired in the night, so that man which looks too far before him in the care of future time has his heart all the day long, gnawed on by fear of death, poverty, or other calamity, and has no repose nor pause of his anxiety but in sleep.

This perpetual fear, always accompanying mankind in the ignorance of causes, as it were in the dark, must needs have for object something. And therefore when there is nothing to be seen there is nothing to accuse, either of their good or evil fortune, but some *power* or agent *invisible;* in which sense perhaps it was that some of the old poets said that the gods were at first created by human fear; which, spoken of the gods—that is to say, of the many gods of the Gentiles—is very true. But the acknowledging of one God, eternal, infinite, and omnipotent, may more easily be derived from the desire men have to know the causes of natural bodies and their several virtues and operations than from the fear of what was to befall them in time to come. For he that from any effect he sees come to pass should reason to the next and immediate cause thereof, and from thence to the cause of that cause, and plunge himself profoundly in the pursuit of causes, shall at last come to this: that there must be, as even the heathen philosophers confessed, one first mover—that is, a first and an eternal cause of all things—which is that which men mean by the name of God; and all this without thought of their fortune, the solicitude whereof both inclines to fear and hinders them from the search of the causes of other things, and thereby gives occasion of feigning of as many gods as there be men that feign them.

And for the matter or substance of the invisible agents, so fancied, they could not by natural cogitation fall upon any other conceit but that it was the same with that of the soul of man; and that the soul of man was of the same substance with that which appears in a dream to one that sleeps, or in a looking glass to one that is awake; which men, not knowing that such apparitions are nothing else but creatures of the fancy, think to be real and external substances, and therefore call them ghosts; as the Latins called them *imagines* and *umbrae,* and thought them spirits—that is, thin aerial bodies—and those invisible agents, which they feared, to be like them, save that they appear and vanish when they please. But the opinion that such spirits were incorporeal or immaterial could never enter into the mind of any man by nature because, though men may put together words of contradictory signification, as *spirit* and *incorporeal,* yet they can never have the imagination of anything answering to them; and therefore men that by their own meditation arrive to the acknowledgment of one infinite, omnipotent, and eternal God choose rather to confess he is incomprehensible and above their understanding than to define his nature by *spirit incorporeal* and then confess their definition to be unintelligible; or if they give him such a title, it is not *dogmatically,* with intention to make the divine nature understood, but *piously,* to honor him with attributes of significations as remote as they can from the grossness of bodies visible.

Then, for the way by which they think these invisible agents wrought their effects—that is to say, what immediate causes they used in bringing things to pass —men that know not what it is that we call *causing*—that is, almost all men—have no other rule to guess by but by observing and remembering what they have seen to precede the like effect at some other time or times before, without seeing between the antecedent and subsequent event any dependence or connection at all; and therefore from the like things past they expect the like things to come, and hope for good or evil luck, superstitiously, from things that have no part at all in the causing of it. They attribute their fortune to a stander by, to a lucky or unlucky place, to words spoken, especially if the name of God be among them—as charming and conjuring (the liturgy of witches)—insomuch as to believe they have power to turn a stone into bread, bread into a man, or anything into anything.

Thirdly, for the worship which naturally men exhibit to powers invisible, it can be no other but such expressions of their reverence as they would use toward men: gifts, petitions, thanks, submission of body, considerate addresses, sober behavior, premeditated words, swearing—that is, assuring one another of their promises—by invoking them. Beyond that reason suggests nothing, but leaves them either to rest there or, for further ceremonies, to rely on those they believe to be wiser than themselves.

Lastly, concerning how these invisible powers declare to men the things which shall hereafter come to pass, especially concerning their good or evil fortune in general, or good or ill success in any particular undertaking, men are naturally at a stand; save that using to conjecture of the time to come by the time past, they are very apt, not only to take casual things, after one or two encounters, for prognostics of the like encounter ever after, but also to believe the like prognostics from other men of whom they have once conceived a good opinion.

And in these four things—opinion of ghosts, ignorance of second causes, devotion toward what men fear, and taking of things casual for prognostics—consists the natural seed of *religion,* which, by reason of the different fancies, judgments, and passions of several men, has grown up into ceremonies so different that those which are used by one man are for the most part ridiculous to another.

From the propagation of religion it is not hard to understand the causes of the resolution of the same into its first seeds or principles—which are only an opinion of a deity and powers invisible and supernatural—that can never be so abolished out of human nature but that new religions may again be made to spring out of them by the culture of such men as for such purpose are in reputation.

For seeing all formed religion is founded at first upon the faith which a multitude has in some one person, whom they believe not only to be a wise man and to labor to procure their happiness, but also to be a holy man to whom God himself vouchsafes to declare his will supernaturally, it follows necessarily when they that have the government of religion shall come to have either the wisdom of those men, their sincerity, or their love suspected, or when they shall be unable to show any probable token of divine revelation, that the religion which they desire to uphold must be suspected likewise, and, without the fear of the civil sword, contradicted and rejected.

That which takes away the reputation of wisdom in him that forms a religion or adds to it when it is already formed is the enjoining of a belief of contradictories; for both parts of a contradiction cannot possibly be true, and therefore to enjoin the belief of them is an argument of ignorance, which detects the author in that and discredits him in all things else he shall propound as from revelation supernatural; which revelation a man may indeed have of many things above, but of nothing against natural reason.

That which takes away the reputation of sincerity is the doing or saying of such things as appear to be signs that what they require other men to believe is not believed by themselves; all which doings or sayings are therefore called scandalous, because they be stumbling blocks that make men to fall in the way of religion—as injustice, cruelty, profaneness, avarice, and luxury. For who can believe that he that does ordinarily such actions as proceed from any of these roots believes there is any such invisible power to be feared as he affrights other men withal for lesser faults?

That which takes away the reputation of love is the being detected of private ends, as when the belief they require of others conduces or seems to conduce to the acquiring of dominion, riches, dignity, or secure pleasure to themselves only or specially. For that which men reap benefit by to themselves they are thought to do for their own sakes, and not for love of others.

Lastly, the testimony that men can render of divine calling can be no other than the operation of miracles, or true prophecy, which also is a miracle, or extraordinary felicity. And therefore, to those points of religion which have been received from them that did such miracles, those that are added by such as approve not their calling by some miracle obtain no greater belief than what the custom and laws of the places in which they be educated have wrought into them. For as in natural things men of judgment require natural signs and arguments, so in supernatural things they require signs supernatural, which are miracles, before they consent inwardly and from their hearts.

OF THE NATURAL CONDITION OF MANKIND AS CONCERNING THEIR FELICITY AND MISERY

Nature has made men so equal in the faculties of the body and mind as that, though there be found one man sometimes manifestly stronger in body or of quicker mind than another, yet, when all is reckoned together, the difference between man and man is not so considerable as that one man can thereupon claim to himself any benefit to which another may not pretend as well as he. For as to the strength of body, the weakest has strength enough to kill the strongest, either by secret machination or by confederacy with others that are in the same danger with himself.

And as to the faculties of the mind, setting aside the arts grounded upon words, and especially that skill of proceeding upon general and infallible rules called science—which very few have and but in few things, as being not a native faculty born with us, nor attained, as prudence, while we look after somewhat else—I find yet a greater equality among men than that of strength. For prudence is but experience, which equal time equally bestows on all men in those things they equally apply themselves unto. That which may perhaps make such equality incredible is but a vain conceit of one's own wisdom, which almost all men think they have in greater degree than the vulgar—that is, than all men but themselves and a few others whom, by fame or for concurring with themselves, they approve. For such is the nature of men that howsoever they may acknowledge many others to be more witty or more eloquent or more learned, yet they will hardly believe there be many so wise as themselves; for they see their own wit at hand and other men's at a distance. But this proves rather that men are in that point equal than unequal. For there is not ordinarily a greater sign of equal distribution of anything than that every man is contented with his share.

From this equality of ability arises equality of hope in the attaining of our ends. And therefore if any two men desire the same thing, which nevertheless they cannot both enjoy, they become enemies; and in the way to their end, which is principally their own conservation, and sometimes their delectation only, endeavor to destroy or subdue one another. And from hence it comes to pass that where an invader has no more to fear than another man's single power, if one plant, sow, build, or possess a convenient seat, others may probably be expected to come prepared with forces united to dispossess and deprive him, not only of the fruit of his labor, but also of his life or liberty. And the invader again is in the like danger of another.

So that in the nature of man we find three principal causes of quarrel: first, competition; secondly, diffidence; thirdly, glory.

The first makes men invade for gain, the second for safety, and the third for reputation. The first use violence to make themselves masters of other men's persons, wives, children, and cattle; the second, to defend them; the third, for trifles, as a word, a smile, a different opinion, and any other sign of undervalue, either direct in their persons or by reflection in their kindred, their friends, their nation, their profession, or their name.

Hereby it is manifest that, during the time men live without a common power to keep them all in awe, they are in that condition which is called war, and such a war as is of every man against every man. For WAR consists not in battle only, or the act of fighting, but in a tract of time wherein the will to contend by battle is sufficiently known; and therefore the notion of *time* is to be considered in the nature of war as it is in the nature of weather. For as the nature of foul weather lies not in a shower or two of rain but in an inclination thereto of many days together, so the nature of war consists not in actual fighting but in the known disposition thereto during all the time there is no assurance to the contrary.

In such condition there is no place for industry, because the fruit thereof is uncertain: and consequently no culture of the earth; no navigation nor use of the commodities that may be imported by sea; no commodious building; no instruments of moving and removing such things as require much force; no knowledge of the face of the earth; no account of time; no arts; no letters; no society; and, which is worst of all, continual fear and danger of violent death; and the life of man solitary, poor, nasty, brutish, and short.

To this war of every man against every man, this also is consequent: that nothing can be unjust. The notions of right and wrong, justice and injustice, have there no place. Where there is no common power, there is no law; where no law, no injustice. Force and fraud are in war the two cardinal virtues. Justice and injustice are none of the faculties neither of the body nor mind. If they were, they might be in a man that were alone in the world, as well as his senses and passions. They are qualities that relate to men in society, not in solitude. It is consequent also to the same condition that there be no propriety, no dominion, no *mine* and *thine* distinct; but only that to be every man's that he can get, and for so long as he can keep it. And thus much for the ill condition which man by mere nature is actually placed in, though with a possibility to come out of it consisting partly in the passions, partly in his reason.

The passions that incline men to peace are fear of death, desire of such things as are necessary to commodious living, and a hope by their industry to obtain them. And reason suggests convenient articles of peace, upon which men may be drawn to agreement. These articles are they which otherwise are called the Laws of Nature, whereof I shall speak more particularly in the two following chapters.

OF THE FIRST AND SECOND NATURAL LAWS, AND OF CONTRACTS

The RIGHT OF NATURE, which writers commonly call *jus naturale,* is the liberty each man has to use his own power, as he will himself, for the preservation of his own nature—that is to say, of his own life—and consequently of doing anything which, in his own judgment and reason, he shall conceive to be the aptest means thereunto.

By LIBERTY is understood, according to the proper signification of the word, the absence of external impediments; which impediments may oft take away part of a man's power to do what he would, but cannot hinder him from using the power left him according as his judgment and reason shall dictate to him.

A LAW OF NATURE, *lex naturalis,* is a precept or general rule, found out by reason, by which a man is forbidden to do that which is destructive of his life or takes away the means of preserving the same and to omit that by which he thinks it may be best preserved. For though they that speak of this subject use to confound *jus* and *lex, right* and *law,* yet they ought to be distinguished; because RIGHT consists in liberty to do or to forbear, whereas LAW determines and binds to one of them; so that law and right differ as much as obligation and liberty, which in one and the same matter are inconsistent. And because the condition of man, as has been declared in the precedent chapter, is a condition of war of every one against every one—in which case everyone is governed by his own reason and there is nothing he can make use of that may not be a help unto him in preserving his life against his enemies—it follows that in such a condition every man has a right to everything, even to one another's body. And therefore, as long as this natural right of every man to everything endures, there can be no security to any man, how strong or wise soever he be, of living out the time which nature ordinarily allows men to live. And consequently it is a precept or general rule of reason *that every man ought to endeavor peace, as far as he has hope of obtaining it; and when he cannot obtain it, that he may seek and use all helps and advantages of war.* The first branch of which rule contains the first and fundamental law of nature, which is *to seek peace and follow it.* The second, the sum of the right of nature, which is, *by all means we can to defend ourselves.*

From this fundamental law of nature, by which men are commanded to endeavor peace, is derived this second law: *that a man be willing, when others are so too, as far forth as for peace and defense of himself he shall think it necessary, to lay down this right to all things, and be contented with so much liberty against other men as he would allow other men against himself.* For as long as every man holds this right of doing anything he likes, so long are all men in the condition of war. But if other men will not lay down their right as well as he, then there is no reason for anyone to divest himself of his, for that were to expose himself to prey, which no man is bound to, rather than to dispose himself to peace. This is that law of the gospel: *whatsoever you require that others should do to you, that do ye to them.* And that law of all men, *quod tibi fieri non vis, alteri ne feceris.*

To *lay down* a man's *right* to anything is to *divest* himself of the *liberty* of hindering another of the benefit of his own right to the same. For he that renounces or passes away his right gives not to any other man a right which he had not before—because there is nothing to which every man had not right by nature—but only stands out of his way, that he may enjoy his own original right without hindrance from him, not without hindrance from another. So that the effect which redounds to one man by another man's defect of right is but so much diminution of impediments to the use of his own right original. Right is laid aside either by simply renouncing it or by transferring it to another. By *simply* RENOUNCING, when he cares not to whom the benefit thereof redounds. By TRANSFERRING, when he intends the benefit thereof to some certain person or persons. And when a man has in either manner abandoned or granted away his right, then he is said to be OBLIGED OR BOUND not to hinder those to whom such right is granted or abandoned from the benefit of it; and that he *ought,* and it is his DUTY, not to make void that voluntary act of his own; and that such hindrance is INJUSTICE and INJURY as being *sine jure,* the right being before renounced or transferred. So that *injury* or *injustice* in the controversies of the world is somewhat like to that which in the disputations of scholars is called *absurdity.* For as it is there called an absurdity to contradict what one maintained in the beginning, so in the world it is called injustice and injury voluntarily to undo that which from the beginning he had voluntarily done.

Whensoever a man transfers his right or renounces it, it is either in consideration of some right reciprocally transferred to himself or for some other good he hopes for thereby. For it is a voluntary act; and of the voluntary acts of every man, the object is some *good to himself.* And therefore there be some rights which no man can be understood by any words or other signs to have abandoned or transferred. As, first, a man cannot lay down the right of resisting them that assault him by force to take away his life, because he cannot be understood to aim thereby at any good to himself. The same may be said of wounds and chains and imprisonment, both because there is no benefit consequent to such patience as there is to the patience of suffering another to be wounded or imprisoned, as also because a man cannot tell, when he sees men proceed against him by violence, whether they intend his death or not. And, lastly, the motive and end for which this renouncing and transferring of right is introduced is nothing else but the security of a man's person in his life and in the means of so preserving life as not to be weary of it. And therefore if a man by words or other signs seem to despoil himself of the end for which those signs were intended, he is not to be understood as if he meant it or that it was his will, but that he was ignorant of how such words and actions were to be interpreted.

The mutual transferring of right is that which men call CONTRACT.

When the transferring of right is not mutual, but one of the parties transfers in hope to gain thereby friendship or service from another or from his friends, or in hope to gain the reputation of charity or magnanimity, or to deliver his mind from the pain of compassion, or in hope of reward in heaven—this is not contract but GIFT, FREE GIFT, GRACE, which words signify one and the same thing.

If a covenant be made wherein neither of the parties perform presently but trust one another, in the condition of mere nature, which is a condition of war of every man against every man, upon any reasonable suspicion, it is void; but if there be a common power set over them both, with right and force sufficient to compel performance, it is not void.

OF OTHER LAWS OF NATURE

From that law of nature by which we are obliged to transfer to another such rights as, being retained, hinder the peace of mankind, there follows a third, which is this: *that men perform their covenants made;* without which covenants are in vain and but empty words, and, the right of all men to all things remaining, we are still in the condition of war.

And in this law of nature consists the fountain and original of JUSTICE. For where no covenant has preceded there has no right been transferred, and every man has right to every thing; and consequently no action can be unjust. But when a covenant is made, then to break it is *unjust;* and the definition of INJUSTICE is no other than *the not performance of covenant.* And whatsoever is not unjust is *just.*

Before the names of just and unjust can have place, there must be some coercive power to compel men equally to the performance of their covenants by the terror of some punishment greater than the benefit they expect by the breach of their covenant, and to make good that propriety which by mutual contract men acquire in recompense of the universal right they abandon; and such power there is none before the erection of a commonwealth.

As justice depends on antecedent covenant, so does GRATITUDE depend on antecedent grace—that is to say, antecedent free gift—and is the fourth law of nature, which may be conceived in this form: *that a man which receives benefit from another of mere grace endeavor that he which gives it have no reasonable cause to repent him of his good will.* For no man gives but with intention of good to himself, because gift is voluntary, and of all voluntary acts the object is to every man his own good; of which if men see they shall be frustrated, there will be no beginning of benevolence or trust nor consequently of mutual help nor of reconciliation of one man to another; and therefore they are to remain still in the condition of *war,* which is contrary to the first and fundamental law of nature, which commands men to *seek peace.* The breach of this law is called *ingratitude,* and has the same relation to grace that injustice has to obligation by covenant.

A fifth law of nature is COMPLAISANCE—that is to say, *that every man strive to accommodate himself to the rest.* For the understanding whereof we may consider that there is in men's aptness to society a diversity of nature arising from their diversity of affections not unlike to that we see in stones brought together for building an edifice. For as that stone which by the asperity and irregularity of figure takes more room from others than itself fills, and for the hardness cannot be easily made plain and thereby hinders the building, is by the builders cast away as unprofitable and troublesome, so also a man that by asperity of nature will strive to retain those things which to himself are superfluous and to others necessary, and for the stubbornness of his passions cannot be corrected, is to be left or cast out of society as cumbersome thereunto. For seeing every man, not only by right but also by necessity of nature, is supposed to endeavor all he can to obtain that which is necessary for his conservation, he that shall oppose himself against it for things superfluous is guilty of the war that thereupon is to follow, and therefore does that which is contrary to the fundamental law of nature, which commands *to seek peace.*

A sixth law of nature is this: *that upon caution of the future time; a man ought to pardon the offenses past of them that, repenting, desire it.* For PARDON is nothing but granting of peace, which, though granted to them that persevere in their hostility, be not peace but fear, yet, not granted to them that give caution of the future time, is sign of an aversion to peace, and therefore contrary to the law of nature.

A seventh is *that in revenges*—that is, retribution of evil for evil—*men look not at the greatness of the evil past, but the greatness of the good to follow.* Whereby we are forbidden to inflict punishment with any other design than for correction of the offender or direction of others. For this law is consequent to the next before it that commands pardon upon security of the future time.

And because all signs of hatred or contempt provoke to fight, insomuch as most men choose rather to hazard their life than not to be revenged, we may in the eighth place for a law of nature set down this precept: *that no man by deed, word, countenance, or gesture declare hatred or contempt of another.* The breach of which law is commonly called *contumely.*

The question who is the better man has no place in the condition of mere nature, where, as has been shown before, all men are equal. And therefore for the ninth law of nature, I put this: *that every man acknowledge another for his equal by nature.* The breach of this precept is *pride.*

On this law depends another: *that at the entrance into conditions of peace, no man require to reserve to himself any right which he is not content should be reserved to every one of the rest.* As it is necessary for all men that seek peace to lay down certain rights of nature—that is to say, not to have liberty to do all they list—so is it necessary for man's life to retain some, as right to govern their own bodies, enjoy air, water, motion, ways to go from place to place, and all things else without which a man cannot live or not live well. If in this case, at the making of peace, men require for themselves that which they would not have to be granted to others, they do contrary to the precedent law that commands the acknowledgment of natural equality and therefore also against the law of nature. The observers of this law are those we call *modest,* and the breakers *arrogant* men.

Also if *a man be trusted to judge between man and man,* it is a precept of the law of nature *that he deal equally between them.* For without that, the controversies of men cannot be determined but by war. He, therefore, that is partial in judgment does what in him lies to deter men from the use of judges and arbitrators, and consequently, against the fundamental law of nature, is the cause of war.

And from this follows another law: *that such things as cannot be divided be enjoyed in common, if it can be; and if the quantity of the thing permit, without stint; otherwise proportionably to the number of them that have right.* For otherwise the distribution is unequal and contrary to equity.

But some things there be that can neither be divided nor enjoyed in common. Then the law of nature, which prescribes equity, requires *that the entire right, or else—making the use alternate—the first possession, be determined by lot.* For equal distribution is of the law of nature; and other means of equal distribution cannot be imagined.

Of *lots* there be two sorts: *arbitrary* and *natural.* Arbitrary is that which is agreed on by the competitors; natural is either *primogeniture* or *first seizure.*

And therefore those things which cannot be enjoyed in common, nor divided, ought to be adjudged to the first possessor; and in some cases to the first-born, as acquired by lot.

It is also a law of nature *that all men*

that mediate peace be allowed safe conduct. For the law that commands peace, as the *end,* commands intercession, as the *means;* and to intercession the means is safe conduct.

And because, though men be never so willing to observe these laws, there may nevertheless arise questions concerning a man's action—first, whether it were done or not done; secondly, if done, whether against the law or not against the law; the former whereof is called a question of *fact,* the latter a question of *right*—therefore, unless the parties to the question covenant mutually to stand to the sentence of another, they are as far from peace as ever. This other to whose sentence they submit is called an ARBITRATOR. And therefore it is of the law of nature *that they that are at controversy submit their right to the judgment of an arbitrator.*

And seeing every man is presumed to do all things in order to his own benefit, no man is a fit arbitrator in his own cause; and if he were never so fit, yet, equity allowing to each party equal benefit, if one be admitted to be judge the other is to be admitted also; and so the controversy—that is, the cause of war—remains against the law of nature.

For the same reason no man in any cause ought to be received for arbitrator to whom greater profit or honor or pleasure apparently arises out of the victory of one party than of the other; for he has taken, though an unavoidable bribe, yet a bribe, and no man can be obliged to trust him. And thus also the controversy and the condition of war remains, contrary to the law of nature.

And in a controversy of *fact,* the judge being to give no more credit to one than to the other, if there be no other arguments, must give credit to a third, or to a third and fourth, no more; for else the question is undecided and left to force, contrary to the law of nature.

These are the laws of nature dictating peace for a means of the conservation of men in multitudes, and which only concern the doctrine of civil society. And the science of them is the true and only moral philosophy. For moral philosophy is nothing else but the science of what is *good* and *evil* in the conversation and society of mankind. *Good* and *evil* are names that signify our appetites and aversions, which in different tempers, customs, and doctrines of men are different; and divers men differ not only in their judgment on the senses of what is pleasant and unpleasant to the taste, smell, hearing, touch, and sight but also of what is conformable or disagreeable to reason in the actions of common life. Nay, the same man in divers times differs from himself, and one time praises—that is, calls good—what another time he dispraises and calls evil; from whence arise disputes, controversies, and at last war. And therefore so long as a man is in the condition of mere nature, which is a condition of war, private appetite is the measure of good and evil; and consequently all men agree on this; that peace is good, and therefore also the way or means of peace, which, as I have showed before, are *justice, gratitude, modesty, equity, mercy,* and the rest of the laws of nature, are good—that is to say, *moral virtues*—and their contrary *vices* evil. Now the science of virtue and vice is moral philosophy; and therefore the true doctrine of the laws of nature is the true moral philosophy.

BENEDICT SPINOZA

Benedict Spinoza (1632–1677) was the son of a Jewish family that had settled in Amsterdam after fleeing the Portuguese Inquisition. He received a traditional rabbinical education, but at the age of twenty-four he was expelled from the Jewish community for heresy. His subsequent life was spent quietly in further studies and writing and in the practice of his craft, making optical lenses.

The Ethics *is Spinoza's major work. Its central theme is ethics—the nature of good and evil, virtue and vice, freedom and bondage, ultimate blessedness—but its spirit is religious and its setting a comprehensive metaphysical account of the nature of God and man. Though the following selections are mainly from its specifically ethical parts, they include enough of the metaphysical setting to indicate the unity of Spinoza's thought.*

*Ethics**

Demonstrated in Geometrical Order and Divided into Five Parts Which Treat (1) of God; (2) of the Nature and Origin of the Mind; (3) on the Nature and Origin of Emotions; (4) of Human Bondage; or of the Strength of the Emotions; (5) of the Power of the Intellect; or of Human Liberty

* By permission. From Benedict Spinoza, *Ethics*, trans. by W. H. White (1883), revised by A. H. Sterling (1899) and J. Gutmann (1949), Hafner Publishing Company, New York, 1949. Deletions are not noted in the text.

Part I
Of God

DEFINITIONS

I. By cause of itself I understand that whose essence involves existence, or that whose nature cannot be conceived unless existing.

II. That thing is called finite in its own kind (*in suo genere*) which can be limited by another thing of the same nature. For example, a body is called finite because we always conceive another which is greater. So a thought is limited by another thought; but a body is not limited by a thought, nor a thought by a body.

III. By substance I understand that which is in itself and is conceived through itself; in other words, that the conception of which does not need the conception of another thing from which it must be formed.

IV. By attribute I understand that which the intellect perceives of substance as constituting its essence.

V. By mode I understand the modifications of substance, or that which is in another thing through which also it is conceived.

VI. By God I understand Being absolutely infinite, that is to say, substance consisting of infinite attributes, each one of which expresses eternal and infinite essence.

Explanation. I say absolutely infinite but not infinite in its own kind, for of whatever is infinite only in its own kind, we can deny infinite attributes; but to the essence of that which is absolutely infinite pertains whatever expresses essence and involves no negation.

VII. That thing is called free which exists from the necessity of its own nature alone and is determined to action by itself alone. That thing, on the other hand, is called necessary or rather compelled which by another is determined to existence and action in a fixed and prescribed manner.

VIII. By eternity I understand existence itself, so far as it is conceived necessarily to follow from the definition alone of the eternal thing.

Explanation. For such existence, like the essence of the thing, is conceived as an eternal truth. It cannot therefore be explained by duration or time, even if the duration be conceived without beginning or end.

AXIOMS

I. Everything which is, is either in itself or in another.

II. That which cannot be conceived through another must be conceived through itself.

III. From a given determinate cause an effect necessarily follows; and, on the other hand, if no determinate cause be given it is impossible that an effect can follow.

IV. The knowledge (*cognitio*) of an effect depends upon and involves the knowledge of the cause.

V. Those things which have nothing mutually in common with one another cannot through one another be mutually understood, that is to say, the conception of the one does not involve the conception of the other.

VI. A true idea must agree with that of which it is the idea (*cum suo ideato*).

VII. The essence of that thing which can be conceived as not existing does not involve existence.

PROPOSITIONS

PROPOSITION I. *Substance is by its nature prior to its modifications.*

Demonstration. This is evident from Defs. 3 and 5.

PROPOSITION II. *Two substances having different attributes have nothing in common with one another.*

Demonstration. This is also evident from Def. 3. For each substance must be in itself and must be conceived through itself, that is to say, the conception of one does not involve the conception of the other. —Q.E.D.

PROPOSITION III. *If two things have nothing in common with one another, one cannot be the cause of the other.*

Demonstration. If they have nothing mutually in common with one another, they cannot (Ax. 5) through one another be mutually understood, and therefore (Ax. 4) one cannot be the cause of the other. —Q.E.D.

PROPOSITION IV. *Two or more distinct*

things are distinguished from one another, either by the difference of the attributes of the substances or by the difference of their modifications.

Demonstration. Everything which is, is either in itself or in another (Ax. 1), that is to say (Defs. 3 and 5), outside the intellect there is nothing but substances and their modifications. There is nothing therefore outside the intellect by which a number of things can be distinguished one from another, but substances or (which is the same thing by Def. 4) their attributes and their modifications.—Q.E.D.

PROPOSITION V. *In nature there cannot be two or more substances of the same nature or attribute.*

Demonstration. If there were two or more distinct substances, they must be distinguished one from the other by difference of attributes or difference of modifications (Prop. 4). If they are distinguished only by difference of attributes, it will be granted that there is but one substance of the same attribute. But if they are distinguished by difference of modifications, since substance is prior by nature to its modifications (Prop. 1), the modifications therefore being placed on one side, and the substance being considered in itself, or, in other words (Def. 3 and Ax. 6), truly considered, it cannot be conceived as distinguished from another substance, that is to say (Prop. 4), there cannot be two or more substances, but only one possessing the same nature or attribute.—Q.E.D.

PROPOSITION VI. *One substance cannot be produced by another substance.*

Demonstration. There cannot in nature be two substances of the same attribute (Prop. 5), that is to say (Prop. 2), two which have anything in common with one another. And therefore (Prop. 3), one cannot be the cause of the other, that is to say, one cannot be produced by the other.—Q.E.D.

Corollary. Hence it follows that there is nothing by which substance can be produced, for in Nature there is nothing but substances and their modifications (as is evident from Ax. 1 and Defs. 3 and 5). But substance cannot be produced by substance (Prop. 6). Therefore absolutely there is nothing by which substance can be produced.—Q.E.D.

PROPOSITION VII. *It pertains to the nature of substance to exist.*

Demonstration. There is nothing by which substance can be produced (Corol., Prop. 6). It will therefore be the cause of itself, that is to say (Def. 1), its essence necessarily involves existence, or, in other words, it pertains to its nature to exist. —Q.E.D.

PROPOSITION VIII. *Every substance is necessarily infinite.*

Demonstration. Substance which has only one attribute cannot exist except as one substance (Prop. 5), and to the nature of this one substance it pertains to exist (Prop. 7). It must therefore from its nature exist as finite or infinite. But it cannot exist as finite substance, for (Def. 2) it must (if finite) be limited by another substance of the same nature, which also must necessarily exist (Prop. 7), and therefore there would be two substances of the same attribute, which is absurd (Prop. 5). It exists therefore as infinite substance.—Q.E.D.

PROPOSITION XIV. *Besides God no substance can be nor can be conceived.*

PROPOSITION XV. *Whatever is, is in God, and nothing can either be or be conceived without God.*

Demonstration. Besides God there is no substance, nor can any be conceived, that is to say (Def. 3), nothing which is in itself and is conceived through itself. But modes (Def. 5) can neither be nor be conceived without substance; therefore in the divine nature only can they be, and through it alone can they be conceived. But besides substances and modes nothing is assumed (Ax. 1). Therefore, nothing can be or be conceived without God.—Q.E.D.

PROPOSITION XVI. *From the necessity of the divine nature infinite numbers of things in infinite ways (that is to say, all things which can be conceived by the infinite intellect) must follow.*

Corollary 1. Hence it follows that God is the efficient cause of all things which can fall under the infinite intellect.

Corollary 2. It follows, secondly, that God is cause through Himself, and not through that which is contingent (*per accidens*).

Corollary 3. It follows, thirdly, that God is absolutely the first cause.

PROPOSITION XVII. *God acts from the laws of His own nature only, and is compelled by no one.*

PROPOSITION XVIII. *God is the immanent and not the transient cause of all things.*

Demonstration. All things which are, are in God and must be conceived through Him (Prop. 15), and therefore (Corol. 1, Prop. 16) He is the cause of the things which are in Himself. This is the first thing which was to be proved. Moreover, outside God there can be no substance (Prop. 14), that is to say (Def. 3), outside Him nothing can exist which is in itself. This was the second thing to be proved. God, therefore, is the immanent, but not the transient, cause of all things.—Q.E.D.

PROPOSITION XXIX. *In Nature there is nothing contingent, but all things are determined from the necessity of the divine nature to exist and act in a certain manner.*

PROPOSITION XXXIII. *Things could have been produced by God in no other manner and in no other order than that in which they have been produced.*

Note 1. Since I have thus shown, with greater clearness than that of noonday light, that in things there is absolutely nothing by virtue of which they can be called contingent, I wish now to explain in a few words what is to be understood by "contingent," but firstly what is to be understood by "necessary" and "impossible." A thing is called necessary either in reference to its essence or its cause. For the existence of a thing necessarily follows either from the essence and definition of the thing itself or from a given efficient cause. In the same way a thing is said to be impossible either because the essence of the thing itself or its definition involves a contradiction, or because no external cause exists determinate to the production of such a thing. But a thing cannot be called contingent unless with reference to a deficiency in our knowledge. For if we do not know that the essence of a thing involves a contradiction, or if we actually know that it involves no contradiction, and nevertheless we can affirm nothing with certainty about its existence because the order of causes is concealed from us, that thing can never appear to us either as necessary or impossible, and therefore we call it either contingent or possible.

Note 2. From what has gone before it clearly follows that things have been produced by God in the highest degree of perfection, since they have necessarily followed from the existence of a most perfect nature. Nor does this doctrine accuse God of any imperfection, but, on the contrary, His perfection has compelled us to affirm it. Indeed, from its contrary would clearly follow, as I have shown above, that God is not absolutely perfect, since, if things had been produced in any other fashion, another nature would have had to be assigned to Him, different from that which the consideration of the most perfect Being compels us to assign to Him.

APPENDIX

I have now explained the nature of God and its properties. I have shown that He necessarily exists; that He is one God; that from the necessity alone of His own nature He is and acts; that He is, and in what way He is, the free cause of all things; that all things are in Him, and so depend upon Him that without Him they can neither be nor can be conceived; and, finally, that all things have been predetermined by Him, not indeed from freedom of will or from absolute good pleasure, but from His absolute nature or infinite power.

Moreover, wherever an opportunity was afforded, I have endeavored to remove prejudices which might hinder the perception of the truth of what I have demonstrated; but because not a few still remain which have been and are now sufficient to prove a very great hindrance to the comprehension of the connection of things in the manner in which I have explained it, I have thought it worth while to call them up to be examined by reason. But all these prejudices which I here undertake to point out depend upon this solely: that it is commonly supposed that all things in Nature, like men, work to some end; and, indeed, it is thought to be certain that God Himself directs all things to some sure end, for it is said that God has made all things for man, and man that he may worship God. This, therefore, I will first investigate by inquiring, first, why so many rest in this prejudice, and why all are so naturally inclined to embrace it. I shall then show its falsity, and, finally, the manner in which there have arisen from its prejudices concerning *good* and *evil, merit* and *sin, praise* and *blame, order* and *disorder, beauty* and *deformity,* and so forth. This, however, is not the place to deduce these things from the nature of the human mind. It will be sufficient if I here take as an axiom that which no one ought to dispute, namely, that man is born ignorant of the causes of things, and that he has a desire, of which he is conscious, to seek that which is profitable to him. From this it follows, first, that he thinks himself free because he is conscious of his wishes and appetites, whilst at the same time he is ignorant of the causes by which he is led to wish and desire, not dreaming what they are; and secondly, it follows that man does everything for an end, namely, for that which is profitable to him, which is what he seeks. Hence it happens that he attempts to discover merely the final causes of that which has happened; and when he has heard them he is satisfied, because there is no longer any cause for further uncertainty. But if he cannot hear from another what these final causes are, nothing remains but to turn to himself and reflect upon the ends which usually determine him to the like actions, and thus by his own mind he necessarily judges that of another. Moreover, since he discovers, both within and without himself, a multitude of means which contribute not a little to the attainment of what is profitable to himself—for example, the eyes, which are useful for seeing, the teeth for mastication, plants and animals for nourishment, the sun for giving light, the sea for feeding fish, etc.—it comes to pass that all natural objects are considered as means for obtaining what is profitable. These, too, being evidently discovered and not created by man, hence he has a cause for believing that some other person exists who has prepared them for man's use. For having considered them as means it was impossible to believe that they had created themselves, and so he was obliged to infer from the means which he was in the habit of providing for himself that some ruler or rulers of Nature exist, endowed with human liberty, who have taken care of all things for him, and have made all things for his use. Since he never heard anything about the mind of these rulers, he was compelled to judge of it from his own, and hence he affirmed that the gods direct everything for his advantage in order that he may be bound to them and hold them in the highest honor. This is the reason why each man has devised for himself, out of his own brain, a different mode of worshipping God, so that God might love him above others, and direct all Nature to the service of his blind cupidity and insatiable avarice.

Thus has this prejudice been turned

into a superstition and has driven deep roots into the mind—a prejudice which was the reason why everyone has so eagerly tried to discover and explain the final causes of things. The attempt, however, to show that Nature does nothing in vain (that is to say, nothing which is not profitable to man) seems to end in showing that Nature, the gods, and man are alike mad.

Do but see, I pray, to what all this has led. Amidst so much in Nature that is beneficial, not a few things must have been observed which are injurious, such as storms, earthquakes, diseases, and it was affirmed that these things happened either because the gods were angry because of wrongs which had been inflicted on them by man, or because of sins committed in the method of worshipping them; and although experience daily contradicted this, and showed by an infinity of examples that both the beneficial and the injurious were indiscriminately bestowed on the pious and the impious, the inveterate prejudices on this point have not therefore been abandoned. For it was much easier for a man to place these things aside with others of the use of which he was ignorant, and thus retain his present and inborn state of ignorance, than to destroy the whole superstructure and think out a new one. Hence it was looked upon as indisputable that the judgments of the gods far surpass our comprehension; and this opinion alone would have been sufficient to keep the human race in darkness to all eternity if mathematics, which does not deal with ends but with the essences and properties of forms, had not placed before us another rule of truth. In addition to mathematics, other causes also might be assigned, which it is superfluous here to enumerate, tending to make men reflect upon these universal prejudices, and leading them to a true knowledge of things.

After man has persuaded himself that all things which exist are made for him, he must in everything adjudge that to be of the greatest importance which is most useful to him, and he must esteem that to be of surpassing worth by which he is most beneficially affected. In this way he is compelled to form those notions by which he explains Nature, such, for instance, as *good, evil, order, confusion, heat, cold, beauty,* and *deformity,* etc.; and because he supposes himself to be free, notions like those of *praise* and *blame, sin* and *merit,* have arisen. We see, therefore, that all those methods by which the common people are in the habit of explaining Nature are only different sorts of imaginations, and do not reveal the nature of anything in itself, but only the constitution of the imagination; and because they have names as if they were entities existing apart from the imagination, I call them entities not of the reason but of the imagination. All argument, therefore, urged against us based upon such notions can be easily refuted. Many people, for instance, are accustomed to argue thus: If all things have followed from the necessity of the most perfect nature of God, how is it that so many imperfections have arisen in Nature—corruption, for instance, of things till they stink; deformity, exciting disgust; confusion, evil, crime, etc.? But, as I have just observed, all this is easily answered. For the perfection of thing is to be judged by their nature and power alone; nor are they more or less perfect because they delight or offend the human senses, or because they are beneficial or prejudicial to human nature. But to those who ask why God has not created all men in such a manner that they might be controlled by the dictates of reason alone, I give but this answer: because to Him material was not wanting for the creation of everything, from the highest down to the very lowest grade of perfection; or, to speak more properly, because the laws of His nature were so ample that they sufficed for the production of everything which can be conceived by an infinite intellect, as I have demonstrated in Prop. 16.

These are the prejudices which I undertook to notice here. If any others of a similar character remain, they can easily be rectified with a little thought by anyone.

Part Three
On the Origin and Nature of the Emotions

Most persons who have written about the emotions and man's conduct of life seem to discuss, not the natural things which follow the common laws of Nature, but things which are outside her. They seem indeed to consider man in Nature as a kingdom within a kingdom. For they believe that man disturbs rather than follows her order, that he has an absolute power over his own actions, and that he is altogether self-determined. They then proceed to attribute the cause of human weakness and changeableness, not to the common power of Nature, but to some vice of human nature which they therefore bewail, laugh at, mock, or, as is more generally the case, detest; whilst he who knows how to revile most eloquently or subtly the weakness of the mind is looked upon as divine. It is true that very eminent men have not been wanting, to whose labor and industry we confess ourselves much indebted, who have written many excellent things about the right conduct of life, and who have given to mortals counsels full of prudence, but no one, so far as I know, has determined the nature and strength of the emotions, and what the mind is able to do toward controlling them.

Nothing happens in Nature which can be attributed to any vice of Nature, for she is always the same and everywhere one. Her virtue is the same, and her power of acting, that is to say, her laws and rules, according to which all things are and are changed from form to form, are everywhere and always the same, so that there must also be one and the same method of understanding the nature of all things whatsoever, that is to say, by the universal laws and rules of Nature. The emotions, therefore, of hatred, anger, envy, considered in themselves, follow from the same necessity and virtue of Nature as other individual things; they have therefore certain causes through which they are to be understood, and certain properties which are just as worthy of being known as the properties of any other thing in the contemplation alone of which we delight. I shall, therefore, pursue the same method in considering the nature and strength of the emotions and the power of the mind over them which I pursued in our previous discussion of God, and I shall consider human actions and appetites just as if I were considering lines, planes, or bodies.

DEFINITIONS AND POSTULATES

DEF. I. I call that an *adequate* cause whose effect can be clearly and distinctly perceived by means of the cause. I call that an *inadequate* or partial cause whose effect cannot be understood by means of the cause alone.

DEF. II. I say that we act when anything is done, either within us or without us, of which we are the adequate cause, that is to say (by the preceding Def.), when from our nature anything follows, either within us or without us, which by that nature alone can be clearly and distinctly understood. On the other hand, I say that we suffer when anything is done within us, or when anything follows from our nature of which we are not the cause except partially.

DEF. III. By emotion I understand the modifications of the body by which the power of acting of the body itself is increased, diminished, helped, or hindered, together with the ideas of these modifications.

If, therefore, we can be the adequate cause of any of these modifications, I understand the emotion to be an action, otherwise it is a passive state.

Postulate 1. The human body can be affected in many ways by which its power of acting is increased or diminished, and also in other ways which make its power of acting neither greater nor less.

This postulate or axiom is based upon Post. 1 and Lems. 5 and 7, following Prop. 13, pt. 2.

Postulate 2. The human body is capable of suffering many changes, and, nevertheless, can retain the impressions or traces of objects (Post. 5, pt. 2), and consequently the same images of things.

PROPOSITIONS

PROPOSITION I. *Our mind acts at times and at times suffers: in so far as it has adequate ideas, it necessarily acts; and in so far as it has inadequate ideas, it necessarily suffers.*

Demonstration. From any given idea some effect must necessarily follow, of which God is the adequate cause (Def. 1, pt. 3), not in so far as He is infinite, but in so far as He is considered as affected with the given idea. But of that effect of which God is the cause, in so far as He is affected by an idea which is adequate in any mind, that same mind is the adequate cause. Our mind, therefore (Def. 2, pt. 3), in so far as it has adequate ideas, necessarily at times acts, which is the first thing we had to prove. Again, if there be anything which necessarily follows from an idea which is adequate in God, not in so far as He contains within Himself the mind of one man only, but also, together with this, the ideas of other things, then the mind of that man is not the adequate cause of that thing, but is only its partial cause, and therefore (Def. 2, pt. 3). in so far as the mind has inadequate ideas, it necessarily at times suffers. This was the second thing to be proved. Therefore our mind etc.—Q.E.D.

Corollary. Hence it follows that the mind is subject to passions in proportion to the number of inadequate ideas which it has, and that it acts in proportion to the number of adequate ideas which it has.

PROPOSITION III. *The actions of the mind arise from adequate ideas alone, but the passive states depend upon those alone which are inadequate.*

PROPOSITION IV. *A thing cannot be destroyed except by an external cause.*

PROPOSITION V. *In so far as one thing is able to destroy another are they of contrary natures, that is to say, they cannot exist in the same subject.*

PROPOSITION VI. *Each thing, in so far as it is in itself, endeavors to persevere in its being.*

Demonstration. A thing has nothing in itself through which it can be destroyed, or which can negate its existence (Prop. 4, pt. 3), but, on the contrary, it is opposed to everything which could negate its existence (Prop. 5, pt. 3). Therefore, in so far as it can, and in so far as it is in itself, it endeavors to persevere in its own being. —Q.E.D.

PROPOSITION VII. *The effort by which each thing endeavors to persevere in its own being is nothing but the actual essence of the thing itself.*

By virtue and power I understand the same thing, that is to say, virtue, in so far as it is related to man, is the essence itself or nature of the man in so far as it has the power of effecting certain things which can be understood through the laws of its nature alone.[1]

PROPOSITION IX. *The mind, both in so far as it has clear and distinct ideas and in so far as it has confused ideas, endeavors to persevere in its being for an indefinite time, and is conscious of this effort.*

Note. This effort, when it is related to the mind alone, is called "will," but when it is related at the same time both to the mind and the body is called "appetite," which is therefore nothing but the very es-

[1] Part IV, Definition VIII.

sence of man, from the nature of which necessarily follow those things which promote his preservation, and thus he is determined to do those things. Hence there is no difference between appetite and desire, unless in this particular that desire is generally related to men in so far as they are conscious of their appetites, and it may therefore be defined as appetite of which we are conscious. From what has been said it is plain, therefore, that we neither strive for, wish, seek, nor desire anything because we think it to be good, but, on the contrary, we adjudge a thing to be good because we strive for, wish, seek or desire it.

PROPOSITION XI. *If anything increases, diminishes, helps, or limits our body's power of action, the idea of that thing increases, diminishes, helps, or limits our mind's power of thought.*

Note. We thus see that the mind can suffer great changes, and can pass now to a greater and now to a lesser perfection; these passive states explaining to us the emotions of joy and sorrow. By "joy," therefore, in what follows, I shall understand the passive states through which the mind passes to a greater perfection; by "sorrow," on the other hand, the passive states through which it passes to a less perfection. The emotion of joy, related at the same time both to the mind and the body, I call "pleasurable excitement" (*titillatio*) or "cheerfulness"; that of sorrow I call "pain" or "melancholy." It is, however, to be observed that pleasurable excitement and pain are related to a man when one of his parts is affected more than the others; cheerfulness and melancholy, on the other hand, when all parts are equally affected. What the nature of desire is I have explained in the note of Prop. 9, pt. 3; and besides these three—joy, sorrow, and desire—I know of no other primary emotion; the others springing from these, as I shall show in what follows.

Note. From what has been said we can clearly see what love is and what hatred is. *Love* is nothing but joy accompanied with the idea of an external cause, and *hatred* is nothing but sorrow with the accompanying idea of an external cause. We see, too, that he who loves a thing necessarily endeavors to keep it before him and to preserve it, and, on the other hand, he who hates a thing necessarily endeavors to remove and destroy it.

A few things remain to be said about the definitions of the emotions, and I will therefore here repeat the definitions in order, appending to them what is necessary to be observed in each.

DEFINITIONS OF THE EMOTIONS

I. *Desire* is the essence itself of man in so far as it is conceived as determined to any action by any one of his modifications.

Explanation. We have said above, in the Note of Prop. 9, pt. 3, that desire is appetite which is self-conscious, and that appetite is the essence itself of man in so far as it is determined to such acts as contribute to his preservation. But in the same note I have taken care to remark that in truth I cannot recognize any difference between human appetite and desire. For whether a man be conscious of his appetite or not, it remains one and the same appetite, and so, lest I might appear to be guilty of tautology, I have not explained desire by appetite, but have tried to give such a definition of desire as would include all the efforts of human nature to which we give the name of appetite, desire, will, or impulse. By the word "desire," therefore, I understand all the efforts, impulses, appetites, and volitions of a man, which vary according to his changing disposition, and not infrequently are so opposed to one another that he is drawn hither and thither, and knows not whither he ought to turn.

II. *Joy* is man's passage from a less to a greater perfection.

III. *Sorrow* is man's passage from a greater to a less perfection.

Explanation. I say passage, for joy is not perfection itself. If a man were born with the perfection to which he passes, he would possess it without the emotion of joy—a truth which will appear the more clearly from the emotion of sorrow, which is the opposite to joy. For that sorrow consists in the passage to a less perfection, but not in the less perfection itself, no one can deny, since in so far as a man shares any perfection he cannot be sad. Nor can we say that sorrow consists in the privation of a greater perfection, for privation is nothing. But the emotion of sorrow is a reality, and it therefore must be the reality of the passage to a lesser perfection, or the reality by which man's power of acting is diminished or limited (Note, Prop. 11, pt. 3).

VI. *Love* is joy with the accompanying idea of an external cause.

VII. *Hatred* is sorrow with the accompanying idea of an external cause.

VIII. *Inclination* (*propensio*) is joy with the accompanying idea of some object as being accidentally the cause of the joy.

XII. *Hope* is a joy not constant, arising from the idea of something future or past, about the issue of which we sometimes doubt.

XIII. *Fear* is a sorrow not constant, arising from the idea of something future or past, about the issue of which we sometimes doubt.

XIV. *Confidence* is joy arising from the idea of a past or future object from which cause for doubting is removed.

XV. *Despair* is sorrow arising from the idea of a past or future object from which cause for doubting is removed.

Explanation. Confidence, therefore, springs from hope and despair from fear, whenever the reason for doubting the issue is taken away—a case which occurs either because we imagine a thing past or future to be present and contemplate it as present, or because we imagine other things which exclude the existence of those which made us to doubt.

XVIII. *Commiseration* is sorrow with the accompanying idea of evil which has happened to some one whom we imagine like ourselves.

XXV. *Self-satisfaction* is the joy which is produced by contemplating ourselves and our own power of action.

XXVI. *Humility* is the sorrow which is produced by contemplating our impotence or helplessness.

Self-satisfaction is opposed to humility in so far as we understand by the former the joy which arises from contemplating our power of action, but in so far as we understand by it joy attended with the idea of something done, which we believe has been done by a free decree of our mind, it is opposed to repentance, which we may thus define:

XXVII. *Repentance* is sorrow accompanied with the idea of something done which we believe has been done by a free decree of our mind.

Explanation. Here, I must observe that it is not to be wondered at that sorrow should always follow all those actions which are from custom called wicked, and that joy should follow those which are called good. But that this is chiefly the effect of education will be evident from what we have before said. Parents, by reprobating what are called bad actions, and frequently blaming their children whenever they commit them, while they persuade them to what are called good actions, and praise their children when they perform them, have caused the emotions of sorrow to connect themselves with the former, and those of joy with the latter. Experience proves this, for custom and religion are not the same everywhere; but, on the contrary, things which are sacred to some are profane to others, and what are honorable with some are disgraceful with others. Education alone, therefore, will determine whether a man will repent of any deed or boast of it.

XXVIII. *Pride* is thinking too much of ourselves, through self-love.

XXIX. *Despondency* is thinking too little of ourselves through sorrow.

Explanation. We are often in the habit of opposing humility to pride, but only when we attend to their emotions rather than to their nature. For we are accustomed to call a man proud who boasts too much, who talks about nothing but his own virtues and other people's vices, who wishes to be preferred to everybody else, and who marches along with that stateliness and pomp which belong to others whose position is far above his. On the other hand, we call a man humble who often blushes, who confesses his own faults and talks about the virtues of others, who yields to every one, who walks with bended head, and who neglects to adorn himself. These emotions—humility and despondency—are very rare, for human nature, considered in itself, struggles against them as much as it can, and hence those who have the most credit for being abject and humble are generally the most ambitious and envious.

The definitions of jealousy and the other vacillations of the mind I pass over in silence, both because they are compounded of the emotions which we have already defined, and also because many of them have no names—a fact which shows that, for the purposes of life, it is sufficient to know these combinations generally. Moreover, it follows from the definitions of the emotions which we have explained that they all arise from desire, joy, or sorrow, or rather that there are none but these three, which pass under names varying as their relations and external signs vary. If, therefore, we attend to these primitive emotions and to what has been said above about the nature of the mind, we shall be able here to define the emotions in so far as they are related to the mind alone.

General definition of the emotions. Emotion which is called *animi pathema* is a confused idea by which the mind affirms of its body, or any part of it, a greater or less power of existence than before; and this increase of power being given, the mind itself is determined to one particular thought rather than to another.

Explanation. I say, in the first place, that an emotion or passion of the mind *is a confused idea.* For we have shown (Prop. 3, pt. 3) that the mind suffers only in so far as it has inadequate or confused ideas. I say again, *by which the mind affirms of its body, or any part of it, a greater or less power of existence than before.* For all ideas which we possess of bodies indicate the actual constitution of our body rather than the nature of the external body; but this idea which constitutes the reality of an emotion must indicate or express the constitution of the body or of some part of it; which constitution the body or any part of it possesses from the fact that its power of action or force of existence is increased or diminished, helped or limited. But it is to be observed that when I say "a greater or less power of existence than before," I do not mean that the mind compares the present with the past constitution of the body, but that the idea which constitutes the reality of an emotion affirms something of the body which actually involves more or less reality than before. Moreover, since the essence of the mind consists in its affirmation of the actual existence of its body, and since we understand by perfection the essence itself of the thing, it follows that the mind passes to a greater or less perfection when it is able to affirm of its body, or some part of it, something which involves a greater or less reality than before. When, therefore, I have said that the mind's power of thought is increased or diminished, I have wished to be understood as meaning nothing else than that the mind has formed an idea of its body, or some part of its body, which expresses more or less reality than it had hitherto affirmed of the body. For the value of ideas and the actual power of thought are measured by the value of the object. Finally, I added, "which being given, the mind itself is determined to one particular thought rather than to another," that I might also express the nature of desire in addition to that of joy and sorrow, which is explained by the first part of the definition.

Part Four
Of Human Bondage; or of the Strength of the Emotions

PREFACE

The impotence of man to govern or restrain the emotions I call "bondage," for a man who is under their control is not his own master, but is mastered by fortune, in whose power he is, so that he is often forced to follow the worse, although he sees the better before him. I propose in this part to demonstrate why this is, and also to show what of good and evil the emotions possess. But before I begin I should like to say a few words about perfection and imperfection, and about good and evil. If a man has proposed to do a thing and has accomplished it, he calls it perfect, and not only he, but every one else who has really known or has believed that he has known the mind and intention of the author of that work will call it perfect too. For example, having seen some work (which I suppose to be as yet not finished), if we know that the intention of the author of that work is to build a house, we shall call the house imperfect; while, on the other hand, we shall call it perfect as soon as we see the work has been brought to the end which the author had determined for it. But if we see any work such as we have never seen before, and if we do not know the mind of the workman, we shall then not be able to say whether the work is perfect or imperfect. This seems to have been the first signification of these words; but afterwards men began to form universal ideas—to think out for themselves types of houses, buildings, castles, and to prefer some types of things to others; and so it happened that each person called a thing perfect which seemed to agree with the universal idea which he had formed of that thing, and, on the other hand, he called a thing imperfect which seemed to agree less with his typal conception, although, according to the intention of the workman, it had been entirely completed. This appears to be the only reason why the words "perfect" and "imperfect" are commonly applied to natural objects which are not made with human hands; for men are in the habit of forming, both of natural as well as of artificial objects, universal ideas which they regard as types of things, and which they think Nature has in view, setting them before herself as types, too; it being the common opinion that she does nothing except for the sake of some end. When, therefore, men see something done by Nature which does not altogether answer to that typal conception which they have of the thing, they think that Nature herself has failed or committed an error, and that she has left the thing imperfect. Thus we see that the custom of applying the words "perfect" and "imperfect" to natural objects has arisen rather from prejudice than from true knowledge of them. For we have shown in the Appendix to the First Part of this work that Nature does nothing for the sake of an end, for that eternal and infinite Being whom we call God or Nature acts by the same necessity by which He exists; for we have shown that He acts by the same necessity of Nature as that by which He exists (Prop. 16, pt. 1). The reason or cause, therefore, why God or Nature acts and the reason why He exists are one and the same. Since, therefore, He exists for no end, He acts for no end; and since He has no principle or end of existence, He has no principle or end of action.

With regard to good and evil, these terms indicate nothing positive in things, considered in themselves, nor are they anything else than modes of thought, or notions which we form from the comparison of one thing with another. For one and the same thing may at the same time be both good and evil or indifferent. Music, for example, is good to a melancholy person, bad to one mourning, while to a deaf man it is neither good nor bad. But although things are so, we must retain these words. For since we desire to form for ourselves an idea of man upon which we may look as a model of human nature, it will be of service to us to retain these expressions in the sense I have mentioned. By "good," therefore, I understand in the following pages everything which we are certain is a means by which we may approach nearer and nearer to the model of human nature we set before us. By "evil," on the contrary, I understand everything which we are certain hinders us from reaching that model. Again, I shall call men more or less perfect or imperfect in so far as they approach more or less nearly to this same model. For it is to be carefully observed that when I say that an individual passes from a less to a greater perfection and *vice versa,* I do not understand that from one essence or form he is changed into another (for a horse, for instance, would be as much destroyed if it were changed into a man as if it were changed into an insect), but rather we conceive that his power of action, in so far as it is understood by his own nature, is increased or diminished. Finally, by "perfection" generally, I understand as I have said, reality, that is to say, the essence of any object in so far as it exists and acts in a certain manner, no regard being paid to its duration. For no individual thing can be said to be more perfect because for a longer time it has persevered in existence; inasmuch as the duration of things cannot be determined by their essence, the essence of things involving no fixed or determined period of existence; any object, whether it be more or less perfect, always being able to persevere in existence with the same force as that with which it commenced existence. All things, therefore, are equal in this respect.

APPENDIX

My observations in this part concerning the true method of life have not been arranged so that they could be seen at a glance. I have determined, therefore, here to collect them, and reduce them under principal heads.

I. All our efforts or desires follow from the necessity of our nature in such a manner that they can be understood either through it alone as their proximate cause, or in so far as we are a part of Nature, which part cannot be adequately conceived through itself and without the other individuals.

II. The desires which follow from our nature in such a manner that they can be understood through it alone are those which are related to the mind, in so far as it is conceived to consist of adequate ideas. The remaining desires are not related to the mind, unless in so far as it conceives things inadequately, whose power and increase cannot be determined by human power, but by the power of objects which are without us. The first kind of desires, therefore, are properly called actions, but the latter passive states, for the first always indicate our power, and the latter, on the contrary, indicate our impotence and imperfect knowledge.

III. Our actions, that is to say, those desires which are determined by man's power or reason, are always good; the others may be good as well as evil.

IV. It is therefore most profitable to us in life to make perfect the intellect or reason as far as possible, and in this one thing consists the highest happiness or blessedness of man; for blessedness is nothing but the peace of mind which springs from the intuitive knowledge of God, and to perfect the intellect is nothing but to understand God, together with the attributes and actions of God which flow from the necessity of His nature. The final aim, therefore, of a man who is guided by reason, that is to say, the chief desire by which he strives to govern all his other desires, is that by which he is led adequately to conceive himself and all things which can be conceived by his intelligence.

V. There is no rational life therefore, without intelligence, and things are good only in so far as they assist man to enjoy that life of the mind which is determined by intelligence. Those things alone, on the other hand, we call evil which hinder man from perfecting his reason and enjoying a rational life.

VI. But because all those things of which man is the efficient cause are necessarily good, it follows that no evil can happen to man except from external causes, that is to say, except in so far as he is a part of the whole of Nature, whose laws human nature is compelled to obey—compelled also to accommodate himself to this whole of Nature in almost an infinite number of ways.

VII. It is impossible that a man should not be a part of Nature and follow her common order; but if he be placed amongst individuals who agree with his nature, his power of action will by that very fact be assisted and supported. But if, on the contrary, he be placed amongst individuals who do not in the least agree with his nature, he will scarcely be able without great change on his part to accommodate himself to them.

VIII. Anything that exists in Nature which we judge to be evil or able to hinder us from existing and enjoying a rational life, we are allowed to remove from us in that way which seems the safest; and whatever, on the other hand, we judge to be good or to be profitable for the preservation of our being or the enjoyment of a rational life, we are permitted to take for our use and use in any way we may think proper; and absolutely, everyone is allowed by the highest right of Nature to do that which he believes contributes to his own profit.

IX. Nothing, therefore, can agree better with the nature of any object than other individuals of the same kind, and so (see § 7) there is nothing more profitable to man for the preservation of his being and the enjoyment of a rational life than a man who is guided by reason. Again, since there is no single thing we know which is more excellent than a man who is guided by reason, it follows that there is nothing by which a person can better show how much skill and talent he possesses than by so educating men that at last they will live under the direct authority of reason.

X. In so far as men are carried away by envy or any emotion of hatred toward one another, so far are they contrary to one another, and, consequently, so much the more are they to be feared, as they have more power than other individual parts of Nature.

XI. Minds, nevertheless, are not conquered by arms, but by love and generosity.

XII. Above all things it is profitable to men to form communities and to unite themselves to one another by bonds which may make all of them as one man; and, absolutely, it is profitable for them to do whatever may tend to strengthen their friendships.

XIII. But to acomplish this, skill and watchfulness are required; for men are changeable (those being very few who live according to the laws of reason), and nevertheless generally envious and more inclined to vengeance than pity. To bear with each, therefore, according to his disposition and to refrain from imitating his emotions requires a singular power of mind. But those, on the contrary, who know how to revile men, to denounce vices rather than teach virtues, and not to strengthen men's minds but to weaken them, are injurious both to themselves and others, so that many of them, through an excess of impatience and a false zeal for religion, prefer living with brutes rather than amongst men; just as boys or youths, unable to endure with equanimity the rebukes of their parents, fly to the army, choosing the discomforts of war and the rule of a tyrant rather than the comforts of home and the admonitions of a father, suffering all kinds of burdens to be imposed upon them in order that they may revenge themselves upon their parents.

XIV. Although, therefore, men generally determine everything by their pleasure, many more advantages than disadvantages arise from their common union. It is better, therefore, to endure with equanimity the injuries inflicted by them, and to apply our minds to those things which subserve concord and the establishment of friendship.

XV. The things which beget concord are those which are related to justice, integrity, and honor; for besides that which is unjust and injurious, men take ill also anything which is esteemed base, or that anyone should despise the received customs of the State. But in order to win love, those things are chiefly necessary which have reference to religion and piety.

XVI. Concord, moreover, is often produced by fear, but it is without good faith. It is to be observed, too, that fear arises from impotence of mind, and therefore is of no service to reason; nor is pity, although it seems to present an appearance of piety.

XVII. Men also are conquered by liberality, especially those who have not the means wherewith to procure what is necessary for the support of life. But to assist every one who is needy far surpasses the strength or profit of a private person, for the wealth of a private person is altogether insufficient to supply such wants. Besides, the power of any one man is too limited for him to be able to unite every one with himself in friendship. The care, therefore, of the poor is incumbent on the whole of society and concerns only the general profit.

XIX. The love of a harlot, that is to say, the lust of sexual intercourse, which arises from mere external form, and absolutely all love which recognizes any other cause than the freedom of the mind, easily passes into hatred unless, which is worse, it becomes a species of delirium.

XX. With regard to marriage, it is plain that it is in accordance with reason if the desire of connection is engendered not merely by external form, but by a love of begetting children and wisely educating them; and if, in addition, the love both of the husband and wife has for its cause not external form merely, but chiefly liberty of mind.

XXVI. Except man, we know no individual thing in Nature in whose mind we can take pleasure, nor anything which we can unite with ourselves by friendship or any kind of intercourse, and therefore regard to our own profit does not demand that we should preserve anything which exists in Nature except men, but teaches us to preserve it or destroy it in accordance with its varied uses, or to adapt it to our own service in any way whatever.

XXVII. The profit which we derive from objects without us, over and above the experience and knowledge which we obtain because we observe them and change them from their existing forms into others, is chiefly the preservation of the body, and for this reason those objects are the most profitable to us which can feed and nourish the body, so that all its parts are able properly to perform their functions. For the more capable the body is of being affected in many ways, and affecting external bodies in many ways, the more capable of thinking is the mind (Props. 38 and 39, pt. 4). But there seem to be very few things in Nature of this kind, and it is consequently necessary for the requisite nourishment of the body to use many different kinds of food, for the human body is composed of a great number of parts of different nature, which need constant and varied food in order that the whole of the body may be equally adapted for all those things which can follow from its nature, and consequently that the mind also may be equally adapted to conceive many things.

XXVIII. The strength of one man would scarcely suffice to obtain these things if men did not mutually assist one another. As money has presented us with an abstract of everything, it has come to pass that its image above every other usually occupies the mind of the multitude because they can imagine hardly any kind of joy without the accompanying idea of money as its cause.

XXIX. This, however, is a vice only in those who seek money not from poverty or necessity, but because they have learned the arts of gain by which they keep up a grand appearance. As for the body itself, they feed it in accordance with custom, but sparingly because they believe that they lose so much of their goods as they spend upon the preservation of their body. Those, however, who know the true use of money, and regulate the measure of wealth according to their needs, live contented with few things.

XXX. Since, therefore, those things are good which help the parts of the body to perform their functions, and since joy consists in this that the power of man, in so far as he is made up of mind and body, is helped or increased, it follows that all those things which bring joy are good. But inasmuch as things do not work to this end—that they may affect us with joy—nor is their power of action guided in accordance with our profit, and finally, since joy is generally related chiefly to some one part of the body, it follows that generally the emotions of joy (unless reason and watchfulness be present), and consequently the desires which are begotten from them, are excessive. It is to be added that an emotion causes us to put that thing first which is sweet to us in the present, and that we are not able to judge the future with an equal emotion.

XXXI. Superstition, on the contrary, seems to affirm that what brings sorrow is good, and, on the contrary, that what brings joy is evil. But no one except an envious man is delighted at my impotence or disadvantage, for the greater the joy with which we are affected, the greater the perfection to which we pass, and consequently the more do we participate in the divine nature; nor can joy ever be evil which is controlled by a true consideration for our own profit. On the other hand, the man who is led by fear and does what is good that he may avoid what is evil, is not guided by reason.

XXXII. But human power is very limited and is infinitely surpassed by the power of external causes, so that we do not possess an absolute power to adapt to our service the things which are without us. Nevertheless we shall bear with equanimity those things which happen to us contrary to what a consideration of our own profit demands if we are conscious that we have performed our duty, that the power we have could not reach so far as to enable us to avoid those things, and that we are a part of the whole of Nature, whose order we follow. If we clearly and distinctly understand this, the part of us which is determined by intelligence, that is to say, the better part of us, will be entirely satisfied therewith, and in that satisfaction will endeavor to persevere; for, in so far as we understand, we cannot desire anything except what is necessary, nor, absolutely, can we be satisfied with anything but the truth. Therefore, in so far as we understand these things properly, will the efforts of the better part of us agree with the order of the whole of Nature.

Part Five
Of the Power of the Intellect; or of Human Freedom

PREFACE

I pass at length to the other part of Ethics which concerns the method or way which leads to freedom. In this part, therefore, I shall treat of the power of reason, showing how much reason itself can control the emotions, and then what is freedom of mind or blessedness. Thence we shall see how much stronger the wise man is than the ignorant. In what manner and in what way the intellect should be rendered perfect, and with what art the body is to be cared for in order that it may properly perform its functions, I have nothing to do with here; for the former belongs to logic, the latter to medicine. I shall occupy myself here, as I have said, solely with the power of the mind or of reason, first of all showing the extent and nature of the authority which it has over the emotions in restraining them and governing them; for that we have not absolute authority over them we have already demonstrated. The Stoics indeed thought that the emotions depend absolutely on our will, and that we are absolutely masters over them; but they were driven, by the contradiction of experience, though not by their own principles, to confess that not a little practice and study are required in order to restrain and govern the emotions. This one of them attempted to illustrate, if I remember rightly, by the example of two dogs, one of a domestic and the other of a hunting breed; for he was able by habit to make the housedog hunt, and the hunting dog, on the contrary, to desist from running after hares. Inasmuch as the power of the mind, as I have shown above, is determined by intelligence alone, we shall determine by the knowledge of the mind alone the remedies against the emotions—remedies which every one, I believe, has experienced, although there may not have been any accurate observation or distinct perception of them, and from this knowledge of the mind alone shall we deduce everything which relates to its blessedness.

AXIOMS

1. If two contrary actions be excited in the same subject, a change must necessarily take place in both, or in one alone, until they cease to be contrary.

2. The power of an emotion is limited by the power of its cause, in so far as the essence of the emotion is manifested or limited by the essence of the cause itself.

PROPOSITIONS

PROPOSITION I. *As thoughts and the ideas of things are arranged and connected in the mind, exactly so are the modifications of the body or the images of things arranged and connected in the body.*

PROPOSITION II. *If we detach a perturbation of the mind or an emotion from the thought of an external cause and connect it with other thoughts, then the love or hatred toward the external cause and the fluctuations of the mind which arise from these emotions will be destroyed.*

PROPOSITION III. *An emotion which is a passion ceases to be a passion as soon as we form a clear and distinct idea of it.*

Corollary. In proportion, then, as we we know an emotion better is it more within our control, and the less does the mind suffer from it.

PROPOSITION IV. *There is no modification of the body of which we cannot form some clear and distinct conception.*

Corollary. Hence it follows that there is no emotion of which we cannot form some clear and distinct conception. For an emotion is an idea of a modification of the body (by the general definition of the emotions), and this idea therefore (Prop. 4, pt. 5) must involve some clear and distinct conception.

Note. Since nothing exists from which some effect does not follow, and since we understand clearly and distinctly everything which follows from an idea which is adequate in us, it is a necessary consequence that everyone has the power, partly at least, if not absolutely, of understanding clearly and distinctly himself and his emotions, and consequently of bringing it to pass that he suffers less from them. We have therefore mainly to strive to acquire a clear and distinct knowledge as far as possible of each emotion, so that the mind may be led to pass from the emotion to think those things which it perceives clearly and distinctly, and with which it is entirely satisfied, and to strive also that the emotion may be separated from the thought of an external cause and connected with true thoughts. Thus not only love, hatred, etc. will be destroyed (Prop. 2, pt. 5), but also the appetites or desires to which the emotion gives rise cannot be excessive. For it is above everything to be observed that the appetite by which a man is said to act is one and the same appetite as that by which he is said to suffer. All the appetites or desires are passions only in so far as they arise from inadequate ideas, and are classed among the virtues whenever they are excited or begotten by adequate ideas; for all the desires by which we are determined to any action may arise either from adequate or inadequate ideas. To return, therefore, to the point from which we set out: there is no remedy within our power which can be conceived more excellent for the emotions than that which consists in a true knowledge of them, since the mind possesses no other power than that of thinking and forming adequate ideas, as we have shown above (Prop. 3, pt. 3).

PROPOSITION VI. *In so far as the mind understands all things as necessary, so far has it greater power over the emotions, or suffers less from them.*

Note. The more this knowledge that things are necessary is applied to individual things which we imagine more distinctly and more vividly, the greater is this power of the mind over the emotions—a fact to which experience also testifies. For we see that sorrow for the loss of anything good is diminished if the person who has lost it considers that it could not by any possibility have been preserved. So also we see that nobody pities an infant because it does not know how to speak, walk, or reason, and lives so many years not conscious, as it were, of itself; but if a number of human beings were born adult, and only a few here and there were born infants, everyone would pity the infants because we should then consider infancy not as a thing natural and necessary, but as a defect or fault of Nature. Many other facts of a similar kind we might observe.

PROPOSITION XIV. *The mind can cause all the modification of the body or the images of things to be related to the idea of God (ideam Dei).*

Demonstration. There is no modification of the body of which the mind cannot form some clear and distinct conception (Prop. 4, pt. 5), and therefore (Prop. 15, pt. 1) it can cause all the modifications of the body to be related to the idea of God. —Q.E.D.

PROPOSITION XV. *He who clearly and distinctly understands himself and his emotions loves God, and loves Him better the better he understands himself and his emotions.*

Demonstration. He who clearly and distinctly understands himself and his emotions rejoices, and his joy is attended with the idea of God (Prop. 14, pt. 5), therefore he loves God, and (by the same reasoning) loves Him better the better he understands himself and his emotions.—Q.E.D.

PROPOSITION XVI. *This love of God above everything else ought to occupy the mind.*

Demonstration. For this love is connected with all the modifications of the body (Prop. 14, pt. 5), by all of which it is cherished (Prop. 15, pt. 5), and therefore above everything else ought to occupy the mind.—Q.E.D.

PROPOSITION XVII. *God is free from passions, nor is He affected with any emotion of joy or sorrow.*

PROPOSITION XIX. *He who loves God cannot strive that God should love him in return.*

PROPOSITION XX. *This love of God cannot be defiled either by the emotion of envy or jealousy, but is the more strengthened, the more people we imagine to be connected with God by the same bond of love.*

Note. There is no emotion directly contrary to this love and able to destroy it, and so we may conclude that this love of God is the most constant of all the emotions, and that, in so far as it is related to the body, it cannot be destroyed unless with the body itself.

I have, in what has preceded, included all the remedies for the emotions, that is to say, everything which the mind, considered in itself alone, can do against them. It appears therefrom that the power of the mind over the emotions consists—

1. In the knowledge itself of the emotions. (See Note, Prop. 4, pt. 5.)

2. In the separation by the mind of the emotions from the thought of an external cause, which we imagine confusedly. (See Prop. 2, pt. 5, and Note, Prop. 4, pt. 5.)

3. In duration, in which the modifications which are related to objects we understand surpass those related to objects conceived in a multilated or confused manner.

4. In the multitude of causes by which the modifications which are related to the common properties of things or to God are nourished.

5. In the order in which the mind can arrange its emotions and connect them one with the other.

But that this power of the mind over the emotions may be better understood, it is to be carefully observed that we call the emotions great when we compare the emotion of one man with that of another, and see that one man is agitated more than another by the same emotion, or when we compare the emotions of one and the same man with one another, and discover that he is affected or moved by one emotion more than by another.

For the power of any emotion is limited by the power of the external cause as compared with our own power. But the power of the mind is limited solely by knowledge, whilst impotence or passion is estimated solely by privation of knowledge or, in other words, by that through which ideas are called inadequate; and it therefore follows that that mind suffers the most whose largest part consists of inadequate ideas, so that it is distinguished by what it suffers rather than by what it does, while, on the contrary, that mind acts the most whose largest part consists of adequate ideas, so that, although it may possess as many inadequate ideas as the first, it is nevertheless distinguished by those which belong to human virtue rather than by those which are a sign of human impotence. Again, it is to be observed that our sorrows and misfortunes mainly proceed from too much love toward an object which is subject to many changes, and which we can never possess. For no one is troubled or anxious about any object he does not love, neither do wrongs, suspicions, hatreds, etc., arise except from love toward objects of which no one can be truly the possessor.

From all this we easily conceive what is the power which clear and distinct knowledge possesses over the emotions—the power, namely, by which it is able, in so far as they are passions, if not actually to destroy them (Note to Prop. 4, pt. 5), at least to make them constitute the smallest part of the mind (see Prop. 14, pt. 5). Moreover, it begets a love toward an immutable and eternal object (see Prop. 15, pt. 5) of which we are really partakers—a love which therefore cannot be vitiated by the defects which are in common love, but which can always become greater and greater (Prop. 15, pt. 5), occupy the largest part of the mind (Prop. 16, pt. 5) and thoroughly affect it.

I have now concluded all that I had to say relating to this present life. For any one who will attend to what has been urged in this Note, and to the definition of the mind and its emotions, and to Props. 1 and 3, pt. 3, will easily be able to see the truth of what I said in the beginning of the Note—that in these few words all the remedies for the emotions are comprehended.

JOSEPH BUTLER

Educated at Oxford, Joseph Butler (1692–1752) was a respected member of the Church of England and held a series of important positions within the Church. He began his career as a preacher at the Rolls Chapel in London and went on to become Bishop of Bristol, Dean of St. Paul's, and finally Bishop of Durham.

The first selection, on human nature and conscience, is taken from his major work, The Analogy of Religion. *The other selections are drawn from* Fifteen Sermons Preached at the Rolls Chapel, *a collection of early sermons to which was added a preface summarizing their contents and showing relationships between them. These works are remarkable not only for their defense of the Christian faith, but also for the subtlety of their treatment of central problems in ethical theory.*

In these works Butler returns to the ancient dictum that virtue consists in living in accordance with nature, and argues that conscience is the distinctive and central aspect of human nature. No less important are his critique of psychological egoism and his doctrine that self-love and benevolence, if rationally pursued, are in harmony.

*A Dissertation upon the Nature of Virtue**

That which renders beings capable of moral government is their having a moral nature and moral faculties of perception and of action. Brute creatures are impressed and actuated by various instincts and propensions; so also are we. But additional to this, we have a capacity of reflecting upon actions and characters, and making them an object to our thought; and in doing this, we naturally and unavoidably approve some actions, under the peculiar view of their being virtuous and of good desert, and disapprove others as vicious and of ill desert. That we have this moral approving and disapproving faculty is certain from our experiencing it in ourselves,

* From *The Analogy of Religion*, London, 1736.

and recognizing it in each other. It appears from our exercising it unavoidably, in the approbation and disapprobation even of feigned characters; from the words "right" and "wrong," "odious" and "amiable," "base" and "worthy," with many others of like signification in all languages applied to actions and characters; from the many written systems of morals which suppose it, since it cannot be imagined that all these authors, throughout all these treatises, had absolutely no meaning at all to their words, or a meaning merely chimerical; from our natural sense of gratitude, which implies a distinction between merely being the instrument of good and intending it; from the like distinction every one makes between injury and mere harm, which Hobbes says is peculiar to mankind, and between injury and just punishment, a distinction plainly natural, prior to the consideration of human laws. It is manifest [that a] great part of common language, and of common behavior over the world, is formed upon supposition of such a moral faculty, whether called conscience, moral reason, moral sense, or divine reason; whether considered as a sentiment of the understanding or as a perception of the heart, or, which seems the truth, as including both. Nor is it at all doubtful in the general what course of action this faculty, or practical discerning power within us, approves and what it disapproves. For, as much as it has been disputed wherein virtue consists, or whatever ground for doubt there may be about particulars, yet in general, there is in reality an universally acknowledged standard of it. It is that which all ages and all countries have made profession of in public; it is that which every man you meet puts on the show of; it is that which the primary and fundamental laws of all civil constitutions over the face of the earth make it their business and endeavor to enforce the practice of upon mankind, namely, justice, veracity and regard to common good. It being manifest then, in general, that we have such a faculty or discernment as this, it may be of use to remark some things more distinctly concerning it.

First, it ought to be observed that the object of this faculty is actions, comprehending under that name active or practical principles—those principles from which men would act if occasions and circumstances gave them power; and which, when fixed and habitual in any person, we call his character. It does not appear that brutes have the least reflex sense of actions, as distinguished from events, or that will and design, which constitute the very nature of actions as such, are at all an object to their perception. But to ours they are; and they are the object, and the only one, of the approving and disapproving faculty. Acting, conduct, behavior, abstracted from all regard to what is in fact and event the consequence of it, is itself the natural object of the moral discernment, as speculative truth and falsehood is of speculative reason. Intention of such and such consequences, indeed, is always included, for it is part of the action itself; but though the intended good or bad consequences do not follow, we have exactly the same sense of the action as if they did. In like manner we think well or ill of characters, abstracted from all consideration of the good or the evil, which persons of such characters have it actually in their power to do. We never, in the moral way, applaud or blame either ourselves or others for what we enjoy or what we suffer, or for having impressions made upon us, which we consider as altogether out of our power, but only for what we do or would have done had it been in our power; or for what we leave undone, which we might have done or would have left undone, though we could have done it.

Secondly, our sense or discernment of actions as morally good or evil implies in it a sense or discernment of them as of good or ill desert. It may be difficult to explain this perception so as to answer all the questions which may be asked concerning it; but everyone speaks of such and such actions as deserving punishment; and it is not, I suppose, pretended that they have absolutely no meaning at all to the expression. Now the meaning plainly is not that we conceive it for the good of society that the doer of such actions should be made to suffer. For if, unhappily, it were resolved that a man who, by some innocent action, was infected with the plague should be left to perish lest, by other people's coming near him, the infection should spread, no one would say he deserved this treatment. Innocence and ill desert are inconsistent ideas. Ill desert always supposes guilt; and if one be no part of the other, yet they are evidently and naturally connected in our mind. The sight of a man in misery raises our compassion toward him, and, if this misery be inflicted on him by another, our indignation against the author of it. But when we are informed that the sufferer is a villain and is punished only for his treachery or cruelty, our compassion exceedingly lessens, and in many instances our indignation wholly subsides. Now what produces this effect is the conception of that in the sufferer which we call ill desert. Upon considering then, or viewing together, our notion of vice and that of misery, there results a third—that of ill desert. And thus there is in human creatures an association of the two ideas, natural and moral evil, wickedness and punishment. If this association were merely artificial or accidental, it were nothing; but most unquestionably natural, it greatly concerns us to attend to it, instead of endeavoring to explain it away.

It may be observed further, concerning our perception of good and of evil desert, that the former is very weak with respect to common instances of virtue. One reason of which may be that it does not appear to a spectator, how far such instances of virtue proceed from a virtuous principle, or in what degree this principle is prevalent; since a very weak regard to virtue may be sufficient to make men act well in many common instances. And on the other hand, our perception of ill desert in vicious actions lessens, in proportion to the temptations men are thought to have had to such vices. For vice in human creatures consisting chiefly in the absence or want of the virtuous principle, though a man be overcome, suppose, by tortures, it does not from thence appear to what degree the virtuous principle was wanting. All that appears is that he had it not in such a degree as to prevail over the temptation; but possibly he had it in a degree which would have rendered him proof against common temptations.

Thirdly, our perception of vice and ill desert arises from, and is the result of, a comparison of actions with the nature and capacities of the agent. For the mere neglect of doing what we ought to do would, in many cases, be determined by all men to be in the highest degree vicious. And his determination must arise from such comparison, and be the result of it; because such neglect would not be vicious in creatures of other natures and capacities, as brutes. And it is the same also with respect to positive vices, or such as consist in doing what we ought not. For every one has a different sense of harm done by an idiot, madman, or child, and by one of mature and common understanding, though the action of both, including the intention, which is part of the action, be the same; as it may be, since idiots and madmen, as well as children, are capable not only of doing mischief, but also of intending it. Now this difference must arise from somewhat discerned in the nature or capacities of one, which renders the action vicious; and the want of which, in the other, renders the same action innocent or less vicious; and this plainly supposes a comparison, whether reflected upon or not, between the action and capacities of the agent, previous to our determining an action to be vicious. And hence arises a proper application of the epithets "incongruous," "unsuitable," "disproportionate," "unfit" to actions which our moral faculty determines to be vicious.

Fourthly, it deserves to be considered whether men are more at liberty, in point of morals, to make themselves miserable without reason than to make other people so, or dissolutely to neglect their own greater good, for the sake of a present lesser gratification, than they are to neglect the good of others whom nature has committed to their care. It should seem that a due concern about our own interest or happiness, and a reasonable endeavor to secure and promote it, which is, I think, very much the meaning of the word "prudence" in our language—it should seem that this is virtue, and the contrary behavior faulty and blameable, since, in the calmest way of reflection, we approve of the first, and condemn the other conduct, both in ourselves and others. This approbation and disapprobation are altogether different from mere desire of our own or of their happiness, and from sorrow upon missing it. For the object or occasion of this last kind of perception is satisfaction or uneasiness, whereas the object of the first is active behavior. In one case, what our thoughts fix upon is our condition, in the other, our conduct. It is true, indeed, that nature has not given us so sensible a disapprobation of imprudence and folly, either in *ourselves* or *others,* as of falsehood, injustice and cruelty; I suppose, because that constant habitual sense of private interest and good, which we always carry about with us, renders such sensible disapprobation less necessary, less wanting, to keep us from imprudently neglecting our own happiness and foolishly injuring ourselves, than it is necessary and wanting to keep us from injuring others to whose good we cannot have so strong and constant a regard; and also because imprudence and folly appearing to bring its own punishment more immediately and constantly than injurious behavior, it less needs the additional punishment which would be inflicted upon it by others had they the same sensible indignation against it as against injustice and fraud and cruelty. Besides, unhappiness being in itself the natural object of compassion, the unhappiness which people bring upon themselves, though it be willfully, excites in us some pity for them; and this, of course, lessens our displeasure against them. But still it is matter of experience that we are formed so as to reflect very severely upon the greater instances of imprudent neglect and foolish rashness, both in ourselves and others. In instances of this kind, men often say of themselves with remorse, and of others with some indignation, that they deserved to suffer such calamities because they brought them upon themselves and would not take warning. Particularly when persons come to poverty and distress by a long course of extravagance and after frequent admonitions, though without falsehood or injustice; we plainly do not regard such people as alike objects of compassion with those who are brought into the same condition by unavoidable accidents. From these things it appears that prudence is a species of virtue, and folly of vice, meaning by "folly" somewhat quite different from mere incapacity—a thoughtless want of that regard and attention to our own happiness which we had capacity for. And this the word properly includes, and, as it seems, in its usual acceptation, for we scarcely apply it to brute creatures.

However, if any person be disposed to dispute the matter, I shall very willingly give him up the words "virtue" and "vice," as not applicable to prudence and folly, but must beg leave to insist that the faculty within us, which is the judge of actions, approves of prudent actions, and disapproves imprudent ones; I say prudent and imprudent *actions* as such, and considered distinctly from the happiness or misery which they occasion. And, by the way, this observation may help to determine what justness there is in that objection against religion, that it teaches us to be interested and selfish.

Fifthly, without inquiring how far, and in what sense, virtue is resolvable into benevolence, and vice into the want of it, it may be proper to observe that benevolence and the want of it, singly considered, are in no sort the whole of virtue and vice. For if this were the case, in the review of one's own character, or that of others, our moral understanding and moral sense would be indifferent to everything but the degrees in which benevolence prevailed, and the degrees in which it was wanting. That is, we should neither approve of benevolence to some persons rather than to others, nor disapprove injustice and falsehood upon any other account than merely as an overbalance of happiness was foreseen likely to be produced by the first, and of misery by the second. But now, on the contrary, suppose two men competitors for anything whatever, which would be of equal advantage to each of them; though nothing indeed would be more impertinent than for a stranger to busy himself to get one of them preferred to the other, yet such endeavor would be virtue, in behalf of a friend or benefactor, abstracted from all consideration of distant consequences, as that examples of gratitude, and the cultivation of friendship, would be of general good to the world. Again, suppose one man should, by fraud or violence, take from another the fruit of his labor, with intent to give it to a third who he thought would have as much pleasure from it as would balance the pleasure which the first possessor would have had in the enjoyment, and his vexation in the loss of it; suppose also that no bad consequences would follow, yet such an action would surely be vicious. Nay further, were treachery, violence and injustice not otherwise vicious than as foreseen likely to produce an overbalance of misery to society, then, if in any case a man could procure to himself as great advantage by an act of injustice as the whole foreseen inconvenience, likely to be brought upon others by it, would amount to, such a piece of injustice would not be faulty or vicious at all; because it would be no more than, in any other case, for a man to prefer his own satisfaction to another's in equal degrees. The fact then appears to be that we are constituted so as to condemn falsehood, unprovoked violence, injustice, and to approve of benevolence to some, preferably to others, abstracted from all consideration which conduct is likeliest to produce an overbalance of happiness or misery. And therefore, were the Author of Nature to propose nothing to himself as an end but the production of happiness, were his moral character merely that of benevolence, yet ours is not so. Upon that supposition, indeed, the only reason of his giving us the abovementioned approbation of benevolence to some persons rather than others, and disapprobation of falsehood, unprovoked violence, and injustice, must be that he foresaw this constitution of our nature would produce more happiness than forming us with a temper of mere general benevolence. But still, since this is our constitution, falsehood, violence, injustice must be vice in us, and benevolence to some, preferably to others, virtue, abstracted from all consideration of the overbalance of evil or good, which they may appear likely to produce.

Now if human creatures are endued with such a moral nature as we have been explaining, or with a moral faculty the natural object of which is actions, moral government must consist in rendering them happy and unhappy, in rewarding and punishing them as they follow, neglect or depart from, the moral rule of action interwoven in their nature, or suggested and enforced by this moral faculty—in rewarding and punishing them upon account of their so doing.

I am not sensible that I have, in this fifth observation, contradicted what any author designed to assert. But some of great and distinguished merit have, I think, expressed themselves in a manner which may occasion some danger to careless readers, of imagining the whole of virtue to consist in singly aiming, according to the best of their judgment, at promoting the happiness of mankind in the present state; and the whole of vice in doing what they foresee, or might foresee, is likely to produce an overbalance of unhappiness in it; than which mistakes, none can be conceived more terrible. For it is certain that some of the most shocking instances of injustice, adultery, murder, perjury, and even of persecution, may, in many supposable cases, not have the appearance of being likely to produce an overbalance of misery in the present state; perhaps sometimes may have the contrary appearance. For this reflection might easily be carried on, but I forbear. The happiness of the world is the concern of him who is the Lord and the Proprietor of it; nor do we know what we are about when we endeavor to promote the good of mankind in any ways but those which he has directed—that is indeed in all ways not contrary to veracity and justice. I speak thus upon supposition of persons really endeavoring, in some sort, to do good without regard to these. But the truth seems to be that such supposed endeavors proceed, almost always, from ambition, the spirit of the party, or some indirect principle, concealed perhaps in great measure from persons themselves. And though it is our business and our duty to endeavor, within the bounds of veracity and justice, to contribute to the ease, convenience, and even cheerfulness and diversion of our fellow creatures, yet, from our short views, it is greatly uncertain whether this endeavor will in particular instances produce an overbalance of happiness upon the whole, since so many and distant things must come into the account. And that which makes it our duty is that there is some appearance that it will, and no positive appearance sufficient to balance this, on the contrary side; and also, that such benevolent endeavor is a cultivation of that most excellent of all virtuous principles, the active principle of benevolence.

However, though veracity as well as justice is to be our rule of life, it must be added, otherwise a snare will be laid in the way of some plain men, that the use of common forms of speech, generally understood, cannot be falsehood; and in general, that there can be no designed falsehood without designing to deceive. It must likewise be observed that, in numberless cases, a man may be under the strictest obligations to what he foresees will deceive, without his intending it. For it is impossible not to foresee that the words and actions of men, in different ranks and employments, and of different educations, will perpetually be mistaken by each other; and it cannot but be so whilst they will judge with the utmost carelessness, as they daily do, of what they are not, perhaps, enough informed to be competent judges of, even though they considered it with great attention.

*Sermons**

Preface: Critique of Psychological Egoism

There is a strange affection in many people of explaining away all particular affections, and representing the whole of life as nothing but one continued exercise of self-love. Hence arises that surprising confusion and perplexity in the Epicureans of old, Hobbes, and this whole set of writers—the confusion of calling actions

* Joseph Butler, *Fifteen Sermons Preached at the Rolls Chapel*, London, 1926. Section headings have been added by the editors.

interested which are done in contradiction to the most manifest known interest, merely for the gratification of a present passion. Now all this confusion might easily be avoided, by stating to ourselves wherein the idea of self-love in general consists, as distinguished from all particular movements toward particular external objects—the appetites of sense, resentment, compassion, curiosity, ambition, and the rest. When this is done, if the words "selfish" and "interested" cannot be parted with but must be applied to everything, yet, to avoid such total confusion of all language, let the distinction be made by epithets: and the first may be called cool or settled selfishness, and the other passionate or sensual selfishness. But the most natural way of speaking plainly is to call the first only "self-love," and the actions proceeding from it "interested"; and to say of the latter that they are not love to ourselves, but movements toward somewhat external: honor, power, the harm or good of another; and that the pursuit of these external objects, so far as it proceeds from these movements (for it may proceed from self-love), is no otherwise interested than as every action of every creature must, from the nature of the thing, be; for no one can act but from a desire or choice or preference of his own.

DEVELOPMENT IN SERMON ONE

Suppose a man of learning to be writing a grave book upon *human nature*, and to show in several parts of it that he had an insight into the subject he was considering; amongst other things, the following one would require to be accounted for: the appearance of benevolence or goodwill in men toward each other in the instances of natural relation, and in others (Hobbes, *Of Human Nature*, c. ix. § 7). Cautious of being deceived with outward show, he retires within himself to see exactly what that is in the mind of man from whence this appearance proceeds; and, upon deep reflection, asserts the principle in the mind to be only the love of power, and delight in the exercise of it. Would not everybody think here was a mistake of one word for another; that the philosopher was contemplating and accounting for some other human actions, some other behavior of man to man? And could anyone be thoroughly satisfied that what is commonly called benevolence or goodwill was really the affection meant, but only by being made to understand that this learned person had a general hypothesis to which the appearance of goodwill could not otherwise be reconciled? That what has this appearance is often nothing but ambition; that delight in superiority often (suppose always) mixes itself with benevolence, only makes it more specious to call it ambition than hunger, of the two: but in reality that passion does no more account for the whole appearances of goodwill than this appetite does. Is there not often the appearance of one man's wishing that good to another which he knows himself unable to procure him; and rejoicing in it, though bestowed by a third person? And can love of power anyway possibly come into account for this desire or delight? Is there not often the appearance of men's distinguishing between two or more persons, preferring one before another, to do good to, in cases where love of power cannot in the least account for the distinction and preference? For this principle can no otherwise distinguish between objects than as it is a greater instance and exertion of power to do good to one rather than to another. Again, suppose goodwill in the mind of man to be nothing but delight in the exercise of power; men might indeed be restrained by distant and accidental considerations; but these restraints being removed, they would have a disposition to, and delight in, mischief as an exercise and proof of power: and this disposition and delight would arise from or be the same principle in the mind, as a disposition to, and delight in, charity. Thus cruelty, as distinct from envy and resentment, would be exactly the same in the mind of man as goodwill—that one tends to the happiness, the other to the misery of our fellow creatures, is, it seems, merely an accidental circumstance, which the mind has not the least regard to. These are the absurdities which even men of capacity run into when they have occasion to belie their nature, and will perversely disclaim that image of God which was originally stamped upon it, the traces of which, however faint, are plainly discernible upon the mind of man.

If any person can in earnest doubt whether there be such a thing as goodwill in one man toward another (for the question is not concerning either the degree or extensiveness of it, but concerning the affection itself), let it be observed that whether man be thus or otherwise constituted, what is the inward frame in this particular, is a mere question of fact or natural history, not provable immediately by reason. It is therefore to be judged of and determined in the same way other facts or matters of natural history are: by appealing to the external senses or inward perceptions respectively, as the matter under consideration is cognizable by one or the other; by arguing from acknowledged facts and actions; for a great number of actions in the same kind, in different circumstances, and respecting different objects, will prove, to a certainty, what principles they do not, and, to the greatest probability, what principles they do proceed from; and lastly, by the testimony of mankind. Now that there is some degree of benevolence amongst men may be as strongly and plainly proved in all these ways, as it could possibly be proved, supposing there was this affection in our nature. And should anyone think fit to assert that resentment in the mind of man was absolutely nothing but reasonable concern for our own safety, the falsity of this, and what is the real nature of that passion, could be shown in no other ways than those in which it may be shown, that there is such a thing in some degree as real goodwill in man toward man. It is sufficient that the seeds of it be implanted in our nature by God. There is, it is owned, much left for us to do upon our own heart and temper; to cultivate, to improve, to call it forth, to exercise it in a steady, uniform manner. This is our work; this is virtue and religion.

Preface: Compatibility of Self-love and Benevolence

Self-love and any particular passion may be joined together; and from this complication it becomes impossible in numberless instances to determine precisely how far an action, perhaps even of one's own, has for its principle general self-love or some particular passion. But this need create no confusion in the ideas themselves of self-love and particular passions. We distinctly discern what one is and what the others are, though we may be uncertain how far one or the other influences us. And though, from this uncertainty, it cannot but be that there will be different opinions concerning mankind as more or less governed by interest, and some will ascribe actions to self-love, which others will ascribe to particular passions; yet it is absurd to say that mankind are wholly actuated by either, since it is manifest that both have their influence. For as, on the one hand, men form a general notion of interest, some placing it in one thing, and some in another, and have a considerable regard to it throughout the course of their life, which is owing to self-love; so, on the other hand, they are often set on work by the particular passions themselves, and a considerable part of life is spent in the actual gratification of them, that is, is employed, not by self-love, but by the passions.

Besides, the very idea of an interested pursuit necessarily presupposes particular passions or appetites, since the very idea of interest or happiness consists in this that an appetite or affection enjoys its object. It is not because we love ourselves that we find delight in such and such objects, but because we have particular affections toward them. Take away these affections and you leave self-love absolutely nothing at all to employ itself about; no end or object for it to pursue except only that of avoiding pain. Indeed, the Epicureans, who maintained that absence of pain was the highest happiness, might, consistently with themselves, deny all affection and, if they had so pleased, every sensual appetite, too; but the very idea of interest or happiness other than absence of pain implies particular appetites or passions, these being necessary to constitute that interest or happiness.

The observation that benevolence is no more disinterested than any of the common particular passions seems in itself worth being taken notice of; but is insisted upon to obviate that scorn which one sees rising upon the faces of people who are said to know the world, when mention is made of a disinterested, generous, or public-spirited action. The truth of that observation might be made appear in a more formal manner of proof; for whoever will consider all the possible respects and relations which any particular affection can have to self-love and private interest, will, I think, see demonstrably that benevolence is not in any respect more at variance with self-love than any other particular affection whatever, but that it is in every respect, at least, as friendly to it.

If the observation be true, it follows that self-love and benevolence, virtue and interest, are not to be opposed but only to be distinguished from each other, in the same way as virtue and any other particular affection, love of arts, suppose, are to be distinguished. Everything is what it is, and not another thing. The goodness or badness of actions does not arise from hence that the epithet "interested" or "disinterested" may be applied to them any more than that any other indifferent epithet, suppose "inquisitive" or "jealous," may or may not be applied to them, not from their being attended with present or future pleasure or pain, but from their being what they are, namely, what becomes such creatures as we are, what the state of the case requires, or the contrary. Or in other words, we may judge and determine that an action is morally good or evil before we so much as consider whether it be interested or disinterested. This consideration no more comes in to determine whether an action be virtuous than to determine whether it be resentful. Self-love in its due degree is as just and morally good as any affection whatever. Benevolence toward particular persons may be to a degree of weakness, and so be blamable; and disinterestedness is so far from being in itself commendable that the utmost possible depravity which we can in imagination conceive is that of disinterested cruelty. . . .

DEVELOPMENT IN SERMON ELEVEN

Since there is generally thought to be some peculiar kind of contrariety between self-love and the love of our neighbor, between the pursuit of public and of private good, insomuch that when you are recommending one of these, you are supposed to be speaking against the other; and from hence arises a secret prejudice against and frequently open scorn of all talk of public spirit and real goodwill to our fellow creatures; it will be necessary to inquire what respect benevolence hath to self-love, and the pursuit of private interest to the pursuit of public; or whether there be anything of that peculiar inconsistency and contrariety between them, over and above what there is between self-love and other passions and particular affections, and their respective pursuits. . . .

Every man hath a general desire of his own happiness, and likewise a variety of particular affections, passions, and appetites to particular external objects. The former proceeds from or is self-love, and seems inseparable from all sensible creatures who can reflect upon themselves and their own interest or happiness, so as to have that interest an object to their minds; what is to be said of the latter is that they proceed from, or together make up, that particular nature according to which man is made. The object the former pursues is somewhat internal—our own happiness, enjoyment, satisfaction; whether we have or have not a distinct particular perception what it is or wherein it consists, the objects of the latter are this or that particular external thing which the affections tend toward, and of which it hath always a particular idea or perception. The principle we call "self-love" never seeks anything external for the sake of the thing, but only as a means of happiness or good; particular affections rest in the external things themselves. One belongs to man as a reasonable creature reflecting upon his own interest or happiness. The other, though quite distinct from reason, are as much a part of human nature.

That all particular appetites and passions are toward *external things themselves,* distinct from the *pleasure arising from them,* is manifested from hence—that there could not be this pleasure were it not for that prior suitableness between the object and the passion; there could be no enjoyment or delight from one thing more than another, from eating food more than from swallowing a stone, if there were not an affection or appetite to one thing more than another.

Every particular affection, even the love of our neighbor, is as really our own affection as self-love; and the pleasure arising from its gratification is as much my own pleasure as the pleasure self-love would have from knowing I myself should be happy some time hence, would be my own pleasure. And if, because every particular affection is a man's own, and the pleasure arising from its gratification his own pleasure, or pleasure to himself, such particular affection must be called self-love, according to this way of speaking no creature whatever can possibly act but merely from self-love; and every action and every affection whatever is to be resolved up into this one principle. But then this is not the language of mankind; or if it were, we should want words to express the difference between the principle of an action proceeding from cool consideration that it will be to my own advantage, and an action, suppose of revenge or of friendship, by which a man runs upon certain ruin to do evil or good to another. It is manifest the principles of these actions are totally different, and so want different words to be distinguished by; all that they agree in is that they both proceed from and are done to gratify an inclination in a man's self. But the principle or inclination in one case is self-love, in the other, hatred or love of another. There is then a distinction between the cool principle of self-love or general desire of our happiness, as one part of our nature and one principle of action, and the particular affections toward particular external objects, as another part of our nature and another principle of action. How much soever therefore is to be allowed to self-love, yet it cannot be allowed to be the whole of our inward constitution, because, you see, there are other parts or principles which come into it.

Further, private happiness or good is all which self-love can make us desire or be concerned about; in having this consists its gratification: it is an affection to ourselves, a regard to our own interest, happiness, and private good; and in the proportion a man hath this, he is interested, or a lover of himself. Let this be kept in mind; because there is commonly, as I shall presently have occasion to observe, another sense put upon these words. On the other hand, particular affections tend toward particular external things; these are their objects; having these is their end—in this consists their gratification, no matter whether it be, or be not, upon the whole, our interest or happiness. An action done from the former of these principles is called an interested action. An action proceeding from any of the latter has its denomination of passionate, ambitious, friendly, revengeful, or any other, from the particular appetite or affection from which it proceeds. Thus self-love as one part of human nature and the several particular principles as the other part are, themselves, their objects and ends, stated and shown.

From hence it will be easy to see how far, and in what ways, each of these can contribute and be subservient to the private good of the individual. Happiness does not consist in self-love. The desire of happiness is no more the thing itself than the desire of riches is the possession or enjoyment of them. People may love themselves with the most entire and unbounded affection, and yet be extremely miserable. Neither can self-love anyway help them out, but by setting them on work to get rid of the causes of their misery, to gain or make use of those objects which are by nature adapted to afford satisfaction. Happiness or satisfaction consists only in the enjoyment of those objects which are by nature suited to our several particular appetites, passions, and affections. So that if self-love wholly engrosses us, and leaves no room for any other principle, there can be absolutely no such thing at all as happiness, or enjoyment of any kind whatever, since happiness consists in the gratification of particular passions, which supposes the having of them. Self-love then does not constitute *this* or *that* to be our interest or good; but, our interest or good being constituted by nature and supposed, self-love only puts us upon obtaining and securing it. Therefore, if it be possible that self-love may prevail and exert itself in a degree or manner which is not subservient to this end, then it will not follow that our interest will be promoted in proportion to the degree in which that principle engrosses us, and prevails over others. Nay further, the private and contracted affection, when it is not subservient to this end, private good, may, for anything that appears, have a direct contrary tendency and effect. And if we will consider the matter, we shall see that it often really has. *Disengagement* is absolutely necessary to enjoyment; and a person may have so steady and fixed an eye upon his own interest, whatever he places it in, as may hinder him from *attending* to many gratifications within his reach, which others have their minds free and open to. Overfondness for a child is not generally thought to be for its advantage; and if there be any guess to be made from appearances, surely that character we call selfish is not the most promising for happiness. Such a temper may plainly be, and exert itself in a degree and manner which may prevent obtaining the means and materials of enjoyment, as well as the making use of them. Immoderate self-love does very ill consult its own interest; and how much soever a paradox it may appear, it is certainly true that even from self-love we should endeavor to get over all inordinate regard to and consideration of ourselves. Every one of our passions and affections hath its natural stint and bound, which may easily be exceeded; whereas our enjoyments can possibly be but in a determinate measure and degree. Therefore such excess of the affection, since it cannot procure any enjoyment, must in all cases be useless, but is generally attended with inconveniences, and often is downright pain and misery. This holds as much with regard to self-love as to all other affections. The natural degree of it, so far as it sets us on work to gain and make use of the materials of satisfaction, may be to our real advantage; but beyond or besides this, it is in several respects an inconvenience and disadvantage. Thus is appears that private interest is so far from being likely to be promoted in proportion to the degree in which self-love engrosses us, and prevails over all other principles, that the contracted affection may be so prevalent as to disappoint itself, and even contradict its own end, private good.

"But who, except the most sordidly covetous, ever thought there was any rivalship between the love of greatness, honor, power, or between sensual appetites and self-love? No, there is a perfect harmony between them. It is by means of these particular appetites and affections that self-love is gratified in enjoyment, happiness, and satisfaction. The competition and rivalship is between self-love and the love of our neighbor, that affection which leads us out of ourselves, makes us regardless of our own interest, and substitute that of another in its stead." Whether then there be any peculiar competition and contrariety in this case, shall now be considered.

Self-love and interestedness was stated to consist in or be an affection to ourselves, a regard to our own private good; it is therefore distinct from benevolence, which is an affection to the good of our fellow creatures. But that benevolence is distinct from, that is, not the same thing with self-love, is no reason for its being looked upon with any peculiar suspicion; because every principle whatever, by means of which self-love is gratified, is distinct from it; and all things which are distinct from each other are equally so. . . .

The object of self-love is expressed in the term "self"; and every appetite of sense and every particular affection of the heart are equally interested or disinterested, because the objects of them are all equally self or somewhat else. Whatever ridicule therefore the mention of a disinterested principle or action may be supposed to lie open to, must, upon the matter being thus stated, relate to ambition and every appetite and particular affection, as much as to benevolence. And indeed all the ridicule and all the grave perplexity, of which this subject hath had its full share, is merely from words. The most intelligible way of speaking of it seems to be this: that self-love and the actions done in consequence of it are interested; that particular affections toward external objects, and the actions done in consequence of those affections, are not so. But everyone is at liberty to use words as he pleases. All that is here insisted upon is that ambition, revenge, benevolence, all particular passions whatever, and the actions they produce, are equally interested or disinterested.

Thus it appears that there is no peculiar contrariety between self-love and benevolence, no greater competition between these than between any other particular affections and self-love. This relates to the affections themselves. Let us now see whether there be any peculiar contrariety between the respective courses of life which these affections lead to, whether there be any greater competition between the pursuit of private and of public good than between any other particular pursuits and that of private good. . . .

The short of the matter is no more than this: happiness consists in the gratification of certain affections, appetites, passions, with objects which are by nature adapted to them. Self-love may indeed set us on work to gratify these, but happiness or enjoyment has no immediate connection with self-love, but arises from such gratification alone. Love of our neighbor is one of those affections. This, considered as a *virtuous principle,* is gratified by a consciousness of endeavoring to promote the good of others; but considered as a *natural affection,* its gratification consists in the actual accomplishment of this endeavor. Now indulgence or gratification of this affection, whether in that consciousness or this accomplishment, has the same respect to interest as indulgence of any other affection; they equally proceed from or do not proceed from self-love; they equally include or equally exclude this principle. Thus it appears that benevolence and the pursuit of public good hath at least as great respect to self-love and the pursuit of private good as any other particular passions, and their respective pursuits. . . .

And to all these things may be added that religion, from whence arises our strongest obligation to benevolence, is so far from disowning the principle of self-love that it often addresses itself to that very principle, and always to the mind in that state when reason presides; and there can no access be had to the understanding but by convincing men that the course of life we would persuade them to is not contrary to their interest. It may be allowed, without any prejudice to the cause of virtue and religion, that our ideas of happiness and misery are of all our ideas the nearest and most important to us, that they will, nay, if you please, that they ought to prevail over those of order and beauty and harmony and proportion if there should ever be, as it is impossible there ever should be, any inconsistency between them, though these last, too, as expressing the fitness of actions, are real as truth itself. Let it be allowed, though virtue or moral rectitude does indeed consist in affection to and pursuit of what is right and good, as such, yet, that when we sit down in a cool hour, we can neither justify to ourselves this or any other pursuit till we are convinced that it will be for our happiness or at least not contrary to it.

DAVID HUME

David Hume (1711–1776) candidly admits that a "love of literary fame" was his "ruling passion." Unfortunately his central philosophical works were largely ignored during his lifetime, and when noted, they were misunderstood and treated with scorn. Still pursuing a literary reputation, he retired to his native Scotland and wrote a history of England which met, in his own words, with "tolerable, and but tolerable, success."

Hume drew inspiration, as did many others of the time, from Newton's striking achievements. If it is possible to reduce physical activities to a few simple laws, Hume saw no reason why the same could not be done for mental activities. Thus his first published work, the Treatise of Human Nature, *bears the subtitle: "An Attempt to Introduce the Experimental Method of Reasoning into Moral Subjects."*

In the first selection, drawn from the Treatise, *Hume discusses the psychological foundations of all moral judgments. The second selection is from* An Enquiry Concerning the Principles of Morals. *Here Hume argues that moral rules, and in particular those concerning justice, are based upon the principle of utility. The final selection is an essay in which Hume critically examines the perennial notion that societies are based upon some form of a social contract. The essay is an example of Hume's brilliance as an analytic thinker.*

*Treatise of Human Nature**

Of Virtue and Vice in General

SECTION I. MORAL DISTINCTIONS NOT DERIVED FROM REASON

It has been observed that nothing is ever present to the mind but its perceptions; and that all the actions of seeing, hearing, judging, loving, hating, and thinking, fall under this denomination. The mind can never exert itself in any action which we may not comprehend under the term of *perception;* and consequently that term is no less applicable to those judgments by which we distinguish moral good and evil, than to every other operation of the mind. To approve of one character, to condemn another, are only so many different perceptions.

Now, as perceptions resolve themselves into two kinds, viz., *impressions* and *ideas,* this distinction gives rise to a ques-

* David Hume, *Treatise of Human Nature,* London, 1739.

tion, with which we shall open up our present inquiry concerning morals, whether it is by means of our *ideas* or *impressions* we distinguish betwixt vice and virtue, and pronounce an action blamable or praiseworthy? This will immediately cut off all loose discourses and declamations, and reduce us to something precise and exact on the present subject.

Those who affirm that virtue is nothing but a conformity to reason; that there are eternal fitnesses and unfitnesses of things which are the same to every rational being that considers them; that the immutable measure of right and wrong imposes an obligation, not only on human creatures, but also on the Deity himself: all these systems concur in the opinion that morality, like truth, is discerned merely by ideas, and by their juxtaposition and comparison. In order, therefore, to judge of these systems, we need only consider whether it be possible from reason alone to distinguish betwixt moral good and evil, or whether there must concur some other principles to enable us to make that distinction.

If morality had naturally no influence on human passions and actions, it were in vain to take such pains to inculcate it; and nothing would be more fruitless than that multitude of rules and precepts with which all moralists abound. Philosophy is commonly divided into *speculative* and *practical;* and as morality is always comprehended under the latter division, it is supposed to influence our passions and actions, and to go beyond the calm and indolent judgments of the understanding. And this is confirmed by common experience, which informs us that men are often governed by their duties, and are deterred from some actions by the opinion of injustice, and impelled to others by that of obligation.

Since morals, therefore, have an influence on the actions and affections, it follows that they cannot be derived from reason. . . . Morals excite passions, and produce or prevent actions. Reason of itself is utterly impotent in this particular. The rules of morality, therefore, are not conclusions of our reason.

No one, I believe, will deny the justness of this inference; nor is there any other means of evading it than by denying that principle on which it is founded. As long as it is allowed that reason has no influence on our passions and actions, it is in vain to pretend that morality is discovered only by a deduction of reason. An active principle can never be founded on an inactive; and if reason be inactive in itself, it must remain so in all its shapes and appearances, whether it exerts itself in natural or moral subjects, whether it considers the powers of external bodies or the actions of rational beings. . . .

Reason is the discovery of truth or falsehood. Truth or falsehood consists in an agreement or disagreement either to the *real* relations of ideas, or to *real* existence and matter of fact. Whatever, therefore, is not susceptible of this agreement or disagreement is incapable of being true or false, and can never be an object of our reason. Now, it is evident our passions, volitions, and actions, are not susceptible of any such agreement or disagreement; being original facts and realities, complete in themselves, and implying no reference to other passions, volitions, and actions. It is impossible, therefore, they can be pronounced either true or false, and be either contrary or conformable to reason.

This argument is of double advantage to our present purpose. For it proves *directly* that actions do not derive their merit from a conformity to reason, nor their blame from a contrariety to it; and it proves the same truth more *indirectly*, by showing us that as reason can never immediately prevent or produce any action by contradicting or approving of it, it cannot be the source of moral good and evil, which are found to have that influence. Actions may be laudable or blamable, but they cannot be reasonable or unreasonable: laudable or blamable, therefore, are not the same with reasonable or unreasonable. The merit and demerit of actions frequently contradict, and sometimes control our natural propensities. But reason has no such influence. Moral distinctions, therefore, are not the offspring of reason. Reason is wholly inactive, and can never be the source of so active a principle as conscience, or a sense of morals. . . .

It has been observed that reason, in a strict and philosophical sense, can have an influence on our conduct only after two ways: either when it excites a passion by informing us of the existence of something which is a proper object of it; or when it discovers the connection of causes and effects so as to afford us means of exerting any passion. These are the only kinds of judgment which can accompany our actions, or can be said to produce them in any manner; and it must be allowed that these judgments may often be false and erroneous. A person may be affected with passion, by supposing a pain or pleasure to lie in an object which has no tendency to produce either of these sensations, or which produces the contrary to what is imagined. A person may also take false measures for the attaining of his end, and may retard by his foolish conduct instead of forwarding the execution of any object. These false judgments may be thought to affect the passions and actions, which are connected with them, and may be said to render them unreasonable, in a figurative and improper way of speaking. But though this be acknowledged, it is easy to observe that these errors are so far from being the source of all immorality that they are commonly very innocent, and draw no manner of guilt upon the person who is so unfortunate as to fall into them. They extend not beyond a mistake of *fact*, which moralists have not generally supposed criminal, as being perfectly involuntary. I am more to be lamented than blamed if I am mistaken with regard to the influence of objects in producing pain or pleasure, or if I know not the proper means of satisfying my desires. No one can ever regard such errors as a defect in my moral character. A fruit, for instance, that is really disagreeable appears to me at a distance, and, through mistake, I fancy it to be pleasant and delicious. Here is one error. I choose certain means of reaching this fruit which are not proper for my end. Here is a second error; nor is there any third one which can ever possibly enter into our reasonings concerning actions. I ask, therefore, if a man in this situation, and guilty of these two errors, is to be regarded as vicious and criminal, however unavoidable they might have been? Or if it be possible to imagine that such errors are the sources of all immorality? . . .

Thus, upon the whole, it is impossible that the distinction betwixt moral good and evil can be made by reason; since that distinction has an influence upon our actions, of which reason alone is incapable. Reason and judgment may, indeed, be the mediate cause of an action, by prompting or by directing a passion; but it is not pretended that a judgment of this kind, either in its truth or falsehood, is attended with virtue or vice. And as to the judgments which are caused by our judgments, they can still less bestow those moral qualities on the actions which are their causes.

But, to be more particular, and to show that those eternal immutable fitnesses and unfitnesses of things cannot be defended by sound philosophy, we may weigh the following considerations.

If the thought and understanding were alone capable of fixing the boundaries of right and wrong, the character of virtuous and vicious either must lie in some relations of objects, or must be a matter of fact which is discovered by our reasoning. This consequence is evident. As the operations of human understanding divide themselves into two kinds—the comparing of ideas and the inferring of matter of fact—

were virtue discovered by the understanding, it must be an object of one of these operations; nor is there any third operation of the understanding which can discover it. There has been an opinion very industriously propagated by certain philosophers that morality is susceptible of demonstration; and though no one has ever been able to advance a single step in those demonstrations, yet it is taken for granted that this science may be brought to an equal certainty with geometry or algebra. Upon this supposition vice and virtue must consist in some relations, since it is allowed on all hands that no matter of fact is capable of being demonstrated. Let us therefore begin with examining this hypothesis. . . .

Of all crimes that human creatures are capable of committing, the most horrid and unnatural is ingratitude, especially when it is committed against parents, and appears in the more flagrant instances of wounds and death. This is acknowledged by all mankind, philosophers as well as the people. The question only arises among philosophers, whether the guilt or moral deformity of this action be discovered by demonstrative reasoning, or be felt by an internal sense and by means of some sentiment which the reflecting on such an action naturally occasions. This question will soon be decided against the former opinion, if we can show the same relations in other objects without the notion of any guilt or iniquity attending them. Reason or science is nothing but the comparing of ideas, and the discovery of their relations; and if the same relations have different characters it must be evidently follow that those characters are not discovered merely by reason. To put the affair, therefore, to this trial, let us choose any inanimate object, such as an oak or elm, and let us suppose that by the dropping of its seed it produces a sapling below it which, springing up by degrees, at last overtops and destroys the parent tree: I ask if in this instance there be wanting any relation which is discoverable in parricide or ingratitude? Is not the one tree the cause of the other's existence; and the latter the cause of the destruction of the former in the same manner as when a child murders his parent? It is not sufficient to reply that a choice or will is wanting. For in the case of parricide, a will does not give rise to any *different* relations, but is only the cause from which the action is derived; and consequently produces the *same* relations that in the oak or elm arise from some other principles. It is a will or choice that determines a man to kill his parent; and they are the laws of matter and motion that determine a sapling to destroy the oak from which it sprung. Here then the same relations have different causes; but still the relations are the same; and as their discovery is not in both cases attended with a notion of immorality, it follows that that notion does not arise from such a discovery.

But to choose an instance still more resembling; I would fain ask anyone why incest in the human species is criminal, and why the very same action and the same relations in animals have not the smallest moral turpitude and deformity? If it be answered that this action is innocent in animals, because they have not reason sufficient to discover its turpitude, but that man being endowed with that faculty which *ought* to restrain him to his duty, the same action instantly becomes criminal to him. Should this be said, I would reply that this is evidently arguing in a circle. For before reason can perceive this turpitude, the turpitude must exist, and consequently is independent of the decisions of our reason, and is their object more properly than their effect. According to this system, then, every animal that has sense, and appetite, and will, that is, every animal must be susceptible of all the same virtues and vices for which we ascribe praise and blame to human creatures. All the difference is that our superior reason may serve to discover the vice or virtue, and by that means may augment the blame or praise; but still this discovery supposes a separate being in these moral distinctions, and a being which depends only on the will and appetite, and which, both in thought and reality, may be distinguished from reason. Animals are susceptible of the same relations with respect to each other as the human species, and therefore would also be susceptible of the same morality if the essence of morality consisted in these relations. Their want of a sufficient degree of reason may hinder them from perceiving the duties and obligations of morality; but can never hinder these duties from existing; since they must antecedently exist in order to their being perceived. Reason must find them, and can never produce them. This argument deserves to be weighed as being, in my opinion, entirely decisive.

Nor does this reasoning only prove that morality consists not in any relations that are the objects of science; but, if examined, will prove with equal certainty that it consists not in any *matter of fact* which can be discovered by the understanding. This is the *second* part of our argument; and if it can be made evident, we may conclude that morality is not an object of reason. But can there be any difficulty in proving that vice and virtue are not matters of fact whose existence we can infer by reason? Take any action allowed to be vicious—wilful murder, for instance. Examine it in all lights, and see if you can find that matter of fact or real existence which you call *vice.* In whichever way you take it, you find only certain passions, motives, volitions, and thoughts. There is no other matter of fact in the case. The vice entirely escapes you, as long as you consider the object. You never can find it till you turn your reflection into your own breast and find a sentiment of disapprobation which arises in you towards this action. Here is a matter of fact; but it is the object of feeling, not of reason. It lies in yourself, not in the object. So that when you pronounce any action or character to be vicious, you mean nothing, but that from the constitution of your nature you have a feeling or sentiment of blame from the contemplation of it. Vice and virtue, therefore, may be compared to sounds, colours, heat, and cold, which, according to modern philosophy, are not qualities in objects but perceptions in the mind: and this discovery in morals, like that other in physics, is to be regarded as a considerable advancement of the speculative sciences; though, like that too, it has little or no influence on practice. Nothing can be more real, or concern us more, than our own sentiments of pleasure and uneasiness; and if these be favourable to virtue, and unfavourable to vice, no more can be requisite to the regulation of our conduct and behaviour.

I cannot forbear adding to these reasonings an observation which may, perhaps, be found of some importance. In every system of morality which I have hitherto met with, I have always remarked that the author proceeds for some time in the ordinary way of reasoning, and establishes the being of a god, or makes observations concerning human affairs; when of a sudden I am surprised to find that instead of the usual copulations of propositions *is* and *is not,* I meet with no proposition that is not connected with an *ought* or an *ought not.* This change is imperceptible, but is, however, of the last consequence. For as this *ought* or *ought not* expresses some new relation or affirmation, it is necessary that it should be observed and explained; and at the same time that a reason should be given for what seems altogether inconceivable, how this new relation can be a deduction from others which are entirely different from it. But as authors do not commonly use this precaution, I shall presume to recommend it to the readers; and am persuaded that this small attention would subvert all the vulgar systems of morality and let us see that the distinction of vice and virtue is not founded merely on the relations of objects, nor is perceived by reason.

SECTION II. MORAL DISTINCTIONS DERIVED FROM A MORAL SENSE

Thus the course of the argument leads us to conclude that since vice and virtue are not discoverable merely by reason, or the comparison of ideas, it must be by means of some impression or sentiment they occasion, that we are able to mark the difference betwixt them. Our decisions concerning moral rectitude and depravity are evidently perceptions; and as all perceptions are either impressions or ideas, the exclusion of the one is a convincing argument for the other. Morality, therefore, is more properly felt than judged of; though this feeling or sentiment is commonly so soft and gentle that we are apt to confound it with an idea, according to our common custom of taking all things for the same which have any near resemblance to each other.

The next question is of what nature are these impressions, and after what manner do they operate upon us? Here we cannot remain long in suspense, but must pronounce the impression arising from virtue to be agreeable, and that proceeding from vice to be uneasy. Every moment's experience must convince us of this. There is no spectacle so fair and beautiful as a noble and generous action; nor any which gives us more abhorrence than one that is cruel and treacherous. No enjoyment equals the satisfaction we receive from the company of those we love and esteem; as the greatest of all punishments is to be obliged to pass our lives with those we hate or contemn. A very play or romance may afford us instances of this pleasure which virtue conveys to us; and pain which arises from vice.

Now, since the distinguishing impressions by which moral good or evil is known are nothing but *particular* pains or pleasures, it follows that in all inquiries concerning these moral distinctions it will be sufficient to show the principles which make us feel a satisfaction or uneasiness from the survey of any character, in order to satisfy us why the character is laudable or blamable. An action, or sentiment, or character, is virtuous or vicious; why? because its view causes a pleasure or uneasiness of a particular kind. In giving a reason, therefore, for the pleasure or uneasiness, we sufficiently explain the vice or virtue. To have the sense of virtue is nothing but to *feel* a satisfaction of a particular kind from the contemplation of a character. The very *feeling* constitutes our praise or admiration. We go no further; nor do we inquire into the cause of the satisfaction. We do not infer a character to be virtuous because it pleases; but in feeling that it pleases after such a particular manner we in effect feel that it is virtuous. The case is the same as in our judgments concerning all kinds of beauty, and tastes, and sensations. Our approbation is implied in the immediate pleasure they convey to us.

I have objected to the system, which establishes eternal rational measures of right and wrong, that 'tis impossible to shew, in the actions of reasonable creatures, any relations, which are not found in external objects; and therefore, if morality always attended these relations, 'twere possible for inanimate matter to become virtuous or vicious. Now it may, in like manner, be objected to the present system, that if virtue and vice be determin'd by pleasure and pain, these qualities must, in every case, arise from the sensations; and consequently any object, whether animate or inanimate, rational or irrational, might become morally good or evil, provided it can excite a satisfaction or uneasiness. But tho' this objection seems to be the very same, it has by no means the same force, in the one case as in the other. For, *first*, 'tis evident, that under the term *pleasure,* we comprehend sensations, which are very different from each other, and which have only such a distant resemblance, as is requisite to make them be express'd by the same abstract term. A good composition of music and a bottle of good wine equally produce pleasure; and what is more, their goodness is determin'd merely by the pleasure. But shall we say upon that account, that the wine is harmonious, or the music of a good flavour? In like manner an inanimate object, and the character or sentiments of any person may, both of them, give satisfaction; but as the satisfaction is different, this keeps our sentiments concerning them from being confounded, and makes us ascribe virtue to the one, and not to the other. Nor is every sentiment of pleasure or pain, which arises from characters and actions, of that *peculiar* kind, which makes us praise or condemn. The good qualities of an enemy are hurtful to us; but may still command our esteem and respect. 'Tis only when a character is considered in general, without reference to our particular interest, that it causes such a feeling or sentiment, as denominates it morally good or evil. 'Tis true, those sentiments, from interest and morals, are apt to be confounded, and naturally run into one another. It seldom happens, that we do not think an enemy vicious, and can distinguish betwixt his opposition to our interest and real villainy or baseness. But this hinders not, but that the sentiments are, in themselves, distinct; and a man of temper and judgment may preserve himself from these illusions, In like manner, tho' 'tis certain a musical voice is nothing but one that naturally gives a *particular* kind of pleasure; yet 'tis difficult for a man to be sensible, that the voice of an enemy is agreeable, or to allow it to be musical. But a person of a fine ear, who has the command of himself, can separate these feelings, and give praise to what deserves it. . . .

It may be asked in *general* concerning this pain or pleasure that distinguishes moral good and evil, *from what principle is it derived, and whence does it arise in the human mind?* To this I reply, *first,* that it is absurd to imagine that, in every particular instance, these sentiments are produced by an *original* quality and *primary* constitution. For as the number of our duties is in a manner infinite, it is impossible that our original instincts should extend to each of them, and from our very first infancy impress on the human mind all that multitude of precepts which are contained in the completest system of ethics. Such a method of proceeding is not conformable to the usual maxims by which nature is conducted, where a few principles produce all that variety we observe in the universe, and everything is carried on in the easiest and most simple manner. It is necessary, therefore, to abridge these primary impulses and find some more general principles upon which all our notions of morals are founded.

But, in the *second* place, should it be asked, whether we ought to search for these principles in *nature,* or whether we must look for them in some other origin? I would reply that our answer to this question depends upon the definition of the word *nature,* than which there is none more ambiguous and equivocal. If *nature* be opposed to miracles, not only the distinction betwixt vice and virtue is natural, but also every event which has ever happened in the world, *excepting those miracles on which our religion is founded.* In saying, then, that the sentiments of vice and virtue are natural in this sense, we make no very extraordinary discovery.

But *nature* may also be opposed to rare and unusual; and in this sense of the word, which is the common one, there may often rise disputes concerning what is natural or unnatural; and one may in general affirm that we are not possessed of any very precise standard by which these disputes can be decided. Frequent and rare depend upon the number of examples we have observed; and as this number may gradually increase or diminish, it will be impossible to fix any exact boundaries betwixt them. We may only affirm on this head that if ever there was anything which could be called natural in this sense, the sentiments of morality certainly may; since there never was any nation of the world, nor any single person in any nation, who was utterly deprived of them, and who never, in any instance, showed the least approbation or dislike of manners. These sentiments are so rooted in our constitution and temper that, without entirely confounding the human mind by disease or madness, it is impossible to extirpate and destroy them.

But *nature* may also be opposed to artifice as well as to what is rare and unusual; and in this sense it may be disputed whether the notions of virtue be natural or not. We readily forget that the designs, and projects, and views of men are principles as necessary in their operation as heat and cold, moist and dry; but, taking them to be free and entirely our own, it is usual for us to set them in opposition to the other principles of nature. Should it therefore be demanded whether the sense of virtue be natural or artificial, I am of opinion that it is impossible for me at present to give any precise answer to this question. Perhaps it will appear afterwards that our sense of some virtues is artificial, and that of others natural. The discussion of this question will be more proper, when we enter upon an exact detail of each particular vice and virtue.

Meanwhile, it may not be amiss to observe from these definitions of *natural* and *unnatural* that nothing can be more unphilosophical than those systems which assert that virtue is the same with what is natural, and vice with what is unnatural. For in the first sense of the word "nature," as opposed to miracles, both vice and virtue are equally natural; and in the second sense, as opposed to what is unusual, perhaps virtue will be found to be the most unnatural. At least it must be owned that heroic virtue, being as unusual, is as little natural as the most brutal barbarity. As to the third sense of the word, it is certain that both vice and virtue are equally artificial and out of nature. For, however it may be disputed whether the notion of a merit or demerit in certain actions be natural or artificial, it is evident that the actions themselves are artificial, and performed with a certain design and intention; otherwise they could never be ranked under any of these denominations. It is impossible, therefore, that the character of natural and unnatural can ever, in any sense, mark the boundaries of vice and virtue.

Thus we are still brought back to our first position that virtue is distinguished by the pleasure, and vice by the pain, that any action, sentiment, or character, gives us by the mere view and contemplation. This decision is very commodious; because it reduces us to this simple question, *why any action or sentiment, upon the general view or survey, gives a certain satisfaction or uneasiness,* in order to show the origin of its moral rectitude or depravity, without looking for any incomprehensible relations and qualities which never did exist in nature, nor even in our imagination, by any clear and distinct conception? I flatter myself I have executed a great part of my present design by a statement of the question which appears to me so free from ambiguity and obscurity.

Of the Other Virtues and Vices

SECTION I. OF THE ORIGIN OF THE NATURAL VIRTUES AND VICES

We come now to the examination of such virtues and vices as are entirely natural, and have no dependence on the artifice and contrivance of men. The examination of these will conclude this system of morals. . . .

We have already observ'd, that moral distinctions depend entirely on certain peculiar sentiments of pain and pleasure, and that whatever mental quality in ourselves or others gives us a satisfaction, by the survey or reflection, is of course virtuous; as every thing of this nature, that gives uneasiness, is vicious. Now since every quality in ourselves or others, which gives pleasure, always causes pride or love; as every one, that produces uneasiness, excites humility or hatred: It follows, that these two particulars are to be consider'd as equivalent, with regard to our mental qualities, *virtue* and the power of producing love or pride, *vice* and the power of producing humility or hatred. In every case, therefore, we must judge of the one by the other; and may pronounce any *quality* of the mind virtuous, which causes love or pride; and any one vicious, which causes hatred or humility.

If any *action* be either virtuous or vicious, 'tis only as a sign of some quality or character. It must depend upon durable principles of the mind, which extend over the whole conduct, and enter into the personal character. Actions themselves, not proceeding from any constant principle, have no influence on love or hatred, pride or humility; and consequently are never consider'd in morality.

This reflexion is self-evident, and deserves to be attended to, as being of the utmost importance in the present subject. We are never to consider any single action in our enquiries concerning the origin of morals; but only the quality or character from which the action proceeded. These alone are *durable* enough to affect our sentiments concerning the person. Actions are, indeed, better indications of a character than words, or even wishes and sentiments; but 'tis only so far as they are such indications, that they are attended with love or hatred, praise or blame.

To discover the true origin of morals, and of that love or hatred, which arises from mental qualities, we must take the matter pretty deep, and compare some principles, which have been already examin'd and explain'd.

We may begin with considering a-new the nature and force of *sympathy*. The minds of all men are similar in their feelings and operations, nor can any one be actuated by any affection, of which all others are not, in some degree susceptible. As in strings equally wound up, the motion of one communicates itself to the rest; so all the affections readily pass from one person to another, and beget correspondent movements in every human creature. When I see the *effects* of passion in the voice and gesture of any person, my mind immediately passes from these effects to their causes, and forms such a lively idea of the passion, as is presently converted into the passion itself. In like manner, when I perceive the *causes* of any emotion, my mind is convey'd to the effects, and is actuated with a like emotion. Were I present at any of the more terrible operations of surgery, 'tis certain, that even before it begun, the preparation of the instruments, the laying of the bandages in order, the heating of the irons, with all the signs of anxiety and concern in the patients and assistants, wou'd have a great effect upon my mind, and excite the strongest sentiments of pity and terror. No passion of another discovers itself immediately to the mind. We are only sensible of its causes or effects. From *these* we infer the passion: And consequently *these* give rise to our sympathy. . . .

No virtue is more esteem'd than justice, and no vice more detested than injustice; nor are there any qualities, which go farther to the fixing the character, either as amiable or odious. Now justice is a moral virtue, merely because it has that tendency to the good of mankind; and, indeed, is nothing but an artificial invention to that purpose. The same may be said of allegiance, of the laws of nations, of modesty, and of good-manners. All these are mere human contrivances for the interest of society. And since there is a very strong sentiment of morals, which in all nations, and all ages, has attended them, we must allow, that the reflecting on the tendency of characters and mental qualities, is sufficient to give us the sentiments of approbation and blame. Now as the means to an end can only be agreeable, where the end is agreeable; and as the good of society, where our own interest is not concern'd, or that of our friends, pleases only by sympathy: It follows, that sympathy is the source of the esteem, which we pay to all the artificial virtues.

Thus it appears, *that* sympathy is a very powerful principle in human nature, . . . and *that* it produces our sentiment of morals in all the artificial virtues. From thence we may presume, that it also gives rise to many of the other virtues; and that qualities acquire our approbration, because of their tendency to the good of mankind. This presumption must become a certainty, when we find that most of those qualities, which we *naturally* approve of, have actually that tendency, and render a man a proper member of society: While the qualities, which we *naturally* disapprove of, have a contrary tendency, and render any intercourse with the person dangerous or disagreeable. For having found, that such tendencies have force enough to produce the strongest sentiment of morals, we can never reasonably, in these cases, look for any other cause of approbation or blame; it being an inviolable maxim in philosophy, that where any particular cause is sufficient for an effect, we ought to rest satisfied with it, and ought not to multiply causes without necessity. We have happily attain'd experiments in the artificial virtues, where the tendency of qualities to the good of society, is the *sole* cause of our approbation, without any suspicion of the concurrence of another principle. From thence we learn the force of that principle. And where that principle may take place, and the quality approv'd of is really beneficial to society, a true philosopher will never require any other principle to account for the strongest approbation and esteem.

That many of the natural virtues have this tendency to the good of society, no one can doubt of. Meekness, beneficence, charity, generosity, clemency, moderation, equity, bear the greatest figure among the moral qualities, and are commonly denominated the *social* virtues, to mark their tendency to the good of society. This goes so far, that some philosophers have represented all moral distinctions as the effect of artifice and education, when skillful politicians endeavour'd to restrain the turbulent passions of men, and make them operate to the public good, by the notions of honour and shame. This system, however, is not consistent with experience. For, *first*, there are other virtues and vices beside those which have this tendency to the public advantage and loss. *Secondly*, had not men a natural sentiment of approbation and blame, it cou'd never be excited by politicians; nor wou'd the words *laudable* and *praise-worthy*, *blameable* and *odious*, be any more intelligible, than if they were a language perfectly unknown to us, as we have already observ'd. But tho' this system be erroneous, it may teach us, that moral distinctions arise, in a great measure, from the tendency of qualities and characters to the interests of society, and that 'tis our concern for that interest, which makes us approve or disapprove of them. Now we have no such extensive concern for society but from sympathy; and consequently 'tis that principle, which takes us so far out of ourselves, as to give us the same pleasure or uneasiness in the characters of others, as if they had a tendency to our own advantage or loss.

The only difference betwixt the natural virtues and justice lies in this, that the good, which results from the former, arises from every single act, and is the object of some natural passion: Whereas a single act of justice, consider'd in itself, may often be contrary to the public good; and 'tis only the concurrence of mankind, in a general scheme or system of action, which is advantageous. When I relieve persons in distress, my natural humanity is my motive; and so far as my succour extends, so far have I promoted the happiness of my fellow-creatures. But if we examine all the questions, that come before any tribunal of justice, we shall find, that, considering each case apart, it wou'd as often be an instance of humanity to decide contrary to the laws of justice as conformable to them. Judges take from a poor man to give to a rich; they bestow on the dissolute the labour of the industrious; and put into the hands of the vicious the means of harming both themselves and others. The whole scheme, however, of law and justice is advantageous to the society; and 'twas with a view to this advantage, that men, by their voluntary conventions, establish'd it. After it is once establish'd by these conventions, it is *naturally* attended with a strong sentiment of morals; which can proceed from nothing but our sympathy with the interests of society. We need no other explication of that esteem, which attends such of the natural virtues, as have a tendency to the public good.

I must farther add, that there are several circumstances, which render this hypothesis much more probable with regard to the natural than the artificial virtues. 'Tis certain, that the imagination is more affected by what is particular, than by what is general; and that the sentiments are always mov'd with difficulty, where their objects are, in any degree, loose and undetermin'd; Now every particular act of justice is not beneficial to society, but the whole scheme or system: And it may not, perhaps, be any individual person, for whom we are concern'd, who receives benefit from justice, but the whole society alike. On the contrary, every particular act of generosity, or relief of the industrious and indigent, is beneficial; and is beneficial to a particular person, who is not undeserving of it. 'Tis more natural, therefore, to think, that the tendencies of the latter virtue will affect our sentiments, and command our approbation, than those of the former; and therefore, since we find, that the approbation of the former arises from their tendencies, we may ascribe, with better reason, the same cause to the approbation of the latter. In any number of similar effects, if a cause can be discover'd for one, we ought to extend that cause to all the other effects, which can be accounted for by it: But much more, if these other effects be attended with peculiar circumstances, which facilitate the operation of that cause.

Before I proceed farther, I must observe two remarkable circumstances in this affair, which may seem objections to the present system. The first may be thus explain'd. When any quality, or character, has a tendency to the good of mankind, we are pleas'd with it, and approve of it; because it presents the lively idea of pleasure; which idea affects us by sympathy, and is itself a kind of pleasure. But as this sympathy is very variable, it may be thought, that our sentiments of morals must admit of all the same variations. We sympathize more with persons contiguous with us, than with persons remote from us: With our acquaintance, than with strangers: With our countrymen, than with foreigners. But notwithstanding this variation of our sympathy, we give the same approbation to the same moral qualities in *China* as in *England*. They appear equally virtuous, and recommend themselves equally to the esteem of a judicious spectator. The sympathy varies without a variation in our esteem. Our esteem, therefore, proceeds not from sympathy.

To this I answer: The approbation of moral qualities most certainly is not deriv'd from reason, or any comparison of ideas; but proceeds entirely from a moral taste, and from certain sentiments of pleasure or disgust, which arise upon the contemplation and view of particular qualities or characters. Now 'tis evident, that those sentiments, whence-ever they are deriv'd, must vary according to the distance or contiguity of the objects; nor can I feel the same lively pleasure from the virtues of a person, who liv'd in *Greece* two thousand years ago, that I feel from the virtues of a familiar friend and acquaintance. Yet I do not say, that I esteem the one more than the other: And therefore, if the variation of the sentiment, without a variation of the esteem, be an objection, it must have equal force against every other system, as against that of sympathy. But to consider the matter a-right, it has no force at all; and 'tis the easiest matter in the world to account for it. Our situation, with regard both to persons and things, is in continual fluctuation; and a man, that lies at a distance from us, may, in a little time, become a familiar acquaintance. Besides, every particular man has a peculiar position with regard to others; and 'tis impossible we cou'd ever converse together on any reasonable terms, were each of us to consider characters and persons, only as they appear from this peculiar point of view. In order, therefore, to prevent those continual *contradictions*, and arrive at a more *stable* judgment of things, we fix on some *steady* and *general* points of view; and always, in our thoughts, place ourselves in them, whatever may be our present situation. In like manner, external beauty is determin'd merely by pleasure; and 'tis evident, a beautiful countenance cannot give so much pleasure, when seen at the distance of twenty paces, as when it is brought nearer us. We say not, however, that it appears to us less beautiful: Because we know what effect it will have in such a position, and by that reflexion we correct its momentary appearance.

In general, all sentiments of blame or praise are variable, according to our situation of nearness or remoteness, with regard to the person blam'd or prais'd, and according to the present disposition of our mind. But these variations we regard not in our general decisions, but still apply the terms expressive of our liking or dislike, in the same manner, as if we remain'd in one point of view. Experience soon teaches us this method of correcting our sentiments, or at least, of correcting our language, where the sentiments are more stubborn and inalterable. Our servant, if diligent and faithful, may excite stronger sentiments of love and kindness than *Marcus Brutus*, as represented in history; but we say not upon that account, that the former character is more laudable than the latter. We know, that were we to approach equally near to that renown'd patriot, he wou'd command a much higher degree of affection and admiration. Such corrections are common with regard to all the senses; and indeed 'twere impossible we cou'd ever make use of language, or communicate our sentiments to one another, did we not correct the momentary appearances of things, and overlook our present situation.

'Tis therefore from the influence of characters and qualities, upon those who have an intercourse with any person, that we blame or praise him. We consider not whether the persons, affected by the qualities, be our acquaintance or strangers, countrymen or foreigners. Nay, we overlook our own interest in those general judgments; and blame not a man for opposing us in any of our pretensions, when his own interest is particularly concern'd. We make allowance for a certain degree of selfishness in men; because we know it to be inseparable from human nature, and inherent in our frame and constitution. By this reflexion we correct those sentiments of blame, which so naturally arise upon any opposition.

But however the general principle of

our blame or praise may be corrected by those other principles, 'tis certain, they are not altogether efficacious, nor do our passions often correspond entirely to the present theory. 'Tis seldom men heartily love what lies at a distance from them, and what no way redounds to their particular benefit; as 'tis no less rare to meet with persons, who can pardon another any opposition he makes to their interest, however justifiable that opposition may be by the general rules of morality. Here we are contented with saying, that reason requires such an impartial conduct, but that 'tis seldom we can bring ourselves to it, and that our passions do not readily follow the determination of our judgment. This language will be easily understood, if we consider what we formerly said concerning that *reason*, which is able to oppose our passion; and which we have found to be nothing but a general calm determination of the passions, founded on some distant view or reflexion. When we form our judgments of persons, merely from the tendency of their characters to our own benefit, or to that of our friends, we find so many contradictions to our sentiments in society and conversation, and such an uncertainty from the incessant changes of our situation, that we seek some other standard of merit and demerit, which may not admit of so great variation. Being thus loosen'd from our first station, we cannot afterwards fix ourselves so commodiously by any means as by a sympathy with those, who have any commerce with the person we consider. This is far from being as lively as when our own interest is concern'd, or that of our particular friends; nor has it such an influence on our love and hatred: But being equally conformable to our calm and general principles, 'tis said to have an equal authority over our reason, and to command our judgment and opinion. We blame equally a bad action, which we read of in history, with one perform'd in our neighborhood t'other day: The meaning of which is, that we know from reflexion, that the former action wou'd excite as strong sentiments of disapprobation as the latter, were it plac'd in the same position.

I now proceed to the *second* remarkable circumstance, which I propos'd to take notice of. Where a person is possess'd of a character, that in its natural tendency is beneficial to society, we esteem him virtuous, and are delighted with the view of his character, even tho' particular accidents prevent its operation, and incapacitate him from being serviceable to his friends and country. Virtue in rags is still virtue; and the love, which it procures, attends a man into a dungeon or desart, where the virtue can no longer be exerted in action, and is lost to all the world. Now this may be esteem'd an objection to the present system. Sympathy interests us in the good of mankind; and if sympathy were the source of our esteem for virtue, that sentiment of approbation cou'd only take place, where the virtue actually attain'd its end, and was beneficial to mankind. Where it fails of its end, 'tis only an imperfect means; and therefore can never acquire any merit from that end. The goodness of an end can bestow a merit on such means alone as are compleat, and actually produce the end.

To this we may reply, that where any object, in all its parts, is fitted to attain any agreeable end, it naturally gives us pleasure, and is esteem'd beautiful, even tho' some external circumstances be wanting to render it altogether effectual. 'Tis sufficient if every thing be compleat in the object itself. A house, that is contriv'd with great judgment for all the commodities of life, pleases us upon that account; tho' perhaps we are sensible, that no-one will ever dwell in it. A fertile soil, and a happy climate, delight us by a reflexion on the happiness which they wou'd afford the inhabitants, tho' at present the country be desart and uninhabited. A man, whose limbs and shape promise strength and activity, is esteem'd handsome, tho' condemn'd to perpetual imprisonment. The imagination has a set of passions belonging to it, upon which our sentiments of beauty much depend. These passions are mov'd by degrees of liveliness and strength, which are inferior to *belief*, and independent of the real existence of their objects. Where a character is, in every respect, fitted to be beneficial to society, the imagination passes easily from the cause to the effect, without considering that there are still some circumstances wanting to render the cause a compleat one. *General rules* create a species of probability, which sometimes influences the judgment, and always the imagination.

'Tis true, when the cause is compleat, and a good disposition is attended with good fortune, which renders it really beneficial to society, it gives a stronger pleasure to the spectator, and is attended with a more lively sympathy. We are more affected by it; and yet we do not say that it is more virtuous, or that we esteem it more. We know, that an alteration of fortune may render the benevolent disposition entirely impotent; and therefore we separate, as much as possible, the fortune from the disposition. The case is the same, as when we correct the different sentiments of virtue, which proceed from its different distances from ourselves. The passions do not always follow our corrections; but these corrections serve sufficiently to regulate our abstract notions, and are alone regarded, when we pronounce in general concerning the degrees of vice and virtue. . . .

Upon these principles we may easily remove any contradiction, which may appear to be betwixt the *extensive sympathy*, on which our sentiments of virtue depend, and that *limited generosity* which I have frequently observ'd to be natural to men, and which justice and property suppose, according to the precedent reasoning. My sympathy with another may give me the sentiment of pain and disapprobation, when any object is presented, that has a tendency to give him uneasiness; tho' I may not be willing to sacrifice any thing of my own interest, or cross any of my passions, for his satisfaction. A house may displease me by being ill-contriv'd for the convenience of the owner; and yet I may refuse to give a shilling towards the rebuilding of it. Sentiments must touch the heart, to make them control our passions: But they need not extend beyond the imagination, to make them influence our taste. When a building seems clumsy and tottering to the eye, it is ugly and disagreeable; tho' we be fully assur'd of the solidity of the workmanship. 'Tis a kind of fear, which causes this sentiment of disapprobation; but the passion is not the same with that which we feel, when oblig'd to stand under a wall, that we really think tottering and insecure. The *seeming tendencies* of objects affect the mind: And the emotions they excite are of a like species with those, which proceed from the *real consequences* of objects, but their feeling is different. Nay, these emotions are so different in their feeling, that they may often be contrary, without destroying each other; as when the fortifications of a city belonging to an enemy are esteem'd beautiful upon account of their strength, tho' we cou'd wish that they were entirely destroy'd. The imagination adheres to the *general* views of things, and distinguishes the feelings they produce, from those which arise from our particular and momentary situation.

If we examine the panegyrics that are commonly made of great men, we shall find, that most of the qualities, which are attributed to them, may be divided into two kinds, *viz.* such as make them perform their part in society; and such as render them serviceable to themselves, and enable them to promote their own interest. Their *prudence, temperance, frugality, industry, assiduity, enterprize, dexterity,* are celecelebrated, as well as their *generosity* and *humanity*. If we ever give an indulgence to any quality, that disables a man from making a figure in life, 'tis to that of *in-*

dolence, which is not suppos'd to deprive one of his parts and capacity, but only suspends their exercise; and that without any inconvenience to the person himself, since 'tis, in some measure, from his own choice. Yet indolence is always allow'd to be a fault, and a very great one, if extreme: Nor do a man's friends ever acknowledge him to be subject to it, but in order to save his character in more material articles. He cou'd make a figure, say they, if he pleas'd to give application: His understanding is sound, his conception quick, and his memory tenacious; but he hates business, and is indifferent about his fortune. And this a man sometimes may make even a subject of vanity; tho' with the air of confessing a fault: Because he may think, that this incapacity for business implies much more noble qualities; such as a philosophical spirit, a fine taste, a delicate wit, or a relish for pleasure and society. But take any other case: Suppose a quality, that without being an indication of any other good qualities, incapacitates a man *always* for business, and is destructive to his interest; such as a blundering understanding, and a wrong judgment of every thing in life; inconstancy and irresolution; or a want of address in the management of men and business: These are all allow'd to be imperfections in a character; and many men wou'd rather acknowledge the greatest crimes, than have it suspected, that they are, in any degree, subject to them.

'Tis very happy, in our philosophical researches, when we find the same phænomenon diversified by a variety of circumstances; and by discovering what is common among them, can the better assure ourselves of the truth of any hypothesis we may make use of to explain it. Were nothing esteem'd virtue but what were beneficial to society, I am persuaded, that the foregoing explication of the moral sense ought still to be receiv'd, and that upon sufficient evidence: But this evidence must grow upon us, when we find other kinds of virtue, which will not admit of any explication except from that hypothesis. Here is a man, who is not remarkably defective in his social qualities; but what principally recommends him is his dexterity in business, by which he has extricated himself from the greatest difficulties, and conducted the most delicate affairs with a singular address and prudence. I find an esteem for him immediately to arise in me: His company is a satisfaction to me; and before I have any farther acquaintance with him, I wou'd rather do him a service than another, whose character is in every other respect equal, but is deficient in that particular. In this case, the qualities that please me are all consider'd as useful to the person, and as having a tendency to promote his interest and satisfaction. They are only regarded as means to an end, and please me in proportion to their fitness for that end. The end, therefore, must be agreeable to me. But what makes the end agreeable? The person is a stranger: I am no way interested in him, nor lie under any obligation to him: His happiness concerns not me, farther than the happiness of every human, and indeed of every sensible creature: That is, it affects me only by sympathy. From that principle, whenever I discover his happiness and good, whether in its causes or effects, I enter so deeply into it, that it gives me a sensible emotion. The appearance of qualities, that have a *tendency* to promote it, have an agreeable effect upon my imagination, and command my love and esteem.

This theory may serve to explain, why the same qualities, in all cases, produce both pride and love, humility and hatred; and the same man is always virtuous or vicious, accomplish'd or despicable to others, who is so to himself. A person, in whom we discover any passion or habit, which originally is only incommodious to himself, becomes always disagreeable to us, merely on its account; as on the other hand, one whose character is only dangerous and disagreeable to others, can never be satisfied with himself, as long as he is sensible of that disadvantage. Nor is this observable only with regard to characters and manners, but may be remark'd even in the most minute circumstances. A violent cough in another gives us uneasiness; tho' in itself it does not in the least affect us. A man will be mortified, if you tell him he has a stinking breath; tho' 'tis evidently no annoyance to himself. Our fancy easily changes its situation; and either surveying ourselves as we appear to others, or considering others as they feel themselves, we enter, by that means, into sentiments, which no way belong to us, and in which nothing but sympathy is able to interest us. And this sympathy we sometimes carry so far, as even to be displeas'd with a quality commodious to us, merely because it displeases others, and makes us disagreeable in their eyes; tho' perhaps we never can have any interest in rendering ourselves agreeable to them.

There have been many systems of morality advanc'd by philosophers in all ages; but if they are strictly examin'd, they may be reduc'd to two, which alone merit our attention. Moral good and evil are certainly distinguish'd by our *sentiments,* not by *reason*: But these sentiments may arise either from the mere species or appearance of characters and passions, or from reflexions on their tendency to the happiness of mankind, and of particular persons. My opinion is, that both these causes are intermix'd in our judgments of morals; after the same manner as they are in our decisions concerning most kinds of external beauty: Tho' I am also of opinion, that reflexions on the tendencies of actions have by far the greatest influence, and determine all the great lines of our duty. There are, however, instances, in cases of less moment, wherein this immediate taste or sentiment produces our approbation. Wit, and a certain easy and disengag'd behaviour, are qualities *immediately agreeable* to others, and command their love and esteem. Some of these qualities produce satisfaction in others by particular *original* principles of human nature, which cannot be accounted for: Others may be resolv'd into principles, which are more general. This will best appear upon a particular enquiry.

As some qualities acquire their merit from their being *immediately agreeable* to others, without any tendency to public interest; so some are denominated virtuous from their being *immediately agreeable* to the person himself, who possesses them. Each of the passions and operations of the mind has a particular feeling, which must be either agreeable or disagreeable. The first is virtuous, the second vicious. This particular feeling constitutes the very nature of the passion; and therefore needs not be accounted for.

But however directly the distinction of vice and virtue may seem to flow from the immediate pleasure or uneasiness, which particular qualities cause to ourselves or others; 'tis easy to observe, that it has also a considerable dependence on the principle of *sympathy* so often insisted on. We approve of a person, who is possess'd of qualities *immediately agreeable* to those, with whom he has any commerce; tho' perhaps we ourselves never reap'd any pleasure from them. We also approve of one, who is possess'd of qualities, that are *immediately agreeable* to himself; tho' they be of no service to any mortal. To account for this we must have recourse to the foregoing principles.

Thus, to take a general review of the present hypothesis: Every quality of the mind is denominated virtuous, which gives pleasure by the mere survey; as every quality, which produces pain, is call'd vicious. This pleasure and this pain may arise from four different sources. For we reap a pleasure from the view of a character, which is naturally fitted to be useful to others, or to the person himself, or which is agreeable to others, or to the person himself. One may, perhaps, be surpriz'd, that amidst all these interests and pleasures, we shou'd forget our own, which touch us so nearly on every other occasion. But we shall easily satisfy ourselves on this head, when we consider, that every particular person's pleasure and interest being different, 'tis impossible men cou'd ever agree in their sentiments and judgments, unless they chose some common point of view, from which they might survey their object, and which might cause it to appear the same to all of them. Now, in judging of characters, the only interest or pleasure, which appears the same to every spectator, is that of the person himself, whose character is examin'd; or that of persons, who have a connexion with him. And tho' such interests and pleasures touch us more faintly than our own, yet being more constant and universal, they counter-balance the latter even in practice, and are alone admitted in speculation as the standard of virtue and morality. They alone produce that particular feeling or sentiment, on which moral distinctions depend.

*An Enquiry Concerning the Principles of Morals**

Of Justice

PART I

That justice is useful to society, and consequently that *part* of its merit, at least, must arise from that consideration, it would be a superfluous undertaking to prove. That public utility is the *sole* origin of justice, and that reflections on the beneficial consequences of this virtue are the *sole* foundation of its merit; this proposition, being more curious and important, will better deserve our examination and enquiry.

* David Hume, *An Enquiry Concerning the Principles of Morals*, London, 1748.

Let us suppose that nature has bestowed on the human race such profuse *abundance* of all *external* conveniences that, without any uncertainty in the event, without any care or industry on our part, every individual finds himself fully provided with whatever his most voracious appetites can want, or luxurious imagination wish or desire. His natural beauty, we shall suppose, surpasses all acquired ornaments; the perpetual clemency of the seasons renders useless all clothes or covering; the raw herbage affords him the most delicious fare; the clear fountain, the richest beverage. No laborious occupation required; no tillage; no navigation. Music, poetry, and contemplation form his sole business; conversation, mirth, and friendship his sole amusement.

It seems evident that in such a happy state every other social virtue would flourish and receive tenfold increase; but the cautious, jealous virtue of justice would never once have been dreamed of. For what purpose make a partition of goods where every one has already more than enough? Why give rise to property where there cannot possibly be any injury? Why call this object *mine* when, upon the seizing of it by another, I need but stretch out my hand to possess myself to what is equally valuable? Justice in that case, being totally useless, would be an idle ceremonial, and could never possibly have place in the catalogue of virtues.

We see, even in the present necessitous condition of mankind, that, wherever any benefit is bestowed by nature in an unlimited abundance, we leave it always in common among the whole human race, and make no subdivisions of right and property. Water and air, though the most necessary of all objects, are not challenged as the property of individuals; nor can any man commit injustice by the most lavish use and enjoyment of these blessings. In fertile extensive countries, with few inhabitants, land is regarded on the same footing. And no topic is so much insisted on by those who defend the liberty of the seas as the unexhausted use of them in navigation. Were the advantages procured by navigation as inexhaustible, these reasoners had never had any adversaries to refute; nor had any claims ever been advanced of a separate, exclusive dominion over the ocean. . . .

Again, suppose that, though the necessities of the human race continue the same as at present, yet the mind is so enlarged, and so replete with friendship and generosity, that every man has the utmost tenderness for every man and feels no more concern for his own interest than for that of his fellows; it seems evident that the use of justice would in this case be suspended by such an extensive benevolence, nor would the divisions and barriers of property and obligation have ever been thought of. Why should I bind another by a deed or promise to do me any good office, when I know that he is already prompted by the strongest inclination to seek my happiness and would of himself perform the desired service, except the hurt he thereby receives be greater than the benefit accruing to me? In which case he knows that, from my innate humanity and friendship, I should be the first to oppose myself to his imprudent generosity. Why raise landmarks between my neighbour's field and mine, when my heart has made no division between our interests, but shares all his joys and sorrows with the same force and vivacity as if originally my own? Every man, upon this supposition, being a second self to another, would trust all his interests to the discretion of every man, without jealousy, without partition, without distinction. And the whole human race would form only one family, where all would lie in common and be used freely, without regard to property; but cautiously too, with as entire regard to the necessities of each individual as if our own interests were most intimately concerned.

In the present disposition of the human heart, it would, perhaps, be difficult to find complete instances of such enlarged affections; but still we may observe that the case of families approaches towards it; and the stronger the mutual benevolence is among the individuals, the nearer it approaches; till all distinction of property be, in a great measure, lost and confounded among them. Between married persons the cement of friendship is by the laws supposed so strong as to abolish all division of possessions, and has often, in reality, the force ascribed to it. And it is observable that during the ardour of new enthusiasms, when every principle is inflamed into extravagance, the community of goods has frequently been attempted; and nothing but experience of its inconveniences, from the returning or disguised selfishness of men, could make the imprudent fanatics adopt anew the ideas of justice and of separate property. So true is it that this virtue derives its existence entirely from its necessary *use* to the intercourse and social state of mankind.

To make this truth more evident, let us reverse the foregoing suppositions and, carrying everything to the opposite extreme, consider what would be the effect of these new situations. Suppose a society to fall into such want of all common necessaries that the utmost frugality and industry cannot preserve the greater number from perishing, and the whole from extreme misery; it will readily, I believe, be admitted that the strict laws of justice are suspended in such a pressing emergency, and give place to the stronger motives of necessity and self-preservation. Is it any crime, after a shipwreck, to seize whatever means or instrument of safety one can lay hold of, without regard to former limitations of property? Or if a city besieged were perishing with hunger, can we imagine that men will see any means of preservation before them, and lose their lives from a scrupulous regard to what, in other situations, would be the rules of equity and justice? The use and tendency of that virtue is to procure happiness and security by preserving order in society; but where the society is ready to perish from extreme necessity, no greater evil can be dreaded from violence and injustice; and every man may now provide for himself by all the means which prudence can dictate or humanity permit.

Thus the rules of equity or justice depend entirely on the particular state and condition in which men are placed, and owe their origin and existence to that utility which results to the public from their strict and regular observance. Reverse, in any considerable circumstance, the condition of men; produce extreme abundance or extreme necessity; implant in the human breast perfect moderation and humanity, or perfect rapaciousness and malice—by rendering justice totally *useless*, you thereby totally destroy its essence and suspend its obligation upon mankind.

The common situation of society is a medium amidst all these extremes. We are naturally partial to ourselves and to our friends; but are capable of learning the advantage resulting from a more equitable conduct. Few enjoyments are given us from the open and liberal hand of nature; but by art, labour, and industry, we can extract them in great abundance. Hence the ideas of property become necessary in all civil society; hence justice derives its usefulness to the public; and hence alone arises its merit and moral obligation. . . .

PART II

If we examine the *particular* laws by which justice is directed and property determined, we shall still be presented with the same conclusion. The good of mankind is the only object of all these laws and regulations. Not only is it requisite for the peace and interest of society that men's possessions should be separated, but the rules which we follow in making the separation are such as can best be contrived to serve further the interests of society.

We shall suppose that a creature, possessed of reason, but unacquainted with human nature, deliberates with himself what rules of justice or property would best promote public interest and establish peace and security among mankind. His most obvious thought would be to assign the largest possessions to the most extensive virtue, and give every one the power of doing good, proportioned to his inclination. In a perfect theocracy, where a being, infinitely intelligent, governs by particular volitions, this rule would certainly have place and might serve to the wisest purposes. But were mankind to execute such a law, so great is the uncertainty of merit, both from its natural obscurity and from the self-conceit of each individual, that no determinate rule of conduct would ever result from it; and the total dissolution of society must be the immediate consequence. Fanatics may suppose *that dominion is founded on grace,* and *that saints alone inherit the earth;* but the civil magistrate very justly puts these sublime theorists on the same footing with common robbers, and teaches them by the severest discipline that a rule, which in speculation may seem the most advantageous to society, may yet be found, in practice, totally pernicious and destructive. . . .

It must, indeed, be confessed that nature is so liberal to mankind that, were all her presents equally divided among the species and improved by art and industry, every individual would enjoy all the necessaries and even most of the comforts of life, nor would ever be liable to any ills, but such as might accidentally arise from the sickly frame and constitution of his body. It must also be confessed that, wherever we depart from this equality, we rob the poor of more satisfaction than we add to the rich, and that the slight gratification of a frivolous vanity in one individual frequently costs more than bread to many families and even provinces. It may appear withal that the rule of equality, as it would be highly *useful,* is not altogether *impracticable,* but has taken place, at least in an imperfect degree, in some republics, particularly that of Sparta, where it was attended, it is said, with the most beneficial consequences. Not to mention that the Agrarian laws, so frequently claimed in Rome, and carried into execution in many Greek cities, proceeded, all of them, from a general idea of the utility of this principle.

But historians, and even common sense, may inform us that, however specious these ideas of *perfect* equality may seem, they are really at bottom *impracticable;* and were they not so, would be extremely *pernicious* to human society. Render possessions ever so equal, men's different degrees of art, care, and industry will immediately break that equality. Or if you check these virtues, you reduce society to the most extreme indigence; and instead of preventing want and beggary in a few, render it unavoidable to the whole community. The most rigorous inquisition too is requisite to watch every inequality on its first appearance; and the most severe jurisdiction, to punish and redress it. But besides that so much authority must soon degenerate into tyranny and be exerted with great partialities, who can possibly be possessed of it in such a situation as is here supposed? Perfect equality of possessions, destroying all subordination, weakens extremely the authority of magistracy, and must reduce all power nearly to a level, as well as property.

We may conclude, therefore, that, in order to establish laws for the regulation of property, we must be acquainted with the nature and situation of man, must reject appearances which may be false though specious, and must search for those rules which are on the whole most *useful* and *beneficial.* Vulgar sense and slight experience are sufficient for this purpose, where men give not way to too selfish avidity or too extensive enthusiasm.

Who sees not, for instance, that whatever is produced or improved by a man's art or industry ought, for ever, to be secured to him, in order to give encouragement to such *useful* habits and accomplishments? That the property ought also to descend to children and relations for the same *useful* purpose? That it may be alienated by consent in order to beget that commerce and intercourse which is so *beneficial* to human society? And that all contracts and promises ought carefully to be fulfilled in order to secure mutual trust and confidence by which the general *interest* of mankind is so much promoted?

Examine the writers on the laws of nature, and you will always find that, whatever principles they set out with, they are sure to terminate here at last, and to assign as the ultimate reason for every rule which they establish, the convenience and necessities of mankind. A concession thus extorted in opposition to systems has more authority than if it had been made in prosecution of them.

What other reason, indeed, could writers ever give why this must be *mine* and that *yours,* since uninstructed nature surely never made any such distinction? The objects which receive those appellations are of themselves foreign to us; they are totally disjoined and separated from us, and nothing but the general interests of society can form the connexion. . . .

In general we may observe that all questions of property are subordinate to the authority of civil laws, which extend, restrain, modify, and alter the rules of natural justice, according to the particular *convenience* of each community. The laws have or ought to have a constant reference to the constitution of government, the manners, the climate, the religion, the commerce, the situation of each society. A late author of genius as well as learning has prosecuted this subject at large, and has established from these principles a system of political knowledge which abounds in ingenious and brilliant thoughts and is not wanting in solidity.

What is a man's property? Anything which it is lawful for him, and for him alone, to use. *But what rule have we by which we can distinguish these objects?* Here we must have recourse to statutes, customs, precedents, analogies, and a hundred other circumstances, some of which are constant and inflexible, some variable and arbitrary. But the ultimate point, in which they all professedly terminate, is the interest and happiness of human society. Where this enters not into consideration, nothing can appear more whimsical, unnatural, and even superstitious, than all or most of the laws of justice and of property. . . .

What alone will beget a doubt concerning the theory on which I insist is the influence of education and acquired habits, by which we are so accustomed to blame injustice that we are not in every instance conscious of any immediate reflection on the pernicious consequences of it. The views the most familiar to us are apt, for that very reason, to escape us; and what we have very frequently performed from certain motives, we are apt likewise to continue mechanically without recalling on every occasion the reflections which first determined us. The convenience or rather necessity which leads to justice is so universal and everywhere points so much to the same rules that the habit takes place in all societies; and it is not without some scrutiny that we are able to ascertain its true origin. The matter, however, is not so obscure, but that even in common life we have every moment recourse to the principle of public utility, and ask, *What must become of the world, if such practices prevail? How could society subsist under such disorders?* Were the distinction or separation of possessions entirely useless, can any one conceive that it ever should have obtained in society?

Thus we seem, upon the whole, to have attained a knowledge of the force of that principle here insisted on, and can determine what degree of esteem or moral approbation may result from reflections on public interest and utility. The necessity of justice to the support of society is the sole foundation of that virtue; and since no moral excellence is more highly esteemed, we may conclude that this circumstance of usefulness has, in general, the strongest energy and most entire command over our sentiments. It must, therefore, be the source of a considerable part of the merit ascribed to humanity, benevolence, friendship, public spirit, and other social virtues of that stamp; as it is the sole source of the moral approbation paid to fidelity, justice, veracity, integrity, and those other estimable and useful qualities and principles. It is entirely agreeable to the rules of philosophy and even of common reason, where any principle has been found to have a great force and energy in one instance, to ascribe to it a like energy in all similar instances. This indeed is Newton's chief rule of philosophizing.

IMMANUEL KANT

Immanuel Kant (1724–1804) was born and educated in Königsberg, East Prussia. He spent all his life there as a professor in the university. Though his life was uneventful (it passed, as one of his biographers has remarked, like the most regular of regular verbs), his philosophical theory was a radical innovation, a major turning point in the history of philosophy. The novelty of his views made it difficult for him to state them clearly; this, coupled with an affection for formal symmetry, which he called "architectonic," makes his major writings formidable reading. His lecture style, however, is happily much simpler. Since his lectures were very popular and much admired, some of his courses were transcribed by his students. Accordingly, we have drawn some of our selections from such a lecture course. Others are taken from the Critique of Practical Reason, *his major work on ethics.*

*Lectures on Ethics**

Universal Practical Philosophy

PROEM

Philosophy is either theoretical or practical. The one concerns itself with knowledge, the other with the conduct of beings possessed of a free will. The one has Theory, the other Practice for its object—and it is the object that differentiates them. There is another distinction of philosophy into speculative and practical. We have, for instance, theoretical geometry and practical geometry, theoretical mechanics and practical mechanics, and so with medicine, and also with jurisprudence. In all these cases the object is the same; it is the form of the science which is different. The theoretical form judges the object; the practical produces it. If, without regard to the object, we draw the distinction between theoretical knowledge and practical knowledge, the differentiation is one of form only; the theoretical form studies, the practical produces the object. But in our present distinction between practical philosophy and theoretical philosophy the dif-

* By permission. From Immanuel Kant, *Lectures on Ethics*, trans. by Louis Infield, Methuen & Co., Ltd., London, and Harper & Brothers, New York, 1930. Deletions are not noted in the text.

ference is not one of form, but of the object. Practical philosophy is such not by its form, but by reference to its object, namely, the voluntary conduct of a free being. The object of practical philosophy is conduct; that of theoretical philosophy cognition. Practical philosophy, being the philosophy of action, is thus the philosophy which provides rules for the proper use of our freedom, irrespective of particular applications of it. Just as logic deals with the use of the understanding in general and not in particular conditions, so does practical philosophy deal with the use of the free will not in specific circumstances but independently of the particular. Logic provides rules concerning the use of the understanding, practical philosophy concerning the use of the will. Understanding and will are the two powers from which springs the whole content of our mental disposition. The understanding is the supreme faculty of knowledge, the free will of desire. We have two disciplines for these two powers: logic for the understanding and practical philosophy for the will; but the lower powers cannot be disciplined, for they are blind.

We thus postulate a being—not only man, but any rational being—which has freedom of will, and we are concerned here with the principles or rules for the use of that freedom. This is general practical philosophy. Its rules are objective. The subjective practical rules are the concern of anthropology. An objective rule lays down what ought to occur, even though it never actually occurs. But the subjective rule deals with actual happenings. Even the wicked have rules of conduct. Thus anthropology observes the actual behaviour of human beings and formulates the practical and subjective rules which that behaviour obeys, whereas moral philosophy alone seeks to formulate rules of right conduct, that is, of what ought to happen, just as logic comprises the rules for the right use of the mind. When we say that something ought to be, we mean that a possible action is capable of being good, it comprises rules for the proper use of the will.

Practical philosophy (that is, the science of how man ought to behave) and anthropology (that is, the science of man's actual behaviour) are closely connected, and the former cannot subsist without the latter: for we cannot tell whether the subject to which our consideration applies is capable of what is demanded of him unless we have knowledge of that subject. It is true that we can pursue the study of practical philosophy without anthropology, that is, without the knowledge of the subject. But our philosophy is then merely speculative, and an Idea. We therefore have to make at least some study of man.

Just as anthropology is a science of the subjective laws of the free will, so practical philosophy is a science of its objective laws. It is a philosophy of the objective necessity of free action, of the Ought—that is, of all possible good actions. Moreover, like logic, practical philosophy does not concern itself with a particular sort of cases of practical activity but deals with the practice of free actions in general without reference to any case whatever.

The objective laws of the free will, the laws which tell us what ought to be, are divisible into three classes: technical, prudential and moral. All of them are expressed by an imperative, unlike subjective practical laws, which are not so expressed.

There are then three kinds of Imperative: the technical, the prudential and the moral. Every imperative expresses an Ought, and thus an objective necessity, and indeed a necessity of the free and good will, for it is a property of the imperative that it necessitates objectively. All imperatives involve an objective necessitation, even on the assumption of a good and free will. The technical imperatives are problematical, the prudential imperatives are pragmatic and the moral imperatives are ethical.

Problematic imperatives imply a necessitation of the will in accordance with a rule to an arbitrarily chosen end. The means are stated assertorically, but the end is problematical. If, for instance, we set ourselves the task of constructing a triangle, a square, or a hexagon, we must proceed in accordance with the rules implied: the problem is at our choice, but having chosen it our means to it are defined. Geometry, mechanics, and, in general, the practical sciences contain technical imperatives. These imperatives are of the greatest utility and must take precedence over all others; for only if we are in a position, and have the means, to fulfil ends of our own choosing can we be sure of fulfilling ends set for us. Technical imperatives are merely hypothetical; for the necessity of using the means arises only on a condition, namely of the end being given.

Practical philosophy contains no technical rules: it contains only rules of prudence and of morality, and it is, therefore, pragmatic and ethical. It is pragmatic in respect of the laws of prudence, and ethical in respect of those of morality.

Prudence is the ability to use the means towards the universal end of man, that is, happiness. We, therefore, have here (as is not the case with technical rules) a determined end. Rules of prudence require us both to define the end and the means to be used to attain it. We need, therefore, a rule for judging what constitutes happiness and the rule for using the means to this happiness. Prudence is thus the ability to determine both the end and the means to the end. First we must establish what happiness is. This is still a matter of controversy: some say it is found in abstinence, others in acquisition. It follows, therefore, that the first object of prudence is to determine the end of happiness and in what it consists, and the second, to determine the means. No problematic condition attaches to the dictates of the prudential imperatives: their condition is assertorical, universal and necessary, inherent in human nature. We do not say to a man: "In so far as you would be happy you must do so and so"; but since every one wishes to be happy, all must observe what is presupposed of all. It is a subjective and not an objective necessary condition. It would be objective if we were to say: "You ought to be happy"; but what we do say is: "Because you want to be happy, you must do this and that."

But we can conceive an imperative where the end is governed by a condition which commands not subjectively but objectively. Moral imperatives are such. Take, for example: "Thou shalt not lie." This is no problematic imperative, for in that case it would mean, "If it harm thee to lie, then do not lie." But the imperative commands simply and categorically: "Thou shalt not lie"; and it does so unconditionally, or under an objective and necessary condition. It is characteristic of the moral imperative that it does not determine an end, and the action is not governed by an end, but flows from the free will and has no regard to ends. The dictates of moral imperatives are absolute and regardless of the end. Our free doing and refraining has an inner goodness, irrespective of its end. Thus moral goodness endues man with an immediate, inner, absolute moral worth. For example, the man who keeps his word has always an immediate inner worth of the free will, apart altogether from the end in view. No such intrinsic worth accrues from any pragmatic goodness.

THE ETHICAL SYSTEMS OF THE ANCIENTS

The ethical systems of the ancients are all based on the question of what constitutes the *summum bonum*—the Supreme Good—and it is in their answers to this question that is to be found the difference between their various systems.

What constitutes the Supreme Good? The supreme created good is the most perfect world, that is, a world in which all rational beings are happy and are worthy of happiness.

The ancients realized that mere happiness could not be the one highest good. For if all men were to obtain this happiness without distinction of just and unjust, the highest good would not be realized, because though happiness would indeed exist, worthiness of it would not.

In mankind therefore we have to look both for happiness and for merit. The combination of the two will be the highest good. Man can hope to be happy only in so far as he makes himself worthy of being happy, for this is the condition of happiness which reason itself proposes.

They further realized that happiness sprang from man's freedom of will, from his intention to make use of everything with which nature so richly endows him. Of the wealthy man we ask to what use he intends to put all those treasures which he has in plenty. Thus the nature and perfectness of the free will, in which dwells the ground of the worthiness to be happy, constitutes ethical perfection. The physical good or well-being, for which health and wealth are requisite, is not by itself the greatest good; the ethical good, right conduct, worthiness of being happy, must be added to the former, and we then have the Supreme Good. Let us imagine a world inhabited by intelligent beings, all of whom behaved well, and so deserved to be happy, but were destitute and lived in the most wretched circumstances. Such beings would have no happiness, and there would, therefore, be no Supreme Good in these conditions. If, on the other hand, all beings were happy but not well-behaved and not worthy of being happy, we should again have no Supreme Good in such circumstances.

The ancients recognized three forms of the ideal of the *summum bonum:*

1. The Cynic ideal of the school of Diogenes.
2. The Epicurean ideal.
3. The Stoic ideal of the school of Zeno.

The Cynic is the ideal of innocence, or rather of simplicity. Diogenes taught that the highest good is to be found in simplicity, in the sober enjoyment of happiness.

The Epicureans set up the ideal of prudence. Epicurus' doctrine was that the highest good was happiness and that well-doing was but a means to happiness.

The ideal of the Stoics was that of wisdom and is in contrast with the ideal of Epicurus. Zeno taught that the highest good is to be found only in morality, in merit (and thus in well-doing), and that happiness is a consequence of morality. Whoever conducts himself well is happy.

We can also conceive a mystical ideal, in which the Supreme Good consists in this; that man sees himself in communion with the highest being. This is the Platonic ideal, a visionary ideal.

The Christian ideal is that of holiness and its pattern is Christ. Christ is also merely an ideal, a standard of moral perfection which is holy by divine aid. This ideal ought not to be confused with those who call themselves Christians. These only seek to come nearer to their ideal pattern.

The ideal of holiness is, philosophically, the most perfect in that it is the ideal of the highest pure and moral perfection; but as it is humanly unattainable it bases itself on the belief in divine aid. Not only does the notion of deserving happiness acquire in this ideal its highest moral perfection, but the ideal itself contains the most potent motive, that of happiness beyond this world. Thus the ideal of the Gospels contains the purest morality as well as the strongest motive—that of happiness or blessedness.

The ancients had no conception of

any higher moral perfection than such as could emanate from human nature. But as human nature is very imperfect, their ethical principles were imperfect. Thus their system of ethics was not pure; it accommodated virtue to man's weakness, and was, therefore, incomplete. But the ideal of the Gospels is complete in every respect. Here we have the greatest purity and the greatest happiness. It sets out the principles of morality in all their holiness. It commands man to be holy, but as he is imperfect it gives him a prop, namely divine aid.

THE GENERAL PRINCIPLE OF MORALITY

Having considered the ideal of the highest moral perfection, we must now see wherein the general principle of morality consists. So far we have said no more than that it rests upon the goodness of the free will. We must now investigate what it essentially is. To establish the general principle of science is by no means easy, particularly if the sciences have already reached a certain stage of development. Thus, for instance, it is difficult to establish the general principle of law or of mechanics. But as we all need a basis for our moral judgments, a principle by which to judge with unanimity what is morally good and what bad, we apprehend that there must exist a single principle having its source in our will. We must therefore set ourselves to discover this principle, upon which we establish morality, and through which we are able to discriminate betwen what is moral and what immoral. However capable and talented a man may be, we still ask about his character. However great his qualities, we still ask about his moral quality. What then is the one principle of morality, the criterion by which to judge everything and in which lies the distinction between moral goodness and all other goodness? Before we decide these questions we must cite and classify the various points of view which lead to the definition of this principle in various ways.

The theoretical concept (not yet a theory, but merely a concept from which a theory can be constructed) is that morality has either an empirical or an intellectual basis, and that it must be derived either from empirical or from intellectual principles. Empirical grounds are derived from the senses, in so far as the senses find satisfaction in them. Intellectual grounds are those in which all morality is derived from the conformity of our actions to the laws of reason.

If an ethical system is based upon empirical grounds, those may be either inner or outer grounds, as they are drawn from the objects of the inner or of the outer sense. Those who derive ethics from the inner grounds of the empirical principle, presuppose a feeling, either physical or ethical.

The physical feeling which they take is self-love. Its aim is advantage to self; it is selfish and aims at satisfying our senses. It is a principle of prudence. Writers who follow the principle of self-love are Epicurus, Helvetius and Mandeville.

The second principle of the inner ground of the empirical system appears when the ground is placed in the ethical feeling whereby we discriminate between good and evil. Among those who build on this basis the foremost are Shaftesbury and Hutcheson.

To the empirical system of the theoretical concept of ethics belong, in the second place, outer grounds. Philosophers who base ethics on these argue that all morality rests upon two things, education and government, which in turn are a matter of custom; we judge all actions in a customary way by what we have been taught or by what the law tells us. Example or legal precept are thus the sources of the moral judgment. While Hobbes takes precept as his thesis and argues that the sovereign power may permit or prohibit any act, Montaigne bases himself on example and points out that in matters of morality men differ with environment, and that the morality of one locality is not that of another. He quotes as instances the permission of theft in Africa, that in China parents may desert their children with impunity, that the Eskimos strangle them, and that in Brazil children are buried alive.

On these grounds it is not permissible for reason to pass ethical judgments on actions. Instead, we act by reference to customary example and the commands of authority, from which it follows that there is no ethical principle, unless it be one borrowed from experience.

But now, in the empirical system, the first principle of ethics is based upon contingent grounds. In the case of self-love, contingent circumstances decide the nature of the action which will advantage or harm us. Where ethical feeling is the basis, and we judge actions by liking or disliking, by repugnance, or in general by taste, the grounds of judgment are again contingent, for what may please one individual may disgust another. (Thus a savage will turn from wine with abhorrence, while we drink it with pleasure.) It is the same with the outer grounds of education and government.

In the second *Systema morale,* which is the intellectual, the philosopher judges that the ethical principle has its ground in the understanding and can be completely apprehended à priori. We say, for instance: "Thou shalt not lie." On the principle of self-love this would mean: "Thou shalt not lie if it harm thee; if it advantage thee then thou mayest lie." If ethical feeling were the basis, then a person so devoid of a refined ethical feeling, that in him lying evoked no disgust, would be at liberty to lie. If it depended on up-bringing and government, then, if we were brought up to telling lies and if the Government so ordained, it would be open to us to tell lies. But if the principle lies in the understanding we say simply: "Thou shalt not lie, be the circumstances what they may." This, if I look into my free will, expresses the consistency of my free will with itself and with that of others; it is a necessary law of the free will. Such principles, which are universal, constant and necessary, have their source in pure reason; they cannot be derived from experience. Every ethical law expresses a categorical necessity, not one drawn from experience, and as every necessary rule must be established à priori, the principles of morality must be intellectual. The moral judgment never occurs at all in virtue of sensuous or empirical principles, for the ethical is never an object of the senses, but purely of the understanding.

The intellectual principle may be of two kinds:

1. Internal—if it depends on the inner nature of the action as apprehended by the understanding.
2. External—where our actions bear some relation to an external being.

But just as we have an ethical theology, so we have theological ethics, and the external intellectual principle is of that kind; but it is false, because discrimination between moral good and evil does not depend on any relation to another being. It follows, therefore, that the basic moral principle is of the first (i.e. the internal) of the above two kinds of intellectual principle. Our aim in what follows will be to discern and determine its constitution.

We have pathological necessitation where the impulse comes from the senses, or from the feeling of what is pleasant or unpleasant. The man who does a thing because it is pleasant is pathologically determined; he who does it because it is good, and because it is good in and for itself, acts on Motives and is practically determined. In so far, therefore, as *causae impulsivae* proceed from what is good, they are of the understanding; in so far as they proceed from what is pleasant, they are of the senses. He who is impelled to action by the former acts *per motiva;* he who is impelled by the latter acts *per stimulos.*

It follows from this argument that all Obligation is not pathological or pragmatic, but moral necessitation. As for the Motives, these have either a pragmatic basis, or else the moral basis of intrinsic goodness.

Pragmatic Motives are conditioned solely by the consideration that actions must be a means to happiness. Actions, being thus a means, do not contain their ground in themselves, and it follows that all *imperativi pragmatici hypothetice necessitant et non absolute.*

Imperativi morales, however, *necessitant absolute* and express a *bonitas absoluta,* just as *imperativi pragmatici* express a *bonitas hypothetica.* Thus honesty may possess a mediated goodness on grounds of prudence, as in commerce, where it is as good as ready money. But from an absolute point of view, to be honest is good in itself, good whatever the end in view, and dishonesty is in itself pernicious. Thus moral necessitation is absolute and the *motivum morale* expresses *bonitas absoluta.* We cannot at this stage explain how it is possible that an action should have *bonitas absoluta;* we must first interpolate the following remarks. If the will is subordinated to the dictate of ends universally valid, it will be in harmony with all human purposes, and herein is to be found its inherent goodness and absolute perfection. To exemplify this is not easy, but truthfulness, for instance, conforms to all my rules; it is in accord with every purpose; it is in harmony with the will of others, and every one can guide his conduct by it; one truth is consistent with another. On the other hand, lies contradict each other and are inconsistent with my purposes and with those of others. Moral goodness consists, therefore, in the submission of our will to rules whereby all our voluntary actions are brought into a harmony which is universally valid. Such a rule, which forms the first principle of the possibility of the harmony of all free wills, is the moral rule. Neither nature nor the laws determine a free action; and freedom, leaving our actions, as it does, quite undetermined, is a terrible thing. Our actions must be regulated if they are to harmonize, and their regulation is effected by the moral law. A pragmatic rule cannot do this. Pragmatic rules may make our actions consistent with our own will, but they will not bring them into harmony with the wills of others: in point of fact they may not even make them consistent with our own will; for the source of such rules is our well-being, and this cannot be determined à priori; rules of prudence can thus be laid down only à posteriori, and they cannot, therefore, apply to all actions, for in order to do that they would have to be à priori rules. Pragmatic rules are not, therefore, consistent with the wills of others and may not be consistent even with our own. But we must have rules to give our actions universal validity and to mould them into a general harmony. These rules are derived from the universal ends of mankind, and they are the moral rules.

The morality of an action is a quite peculiar thing: there is a distinct difference between a moral act and any pragmatic or pathological action; morality is subtle and pure and calls for special consideration on its own. There are actions for which moral Motives are not sufficient to produce moral goodness and for which pragmatic, or even pathological, *causae impulsivae* are wanted in addition; but when considering the goodness of an action we are not concerned with that which moves us to that goodness, but merely with what constitutes the goodness in and for itself.

The *motivum morale* must, therefore, be considered purely in and for itself, as something apart and distinct from other

Motives, whether of prudence or of the senses. Nature has implanted in us the faculty of drawing a subtle but very definite distinction between moral goodness and problematic and pragmatic goodness, and action which has a moral goodness is as pure as if it came from heaven itself.

Prudence requires a good understanding, morality a good will. If our conduct as free agents is to have moral goodness, it must proceed solely from a good will. The will can, therefore, be good in itself. In the case of prudence everything depends, not on the end, since the end is always the same, namely happiness, but on the understanding which apprehends the end and the means to attain it; one individual may be a greater adept at this than another. But while a sound understanding is requisite to prudence, to morality what is requisite is a will which is simply good in itself. Thus, for instance, the will to be rich is good in reference to its end, but not in itself.

We now proceed to examine what exactly constitutes that will, simply good in itself, on which moral goodness depends.

THE SUPREME PRINCIPLE OF MORALITY

In this connexion we must first notice that there are two points to consider; the principle of the discrimination of our obligation and the principle of its performance or execution. We must distinguish between measuring-rod and mainspring. The measuring-rod is the principle of discrimination; the mainspring is the principle of the performance of our obligation. Confusion between these has led to complete falsity in the sphere of ethics. If we ask, "What is morally good and what is not?" it is the principle of discrimination which is in question, in terms of which I decide the goodness of the action. But if we ask, "What is it that moves me to act in accordance with the laws of morality?" we have a question which concerns the principle of the motive.

The supreme principle of all moral judgment lies in the understanding: that of the moral incentive to action lies in the heart. This motive is moral feeling. We must guard against confusing the principle of the judgment with the principle of the motive. The first is the norm; the second the incentive. The motive cannot take the place of the rule. Where the motive is wanting, the error is practical; but when the judgment fails the error is theoretical.

We shall now proceed to indicate shortly and negatively what does not constitute the principle of morality. Firstly, there is nothing pathological about it. It would be pathological if it were derived from subjective grounds, from our inclination and feeling. There is no pathological principle in ethics because its laws are objective, and deal with what we ought to do, not with what we desire to do. Ethics is no analysis of inclination but a prescription which is contrary to all inclination. A pathological principle of morality would consist in an instruction to satisfy all our desires, and this would constitute a bestial, not the real, Epicureanism.

A moral law states categorically what ought to be done, whether it pleases us or not. It is, therefore, not a case of satisfying an inclination. If it were, there would be no moral law, but every one might act according to his own feeling. Even if we assumed that all men had a like degree of feeling, there would still be no Obligation to act according to feeling, for we could not then say that we *ought* to do what pleases us, but only that so-and-so might do such-and-such *because* it pleased him. The moral law, however, commands categorically. Morality cannot, therefore, be based on any pathological principle, neither on a physical nor yet on a moral feeling. Moreover, to have recourse to feeling in the case of a practical rule is quite contrary to philosophy. Every feeling has only a private validity, and no man's feeling can be apprehended by another. There is, therefore, no such thing as a pathological principle of morality, and there must accordingly be an intellectual principle in the sense that it must be derived from the understanding. This principle will consist in a rule of the understanding, either because the understanding provides us with the means so to direct our actions that they conform to our inclinations or because the ground of morality is immediately apprehended by the understanding. If the former, the principle is no doubt intellectual, inasmuch as the understanding provides the means; it is nevertheless evidently rooted in inclination. Such a pseudo-intellectual principle is pragmatic, and depends on the capacity of the rule to satisfy our inclinations. This principle of prudence is the true Epicurean principle. To be told that we ought to promote our happiness is in effect to be told that we ought to employ our understanding to discover the means for satisfying our inclinations and our desire for pleasure. This principle is intellectual in so far as it requires the understanding to provide the rules for the employment of the means to promote our happiness. But as this happiness consists in the satisfaction of all our inclinations, the pragmatic principle is dependent on the inclinations. Morality is, however, independent of all inclination, and it is not, therefore, grounded in any pragmatic principle. Were it so grounded, there could be no agreement amongst men in regard to morality, as every individual would seek to satisfy his own inclinations. Morality cannot, however, be based on the subjective laws of men's inclinations, and so it follows that the principle of morality cannot be pragmatic. It must, to be sure, be intellectual, but not, as in the case of the pragmatic principle, mediately so; it must be an unmediated principle of morality in the sense that the ground of morality is apprehended immediately by the mind. The ethical principle is, therefore, a sheerly intellectual principle of the pure reason. But this pure intellectual principle must not be tautologous. It must not consist in the tautology of pure reason as does, for example, Wolff's rule, "do good and eschew evil," which is empty and unphilosophic.

The pure intellectual principle cannot, however, be a *principium externum,* in terms of the relation of our actions to a foreign being. It does not, therefore, depend on the divine will. It cannot, for instance, take the form: "Thou shalt not lie, because lying is forbidden." Accordingly, as it cannot be external, it cannot be tautological. There are those who argue that we must first have God and then morality—a very convenient principle; but ethics and theology are neither of them a principle of the other. It is true that theology cannot subsist without ethics and vice versa. We are not, however, discussing here the fact that theology is a motive for ethics—which it is, but we are investigating whether the principle of ethical discrimination is theological—and it cannot be that. Were it so, then before a nation could have any concept of duties it would first have to know God. Consequently, nations which had no right concept of God would have no duties, and this is not the case. Nations had a right idea of their duties, and were aware that lies were detestable, without having the proper concept of God. Duties must, therefore, be derived from another source. Men have derived morality from the divine will because the moral laws are expressed in the form "thou shalt," and this has led to the belief that a third being must have promulgated the command. But whilst it is true that the moral laws are commands, and whilst they may be commandments of the divine will, they do not originate in the commandment. God has commanded this or that because it is a moral law, and because His will coincides with the moral law.

Having examined what the principle of morality is not, we must now examine what it is. Now the principle of morality is *intellectuale internum*, and must, therefore, be sought in the action itself by the pure reason. Wherein then does it consist? Morality is the harmony of actions with the universally valid law of the free will: it is always the relation in which actions stand to the general rule. In all our actions that which is called moral is regular. It conforms to a rule. The essence of morality is that our actions are motivated by a general rule, that is, that the reasons for the actions are to be found in such a rule. If we make it the foundation of our conduct that our actions shall be consistent with the universal rule, which is valid at all times and for every one, then our actions have their source in the principle of morality. Take, for example, the keeping of a promise. To break a promise as it please our sensibility is not moral, for if no man were willing to keep his promise simply in terms of the original proposal promises would in the long run become useless. But I may judge the matter in terms of the understanding, to discover whether it is a universal rule that promises should be kept. I then find that as I wish that all others should keep their promises to me, I must keep my promises to others. My action then conforms to the universal rule of will in general. Take again the practice of benevolence. Assume that I meet a man who is in the most distressed circumstances, and though I have the wherewithal to assist him, I am indifferent to his sufferings and prefer to spend my money on my own pleasures. Let me test this by my understanding; let me see whether my conduct can be a universal rule; let me see whether such indifference on the part of another, if I were in distress, would accord with my will; and what do I find? I find that it would not. Such conduct, therefore, is not moral.

Every immoral man has his maxims. While a precept is an objective law in accordance with which we ought to act, a maxim is a subjective law in accordance with which we actually do act. Every one regards the moral law as something which he can publicly profess, but his maxims as something which must be concealed because they are contrary to morality and cannot serve as a universal rule. Take, for example, a man whose maxim is to become rich. He cannot and will not declare it, or else he would fail in his purpose. If it came to be used as a general rule, every one would want to grow rich, and then it would be impossible to become rich, because everyone would know about it and everyone would want to be so. Examples from the sphere of duties towards oneself are the least well known and are, therefore, somewhat more difficult to understand. They are often confused with the pragmatic rules (of which more anon) for promoting one's well-being. May a man, for instance, multilate his body for profit? May he sell a tooth? May he surrender himself at a price to the highest bidder? What is the moral aspect of such questions as these? I apply my understanding to investigate whether the intent of the action is of such a nature that it could be a universal rule. What is that intent in these cases? It is to gain material advantage. It is obvious, therefore, that in so acting man reduces himself to a thing, to an instrument of animal amusements. We are, however, as human beings, not things but persons, and by turning ourselves into things we dishonour human nature in our own persons. The same applies to suicide. By the rules of prudence there might be cases in which, in order to have done with misery, one might commit suicide, but not so by rules of morality. Suicide is immoral; for the intention is to rid oneself of all pains and discomforts attendant upon one's state by sacrificing that state, and this subordinates human nature to animal nature and brings the understanding under the control of animal impulses. In doing this I contradict myself, if I still desire to possess the rights of man.

In all moral judgments the idea which we frame is this, "What is the character of the action taken by itself?" If the intent of the action can without self-contradiction be universalized, it is morally possible; if it cannot be so universalized without contradicting itself, it is morally impossible. Consider, for instance, the case of telling a lie in order to gain a large fortune. If this were made a universal principle, it would be impossible to maintain it, because the end would be known to every one. That action is immoral whose intent cancels and destroys itself when it is made a universal rule. It is moral, if the intent of the action is in harmony with itself when it is made a universal rule. Understanding is the faculty of the rule of our actions, and actions which are in harmony with the universal rule are in harmony with the understanding, and thus their impulsive grounds are in the understanding.

REWARD AND PUNISHMENT

Punishment in general is physical evil accruing from moral evil. It is either deterrent or else retributive. Punishments are deterrent if their sole purpose is to prevent an evil from arising; they are retributive when they are imposed because an evil has been done. Punishments are, therefore, a means of preventing an evil or of punishing it. Those imposed by governments are always deterrent. They are meant to deter the sinner himself or to deter others by making an example of him. But the punishments imposed by a being who is guided by moral standards are retributive.

Punishments appertain either to the lawgiver's justice or to his prudence. In the first case they are moral, in the second pragmatic. Moral punishments are imposed because a sin has been committed. Those which are pragmatic are imposed in order that there should be no sin; they are a means of obviating transgression. All punishments imposed by sovereigns and governments are pragmatic; they are designed either to correct or to make an example. Ruling authorities do not punish because a crime has been committed, but in order that crimes should not be committed. But apart from this actual punishment, every transgression has a penal desert for the reason that it has been committed. Punishment which must follow from the action by such a necessity is moral and therefore a *poena vindicativa.* Just so reward follows a good deed not in order to encourage to further good deeds, but because of the deed itself. If we compare rewards and punishments we notice that neither should be regarded as incentives to action. Just as rewards ought not to be the grounds for doing good deeds, so punishments ought not to be the grounds for avoiding evil deeds. If they are, a mean condition of mind tends to be set up, an *indoles abjecta.* The impulsive ground ought to be moral. The ground for doing a good action should not lie in the reward but the action should be rewarded because it is good; the ground for not doing an evil action should not lie in the punishment but the action should not be done, because it is evil. Reward and punishment are merely subjective incentives, to be used only when the objective ones are no longer effective, and they serve merely to make up for the lack of morality.

The Subject must first be habituated to morality. The moral feeling must be enlivened so that the Subject can be swayed by moral Motives. If this fails, we must then have recourse to the subjective incentives of reward and punishment. A man who is rewarded for good conduct will repeat that conduct not because it is good, but because it is rewarded; one who is punished for evil conduct will hate not the conduct but the punishment; he will repeat the evil deed and try with jesuitical craftiness to escape punishment. It is wrong, therefore, for religion to preach that men should avoid doing evil in order to escape eternal punishment; such preaching will lead to wicked conduct, for men will think that they can escape punishment in the long run by a sudden conversion. Nevertheless, reward and punishment can serve indirectly as a means of moral training. If a man does good for the sake of reward, he will gradually acquire the habit of good deeds and will ultimately do them regardless of reward and merely because they are good. Similarly, a man who refrains from doing evil because of fear of punishment will in the long run get accustomed to it and will feel that it is better to leave such things undone. A drunkard who gives up drink because of the harm it does to him will ultimately acquire the habit of sobriety and will come to see that it is better to be temperate than to be a drunkard. Rewards are an even better means for inculcating good conduct than are punishments for inculcating the avoidance of evil. Reward is pleasant, and we can take pleasure in the law which promises a pleasant result provided we act in a certain way; but we cannot love a law which merely threatens punishment. Rewards are thus more in harmony with morality than are punishments. Love is a stronger ground of impulse to performance. It is, therefore, better in religion to begin with reward rather than with punishment.

Ethics

DUTIES TO ONESELF

We now proceed to deal with essential morality and with our proper duties towards everything in the world. First amongst these duties is the duty we owe to our own selves.

My duty towards myself cannot be treated juridically; the law touches only our relations with other men; I have no legal obligations towards myself; and whatever I do to myself I do to a consenting party; I cannot commit an act of injustice against myself. What we have to discuss is the use we make of liberty in respect of ourselves. By way of introduction it is to be noted that there is no question in moral philosophy which has received more defective treatment than that of the individual's duty towards himself. No one has framed a proper concept of self-regarding duty. The reason for all this is the want of a pure concept, which should form the basis of a self-regarding duty. It was taken for granted that a man's duty towards himself consisted in promoting his own happiness. In fact, the principle of self-regarding duties is a very different one, which has no connexion with our well-being or earthly happiness. Far from ranking lowest in the scale of precedence, our duties towards ourselves are of primary importance and should have pride of place; for (deferring for the moment the definition of what constitutes this duty) it is obvious that nothing can be expected from a man who dishonours his own person. He who transgresses against himself loses his manliness and becomes incapable of doing his duty towards his fellows. A man who performed his duty to others badly, who lacked generosity, kindness and sympathy, but who nevertheless did his duty to himself by leading a proper life, might yet possess a certain inner worth; but he who has transgressed his duty towards himself, can have no inner worth whatever. Thus a man who fails in his duty to himself loses worth absolutely; while a man who fails in his duty to others loses worth only relatively. It follows that the prior condition of our duty to others is our duty to ourselves; we can fulfil the former only in so far as we first fulfil the latter. Let us illustrate our meaning by a few examples of failure in one's duty to oneself. A drunkard does no harm to another, and if he has a strong constitution he does no harm to himself, yet he is an object of contempt. We are not indifferent to cringing servility; man should not cringe and fawn; by so doing he degrades his person and loses his manhood.

A liar, even though by his lies he does no harm to any one, yet becomes an object of contempt, he throws away his personality; his behaviour is vile, he has transgressed his duty towards himself. We can carry the argument further and say that to accept favours and benefits is also a breach of one's duty to oneself. If I accept favours, I contract debts which I can never repay, for I can never get on equal terms with him who has conferred the favours upon me; he has stolen a march upon me, and if I do him a favour I am only returning a *quid pro quo;* I shall always owe him a debt of gratitude, and who will accept such a debt? For to be indebted is to be subject to an unending constraint. The most serious offence against the duty one owes to oneself is suicide. But why should suicide be so abominable? It is no answer to say "because God forbids it." Suicide is not an abomination because God has forbidden it; it is forbidden by God because it is abominable. Suicide is an abomination because it implies the abuse of man's freedom of action: he uses his freedom to destroy himself. His freedom should be employed to enable him to live as a man. He is free to dispose as he pleases of things appertaining to his person, but not of his person; he may not use his freedom against himself. In terms of the rule of prudence suicide may often be the surest and best course; none the less suicide is in itself revolting. The rule of morality, which takes precedence of all rules of reflective prudence, commands apodeictically and categorically that we must observe our duties to ourselves; and in committing suicide and reducing himself to a carcase, man uses his powers and his liberty against himself. Man is free to dispose of his condition but not of his person; he himself is an end and not a means; all else in the world is of value only as a means, but man is a person and not a thing and therefore not a means. It is absurd that a reasonable being, an end for the sake of which all else is means, should use himself as a means. It is true that a person can serve as a means for others (e.g. by his work), but only in a way whereby he does not cease to be a person and an end. Whoever acts in such a way that he cannot be an end, uses himself as a means and treats his person as a thing. Man is not free to dispose of his person as a means; and in what follows we shall have more to say on this score.

The duties we owe to ourselves do not depend on the relation of the action to the ends of happiness. If they did, they would depend on our inclinations and so be governed by rules of prudence. Such rules are not moral. The basis of such obligation is not to be found in the advantages we reap from doing our duty towards ourselves, but in the worth of manhood. This principle does not allow us an unlimited freedom in respect of our own persons. It insists that we must reverence humanity in our own person, because apart from this man becomes an object of contempt, worthless in the eyes of his fellows and worthless in himself. Such faultiness is absolute. Our duties towards ourselves constitute the supreme condition and the principle of all morality; for moral worth is the worth of the person as such; our capacities have a value only in regard to the circumstances in which we find ourselves.

Let us next consider the basis of the principle of all self-regarding duties.

Freedom is, on the one hand, that faculty which gives unlimited usefulness to all other faculties. It is the highest order of life, which serves as the foundation of all perfections and is their necessary condition. All animals have the faculty of using their powers according to will. But this will is not free. It is necessitated through the incitement of *stimuli,* and the actions of animals involve a *bruta necessitas.* If the will of all beings were so bound to sensuous impulse, the world would possess no value. The inherent value of the world, the *summum bonum,* is freedom in accordance with a will which is not necessitated to action. Freedom is thus the inner value of the world. But on the other hand, freedom unrestrained by rules of its conditional employment is the most terrible of all things. The actions of animals are regular; they are performed in accordance with rules which necessitate them subjectively. Mankind apart, nature is not free; through it all there runs a subjectively necessitating principle in accordance with which everything happens regularly. Man alone is free; his actions are not regulated by any such subjectively necessitating principle; if they were, he would not be free. And what then? If the freedom of man were not kept within bounds by objective rules, the result would be the completest savage disorder. There could then be no certainty that man might not use his powers to destroy himself, his fellows, and the whole of nature. I can conceive freedom as the complete absence of orderliness, if it is not subject to an objective determination. The grounds of this objective determination must lie in the understanding, and constitute the restrictions to freedom. Therefore the proper use of freedom is the supreme rule. What then is the condition under which freedom is restricted? It is the law. The universal law is therefore as follows: Let thy procedure be such that in all thine actions regularity prevails. What does this restraint imply when applied to the individual? That he should not follow his inclinations. The fundamental rule, in terms of which I ought to restrain my freedom, is the conformity of free behaviour to the essential ends of humanity. I shall not then follow my inclinations, but bring them under a rule. He who subjects his person to his inclinations, acts contrary to the essential end of humanity; for as a free being he must not be subjected to inclinations, but ought to determine them in the exercise of his freedom; and being a free agent he must have a rule, which is the essential end of humanity. In the case of animals inclinations are already determined by subjectively compelling factors; in their case, therefore, disorderliness is impossible. But if man gives free rein to his inclinations, he sinks lower than an animal because he then lives in a state of disorder which does not exist among animals. A man is then in contradiction with the essential ends of humanity in his own person, and so with himself. All evil in the world springs from freedom. Animals, not being free, live according to rules. But free beings can only act regularly, if they restrict their freedom by rules. Let us reflect upon the actions of man which refer to himself, and consider freedom in them. These spring from impulse and inclinations or from maxims and principles. It is essential, therefore, that man should take his stand upon maxims and restrain by rules the free actions which relate to himself. These are the rules of his self-regarding duties. The supreme rule is that in all the actions which affect himself a man should so conduct himself that every exercise of his power is compatible with the fullest employment of them. Let us illustrate our meaning by examples. If I have drunk too much I am incapable of using my freedom and my powers. Again, if I kill myself, I use my powers to deprive myself of the faculty of using them. That freedom, the principle of the highest order of life, should annul itself and abrogate the use of itself conflicts with the fullest use of freedom. But freedom can only be in harmony with itself under certain conditions; otherwise it comes into collision with itself. If there were no established order in Nature, everything would come to an end, and so is it with unbridled freedom. Evils are to be found, no doubt, in Nature, but the true moral evil, vice, only in freedom. We pity the unfortunate, but we hate the vicious and rejoice at their punishment. The conditions under which alone the fullest use of freedom is possible, and can be in harmony with itself, are the essential ends of humanity. It must conform with these. The principle of all duties is that the use of freedom must be in keeping with the essential ends of humanity.

DUTIES TOWARDS OTHERS

We have only other-regarding duties towards men. Inanimate things are completely subject to our will, and our duties to animals are duties only with reference to ourselves. We shall therefore reduce all these duties to duties towards other men. They are divisible into two main groups:

1. Duties of good-will, or benevolence.

2. Duties of indebtedness or justice.

Actions falling under the first group are benevolent; those falling under the second are righteous and compulsory.

The duties falling under the first heading do not imply any definite obligation upon us to love other human beings and to do them good. The man who loves his neighbour wishes him well, but of his own impulse; he does so willingly and from a voluntary disposition, not because he is bound to. Love is good-will from inclination; but there can also be good-will on principle.

But can a moralist say that we have a duty to love others? Love is good-will from inclination. Now whatever depends upon my inclination and not upon my will, cannot be laid upon me as a duty. I certainly cannot love at will, but only when I have an impulse to love. Duty is always a compulsion, which may be either self-imposed or else imposed upon us by others. If then we are under an obligation to be mindful of the welfare of others, on what is this obligation founded? On principles. For let us consider the world and ourselves. The world is an arena on which nature has provided everything necessary for our temporal welfare, and we are nature's guests. We all have an equal right to the good things which nature has provided. These good things have not, however, been shared out by God. He has left men to do the sharing. Every one of us, therefore, in enjoying the good things of life must have regard to the happiness of others; they have an equal right and ought not to be deprived of it. Since God's providence is universal, I may not be indifferent to the happiness of others. If, for instance, I were to find in the forest a table spread with all manner of dishes, I ought not to conclude that it is all for me; I may eat, but I should also remember to leave some for others to enjoy. I ought not even to consume in its entirety any particular dish in case some one else might fancy it also. Recognizing, therefore, that Providence is universal, I am placed under an obligation to restrict my own consumption, and to bear in mind that nature's preparations are made for all of us. This is the source of the obligation to benevolence.

Let us now consider the second group of duties towards others, namely the duties of indebtedness and justice. Here there is no question of inclination, only of the rights of others. It is not their needs that count in this connexion, but their rights; it is not a question of whether my neighbor is needy, wretchedly poor or the reverse; if his right is concerned, it must be satisfied. This group of duties is grounded in the general rule of right.

The chief of these duties is respect for the rights of others. It is our duty to regard them as sacred and to respect and maintain them as such. There is nothing more sacred in the wide world than the rights of others. They are inviolable. Woe unto him who trespasses upon the right of another and tramples it underfoot! His right should be his security; it should be stronger than any shield or fortress. We have a holy ruler and the most sacred of his gifts to us is the rights of man.

Let us take a man who is guided only by justice and not by charity. He may close his heart to all appeal; he may be utterly indifferent to the misery and misfortune around him; but so long as he conscientiously does his duty in giving to every one what is his due, so long as he respects the rights of other men as the most sacred trust given to us by the ruler of the world, his conduct is righteous; let him give to another no trifle in excess of his due, and yet be equally punctilious to keep no jot nor tittle back, and his conduct is righteous. If all of us behaved in this way, if none of us ever did any act of love and charity, but only kept inviolate the rights of every man, there would be no misery in the world except sickness and misfortune and other such sufferings as do not spring from the violation of rights. The most frequent and fertile source of human misery is not misfortune, but the injustice of man.

Respect for the rights of others is rooted in principle, and as mankind is not rich in principles, Providence has implanted in our bosoms the instinct of benevolence to be the source of actions by which we restore what we have unrighteously procured. We have thus an instinct to benevolence, but not to righteousness. This impulse makes a man merciful and charitable to his neighbour, so that he makes restitution for an injustice of which he is quite unconscious; though unconscious of it only because he does not properly examine his position. Although we may be entirely within our rights, according to the laws of the land and the rules of our social structure, we may nevertheless be participating in general injustice, and in giving to an unfortunate man we do not give him a gratuity but only help to return to him that of which the general injustice of our system has deprived him. For if none of us drew to himself a greater share of the world's wealth than his neighbour, there would be no rich and no poor. Even charity therefore is an act of duty imposed upon us by the rights of others and the debt we owe to them.

THE ULTIMATE DESTINY OF THE HUMAN RACE

The ultimate destiny of the human race is the greatest moral perfection, provided that it is achieved through human freedom, whereby alone man is capable of the greatest happiness. God might have made men perfect and given to each his portion of happiness. But happiness would not then have been derived from the inner principle of the world, for the inner principle of the world is freedom. The end, therefore, for which man is destined is to achieve his fullest perfection through his own freedom. God's will is not merely that we should be happy, but that we should make ourselves happy, and this is the true morality. The universal end of mankind is the highest moral perfection. If we all so ordered our conduct that it should be in harmony with the universal end of mankind, the highest perfection would be attained. We must each of us, therefore, endeavour to guide our conduct to this end; each of us must make such a contribution of his own that if all contributed similarly the result would be perfection. How far has the human race progressed on the road to perfection? If we look at the most enlightened portion of the world, we see the various States armed to the teeth, sharpening their weapons in time of peace the one against the other. The consequences of this are such that they block our approach to the universal end of perfection. The Abbot of St. Pierre has proposed that a senate of the nations should be formed. If this proposal were carried out it would be a great step forward, for the time now occupied by each nation in providing for its own security could then be employed for the advancement of mankind. But the Idea of right has less authority with princes than the Idea of independence and individual sovereignty, or the lust for despotic power, and therefore nothing is to be hoped for from this direction. How then is perfection to be sought? Wherein lies our hope? In education, and in nothing else. Education must be adapted to all the ends of nature, both civil and domestic. Our present education, both in the home and at school, is still very faulty, in respect of discipline, doctrine and the cultivation of talent as much as in respect of the building of character in accordance with moral principles. We care more for skill than for the disposition to use it well. How then can it be hoped that persons improperly educated should rule a State to better advantage? Let education be conceived on right lines, let natural gifts be developed as they should, let character be formed on moral principles, and in time the effects of this will reach even to the seat of government, when princes themselves are educated by teachers fitted for the task. But so far no prince has contributed one iota to the perfection of mankind, to inner happiness, to the worth of humanity; all of them look ever and only to the prosperity of their own countries, making that their chief concern. A proper education would teach them so to frame their minds that conciliation would be promoted. Once planted, the seed would grow; once propagated, conciliation would maintain itself by public opinion. But the ruler cannot do it alone; men of all ranks in the State would have to be similarly trained; then would the State be built on a firm foundation. Can we hope for this? The Basedow institutions give us hope, warm even though small. The realization of the full destiny, the highest possible perfection of human nature —this is the kingdom of God on earth. Justice and equity, the authority, not of governments, but of conscience within us, will then rule the world. This is the destined final end, the highest moral perfection to which the human race can attain; but the hope of it is still distant; it will be many centuries before it can be realized.

*Critique of Practical Reason**

Book I
Analytic of Pure Practical Reason

CHAPTER I. PRINCIPLES OF PURE PRACTICAL REASON

1. *Definition*

Practical principles are propositions which contain a general determination of the will, having under it several practical rules. They are subjective, or maxims, when the condition is regarded by the subject as valid only for his own will. They are objective, or practical laws, when the condition is recognized as objective, i.e., as valid for the will of every rational being.

Assuming that pure reason can contain a practical ground sufficient to determine the will, then there are practical laws. Otherwise all practical principles are mere maxims. In the will of a rational being affected by feeling, there can be a conflict of maxims with the practical laws recognized by this being. For example, someone can take as his maxim not to tolerate any unavenged offense and yet see at the same time that this is only his own maxim and not a practical law and that, if it is taken as a rule for the will of every rational being, it would be inconsistent with itself.

2. *Theorem I*

All practical principles which presuppose an object (material) of the faculty of desire as the determining ground of the will are without exception empirical and can furnish no practical laws.

By the term "material of the faculty of desire," I understand an object whose

* Immanuel Kant, *Critique of Practical Reason*, trans. Lewis White Beck, Copyright © 1956, by The Liberal Arts Press, Inc., reprinted by permission of The Liberal Arts Press Division of The Bobbs-Merrill Company, Inc. Deletions are not noted in the text.

reality is desired. When the desire for this object precedes the practical rule and is the condition under which the latter becomes a principle, I say, first, that this principle is then always empirical. I say this because the determining ground of choice consists in the conception of an object and its relation to the subject, whereby the faculty of desire is determined to seek its realization. Such a relation to the subject is called pleasure in the reality of an object, and it must be presupposed as the condition of the possibility of the determination of choice. But we cannot know, a priori, of the idea of any object, whatever the nature of this idea, whether it will be associated with pleasure or displeasure or will be merely indifferent. Thus any such determining ground of choice must always be empirical, and the practical material principle which has it as a condition is likewise empirical.

Second, a principle which is based only on the subjective susceptibility to a pleasure or displeasure (which is never known except empirically and cannot be valid in the same form for all rational beings) cannot function as a law even to the subject possessing this susceptibility, because it lacks objective necessity, which must be known a priori. For this reason, such a principle can never furnish a practical law. It can, however, be counted among the maxims of a subject thus susceptible.

3. *Theorem II*

All material practical principles are, as such, of one and the same kind and belong under the general principle of self-love or one's own happiness.

4. *Theorem III*

If a rational being can think of its maxims as practical universal laws, he can do so only by considering them as principles which contain the determining grounds of the will because of their form and not because of their matter.

The material of a practical principle is the object of the will. This object either is the determining ground of the will or it is not. If it is, the rule of the will is subject to an empirical condition (to the relation of the determining idea to feelings of pleasure or displeasure), and therefore it is not a practical law. If all material of a law, i.e., every object of the will considered as a ground of its determination, is abstracted from it, nothing remains except the mere form of giving universal law. Therefore, a rational being either cannot think of his subjectively practical principles (maxims) as universal laws, or he must suppose that their mere form, through which they are fitted for being *universal* laws, is alone that which makes them a practical law.

REMARK

What form of a maxim makes it suitable for universal law-giving and what form does not do so can be distinguished without instruction by the most common understanding. I have, for example, made it my maxim to increase my property by every safe means. Now I have in my possession a deposit, the owner of which has died without leaving any record of it. Naturally, this case falls under my maxim. Now I want to know whether this maxim can hold as a universal practical law. I apply it, therefore, to the present case and ask if it could take the form of a law, and consequently whether I could, by the maxim, make the law that every man is allowed to deny that a deposit has been made when no one can prove the contrary. I immediately realize that taking such a principle as a law would annihilate itself, because its result would be that no one would make a deposit. A practical law which I acknowledge as such must qualify for being universal law; this is an identical and therefore a self-evident proposition.

Now, if I say that my will is subject to a practical law, I cannot put forward my inclination (in this case, my avarice) as fit to be a determining ground of a universal practical law. It is so far from being worthy of universal legislation that in the form of a universal law it must destroy itself.

5. *Problem I*

Granted that the mere legislative form of maxims is the sole sufficient determining ground of a will, find the character of the will which is determinable by it alone.

Since the mere form of a law can be thought only by reason and is consequently not an object of the senses and therefore does not belong among appearances, the conception of this form as the determining ground of the will is distinct from all determining grounds of events in nature according to the law of causality, for these grounds must themselves be appearances. Now, as no determining ground of the will except the universal legislative form can serve as a law for it, such a will must be conceived as wholly independent of the natural law of appearances in their mutual relations, i.e., the law of causality. Such independence is called *freedom* in the strictest, i.e., transcendental, sense. Therefore, a will to which only the legislative form of the maxim can serve as a law is a free will.

6. *Problem II*

Granted that a will is free, find the law which alone is competent to determine it necessarily.

Since the material of the practical law, i.e., an object of the maxim, cannot be given except empirically, and since a free will must be independent of all empirical conditions (i.e., those belonging to the world of sense) and yet be determinable, a free will must find its ground of determination in the law, but independently of the material of the law. But besides the latter there is nothing in a law except the legislative form. Therefore, the legislative form, in so far as it is contained in the maxim, is the only thing which can constitute a determining ground of the [free] will. Thus freedom and unconditional practical law reciprocally imply each other.

7. *Fundamental Law of Pure Practical Reason*

So act that the maxim of your will could always hold at the same time as a principle establishing universal law.

REMARK

Pure geometry has postulates as practical propositions, which, however, contain nothing more than the presupposition that one *can* do something and that, when some result is needed, one *should* do it; these are the only propositions of pure geometry which apply to an existing thing. They are thus practical rules under a problematic condition of the will. Here, however, the rule says: One ought absolutely to act in a certain way. The practical rule is therefore unconditional and thus is thought of a priori as a categorically practical proposition. The practical rule, which is thus here a law, absolutely and directly determines the will objectively, for pure reason, practical in itself, is here directly legislative. The will is thought of as independent of empirical conditions and consequently as pure will, determined by the mere form of the law, and this ground of determination is regarded as the supreme condition of all maxims.

The thing is strange enough and has no parallel in the remainder of practical knowledge. For the a priori thought of the possibility of giving universal law, which is thus merely problematic, is unconditionally commanded as a law without borrowing anything from experience or from any external will. It is, however, not a prescription according to which an act should occur in order to make a desired effect possible, for such a rule is always physically conditioned; it is, on the contrary, a rule which determines the will a priori only with respect to the form of its maxims.

COROLLARY

Pure reason is practical of itself alone, and it gives (to man) a universal law, which we call the *moral law.*

REMARK

The fact just mentioned is undeniable. One need only analyze the sentence which men pass upon the lawfulness of their actions to see in every case that their reason, incorruptible and self-constrained, in every action holds up the maxim of the will to the pure will, i.e., to itself regarded as a priori practical; and this it does regardless of what inclination may say to the contrary.

8. *Theorem IV*

The *autonomy* of the will is the sole principle of all moral laws and of the duties conforming to them; *heteronomy* of choice, on the other hand, not only does not establish any obligation but is opposed to the principle of duty and to the morality of the will.

CHAPTER II. THE CONCEPT OF AN OBJECT OF PURE PRACTICAL REASON

By a concept of an object of practical reason I understand the idea of an object as an effect possible through freedom. To be an object of practical knowledge as such signifies, therefore, only the relation of the will to the action whereby it or its opposite is brought into being. To decide whether or not something is an object of the pure practical reason is only to discern the possibility or impossibility of willing the action by which a certain object would be made real, provided we had the ability to bring it about (the latter being a matter which experience must decide). If the object is taken as the determining ground of our faculty of desire, its physical possibility through the free use of our strength must precede the decision as to whether it is or is not an object of the practical reason. But if, on the other hand, the a priori law can be regarded as the determining ground of action, which is consequently seen as determined by the pure practical reason, then the judgment as to whether or not something is an object of the pure practical reason is wholly independent of any question of our physical ability; the only question is whether we should will an action directed to the existence of an object if it were within our power. Consequently, the moral possibility of the action takes precedence, for in this case it is not the object but the law of the will which is its ground of determination.

The sole objects of a practical reason are thus those of the good and the evil. By the former, one understands a necessary object of the faculty of desire, and by the latter, a necessary object of aversion, both according to a principle of reason.

If the concept of the good is not derived from a practical law but rather serves as the ground of the latter, it can only be the concept of something whose existence promises pleasure and thus determines the causality of the subject (the faculty of desire) to produce it. Now, because it is impossible to see a priori which idea will be accompanied with pleasure and which with pain, it would be solely a matter of experience to discern what is immediately good or evil. The property of the subject, by virtue of which such experience could be had, is the feeling of pleasure or displeasure as a receptivity belonging to the inner sense; thus the concept of that which is immediately good would only refer to that with which the sensation of pleasure is immediately associated, and the concept of the absolutely evil would have to be related only to that which directly excites pain.

Even the usage of language is opposed to this, however, since it distinguishes the pleasant from the good and the unpleasant from the evil, and demands that good and evil be judged by reason and thus through concepts which alone can be universally communicated, and not by mere sensation which is limited to the individual subjects and their susceptibility.

The German language has the good fortune to possess expressions which do not permit this difference to be overlooked. It has two very different concepts and equally different expressions for what the Latins named with the single word *bonum.* For *bonum,* it has *das Gute* [the good] and *das Wohl* [well-being]; for *malum, das Böse* [evil, wicked] and *das Übel* [bad, ill] or *das Weh* [woe]. Thus there are two very different judgments if in an action we have regard to its goodness or wickedness or to our weal or woe (ill).

Though one may laugh at the Stoic who in the worst paroxysm of gout cried out, "Pain, however thou tormentest me, I will never admit that thou art anything bad (*κακόν, malum*)!" he was nevertheless right. He felt it was an evil, and he betrayed that in his cry; but that anything [morally] evil attached to him he had no reason to concede, for the pain did not in the least diminish the worth of his person but only the worth of his condition. A single lie of which he was conscious would have struck down his pride, but pain served only as an occasion for raising it when he was conscious that he had not made himself liable to it by an unrighteous action and thus culpable.

What we call good must be, in the judgment of every reasonable man, an object of the faculty of desire, and the evil must be, in everyone's eyes, an object of aversion. Thus, in addition to sense, this judgment requires reason. So it is with truthfulness as opposed to a lie, with justice in contrast to violence, etc. But we can call something an ill, however, which everyone at the same time must acknowledge as good, either directly or indirectly. Whoever submits to a surgical operation feels it without doubt as an ill, but by reason he and everyone else will describe it as good. When, however, someone who delights in annoying and vexing peace-loving folk receives at last a right good beating, it is certainly an ill, but everyone approves of it and considers it as good in itself even if nothing further results from it; nay, even he who gets the beating must acknowledge, in his reason, that justice has been done to him, because he sees the proportion between welfare and well-doing, which reason inevitably holds before him, here put into practice.

Certainly our weal and woe are very important in the estimation of our practical reason; and, as far as our nature as sensible beings is concerned, our happiness is the only thing of importance, provided this is judged, as reason especially requires, not according to transitory sensation but according to the influence which this contingency has on our whole existence and our satisfaction with it. But still not everything depends upon that. Man is a being of needs, so far as he belongs to the world of sense, and to this extent his reason certainly has an inescapable responsibility from the side of his sensuous nature to attend to its interest and to form practical maxims with a view to the happiness of this and, where possible, of a future life. But still he is not so completely an animal as to be indifferent to everything which reason says on its own and to use it merely as a tool for satisfying his needs as a sensuous being. That he has reason does not in the least raise him in worth above mere animality if reason only serves the purposes which, among animals, are taken care of by instinct; if this were so, reason would be only a specific way nature had made use of to equip man for the same purpose for which animals are qualified, without fitting him for any higher purpose. No doubt, as a result of this unique arrangement, he needs reason, to consider at all times his weal and woe. But he has reason for a yet higher purpose, namely, to consider also what is in itself good or evil, which pure and sensuously disinterested reason alone can judge, and furthermore, to distinguish this estimation from a sensuous estimation and to make the former the supreme condition of good and evil.

CHAPTER III. THE INCENTIVES OF PURE PRACTICAL REASON

It is of the utmost importance in all moral judging to pay strictest attention to the subjective principle of every maxim, so that all the morality of actions may be placed in their necessity from duty and from respect for the law, and not from love for or leaning toward that which the action is to produce. For men and all rational creatures, the moral necessity is a constraint, an obligation. Every action based on it is to be considered as duty, and not as a manner of acting which we naturally favor or which we sometime might favor. This would be tantamount to believing we could finally bring it about that, without respect for the law (which is always connected with fear or at least apprehension that we might transgress it) we, like the independent deity, might come into possession of holiness of will through irrefragable agreement of the will with the pure moral law becoming, as it were, our very nature. This pure law, if we could never be tempted to be untrue to it, would finally cease altogether to be a command for us.

It is a very beautiful thing to do good to men because of love and a sympathetic good will, or to do justice because of a love of order. But this is not the genuine moral maxim of our conduct, the maxim which is suitable to our position among rational beings as men, when we presume, like volunteers, to flout with proud conceit the thought of duty and, as independent of command, merely to will of our own good pleasure to do something to which we think we need no command. We stand under a *discipline* of reason, and in all our maxims we must not forget our subjection to it, or withdraw anything from it, or by an egotistical illusion detract from the authority of the law (even though it is given by our own reason), so that we could place the determining ground of our will (even though it is in accordance with the law) elsewhere than in the law itself and in respect for it. Duty and obligation are the only names which we must give to our relation to the moral law. We are indeed legislative members of a moral realm which is possible through freedom and which is presented to us as an object of respect by practical reason; yet we are at the same time subjects in it, not sovereigns, and to mistake our inferior position as creatures and to deny, from self-conceit, respect to the holy law is, in spirit, a defection from it even if its letter be fulfilled.

part 4

THE NINETEENTH CENTURY

Many of the tendencies which we found present, at least implicitly, in the early modern period continued in the nineteenth century. Thus there was an increasing emphasis on welfare, which we said resulted from combining the concept of equality with the concept of plenty. The basic formula of the utilitarians—"the greatest good to the greatest number"—reflects this interest. All of the utilitarians—Bentham, Mill, and Sidgwick—were concerned with the elaboration and refinement of this formula and with reconciling it with theories that stressed other aspects of the ethical situation. Thus one of the characteristics of utilitarian ethics is its concentration on results; it tends to evaluate conduct in terms of the goods actually produced, rather than in terms of the motives of the agent. Motives, according to the utilitarians, are not good or bad in themselves, but simply in so far as certain types of motives tend to be productive of good or bad results. Accordingly, a problem for the utilitarians was the reconciliation of their focus on results with the traditional Christian emphasis (as represented, say, in Kant's theory) on purity of motives regardless of the results accomplished.

Another influence that we found operative in the early modern period was scientific theory. This influence, too, became more pronounced in the nineteenth century and operated in a great diversity of ways. For instance, there was a widespread attempt to treat the data of ethics scientifically—to apply scientific methods to ethics, in the expectation of achieving exact knowledge of correct conduct. This trend is also represented in utilitarian theory. Bentham's hedonic calculus is a notable example of the attempt to quantify ethics and so to render it precise (p. 316). His seven indices for measuring the quantity of pleasure associated with any anticipated line of conduct is a direct ancestor of game theory and similar contemporary attempts by economists and others to put decision making on a formal and rational basis.

Again, in identifying the *summum bonum* as a natural phenomenon—pleasurable psychological states—the utilitarians showed the influence of an empirical and scientific approach, as opposed to the religious transcendentalism that had dominated much of ethical theorizing in the past.

Thirdly, there was the problem of the relation between the citizen and the state. There had been, even in the early modern period, an attempt to strike a balance between the claims of the individual and the claims of the collectivity. In the nineteenth century, as a result of the increasingly massive accumulations of political and economic power, this issue became primary. We may, indeed, draw a spectrum of opinion from those who thought of the group as essentially a set of interacting individuals to those who thought of the individual as simply a fragmentary aspect of the group: Bentham represents a position roughly at the former end of this spectrum; Hegel and (in a sense) Schopenhauer represent positions at the other end. In general, English thinkers (at least those represented in this volume) came down, when they had to choose, on the side of the individual, while thinkers in the Hegelian tradition emphasized the state. In this connection Bradley (p. 418) is particularly interesting, since he shared the biases of his countrymen toward the individual, while he nevertheless sought to formulate these judgments in terms of a Hegelian metaphysics.

A fourth characteristic of the period is the development of considerable skepticism concerning the possibility of making ethics a mere chapter in a grander metaphysical scheme. This is exemplified to some degree in Bentham and Mill, but most clearly in Sidgwick, who carefully distinguishes ethical from metaphysical questions, though he is ultimately unable to assert their complete independence. Both Kierkegaard and Nietzsche, although for very different reasons, likewise object to the attempt to derive standards of conduct from a general world view.

Finally, as a tendency of nineteenth-century ethical theory we must mention a very complex, widespread, and pervasive characteristic which may loosely be called irrationalism. The old conception of man, so well represented in the tradition by Plato, by Aristotle, and by St. Thomas, was certainly of man as an animal, but as very much a rational animal, capable of contemplating eternal truths and acting in accordance with them. Though we can find counterexamples earlier (for instance, in Machiavelli and Hobbes), this tradition survived for a long time; finally, in the nineteenth century, it was seriously weakened. Here we find increasingly the old conception of man replaced by a very different one—man is a creature of passion, of whim, of deep, unconscious desires; will, not reason, was found to be the primary characteristic of man. The culmination of this development was of course the Freudian theory of psychoanalysis, which emerged just at the end of the nineteenth century. But we encounter several remarkable anticipations of it among earlier nineteenth-century thinkers, notably Schopenhauer, Kierkegaard, and Nietzsche. The main effect on ethical theory of these new conceptions was the reopening of the question of the good life. It might be that, as with Schopenhauer (p. 346), it was now defined as surcease from goalless striving; it might be that, as with Nietzsche (p. 406), it was identified with this very striving. But one thing was sure: it could no longer be simply identified with or by rational contemplation.

We may summarize all of these diverse currents and trends under two main heads. On the one hand there was increasing respect for scientific method—empiricism, objectivism, and precision. On the other hand there was a strong reaction against this trend—a reaction in the direction of irrationalism, subjectivity, and uncertainty. The utilitarians may be taken as typical of the former trend; the existentialists and voluntarists of the latter. The history of ethical theory in the nineteenth century can be read as the interplay of these opposing movements.

JEREMY BENTHAM

Jeremy Bentham (1748–1832) was educated at Westminster School and Oxford. Though he subsequently studied law, he never practiced; instead he became the leader of a small group who called themselves the "Philosophical Radicals" and who were deeply committed to reform. Bentham's views were in fact deeply influential on most of the nineteenth-century English legislation aimed at social improvement, and through the Fabians, he had a considerable influence on the Labor Party in the twentieth century.

Bentham wrote extensively on economics, psychology, penology, law, and theology—all areas in which he believed, with justification, that reform was desirable and possible. But, in a way, his writings on ethics are basic to all these studies. For he sought to work out a simple procedure, or calculus, for reaching correct decisions regarding the right line of action to pursue in any circumstances. If it were possible to put ethics on this scientific basis, the foundations would obviously have been laid for supporting the legislative and other reforms he advocated.

*An Introduction to the Principles of Morals and Legislation**

CHAPTER I. OF THE PRINCIPLE OF UTILITY

I. Nature has placed mankind under the governance of two sovereign masters, *pain* and *pleasure*. It is for them alone to point out what we ought to do, as well as to determine what we shall do. On the one hand the standard of right and wrong, on the other the chain of causes and effects, are fastened to their throne. They govern us in all we do, in all we say, in all we think: every effort we can make to throw off our subjection, will serve but to demonstrate and confirm it. In words a man may pretend to abjure their empire: but in reality he will remain subject to it all the

* London, 1789, revised edition, 1823.

while. The *principle of utility*[1] recognises this subjection, and assumes it for the foundation of that system, the object of which is to rear the fabric of felicity by the hands of reason and of law. Systems which attempt to question it, deal in sounds instead of sense, in caprice instead of reason, in darkness instead of light.

But enough of metaphor and declamation: it is not by such means that moral science is to be improved.

II. The principle of utility is the foundation of the present work: it will be proper therefore at the outset to give an explicit and determinate acount of what is meant by it. By the principle of utility is meant that principle which approves or disapproves of every action whatsoever, according to the tendency which it appears to have to augment or diminish the happiness of the party whose interest is in question: or, what is the same thing in other words, to promote or to oppose that happiness. I say of every action whatsoever; and therefore not only of every action of a private individual, but of every measure of government.

III. By utility is meant that property in any object, whereby it tends to produce benefit, advantage, pleasure, good, or happiness (all this in the present case comes to the same thing), or (what comes again to the same thing) to prevent the happening of mischief, pain, evil, or unhappiness to the party whose interest is considered: if that party be the community in general, then the happiness of the community: if a particular individual, then the happiness of that individual.

IV. The interest of the community is one of the most general expressions that can occur in the phraseology of morals: no wonder that the meaning of it is often lost. When it has a meaning, it is this. The community is a fictitious *body*, composed of the individual persons who are considered as constituting as it were its *members.* The interest of the community then is, what?—the sum of the interests of the several members who compose it.

V. It is in vain to talk of the interest of the community, without understanding what is the interest of the individual.[2] A thing is said to promote the interest, or to be *for* the interest, of an individual, when it tends to add to the sum total of his pleasures: or, what comes to the same thing, to diminish the sum total of his pains.

VI. An action then may be said to be conformable to the principle of utility, or, for shortness sake, to utility (meaning with respect to the community at large), when the tendency it has to augment the happiness of the community is greater than any it has to diminish it.

VII. A measure of government (which is but a particular kind of action, performed by a particular person or persons) may be said to be conformable to or dictated by the principle of utility, when in like manner the tendency which it has to augment the happiness of the community is greater than any which it has to diminish it. . . .

IX. A man may be said to be a partizan of the principle of utility, when the

[1] Note by the Author, July 1822: To this denomination has of late been added, or substituted, the *greatest happiness* or *greatest felicity* principle: this for shortness, instead of saying at length *that principle* which states the greatest happiness of all those whose interest is in question, as being the right and proper, and only right and proper and universally desirable, end of human action. . . . The word *utility* does not so clearly point to the ideas of *pleasure* and *pain* as the words *happiness* and *felicity* do: nor does it lead us to the consideration of the *number*, of the interests affected; to the *number*, as being the circumstance, which contributes, in the largest proportion, to the formation of the standard here in question; the *standard of right and wrong*, by which alone the propriety of human conduct, in every situation, can with propriety be tried. . . .

[2] Interest is one of those words, which not having any superior *genus*, cannot in the ordinary way be defined.

approbation or disapprobation he annexes to any action, or to any measure, is determined by and proportioned to the tendency which he conceives it to have to augment or to diminish the happiness of the community: or in other words, to its conformity or unconformity to the laws or dictates of utility.

X. Of an action that is conformable to the principle of utility one may always say either that it is one that ought to be done, or at least that it is not one that ought not to be done. One may say also, that it is right it should be done; at least that it is not wrong it should be done: that it is a right action; at least that it is not a wrong action. When thus interpreted, the words *ought*, and *right* and *wrong*, and others of that stamp, have a meaning: when otherwise, they have none.

XI. Has the rectitude of this principle been ever formally contested? It should seem that it had, by those who have not known what they have been meaning. Is it susceptible of any direct proof? it should seem not: for that which is used to prove every thing else, cannot itself be proved: a chain of proofs must have their commencement somewhere. To give such proof is as impossible as it is needless. . . .

XIII. When a man attempts to combat the principle of utility, it is with reasons drawn, without his being aware of it, from that very principle itself.[3] His arguments, if they prove any thing, prove not that the principle is *wrong*, but that, according to the applications he supposes to be made of it, it is *misapplied*. Is it possible for a man to move the earth? Yes; but he must first find out another earth to stand upon.

XIV. To disprove the propriety of it by arguments is impossible; but, from the causes that have been mentioned, or from some confused or partial view of it, a man may happen to be disposed not to relish it. Where this is the case, if he thinks the settling of his opinions on such a subject worth the trouble, let him take the following steps, and at length, perhaps, he may come to reconcile himself to it.

1. Let him settle with himself, whether he would wish to discard this principle altogether; if so, let him consider what it is that all his reasonings (in matters of politics especially) can amount to?

2. If he would, let him settle with himself, whether he would judge and act without any principle, or whether there is any other he would judge and act by?

3. If there be, let him examine and satisfy himself whether the principle he thinks he has found is really any separate intelligible principle; or whether it be not a mere principle in words, a kind of phrase, which at bottom expresses neither more nor less than the mere averment of his own unfounded sentiments; that is, what in another person he might be apt to call caprice?

4. If he is inclined to think that his own approbation or disapprobation, annexed to the idea of an act, without any regard to its consequences, is a sufficient foundation for him to judge and act upon, let him ask himself whether his sentiment is to be a standard of right and wrong, with respect to every other man, or whether every man's sentiment has the same privilege of being a standard to itself?

5. In the first case, let him ask himself whether his principle is not despotical, and hostile to all the rest of the human race?

6. In the second case, whether it is not anarchial, and whether at this rate there are not as many different standards of right and wrong as there are men? and whether even to the same man, the same thing, which is right to-day, may not (without the least change in its nature) be

[3] "The principle of utility, (I have heard it said) is a dangerous principle: it is dangerous on certain occasions to consult it." This is as much as to say, what? that it is not consonant to utility, to consult utility: in short, that it is *not* consulting it, to consult it. . . .

wrong to-morrow? and whether the same thing is not right and wrong in the same place at the same time? and in either case, whether all argument is not at an end? and whether, when two men have said, "I like this," and "I don't like it," they can (upon such a principle) have any thing more to say?

7. If he should have said to himself, No: for that the sentiment which he proposes as a standard must be grounded on reflection, let him say on what particulars the reflection is to turn? if on particulars having relation to the utility of the act, then let him say whether this is not deserting his own principle, and borrowing assistance from that very one in opposition to which he sets it up: or if not on those particulars, on what other particulars?

8. If he should be for compounding the matter, and adopting his own principle in part, and the principle of utility in part, let him say how far he will adopt it?

9. When he has settled with himself where he will stop, then let him ask himself how he justifies to himself the adopting it so far? and why he will not adopt it any farther?

10. Admitting any other principle than the principle of utility to be a right principle, a principle that it is right for man to pursue; admitting (what is not true) that the word *right* can have a meaning without reference to utility, let him say whether there is any such thing as a *motive* that a man can have to pursue the dictates of it: if there is, let him say what that motive is, and how it is to be distinguished from those which enforce the dictates of utility: if not, then lastly let him say what it is this other principle can be good for?

CHAPTER II. OF PRINCIPLES ADVERSE TO THAT OF UTILITY

XI. Among principles adverse to that of utility, that which at this day seems to have most influence in matters of government, is what may be called the principle of sympathy and antipathy. By the principle of sympathy and antipathy, I mean that principle which approves or disapproves of certain actions, not on account of their tending to augment the happiness, nor yet on account of their tending to diminish the happiness of the party whose interest is in question, but merely because a man finds himself disposed to approve or disapprove of them: holding up that approbation or disapprobation as a sufficient reason for itself, and disclaiming the necessity of looking out for any extrinsic ground. Thus far in the general department of morals; and in the particular department of politics, measuring out the quantum (as well as determining the ground) of punishment, by the degree of the disapprobation.

XII. It is manifest, that this is rather a principle in name than in reality; it is not a positive principle of itself, so much as a term employed to signify the negation of all principle. What one expects to find in a principle is something that points out some external consideration, as a means of warranting and guiding the internal sentiments of approbation and disapprobation; this expectation is but ill fulfilled by a proposition, which does neither more nor less than hold up each of those sentiments as a ground and standard for itself.

XIII. In looking over the catalogue of human actions (says a partizan of this principle) in order to determine which of them are to be marked with the seal of disapprobation, you need but to take counsel of your own feelings: whatever you find in yourself a propensity to condemn, is wrong for that very reason. For the same reason it is also meet for punishment: what proportion it is adverse to utility, or whether it be adverse to utility at all, is a matter that makes no difference. In that same *proportion* also is it meet for punishment; if you hate much, punish much; if you hate little, punish little; punish as you hate. If you hate not at all, punish not at all; the fine feelings of the soul are not to be overborne and tyrannized by the harsh and rugged dictates of political utility.

XIV. The various systems that have been formed concerning the standard of right and wrong, may all be reduced to the principle of sympathy and antipathy. One account may serve for all of them. They consist all of them in so many contrivances for avoiding the obligation of appealing to any external standard, and for prevailing upon the reader to accept of the author's sentiment or opinion as a reason for itself. The phrases different, but the principle the same.[4]

XV. It is manifest, that the dictates of this principle will frequently coincide with those of utility, though perhaps without intending any such thing. Probably more frequently than not: and hence it is that the business of penal justice is carried on upon that tolerable sort of footing upon which we see it carried on in common at this day. For what more natural or more general ground of hatred to a practice can there be, than the mischievousness of such practice? What all men are exposed to suffer by, all men will be disposed to hate. It is far yet, however, from being a constant ground: for when a man suffers, it is not

---

[4] It is curious enough to observe the variety of inventions men have hit upon, and the variety of phrases they have brought forward, in order to conceal from the world, and, if possible, from themselves, this very general and therefore very pardonable self-sufficiency.

1. One man says, he has a thing made on purpose to tell him what is right and what is wrong; and that it is called a *moral sense:* and then he goes to work at his ease, and says, such a thing is right, and such a thing is wrong—why? "because my moral sense tells me it is."

2. Another man comes and alters the phrase: leaving out *moral,* and putting in *common,* in the room of it. He then tells you, that his common sense teaches him what is right and wrong, as surely as the other's moral sense did: meaning by common sense, a sense of some kind or other, which, he says, is possessed by all mankind: the sense of those, whose sense is not the same as the author's, being struck out of the account as not worth taking. This contrivance does better than the other; for a moral sense, being a new thing, a man may feel about him a good while without being able to find it out: but common sense is as old as the creation; and there is no man but would be ashamed to be thought not to have as much of it as his neighbours. It has another great advantage: by appearing to share power, it lessens envy: for when a man gets up upon this ground, in order to anathematize those who differ from him, it is not by a *sic volo sic jubeo,* but by a *velitis jubeatis.*

3. Another man comes, and says, that as to a moral sense indeed, he cannot find that he has any such thing: that however he has an *understanding,* which will do quite as well. This understanding, he says, is the standard of right and wrong: it tells him so and so. All good and wise men understand as he does: if other men's understandings differ in any point from his, so much the worse for them: it is a sure sign they are either defective or corrupt.

4. Another man says, that there is an eternal and immutable Rule of Right: that that rule of right dictates so and so: and then he begins giving you his sentiments upon anything that comes uppermost: and these sentiments (you are to take for granted) are so many branches of the eternal rule of right.

5. Another man, or perhaps the same man (it's no matter) says, that there are certain practices conformable, and others repugnant to the Fitness of Things; and then he tells you, at his leisure, what practices are conformable and what repugnant: just as he happens to like a practice or dislike it.

6. A great multitude of people are continually talking of the Law of Nature; and then they go on giving you their sentiments about what is right and what is wrong: and these sentiments, you are to understand, are so many chapters and sections of the Law of Nature.

7. Instead of the phrase, Law of Nature, you have sometimes, Law of Reason, Right Reason, Natural Justice, Natural Equity, Good Order. Any of them will do equally well. This latter is most used in politics. The last three are much more tolerable than the others, be-

always that he knows what it is he suffers by. A man may suffer grievously, for instance, by a new tax, without being able to trace up the cause of his sufferings to the injustice of some neighbour, who has eluded the payment of an old one.

XVI. The principle of sympathy and antipathy is most apt to err on the side of severity. It is for applying punishment in many cases which deserve none: in many cases which deserve some, it is for applying more than they deserve. There is no incident imaginable, be it ever so trivial, and so remote from mischief, from which this principle may not extract a ground of punishment. Any difference in taste: any difference in opinion: upon one subject as well as upon another. No disagreement so trifling which perseverance and altercation will not render serious. Each becomes in the other's eyes an enemy, and, if laws permit, a criminal. This is one of the circum-

---

cause they do not very explicitly claim to be anything more than phrases; they insist but feebly upon the being looked upon as so many positive standards of themselves, and seem content to be taken, upon occasion, for phrases expressive of the conformity of the thing in question to the proper standard, whatever that may be. On most occasions, however, it will be better to say *utility: utility* is clearer, as referring more explicitly to pain and pleasure.

8. We have one philosopher, who says, there is no harm in anything in the world but in telling a lie: and that if, for example, you were to murder your own father, this would only be a particular way of saying, he was not your father. Of course, when this philosopher sees anything that he does not like, he says, it is a particular way of telling a lie. It is saying, that the act ought to be done, or may be done, when, *in truth,* it ought not to be done.

9. The fairest and openest of them all is that sort of man who speaks out, and says, I am of the number of the Elect: now God himself takes care to inform the Elect what is right: and that with so good effect, that let them strive ever so, they cannot help not only knowing it but practising it. If therefore a man wants to know what is right and what is wrong, he has nothing to do but to come to me.

It is upon the principle of antipathy that such and such acts are often reprobated on the score of their being *unnatural:* the practice of exposing children, established among the Greeks and Romans, was an unnatural practice. Unnatural, when it means any thing, means unfrequent: and there it means something; although nothing to the present purpose. But here it means no such thing: for the frequency of such acts is perhaps the great complaint. It therefore means nothing; nothing, I mean, which there is in the act itself. All it can serve to express is, the disposition of the person who is talking of it: the disposition he is in to be angry at the thoughts of it. Does it merit his anger? Very likely it may: but whether it does or no is a question, which to be answered rightly, can only be answered upon the principle of utility.

Unnatural, is as good a word as moral sense, or common sense; and would be as good a foundation for a system. Such an act is unnatural; that is, repugnant to nature: for I do not like to practise it: and, consequently, do not practise it. It is therefore repugnant to what ought to be the nature of everybody else.

This mischief common to all these ways of thinking and arguing (which, in truth, as we have seen, are but one and the same method, couched in different forms of words) is their serving as a cloke, and pretence, and aliment, to despotism: if not a despotism in practice, a despotism however in disposition: which is but too apt, when pretence and power offer, to show itself in practice. The consequence is, that with intentions very commonly of the purest kind, a man becomes a torment either to himself or his fellow-creatures. If he be of the melancholy cast, he sits in silent grief, bewailing their blindness and depravity: if of the irascible, he declaims with fury and virulence against all who differ from him; blowing up the coals of fanaticism, and branding with the charge of corruption and insincerity, every man who does not think, or profess to think, as he does.

If such a man happens to possess the advantages of style, his book may do a considerable deal of mischief before the nothingness of it is understood.

stances by which the human race is distinguished (not much indeed to its advantage) from the brute creation.

XVII. It is not, however, by any means unexampled for this principle to err on the side of lenity. A near and perceptible mischief moves antipathy. A remote and imperceptible mischief, though not less real, has no effect. Instances in proof of this will occur in numbers in the course of the work. It would be breaking in upon the order of it to give them here.

XVIII. It may be wondered, perhaps, that in all this while no mention has been made of the *theological* principle; meaning that principle which professes to recur for the standard of right and wrong to the will of God. But the case is, this is not in fact a distinct principle. It is never anything more or less than one or other of the

---

These principles, if such they can be called, it is more frequent to see applied to morals than to politics: but their influence extends itself to both. In politics, as well as morals, a man will be at least equally glad of a pretence for deciding any question in the manner that best pleases him, without the trouble of inquiry. If a man is an infallible judge of what is right and wrong in the actions of private individuals, why not in the measures to be observed by public men in the direction of those actions? accordingly (not to mention other chimeras) I have more than once known the pretended law of nature set up in legislative debates, in opposition to arguments derived from the principle of utility.

"But is it never, then, from any other considerations than those of utility, that we derive our notions of right and wrong?" I do not know: I do not care. Whether a moral sentiment can be originally conceived from any other source than a view of utility, is one question: whether upon examination and reflection it can, in point of fact, be actually persisted in and justified on any other ground, by a person reflecting within himself, is another: whether in point of right it can properly be justified on any other ground, by a person addressing himself to the community, is a third. The two first are questions of speculation: it matters not, comparatively speaking, how they are decided. The last is a question of practice: the decision of it is of as much importance as that of any can be.

"I feel in myself," (say you) "a disposition to approve of such or such an action in a moral view: but this is not owing to any notions I have of its being a useful one to the community. I do not pretend to know whether it be an useful one or not: it may be, for aught I know, a mischievous one." "But is it then," (say I) "a mischievous one? examine; and if you can make yourself sensible that it is so, then, if duty means any thing, that is, moral duty, it is your *duty* at least to abstain from it: and more than that, if it is what lies in your power, and can be done without too great a sacrifice, to endeavour to prevent it. It is not your cherishing the notion of it in your bosom, and giving it the name of virtue, that will excuse you."

"I feel in myself," (say you again) "a disposition to detest such or such an action in a moral view; but this is not owing to any notions I have of its being a mischievous one to the community. I do not pretend to know whether it be a mischievous one or not: it may be not a mischievous one: it may be, for aught I know, an useful one."—"May it indeed," (say I) "an useful one? but let me tell you then, that unless duty, and right and wrong, be just what you please to make them, if it really be not a mischievous one, and any body has a mind to do it, it is no duty of yours, but, on the contrary, it would be very wrong in you, to take upon you to prevent him: detest it within yourself as much as you please; that may be a very good reason (unless it be also a useful one) for your not doing it yourself: but if you go about, by word or deed, to do any thing to hinder him, or make him suffer for it, it is you, and not he, that have done wrong: it is not your setting yourself to blame his conduct, or branding it with the name of vice, that will make him culpable, or you blameless. Therefore, if you can make yourself content that he shall be of one mind, and you of another, about that matter, and so continue, it is well: but if nothing will serve you, but that you and he must needs be of the same mind, I'll tell you what you have to do: it is for you to get the better of your antipathy, not for him to truckle to it."

three before-mentioned principles presenting itself under another shape. The *will* of God here meant cannot be his revealed will, as contained in the sacred writings: for that is a system which nobody ever thinks of recurring to at this time of day, for the details of political administration: and even before it can be applied to the details of private conduct, it is universally allowed, by the most eminent divines of all persuasions, to stand in need of pretty ample interpretations; else to what use are the works of those divines? And for the guidance of these interpretations, it is also allowed, that some other standard must be assumed. The will then which is meant on this occasion, is that which may be called the *presumptive* will: that is to say, that which is presumed to be his will on account of the conformity of its dictates to those of some other principle. What then may be this other principle? it must be one or other of the three mentioned above; for there cannot, as we have seen, be any more. It is plain, therefore, that, setting revelation out of the question, no light can ever be thrown upon the standard of right and wrong, by anything that can be said upon the question, what is God's will. We may be perfectly sure, indeed, that whatever is right is conformable to the will of God; but so far is that from answering the purpose of showing us what is right, that it is necessary to know first whether a thing is right, in order to know from thence whether it be conformable to the will of God.

XIX. There are two things which are very apt to be confounded, but which it imports us carefully to distinguish:—the motive or cause, which, by operating on the mind of an individual, is productive of any act, and the ground or reason which warrants a legislator, or other bystander, in regarding that act with an eye of approbation. When the act happens, in the particular instance in question, to be productive of effects which we approve of, much more if we happen to observe that the same motive may frequently be productive, in other instances, of the like effects, we are apt to transfer our approbation to the motive itself, and to assume, as the just ground for the approbation we bestow on the act, the circumstance of its originating from that motive. It is in this way that the sentiment of antipathy has often been considered as a just ground of action. Antipathy, for instance, in such or such a case, is the cause of an action which is attended with good effects; but this does not make it a right ground of action in that case, any more than in any other. Still farther. Not only the effects are good, but the agent sees beforehand that they will be so. This may make the action indeed a perfectly right action: but it does not make antipathy a right ground for action. For the same sentiment of antipathy, if implicitly deferred to, may be, and very frequently is, productive of the very worst effects. Antipathy, therefore, can never be a right ground of action. No more, therefore, can resentment, which, as will be seen more particularly hereafter, is but a modification of antipathy. The only right ground of action, that can possibly subsist, is, after all, the consideration of utility, which, if it is a right principle of action, and of approbation, in any one case, is so in every other. Other principles in abundance, that is, other motives, may be the reasons why such and such an act *has* been done, that is, the reason or causes of its being done; but it is this alone that can be the reason why it might or ought to have been done. Antipathy or resentment requires always to be regulated, to prevent its doing mischief: to be regulated by what? always by the principle of utility. The principle of utility neither requires nor admits of any other regulator than itself.

CHAPTER III. OF THE FOUR SANCTIONS OR SOURCES OF PAIN AND PLEASURE

I. It has been shown that the happiness of the individuals, of whom a community is composed, that is their pleasures and their security, is the end and the sole end which the legislator ought to have in view: the sole standard, in conformity to which each individual ought, as far as depends upon the legislator, to be *made* to fashion his behaviour. But whether it be this or any thing else that is to be *done,* there is nothing by which a man can ultimately be *made* to do it, but either pain or pleasure. Having taken a general view of these two grand objects (*viz.* pleasure, and what comes to the same thing, immunity from pain) in the character of *final* causes; it will be necessary to take a view of pleasure and pain itself, in the character of *efficient* causes or means.

II. There are four distinguishable sources from which pleasure and pain are in use to flow: considered separately, they may be termed the *physical,* the *political,* the *moral,* and the *religious:* and inasmuch as the pleasures and pains belonging to each of them are capable of giving a binding force to any law or rule of conduct, they may all of them be termed *sanctions.*[5]

III. If it be in the present life, and from the ordinary course of nature, not purposely modified by the interposition of the will of any human being, nor by any extraordinary interposition of any superior invisible being, that the pleasure or the pain takes place or is expected, it may be said to issue from or to belong to the *physical sanction.*

IV. If at the hands of a *particular* person or set of persons in the community, who under names correspondent to that of *judge,* are chosen for the particular purpose of dispensing it, according to the will of the sovereign or supreme ruling power in the state, it may be said to issue from the *political sanction.*

V. If at the hands of such *chance* persons in the community, as the party in question may happen in the course of his life to have concerns with, according to each man's spontaneous disposition, and not according to any settled or concerted rule, it may be said to issue from the *moral* or *popular sanction.*[6]

VI. If from the immediate hand of a superior invisible being, either in the present life, or in a future, it may be said to issue from the *religious sanction.*

VII. Pleasures or pains which may be expected to issue from the *physical, political,* or *moral* sanctions, must all of them be expected to be experienced, if ever, in the *present* life: those which may be ex-

[5] Sanctio, in Latin, was used to signify the *act of binding,* and, by a common grammatical transition, *any thing which serves to bind a man:* to wit, to the observance of such or such a mode of conduct. According to a Latin grammarian, the import of the word is derived by rather a far-fetched process (such as those commonly are, and in a great measure indeed must be, by which intellectual ideas are derived from sensible ones) from the word *sanguis,* blood: because, among the Romans, with a view to inculcate into the people a persuasion that such or such a mode of conduct would be rendered obligatory upon a man by the force of what I call the religious sanction (that is, that he would be made to suffer by the extraordinary interposition of some superior being, if he failed to observe the mode of conduct in question) certain ceremonies were contrived by the priests: in the course of which ceremonies the blood of victims was made use of.

A Sanction then is a source of obligatory powers or *motives:* that is, of *pains* and *pleasures;* which, according as they are connected with such or such modes of conduct, operate, and are indeed the only things which can operate, as *motives.* See Chap. x. [Motives].

[6] Better termed *popular,* as more directly indicative of its constituent cause; as likewise of its relation to the more common phrase *public opinion,* in French *opinion publique,* the name there given to that tutelary power, of which of late so much is said, and by which so much is done. The latter appellation is however unhappy and inexpressive; since if *opinion* is material, it is only in virtue of the influence it exercises over action, through the medium of the affections and the will.

pected to issue from the *religious* sanction, may be expected to be experienced either in the *present* life or in a *future*.

CHAPTER IV. VALUE OF A LOT OF PLEASURE OR PAIN, HOW TO BE MEASURED

I. Pleasures then, and the avoidance of pains, are the *ends* which the legislator has in view: it behooves him therefore to understand their *value*. Pleasures and pains are the *instruments* he has to work with: it behooves him therefore to understand their force, which is again, in other words, their value.

II. To a person considered *by himself*, the value of a pleasure or pain considered *by itself*, will be greater or less, according to the four following circumstances:[7]

1. Its *intensity*.
2. Its *duration*.
3. Its *certainty* or *uncertainty*.
4. Its *propinquity* or *remoteness*.

III. These are the circumstances which are to be considered in estimating a pleasure or a pain considered each of them by itself. But when the value of any pleasure or pain is considered for the purpose of estimating the tendency of any *act* by which it is produced, there are two other circumstances to be taken into the account; these are,

5. Its *fecundity*, or the chance it has of being followed by sensations of the *same* kind: that is, pleasures, if it be a pleasure: pains, if it be a pain.

6. Its *purity*, or the chance it has of *not* being followed by sensations of the *opposite* kind: that is, pains, if it be a pleasure: pleasures, if it be a pain. . . .

7. Its *extent;* that is, the number of persons to whom it *extends;* or (in other words) who are affected by it. . . .

V. To take an exact account then of the general tendency of any act, by which the interests of a community are affected, proceed as follows. Begin with any one person of those whose interests seem most immediately to be affected by it: and take an account,

1. Of the value of each distinguishable *pleasure* which appears to be produced by it in the *first* instance.

2. Of the value of each *pain* which appears to be produced by it in the *first* instance.

3. Of the value of each pleasure which appears to be produced by it *after* the first. This constitutes the *fecundity* of the first *pleasure* and the *impurity* of the first *pain*.

4. Of the value of each *pain* which appears to be produced by it after the first. This constitutes the *fecundity* of the first *pain*, and the *impurity* of the first pleasure.

5. Sum up all the values of all the *pleasures* on the one side, and those of all the pains on the other. The balance, if it be on the side of pleasure, will give the *good* tendency of the act upon the whole,

[7] These circumstances have since been denominated *elements* or *dimensions* of *value* in a pleasure or a pain.

Not long after the publication of the first edition, the following memoriter verses were framed, in the view of lodging more effectually, in the memory, these points, on which the whole fabric of morals and legislation may be seen to rest.

Intense, long, certain, speedy, fruitful, pure—
Such marks in *pleasures* and in *pains* endure.
Such pleasures seek if *private* be thy end:
If it be *public,* wide let them *extend.*
Such *pains* avoid, whichever be thy view:
If pains *must* come, let them *extend* to few.

with respect to the interests of that *individual* person; if on the side of pain, the *bad* tendency of it upon the whole.

6. Take an account of the *number* of persons whose interests appear to be concerned; and repeat the above process with respect to each. *Sum up* the numbers expressive of the degrees of *good* tendency, which the act has, with respect to each individual, in regard to whom the tendency of it is *good* upon the whole: do this again with respect to each individual, in regard to whom the tendency of it is *good* upon the whole: do this again with respect to each individual, in regard to whom the tendency of it is *bad* upon the whole. Take the *balance;* which, if on the side of *pleasure,* will give the general *good tendency* of the act, with respect to the total number or community of individuals concerned; if on the side of pain, the general *evil tendency,* with respect to the same community.

VI. It is not to be expected that this process should be strictly pursued previously to every moral judgment, or to every legislative or judicial operation. It may, however, be always kept in view: and as near as the process actually pursued on these occasions approaches to it, so near will such process approach to the character of an exact one. . . .

CHAPTER V. PLEASURES AND PAINS, THEIR KINDS

I. Having represented what belongs to all sorts of pleasures and pains alike, we come now to exhibit, each by itself, the several sorts of pains and pleasures. Pains and pleasures may be called by one general word, interesting perceptions. Interesting perceptions are either simple or complex. The simple ones are those which cannot any one of them be resolved into more: complex are those which are resolvable into divers simple ones. A complex interesting perception may accordingly be composed either, 1. Of pleasures alone: 2. Of pains alone: or, 3. Of a pleasure or pleasures, and a pain or pains together. What determines a lot of pleasure, for example, to be regarded as one complex pleasure, rather than as divers simple ones, is the nature of the exciting cause. Whatever pleasures are excited all at once by the action of the same cause, are apt to be looked upon as constituting all together but one pleasure.

II. The several simple pleasures of which human nature is susceptible, seem to be as follows: 1. The pleasures of sense.* 2. The pleasures of wealth. 3. The pleasures of skill. 4. The pleasures of amity. 5. The pleasures of a good name. 6. The pleasures of power. 7. The pleasures of piety. 8. The pleasures of benevolence. 9. The pleasures of malevolence. 10. The pleasures of memory. 11. The pleasures of imagination. 12. The pleasures of expectation. 13. The pleasures dependent on association. 14. The pleasures of relief.

III. The several simple pains seem to be as follows: 1. The pains of privation. 2. The pains of the senses. 3. The pains of awkwardness. 4. The pains of enmity. 5.

* Bentham gives the following as examples of the pleasures of sense:

"1. The simple pleasures of sight, excited by the perception of agreeable colours and figures, green fields, waving foliage, glistening water, and the like.

"2. The simple pleasures of the ear, excited by the perceptions of the chirping of birds, the murmuring of waters, the rustling of the wind among the trees.

"3. The pleasures of the smell, excited by the perceptions of the fragrance of flowers, of new-mown hay, or other vegetable substances, in the first stages of fermentation.

"4. The agreeable inward sensation, produced by a brisk circulation of the blood, and the ventilation of it in the lungs by a pure air, such as that in the country frequently is in comparison of that which is breathed in towns."

The pains of an ill name. 6. The pains of piety. 7. The pains of benevolence. 8. The pains of malevolence. 9. The pains of the memory. 10. The pains of the imagination. 11. The pains of expectation. 12. The pains dependent on association. . . .

CHAPTER VII. OF HUMAN ACTIONS IN GENERAL

II. The general tendency of an act is more or less pernicious, according to the sum total of its consequences: that is, according to the difference between the sum of such as are good, and the sum of such as are evil. . . .

IV. It is also to be observed, that into the account of the consequences of the act, are to be taken not such only as might have ensued, were intention out of the question, but such also as depend upon the connexion there may be between these first-mentioned consequences and the intention. The connexion there is between the intention and certain consequences is . . . a means of producing other consequences. In this lies the difference between rational agency and irrational.

V. Now the intention, with regard to the consequences of an act, will depend upon two things: 1. The state of the will or intention, with respect to the act itself. And, 2. The state of the understanding, or perceptive faculties, with regard to the circumstances which it is, or may appear to be, accompanied with. Now with respect to these circumstances, the perceptive faculty is susceptible of three states: consciousness, unconsciousness, and false consciousness. Consciousness, when the party believes precisely those circumstances, and no others, to subsist, which really do subsist: unconsciousness, when he fails of perceiving certain circumstances to subsist, which, however, do subsist: false consciousness, when he believes or imagines certain circumstances to subsist, which in truth do not subsist.

VI. In every transaction, therefore, which is examined with a view to punishment, there are four articles to be considered: 1. The *act* itself, which is done. 2. The *circumstances* in which it is done. 3. The *intentionality* that may have accompanied it. 4. The *consciousness,* unconsciousness, or false consciousness, that may have accompanied it.

What regards the act and the circumstances will be the subject of the present chapter: what regards intention and consciousness, that of the two succeeding.

VII. There are also two other articles on which the general tendency of an act depends: and on that, as well as on other accounts, the demand which it creates for punishment. These are, 1. The particular *motive* or motives which gave birth to it. 2. The general *disposition* which it indicates. These articles will be the subject of two other chapters.

VIII. Acts may be distinguished in several ways, for several purposes.

They may be distinguished, in the first place, into *positive* and *negative.* By positive are meant such as consist in motion or exertion: by negative, such as consist in keeping at rest; that is, in forbearing to move or exert one's self in such and such circumstances. Thus, to strike is a positive act: not to strike on a certain occasion, a negative one. . . .

XI. In the second place, acts may be distinguished into *external* and *internal.* By external, are meant corporal acts; acts of the body: by internal, mental acts; acts of the mind. Thus, to strike is an external or exterior[8] act: to intend to strike, an internal or interior one.

XII. Acts of *discourse* are a sort of mixture of the two: external acts, which are no ways material, nor attended with any consequences, any farther than as they serve to express the existence of internal

[8] An exterior act is also called by lawyers *overt.*

ones. To speak to another to strike, to write to him to strike, to make signs to him to strike, are all so many acts of discourse. . . .

XXI. So much with regard to acts considered in themselves: we come now to speak of the *circumstances* with which they may have been accompanied. These must necessarily be taken into the account before any thing can be determined relative to the consequences. . . .

XXII. Now the circumstances of an act, are, what? Any objects whatsoever. Take any act whatsoever, there is nothing in the nature of things that excludes any imaginable object from being a circumstance to it. Any given object may be a circumstance to any other. . . .

XXIV. The consequences of an act are events. A circumstance may be related to an event in point of causality in any one of four ways: 1. In the way of causation or production. 2. In the way of derivation. 3. In the way of collateral connexion. 4. In the way of conjunct influence. It may be said to be related to the event in the way of causation, when it is of the number of those that contribute to the production of such event: in the way of derivation, when it is of the number of the events to the production of which that in question has been contributory: in the way of collateral connexion, where the circumstance in question, and the event in question, without being either of them instrumental in the production of the other, are related, each of them, to some common object, which has been concerned in the production of them both: in the way of conjunct influence, when, whether related in any other way or not, they have both of them concurred in the production of some common consequence. . . .

XXVI. These several relations do not all of them attach upon an event with equal certainty. In the first place, it is plain, indeed, that every event must have some circumstance or other, and in truth, an indefinite multitude of circumstances, related to it in the way of production: it must of course have a still greater multitude of circumstances related to it in the way of collateral connexion. . . . But of the circumstances of all kinds which actually do attach upon an event, it is only a very small number that can be discovered by the utmost exertion of the human faculties: it is a still smaller number that ever actually do attract our notice: when occasion happens, more or fewer of them will be discovered by a man in proportion to the strength, partly of his intellectual powers, partly of his inclination. . . .

CHAPTER VIII. OF INTENTIONALITY

I. So much with regard to the two first of the articles upon which the evil tendency of an action may depend: *viz.* the act itself, and the general assemblage of the circumstances with which it may have been accompanied. We come now to consider the ways in which the particular circumstance of *intention* may be concerned in it.

II. First, then, the intention or will may regard either of two objects: 1. The act itself: or, 2. Its consequences. Of these objects, that which the intention regards may be styled *intentional.* If it regards the act, then the act may be said to be intentional:[9] if the consequences, so also then

[9] On this occasion the words *voluntary* and *involuntary* are commonly employed. These, however, I purposely abstain from, on account of the extreme ambiguity of their signification. By a voluntary act is meant sometimes, any act, in the performance of which the will has had any concern at all; in this sense it is synonymous to *intentional:* sometimes such acts only, in the production of which the will has been determined by motives not of a painful nature; in this sense it is synonymous to unconstrained, or *uncoerced:* sometimes such acts only, in the production of which the will has been determined by motives, which, whether of the pleasurable or painful kind, occurred to a man himself, with-

may the consequences. If it regards both the act and consequences, the whole *action* may be said to be intentional. Whichever of those articles is not the object of the intention, may of course be said to be *unintentional.*

III. The act may very easily be intentional without the consequences; and often is so. Thus, you may intend to touch a man without intending to hurt him: and yet, as the consequences turn out, you may chance to hurt him.

IV. The consequences of an act may also be intentional, without the act's being intentional throughout; that is, without its being intentional in every stage of it: but this is not so frequent a case as the former. You intend to hurt a man, suppose, by running against him, and pushing him down: and you run towards him accordingly: but a second man coming in on a sudden between you and the first man, before you can stop yourself, you run against the second man, and by him push down the first.

V. But the consequences of an act cannot be intentional, without the act's being itself intentional in at least the first stage. If the act be not intentional in the first stage, it is no act of yours: there is accordingly no intention on your part to produce the consequences: that is to say, the individual consequences. . . .

VI. Second. A consequence, when it is intentional, may either be *directly* so, or only *obliquely.* It may be said to be directly or lineally intentional, when the prospect of producing it constituted one of the links in the chain of causes by which the person was determined to do the act. It may be said to be obliquely or collaterally intentional, when, although the consequence was in contemplation, and appeared likely to ensue in case of the act's being performed, yet the prospect of producing such consequence did not constitute a link in the aforesaid chain.

VII. Third. An incident, which is directly intentional, may either be *ultimately* so, or only *mediately.* It may be said to be ultimately intentional, when it stands last of all exterior events in the aforesaid chain of motives. . . . It may be said to be mediately intentional, and no more, when there is some other incident, the prospect of producing which forms a subsequent link in the same chain. . . .

VIII. Fourth. When an incident is directly intentional, it may either be *exclusively* so, or *inexclusively.* It may be exclusively intentional, when no other but that very individual incident would have answered the purpose, insomuch that no other incident had any share in determining the will to the act in question. It may be said to have been inexclusively intentional, when there was some other incident, the prospect of which was acting upon the will at the same time.

IX. Fifth. When an incident is inexclusively intentional, it may be either *con*junctively so, *dis*junctively, or *indiscriminately.* It may be said to be conjunctively intentional with regard to such other incident, when the intention is to produce both: disjunctively, when the intention is to produce either the one or the other indifferently, but not both: indiscriminately, when the intention is indifferently to produce either the one or the other, or both, as it may happen.

X. Sixth. When two incidents are disjunctively intentional, they may be so with or without *preference.* They may be said to be so with preference, when the intention

out being suggested by any body else; in this sense it is synonymous to *spontaneous.* The sense of the word involuntary does not correspond completely to that of the word voluntary. Involuntary is used in opposition to intentional; and to unconstrained: but not to spontaneous. It might be of use to confine the signification of the words voluntary and involuntary to one single and very narrow case.

is, that one of them in particular should happen rather than the other: without preference, when the intention is equally fulfilled, whichever of them happens.

XI. One example will make all this clear. William II, king of England, being out a stag-hunting, received from Sir Walter Tyrrel a wound, of which he died. Let us take this case, and diversify it with a variety of suppositions, correspondent to the distinctions just laid down.

1. First then, Tyrrel did not so much as entertain a thought of the king's death; or, if he did, looked upon it as an event of which there was no danger. In either of these cases the incident of his killing the king was altogether unintentional.

2. He saw a stag running that way, and he saw the king riding that way at the same time: what he aimed at was to kill the stag: he did not wish to kill the king: at the same time he saw, that if he shot, it was as likely he should kill the king as the stag: yet for all that he shot, and killed the king accordingly. In this case the incident of his killing the king was intentional, but obliquely so.

3. He killed the king on account of the hatred he bore him, and for no other reason than the pleasure of destroying him. In this case the incident of the king's death was not only directly but ultimately intentional.

4. He killed the king, intending fully so to do; not for any hatred he bore him, but for the sake of plundering him when dead. In this case the incident of the king's death was directly intentional, but not ultimately: it was mediately intentional.

5. He intended neither more nor less than to kill the king. He had no other aim nor wish. In this case it was exclusively as well as directly intentional: exclusively, to wit, with regard to every other material incident.

6. Sir Walter shot the king in the right leg, as he was plucking a thorn out of it with his left hand. His intention was, by shooting the arrow into his leg through his hand, to cripple him in both those limbs at the same time. In this case the incident of the king's being shot in the leg was intentional: and that conjunctively with another which did not happen; *viz.* his being shot in the hand.

7. The intention of Tyrrel was to shoot the king either in the hand or in the leg, but not in both; and rather in the hand than in the leg. In this case the intention of shooting in the hand was disjunctively concurrent, with regard to the other incident, and that with preference.

8. His intention was to shoot the king either in the leg or the hand, whichever might happen: but not in both. In this case the intention was inexclusive, but disjunctively so: yet that, however, without preference.

9. His intention was to shoot the king either in the leg or the hand, or in both, as it might happen. In this case the intention was indiscriminately concurrent, with respect to the two incidents. . . .

XIII. It is frequent to hear men speak of a good intention, of a bad intention; of the goodness and badness of a man's intention: a circumstance on which great stress is generally laid. It is indeed of no small importance, when properly understood: but the import of it is to the last degree ambiguous and obscure. Strictly speaking, nothing can be said to be good or bad, but either in itself; which is the case only with pain or pleasure: or on account of its effects; which is the case only with things that are the causes or preventives of pain and pleasure. But in a figurative and less proper way of speech, a thing may also be styled good or bad, in consideration of its cause. Now the effects of an intention to do such or such an act, are the same objects which we have been speaking of under the appellation of its *consequences:* and the causes of intention are called *motives.* A man's intention then on any occasion may be styled good or bad, with reference either to the consequences of the act, or with reference to his motives. . . .

CHAPTER X. OF MOTIVES

I. It is an acknowledged truth, that every kind of act whatever, and consequently every kind of offence, is apt to assume a different character, and be attended with different effects, according to the nature of the *motive* which gives birth to it. This makes it requisite to take a view of the several motives by which human conduct is liable to be influenced. . . .

III. By a motive then, in this sense of the word, is to be understood any thing whatsoever, which, by influencing the will of a sensitive being, is supposed to serve as a means of determining him to act, or voluntarily to forbear to act, upon any occasion. . . .

IV. Owing to the poverty and unsettled state of language, the word *motive* is employed indiscriminately to denote two kinds of objects, which, for the better understanding of the subject, it is necessary should be distinguished. On some occasions it is employed to denote any of those really existing incidents from whence the act in question is supposed to take its rise. The sense it bears on these occasions may be styled its literal or *unfigurative* sense. On other occasions it is employed to denote a certain fictitious entity, a passion, an affection of the mind, an ideal being which upon the happening of any such incident is considered as operating upon the mind, and prompting it to take that course, towards which it is impelled by the influence of such incident. Motives of this class are Avarice, Indolence, Benevolence, and so forth; as we shall see more particularly farther on. This latter may be styled the *figurative* sense of the term *motive.*

V. As to the real incidents to which the name of motive is also given, these too are of two very different kinds. They may be either, 1. The *internal* perception of any individual lot of pleasure or pain, the expectation of which is looked upon as calculated to determine you to act in such or such a manner; as the pleasure of acquiring such a sum of money, the pain of exerting yourself on such an occasion, and so forth: or, 2. Any *external* event, the happening whereof is regarded as having a tendency to bring about the perception of such pleasure or such pain; for instance, the coming up of a lottery ticket, by which the possession of the money devolves to you; or the breaking out of a fire in the house you are in, which makes it necessary for you to quit it. The former kind of motives may be termed interior, or internal: the latter exterior, or external. . . .

IX. A motive is substantially nothing more than pleasure or pain, operating in a certain manner.

X. Now, pleasure is in *itself* a good: nay even setting aside immunity from pain, the only good: pain is in itself an evil; and, indeed, without exception, the only evil; or else the words good and evil have no meaning. And this is alike true of every sort of pain, and of every sort of pleasure. It follows, therefore, immediately and incontestably, that *there is no such thing as any sort of motive that is in itself a bad one.*[10]

XI. It is common, however, to speak of actions as proceeding from *good* or *bad* motives: [But] with respect to goodness

[10] Let a man's motive be ill-will; call it even malice, envy, cruelty; it is still a kind of pleasure that is his motive: the pleasure he takes at the thought of the pain which he sees, or expects to see, his adversary undergo. Now even this wretched pleasure, taken by itself, is good: it may be faint; it may be short; it must at any rate be impure: yet while it lasts, and before any bad consequences arrive, it is as good as any other that is not more intense. See ch. iv. [Value].

and badness, as it is with everything else that is not itself either pain or pleasure, so is it with motives. If they are good or bad, it is only on account of their effects: good, on account of their tendency to produce pleasure, or avert pain: bad, on account of their tendency to produce pain, or avert pleasure. Now the case is, that from one and the same motive, and from every kind of motive, may proceed actions that are good, others that are bad, and others that are indifferent. . . .

XXIX. It appears then that there is no such thing as any sort of motive which is a bad one in itself: nor, consequently, any such thing as a sort of motive, which in itself is exclusively a good one. And as to their effects, it appears too that these are sometimes bad, at other times either indifferent or good: and this appears to be the case with every sort of motive. *If any sort of motive then is either good or bad on the score of its effects, this is the case only on individual occasions, and with individual motives;* and this is the case with one sort of motive as well as with another. *If any sort of motive then can, in consideration of its effects, be termed with any propriety a bad one,* it can only be with reference to the balance of all the effects it may have had of both kinds within a given period, that is, of its most usual tendency.

XXX. What then? (it will be said) are not lust, cruelty, avarice, bad motives? Is there so much as any one individual occasion, in which motives like these can be otherwise than bad? No, certainly: and yet the proposition, that there is no one *sort* of motive but what will on many occasions be a good one, is nevertheless true. The fact is, that these are names which, if properly applied, are never applied but in the cases where the motives they signify happen to be bad. The names of these motives, considered apart from their effects, are sexual desire, displeasure, and pecuniary interest. To sexual desire, when the effects of it are looked upon as bad, is given the name of lust. Now lust is always a bad motive. Why? Because if the case be such, that the effects of the motive are not bad, it does not go, or at least ought not to go, by the name of lust. The case is, then, that when I say, "Lust is a bad motive," it is a proposition that merely concerns the import of the word lust; and which would be false if transferred to the other word used for the same motive, sexual desire. Hence we see the emptiness of all those rhapsodies of common-place morality, which consist in the taking of such names as lust, cruelty, and avarice, and branding them with marks of reprobation: applied to the *thing,* they are false; applied to the *name,* they are true indeed, but nugatory. Would you do a real service to mankind, show them the cases in which sexual desire *merits* the name of lust; displeasure, that of cruelty; and pecuniary interest, that of avarice. . . .

XXXVI. Of all these sorts of motives, goodwill is that of which the dictates,[11] taken in a general view, are surest of coinciding with those of the principle of utility. For the dictates of utility are neither more nor less than the dictates of the most extensive and enlightened (that is *well-advised*) benevolence. The dictates of the other motives may be conformable to those of utility, or repugnant, as it may happen. . . .

XXXVIII. After good-will, the motive of which the dictates seem to have the next best chance for coinciding with those of utility, is that of the love of reputation. . . .

XXXIX. After the dictates of the love of reputation come, as it should seem, those of the desire of amity. The former are dis-

[11] When a man is supposed to be prompted by any motive to engage, or not to engage, in such or such an action, it may be of use, for the convenience of discourse, to speak of such motive as giving birth to an imaginary kind of *law* or *dictate,* injoing him to engage, or not to engage, in it. [See ch. i.]

posed to coincide with those of utility, inasmuch as they are disposed to coincide with those of benevolence. Now those of the desire of amity are apt also to coincide, in a certain sort, with those of benevolence. But the sort of benevolence with the dictates of which the love of reputation coincides, is the more extensive; that with which those of the desire of amity coincide, the less extensive. Those of the love of amity have still, however, the advantage of those of the self-regarding motives. The former, at one period or other of his life, dispose a man to contribute to the happiness of a considerable number of persons: the latter, from the beginning of life to the end of it, confine themselves to the care of that single individual. The dictates of the desire of amity, it is plain, will approach nearer to a coincidence with those of the love of reputation, and thence with those of utility, in proportion, *cœteris paribus,* to the number of the persons whose amity a man has occasion to desire: and hence it is, for example, that an English member of parliament, with all his own weaknesses, and all the follies of the people whose amity he has to cultivate, is probably, in general, a better character than the secretary of a visier at Constantinople, or of a naïb in Indostan.

XL. The dictates of religion are, under the infinite diversity of religions, so extremely variable, that it is difficult to know what general account to give of them, or in what rank to place the motive they belong to. Upon the mention of religion, people's first thoughts turn naturally to the religion they themselves profess. This is a source of miscalculation, and has a tendency to place this sort of motive in a higher rank than it deserves. The dictates of religion would coincide, in all cases, with those of utility, were the Being, who is the object of religion, universally supposed to be as benevolent as he is supposed to be wise and powerful; and were the notions entertained of his benevolence, at the same time, as correct as those which are entertained of his wisdom and his power. Unhappily, however, neither of these is the case. He is universally supposed to be all-powerful: for by the Deity, what else does any man mean than the Being, whatever he be, by whom every thing is done? And as to knowledge, by the same rule that he should know one thing he should know another. These notions seem to be as correct, for all material purposes, as they are universal. But among the votaries of religion (of which number the multifarious fraternity of Christians is but a small part) there seem to be but few (I will not say how few) who are real believers in his benevolence. They call him benevolent in words, but they do not mean that he is so in reality. They do not mean, that he is benevolent as man is conceived to be benevolent: they do not mean that he is benevolent in the only sense in which benevolence has a meaning. For if they did, they would recognise that the dictates of religion could be neither more nor less than the dictates of utility: not a tittle different: not a tittle less or more. But the case is, that on a thousand occasions they turn their backs on the principle of utility. They go astray after the strange principles its antagonists: sometimes it is the principle of asceticism: sometimes the principle of sympathy and antipathy. Accordingly, the idea they bear in their minds, on such occasions, is but too often the idea of malevolence; to which idea, stripping it of its own proper name, they bestow the specious appellation of the social motive. . . .[12] The dic-

[12] Sometimes, in order the better to conceal the cheat (from their own eyes doubtless as well as from others) they set up a phantom of their own, which they call Justice: whose dictates are to modify (which being explained, means to oppose) the dictates of benevolence. But justice, in the only sense in which it has a meaning, is an imaginary personage, feigned for the convenience of discourse, whose dictates are the dictates of utility, applied to cer-

tates of religion are in all places intermixed more or less with dictates unconformable to those of utility, deduced from texts, well or ill interpreted, of the writings held for sacred by each sect: unconformable, by imposing practices sometimes inconvenient to man's self, sometimes pernicious to the rest of the community. The sufferings of uncalled martyrs, the calamities of holy wars and religious persecutions, the mischiefs of intolerant laws (objects which can here only be glanced at, not detailed), are so many additional mischiefs over and above the number of those which were ever brought into the world by the love of reputation. On the other hand, it is manifest, that with respect to the power of operating in secret, the dictates of religion have the same advantage over those of the love of reputation, and the desire of amity, as is possessed by the dictates of benevolence.

---

tain particular cases. Justice, then, is nothing more than an imaginary instrument, employed to forward on certain occasions, and by certain means, the purposes of benevolence. The dictates of justice are nothing more than a part of the dictates of benevolence, which, on certain occasions, are applied to certain subjects; to wit, to certain actions.

GEORG WILHELM FRIEDRICH HEGEL

Georg Wilhelm Friedrich Hegel (1770–1831) is one of the dominant intellectual figures of the last two centuries. His thought set the style for philosophy for much of the nineteenth century—he supplied the vocabulary, the problems, and the method for carrying on the philosophic enterprise. Few continental philosophers of the nineteenth century could honestly claim that they owed little to Hegel, and by the end of the nineteenth century his thoughts had taken deep root both in England—note, for instance, the similarities in thought that are evident in the selection from F. H. Bradley—and in America. Hegel continues to exert a profound influence on the twentieth century in such diverse philosophic movements as existentialism, Marxism, and instrumentalism.

Hegel exercises this extensive influence despite the great difficulties of his texts. These difficulties spring essentially from two sources: (1) the terminology, which is now quite foreign to the contemporary reader, and (2) the technique of arguing, or as Hegel calls it, his dialectical method. There is no easy remedy for either of these difficulties. Since the meanings of Hegel's key terms emerge only in context, comprehension can be gained only by examining them in that context.

For these reasons our selection is drawn from Hegel's Early Theological Writings; *it expresses some characteristic Hegelian themes in pretechnical language, but it is easy to catch the "flavor" of the mature Hegel even in these very early writings.*

*Early Theological Writings**

HOW A MORAL OR RELIGIOUS SOCIETY GROWS INTO A STATE

In civil society only those duties are in question which arise out of another's rights, and the only duties the state can impose are of this order. The other's right must be sustained, but I may for moral reasons impose on myself a duty to respect it, or I may not. In the latter event, I am treated forcibly by the state, as if I were a mere natural object. The other's right must first be proved before the duty of respecting it arises. A very conscientious man may decline to regard as valid the claims another may make on the score of his rights until the other has proved them. But, once he is convinced of the other's right, he will also recognize the duty of satisfying the other's claims, and he will do this of his own accord without any judicial pronouncement to that effect. Nevertheless, the recognition that he has this duty arises only out of a recognition of the other's right.

But there are also other duties which do not arise from another's right, e.g., the duty of charity. A man in misfortune has no prima facie right to my purse except on the assumption that I ought to have made it my duty to assist the unfortunate. So far as I am concerned, my duty is not grounded in his right; his right to life, health, etc., belongs to him not as this specific individual but simply as a *man* (the child's right to life belongs to its parents), and it imposes the duty of preserving his life, etc., not on another specific individual but on the state or in general on his immediate circle. . . .

A poor man can demand alms as a right from me as a member of the state; but if he makes his demand to me personally, he is directly making a demand which he should have made indirectly through the state. On me as a moral being there is a moral demand, in the name of the moral law, to impose on myself the duty of charity. On me as a pathological being (i.e., one endowed with sympathetic impulses) the beggar makes no demand; he works on my nature only by arousing my sympathy.

Justice depends on my respecting the rights of others. It is a virtue if I regard it as a duty and make it the maxim of my actions, not because the state so requires but simply because it is a duty, and in that event it is a requirement of the moral law, not of the state. The second kind of duties, e.g., charity whether as a contribution to the poor box or as the foundation of hospitals, cannot be demanded by the state from specific individuals in specific circumstances, but only from the citizens en masse and as a general duty. Charity pure and simple is a duty demanded by morality.

Besides these duties there may also be others which arise neither from rights against me as an individual nor from rights against humanity in general. These do not arise from the rights of others at all. I have simply imposed them on myself voluntarily, not because the moral law so requires. Here the rights I allow to another are equally allowed to him simply from my own free choice. Of this kind are the duties I freely impose on myself by entering a society whose aim is not opposed to that of the state (if it were, I would have trespassed against the state's rights). My entry into such a society gives its members certain rights against me; these are based simply on my voluntary entry into the society and in turn they form the basis of voluntarily accepted duties.

The rights against me which I concede to such a society cannot be rights which the state has against me, or otherwise I would be recognizing a power in the

* Reprinted from *Early Theological Writings* by G. W. F. Hegel, trans. by T. M. Knox, by permission of The University of Chicago Press. Chicago, 1948.

state which, though different from the state, yet had equal rights with it. The state cannot grant me liberty to concede to a society the right of giving a judicial verdict on someone's life or on a dispute about property (though, of course, I may regard the society as a friendly arbiter to whose judgment I am submitting of my own free will). But I may concede to such a society the right to supervise my moral life, to give me moral guidance, to require me to confess my faults, and to impose penances on me accordingly; but these rights can last only so long as my decision to impose on myself the duties from which these rights arise. Since these duties are not grounded in another's rights, I am at liberty to renounce the duties, and together with them, the other's rights; and, moreover, another reason for this liberty is that these duties are assumed voluntarily to such an extent that they are not even commanded by the moral law. Yet I may also cancel another's rights even if they arise originally out of duties imposed on me by the moral law; for example, I may at my pleasure cancel the right I have allowed to a poor man to demand a weekly contribution from me, because his right was not self-subsistent but first arose from my imposing on myself the duty of giving him this contribution.

Not as a state, but only as a moral entity, can the state demand morality of its citizens. It is the state's duty not to make any arrangements which contravene or secretly undermine morality, because it is in its own greatest interest, even for the sake of legality (its proper aim), to insure that its citizens shall also be morally good. But if it sets up institutions with a view to bringing about this result directly, then it might issue laws enacting that its citizens ought to be moral, but they would be improper, contradictory, and laughable. The state could only bring its citizens to submit to these institutions through their trust in them, and this trust it must first arouse. Religion is the best means of doing this, and all depends on the use the state makes of it whether religion is able to attain this end. The end is plain in the religion of all nations; all have this in common, that their efforts always bear on producing a certain attitude of mind, and this cannot be the object of any civil legislation. A religion is better or worse according as, with a view to producing this disposition which gives birth to action in correspondence with the civil or the moral laws, it sets to work through moral motives or through terrorizing the imagination and, consequentially, the will. If the religious ordinances of the state become laws, then once again the state attains no more than the legality which is all that any civil legislation can produce.

It is impossible for the state to bring men to act out of respect for duty even if it calls religion to its aid and thereby seduces men into believing that morality has been satisfied by the observance of these state-regulated religious practices, and persuades them that no more than this is required of anyone. But though this is impossible for the state, it is what good men have always tried to do both on a large and on a small scale. . . .

THE FORM MORALITY MUST ACQUIRE IN A CHURCH

With the spread of Christianity a most important change has taken place in the method of furthering morality. When the church grew from a private society into a state, what was a private affair became a state affair and what was and is by nature a free choice became a duty. To some extent this has led to the growth of an ecclesiastical right over extra-ecclesiastical matters. The church has laid down the principles of morality, provided the means of assimilating these principles, and, in particular, set up a comprehensive science, called casuistry, for the application of these principles to individual cases.

One leading trait in the church's moral system is its erection on religion and our dependence on the deity. Its foundation is not a datum of our own minds, a proposition which could be developed out of our own consciousness, but rather something learned. On this view morality is not a self-subsistent science or one with independent principles; neither is the essence of morality grounded on freedom, i.e., it is not the autonomy of the will.

A start is made with historical facts; and the feelings and the type of disposition —gratitude and fear—they are to produce in order to keep us faithful to our duties are duly prescribed. What is pleasing to God is made the criterion of what our duty is; this is obvious enough where certain duties are concerned, but it takes some ingenious calculation to show how others are derived from that criterion. This arithmetic is so extensive and the multitude of duties is consequentially so infinitely enlarged that little is left to free choice. What in itself is neither commanded nor forbidden as a duty finally becomes important in the asceticism which leaves free no thoughts however private, leaves uncontrolled no action, no involuntary glance, no enjoyment of whatever kind, whether joy, love, friendship, or sociability. It lays claim to every psychical emotion, every association of thought, every idea which flits through the mind from moment to moment, every sense of well-being. It deduces duties by a calculation like that employed in eudaemonism, and it knows how to deduce dangers by a long string of syllogisms. It also prescribes a mass of exercises by which the soul is supposed to be developed. It is a comprehensive science of tactics which teaches artful and regular maneuvers both against every enemy of piety which lurks in everyone's bosom and which may be created out of any situation and any thought, and also and especially against the invisible enemy in hell.

[*a*) On this system], to judge how we ought to act in every individual situation is of course very hard for the laity and the unlearned, because there is such a mass of moral and prudential rules that several of them may clash with one another in the simplest of matters, and it needs a keen and practiced eye to find a happy way out of situations that have thus become so involved. Of course, healthy common sense has taken no thought for all these precautions, and immediate feeling has generally seized on a more correct line of conduct than the most learned casuists, and, unlike what commonly happens with their decisions, it has not lost an opportunity of doing a good action because some occasion for sin is supposed to be its possible and distant result.

In all these moral and prudential rules the procedure is a priori; i.e., a dead letter is laid down as a foundation and on it a system is constructed prescribing how men are to act and feel, what motives are to be produced by this or that "truth." Legislative power is ceded to memory above all the soul's other capacities, even the noblest of them. . . .

[*b*)] If a man has run through the whole course of knowledge, feelings, and dispositions prescribed by the church and has got no farther on than another without all this apparatus (e.g., than so many virtuous men among those who are called the "blind" heathen), if he has made great progress in anxious scrupulosity and prudence, in subjection and obedience, but lags behind or is lacking altogether in courage, decision, strength, and the other virtues which are the essential prerequisites of furthering the individual's and the state's well-being, we may well ask what the human race has gained from the laborious asceticism of the church. . . .

The necessary consequences of proposing to command feelings were, and were bound to be, these: (*a*) self-deception, i.e., the belief that one has the prescribed feeling, that one's feeling corresponds with what one finds described in the books, though a feeling thus artificially produced could not possibly be equivalent to the true and natural feeling either in force or value. (*b*) The result of this self-deception is a false tranquillity which sets a high value on these feelings manufactured in a spiritual hothouse and thinks much of itself on the strength of these; for this reason it is weak where it should be powerful, and, if a man recognizes this for himself, he sinks into helplessness, anxiety, and self-distrust, a psychical state which often develops into madness. Often, too, he falls into despair if he thinks that, despite all his good will and every possible effort, his feelings have still not been intensified to the extent required of him. Since he is in the realm of feeling and can never reach any firm criterion of his perfection (except perhaps via deceptive imaginings), he lapses into a frenzy of anxiety which lacks all strength and decision and which finds a measure of peace only in trusting on the boundless mercy of God. It takes only a slight increase in the intensity of the imagination to turn this condition too into madness and lunacy.

The commonest effect is one form of the self-deception just mentioned, because, despite all his wealth of spiritual feelings, the man retains most of his ordinary character; the ordinary self goes on acting as before alongside the spiritual self and is at best dressed up by the latter with rhetorical phraseology and external gestures. In trade and commerce the ordinary man appears, but he is a different person altogether on Sundays or under the eyes of his coreligionists or in reading his prayer-book. To charge a man like this with hypocrisy is often too harsh, because hypocrisy strictly entails a consciousness of the contradiction betwen the label given to an action and the motives behind it; in this instance this consciousness is altogether lacking, and the man is not a unity at all. If these two sorts of disposition openly collide with each other, and if the flesh, as is very often the case, gets the upper hand, then amid the prodigious mass of moral and ascetic commands it cannot possibly lack for one with which the trespass can be linked and, thus disguised, be made to appear to the agent in a praiseworthy light. . . .

THE MORAL TEACHING OF JESUS

Over against commands which required a bare service of the Lord, a direct slavery, an obedience without joy, without pleasure or love, i.e., the commands in connection with the service of God, Jesus set their precise opposite, a human urge and so a human need. Religious practice is the most holy, the most beautiful, of all things; it is our endeavor to unify the discords necessitated by our development and our attempt to exhibit the unification in the *ideal* as fully *existent,* as no longer opposed to reality, and thus to express and confirm it in a deed. It follows that, if that spirit of beauty be lacking in religious actions, they are the most empty of all; they are the most senseless bondage, demanding a consciousness of one's annihilation, or deeds in which man expresses his nullity, his passivity. The satisfaction of the commonest human want rises superior to actions like these, because there lies directly in such a want the sensing or the preserving of a human being, no matter how empty his being may be. . . .

Against purely objective commands Jesus set something totally foreign to them, namely, the subjective in general; but he took up a different attitude to those laws which from varying points of view we call either moral or else civil commands. Since it is natural relations which these express in the form of commands, it is perverse to make them wholly or partly objective. Since laws are unifications of opposites in a *concept,* which thus leaves them as opposites while it exists itself in opposition to *reality,* it follows that the concept expresses an *ought.* If the concept is treated in accordance with its form, not its content, i.e., if it is treated as a concept made and grasped by men, the command is moral. If we look solely at the content, as the specific unification of specific opposites, and if therefore the "ought" [or "Thou shalt"] does not arise from the property of the concept but is asserted by an external power, the command is civil. Since in the latter case the unification of opposites is not achieved by thinking, is not subjective, civil laws delimit the opposition between several living beings, while purely moral laws fix limits to opposition in one living being. Thus the former restrict the opposition of one living being to others, the latter the opposition of one side, one power, of the living being to other sides, other powers, of that same living being; and to this extent one power of this being lords it over another of its powers. Purely moral commands which are incapable of becoming civil ones, i.e., those in which the opposites and the unification cannot be formally alien to one another, would be such as concern the restriction of those forces whose activity does not involve a relation to other men or is not an activity against them. If the laws are operative as purely civil commands, they are positive, and since in their matter they are at the same time moral, or since the unification of objective entities in the concept also either presupposes a nonobjective unification or else may be such, it follows that their form as *civil* commands would be canceled if they were made moral, i.e., if their "ought" became, not the command of an external power, but reverence for duty, the consequence of their own concept. . . .

We might have expected Jesus to work along these lines against the positivity of moral commands, against sheer legality, and to show that, although the legal is a universal whose entire obligatoriness lies in its universality, still, even if every ought, every command, declares itself as something alien, nevertheless as concept (universality) it is something subjective, and, as subjective, as a product of a human power (i.e., of reason as the capacity for universality), it loses its objectivity, its positivity, its heteronomy, and the thing commanded is revealed as grounded in an autonomy of the human will. By this line of argument, however, positivity is only partially removed; and between the Shaman of the Tungus, the European prelate who rules church and state, the Voguls, and the Puritans, on the one hand, and the man who listens to his own command of duty, on the other, the difference is not that the former make themselves slaves, while the latter is free, but that the former have their lord outside themselves, while the latter carries his lord in himself, yet at the same time is his own slave. For the particular—impulses, inclinations, pathological love, sensuous experience, or whatever else it is called—the universal is necessarily and always something alien and objective. There remains a residuum of indestructible positivity which finally shocks us because the content which the universal command of duty acquires, a specific duty, contains the contradiction of being restricted and universal at the same time and makes the most stubborn claims for its one-sidedness, i.e., on the strength of possessing universality of form. Woe to the human relations which are not unquestionably found in the concept of duty; for this concept (since it is not merely the empty thought of universality but is to manifest itself in an action) excludes or dominates all other relations. . . .

This spirit of Jesus, a spirit raised above morality, is visible, directly attacking laws, in the Sermon on the Mount, which is an attempt, elaborated in numerous examples, to strip the laws of legality, of their legal form. The Sermon does not teach reverence for the laws; on the contrary, it exhibits that which fulfills the law but annuls it as law and so is something higher than obedience to law and makes law superfluous. Since the commands of duty presuppose a cleavage [between reason and inclination] and since the domination of the concept declares itself in a "thou shalt," that which is raised above this cleavage is by contrast an "is," a modification of life, a modification which is exclusive and therefore restricted only if looked at in reference to the object, since the exclusiveness is given only through the restrictedness of the object and only concerns the object. When Jesus expresses in terms of commands what he sets against and above the laws (think not that I wish to destroy the law; let your word be; I tell you not to resist, etc.; love God and your neighbor), this turn of phrase is a command in a sense quite different from that of the "shalt" of a moral imperative. It is only the sequel to the fact that, when life is conceived in thought or given expression, it acquires a *form* alien to it, a conceptual form, while, on the other hand, the moral imperative is, as a universal, in *essence* a concept. . . .

This supplement he goes on to exhibit in several laws. This expanded content we may call an inclination so to act as the laws may command, i.e., a unification of inclination with the law whereby the latter loses its form as law. . . .

The correspondence of inclination with law is such that law and inclination are no longer different; and the expression "correspondence of inclination with the law" is therefore wholly unsatisfactory because it implies that law and inclination are still particulars, still opposites. Moreover, the expression might easily be understood to mean that a support of the moral disposition, of reverence for the law, of the will's determinacy by the law, was forthcoming from the inclination which was other than the law, and since the things in correspondence with one another would on this view be different, their correspondence would be only fortuitous, only the unity of strangers, a unity in thought only. In the "fulfilment" of both the laws and duty, their concomitant, however, the moral disposition, etc., ceases to be the universal, opposed to inclination, and inclination ceases to be particular, opposed to the law, and therefore this correspondence of law and inclination is life and, as the relation of differents to one another, love; i.e., it is an "is" which expressed as (α) concept, as law, is of necessity congruent with law, i.e., with itself, or as (β) reality, as inclination opposed to the concept, is likewise congruent with itself, with inclination.

The command "Thou shalt not kill" is a maxim which is recognized as valid for the will of every rational being and which can be valid as a principle of a universal legislation. Against such a command Jesus sets the higher genius of reconcilability (a modification of love) which not only does not act counter to this law but makes it wholly superfluous; it has in itself a so much richer, more living, fulness that so poor a thing as a law is nothing for it at all. In reconcilability the law loses its form, the concept is displaced by life; but what reconcilability thereby loses in respect of the universality which grips all particulars together in the concept is only a seeming loss and a genuine infinite gain on account of the wealth of living relations with the individuals (perhaps few) with whom it comes into connection. It excludes not a reality but only thoughts and possibilities, while the form of the command and this wealth of possibility in the universality of the concept is itself a rending of life; and the content of the command is so indigent that it permits any transgression except the one it forbids. For reconcilability, on the other hand, even anger is a crime and amounts to the quick reaction of feeling to an oppression, the uprush of the desire to oppress in turn, which is a kind of blind justice and so presupposes equality, though the equality of enemies. Per contra, the spirit of reconcilability, having no inimical disposition of its own, struggles to annul the enmity of the other. If love is the standard of judgment, then by that standard calling one's brother a scoundrel is a crime, a greater crime than anger. Yet a scoundrel in the isolation in which he puts himself by setting himself, a man, over against other men in enmity, and by striving to persist in this disorder, is still of some worth, he still counts since he is hated, and a great scoundrel may be admired. Therefore, it is still more alien to love to call the other a fool, for this annuls not only all relation with the speaker but also all equality, all community of essence. The man called a fool is represented as completely subjugated and is designated a nonentity. . . .

Over against the positivity of the Jews, Jesus set man; over against the laws and their obligatoriness he set the virtues, and in these the immorality of "positive" man is overcome. It is true that "positive" man, in respect of a specific virtue which in him and for him is service, is neither moral nor immoral, and the service whereby he fulfils certain duties is not of necessity a nonvirtuous attitude to these same duties; but from another aspect there is linked with this neutrality of character a measure of immorality, because the agent's specific positive service has a limit which he cannot transcend, and hence beyond it he is immoral. Thus this immorality of positivity does not open on the same aspect of human relations as positive obedience does; within the sphere of the latter the nonmoral [i.e., the morally neutral obedience] is not the immoral (but the opposite of virtue is immorality or vice).

When subjectivity is set against the positive, service's moral neutrality vanishes along with its limited character. Man confronts himself; his character and his deeds become the man himself. He has barriers only where he erects them himself, and his virtues are determinacies which he fixes himself. This possibility of making a clear-cut opposition [between virtue and vice] is freedom, is the "or" in "virtue or vice." In the opposition of law to nature, of the universal to the particular, both opposites are posited, are actual; the one is not unless the other is. In the moral freedom which consists in the opposition of virtue to vice, the attainment of one is the exclusion of the other; and, hence, if one is actual, the other is only possible.

The opposition of duty to inclination has found its unification in the modifications of love, i.e., in the virtues. Since law was opposed to love, not in its content but in its form, it could be taken up into love, though in this process it lost its shape. To a trespass, however, law is opposed in content; trespass precludes it, and yet it *is*. Trespass is a destruction of nature, and since nature is one, there is as much destruction in what destroys as in what is destroyed. If what is one is opposed, then a unification of the opposites is available only in the concept [not in reality]. A law has been made; if the thing opposed to it has been destroyed, there still remains the concept, the law; but it then expresses only the deficiency, only a gap, because its content has in reality been annulled; and it is then called a penal law. This form of law (and the law's content) is the direct opposite of life because it signalizes the destruction of life. But it seems all the more difficult to think how the law in this form as penal justice can be superseded. In the previous supersession of law by the virtues, it was only the form of law, not its content, which had vanished; here, however, the content would be superseded along with the form, since the content is punishment. . . .

Thus the law remains, and a punishment, his desert, remains. But the living being whose might has been united with the law, the executor who deprives the trespasser in reality of the right which he has lost in the concept, i.e., the judge, is not abstract justice, but a living being, and justice is only his special characteristic. Punishment is inevitably deserved; that is inescapable. But the execution of justice is not inevitable, because as a characteristic of a living being it may vanish and another characteristic may come on the scene instead. Justice thus becomes something contingent; there may be a contradiction between it as universal, as thought, and it as real, i.e., in a living being. An avenger can forgive, can forgo his revenge, and a judge can give up acting as a judge, i.e., can pardon. But this does not satisfy justice, for justice is unbending; and, so long as laws are supreme, so long as there is no escape from them, so long must the individual be sacrificed to the universal, i.e., be put to death. For this reason it is also contradictory to contemplate satisfying the law by punishing one man as a representative of many like criminals, since, in so far as the others are looked on as suffering punishment in him, he is their universal, their concept; and the law, as ordering or punishing, is only law by being opposed to a particular. The condition of the law's universality lies in the fact that either men in acting, or else their actions, are particulars; and the actions are particulars in so far as they are considered in their bearing on universality, on the laws, i.e., considered as conforming to them or contravening them. From this point of view, their relation to the law, their specific character, can suffer no alteration; they are realities, they are what they are; what has happened cannot be undone; punishment follows the deed, and that connection is indissoluble. If there is no way to make an action undone, if its reality is eternal, then no reconciliation is possible, not even through suffering punishment. To be sure, the law is satisfied when the trespasser is punished, since thus the contradiction between its declared fiat and the reality of the trespasser is annulled, and along with it the exception which the trespasser wished to make to the universality of the law. Only the trespasser is not reconciled with the law, whether (α) the law is in his eyes something alien, or whether (β) it is present in him subjectively as a bad conscience. (α) The alien power which the trespasser has created and armed against himself, this hostile being, ceases to work on him once it has punished him. When in its turn it has done to him just what he did himself, it then lets go, but it still withdraws to a threatening attitude; it has not lost its shape or been made friendly. (β) In the bad conscience (the consciousness of a bad action, of one's self as a bad man) punishment, once suffered, alters nothing. For the trespasser always sees himself as a trespasser; over his action as a reality he has no power, and this his reality is in contradiction with his consciousness of the law. . . .

The fate in which the man senses what he has lost creates a longing for the lost life. This longing, if we are to speak of bettering and being bettered, may in itself be called a bettering, because, since it is a sense of the loss of life, it recognizes what has been lost as life, as what was once its friend, and this recognition is already itself an enjoyment of life. And the man animated by this longing may be conscientious in the sense that, in the contradiction between the consciousness of his guilt and the renewed sensing of life, he may still hold himself back from returning to the latter; he may prolong his bad conscience and feeling of grief and stimulate it every moment; and thus he avoids being frivolous with life, because he postpones reunion with it, postpones greeting it as a friend again, until his longing for reunion springs from the deepest recesses of his soul. In sacrifices and penances criminals have made afflictions for themselves; as pilgrims in hair shirts and walking every step barefoot on the hot sand, they have prolonged and multiplied their affliction and their consciousness of being evil; what they have lost, this gap in their life, they have felt in their very bones, and yet in this experience, though they sense their loss as something hostile, they yet sense it wholly as life; and this has made it possible for them to resume it again. Opposition is the possibility of reunification, and the extent to which in affliction life is felt as an opposite is also the extent of the possibility of resuming it again. It is in the fact that even the enemy is felt as life that there lies the possibility of reconciling fate. This reconciliation is thus neither the destruction or subjugation of something alien, nor a contradiction between consciousness of one's self and the hoped-for difference in another's idea of one's self, nor a contradiction between desert in the eyes of the law and the actualization of the same, or between man as concept and man as reality. This sensing of life, a sensing which finds itself again, is love, and in love fate is reconciled. Thus considered, the trespasser's deed is no fragment; the action which issues from life, from the whole, also reveals the whole. But the trespass which is a transgression of a law *is* only a fragment, since there is outside it from the start the law which does not belong to it. The trespass which issues from life reveals the whole, but as divided, and the hostile parts can coalesce again into the whole. Justice is satisfied, since the trespasser has sensed as injured in himself the same life that he has injured. The pricks of conscience have become blunt, since the deed's evil spirit has been chased away; there is no longer anything hostile in the man, and the deed remains at most as a soulless carcass lying in the charnel-house of actualities, in memories. . . .

The truth of both opposites, courage and passivity, is so unified in beauty of soul that the life in the former remains though opposition falls away, while the loss of right in the latter remains, but the grief disappears. There thus arises a transcendence of right without suffering, a living free elevation above the loss of right and above struggle. The man who lets go what another approaches with hostility, who ceases to call his what the other assails, escapes grief for loss, escapes handling by the other or by the judge, escapes the necessity of engaging with the other. If any side of him is touched, he withdraws himself therefrom and simply lets go into the other's hands a thing which in the moment of the attack he has alienated. To renounce his relationships in this way is to abstract from himself, but this process has no fixed limits. (The more vital the relations are, out of which, once they are sullied, a noble nature must withdraw himself, since he could not remain in them without himself becoming contaminated, the greater is his misfortune. But this misfortune is neither just nor unjust; it only becomes his fate because his disdain of those relations is his own will, his free choice. Every grief which thus results to him is so far just and is now his unhappy fate, a fate which he himself has consciously wrought; and it is his distinction to suffer justly, because he is raised so far above these rights that he *willed* to have them for enemies. Moreover, since this fate is rooted in himself, he can endure it, face it, because his griefs are not a pure passivity, the predominance of an alien being, but are produced by himself.) To save himself, the man kills himself; to avoid seeing his own being in another's power, he no longer calls it his own, and so he annihilates himself in wishing to maintain himself, since anything in another's power would no longer be the man himself, and there is nothing in him which could not be attacked and sacrificed.

ARTHUR SCHOPENAUER

Arthur Schopenhauer (1788–1860) was born into a family of wealthy and cultivated merchants. Though he was originally destined for business, he persuaded his family to let him seek a university career. At Berlin he sought to compete for students with Hegel, who was then at the height of his popular success. Failing at this, he withdrew from academic life (he had an independent income) and devoted himself to writing and publishing.

Schopenhauer's chief work, The World as Will and Idea, *was written when he was thirty. In it he maintains that, though for perception and reason the world seems a vast collection of diverse objects spread out in space, it is really only a blind, struggling will; that this is the case is supposed to be known in an act of intuition. Since Schopenhauer's ethical theory is based upon this metaphysical doctrine, we have drawn our selections from* The World as Will and Idea. *A book on ethics is available in English with the title* On the Basis of Morality.

*The World as Will and Idea**

Fourth Book
The World as Will

THE ASSERTION AND DENIAL OF THE WILL TO LIVE, WHEN SELF-CONSCIOUSNESS HAS BEEN ATTAINED

54. The world as idea is the complete mirror of the will, in which it knows itself in ascending grades of distinctness and completeness, the highest of which is man. . . .

The will, which, considered purely in itself, is without knowledge, and is merely a blind incessant impulse, as we see it appear in unorganised and vegetable nature and their laws, and also in the vegetative part of our own life, receives through the addition of the world as idea, which is developed in subjection to it, the knowledge of its own willing and of what it is that it wills. And this is nothing else than the world as idea, life, precisely as it exists. Therefore we called the phenomenal world

* Trans. by R. B. Haldane and J. Kemp, Routledge & Kegan Paul, Ltd., London, 1883. Section headings have been added by the editors.

the mirror of the will, its objectivity. And since what the will wills is always life, just because life is nothing but the representation of that willing for the idea, it is all one and a mere pleonism, if, instead of simply saying "the will," we say "the will to live."

Will is the thing-in-itself, the inner content, the essence of the world. Life, the visible world, the phenomenon, is only the mirror of the will. Therefore life accompanies the will inseparably as the shadow accompanies the body.... It is true we see the individual come into being and pass away; but the individual is only phenomenal, exists only for the knowledge which is bound to the principle of sufficient reason, to the principle of individuation....

The whole of nature is the phenomenon and also the fulfilment of the will to live. The form of this phenomenon is time, space, and causality, and by means of these individuation, which carries with it that the individual must come into being and pass away. But this no more affects the will to live, of whose manifestation the individual is, as it were, only a particular example or specimen, than the death of an individual injures the whole of nature. For it is not the individual, but only the species that Nature cares for, and for the preservation of which she so earnestly strives, providing for it with the utmost prodigality through the vast surplus of the seed and the great strength of the fructifying impulse. The individual, on the contrary, neither has nor can have any value for Nature, for her kingdom is infinite time and infinite space, and in these infinite multiplicity of possible individuals.... The man who has comprehended and retained this point of view may well console himself, when contemplating his own death and that of his friends, by turning his eyes to the immortal life of Nature, which he himself is....

But ... this is not to be numbered with the doctrines of immortality. For permanence has no more to do with the will or with the pure subject of knowing, the eternal eye of the world, than transitoriness, for both are predicates that are only valid in time, and the will and the pure subject of knowing lie outside time. Therefore the egoism of the individual (this particular phenomenon of will enlightened by the subject of knowing) can extract as little nourishment and consolation for his wish to endure through endless time from the view we have expressed, as he could from the knowledge that after his death the rest of the eternal world would continue to exist, which is just the expression of the same view considered objectively, and therefore temporally. For every individual is transitory only as phenomenon, but as thing-in-itself is timeless, and therefore endless. But it is also only as phenomenon that an individual is distinguished from the other things of the world; as thing-in-itself he is the will which appears in all, and death destroys the illusion which separates his consciousness from that of the rest: this is immortality.... For the will in itself is absolutely free and entirely self-determining, and for it there is no law. But ... we must first explain and more exactly define this *freedom* and its relation to necessity....

FREEDOM OF THE WILL

55. That the will as such is *free*, follows from the fact that, according to our view, it is the thing-in-itself, the content of all phenomena. The phenomena, on the other hand, we recognise as absolutely subordinate to the principle of sufficient reason in its four forms. And since we know that necessity is throughout identical with following from given grounds, and that these are convertible conceptions, all that belongs to the phenomenon, *i.e.*, all that is object for the knowing subject as individual, is in one aspect reason, and in

another aspect consequent; and in this last capacity is determined with absolute necessity, and can, therefore, in no respect be other than it is. The whole content of Nature, the collective sum of its phenomena, is thus throughout necessary, and the necessity of every part, of every phenomenon, of every event, can always be proved, because it must be possible to find the reason from which it follows as a consequent. This admits of no exception: it follows from the unrestricted validity of the principle of sufficient reason. In another aspect, however, the same world is for us, in all its phenomena, objectivity of will. And the will, since it is not phenomenon, is not idea or object, but thing-in-itself, and is not subordinate to the principle of sufficient reason, the form of all object; thus is not determined as a consequent through any reason, knows no necessity, *i.e.*, is *free*. . . . Now here lies before us in its most distinct form the solution of that great contradiction, the union of freedom with necessity, which has so often been discussed in recent times, yet, so far as I know, never clearly and adequately. Everything is as phenomenon, as object, absolutely necessary; *in itself* it is will, which is perfectly free to all eternity. The phenomenon, the object, is necessarily and unalterably determined in that chain of causes and effects which admits of no interruption. But the existence in general of this object, and its specific nature, *i.e.*, the Idea which reveals itself in it, or, in other words, its character, is a direct manifestation of will. Thus, in conformity with the freedom of this will, the object might not be at all, or it might be originally and essentially something quite different from what it is, in which case, however, the whole chain of which it is a link, and which is itself a manifestation of the same will, would be quite different also. But once there and existing, it has entered the chain of causes and effects, is always necessarily determined in it, and can, therefore, neither become something else, *i.e.*, change itself, nor yet escape from the chain, *i.e.*, vanish. Man, like every other part of Nature, is objectivity of the will; therefore all that has been said holds good of him. As everything in Nature has its forces and qualities, which react in a definite way when definitely affected, and constitute its character, man also has his *character*, from which the motives call forth his actions with necessity. . . .

Kant, whose merit in this respect is specially great, first proved the coexistence of this necessity with the freedom of the will in itself, *i.e.*, apart from the phenomenon, by establishing the distinction between the intelligible and the empirical character. I entirely adhere to this distinction. . . . In order to make the relation of the two comprehensible, the best expression is that . . . the intelligible character of every man is to be regarded as an act of will outside time, and therefore indivisible and unchangeable, and the manifestation of this act of will developed and broken up in time and space and all the forms of the principle of sufficient reason is the empirical character as it exhibits itself for experience in the whole conduct and life of this man. . . .

Apart from the fact that the will as the true thing-in-itself is actually original and independent, and that the feeling of its originality and absoluteness must accompany its acts in self-consciousness, though here they are already determined, there arises the illusion of an empirical freedom of the will (instead of the transcendental freedom which alone is to be attributed to it), and thus a freedom of its particular actions. . . . The intellect knows the conclusions of the will only *a posteriori* and empirically; therefore when a choice is presented, it has no data as to how the will is to decide. For the intelligible character, by virtue of which, when motives are given, only *one* decision is possible and is therefore necessary does not come within the knowledge of the intellect, but merely the empirical character is known to it through the succession of its particular acts. Therefore it seems to the intellect that in a given case two opposite decisions are possible for the will. But this is just the same thing as if we were to say of a perpendicular beam that has lost its balance, and is hesitating which way to fall, "It can fall either to the right hand or the left." This *can* has merely a subjective significance, and really means "as far as the data known to us are concerned." Objectively, the direction of the fall is necessarily determined as soon as the equilibrium is lost. Accordingly, the decision of one's own will is undetermined only to the beholder, one's own intellect, and thus merely relatively and subjectively for the subject of knowing. In itself and objectively, on the other hand, in every choice presented to it, its decision is at once determined and necessary. . . .

The assertion of an empirical freedom of the will, a freedom of indifference, agrees precisely with the doctrine that places the inner nature of man in a *soul,* which is originally a *knowing,* and indeed really an abstract *thinking* nature, and only in consequence of this a *willing* nature— a doctrine which thus regards the will as of a secondary or derivative nature, instead of knowledge which is really so. The will indeed came to be regarded as an act of thought, and to be identified with the judgment, especially by Descartes and Spinoza. According to this doctrine every man must become what he is only through his knowledge; he must enter the world as a moral cipher come to know the things in it, and thereupon determine to be this or that, to act thus or thus, and may also through new knowledge achieve a new course of action, that is to say, become another person. Further, he must first know a thing to be *good,* and in consequence of this will it, instead of first *willing* it, and in consequence of this calling it *good.* According to my fundamental point of view, all this is a reversal of the true relation. Will is first and original; knowledge is merely added to it as an instrument belonging to the phenomenon of will. Therefore every man is what he is through his will, and his character is original, for willing is the basis of his nature. Through the knowledge which is added to it he comes to know in the course of experience *what he is, i.e.,* he learns his character. Thus he *knows* himself in consequence of and in accordance with the nature of his will, instead of *willing* in consequence of and in accordance with his knowing. . . . Therefore he cannot resolve to be this or that, nor can he become other than he is; but he *is* once for all, and he knows in the course of experience *what* he is. According to one doctrine he *wills* what he knows, and according to the other he *knows* what he wills. . . .

Therefore instruction, improved knowledge, in other words, influence from without, may indeed teach the will that it erred in the means it employed, and can therefore bring it about that the end after which it strives once for all according to its inner nature shall be pursued on an entirely different path and in an entirely different object from what has hitherto been the case. But it can never bring about that the will shall will something actually different from what it has hitherto willed; this remains unchangeable, for the will is simply this willing itself, which would have to be abolished. The former, however, the possible modification of knowledge, and through knowledge of conduct, extends so far that the will seeks to attain its unalterable end, for example, Mohammed's paradise, at one time in the real world, at another time in a world of imagination, adapting the means to each, and thus in the first case applying prudence, might, and fraud, and in the second case, abstinence, justice, alms, and pilgrimages to Mecca. But its effort itself has not therefore changed, still less the will itself. Thus, although its action certainly shows itself very different at different times, its willing has yet remained precisely the same. . . .

Repentance never proceeds from a change of the will (which is impossible), but from a change of knowledge. The essential and peculiar in what I have always willed I must still continue to will; for I myself am this will which lies outside time and change. I can therefore never repent of what I have willed, though I can repent of what I have done; because, led by false conceptions, I did something that was not in conformity with my will. The discovery of this through fuller knowledge is *repentance*. This extends not merely to worldly wisdom, to the choice of the means, and the judgment of the appropriateness of the end to my own will, but also to what is properly ethical. For example, I may have acted more egotistically than is in accordance with my character, led astray by exaggerated ideas of the need in which I myself stood, or of the craft, falseness, and wickedness of others. . . .

Knowledge of our own mind and its capacities of every kind, and their unalterable limits, is . . . the surest way to the attainment of the greatest possible contentment with ourselves. For it holds good of inward as of outward circumstances that there is for us no consolation so effective as the complete certainty of unalterable necessity. No evil that befalls us pains us so much as the thought of the circumstances by which it might have been warded off. Therefore nothing comforts us so effectually as the consideration of what has happened from the standpoint of necessity. . . .

The inner being of unconscious nature is a constant striving without end and without rest. And this appears to us much more distinctly when we consider the nature of brutes and man. Willing and striving is its whole being, which may be very well compared to an unquenchable thirst. But the basis of all willing is need, deficiency, and thus pain. Consequently, the nature of brutes and man is subject to pain originally and through its very being. If, on the other hand, it lacks objects of desire, because it is at once deprived of them by a too easy satisfaction, a terrible void and ennui comes over it, *i.e.*, its being and existence itself becomes an unbearable burden to it. Thus its life swings like a pendulum backwards and forwards between pain and ennui. This has also had to express itself very oddly in this way; after man had transferred all pain and torments to hell, there then remained nothing over for heaven but ennui. . . .

ALL SATISFACTION IS MERELY NEGATIVE

58. All satisfaction, or what is commonly called happiness, is always really and essentially only *negative*, and never positive. It is not an original gratification coming to us of itself, but must always be the satisfaction of a wish. The wish, *i.e.*, some want, is the condition which precedes every pleasure. But with the satisfaction the wish and therefore the pleasure cease. Thus the satisfaction or the pleasing can never be more than the deliverance from a pain, from a want. . . .

The human mind, not content with the cares, anxieties, and occupations which the actual world lays upon it, creates for itself an imaginary world also in the form of a thousand different superstitions, then finds all manner of employment with this, and wastes time and strength upon it, as soon as the real world is willing to grant it the rest which it is quite incapable of enjoying. . . . It is the expression and symptom of the actual need of mankind, partly for help and support, partly for occupation and diversion; and if it often works in direct opposition to the first need, because when accidents and dangers arise valuable time and strength, instead of being directed to warding them off, are uselessly wasted on prayers and offerings. . . .

THE MEANING OF GOOD AND BAD

65. In all the preceding investigations of human action, we have been leading up to the final investigation, and have to a considerable extent lightened the task of raising to abstract and philosophical clearness, and exhibiting as a branch of our central thought that special ethical significance of action which in life is with perfect understanding denoted by the words *good* and *bad*.

First, however, I wish to trace back to their real meaning those conceptions of *good* and *bad* which have been treated by the philosophical writers of the day, very extraordinarily, as simple conceptions, and thus incapable of analysis. . . .

The concept *good* . . . is essentially relative, and signifies *the conformity of an object to any definite effort of the will.* Accordingly everything that corresponds to the will in any of its expressions and fulfils its end is thought through the concept *good,* however different such things may be in other respects. Thus we speak of good eating, good roads, good weather, good weapons, good omens, and so on; in short, we call everything good that is just as we wish it to be; and therefore that may be good in the eyes of one man which is just the reverse in those of another. The conception of the good divides itself into two sub-species—that of the direct and present satisfaction of any volition, and that of its indirect satisfaction which has reference to the future, *i.e.,* the agreeable and the useful. The conception of the opposite, so long as we are speaking of unconscious existence, is expressed by the word *bad,* more rarely and abstractly by the word *evil,* which thus denotes everything that does not correspond to any effort of the will. . . .

It follows from what has been said above, that the *good* is, according to its concept, essentially relative, for its being consists in its relation to a desiring will. *Absolute good* is, therefore, a contradiction in terms; highest good, *summum bonum,* really signifies the same thing—a final satisfaction of the will, after which no new desire could arise,—the last motive, the attainment of which would afford enduring satisfaction of the will. But, according to the investigations which have already been conducted in this Fourth Book, such a consummation is not even thinkable. The will can just as little cease from willing altogether on account of some particular satisfaction, as time can end or begin; for if there is no such thing as a permanent fulfilment which shall completely and for ever satisfy its craving. . . . If, however, we wish to give an honorary position, as it were emeritus, to an old expression, which from custom we do not like to discard altogether, we may, metaphorically and figuratively, call the complete self-effacement and denial of the will, the true absence of will, which alone for ever stills and silences its struggle, alone gives that contentment which can never again be disturbed, alone redeems the world, and which we shall now soon consider at the close of our whole investigation —the absolute good, the *summum bonum* —and regard it as the only radical cure of the disease of which all other means are only palliations or anodynes. . . . So much for the words *good* and *bad;* now for the thing itself.

If a man is always disposed to do *wrong* whenever the opportunity presents itself, and there is no external power to restrain him, we call him *bad.* According to our doctrine of wrong, this means that such a man does not merely assert the will to live as it appears in his own body, but in this assertion goes so far that he denies the will which appears in other individuals. This is shown by the fact that he desires their powers for the service of his own will, and seeks to destroy their existence when they stand in the way of its efforts. The ultimate source of this is a high degree of egoism.... Two things are here apparent. In the first place, that in such a man an excessively vehement will to live expresses itself, extending far beyond the assertion of his own body; and, in the second place, that his knowledge, entirely given up to the principle of sufficient reason and involved in the principle of individuation, cannot get beyond the difference which this latter principle establishes between his own person and every one else. Therefore he seeks his own well-being alone, completely indifferent to that of all others, whose existence is to him altogether foreign and divided from his own by a wide gulf, and who are indeed regarded by him as mere masks with no reality behind them. And these two qualities are the constituent elements of the bad character.

This great intensity of will is in itself and directly a constant source of suffering.... Because much intense suffering is inseparable from much intense volition, very bad men bear the stamp of inward suffering in the very expression of the countenance.... From this inward torment, which is absolutely and directly essential to them, there finally proceeds that delight in the suffering of others which does not spring from mere egoism, but is disinterested, and which constitutes *wickedness* proper, rising to the pitch of *cruelty*. For this the suffering of others is not a means for the attainment of the ends of its own will, but an end in itself. The more definite explanation of this phenomenon is as follows:—Since man is a manifestation of will illuminated by the clearest knowledge, he is always contrasting the actual and felt satisfaction of his will with the merely possible satisfaction of it which knowledge presents to him. Hence arises envy: every privation is infinitely increased by the enjoyment of others, and relieved by the knowledge that others also suffer the same privation. Those ills which are common to all and inseparable from human life trouble us little, just as those which belong to the climate, to the whole country. The recollection of greater sufferings than our own stills our pain; the sight of the sufferings of others soothes our own. If, now, a man is filled with an exceptionally intense pressure of will, . . . the suffering of others now becomes for him an end in itself, and is a spectacle in which he delights; and thus arises the phenomenon of pure cruelty, blood-thirstiness, which history exhibits so often in the Neros and Domitians, in the African Deis, in Robespierre, and the like. . . .

Besides the suffering which has been described, and which is inseparable from wickedness, because it springs from the same root, excessive vehemence of will, another specific pain quite different from this is connected with wickedness, which is felt in the case of every bad action, whether it be merely in justice proceeding from egoism or pure wickedness, and according to the length of its duration is called *the sting of conscience* or *remorse*....

However closely the veil of Mâyâ may envelop the mind of the bad man, *i.e.*, however firmly he may be involved in the principle of individuation, according to which he regards his person as absolutely different and separated by a wide gulf from all others, a knowledge to which he clings with all his might, as it alone suits and supports his egoism, so that knowledge is almost always corrupted by will, yet there arises in the inmost depths of his consciousness the secret presentiment that such an order of things is only phenomenal, and that their real constitution is quite different. He has a dim foreboding that, however much time and space may separate him from other individuals and the innumerable miseries which they suffer, and even suffer through him, and may represent them as quite foreign to him, yet in themselves, and apart from the idea and its forms, it is the one will to live appearing in them all, which here failing to recognize itself, turns its weapons against itself, and, by seeking increased happiness in one of its phenomena, imposes the greatest suffering upon another. He dimly sees that he, the bad man, is himself this whole will; that consequently he is not only the inflicter of pain but also the endurer of it, from whose suffering he is only separated and exempted by an illusive dream, the form of which is space and time. . . . Beginning and end only concern the individual through time, the form of the phenomenon for the idea. Outside time lies only the will, Kant's thing-in-itself, and its adequate objectification, the Idea of Plato. Therefore suicide affords no escape; what every one in his inmost consciousness *wills,* that must he *be;* and what every one *is,* that he *wills.* . . .

This exposition of the significance and inner nature of the *bad,* which as mere feeling, *i.e.,* not as distinct, abstract knowledge, is the content of *remorse,* will gain distinctness and completeness by the similar consideration of the *good* as a quality of human will, and finally of absolute resignation and holiness which proceeds from it when it has attained its highest grade. . . .

JUSTICE

66. Before we speak of the *good* proper, in opposition to the *bad,* which has been explained, we must touch on an intermediate grade, the mere negation of the bad; this is *justice.* . . . He who voluntarily recognises and observes those merely moral limits between wrong and right, even where this is not secured by the state or any other external power, thus he who, according to our explanation, never carries the assertion of his own will so far as to deny the will appearing in another individual, is *just.* Thus, in order to increase his own well-being, he will not inflict suffering upon others, *i.e.,* he will commit no crime, he will respect the rights and the property of others. We see that for such a just man the principle of individuation is no longer, as in the case of the bad man, an absolute wall of partition. We see that he does not, like the bad man, merely assert his own manifestation of will and deny all others; that other persons are not for him mere masks, whose nature is quite different from his own; but he shows in his conduct that he also recognises his own nature—the will to live as a thing-in-itself, in the foreign manifestation which is only given to him as idea. . . . To this extent, therefore, he sees through the principle of individuation, the veil of Mâyâ; so far he sets the being external to him on a level with his own—he does it no injury.

If we examine the inmost nature of this justice, there already lies in it the resolution not to go so far in the assertion of one's own will as to deny the manifestations of will of others, by compelling them to serve one's own. . . .

Voluntary justice has its inmost source in a certain degree of penetration of the principle of individuation, while the unjust remain entirely involved in this principle. This penetration may exist not only in the degree which is required for justice, but also in the higher degree which leads to benevolence and well-doing, to love of mankind. . . . The good man is by no means to be regarded as originally a weaker manifestation of will than the bad man, but it is knowledge which in him masters the blind striving of will. *He makes less distinction than is usually made between himself and others.* . . . The principle of individuation, the form of the phenomenon, no longer holds him so tightly in its grasp, but the suffering which he sees in others touches him almost as closely as his own. He therefore tries to strike a balance between them, denies himself pleasures, practises renunciation, in order to mitigate the suffering of others. He sees that the distinction between himself and others, which to the bad man is so great a gulf, only belongs to a fleeting and illusive phenomenon. He recognises directly and without reasoning that the in-itself of his own manifestation is also that of others, the will to live, which constitutes the inner nature of everything and lives in all; indeed, that this applies also to the brutes and the whole of nature, and therefore he will not cause suffering even to a brute. . . .

The opposite of the sting of conscience, the origin and significance of which is explained above, is the *good conscience,* the satisfaction which we experience after every disinterested deed. It arises from the fact that such a deed, as it proceeds from the direct recognition of our own inner being in the phenomenon of another, affords us also the verification of this knowledge, the knowledge that our true self exists not only in our own person, this particular manifestation, but in everything that lives. . . . The knowledge that everything living is just as much our own inner nature, as is our own person, extends our interest to everything living; and in this way the heart is enlarged. . . .

Thus, though others have set up moral principles which they give out as prescriptions for virtue, and laws which it was necessary to follow, I, as has already been said, cannot do this because I have no "ought" or law to prescribe to the eternally free-will. Yet on the other hand, in the connection of my system, what to a certain extent corresponds and is analogous to that undertaking is the purely theoretical truth, of which my whole exposition may be regarded as merely an elaboration, that the will is the in-itself of every phenomenon, but itself, as such, is free from the forms of the phenomenal, and consequently from multiplicity; a truth, which, with reference to action, I do not know how to express better than by the formula of the Vedas . . . : "Tat twam asi!" (This thou art!) Whoever is able to say this to himself, with regard to every being with whom he comes in contact, with clear knowledge and firm inward conviction, is certain of all virtue and blessedness, and is on the direct road to salvation. . . .

ASCETICISM

68. If this penetration of the principle of individuation, this direct knowledge of the identity of will in all its manifestations, is present in a high degree of distinctness, it will at once show an influence upon the will which extends still further. If that veil of Mâyâ, the principle of individuation, is lifted from the eyes of a man to such an extent that he no longer makes the egotistical distinction between his person and that of others, but takes as much interest in the sufferings of other individuals as in his own, and therefore is not only benevolent in the highest degree, but even ready to sacrifice his own individuality whenever such a sacrifice will save a number of other persons, then it clearly follows that such a man, who recognises in all beings his own inmost and true self, must also regard the infinite suffering of all suffering beings as his own, and take on himself the pain of the whole world. No suffering is any longer strange to him. . . . But . . . why should he now, with such knowledge of the world, assert this very life through constant acts of will, and thereby bind himself ever more closely to it, press it ever more firmly to himself? . . . That knowledge of the whole, of the nature of the thing-in-itself which has been described, becomes a *quieter* of all and every volition. The will now turns away from life; it now shudders at the pleasures in which it recognises the assertion of life.

Man now attains to the state of voluntary renunciation, resignation, true indifference, and perfect will-lessness. . . .

He who sees through the principle of individuation, and recognises the real nature of the thing-in-itself, and thus the whole, is no longer susceptible of such consolation; he sees himself in all places at once, and withdraws. His will turns round, no longer asserts its own nature, which is reflected in the phenomenon, but denies it. The phenomenon by which this change is marked, is the transition from virtue to asceticism. That is to say, it no longer suffices for such a man to love others as himself, and to do as much for them as for himself; but there arises within him a horror of the nature of which his own phenomenal existence is an expression, the will to live, the kernel and inner nature of that world which is recognised as full of misery. He therefore disowns this nature which appears in him. . . . Voluntary and complete chastity is the first step in asceticism or the denial of the will to live. . . . Nature, always true and naïve, declares that if this maxim became universal, the human race would die out; and I think I may assume . . . that with its highest manifestation, the weaker reflection of it would also pass away, as the twilight vanishes along with the full light. With the entire abolition of knowledge, the rest of the world would of itself vanish into nothing; for without a subject there is no object.

Asceticism then shows itself further in voluntary and intentional poverty, which not only arises *per accidens,* because the possessions are given away to mitigate the sufferings of others, but is here an end in itself, is meant to serve as a constant mortification of will, so that the satisfaction of the wishes, the sweet of life, shall not again arouse the will, against which self-knowledge has conceived a horror. . . . And he mortifies not only the will itself, but also its visible form, its objectivity, the body. He nourishes it sparingly, lest its excessive vigour and prosperity should animate and excite more strongly the will, of which it is merely the expression and the mirror. So he practises fasting, and even resorts to chastisement and self-inflicted torture, in order that, by constant privation and suffering, he may more and more break down and destroy the will, which he recognises and abhors as the source of his own suffering existence and that of the world. . . .

And what I have here described with feeble tongue and only in general terms, is no philosophical fable, invented by myself, and only of to-day; no, it was the enviable life of so many saints and beautiful souls among Christians, and still more among Hindus and Buddhists, and also among the believers of other religions. However different were the dogmas impressed on their reason, the same inward, direct, intuitive knowledge, from which alone all virtue and holiness proceed, expressed itself in precisely the same way in the conduct of life. For here also the great distinction between intuitive and abstract knowledge shows itself. . . . Intuitively or *in concreto,* every man is really conscious of all philosophical truths, but to bring them to abstract knowledge, to reflection, is the work of philosophy, which neither ought nor is able to do more than this.

Thus it may be that the inner nature of holiness, self-renunciation, mortification of our own will, asceticism, is here for the first time expressed abstractly, and free from all mythical elements, as *denial of the will to live,* appearing after the complete knowledge of its own nature has become a quieter of all volition. On the other hand, it has been known directly and realised in practice by saints and ascetics, who had all the same inward knowledge, though they used very different language with regard to it, according to the dogmas which their reason had accepted. . . .

I now end the general account of

ethics, and . . . I by no means desire to conceal here an objection which concerns this last part of my exposition. . . . It is this, that after our investigation has brought us to the point at which we have before our eyes perfect holiness, the denial and surrender of all volition, and thus the deliverance from a world whose whole existence we have found to be suffering, this appears to us as a passing away into empty nothingness.

Before us there is certainly only nothingness. But that which resists this passing into nothing, our nature, is indeed just the will to live, which we ourselves are as it is our world. That we abhor annihilation so greatly, is simply another expression of the fact that we so strenuously will life, and are nothing but this will, and know nothing besides it. . . . What remains after the entire abolition of will is for all those who are still full of will certainly nothing; but, conversely, to those in whom the will has turned and has denied itself, this our world, which is so real, with all its suns and milky-ways—is nothing.

JOHN STUART MILL

John Stuart Mill (1806–1873) was a child prodigy whose education, carried out under the personal direction of his father and with the advice of Jeremy Bentham, had made of him, by the age of twenty-one, a "bottomless pit of learning" and a close adherent to utilitarianism. In 1822 he began a successful career in India House (the London headquarters of the East India Company); all his life he maintained a deep interest in public affairs. He served one term in Parliament and was the founder of the first women's suffrage society in England.

In his Utilitarianism *(1863) Mill develops and applies a version of the utilitarian doctrine. The most striking feature of this work is the introduction of fundamental changes in the Benthamite position. Over against Bentham, he admits that some pleasures are intrinsically higher than others; he hints that virtue may have a value apart from the good consequences of virtuous action; and finally, he gives conscience a basic position in the foundation of ethics. Thus Mills's defense of his own version of utilitarianism is an implicit criticism of Bentham's formulation of this doctrine.*

*Utilitarianism**

CHAPTER II. WHAT UTILITARIANISM IS

The creed which accepts as the foundation of morals "utility" or the "greatest happiness principle" holds that actions are right in proportion as they tend to promote happiness, wrong as they tend to produce the reverse of happiness. By happiness is intended pleasure, and the absence of pain; by unhappiness, pain, and the privation of pleasure. To give a clear view of the moral standard set up by the theory, much more requires to be said; in particular, what things it includes in the ideas of pain and pleasure; and to what extent this is left an open question. But these supplementary explanations do not affect the theory of life on which this theory of morality is grounded—namely, that pleasure and freedom from pain are the only things desirable as ends; and that all desirable things (which are as numerous in

* *Utilitarianism,* London, 1863.

the utilitarian as in any other scheme) are desirable either for the pleasure inherent in themselves, or as means to the promotion of pleasure and the prevention of pain.

Now such a theory of life excites in many minds, and among them in some of the most estimable in feeling and purpose, inveterate dislike. To suppose that life has (as they express it) no higher end than pleasure—no better and nobler object of desire and pursuit—they designate as utterly mean and groveling; as a doctrine worthy only of swine, to whom the followers of Epicurus were, at a very early period, contemptuously likened; and modern holders of the doctrine are occasionally made the subject of equally polite comparisons by its German, French, and English assailants.

When thus attacked, the Epicureans have always answered that it is not they, but their accusers, who represent human nature in a degrading light, since the accusation supposes human beings to be capable of no pleasures except those of which swine are capable. If this supposition were true, the charge could not be gainsaid, but would then be no longer an imputation; for if the sources of pleasure were precisely the same to human beings and to swine, the rule of life which is good enough for the one would be good enough for the other. The comparison of the Epicurean life to that of beasts is felt as degrading, precisely because a beast's pleasures do not satisfy a human being's conceptions of happiness. Human beings have faculties more elevated than the animal appetites and, when once made conscious of them, do not regard anything as happiness which does not include their gratification. I do not, indeed, consider the Epicureans to have been by any means faultless in drawing out their scheme of consequences from the utilitarian principle. To do this in any sufficient manner, many Stoic, as well as Christian, elements require to be included. But there is no known Epicurean theory of life which does not assign to the pleasures of the intellect, of the feelings and imagination, and of the moral sentiments, a much higher value of pleasures than to those of mere sensation. It must be admitted, however, that utilitarian writers in general have placed the superiority of mental over bodily pleasures chiefly in the greater permanency, safety, uncostliness, etc., of the former—that is, in their circumstantial advantages rather than in their intrinsic nature. And on all these points utilitarians have fully proved their case; but they might have taken the other and, as it may be called, higher ground with entire consistency. It is quite compatible with the principle of utility to recognize the fact that some kinds of pleasure are more desirable and more valuable than others. It would be absurd that, while, in estimating all other things, quality is considered as well as quantity, the estimation of pleasures should be supposed to depend on quantity alone.

If I am asked what I mean by difference of quality in pleasures, or what makes one pleasure more valuable than another, merely as a pleasure, except its being greater in amount, there is but one possible answer. Of two pleasures, if there be one to which all or almost all who have experience of both give a decided preference, irrespective of a feeling of moral obligation to prefer it, that is the more desirable pleasure. If one of the two is, by those who are competently acquainted with both, placed so far above the other that they prefer it, even though knowing it to be attended with a greater amount of discontent, and would not resign it for any quantity of the other pleasure which their nature is capable of, we are justified in ascribing to the preferred enjoyment a superiority in quality so far outweighing quantity as to render it, in comparison, of small account.

Now it is an unquestionable fact that

those who are equally acquainted with and equally capable of appreciating and enjoying both, do give a most marked preference to the manner of existence which employs their higher faculties. Few human creatures would consent to be changed into any of the lower animals for a promise of the fullest allowance of a beast's pleasures; no intelligent human being would consent to be a fool, no instructed person would be an ignoramus, no person of feeling and conscience would be selfish and base, even though they should be persuaded that the fool, the dunce, or the rascal is better satisfied with his lot than they are with theirs. They would not resign what they possess more than he for the most complete satisfaction of all the desires which they have in common with him. . . . It is better to be a human being dissatisfied than a pig satisfied; better to be Socrates dissatisfied than a fool satisfied. And if the fool, or the pig, are of a different opinion, it is because they only know their own side of the question. The other party to the comparison knows both sides. . . .

From this verdict of the only competent judges, I apprehend there can be no appeal. On the question which is the best worth having of two pleasures, or which of two modes of existence is the most grateful to the feelings, apart from its moral attributes and from its consequences, the judgment of those who are qualified by knowledge of both, or, if they differ, that of the majority of them, must be admitted as final. And there needs be the less hesitation to accept this judgment respecting the quality of pleasures, since there is no other tribunal to be referred to even on the question of quantity. What means are there of determining which is the acutest of two pains, or the intensest of two pleasurable sensations, except the general suffrage of those who are familiar with both? Neither pains nor pleasures are homogeneous, and pain is always heterogeneous with pleasure. What is there to decide whether a particular pleasure is worth purchasing at the cost of a particular pain, except the feelings and judgment of the experienced? When, therefore, those feelings and judgment declare the pleasures derived from the higher faculties to be preferable *in kind,* apart from the question of intensity, to those of which the animal nature, disjoined from the higher faculties, is susceptible, they are entitled on this subject to the same regard.

I have dwelt on this point, as being a necessary part of a perfectly just conception of utility or happiness considered as the directive rule of human conduct. But it is by no means an indispensable condition to the acceptance of the utilitarian standard; for that standard is not the agent's own greatest happiness, but the greatest amount of happiness altogether; and character is always the happier for its nobleness, there can be no doubt that it makes other people happier, and that the world in general is immensely a gainer by it. Utilitarianism, therefore, could only attain its end by the general cultivation of nobleness of character, even if each individual were only benefited by the nobleness of others, and his own, so far as happiness is concerned, were a sheer deduction from the benefit. But the bare enunciation of such an absurdity as this last renders refutation superfluous.

According to the greatest happiness principle, as above explained, the ultimate end, with reference to and for the sake of which all other things are desirable—whether we are considering our own good or that of other people—is an existence exempt as far as possible from pain, and as rich as possible in enjoyments, both in point of quantity and quality; the test of quality and the rule for measuring it against quantity being the preference felt by those who, in their opportunities of experience, to which must be added their habits of self-consciousness and self-observation, are best furnished with the means of comparison. This, being, according to the utilitarian opinion, the end of human action, is necessarily also the standard of morality, which may accordingly be defined "the rules and precepts for human conduct," by the observance of which an existence such as has been described might be, to the greatest extent possible, secured to all mankind; and not to them only, but, so far as the nature of things admits, to the whole sentient creation. . . .

The main constituents of a satisfied life appear to be two, either of which by itself is often found sufficient for the purpose: tranquility and excitement. With much tranquility, many find that they can be content with very little pleasure; with much excitement, many can reconcile themselves to a considerable quantity of pain. There is assuredly no inherent impossibility of enabling even the mass of mankind to unite both, since the two are so far from being incompatible that they are in natural alliance, the prolongation of either being a preparation for, and exciting a wish for, the other. It is only those in whom indolence amounts to a vice that do not desire excitement after an interval of repose; it is only those in whom the need of excitement is a disease that feel the tranquility which follows excitement dull and insipid, instead of pleasurable in direct proportion to the excitement which preceded it. When people who are tolerably fortunate in their outward lot do not find in life sufficient enjoyment to make it valuable to them, the cause generally is caring for nobody but themselves. To those who have neither public nor private affections, the excitements of life are much curtailed, and in any case dwindle in value as the time approaches when all selfish interests must be terminated by death; while those who leave after them objects of personal affection, and especially those who have also cultivated a fellow-feeling with the collective interests of mankind, retain as lively an interest in life on the eve of death as in the vigor of youth and health. Next to selfishness, the principal cause which makes life unsatisfactory is want of mental cultivation. A cultivated mind—I do not mean that of a philosopher, but any mind to which the fountains of knowledge have been opened, and which has been taught, in any tolerable degree, to exercise its faculties—finds sources of inexhaustible interest in all that surrounds it: in the objects of nature, the achievements of art, the imaginations of poetry, the incidents of history, the ways of mankind, past and present, and their prospects in the future. It is possible, indeed, to become indifferent to all this, and that too without having exhausted a thousandth part of it, but only when one has had from the beginning no moral or human interest in these things, and has sought in them only the gratification of curiosity.

Now there is absolutely no reason in the nature of things why an amount of mental culture sufficient to give an intelligent interest in these objects of contemplation should not be the inheritance of every one born in a civilized country. As little is there an inherent necessity that any human being should be a selfish egotist, devoid of every feeling or care but those which center in his own miserable individuality. Something far superior to this is sufficiently common even now, to give ample earnest of what the human species may be made. Genuine private affections and a sincere interest in the public good are possible, though in unequal degrees, to every rightly brought up human being. In a world in which there is so much to interest, so much to enjoy, and so much also to correct and improve, every one who has this moderate amount of moral and intellectual requisites is capable of an existence which may be called enviable; and unless such a person, through bad laws or subjection to the will of others, is denied the liberty to use the sources of happiness within his reach, he will not fail to find this enviable existence, if he escape the positive evils of life, the great sources of physical and mental suffering—such as indigence, disease, and the unkindness, worthlessness, or premature loss of objects of affection. The main stress of the problem lies, therefore, in the contest with these calamities from which it is a rare good fortune entirely to escape; which, as things now are, cannot be obviated, and often cannot be in any material degree mitigated. Yet no one whose opinion deserves a moment's consideration can doubt that most of the great positive evils of the world are in themselves removable, and will, if human affairs continue to improve, be in the end reduced within narrow limits. Poverty, in any sense implying suffering, may be completely extinguished by the wisdom of society combined with the good sense and providence of individuals. Even that most intractable of enemies, disease, may be indefinitely reduced in dimensions by good physical and moral education and proper control of noxious influences, while the progress of science holds out a promise for the future of still more direct conquests over this detestable foe. And every advance in that direction relieves us from some, not only of the chances which cut short our own lives, but, what concerns us still more, which deprive us of those in whom our happiness is wrapt up. As for vicissitudes of fortune and other disappointments connected with worldly circumstances, these are principally the effect either of gross imprudence, of ill-regulated desires, or of bad or imperfect social institutions. All the grand sources, in short, of human suffering are in a great degree, many of them almost entirely, conquerable by human care and effort; and though their removal is grievously slow—though a long succession of generations will perish in the breach before the conquest is completed, and this world becomes all that, if will and knowledge were not wanting, it might easily be made—yet every mind sufficiently intelligent and generous to bear a part, however small and inconspicuous, in the endeavour will draw a noble enjoyment from the contest itself, which he would not for any bribe in the form of selfish indulgence consent to be without. . . .

The objectors to utilitarianism cannot always be charged with representing it in a discreditable light. On the contrary, those among them who entertain anything like a just idea of its disinterested character sometimes find fault with its standard as being too high for humanity. They say it is exacting too much to require that people shall always act from the inducement of promoting the general interests of society. But this is to mistake the very meaning of a standard of morals, and confound the business of ethics to tell us what are our duties, or by what test we may know them; but no system of ethics requires that the sole motive of all we do shall be a feeling of duty; on the contrary, ninety-nine hundredths of all our actions are done from other motives, and rightly so done if the rule of duty does not condemn them. It is the more unjust to utilitarianism that this particular misapprehension should be made a ground of objection to it, inasmuch as utilitarian moralists have gone beyond almost all others in affirming that the motive has nothing to do with the morality of the action, though much with the worth of the agent. He who saves a fellow creature from drowning does what is morally right, whether his motive be duty or the hope of being paid for his trouble; he who betrays the friend that trusts him is guilty of a crime, even if his object be to serve another friend to whom he is under greater obligations. But to speak only of actions done from the motive of duty, and in direct obedience to principle: it is a misapprehension of the utilitarian mode of thought to conceive it as implying that people should fix their minds upon so wide a generality as the world, or society at large. The great majority of good actions are intended not for the benefit of the world, but for that of individuals, of which the good of the world is made up; and the thoughts of the most virtuous man need not on these occasions travel beyond the particular persons concerned, except so far as is necessary to assure himself that in benefiting them he is not violating the rights, that is, the legitimate and authorized expectations, of any one else. The multiplication of happiness is, according to the utilitarian ethics, the object of virtue: the occasions on which any person (except one in a thousand) has it in his power to do this on an extended scale, in other words, to be a public benefactor, are but exceptional; and on these occasions alone is he called on to consider public utility; in every other case, private utility, the interest or happiness of some few persons, is all he has to attend to. Those alone the influence of whose actions extends to society in general need concern themselves habitually about so large an object. In the case of abstinences indeed—of things which people forbear to do from moral considerations, though the consequences in the particular case might be beneficial—it would be unworthy of an intelligent agent not to be consciously aware that the action is of a class which, if practiced generally, would be generally injurious, and that this is the ground of the obligation to abstain from it. The amount of regard for the public interest implied in this recognition is no greater than is demanded by every system of morals, for they all enjoin to abstain from whatever is manifestly pernicious to society.

The same considerations dispose of another reproach against the doctrine of utility, founded on a still grosser misconception of the purpose of a standard of morality, and of the very meaning of the words "right" and "wrong." It is often affirmed that utilitarianism renders men cold and unsympathizing; that it chills their moral feelings towards individuals; that it makes them regard only the dry and hard consideration of the consequences of actions, not taking into their moral estimate the qualities from which those actions emanate. . . .

If no more be meant by the objection than that many utilitarians look on the morality of actions, as measured by the utilitarian standards, with too exclusive a regard, and do not lay sufficient stress upon the other beauties of character which go towards making a human being lovable or admirable, this may be admitted. Utilitarians who have cultivated their moral feelings, but not their sympathies, nor their artistic perceptions, do fall into this mistake; and so do all other moralists under the same conditions. What can be said in excuse for other moralists is equally available for them, namely, that, if there is to be any error, it is better that it should be on that side. As a matter of fact, we may affirm that among utilitarians, as among adherents of other systems, there is every imaginable degree of rigidity and of laxity in the application of their standard; some are even puritanically rigorous, while others are as indulgent as can possibly be desired by sinner or by sentimentalist. But on the whole, a doctrine which brings prominently forward the interest that mankind have in the repression and prevention of conduct which violates the moral law, is likely to be inferior to no other in turning the sanctions of opinion against such violations. It is true, the question, "What does violate the moral law?" is one on which those who recognize different standards of morality are likely now and then to differ. But difference of opinion on moral questions was not first introduced into the world by utilitarianism, while that doctrine does supply, if not always an easy, at all events a tangible and intelligible, mode of deciding such differences. . . .

We not uncommonly hear the doctrine of utility inveighed against as a *godless* doctrine. If it be necessary to say anything at all against so mere an assumption, we may say that the question depends upon what idea we have formed of the moral character of the Deity. If it be a true belief that God desires, above all things, the happiness of his creatures, and that this was his purpose in their creation, utility is not only not a godless doctrine, but more profoundly religious than any other. If it be meant that utilitarianism does not recognize the revealed will of God as the supreme law of morals, I answer that a utilitarian who believes in the perfect goodness and wisdom of God necessarily believes that whatever God has thought fit to reveal on the subject of morals must fulfil the requirements of utility in a supreme degree. But others besides utilitarians have been of opinion that the Christian revelation was intended, and is fitted, to inform the hearts and minds of mankind with a spirit which should enable them to find for themselves what is right, and incline them to do it when found, rather than to tell them, except in a very general way, what it is; and that we need a doctrine of ethics, carefully followed out, to *interpret* to us the will of God. Whether this opinion is correct or not, it is superfluous here to discuss; since whatever aid religion, either natural or revealed, can afford to ethical investigation, is as open to the utilitarian moralist as to any other. He can use it as the testimony of God to the usefulness or hurtfulness of any given course of action, by as good a right as others can use it for the indication of a transcendental law, having no connection with usefulness or with happiness. . . .

Again, defenders of utility often find themselves called upon to reply to such objections as this—that there is not time, previous to action, for calculating and weighing the effects of any line of conduct on the general happiness. This is exactly as if any one were to say that it is impossible to guide our conduct by Christianity because there is not time, on every occasion on which anything has to be done, to read through the Old and New Testaments. The answer to the objection is that there has been ample time, namely, the whole past duration of the human species. During all that time, mankind have been learning by experience the tendencies of actions; on which experience all the prudence, as well as all the morality, of life are dependent. People talk as if the commencement of this course of experience had hitherto been put off, and as if, at the moment when some man feels tempted to meddle with the property or life of another, he had to begin considering for the first time whether murder and theft are injurious to human happiness. Even then I do not think that he would find the question very puzzling; but, at all events, the matter is now done to his hand. It is truly a whimsical supposition that, if mankind were agreed in considering utility to be the test of morality, they would remain without any agreement as to what *is* useful, and would take no measures for having their notions on the subject taught to the young, and enforced by law and opinion. There is no difficulty in proving any ethical standard whatever to work ill if we suppose universal idiocy to be conjoined with it; but on any hypothesis short of that, mankind must by this time have acquired positive beliefs as to the effects of some actions on their happiness; and the beliefs which have thus come down are the rules of morality for the multitude, and for the philosopher until he has succeeded in finding better. That philosophers might easily do this, even now, on many subjects; that the received code of ethics is by no means of divine right; and that mankind have still much to learn as to the effects of actions on the general happiness, I admit or rather earnestly maintain. The corollaries from the principle of utility, like the precepts of every practical art, admit of indefinite improvement, and, in a progressive state of the human mind, their improvement is perpetually going on. But to consider the rules of morality as improvable is one thing; to pass over the intermediate generalization entirely and endeavor to test each individual action directly by the first principle is another. . . . Nobody argues that the art of navigation is not founded on astronomy because sailors cannot wait to calculate the Nautical Almanac. Being rational creatures, they go to sea with it ready calculated; and all rational creatures go out upon the sea of life with their minds made up on the common questions of right and wrong, as well as on many of the far more difficult questions of wise and foolish. And this, as long as foresight is a human quality, it is to be presumed they will continue to do. Whatever we adopt as the fundamental principle of morality, we require subordinate principles to apply it by; the impossibility of doing without them, being common to all systems, can afford no argument against any one in particular; but gravely to argue as if no such secondary principles could be had, and as if mankind had remained till now, and always must remain, without drawing any general conclusions from the experience of human life, is as high a pitch, I think, as absurdity has ever reached in philosophical controversy. . . .

CHAPTER III. OF THE ULTIMATE SANCTION OF THE PRINCIPLE OF UTILITY

The question is often asked, and properly so, in regard to any supposed moral standard—What is its sanction? what are the motives to obey? or more specifically, what is the source of its obligation? whence does it derive its binding force? . . .

The principle of utility either has, or there is no reason why it might not have, all the sanctions which belong to any other system of morals. Those sanctions are either external or internal. Of the external sanctions it is not necessary to speak at any length. They are the hope of favor and the fear of displeasure from our fellow creatures or from the Ruler of the universe, along with whatever we may have of sympathy or affection for them, or of love and awe of Him, inclining us to do His will independently of selfish consequences. There is evidently no reason why all these motives for observance should not attach themselves to the utilitarian morality as completely and as powerfully as to any other. Indeed, those of them which refer to our fellow creatures are sure to do so, in proportion to the amount of general intelligence; for whether there be any other ground of moral obligation than the general happiness or not, men do desire happiness; and however imperfect may be their own practice, they desire and commend all conduct in others towards themselves by which they think their happiness is promoted. With regard to the religious motive, if men believe, as most profess to do, in the goodness of God, those who think that conduciveness to the general happiness is the essence or even only the criterion of good must necessarily believe that it is also that which God approves. The whole force therefore of external reward and punishment, whether physical or moral, and whether proceeding from God or from our fellow men, together with all that the capacities of human nature admit of disinterested devotion to either, become available to enforce the utilitarian morality, in proportion as that morality is recognized; and the more powerfully, the more the appliances of education and general cultivation are bent to the purpose.

So far as to external sanctions. The internal sanction of duty, whatever our standard of duty may be, is one and the same—a feeling in our own mind; a pain, more or less intense, attendant on violation of duty, which in properly cultivated moral natures rises, in the more serious cases, into shrinking from it as an impossibility. This feeling, when disinterested and connecting itself with the pure idea of duty, and not with some particular form of it, or with any of the merely accessory circumstances, is the essence of conscience; though in that complex phenomenon as it actually exists, the simple fact is in general all encrusted over with collateral associations derived from sympathy, from love, and still more from fear; from all the forms of religious feeling; from the recollections of childhood and of all our past life; from self-esteem, desire of the esteem of others, and occasionally even self-abasement. This extreme complication is, I apprehend, the origin of the sort of mystical character which, by a tendency of the human mind of which there are many other examples, is apt to be attributed to the idea of moral obligation, and which leads people to believe that the idea cannot possibly attach itself to any other objects than those which, by a supposed mysterious law, are found in our present experience to excite it. Its binding force, however, consists in the existence of a mass of feeling which must be broken through in order to do what violates our standard of right, and which, if we do nevertheless violate that standard, will probably have to be encountered afterwards in the form of remorse. Whatever theory we have of the nature or origin of conscience, this is what essentially constitutes it.

The ultimate sanction, therefore, of all morality (external motives apart) being a subjective feeling in our own minds, I see nothing embarrassing to those whose standard is utility in the question. What is the sanction of that particular standard? We may answer, the same as of all other moral standards—the conscientious feelings of mankind. Undoubtedly this sanction has no binding efficacy on those who do not possess the feelings it appeals to; but neither will these persons be more obedient to any other moral principle than to the utilitarian one. On them morality of any kind has no hold but through the external sanctions. Meanwhile the feelings exist, a fact in human nature, the reality of which, and the great power with which they are capable of acting on those in whom they have been duly cultivated, are proved by experience. No reason has ever been shown why they may not be cultivated to as great intensity in connection with the utilitarian, as with any other rule of morals. . . .

Moral associations which are wholly of artificial creation, when intellectual culture goes on, yield by degrees to the dissolving force of analysis; and if the feeling of duty, when associated with utility, would appear equally arbitrary; if there were no leading department of our nature, no powerful class of sentiments, with which that association would harmonize, which would make us feel it congenial and incline us not only to foster it in others (for which we have abundant interested motives), but also to cherish it in ourselves—if there were not, in short, a natural basis of sentiment for utilitarian morality, it might well happen that this association also, even after it had been implanted by education, might be analyzed away.

But there *is* this basis of powerful natural sentiment; and this it is which, when once the general happiness is recognized as the ethical standard, will constitute the strength of the utilitarian morality. This firm foundation is that of the social feelings of mankind; the desire to be in unity with our fellow creatures, which is already a powerful principle in human nature, and happily one of those which tend to become stronger, even without express inculcation, from the influences of advancing civilization. The social state is at once so natural, so necessary, and so habitual to man, that, except in some unusual circumstances or by an effort of voluntary abstraction, he never conceives himself otherwise than as a member of a body; and this association is riveted more and more, as mankind are further removed from the state of savage independence. Any condition, therefore, which is essential to a state of society, becomes more and more an inseparable part of every person's conception of the state of things which he is born into, and which is the destiny of a human being. Now society between human beings, except in the relation of master and slave, is manifestly impossible on any other footing than that the interests of all are to be consulted. Society between equals can only exist on the understanding that the interests of all are to be regarded equally. And since in all states of civilization, every person, except an absolute monarch, has equals, everyone is obliged to live on these terms with somebody; and in every age some advance is made towards a state in which it will be impossible to live permanently on other terms with anybody. In this way people grow up unable to conceive as possible to them a state of total disregard of other people's interests. . . . Not only does all strengthening of social ties, and all healthy growth of society, give to each individual a stronger personal interest in practically consulting the welfare of others, it also leads him to identify his *feelings* more and more with their good, or at least with an even greater degree of practical consideration for it. He comes, as though instinctively, to be conscious of himself as a being who *of course* pays regard to others. The good of others becomes to him a thing naturally and necessarily to be attended to, like any of the physical conditions of our existence. Now, whatever amount of this feeling a person has, he is urged by the strongest motive both of interest and of sympathy to demonstrate it, and to the utmost of his power encourage it in others; and even if he has none of it himself, he is as greatly interested as any one else that others should have it. Consequently the smallest germs of the feeling are laid hold of and nourished by the contagion of sympathy and the influences of education; and a complete web of corroborative association is woven round it, by the powerful agency of the external sanctions. This mode of conceiving ourselves and human life, as civilization goes on, is felt to be more and more natural. Every step in political improvement renders it more so, by removing the sources of opposition of interest and levelling those inequalities of legal privilege between individuals or classes, owing to which there are large portions of mankind whose happiness it is still practicable to disregard. In an improving state of the human mind, the influences are constantly on the increase which tend to generate in each individual a feeling of unity with all the rest; which, if perfect, would make him never think of, or desire, any beneficial condition for himself, in the benefits of which they are not included. If we now suppose this feeling of unity to be taught as a religion, and the whole force of education, of institutions, and of opinion, directed, as it once was in the case of religion, to make every person grow up from infancy surrounded on all sides both by the profession and the practice of it, I think that no one who can realize this conception will feel any misgiving about the sufficiency of the ultimate sanction for the happiness morality.

CHAPTER IV. OF WHAT SORT OF PROOF THE PRINCIPLE OF UTILITY IS SUSCEPTIBLE

To be incapable of proof by reasoning is common to all first principles, to the first premises of our knowledge, as well as to those of our conduct. But the former, being matters of fact, may be the subject of a direct appeal to the faculties which judge of fact—namely, our senses and our internal consciousness. Can an appeal be made to the same faculties on questions of practical ends? Or by what other faculty is cognizance taken of them?

Questions about ends are, in other words, questions about what things are desirable. The utilitarian doctrine is that happiness is desirable, and the only thing desirable, as an end; all other things being only desirable as means to that end. What ought to be required of this doctrine, what conditions is it requisite that the doctrine should fulfill—to make good its claim to be believed?

The only proof capable of being given that an object is visible is that people actually see it. The only proof that a sound is audible is that people hear it; and so of the other sources of our experience. In like manner, I apprehend, the sole evidence it is possible to produce that anything is desirable is that people do actually desire it. If the end which the utilitarian doctrine proposes to itself were not, in theory and in practice, acknowledged to be an end, nothing could ever convince any person that it was so. No reason can be given why the general happiness is desirable, except that each person, so far as he believes it to be attainable, desires his own happiness. This, however, being a fact, we have not only all the proof which the case admits of, but all which it is possible to require, that happiness is a good; that each person's happiness is a good to that person, and the general happiness, therefore, a good to the aggregate of all persons. Happiness has made out its title as *one* of the ends of conduct, and consequently one of the criteria of morality.

But it has not, by this alone, proved itself to be the sole criterion. To do that, it would seem, by the same rule, necessary to show, not only that people desire happiness, but that they never desire anything else. Now it is palpable that they do desire things which, in common language, are decidedly distinguished from happiness. They desire, for example, virtue and the absence of vice, no less really than pleasure and the absence of pain. The desire of virtue is not as universal, but it is as authentic a fact as the desire of happiness. And hence the opponents of the utilitarian standard deem that they have a right to infer that there are other ends of human action besides happiness, and that happiness is not the standard of approbation and disapprobation.

But does the utilitarian doctrine deny that people desire virtue, or maintain that virtue is not a thing to be desired? The very reverse. It maintains not only what virtue is to be desired, but that it is to be desired distinterestedly, for itself. Whatever may be the opinion of utilitarian moralists as to the original conditions by which virtue is made virtue, however they may believe (as they do) that actions and dispositions are only virtuous because they promote another end than virtue, yet this being granted, and it having been decided, from considerations of this description, what *is* virtuous, they not only place virtue at the very head of the things which are good as means to the ultimate end, but they also recognize as a psychological fact the possibility of its being, to the individual, a good in itself, without looking to any end beyond it; and hold that the mind is not in a right state, not in a state conformable to utility, not in the state most conducive to the general happiness, unless it does love virtue in this manner—as a thing desirable in itself, even although, in the individual instance, it should not produce those other desirable consequences which it tends to produce, and on account of which it is held to be virtue. This opinion is not, in the smallest degree, a departure from the happiness principle. The ingredients of happiness are very various, and each of them is desirable in itself, and not merely when considered as swelling an aggregate. The principle of utility does not mean that any given pleasure, as music, for instance, or any given exemption from pain, as for example health, is to be looked upon as means to a collective something termed happiness, and to be desired on that account. They are desired and desirable in and for themselves; besides being means, they are a part of the end. Virtue, according to the utilitarian doctrine, is not naturally and originally part of the end, but it is capable of becoming so; and in those who love it disinterestedly it has become so, and is desired and cherished, not as a means to happiness, but as a part of their happiness. . . .

Virtue, according to the utilitarian conception, is a good of this description. There was no original desire of it, or motive to it, save its conduciveness to pleasure, and especially to protection from pain. But through the association thus formed it may be felt a good in itself, and desired as such with as great intensity as any other good; and with this difference between it and the love of money, of power, or of fame, that all of these may, and often do, render the individual noxious to the other members of the society to which he belongs, whereas there is nothing which makes him so much a blessing to them as the cultivation of the disinterested love of virtue. And consequently, the utilitarian standard, while it tolerates and approves those other acquired desires, up to the point beyond which they would be more injurious to the general happiness than promotive of it, enjoins and requires the cultivation of the love of virtue up to the greatest strength possible, as being above all things important to the general happiness.

It results from the preceding considerations that there is in reality nothing desired except happiness. Whatever is desired otherwise than as a means to some end beyond itself, and ultimately to happiness, is desired as itself a part of happiness, and is not desired for itself until it has become so. Those who desire virtue for its own sake desire it either because the consciousness of it is a pleasure, or because the consciousness of being without it is a pain, or for both reasons united; as in truth the pleasure and pain seldom exist separately, but almost always together—the same person feeling pleasure in the degree of virtue attained, and pain in not having attained more. If one of these gave him no pleasure, and the other no pain, he would not love or desire virtue, or would desire it only for the other benefits which it might produce to himself or to persons whom he cared for.

We have now, then, an answer to the question, of what sort of proof the principle of utility is susceptible. If the opinion which I have now stated is psychologically true—if human nature is so constituted as to desire nothing which is not either a part of happiness or a means of happiness, we can have no other proof, and we require no other, that these are the only things desirable. If so, happiness is the sole end of human action, and the promotion of it the test by which to judge of all human conduct; from whence it necessarily follows that it must be the criterion of morality, since a part is included in the whole.

And now to decide whether this is really so, whether mankind do desire nothing for itself but that which is a pleasure to them, or of which the absence is a pain, we have evidently arrived at a question of fact and experience, dependent, like all similar questions, upon evidence. It can only be determined by practised self-consciousness and self-observation, assisted by observation of others. I believe that these sources of evidence, impartially consulted, will declare that desiring a thing and finding it pleasant, aversion to it and thinking of it as painful, are phenomena entirely inseparable or rather two parts of the same phenomenon; in strictness of language, two different modes of naming the same psychological fact; that to think of an object as desirable (unless for the sake of its consequences) and to think of it as pleasant are one and the same thing; and that to desire anything except in proportion as the idea of it is pleasant, is a physical and metaphysical impossibility.

So obvious does this appear to me that I expect it will hardly be disputed; and the objection made will be, not that desire can possibly be directed to anything ultimately except pleasure and exemption from pain, but that the will is a different thing from desire; that a person of confirmed virtue or any other person whose purposes are fixed carries out his purposes without any thought of the pleasure he has in contemplating them or expects to derive from their fulfilment, and persists in acting on them, even though these pleasures are much diminished by changes in his character or decay of his passive sensibilities, or are outweighed by the pains which the pursuit of the purposes may bring upon him. All this I fully admit and have stated it elsewhere as positively and empathically as anyone. Will, the active phenomenon, is a different thing from desire, the state of passive sensibility, and, though originally an offshoot from it, may in time take root and detach itself from the parent stock, so much so that in the case of an habitual purpose, instead of willing the thing because we desire it, we often desire it only because we will it. This, however, is but an instance of that familiar fact, the power of habit, and is nowise confined to the case of virtuous actions. Many indifferent things which men originally did from a motive of some sort, they continue to do from habit. Sometimes this is done unconsciously; the consciousness coming only after the action; at other times with conscious volition, but volition which has become habitual is put in operation by the force of habit, in opposition perhaps to the deliberate preference, as often happens to those who have contracted habits of vicious or hurtful indulgence. Third and last comes the case in which the habitual act of will in the individual instance is not in contradiction to the general intention prevailing at other times, but in fulfilment of it; as in the case of the person of confirmed virtue and of all who pursue deliberately and consistently any determinate end. The distinction between will and desire thus understood is an authentic and highly important psychological fact; but the fact consists solely in this—that will, like all other parts of our constitution, is amenable to habit, and that we may will from habit what we no longer desire for itself, or desire only because we will it. It is not the less true that will, in the beginning, is entirely produced by desire; including in that term the repelling influence of pain as well as the attractive one of pleasure. Let us take into consideration no longer the person who has a confirmed will to do right, but him in whom that virtuous will is still feeble, conquerable by temptation, and not to be fully relied on; by what means can it be strengthened? How can the will to be virtuous, where it does not exist in sufficient force, be implanted or awakened? Only by making the person *desire* virtue—by making him think of it in a pleasurable light, or of its absence in a painful one. It is by associating the doing right with pleasure, or the doing wrong with pain, or by eliciting and impressing and bringing home to the person's experience the pleasure naturally involved in the one or the pain in the other that it is possible to call forth that will to be virtuous which, when confirmed, acts without any thought of either pleasure or pain. Will is the child of desire, and passes out of the dominion of its parent only to come under that of habit. That which is the result of habit affords no presumption of being intrinsically good; and there would be no reason for wishing that the purpose of virtue should become independent of pleasure and pain were it not that the influence of the pleasurable and painful associations which prompt to virtue is not sufficiently to be depended on for unerring constancy of action until it has acquired the support of habit. Both in feeling and in conduct, habit is the only thing which imparts certainty; and it is because of the importance to others of being able to rely absolutely on one's feelings and conduct, and to oneself of being able to rely on one's own, that the will to do right ought to be cultivated into this habitual independence. In other words, this state of the will is a means to good, not intrinsically a good; and does not contradict the doctrine that nothing is a good to human beings but in so far as it is either itself pleasurable or a means of attaining pleasure or averting pain.

But if this doctrine be true, the principle of utility is proved. Whether it is so or not, must now be left to the consideration of the thoughtful reader.

SØREN KIERKEGAARD

Søren Kierkegaard (1813–1855) is usually regarded as the father of modern existentialism. It was not, however, until the start of World War II that his works began to circulate in translation and his name became well known. Most of the leading figures of contemporary existentialism now acknowledge their debt to him as the inspirer of their innovations.

Though he was the son of a successful merchant and was nurtured in a conservative and conventional society, Kierkegaard was a caustic critic of the church, the society, and the dominant Hegelian philosophy of his day. Despite his short life, his writings are extensive; they are also repetitious and hastily written. In 1843, for instance, he published no fewer than six books, including his longest. Frantic intensity seems to have driven him; this is evident in the autobiographical and psychological elements so often at the forefront in his work.

The short opening selection from his Journals *is typical of the way in which existentialist writing is intimately connected to the writer's personal life. Like the other selections, it indicates the crucial role that decision plays in the formation of personality; it reveals the psychological tone of "despair" and the stress on the importance of "subjectivity," which are so characteristic of all existentialism.*

*The Journals: What I Am to Do**

Gilleleie, August 1, 1835

What I really lack is to be clear in my mind *what I am to do,* not what I am to know, except in so far as a certain understanding must precede every action. The thing is to understand myself, to see what God really wishes *me* to do; the thing is to find a truth which is true *for me,* to find *the idea for which I can live and die.* What would be the use of discovering so-called objective truth, of working through all the systems of philosophy and of being able, if required, to review them

* By permission. *The Journals of Kierkegaard,* trans. and ed. by Alexander Dru. Harper & Brothers, New York, 1959.

all and show up the inconsistencies within each system;—what good would it do me to be able to develop a theory of the state and combine all the details into a single whole, and so construct a world in which I did not live, but only held up to the view of others;—what good would it do me to be able to explain the meaning of Christianity if it had *no* deeper significance *for me and for my life;*—what good would it do me if truth stood before me, cold and naked, not caring whether I recognised her or not, and producing in me a shudder of fear rather than a trusting devotion? I certainly do not deny that I still recognise an *imperative of understanding* and that through it one can work upon men, *but it must be taken up into my life,* and *that is* what I now recognise as the most important thing. That is what my soul longs after, as the African desert thirsts for water.

Either / Or*

The Unhappiest Man

In each of Hegel's systematic writings there is a section which treats of the unhappy consciousness. One approaches the reading of such inquiries with an inner restlessness, with a trembling of the heart, with a fear lest one learn too much, or too little. The unhappy consciousness is a term which, when casually introduced, almost makes the blood run cold, and the nerves to quiver; and then to see it so expressly emphasized, like the mysterious sentence in a story of Clemens Brentano's, *tertia nux mors est*[1]—it is enough make one tremble like a sinner. Ah, happy he who has nothing more to do with it than to write a paragraph on the subject, happier still, he who can write the next. The unhappy person is one who has his ideal, the content of his life, the fullness of his consciousness, the essence of his being, in some manner outside of himself. He is always absent, never present to himself. But it is evident that it is possible to be absent from one's self either in the past or in the future. This, then, at once circumscribes the entire territory of the unhappy consciousness. For this rigid limitation we are grateful to Hegel; and now, since we are not merely philosophers beholding the kingdom from afar, we shall as native inhabitants give our attention in detail to the various types which are implied herein. The unhappy person is consequently absent. But one is absent when living either in the past or in the future. The form of expression must here be carefully noted; for it is clear, as philology also teaches us, that there is a tense which expresses presence in the past, and a tense which expresses presence in the future; but the same science also teaches us that there is a tense which is *plus quam perfectum,* in which there is no present, as well as a *futurum exactum* of an analogous character. Now there are some individuals who live in hope, and others who live in memory. These are indeed in a sense unhappy individuals, in so far, namely, as they live solely in hope or in memory, if ordinarily only he is happy who is present to himself. However, one cannot in a strict sense be called an unhappy individual, who is present in hope or in memory. That which must here be emphasized is that he is present to himself in one or the other of these forms of consciousness. We shall also see from this that a single blow, be it ever so heavy, cannot possibly make a man the unhappiest of all. For one blow can either deprive him of hope, thereby leaving him present in memory, or of memory, thus leaving him present in hope. We now go

* By permission. From Søren Kierkegaard, *Either/Or,* trans. by David F. Swenson and Lillian Swenson, rev. Howard A. Johnson, Princeton University Press, Princeton, N.J. 1959.

[1] "The third nut is death." (Clemens Brentano, *The Three Nuts.*)

on to get a more detailed description of the unhappy individual.

First we shall consider the man of hope. When he as a hoping individual (and in so far, of course, unhappy) is not present to himself in his hope, then he becomes in the stricter sense unhappy. An individual who hopes for an eternal life is, indeed, in a certain sense unhappy, since he has renounced the present, but not yet in the strict sense, because he is himself present in this hope, and does not come into conflict with the individual moments of the finite life. But if he does not become present to himself in this hope, but loses his hope and then hopes again and again loses, and so on, he is absent from himself, not only with respect to the present, but also with respect to the future; this gives us one type of the unhappy consciousness. In the case of the man of memory the case is parallel. If he can find himself present in the past, he is not in the strict sense unhappy; but if he cannot, but is constantly absent from himself in the past, then we have another type of unhappiness.

Memory is emphatically the real element of the unhappy, as is natural, because the past has the remarkable characteristic that it is past, the future, that it is yet to come, whence one may say that in a certain sense the future is nearer the present than is the past. In order that the man of hope may be able to find himself in the future, the future must have reality, or, rather, it must have reality for him; in order that the man of memory may find himself in the past, the past must have had reality for him. But when the man of hope would have a future which can have no reality for him, or the man of memory would remember a past which has had no reality, then we have the essentially unhappy individuals. It might seem as if the first supposition were impossible, or sheer lunacy; however, it is not so; for though the hoping individual does not hope for something which has no reality for him, he may nevertheless hope for something which he himself knows cannot be realized. For when an individual loses his hope, and then instead of taking refuge in memory, continues to hope, then we have such a type. When an individual who loses his memory, or who has nothing to remember, will not become a hoping individual, but continues to be a man of memory, then we have one type of unhappiness. If thus an individual buried himself in antiquity, or in the Middle Ages, or in any other period of time so that this had an authentic reality for him, or if he lost himself in his own childhood or youth, so that these things had an authentic reality for him, then he would not in a strict sense be an unhappy individual. On the other hand, if I imagine a man who himself had had no childhood, this age having passed him by without attaining essential significance for him, but who now, perhaps by becoming a teacher of youth, discovered all the beauty that there is in childhood, and who would now remember his own childhood, constantly staring back at it, then I should have an excellent illustration of this type of unhappiness. Too late he would have discovered the significance of that which was past for him but which he still desired to remember in its significance. If I imagined a man who had lived without real appreciation of the pleasures or joy of life, and who now on his deathbed gets his eyes opened to these things, if I imagined that he did not die (which would be the most fortunate thing) but lived on, though without living his life over again—such a man would have to be considered in our quest for the unhappiest man.

The unhappiness of hope is never so painful as the unhappiness of memory. The man of hope always has a more tolerable disappointment to bear. It follows that the unhappiest man will have to be sought among the unhappy individuals of memory.

Let us proceed. Let us imagine a combination of the two stricter types of unhappiness already described. The unhappy man of hope could not find himself present in his hope, just as the unhappy man of memory could not find himself present in his memory. There can be but one combination of these two types, and this happens when it is memory which prevents the unhappy individual from finding himself in his hope, and hope which prevents him from finding himself in his memory. When this happens, it is, on the one hand, due to the fact that he constantly hopes something that should be remembered; his hope constantly disappoints him and, in disappointing him, reveals to him that it is not because the realization of his hope is postponed, but because it is already past and gone, has already been experienced, or should have been experienced, and thus has passed over into memory. On the other hand, it is due to the fact that he always remembers that for which he ought to hope; for the future he has already anticipated in thought, in thought already experienced it, and this experience he now remembers, instead of hoping for it. Consequently, what he hopes for lies behind him, what he remembers lies before him. His life is not so much lived regressively as it suffers a two-fold reversal. He will soon notice his misfortune even if he is not able to understand the reason for it. To make sure, however, that he really shall have opportunity to feel it, misunderstanding puts in its appearance to mock him at each moment in a curious way.

In the ordinary course of things, he enjoys the reputation of being in full possession of his five senses, and yet he knows that if he were to explain to a single person just how it is with him, he would be declared mad. This is quite enough to drive a man mad, and yet he does not become so, and this is precisely his misfortune. His misfortune is that he has come into the world too soon, and therefore he always comes too late. He is constantly quite near his goal, and in the same moment he is far away from it; he finds that what now makes him unhappy because he has it, or because he is this way, is just what a few years ago would have made him happy if he had had it then, while then he was unhappy because he did not have it. His life is empty, like that of Ancaeus, of whom it is customary to say that nothing is known about him except that he gave rise to the proverb: "There's many a slip 'twixt the cup and the lip"—as if this was not more than enough. His life is restless and without content; he does not live in the present, he does not live in the future, for the future has already been experienced; he does not live in the past, for the past has not yet come. So like Latona, he is driven about in the Hyperborean darkness, or to the bright isles of the equator, and cannot bring to birth though he seems constantly on the verge. Alone by himself he stands in the wide world. He has no contemporary time to support him; he has no past to long for, since his past has not yet come; he has no future to hope for, since his future is already past. Alone, he has the whole world over against him as the *alter* with which he finds himself in conflict; for the rest of the world is to him only one person, and this person, this inseparable, importunate friend, is Misunderstanding. He cannot become old, for he has never been young; he cannot become young, for he is already old. In one sense of the word he cannot die, for he has not really lived; in another sense he cannot live, for he is already dead. He cannot love, for love is in the present, and he has no present, no future, and no past; and yet he has a sympathetic nature, and he hates the world only because he loves it. He has no passion, not because he is destitute of it, but because simultaneously he has the opposite passion. He has no time for anything, not because his time is taken up with something else, but because he has no time at all. He is impotent, not because he has no energy, but because his own energy makes him impotent.

Equilibrium between the Aesthetical and the Ethical in the Composition of Personality

My Friend,

What I have so often said to you I say now once again, or rather I shout it: Either/or. . . . I think of my early youth, when without clearly comprehending what it is to make a choice I listened with childish trust to the talk of my elders and the instant of choice was solemn and venerable, although in choosing I was only following the instructions of another person. I think of the occasions in my later life when I stood at the crossways, when my soul was matured in the hour of decision. I think of the many occasions in life less important but by no means indifferent to me, when it was a question of making a choice. For although there is only one situation in which either/or has absolute significance, namely, when truth, righteousness and holiness are lined up on one side, and lust and base propensities and obscure passions and perdition on the other; yet, it is always important to choose rightly, even as between things which one may innocently choose; it is important to test oneself, lest some day one might have to beat a painful retreat to the point from which one started, and might have reason to thank God if one had to reproach oneself for nothing worse than a waste of time. In common parlance I use these words as others use them, and it would indeed be a foolish pedantry to give up using them. But sometimes it occurs, nevertheless, that I become aware of using them with regard to things entirely indifferent. Then they lay aside their humble dress, I forget the insignificant thoughts they discriminated, they advance to meet me with all their dignity, in their official robes. As a magistrate in common life may appear in plain clothes and mingle without distinction in the crowd, so do these words mingle in common speech—when, however, the magistrate steps forward with authority he distinguishes himself from all. Like such a magistrate whom I am accustomed to see only on solemn occasions, these words appear before me, and my soul always becomes serious. And although my life now has to a certain degree its either/or behind it, yet I know well that it may still encounter many a situation where the either/or will have its full significance. I hope, however, that these words may find me in a worthy state of mind when they check me on my path, and I hope that I may be successful in choosing the right course; at all events, I shall endeavor to make the choice with real earnestness, and with that I venture, at least, to hope that I shall the sooner get out of the wrong path. . . .

But now mark well what I would say to you, young man—for though you are not young, one is always compelled to address you as such. Now what did you do in this case? You acknowledged, as ordinarily you are not willing to do, the importance of an either/or. And why? Because your soul was moved by love for the young man. And yet in a way you deceived him, for he will, perhaps, encounter you at another time when it by no means suits your convenience to acknowledge this importance. Here you see one of the sorry consequences of the fact that a man's nature cannot harmoniously reveal itself. You thought you were doing the best for him, and yet perhaps you have harmed him; perhaps he would have been better able to maintain himself over against your distrust of life than to find repose in the subjective, deceitful trust you conveyed to him. Imagine that after the lapse of several years you again encountered him; he was lively, witty, intellectual, daring in his thought, bold in his expression, but your ear easily detected doubt in his soul, you conceived a suspicion that he had acquired the questionable wisdom: I say merely either/or. It is true, is it not, that you would be sorry for him, would feel that he had lost something, and something very essential. But for yourself you will not sorrow, you are content with your ambiguous wisdom, yea, proud of it, so proud that you will not suffer another to share it, since you wish to be alone with it. And yet you find it deplorable in another connection, and it is your sincere opinion that it was deplorable for the young man to have reached the same wisdom. What a monstrous contradiction! Your whole nature contradicts itself. But you can only get out of this contradiction by an either/or, and I, who love you more sincerely than you loved this young man, I, who in my life have experienced the significance of choice, I congratulate you upon the fact that you are still so young, that even though you always will be sensible of some loss, yet, if you have, or rather if you will to have the requisite energy, you can win what is the chief thing in life, win yourself, acquire your own self.

Now in case a man were able to maintain himself upon the pinnacle of the instant of choice, in case he could cease to be a man, in case he were in his inmost nature only an airy thought, in case personality meant nothing more than to be a kobold, which takes part, indeed, in the movements but nevertheless remains unchanged; in case such were the situation, it would be foolish to say that it might ever be too late for a man to choose, for in a deeper sense there could be no question of a choice. The choice itself is decisive for the content of the personality, through the choice the personality immerses itself in the thing chosen, and when it does not choose it withers away in consumption. For an instant it is so, for an instant it may seem as if the things between which a choice is to be made lie outside of the chooser, that he stands in no relationship to it, that he can preserve a state of indifference over against it. This is the instant of deliberation, but this, like the Platonic instant, has no existence, least of all in the abstract sense in which you would hold it fast, and the longer one stares at it the less it exists. That which has to be chosen stands in the deepest relationship to the chooser, and when it is a question of a choice involving a life problem the individual must naturally be living in the meantime, and hence, it comes about that the longer he postpones the choice the easier it is for him to alter its character, notwithstanding that he is constantly deliberating and deliberating and believes that thereby he is holding the alternatives distinctly apart. When life's either/or is regarded in this way one is not easily tempted to jest with it. One sees, then, that the inner drift of the personality leaves no time for thought experiments, that it constantly hastens onward and in one way or another posits this alternative or that, making the choice more difficult the next instant because what has thus been posited must be revoked. Think of the captain on his ship at the instant when it has to come about. He will perhaps be able to say, "I can either do this or that"; but in case he is not a pretty poor navigator, he will be aware at the same time that the ship is all the while making its usual headway, and that therefore it is only an instant when it is indifferent whether he does this or that. So it is with a man. If he forgets to take account of the headway, there comes at last an instant when there no longer is any question of an either/or, not because he has chosen but because he has neglected to choose, which is equivalent to saying, because others have chosen for him, because he has lost his self.

You will perceive also in what I have just been saying how essentially my view of choice differs from yours (if you can properly be said to have any view), for yours differs precisely in the fact that it prevents you from choosing. For me the instant of choice is very serious, not so much on account of the rigorous cogitation involved in weighing the alternatives, not on account of the multiplicity of thoughts which attach themselves to every link in the chain, but rather because there is danger afoot, danger that the next instant it may not be equally in my power to choose, that something already has been lived which must be lived over again. For to think that for an instant one can keep one's personality a blank, or that strictly speaking one can break off and bring to a halt the course of the personal life, is a delusion. The personality is already interested in the choice before one chooses, and when the choice is postponed the personality chooses unconsciously, or the choice is made by obscure powers within it. So when at last the choice is made one discovers (unless, as I remarked before, the personality has been completely volatilized) that there is something which must be done over again, something which must be revoked, and this is often very difficult. We read in fairy tales about human beings whom mermaids and mermen enticed into their power by means of demoniac music. In order to break the enchantment it was necessary in the fairy tale for the person who was under the spell to play the same piece of music backwards without making a single mistake. This is very profound, but very difficult to perform, and yet so it is: the errors one has taken into oneself one must eradicate in this way, and every time one makes a mistake one must begin all over. Therefore, it is important to choose and to choose in time. You, on the contrary, have another method—for I know very well that the polemical side you turn towards the world is not your true nature. Yea, if to deliberate were the proper task for a human life, you would be pretty close to perfection. I will adduce an example. To fit your case the contrasts must be bold: either a parson/or an actor. Here is the dilemma. Now all your passionate energy is awakened, reflection with its hundred arms lays hold of the thought of being a parson. You find no repose, day and night you think about it, you read all the books you can lay your hands on, you go to church three times every Sunday, pick up acquaintance with parsons, write sermons yourself, deliver them to yourself; for half a year you are dead to the whole world. You can now talk of the clerical calling with more insight and apparently with more experience than many who have been parsons for twenty years. When you encounter such men it arouses your indignation that they do not know how to get the thing off their chests with more eloquence. "Is this enthusiasm?" you say. "Why I who am not a parson, who have not consecrated myself to this calling, speak with the voice of angels as compared with them." That, perhaps, is true enough, but neverthless, you have not become a parson. Then you act in the same way with respect to the other task, and your enthusiasm for art almost surpasses your clerical eloquence. Then you are ready to choose. However, one may be sure that in the prodigious thought-production you were engaged in there must have been lots of waste products, many incidental reflections and observations. Hence, the instant you have to choose, life and animation enter into this waste mass, a new either/or presents itself—jurist, perhaps advocate, this has something in common with both the other alternatives. Now you are lost. For that same moment you are at once advocate enough to be able to prove the reasonableness of taking the third possibility into account. So your life drifts on.

After you have wasted a year and a half on such deliberations, after you have with admirable energy exerted to the utmost the powers of your soul, you have not got one step further. You break the thread of thought, you become impatient, passionate, scolding and storming, and then you continue: "Either hairdresser/or bank teller; I say merely either/or." What wonder, then, that this saying has become for you an offense and foolishness, that it seems, as you say, as if it were like the arms attached to the iron maiden whose embrace was the death penalty. You treat people superciliously, you make sport of them, and what you have become is what you most abhor: a critic, a universal critic in all faculties. Sometimes I cannot help smiling at you, and yet it is pitiful to see how your really excellent intellectual gifts are thus dissipated. But here again there is the same contradiction in your nature; for you see the ludicrous very clearly, and God help him who falls into your hands if his case is similar to yours. And yet the whole difference is that he perhaps becomes downcast and broken, while you on the contrary become light and erect and merrier than ever, making yourself and others blissful with the gospel: *vanitas vanitatum vanitas,* hurrah! But this is no choice, it is what we call in Danish letting it go, or it is mediation like letting five count as an even number. Now you feel yourself free, you say to the world, farewell.

> *So zieh' ich hin in alle Ferne,*
> *Uber meiner Mütze nur die Sterne.*[2]

Therewith you have chosen . . . not to be sure, as you yourself will admit, the better part. But in reality you have not chosen at all, or it is in an improper sense of the word you have chosen. Your choice is an aesthetic choice, but an aesthetic choice is no choice. The act of choosing is essentially a proper and stringent expression of the ethical. Whenever in a stricter sense there is question of an either/or, one can always be sure that the ethical is involved. The only absolute either/or is the choice between good and evil, but that is also absolutely ethical. The aesthetic choice is either entirely immediate and to that extent no choice, or it loses itself in the multifarious. Thus, when a young girl follows the choice of her heart, this choice, however beautiful it may be, is in the strictest sense no choice, since it is entirely immediate. When a man deliberates aesthetically upon a multitude of life's problems, as you did in the foregoing, he does not easily get one either/or, but a whole multiplicity, because the self-determining factor in the choice is not ethically accentuated, and because when one does not choose absolutely one chooses only for the moment, and therefore can choose something different the next moment. The ethical choice is therefore in a certain sense much easier, much simpler, but in another sense it is infinitely harder. He who would define his life task ethically has ordinarily not so considerable a selection to choose from; on the other hand, the act of choice has far more importance for him. If you will understand me aright, I should like to say that in making a choice it is not so much a question of choosing the right as of the energy, the earnestness, the pathos with which one chooses. Thereby the personality announces its inner infinity, and thereby, in turn, the personality is consolidated. Therefore, even if a man were to choose the wrong, he will nevertheless discover, precisely by reason of the energy with which he chose, that he had chosen the wrong. For the choice being made with the whole inwardness of his personality, his nature is purified and he himself brought into immediate relation to the eternal Power whose omnipresence interpenetrates the whole of existence. This transfiguration, this higher consecration, is never attained by that man who chooses merely aestheti-

[2] Goethe, *West-östlicher Divan,* "Freiheit." The meaning of the couplet may be suggested by a free translation:

> *I give myself up to infinite space.*
> *And nothing but the stars are above my head.*

cally. The rhythm in that man's soul, in spite of all its passion, is only a *spiritus lenis*.

So, like a Cato I shout at you my either/or, and yet not like a Cato, for my soul has not yet acquired the resigned coldness which he possessed. But I know that only this incantation, if I have the strength for it, will be capable of rousing you, not to an activity of thought, for of that you have no lack, but to earnestness of spirit. Perhaps you will succeed without that in accomplishing much, perhaps even in astonishing the world (for I am not niggardly), and yet you will miss the highest thing, the only thing which truly gives meaning to life; perhaps you will gain the whole world and lose your own self.

What is it, then, that I distinguish in my either/or? Is it good and evil? No, I would only bring you up to the point where the choice between the evil and the good acquires significance for you. Everything hinges upon this. As soon as one can get a man to stand at the crossways in such a position that there is no recourse but to choose, he will choose the right. Hence, if it should chance that, while you are in the course of reading this somewhat lengthy dissertation, which again I send you in the form of a letter, you were to feel that the instant for choice had come, then throw the rest of this away, never concern yourself about it, you have lost nothing—but choose, and you shall see what validity there is in this act, yea, no young girl can be so happy with the choice of her heart as is a man who knows how to choose. So then, one either has to live aesthetically or one has to live ethically. In this alternative, as I have said, there is not yet in the strictest sense any question of a choice; for he who lives aesthetically does not choose, and he who after the ethical has manifested itself to him chooses the aesthetical is not living aesthetically, for he is sinning and is subject to ethical determinants even though his life may be described as unethical. Lo, this is, as it were, a *character indelebilis* impressed upon the ethical, that though it modestly places itself on a level with the aesthetical, it is nevertheless that which makes the choice a choice. And this is the pitiful thing to one who contemplates human life, that so many live on in a quiet state of perdition; they outlive themselves, not in the sense that the content of life is successively unfolding and now is possessed in this expanded state, but they live their lives, as it were, outside of themselves, they vanish like shadows, their immortal soul is blown away, and they are not alarmed by the problem of its immortality, for they are already in a state of dissolution before they die. They do not live aesthetically, but neither has the ethical manifested itself in its entirety, so they have not exactly rejected it either, they therefore are not sinning, except in so far as it is sin not to be either one thing or the other; neither are they ever in doubt about their immortality, for he who deeply and sincerely is in doubt of it on his own behalf will surely find the right. *On his own behalf*, I say, and surely it is high time to utter a warning against the greathearted, heroic objectivity with which many thinkers think on behalf of others and not on their own behalf. If one would call this which I here require selfishness, I would reply that this comes from the fact that people have no conception of what this "self" is, and that it would be of very little use to a man if he were to gain the whole world and lose himself, and that it must necessarily be a poor proof which does not first of all convince the man who presents it.

My either/or does not in the first instance denote the choice between good and evil; it denotes the choice whereby one chooses good *and* evil/or excludes them. Here the question is under what determinants one would contemplate the whole of existence and would himself live.

That the man who chooses good and evil chooses the good is indeed true, but this becomes evident only afterwards; for the aesthetical is not the evil but neutrality, and that is the reason why I affirmed that it is the ethical which constitutes the choice. It is, therefore, not so much a question of choosing between willing the good *or* the evil, as of choosing to will, but by this in turn the good and the evil are posited. He who chooses the ethical chooses the good, but here the good is entirely abstract, only its being is posited, and hence it does not follow by any means that the chooser cannot in turn choose the evil, in spite of the fact that he chose the good. Here you see again how important it is that a choice be made, and that the crucial thing is not deliberation but the baptism of the will which lifts up the choice into the ethical. The longer the time that elapses, the more difficult it is to choose, for the soul is constantly attached to one side of the dilemma, and it becomes more and more difficult, therefore, to tear oneself loose. . . .

*The Sickness unto Death: A Christian Psychological Exposition for Edification and Awakening**

The Universality of this Sickness (Despair)

Just as the physician might say that there lives perhaps not one single man who is in perfect health, so one might say perhaps that there lives not one single man who after all is not to some extent in despair, in whose inmost parts there does not dwell a disquietude, a perturbation, a discord, an anxious dread of an unknown something, or of a something he does not even dare to make acquaintance with, dread of a possibility of life, or dread of himself, so that, after all, as physicians speak of a man going about with a disease in him, this man is going about and carrying a sickness of the spirit, which only rarely and in glimpses, by and with a dread which to him is inexplicable, gives evidence of its presence within. At any rate there has lived no one and there lives no one outside of Christendom who is not in despair, and no one in Christendom, unless he be a true Christian, and if he is not quite that, he is somewhat in despair after all.

This view will doubtless seem to many a paradox, an exaggeration, and a gloomy and depressing view at that. Yet it is nothing of the sort. It is not gloomy; on the contrary, it seeks to throw light upon a subject which ordinarily is left in obscurity. It is not depressing; on the contrary it is uplifting, since it views every man in the aspect of the highest demand made upon him, that he be spirit. Nor is it a paradox; on the contrary, it is a fundamental apprehension consistently carried through, and hence it is no exaggeration.

On the other hand, the ordinary view of despair remains content with appearances, and so it is a superficial view, that is, no view at all. It assumes that every man must know by himself better than anyone else whether he is in despair or not. So whoever says that he is in despair is regarded as being in despair, but whoever thinks he is not in despair is not so regarded. Consequently despair becomes a rather rare phenomenon, whereas in fact it is quite universal. It is not a rare exception that one is in despair; no, the rare, the very rare exception is that one is not in despair.

But the vulgar view has a very poor understanding of despair. Among other things (to mention only one which, if rightly understood, would bring thousands, yea, millions under this category), it completely overlooks the fact that one form of despair is precisely this of not being in despair, that is, not being aware of it. The

* By permission. From Soren Kierkegaard, *The Sickness unto Death*, trans. by Walter Lowrie, Anchor Books, Doubleday & Company, Inc., New York, 1954.

vulgar view is exposed, though in a much deeper sense, to the same fallacy it sometimes falls into when it would determine whether a man is sick or not. In a much deeper sense, I say, for the vulgar view has a far more inadequate notion of spirit than of sickness and health—and without understanding spirit it is impossible to understand despair. It is ordinarily assumed that a man is well when he does not himself say that he is sick, and still more confidently when he says that he is well. The physician on the other hand regards sickness differently. And why? Because he has a definite and well thought out conception of what it is to be in sound health, and by this he tests the man's condition. The physician knows that just as there is sickness which is only imaginary, so also there is such a thing as fictitious health. In the latter case, therefore, the physician first employs medicines to cause the disease to become manifest. Generally the physician, just because he is a physician, i.e. the competent man, has no unconditional faith in a person's own assertion about the state of his health. If it were true that what every man says about the state of his health (as to whether he is sick or well, where he suffers, etc.) were absolutely to be relied upon, it would be an illusion to be a physician. For a physician does not merely have to prescribe medicines, but first and foremost he has to be acquainted with sickness, and so first and foremost to know whether a supposedly sick man really is sick, or whether a supposedly well man is not really sick. So it is also with the physician of souls when dealing with despair. He knows what despair is, he is acquainted with it, and hence he is not satisfied with a man's assertion that he is in despair or that he is not. For it must be observed that in a certain sense not even all who say they are in despair always are so. One may affect despair, and one may make a mistake and confuse despair with all sorts of transitory dejection or grief which pass away without coming to the point of despair. However, the physician of souls does, it is true, regard these states also as forms of despair. He perceives very well that this is affectation—but precisely this affectation is despair. He perceives very well that this dejection etc. does not mean much—but precisely this fact, that it does not mean much, is despair. . . .

The Forms of This Sickness, i.e. of Despair

The forms of despair must be discoverable abstractly by reflecting upon the factors which compose the self as a synthesis. The self is composed of infinity and finiteness. But the synthesis is a relationship, and it is a relationship which, though it is derived, relates itself to itself, which means freedom. The self is freedom. But freedom is the dialectical element in the terms possibility and necessity.

Principally, however, despair must be viewed under the category of consciousness: the question whether despair is conscious or not, determines the qualitative difference between despair and despair. In its concept all despair is doubtless conscious; but from this it does not follow that he in whom it exists, he to whom it can rightly be attributed in conformity with the concept, is himself conscious of it. It is in this sense that consciousness is decisive. Generally speaking, consciousness, i.e. consciousness of self, is the decisive criterion of the self. The more consciousness, the more self; the more consciousness, the more will, and the more will the more self. A man who has no will at all is no self; the more will he has, the more consciousness of self he has also. . . .

DESPAIR VIEWED UNDER THE ASPECT OF CONSCIOUSNESS

With every increase in the degree of consciousness, and in proportion to that increase, the intensity of despair increases: the more consciousness, the more intense the despair. This is everywhere to be seen, most clearly in the maximum and minimum of despair. The devil's despair is the most intense despair, for the devil is sheer spirit, and therefore absolute consciousness and transparency; in the devil there is no obscurity which might serve as a mitigating excuse, his despair is therefore absolute defiance. This is the maximum of despair. The minimum of despair is a state which (as one might humanly be tempted to express it) by reason of a sort of innocence does not even know that there is such a thing as despair. So when consciousness is at its minimum the despair is least; it is almost as if it were a dialectical problem whether one is justified in calling such a state despair.

THE DESPAIR WHICH IS UNCONSCIOUS THAT IT IS DESPAIR, OR THE DESPAIRING UNCONSCIOUSNESS OF HAVING A SELF AND AN ETERNAL SELF

That this condition is nevertheless despair and is rightly so denominated may be taken as an expression for a trait which we may call, in a good sense, the opinionativeness of truth. *Veritas est index sui et falsi.*[3] But this opinionativeness of truth is, to be sure, held in scant honor, as also it is far from being the case that men in general regard relationship to the truth, the fact of standing in relationship to the truth, as the highest good, and it is very far from being the case that they, Socratically, regard being under a delusion as the greatest misfortune; their sensuous nature is generally predominant over their intellectuality. So when a man is supposed to be happy, he imagines that he is happy (whereas viewed in the light of the truth he is unhappy), and in this case he is generally very far from wishing to be torn away from that delusion. On the contrary, he becomes furious, he regards the man who does this as his most spiteful enemy, he considers it an insult, something near to murder, in the sense that one speaks of killing joy. What is the reason of this? The reason is that the sensuous nature and the psycho-sensuous completely dominate him; the reason is that he lives in the sensuous categories agreeable/disagreeable, and says goodbye to truth etc.; the reason is that he is too sensuous to have the courage to venture to be spirit or to endure it. However vain and conceited men may be, they have nevertheless for the most part a very lowly conception of themselves, that is to say, they have no conception of being spirit, the absolute of all that a man can be—but vain and conceited they are . . . by way of comparison. In the case one were to think of a house, consisting of cellar, ground-floor and *premier étage,* so tenanted, or rather so arranged, that it was planned for a distinction of rank between the dwellers on the several floors; and in case one were to make a comparison between such a house and what it is to be a man—then unfortunately this is the sorry and ludicrous condition of the majority of men, that in their own house they prefer to live in the cellar. The soulish-bodily synthesis in every man is planned with a view to being spirit, such is the building; but the man prefers to dwell in the cellar, that is, in the determinants of sensuousness. And not only does he prefer to dwell in the cellar; no, he loves that to such a degree that he becomes furious if anyone would propose to him to occupy the *bel étage* which stands empty at his disposition—for in fact he is dwelling in his own house.

No, to be in error or delusion is (quite un-Socratically) the thing they fear the least. One may behold amazing examples which illustrate this fact on a prodigious scale. A thinker erects an immense building, a system, a system which embraces the whole of existence and world-history etc.—and if we contemplate his

[3] Truth is the criterion of itself and of falsehood—quoted loosely from Spinoza's *Ethics,* Propositio 11, Scholium 43.

personal life, we discover to our astonishment this terrible and ludicrous fact, that he himself personally does not live in this immense high-vaulted palace, but in a barn alongside of it, or in a dog kennel, or at the most in the porter's lodge. If one were to take liberty of calling his attention to this by a single word, he would be offended. For he has not fear of being under a delusion, if only he can get the system completed . . . by means of the delusion.

So then, the fact that the man in despair is unaware that his condition is despair, has nothing to do with the case, he is in despair all the same. If despair is bewilderment (*Forvildelse*), then the fact that one is unconscious of it is the additional aggravation of being at the same time under a delusion (*Vildfarelse*). . . .

The despairing man who is unconscious of being in despair is, in comparison with him who is conscious of it, merely a negative step further from the truth and from salvation. Despair itself is a negativity, unconsciousness of it is a new negativity. But to reach truth one must pierce through every negativity. For here applies what the fairy-tale recounts about a certain enchantment: the piece of music must be played through backwards; otherwise the enchantment is not broken. However, it is only in one sense, in a purely dialectical sense, that he who is unconscious of despair is further away from truth and salvation than the man who is conscious of his despair and yet remains in it. For in another sense, an ethical-dialectic sense, the despairing man who consciously remains in despair is further from salvation, since his despair is more intense. But unawareness is so far from removing despair, or of transforming despair into non-despair, that, on the contrary, it may be the most dangerous form of despair. By unconsciousness the despairing man is in a way secured (but to his own destruction) against becoming aware—that is, he is securely in the power of despair.

In unconsciousness of being in despair a man is furthest from being conscious of himself as spirit. But precisely the thing of not being conscious of oneself as spirit is despair, which is spiritlessness—whether the condition be that of complete deadness, a merely vegetative life, or a life of higher potency the secret of which is nevertheless despair. In the latter instance the man is like the sufferer from consumption: he feels well, considers himself in the best of health, seems perhaps to others to be in florid health, precisely when the sickness is most dangerous.

This form of despair (i.e. unconsciousness of it) is the commonest in the world—yes, in what people call the world, or, to define it more exactly, what Christianity calls "the world," i.e. paganism, and the natural man in Christendom. Paganism as it historically was and is, and paganism within Christendom, is precisely this sort of despair, it is despair but does not know it. . . .

*Concluding Unscientific Postscript**

Part Two
How the Subjectivity of the Individual Must be Qualified in Order That the Problem May Exist for Him

THE TASK OF BECOMING SUBJECTIVE

Objectively we consider only the matter at issue, subjectively we have regard to the subject and his subjectivity; and behold, precisely this subjectivity is the matter at issue. This must constantly be borne in mind, namely, that the subjective problem is not something about an objective

* By permission. From Søren Kierkegaard, *Concluding Unscientific Postscript*, trans. by David F. Swenson and Walter Lowrie, Princeton University Press, Princeton, N.J., 1944.

issue, but is the subjectivity itself. For since the problem in question poses a decision, and since all decisiveness inheres in subjectivity, it is essential that every trace of an objective issue should be eliminated. If any such trace remains, it is at once a sign that the subject seeks to shirk something of the pain and crisis of the decision; that is, he seeks to make the problem to some degree objective. If the Introduction still awaits the appearance of another work before bringing the matter up for judgment, if the System still lacks a paragraph, if the speaker has still another argument up his sleeve, it follows that the decision is postponed. Hence we do not here raise the question of the truth of Christianity in the sense that when this has been determined, the subject is assumed ready and willing to accept it. No, the question is as to the mode of the subject's acceptance; and it must be regarded as an illusion rooted in the demoralization which remains ignorant of the subjective nature of the decision, or as an evasion springing from the disingenuousness which seeks to shirk the decision by an objective mode of approach, wherein there can in all eternity be no decision, to assume that the transition from something objective to the subjective acceptance is a direct transition, following upon the objective deliberation as a matter of course. On the contrary, the subjective acceptance is precisely the decisive factor; and an objective acceptance of Christianity (*sit venia verbo*) is paganism or thoughtlessness. . . .

The objective tendency, which proposes to make everyone an observer, and in its maximum to transform him into so objective an observer that he becomes almost a ghost, scarcely to be distinguished from the tremendous spirit of the historical past—this tendency naturally refuses to know or listen to anything except what stands in relation to itself. If one is so fortunate as to be of service within the given presupposition, by contributing one or another item of information concerning a tribe perhaps hitherto unknown, which is to be provided with a flag and given a place in the paragraph parade; if one is competent within the given presupposition to assign China a place different from the one it has hitherto occupied in the systematic procession,—in that case one is made welcome. But everything else is divinity-school prattle. For it is regarded as a settled thing, that the objective tendency in direction of intellectual contemplation is, in the newer linguistic usage, the *ethical* answer to the question of what I *ethically* have to do; and the task assigned to the contemplative nineteenth century is world history. The objective tendency is the way and the truth; the ethical is, becoming an observer! That the individual must become an observer, is the *ethical* answer to the problem of life —or else one is compelled to assume that there is no ethical question at all, and in so far no ethical answer.

Let us here in all simplicity seek to bring clearly before our minds a little subjective doubt with respect to the tendency toward objectivity. . . . The question I would ask is this: *What conclusion would inevitably force itself upon Ethics, if the becoming a subject were not the highest task confronting a human being?* And to what conclusion would Ethics be forced? Aye, it would, of course, be driven to despair. But what does the System care about that? It is consistent enough not to include an Ethic in its systematic scheme.

The Idea of a universal history tends to a greater and greater systematic concentration of everything. A Sophist has said that he could carry the whole world in a nutshell, and this is what modern surveys of world history seem to realize: the survey becomes more and more compendious. It is not my intention to show how comical this is, but rather to try to make it clear, through the elaboration of several different thoughts all leading to the same end, what objection Ethics and the ethical have to raise against this entire order of things. For in our age it is not merely an individual scholar or thinker here and there who concerns himself with universal history; the whole age loudly demands it. Nevertheless, Ethics and the ethical, as constituting the essential anchorage for all individual existence, have an indefeasible claim upon every existing individual; so indefeasible a claim, that whatever a man may accomplish in the world, even to the most astonishing of achievements, it is none the less quite dubious in its significance, unless the individual has been ethically clear when he made his choice, has ethically clarified his choice to himself. The ethical quality is jealous for its own integrity, and is quite unimpressed by the most astounding quantity.

It is for this reason that Ethics looks upon all world-historical knowledge with a degree of suspicion, because it may so easily become a snare, a demoralizing aesthetic diversion for the knowing subject, in so far as the distinction between what does or does not have historical significance obeys a quantitative dialectic. As a consequence of this fact, the absolute ethical distinction between good and evil tends for the historical survey to be neutralized in the aesthetic-metaphysical determination of the great and significant, to which category the bad has equal admittance with the good. In the case of what has world-historic significance, another set of factors plays an essential rôle, factors which do not obey an ethical dialectic: accidents, circumstances, the play of forces entering into the historic totality that modifyingly incorporates the deed of the individual so as to transform it into something that does not directly belong to him. Neither by willing the good with all his strength, nor by satanic obduracy in willing what is evil, can a human being be assured of historical significance. Even in the case of misfortune the principle holds, that it is necessary to be fortunate in order that one's misfortune may obtain world-historical significance. How then does an individual acquire historical significance? By means of what from the ethical point of view is accidental. But Ethics regards as unethical the transition by which an individual renounces the ethical quality in order to try his fortune, longingly, wishingly, and so forth, in the quantitative and non-ethical.

An age or an individual may be immoral in many different ways. It is also a form of immorality, or at any rate constitutes a temptation, for an individual to practise too assiduous an intercourse with the historical, since this may readily lead him to crave world-historical significance when the time comes for him to act for himself. Through an absorption in constant contemplation of the accidental, of that *accessorium* through which historical figures become historical, one may easily be misled into confusing this with the ethical; and instead of concerning oneself infinitely with the ethical, one may existentially be betrayed into developing an unwholesome, frivolous and cowardly concern for the accidental. This is possibly the reason why the contemporary age is seized with discontent when it confronts the necessity of action, because it has been spoiled by the habit of contemplation; and from this proceed, perhaps, the many sterile attempts to count for more than one by socially clubbing together, hoping thus numerically to overawe the spirit of history. Demoralized by too assiduous an absorption in world-historical considerations, people no longer have any will for anything except what is world-historically significant, no concern for anything but the accidental, the world-historical outcome, instead of concerning themselves solely with the essential, the inner spirit, the ethical, freedom. . . .

For the study of the ethical, every man is assigned to himself. His own self is as material for this study more than sufficient; aye, this is the only place where *he* can study it with any assurance of certainty. Even another human being with whom he lives can reveal himself to his observation only through the external; and in so far the interpretation is necessarily affected with ambiguities. But the more complicated the externality in which the ethical inwardness is reflected, the more difficult becomes the problem of observation, until it finally loses its way in something quite different, namely, in the aesthetic. . . .

*Fear and Trembling**

Is There Such a Thing as a Teleological Suspension of the Ethical?

The ethical as such is the universal, and as the universal it applies to everyone, which may be expressed from another point of view by saying that it applies every instant. It reposes immanently in itself, it has nothing without itself which is its *telos,* but is itself *telos* for everything outside it, and when this has been incorporated by the ethical it can go no further. Conceived immediately as physical and psychical, the particular individual is the individual who has his *telos* in the universal, and his ethical task is to express himself constantly in it, to abolish his particularity in order to become the universal. As soon as the individual would assert himself in his particularity over against the universal he sins, and only by recognizing this can he again reconcile himself with the universal. Whenever the individual after he has entered the universal feels an impulse to assert himself as the particular, he is in temptation (*Anfechtung*), and he can labor himself out of this only by penitently abandoning himself as the particular in the universal. If this be the highest thing that can be said of man and of his existence, then the ethical has the same character as man's eternal blessedness, which to all eternity and at every instant is his *telos,* since it would be a contradiction to say that this might be abandoned (i.e. teleologically suspended), inasmuch as this is no sooner suspended than it is forfeited, whereas in other cases what is suspended is not forfeited but is preserved precisely in that higher thing which is its *telos.*

If such be the case, then Hegel is right when in his chapter on "The Good and the Conscience," he characterizes man merely as the particular and regards this character as "a moral form of evil" which is to be annulled in the teleology of the moral, so that the individual who remains in this stage is either sinning or subjected to temptation (*Anfechtung*). On the other hand, Hegel is wrong in talking of faith, wrong in not protesting loudly and clearly against the fact that Abraham enjoys honor and glory as the father of faith, whereas he ought to be prosecuted and convicted of murder.

For faith is this paradox, that the particular is higher than the universal—yet in such a way, be it observed, that the movement repeats itself, and that consequently the individual, after having been in the universal, now as the particular isolates himself as higher than the universal. If this be not faith, then Abraham is lost, then faith has never existed in the world . . . because it has always existed. For if the ethical (i.e. the moral) is the highest thing, and if nothing incommensurable remains in man in any other way but as the evil (i.e. the particular which has to be expressed in the universal), then one needs no other categories besides those which the Greeks possessed or which by consistent thinking can be derived from them. . . . This position cannot be mediated, for all

* By permission. Søren Kierkegaard. *Fear and Trembling,* trans. Walter Lowrie. Copyright 1941 by Princeton University Press, Princeton, N.J.

mediation comes about precisely by virtue of the universal; it is and remains to all eternity a paradox, inaccessible to thought. And yet faith is this paradox—or else (these are the logical deductions which I would beg the reader to have *in mente* at every point, though it would be too prolix for me to reiterate them on every occasion) —or else there never has been faith . . . precisely because it always has been. In other words, Abraham is lost. . . .

Now the story of Abraham contains such a teleological suspension of the ethical. There have not been lacking clever pates and profound investigators who have found analogies to it. Their wisdom is derived from the pretty proposition that at bottom everything is the same. If one will look a little more closely, I have not much doubt that in the whole world one will not find a single analogy (except a later instance which proves nothing), if it stands fast that Abraham is the representative of faith, and that faith is normally expressed in him whose life is not merely the most paradoxical that can be thought but so paradoxical that it cannot be thought at all. He acts by virtue of the absurd, for it is precisely absurd that he as the particular is higher than the universal. This paradox cannot be mediated; for as soon as he begins to do this he has to admit that he was in temptation (*Anfechtung*), and if such was the case, he never gets to the point of sacrificing Isaac, or, if he has sacrificed Isaac, he must turn back repentantly to the universal. By virtue of the absurd he gets Isaac again. Abraham is therefore at no instant a tragic hero but something quite different, either a murderer or a believer. The middle term which saves the tragic hero, Abraham has not. Hence it is that I can understand the tragic hero but cannot understand Abraham, though in a certain crazy sense I admire him more than all other men.

Abraham's relation to Isaac, ethically speaking, is quite simply expressed by saying that a father shall love his son more dearly than himself. Yet within its own compass the ethical has various gradations. Let us see whether in this story there is to be found any higher expression for the ethical such as would ethically explain his conduct, ethically justify him in suspending the ethical obligation toward his son, without in this search going beyond the teleology of the ethical. . . .

The difference between the tragic hero and Abraham is clearly evident. The tragic hero still remains within the ethical. He lets one expression of the ethical find its *telos* in a higher expression of the ethical, the ethical relation between father and son, or daughter and father, he reduces to a sentiment which has its dialectic in its relation to the idea of morality. Here there can be no question of a teleological suspension of the ethical itself.

With Abraham the situation was different. By his act he overstepped the ethical entirely and possessed a higher *telos* outside of it, in relation to which he suspended the former. For I should very much like to know how one would bring Abraham's act into relation with the universal, and whether it is possible to discover any connection whatever between what Abraham did and the universal . . . except the fact that he transgressed it. It was not for the sake of saving a people, not to maintain the idea of the state, that Abraham did this, and not in order to reconcile angry deities. If there could be a question of the deity being angry, he was angry only with Abraham, and Abraham's whole action stands in no relation to the universal, is a purely private undertaking. Therefore, whereas the tragic hero is great by reason of his moral virtue, Abraham is great by reason of a purely personal virtue. In Abraham's life there is no higher expression for the ethical than this, that the father shall love his son. Of the ethical in the sense of morality there can be no question in this instance. In so far as the universal was present, it was indeed cryptically present in Isaac, hidden as it were in Isaac's loins, and must therefore cry out with Isaac's mouth, "Do it not! Thou art bringing everything to naught."

Why then did Abraham do it? For God's sake, and (in complete identity with this) for his own sake. He did it for God's sake because God required this proof of his faith; for his own sake he did it in order that he might furnish the proof. The unity of these two points of view is perfectly expressed by the word which has always been used to characterize this situation: it is a trial, a temptation (*Frietelse*). A temptation—but what does that mean? What ordinarily tempts a man is that which would keep him from doing his duty, but in this case the temptation is itself the ethical . . . which would keep him from doing God's will. But what then is duty? Duty is precisely the expression for God's will.

Here is evident the necessity of a new category if one would understand Abraham. Such a relationship to the deity paganism did not know. The tragic hero does not enter into any private relationship with the deity, but for him the ethical is the divine, hence the paradox implied in his situation can be mediated in the universal.

Abraham cannot be mediated, and the same thing can be expressed also by saying that he cannot talk. So soon as I talk I express the universal, and if I do not do so, no one can understand me. Therefore if Abraham would express himself in terms of the universal, he must say that his situation is a temptation (*Anfechtung*), for he has no higher expression for that universal which stands above the universal which he transgresses.

KARL MARX

Karl Marx (1818–1883) was undoubtedly one of the most influential writers in the history of thought. His extensive work in economics, sociology, and the philosophy of politics and history has served as the intellectual basis of twentieth-century communism and socialism, but many of his doctrines have been assimilated by scholars who do not represent the political left.

Marx was born in Trier, Germany. Although he intended to enter the profession of law, his studies as a young man led him increasingly into philosophy and into revolutionary political activity. A series of clashes with the authorities led in 1850 to his exile from Germany; he settled in London, where he devoted the rest of his life to the studies that were eventually to reshape the modern world.

Although Marx had much to say on ethical questions, his discussions are scattered throughout works that are primarily on economics and politics. Our first selection summarizes his theory of the economic determination of history —the basis of all the rest of his thought. The other two selections present his theory of man's estrangement from society and the overcoming of this estrangement through communism.

*A Contribution to the Critique of Political Economy**

The general conclusion at which I arrived and which, once reached, continued to serve as the leading thread in my studies may be briefly summed up as follows: In the social production which men carry on they enter into definite relations that are indispensable and independent of their will; these relations of production correspond to a definite stage of development of their material powers of production. The sum total of these relations of production constitutes the economic structure of society—the real foundation, on which rise legal and political superstructures and to which correspond definite forms of social consciousness. The mode of production in material life determines the general character of the social, political, and spiritual processes of life. It is not the consciousness of men that determines their existence, but,

* By permission. Karl Marx, *A Contribution to the Critique of Political Economy.* Trans. by N. I. Stone, Charles H. Kerr & Co., Chicago, 1904.

on the contrary, their social existence determines their consciousness. At a certain stage of their development the material forces of production in society come into conflict with the existing relations of production, or—what is but a legal expression for the same thing—with the property relations within which they had been at work before. From forms of development of the forces of production these relations turn into their fetters. Then comes the period of social revolution. With the change of the economic foundation the entire immense superstructure is more or less rapidly transformed. In considering such transformations the distinction should always be made between the material transformation of the economic conditions of production, which can be determined with the precision of natural science, and the legal, political, religious, aesthetic, or philosophic—in short, ideological—forms in which men become conscious of this conflict and fight it out. Just as our opinion of an individual is not based on what he thinks of himself, so can we not judge such a period of transformation by its own consciousness; on the contrary, this consciousness must rather be explained from the contradictions of material life, from the existing conflict between the social forces of production and the relations of production. No social order ever disappears before all the productive forces for which there is room in it have been developed, and new, higher relations of production never appear before the material conditions of their existence have matured in the womb of the old society. Therefore mankind always takes up only such problems as it can solve, since, looking at the matter more closely, we will always find that the problem itself arises only when the material conditions necessary for its solution already exist or are at least in the process of formation. In broad outlines we can designate the Asiatic, the ancient, the feudal, and the modern bourgeois methods of production as so many epochs in the progress of the economic formation of society. The bourgeois relations of production are the last antagonistic form of the social process of production—antagonistic not in the sense of individual antagonism, but of one arising from conditions surrounding the life of individuals in society; at the same time the productive forces developing in the womb of bourgeois society create the material conditions for the solution of that antagonism. This social formation constitutes, therefore, the closing chapter of the prehistoric stage of human society.

*Alienated Labour**

. . . We have to grasp the real connexion between this whole system of alienation—private property, acquisitiveness, the separation of labour, capital and land, exchange and competition, value and the devaluation of man, monopoly and competition—and the system of *money*.

Let us not begin our explanation, as does the economist, from a legendary primordial condition. Such a primordial condition does not explain anything; it merely removes the question into a grey and nebulous distance. It asserts as a fact or event what it should deduce, namely, the necessary relation between two things; for example, between the division of labour and exchange. In the same way theology explains the origin of evil by the fall of man; that is, it asserts as a historical fact what it should explain.

We shall begin from a *contemporary* economic fact. The worker becomes poorer the more wealth he produces and the more his production increases in power and extent. The worker becomes an ever cheaper commodity the more goods he creates. The

* By permission. Karl Marx, *Alienated Labour*, in *Karl Marx: Early Writings*, trans. and ed. by T. B. Bottomore, C. A. Watts & Co. Ltd., London, 1963.

devaluation of the human world increases in direct relation with the *increase in value* of the world of things. Labour does not only create goods; it also produces itself and the worker as a *commodity,* and indeed in the same proportion as it produces goods.

This fact simply implies that the object produced by labour, its product, now stands opposed to it as an *alien being,* as a *power independent* of the producer. The product of labour is labour which has been embodied in an object and turned into a physical thing; this product is an *objectification* of labour. The performance of work is at the same time its objectification. The performance of work appears in the sphere of political economy as a *vitiation* of the worker, objectification as a *loss* and as *servitude to the object,* and appropriation as *alienation.*

So much does the performance of work appear as vitiation that the worker is vitiated to the point of starvation. So much does objectification appear as loss of the object that the worker is deprived of the most essential things not only of life but also of work. Labour itself becomes an object which he can acquire only by the greatest effort and with unpredictable interruptions. So much does the appropriation of the object appear as alienation that the more objects the worker produces the fewer he can possess and the more he falls under the domination of his product, of capital.

All these consequences follow from the fact that the worker is related to the *product of his labour* as to an *alien* object. For it is clear on this presupposition that the more the worker expends himself in work the more powerful becomes the world of objects which he creates in face of himself, the poorer he becomes in his inner life, and the less he belongs to himself. It is just the same as in religion. The more of himself man attributes to God the less he has left in himself. The worker puts his life into the object, and his life then belongs no longer to himself but to the object. The greater his activity, therefore, the less he possesses. What is embodied in the product of his labour is no longer his own. The greater this product is, therefore, the more he is diminished. The *alienation* of the worker in his product means not only that his labour becomes an object, assumes an *external* existence, but that it exists independently, *outside himself,* and alien to him, and that it stands opposed to him as an autonomous power. The life which he has given to the object sets itself against him as an alien and hostile force.

Let us now examine more closely the phenomenon of *objectification;* the worker's production and the *alienation* and *loss* of the object it produces, which is involved in it. The worker can create nothing without *nature,* without the *sensuous external world.* The latter is the material in which his labour is realized, in which it is active, out of which and through which it produces things.

But just as nature affords the *means of existence* of labour, in the sense that labour cannot *live* without objects upon which it can be exercised, so also it provides the *means of existence* in a narrower sense; namely the means of physical existence for the *worker himself.* Thus, the more the worker *appropriates* the external world of sensuous nature by his labour the more he deprives himself of *means of existence,* in two respects: first, that the sensuous external world becomes progressively less an object belonging to his labour or a means of existence of his labour, and secondly, that it becomes progressively less a means of existence in the direct sense, a means for the physical subsistence of the worker.

In both respects, therefore, the worker becomes a slave of the object; first, in that he receives an *object of work,* i.e. receives *work,* and secondly, in that he receives *means of subsistence.* Thus the object enables him to exist, first as a *worker* and secondly, as a *physical subject*. The culmination of this enslavement is that he can only maintain himself as a *physical subject* so far as he is a *worker*, and that it is only as a *physical subject* that he is a worker. . . .

Labour certainly produces marvels for the rich but it produces privation for the worker. It produces palaces, but hovels for the worker. It produces beauty, but deformity for the worker. It replaces labour by machinery, but it casts some of the workers back into a barbarous kind of work and turns the others into machines. It produces intelligence, but also stupidity and cretinism for the workers.

The direct relationship of labour to its products is the relationship of the worker to the objects of his production. The relationship of property owners to the objects of production and to production itself is merely a *consequence* of this first relationship and confirms it. We shall consider this second aspect later.

Thus, when we ask what is the important relationship of labour we are concerned with the relationship of the *worker* to production.

So far we have considered the alienation of the worker only from one aspect; namely, *his relationship with the products of his labour.* However, alienation appears not merely in the result but also in the *process* of *production,* within *productive activity* itself. How could the worker stand in an alien relationship to the product of his activity if he did not alienate himself in the act of production itself? The product is indeed only the *résumé* of activity, of production. Consequently, if the product of labour is alienation, production itself must be active alienation—the alienation of activity and the activity of alienation. The alienation of the object of labour merely summarizes the alienation in the work activity itself.

What constitutes the alienation of labour? First, that the work is *external* to the worker, that it is not part of his nature; and that, consequently, he does not fulfil himself in his work but denies himself, has a feeling of misery rather than well-being, does not develop freely his mental and physical energies but is physically exhausted and mentally debased. The worker, therefore, feels himself at home only during his leisure time, whereas at work he feels homeless. His work is not voluntary but imposed, *forced labour.* It is not the satisfaction of a need, but only a *means* for satisfying other needs. Its alien character is clearly shown by the fact that as soon as there is no physical or other compulsion it is avoided like the plague. External labour, labour in which man alienates himself, is a labour of self-sacrifice, of mortification. Finally, the external character of work for the worker is shown by the fact that it is not his own work but work for someone else, that in work he does not belong to himself but to another person.

Just as in religion the spontaneous activity of human fantasy, of the human brain and heart, reacts independently as an alien activity of gods or devils upon the individual, so the activity of the worker is not his own spontaneous activity. It is another's activity and a loss of his own spontaneity.

We arrive at the result that man (the worker) feels himself to be freely active only in his animal functions—eating, drinking and procreating, or at most also in his dwelling and in personal adornment—while in his human functions he is reduced to an animal. The animal becomes human and the human becomes animal.

Eating, drinking and procreating are of course also genuine human functions. But abstractly considered, apart from the environment of human activities, and turned into final and sole ends, they are animal functions.

We have now considered the act of alienation of practical human activity, labour, from two aspects: (1) the relationship of the worker to the *product of labour* as an alien object which dominates him. This relationship is at the same time the relationship to the sensuous external world, to natural objects, as an alien and hostile world; (2) the relationship of labour to the *act of production* within *labour*. This is the relationship of the worker to his own activity as something alien and not belonging to him, activity as suffering (passivity), strength as powerlessness, creation as emasculation, the *personal* physical and mental energy of the worker, his personal life (for what is life but activity?), as an activity which is directed against himself, independent of him and not belonging to him. This is *self-alienation* as against the above-mentioned alienation of the *thing*.

We have now to infer a third characteristic of *alienated labour* from the two we have considered.

Man is a species-being not only in the sense that he makes the community (his own as well as those of other things) his object both practically and theoretically, but also (and this is simply another expression for the same thing) in the sense that he treats himself as the present, living species, as a *universal* and consequently free being.

Species-life, for man as for animals, has its physical basis in the fact that man (like animals) lives from inorganic nature, and since man is more universal than an animal so the range of inorganic nature from which he lives is more universal. Plants, animals, minerals, air, light, etc. constitute, from the theoretical aspect, a part of human consciousness as objects of natural science and art; they are man's spiritual inorganic nature, his intellectual means of life, which he must first prepare for enjoyment and perpetuation. So also, from the practical aspect, they form a part of human life and activity. In practice man lives only from these natural products, whether in the form of food, heating, clothing, housing, etc. The universality of man appears in practice in the universality which makes the whole of nature into his inorganic body: (1) as a direct means of life; and equally (2) as the material object and instrument of his life activity. Nature is the inorganic body of man; that is to say nature, excluding the human body itself. To say that man *lives* from nature means that nature is his *body* with which he must remain in a continuous interchange in order not to die. The statement that the physical and mental life of man, and nature, are interdependent means simply that nature is interdependent with itself, for man is a part of nature.

Since alienated labour: (1) alienates nature from man; and (2) alienates man from himself, from his own active function, his life activity; so it alienates him from the species. It makes *species-life* into a means of individual life. In the first place it alienates species-life and individual life, and secondly, it turns the latter, as an abstraction, into the purpose of the former, also in its abstract and alienated form.

For labour, *life activity, productive life,* now appear to man only as *means* for the satisfaction of a need, the need to maintain his physical existence. Productive life is, however, species-life. It is life creating life. In the type of life activity resides the whole character of a species, its species-character; and free, conscious activity is the species-character of human beings. Life itself appears only as a *means of life*.

The animal is one with its life activity. It does not distinguish the activity from itself. It is *its activity*. But man makes his life activity itself an object of his will and consciousness. He has a conscious life activity. It is not a determination with which he is completely identified. Conscious life activity distinguishes man from the life activity of animals. Only for this reason is he a species-being. Or rather, he is only a self-conscious being, i.e. his own life is an object for him, because he is a species-being. Only for this reason is his activity free activity. Alienated labour reverses the relationship, in that man because he is a self-conscious being makes his life activity, his *being*, only a means for his *existence*.

The practical construction of an *objective world*, the *manipulation* of inorganic nature, is the confirmation of man as a conscious species-being, i.e. a being who treats the species as his own being or himself as a species-being. Of course, animals also produce. They construct nests, dwellings, as in the case of bees, beavers, ants, etc. But they only produce what is strictly necessary for themselves or their young. They produce only in a single direction, while man produces universally. They produce only under the compulsion of direct physical needs, while man produces when he is free from physical need and only truly produces in freedom from such need. Animals produce only themselves, while man reproduces the whole of nature. The products of animal production belong directly to their physical bodies, while man is free in face of his product. Animals construct only in accordance with the standards and needs of the species to which they belong, while man knows how to produce in accordance with the standards of every species and knows how to apply the appropriate standard to the object. Thus man constructs also in accordance with the laws of beauty.

It is just in his work upon the objective world that man really proves himself as a *species-being*. This production is his active species-life. By means of it nature appears as *his* work and his reality. The object of labour is, therefore, the *objectification of man's species-life;* for he no longer reproduces himself merely intellectually, as in consciousness, but actively and in a real sense, and he sees his own reflection in a world which he has constructed. While, therefore, alienated labour takes away the object of production from man, it also takes away his *species-life*, his real objectivity as a species-being, and changes his advantage over animals into a disadvantage in so far as his inorganic body, nature, is taken from him.

Just as alienated labour transforms free and self-directed activity into a means, so it transforms the species-life of man into a means of physical existence.

Consciousness, which man has from his species, is transformed through alienation so that species-life becomes only a means for him. (3) Thus alienated labour turns the *species-life of man*, and also nature as his mental species-property, into an *alien* being and into a *means* for his *individual existence*. It alienates from man his own body, external nature, his mental life and his *human* life. (4) A direct consequence of the alienation of man from the product of his labour, from his life activity and from his species-life, is that *man* is *alienated* from other *men*. When man confronts himself he also confronts *other* men. What is true of man's relationship to his work, to the product of his work and to himself, is also true of his relationship to other men, to their labour and to the objects of their labour.

In general, the statement that man is alienated from his species-life means that each man is alienated from others, and that each of the others is likewise alienated from human life.

Human alienation, and above all the relation of man to himself, is first realized and expressed in the relationship between each man and other men. Thus in the relationship of alienated labour every man regards other men according to the standards and relationships in which he finds himself placed as a worker.

We began with an economic fact, the alienation of the worker and his production. We have expressed this fact in conceptual terms as *alienated labour*, and in analysing the concept we have merely analysed an economic fact.

Let us now examine further how this concept of alienated labour must express and reveal itself in reality. If the product of labour is alien to me and confronts me as an alien power, to whom does it belong? If my own activity does not belong to me but is an alien, forced activity, to whom does it belong? To a being *other* than myself. And who is this being? The *gods*? It is apparent in the earliest stages of advanced production, e.g. temple building, etc. in Egypt, India, Mexico, and in the service rendered to gods, that the product belonged to the gods. But the gods alone were never the lords of labour. And no more was *nature*. What a contradiction it would be if the more man subjugates nature by his labour, and the more the marvels of the gods are rendered superfluous by the marvels of industry, the more he should abstain from his joy in producing and his enjoyment of the product for love of these powers.

The *alien* being to whom labour and the product of labour belong, to whose service labour is devoted, and to whose enjoyment the product of labour goes, can only be *man* himself. If the product of labour does not belong to the worker, but confronts him as an alien power, this can only be because it belongs to *a man other than the worker*. If his activity is a torment to him it must be a source of *enjoyment* and pleasure to another. Not the gods, nor nature, but only man himself can be this alien power over men.

Consider the earlier statement that the relation of man to himself is first *realized, objectified*, through his relation to other men. If he is related to the product of his labour, his objectified labour, as to an *alien*, hostile, powerful and independent object, he is related in such a way that another alien, hostile, powerful and independent man is the lord of this object. If he is related to his own activity as to unfree activity, then he is related to it as activity in the service, and under the domination, coercion and yoke, of another man.

Every self-alienation of man, from himself and from nature, appears in the relation which he postulates between other men and himself and nature. Thus religious self-alienation is necessarily exemplified in the relation between laity and priest, or, since it is here a question of the spiritual world, between the laity and a mediator. In the real world of practice this self-alienation can only be expressed in the real, practical relation of man to his fellow men. The medium through which alienation occurs is itself a *practical* one. Through alienated labour, therefore, man not only produces his relation to the object and to the process of production as to alien and hostile men; he also produces the relation of other men to his production and his product, and the relation between himself and other men. Just as he creates his own production as a vitiation, a punishment, and his own product as a loss, as a product which does not belong to him, so he creates the domination of the non-producer over production and its product. As he alienates his own activity, so he bestows upon the stranger an activity which is not his own.

We have so far considered this relation only from the side of the worker, and later on we shall consider it also from the side of the non-worker.

Thus, through alienated labour the worker creates the relation of another man, who does not work and is outside the work process, to this labour. The relation of the worker to work also produces the relation of the capitalist (or whatever one likes to call the lord of labour) to work. *Private property* is, therefore, the product, the necessary result, of *alienated labour*, of the external relation of the worker to nature and to himself.

Private property is thus derived from the analysis of the concept of *alienated labour;* that is, alienated man, alienated labour, alienated life, and estranged man. . . .

Only in the final stage of the development of private property is its secret revealed, namely, that it is on one hand the *product* of alienated labour, and on the other hand the *means* by which labour is alienated, *the realization of this alienation.*

*Private Property and Communism**

The supersession of self-estrangement follows the same course as self-estrangement. *Private property* is first considered only from its objective aspect, but with labour conceived as its essence. Its mode of existence is, therefore, *capital* which it is necessary to abolish "as such". . . .

Finally, *communism* is the positive expression of the abolition of private property, and in the first place of universal private property. In taking this relation in its *universal aspect* communism is, in its first form, only the generalization and fulfilment of the relation. As such it appears in a double form; the domination of material property looms so large that it aims to destroy everything which is incapable of being possessed by everyone as private property. It wishes to eliminate talent, etc. by *force.* Immediate physical possession seems to it the unique goal of life and existence. The role of *worker* is not abolished, but is extended to all men. The relation of private property remains the relation of the community to the world of things. Finally, this tendency to oppose general private property to private property is expressed in an animal form; *marriage* (which is incontestably a form of *exclusive private property*) is contrasted with the community of women, in which women become communal and common property. One may say that this idea of the *community of women* is the *open secret* of this entirely crude and unreflective communism. Just as women are to pass from marriage to universal prostitution, so the whole world of wealth (i.e. the objective being of man) is to pass from the relation of exclusive marriage with the private owner to the relation of universal prostitution with the community. This communism, which negates the *personality* of man in every sphere, is only the logical expression of private property, which is this negation. Universal *envy* setting itself up as a power is only a camouflaged form of cupidity which re-establishes itself and satisfies itself in a different way. The thoughts of every individual private property are *at least* directed against any *wealthier* private property, in the form of envy and the desire to reduce everything to a common level; so that this envy and levelling in fact constitute the essence of competition. Crude communism is only the culmination of such envy and levelling-down on the basis of a *preconceived* minimum. How little this abolition of private property represents a genuine appropriation is shown by the abstract negation of the whole world of culture and civilization, and the regression to the *unnatural* simplicity of the poor and wantless individual who has not only not surpassed private property but has not yet even attained to it.

The community is only a community of *work* and of *equality of wages* paid out by the communal capital, by the *community* as universal capitalist. The two sides of the relation are raised to a *supposed* universality; *labour* as a condition in which everyone is placed, and *capital* as the acknowledged universality and power of the community.

* By permission. Karl Marx, *Private Property and Communism,* in *Karl Marx: Early Writings,* trans. and ed. by T. B. Bottomore, C. A. Watts & Co. Ltd., London, 1963.

In the relationship with *woman,* as the prey and the handmaid of communal lust, is expressed the infinite degradation in which man exists for himself; for the secret of this relationship finds its *unequivocal,* incontestable, *open* and revealed expression in the relation of man to woman and in the way in which the *direct* and *natural* species-relationship is conceived. The immediate, natural and necessary relation of human being to human being is also the *relation* of *man* to *woman.* In this *natural* species-relationship man's relation to nature is directly his relation to man, and his relation to man is directly his relation to nature, to his own *natural* function. Thus, in this relation is *sensuously revealed,* reduced to an observable *fact,* the extent to which human nature has become nature for man and to which nature has become human nature for him. From this relationship man's whole level of development can be assessed. It follows from the character of this relationship how far *man* has become, and has understood himself as, a *species-being,* a *human being.* The relation of man to woman is the *most natural* relation of human being to human being. It indicates, therefore, how far man's *natural* behaviour has become *human,* and how far his *human* essence has become a *natural* essence for him, how far his *human nature* has become *nature* for him. It also shows how far man's needs have become *human* needs, and consequently how far the other person, as a person, has become one of his needs, and to what extent he is in his individual existence at the same time a social being. The first positive annulment of private property, crude communism, is, therefore, only a *phenomenal form* of the infamy of private property representing itself as positive community.

2. Communism (*a*) still political in nature, democratic or despotic; (*b*) with the abolition of the state, yet still incomplete and influenced by private property, that is, by the alienation of man. In both forms communism is already aware of being the reintegration of man, his return to himself, the supersession of man's self-alienation. But since it has not yet grasped the positive nature of private property, or the *human* nature of needs, it is still captured and contaminated by private property. It has well understood the concept, but not the essence.

3. *Communism* is the *positive* abolition of *private property,* of *human self-alienation,* and thus the real *appropriation* of *human* nature through and for man. It is, therefore, the return of man himself as a *social,* i.e. really human, being, a complete and conscious return which assimilates all the wealth of previous development. Communism as a fully developed naturalism is humanism and as a fully developed humanism is naturalism. It is the *definitive* resolution of the antagonism between man and nature, and between man and man. It is the true solution of the conflict between existence and essence, between objectification and self-affirmation, between freedom and necessity, between individual and species. It is the solution of the riddle of history and knows itself to be this solution.

It is easy to understand the necessity which leads the whole revolutionary movement to find its empirical, as well as its theoretical, basis in the development of *private property,* and more precisely of the economic system.

This material, directly *perceptible* private property is the material and sensuous expression of *alienated human* life. Its movement—production and consumption—is the *sensuous* manifestation of the movement of all previous production, i.e. the realization or reality of man. Religion, the family, the state, law, morality, science, art, etc. are only *particular* forms of production and come under its general law. The positive supersession of *private property,* as the appropriation of *human* life, is, therefore, the positive supersession of all alienation, and the return of man from religion, the family, the state, etc. to his *human*, i.e. social life. Religious alienation as such occurs only in the sphere of *consciousness*, in the inner life of man, but economic alienation is that of *real life* and its supersession, therefore, affects both aspects. Of course, the development in different nations has a different beginning according to whether the actual and *established* life of the people is more in the realm of mind or more in the external world, is a real or ideal life. Communism begins where atheism begins (Owen), but atheism is at the outset still far from being *communism*; indeed it is still for the most part an abstraction.

Thus the philanthropy of atheism is at first only an abstract *philosophical* philanthropy, whereas that of communism is at once *real* and oriented towards *action*.

We have seen how, on the assumption that private property has been positively superseded, man produces man, himself and then other men; how the object which is the direct activity of his personality is at the same time his existence for other men and their existence for him. Similarly, the material of labour and man himself as a subject are the starting-point as well as the result of this movement (and because there must be this starting-point private property is a historical necessity). Therefore, the *social* character is the universal character of the whole movement; *as* society itself produces *man* as *man*, so it is *produced* by him. Activity and mind are social in their content as well as in their *origin*; they are *social* activity and social mind. The *human* significance of nature only exists for *social* man, because only in this case is nature a *bond* with other *men*, the basis of his existence for others and of their existence for him. Only then is nature the *basis* of his own *human* experience and a vital element of human reality. The *natural* existence of man has here become his *human* existence and nature itself has become human for him. Thus *society* is the accomplished union of man with nature, the veritable resurrection of nature, the realized naturalism of man and the realized humanism of nature.

HENRY SIDGWICK

The Methods of Ethics *is Henry Sidgwick's (1838–1900) major contribution to ethical theory, and there is no better introduction to his thought than an explanation of this title. "A 'Method of Ethics,'" in his own words, "is any rational procedure by which we determine what individual human beings 'ought' to do."*

Through an examination of the history of ethical theory he comes to the conclusion that there are only three such methods: (1) egotistic hedonism—consideration of the act's tendency to benefit the agent; (2) universalistic hedonism —consideration of the act's tendency to benefit everyone affected by it; and (3) intuitionism—appeal to self-evident moral axioms that hold without reference to consequences.

In The Methods of Ethics *Sidgwick grants the legitimacy of all three methods and examines the relationships that obtain between them. He argues that there is no incompatibility between intuitionism and universalistic hedonism, and in fact utilitarianism (the more common name for universalistic hedonism) is "the final form into which intuitionism tends to pass."*

But in the final analysis he can find no self-evident compatibility between the demands of private interest and public interest. Thus in the concluding chapter he suggests that we may have to postulate a deity to guarantee the consistency of the three methods.

*The Methods of Ethics**

PHILOSOPHICAL INTUITIONISM. AXIOMS OF PRUDENCE, JUSTICE, AND BENEVOLENCE

. . . We conceive it as the aim of a philosopher, as such, to do somewhat more than define and formulate the common moral opinions of mankind. His function is to tell men what they ought to think, rather than what they do think: he is expected to transcend Common Sense in his premises, and is allowed a certain divergence from Common Sense in his conclusions. It is true that the limits of this deviation are firmly, though indefinitely, fixed: the truth of a philosopher's premises will always be tested by the acceptability of his conclusions: if in any important point he be found in flagrant conflict with common opinion, his method is likely to be declared invalid. Still, though he is expected to establish and concatenate at least the main part of the commonly accepted moral rules, he is not necessarily bound to take them as the basis on which his own system is constructed. Rather, we should expect that the history of Moral Philosophy—so far at least as those whom we may call orthodox thinkers are concerned—would be a history of attempts to enunciate, in full breadth and clearness, those primary intuitions of Reason, by the scientific application of which the common moral thought of mankind may be at once systematised and corrected.

But here a word of caution seems required: . . . against a certain class of sham-axioms, which are very apt to offer themselves to the mind that is earnestly seeking for a philosophical synthesis of practical rules, and to delude the unwary with a tempting aspect of clear self-evidence. These are principles which appear certain and self-evident because they are substantially tautological: because, when examined, they are found to affirm no more than that it is right to do that which is—in a certain department of life, under certain circumstances and conditions—right to be done. One important lesson which the history of moral philosophy teaches is that, in this region, even powerful intellects are liable to acquiesce in tautologies of this kind; sometimes expanded into circular reasonings, sometimes hidden in the recesses of an obscure notion, often lying so near the surface that, when once they have been exposed, it is hard to understand how they could ever have presented themselves as important.

Let us turn, for illustration's sake, to the time-honoured Cardinal Virtues. If we are told that the dictates of Wisdom and Temperance may be summed up in clear and certain principles, and that these are respectively,

1. It is right to act rationally,
2. It is right that the Lower parts of our nature should be governed by the Higher,

we do not at first feel that we are not obtaining valuable information. But when we find that "acting rationally" is merely another phrase for "doing what we see to be right," and, again, that the "higher part" of our nature to which the rest are to submit is explained to be Reason, so that "acting temperately" is only "acting rationally" under the condition of special non-rational impulses needing to be resisted, the tautology of our "principles" is obvious. Similarly when we are asked to accept as the principle of Justice "that we ought to give every man his own," the definition seems plausible—until it appears that we cannot define "his own" except as equivalent to "that which it is right he should have."

The definitions quoted may be found in modern writers: but it seems worthy of remark that throughout the ethical speculation of Greece, such universal affirmations as are presented to us concerning

* Henry Sidgwick, *The Methods of Ethics*, 7th edition, London, 1893.

Virtue or Good conduct seem almost always to be propositions which can only be defended from the charge of tautology, if they are understood as definitions of the problem to be solved, and not as attempts at its solution. For example, Plato and Aristotle appear to offer as constructive moralists the scientific knowledge on ethical matters of which Socrates proclaimed the absence; knowledge, that is, of the Good and Bad in human life. And they seem to be agreed that such Good as can be realised in the concrete life of men and communities is chiefly Virtue,—or (as Aristotle more precisely puts it) the *exercise* of Virtue: so that the practical part of ethical science must consist mainly in the knowledge of Virtue. If, however, we ask how we are to ascertain the kind of conduct which is properly to be called Virtuous, it does not seem that Plato can tell us more of each virtue in turn than that it consists in (1) the knowledge of what is Good in certain circumstances and relations, and (2) such a harmony of the different elements of man's appetitive nature, that their resultant impulse may be always in accordance with this knowledge. But it is just this knowledge (or at least its principles and method) that we are expecting him to give us: and to explain to us instead the different exigencies under which we need it, in no way satisfies our expectation. Nor, again, does Aristotle bring us much nearer such knowledge by telling us that the Good in conduct is to be found somewhere between different kinds of Bad. This at best only indicates the *whereabouts* of Virtue: it does not give us a method for finding it.

On the Stoic system, . . . we must pronounce the exposition of its general principles a complicated enchainment of circular reasonings, by which the inquirer is continually deluded with an apparent approach to practical conclusions, and continually led back to the point from which he set out.

The most characteristic formula of Stoicism seems to have been that declaring "Life according to Nature" to be the ultimate end of action. The spring of the motion that sustained this life was in the vegetable creation a mere unfelt impulse: in animals it was impulse accompanied with sensation: in man it was the direction of Reason, which in him was naturally supreme over all merely blind irrational impulses. What then does Reason direct? "To live according to Nature" is one answer: and thus we get the circular exposition of ethical doctrine in its simplest form. Sometimes, however, we are told that it is "Life according to Virtue": which leads us into the circle already noticed in the Platonic-Aristotelian philosophy; as Virtue, by the Stoics also, is only defined as knowledge of Good and Bad in different circumstances and relations. Indeed, this latter circle is given by the Stoics more neatly and perfectly: for with Plato and Aristotle Virtue was not the *sole*, but only the *chief* content of the notion Good, in its application to human life: but in the view of Stoicism the two notions are absolutely coincident. The result, then, is that Virtue is knowledge of what is good and ought to be sought or chosen, and of what is bad and ought to be shunned or rejected: while at the same time there is nothing good or properly choice-worthy, nothing bad or truly formidable, except Virtue and Vice respectively. But if Virtue is thus declared to be a science that has no object except itself, the notion is inevitably emptied of all practical content. In order, therefore, to avoid this result and to reconcile their system with common sense, the Stoics explained that there were other things in human life which were in a manner preferable, though not strictly good, including in this class the primary objects of men's normal impulses. On what principle then are we to select these objects when our impulses are conflicting or ambiguous? If we can get an answer to this question, we shall at length have come to something practical. But here again the Stoic could find no other general answer except either that we were to choose what was Reasonable, or that we were to act in accordance with Nature: each of which answers obviously brings us back into the original circle at a different point.

In Butler's use of the Stoic formula, this circular reasoning seems to be avoided: but it is so only so long as the intrinsic reasonableness of right conduct is ignored or suppressed. Butler assumes with his opponents that it is reasonable to live according to Nature, and argues that Conscience or the faculty that imposes moral rules is naturally supreme in man. It is therefore reasonable to obey Conscience. But are the rules that Conscience lays down merely known to us as the dictates of arbitrary authority, and not as in themselves reasonable? This would give a surely dangerous absoluteness of authority to the possibly unenlightened conscience of any individual: and Butler is much too cautious to do this: in fact, . . . he expressly adopts the doctrine that the true rules of morality are essentially reasonable. But if Conscience is, after all, Reason applied to Practice, then Butler's argument seems to bend itself into the old circle: "it is reasonable to live according to Nature, and it is natural to live according to Reason."

Can we then, between this Scylla and Charybdis of ethical inquiry, avoiding on the one hand doctrines that merely bring us back to common opinion with all its imperfections, and on the other hand doctrines that lead us round in a circle, find any way of obtaining self-evident moral principles of real significance? It would be disheartening to have to regard as altogether illusory the strong instinct of Common Sense that points to the existence of such principles, and the deliberate convictions of the long line of moralists who have enunciated them. At the same time, the more we extend our knowledge of man and his environment, the more we realise the vast variety of human natures and circumstances that have existed in different ages and countries, the less disposed we are to believe that there is any definite code of absolute rules, applicable to all human beings without exception. And we shall find, I think, that the truth lies between these two conclusions. There are certain absolute practical principles, the truth of which, when they are explicitly stated, is manifest; but they are of too abstract a nature, and too universal in their scope, to enable us to ascertain by immediate application of them what we ought to do in any particular case; particular duties have still to be determined by some other method.

One such principle was . . . that whatever action any of us judges to be right for himself, he implicitly judges to be right for all similar persons in similar circumstances. Or, as we may otherwise put it, "if a kind of conduct that is right (or wrong) for me is not right (or wrong) for some one else, it must be on the ground of some difference between the two cases, other than the fact that I and he are different persons." A corresponding proposition may be stated with equal truth in respect of what ought to be done *to*—not *by*—different individuals. These principles have been most widely recognised, not in their most abstract and universal form, but in their special application to the situation of two (or more) individuals similarly related to each other: as so applied, they appear in what is popularly known as the Golden Rule, "Do to others as you would have them do to you." This formula is obviously unprecise in statement; for one might wish for another's co-operation in sin, and be willing to reciprocate it. Nor is it even true to say that we ought to do to others only what we think it right for them to do to us; for no one will deny that there may be differences in the circumstances—and even in the natures—of two individuals, *A* and *B*, which would make it wrong for *A* to treat *B* in the way in which it is right for *B* to treat *A*. In short the self-evident principle strictly stated must take some such negative form as this; "it cannot be right for *A* to treat *B* in a manner in which it would be wrong for *B* to treat *A*, merely on the ground that they are two different individuals, and without there being any difference between the natures or circumstances of the two which can be stated as a reasonable ground for difference of treatment." Such a principle manifestly does not give complete guidance—indeed its effect, strictly speaking, is merely to throw a definite *onus probandi* on the man who applies to another a treatment of which he would complain if applied to himself; but Common Sense has amply recognised the practical importance of the maxim: and its truth, so far as it goes, appears to me self-evident.

A somewhat different application of the same fundamental principle that individuals in similar conditions should be treated similarly finds its sphere in the ordinary administration of Law, or (as we say) of "Justice." Accordingly, . . . "impartiality in the application of general rules," is an important element in the common notion of Justice; indeed, there ultimately appeared to be no other element which could be intuitively known with perfect clearness and certainty. Here again it must be plain that this precept of impartiality is insufficient for the complete determination of just conduct, as it does not help us to decide what kind of rules should be thus impartially applied; though all admit the importance of excluding from government, and human conduct generally, all conscious partiality and "respect of persons."

The principle just discussed, which seems to be more or less clearly implied in the common notion of "fairness" or "equity," is obtained by considering the similarity of the individuals that make up a Logical Whole or Genus. There are others, no less important, which emerge in the consideration of the similar parts of a Mathematical or Quantitative Whole. Such a Whole is presented in the common notion of the Good—or, as is sometimes said, "good on the whole"—of any individual human being. The proposition "that one ought to aim at one's own good" is sometimes given as the maxim of Rational Self-love or Prudence: but as so stated it does not clearly avoid tautology; since we may define "good" as "what one ought to aim at." If, however, we say "one's good on the whole," the addition suggests a principle which, when explicitly stated, is, at any rate, not tautological. . . . This principle is that "of impartial concern for all parts of our conscious life":—we might express it concisely by saying "that Hereafter *as such* is to be regarded neither less nor more than Now." It is not, of course, meant that the good of the present may not reasonably be preferred to that of the future on account of its greater certainty: or again, that a week ten years hence may not be more important to us than a week now, through an increase in our means or capacities of happiness. All that the principle affirms is that the mere difference of priority and posterity in time is not a reasonable ground for having more regard to the consciousness of one moment than to that of another. The form in which it practically presents itself to most men is "that a smaller present good is not to be preferred to a greater future good" (allowing for difference of certainty): since Prudence is generally exercised in restraining a present desire (the object or satisfaction of which we commonly regard as *pro tanto* "a good"), on account of the remoter consequences of gratifying it. The commonest view of the principle would no doubt be that the present *pleasure* or *happiness* is reasonably to be foregone with the view of obtaining greater pleasure or happiness hereafter: but the principle need not be restricted to a hedonistic application; it is equally applicable to any other interpretation of "one's own good," in which good is conceived as a mathematical whole, of which the integrant parts are realised in different parts or moments of a lifetime. And therefore it is perhaps better to distinguish it here from the principle "that Pleasure is the sole Ultimate Good," which does not seem to have any logical connexion with it.

So far we have only been considering the "Good on the Whole" of a single individual: but just as this notion is constructed by comparison and integration of the different "goods" that succeed one another in the series of our conscious states, so we have formed the notion of Universal Good by comparison and integration of the goods of all individual human—or sentient—existences. And here again, just as in the former case, by considering the relation of the integrant parts to the whole and to each other, I obtain the self-evident principle that the good of any one individual is of no more importance, from the point of view (if I may say so) of the Universe, than the good of any other; unless, that is, there are special grounds for believing that more good is likely to be realised in the one case than in the other. And it is evident to me that as a rational being I am bound to aim at good generally,—so far as it is attainable by my efforts,—not merely a particular part of it.

From these two rational intuitions we may deduce, as a necessary inference, the maxim of Benevolence in an abstract form: viz. that each one is morally bound to regard the good of any other individual as much as his own, except in so far as he judges it to be less, when impartially viewed, or less certainly knowable or attainable by him. . . . The duty of Benevolence as recognised by common sense seems to fall somewhat short of this. But I think it may be fairly urged in explanation of this that *practically* each man, even with a view to universal Good, ought chiefly to concern himself with promoting the good of a limited number of human beings, and that generally in proportion to the closeness of their connexion with him. I think that a "plain man," in a modern civilised society, if his conscience were fairly brought to consider the hypothetical question, whether it would be morally right for him to seek his own happiness on any occasion if it involved certain sacrifice of the greater happiness of some other human being,—without any counterbalancing gain to any one else,—would answer unhesitatingly in the negative.

I have tried to show how in the principles of Justice, Prudence, and Rational Benevolence as commonly recognised there is at least a self-evident element, immediately cognisable by abstract intuition; depending in each case on the relation which individuals and their particular ends bear as parts to their wholes, and to other parts of these wholes. I regard the apprehension, with more or less distinctness, of these abstract truths, as the permanent basis of the common conviction that the fundamental precepts of morality are essentially reasonable. No doubt these principles are often placed side by side with other precepts to which custom and general consent have given a merely illusory air of self-evidence: but the distinction between the two kinds of maxims appears to me to become manifest by merely reflecting upon them. I know by direct reflection that the propositions, "I ought to speak the truth," "I ought to keep my promises"—however true they may be—are not self-evident to me; they present themselves as propositions requiring rational justification of some kind. On the other hand, the propositions, "I ought not to prefer a present lesser good to a future greater good," and "I ought not to prefer my own lesser good to the greater good of another," do present themselves as self-evident; as much (*e.g.*) as the mathematical axiom that "if equals be added to equals the wholes are equal."

I must now point out—if it has not long been apparent to the reader—that the self-evident principles laid down do not specially belong to Intuitionism in the restricted sense which, for clear distinction of methods, I gave to this term at the outset of our investigation. The axiom of Prudence, as I have given it, is a self-evident principle, implied in Rational Egoism as commonly accepted. Again, the axiom of Justice or Equity as above stated—"that similar cases ought to be treated similarly" —belongs in all its applications to Utilitarianism as much as to any system commonly called Intuitional: while the axiom of Rational Benevolence is, in my view, required as a rational basis for the Utilitarian system.

Accordingly, I find that I arrive, in my search for really clear and certain ethical intuitions, at the fundamental principle of Utilitarianism. . . .

Utilitarianism is thus presented as the final form into which Intuitionism tends to pass, when the demand for really self-evident first principles is rigorously pressed. In order, however, to make this transition logically complete, we require to interpret "Universal Good" as "Universal Happiness." And this interpretation cannot, in my view, be justified by arguing . . . from the psychological fact that Happiness is the sole object of men's actual desires, to the ethical conclusion that it alone is desirable or good; because . . . Happiness or Pleasure is not the only object that each for himself actually desires. The identification of Ultimate Good with Happiness is properly to be reached, I think, by a more indirect mode of reasoning; which I will endeavour to explain in the next Chapter.

ULTIMATE GOOD

. . . There are two forms in which the object of ethical inquiry is considered; it is sometimes regarded as a Rule or Rules of Conduct, "the Right," sometimes as an end or ends, "the Good." I pointed out that in the moral consciousness of modern Europe the two notions are *prima facie* distinct; since while it is commonly thought that the obligation to obey moral rules is absolute, it is not commonly held that the whole Good of man lies in such obedience; this view, we may say, is—vaguely and respectfully but unmistakably—repudiated as a Stoical paradox. The ultimate Good or Wellbeing of man is rather regarded as an ulterior result, the connexion of which with his Right Conduct is indeed commonly held to be certain, but is frequently conceived as supernatural, and so beyond the range of independent ethical speculation. But now, if the conclusions of the preceding chapters are to be trusted, it would seem that the practical determination of Right Conduct depends on the determination of Ultimate Good. For we have seen (*a*) that most of the commonly received maxims of Duty—even of those which at first sight appear absolute and independent—are found when closely examined to contain an implicit subordination to the more general principles of Prudence and Benevolence: and (*b*) that no principles except these, and the formal principle of Justice or Equity can be admitted as at once intuitively clear and certain; while, again, these principles themselves, so far as they are self-evident, may be stated as precepts to seek (1) one's own good on the whole, repressing all seductive impulses prompting to undue preference of particular goods, and (2) others' good no less than one's own, repressing any undue preference for one individual over another. Thus we are brought round to the old question with which ethical speculation in Europe began, "What is the Ultimate Good for man?"—though not in the egoistic form in which the old question was raised. When, however, we examine the controversies to which this question originally led, we see that the investigation which has brought us round to it has tended definitely to exclude one of the answers which early moral reflection was disposed to give to it. For to say that "General Good" consists solely in general Virtue,—if we mean by Virtue conformity to such prescriptions and prohibitions as make up the main part of the morality of Common Sense—would obviously involve us in a logical circle; since we have seen that the exact determination of these prescriptions and prohibitions must depend on the definition of this General Good. . . .

It must be allowed that we find in Common Sense an aversion to admit Happiness (when explained to mean a sum of pleasures) to be the sole ultimate end and standard of right conduct. But this, I think, can be fully accounted for by the following considerations.

I. The term Pleasure is not commonly used so as to include clearly *all* kinds of consciousness which we desire to retain or reproduce: in ordinary usage it suggests too prominently the coarser and commoner kinds of such feelings; and it is difficult even for those who are trying to use it scientifically to free their minds altogether from the associations of ordinary usage, and to mean by Pleasure only Desirable Consciousness or Feeling of whatever kind. Again, our knowledge of human life continually suggests to us instances of pleasures which will inevitably involve as concomitant or consequent either a greater amount of pain or a loss of more important pleasures: and we naturally shrink from including even hypothetically in our conception of ultimate good these—in Bentham's phrase—"impure" pleasures; especially since we have, in many cases, moral or æsthetic instincts warning us against such pleasures.

II. . . . Many important pleasures can only be felt on condition of our experiencing desires for other things than pleasure. Thus the very acceptance of Pleasure as the ultimate end of conduct involves the practical rule that it is not always to be made the conscious end. Hence, even if we are considering merely the good of one human being taken alone, excluding from our view all effects of his conduct on others, still the reluctance of Common Sense to regard pleasure as the sole thing ultimately desirable may be justified by the consideration that human beings tend to be less happy if they are exclusively occupied with the desire of personal happiness. *E.g.* . . . we shall miss the valuable pleasures which attend the exercise of the benevolent affections if we do not experience genuinely disinterested impulses to procure happiness for others (which are, in fact, implied in the notion of "benevolent affections").

III. But again, I hold . . . that disinterested benevolence is not only thus generally in harmony with rational Self-love, but also in another sense and independently rational: that is, Reason shows me that if my happiness is desirable and a good, the equal happiness of any other person must be equally desirable. Now, when Happiness is spoken of as the sole ultimate good of man, the idea most commonly suggested is that each individual is to seek his own happiness at the expense (if necessary) or, at any rate, to the neglect of that of others: and this offends both our sympathetic and our rational regard for others' happiness. It is, in fact, rather the end of Egoistic than of Universalistic Hedonism, to which Common Sense feels an aversion. And certainly one's individual happiness is, in many respects, an unsatisfactory mark for one's supreme aim, apart from any direct collision into which the exclusive pursuit of it may bring us with rational or sympathetic Benevolence. It does not possess the characteristics which, as Aristotle says, we "divine" to belong to Ultimate Good: being (so far, at least, as it can be empirically foreseen) so narrow and limited, of such necessarily brief duration, and so shifting and insecure while it lasts. But Universal Happiness, desirable consciousness or feeling for the innumerable multitude of sentient beings, present and to come, seems an End that satisfies our imagination by its vastness, and sustains our resolution by its comparative security.

It may, however, be said that if we require the individual to sacrifice his own happiness to the greater happiness of others on the ground that it is reasonable to do so, we really assign to the individual a different ultimate end from that which we lay down as the ultimate Good of the universe of sentient beings: since we direct him to take, as ultimate, Happiness for the Universe, but Conformity to Reason for himself. I admit the substantial truth of this statement. . . . But granting the alleged difference, I do not see that it constitutes an argument against the view here maintained, since the individual is essentially and fundamentally different from the larger whole—the universe of sentient beings—of which he is conscious of being a part; just because he has a known relation to similar parts of the same whole, while the whole itself has no such relation. I accordingly see no inconsistency in holding that while it *would* be reasonable for the aggregate of sentient beings, if it could act collectively, to aim at its own happiness only as an ultimate end—and would be reasonable for any individual to do the same, if he were the only sentient being in the universe—it may yet be *actually* reasonable for an individual to sacrifice his own Good or happiness for the greater happiness of others.[1]

At the same time I admit that, in the earlier age of ethical thought which Greek philosophy represents, men sometimes judged an act to be "good" *for the agent,* even while recognising that its consequences would be on the whole painful to him,—as (*e.g.*) a heroic exchange of a life full of happiness for a painful death at the call of duty. I attribute this partly to a confusion of thought between what it is reasonable for an individual to desire, when he considers his own existence alone, and what he must recognise as reasonably to be desired, when he takes the point of view of a larger whole: partly, again, to a faith deeply rooted in the moral consciousness of mankind, that there cannot be really and ultimately any conflict between the two kinds of reasonableness. But when "Reasonable Self-love" has been clearly distinguished from Conscience, as it is by Butler and his followers, we find it is naturally understood to mean desire for one's own Happiness: so that in fact the interpretation of "one's own good," which was almost peculiar in ancient thought to the Cyrenaic and Epicurean heresies, is adopted by some of the most orthodox of modern moralists. Indeed it often does not seem to have occurred to these latter that this notion can have any other interpretation. If, then, when any one hypothetically concentrates his attention on himself, Good is naturally and almost inevitably conceived to be Pleasure, we may reasonably conclude that the Good of any number of similar beings, whatever their mutual relations may be, cannot be essentially different in quality.

IV. But lastly, from the universal point of view no less than from that of the individual, it seems true that Happiness is likely to be better attained if the extent to which we set ourselves consciously to aim at it be carefully restricted. And this not only because action is likely to be more effective if our effort is temporarily concentrated on the realisation of more limited ends—though this is no doubt an important reason:—but also because the fullest development of happy life for each individual seems to require that he should have other external objects of interest besides the happiness of other conscious beings. And thus we may conclude that the pursuit of the ideal objects, Virtue, Truth, Freedom, Beauty, etc., *for their own sakes,* is indirectly and secondarily, though not primarily and absolutely, rational; on ac-

[1] I ought at the same time to say that I hold it no less reasonable for an individual to take his own happiness as his ultimate end. This "Dualism of the Practical Reason" will be further discussed in the concluding chapter of the treatise.

count not only of the happiness that will result from their attainment, but also of that which springs from their disinterested pursuit. While yet if we ask for a final criterion of the comparative value of the different objects of men's enthusiastic pursuit, and of the limits within which each may legitimately engross the attention of mankind, we shall none the less conceive it to depend upon the degree in which they respectively conduce to Happiness.

If, however, this view be rejected, it remains to consider whether we can frame any other coherent account of Ultimate Good. If we are not to systematise human activities by taking Universal Happiness as their common end, on what other principles are we to systematise them? It should be observed that these principles must not only enable us to compare among themselves the values of the different non-hedonistic ends which we have been considering, but must also provide a common standard for comparing these values with that of Happiness; unless we are prepared to adopt the paradoxical position of rejecting happiness as absolutely valueless. For we have a practical need of determining not only whether we should pursue Truth rather than Beauty, or Freedom or some ideal constitution of society rather than either, or perhaps desert all of these for the life of worship and religious contemplation; but also how far we should follow any of these lines of endeavour, when we foresee among its consequences the pains of human or other sentient beings, or even the loss of pleasures that might otherwise have been enjoyed by them.

I have failed to find—and am unable to construct—any systematic answer to this question that appears to me deserving of serious consideration: and hence I am finally led to the conclusion (which at the close of the last chapter seemed to be premature) that the Intuitional method rigorously applied yields as its final result the doctrine of pure Universalistic Hedonism,—which it is convenient to denote by the single word, Utilitarianism. . . .

CAN WE RECONCILE EGOISTIC AND UNIVERSALISTIC HEDONISM?

. . . It would be contrary to Common Sense to deny that the distinction between any one individual and any other is real and fundamental, and that consequently "I" am concerned with the quality of my existence as an individual in a sense, fundamentally important, in which I am not concerned with the quality of the existence of other individuals: and this being so, I do not see how it can be proved that this distinction is not to be taken as fundamental in determining the ultimate end of rational action for an individual. And it may be observed that most Utilitarians, however anxious they have been to convince men of the reasonableness of aiming at happiness generally, have not commonly sought to attain this result by any logical transition from the Egoistic to the Universalistic principle. They have relied almost entirely on the Sanctions of Utilitarian rules; that is, on the pleasures gained or pains avoided by the individual conforming to them. Indeed, if an Egoist remains impervious to the principle of Rational Benevolence, the only way of rationally inducing him to aim at the happiness of all, is to show him that his own greatest happiness can be best attained by so doing. And further, even if a man admits the self-evidence of the principle of Rational Benevolence, he may still hold that his own happiness is an end which it is irrational for him to sacrifice to any other; and that therefore a harmony between the maxim of Prudence and the maxim of Rational Benevolence must be somehow demonstrated, if morality is to be made completely rational. This latter view, indeed appears to me, on the whole, the view of Common Sense: and it is that which I myself hold. It thus becomes needful to examine how far and in what way the required demonstration can be effected. . . .

While in any tolerable state of society the performance of duties towards others and the exercise of social virtues seem *generally* likely to coincide with the attainment of the greatest possible happiness in the long run for the virtuous agent, still the *universality* and *completeness* of this coincidence are at least incapable of empirical proof. Indeed, the more carefully we analyse and estimate the different sanctions —Legal, Social, and Conscientious—considered as operating under the actual conditions of human life, the more difficult it seems to believe that they can be always adequate to produce this coincidence. The natural effect of this argument upon a convinced Utilitarian is merely to make him anxious to alter the actual conditions of human life: and it would certainly be a most valuable contribution to the actual happiness of mankind, if we could so improve the adjustment of the machine of Law in any society, and so stimulate and direct the common awards of praise and blame, and so develop and train the moral sense of the members of the community, as to render it clearly prudent for every individual to promote as much as possible the general good. However, we are not now considering what a consistent Utilitarian will try to effect for the future, but what a consistent Egoist is to do in the present. And it must be admitted that, as things are, whatever difference exists between Utilitarian morality and that of Common Sense is of such a kind as to render the coincidence with Egoism still more improbable in the case of the former. For Utilitarianism is more rigid than Common Sense in exacting the sacrifice of the agent's private interests where they are incompatible with the greatest happiness of the greatest number: and of course in so far as the Utilitarian's principles bring him into conflict with any of the commonly accepted rules of morality, the whole force of the Social Sanction operates to deter him from what he conceives to be his duty. . . .

The effectiveness of Butler's famous argument against the vulgar antithesis between Self-love and Benevolence is undeniable: and it seems scarcely extravagant to say that, amid all the profuse waste of the means of happiness which men commit, there is no imprudence more flagrant than that of Selfishness in the ordinary sense of the term,—that excessive concentration of attention on the individual's own happiness which renders it impossible for him to feel any strong interest in the pleasures and pains of others. The perpetual prominence of self that hence results tends to deprive all enjoyments of their keenness and zest, and produce rapid satiety and *ennui:* the selfish man misses the sense of elevation and enlargement given by wide interests; he misses the more secure and serene satisfaction that attends continually on activities directed towards ends more stable in prospect than an individual's happiness can be; he misses the peculiar rich sweetness, depending upon a sort of complex reverberation of sympathy, which is always found in services rendered to those whom we love and who are grateful. He is made to feel in a thousand various ways, according to the degree of refinement which his nature has attained, the discord between the rhythms of his own life and of that larger life of which his own is but an insignificant fraction.

But allowing all this, it yet seems to me as certain as any conclusion arrived at by hedonistic comparison can be, that the utmost development of sympathy, intensive and extensive, which is now possible to any but a very few exceptional persons, would not cause a perfect coincidence between Utilitarian duty and self-interest. . . . Suppose a man finds that a regard for the general good—Utilitarian Duty—demands from him a sacrifice, or extreme risk, of life. There are perhaps one or two human beings so dear to him that the remainder of a life saved by sacrificing their happiness to his own would be worthless to him from an egoistic point of view. But it is doubtful whether many men, "sitting down in a cool hour" to make the estimate, would affirm even this: and of course that particular portion of the general happiness, for which one is called upon to sacrifice one's own, may easily be the happiness of persons not especially dear to one. But again, from this normal limitation of our keenest and strongest sympathy to a very small circle of human beings, it results that the very development of sympathy may operate to increase the weight thrown into the scale against Utilitarian duty. There are very few persons, however strongly and widely sympathetic, who are so constituted as to feel for the pleasures and pains of mankind generally a degree of sympathy at all commensurate with their concern for wife or children, or lover, or intimate friend: and if any training of the affections is at present possible which would materially alter this proportion in the general distribution of our sympathy, it scarcely seems that such a training is to be recommended as on the whole felicific. And thus when Utilitarian Duty calls on us to sacrifice not only our own pleasures but the happiness of those we love to the general good, the very sanction on which Utilitarianism most relies must act powerfully in opposition to its precepts.

It seems, then, that we must conclude . . . that the inseparable connexion between Utilitarian Duty and the greatest happiness of the individual who conforms to it cannot be satisfactorily demonstrated on empirical grounds. Hence another section of the Utilitarian school has preferred to throw the weight of Duty on the Religious Sanction. . . .

If—as all theologians agree—we are to conceive God as acting for some end, we must conceive that end to be Universal Good, and, if Utilitarians are right, Universal Happiness: and we cannot suppose that in a world morally governed it can be prudent for any man to act in conscious opposition to what we believe to be the Divine Design. Hence if in any case after calculating the consequences of two alternatives to be less conducive to Happiness generally, we shall be acting in a manner for which we cannot but expect to suffer.

If, then, we may assume the existence of such a Being as God, by the *consensus* of theologians, is conceived to be, it seems that Utilitarians may legitimately infer the existence of Divine sanctions to the code of social duty as constructed on a Utilitarian basis; and such sanctions would, of course, suffice to make it always every one's interest to promote universal happiness to the best of his knowledge. It is, however, desirable, before we conclude, to examine carefully the validity of this assumption, in so far as it is supported on ethical grounds alone. For by the result of such an examination will be determined, as we now see, the very important question whether ethical science can be constructed on an independent basis; or whether it is forced to borrow a fundamental and indispensable premise from Theology or some similar source. In order fairly to perform this examination, let us reflect upon the clearest and most certain of our moral intuitions. I find that I undoubtedly seem to perceive, as clearly and certainly as I see any axiom in Arithmetic or Geometry, that it is "right" and "reasonable" for me to treat others as I should think that I myself ought to be treated under similar conditions, and to do what I believe to be ultimately conducive to universal Good or Happiness. But I cannot find inseparably connected with this conviction, and similarly attainable by mere reflective intuition, any cognition that there actually is a Supreme Being who will adequately reward me for obeying these rules of duty, or punish me for violating them. Or,—omitting the strictly theological element of the proposition,—I may say that I do not find in my moral consciousness any intuition, claiming to be clear and certain, that the performance of duty will be adequately rewarded and its violation punished. I feel indeed a desire, apparently inseparable from the moral sentiments, that this result may be realised not only in my own case but universally; but the mere existence of the desire would not go far to establish the probability of its fulfilment, considering the large proportion of human desires that experience shows to be doomed to disappointment. I also judge that in a certain sense this result *ought* to be realised: in this judgment, however, "ought" is not used in a strictly ethical meaning; it only expresses the vital need that our Practical Reason feels of proving or postulating this connexion of Virtue and self-interest, if it is to be made consistent with itself. For the negation of the connexion must force us to admit an ultimate and fundamental contradiction in our apparent intuitions of what is Reasonable in conduct; and from this admission it would seem to follow that the apparently intuitive operation of the Practical Reason, manifested in these contradictory judgments, is after all illusory.

I do not mean that if we gave up the hope of attaining a practical solution of this fundamental contradiction, through any legitimately obtained conclusion or postulate as to the moral order of the world, it would become reasonable for us to abandon morality altogether: but it would seem necessary to abandon the idea of rationalising it completely. We should doubtless still, not only from self-interest, but also through sympathy and sentiments protective of social well being, imparted by education and sustained by communication with other men, feel a desire for the general observance of rules conducive to general happiness; and practical reason would still impel us decisively to the performance of duty in the more ordinary cases in which what is recognised as duty is in harmony with self-interest properly understood. But in the rarer cases of a recognised conflict between self-interest and duty, practical reason, being divided against itself, would cease to be a motive on either side; the conflict would have to be decided by the comparative preponderance of one or other of two groups of non-rational impulses.

If then the reconciliation of duty and self-interest is to be regarded as a hypothesis logically necessary to avoid a fundamental contradiction in one chief department of our thought, it remains to ask how far this necessity constitutes a sufficient reason for accepting this hypothesis. This, however, is a profoundly difficult and controverted question, the discussion of which belongs rather to a treatise on General Philosophy than to a work on the Methods of Ethics: as it could not be satisfactorily answered, without a general examination of the criteria of true and false beliefs. Those who hold that the edifice of physical science is really constructed of conclusions logically inferred from self-evident premises, may reasonably demand that any practical judgments claiming philosophic certainty should be based on an equally firm foundation. If on the other hand we find that in our supposed knowledge of the world of nature propositions are commonly taken to be universally true, which yet seem to rest on no other grounds that that we have a strong disposition to accept them, and that they are indispensable to the systematic coherence of our beliefs,—it will be more difficult to reject a similarly supported assumption in ethics, without opening the door to universal scepticism.

FRIEDRICH NIETZCHE

Friedrich Nietzsche (1844–1900), the son of a Lutheran minister, was born in Röcken, Germany. He studied at Bonn and later at Leipzig Universities, and was appointed to a professorship in classical philology at the University of Basel, Switzerland, in 1870. He retired from the academic profession in 1879, devoting himself to writing, until he succumbed to mental illness, caused probably by an infection of the nervous system. There is no evidence, despite allegations of Nietzsche's critics, that he had become insane even before his breakdown.

Nowadays Nietzsche is probably best known for his doctrine of nobility, with its related themes of the Superman and the Will to Power; his vitriolic attack upon all aspects of Christianity and especially upon Christian morals as he understood them; and his development of the problems and what may be called the style of thought of twentieth-century existentialism. These three sides of Nietzsche are illustrated briefly in the following selections. The Genealogy of Morals *was published in 1887;* Twilight of the Idols *and* The Antichrist *were completed in 1888, the year before his mental breakdown.*

Sounding Out Idols

PREFACE*

. . . A maxim, the origin of which I withhold from scholarly curiosity, has long been my motto:

Increscunt animi, virescit vulnere virtus[1]

Another mode of convalescence—under certain circumstances even more to my liking—is *sounding out idols.* There are more idols than realities in the world: that is *my* "evil eye" for this world; that is

* From "Twilight of the Idols," *The Portable Nietzsche* edited and translated by Walter Kaufman. Copyright 1954. Reprinted by permission of The Viking Press, Inc., New York.

[1] "The spirits increase, vigor grows through a wound."

also my "evil *ear*." For once to pose questions here with a *hammer*, and, perhaps, to hear as a reply that famous hollow sound which speaks of bloated entrails—what a delight for one who has ears even behind his ears, for me, an old psychologist and pied piper before whom just that which would remain silent must become outspoken. . . .

Regarding the sounding out of idols, this time they are not just idols of the age, but eternal idols, which are here touched with a hammer as with a tuning fork: there are altogether no older, no more convinced, no more puffed-up idols—and none more hollow. That does not prevent them from being those in which people have the most faith; nor does one ever say "idol," especially not in the most distinguished instance.

MAXIMS AND ARROWS*

"All truth is simple." Is that not doubly a lie?

I want, once and for all, *not* to know many things. Wisdom sets limits to knowledge too.

In our own wild nature we find the best recreation from our un-nature, from our spirituality.

What? Is man merely a mistake of God's? Or God merely a mistake of man's?

Help yourself, then everyone will you. Principle of neighbor-love.

Not to perpetrate cowardice against one's own acts! Not to leave them in the lurch afterward! The bite of conscience is indecent.

What? You search? You would multiply yourself by ten, by a hundred? You seek followers? Seek *zeros!*

Posthumous men—I, for example—are understood worse than timely ones, but *heard* better. More precisely: we are never understood—*hence* our authority.

Whoever does not know how to lay his will into things, at least lays some *meaning* into them: that means, he has the faith that they already obey a will. (Principle of "faith.")

I mistrust all systematizers and I avoid them. The will to a system is a lack of integrity.

When stepped on, a worm doubles up. That is clever. In that way he lessens the probability of being stepped on again. In the language of morality: *humility.*

There is a hatred of lies and simulation, stemming from an easily provoked sense of honor. There is another such hatred, from cowardice, since lies are *forbidden* by a divine commandment. Too cowardly to lie.

You run *ahead?* Are you doing it as a shepherd? Or as an exception? A third case would be the fugitive. *First* question of conscience.

Are you genuine? Or merely an actor? A representative? Or that which is represented? In the end, perhaps you are merely a copy of an actor. *Second* question of conscience.

The disappointed one speaks. I searched for great human beings; I always found only the *apes* of their ideals.

Are you one who looks on? Or one who lends a hand? Or one who looks away and walks off? *Third* question of conscience.

Do you want to walk along? Or walk ahead? Or walk by yourself? One must know *what* one wants and *that* one wants. *Fourth* question of conscience.

Those were steps for me, and I have climbed up over them: to that end I had to pass over them. Yet they thought that I wanted to retire on them.

What does it matter if *I* remain right. I am much too right. And he who laughs best today will also laugh last.

The formula of my happiness: a Yes, a No, a straight line, a *goal.*

* *Ibid.*

THE GENEALOGY OF MORALS*

We knowers are unknown to ourselves, and for a good reason: how can we ever hope to find what we have never looked for? There is a sound adage which runs: "Where a man's treasure lies, there lies his heart." Our treasure lies in the beehives of our knowledge. We are perpetually on our way thither, being by nature winged insects and honey gatherers of the mind. The only thing that lies close to our heart is the desire to bring something home to the hive. As for the rest of life—so called "experience"—who among us is serious enough for that? Or has time enough? When it comes to such matters, our heart is simply not in it—we don't even lend our ear. Rather, as a man divinely abstracted and self-absorbed into whose ears the bell has just drummed the twelve strokes of noon will suddenly awake with a start and ask himself what hour has actually struck, we sometimes rub our ears after the event and ask ourselves, astonished and at a loss, "What have we really experienced?"—or rather, "Who are we, really?" And we recount the twelve tremulous strokes of our experience, our life, our being, but unfortunately count wrong. The sad truth is that we remain necessarily strangers to ourselves, we don't understand our own substance, we *must* mistake ourselves; the axiom, "Each man is farthest from himself," will hold for us to all eternity. . . .

Now it is obvious to me [that the Utilitarian] looks for the genesis of the concept *good* in the wrong place: the judgment *good* does not originate with those to whom the good has been done. Rather it was the "good" themselves, that is to say the noble, mighty, highly placed, and high-minded who decreed themselves and their actions to be good, i.e., belonging to the highest rank, in contradistinction to all that was base, low-minded and plebeian. It was only this *pathos of distance* that authorized them to create values and name them—what was utility to them? The notion of utility seems singularly inept to account for such a quick jetting forth of supreme value judgments. Here we come face to face with the exact opposite of that lukewarmness which every scheming prudence, every utilitarian calculus presupposes—and not for a time only, for the rare, exceptional hour, but permanently. The origin of the opposites *good* and *bad* is to be found in the pathos of nobility and distance, representing the dominant temper of a higher, ruling class in relation to a lower, dependent one. (The lordly right of bestowing names is such that one would almost be justified in seeing the origin of language itself as an expression of the rulers' power. They say, "This *is* that or that"; they seal off each thing and action with a sound and thereby take symbolic possession of it.) Such an origin would suggest that there is no *a priori* necessity associating the word *good* with altruistic deeds, as those moral psychologists are fond of claiming. In fact, it is only after aristocratic values have begun to decline that the egotism-altruism dichotomy takes possession of the human conscience; to use my own terms, it is the herd instinct that now asserts itself. Yet it takes quite a while for this instinct to assume such sway that it can reduce all moral valuations to that dichotomy—as is currently happening throughout Europe, where the prejudice equating the terms *moral, altruistic,* and

* From *The Birth of Tragedy and the Genealogy of Morals* by Friedrich Nietzsche, in new translation by Francis Golffing.

disinterested has assumed the obsessive force of an *idée fixe*. . . .

The slave revolt in morals begins by rancor turning creative and giving birth to values—the rancor of beings who, deprived of the direct outlet of action, compensate by an imaginary vengeance. All truly noble morality grows out of triumphant self-affirmation. Slave ethics, on the other hand, begins by saying *no* to an "outside," an "other," a non-self, and that *no* is its creative act. This reversal of direction of the evaluating look, this invariable looking outward instead of inward, is a fundamental feature of rancor. Slave ethics requires for its inception a sphere different from and hostile to its own. Physiologically speaking, it requires an outside stimulus in order to act at all; all its action is reaction. The opposite is true of aristocratic valuations: such values grow and act spontaneously, seeking out their contraries only in order to affirm themselves even more gratefully and delightedly. Here the negative concepts, *humble, base, bad,* are late, pallid counterparts of the positive, intense and passionate credo, "We noble, good, beautiful, happy ones." Aristocratic valuations may go amiss and do violence to reality, but this happens only with regard to spheres which they do not know well, or from the knowledge of which they austerely guard themselves: the aristocrat will, on occasion, misjudge a sphere which he holds in contempt, the sphere of the common man, the people. On the other hand we should remember that the emotion of contempt, of looking down, provided that it falsifies at all, is as nothing compared with the falsification which suppressed hatred, impotent vindictiveness, effects upon its opponent, though only in effigy. There is in all contempt too much casualness and nonchalance, too much blinking of facts and impatience, and too much inborn gaiety for it ever to make of its object a downright caricature and monster. . . .

All this stands in utter contrast to what is called happiness among the impotent and oppressed, who are full of bottled-up aggressions. Their happiness is purely passive and takes the form of drugged tranquillity, stretching and yawning, peace, "sabbath," emotional slackness. Whereas the noble lives before his own conscience with confidence and frankness (*gennaīos* "nobly bred" emphasizes the nuance "truthful" and perhaps also "ingenuous"), the rancorous person is neither truthful nor ingenuous nor honest and forthright with himself. His soul squints; his mind loves hide-outs, secret paths, and back doors; everything that is hidden seems to him his own world, his security, his comfort; he is expert in silence, in long memory, in waiting, in provisional self-depreciation, and in self-humiliation. A race of such men will, in the end, inevitably be cleverer than a race of aristocrats, and it will honor sharp-wittedness to a much greater degree, i.e., as an absolutely vital condition for its existence. Among the noble, mental acuteness always tends slightly to suggest luxury and overrefinement. The fact is that with them it is much less important than is the perfect functioning of the ruling, unconscious instincts or even a certain temerity to follow sudden impulses, court danger, or indulge spurts of violent rage, love, worship, gratitude, or vengeance. When a noble man feels resentment, it is absorbed in his instantaneous reaction and therefore does not poison him. Moreover, in countless cases where we might expect it, it never arises, while with weak and impotent people it occurs without fail. It is a sign of strong, rich temperaments that they cannot for long take seriously their enemies, their misfortunes, their *misdeeds;* for such characters have in them an excess of plastic curative power, and also a power of oblivion. (A good modern example of the latter is Mirabeau, who lacked all memory for insults and meannesses done him, and who was unable to forgive because he had forgotten.) Such a man simply shakes off vermin which would get beneath another's skin—and only here, if anywhere on earth, is it possible to speak of "loving one's enemy." The noble person will respect his enemy, and respect is already a bridge to love. . . . Indeed he requires his enemy for himself, as his mark of distinction, nor could he tolerate any other enemy than one in whom he finds nothing to despise and much to esteem. Imagine, on the other hand, the "enemy" as conceived by the rancorous man! For this is his true creative achievement: he has conceived the "evil enemy," The Evil One, as a fundamental idea, and then as a pendant he has conceived a Good One—himself.

⁂

The exact opposite is true of the nobleminded, who spontaneously creates the notion *good,* and later derives from it the conception of the *bad*. How ill-matched these two concepts look, placed side by side: the bad of noble origin, and the *evil* that has risen out of the cauldron of unquenched hatred! The first is a by-product, a complementary color, almost an afterthought; the second is the beginning, the original creative act of slave ethics. But neither is the conception of good the same in both cases, as we soon find out when we ask ourselves who it is that is really evil according to the code of rancor. The answer is: precisely the good one of the opposite code, that is the noble, the powerful—only colored, reinterpreted, reenvisaged by the poisonous eye of resentment. And we are the first to admit that anyone who knew these "good" ones only as enemies would find them evil enemies indeed. For these same men who, amongst themselves, are so strictly constrained by custom, worship, ritual, gratitude, and by mutual surveillance and jealously, who are so resourceful in consideration, tenderness, loyalty, pride and friendship, when once they step outside their circle become little better than uncaged beasts of prey. Once abroad in the wilderness, they revel in the freedom from social constraint and compensate for their long confinement in the quietude of their own community. They revert to the innocence of wild animals: we can imagine them returning from an orgy of murder, arson, rape, and torture, jubilant and at peace with themselves as though they had committed a fraternity prank—convinced, moreover, that the poets for a long time to come will have something to sing about and to praise. Deep within all these noble races there lurks the beast of prey, bent on spoil and conquest. This hidden urge has to be satisfied from time to time, the beast let loose in the wilderness. This goes as well for the Roman, Arabian, German, Japanese nobility as for the Homeric heroes and the Scandinavian vikings. The noble races have everywhere left in their wake the catchword "barbarian." And even their highest culture shows an awareness of this trait and a certain pride in it (as we see, for example, in Pericles' famous funeral oration, when he tells the Athenians: "Our boldness has gained us access to every land and sea, and erected monuments to itself *for both good and evil.*") This "boldness" of noble races, so headstrong, absurd, incalculable, sudden, improbable (Pericles commends the Athenians especially for their *rathumia*), their utter indifference to safety and comfort, their terrible pleasure in destruction, their taste for cruelty—all these traits are embodied by their victims in the image of the "barbarian," the "evil enemy," the Goth or the Vandal. . . . If it were true, as passes current nowadays, that the real meaning of culture resides in its power to domesticate man's savage instincts, then we might be justified in viewing all those rancorous machinations by which the noble tribes, and their ideals, have been laid low as the true instruments of culture. But this would still not amount to saying that the *organizers* themselves represent culture. Rather, the exact opposite would be true, as is vividly shown by the current state of affairs. These carriers of the leveling and retributive instincts, these descendants of every European and extra-European slavedom, and especially of the pre-Aryan populations, represent human retrogression most flagrantly. Such "instruments of culture" are a disgrace to man and might make one suspicious of culture altogether. One might be justified in fearing the wild beast lurking within all noble races and in being on one's guard against it, but who would not a thousand times prefer fear when it is accompanied with admiration to security accompanied by the loathsome sight of perversion, dwarfishness, degeneracy? And is not the latter our predicament today? What accounts for our repugnance to man—for there is no question that he makes us suffer? Certainly not our fear of him, rather the fact that there is no longer anything to be feared from him; that the vermin "man" occupies the entire stage; that, tame, hopelessly mediocre, and savorless, he considers himself the apex of historical evolution; and not entirely without justice, since he is still somewhat removed from the mass of sickly and effete creatures whom Europe is beginning to stink of today.

MORALITY AS ANTI-NATURE*

All passions have a phase when they are merely disastrous, when they drag down their victim with the weight of stupidity—and a later, very much later phase when they wed the spirit, when they "spiritualize" themselves. Formerly, in view of the element of stupidity in passion, war was declared on passion itself, its destruction was plotted; all the old moral monsters are agreed on this: *il faut tuer les passions.*[2] The most famous formula for this is to be found in the New Testament, in that Sermon on the Mount, where, incidentally, things are by no means looked at from a height. There it is said, for example, with particular reference to sexuality: "If thy eye offend thee, pluck it out." Fortunately, no Christian acts in accordance with this precept. *Destroying* the passions and cravings, merely as a preventive measure against their stupidity and the unpleasant consequences of this stupidity—today this itself strikes us as merely another acute form of stupidity. We no longer admire dentists who "pluck out" teeth so that they will not hurt any more.

To be fair, it should be admitted, however, that on the ground out of which Christianity grew, the concept of the "*spiritualization* of passion" could never have been formed. After all the first church, as is well known, fought *against* the "intelligent" in favor of the "poor in spirit." How could one expect from it an intelligent war against passion? The church fights passion with excision in every sense: its practice, its "cure," is *castratism.* It never asks: "How can one spiritualize, beautify, deify a craving?" It has at all times laid the stress of discipline on extirpation (of sensuality, of pride, of the lust to rule, of avarice, of vengefulness). But an attack on the roots of passion means an attack on the roots of life: the practice of the church is *hostile to life.*

✲ ✲

The same means in the fight against a craving—castration, extirpation—is instinctively chosen by those who are too

* From "Twilight of the Idols."

[2] "One must kill the passions."

weak-willed, too degenerate, to be able to impose moderation on themselves; by those who are so constituted that they require *La Trappe*,[3] to use a figure of speech, or (without any figure of speech) some kind of definitive declaration of hostility, a *cleft* between themselves and the passion. Radical means are indispensable only for the degenerate; the weakness of the will—or, to speak more definitely, the inability *not* to respond to a stimulus—is itself merely another form of degeneration. The radical hostility, the deadly hostility against sensuality, is always a symptom to reflect on: it entitles us to suppositions concerning the total state of one who is excessive in this manner. . . .

The spiritualization of sensuality is called *love:* it represents a great triumph over Christianity. Another triumph is our spiritualization of *hostility.* It consists in a profound appreciation of the value of having enemies: in short, it means acting and thinking in the opposite way from that which has been the rule. . . .

The price of fruitfulness is to be rich in internal opposition; one remains young only as long as the soul does not stretch itself and desire peace. Nothing has become more alien to us than that desideratum of former times, "peace of soul," the *Christian* desideratum; there is nothing we envy less than the moralistic cow and the fat happiness of the good conscience. One has renounced the *great* life when one renounces war.

In many cases, to be sure, "peace of soul" is merely a misunderstanding—something else, which lacks only a more honest name. Without further ado or prejudice, a few examples. "Peace of soul" can be, for one, the gentle radiation of a rich animality into the moral (or religious) sphere. Or the beginning of weariness, the first shadow of evening, of any kind of evening. Or a sign that the air is humid, that south winds are approaching. Or unrecognized gratitude for a good digestion (sometimes called "love of man"). Or the attainment of calm by a convalescent who feels a new relish in all things and waits. Or the state which follows a thorough satisfaction of our dominant passion, the well-being of a rare repletion. Or the senile weakness of our will, our cravings, our vices. Or laziness, persuaded by vanity to give itself moral airs. Or the emergence of certainty, even a dreadful certainty, after long tension and torture by uncertainty. Or the expression of maturity and mastery in the midst of doing, creating, working, and willing—calm breathing, *attained* "freedom of the will." *Twilight of the Idols*—who knows? perhaps also only a kind of "peace of soul."

I reduce a principle to a formula. Every naturalism in morality—that is, every healthy morality—is dominated by an instinct of life; some commandment of life is fulfilled by a determinate canon of "shalt" and "shalt not"; some inhibition and hostile element on the path of life is thus removed. *Anti-natural* morality—that is, almost every morality which has so far been taught, revered, and preached—turns, conversely, *against* the instincts of life: it is *condemnation* of these instincts, now secret, now outspoken and impudent. When it says, "God looks at the heart," it says No to both the lowest and the highest desires of life, and posits God as the *enemy of life.* The saint in whom God delights is the ideal eunuch. Life has come to an end where the "kingdom of God" begins.

Once one has comprehended the outrage of such a revolt against life as has become almost sacrosanct in Christian moral-

[3] The Trappist Order.

ity, one has, fortunately, also comprehended something else: the futility, apparentness, absurdity, and *mendaciousness* of such a revolt. A condemnation of life by the living remains in the end a mere symptom of a certain kind of life: the question whether it is justified or unjustified is not even raised thereby. One would require a position *outside* of life, and yet have to know it as well as one, as many, as all who have lived it, in order to be permitted even to touch the problem of the *value* of life: reasons enough to comprehend that this problem is for us an unapproachable problem. When we speak of values, we speak with the inspiration, with the way of looking at things, which is part of life: life itself forces us to posit values; life itself values through us when we posit values. From this it follows that even that anti-natural morality which conceives of God as the counterconcept and condemnation of life is only a value judgment of life—but of what life? of what kind of life? I have already given the answer: of declining, weakened, weary, condemned life. Morality, as it has so far been understood—as it has in the end been formulated once more by Schopenhauer, as "negation of the will to life"—is the very *instinct of decadence*, which makes in imperative of itself. It says: *"Perish!"* It is a condemnation pronounced by the condemned.

Let us finally consider how naïve it is altogether to say: "Man *ought* to be such and such!" Reality shows us an enchanting wealth of types, the abundance of a lavish play and change of forms—and some wretched loafer of a moralist comments: "No! Man ought to be different." He even knows what man should be like, this wretched bigot and prig: he paints himself on the wall and comments, *"Ecce homo!"* But even when the moralist addresses himself only to the single human being and says to him, "You ought to be such and such!" he does not cease to make himself ridiculous. The single human being is a piece of *fatum* from the front and from the rear, one law more, one necessity more for all that is yet to come and to be. To say to him, "Change yourself!" is to demand that everything be changed, even retroactively. And indeed there have been consistent moralists who wanted man to be different, that is, virtuous—they wanted him remade in their own image, as a prig: to that end, they *negated* the world! No small madness! No modest kind of immodesty!

Morality, insofar as it *condemns* for its own sake, and *not* out of regard for the concerns, considerations, and contrivances of life, is a specific error with which one ought to have no pity—an *idiosyncrasy of degenerates* which has caused immeasurable harm.

We others, we immoralists, have, conversely, made room in our hearts for every kind of understanding, comprehending, and *approving*. We do not easily negate; we make it a point of honor to be *affirmers*. More and more, our eyes have opened to that economy which needs and knows how to utilize all that the holy witlessness of the priest, of the *diseased* reason in the priest, rejects—that economy in the law of life which finds an advantage even in the disgusting species of the prigs, the priests, the virtuous. *What* advantage? But we ourselves, we immoralists, are the answer. . . .

THE ERROR OF FREE WILL

Today we no longer have any pity for the concept of "free will": we know only too well what it really is—the foulest of all theologians' artifices, aimed at making mankind "responsible" in their sense, that is, *dependent upon them*. Here I simply supply the psychology of all "making responsible."

Wherever responsibilities are sought, it is usually the instinct of wanting to judge and punish which is at work. Becoming has been deprived of its innocence when any being-such-and-such is traced back to will, to purposes, to acts of responsibility: the doctrine of the will has been invented essentially for the purpose of punishment, that is, because one wanted to impute guilt. The entire old psychology, the psychology of will, was conditioned by the fact that its originators, the priests at the head of ancient communities, wanted to create for themselves the right to punish—or wanted to create this right for God. Men were considered "free" so that they might be judged and punished—so that they might become *guilty:* consequently, every act had to be considered as willed, and the origin of every act had to be considered as lying within the consciousness (and thus the most fundamental counterfeit *in psychologicis* was made the principle of psychology itself).

Today, as we have entered into the reverse movement and we immoralists are trying with all our strength to take the concept of guilt and the concept of punishment out of the world again, and to cleanse psychology, history, nature, and social institutions and sanctions of them, there is in our eyes no more radical opposition than that of the theologians, who continue with the concept of a "moral world-order" to infect the innocence of becoming by means of "punishment" and "guilt." Christianity is a metaphysics of the hangman.

❧ ❧

What alone can be *our* doctrine? That no one *gives* man his qualities—neither God, nor society, nor his parents and ancestors, nor he himself. (The nonsense of the last idea was taught as "intelligible freedom" by Kant—perhaps by Plato already.) No one is responsible for man's being there at all, for his being such-and-such, or for his being in these circumstances or in this environment. The fatality of his essence is not to be disentangled from the fatality of all that has been and will be. Man is not the effect of some special purpose, of a will, and end; nor is he the object of an attempt to attain an "ideal of humanity" or an "ideal of happiness" or an "ideal of morality." It is absurd to wish to devolve one's essence on some end or other. We have invented the concept of "end": in reality there is no end.

One is necessary, one is a piece of fatefulness, one belongs to the whole, one is in the whole; there is nothing which could judge, measure, compare, or sentence our being, for that would mean judging, measuring comparing, or sentencing the whole. But there is nothing besides the whole. That nobody is held responsible any longer, that the mode of being may not be traced back to a *causa prima,* that the world does not form a unity either as a sensorium or as "spirit"—that alone is the great liberation; with this alone is the innocence of becoming restored. The concept of "God" was until now the greatest objection to existence. We deny God, we deny the responsibility in God: only thereby do we redeem the world.

THE "IMPROVERS" OF MANKIND

My demand upon the philosopher is known, that he take his stand *beyond* good and evil and leave the illusion of moral judgment *beneath* himself. This demand follows from an insight which I was the first to formulate: that *there are altogether no moral facts.* Moral judgments agree with religious ones in believing in realities which are no realities. Morality is merely an interpretation of certain phenomena—more precisely, a misinterpretation. Moral judgments, like religious ones, belong to a stage of ignorance at which the very concept of the real and the distinction between what is real and imaginary, are still lacking; thus "truth," at this stage, designates all sorts of things which we today call "imaginings." Moral judgments are therefore never to be taken literally: so understood, they always contain mere absurdity. Semeiotically, however, they remain invaluable: they reveal, at least for those who know, the most valuable realities of cultures and inwardnesses which did not know enough to "understand" themselves. Morality is mere sign language, mere symptomatology; one must know what it is all about to be able to profit from it.

A first example, quite provisional. At all times they have wanted to "improve" men: this above all was called morality. Under the same word, however, the most divergent tendencies are concealed. Both the *taming* of the beast, man, and the *breeding* of a particular kind of man have been called "improvement." Such zoological terms are required to express the realities —realities, to be sure, of which the typical "improver," the priest, neither knows anything, nor wants to know anything.

To call the taming of an animal its "improvement" sounds almost like a joke to our ears. Whoever knows what goes on in menageries doubts that the beasts are "improved" there. They are weakened, they are made less harmful, and through the depressive effect of fear, through pain, through wounds, and through hunger they become sickly beasts. It is no different with the tamed man whom the priest has "improved." In the early Middle Ages, when the church was indeed, above all, a menagerie, the most beautiful specimens of the "blond beast" were hunted down everywhere; and the noble Teutons, for example, were "improved." But how did such an "improved" Teuton who had been seduced into a monastery look afterward? Like a caricature of man, like a miscarriage: he had become a "sinner," he was stuck in a cage, imprisoned among all sorts of terrible concepts. And there he lay, sick, miserable, malevolent against himself: full of hatred against the springs of life, full of suspicion against all that was still strong and happy. In short, a "Christian." . . .

REVALUATION OF ALL VALUES: THE ANTICHRIST*

What is good? Everything that heightens the feeling of power in man, the will to power, power itself.

What is bad? Everything that is born of weakness.

What is happiness? The feeling that power is *growing,* that resistance is overcome.

Not contentedness but more power; not peace but war; not virtue but fitness (Renaissance virtue, *virtù,* virtue that is moraline-free).

The weak and the failures shall perish: first principle of *our* love of man. And they shall even be given every possible assistance.

What is more harmful than any vice? Active pity for all the failures and all the weak: Christianity.

The problem I thus pose is not what shall succeed mankind in the sequence of living beings (man is an *end*), but what type of man shall be *bred,* shall be *willed,* for being higher in value, worthier of life, more certain of a future.

Even in the past this higher type has appeared often—but as a fortunate accident, as an exception, never as something *willed.* In fact, this has been the type most dreaded—almost *the* dreadful—and from dread the opposite type was willed, bred,

* From "The Antichrist," *The Portable Nietzsche,* edited and translated by Walter Kaufman. Copyright 1954. Reprinted by permission of The Viking Press, Inc., New York.

and *attained:* the domestic animal, the herd, the sick human animal—the Christian. . . .

Christianity should not be beautified and embellished: it has waged deadly war against this higher type of man; it has placed all the basic instincts of this type under the ban; and out of these instincts it has distilled evil and the Evil One: the strong man as the typically reprehensible man, the "reprobate." Christianity has sided with all that is weak and base, with all failures; it has made an ideal of whatever *contradicts* the instinct of the strong life to preserve itself; it has corrupted the reason even of those strongest in spirit by teaching men to consider the supreme values of the spirit as something sinful, as something that leads into error—as temptations. The most pitiful example: the corruption of Pascal, who believed in the corruption of his reason through original sin when it had in fact been corrupted only by his Christianity.

It is a painful, horrible spectacle that has dawned on me: I have drawn back the curtain from the *corruption* of man. In my mouth, this word is at least free from one suspicion: that it might involve a moral accusation of man. It is meant—let me emphasize this once more—*moraline-free.* So much so that I experience this corruption most strongly precisely where men have so far aspired most deliberately to "virtue" and "godliness." I understand corruption, as you will guess, in the sense of decadence: it is my contention that all the values in which mankind now sums up its supreme desiderata are *decadence-values.*

I call an animal, a species, or an individual corrupt when it loses its instincts, when it chooses, when it prefers, what is disadvantageous for it. A history of "lofty sentiments," of the "ideals of mankind"—and it is possible that I shall have to write it—would almost explain too *why* man is so corrupt. Life itself is to my mind the instinct for growth, for durability, for an accumulation of forces, for *power:* where the will to power is lacking there is decline. It is my contention that all the supreme values of mankind *lack* this will—that the values which are symptomatic of decline, *nihilistic* values, are lording it under the holiest names.

Christianity is called the religion of *pity.* Pity stands opposed to the tonic emotions which heighten our vitality: it has a depressing effect. We are deprived of strength when we feel pity. That loss of strength which suffering as such inflicts on life is still further increased and multiplied by pity. Pity makes suffering contagious. Under certain circumstances, it may engender a total loss of life and vitality out of all proportion to the magnitude of the cause (as in the case of the death of the Nazarene). That is the first consideration, but there is a more important one.

Suppose we measure pity by the value of the reactions it usually produces; then its perilous nature appears in an even brighter light. Quite in general, pity crosses the law of development, which is the law of *selection.* It preserves what is ripe for destruction; it defends those who have been disinherited and condemned by life; and by the abundance of the failures of all kinds which it keeps alive, it gives life itself a gloomy and questionable aspect. . . .

In Christianity neither morality nor religion has even a single point of contact with reality. Nothing but imaginary *causes*

("God," "soul," "ego," "spirit," "free will" —for that matter, "unfree will"), nothing but imaginary *effects* ("sin," "redemption," "grace," "punishment," "forgiveness of sins"). Intercourse between imaginary *beings* ("God," "spirits," "souls"); an imaginary *natural* science (anthropocentric; no trace of any concept of natural causes); an imaginary *psychology* (nothing but self-misunderstandings, interpretations of agreeable or disagreeable general feelings—for example, of the states of the *nervus sympathicus*—with the aid of the sign language of the religio-moral idiosyncrasy: "repentance," "pangs of conscience," "temptation by the devil," "the presence of God"); an imaginary *teleology* ("the kingdom of God," "the Last Judgment," "eternal life").

This *world of pure fiction* is vastly inferior to the world of dreams insofar as the latter *mirrors* reality, whereas the former falsifies, devalues, and negates reality. Once the concept of "nature" had been invented as the opposite of "God," "natural" had to become a synonym of "reprehensible": this whole world of fiction is rooted in *hatred* of the natural (of reality!); it is the expression of a profound vexation at the sight of reality.

But this explains everything. Who alone has good reason to lie his way out of reality? He who suffers from it. But to suffer from reality is to be a piece of reality that has come to grief. The preponderance of feelings of displeasure over feelings of pleasure is the cause of this fictitious morality and religion; but such a preponderance provides the very formula for decadence. . . .

Wherever the will to power declines in any form, there is invariably also a physiological retrogression, decadence. The deity of decadence, gelded in his most virile virtues and instincts, becomes of necessity the god of the physiologically retrograde, of the weak. Of course, they do not *call* themselves the weak; they call themselves "the good." . . .

The Christian conception of God—God as god of the sick, God as a spider, God as spirit—is one of the most corrupt conceptions of the divine ever attained on earth. It may even represent the low-water mark in the descending development of divine types. God degenerated into the *contradiction* of life, instead of being its transfiguration and eternal Yes! God as the declaration of war against life, against nature, against the will to live! God—the formula for every slander against "this world," for every lie about the "beyond"! God—the deification of nothingness, the will to nothingness pronounced holy! . . .

The instinctive hatred of reality: a consequence of an extreme capacity for suffering and excitement which no longer wants any contact at all because it feels every contact too deeply.

The instinctive exclusion of any antipathy, any hostility, any boundaries or divisions in man's feelings: the consequence of an extreme capacity for suffering and excitement which experiences any resistance, even any compulsion to resist, as unendurable *displeasure* (that is, as *harmful,* as something against which the instinct of self-preservation *warns* us); and finds blessedness (pleasure) only in no longer offering any resistance to anybody, neither to evil nor to him who is evil—love as the only, as the *last* possible, way of life.

These are the two *physiological realities* on which, out of which, the doctrine of redemption grew. I call this a sublime further development of hedonism on a thoroughly morbid basis. Most closely related to it, although with a generous admixture of Greek vitality and nervous energy, is Epicureanism, the pagan doctrine of redemption. Epicurus, a *typical decadent*—first recognized as such by me. The fear of pain, even of infinitely minute pain—that can end in no other way than in a *religion of love.*

⁂ ⁂

The Gospels are valuable as testimony to the irresistible corruption *within* the first community. What Paul later carried to its conclusion, with the logician's cynicism of a rabbi, was nevertheless nothing other than that process of decay which had begun with the death of the Redeemer.

One cannot read these Gospels cautiously enough; every word poses difficulties. I confess—one will pardon me—that precisely on this account they are a first-rate delight for a psychologist—as the *opposite* of all naïve corruption, as subtlety par excellence, as artistry in psychological corruption. The Gospels stand apart. The Bible in general suffers no comparison. . . .

⁂ ⁂

I give some examples of what these little people put into their heads, what they *put into the mouth* of their master: without exception, confessions of "beautiful souls":

"And whosoever shall not receive you, nor hear you, when ye depart thence, shake off the dust under your feet for a testimony against them. Verily I say unto you, It shall be more tolerable for Sodom and Gomorrah in the day of judgment, than for that city" (Mark 6:11). How *evangelical!* . . .

"Whosoever will come after me, let him deny himself, and take up his cross, and follow me. *For—*" (*Note of a psychologist.* Christian morality is refuted by its *For's:* its "reasons" refute—thus is it Christian.) (Mark 8:34.)

"Judge not, that ye be not judged. . . . With what measure ye mete, it shall be measured to you again" (Matt. 7:1 ff.). What a conception of justice and of a "just" judge!

"For if ye love them which love you, what reward have ye? do not even the publicans the same? And if ye salute your brethren only, what do ye more *than others?* do not even the publicans so?" (Matt. 5:46 *f.*). The principle of "Christian love": in the end it wants to be *paid* well. . . .

"Know ye not that ye are the temple of God, and that the Spirit of God dwelleth in you? If any man defile the temple of God, him shall God destroy; for the temple of God is holy, which temple ye are" (Paul, I Cor. 3:16 *f.*). This sort of thing one cannot despise enough .

"Do ye not know that the saints shall judge the world? and if the world shall be judged by you, are ye unworthy to judge the smallest matters?" (Paul, I Cor. 6:2). Unfortunately not merely the talk of a lunatic. This *frightful swindler* continues literally: "Know ye not that we shall judge angels? how much more things that pertain to this life!"

"Hath not God made foolish the wisdom of this world? For after that the world by its wisdom knew not God in his wisdom, it pleased God by foolish preaching to make blessed them that believe in it. . . . Not many wise men after the flesh, not many mighty, not many noble, are called. But God hath chosen the foolish things of the world to ruin the wise; and God hath chosen the weak things of the world to ruin what is strong; And base things of the world, and things which are despised, hath God chosen, yea, and what is nothing, to bring to nought what is something: That no flesh should glory in his presence" (Paul, I Cor. 1:20 ff.). . . .

⁂ ⁂

What follows from this? That one does well to put on gloves when reading the

New Testament. The proximity of so much uncleanliness almost forces one to do this.

❧ ❧

One should not be deceived: great spirits are skeptics. . . . Strength, *freedom* which is born of the strength and over-strength of the spirit, proves itself by skepticism. Men of conviction are not worthy of the least consideration in fundamental questions of value and disvalue. Convictions are prisons. Such men do not look far enough, they do not look *beneath* themselves: but to be permitted to join in the discussion of value and disvalue, one must see five hundred convictions *beneath* onself—*behind* oneself.

A spirit who wants great things, who also wants the means to them, is necessarily a skeptic. Freedom from all kinds of convictions, to be able to see freely, is part of strength. Great passion, the ground and the power of his existence, even more enlightened, even more despotic than he is himself, employs his whole intellect; it makes him unhesitating; it gives him courage even for unholy means; under certain circumstances it does not begrudge him convictions. Conviction as a *means:* many things are attained only by means of a conviction. Great passion uses and uses up convictions, it does not succumb to them—it knows itself sovereign.

Conversely: the need for faith, for some kind of unconditional Yes and No, this Carlylism, if one will forgive me this word, is a need born of *weakness*. The man of faith, the "believer" of every kind, is necessarily a dependent man—one who cannot posit *himself* as an end, one who cannot posit any end at all by himself. The "believer" does not belong to *himself,* he can only be a means, he must be *used up,* he requires somebody to use him up. His instinct gives the highest honor to a morality of self-abnegation; everything persuades him in this direction: his prudence, his experience, his vanity. Every kind of faith is itself an expression of self-abnegation, of self-alienation.

❧ ❧

I pronounce my judgment. I *condemn* Christianity. I raise against the Christian church the most terrible of all accusations that any accuser ever uttered. It is to me the highest of all conceivable corruptions. It has had the will to the last corruption that is even possible. The Christian church has left nothing untouched by its corruption; it has turned every value into an un-value, every truth into a lie, every integrity into a vileness of the soul. Let anyone dare to speak to me of its "humanitarian" blessings! To *abolish* any distress ran counter to its deepest advantages: it lived on distress, it *created* distress to eternalize *itself*.

The worm of sin, for example: with this distress the church first enriched mankind. The "equality of souls before God," this falsehood, this *pretext* for the rancor of all the base-minded, this explosive of a concept which eventually became revolution, modern idea, and the principle of decline of the whole order of society—is *Christian* dynamite. "Humanitarian" blessings of Christianity! To breed out of *humanitus* a self-contradiction, an art of self-violation, a will to lie at any price, a repugnance, a contempt for all good and honest instincts! Those are some of the blessings of Christianity!

Parasitism as the *only* practice of the church; with its ideal of anemia, of "holiness," draining all blood, all love, all hope for life; the beyond as the will to negate every reality; the cross as the mark of recognition for the most subterranean conspiracy that ever existed—against health, beauty, whatever has turned out well, courage, spirit, *graciousness* of the soul, *against life itself*.

This eternal indictment of Christianity I will write on all walls, wherever there are walls—I have letters to make even the blind see.

I call Christianity the one great curse, the one great innermost corruption, the one great instinct of revenge, for which no means is poisonous, stealthy, subterranean, *small* enough—I call it the one immortal blemish of mankind.

And time is reckoned from the *dies nefastus* with which this calamity began—after the *first* day of Christianity! *Why not rather after its last day? After today?* Revaluation of all values!

THE HAMMER SPEAKS*

"Why so hard?" the kitchen coal once said to the diamond. "After all, are we not close kin?"

Why so soft? O my brothers, thus I ask you: are you not after all my brothers?

Why so soft, so pliant and yielding? Why is there so much denial, self-denial, in your hearts? So little destiny in your eyes?

And if you do not want to be destinies and inexorable ones, how can you one day triumph with me?

And if your hardness does not wish to flash and cut and cut through, how can you one day create with me?

For all creators are hard. And it must seem blessedness to you to impress your hand on millennia as on wax,

Blessedness to write on the will of millennia as on bronze—harder than bronze, nobler than bronze. Only the noblest is altogether hard.

This new tablet, O my brothers, I place over you: become hard!

Zarathustra, III

* From "Twilight of the Idols."

FRANCIS HERBERT BRADLEY

Francis Herbert Bradley (1846–1924) was elected to a fellowship at Merton College shortly after graduating from Oxford. Though he remained a fellow for fifty-four years, he never taught. Partly because of illness but possibly also as a matter of choice, he lived the life of a recluse, rarely entertaining, and performing only those few duties associated with his fellowship in the college.

Seclusion did not prevent him from having a wide impact on his age. He was one of the leaders of the revolt against the traditional British empiricism, carrying on the battle by introducing the insights of German philosophy into the stream of British thought. But in one respect he was a member of the British philosophical tradition, for in spite of the difficulty of his subject matter, he endeavored to write with clarity, with precision, and not least important, with wit.

Though Bradley drew inspiration from many sources, his chief indebtedness is to Hegel, as is exhibited by the selections given below. But Bradley was no mere "popularizer" of Hegel, for while he relied heavily upon Hegelian doctrines, the clarification, emendation, and final synthesis of these doctrines transform them into a distinctive philosophic position of his own.

*Ethical Studies**

Self-realization as the Ethical End†

How can it be proved that self-realization is the end? There is only one way to do that. This is to know what we mean when we say "self" and "real" and "realize" and "end"; and to know that is to have something like a system of metaphysic, and to say it would be to exhibit that system. Instead of remarking then that we lack space to develop our views, let us frankly confess that, properly speaking, we have no such views to develop, and therefore we cannot *prove* our thesis. All that we can do is partially to explain it, and try to render it plausible. . . .

An objection will occur at once. "There surely are ends," it will be said, "which are not myself, which fall outside my activity, and which, nevertheless, I do realize and think I ought to realize." We must try to show that the objection rests upon a misunderstanding; and, as a statement of fact, brings with it insuperable difficulties.

Let us first go to the moral consciousness and see what that tells us about its end.

Morality implies an end in itself—we take that for granted. Something is to be done, a good is to be realized. But that result is, by itself, not morality; morality differs from art in that it cannot make the act a *mere* means of the result. Yet there is a means. There is not only something to be done, but something to be done by me—*I* must do the act, must realize the end. Morality implies both the something to be done and the doing of it by me; and if you consider them as end and means, you cannot separate the end and the means. If you chose to change the position of end and means and say my doing is the end and the "to be done" is the means, you would not violate the moral consciousness; for the truth is that means and end are not applicable here. The act for me means my act, and there is no end beyond the act. This we see in the belief that failure may be equivalent morally to success—in the saying that there is nothing good except a good will. In short, for morality the end implies the act, and the act implies self-realization. This, if it were doubtful, would be shown (we may remark in passing) by the feeling of pleasure which attends the putting forth of the act. For if pleasure be the feeling of self and accompany the act, this indicates that the putting forth of the act is also the putting forth of the self.

But we must not lay too much stress on the moral consciousness, for we shall be reminded, perhaps, that not only can it be, but, like the miser's consciousness, it frequently has been explained; and that both states of mind are illusions generated on one and the same principle.

Let us then dismiss the moral consciousness and not trouble ourselves about what we think we ought to do; let us try to show that what we do is, perfectly or imperfectly, to realize ourselves, and that we cannot possibly do anything else; that all we can realize is (accident apart) our ends, or the objects we desire; and that all we can desire is, in a word, self.

This, we think, will be readily admitted by our main psychological party. What we wish to avoid is that it should be admitted in a form which makes it unmeaning; and of this there is perhaps some danger. We do not want the reader to say, "Oh yes, of course, relativity of knowledge—everything is a state of consciousness," and so dismiss the question. If the reader believes that a steam engine, after it is made, is nothing but a state of the mind of the person or persons who have made it, or who are looking at it, we do not hold what we feel tempted to call such a silly

* By permission. F. H. Bradley, *Ethical Studies*, The Claredon Press, Oxford, 1927. Some section headings added by the Editors.

† From "Why Should I Be Moral?"

doctrine; and would point out to those who do hold it that, at all events, the engine is a very different state of mind after it is made to what it was before.

Again, we do not want the reader to say, "Certainly, every object or end which I propose to myself is, as such, a mere state of my mind—it is a thought in my head, or a state of me; and so, when it becomes real, I become real"; because, though it is very true that my thought, as my thought, cannot exist apart from me thinking it, and therefore my proposed end must, as such, be a state of me, yet this is not what we are driving at. All my ends are my thoughts, but all my thoughts are not my ends; and if what we meant by self-realization was that I have in my head the idea of any future external event, then I should realize myself practically when I see that the engine is going to run off the line, and it does so.

A desired object (as desired) is a thought, and my thought, but it is something more and that something more is, in short, that it is desired by me. And we ought by right, before we go further, to exhibit a theory of desire; but, if we could do that, we could not stop to do it. However, we say with confidence that, in desire, what is desired must in all cases be self.

If we could accept the theory that the end or motive is always the idea of a pleasure (or pain) of our own, which is associated with the object presented, and which is that in the object which moves us, and the only thing which does move us, then from such a view it would follow at once that all we can aim at is a state of ourselves.

We cannot, however, accept the theory, since we believe it both to ignore and to be contrary to facts; but, though we do not admit that the motive is always, or in most cases, the idea of a state of our feeling self, yet we think it is clear that nothing moves unless it be desired and that what is desired is ourself. For all objects or ends have been associated with our satisfaction, or (more correctly) have been felt in and as ourselves, or we have felt ourselves therein; and the only reason why they move us now is that when they are presented to our minds as motives we do now feel ourselves asserted or affirmed in them. The essence of desire for an object would thus be the feeling of our affirmation in the idea of something not ourself, felt against the feeling of ourself as, without the object, void and negated; and it is the tension of this relation which produces motion. If so, then nothing is desired except that which is identified with ourselves, and we can aim at nothing except so far as we aim at ourselves in it.

But passing by the above, which we cannot here expound and which we lay no stress on, we think that the reader will probably go with us so far as this, that in desire what we want, so far as we want it, is ourselves in some form, or is some state of ourselves; and that our wanting anything else would be psychologically inexplicable.

Let us take this for granted then; but is this what we mean by self-realization? Is the conclusion that, in trying to realize, we try to realize some state of ourself, all that we are driving at? No, the self we try to realize is for us a whole, it is not a mere collection of states.

If we may presuppose in the reader a belief in the doctrine that what is wanted is a state of self, we wish, standing upon that, to urge further that the whole self is present in its states, and that therefore the whole self is the object aimed at; and this is what we mean by self-realization. If a state of self is what is desired, can you, we wish to ask, have states of self which are states of nothing; can you possibly succeed in regarding the self as a collection or stream or train or series or aggregate? If you cannot think of it as a mere one, can you on the other hand think of it as a mere many, as mere ones; or are you not driven, whether you wish it or not, to regard it as a one in many, or a many in one? Are we not forced to look on the self as a whole which is not merely the sum of its parts, nor yet some other particular beside them? And must we not say that to realize self is always to realize a whole, and that the question in morals is to find the true whole, realizing which will practically realize the true self? . . .

Contenting ourselves with the proposition that to realize is to realize self, let us now, apart from questions of psychology or metaphysics, see what ends they are, in fact, which living men do propose to themselves and whether these do not take the form of a whole.

Upon this point there is no need, I think, to dwell at any length; for it seems clear that if we ask ourselves what it is we should most wish for, we find some general wish which would include and imply our particular wishes. And if we turn to life we see that no man has disconnected particular ends; he looks beyond the moment, beyond this or that circumstance or position; his ends are subordinated to wider ends; each situation is seen (consciously or unconsciously) as part of a broader situation, and in this or that act he is aiming at and realizing some larger whole which is not real in any particular act as such, and yet is realized in the body of acts which carry it out. We need not stop here because the existence of larger ends, which embrace smaller ends, cannot be doubted; and so far we may say that the self we realize is identified with wholes, or that the ideas of the states of self we realize are associated with ideas that stand for wholes.

But is it also true that these larger wholes are included in one whole? I think that it is. I am not forgetting that we act, as a rule, not *from* principle or with the principle before us, and I wish the reader not to forget that the principle may be there and may be our basis or our goal, without our knowing anything about it. And here, of course, I am not saying that it has occurred to every one to ask himself whether he aims at a whole, and what that is; because considerable reflection is required for this, and the amount need not have been reached. Nor again am I saying that every man's actions are consistent, that he does not wander from his end, and that he has not particular ends which will not come under his main end. Nor further do I assert that the life of every man does form a whole; that in some men there are not co-ordinated ends which are incompatible and incapable of subordination into a system. What I am saying is that if the life of the normal man be inspected and the ends he has in view (as exhibited in his acts) be considered, they will, roughly speaking, be embraced in one main end or whole of ends. It has been said that "every man has a different notion of happiness," but this is scarcely correct unless mere detail be referred to. Certainly, however, every man has *a* notion of happiness, and *his* notion, though he may not quite know what it is. Most men have a life which they live and with which they are tolerably satisfied, and that life, when examined, is seen to be fairly systematic; it is seen to be a sphere including spheres, the lower spheres subordinating to themselves and qualifying particular actions, and themselves subordinated to and qualified by the whole. And most men have more or less of an ideal of life—a notion of perfect happiness which is never quite attained in real life; and if you take (not of course any one, but) the normal decent and serious man, when he has been long enough in the world to know what he wants, you will find that his notion of perfect happiness or ideal life is not something straggling, as it were, and discontinuous, but is brought before the mind as an unity, and, if imagined more in detail, is a system where particulars subserve one whole. . . .

All we know at present is that we are to realize self as *a* whole; but as to *what* whole it is, we know nothing and must further consider.

The end we desire (to repeat it) is the finding and possessing ourselves as a whole. We aim at this both in theory and practice. What we want in theory is to understand the object; we want neither to remove nor alter the world of sensuous fact, but we want to get at the truth of it. The whole of science takes it for granted that the "not-ourself" is really intelligible; it stands and falls with this assumption. So long as our theory strikes on the mind as strange and alien, so long do we say we have not found truth; we feel the impulse to go beyond and beyond, we alter and alter our views till we see them as a consistent whole. There we rest because then we have found the nature of our own mind and the truth of facts in one. And in practice again, with a difference, we have the same want. Here our aim is not, leaving the given as it is, to find the truth of it; but here we want to force the sensuous fact to correspond to the truth of ourselves. We say, "My sensuous existence is thus, but I truly am not thus; I am different." On the one hand, as a matter of fact, I and my existing world are discrepant; on the other hand, the instinct of my nature tells me that the world is mine. On that impulse I act, I alter and alter the sensuous facts till I find in them nothing but myself carried out. Then I possess my world, and I do not possess it until I find my will in it; and I do not find that until what I have is a harmony or a whole in system.

Both in theory and practice my end is to realize myself as a whole. But is this all? Is a *consistent* view all that we want in theory? Is a *harmonious* life all that we want in practice? Certainly not. A doctrine must not only hold together, but it must hold the facts together as well. We cannot rest in it simply because it does not contradict itself. The theory must take in the facts, and an ultimate theory must take in all the facts. So again in practice. It is no human ideal to lead "the life of an oyster." We have no right first to find out just what we happen to be and to have, and then to contract our wants to that limit. We cannot do it if we would, and morality calls to us that, if we try to do it, we are false to ourselves. Against the sensuous facts around us and within us we must forever attempt to widen our empire; we must at least try to go forward or we shall certainly be driven back.

So self-realization means more than the mere assertion of the self as a whole. . . . Our true being is not the extreme of unity, nor of diversity, but the perfect identity of both. And "Realize yourself" does not mean merely "Be a whole," but "Be an infinite whole."

At this word I am afraid the reader who has not yet despaired of us will come to a stop and refuse to enter into the region of nonsense. But why should it be nonsense? When the poet and the preacher tell us the mind is infinite, most of us feel that it is so; and has our science really come to this that the beliefs which answer to our highest feelings must be theoretical absurdities? Should not the philosophy which tells us such a thing be very sure of the ground it goes upon? But if the reader will follow me I think I can show him that the mere finitude of the mind is a more difficult thesis to support than its infinity. . . .

Finite means limited from the outside and by the outside. The finite is to know itself as this, or not as finite. If its knowledge ceases to fall wholly within itself, then so far it is not finite. It knows that it is limited from the outside and by the outside, and that means it knows the outside. But if so, then it is so far not finite. If its whole being fell within itself, then in knowing itself it coud not know that there was anything outside itself. It does do the latter; hence the former supposition is false.

Imagine a man shut up in a room, who said to us, "My faculties are entirely confined to the *inside* of this room. The limit of the room is the limit of my mind and so I can have no knowledge whatever of the outside"; should we not answer, "My dear sir, you contradict yourself. If it were as you say, you could not know of an outside, and so, by consequence, not of an inside, as such. You should be in earnest and go through with your doctrine of 'relativity.' "

To the above simple argument I fear we may not have done justice. However that be, I know of no answer to it; and until we find one, we must say that it is not true that the mind is finite.

If I am to realize myself it must be as infinite; and now the question is, What does infinite mean? . . . The infinite is "the unity of the finite and infinite." The finite was determined from the outside, so that everywhere to characterize and distinguish it was in fact to divide it. Wherever you defined anything you were at once carried beyond to something else and something else, and this because the negative, required for distinction, was an outside other. In the infinite you can distinguish without dividing; for this is an unity holding within itself subordinated factors which are negative of, and so distinguishable from, each other; while at the same time the whole is so present in each that each has its own being in its opposite, and depends on that relation for its own life. The negative is also its affirmation. Thus the infinite has a distinction, and so a negation, in itself, but is distinct from and negated by nothing but itself. Far from being one something which is *not* another something, it is a whole in which both one and the other are mere elements. This whole is hence "relative" utterly and through and through, but the relation does not fall outside it; the relatives are moments in which it is the relation of itself to itself, and so is above the relation, and is absolute reality. The finite is relative to something *else;* the infinite is *self*-related. It is this sort of infinite which the mind is. The simplest symbol of it is the circle, the line which returns into itself, not the straight line produced indefinitely; and the readiest way to find it is to consider the satisfaction of desire. There we have myself and its opposite, and the return from the opposite, the finding in the other nothing but self. And here it would be well to recall what we said above on the form of the will.

If the reader to whom this account of the infinite is new has found it in any way intelligible, I think he will see that there is some sense in it when we say, "Realize yourself as an infinite whole"; or, in other words, "Be specified in yourself, but not specified by anything foreign to yourself."

But the objection comes: "Morality tells us to progress; it tells us we are not concluded in ourselves nor perfect, but that there exists a not-ourself which never does wholly become ourself. And apart from morality, it is obvious that I and you, this man and the other man, are finite beings. We are not one another; more or less we must limit each other's sphere; I am what I am more or less by external relations, and I do not fall wholly within myself. Thus I am to be infinite, to have no limit from the outside; and yet I am one among others, and therefore am finite. It is all very well to tell me that in me there is infinity, the perfect identity of subject and object—that I may be willing perhaps to believe, but nonetheless I am finite."

We admit the full force of the objection. I *am* finite; I am both infinite *and* finite and that is why my moral life is a perpetual progress. I must progress because I have an other which is to be, and yet never quite is, myself; and so, as I am, am in a state of contradiction.

It is not that I wish to increase the mere quantity of my true self. It is that I wish to be nothing *but* my true self, to be rid of all external relations, to bring them all within me, and so to fall wholly within myself.

I am to be perfectly homogeneous; but I cannot be unless fully specified, and the question is, How can I be extended so as to take in my external relations? Goethe has said, "Be a whole *or* join a whole," but to that we must answer, "You cannot be a whole, *unless* you join a whole."

The difficulty is: being limited and so not a whole, how extend myself so as to be a whole? The answer is, be a member in a whole. Here your private self, your finitude, ceases as such to exist; it becomes the function of an organism. You must be, not a mere piece of, but a member in, a whole, and as this must know and will yourself.

The whole to which you belong specifies itself in the detail of its functions, and yet remains homogeneous. It lives not many lives but one life, and yet cannot live except in its many members. Just so, each one of the members is alive, but not apart from the whole which lives in it. The organism is homogeneous because it is specified, and specified because it is homogeneous.

"But," it will be said, "what is that to me? I remain one member, and I am not other members. The more perfect the organism, the more it is specified, and so much the intenser becomes its homogeneity. But its 'more' means my 'less.' The unity falls in the whole and so outside me; and the greater specification of the whole means the making me more special, more narrowed and limited, and less developed within myself."

We answer that this leaves out of sight a fact quite palpable and of enormous significance, viz., that in the moral organism the members are aware of themselves, and aware of themselves as members. I do not know myself as mere this, against something else which is not myself. The relations of the others to me are not mere external relations. I know myself as a member; that means I am aware of my own function; but it means also that I am aware of the whole as specifying itself in me. The will of the whole knowingly wills itself in me; the will of the whole is the will of the members, and so, in willing my own function, I do know that the others will themselves in me. I do know again that I will myself in the others, and in them find my will once more as not mine, and yet as mine. It is false that the homogeneity falls outside me; it is not only in me, but for me too; and apart from my life in it, my knowledge of it, and devotion to it, I am not myself. When it goes out my heart goes out with it, where it triumphs I rejoice, where it is maimed I suffer; separate me from the love of it and I perish.

No doubt the distinction of separate selves remains, but the point is this. In morality the existence of my mere private self, as such, is something which ought not to be, and which, so far as I am moral, has already ceased. I am morally realized, not until my personal self has utterly ceased to be my exclusive self, is no more a will which is outside others' wills, but finds in the world of others nothing but self.

"Realize yourself as an infinite whole" means "Realize yourself as the self-conscious member of an infinite whole, by realizing that whole in yourself." When that whole is truly infinite, and when your personal will is wholly made one with it, then you also have reached the extreme of homogeneity and specification in one, and have attained a perfect self-realization. . . .

*The Will as the Ethical End**

Explicitly or by implication, all Ethics presupposed something which is the good, and this good (whatever else may be its nature) has always the character of an end. The moral good is an end in itself, is to be pursued for its own sake. . . .

What is the moral end? . . . To know what it is we must go to the moral consciousness. We find there that the end is for me as active, is a practical end. It is not something merely to be felt, it is something to be done.

And it is not something to be done, in which, when done, the doer is not to be

* From "Duty For Duty's Sake."

involved. The end does not fall outside the doer. I am to realize myself; and, as we saw, I cannot make an ultimate end of anything except myself, cannot make myself a mere means to something else. Nor, again, does the end fall outside the activity. If the production in me of a mere passive state were the end, the activity would be a mere means to that. But the moral consciousness assures us that the activity is an end in itself. The end is a doing which is to be done; the activity is good in itself, not for the sake of a result beyond. The end, then, is not to be felt, but is to be done; it is to be done and not made; it falls not outside the self of the doer, nor further outside his activity.

In short, the good is the Good Will. The end is will for the sake of will; and, in its relation to me, it is the realization of the good will in myself, or of myself as the good will. In this character I am an end to myself, and I am an absolute and ultimate end. There is nothing which is good unless it be a good will.

This is no metaphysical fiction. It is the truth of life and of the moral consciousness. A man is not called good because he is rich, nor because he is handsome or clever. He is good when he is moral, and he is moral when his actions are conformed to and embody a good will, or when his will is good.

But "good will" tells us little or nothing. It says only *that* will is the end. It does not say *what* will is the end; and we want to know what the good will is.

What is the good will? We may call it indifferently the free will or the universal will, or the autonomous will, or finally the formal will.

1. It is the universal will. The very notion of the moral end is that it should be an end absolutely, not conditionally. It is not an end for me without being one also for you, or for you and me and not for a third person; but it is, without limitation to any this or that, an end for us all. And so the will, as end, is not the particular will of particular men, existing as this, that, and the other series of states of mind. It is the same for you and me and in the character of our common standard and aim it is above you and me. It is thus objective and universal.

2. It is the free will. It is not conditioned by it, it does not owe its existence and attributes to, it is not made what it is by, and hence it cannot (properly speaking) be called forth by, anything which is not itself. It exists because of itself and for the sake of itself. It has no end or aim beyond itself, is not constituted or determined by anything else.

Hence we see it is not determined by anything in particular. For, as we saw, it was universal, and universal means not particular; and so no more than a verbal conclusion is wanted to show that, if determined by something particular, it would be determined by something not itself. And this we have already taken to be false.

3. It is autonomous. For it is universal and an end to itself. The good will is the will which wills the universal as itself and itself as the universal, and hence may be said to be a law to itself and to will its own law. And, because it is universal, hence in willing what is valid for itself it wills what is valid for all. It legislates universally in legislating for itself, since it would not legislate for itself did it not legislate universally.

4. And lastly, it is formal. For, in willing itself, it wills the universal, and that is not-particular. Any possible object of desire, any wished-for event, any end in the shape of a result to be attained in the particular existence of myself or another, all are this or that something—they have a content, they are "material." Only that will is good which wills itself as not-particular, as without content or matter, in a word, which wills itself as form.

The good will, then, is the will which is determined by the form only, which realizes itself as the bare form of the will.

My Station and Its Duties*

The self is to be realized . . . as will, will not being merely the natural will, or the will as it happens to exist and finds itself here or there, but the will as the *good* will, *i.e.*, the will that realizes an end which is above this or that man, superior to them, and capable of confronting them in the shape of a law or an ought. This superior something further, which is a possible law or ought to the individual man, does not depend for its existence on his choice or opinion. Either there is no morality, so says the moral consciousness, or moral duties exist independently of their position by this or that person—my duty may be mine and no other man's, but I do not make it mine. If it is duty, it would be the duty of any person in my case and condition, whether they thought so or not—in a word, duty is "objective," in the sense of not being contingent on the opinion or choice of this or that subject.

What we have left then (to resume it) is this—the end is the realization of the good will which is superior to ourselves; and again the end is self-realization. Bringing these together we see the end is the realization of ourselves as the will which is above ourselves. And this will (if morality exists) we saw must be "objective," because not dependent on "subjective" liking; and "universal," because not identifiable with any particular, but standing above all actual and possible particulars. Further, though universal it is not abstract since it belongs to its essence that it should be realized, and it has no real existence except in and through its particulars. The good will (for morality) is meaningless, if, whatever else it be, it be not the will of living human beings. It is a concrete universal because it not only is above but is within and throughout its details, and is so far only as they are. It is the life which can live only in and by them, as they are dead unless within it; it is the whole soul which lives so far as the body lives, which makes the body a living body and which without the body is as unreal an abstraction as the body without it. It is an organism and a moral organism; and it is conscious self-realization because only by the will of its self-conscious members can the moral organism give itself reality. It is the self-realization of the whole body because it is one and the same will which lives and acts in the life and action of each. It is the self-realization of each member because each member cannot find the function which makes him himself, apart from the whole to which he belongs; to be himself he must go beyond himself, to live his life he must live a life which is not *merely* his own, but which, none the less, but on the contrary all the more, is intensely and emphatically his own individuality. . . . Here is a universal which can confront our wandering desires with a fixed and stern imperative, but which yet is no unreal form of the mind but a living soul that penetrates and stands fast in the detail of actual existence. It is real, and real for me. It is in its affirmation that I affirm myself, for I am but as a "heart-beat in its system." And I am real in it, for, when I give myself to it, it gives me the fruition of my own personal activity, the accomplished ideal of my life which is happiness. In the realized idea which, superior to me and yet here and now in and by me, affirms itself in a continuous process, we have found the end, we have found self-realization, duty, and happiness in one—yes, we have found ourselves when we have found our station and its duties, our function as an organ in the social organism. . . .

Let us take a man, an Englishman as he is now, and try to point out that apart from what he has in common with others, apart from his sameness with others, he is not an Englishman—nor a man at all; that if you take him as something by himself, he is not what he is. Of course we do not mean

* From "My Station and Its Duties."

to say that he cannot go out of England without disappearing, nor, even if all the rest of the nation perished that he would not survive. What we mean to say is that he is what he is because he is a born and educated social being, and a member of an individual social organism; that if you make abstraction of all this, which is the same in him and in others, what you have left is not an Englishman, nor a man, but some I know not what residuum, which never has existed by itself and does not so exist. If we suppose the world of relations, in which he was born and bred, never to have been, then we suppose the very essence of him not to be; if we take that away, we have taken him away; and hence he now is not an individual, in the sense of owing nothing to the sphere of relations in which he finds himself, but does contain those relations within himself as belonging to his very being; he is what he is, in brief, so far as he is what others also are. . . .

The "individual" man, the man into whose essence his community with others does not enter, who does not include relation to others in his very being, is, we say, a fiction, and in the light of facts we have to examine him. Let us take him in the shape of an English child as soon as he is born; for I suppose we ought not to go further back. Let us take him as soon as he is separated from his mother and occupies a space clear and exclusive of all other human beings. At this time, education and custom will, I imagine, be allowed to have not as yet operated on him or lessened his "individuality." But is he now a mere "individual," in the sense of not implying in his being identity with others? We cannot say that if we hold to the teaching of modern physiology. Physiology would tell us, in one language or another, that even now the child's mind is no passive "tabula rasa"; he has an inner, a yet undeveloped nature, which must largely determine his future individuality. What is this inner nature? Is it particular to himself? Certainly not all of it, will have to be the answer. The child is not fallen from heaven. He is born of certain parents who come of certain families, and he has in him the qualities of his parents, and, as breeders would say, of the strains from both sides. Much of it we can see and more we believe to be latent and, given certain (possible or impossible) conditions, ready to come to light. On the descent of mental qualities modern investigation and popular experience, as expressed in uneducated vulgar opinion, altogether, I believe, support one another, and we need not linger here. But if the intellectual and active qualities do descend from ancestors, is it not, I would ask, quite clear that a man may have in him the same that his father and mother had, the same that his brothers and sisters have? And if anyone objects to the word "same," I would put this to him. If, concerning two dogs allied in blood, I were to ask a man, "Is that of the same strain of stock as this?" and were answered, "No, not the same, but similar," should I not think one of these things, that the man either meant to deceive me, or was a "thinker," or a fool?

But the child is not merely the member of a family; he is born into other spheres, and (passing over the subordinate wholes which nevertheless do in many cases qualify him) he is born a member of the English nation. It is, I believe, a matter of fact that at birth the child of one race is not the same as the child of another; that in the children of the one race there is a certain identity, a developed or undeveloped national type which may be hard to recognize, or which at present may even be unrecognizable, but which nevertheless in some form will appear. If that be the fact, then again we must say that one English child is in some points, though perhaps it does not as yet show itself, the same as another. His being is so far common to him with others; he is not a mere "individual." . . .

What is it then that I am to realize? We have said it in "my station and its duties." To know what a man is (as we have seen) you must not take him in isolation. He is one of a people, he was born in a family, he lives in a certain society, in a certain state. What he has to do depends on what his place is, what his function is, and that all comes from his station in the organism. Are there then such organisms in which he lives, and if so, what is their nature? Here we come to questions which must be answered in full by any complete system of Ethics, but which we cannot enter on. We must content ourselves by pointing out that there are such facts as the family, then in a middle position a man's own profession and society, and, over all, the larger community of the state. Leaving out of sight the question of a society wider than the state, we must say that a man's life with its moral duties is in the main filled up by his station in that system of wholes which the state is, and that this, partly by its laws and institutions and still more by its spirit, gives him the life which he does live and ought to live. That objective institutions exist is of course an obvious fact; and it is a fact which every day is becoming plainer that these institutions are organic, and further, that they are moral. The assertion that communities have been manufactured by the addition of exclusive units is a mere fable; and if, within the state, we take that which seems wholly to depend on individual caprice, *e.g.*, marriage, yet even here we find that a man does give up his self so far as it excludes others, he does bring himself under a unity which is superior to the particular person and the impulses that belong to his single existence, and which makes him fully as much as he makes it. In short, man is a social being; he is real only because he is social, and can realize himself only because it is as social that he realizes himself. The mere individual is a delusion of theory; and the attempt to realize it in practice is the starvation and mutilation of human nature, with total sterility or the production of monstrosities. . . .

The non-theoretical person, if he be not immoral, is at peace with reality; and the man who in any degree has made this point of view his own becomes more and more reconciled to the world and to life, and the theories of "advanced thinkers" come to him more and more as the thinnest and most miserable abstractions. He sees evils which cannot discourage him, since they point to the strength of the life which can endure such parasites and flourish in spite of them. If the popularizing of superficial views inclines him to bitterness, he comforts himself when he sees that they live in the head, and but little, if at all, in the heart and life; that still at the push the doctrinaire and the quacksalver go to the wall, and that even that too is as it ought to be. He sees the true account of the state (which holds it to be neither mere force nor convention, but the moral organism, the real identity of might and right) unknown or "refuted," laughed at and despised, but he sees the state every day in its practice refute every other doctrine, and do with the moral approval of all what the explicit theory of scarcely one will morally justify. He sees instincts are better and stronger than so-called "principles." He sees in the hour of need what are called "rights" laughed at, "freedom," the liberty to do what one pleases, tramped on, the claims of the individual trodden under foot, and theories burst like cobwebs. And he sees, as of old, the heart of a nation rise high and beat in the breast of each one of her citizens till her safety and her honor are dearer to each than life, till to those who live her shame and sorrow, if such is allotted, outweigh their loss, and death seems a little thing to those who go for her to their common and nameless grave. And he knows that what is stronger than death is hate or love, hate here for love's sake, and that love does not fear death because already it is the death into life of what our philosophers tell us is the only life and reality.

Yes, the state is not put together, but

it lives; it is not a heap nor a machine; it is no mere extravagance when a poet talks of a nation's soul. It is the objective mind which is subjective and self-conscious in its citizens—it feels and knows itself in the heart of each. It speaks the word of command and gives the field of accomplishment, and in the activity of obedience it has and bestows individual life and satisfaction and happiness. . . .

Once let us take the point of view which regards the community as the real moral organism, which in its members knows and wills itself and sees the individual to be real just so far as the universal self is in his self, as he in it, and we get the solution of most, if not all, of our previous difficulties. There is here no need to ask and by some scientific process find out what is moral, for morality exists all round us, and faces us, if need be, with a categorical imperative, while it surrounds us on the other side with an atmosphere of love.

The belief in this real moral organism is the one solution of ethical problems. It breaks down the antithesis of despotism and individualism; it denies them, while it preserves the truth of both. The truth of individualism is saved, because unless we have intense life and self-consciousness in the members of the state, the whole state is ossified. The truth of despotism is saved, because unless the member realizes the whole by and in himself, he fails to reach his own individuality. Considered in the main, the best communities are those which have the best men for their members, and the best men are the members of the best communities. Circle as this is, it is not a vicious circle. The two problems of the best man and best state are two sides, two distinguishable aspects of the one problem, how to realize in human nature the perfect unity of homogeneity and specification; and when we see that each of these without the other is unreal, then we see that (speaking in general) the welfare of the state and the welfare of its individuals are questions which it is mistaken and ruinous to separate. Personal morality and political and social institutions cannot exist apart, and (in general) the better the one the better the other. The community is moral because it realizes personal morality; personal morality is moral because and in so far as it realizes the moral whole.

It is here we find an answer to the complaint of our day on the dwindling of human nature. The higher the organism (we are told), the more are its functions specified, and hence narrowed. The man becomes a machine, or the piece of a machine; and, though the world grows, "the individual withers." On this we may first remark that, if what is meant is that the more centralized the system, the more narrow and monotonous is the life of the member, that is a very questionable assertion. If it be meant that the individual's life can be narrowed to "file-packing," or the like, without detriment to the intensity of the life of the whole, that is even more questionable. If again it be meant that in many cases we have a one-sided specification, which, despite the immediate stimulus of particular function implies ultimate loss of life to the body, that, I think, probably is so, but it is doubtful if we are compelled to think it always must be so. But the root of the whole complaint is a false view of things, which we have briefly noticed above. The moral organism is not a mere animal organism. In the latter (it is no novel remark) the member is not aware of itself as such, while in the former it knows itself, and therefore knows the whole in itself. The narrow external function of the man is not the whole man. He has a life which we cannot see with our eyes; and there is no duty so mean that it is not the realization of this, and knowable as such. What counts is not the visible outer work so much as the spirit in which it is done. The breadth of my life is not measured by the multitude of my pursuits, nor the space I take up amongst other men, but by the fullness of the whole life which I know as mine. It is true that less now depends on each of us, as this or that man; it is not true that our individuality is therefore lessened, that therefore we have less in us. . . .

The next point we come to is the question, How do I get to know in particular what is right and wrong? and here we find a strangely erroneous preconception. It is thought that moral philosophy has to accomplish this task for us, and the conclusion lies near at hand that any system which will not do this is worthless. Well, we first remark, and with some confidence, that there cannot be a moral philosophy which will tell us what in particular we are to do, and also that it is not the business of philosophy to do so. All philosophy has to do is "to understand what is," and moral philosophy has to understand morals which exist, not to make them or give directions for making them. Such a notion is simply ludicrous. Philosophy in general has not to anticipate the discoveries of the particular sciences nor the evolution of history; the philosophy of religion has not to make a new religion or teach an old one, but simply to understand the religious consciousness; and aesthetic has not to produce works of fine art, but to theorize the beautiful which it finds; political philosophy has not to play tricks with the state, but to understand it; and ethics has not to make the world moral, but to reduce to theory the morality current in the world. If we want it to do anything more, so much the worse for us; for it cannot possibly construct new morality, and, even if it could to any extent codify what exists (a point on which I do not enter), yet it surely is clear that in cases of collision of duties it would not help you to know what to do. . . . In short, the view which thinks moral philosophy is to supply us with particular moral prescriptions confuses science with art, and confuses, besides, reflective with intuitive judgment. That which tells us what in particular is right and wrong is not reflection but intuition.

We know what is right in a particular case by what we may call an immediate judgment, or an intuitive subsumption. These phrases are perhaps not very luminous, and the matter of the "intuitive understanding" in general is doubtless difficult, and the special character of moral judgments not easy to define; and I do not say that I am in a position to explain these subjects at all, nor, I think, could anyone do so, except at considerable length. But the point that I do wish to establish here is, I think, not at all obscure. The reader has first to recognize that moral judgments are not discursive; next, that nevertheless they do start from and rest on a certain basis; and then if he puts the two together, he will see that they involve what he may call the "intuitive understanding," or any other name, so long as he keeps in sight the two elements and holds them together.

On the head that moral judgments are not discursive, no one, I think, will wish me to stay long. If the reader attends to the facts he will not want anything else; and if he does not, I confess I cannot prove my point. In practical morality, no doubt, we *may* reflect on our principles, but I think it is not too much to say that we *never* do so, except where we have come upon a difficulty of particular application. If anyone thinks that a man's *ordinary* judgment, "this is right or wrong," comes from the having a rule *before* the mind and bringing the particular case under it, he may be right, and I cannot try to show that he is wrong. I can only leave it to the reader to judge for himself. We say we "see" and we "feel" in these cases, not we "conclude."

Taking for granted then that our ordinary way of judging in morals is not by reflection and explicit reasoning, we have now to point to the other side of the fact, viz., that these judgments are not mere isolated impressions, but stand in an intimate and vital relation to a certain system, which is their basis. Here again we must ask the reader to pause, if in doubt, and consider the facts for himself. Different men, who have lived in different times and countries, judge a fresh case in morals differently. Why is this? There is probably no "why" before the mind of either when he judges; but *we* perhaps can say, "I know why A said so and B so," because we find some general rule or principle different in each, and in each the basis of the judgment. Different people in the same society may judge points differently, and we sometimes know why. It is because A is struck by one aspect of the case, B by another; and one principle is (not *before*, but) *in* A's mind when he judges, and another in B's. Each has subsumed, but under a different head; the one perhaps justice, the other gratitude. Every man has the morality he has made his own in his mind, and he "sees" or "feels" or "judges" accordingly, though he does not reason explicitly from data to a conclusion.

I think this will be clear to the reader; and so we must say that on their perceptive or intellectual side (and that, the reader must not forget, is the one side that we are considering) our moral judgments are intuitive subsumptions.

If a man is to know what is right, he should have imbibed by precept, and still more by example, the spirit of his community, its general and special beliefs as to right and wrong, and, with this whole embodied in his mind should particularize it in any new case, not by a reflective deduction, but by an intuitive subsumption, which does not know that it is a subsumption;[1] by a carrying out of the self into a new case, wherein what is before the mind is the case and not the self to be carried out, and where it is indeed the whole that feels and sees, but all that is seen is seen in the form of *this* case, *this* point, *this* instance. Precept is good, but example is better; for by a series of particulars (as such forgotten) we get the general spirit, we identify ourselves both on the side of will and judgment with the basis, which basis (be it remembered) has not got to be explicit.

* *

There is nothing better than my station and its duties, nor anything higher or more truly beautiful. It holds and will hold its own against the worship of the "individual," whatever form that may take. It is strong against frantic theories and vehement passions, and in the end it triumphs over the fact and can smile at the literature, even of sentimentalism, however fulsome in its impulsive setting out, or sour in its disappointed end. It laughs at its frenzied apotheosis of the yet unsatisfied passion it calls love; and at that embitterment too which has lost its illusions, and yet cannot let them go—with its kindness for the genius too clever in general to do anything in particular, and its adoration of stargazing virgins with souls above their spheres, whose wish to be something in the world takes the form of wanting to do something with it, and who in the end do badly what they might have done in the beginning

[1] Every act has, of course, many sides, many relations, many "points of view from which it may be regarded," and so many qualities. There are always several principles under which you can bring it, and hence there is not the smallest difficulty in exhibiting it as the realization of either right or wrong. No act in the world is without *some* side capable of being subsumed under a good rule, *e.g.*, theft is economy, care for one's relations, protest against bad institutions, really doing oneself but justice, etc.; and, if all else fails, it probably saves us from something worse, and therefore is good. Cowardice is prudence and a duty, courage rashness and a vice, and so on. The casuist must have little ingenuity, if there is anything he fails to justify or condemn according to his order. And the vice of casuistry is that, attempting to decide the particulars of morality by the deductions of the reflective

well; and, worse than all, its cynical contempt for what deserves only pity, sacrifice of a life for work to the best of one's lights, a sacrifice despised not simply because it has failed, but because it is stupid, and uninteresting, and altogether unsentimental.

Concluding Remarks

Reflection on morality leads us beyond it. It leads us, in short, to see the necessity of a religious point of view. It certainly does not tell us that morality comes first in the world and then religion. What it tells us is that morality is imperfect and imperfect in such a way as implies a higher, which is religion.

Morality issues in religion; and at this word "religion" the ordinary reader is upon us with cries and questions, and with all the problems of the day—God, and personal God, immortality of the soul, the conflict of revelation and science, and who knows what beside? He must not expect any answer to these questions here; we are writing a mere appendix; and in that our object is to show that religion, as a matter of fact, does give us what morality does not give; and our method is simply, so far as our purpose requires, to point to the facts of the religious consciousness without drawing conclusions to the right or left, without trying to go much below the surface, or doing anything beyond what is wanted in this connection with morality.

We purpose to say nothing about the ultimate truth of religion—nothing again about its origin in the world, or in the individual. We are to take the religious consciousness as an existing fact, and to take it as we find it now in the modern Christian mind, whether that mind recognizes it or whether it does not. And lastly, space compels us to do no more than dogmatically assert what seems to us to be true in respect of it.

That there is some connection between true religion and morality everyone we need consider sees. A man who is "religious" and does not act morally, is an

---

understanding, it at once degenerates into finding a good reason for what you mean to do. You have principles of all sorts, and the case has all sorts of sides; *which* side is the essential side, and which principle is *the* principle *here,* rests in the end on your mere private choice, and that is determined by heaven knows what. No *reasoning* will tell which the moral point of view *here* is. Hence the necessary immorality and the ruinous effects of practical casuistry. (Casuistry used not as a guide to conduct, but as a means to the theoretical investigation of moral principles, the casuistry used to discover the principle *from* the fact, and not to deduce the fact from the principle—is, of course, quite another thing.) Our moralists do not like casuistry; but if the current notion that moral philosophy has to tell you what to do is well founded, then casuistry, so far as I can see, at once follows, or should follow.

But the ordinary moral judgment is not discursive. It does not look to the right or left, and considering the case from all its sides, consciously subsume under one principle. When the case is presented, it fixes on one quality in the act, referring that unconsciously to one principle in which it feels the whole of itself, and sees that whole in a single side of the act. So far as right and wrong are concerned it can perceive nothing but *this* quality of *this* case, and anything else it refuses to try to perceive. Practical morality means single-mindedness, the having one idea; it means what in other spheres would be the greatest narrowness. Point out to a man of simple morals that the case has other sides than the one he instinctively fixes on and he suspects you wish to corrupt him. And so you probably would if you went on. Apart from bad example, the readiest way to debauch the morality of any one is, on the side of principle, to confuse them by forcing them to see in all moral and immoral acts other sides and points of view, which alter the character of each; and, on the side of particulars, to warp their instinctive apprehension through personal affection for yourself or some other individual.

impostor, or his religion is a false one. This does not hold good elsewhere. A philosopher may be a good philosopher, and yet, taking him as a whole, may be immoral; and the same thing is true of an artist, or even of a theologian. They may all be good, and yet not good men; but no one who knew what true religion was would call a man, who on the whole was immoral, a religious man. For religion is not the mere knowing or contemplating of any object, however high. It is not mere philosophy nor art because it is not mere seeing, no mere theoretic activity, considered as such or merely from its theoretical side. The religious consciousness tells us that a man is not religious, or more religious, because the matter of his theoretic activity is religious; just as the moral consciousness told us that a man was not moral, or more moral, simply because he was a moral philosopher. Religion is essentially a doing, and a doing which is moral. It implies a realizing, and a realizing of the good self.

Are we to say then that morality is religion? Most certainly not. In morality the ideal is not: it forever remains a "to be." The reality in us or the world is partial and inadequate; and no one could say that it answers to the ideal, that, morally considered, both we and the world are all we ought to be, and ought to be just what we are. We have at furthest the belief in an ideal which in its pure completeness is never real; which, as an ideal, is a mere "should be." And the question is, Will that do for religion? No knower of religion, who was not led away by a theory, would answer Yes. Nor does it help us to say that religion is "morality touched by emotion"; for loose phrases of this sort may suggest to the reader what he knows already without their help, but, properly speaking, they *say* nothing. *All* morality is, in one sense or another, "touched by emotion." Most emotions, high or low, can go with and "touch" morality; and the moment we leave our phrase-making, and begin to reflect, we see all that is meant is that morality "touched" by *religious* emotion is religious; and so, as answer to the question What is religion? all that we have said is "It is religion when with morality you have—religion." I do not think we learn a very great deal from this.

Religion is more than morality. In the religious consciousness we find the belief, however vague and indistinct, in an object, a not-myself; an object, further, which is real. An ideal which is not real, which is only in our heads, cannot be the object of religion; and in particular the ideal self, as the "is to be" which is real only so far as we put it forth by our wills, and which, as an ideal, we cannot put forth, is not a real object, and so not the object for religion. Hence, because it is unreal, the ideal of personal morality is not enough for religion. And we have seen before that the ideal is not realized in the objective world of the state; so that, apart from other objections, here again we cannot find the religious object. For the religious consciousness that object is real; and it is not to be found in the mere moral sphere. . . .

Religion must have an object; and that object is neither an abstract idea in the head, nor one particular thing or quality, nor any collection of such things or qualities, nor any phrase which stands for one of them or a collection of them. In short, it is nothing finite. It cannot be a thing or person in the world; it cannot exist in the world, as a part of it, or as this or that course of events in time; it cannot be the "All," the sum of things or persons—since, if one is not divine, no putting of ones together will beget divinity. All this it is not. Its positive character is that it is real; and further, on examining what we find in the religious consciousness,[2] we discover that it is the ideal self

[2] The reader must carefully distinguish what is *for* (or before) the religious consciousness, and what is only *in* it, and *for us* as we investigate it.

considered as realized and real. The ideal self, which in morality is to be, is here the real ideal which truly is.

For morals the ideal self was an "ought," an "is to be" that is not; the object of religion is that same ideal self, but here it no longer only ought to be, but also is. This is the nature of the religious object, though the manner of apprehending it may differ widely, may be anything from the vaguest instinct to the most thoughtful reflection.

With religion we may here compare science and art. The artist and poet, however obscurely, do feel and believe that beauty, where it is not seen, yet somehow and somewhere is and is real; though not as a mere idea in people's heads, nor yet as anything in the visible world. And science, however dimly, starts from and rests upon the preconception that, even against appearances, reason not only ought to be, but really is.

Is then religion a mere mode of theoretic creation and contemplation, like art and science? Is it a lower form or stage of philosophy, or another sort of art, or some kind of compound mixture? It is none of these, and between it and them there is a vital difference.

In the very essence of the religious consciousness we find the relation of our *will* to the real ideal self. We find ourselves, as this or that will, against the object as the real ideal will, which is not ourselves, and which stands to us in such a way that, *though real, it is to be realized, because it is all and the whole reality*.

A statement, no doubt, which may stagger us; but the statement, we maintain, of a simple fact of the religious consciousness. If anyone likes to call it a delusion, that makes no difference; unless, as some people seem to think, you can get rid of facts by applying phrases to them. And, however surprising the fact may be to the reader, it certainly ought not to be new to him.

We find the same difficulty, that the real is to be realized, both in art and science. The self dimly feels, or forefeels, itself as full of truth and beauty, and unconsciously sets that fullness before it as an object, a not-itself which is against itself as this or that man. And so the self goes on to realize what it obscurely foreknows as real; it realizes it, although, and because, it is aware of it as real. . . .

The object, which by faith the self appropriates, is in Christianity nothing alien from and outside the world, not an abstract divine which excludes the human; but it is the inseparable unity of human[3] and divine. It is the ideal which, as will, affirms itself in and by will; it is will which is one with the ideal. And this whole object, while presented in a finite individual form, is not yet truly presented. It is known, in its truth, not until it is apprehended as an organic human-divine totality; as one body with diverse members, as one self which, in many selves, realizes, wills, and loves itself, as they do themselves in it.

And for faith this object is the real, and the only real. What seems to oppose it is, if fact, not reality: and this seeming fact has two forms: one the imperfection and evil in the heart, the inner self; and the other the imperfection and evil in the world of which my external self is a part. In both these spheres, the inner and outer, the object of religion is real; and the object has two corresponding sides, the inner and personal, and the external side; which two sides are sides of a single whole.

Faith involves the belief (1) that the course of the external world, despite appearances, is the realization of the ideal will; (2) that on the inner side the human and divine are one: or the belief (1) that

[3] By the term "human" we understand all rational finite mind. Whether that exists or not outside our planet is not a matter which concerns us, though it does touch very nearly certain forms of Christian belief.

the world is the realization of humanity as a divine organic whole; and (2) that with that whole the inner wills of particular persons are identified. Faith must hold that, in biblical language, there is "a kingdom of God," that there is an organism which realizes itself in its members, and also in those members, on the subjective side, wills and is conscious of itself, as they will and are conscious of themselves in it. . . .

Has the divine will of the religious consciousness any other content than the moral ideal? We answer, Certainly not. Religion is practical; it means doing something which is a duty. Apart from duties, there is no duty; and as all moral duties are also religious, so all religious duties are also moral.

In order to be, religion must do. Its practice is the realization of the ideal in me and in the world. Separate religion from the real world, and you will find it has nothing left it to do; it becomes a form, and so ceases. The practical content which religion carries out comes from the state, society, art, and science. But the whole of this sphere is the world of morality, and all our duties there are moral duties. And if this is so, then this religious duty may collide with that religious duty, just as one moral duty may be contrary to another; but that religion, as such, should be in collision with morality, as such, is out of the question.

So far religion and morality are the same; though, as we have seen, they are also different. The main difference is that what in morality only is to be, in religion somehow and somewhere really is, and what we are to do is done. Whether it is thought of as what is done now, or what will be done hereafter, makes in this respect no practical difference. They are different ways of looking at the same thing; and, whether present or future, the reality is equally certain. The importance for practice of this religious point of view is that what is to be done is approached, not with the knowledge of a doubtful success, but with the forefelt certainty of already accomplished victory.

Morality, the process of realization, thus survives within religion. It is only as mere morality that it vanishes; as an element it remains and is stimulated. . . .

The sum of the matter is this. Practical faith is the end, and what helps that is good because that is good; and where a religious ordinance does not help that, there it is not good. And often it may do worse than not help, and then it is positively hurtful.

So with religious exercises, and what too exclusively is called personal piety. They are religious if they are the simple expression of, or helps to, religion; and if not, then they are not religious, and perhaps even irreligious. Religion issues in the practical realizing of the reconcilement; and where there is no such realization, there is no faith, and no religion. . . .

If this is so, then our Essays have, in a way too imperfect, yet brought us to the end, where morality is removed and survives in its fulfillment. In our journey we have not seen much, and much that we have seen was perhaps little worth the effort, or might have been had without it. Be that as it may, the hunt after pleasure in any shape has proved itself a delusion, and the form of duty a snare, and the finite realization of "my station" was truth indeed, and a happiness that called to us to stay, but was too narrow to satisfy wholly the spirit's hunger; and ideal morality brought the sickening sense of inevitable failure. Here where we are landed at last, the process is at an end, though the best activity here first begins. Here our morality is consummated in oneness with God, and everywhere we find that "immortal Love," which builds itself forever on contradiction, but in which the contradiction is eternally resolved.

part 5

THE TWENTIETH CENTURY

In considering the main currents of philosophy in any historical period, it is well to keep in mind that so-called "schools of thought" such as positivism and existentialism are affected by two kinds of factors. The first factor consists of the actual writings of the philosopher in which an idea is stated, developed, and applied. The second is the general cultural background which influenced both the philosopher himself and the spread and popularity of his idea. We may call these respectively the "intellectual" and "cultural" components of a trend or school of thought. For example, G. E. Moore's *Principia Ethica* is a major intellectual landmark in the whole development of contemporary ethical analysis. In it Moore argues on purely rational grounds, without explicit reference to any cultural features of the twentieth century, that "good" cannot be defined at all and that, consequently, every naturalistic theory of value is foredoomed to failure. On the other hand, the experience of two world wars, with its attendant disillusionment with science as an instrument for the solution of moral ills, was one of the cultural components that made for the spread of such a critique of scientific reason in ethics.

Again, A. J. Ayer and C. L. Stevenson argue that it is not possible to prove that any particular set of values—including one's own—is superior to any other set. These arguments are now part of the intellectual tradition of positivism. But the appeal of this tradition is certainly due in part to a cultural fact, namely, that nowadays every educated person is aware of, and has to take seriously, the actual diversity in moral beliefs.

Together with the decline of the rather smug assumption that one's own codes of conduct are as a matter of course the best, there is also the decline of the view that man is in essence morally upright—a view often expressed and even more often implicitly believed in the nineteenth century. This is in fact the classical view, inherited from both Plato and Aristotle. It assumes that moral evil is a superficial aspect of man's nature and would disappear if man's circumstances were suitably altered. This assumption was shaken by any number of recent events, but above all by the spectacle of Nazism. The loss of this optimistic theory of evil and return to a more nearly medieval conception of sinful man are a cultural factor in those current theories, e.g., those of Sartre and Tillich, which emphasize the capacity for evil as a definitive trait of man. Freud's conception of aggression makes the same point within a naturalistic perspective.

But the disenchantment with the sovereignty of scientific reason no doubt has had the most far-reaching consequences for contemporary ethical theory. This attitude is directed primarily toward the sciences as such, but it carries over to disinterested rationality in general. Many have concluded that science has failed to alleviate social troubles, that the application of scientific methods is obviously no guarantee against prejudice, and that scientists are irresponsible weaponmakers. To state the attitude in extreme form: science cannot distinguish between good and evil; even if it could, it cannot induce us to pursue the good; and it is largely enlisted on the side of those forces that are working for the destruction or dehumanization of man.

This attitude, in some form or other, has helped suggest and prepare the ground for the following point of view: human reason can make no moral *discoveries.* Ethical theorists of very different persuasions are united on this. Ayer argues that there is really nothing to discover, since specifically ethical statements have no factual content. The existentialists hold that a theory of value, either as a set of principles or as a description of a procedure that will distinguish right and wrong, good and evil, is impossible, since each man's values are his own free creation. It is, however, possible to *describe* the phenomena of valuation; Sartre's description of bad faith is a case in point.

So far we have emphasized the negative side of our cultural scene. It is necessary therefore to point out, first, that scientific naturalism remains a vigorous tradition in the twentieth century. Dewey and Perry, in spite of differences between them, represent the view that scientific methods can be employed in the critical evaluation of ethical beliefs. Moreover, the critiques of ethical theory that were developed by Moore, Prichard, and the positivists have led to considerable methodological clarification.

SIGMUND FREUD

Sigmund Freud (1856–1939) lived most of his life in Vienna but died in England, where he had taken refuge after the Nazi occupation of Austria. He studied medicine and began his career as a practicing physician. His interest in mental illness and his studies of hysteria and of other neuroses led him gradually to the formulation of his theory of psychoanalysis.

There is no doubt that Freud is one of the most influential minds of our time—in literature and the arts, in the social sciences, and in philosophy, as well as in psychology proper. The following selections are drawn from Civilization and Its Discontents, *one of the works of his later years. They illustrate the underlying ethical and cultural implications of psychoanalysis as Freud himself saw them.*

*Civilization and Its Discontents**

THE PLEASURE PRINCIPLE

The question of the purpose of human life has been raised countless times; it has never yet received a satisfactory answer and perhaps does not admit of one. Some of those who have asked it have added that if it should turn out that life has *no* purpose, it would lose all value for them. But this threat alters nothing. It looks, on the contrary, as though one had a right to dismiss the question, for it seems to derive from the human presumptuousness, many other manifestations of which are already familiar to us. Nobody talks about the purpose of the life of animals, unless, perhaps, it may be supposed to lie in being of service to man. But this view is not tenable either, for there are many animals of which man can make nothing, except to describe, classify and study them; and innumerable species of animals have escaped even this use, since they existed and became extinct before man set eyes on them. Once again, only religion can answer the question of the purpose of life. One can hardly be wrong in concluding that the idea of life having a purpose stands and falls with the religious system.

We will therefore turn to the less

* By permission. From Sigmund Freud, *Civilization and Its Discontents*, Hogarth Press, Ltd., London. Reprinted from *Civilization and Its Discontents* by Sigmund Freud. Published by W. W. Norton & Company, Inc., New York, 1962. Copyright © 1961 by James Strachey. Reprinted by permission of the publisher.

ambitious question of what men themselves show by their behaviour to be the purpose and intention of their lives. What do they demand of life and wish to achieve in it? The answer to this can hardly be in doubt. They strive after happiness; they want to become happy and to remain so. This endeavour has two sides, a positive and a negative aim. It aims, on the one hand, at an absence of pain and unpleasure, and, on the other, at the experiencing of strong feelings of pleasure. In its narrower sense the word "happiness" only relates to the last. In conformity with this dichotomy in his aims, man's activity develops in two directions, according as it seeks to realize—in the main, or even exclusively—the one or the other of these aims.

As we see, what decides the purpose of life is simply the programme of the pleasure principle. This principle dominates the operation of the mental apparatus from the start. There can be no doubt about its efficacy, and yet its programme is at loggerheads with the whole world, with the macrocosm as much as with the microcosm. There is no possibility at all of its being carried through; all the regulations of the universe run counter to it. One feels inclined to say that the intention that man should be "happy" is not included in the plan of "Creation." What we call happiness in the strictest sense comes from the (preferably sudden) satisfaction of needs which have been dammed up to a high degree, and it is from its nature only possible as an episodic phenomenon. When any situation that is desired by the pleasure principle is prolonged, it only produces a feeling of mild contentment. We are so made that we can derive intense enjoyment only from a contrast and very little from a state of things. Thus our possibilities of happiness are already restricted by our constitution. Unhappiness is much less difficult to experience. We are threatened with suffering from three directions: from our own body, which is doomed to decay and dissolution and which cannot even do without pain and anxiety as warning signals; from the external world, which may rage against us with overwhelming and merciless forces of destruction; and finally from our relations to other men. The suffering which comes from this last source is perhaps more painful to us than any other. We tend to regard it as a kind of gratuitous addition, although it cannot be any less fatefully inevitable than the suffering which comes from elsewhere.

It is no wonder if, under the pressure of these possibilities of suffering, men are accustomed to moderate their claims to happiness. . . . Reflection shows that the accomplishment of this task can be attempted along very different paths; and all these paths have been recommended by the various schools of worldly wisdom and put into practice by men. An unrestricted satisfaction of every need presents itself as the most enticing method of conducting one's life, but it means putting enjoyment before caution, and soon brings its own punishment. The other methods, in which avoidance of unpleasure is the main purpose, are differentiated according to the source of unpleasure to which their attention is chiefly turned. Some of these methods are extreme and some moderate; some are one-sided and some attack the problem simultaneously at several points. Against the suffering which may come upon one from human relationships the readiest safeguard is voluntary isolation, keeping oneself aloof from other people. The happiness which can be achieved along this path is, as we see, the happiness of quietness. Against the dreaded external world one can only defend oneself by some kind of turning away from it, if one intends to solve the task by oneself. There is, indeed, another and better path: that of becoming a member of the human community, and, with the help of a technique guided by science, going over to the attack against nature and subjecting her to the human will. Then one is working with all for the good of all. But the most interesting methods of averting suffering are those which seek to influence our own organism. In the last analysis, all suffering is nothing else than sensation; it only exists in so far as we feel it, and we only feel it in consequence of certain ways in which our organism is regulated.

The crudest, but also the most effective among these methods of influence is the chemical one—intoxication. . . . The service rendered by intoxicating media in the struggle for happiness and in keeping misery at a distance is so highly prized as a benefit that individuals and peoples alike have given them an established place in the economics of their libido. We owe to such media not merely the immediate yield of pleasure, but also a greatly desired degree of independence from the external world. For one knows that, with the help of this "drowner of cares" one can at any time withdraw from the pressure of reality and find refuge in a world of one's own with better conditions of sensibility. As is well known, it is precisely this property of intoxicants which also determines their danger and their injuriousness. They are responsible, in certain circumstances, for the useless waste of a large quota of energy which might have been employed for the improvement of the human lot.

The complicated structure of our mental apparatus admits, however, of a whole number of other influences. Just as a satisfaction of instinct spells happiness for us, so severe suffering is caused us if the external world lets us starve, if it refuses to sate our needs. One may therefore hope to be freed from a part of one's sufferings by influencing the instinctual impulses. This type of defence against suffering is no longer brought to bear on the sensory apparatus; it seeks to master the internal sources of our needs. The extreme form of this is brought about by killing off the instincts, as is prescribed by the worldly wisdom of the East and practised by Yoga. If it succeeds, then the subject has, it is true, given up all other activities as well—he has sacrificed his life; and, by another path, he has once more only achieved the happiness of quietness. We follow the same path when our aims are less extreme and we merely attempt to *control* our instinctual life. In that case, the controlling elements are the higher psychical agencies, which have subjected themselves to the reality principle. Here the aim of satisfaction is not by any means relinquished; but a certain amount of protection against suffering is secured, in that non-satisfaction is not so painfully felt in the case of instincts kept in dependence as in the case of uninhibited ones. As against this, there is an undeniable diminution in the potentialities of enjoyment. The feeling of happiness derived from the satisfaction of a wild instinctual impulse untamed by the ego is incomparably more intense than that derived from sating an instinct that has been tamed. The irresistibility of perverse instincts, and perhaps the attraction in general of forbidden things finds an economic explanation here.

Another technique for fending off suffering is . . . shifting the instinctual aims in such a way that they cannot come up against frustration from the external world. In this, sublimation of the instincts lends its assistance. One gains the most if one can sufficiently heighten the yield of pleasure from the sources of psychical and intellectual work. When that is so, fate can do little against one. A satisfaction of this kind, such as an artist's joy in creating, in giving his phantasies body, or a scientist's in solving problems or discovering truths, has a special quality which we shall certainly one day be able to characterize in metapsychological terms. At present we can only say figuratively that such satisfactions seem "finer and higher." But their intensity is mild as compared with that derived from the sating of crude and primary instinctual impulses; it does not convulse our physical being. And the weak point of this method is that it is not applicable generally: it is accessible to only a few people. It presupposes the possession of special dispositions and gifts which are far from being common to any practical degree. And even to the few who do possess them, this method cannot give complete protection from suffering. It creates no impenetrable armour against the arrows of fortune, and it habitually fails when the source of suffering is a person's own body.

While this procedure already clearly shows an intention of making oneself independent of the external world by seeking satisfaction in internal, psychical processes, the next procedure brings out those features yet more strongly. In it, the connection with reality is still further loosened; satisfaction is obtained from illusions, which are recognized as such without the discrepancy between them and reality being allowed to interfere with enjoyment. The region from which these illusions arise is the life of the imagination; at the time when the development of the sense of reality took place, this region was expressly exempted from the demands of reality-testing and was set apart for the purpose of fulfilling wishes which were difficult to carry out. At the head of these satisfactions through phantasy stands the enjoyment of works of art —an enjoyment which, by the agency of the artist, is made accessible even to those who are not themselves creative. People who are receptive to the influence of art cannot set too high a value on it as a source of pleasure and consolation in life. Nevertheless the mild narcosis induced in us by art can do no more than bring about a transient withdrawal from the pressure of vital needs, and it is not strong enough to make us forget real misery.

Another procedure operates more energetically and more thoroughly. It regards reality as the sole enemy and as the source of all suffering, with which it is impossible to live, so that one must break off all relations with it if one is to be in any way happy. The hermit turns his back on the world and will have no truck with it. But one can do more than that; one can try to re-create the world, to build up in its stead another world in which its most unbearable features are eliminated and replaced by others that are in conformity with one's own wishes. But whoever, in desperate defiance, sets out upon this path to happiness will as a rule attain nothing. Reality is too strong for him. He becomes a madman, who for the most part finds no one to help him in carrying through his delusion. It is asserted, however, that each one of us behaves in some one respect like a paranoic, corrects some aspect of the world which is unbearable to him by the construction of a wish and introduces this delusion into reality. A special importance attaches to the case in which this attempt to procure a certainty of happiness and a protection against suffering through a delusional remoulding of reality is made by a considerable number of people in common. The religions of mankind must be classed among the mass-delusions of this kind. No one, needless to say, who shares a delusion ever recognizes it as such.

I do not think that I have made a complete enumeration of the methods by which men strive to gain happiness and keep suffering away and I know, too, that the material might have been differently arranged. One procedure I have not yet mentioned—not because I have forgotten it but because it will concern us later in another connection. And how could one possibly forget, of all others, this technique in the art of living? It is conspicuous for a most remarkable combination of characteristic features. It, too, aims of course at making the subject independent of Fate (as it is best to call it), and to that end it locates satisfaction in internal mental processes. . . . But it does not turn away from the external world; on the contrary, it clings to the objects belonging to that world and obtains happiness from an emotional relationship to them. Nor is it content to aim at an avoidance of unpleasure—a goal, as we might call it, of weary resignation; it passes this by without heed and holds fast to the original, passionate striving for a positive fulfilment of happiness. And perhaps it does in fact come nearer to this goal than any other method. I am, of course, speaking of the way of life which makes love the centre of everything, which looks for all satisfaction in loving and being loved. A psychical attitude of this sort comes naturally enough to all of us; one of the forms in which love manifests itself—sexual love—has given us our most intense experience of an overwhelming sensation of pleasure and has thus furnished us with a pattern for our search for happiness. What is more natural than that we should persist in looking for happiness along the path on which we first encountered it? The weak side of this technique of living is easy to see; otherwise no human being would have thought of abandoning this path to happiness for any other. It is that we are never so defenceless against suffering as when we love, never so helplessly unhappy as when we have lost our loved object or its love. . . .

I will venture on a few remarks as a conclusion to our enquiry. The programme of becoming happy, which the pleasure principle imposes on us, cannot be fulfilled; yet we must not—indeed, we cannot—give up our efforts to bring it nearer to fulfilment by some means or other. Very different paths may be taken in that direction, and we may give priority either to the positive aspect of the aim, that of gaining pleasure, or to its negative one, that of avoiding unpleasure. By none of these paths can we attain all that we desire. Happiness, in the reduced sense in which we recognize it as possible, is a problem of the economics of the individual's libido. There is no golden rule which applies to everyone: every man must find out for himself in what particular fashion he can be saved. All kinds of different factors will operate to direct his choice. It is a question of how much real satisfaction he can expect to get from the external world, how far he is led to make himself independent of it, and, finally, how much strength he feels he has for altering the world to suit his wishes. In this, his psychical constitution will play a decisive part, irrespectively of the external circumstances. The man who is predominantly erotic will give first preference to his emotional relationships to other people; the narcissistic man, who inclines to be self-sufficient, will seek his main satisfaction in his internal mental processes; the man of action will never give up the external world on which he can try out his strength. . . . A person who is born with a specially unfavourable instinctual constitution, and who has not properly undergone the transformation and rearrangement of his libidinal components which is indispensable for later achievements, will find it hard to obtain happiness from his external situation, especially if he is faced with tasks of some difficulty. As a last technique of living, which will at least bring him substitutive satisfaction, he is offered that of a flight into neurotic illness—a flight which he usually accomplishes when he is still young. The man who sees his pursuit of happiness come to nothing in later years can still find consolation in the yield of pleasure of chronic intoxication; or he can embark on the desperate attempt at rebellion seen in a psychosis.

Religion restricts this play of choice and adaptation, since it imposes equally on everyone its own path to the acquisition of happiness and protection from suffering. Its technique consists in depressing the value of life and distorting the picture of the real world in a delusional manner—which presupposes an intimidation of the intelligence. At this price, by forcibly fixing them in a state of psychical infantilism and by drawing them into a mass-delusion, religion succeeds in sparing many people an individual neurosis. But hardly anything more. There are, as we have said, many paths which *may* lead to such happiness as is attainable by men, but there is none which does so for certain. Even religion cannot keep its promise. If the believer finally sees himself obliged to speak of God's "inscrutable decrees," he is admitting that all that is left to him as a last possible consolation and source of pleasure in his suffering is an unconditional submission. And if he is prepared for that, he could probably have spared himself the *détour* he has made. . . .

AGGRESSION, GUILT, AND CONSCIENCE

"Thou shalt love thy neighbour as thyself" . . . is known throughout the world and is undoubtedly older than Christianity, which puts it forward as its proudest claim. Yet it is certainly not very old; even in historical times it was still strange to mankind. Let us adopt a naïve attitude towards it, as though we were hearing it for the first time; we shall be unable then to suppress a feeling of surprise and bewilderment. Why should we do it? What good will it do us? But, above all, how shall we achieve it? How can it be possible? My love is something valuable to me which I ought not to throw away without reflection. It imposes duties on me for whose fulfilment I must be ready to make sacrifices. If I love someone, he must deserve it in some way. (I leave out of account the use he may be to me, and also his possible significance for me as a sexual object, for neither of these two kinds of relationship comes into question where the precept to love my neighbour is concerned.) He deserves it if he is so like me in important ways that I can love myself in him; and he deserves it if he is so much more perfect than myself that I can love my ideal of my own self in him. Again, I have to love him if he is my friend's son, since the pain my friend would feel if any harm came to him would be my pain too—I should have to share it. But if he is a stranger to me and if he cannot attract me by any worth of his own or any significance that he may already have acquired for my emotional life, it will be hard for me to love him. Indeed, I should be wrong to do so, for my love is valued by all my own people as a sign of my preferring them, and it is an injustice to them if I put a stranger on a par with them. But if I am to love him (with this universal love) merely because he, too, is an inhabitant of this earth, like an insect, an earth-worm or a grass-snake, then I fear that only a small modicum of my love will fall to his share —not by any possibility as much as, by the judgement of my reason, I am entitled to retain for myself. What is the point of a precept enunciated with so much solemnity if its fulfilment cannot be recommended as reasonable?

On closer inspection, I find still further difficulties. Not merely is this stranger in general unworthy of my love; I must honestly confess that he has more claim to my hostility and even my hatred. He seems not to have the least trace of love for me and shows me not the slightest consideration. If it will do him any good he has no hesitation in injuring me, nor does he ask himself whether the amount of advantage he gains bears any proportion to the extent of the harm he does to me. Indeed, he need not even obtain an advantage; if he can satisfy any sort of desire by it, he thinks nothing of jeering at me, insulting me, slandering me and showing his superior power; and the more secure he feels and the more helpless I am, the more certainly I can expect him to behave like this to me. If he behaves differently, if he shows me consideration and forbearance as a stranger, I am ready to treat him in the same way, in any case and quite apart from any precept. Indeed, if this grandiose commandment had run "Love thy neighbour as thy neighbour loves thee," I should not take exception to it. And there is a second commandment, which seems to me even more incomprehensible and arouses still stronger opposition in me. It is "Love thine enemies."

Men are not gentle creatures who want to be loved, and who at the most can defend themselves if they are attacked; they are, on the contrary, creatures among whose instinctual endowments is to be reckoned a powerful share of aggressiveness. As a result, their neighbour is for them not only a potential helper or sexual object, but also someone who tempts them to satisfy their aggressiveness on him, to exploit his capacity for work without compensation, to use him sexually without his consent, to seize his possessions, to humiliate him, to cause him pain, to torture and to kill him. *Homo homini lupus.* Who, in the face of all his experience of life and of history, will have the courage to dispute this assertion? As a rule this cruel aggressiveness waits for some provocation or puts itself at the service of some other purpose, whose goal might also have been reached by milder measures. In circumstances that are favourable to it, when the mental counter-forces which ordinarily inhibit it are out of action, it also manifests itself spontaneously and reveals man as a savage beast to whom consideration towards his own kind is something alien. Anyone who calls to mind the atrocities committed during the racial migrations or the invasions of the Huns, or by the people known as Mongols under Jenghiz Khan and Tamerlane, or at the capture of Jerusalem by the pious Crusaders, or even, indeed, the horrors of the recent World War—anyone who calls these things to mind will have to bow humbly before the truth of this view.

The existence of this inclination to aggression, which we can detect in ourselves and justly assume to be present in others, is the factor which disturbs our relations with our neighbour and which forces civilization into such a high expenditure [of energy]. In consequence of this primary mutual hostility of human beings, civilized society is perpetually threatened with disintegration. The interest of work in common would not hold it together; instinctual passions are stronger than reasonable interests. Civilization has to use its utmost efforts in order to set limits to man's aggressive instincts and to hold the manifestations of them in check by psychical reaction-formations. Hence, therefore, the use of methods intended to incite people into identifications and aim-inhibited relationships of love, hence the restriction upon sexual life, and hence too the ideal's commandment to love one's neighbour as oneself—a commandment which is really justified by the fact that nothing else runs so strongly counter to the original nature of man. In spite of every effort, these endeavours of civilization have not so far achieved very much....

According to [the Communists], man is wholly good and is well-disposed to his neighbour; but the institution of private property has corrupted his nature.... I have no concern with any economic criticisms of the communist system; I cannot enquire into whether the abolition of private property is expedient or advantageous. But I am able to recognize that the psychological premises on which the system is based are an untenable illusion. In abolishing private property we deprive the human love of aggression of one of its instruments, certainly a strong one, though certainly not the strongest; but we have in no way altered the differences in power and influence which are misused by aggressiveness, nor have we altered anything in its nature. Aggressiveness was not created by property. It reigned almost without limit in primitive times, when property was still very scanty, and it already shows itself in the nursery almost before property has given up its primal, anal form; it forms the basis of every relation of affection and love among people (with the single exception, perhaps, of the mother's relation to her male child). If we do away with personal rights over material wealth, there still remains prerogative in the field of sexual relationships, which is bound to become the source of the strongest dislike and the most violent hostility among men who in other respects are on an equal footing. If we were to remove this factor, too, by allowing complete freedom of sexual life and thus abolishing the family, the germ-cell of civilization, we cannot, it is true, easily foresee what new paths the development of civilization could take; but one thing we can expect, and that is that this indestructible feature of human nature will follow it there.

It is clearly not easy for men to give up the satisfaction of this inclination to aggression. They do not feel comfortable without it. The advantage which a comparatively small-cultural group offers of allowing this instinct an outlet in the form of hostility against intruders is not to be despised. It is always possible to bind together a considerable number of people in love, so long as there are other people left over to receive the manifestations of their aggressiveness. . . .

What means does civilization employ in order to inhibit the aggressiveness which opposes it, to make it harmless, to get rid of it, perhaps? We have already become acquainted with a few of these methods, but not yet with the one that appears to be the most important. This we can study in the history of the development of the individual. What happens in him to render his desire for aggression innocuous? Something very remarkable, which we should never have guessed and which is nevertheless quite obvious. His aggressiveness is introjected, internalized; it is, in point of fact, sent back to where it came from—that is, it is directed towards his own ego. There it is taken over by a portion of the ego, which sets itself over against the rest of the ego as super-ego, and which now, in the form of "conscience," is ready to put into action against the ego the same harsh aggressiveness that the ego would have liked to satisfy upon other, extraneous individuals. The tension between the harsh super-ego and the ego that is subjected to it, is called by us the sense of guilt; it expresses itself as a need for punishment. Civilization, therefore, obtains mastery over the individual's dangerous desire for aggression by weakening and disarming it and by setting up an agency within him to watch over it, like a garrison in a conquered city. . . .

If we ask how a person comes to have a sense of guilt, we arrive at an answer which cannot be disputed: a person feels guilty (devout people would say "sinful") when he has done something which he knows to be "bad." But then we notice how little this answer tells us. Perhaps, after some hesitation, we shall add that even when a person has not actually *done* the bad thing but has only recognized in himself an *intention* to do it, he may regard himself as guilty; and the question then arises of why the intention is regarded as equal to the deed. Both cases, however, presuppose that one had already recognized that what is bad is reprehensible, is something that must not be carried out. How is this judgement arrived at? We may reject the existence of an original, as it were natural, capacity to distinguish good from bad. What is bad is often not at all what is injurious or dangerous to the ego; on the contrary, it may be something which is desirable and enjoyable to the ego. Here, therefore, there is an extraneous influence at work, and it is this that decides what is to be called good or bad. Since a person's own feelings would not have led him along this path, he must have had a motive for submitting to this extraneous influence. Such a motive is easily discovered in his helplessness and his dependence on other people, and it can best be designated as fear of loss of love. If he loses the love of another person upon whom he is dependent, he also ceases to be protected from a variety of dangers. Above all, he is exposed to the danger that this stronger person will show his superiority in the form of punishment. At the beginning, therefore, what is bad is whatever causes one to be threatened with loss of love. For fear of that loss, one must avoid it. This, too, is the reason why it makes little difference whether one has already done the bad thing or only intends to do it. In either case the danger only sets in if and when the authority discovers it, and in either case the authority would behave in the same way.

This state of mind is called a "bad conscience"; but actually it does not deserve this name, for at this stage the sense of guilt is clearly only a fear of loss of love, "social" anxiety. In small children it can never be anything else, but in many adults, too, it has only changed to the extent that the place of the father or the two parents is taken by the larger human community. Consequently, such people habitually allow themselves to do any bad thing which promises them enjoyment, so long as they are sure that the authority will not know anything about it or cannot blame them for it; they are afraid only of being found out. Present-day society has to reckon in general with this state of mind.

A great change takes place only when the authority is internalized through the establishment of a super-ego. The phenomena of conscience then reach a higher stage. Actually, it is not until now that we should speak of conscience or a sense of guilt. At this point, too, the fear of being found out comes to an end; the distinction, moreover, between doing something bad and wishing to do it disappears entirely, since nothing can be hidden from the super-ego, not even thoughts. It is true that the seriousness of the situation from a real point of view has passed away, for the new authority, the super-ego, has no motive that we know of for ill-treating the ego, with which it is intimately bound up; but genetic influence, which leads to the survival of what is past and has been surmounted, makes itself felt in the fact that fundamentally things remain as they were at the beginning. The super-ego torments the sinful ego with the same feeling of anxiety and is on the watch for opportunities of getting it punished by the external world.

At this second stage of development, the conscience exhibits a peculiarity which was absent from the first stage and which is no longer easy to account for. For the more virtuous a man is, the more severe and distrustful is its behaviour, so that ultimately it is precisely those people who have carried saintliness furthest who reproach themselves with the worst sinfulness. This means that virtue forfeits some part of its promised reward; the docile and continent ego does not enjoy the trust of its mentor, and strives in vain, it would seem, to acquire it. The objection will at once be made that these difficulties are artificial ones, and it will be said that a stricter and more vigilant conscience is precisely the hallmark of a moral man. Moreover, when saints call themselves sinners, they are not so wrong, considering the temptations to instinctual satisfaction to which they are exposed in a specially high degree—since, as is well known, temptations are merely increased by constant frustration, whereas an occasional satisfaction of them causes them to diminish, at least for the time being. The field of ethics, which is so full of problems, presents us with another fact: namely that ill-luck—that is, external frustration—so greatly enhances the power of the conscience in the super-ego. As long as things go well with a man, his conscience is lenient and lets the ego do all sorts of things; but when misfortune befalls him, he searches his soul, acknowledges his sinfulness, heightens the demands of his conscience, imposes abstinences on himself and punishes himself with penances. Whole peoples have behaved in this way, and still do. This, however, is easily explained by the original infantile stage of conscience, which, as we see, is not given up after the introjection into the super-ego, but persists alongside of it and behind it. Fate is regarded as a substitute for the parental agency. If a man is unfortunate it means that he is no longer loved by this highest power; and, threatened by such a loss of love, he once more bows to the parental representative in his super-ego—a representative whom, in his days of good fortune, he was ready to neglect. This becomes especially clear where Fate is looked upon in the strictly religious sense of being nothing else than an expression of the Divine Will. The people of Israel had believed themselves to be the favourite child of God, and when the great Father caused misfortune after misfortune to rain down upon this people of his, they were never shaken in their belief in his relationship to them or questioned his power or righteousness. Instead, they produced the prophets, who held up their sinfulness before them; and out of their sense of guilt they created the over-strict commandments of their priestly religion. It is remarkable how differently a primitive man behaves. If he has met with a misfortune, he does not throw the blame on himself but on his fetish, which has obviously not done its duty, and he gives it a thrashing instead of punishing himself.

Thus we know of two origins of the sense of guilt: one arising from fear of an authority, and the other, later on, arising from fear of the super-ego. The first insists upon a renunciation of instinctual satisfactions; the second, as well as doing this presses for punishment, since the continuance of the forbidden wishes cannot be concealed from the super-ego. . . . We now see in what relationship the renunciation of instinct stands to the sense of guilt. Originally, renunciation of instinct was the result of fear of an external authority: one renounced one's satisfactions in order not to lose its love. If one has carried out this renunciation, one is, as it were, quits wtih the authority and no sense of guilt should remain. But with fear of the super-ego the case is different. Here, instinctual renunciation is not enough, for the wish persists and cannot be concealed from the super-ego. Thus, in spite of the renunciation that has been made, a sense of guilt comes about. This constitutes a great economic disadvantage in the erection of a super-ego, or, as we may put it, in the formation of a conscience. Instinctual renunciation now no longer has a completely liberating effect; virtuous continence is no longer rewarded with the assurance of love. A threatened external unhappiness—loss of love and punishment on the part of the external authority—has been exchanged for a permanent internal unhappiness, for the tension of the sense of guilt. . . .

THE CULTURAL SUPER-EGO

It can be asserted that the community, too, evolves a super-ego under whose influence cultural development proceeds. It would be a tempting task for anyone who has a knowledge of human civilizations to follow out this analogy in detail. I will confine myself to bringing forward a few striking points. The super-ego of an epoch of civilization has an origin similar to that of an individual. It is based on the impression left behind by the personalities of great leaders—men of overwhelming force of mind or men in whom one of the human impulsions has found its strongest and purest, and therefore often its most one-sided, expression. In many instances the analogy goes still further, in that during their lifetime these figures were—often enough, even if not always—mocked and maltreated by others and even despatched in a cruel fashion. In the same way, indeed, the primal father did not attain divinity until long after he had met his death by violence. The most arresting example of this fateful conjunction is to be seen in the figure of Jesus Christ—if, indeed, that figure is not a part of mythology, which called it into being from an obscure memory of that primal event. Another point of agreement between the cultural and the individual super-ego is that the former, just like the latter, sets up strict ideal demands, disobedience to which is visited with "fear of conscience". . . . At this point the two processes, that of the cultural development of the group and that of the cultural development of the individual, are, as it were, always interlocked. . . .

The cultural super-ego has developed its ideals and set up its demands. Among the latter, those which deal with the relations of human beings to one another are comprised under the heading of ethics. People have at all times set the greatest value on ethics, as though they expected that it in particular would produce especially important results. And it does in fact deal with a subject which can easily be recognized as the sorest spot in every civilization. Ethics is thus to be regarded as a therapeutic attempt—as an endeavour to achieve, by means of a command of the super-ego, something which has so far not been achieved by means of any other cultural activities. As we already know, the problem before us is how to get rid of the greatest hindrance to civilization—namely, the constitutional inclination of human beings to be aggressive towards one another; and for that very reason we are especially interested in what is probably the most recent of the cultural commands of the super-ego, the commandment to love one's neighbour as oneself [Cf. pp. 444 ff. above.] In our research into, and therapy of, a neurosis, we are led to make two reproaches against the super-ego of the individual. In the severity of its commands and prohibitions it troubles itself too little about the happiness of the ego, in that it takes insufficient account of the resistances against obeying them—of the instinctual strength of the id [in the first place], and of the difficulties presented by the real external environment [in the second]. Consequently we are very often obliged, for therapeutic purposes, to oppose the super-ego, and we endeavour to lower its demands. Exactly the same objections can be made against the ethical demands of the cultural super-ego. It, too, does not trouble itself enough about the facts of the mental constitution of human beings. It issues a command and does not ask whether it is possible for people to obey it. On the contrary, it assumes that a man's ego is psychologically capable of anything that is required of it, that his ego has unlimited mastery over his id. This is a mistake; and even in what are known as normal people the id cannot be controlled beyond certain limits. If more is demanded of a man, a revolt will be produced in him or a neurosis, or he will be made unhappy. The commandment, "Love thy neighbour as thyself," is the strongest defence against human aggressiveness and an excellent example of the unpsychological proceedings of the cultural super-ego. The commandment is impossible to fulfil; such an enormous inflation of love can only lower its value, not get rid of the difficulty. Civilization pays no attention to all this; it merely admonishes us that the harder it is to obey the precept the more meritorious it is to do so. But anyone who follows such a precept in present-day civilization only puts himself at a disadvantage *vis-à-vis* the person who disregards it. What a potent obstacle to civilization aggressiveness must be, if the defence against it can cause as much unhappiness as aggressiveness itself! "Natural" ethics, as it is called, has nothing to offer here except the narcissistic satisfaction of being able to think oneself better than others. At this point the ethics based on religion introduces its promises of a better after-life. But so long as virtue is not rewarded here on earth, ethics will, I fancy, preach in vain. I too think it quite certain that a real change in the relations of human beings to possessions would be of more help in this direction than any ethical commands; but the recognition of this fact among socialists has been obscured and made useless for practical purposes by a fresh idealistic misconception of human nature.

The fateful question for the human species seems to me to be whether and to what extent their cultural development will succeed in mastering the disturbance of their communal life by the human instinct of aggression and self-destruction. It may be that in this respect precisely the present time deserves a special interest. Men have gained control over the forces of nature to such an extent that with their help they would have no difficulty in exterminating one another to the last man. They know this, and hence comes a large part of their current unrest, their unhappiness and their mood of anxiety. And now it is to be expected that the other of the two "Heavenly Powers," eternal Eros, will make an effort to assert himself in the struggle with his equally immortal adversary. But who can foresee with what success and with what result?

JOHN DEWEY

John Dewey (1859–1952) was born in Burlington, Vermont, and educated at the University of Vermont and Johns Hopkins University. He taught at the University of Michigan, at the University of Chicago (where he directed an experimental school for testing his educational theories), and finally, from 1904 to 1929, at Columbia University.

He is America's most distinguished—and most controversial—philosopher. His numerous writings have exerted a profound influence on contemporary philosophy, especially in the theory of knowledge and theory of value. But his impact outside philosophy is also large: contemporary jurisprudence, education, psychology, and social theory all bear the stamp of his thought. He is often regarded as a classical spokesman for democratic liberalism.

*Reconstruction in Philosophy**

RECONSTRUCTION IN MORAL CONCEPTIONS

Ethical theory began among the Greeks as an attempt to find a regulation for the conduct of life which should have a rational basis and purpose instead of being derived from custom. But reason as a substitute for custom was under the obligation of supplying objects and laws as fixed as those of custom had been. Ethical theory ever since has been singularly hypnotized by the notion that its business is to discover some final end or good or some ultimate and supreme law. This is the common element among the diversity of theories. Some have held that the end is loyalty or obedience to a higher power or authority; and they have variously found this higher principle in Divine Will, the will of the secular ruler, the maintenance of institutions in which the purpose of superiors is embodied, and the rational consciousness of duty. But they have differed from one another because there was one point in which they were agreed: a single and final source of law. Others have asserted that it is impossible to locate morality in conformity to law-giving power, and that it must be sought in ends that are goods. And some have sought the good in self-realization, some in holiness, some in happiness, some in the greatest possible aggregate of pleasures. And yet these schools have agreed in the assumption that there is a single, fixed and final good. They have been able to dispute with one another only because of their common premise.

The question arises whether the way

* John Dewey, *Reconstruction in Philosophy.* Reprinted by permission of Beacon Press, copyright © 1948 by Beacon Press, Boston.

out of the confusion and conflict is not to go to the root of the matter by questioning this common element. Is not the belief in the single, final and ultimate (whether conceived as good or as authoritative law) an intellectual product of that feudal organization which is disappearing historically and of that belief in a bounded, ordered cosmos, wherein rest is higher than motion, which has disappeared from natural science? It has been repeatedly suggested that the present limit of intellectual reconstruction lies in the fact that it has not as yet been seriously applied in the moral and social disciplines. Would not this further application demand precisely that we advance to a belief in a plurality of changing, moving, individualized goods and ends, and to a belief that principles, criteria, laws are intellectual instruments for analyzing individual or unique situations?

The blunt assertion that every moral situation is a unique situation having its own irreplaceable good may seem not merely blunt but preposterous. For the established tradition teaches that it is precisely the irregularity of special cases which makes necessary the guidance of conduct by universals, and that the essence of the virtuous disposition is willingness to subordinate every particular case to adjudication by a fixed principle. It would then follow that submission of a generic end and law to determination by the concrete situation entails complete confusion and unrestrained licentiousness. Let us, however, follow the pragmatic rule, and in order to discover the meaning of the idea ask for its consequences. Then it surprisingly turns out that the primary significance of the unique and morally ultimate character of the concrete situation is to transfer the weight and burden of morality to intelligence. It does not destroy responsibility; it only locates it. A moral situation is one in which judgment and choice are required antecedently to overt action. The practical meaning of the situation—that is to say the action needed to satisfy it—is not self-evident. It has to be searched for. There are conflicting desires and alternative apparent goods. What is needed is to find the right course of action, the right good. Hence, inquiry is exacted: observation of the detailed makeup of the situation; analysis into its diverse factors; clarification of what is obscure; discounting of the more insistent and vivid traits; tracing the consequences of the various modes of action that suggest themselves; regarding the decision reached as hypothetical and tentative until the anticipated or supposed consequences which led to its adoption have been squared with actual consequences. This inquiry is intelligence. Our moral failures go back to some weakness of disposition, some absence of sympathy, some one-sided bias that makes us perform the judgment of the concrete case carelessly or perversely. Wide sympathy, keen sensitiveness, persistence in the face of the disagreeable, balance of interests enabling us to undertake the work of analysis and decision intelligently are the distinctively moral traits—the virtues or moral excellencies.

It is worth noting once more that the underlying issue is, after all, only the same as that which has been already threshed out in physical inquiry. There too it long seemed as if rational assurance and demonstration could be attained only if we began with universal conceptions and subsumed particular cases under them. The men who initiated the methods of inquiry that are now everywhere adopted were denounced in their day (and sincerely) as subverters of truth and foes of science. If they have won in the end, it is because, as has already been pointed out, the method of universals confirmed prejudices and sanctioned ideas that had gained currency irrespective of evidence for them; while placing the initial and final weight upon the individual case stimulated painstaking inquiry into facts and examination of principles. In the end, loss of eternal truths was more than compensated for in the accession of quotidian facts. The loss of the system of superior and fixed definitions and kinds was more than made up for by the growing system of hypotheses and laws used in classifying facts. After all, then, we are only pleading for the adoption in moral reflection of the logic that has been proved to make for security, stringency and fertility in passing judgments upon physical phenomena. And the reason is the same. The old method in spite of its nominal and esthetic worship of reason discouraged reason, because it hindered the operation of scrupulous and unremitting inquiry.

More definitely, the transfer of the burden of the moral life from following rules or pursuing fixed ends over to the detection of the ills that need remedy in a special case and the formation of plans and methods for dealing with them, eliminates the causes which have kept moral theory controversial, and which have also kept it remote from helpful contact with the exigencies of practice. The theory of fixed ends inevitably leads thought into the bog of disputes that cannot be settled. If there is one *summum bonum,* one supreme end, what is it? To consider this problem is to place ourselves in the midst of controversies that are as acute now as they were two thousand years ago. Suppose we take a seemingly more empirical view, and say that while there is not a single end, there also are not as many as there are specific situations that require amelioration; but there are a number of such natural goods as health, wealth, honor, or good name, friendship, esthetic appreciation, learning and such moral goods as justice, temperance, benevolence, etc. What or who is to decide the right of way when these ends conflict with one another, as they are sure to do? Shall we resort to the method that once brought such disrepute upon the whole business of ethics: Casuistry? Or shall we have recourse to what Bentham well called the *ipse dixit* method: the arbitrary preference of this or that person for this or that end? Or shall we be forced to arrange them all in an order of degrees from the highest good down to the least precious? Again we find ourselves in the middle of unreconciled disputes with no indication of the way out.

Meantime, the special moral perplexities where the aid of intelligence is required go unenlightened. We cannot seek or attain health, wealth, learning, justice or kindness in general. Action is always specific, concrete, individualized, unique. And consequently judgments as to acts to be performed must be similarly specific. To say that a man seeks health or justice is only to say that he seeks to live healthily or justly. These things, like truth, are abverbial. They are modifiers of action in special cases. How to live healthily or justly is a matter which differs with every person. It varies with his past experience, his opportunities, his temperamental and acquired weaknesses and abilities. Not man in general but a particular man suffering from some particular disability aims to live healthily, and consequently health cannot mean for him exactly what it means for any other mortal. Healthy living is not something to be attained by itself apart from other ways of living. A man needs to be healthy *in* his life, not apart from it, and what does life mean except the aggregate of his pursuits and activities? A man who aims at health as a distinct end becomes a valetudinarian or a fanatic, or a mechanical performer of exercises, or an athlete so one-sided that his pursuit of bodily development injures his heart. When the endeavor to realize a so-called end does not temper and color all other activities, life is portioned out into strips and fractions. Certain acts and times are devoted to getting health, others to cultivating religion, others to seeking learning, to being a good citizen, a devotee of fine art and so on. This is the only logical alternative to subordinating all aims to the accomplishment of one alone—fanaticism. This is out of fashion at present, but who can say how much of distraction and dissipation in life, and how much of its hard and narrow rigidity is the outcome of men's failure to realize that each situation has its own unique end and that the whole personality should be concerned with it? Surely, once more, what a man needs is to live healthily, and this result so affects all the activities of his life that it cannot be set up as a separate and independent good.

Nevertheless the general notions of health, disease, justice, artistic culture are of great importance: Not, however, because this or that case may be brought exhaustively under a single head and its specific traits shut out, but because generalized science provides a man as physician and artist and citizen, with questions to ask, investigations to make, and enables him to understand the meaning of what he sees. Just in the degree in which a physician is an artist in his work he uses his science, no matter how extensive and accurate, to furnish him with tools of inquiry into the individual case, and with methods of forecasting a method of dealing with it. Just in the degree in which, no matter how great his learning, he subordinates the individual case to some classification of diseases and some generic rule of treatment, he sinks to the level of the routine mechanic. His intelligence and his action become rigid, dogmatic, instead of free and flexible.

Moral goods and ends exist only when something has to be done. The fact that something has to be done proves that there are deficiencies, evils in the existent situation. This ill is just the specific ill that it is. It never is an exact duplicate of anything else. Consequently the good of the situation has to be discovered, projected and attained on the basis of the exact defect and trouble to be rectified. It cannot intelligently be injected into the situation from without. Yet it is the part of wisdom to compare different cases, to gather together the ills from which humanity suffers, and to generalize the corresponding goods into classes. Health, wealth, industry, temperance, amiability, courtesy, learning, esthetic capacity, initiative, courage, patience, enterprise, thoroughness and a multitude of other generalized ends are acknowledged as goods. But the *value* of this systematization is intellectual or analytic. Classifications *suggest* possible traits to be on the lookout for in studying a particular case; they suggest methods of action to be tried in removing the inferred causes of ill. They are tools of insight; their value is in promoting an individualized response in the individual situation.

Morals is not a catalogue of acts nor a set of rules to be applied like drugstore prescriptions or cook-book recipes. The need in morals is for specific methods of inquiry and of contrivance: Methods of inquiry to locate difficulties and evils; methods of contrivance to form plans to be used as working hypotheses in dealing with them. And the pragmatic import of the logic of individualized situations, each having its own irreplaceable good and principle, is to transfer the attention of theory from preoccupation with general conceptions to the problem of developing effective methods of inquiry.

Two ethical consequences of great moment should be remarked. The belief in fixed values has bred a division of ends into intrinsic and instrumental, of those that are really worth while in themselves and those that are of importance only as means to intrinsic goods. Indeed, it is often thought to be the very beginning of wisdom, of moral discrimination, to make this distinction. Dialectically, the distinction is interesting and seems harmless. But carried into practice it has an import that is tragic. Historically, it has been the source and justification of a hard and fast difference between ideal goods on one side and material goods on the other. At present those who would be liberal conceive intrinsic goods as esthetic in nature rather than as exclusively religious or as intellectually contemplative. But the effect is the same. So-called intrinsic goods, whether religious or esthetic, are divorced from those interests of daily life which because of their constancy and urgency form the preoccupation of the great mass. Aristotle used this distinction to declare that slaves and the working class though they are necessary *for* the state—the commonweal—are not constituents *of* it. That which is regarded as *merely* instrumental must approach drudgery; it cannot command either intellectual, artistic or moral attention and respect. Anything becomes *unworthy* whenever it is thought of as intrinsically lacking worth. So men of "ideal" interests have chosen for the most part the way of neglect and escape. The urgency and pressure of "lower" ends have been covered up by polite conventions. Or, they have been relegated to a baser class of mortals in order that the few might be free to attend to the goods that are really or intrinsically worth while. This withdrawal, in the name of higher ends, has left, for mankind at large and especially for energetic "practical" people the lower activities in complete command.

No one can possibly estimate how much of the obnoxious materialism and brutality of our economic life is due to the fact that economic ends have been regarded as *merely* instrumental. When they are recognized to be as intrinsic and final in their place as any others, then it will be seen that they are capable of idealization, and that if life is to be worth while, they must acquire ideal and intrinsic value. Esthetic, religious and other "ideal" ends are now thin and meagre or else idle and luxurious because of the separation from "instrumental" or economic ends. Only in connection with the latter can they be woven into the texture of daily life and made substantial and pervasive. The vanity and irresponsibility of values that are merely final and not also in turn means to the enrichment of other occupations of life ought to be obvious. But now the doctrine of "higher" ends gives aid, comfort and support to every socially isolated and socially irresponsible scholar, specialist, esthete and religionist. It protects the vanity and irresponsibility of his calling from observation by others and by himself. The moral deficiency of the calling is transformed into a cause of admiration and gratulation.

The other generic change lies in doing away once for all with the traditional distinction between moral goods, like the virtues, and natural goods like health, economic security, art, science and the like. The point of view under discussion is not the only one which has deplored this rigid distinction and endeavoured to abolish it. Some schools have even gone so far as to regard moral excellencies, qualities of character as of value only because they promote natural goods. But the experimental logic when carried into morals makes every quality that is judged to be good according as it contributes to amelioration of existing ills. And in so doing, it enforces the moral meaning of natural science. When all is said and done in criticism of present social deficiencies, one may well wonder whether the root difficulty does not lie in the separation of natural and moral science. When physics, chemistry, biology, medicine, contribute to the detection of concrete human woes and to the development of plans for remedying them and relieving the human estate, they become moral; they become part of the apparatus of moral inquiry or science. The latter then loses its peculiar flavor of the didactic and pedantic; its ultra-moralistic and hortatory tone. It loses its thinness and shrillness as well as its vagueness. It gains agencies that are efficacious. But the gain is not confined to the side of moral science. Natural science loses its divorce from humanity; it becomes itself humanistic in quality. It is something to be pursued not in a technical and specialized way for what is called truth for its own sake, but with the sense of its social bearing, its intellectual indispensableness. It is technical only in the sense that it provides the technique of social and moral engineering.

When the consciousness of science is fully impregnated with the consciousness of human value, the greatest dualism which now weighs humanity down, the split between the material, the mechanical, the scientific and the moral and ideal will be destroyed. Human forces that now waver because of this division will be unified and reinforced. As long as ends are not thought of as individualized according to specific needs and opportunities, the mind will be content with abstractions, and the adequate stimulus to the moral or social use of natural science and historical data will be lacking. But when attention is concentrated upon the diversified concretes, recourse to all intellectual materials needed to clear up the special cases will be imperative. At the same time that morals are made to focus in intelligence, things intellectual are moralized. The vexatious and wasteful conflict between naturalism and humanism is terminated. . . .

*The Quest for Certainty**

THE CONSTRUCTION OF GOOD

The scientific revolution came about when material of direct and uncontrolled experience was taken as problematic; as supplying material to be transformed by reflective operations into known objects. The contrast between experienced and known objects was found to be a temporal one; namely, one between empirical subject-matters which were had or "given" prior to the acts of experimental variation and redisposition and those which succeed these acts and issued from them. The notion of an act whether of sense or thought which supplied a valid measure of thought in immediate knowledge was discredited. Consequences of operations became the important thing. The suggestion almost imperatively follows that escape from the defects of transcendental absolutism is not to be had by setting up as values enjoyments that happen anyhow, but in defining value by enjoyments which are the consequences of intelligent action. Without the intervention of thought, enjoyments are not values but problematic goods, becoming values when they re-issue in a changed form from intelligent behavior. The fundamental trouble with the current empirical theory of values is that it merely formulates and justifies the socially prevailing habit of regarding enjoyments as they are actually experienced as values in and of themselves. It completely side-steps the question of regulation of these enjoyments. This issue involves nothing less than the problem of the directed reconstruction of economic, political and religious institutions.

There was seemingly a paradox involved in the notion that if we turned our backs upon the immediately perceived qualities of things, we should be enabled to form valid conceptions of objects, and that these conceptions could be used to bring about a more secure and more significant experience of them. But the method terminated in disclosing the connections or interactions upon which perceived objects, viewed as events, depend. Formal analogy suggests that we regard our direct and original experience of things liked and enjoyed as only possibilities of values to be achieved; that enjoyment becomes a value when we discover the relations upon which

* Reprinted by permission of G. P. Putnam's Sons, New York, from *The Quest for Certainty* by John Dewey. Copyright 1929, ® 1957 by Mrs. Roberta Dewey.

its presence depends. Such a causal and operational definition gives only a conception of a value, not a value itself. But the utilization of the conception in action results in an object having secure and significant value.

The formal statement may be given concrete content by pointing to the difference between the enjoyed and the enjoyable, the desired and the desirable, the satis*fying* and the satis*factory*. To say that something is enjoyed is to make a statement about a fact, something already in existence; it is not to judge the value of that fact. There is no difference between such a proposition and one which says that something is sweet or sour, red or black. It is just correct or incorrect and that is the end of the matter. But to call an object a value is to assert that it satisfies or fulfills certain conditions. Function and status in meeting conditions is a different matter from bare existence. The fact that something is desired only raises the *question* of its desirability; it does not settle it. Only a child in the degree of his immaturity thinks to settle the question of desirability by reiterated proclamation: "I want it, I want it, I want it." What is objected to in the current empirical theory of values is not connection of them with desire and enjoyment but failure to distinguish between enjoyments of radically different sorts. There are many common expressions in which the difference of the two kinds is clearly recognized. Take for example the difference between the ideas of "satisfying" and "satisfactory." To say that something satisfies is to report something as an isolated finality. To assert that it is satis*factory* is to define it in its connections and interactions. The fact that it pleases or is immediately congenial poses a problem to judgment. How shall the satisfaction be rated? Is it a value or is it not? Is it something to be prized and cherished, *to be* enjoyed? Not stern moralists alone but everyday experience informs us that finding satisfaction in a thing may be a warning, a summons to be on the lookout for consequences. To declare something satis*factory* is to assert that it meets specifiable conditions. It is, in effect, a judgment that the thing "will do." It involves a prediction; it contemplates a future in which the thing will continue to serve; it *will* do. It asserts a consequence the thing will actively institute; it will *do*. That it is satisfying is the content of a proposition of fact; that it is satisfactory is a judgment, an estimate, an appraisal. It denotes an attitude *to be* taken, that of striving to perpetuate and to make secure.

It is worth notice that besides the instances given, there are many other recognitions in ordinary speech of the distinction. The endings "able," "worthy" and "ful" are cases in point. Noted and notable, noteworthy; remarked and remarkable; advised and advisable; wondered at and wonderful; pleasing and beautiful; loved and lovable; blamed and blameable, blameworthy; objected to and objectionable; esteemed and estimable; admired and admirable; shamed and shameful; honored and honorable; approved and approvable, worthy of approbation, etc. The multiplication of words adds nothing to the force of the distinction. But it aids in conveying a sense of the fundamental character of the distinction; of the difference between mere report of an already existent fact and judgment as to the importance and need of bringing a fact into existence; or, if it is already there, of sustaining it in existence. The latter is a genuine practical judgment, and marks the only type of judgment that has to do with the direction of action. Whether or no we reserve the term "value" for the latter (as seems to me proper), is a minor matter; that the distinction be acknowledged as the key to understanding the relation of values to the direction of conduct is the important thing.

This element of direction by an idea of value applies to science as well as anywhere else. For in every scientific undertaking, there is passed a constant succession of estimates; such as "it is worth treating these facts as data or evidence; it is advisable to try this experiment; to make that observation; to entertain such and such a hypothesis; to perform this calculation," etc.

The word "taste" has perhaps got too completely associated with arbitrary liking to express the nature of judgments of value. But if the word be used in the sense of an appreciation at once cultivated and active, one may say that the formation of taste is the chief matter wherever values enter in, whether intellectual, esthetic or moral. Relatively immediate judgments, which we call tact or to which we give the name of intuition, do not precede reflective inquiry, but are the funded products of much thoughtful experience. Expertness of taste is at once the result and the reward of constant exercise of thinking. Instead of there being no disputing about tastes, they are the one thing worth disputing about, if by "dispute" is signified discussion involving reflective inquiry. Taste, if we use the word in its best sense, is the outcome of experience brought cumulatively to bear on the intelligent appreciation of the real worth of likings and enjoyments. There is nothing in which a person so completely reveals himself as in the things which he judges enjoyable and desirable. Such judgments are the sole alternative to the domination of belief by impulse, chance, blind habit and self-interest. The formation of a cultivated and effectively operative good judgment or taste with respect to what is esthetically admirable, intellectually acceptable and morally approvable is the supreme task set to human beings by the incidents of experience.

Propositions about what is or has been liked are of instrumental value in reaching judgments of value, in as far as the conditions and consequences of the thing liked are thought about. In themselves they make no claims; they put forth no demand upon subsequent attitudes and acts; they profess no authority to direct. If one likes a thing he likes it; that *is* a point about which there can be no dispute: —although it is not so easy to state just *what* is liked as is frequently assumed. A judgment about what is *to be* desired and enjoyed is, on the other hand, a claim on future action; it possesses *de jure* and not merely *de facto* quality. It is a matter of frequent experience that likings and enjoyments are of all kinds, and that many are such as reflective judgments condemn. By way of self-justification and "rationalization," an enjoyment creates a tendency to assert that the thing enjoyed is a value. This assertion of validity adds authority to the fact. It is a decision that the object has a right to exist and hence a claim upon action to further its existence. . . .

Not even the most devoted adherents of the notion that enjoyment and value are equivalent facts would venture to assert that because we have once liked a thing we should go on liking it; they are compelled to introduce the idea that *some* tastes are to be cultivated. Logically, there is no ground for introducing the idea of cultivation; liking is liking, and one is as good as another. If enjoyments *are* values, the judgment of value cannot regulate the form which liking takes; it cannot regulate its own conditions. Desire and purpose, and hence action, are left without guidance, although the question of regulation of their formation is the supreme problem of practical life. Values (to sum up) may be connected inherently with liking, and yet not with *every* liking but only with those that judgment has approved, after examination of the relation upon which the object liked depends. A casual liking is one that happens without knowledge of how it occurs nor to what effect. The difference between it and one which is sought because of a judgment that is worth having and is to be striven for, makes just the difference between enjoyments which are accidental and enjoyments that have value and hence a claim upon our attitude and conduct. . . .

When theories of values do not afford intellectual assistance in framing ideas and beliefs about values that are adequate to direct action, the gap must be filled by other means. If intelligent method is lacking, prejudice, the pressure of immediate circumstance, self-interest and class-interest, traditional customs, institutions of accidental historic origin, are *not* lacking, and they tend to take the place of intelligence. Thus we are led to our main proposition: *Judgments about values are judgments about the conditions and the results of experienced objects; judgments about that which should regulate the formation of our desires, affections and enjoyments.* For whatever decides their formation will determine the main course of our conduct, personal and social.

If it sounds strange to hear that we should frame our judgments as to what has value by considering the connections in existence of what we like and enjoy, the reply is not far to seek. As long as we do not engage in this inquiry enjoyments (values if we choose to apply that term) are casual; they are given by "nature," not constructed by art. Like natural objects in their qualitative existence, they at most only supply material for elaboration in rational discourse. A *feeling* of good or excellence is as far removed from goodness in fact as a feeling that objects are intellectually thus and so is removed from their being actually so. To recognize that the truth of natural objects can be reached only by the greatest care in selecting and arranging directed operations, and then to suppose that values can be truly determined by the mere fact of liking seems to leave us in an incredible position. All the serious perplexities of life come back to the genuine difficulty of forming a judgment as to the values of the situation; they come back to a conflict of goods. Only dogmatism can suppose that serious moral conflict is between something clearly bad and something known to be good, and that uncertainty lies wholly in the will of the one choosing. Most conflicts of importance are conflicts between things which are or have been satisfying, not between good and evil. And to suppose that we can make a hierarchical table of values at large once for all, a kind of catalogue in which they are arranged in an order of ascending or descending worth, is to indulge in a gloss on our inability to frame intelligent judgments in the concrete. Or else it is to dignify customary choice and prejudice by a title of honor.

The alternative to definition, classification and systematization of satisfactions just as they happen to occur is judgment of them by means of the relations under which they occur. If we know the conditions under which the act of liking, of desire and enjoyment, takes place, we are in a position to know what are the consequences of that act. The difference between the desired and the desirable, admired and the admirable, becomes effective at just this point. Consider the difference between the proposition "That thing has been eaten," and the judgment "That thing is edible." The former statement involves no knowledge of any relation except the one stated; while we are able to judge of the edibility of anything only when we have a knowledge of its interactions with other things sufficient to enable us to foresee its probable effects when it is taken into the organism and produces effects there.

To assume that anything can be known in isolation from its connections with other things is to identify knowing with merely having some object before perception or in feeling, and is thus to lose the key to the traits that distinguish an object as known. It is futile, even silly, to suppose that some quality that is directly present constitutes the whole of the thing presenting the quality. It does not do so when the quality is that of being hot or fluid or heavy, and it does not when the quality is that of giving pleasure, or being enjoyed. Such qualities are, once more, effects, ends in the sense of closing termini of processes involving causal connections. They are something to be investigated, challenges to inquiry and judgment. The more connections and interactions we ascertain, the more we *know* the object in question. Thinking is search for these connections. Heat experienced as a consequence of directed operations has a meaning quite different from the heat that is casually experienced without knowledge of how it came about. The same is true of enjoyments. Enjoyments that issue from conduct directed by insight into relations have a meaning and a validity due to the way in which they are experienced. Such enjoyments are not repented of; they generate no after-taste of bitterness. Even in the midst of direct enjoyment, there is a sense of validity, of authorization, which intensifies the enjoyment. There is solicitude for perpetuation of the *object* having value which is radically different from mere anxiety to perpetuate the *feeling* of enjoyment.

Such statements as we have been making are, therefore, far from implying that there are values apart from things actually enjoyed as good. To find a thing enjoy*able* is, so to say, a *plus* enjoyment. We saw that it was foolish to treat the scientific object as a rival to or substitute for the perceived object, since the former is intermediate between uncertain and settled situations and those experienced under conditions of greater control. In the same way, judgment of the value of an object to be experienced is instrumental to appreciation of it when it is realized. But the notion that every object that happens to satisfy has an equal claim with every other to be a value is like supposing that every object of perception has the same cognitive force as every other. There is no knowledge without perception; but objects perceived are *known* only when they are determined as consequences of connective operations. There is no value except where there is satisfaction, but there have to be certain conditions fulfilled to transform a satisfaction into a value.

The time will come when it will be found passing strange that we of this age should take such pains to control by every means at command the formation of ideas of physical things, even those most remote from human concern, and yet are content with haphazard beliefs about the qualities of objects that regulate our deepest interests; that we are scrupulous as to methods of forming ideas of natural objects, and either dogmatic or else driven by immediate conditions in framing those about values. There is, by implication, if not explicitly, a prevalent notion that values are already well known and that all which is lacking is the will to cultivate them in the order of their worth. In fact the most profound lack is not the will to act upon goods already known but the will to know what they are. . . .

This distinction between higher and lower types of value is itself something to be looked into. Why should there be a sharp division made between some goods as physical and material and others as ideal and "spiritual"? The question touches the whole dualism of the material and the ideal at its root. To denominate anything "matter" or "material" is not in truth to disparage it. It is, if the designation is correctly applied, a way of indicating that the thing in question is a condition or means of the existence of something else. And disparagement of effective means is practically synonymous with disregard of the things that are termed, in eulogistic fashion, ideal and spiritual. For the latter terms if they have any concrete application at all signify something which is a desirable consummation of conditions, a cherished fulfillment of means. The sharp separation between material and ideal good thus deprives the latter of the underpinning of effective support while it opens the way for treating things which should be employed as means as ends in themselves. For since men cannot after all live without some measure of possession of such matters as health and wealth, the latter things will be viewed as values and ends in isolation unless they are treated as integral constituents of the goods that are deemed supreme and final.

Where will regulation come from if we surrender familiar and traditionally prized values as our directive standards? Very largely from the findings of the natural sciences. For one of the effects of the separation drawn between knowledge and action is to deprive scientific knowledge of its proper service as a guide of conduct—except once more in those technological fields which have been degraded to an inferior rank. Of course, the complexity of the conditions upon which objects of human and liberal value depend is a great obstacle, and it would be too optimistic to say that we have as yet enough knowledge of the scientific type to enable us to regulate our judgments of value very extensively. But we have more knowledge than we try to put to use, and until we try more systematically we shall not know what are the important gaps in our sciences judged from the point of view of their moral and humane use.

For moralists usually draw a sharp line between the field of the natural sciences and the conduct that is regarded as moral. But a moral that frames its judgments of value on the basis of consequences must depend in a most intimate manner upon the conclusions of science. For the knowledge of the relations between changes which enable us to connect things as antecedents and consequences *is* science. The narrow scope which moralists often give to morals, their isolation of some conduct as virtuous and vicious from other large ranges of conduct, those having to do with health and vigor, business, education, with all the affairs in which desires and affection are implicated, is perpetuated by this habit of exclusion of the subject-matter of natural science from a rôle in formation of moral standards and ideals. The same attitude operates in the other direction to keep natural science a technical specialty, and it works unconsciously to encourage its use exclusively in regions where it can be turned to personal and class advantage, as in war and trade.

Another great difference to be made by carrying the experimental habit into all matter of practice is that it cuts the roots of what is often called subjectivism, but which is better termed egoism. The subjective attitude is much more widespread than would be inferred from the philosophies which have that label attached. It is as rampant in realistic philosophies as in any others, sometimes even more so, although disguised from those who hold these philosophies under the cover of reverence for and enjoyment of ultimate values. For the implication of placing the standard of thought and knowledge in antecedent existence is that our thought makes no difference in what is significantly real. It then affects only our own attitude toward it.

This constant throwing of emphasis back upon a change made in ourselves instead of one made in the world in which we live seems to me the essence of what is objectionable in "subjectivism." Its taint hangs about even Platonic realism with its insistent evangelical dwelling upon the change made within the mind by contemplation of the realm of essence, and its depreciation of action as transient and all but sordid—a concession to the necessities of organic existence. All the theories which put conversion "of the eye of the soul" in the place of a conversion of natural and social objects that modifies goods actually experienced, is a retreat and escape from existence—and this retraction into self is, once more, the heart of subjective egoisms. The typical example is perhaps the other-worldliness found in religions whose chief concern is with the salvation of the personal soul. But other-worldliness is found as well in estheticism and in all seclusion within ivory towers. . . .

A third significant change that would issue from carrying over experimental method from physics to man concerns the import of standards, principles, rules. With the transfer, these, and all tenents and creeds about good and goods, would be recognized to be hypotheses. Instead of being rigidly fixed, they would be treated as intellectual instruments to be tested and confirmed—and altered—through consequences effected by acting upon them. They would lose all pretence of finality—the ulterior source of dogmatism. It is both astonishing and depressing that so much of the energy of mankind has gone into fighting for (with weapons of the flesh as well as of the spirit) the truth of creeds, religious, moral and political, as distinct from what has gone into effort to try creeds by putting them to the test of acting upon them. The change would do away with the intolerance and fanaticism that attend the notion that beliefs and judgments are capable of inherent truth and authority; inherent in the sense of being independent of what they lead to when used as directive principles. The transformation does not imply merely that men are responsible for acting upon what they profess to believe; that is an old doctrine. It goes much further. Any belief as such is tentative, hypothetical; it is not just to be acted upon, but is to be *framed* with reference to its office as a guide to action. Consequently, it should be the last thing in the world to be picked up casually and then clung to rigidly. When it is apprehended as a tool and only a tool, an instrumentality of direction, the same scrupulous attention will go to its formation as now goes into the making of instruments of precision in technical fields. Men, instead of being proud of accepting and asserting beliefs and "principles" on the ground of loyalty, will be as ashamed of that procedure as they would now be to confess their assent to a scientific theory out of reverence for Newton or Helmholz or whomever, without regard to evidence.

*Theory of Valuation**

THE CONTINUUM OF ENDS-MEANS

Those who have read and enjoyed Charles Lamb's essay on the origin of roast pork have probably not been conscious that their enjoyment of its absurdity was due to perception of the absurdity of any "end" which is set up apart from the means by which it is to be attained and apart from its own further function as means. Nor is it probable that Lamb himself wrote the story as a deliberate travesty of the theories that make such a separation. Nonetheless, that is the whole point of the tale. The story, it will be remembered, is that roast pork was first enjoyed when a house in which pigs were confined was accidentally burned down. While searching in the ruins, the owners touched the pigs that had been roasted in the fire and scorched their fingers. Impulsively bringing their fingers to their mouths to cool them, they experienced a new taste. Enjoying the taste, they henceforth set themselves to building houses, inclosing pigs in them, and then burning the houses down. Now, if ends-in-view are what they are entirely apart for means, and have their value independently of valuation of means, there is nothing ab-

* John Dewey, *Theory of Valuation.* Reprinted by permission of Beacon Press, Boston, copyright © 1948 by Beacon Press.

surd, nothing ridiculous, in this procedure, for the end attained, the *de facto* termination, *was* eating and enjoying roast pork, and that was just the end desired. Only when the end attained is estimated in terms of the means employed—the building and burning-down of houses in comparison with other available means by which the desired result in view might be attained—is there anything absurd or unreasonable about the method employed.

The story has a direct bearing upon another point, the meaning of "intrinsic." *Enjoyment* of the taste of roast pork may be said to be immediate, although even so the enjoyment would be a somewhat troubled one, for those who have memory, by the thought of the needless cost at which it was obtained. But to pass from immediacy of enjoyment to something called "intrinsic value" is a leap for which there is no ground. The *value* of enjoyment of an object *as* an attained end is a value of something which in being an end, an outcome, stands in relation to the means of which it is the consequence. Hence if the object in question is prized *as* an end or "final" value, it is valued *in this relation* or as mediated. The first time roast pork was enjoyed, it was *not* an end-value, since by description is was not the result of desire, foresight, and intent. Upon subsequent occasions it was, by description, the outcome of prior foresight, desire, and effort, and hence occupied the position of an end-in-view. There are occasions in which previous effort enhances enjoyment of what is attained. But there are also many occasions in which persons find that, when they have attained something as an end, they have paid too high a price in effort and in sacrifice of other ends. In such situations *enjoyment* of the end attained is itself *valued,* for it is not taken in its immediacy but in terms of its cost—a fact fatal to its being regarded as "an end-in-itself," a self-contradictory term in any case.

The story throws a flood of light upon what is usually meant by the maxim "the end justifies the means" and also upon the popular objection to it. Applied in this case, it would mean that the value of the attained end, the eating of roast pork, was such as to warrant the price paid in the means by which it was attained—destruction of dwelling-houses and sacrifice of the values to which they contribute. The conception involved in the maxim that "the end justifies the means" is basically the same as that in the notion of ends-in-themselves; indeed, from a historical point of view, it is the fruit of the latter, for only the conception that certain things are ends-in-themselves can warrant the belief that the relation of ends-means is unilateral, proceeding exclusively from end to means. When the maxim is compared with empirically ascertained facts, it is equivalent to holding one of two views, both of which are incompatible with the facts. One of the views is that only the specially selected "end" held in view will actually be brought into existence by the means used, something miraculously intervening to prevent the means employed from having their other usual effects; the other (and more probable) view is that, as compared with the importance of the selected and uniquely prized end, other consequences may be completely ignored and brushed aside no matter how intrinsically obnoxious they are. This arbitrary selection of some one part of the attained consequences as *the* end and hence as the warrant of means used (no matter how objectionable are their *other* consequences) is the fruit of holding that *it,* as *the* end, is an end-in-itself, and hence possessed of "value" irrespective of all its existential relations. And this notion is inherent in *every* view that assumes that "ends" can be valued apart from appraisal of the things used as means in attaining them. The sole alternative to the view that *the* end is an arbitrarily selected part of actual consequences which *as* "the end" then justifies the use of means irrespective of the other consequences they produce, is that desires, ends-in-view, and consequences achieved be valued in turn as means of further consequences. The maxim referred to, under the guise of saying that ends, in the sense of actual consequences, provide the warrant for means employed—a correct position—actually says that some fragment of these actual consequences—a fragment arbitrarily selected because the heart has been set upon it—authorizes the use of means to obtain *it,* without the need of foreseeing and weighing other ends as consequences of the means used. It thus discloses in a striking manner the fallacy involved in the position that ends have value independent of appraisal of means involved and independent of their own further causal efficacy. . . .

In all the physical sciences (using "physical" here as a synonym for *nonhuman*) it is now taken for granted that all "effects" are also "causes," or, stated more accurately, that nothing happens which is *final* in the sense that it is not part of an ongoing stream of events. If this principle, with the accompanying discrediting of belief in objects that are ends but not means, is employed in dealing with distinctive human phenomena, it necessarily follows that the distinction between ends and means is temporal and relational. Every condition that has to be brought into existence in order to serve as means is, *in that connection,* an object of desire and an end-in-view, while the end actually reached is a means to future ends as well as a test of valuations previously made. Since the end attained is a condition of further existential occurrences, it must be appraised as a potential obstacle and potential resource. If the notion of some objects as ends-in-themselves were abandoned, not merely in words but in all practical implications, human beings would for the first time in history be in a position to frame ends-in-view and form desires on the basis of empirically grounded propositions of the temporal relations of events to one another.

At any given time an adult person in a social group has certain ends which are so standardized by custom that they are taken for granted without examination, so that the only problems arising concern the best means for attaining them. In one group money-making would be such an end; in another group, possession of political power; in another group, advancement of scientific knowledge; in still another group, military prowess, etc. But such ends in any case are (i) more or less blank frameworks where the nominal "end" sets limits within which definite ends will fall, the latter being determined by appraisal of things as means; while (ii) as far as they simply express habits that have become established without critical examination of the relation of means and ends, they do not provide a model for a theory of valuation to follow. If a person moved by an experience of intense cold, which is highly objectionable, should momentarily judge it worth while to get warm by burning his house down, all that saves him from an act determined by a "compulsion neurosis" is the intellectual realization of what other consequences would ensue with the loss of his house. It is not necessarily a sign of insanity (as in the case cited) to isolate some event projected as an end out of the context of a world of moving changes in which it will in fact take place. But it is at least a sign of immaturity when an individual fails to view his end as also a moving condition of further consequences, thereby treating it as *final* in the sense in which "final" signifies that the course of events has come to a complete stop. Human beings do indulge in such arrests. But to treat them as models for forming a theory of ends is to substitute a manipulation of ideas, abstracted from the contexts in which they arise and function, for the conclusions of observation of concrete facts. It is a sign either of insanity, immaturity, indurated routine, or of a fanaticism that is a mixture of all three.

Generalized ideas of ends and values undoubtedly exist. They exist not only as expressions of habit and as uncritical and probably invalid ideas but also in the same way as valid general ideas arise in any subject. Similar situations recur; desires and interests are carried over from one situation to another and progressively consolidated. A schedule of general ends results, the involved values being "abstract" in the sense of not being directly connected with any particular existing case but not in the sense of independence of all empirically existent cases. As with general ideas in the conduct of any natural science, these general ideas are used as intellectual instrumentalities in judgment of particular cases as the latter arise; they are, in effect, tools that direct and facilitate examination of things in the concrete while they are also developed and tested by the results of their application in these cases. Just as the natural sciences began a course of sure development when the dialectic of concepts ceased to be employed to arrive at conclusions about existential affairs and was employed instead as a means of arriving at a hypothesis fruitfully applicable to particulars, so it will be with the theory of human activities and relations. There is irony in the fact that the very continuity of experienced activities which enables general ideas of value to function as rules for evaluation of particular desires and ends should have become the source of a belief that desires, by the bare fact of their occurrence, confer value upon objects as ends, entirely independent of their contexts in the continuum of activities. . . .

The objection always brought against the view set forth is that, according to it, valuation activities and judgments are involved in a hopeless *regressus ad infinitum.* If, so it is said, there is no end which is not in turn a means, foresight has no place at which it can stop, and no end-in-view can be formed except by the most arbitrary of acts—an act so arbitrary that it mocks the claim of being a genuine valuation-proposition.

This objection brings us back to the conditions under which desires take shape and foreseen consequences are projected as ends to be reached. These conditions are those of need, deficit, and conflict. Apart from a condition of tension between a person and environing conditions there is, as we have seen, no occasion for evocation of desire for something else; there is nothing to induce the formation of an end, much less the formation of one end rather than any other out of the indefinite number of ends theoretically possible. Control of transformation of active tendencies into a desire in which a particular end-in-view is incorporated, is exercised by the needs or privations of an actual situation as its requirements are disclosed to observation. The "value" of different ends that suggest themselves is estimated or measured by the capacity they exhibit to guide action in making good, *satisfying,* in its literal sense, existing lacks. Here is the factor which cuts short the process of foreseeing and weighing ends-in-view in their function as means. Sufficient unto the day is the evil thereof and sufficient also is the *good* of that which does away with the existing evil. Sufficient because it is the means of instituting a complete situation or an integrated set of conditions. . . .

A physician has to determine the value of various courses of action and their results in the case of a particular patient. He forms ends-in-view having the value that justifies their adoption, on the ground of what his examination discloses is the "matter" or "trouble" with the patient. He estimates the worth of what he undertakes on the ground of its capacity to produce a condition in which these troubles will not exist, in which, as it is ordinarily put, the patient will be "restored to health." He does not have an idea of health as an absolute end-in-itself, an absolute good by which to determine what to do. On the contrary, he forms his general idea of health as an end and a good (value) for the patient on the ground of what his techniques of examination have shown to be the troubles from which patients suffer and the means by which they are overcome. There is no need to deny that a general and abstract conception of health finally develops. But it is the outcome of a great number of definite, empirical inquiries, not an a priori preconditioning "standard" for carrying on inquiries. . . .

While there is no a priori standard of health with which the actual state of human beings can be compared so as to determine whether they are well or ill, or in what respect they are ill, there have developed, out of past experience, certain criteria which are operatively applicable in new cases as they arise. Ends-in-view are appraised or valued as *good* or *bad* on the ground of their serviceability in the direction of behavior dealing with states of affairs found to be objectionable because of some lack or conflict in them. They are appraised as fit or unfit, proper or improper, *right or wrong,* on the ground of their *requiredness* in accomplishing this end.

The attained end or consequence is always an organization of activities, where organization is a co-ordination of all activities which enter as factors. The *end-in-view* is that particular activity which operates as a co-ordinating factor of all other subactivities involved. Recognition of the end as a co-ordination or unified organization of activities, and of the end-in-view as the special activity which is the means of effecting this co-ordination, does away with any appearance of paradox that seems to be attached to the idea of a temporal continuum of activities in which each successive stage is equally end and means. The *form* of an attained end or consequence is always the same: that of adequate co-ordination. The content or involved matter of each successive result differs from that of its predecessors; for, while it is a *reinstatement* of a unified ongoing action, after a period of interruption through conflict and need, it is also an *enactment* of a new state of affairs. It has the qualities and properties appropriate to its being the consummatory resolution of a previous state of activity in which there was a peculiar need, desire, and end-in-view. In the continuous temporal process of organizing activities into a co-ordinated and co-ordinating unity, a constituent activity is both an end and a means: an end, in so far as it is temporally and relatively a close; a means, in so far as it provides a condition to be taken into account in further activity.

Instead of there being anything strange or paradoxical in the existence of situations in which means are constituents of the very end-objects they have helped to bring into existence, such situations occur whenever behavior succeeds in intelligent projection of ends-in-view that direct activity to resolution of the antecedent trouble. The cases in which ends and means fall apart are the abnormal ones, the ones which deviate from activity which is intelligently conducted. Wherever, for example, there is sheer drudgery, there is separation of the required and necessary means from both the end-in-view and the end attained. Wherever, on the other side, there is a so-called "ideal" which is utopian and a matter of fantasy, the same separation occurs, now from the side of the so-called *end.* Means that do not become constituent elements of the very ends or consequences they produce form what are called "necessary evils," their "necessity" being relative to the existing state of knowledge and art. They are comparable to scaffoldings that had to be later torn down, but which were necessary in erection of buildings until elevators were introduced. The latter remained for use in the building erected and were employed as means of transporting materials that in turn became an integral part of the building. Results or consequences which at one time were necessarily waste products in the production of the particular thing desired were utilized in the light of the development of human experience and intelligence as means for further desired consequences. The generalized ideal and standard of economy-efficiency which operates in every advanced art and technology is equivalent, upon analysis, to the conception of means that are constituents of ends attained and of ends that are usable as means to further ends.

It must also be noted that *activity* and *activities*, as these words are employed in the foregoing account, involve, like any actual behavior, existential material, as breathing involves air; walking, the earth; buying and selling, commodities; inquiry, things investigated, etc. No human activity operates in a vacuum; it acts in the world and has materials upon which and through which it produces results. On the other hand, no material—air, water, metal, wood, etc.—is *means* save as it is employed in some human activity to accomplish something. When "organization of activities" is mentioned, it always includes within itself organization of the materials existing in the world in which we live. That organization which is the "final" value for each concrete situation of valuation thus forms part of the existential conditions that have to be taken into account in further formation of desires and interests or valuations. In the degree in which a particular valuation is invalid because of inconsiderate shortsighted investigation of things in their relation of means-end, difficulties are put in the way of subsequent reasonable valuations. To the degree in which desires and interests are formed after critical survey of the conditions which as means determine the actual outcome, the more smoothly continuous become subsequent activities, for consequences attained are then such as are evaluated more readily as means in the continuum of action.

*Reconstruction in Philosophy**

EDUCATION AND MORALITY

If a few words are added upon the topic of education, it is only for the sake of suggesting that the educative process is all one with the moral process, since the latter is a continuous passage of experience from worse to better. Education has been traditionally thought of as preparation: as learning, acquiring certain things because they will later be useful. The end is remote, and education is getting ready, is a preliminary to something more important to happen later on. Childhood is only a preparation for adult life, and adult life for another life. Always the future, not the present, has been the significant thing in education: Acquisition of knowledge and skill for future use and enjoyment; formation of habits required later in life in business, good citizenship and pursuit of science. Education is thought of also as something needed by some human beings merely because of their dependence upon others. We are born ignorant, unversed, unskilled, immature, and consequently in a state of social dependence. Instruction, training, moral discipline are processes by which the mature, the adult, gradually raise the helpless to the point where they can look out for themselves. The business of childhood is to grow into the independence of adulthood by means of the guidance of those who have already attained it. Thus the process of education as the main business of life ends when the young have arrived at emancipation from social dependence.

These two ideas, generally assumed

* *Supra*, p. 451.

but rarely explicitly reasoned out, contravene the conception that growing, or the continuous reconstruction of experience, is the only end. If at whatever period we choose to take a person, he is still in process of growth, then education is not, save as a by-product, a preparation for something coming later. Getting from the present the degree and kind of growth there is in it is education. This is a constant function, independent of age. The best thing that can be said about any special process of education, like that of the formal school period, is that it renders its subject capable of further education: more sensitive to conditions of growth and more able to take advantage of them. Acquisition of skill, possession of knowledge, attainment of culture are not ends: they are marks of growth and means to its continuing.

The contrast usually assumed between the period of education as one of social dependence and of maturity as one of social independence does harm. We repeat over and over that man is a social animal, and then confine the significance of this statement to the sphere in which sociality usually seems least evident, politics. The heart of the sociality of man is in education. The idea of education as preparation and of adulthood as a fixed limit of growth are two sides of the same obnoxious untruth. If the moral business of the adult as well as the young is a growing and developing experience, then the instruction that comes from social dependencies and interdependencies is as important for the adult as for the child. Moral independence for the adult means arrest of growth, isolation means induration. We exaggerate the intellectual dependence of childhood so that children are too much kept in leading strings, and then we exaggerate the independence of adult life from intimacy of contacts and communication with others. When the identity of the moral process with the processes of specific growth is realized, the more conscious and formal education of childhood will be seen to be the most economical and efficient means of social advance and reorganization, and it will also be evident that the test of all the institutions of adult life is their effect in furthering continued education. Government, business, art, religion, all social institutions have a meaning, a purpose. That purpose is to set free and to develop the capacities of human individuals without respect to race, sex, class or economic status. And this is all one with saying that the test of their value is the extent to which they educate every individual into the full stature of his possibility. Democracy has many meanings, but if it has a moral meaning, it is found in resolving that the supreme test of all political institutions and industrial arrangements shall be the contribution they make to the all-around growth of every member of society.

H. A. PRICHARD

For many years H. A. Prichard (1871–1947) taught at Oxford and in this position exerted important influence upon his students and colleagues alike. He published little, but the clarity and economy of his thought allowed him to present his views within the boundaries of brief articles.

Prichard's relationship to Moore reveals the main lines of his position. Moore had attacked a cardinal tenet of Bentham's and Mill's utilitarianism—the doctrine of ethical hedonism. He argued that goodness could not be identified with pleasure, or for that matter with any natural property. He therefore maintained that goodness is a simple non-natural property that is apprehended intuitively.

Prichard accepted this much of Moore's position but carried intuitionism a step further. Moore, though an opponent of ethical hedonism, remained a utilitarian. He believed the rightness of an act could be defined in terms of the goodness of the consequences of that act. On this point Prichard disagreed, employing an argument closely paralleling Moore's critique of naturalism. He argued that rightness cannot be defined in terms of goodness, for rightness is a simple irreducible notion, not only distinct from any natural property, but also distinct from goodness as well. Thus Prichard argues for deontological *intuitionism in place of Moore's* teleological *intuitionism.*

*Does Moral Philosophy Rest on a Mistake?**

Probably to most students of Moral Philosophy there comes a time when they feel a vague sense of dissatisfaction with the whole subject. And the sense of dissatisfaction tends to grow rather than to diminish. It is not so much that the positions, and still more the arguments, of particular thinkers seem unconvincing, though this is true. It is rather that the aim of the subject becomes increasingly obscure. "What," it is asked, "are we really going to learn by Moral Philosophy?" "What are books on Moral Philosophy really trying to show, and when their aim is clear, why are they so unconvincing and artificial?" And again: "Why is it so difficult to substitute anything better?"

* With permission of the Editor of *Mind*. H. A. Prichard, "Does Moral Philosophy Rest on a Mistake?" *Mind*, N.S., Vol. 21, 1912.

Personally, I have been led by growing dissatisfaction of this kind to wonder whether the reason may not be that the subject, at any rate as usually understood, consists in the attempt to answer an improper question. And in this article, I shall venture to contend that the existence of the whole subject, as usually understood, rests on a mistake, and on a mistake parallel to that on which rests, as I think, the subject usually called the Theory of Knowledge.

If we reflect on our own mental history or on the history of the subject, we feel no doubt about the nature of the demand which originates the subject. Any one who, stimulated by education, has come to feel the force of the various obligations in life, at some time or other comes to feel the irksomeness of carrying them out, and to recognise the sacrifice of interest involved; and, if thoughtful, he inevitably puts to himself the question: "Is there really a reason why I should act in the ways in which hitherto I have thought I ought to act? May I not have been all the time under an illusion in so thinking? Should not I really be justified in simply trying to have a good time?" Yet, like Glaucon, feeling that somehow he ought after all to act in these ways, he asks for a *proof* that this feeling is justified. In other words, he asks "*Why* should I do these things?" and his and other people's moral philosophising is an attempt to supply the answer, *i.e.* to supply by a process of reflexion a proof of the truth of what he and they have prior to reflexion believed immediately or without proof. This frame of mind seems to present a close parallel to the frame of mind which originates the Theory of Knowledge. Just as the recognition that the doing of our duty often vitally interferes with the satisfaction of our inclinations leads us to wonder whether we really ought to do what we usually call our duty, so the recognition that we and others are liable to mistakes in knowledge generally leads us, as it did Descartes, to wonder whether hitherto we may not have been always mistaken. And just as we try to find a proof, based on the general consideration of action and of human life, that we ought to act in the ways usually called moral, so we, like Descartes, propose by a process of reflexion on our thinking to find a test of knowledge, *i.e.* a principle by applying which we can show that a certain condition of mind was really knowledge, a condition which *ex hypothesi* existed independently of the process of reflexion.

Now, how has the moral question been answered? So far as I can see, the answers all fall, and fall from the necessities of the case, into one of two species. *Either* they state that we ought to do so and so, because as we see when we fully apprehend the facts, doing so will be for our good, *i.e.* really, as I would rather say, for our advantage, or, better still, for our happiness; *or* they state that we ought to do so and so, because something realised either in or by the action is good. In other words, the reason "why" is stated in terms either of the agent's happiness or of the goodness of something involved in the action.

To see the prevalence of the former species of answer, we have only to consider the history of Moral Philosophy. To take obvious instances, Plato, Butler, Hutcheson, Paley, Mill, each in his own way seeks at bottom to convince the individual that he ought to act in so-called moral ways by showing that to do so will really be for his happiness. Plato is perhaps the most significant instance, because of all philosophers he is the one to whom we are least willing to ascribe a mistake on such matters, and a mistake on his part would be evidence of the deep-rootedness of the tendency to make it. To show that Plato really justifies morality by its profitableness, it is only necessary to point out (1) that the very formulation of the thesis to be met, viz., that justice is ἀλλότριον ἀγαθόν, implies that any refutation must consist in showing that justice is οἴκειον ἀγαθόν, *i.e.* really, as the context shows, one's own advantage, and (2) that the term λυσιτελεῖν supplies the keynote not only to the problem but also to its solution.

The tendency to justify acting on moral rules in this way is natural. For if, as often happens, we put to ourselves the question "Why should we do so and so?" we are satisfied by being convinced either that the doing so will lead to something which we want (*e.g.* that taking certain medicine will heal our disease), or that the doing so itself, as we see when we appreciate its nature, is something that we want or should like, *e.g.* playing golf. The formulation of the question implies a state of unwillingness or indifference towards the action, and we are brought into a condition of willingness by the answer. And this process seems to be precisely what we desire when we ask, *e.g.*, "Why should we keep our engagements to our own loss?" for it is just the fact that the keeping our engagements runs counter to the satisfaction of our desires which produced the question.

The answer is, of course, not an answer, for it fails to convince us that we ought to keep our engagements; even if successful on its own lines, it only makes us *want* to keep them. And Kant was really only pointing out this fact when he distinguished hypothetical and categorical imperatives, even though he obscured the nature of the fact by wrongly describing his so-called "hypothetical imperatives" as imperatives. But if this answer be no answer, what other can be offered? Only, it seems, an answer which bases the obligation to do something on the *goodness* either of something to which the act leads or of the act itself. Suppose, when wondering whether we really ought to act in the ways usually called moral, we are told as a means of resolving our doubt that those acts are right which produce happiness. We at once ask "Whose happiness?" If we are told "Our own happiness," then, though we shall lose our hesitation to act in these ways, we shall not recover our sense that we ought to do so. But how can this result be avoided? Apparently, only by being told one of two things; *either* that any one's happiness is a thing good in itself, and that *therefore* we ought to do whatever will produce it, *or* that the working for happiness is itself good, and that the intrinsic goodness of such an action is the reason why we ought to do it. The advantage of this appeal to the goodness of something consists in the fact that it avoids reference to desire, and, instead, refers to something impersonal and objective. In this way it seems possible to avoid the resolution of obligation into inclination. But just for this reason it is of the essence of the answer, that, to be effective, it must neither include nor involve the view that the apprehension of the goodness of anything necessarily arouses the desire for it. Otherwise the answer resolves itself into a form of the former answer by substituting desire or inclination for the sense of obligation, and in this way it loses what seems its special advantage.

Now it seems to me that both forms of this answer break down, though each for a different reason.

Consider the first form. It is what may be called Utilitarianism in the generic sense in which what is good is not limited to pleasure. It takes its stand upon the distinction between something which is not itself an action but which can be produced by an action and the action which will produce it, and contends that if something which is not an action is good, then we *ought* to undertake the action which will, directly or indirectly, originate it.

But this argument, if it is to restore the sense of obligation to act, must presuppose an intermediate link, *viz.*, the further thesis that what is good ought to be. The necessity of this link is obvious. An "ought," if it is to be derived at all, can only be derived from another "ought." Moreover this link tacitly presupposes another, *viz.*, that the apprehension that something good which is not an action ought to be involves just the feeling of imperativeness or obligation which is to be aroused by the thought of the action which will originate it. Otherwise the argument will not lead us to feel the obligation to produce it by the action. And, surely, both this link and its implication are false.[1] The word "ought" refers to actions and to actions alone. The proper language is never "So and so ought to be," but "I ought to do so and so." Even if we are sometimes moved to say that the world or something in it is not what it ought to be, what we really mean is that God or some human being has not made something what he ought to have made it. And it is merely stating another side of this fact to urge that we can only feel the imperativeness upon us of something which is in our power; for it is actions and actions alone which, directly at least, are in our power.

Perhaps, however, the best way to see the failure of this view is to see its failure to correspond to our actual moral convictions. Suppose we ask ourselves whether our sense that we ought to pay our debts or to tell the truth arises from our recognition that in doing so we should be originating something good, *e.g.*, material comfort in A or true belief in B, *i.e.*, suppose we ask ourselves whether it is this aspect of the action which leads to our recognition that we ought to do it. We, at once, and without hesitation answer "No." Again, if we take as our illustration our sense that we ought to act justly as between two parties, we have, if possible, even less hesitation in giving a similar answer; for the balance of resulting good may be, and often is, not on the side of justice.

At best it can only be maintained that there is this element of truth in the Utilitarian view that unless we recognised that something which an act will originate is good, we should not recognise that we ought to do the action. Unless we thought knowledge a good thing, it may be urged, we should not think that we ought to tell the truth; unless we thought pain a bad thing, we should not think the infliction of it, without special reason, wrong. But this is not to imply that the badness of error is the reason why it is wrong to lie, or the badness of pain the reason why we ought not to inflict it without special cause.[2]

It is, I think, just because this form of the view is so plainly at variance with our moral consciousness, that we become driven to adopt the other form of the view, *viz.*, that the act is good in itself and that its intrinsic goodness is the reason why it ought to be done. It is this form which has always made the most serious appeal; for the goodness of the act itself seems more closely related to the obligation to do it than that of its mere consequences or results, and therefore, if obligation is to be based on the goodness of something, it would seem that this goodness should be that of the act itself. Moreover, the view gains plausibility from the fact that moral actions are most conspicuously those to which the term "intrinsically good" is applicable.

Nevertheless this view, though perhaps less superficial, is equally untenable. For it leads to precisely the dilemma which

[1] When we speak of anything, *e.g.*, of some emotion or of some quality of a human being, as good, we never dream in our ordinary consciousness of going on to say that therefore it ought to be.

[2] It may be noted that if the badness of pain were the reason why we ought not to inflict pain on another, it would equally be a reason why we ought not to inflict pain on ourselves; yet, though we should allow the wanton infliction of pain on ourselves to be foolish, we should not think of describing it as wrong.

faces every one who tries to solve the problem raised by Kant's theory of the good will. To see this, we need only consider the nature of the acts to which we apply the term "intrinsically good."

There is, of course, no doubt that we approve and even admire certain actions, and also that we should describe them as good, and as good in themselves. But it is, I think, equally unquestionable that our approval and our use of the term "good" is always in respect of the motive and refers to actions which have been actually done and of which we think we know the motive. Further, the actions of which we approve and which we should describe as intrinsically good are of two and only two kinds. They are either actions in which the agent did what he did because he thought he ought to do it, or actions of which the motive was a desire prompted by some good emotion, such as gratitude, affection, family feeling, or public spirit, the most prominent of such desires in books on Moral Philosophy being that ascribed to what is vaguely called benevolence. For the sake of simplicity I omit the case of actions done partly from some such desire and partly from a sense of duty; for even if all good actions are done from a combination of these motives, the argument will not be affected. The dilemma is this. If the motive in respect of which we think an action good is the sense of obligation, then so far from the sense that we ought to do it being derived from our apprehension of its goodness, our apprehension of its goodness will presuppose the sense that we ought to do it. In other words, in this case the recognition that the act is good will plainly *presuppose* the recognition that the act is right, whereas the view under consideration is that the recognition of the goodness of the act *gives rise* to the recognition of its rightness. On the other hand, if the motive in respect of which we think an action good is some intrinsically good desire, such as the desire to help a friend, the recognition of the goodness of the act will equally fail to give rise to the sense of obligation to do it. For we cannot feel that we ought to do that the doing of which is *ex hypothesi* prompted solely by the desire to do it.

The fallacy underlying the view is that while to base the rightness of an act upon its intrinsic goodness implies that the goodness in question is that of the motive, in reality the rightness or wrongness of an act has nothing to do with any question of motives at all. For, as any instance will show, the rightness of an action concerns an action not in the fuller sense of the term in which we include the motive in the action, but in the narrower and commoner sense in which we distinguish an action from its motive and mean by an action merely the conscious origination of something, an origination which on different occasions or in different people may be prompted by different motives. The question "Ought I to pay my bills?" really means simply "Ought I to bring about my tradesmen's possession of what by my previous acts I explicitly or implicitly promised them?" There is, and can be, no question of whether I ought to pay my debts from a particular motive. No doubt we know that if we pay our bills we shall pay them with a motive, but in considering whether we ought to pay them we inevitably think of the act in abstraction from the motive. Even if we knew what our motive would be if we did the act, we should not be any nearer an answer to the question.

Moreover, if we eventually pay our bills from fear of the county court, we shall still have done *what* we ought, even though we shall not have done it *as* we ought. The attempt to bring in the motive involves a mistake similar to that involved in supposing that we can will to will. To feel that I ought to pay my bills is to be *moved towards* paying them. But what I can be moved towards must always be an action and not an action in which I am moved in a particular way, *i.e.* an action from a particular motive; otherwise I should be moved towards being moved, which is impossible. Yet the view under consideration involves this impossibility; for it really resolves the sense that I ought to do so and so, into the sense that I ought to be moved to do it in a particular way.[3]

So far my contentions have been mainly negative, but they form, I think, a useful, if not a necessary, introduction to what I take to be the truth. This I will now endeavour to state, first formulating what, as I think, is the real nature of our apprehension or appreciation of moral obligations, and then applying the result to elucidate the question of the existence of Moral Philosophy.

The sense of obligation to do, or of the rightness of, an action of a particular kind is absolutely underivative or immediate. The rightness of an action consists in its being the origination of something of a certain kind A in a situation of a certain kind, a situation in a certain relation B of the agent to others or to his own nature. To appreciate its rightness two preliminaries may be necessary. We may have to follow out the consequences of the proposed action more fully than we have hitherto done, in order to realise that in the action we should originate A. Thus we may not appreciate the wrongness of telling a certain story until we realise that we should thereby be hurting the feelings of one of our audience. Again, we may have to take into account the relation B involved in the situation, which we had hitherto failed to notice. For instance, we may not appreciate the obligation to give X a present, until we remember that he has done us an act of kindness. But, given that by a process which is, of course, merely a process of general and not of moral thinking we come to recognise that the proposed act is one by which we shall originate A in a relation B, then we appreciate the obligation immediately or directly, the appreciation being an activity of *moral* thinking. We recognise, for instance, that this performance of a service to X, who has done us a service, just in virtue of its being the performance of a service to one who has rendered a service to the would-be agent, ought to be done by us. This apprehension is immediate, in precisely the sense in which a mathematical apprehension is immediate, *e.g.*, the apprehension that this three-sided figure, in virtue of its being three-sided, must have three angles. Both apprehensions are immediate in the sense that in both insight into the nature of the subject directly leads us to recognise its possession of the predicate; and it is only stating this fact from the other side to say that in both cases the fact apprehended is self-evident.

The plausibility of the view that obligations are not self-evident but need proof lies in the fact that an act which is referred to as an obligation may be incompletely stated, what I have called the preliminaries to appreciating the obligation being incomplete. If, *e.g.*, we refer to the act of repaying X by a present merely as giving X a present, it appears, and indeed is, necessary to give a reason. In other words, wherever a moral act is regarded in this incomplete way the question, "*Why* should I do it?" is perfectly legitimate. This fact suggests, but suggests wrongly, that even if the nature of the act is completely stated, it is still necessary to give a reason, or, in other words, to supply a proof.

The relations involved in obligations of various kinds, are, of course, very different. The relation in certain cases is a relation to others due to a past act of theirs or ours. The obligation to repay a benefit

[3] It is of course not denied here than an action done from a particular motive may be good; it is only denied that the *rightness* of an action depends on its being done with a particular motive.

involves a relation due to a past act of the benefactor. The obligation to pay a bill involves a relation due to a past act of ours in which we have either said or implied that we would make a certain return, for something which we have asked for and received. On the other hand the obligation to speak the truth implies no such definite act; it involves a relation consisting in the fact that others are trusting us to speak the truth, a relation the apprehension of which gives rise to the sense that communication of the truth is something owing by us to them. Again the obligation not to hurt the feelings of another, involves no special relation of us to that other, *i.e.*, no relation other than that involved in our both being men and men in one and the same world. Moreover, it seems that the relation involved in an obligation need not be a relation to another at all. Thus we should admit that there is an obligation to overcome our natural timidity or greediness, and that this involves no relations to others. Still there is a relation involved, *viz.*, a relation to our own disposition. It is simply because we can and because others cannot directly modify our disposition that it is our business to improve it, and that it is not theirs, or, at least, not theirs to the same extent.

The negative side of all this is, of course, that we do not come to appreciate an obligation by an *argument, i.e.* by a process of non-moral thinking, and that, in particular, we do not do so by an argument of which a premise is the ethical but not moral activity of appreciating the goodness either of the act or of a consequence of the act; *i.e.* that our sense of the rightness of an act is not a conclusion from our appreciation of the goodness either of it or of anything else.

It will probably be urged that on this view our various obligations form, like Aristotle's categories, an unrelated chaos in which it is impossible to acquiesce. For, according to it, the obligation to repay a benefit, or to pay a debt, or to keep a promise, presupposes a previous act of another; whereas the obligation to speak the truth or not to harm another does not; and, again, the obligation to remove our timidity involves no relations to others at all. Yet, at any rate, an effective *argumentum ad hominem* is at hand in the fact that the various qualities which we recognise as good are equally unrelated; *e.g.* courage, humility, and interest in knowledge. If, as is plainly the case, ἀγαθά differ ᾗ ἀγαθά, why should not obligations equally differ *qua* their obligatoriness? Moreover if this were not so, there could in the end be only one obligation, which is palpably contrary to fact.[4]

Certain observations will help to make the view clearer.

In the first place, it may seem that the

[4] Two other objections may be anticipated: (1) that obligations cannot be self-evident, since many actions regarded as obligations by some are not so regarded by others; and (2) that if obligations are self-evident, the problem of how we ought to act in the presence of conflicting obligations is insoluble.

To the first I should reply:—

(a) That the appreciation of an obligation is, of course, only possible for a developed moral being, and that different degrees of development are possible.

(b) That the failure to recognize some particular obligation is usually due to the fact that, owing to a lack of thoughtfulness, what I have called the preliminaries to this recognition are incomplete.

(c) That the view put forward is consistent with the admission that, owing to a lack of thoughtfulness, even the best men are blind to many of their obligations, and that in the end our obligations are seen to be co-extensive with almost the whole of our life.

To the second objection I should reply that obligation admits of degrees, and that where obligations conflict, the decision of what we ought to do turns not on the question "Which of the alternative courses of action will originate the greater good?" but on the question "Which is the greater obligation?"

view, being—as it is—avowedly put forward in opposition to the view that what is right is derived from what is good, must itself involve the opposite of this, *viz.*, the Kantian position that what is good is based upon what is right, *i.e.*, that an act, if it be good, is good because it is right. But this is not so. For, on the view put forward, the rightness of a right action lies solely in the origination in which the act consists, whereas the intrinsic goodness of an action lies solely in its motive; and this implies that a morally good action is morally good not simply because it is a right action but because it is a right action done because it is right, *i.e.*, from a sense of obligation. And this implication, it may be remarked incidentally, seems plainly true.

In the second place the view involves that when, or rather so far as, we act from a sense of obligation, we have no purpose or end. By a "purpose" or "end" we really mean something the existence of which we desire, and desire of the existence of which leads us to act. Usually our purpose is something which the act will originate, as when we turn round in order to look at a picture. But it may be the action itself, *i.e.*, the origination of something, as when we hit a golf ball into a hole or kill some one out of revenge.[5] Now if by a purpose we mean something the existence of which we desire and desire for which leads us to act, then plainly so far as we act from a sense of obligation, we have no purpose, consisting either in the action itself or in anything which it will produce. This is so obvious that it scarcely seems worth pointing out. But I do so for two reasons. (1) If we fail to scrutinise the meaning of the terms "end" and "purpose," we are apt to assume uncritically that all deliberate action, *i.e.*, action proper, must have a purpose; we then become puzzled both when we look for the purpose of an action done from a sense of obligation, and also when we try to apply to such an action the distinction of means and end, the truth all the time being that since there is no end, there is no means either. (2) The attempt to base the sense of obligation on the recognition of the goodness of something is really an attempt to find a purpose in a moral action in the shape of something good which, as good, we want. And the expectation that the goodness of something underlies an obligation disappears as soon as we cease to look for a purpose.

The thesis, however, that, so far as we act from a sense of obligation, we have no purpose must not be misunderstood. It must not be taken either to mean or to imply that so far as we so act we have no *motive*. No doubt in ordinary speech the words "motive" and "purpose" are usually treated as correlatives, "motive" standing for the desire which induces us to act, and "purpose" standing for the object of this desire. But this is only because, when we are looking for the motive of some action, say some crime, we are usually presupposing that the act in question is prompted by a desire and not by the sense of obligation. At bottom, however, we mean by a motive what moves us to act; a sense of obligation does sometimes move us to act; and in our ordinary consciousness we should not hesitate to allow that the action we were considering might have had as its motive a sense of obligation. Desire and the sense of obligation are co-ordinate forms or species of motive.

In the third place, if the view put forward be right, we must sharply distinguish morality and virtue as independent, though related, species of goodness, neither being an aspect of something of which the other is an aspect, nor again a form or species of the other, nor again something

[5] It is no objection to urge that an action cannot be its own purpose, since the purpose of something cannot be the thing itself. For, speaking strictly, the purpose is not the *action's* purpose but *our* purpose, and there is no contradiction in holding that our purpose in acting may be the action.

deducible from the other; and we must at the same time allow that it is possible to do the same act either virtuously or morally or in both ways at once. And surely this is true. An act, to be virtuous, must, as Aristotle saw, be done willingly or with pleasure; as such it is just not done from a sense of obligation but from some desire which is intrinsically good, as arising from some intrinsically good emotion. Thus in an act of generosity the motive is the desire to help another arising from sympathy with that other; in an act which is courageous and no more, *i.e.* in an act which is not at the same time an act of public spirit or family affection or the like, we prevent ourselves from being dominated by a feeling of terror, desiring to do so from a sense of shame at being terrified. The goodness of such an act is different from the goodness of an act to which we apply the term moral in the strict and narrow sense, *viz.* an act done from a sense of obligation. Its goodness lies in the intrinsic goodness of the emotion and the consequent desire under which we act, the goodness of this motive being different from the goodness of the moral motive proper, *viz.*, the sense of duty or obligation. Nevertheless, at any rate in certain cases, an act can be done either virtuously or morally or in both ways at once. It is possible to repay a benefit either from desire to repay it or from the feeling that we ought to do so or from both motives combined. A doctor may tend his patients either from a desire arising out of interest in his patients or in the exercise of skill or from a sense of duty, or from a desire and a sense of duty combined. Further, although we recognise that in each case the act possesses an intrinsic goodness, we regard that action as the best in which both motives are combined; in other words, we regard as the really best man the man in whom virtue and morality are united.

It may be objected that the distinction between the two kinds of motive is untenable on the ground that the *desire* to repay a benefit, for example, is only the manifestation of that which manifests itself as the *sense of obligation* to repay whenever we think of something in the action which is other than the repayment and which we should not like, such as the loss or pain involved. Yet the distinction can, I think, easily be shown to be tenable. For, in the analogous case of revenge, the desire to return the injury and the sense that we ought not to do so, leading, as they do, in opposite directions, are plainly distinct; and the obviousness of the distinction here seems to remove any difficulty in admitting the existence of a parallel distinction between the desire to return a benefit and the sense that we ought to return it.[6]

Further the view implies that an obligation can no more be based on or derived from a virtue than a virtue can be derived from an obligation, in which latter case a virtue would consist in carrying out an obligation. And the implication is surely true and important. Take the case of courage. It is untrue to urge that, since courage is a virtue, we ought to act courageously. It is and must be untrue, because, as we see in the end, to feel an obligation to act courageously would involve a contradiction. For, as I have urged before, we can only feel an obligation to *act;* we cannot feel

[6] This sharp distinction of virtue and morality as co-ordinate and independent forms of goodness will explain a fact which otherwise it is difficult to account for. If we turn from books on Moral Philosophy to any vivid account of human life and action such as we find in Shakespeare, nothing strikes us more than the comparative remoteness of the discussions of Moral Philosophy from the facts of actual life. Is not this largely because, while Moral Philosophy has, quite rightly, concentrated its attention on the fact of obligation, in the case of many of those whom we admire most and whose lives are of the greatest interest, the sense of obligation, though it may be an important, is not a dominating factor in their lives?

an obligation to *act from a certain desire,* in this case the desire to conquer one's feelings of terror arising from the sense of shame which they arouse. Moreover, if the sense of obligation to act in a particular way leads to an action, the action will be an action done from a sense of obligation, and therefore not, if the above analysis of virtue be right, an act of courage.

The mistake of supposing that there can be an obligation to act courageously seems to arise from two causes. In the first place, there is often an obligation to do that which involves the conquering or controlling our fear in the doing of it, *e.g.*, the obligation to walk along the side of a precipice to fetch a doctor for a member of our family. Here the acting on the obligation is externally, though only externally, the same as an act of courage proper. In the second place there is an obligation to acquire courage, *i.e.*, to do such things as will enable us afterwards to act courageously, and this may be mistaken for an obligation to act courageously. The same considerations can, of course, be applied, *mutatis mutandis,* to the other virtues.

The fact, if it be a fact, that virtue is no basis for morality will explain what otherwise it is difficult to account for, *viz.*, the extreme sense of dissatisfaction produced by a close reading of Aristotle's *Ethics*. Why is the *Ethics* so disappointing? Not, I think, because it really answers two radically different questions as if they were one: (1) "What is the happy life?" (2) "What is the virtuous life?" It is, rather, because Aristotle does not do what we as Moral Philosophers want him to do, *viz.*, to convince us that we really ought to do what in our non-reflective consciousness we have hitherto believed we ought to do, or, if not, to tell us what, if any, are the other things which we really ought to do, and to prove to us that he is right. Now, if what I have just been contending is true, a systematic account of the virtuous character cannot possibly satisfy this demand. At best it can only make clear to us the details of one of our obligations, *viz.*, the obligation to make ourselves better men; but the achievement of this does not help us to discover what we ought to do in life as a whole and why; to think that it did would be to think that our only business in life was self-improvement. Hence it is not surprising that Aristotle's account of the good man strikes us as almost wholly of academic value, with little relation to our real demand, which is formulated in Plato's words: *οὐ γὰρ περὶ τοῦ ἐπιτύχοντος ὁ λόγος ἀλλά περὶ τοῦ ὅντινα τρόπον χρῆ ξῆν.*

I am not, of course, *criticising* Aristotle for failing to satisfy this demand, except so far as here and there he leads us to think that he intends to satisfy it. For my main contention is that the demand cannot be satisfied and cannot be satisfied because it is illegitimate. Thus we are brought to the question: "Is there really such a thing as Moral Philosophy, and, if there is, in what sense?"

We should first consider the parallel case—as it appears to be—of the Theory of Knowledge. As I urged before, at some time or other in the history of all of us, if we are thoughtful, the frequency of our own and of others' mistakes is bound to lead to the reflexion that possibly we and others have *always* been mistaken in consequence of some radical defect of our faculties. In consequence certain things which previously we should have said without hesitation that we *knew,* as *e.g.*, that $4 \times 7 = 28$, become subject to doubt; we become able only to say that we thought we knew these things. We inevitably go on to look for some general procedure by which we can ascertain that a given condition of mind is really one of knowledge. And this involves the search for a criterion of knowledge, *i.e.* for a principle by applying which we can settle that a given state of mind is really knowledge. The search for this criterion and the application of it, when found, is what is called the Theory of

Knowledge. The search implies that instead of its being the fact that the knowledge that A is B is obtained directly by consideration of the nature of A and B, the knowledge that A is B, in the full or complete sense, can only be obtained by first knowing that A is B, and then knowing that we knew it, by applying a criterion, such as Descartes' principle that what we clearly and distinctly conceive is true.

Now it is easy to show that the doubt whether A is B based on this speculative or general ground, could, if genuine, never be set at rest. For if, in order really to know that A is B, we must first know that we knew it, then really to know that we knew it, we must first know that we knew that we knew it. But—what is more important—it is also easy to show that this doubt is not a genuine doubt but rests on a confusion the exposure of which removes the doubt. For when we *say* we doubt whether our previous condition was one of knowledge, what we *mean*, if we mean anything at all, is that we doubt whether our previous *belief* was *true*, a belief which we should express as the *thinking* that A is B. For in order to doubt whether our previous condition was one of knowledge, we have to think of it not as knowledge but as only belief, and our only question can be "Was this belief true?" But as soon as we see that we are thinking of our previous condition as only one of belief, we see that what we are now doubting is not what we first *said* we were doubting, *viz.*, whether a previous condition of knowledge was really knowledge. Hence, to remove the doubt, it is only necessary to appreciate the real nature of our consciousness in apprehending, *e.g.*, that $7 \times 4 = 28$, and thereby see that it was no mere condition of believing but a condition of knowing, and then to notice that in our subsequent doubt what we are really doubting is not whether this consciousness was really knowledge, but whether a consciousness of another kind, *viz.* a belief that $7 \times 4 = 28$, was true. We thereby see that though a doubt based on speculative grounds is possible, it is not a doubt concerning what we believed the doubt concerned, and that a doubt concerning this latter is impossible.

Two results follow. In the first place, if, as is usually the case, we mean by the "Theory of Knowledge" the knowledge which supplies the answer to the question "Is what we have hitherto thought knowledge really knowledge?" there is and can be no such thing, and the supposition that there can is simply due to a confusion. There can be no answer to an illegitimate question, except that the question is illegitimate. Nevertheless the question is one which we continue to put until we realise the inevitable immediacy of knowledge. And it is positive knowledge that knowledge is immediate and neither can be, nor needs to be, improved or vindicated by the further knowledge that it was knowledge. This positive knowledge sets at rest the inevitable doubt, and, so far as by the "Theory of Knowledge" is meant this knowledge, then even though this knowledge be the knowledge that there is no Theory of Knowledge in the former sense, to that extent the Theory of Knowledge exists.

In the second place, suppose we come genuinely to doubt whether, *e.g.*, $7 \times 4 = 28$ owing to a genuine doubt whether we were right in believing yesterday that $7 \times 4 = 28$, a doubt which can in fact only arise if we have lost our hold of, *i.e.*, no longer remember, the real nature of our consciousness of yesterday, and so think of it as consisting in believing. Plainly, the only remedy is to do the sum again. Or, to put the matter generally, if we do come to doubt whether it is true that A is B, as we once thought, the remedy lies not in any process of reflection but in such a reconsideration of the nature of A and B as leads to the knowledge that A is B.

With these considerations in mind,

consider the parallel which, as it seems to me, is presented—though with certain differences—by Moral Philosophy. The sense that we ought to do certain things arises in our unreflective consciousness, being an activity of moral thinking occasioned by the various situations in which we find ourselves. At this stage our attitude to these obligations is one of unquestioning confidence. But inevitably the appreciation of the degree to which the execution of these obligations is contrary to our interest raises the doubt whether after all these obligations are really obligatory, *i.e.*, whether our sense that we ought not to do certain things is not illusion. We then want to have it *proved* to us that we ought to do so, *i.e.*, to be convinced of this by a process which, as an argument, is different in kind from our original and unreflective appreciation of it. This demand is, as I have argued, illegitimate.

Hence in the first place, if, as is almost universally the case, by Moral Philosophy is meant the knowledge which would satisfy this demand, there is no such knowledge, and all attempts to attain it are doomed to failure because they rest on a mistake, the mistake of supposing the possibility of proving what can only be apprehended directly by an act of moral thinking. Nevertheless the demand, though illegitimate, is inevitable until we have carried the process of reflexion far enough to realise the self-evidence of our obligations, *i.e.*, the immediacy of our apprehension of them. This realisation of their self-evidence is positive knowledge, and so far, and so far only, as the term Moral Philosophy is confined to this knowledge and to the knowledge of the parallel immediacy of the apprehension of the goodness of the various virtues and of good dispositions generally, is there such a thing as Moral Philosophy. But since this knowledge may allay doubts which often affect the whole conduct of life, it is, though not extensive, important and even vitally important.

In the second place, suppose we come genuinely to doubt whether we ought, for example, to pay our debts owing to a genuine doubt whether our previous conviction that we ought to do so is true, a doubt which can, in fact only arise if we fail to remember the real nature of what we now call our past conviction. The only remedy lies in actual getting into a situation which occasions the obligation, or —if our imagination be strong enough—in imagining ourselves in that situation, and then letting our moral capacities of thinking do their work. Or, to put the matter generally, if we do doubt whether there is really an obligation to originate A in a situation B, the remedy lies not in any process of general thinking, but in getting face to face with a particular instance of the situation B, and then directly appreciating the obligation to originate A in that situation.

G. E. MOORE

G. E. Moore (1873–1958) entered Cambridge in 1892 and taught there until he retired in 1939. Throughout this period he was a leading figure in the university, influencing others through his writing, teaching, and, not least important, conversation.

In ethics, Moore was a utilitarian, a student of Sidgwick; he never abandoned the basic principle that the rightness of an act is measured by the goodness of its consequences. But so far from being a mere disciple of Bentham, Mill, and Sidgwick, Moore's major contribution to ethical theory consists of an attack upon the doctrines of his predecessors. For while Moore was a utilitarian, he rejected ethical hedonism, i.e., the claim that pleasure is the sole good, or that goodness and pleasure are identical.

Moore argued that good is a simple indefinable non-natural property, and hence any attempt to define it or to identify it with a natural property involves a fallacy. This argument had a wide impact. Many philosophers abandoned hedonistic utilitarianism in favor of a non-hedonistic, or ideal, utilitarianism. Later, a similar argument was stated by Prichard and others as an attack upon the utilitarian principle itself. Finally, the logical positivists (e.g., Ayer and Stevenson) employed this argument as a key weapon in their attack upon the possibility of any ethical theory at all.

*Principia Ethica**

CAN GOOD BE DEFINED?

5. How "good" is to be defined, is the most fundamental question in all Ethics. That which is meant by "good" is, in fact, except its converse "bad," the *only* simple object of thought which is peculiar to Ethics. Its definition is, therefore, the most essential point in the definition of Ethics; and moreover a mistake with regard to it entails a far larger number of erroneous ethical judgments than any other. Unless this first question be fully understood, and its true answer clearly recognised, the rest of Ethics is as good as useless from the point of view of systematic knowledge. True ethical judgments . . . may indeed be

* From G. E. Moore, *Principia Ethica*, by permission of the Cambridge University Press, 1903. Section headings have been added by the editors.

made by those who do not know the answer to this question as well as by those who do; and it goes without saying that the two classes of people may lead equally good lives. But it is extremely unlikely that the *most general* ethical judgments will be equally valid, in the absence of a true answer to this question: I shall presently try to shew that the gravest errors have been largely due to beliefs in a false answer. And, in any case, it is impossible that, till the answer to this question be known, any one should know *what is the evidence* for any ethical judgment whatsoever. But the main object of Ethics, as a systematic science, is to give correct *reasons* for thinking that this or that is good; and, unless this question be answered, such reasons cannot be given. Even, therefore, apart from the fact that a false answer leads to false conclusions, the present enquiry is a most necessary and important part of the science of Ethics.

6. What, then, is good? How is good to be defined? Now, it may be thought that this is a verbal question. A definition does indeed often mean the expressing of one word's meaning in other words. But this is not the sort of definition I am asking for. Such a definition can never be of ultimate importance in any study except lexicography. If I wanted that kind of definition I should have to consider in the first place how people generally used the word "good"; but my business is not with its proper usage, as established by custom. I should, indeed, be foolish, if I tried to use it for something which it did not usually denote: if, for instance, I were to announce that, whenever I used the word "good," I must be understood to be thinking of that object which is usually denoted by the word "table." I shall, therefore, use the word in the sense in which I think it is ordinarily used; but at the same time I am not anxious to discuss whether I am right in thinking that it is so used. My business is solely with that object or idea, which I hold, rightly or wrongly, that the word is generally used to stand for. What I want to discover is the nature of that object or idea, and about this I am extremely anxious to arrive at an agreement.

But, if we understand the question in this sense, my answer to it may seem a very disappointing one. If I am asked "What is good?" my answer is that good is good, and that is the end of the matter. Or if I am asked "How is good to be defined?" my answer is that it cannot be defined, and that is all I have to say about it. But disappointing as these answers may appear, they are of the very last importance. To readers who are familiar with philosophic terminology, I can express their importance by saying that they amount to this: That propositions about the good are all of them synthetic and never analytic; and that is plainly no trivial matter. And the same thing may be expressed more popularly, by saying that, if I am right, then nobody can foist upon us such an axiom as that "Pleasure is the only good" or that "The good is the desired" on the pretence that this is "the very meaning of the word."

7. Let us, then, consider this position. My point is that "good" is a simple notion, just as "yellow" is a simple notion; that, just as you cannot, by any manner of means, explain to any one who does not already know it, what yellow is, so you cannot explain what good is. Definitions of the kind that I was asking for, definitions which describe the real nature of the object or notion denoted by a word, and which do not merely tell us what the word is used to mean, are only possible when the object or notion in question is something complex. You can give a definition of a horse, because a horse has many different properties and qualities, all of which you can enumerate. But when you have enumerated them all, when you have reduced a horse to his simplest terms, then you can no longer define those terms. They are simply something which you think of or perceive,

and to any one who cannot think of or perceive them, you can never, by any definition, make their nature known. It may perhaps be objected to this that we are able to describe to others, objects which they have never seen or thought of. We can, for instance, make a man understand what a chimaera is, although he has never heard of one or seen one. You can tell him that it is an animal with a lioness's head and body, with a goat's head growing from the middle of its back, and with a snake in place of a tail. But here the object which you are describing is a complex object; it is entirely composed of parts, with which we are all perfectly familiar—a snake, a goat, a lioness; and we know, too, the manner in which those parts are to be put together, because we know what is meant by the middle of a lioness's back, and where her tail is wont to grow. And so it is with all objects, not previously known, which we are able to define: they are all complex; all composed of parts, which may themselves, in the first instance, be capable of similar definition, but which must in the end be reducible to simplest parts, which can no longer be defined. But yellow and good, we say, are not complex: they are notions of that simple kind, out of which definitions are composed and with which the power of further defining ceases.

8. When we say, as Webster says, "The definition of horse is 'A hoofed quadruped of the genus Equus,'" we may, in fact, mean three different things. (1) We may mean merely: "When I say 'horse,' you are to understand that I am talking about a hoofed quadruped of the genus Equus." This might be called the arbitrary verbal definition: and I do not mean that good is indefinable in that sense. (2) We may mean, as Webster ought to mean: "When most English people say 'horse,' they mean a hoofed quadruped of the genus Equus." This may be called the verbal definition proper, and I do not say that good is indefinable in this sense either; for it is certainly possible to discover how people use a word: otherwise, we could never have known that "good" may be translated by "gut" in German and by "bon" in French. But (3) we may, when we define horse, mean something much more important. We may mean that a certain object, which we all of us know, is composed in a certain manner: that it has four legs, a head, a heart, a liver, etc., etc., all of them arranged in definite relations to one another. It is in this sense that I deny good to be definable. I say that it is not composed of any parts, which we can substitute for it in our minds when we are thinking of it. We might think just as clearly and correctly about a horse, if we thought of all its parts and their arrangement instead of thinking of the whole: we could, I say, think how a horse differed from a donkey just as well, just as truly, in this way, as now we do, only not so easily; but there is nothing whatsoever which we could so substitute for good; and that is what I mean, when I say that good is indefinable.

9. But I am afraid I have still not removed the chief difficulty which may prevent acceptance of the proposition that good is indefinable. I do not mean to say that *the* good, that which is good, is thus indefinable; if I did think so, I should not be writing on Ethics, for my main object is to help towards discovering that definition. It is just because I think there will be less risk of error in our search for a definition of "the good," that I am now insisting that *good* is indefinable. I must try to explain the difference between these two. I suppose it may be granted that "good" is an adjective. Well "the good," "that which is good," must therefore be the substantive to which the adjective "good" will apply: it must be the whole of that to which the adjective will apply, and the adjective must *always* truly apply to it. But if it is that to which the adjective will apply, it must be something different

from the adjective itself; and the whole of that something different, whatever it is, will be our definition of *the* good. Now it may be that this something will have other adjectives, beside "good," that will apply to it. It may be full of pleasure, for example; it may be intelligent: and if these two adjectives are really part of its definition, then it will certainly be true, that pleasure and intelligence are good. And many people appear to think that, if we say "Pleasure and intelligence are good," or if we say "Only pleasure and intelligence are good," we are defining "good." Well, I cannot deny that propositions of this nature may sometimes be called definitions; I do not know well enough how the word is generally used to decide upon this point. I only wish it to be understood that that is not what I mean when I say there is no possible definition of good, and that I shall not mean this if I use the word again. I do most fully believe that some true proposition of the form "Intelligence is good and intelligence alone is good" can be found; if none could be found, our definition of *the* good would be impossible. As it is, I believe *the* good to be definable; and yet I still say that good itself is indefinable.

10. "Good," then, if we mean by it that quality which we assert to belong to a thing, when we say that the thing is good, is incapable of any definition, in the most important sense of that word. The most important sense of "definition" is that in which a definition states what are the parts which invariably compose a certain whole; and in this sense "good" has no definition because it is simple and has no parts. It is one of those innumerable objects of thought which are themselves incapable of definition, because they are the ultimate terms by reference to which whatever *is* capable of definition must be defined. That there must be an indefinite number of such terms is obvious, on reflection; since we cannot define anything except by an analysis, which, when carried as far as it will go, refers us to something, which is simply different from anything else, and which by that ultimate difference explains the peculiarity of the whole which we are defining: for every whole contains some parts which are common to other wholes also. There is, therefore, no intrinsic difficulty in the contention that "good" denotes a simple and indefinable quality. There are many other instances of such qualities.

Consider yellow, for example. We may try to define it, by describing its physical equivalent; we may state what kind of light-vibrations must stimulate the normal eye, in order that we may perceive it. But a moment's reflection is sufficient to shew that those light-vibrations are not themselves what we mean by yellow. *They* are not what we perceive. Indeed we should never have been able to discover their existence, unless we had first been struck by the patent difference of quality between the different colours. The most we can be entitled to say of those vibrations is that they are what corresponds in space to the yellow which we actually perceive.

Yet a mistake of this simple kind has commonly been made about "good." It may be true that all things which are good are *also* something else, just as it is true that all things which are yellow produce a certain kind of vibration in the light. And it is a fact, that Ethics aims at discovering what are those other properties belonging to all things which are good. But far too many philosophers have thought that when they named those other properties they were actually defining good; that these properties, in fact, were simply not "other," but absolutely and entirely the same with goodness. This view I propose to call the "naturalistic fallacy" and of it I shall now endeavour to dispose.

11. Let us consider what it is such philosophers say. And first it is to be noticed that they do not agree among themselves. They not only say that they

are right as to what good is, but they endeavour to prove that other people who say that it is something else, are wrong. One, for instance, will affirm that good is pleasure, another, perhaps, that good is that which is desired; and each of these will argue eagerly to prove that the other is wrong. But how is that possible? One of them says that good is nothing but the object of desire, and at the same time tries to prove that it is not pleasure. But from his first assertion, that good just means the object of desire, one of two things must follow as regards his proof:

(1) He may be trying to prove that the object of desire is not pleasure. But, if this be all, where is his Ethics? The position he is maintaining is merely a psychological one. Desire is something which occurs in our minds, and pleasure is something else which so occurs; and our would-be ethical philosopher is merely holding that the latter is not the object of the former. But what has that to do with the question in dispute? His opponent held the ethical proposition that pleasure was the good, and although he should prove a million times over the psychological proposition that pleasure is not the object of desire, he is no nearer proving his opponent to be wrong. The position is like this. One man says a triangle is a circle: another replies "A triangle is a straight line, and I will prove to you that I am right: *for*" (this is the only argument) "a straight line is not a circle." "That is quite true," the other may reply; "but nevertheless a triangle is a circle, and you have said nothing whatever to prove the contrary. What is proved is that one of us is wrong, for we agree that a triangle cannot be both a straight line and a circle: but which is wrong, there can be no earthly means of proving, since you define triangle as straight line and I define it as circle."—Well, that is one alternative which any naturalistic Ethics has to face; if good is *defined* as something else, it is then impossible either to prove that any other definition is wrong or even to deny such definiton.

(2) The other alternative will scarcely be more welcome. It is that the discussion is after all a verbal one. When A says "Good means pleasant" and B says "Good means desired," they may merely wish to assert that most people have used the word for what is pleasant and for what is desired respectively. And this is quite an interesting subject for discussion: only it is not a whit more an ethical discussion than the last was. Nor do I think that any exponent of naturalistic Ethics would be willing to allow that this was all he meant. They are all so anxious to persuade us that what they call the good is what we really ought to do. "Do, pray, act so, because the word 'good' is generally used to denote actions of this nature": such, on this view, would be the substance of their teaching. And in so far as they tell us how we ought to act, their teaching is truly ethical, as they mean it to be. But how perfectly absurd is the reason they would give for it! "You are to do this, because most people use a certain word to denote conduct such as this." "You are to say the thing which is not, because most people call it lying." That is an argument just as good!—My dear sirs, what we want to know from you as ethical teachers, is not how people use a word; it is not even, what kind of actions they approve, which the use of this word "good" may certainly imply: what we want to know is simply what *is* good. We may indeed agree that what most people do think good, is actually so; we shall at all events be glad to know their opinions: but when we say their opinions about what *is* good, we do mean what we say; we do not care whether they call that thing which they mean "horse" or "table" or "chair," "gut" or "bon" or "ἀγαθος"; we want to know what it is that they so call. When they say "Pleasure is good," we cannot believe that they merely mean "Pleasure is pleasure" and nothing more than that.

12. Suppose a man says "I am pleased"; and suppose that is not a lie or a mistake but the truth. Well, if it is true, what does that mean? It means that his mind, a certain definite mind, distinguished by certain definite marks from all others, has at this moment a certain definite feeling called pleasure. "Pleased" *means* nothing but having pleasure, and though we may be more pleased or less pleased, and even, we may admit for the present, have one or another kind of pleasure; yet in so far as it is pleasure we have, whether there be more or less of it, and whether it be of one kind or another, what we have is one definite thing, absolutely indefinable, some one thing that is the same in all the various degrees and in all the various kinds of it that there may be. We may be able to say how it is related to other things: that, for example, it is in the mind, that it causes desire, that we are conscious of it, etc., etc. We can, I say, describe its relations to other things, but define it we can *not*. And if anybody tried to define pleasure for us as being any other natural object; if anybody were to say, for instance, that pleasure *means* the sensation of red, and were to proceed to deduce from that that pleasure is a colour, we should be entitled to laugh at him and to distrust his future statements about pleasure. Well, that would be the same fallacy which I have called the naturalistic fallacy. That "pleased" does not mean "having the sensation of red," or anything else whatever, does not prevent us from understanding what it does mean. It is enough for us to know that "pleased" does mean "having the sensation of pleasure," and though pleasure is absolutely indefinable, though pleasure is pleasure and nothing else whatever, yet we feel no difficulty in saying that we are pleased. The reason is, of course, that when I say "I am pleased," I do *not* mean that "I" am the same thing as "having pleasure." And similarly no difficulty need be found in my saying that "pleasure is good" and yet not meaning that "pleasure" is the same thing as "good," that pleasure *means* good, and that good *means* pleasure. If I were to imagine that when I said "I am pleased," I meant that I was exactly the same thing as "pleased," I should not indeed call that a naturalistic fallacy, although it would be the same fallacy as I have called naturalistic with reference to Ethics. The reason of this is obvious enough. When a man confuses two natural objects with one another, defining the one by the other, if for instance, he confuses himself, who is one natural object, with "pleased" or with "pleasure" which are others, then there is no reason to call the fallacy naturalistic. But if he confuses "good," which is not in the same sense a natural object, with any natural object whatever, then there is a reason for calling that a naturalistic fallacy; its being made with regard to "good" marks it as something quite specific, and this specific mistake deserves a name because it is so common. As for the reasons why good is not to be considered a natural object, they may be reserved for discussion in another place. But, for the present, it is sufficient to notice this: Even if it were a natural object, that would not alter the nature of the fallacy nor diminish its importance one whit. All that I have said about it would remain quite equally true: only the name which I have called it would not be so appropriate as I think it is. And I do not care about the name: what I do care about is the fallacy. It does not matter what we call it, provided we recognise it when we meet with it. It is to be met with in almost every book on Ethics; and yet it is not recognised: and that is why it is necessary to multiply illustrations of it, and convenient to give it a name. It is a very simple fallacy indeed. When we say that an orange is yellow, we do not think our statement binds us to hold that "orange" means nothing else than "yellow," or that nothing can be yellow but an orange. Supposing the orange is also sweet! Does that bind

us to say that "sweet" is exactly the same thing as "yellow," that "sweet" must be defined as "yellow"? And supposing it be recognised that "yellow" just means "yellow" and nothing else whatever, does that make it any more difficult to hold that oranges are yellow? Most certainly it does not: on the contrary, it would be absolutely meaningless to say that oranges were yellow, unless yellow did in the end mean just "yellow" and nothing else whatever—unless it was absolutely indefinable. We should not get any very clear notion about things, which are yellow—we should not get very far with our science, if we were bound to hold that everything which was yellow, *meant* exactly the same thing as yellow. We should find we had to hold that an orange was exactly the same thing as a stool, a piece of paper, a lemon, anything you like. We could prove any number of absurdities; but should we be the nearer to the truth? Why, then, should it be different with "good"? Why, if good is good and indefinable, should I be held to deny that pleasure is good? Is there any difficulty in holding both to be true at once? On the contrary, there is no meaning in saying that pleasure is good, unless good is something different from pleasure. It is absolutely useless, so far as Ethics is concerned, to prove, as Mr. Spencer tries to do, that increase of pleasure coincides with increase of life, unless good *means* something different from either life or pleasure. He might just as well try to prove that an orange is yellow by shewing that it always is wrapped up in paper.

13. In fact, if it is not the case that "good" denotes something simple and indefinable, only two alternatives are possible: either it is a complex, a given whole, about the correct analysis of which there may be disagreement; or else it means nothing at all, and there is no such subject as Ethics. In general, however, ethical philosophers have attempted to define good, without recognising what such an attempt must mean. They actually use arguments which involve one or both of the absurdities considered in § 11. We are, therefore, justified in concluding that the attempt to define good is chiefly due to want of clearness as to the possible nature of definition. There are, in fact, only two serious alternatives to be considered, in order to establish the conclusion that "good" does denote a simple and indefinable notion. It might possibly denote a complex, as "horse" does; or it might have no meaning at all. Neither of these possibilities has, however, been clearly conceived and seriously maintained, as such, by those who presume to define good; and both may be dismissed by a simple appeal to facts.

(1) The hypothesis that disagreement about the meaning of good is disagreement with regard to the correct analysis of a given whole, may be most plainly seen to be incorrect by consideration of the fact that, whatever definition be offered, it may be always asked, with significance, of the complex so defined, whether it is itself good. To take, for instance, one of the more plausible, because one of the more complicated, of such proposed definitions, it may easily be thought, at first sight, that to be good may mean to be that which we desire to desire. Thus if we apply this definition to a particular instance and say "When we think that A is good, we are thinking that A is one of the things which we desire to desire," our proposition may seem quite plausible. But, if we carry the investigation further, and ask ourselves "Is it good to desire to desire A?" it is apparent, on a little reflection, that this question is itself as intelligible, as the original question "Is A good?"—that we are, in fact, now asking for exactly the same information about the desire to desire A, for which we formerly asked with regard to A itself. But it is also apparent that the meaning of this second question cannot be correctly analysed into "Is the desire to desire A one of the things which we desire to desire?": we

have not before our minds anything so complicated as the question "Do we desire to desire to desire to desire A?" Moreover any one can easily convince himself by inspection that the predicate of this proposition—"good"—is positively different from the notion of "desiring to desire" which enters into its subject: "That we should desire to desire A is good" is *not* merely equivalent to "That A should be good is good." It may indeed be true that what we desire to desire is always also good; perhaps, even the converse may be true: but it is very doubtful whether this is the case, and the mere fact that we understand very well what is meant by doubting it, shews clearly that we have two different notions before our minds.

(2) And the same consideration is sufficient to dismiss the hypothesis that "good" has no meaning whatsoever. It is very natural to make the mistake of supposing that what is universally true is of such a nature that its negation would be self-contradictory: the importance which has been assigned to analytic propositions in the history of philosophy shews how easy such a mistake is. And thus it is very easy to conclude that what seems to be a universal ethical principle is in fact an identical proposition; that, if, for example, whatever is called "good" seems to be pleasant, the proposition "Pleasure is the good" does not assert a connection between two different notions, but involves only one, that of pleasure, which is easily recognised as a distinct entity. But whoever will attentively consider with himself what is actually before his mind when he asks the question 'Is pleasure (or whatever it may be) after all good?" can easily satisfy himself that he is not merely wondering whether pleasure is pleasant. And if he will try this experiment with each suggested definition in succession, he may become expert enough to recognise that in every case he has before his mind a unique object, with regard to the connection of which with any other object, a distinct question may be asked. Every one does in fact understand the question "Is this good?" When he thinks of it, his state of mind is different from what it would be, were he asked "Is this pleasant, or desired, or approved?" It has a distinct meaning for him, even though he may not recognise in what respect it is distinct. Whenever he thinks of "intrinsic value," or "intrinsic worth," or says that a thing "ought to exist," he has before his mind the unique object—the unique property of things—which I mean by "good." Everybody is constantly aware of this notion, although he may never become aware at all that it is different from other notions of which he is also aware. But, for correct ethical reasoning, it is extremely important that he should become aware of this fact; and, as soon as the nature of the problem is clearly understood, there should be little difficulty in advancing so far in analysis.

14. "Good," then, is indefinable; and yet, so far as I know, there is only one ethical writer, Prof. Henry Sidgwick, who has clearly recognised and stated this fact. We shall see, indeed, how far many of the most reputed ethical systems fall short of drawing the conclusions which follow from such a recognition. At present I will only quote one instance, which will serve to illustrate the meaning and importance of this principle that "good" is indefinable, or, as Prof. Sidgwick says, an "unanalysable notion." It is an instance to which Prof. Sidgwick himself refers in a note on the passage, in which he argues that "ought" is unanalysable.

"Bentham," says Sidgwick, "explains that his fundamental principle 'states the greatest happiness of all those whose interest is in question as being the right and proper end of human action' "; and yet "his language in other passages of the same chapter would seem to imply" that he *means* by the word "right" "conducive to the general happiness." Prof. Sidgwick sees that, if you take these two statements together, you get the absurd result that "greatest happiness is the end of human action, which is conducive to the general happiness"; and so absurd does it seem to him to call this result, as Bentham calls it, "the fundamental principle of a moral system," that he suggests that Bentham cannot have meant it. Yet Prof. Sidgwick himself states elsewhere that Psychological Hedonism is "not seldom confounded with Egoistic Hedonism"; and that confusion, as we shall see, rests chiefly on that same fallacy, the naturalistic fallacy, which is implied in Bentham's statements. Prof. Sidgwick admits therefore that this fallacy is sometimes committed, absurd as it is; and I am inclined to think that Bentham may really have been one of those who committed it. Mill . . . certainly did commit it. In any case, whether Bentham committed it or not, his doctrine, as above quoted, will serve as a very good illustration of this fallacy, and of the importance of the contrary proposition that good is indefinable.

Let us consider this doctrine. Bentham seems to imply, so Prof. Sidgwick says, that the word "right" *means* "conducive to general happiness." Now this, by itself, need not necessarily involve the naturalistic fallacy. For the word "right" is very commonly appropriated to actions which lead to the attainment of what is good; which are regarded as *means* to the ideal and not as ends-in-themselves. This use of "right," as denoting what is good as a means, whether or not it be also good as an end, is indeed the use to which I shall confine the word. Had Bentham been using "right" in this sense, it might be perfectly consistent for him to *define* right as "conducive to the general happiness," *provided only* (and notice this proviso) he had already proved, or laid down as an axiom, that general happiness was *the* good, or (what is equivalent to this) that general happiness alone was good. For in that case he would have already defined *the* good as general happiness (a position perfectly consistent, as we have seen, with the contention that "good" is indefinable), and, since right was to be defined as "conducive to *the* good," it would actually *mean* "conducive to general happiness." But this method of escape from the charge of having committed the naturalistic fallacy has been closed by Bentham himself. For his fundamental principle is, we see, that the greatest happiness of all concerned is the *right* and proper *end* of human action. He applies the word "right," therefore, to the end as such, not only to the means which are conducive to it; and, that being so, right can no longer be defined as "conducive to the general happiness," without involving the fallacy in question. For now it is obvious that the definition of right as conducive to general happiness can be used by him in support of the fundamental principle that general happiness is the right end; instead of being itself derived from that principle. If right, by definition, means conducive to general happiness, then it is obvious that general happiness is the right end. It is not necessary now first to prove or assert that general happiness is the right end, before right is defined as conducive to general happiness—a perfectly valid procedure; but on the contrary the definition of right as conducive to general happiness proves general happiness to be the right end—a perfectly invalid procedure, since in this case the statement that "general happiness is the right end of human action" is not an ethical principle at all, but either, as we have seen, a proposition about the meaning of words, or else a proposition about the *nature* of general happiness, not about its rightness or goodness.

Now, I do not wish the importance I assign to this fallacy to be misunderstood. The discovery of it does not at all refute Bentham's contention that greatest happiness is the proper end of human action, if that be understood as an ethical proposition, as he undoubtedly intended it. That principle may be true all the same; we shall consider whether it is so in succeeding chapters. Bentham might have maintained it, as Professor Sidgwick does, even if the fallacy had been pointed out to him. What I am maintaining is that the *reasons* which he actually gives for his ethical proposition are fallacious ones, so far as they consist in a definition of right. What I suggest is that he did not perceive them to be fallacious; that, if he had done so, he would have been led to seek for other reasons in support of his Utilitarianism; and that, had he sought for other reasons, he *might* have found none which he thought to be sufficient. In that case he would have changed his whole system—a most important consequence. It is undoubtedly also possible that he would have thought other reasons to be sufficient, and in that case his ethical system, in its main results, would still have stood. But, even in this latter case, his use of the fallacy would be a serious objection to him as an ethical philosopher. For it is the business of Ethics, I must insist, not only to obtain true results, but also to find valid reasons for them. The direct object of Ethics is knowledge and not practice; and any one who uses the naturalistic fallacy has certainly not fulfilled this first object, however correct his practical principles may be.

My objections to Naturalism are then, in the first place, that it offers no reason at all, far less any valid reason, for any ethical principle whatever; and in this it already fails to satisfy the requirements of Ethics, as a scientific study. But in the second place I contend that, though it gives a reason for no ethical principle, it is a *cause* of the acceptance of false principles—it deludes the mind into accepting ethical principles, which are false; and in this it is contrary to every aim of Ethics. It is easy to see that if we start with a definition of right conduct as conduct conducive to general happiness; then, knowing that right conduct is universally conduct conducive to the good, we very easily arrive at the result that the good is general happiness. If, on the other hand, we once recognise that we must start our Ethics without a definition, we shall be much more apt to look about us, before we adopt any ethical principle whatever; and the more we look about us, the less likely are we to adopt a false one. It may be replied to this: Yes, but we shall look about us just as much, before we settle on our definition, and are therefore just as likely to be right. But I will try to shew that this is not the case. If we start with the conviction that a definition of good can be found, we start with the conviction that good *can mean* nothing else than some one property of things; and our only business will then be to discover what that property is. But if we recognise that, so far as the meaning of good goes, anything whatever may be good, we start with a much more open mind. Moreover, apart from the fact that, when we think we have a definition, we cannot logically defend our ethical principles in any way whatever, we shall also be much less apt to defend them well, even if illogically. For we shall start with the conviction that good must mean so and so, and shall therefore be inclined either to misunderstand our opponent's arguments or to cut them short with the reply, "This is not an open question: the very meaning of the word decides it; no one can think otherwise except through confusion."

DEFINITION OF NATURAL PROPERTY

I have appropriated the name Naturalism to a particular method of approaching Ethics—a method which, strictly understood, is inconsistent with the possibility of any Ethics whatsoever. This method consists in substituting for "good" some one property of a natural object or of a collection of natural objects; and in thus replacing Ethics by some one of the natural sciences. . . . The name then is perfectly general; for, no matter what the something is that good is held to mean, the theory is still Naturalism. Whether good be defined as yellow or green or blue, as loud or soft, as round or square, as sweet or bitter, as productive of life or productive of pleasure, as willed or desired or felt: whichever of these or of any other object in the world, good may be held to *mean*, the theory, which holds it to *mean* them, will be a naturalistic theory. I have called such theories naturalistic because all of these terms denote properties, simple or complex, of some simple or complex natural object; and, before I proceed to consider them, it will be well to define what is meant by "nature" and by "natural objects."

By "nature," then, I do mean and have meant that which is the subject-matter of the natural sciences and also of psychology. It may be said to include all that has existed, does exist, or will exist in time. If we consider whether any object is of such a nature that it may be said to exist now, to have existed, or to be about to exist, then we may know that that object is a natural object, and that nothing, of which this is not true, is a natural object. Thus, for instance, of our minds we should say that they did exist yesterday, that they do exist to-day, and probably will exist in a minute or two. We shall say that we had thoughts yesterday, which have ceased to exist now, although their effects may remain: and in so far as those thoughts did exist, they too are natural objects.

There is, indeed, no difficulty about the "objects" themselves, in the sense in which I have just used the term. It is easy to say which of them are natural, and which (if any) are not natural. But when we begin to consider the properties of objects, then I fear the problem is more difficult. Which among the properties of natural objects are natural properties and which are not? For I do not deny that good is a property of certain natural objects: certain of them, I think, *are* good; and yet I have said that "good" itself is not a natural property. Well, my test for these too also concerns their existence in time. Can we imagine "good" as existing *by itself* in time, and not merely as a property of some natural object? For myself, I cannot so imagine it, whereas with the greater number of properties of objects—those which I call the natural properties—their existence does seem to me to be independent of the existence of those objects. They are, in fact, rather parts of which the object is made up than mere predicates which attach to it. If they were all taken away, no object would be left, not even a bare substance: for they are in themselves substantial and give to the object all the substance that it has. But this is not so with good. If indeed good were a feeling, as some would have us believe, then it would exist in time. But that is why to call it so is to commit the naturalistic fallacy. It will always remain pertinent to ask, whether the feeling itself is good; and if so, then good cannot itself be identical with any feeling.*

* In "A Reply to My Critics" (*The Philosophy of G. E. Moore*, Paul Arthur Schilpp ed., Northwestern University, 1942, p. 591), Moore rejected the above discussion in favor of the following:

". . . An intrinsic property is 'natural' if and only if, in ascribing it to a natural object, you are to some extent 'describing' that object (where 'describe' is used in one particular sense); and that hence an intrinsic property, e.g., the sense of 'good' with which we are concerned, is not 'natural' if, in ascribing it to a natural object you are not (in the same sense of 'describe') describing that object to any extent at all. It is certainly the case that this account is vague and not clear. To make it clear it would be necessary to specify the sense of 'describe' in question; and I am no more able to do this now than I was then."

RALPH BARTON PERRY

Ralph Barton Perry (1876–1957) was, for many years, a distinguished scholar at Harvard. Under the influence of William James he became a staunch defender of naturalism—the doctrine that the scientific method is the sole means for gaining truth and consequently should be applied in all areas of human endeavor. For this reason, Perry referred to his own work in ethics as "science applied to life."

Perry's first major work in ethics, his General Theory of Value *(1926), is an attempt to employ scientific procedures to discover the common features of all values. We have included a large portion of Chapter Five, where he defines value in terms of interest.* Realms of Value, *which appeared twenty-eight years later (1954), is a detailed application of the general theory to specific areas. We have presented most of Chapter Six of this work, where he discusses the meaning of morality.*

General Theory of Value*

VALUE AS ANY OBJECT OF ANY INTEREST

It is characteristic of living mind to be *for* some things and *against* others. This polarity is not reducible to that between "yes" and "no" in the logical or in the purely cognitive sense, because one can say "yes" with reluctance or be glad to say "no." To be "for" or "against" is to view with favor or disfavor; it is a bias of the subject toward or away from. It implies, as we shall see more clearly in the sequel, a tendency to create or conserve, or an opposite tendency to prevent or destroy. This duality appears in many forms, such as liking and disliking, desire and aversion, will and refusal, or seeking and avoiding. It is to this all-pervasive characteristic of the motor-affective life, this *state, act, attitude or disposition of favor or disfavor*, to which we propose to give the name of *interest*.

This, then, we take to be the original source and constant feature of all value. That which is an object of interest is *eo*

* Reprinted by permission of the publishers from Ralph Barton Perry, *General Theory of Value: Its Meaning and Basic Principles Construed in Terms of Interest*, Cambridge, Mass.: Harvard University Press, Copyright, 1926, by The President and Fellows of Harvard College—1954 by Ralph Barton Perry.

ipso invested with value. Any object, whatever it be, acquires value when any interest, whatever it be, is taken in it; just as anything whatsoever becomes a target when anyone whosoever aims at it. In other words, Aristotle was fundamentally mistaken when he said, that as a thing's "apparent good" makes it an object of appetite, so its real good makes it the object of 'rational desire."[1] By the same token Spinoza was fundamentally correct when he said that

> *in no case do we strive for, wish for, long for, or desire anything, because we deem it to be good, but on the other hand we deem a thing to be good, because we strive for it, wish for it, long for it, or desire it.*[2]

The view may otherwise be formulated in the equation: x is valuable = interest is taken in x. Value is thus a specific relation into which things possessing any ontological status whatsoever, whether real or imaginary, may enter with interested subjects.

This is value *simpliciter*,—value in the elementary, primordial and generic sense. It follows that any variation of interest or of its object will determine a variety of value; that any derivative of interest or its object will determine value in a derived sense; and that any condition of interest or its object will determine a conditional value. In short, interest being constitutive of value in the basic sense, theory of value will take this as its point of departure and centre of reference; and will classify and systematize values in terms of the different forms which interests and their objects may be found to assume. . . .

It may appear surprising that a doctrine so familiar, if not banal, as that just stated, should have received so little authoritative support. Rarity is the last thing that would have been expected of it, either by its advocates who regard it as sound common-sense, or by its opponents who regard it as vulgar error. It is none the less a fact that this doctrine has rarely been explicitly avowed by philosophers. The reasons for this fact are extremely illuminating, and although they have been repeatedly alluded to, a brief recapitulation of them at this point will serve to sharpen the meaning of our definition.

All of these reasons are traceable to an imperfect conception of the problem itself. Theory of value in the contemporary sense has asked a new question, to which none of the traditional philosophical doctrines is precisely relevant. It may, perhaps, be fair to say that this question has been *tacitly* asked and answered; but it is evident that a tacit answer cannot be quoted. This new question, is the question, *In what consists value in the generic sense?* It is because neither philosophy nor common-sense has ordinarily been explicitly and unambiguously concerned with this question that so few explicit and unambiguous answers to it can be found. Most theories of value are intended not as answers to this question, but as answers to some one or more of the following questions: What is uniquely valuable? What is superlatively valuable? What is reflectively or consciously valuable? The history of thought abounds in opinions which identify value with interest, but in nearly all cases these opinions are formulated in terms of one of these questions, and cannot, therefore, be cited as generic definitions of value in the sense here proposed.

Perhaps the most ancient and persistent notion of value is *hedonism*, which construes good in terms of pleasure, and evil in terms of pain. But hedonistic writers cannot be cited in support of the doctrine here proposed, because they have been

[1] *Metaphysica*, XII, Ch. 7, trans. by W. D. Ross, 1072a.

[2] *Ethics*, Part III, Prop. IX, Note, trans. by R. H. M. Elwes, 1901.

primarily concerned to show that only pleasure and pain *possess* value. If we turn to the authoritative formulation of this doctrine by Bentham, we read that "nature has placed mankind under the governance of two sovereign masters, *pain* and *pleasure*."[3] John Stuart Mill begins with the assertion that "questions about ends are . . . questions what things are desirable"; adds that "the sole evidence it is possible to produce that anything is desirable, is that people do actually desire it"; and presently concludes "that there is in reality nothing desired except happiness." Bentham, in other words, asserts that pleasure and pain are the only governing motives in human action; and Mill, that only happiness is desired. They are both concerned to show that pleasure and pain are the *unique objects* of interest. It is doubtless true that they both assume a more fundamental principle, to the effect that value means motive-power, or object-of-desire-and-avoidance. Without such a major premise the argument would be palpably incomplete, and would have none of the moral implications which they impute to it. But since this major premise is only tacitly or dogmatically avowed by the utilitarian school, and since it is the very question at issue in a general theory of value, the members of this school cannot be cited as in clear and explicit agreement with the view here proposed.

Philosophers, like the average man, have been as a rule more interested in the scale of values than in the generic nature of value. . . . Most theory of value that has emanated from "high metaphysics," or from the grand tradition, has been wholly preoccupied with the former of these questions. It has preferred to discuss the Highest Good, rather than low and middling goods; or to deal with value in a eulogistic and edifying manner, rather than simply to describe it. It is astonishing how persistent, how almost ineradicable, is this tendency even among contemporary and otherwise emanicipated philosophers. . . .

How is the view here proposed to be proved? What is the evidence upon which it rests? . . .

A certain positive plausibility is given to this hypothesis by the fact that in order to create values where they did not exist before it seems to be sufficient to introduce an interest. The silence of the desert is without value, until some wanderer finds it lonely and terrifying; the cataract, until some human sensibility finds it sublime, or until it is harnessed to satisfy human needs. Natural substances or the by-products of manufacture are without value until a use is found for them, whereupon their value may increase to any degree of preciousness according to the eagerness with which they are coveted. There is no entity that can be named that does not, in the very naming of it, take on a certain value through the fact that it is selected by the cognitive purpose of some interested mind. As interests grow and expand, multiplying in number and extending their radius through experience and imagination, the store of cosmic values is enriched and diversified.

But it may be contended that such proof is redundant or verbal. It proves only that objects of interest appear whenever interest is taken in objects; or, it proves at most that what is added to a given situation when interests are introduced corresponds closely to what it is customary to *call* value. It does not add to our knowledge by demonstrating the existence of value where it was not suspected, or by resolving doubts as to what is *really* valuable.

This objection again brings to light the difference between the general definition of value and the solution of special questions of value. The doubts and perplexities of everyday life, as well as the limited theoretical problems of the several value sciences, commonly asume a general defini-

[3] *Principles of Morals and Legislation*, Ch. I.

tion of value, and turn upon some question of fact. Is this distant island worth annexing and defending? The answer depends upon the existence of mineral deposits or a good harbor, assuming that it is worth annexing if the satisfactions and utilities which it affords outweigh the sacrifices which it costs. Ought I to surrender my position for the sake of my scruples, or compromise temporarily in the hope of converting others to my way of thinking? The answer depends on certain probable trains of consequences following from each of the alternatives, assuming that the one or the other ought to be adopted in accordance with the principle of human happiness, broadly applied. Is recent American verse to be ranked as genuine poetry? The answer depends experimentally on the sort of feeling aroused in certain persons, such as the critic himself, by the prolonged and attentive reading of it, on the assumption that such a judgment of taste is decisive. Is the economic worth or the aesthetic superiority of a work of art dependent on its moral wholesomeness? The answer is assumed to depend on the record of market transactions, or the reported sentiments of connoisseurs.

Now the general definition of value does not directly answer any such question, because it does not ascertain the specific facts and probabilities upon which they turn. It concerns itself with the *assumption*, and must therefore always appear to deal with the obvious rather than with the questionable. Its proper task is to make these asumptions explicit and consistent. By so doing it will inevitably affect the solution of such special questions, since it will prescribe the terms or the principle of their solution. But it has to do with the use which is to be made of evidence, rather than with the uncovering of new facts.

It follows that there can be no conclusive proof of a general definition of value, short of its success in facilitating the solution of all special questions of value. Such a definition is *an experiment in generalization*. If we adopt the fact of interest as our centre of reference, and view other facts of the surrounding field *in that relation*—if, in short, we take life *interest-wise*, as it can, in fact, be taken—do the data and the perplexities denoted by "good" and "evil," "right" and "wrong," "better" and "worse," or grouped within the special fields of morality, art, religion and kindred institutions, then fall into place and form a comprehensive system? It is evident that the only proof of which such a hypothesis is capable lies in its complete elaboration. . . .

REPLY TO THE CHARGE OF RELATIVISM

Although no conclusive proof of the present view is possible until it is completely elaborated, it has been supposed that there is a conclusive *disproof* which can be urged without further ado. To attribute value to any object of any interest is at once to expose oneself to the charge of *relativism*, whatever the psychological details, and however successful such a definition may prove for purposes of systematic generalization.

No one can afford to disregard this charge. Relativism is an epithet which implies disparagement, when, as is often the case, it implies nothing more. Even the respectable scientific authority which has pronounced in its favor has not saved the physical theory of relativity from being regarded as somewhat *risqué*,—as evidence of the corruption of the times or of the malicious influence of the Semitic mind. There is no man who would not rather be absolute than relative, even though he has not the faintest conception of the meaning of either term.

This sentiment is peculiarly strong in the field of values, and preëminently in the province of morals. Nothing could be more scandalous than these lines of Sir Richard Burton:

There is no good, there is no bad, these
be the whims of mortal will;
What works me weal that call I good,
what harms and hurts I hold as ill.
They change with space, they shift with
race, and in the veriest space of time,
Each vice has worn a virtue's crown, all
good been banned as sin or crime.

How much nobler and more edifying in tone are such utterances as these of Froude and Carlyle:

> *The eternal truths and rights of things exist, fortunately, independent of our thoughts or wishes, fixed as mathematics, inherent in the nature of man and the world. They are no more to be trifled with than gravitation.*
>
> *What have men to do with interests? There is a right way and a wrong way. That is all we need think about it.*[4]

Yet there can scarcely be more offence in the adjective "relative" than there is in the substantive "relation"; and when we investigate the world in which we live, we discover as a rule that what we took to be an absolute does as a matter of fact both stand in relations and comprise relations. In any case we shall be influenced only by such *theoretical* difficulties as may be urged against a relativistic theory of value, and not in the least by practical or sentimental objections. . . .

There is unquestionably one form of relativism which is theoretically objectionable. He who identifies the act of *cognizing* values with that act of the subject which *constitutes* them, or holds that values are both known and created in one and the same act, does imply the impossibility of knowing anything whatsoever about value, and thus belies any statements that he himself may make about it. This objection holds against certain philosophers who have identified value with interest, and it therefore behooves us to discover whether our own view is similarly objectionable.

Professor G. E. Moore distinguishes two forms in which this vicious relativism may be stated. In the first place, "it may be held that whenever any man asserts an action to be right or wrong, what he is asserting is merely that he *himself* has some particular feeling toward the action in question."[5] In this case the act of knowing or judging value, is construed as simply an expression of the judge's own interest. The following famous passage from Hobbes is a case in point:

> *But whatsoever is the object of any man's appetite or desire, that is it which he for his part calleth "good"; and the object of his hate and aversion, "evil"; and of his contempt "vile" and "inconsiderable." For these words of good, evil, and contemptible, are ever used with relation to the person that useth them: there being nothing simply and absolutely so; nor any common rule of good and evil, to be taken from the nature of the objects themselves.*[6]

The *reductio ad absurdum* of such a view, lies, as Professor Moore points out, in the fact that it would lead to the mutual irrelevance of all judgments in which the value-predicates are employed. If in affirming an act to be right or wrong, good or evil, a judge were always referring to *his own present feeling* about it, then no two judges could ever agree or disagree with one another, nor could the same judge ever reaffirm or correct his own past opinions.[7] In other words, on questions of value there could not be any such thing as judgment or opinion in the ordinary sense of these terms. This is not only contrary to

[4] J. A. Froude, *Inaugural Lecture at St. Andrews,* 1869, p. 41; Letter of Carlyle to Froude, *Longman's Magazine,* 1892, p. 151.

[5] *Ethics.* Home University Library, p. 89.

[6] *Leviathan,* Part I, Ch. VI.

[7] Cf. G. E. Moore, *op. cit.,* pp. 100–103.

fact, but it is inevitably contradicted by the very man who makes the assertion.

A second statement of this vicious relativism is the assertion "that when we judge an action to be right or wrong what we are asserting is merely that somebody or other thinks it to be right or wrong." Generalized and simplified, this assertion is to the effect that value consists in being thought to be valuable—"There is nothing either good or bad, but thinking makes it so." Now the fundamental difficulty with this view lies in the fact that one would then have nothing to think about. If a thing is valuable by virtue of being believed to be valuable, then when one believes a thing to be valuable, one believes that it is believed to be valuable, or one believes that it is believed to be believed to be valuable, and so on *ad infinitum.*[8] In short, there can be no judgment about value, or about anything else, unless there is some content or object other than the act of judgment itself, —a judged as well as a judging.

It is this error or confusion which vitiates the work of Westermarck and others who, not content with a history of moral opinion, have attempted to *define* moral values in *terms* of moral opinion.[9] It is the characteristic and besetting error of all anthropological and sociological theories of value, which aim to be scientific or "positive."[10] What has been judged with unanimity to be good or evil by members of a social group, is a matter of record; and is thus a fact ascertainable by archaeological or historical methods, and with a precision and indubitableness peculiar to these methods. But such methodological preferences do not alter the fact that these judgments, if judgments at all, must have been *about* something; and in theory of value it is this *object,* and not the acts of judgment themselves, which is primarily in question. There are also recorded opinions about the stars, and anthropologists may and do investigate these opinions; but one does not therefore propose to substitute a history of astronomical opinions for astronomy.

Let us now inquire whether the view here proposed is guilty of a vicious or sceptical relativism in either or both of these two senses. In the first place, although defining value as relative to interest, we have not defined value as exclusively relative to the present interest of the judge. Thus if Caesar was ambitious when he waged war upon Pompey, the definition implies that power was in fact good, as being coveted by Caesar. But this fact may have been affirmed by Mark Antony, or afterwards denied by Caesar himself in his own defence. Value, therefore, lends itself to judgment in the ordinary sense,—to judgments which are true or false, and which may agree or disagree.

In the second place, having defined value as constituted by interests, such judgments have a content or object other than themselves. They may refer to the interest of the judge, or to any other interests, past or present, common or unique; but the interest that creates the value is always other than the judgment that cognizes it. Theory of value is not a history of opinion about values, but deals with that to which such opinion refers.

The view here proposed may properly be termed a bio-centric or psycho-centric theory of value, in the sense that values are held to be functions of certain acts of living mind to which we have given the name of interest. Interests and their objects,

[8] Cf. G. E. Moore, *op. cit.*, pp. 122–124.

[9] E. Westermarck, *Origin and Development of Moral Ideas,* 1906, Vol. I, *passim.* Westermarck's confusion is largely due to the ambiguity of the term "approval," and the absence of any clear notion of judgment.

[10] For a general statement of this position, cf. L. Lévy-Bruhl, *La Morale et la Science des Mœurs,* 1910.

or the complex facts, objects-of-interest, can be known like any other facts. But they do not have to obtain from anybody's knowledge of them, permission either to exist or to be what they are. No subject whatsoever, human or divine, has the power to make or unmake them by his own simple affirmation or denial. When value is defined in terms of these facts it possesses the same independence. A value acquires existence when an interest is generated, regardless of any knowledge about it. A value will cease to exist when its own sustaining interest is destroyed or altered; but it does not cease to exist simply because it is cognitively excommunicated. He who knows values, and takes account of them, profits from that knowledge through his better adaptation to the environment in which he lives; and he who ignores them does so at his peril.

*Realms of Value**

THE MEANING OF MORALITY

Morality is man's endeavor to harmonize conflicting interests: to prevent conflict when it threatens, to remove conflict when it occurs, and to advance from the negative harmony of non-conflict to the positive harmony of coöperation. Morality is the solution of the problem created by conflict—conflict among the interests of the same or of different persons. The solution of the personal problem lies in the substitution for a condition of warring and mutually destructive impulses a condition in which each impulse, being assigned a limited place, may be innocent and contributory. For the weakness of inner discord it substitutes the strength of a unified life in which the several interests of an individual make common cause together. The same description applies to the morality of a social group, all along the line from the domestic family to the family of nations.

Such a moralization of life takes place, insofar as it does take place, through organization—personal and social. This crucial idea of organization must not be conceived loosely, or identified with organism. In organism, as in a work of art, the part serves the whole; in moral organization the whole serves the parts, or the whole only for the sake of the parts. The parts are interests, and they are organized in order that they, the constituent interests themselves, may be saved and fulfilled.

When interests are thus organized there emerges an interest of the totality, or moral interest, whose superiority lies in its being greater than any of its parts—greater by the principle of inclusiveness. It is authorized to speak for all of the component interests when its voice is their joint voice. The height of any claim in the moral scale is proportional to the breadth of its representation. What suits all of a person's interests is exalted above what merely suits a fraction; what suits everybody is exalted above what merely suits somebody.

Certain philosophies and religions of the past have conceived the world as originally a moral order, that is, as *constitutionally* harmonious, all desires and wills being so fitted to one another that each acting for itself is at the same time harmless or helpful to the rest. Such a guarantee of cosmic harmony has been an article of faith in Christian theism, as exemplified in the terrestrial and celestial paradises. In the thought of the eighteenth century this was represented in terms of an idyllic "state of nature." In Kant it was a "kingdom of ends" ruled by the moral imperative. After Kant it assumed another form in the idealistic doctrine of an "abso-

* Reprinted by permission of the publishers. Ralph Barton Perry, *Realms of Value: A Critique of Human Civilization*, Cambridge, Mass.: Harvard University Press, Copyright, 1954, by The President and Fellows of Harvard College.

lute spirit." Still later it found expression in the Spencerian doctrine of a "perfectly adjusted society," conceived as the end product of natural evolution.

But Christian theism and the eighteenth century doctrine of nature both found it necessary to acknowledge an unfortunate lapse or "fall," from which men must be redeemed through salvation or through civil institutions. The Kantian kingdom of ends was assigned to a "noumenal" world beyond the reach of knowledge, and affirmed by an act of faith. The idealistic philosophy found it necessary to acknowledge the disharmony of the phenomenal world and to transpose the realization of harmony to a supersensible realm. And science has long since abandoned the idea that harmony is a predetermined outcome of the evolutionary process. Whether as recovery from a fall, or as a bridge from the temporal to the eternal, or as a conscious control of natural forces, it is now recognized as necessary to invoke the human will in order that harmony shall be *made out of* disharmony. Harmony thus becomes an ideal future good; a goal the attainment of which is conditioned by plasticity of circumstance, fidelity of purpose, efficiency of control, and growth of enlightenment.

Morality conceived as the harmonization of interests for the sake of the interests harmonized can be described as a cult of freedom. It does not force interests into a procrustean bed, but gives interests space and air in which to be more abundantly themselves. Its purpose is to provide room. And ideally the benefits of morality are extended to all interests. Hence moral progress takes the double form, of liberalizing the existing organization, and of extending it to interests hitherto excluded. Both of these principles have important applications to the "dynamics" of morality, or to the moral force in human history. The extension of moral organization is made possible by increase of contact and interaction, which, however, then multiplies the possibilities of conflict. Hence the peculiar destiny of man, whose ascent is rendered possible by the same conditions which make possible his fall. There can be no development of a unified personality or society without the risk of inner tensions; no neighborhood, nation or society of all mankind, without the risk of war.

Morality as progressive achievement requires the integration of interests. They cannot be simply added together. If they are to compose a harmonious will that represents them all, they must be brought into line. At the same time, if such a will is truly to embrace them, which is the ground of its higher claim, they must themselves accept the realignment. Morality is an integration of interests, in which they are rendered harmonious without losing their identity. The procedure by which this is effected is the method of *reflective agreement*, appearing in the personal will, and in the social will.

Interests are integrated by reflection. In the creation of the personal will there occurs a thinking over, in which the several interests of the same person are reviewed, and invited to present their claims. Reflection overcomes the effects of forgetfulness and disassociation. It corrects the perspectives of time and immediacy, anticipating the interests of tomorrow, and giving consideration to the interests which at the moment are cold or remote. It brings to light the causal relations between one interest and another. From reflection there emerge decisions which fulfill, in some measure, the purpose of harmony: plans, schedules, quotas, substitutions, and other arrangements by which the several interests avoid collision and achieve mutual reinforcement.

The personal will which emerges from reflection is not, as has sometimes been held, merely the strongest among existing interests, prevailing after a struggle of opposing forces. It is not a mere survivor, other contestants having been eliminated. It does not intervene on one side or the other, but takes a line down the middle, analogous to the resultant or vector in a field of forces. It makes its own choices, and sets its own precedents. Its accumulated decisions, having become permanent dispositions, form a character, or unwritten personal constitution.

The achievement of such a personal will cannot be indefinitely postponed. The exigencies of life are imperative, and have to be met with whatever personal will can be achieved. There is always a dateline for action. Any given personal will is thus inevitably premature, provisional, and subject to improvement. But insofar as it is enlightened and circumspect this personal will is considered as finally justified, except insofar as it neglects the similar personal wills of others. Within the domain of its included interests it is a moral ultimate. The several interests which it embraces have no moral cause for complaint insofar as they have been given the opportunity of contributing to the purpose to which they are subordinated.

The relation of the personal will to the person's several interests is primarily one of government, overruling, or dominance. It serves as a check or censor called into play when any of the particular interests tends to exceed bounds. Like a sentinel it challenges each passing interest and requires it to show its credentials.

The similarity between the personal and social forms of the moral will must not be allowed to obscure their profound difference. It is true that as the personal will emerges from reflection so the social will emerges from communication and discussion. In both cases the emergent will represents a totality of interests, and achieves by organization a substitution of harmony for conflict. The difference lies in the fact that whereas the personal will is composed of sub-personal interests, the social will is composed of persons.

But while the social moral will is a will of persons, society is not a person. Excluding fictitious persons, corporate persons, legal persons, and every metaphorical or figurative use of the term, the only real person is that being which is capable of reflecting, choosing, relating means to ends, making decisions, and subordinating particular interests to an overruling purpose. It follows that there can be no moral will on the social level except as composed of several personal wills which are peculiarly modified and interrelated.

The ramifications of this fact pervade the whole domain of morality and moral institutions. It is echoed in all of those doctrines which exalt the person as an end in himself. It gives meaning to fraternity as the acknowledgment of person by fellow-persons. It gives to the individual man that "dignity" of which we hear so much. It provides for that unique role of the person as thinker, judge, and chooser, which lies at the basis of all representative institutions, and determines the moral priority of individuals to society.

The creation of a social moral will out of personal wills depends on benevolence, that is, one person's positive interest in another person's interest. To be benevolent here means not that I treat you well so far as it happens to suit my existing interests to do so; my concern for your interests is an independent interest. Taking your desires and aversions, your hopes and fears, your pleasures and pains, in short, the interests by which you are actually moved, I act as though these interests were my own. Though I cannot, strictly speaking, *feel* your interests, I can acknowledge them, wish them well, and allow for them in addition to the interests which are already embraced within me. When you are at the same time benevolently disposed to my interests, we then have the same problem of reconciling the same interests, except that my original interests form the content of your benevolence and your original interests the content of mine.

In this pooling of interests I am ordinarily concerned that your benevolence shall actually embrace my original interests; and you are similarly concerned to accent yours. Each of us assumes that the other can safely be trusted to look out for his own. Assuming that each will be biased in favor of his own interests, the bias of each will tend to correct the bias of the other. Each will be the special pleader of his own interests, and his insistence on them will reinforce the other's weaker benevolence.

There will be a further difference. Your interests are best and most immediately served by you, and mine by me. I can for the most part serve you best by letting you serve yourself. The greater part of my benevolence, therefore, will take a permissive form. I will sometimes help you, but more often will abstain from hurting you; or will so follow my own inclinations as to make it possible for you also to follow yours; or accept your inclinations as setting a limit to mine.

No will is here introduced over and above the wills of the two persons, but since the two wills now represent the same interests, they will have achieved a community of end and a coöperative relation of means. In each person the new socialized purpose will have become dominant over his original interests. Neither will have become the mere means to the other since the common end is now each person's governing end. Each can speak with equal authority for that end, and may legitimately use the pronouns "we" and "our" in behalf of both. Each, speaking for the common end, can approve or disapprove the other's conduct without arrogance or impertinence.

The social form of the moral will is an agreement of personal wills of which independent benevolence is the essential condition. There are many other factors which conduce to such agreement, and which in their totality make up the method or art of agreement. The first prerequisite of agreement is a desire to agree, rather than to "get the better" of the other party. To induce this attitude it is necessary that both parties should be conscious of the wastefulness of conflict, and the gains, even if they be selfish gains, of peace. The Quaker idea of achieving unanimity, or a "sense of the meeting," which leaves no slumbering grievances and seeds of fresh dispute, is precisely the moral norm which is here defined. The further Quaker idea of periods of silence may or may not be taken to imply a religious doctrine of "inner light"; it may be taken to mean only that an interval of meditation will serve to cool the temper of acrimony.

Agreement is often promoted by shifting the emphasis from points of disagreement to matters in which there is already agreement. This area of agreement may be found either in subsidiary matters or in a common ideal goal. In either case there is created a mood of agreement which is favorable to further agreement. Since interests embrace a factor of cognitive mediation it is always possible to find occasions for cognitive agreement. There are always questions of fact and logic which can be made the focus of discussion. But though this conduces to an agreement of wills, it does not suffice. For practical or moral agreement it is necessary that each person should be *moved* as the other is moved, so as to achieve a harmony of purpose and action. . . .

Reflective agreement between persons confers on each the right to speak for all. But there are degrees of reflection. It may be comparatively hasty, shallow, impulsive, irrational; or it may be comparatively deliberate, deep, wholehearted, rational. These different levels of reflection define a norm by which the social will can be appraised. Since the person is the seat of reflection it is to the personal will that we must look for an understanding of this difference of level.

If the word "we" is the most presumptuous word in the English language, the word "I" is a close rival. The word "I" claims to speak for the whole of the person to which the moment of its utterance belongs. When my hunger speaks, it says, "*I* am hungry"; momentary appetites and impulses say "I" even more carelessly and shamelessly than persons say "we." But the first person singular means, ideally, the totality of the person who is the user of that pronoun. It claims agreement on the part of the whole company of his interests, most of which will at any given moment be unconscious. This claim is warranted only insofar as these interests have been consulted and, after whatever transformations may have been necessary, have acquiesced.

In the light of this norm it may now be seen that social agreement will vary in the extent to which it expresses the total persons of the agreeing parties; and this will depend on the process, whether *more or less* reflective, by which the agreement is made. By the same token, representative agreement will vary in the degree to which the spokesman, when he uses the pronoun "we," can speak not only for all, but for all of all—that is, with the "full consent" of all. . . .

Since the unscrupulous propagandist is usually concerned with *immediate* support and control, he is inclined to be indifferent to the *manner* in which the consent of others is obtained, provided it *is* obtained. It is comparatively easy for men to agree superficially; when men think for themselves they tend for a time to take divergent paths. The method best calculated to secure a prompt unanimity is the one way passage—the spoken or written word by which the propagandist "holds the floor," while his spellbound victim assumes a passive role. He who would quickly possess men's minds will not stir their depths. The unscrupulous propagandist will not excite the critical faculties. He will appeal to ready-made opinions and to common appetites. When these existing agreements do not suffice he will induce a state of suggestibility. The essential condition of suggestibility is dissociation; which isolates some part of the person, and exposes this part helplessly to contagion and fixation by cutting its interior controls.

In short, by non-reflective propaganda men are united with one another by being divided from themselves. It is true that the effects of such suggested or passionate unanimity are sometimes benign, and its motive may be noble. But whether it be a lynching party or a crusade, a drunken debauch or a religious revival, agreement obtained by methods thus deliberately contrived to inhibit reflection does violence to personal integrity. Of such agreement it is not strictly correct to say "you agree" or "we agree." It would be more correct to say "it agrees"—referring to some fragmentary item, some accidental part, some particular impulse, some isolated idea.

It is commonly supposed that there is virtue in passionate unanimity. As a matter of fact there is more of the substance of the moral will in conflicting egoisms, where each ego is at least a reflective person. The spread of identical passions instead of justifying these passions only renders them more resistant to reason and conscience, increasing the very blindness, narrow insistence, and ruthlessness which constitute the essence of original sin. The complete social agreement which takes the supreme place in the moral order requires two components, the horizontal component of spread and the vertical component of depth.

Morality may be illustrated by the actual complexities of social life arranged in spheres of expanding inclusiveness. In the more intimate family or local circle there are several persons within the range of familiar acquaintance, each with interests of his own. Through communication and benevolence each adopts as his own the interest of father, mother, son, daughter, brother, sister, friend, neighbor; integrates them, speaks for the family or local group as a whole, and himself accepts this voice as authoritative over his original interests.

When representatives of capital and labor sit around a table and engage in what is called "collective bargaining," and insofar as this is a *moral* transaction which achieves a "right" solution of the problem of conflict, the process is similar except that the interests are represented, instead of being immediately present "in person." Each representative enters the conference as the advocate of one of the conflicting economic interests, and he is expected to advocate it. But he is also expected to take the view of the opposing advocate. He must listen to him, be impressed, concede his point, acknowledge his claims. In proportion as there is this exchange of interests, both parties tend to be actuated by both interests. Their two attitudes tend to converge and to approximate that of a third party, such as "the representative of the public," the judge, or the arbitrator, whose role it is to be equally considerate of both interests, and the partisan advocate of neither. . . .

A political will differs from more limited collective wills only in its complexity and in the comparatively long chain of intermediate steps which it requires. It is achieved by discussion, taken as an interchange of personal interests, and of the collective interests of classes or groups. The ruler is the guardian not only of his individual interests and the interests of his group, but also, through benevolence, of the interests of all fellow-nationals. Whether it be the private citizen or the public official in whom this multiplicity of interests is assembled and harmonized, the ultimate decisions are made by a person. The political will is a political form of personal will, repeated among the members. When all agree, each can speak for the rest, and the authority for all; but the voice which speaks is a personal voice, and the agreement must be a personal aceptance. This is the moral core of politics, and the germ of political democracy.

In the judicial process the presiding judge, and the law which he applies and interprets, are supposed to represent both the defendant and the plaintiff. But it is demed important that each litigant should plead his own case, directly or through an attorney who has identified himself with his client's case. When the decision is left to a judge he must be disinterested not only in the sense of excluding his own personal interest, but in the sense of taking account of all the interests at stake. When the decision is left to a jury it is assumed that this will afford the best guarantee that the interests at stake are sympathetically understood and have reached a unanimous agreement.

What reciprocal and sympathetic acquaintance achieves in the narrower circles of home and neighborhood, what collective bargaining achieves in the reconciliation of economic groups, what popular discussion, campaigning, and elections achieve in the civil polity, what pleading, argument, and judicial decision achieve in the field of law, is achieved in the international area by diplomacy, negotiation, treaty-making, and conference.

In this area one is painfully aware of a mixture of methods. Nations still practice war and power politics. But intermingled with this non-moral heritage from the past there is now an increasing and not wholly unsuccessful atempt to find a moral remedy. This remedy is achieved insofar as nations and peoples "understand one another," that is, benevolently share one another's interests, and seek a harmonizing purpose in which all the interests of mankind are embraced. Insofar as this occurs there can be said to be an international will or a will of mankind; which by virtue of its maximum breadth of representation stands at the summit of the moral hierarchy.

Such a will, like every lesser will, is a will of persons. International will consists of international-mindedness on the part of nations whose national wills consist in turn of the national-mindness of their subgroups and individual members. It is insofar as each person is directly or indirectly represented that the inclusive requirements of international organization can be said to take precedence of those of any lesser group. Morally speaking international organization is a community of persons, in which because of the identity of their ends millions of men agree upon means; and are thus brought into relations of innocence and mutual aid. Each member of such a universal community of persons would be authorized to say "we" or "our" for all men. There is no other being, unless it be God, that can speak for mankind; no other situation in which this pretension is warranted.

Such is the principle of reflective agreement. No claim is here made for the frequency or success of its application. But it means something, it is humanly possible, and it is successfully applied in some measure. If reflective inter-personal agreement be the moral principle, one must be prepared to admit that there is not always a moral solution of a problem of conflict. There is, however, a *way* to such a solution—a *line of effort*. Morality is a *pursuit*, not an infallible recipe. The conflicting parties may not try at all, or they may try and fail. All that moral philosophy can do is to define the moral goal; all that moral prophets can do is to exhort men to aim at the goal; all that moral sages can do is to cite the experience of those who have been successful. If the conflicting parties do not look for agreement, there is no moral solution; if they do not succeed in reaching agreement, there is no moral solution. In case of unwillingness to agree, or in case of failure to agree, the action of the parties in question must take other grounds—partisanship, egoism, passion, whatever it be.

Morality is like a cultivated field in the midst of the desert. It is a partial and precarious conquest. Ground that is conquered has to be protected against the resurgence of original divisive forces. The moralized life is never immune against *de*moralization. At the same time that morality gains ground in one direction it may lose ground in another. Changes in the natural and historical environment and the development of man himself are perpetually introducing new factors and requiring a moral reorganization to embrace them. In the last analysis all depends on the energy, perseverance, and perpetual vigilance of the human person.

PAUL TILLICH

Paul Tillich (1886–1965) was one of the leading theologians of this century. What Reinhold Niebuhr did to revolutionize the ethical and political outlook of American Protestantism, Tillich did for systematic theological construction. Tillich achieved fame as a social thinker in Germany before being forced to flee by the Nazis. He admits that his thinking underwent considerable change as a result of living in America. He taught at Union Theological Seminary and at Harvard.

Tillich readily acknowledged the influence which existentialism had upon his thought, as the following selections indicate. The first (from his Systematic Theology*) shows the value of existentialism for Christian theology; the second (from his Terry Lectures, entitled* The Courage to Be*) discusses faith as a solution to the discovery of existential meaninglessness; the third (from* Theology of Culture*) draws the implications of existentialism for the interpretation of ethics; the fourth (from* Morality and Beyond*) examines the relation between choice and moral imperatives.*

*Systematic Theology**

Existence and Existentialism

EXISTENTIALISM AGAINST ESSENTIALISM

. . . The common point in all existentialist attacks is that man's existential situation is a state of estrangement from his essential nature. Hegel is aware of this estrangement, but he believes that it has been overcome and that man has been reconciled with his true being. According to all the existentialists, this belief is Hegel's basic error. Reconciliation is a matter of anticipation and expectation, but not of reality. The world is not reconciled, either in the individual—as Kierkegaard shows—or in society—as Marx shows—or in life as such—as Schopenhauer and Nietzsche show. Existence is estrangement and not reconciliation; it is dehumanization and not the expression of essential humanity. It is the process in which man becomes a thing and ceases to be a person. History is not the divine self-manifestation but a series of unreconciled conflicts, threatening man with self-destruction. The existence of the individual is filled with anxiety and threatened by meaninglessness. With this description of man's predicament all existen-

* By permission. From Paul Tillich, *Systematic Theology*, vol. II, The University of Chicago Press, Chicago, 1957.

tialists agree and are therefore opposed to Hegel's essentialism. They feel that it is an attempt to hide the truth about man's actual state.

The distinction has been made between atheistic and theistic existentialism. Certainly there are existentialists who could be called "atheistic," at least according to their intention; and there are others who can be called "theistic." But, in reality, there is no atheistic or theistic existentialism. Existentialism gives an analysis of what it means to exist. It shows the contrast between an essentialist description and an existentialist analysis. It develops the question implied in existence, but it does not try to give the answer, either in atheistic or in theistic terms. Whenever existentialists give answers, they do so in terms of religious or quasi-religious traditions which are not derived from their existentialist analysis. Pascal derives his answers from the Augustinian tradition, Kierkegaard from the Lutheran, Marcel from the Thomist, Dostoevski from the Greek Orthodox. Or the answers are derived from humanistic traditions, as with Marx, Sartre, Nietzsche, Heidegger, and Jaspers. None of these men was able to develop answers out of his questions. The answers of the humanists come from hidden religious sources. They are matters of ultimate concern or faith, although garbed in a secular gown. Hence the distinction between atheistic and theistic existentialism fails. Existentialism is an analysis of the human predicament. And the answers to the questions implied in man's predicament are religious, whether open or hidden.

EXISTENTIAL AND EXISTENTIALIST THINKING

For the sake of further philological clarification, it is useful to distinguish between existential and existentialist. The former refers to a human attitude, the latter to a philosophical school. The opposite of existential is detached; the opposite of existentialist is essentialist. In existential thinking, the object is involved. In non-existential thinking, the object is detached. By its very nature, theology is existential; by its very nature, science is non-existential. Philosophy unites elements of both. In intention, it is non-existential; in reality, it is an ever changing combination of elements of involvement and detachment. This makes futile all attempts to create a so-called "scientific philosophy."

Existential is not existentialist, but they are related in having a common root, namely, "existence." Generally speaking, one can describe essential structures in terms of detachment, and existential predicament in terms of involvement. But this statement needs drastic qualifications. There is an element of involvement in the construction of geometrical figures; and there is an element of detachment in the observation of one's own anxiety and estrangement. The logician and mathematician are driven by *eros*, including desire and passion. The existentialist theologian, who analyzes existence, discovers structures through cognitive detachment, even if they are structures of destruction. And between these poles there are many mixtures of detachment and involvement, as in biology, history, and psychology. Nevertheless, a cognitive attitude in which the element of involvement is dominant is called "existential." The converse is also true. Since the element of involvement is so dominant, the most striking existentialist analyses have been made by novelists, poets, and painters. But even they could escape irrelevant subjectivity only by submitting themselves to detached and objective observation. As a result, the materials brought out by the detached methods of therapeutic psychology are used in existentialist literature and art. Involvement and detachment are poles, not conflicting alternatives; there is no existentialist analysis without non-existential detachment.

EXISTENTIALISM AND CHRISTIAN THEOLOGY

. . . Existentialism has analyzed the "old eon," namely, the predicament of man and his world in the state of estrangement. In doing so, existentialism is a natural ally of Christianity. Immanuel Kant once said that mathematics is the good luck of human reason. In the same way, one could say that existentialism is the good luck of Christian theology. It has helped to rediscover the classical Christian interpretation of human existence. Any theological attempt to do this would not have had the same effect. This positive use refers not only to existentialist philosophy but also to analytic psychology, literature, poetry, drama, and art. In all these realms there is an immense amount of material which the theologian can use and organize in the attempt to present Christ as the answer to the questions implied within existence. In earlier centuries a similar task was undertaken mainly by monastic theologians, who analyzed themselves and the members of their small community so penetratingly that there are few present-day insights into the human predicament which they did not anticipate. The penitential and devotional literature impressively shows this. But this tradition was lost under the impact of the philosophies and theologies of pure consciousness, represented, above all, my Cartesianism and Calvinism. Notwithstanding differences, they were allies in helping to repress the unconscious and half-conscious sides of human nature, thus preventing a full understanding of man's existential predicament (in spite of Calvin's doctrine of man's total depravity and the Augustinianism of the Cartesian school). In recovering the elements of man's nature which were suppressed by the psychology of consciousness, existentialism and contemporary theology should become allies and analyze the character of existence in all its manifestations, the unconscious as well as the conscious. . . .

ESTRANGEMENT AND SIN

The state of existence is the state of estrangement. Man is estranged from the ground of his being, from other beings, and from himself. The transition from essence to existence results in personal guilt and universal tragedy. It is now necessary to give a description of existential estrangement and its self-destructive implications. But, before doing so, we must answer the question which has already arisen: What is the relation of the concept of estrangement to the traditional concept of sin? . . .

Estrangement is not a biblical term but is implied in most of the biblical descriptions of man's predicament. It is implied in the symbols of the expulsion from paradise, in the hostility between man and nature, in the deadly hostility of brother against brother, in the estrangement of nation from nation through the confusion of language, and in the continuous complaints of the prophets against their kings and people who turn to alien gods. Estrangement is implied in Paul's statement that man perverted the image of God into that of idols, in his classical description of "man against himself," in his vision of man's hostility against man as combined with his distorted desires. In all these interpretations of man's predicament, estrangement is implicitly asserted. Therefore, it is certainly not unbiblical to use the term "estrangement" in describing man's existential situation.

Nevertheless, "estrangement" cannot replace "sin." Yet the reasons for attempts to replace the word "sin" with another word are obvious. The term has been used in a way which has little to do with its genuine biblical meaning. Paul often spoke of "Sin" in the singular and without an article. He saw it as a quasi-personal power which ruled this world. But in the Christian churches, both Catholic and Protestant, sin has been used predominantly in the plural, and "sins" are deviations from moral laws. This has little to do with "sin" as the state of estrangement from that to which one belongs—God, one's self, one's world. Therefore, the characteristics of sin are here considered under the heading of "estrangement." And the word "estrangement" itself implies a reinterpretation of sin from a religious point of view.

Nevertheless, the word "sin" cannot be overlooked. It expresses what is not implied in the term "estrangement," namely, the personal act of turning away from that to which one belongs. Sin expresses most sharply the personal character of estrangement over against its tragic side. It expresses personal freedom and guilt in contrast to tragic guilt and the universal destiny of estrangement. The word "sin" can and must be saved, not only because classical literature and liturgy continuously employ it but more particularly because the word has a sharpness which accusingly points to the element of personal responsibility in one's estrangement. Man's predicament is estrangement, but his estrangement is sin. It is not a state of things, like the laws of nature, but a matter of both personal freedom and universal destiny. For this reason the term "sin" must be used after it has been reinterpreted religiously. An important tool for this reinterpretation is the term "estrangement."

Reinterpretation is also needed for the terms "original" or "hereditary" with respect to sin. But in this case reinterpretation may demand the rejection of the terms. Both point to the universal character of estrangement, expressing the element of destiny in estrangement. But both words are so much burdened with literalistic absurdities that it is practically impossible to use them any longer.

If one speaks of "sins" and refers to special acts which are considered as sinful, one should always be conscious of the fact that "sins" are the expressions of "sin." It is not the disobedience to a law which makes an act sinful but the fact that it is an expression of man's estrangement from God, from men, from himself. Therefore, Paul calls everything sin which does not result from faith, from the unity with God. And in another context (following Jesus) all laws are summed up in the law of love by which estrangement is conquered. Love as the striving for the reunion of the separated is the opposite of estrangement. In faith and love, sin is conquered because estrangement is overcome by reunion.

*The Courage to Be**

ABSOLUTE FAITH AND THE COURAGE TO BE

The question is this: Is there a courage which can conquer the anxiety of meaninglessness and doubt? Or in other words, can the faith which accepts acceptance resist the power of nonbeing in its most radical form? Can faith resist meaninglessness? Is there a kind of faith which can exist together with doubt and meaninglessness? These questions lead to the . . . one most relevant to our time: How is the courage to be possible if all the ways to create it are barred by the experience of their ultimate insufficiency? If life is as meaningless as death, if guilt is as questionable as perfection, if being is no more

* By permission. From Paul Tillich, *The Courage to Be*, Yale University Press, New Haven, Conn., and John Nesbitt Inc., Ltd., Welwyn, Hertfordshire, 1952.

meaningful than nonbeing, on what can one base the courage to be?

There is an inclination in some Existentialists to answer these questions by a leap from doubt to dogmatic certitude, from meaninglessness to a set of symbols in which the meaning of a special ecclesiastical or political group is embodied. This leap can be interpreted in different ways. It may be the expression of a desire for safety; it may be as arbitrary as, according to Existentialist principles, every decision is; it may be the feeling that the Christian message is the answer to the questions raised by an analysis of human existence; it may be a genuine conversion, independent of the theoretical situation. In any case it is not a solution of the problem of radical doubt. It gives the courage to be to those who are converted but it does not answer the question as to how such a courage is possible in itself. The answer must accept, as its precondition, the state of meaninglessness. It is not an answer if it demands the removal of this state; for that is just what cannot be done. He who is in the grip of doubt and meaninglessness cannot liberate himself from this grip; but he asks for an answer which is valid within and not outside the situation of his despair. He asks for the ultimate foundation of what we have called the "courage of despair." There is only one possible answer, if one does not try to escape the question: namely that the acceptance of despair is in itself faith and on the boundary line of the courage to be. In this situation the meaning of life is reduced to despair about the meaning of life. But as long as this despair is an act of life it is positive in its negativity. Cynically speaking, one could say that it is true to life to be cynical about it. Religiously speaking, one would say that one accepts oneself as accepted in spite of one's despair about the meaning of this acceptance. The paradox of every radical negativity, as long as it is an active negativity, is that it must affirm itself in order to be able to negate itself. No actual negation can be without an implicit affirmation. The hidden pleasure produced by despair witnesses to the paradoxical character of self-negation. The negative lives from the positive it negates.

The faith which makes the courage of despair possible is the acceptance of the power of being, even in the grip of nonbeing. Even in the despair about meaning being affirms itself through us. The act of accepting meaninglessness is in itself a meaningful act. It is an act of faith. . . . He who has the courage to affirm his being in spite of fate and guilt has not removed them. He remains threatened and hit by them. But he accepts his acceptance by the power of being-itself in which he participates and which gives him the courage to take the anxieties of fate and guilt upon himself. The same is true of doubt and meaninglessness. The faith which creates the courage to take them into itself has no special content. It is simply faith, undirected, absolute. It is undefinable, since everything defined is dissolved by doubt and meaninglessness. Nevertheless, even absolute faith is not an eruption of subjective emotions or a mood without objective foundation.

An analysis of the nature of absolute faith reveals the following elements in it. The first is the experience of the power of being which is present even in face of the most radical manifestation of nonbeing. If one says that in this experience vitality resists despair one must add that vitality in man is proportional to intentionality. The vitality that can stand the abyss of meaninglessness is aware of a hidden meaning within the destruction of meaning. The second element in absolute faith is the dependence of the experience of nonbeing on the experience of being and the dependence of the experience of meaninglessness on the experience of meaning. Even in the state of despair one has enough being to make despair possible. There is a third element in absolute faith, the acceptance of being accepted. Of course, in the state of despair there is nobody and nothing that accepts. But there is the power of acceptance itself which is experienced. Meaninglessness, as long as it is experienced, includes an experience of the "power of acceptance." To accept this power of acceptance consciously is the religious answer of absolute faith, of a faith which has been deprived by doubt of any concrete content, which nevertheless is faith and the source of the most paradoxical manifestation of the courage to be.

This faith transcends both the mystical experience and the divine-human encounter. The mystical experience seems to be nearer to absolute faith but it is not. Absolute faith includes an element of skepticism which one cannot find in the mystical experience. Certainly mysticism also transcends all specific contents, but not because it doubts them or has found them meaningless; rather it deems them to be preliminary. Mysticism uses the specific contents as grades, stepping on them after having used them. The experience of meaninglessness, however, denies them (and everything that goes with them), without having used them. The experience of meaninglessness is more radical than mysticism. Therefore it transcends the mystical experience.

Absolute faith also transcends the divine-human encounter. In this encounter the subject-object scheme is valid: a definite subject (man) meets a definite object (God). One can reverse this statement and say that a definite subject (God) meets a definite object (man). But in both cases the attack of doubt undercuts the subject-object structure. The theologians who speak so strongly and with such self-certainty about the divine-human encounter should be aware of a situation in which this encounter is prevented by radical doubt and nothing is left but absolute faith. The acceptance of such a situation as religiously valid has, however, the consequence that the concrete contents of ordinary faith must be subjected to criticism and transformation. The courage to be in its radical form is a key to an idea of God which transcends both mysticism and the person-to-person encounter.

The Courage to Be as the Key to Being-itself

NONBEING OPENING UP BEING

The courage to be in all its forms has, by itself, revelatory character. It shows the nature of being, it shows that the self-affirmation of being is an affirmation that overcomes negation. In a metaphorical statement (and every assertion about being-itself is either metaphorical or symbolic) one could say that being includes nonbeing but nonbeing does not prevail against it. "Including" is a spatial metaphor which indicates that being embraces itself and that which is opposed to it, nonbeing. Nonbeing belongs to being, it cannot be separated from it. We could not even think "being" without a double negation: being must be thought as the negation of the negation of being. This is why we describe being best by the metaphor "power of being." Power is the possibility a being has to actualize itself against the resistance of other beings. . . . The self-affirmation of being without nonbeing would not even be self-affirmation but an immovable self-identity. Nothing would be manifest, nothing expressed, nothing revealed. But nonbeing drives being out of its seclusion, it forces it to affirm itself dynamically. . . . Nonbeing (that in God which makes his self-affirmation dynamic) opens up the divine self-seclusion and reveals him as power and love. Nonbeing makes God a living God. Without the No he has to overcome in himself and in his creature, the divine Yes to himself would be lifeless. There would be no revelation of the ground of being, there would be no life.

But where there is nonbeing there is finitude and anxiety. If we say that nonbeing belongs to being-itself, we say that finitude and anxiety belong to being-itself. Wherever philosophers or theologians have spoken of the divine blessedness they have implicitly (and sometimes explicitly) spoken of the anxiety of finitude which is eternally taken into the blessedness of the divine infinity. . . .

The divine self-affirmation is the power that makes the self-affirmation of the finite being, the courage to be, possible. Only because being-itself has the character of self-affirmation in spite of nonbeing is courage possible. Courage participates in the self-affirmation of being-itself, it participates in the power of being which prevails against nonbeing. He who receives this power in an act of mystical or personal or absolute faith is aware of the source of his courage to be.

Man is not necessarily aware of this source. In situations of cynicism and indifference he is not aware of it. But it works in him as long as he maintains the courage to take his anxiety upon himself. In the act of the courage to be the power of being is effective in us, whether we recognize it or not. Every act of courage is a manifestation of the ground of being, however questionable the content of the act may be. The content may hide or distort true being, the courage in it reveals true being. Not arguments but the courage to be reveals the true nature of being-itself. By affirming our being we participate in the self-affirmation of being-itself. There are no valid arguments for the "existence" of God, but there are acts of courage in which we affirm the power of being, whether we know it or not. If we know it, we accept acceptance consciously. If we do not know it, we nevertheless accept it and participate in it. And in our acceptance of that which we do not know the power of being is manifest to us. Courage has revealing power, the courage to be is the key to being-itself.

*Theology of Culture**

Moralisms and Morality: Theonomous Ethics

The title of this chapter requires a few "semantic" considerations, for neither the word "moralisms" nor the word "morality" is unambiguous. "Moralism" designates an attitude toward life, an attitude which is widespread in this country. It is the distortion of the moral imperative into an oppressive law. One can find a puritan, an evangelistic, a nationalistic, and simply a conventional moralism (which is not conscious of its historical roots). Moralism as the distortion of the moral imperative has no plural. It is an attitude, a negative one, against which theology and psychology should wage a common war.

"Moralisms" (in plural) does not mean something negative. It points to systems of moral imperatives as they have developed in special cultures and are dependent upon the relativities and limitations of these cultures. There is, however, an essential relation between the meaning of the plural and the singular of moralism: Moral systems, just because of their intimate connection with a cultural system, have the tendency to become oppressive if the general cultural scheme changes. They tend to produce moralism as an attitude. The distinction between moralisms as ethical systems and moralism as a negative attitude is identical with the distinction between the creative and the oppressive character of moral im-

* By permission. From Paul Tillich, *Theology of Culture*, edited by Robert C. Kimball, International Universities Press, New York, 1959.

peratives, and each ethical system has both characteristics.

The other term to be considered is morality. It is as ambiguous as the term moralism. Morality, in the first place, is the experience of the moral imperative. It is a function of man as man. Without it he would not be man. A being without the consciousness of a moral demand is not human. If a feeble-minded child behaves as if he were unaware of any moral demand, he is sub-human, which does not mean that he is an animal. He is both more and less than an animal. In contrast to him, a criminal is aware of the moral imperative, while defying its commands. He is human although he fights against an essential element in human nature. For man as man has the potentiality to contradict himself.

Morality can also mean "moral behavior," the attempt to be obedient to a system of moral rules. The contrast to morality in this sense should be immorality (in difference to the amorality of sub-human beings). But unfortunately the word "immoral" can hardly be used since, through the special Anglo-Saxon moralism, it has received an almost exclusively sexual connotation. Immorality in the general sense of anti-moral behavior is possible only in a limited way. Even the criminal shows morality, although he follows a moralistic code which contradicts the accepted moralism of a society.

After this attempt at semantic clarification, there are now four central questions which this chapter should raise under the following four headings:

I. Moralisms Conditioned, Morality Unconditional
II. Moralisms of Authority and Morality of Risk
III. Moralisms of Law and Morality of Grace
IV. Moralisms of Justice and Morality of Love

I. MORALISMS CONDITIONED, MORALITY UNCONDITIONAL

People today are afraid of the term "unconditional." This is understandable if one considers the way in which many rather conditioned ideas and methods have been imposed on individuals and groups in the name of an unconditional truth, authoritatively and through suppression. The destructive consequences of such a demonic absolutism have produced a reaction even against the term unconditional. The mere word provokes passionate resistance. But not everything which is psychologically understandable is for this reason true. Even the most outspoken relativists cannot avoid something absolute. They acknowledge the unconditional quest to follow logical rules in their reasoning, and to act according to the law of scientific honesty in their thinking and speaking. Their character as scientific personalities is dependent on the unconditional acceptance of these principles.

This leads us to a more general understanding of the unconditional character of the moral imperative. What Immanuel Kant has called the "categorical imperative" is nothing more than the unconditional character of the "ought-to-be," the moral commandment. Whatever its content may be, its form is unconditional. One can rightly criticize Kant because he establishes a system of ethical forms without ethical contents. But just this limitation is his greatness. It makes as sharp as possible the distinction between morality which is unconditional, and moralisms which are valid only conditionally and within limits. If this is understood, the relativity of all concrete ethics (moralisms) is accepted and emphasized. The material cited by the sociologist, anthropologist, and psychologist showing the endless differences of ethical ideals is no argument against the unconditional validity of the moral imperative. If we disregard this distinction, we either fall into an absolute skepticism which, in the long run, undermines morality as such, or we fall into an absolutism which attributes unconditional validity to one of the many possible moralisms. Since, however, each of these moralisms has to maintain itself against others, it becomes fanatical, for fanaticism is the attempt to repress elements of one's own being for the sake of others. If the fanatic encounters these elements in somebody else, he fights against them passionately, because they endanger the success of his own repression.

The reason for the unconditional character of the moral imperative is that it puts our essential being as a demand against us. The moral imperative is not a strange law, imposed on us, but it is the law of our own being. In the moral imperative we ourselves, in our essential being, are put against ourselves, in our actual being. No outside command can be unconditional, whether it comes from a state, or a person, or God—if God is thought of as an outside power, establishing a law for our behavior. A stranger, even if his name were God, who imposes commands upon us must be resisted or, as Nietzsche has expressed it in his symbol of the "ugliest man," he must be killed because nobody can stand him. We cannot be obedient to the commands of a stranger even if he is God. Nor can we take unconditionally the content of the moral imperative from human authorities like traditions, conventions, political or religious authorities. There is no ultimate authority in them. One is largely dependent on them, but none of them is unconditionally valid.

The moral command is unconditional because it is we ourselves commanding ourselves. Morality is the self-affirmation of our essential being. This makes it unconditional, whatever its content may be. This is quite different from an affirmation of one's self in terms of one's desires and fears. Such a self-affirmation has no unconditional character; ethics based on it are ethics of calculation, describing the best way of getting fulfillment of desires and protection against fears. There is nothing absolute in technical calculation. But morality as the self-affirmation of one's essential being is unconditional.

The contents, however, of the moral self-affirmation are conditioned, relative, dependent on the social and psychological constellation. While morality as the pure form of essential self-affirmation is absolute, the concrete systems of moral imperatives, the "moralisms," are relative. This is not relativism (which as a philosophical attitude is self-contradictory), but it is the acknowledgment of man's finitude and his dependence on the contingencies of time and space. No conflict between the ethicist, theological or philosophical, and the anthropologist or sociologist is necessary. No theologian should deny the relativity of the moral contents; no ethnologist should deny the absolute character of the ethical demand.

Against the doctrine of the relativity of moral contents, the concept of "natural law" seems to stand. But it is only in the Roman Catholic interpretation of the moral law that a conflict exists. Natural, according to classical doctrine, is the law which is implied in man's essential nature. It has been given in creation, it has been lost by "the fall," it has been restated by Moses and Jesus (there is no difference between natural and revealed law in Bible and classical theology). The restatement of the natural law was, at the same time, its formalization and its concentration into one all-embracing law, the "Great Commandment," the commandment of love.

There is, however, a difference between the Protestant and the Catholic doctrine of the natural law. Catholicism believes that the natural law has definite contents, which are unchangeable and are authoratively stated by the Church (e.g. the fight of the Roman Church against birth control). Protestantism, on the other hand, at least today and in this country, determines the contents of the natural law largely by ethical traditions and conventions; but this is done without a supporting theory, and therefore Protestantism has the possibility of a dynamic concept of natural law. It can protest against each moral content which claims unconditional character. This whole chapter is an attempt to protest, in the name of the Protestant principle, against the Protestant moralism as it has developed in Protestant countries.

II. MORALISMS OF AUTHORITY AND MORALITY OF RISK

Systems of ethical rules, that is moralisms, are imposed on the masses by authorities: religious authorities as the Roman Church, quasi-religious authorities as the totalitarian governments, secular authorities as the givers of positive laws, conventional, family, and school authorities. "Imposing" in a radical sense means forming a conscience. External imposition is not sufficient for the creation of a moral system. It must be internalized. Only a system which is internalized is safe. Only commands which have become natural will be obeyed in extreme situations. The obedience is complete if it works automatically.

Conscience has been interpreted in different ways. The concept of internalization points to the fact that even conscience is not above the relativity which characterizes all ethical contents. It is neither the infallible voice of God, nor the infallible awareness of the natural law. It is, as the German philosopher Heidegger has said, the call, often the silent call, of man to be himself. But the self to which the conscience calls is the essential, not as Heidegger believes, the existential self. It calls us to what we essentially are, but it does not tell with certainty what that is. Even the conscience can judge us erroneously. It does not help us to a valid moral decision if one says with many theologians and philosophers: Always follow your conscience. This does not say, for example, what to do if the conscience is split. As long as the conscience points unambiguously in one direction, it is comparatively safe to follow it. Split authority destroys authority, in human relations, as well as in one's conscience.

Authority has a double meaning and a double function in the context of our problem. One is born into a moral universe, produced by the experience of all former generations. It is a mixture of natural interest, especially of the ruling classes, and wisdom, acquired by the leading people. A moral universe is not only an ideology, that is, a product of the will to gain and to preserve power. It is also a result of experience and real wisdom. It gives the material in which moral decisions are made. And every single decision adds to the experience and the wisdom of the whole. In this sense, we all are dependent on authority, on factual authority, or, as Erich Fromm has called it, rational authority. Everyone has, in some realm, rational authority above the others. For everyone contributes in a unique way to the life of the whole. And his unique experience gives, even to the least educated man, some authority over the highest educated one.

But besides this factual authority which is mutual and exercised by everybody, there is the established authority which is one-sided and exercised by selected individuals or groups. If they represent the ethical realm, they participate in the unconditional character of the moral imperative. These authorities gain absolute authority because of the absolute character of what they stand for. This analysis contradicts the way in which the idea of God is derived by some philosophers and psychologists from the unconditional impact of the father image on the child. One calls God the projection of the father image. But every projection is not only a projection *of* something, but it is also a projection *upon* something. What is this "something" upon which the image of the father is "projected" so that it becomes divine? The answer can only be: It is projected upon the "screen" of the unconditional! And this screen is not projected. It makes projection possible. So we do not reject the theory of projection (which is as old as philosophical thought), but we try to refine it. It has to be constructed in three steps. The first and basic step is the assertion that man, as man, experiences something unconditional in terms of the unconditional character of the moral imperative.

The second step is the recognition that the early dependence on the father, or on father figures, drives to a projection of the father image upon the screen of the unconditional.

The third step is the insight that this identification of the concrete media of the unconditional with the unconditional itself is, religiously speaking, demonic, psychologically speaking, neurotic. Education and psychotherapy can and must dissolve this kind of father image, but they cannot dissolve the element of the unconditional itself, for this is essentially human.

Since the ethical authorities are not absolute (in spite of the absolute character of the moral imperative), every moral act includes a risk. The human situation itself is such a risk. In order to become human, man must trespass the "state of innocence," but when he has trespassed it he finds himself in a state of self-contradiction. This situation, which is a permanent one, is symbolized in the story of the Paradise. Man must always trespass the safety regions which are circumscribed by ethical authorities. He must enter the spheres of unsafety and uncertainty. A morality which plays safe, by subjecting itself to an unconditional authority, is suspect. It has not the courage to take guilt and tragedy upon itself. True morality is a morality of risk. It is a morality which is based on the "courage to be," the dynamic self-affirmation of man as man. This self-affirmation must take the threat of nonbeing, death, guilt, and meaninglessness into itself. It risks itself, and through the courage of risking itself, it wins itself. Moralisms give safety, morality lives in the unsafety of risk and courage.

III. MORALISMS OF LAW AND MORALITY OF GRACE

Because the moral imperative puts our essential against our actual being, it appears to us as law. A being which lives out of its essential nature is law to itself. It follows its natural structure. But this is not the human situation. Man is estranged from his essential being and, therefore, the moral imperative appears as law to him: Moralism is legalism!

The law is first of all "natural law." In the Stoic tradition this term does not mean the physical laws but the natural laws which constitute our essential nature. These laws are the background of all positive laws in states and other groups. They are also the background of the moral law, which is our problem today. The moral law is more oppressive than the severest positive law, just because it is internalized. It creates conscience and the feeling of guilt.

So we must ask: What is the power inducing us to fulfill the law? The power behind the positive laws is rewards and punishments. What is the power behind the moral law? One could say: the reward of the good and the punishment of the uneasy conscience, often projected as heavenly rewards and punishments in purgatory or hell. (Cf. Hamlet's words about the conscience, which makes cowards of us.) But this answer is not sufficient. It does not explain the insuperable resistance the law provokes against itself, in spite of punishments and rewards. The law is not able to create its own fulfillment.

The reason for this is visible when we consider the words of Jesus, Paul, and Luther saying that the law is only fulfilled if it is fulfilled with joy, and not with resentment and hate. But joy cannot be commanded. The law brings us into a paradoxical situation: It commands, which means that it stands against us. But it commands something which can be done only if it does *not* stand against us, if we are united with what it commands. This is the point where the moral imperative drives towards something which is not command but reality. Only the "good tree" brings "good fruits." Only if being precedes that which ought-to-be, can the ought-to-be be fulfilled. Morality can be maintained only through that which is given and not through that which is demanded; in religious terms, through grace and not through law. Without the reunion of man with his own essential nature no perfect moral act is possible. Legalism drives either to self-complacency (I have kept *all* commandments) or to despair (I cannot keep *any* commandment). Moralism of law makes pharisees or cynics, or it produces in the majority of people an indifference which lowers the moral imperative to conventional behavior. Moralism necessarily ends in the quest for grace.

Grace unites two elements: the overcoming of guilt and the overcoming of estrangement. The first element appears in theology as the "forgiveness of sins," or in more recent terminology, as "accepting acceptance though being unacceptable." The second element appears in theology as "regeneration" or in more recent terminology, as the "entering into the new being" which is above the split between what we are and what we ought to be. Every religion, even if seemingly moralistic, has a doctrine of salvation in which these two elements are present.

And psychotherapy is involved in the same problems. Psychotherapy is definitely antimoralistic. It avoids commandments because it knows that neurotics cannot be healed by moral judgments and moral demands. The only help is to accept him who is unacceptable, to create a communion with him, a sphere of participation in a new reality. Psychotherapy must be a therapy of grace or it cannot be therapy at all. There are striking analogies between the recent methods of mental healing and the traditional ways of personal salvation. But there is also one basic difference. Psychotherapy can liberate one from a special difficulty. Religion shows to him who is liberated, and has to decide about the meaning and aim of his existence, a final way. This difference is decisive for the independence as well as for the co-operation of religion and psychotherapy.

IV. MORALISMS OF JUSTICE AND MORALITY OF LOVE

The moral imperative expresses itself in laws which are supposed to be just. Justice, in Greek thinking, is the unity of the whole system of morals. Justice, in the Old Testament, is that quality of God which makes Him the Lord of the Universe. In Islam, morality and law are not distinguished, and in the philosophy of Hegel, ethics are treated as a section of the philosophy of law (*Recht*). Every system of moral commandments is, at the same time, the basis for a system of laws. In all moralisms the moral imperative has the tendency to become a legal principle. Justice, in Aristotle, is determined by proportionality. Everybody gets what he deserves according to quantitative measurements. This is not the Christian point of view. Justice, in the Old Testament, is the activity of God toward the fulfillment of His promises. And justice, in the New Testament, is the unity of judgment and forgiveness. Justification by grace is the highest form of divine justice. This means that proportional justice is not the answer to the moral problem. Not proportional, but transforming justice has divine character. In other words: Justice is fulfilled in love. The moralisms of justice drive toward the morality of love.

Love, in the sense of this statement, is not an emotion, but a principle of life. If love were primarily emotion it would inescapably conflict with justice, it would add something to justice which is not justice. But love does not add something strange to justice. Rather it is the ground, the power, and the aim of justice. Love is the life which separates itself from itself and drives toward reunion with itself. The norm of justice is reunion of the estranged. Creative justice—justice, creative as love—is the union of love and justice and the ultimate principle of morality.

From this it follows that there is a just self-love, namely the desire of reunion of oneself with oneself. One can be loveless toward oneself. But if this is the case, one is not only without love but also without justice toward oneself—and toward others. One must accept oneself just as one is accepted in spite of being unacceptable. And in doing so one has what is called the right self-love, the opposite of the wrong self-love. In order to avoid many confusions one should replace the word self-love completely. One may call the right self-love self-acceptance, the wrong self-love selfishness, and the natural self-love self-affirmation. In all cases the word "self," as such, has no negative connotations. It is the structure of the most developed form of reality, the most individualized and the most universal being. Self is good, self-affirmation is good, self-acceptance is good, but selfishness is bad because it prevents both self-affirmation and self-acceptance.

Love is the answer to the problem of moralisms and morality. It answers the questions implied in all four confrontations of moralism and morality. Love is unconditional. There is nothing which could condition it by a higher principle. There is nothing above love. And love conditions itself. It enters every concrete situation and works for the reunion of the separated in a unique way.

Love transforms the moralisms of authority into a morality of risk. Love is creative and creativity includes risk. Love does not destroy factual authority but it liberates from the authority of a special place, from an irrational hypostatized authority. Love participates, and participation overcomes authority.

Love is the source of grace. Love accepts that which is unacceptable and love renews the old being so that it becomes a new being. Medieval theology almost identified love and grace, and rightly so, for that which makes one graceful is love. But grace is, at the same time, the love which forgives and accepts.

Nevertheless, love includes justice. Love without justice is a body without a backbone. The justice of love includes that no partner in this relation is asked to annihilate himself. The self which enters a love relation is preserved in its independence. Love includes justice to others and to oneself. Love is the solution of the problem: moralisms and morality.

*Morality and Beyond**

The Religious Dimension of the Moral Imperative

. . . To understand the meaning of the phrase "moral imperative," we must distinguish the three basic functions of the human spirit: morality, culture, and religion. When we call them functions of man's "spirit," we point to the dynamic unity of body and mind, of vitality and rationality, of the conscious and the unconscious, of the emotional and the intellectual. In every function of the human spirit the whole person is involved, and not merely one part or one element. As I have often insisted, we must revive the term "spirit" as designating a natural quality of man. It cannot be replaced by "mind" because "mind" is overweighted by its intellectual aspect.

None of the three functions of the spirit ever appears in isolation from the other two. They must be distinguished, nonetheless, because they are able to relate to each other in many different ways. Most concisely, we might say: morality is the constitution of the bearer of the spirit, the centered person; culture points to the creativity of the spirit and also to the totality of its creations; and religion is the self-transcendence of the spirit toward what is ultimate and unconditioned in being and meaning. . . .

The moral act establishes man as a person, and as a bearer of the spirit. It is the unconditional character of the moral imperative that gives ultimate seriousness both to culture and to religion. Without it culture would deteriorate into an aesthetic or utilitarian enterprise, and religion into an emotional distortion of mysticism. It was the prophetic message, as recorded in the Old Testament, that contrasted the moral imperative, in terms of the demand for justice, with both the culture and the religion of its time. The message is one of ultimate seriousness and has no equivalent in any other religion. The seriousness of Christianity depends upon it, as does also any ultimate seriousness in Western culture. Science and the arts, politics, education—all become empty and self-destructive if, in their creation, the moral imperative is disregarded. The imperative exhibits itself in scientific and artistic honesty to the extent of self-sacrifice; in one's commitment to humanity and justice in social relations and political actions; and in the love of one toward the other, as a consequence of experiencing the divine love. These are examples which demonstrate that, without the immanence of the moral imperative, both culture and religion disintegrate because of lack of ultimate seriousness.

The moral imperative is the command to become what one potentially is, a *person* within a community of persons. Only man, in the limit of our experience, can become a person, because only man is a completely centered self, having himself as a self in the face of a world to which he belongs and from which he is, at the same time, separated. This dual relation to his world, belongingness and separation, makes it possible for him to ask questions and find answers, to receive and make demands. As a centered self and individual, man can respond in knowledge and action to the stimuli that reach him from the world to which he belongs; but because he also *confronts* his world, and in this sense is free from it, he can respond "responsibly," namely, after deliberation and decision rather than through a determined compulsion. This is his greatness, but also his danger: it enables him to act *against* the moral demand. He can surrender to the disintegrating forces which tend to control the personal center and to destroy its unity. . . .

Man has a world, namely, a structured whole of innumerable parts, a *cosmos,* as the Greeks called it, because of its structured character which makes it accessible to man through acts of creative receiving and transforming. Having a world is more than having environment. Of course, man, like any other being, has environment; but in contrast to the higher animals, for example, he is not bound to it. He can transcend it in any direction, in imagination, thought and action (e.g., social utopias or ontological concepts or space exploration). Man has "world" through every part of his environment. His encounter with any of the objects surrounding him is always an encounter with the universe manifest in a particular object. Man never encounters *this* tree only as *this* tree, but also as *tree,* one of many trees, as an example of the species tree (in itself a special manifestation of the universal power of being).

Such an encounter presupposes freedom from the particular, and the ability to see the universal within the particular. The manifestation of this freedom is language. Language lives in universals. It is one and the same thing to have world, to transcend environment, and to speak in concepts and meaningful propositions. All this constitutes man's essential freedom and is the presupposition of man's experience of the moral imperative.

The moral imperative is the demand to become actually what one is essentially and therefore potentially. It is the power of man's being, given to him by nature, which he shall actualize in time and space. His true being shall become his actual being—this is the moral imperative. And since his true being is the being of a person in a community of persons, the moral imperative has this content: to become a person. Every moral act is an act in which an individual self establishes itself as a person.

Therefore, a moral act is not an act in obedience to an external law, human or divine. It is the inner law of our true being, of our essential or created nature, which demands that we actualize what follows from it. And an antimoral act is not the transgression of one or several precisely circumscribed commands, but an act that contradicts the self-realization of the person as a person and drives toward disintegration. It disrupts the centeredness of the person by giving predominance to partial trends, passions, desires, fears, and anxieties. The central control is weakened, often almost removed. And when this happens, and other partial trends also aspire to predominance, the self is split, and the conflicting trends make it their battlefield. The "will," in the sense of a self that acts from the centered totality of its being, is enslaved. Freedom is replaced by compulsion. Deliberation and decision, the hallmarks of freedom, become façades for overwhelming drives that predetermine the decision. The voice of man's essential being is silenced, step by step; and his disintegrating self, his depersonalization, shows the nature of the antimoral act and, by contrast, the nature of the moral act.

The moral act as the self-actualization of the centered self or the constitution of the person as a person, has analogies in the realm of all living beings, including man from the biological point of view. The analogy to the diminution or loss of centeredness in man is the psychosomatic phenomenon of disease. In disease, some processes that are necessary elements in the whole of a life process take an independent course and endanger the functioning of the whole. The cancerous growth of parts of the body is the most illuminating analogy to what happens in the centered self when particular trends conquer the center and destroy the unity of balanced trends. The analogy between the antimoral act and bodily disease is in many (somehow in all) cases more than an analogy. Both are expressions of the universal ambiguity of life, according to which the processes of self-integration are continuously combated by movements toward disintegration. For the ethical problem this means that the moral act is always a victory over disintegrating forces and that its aim is the actualization of man as a centered and therefore free person. . . .

The "Will of God" for us is precisely our essential being with all its potentialities, our created nature declared as "very good" by God, as, in terms of the Creation myth, He "saw everything that he made." For us the "Will of God" is manifest in our essential being; and only because of this can we accept the moral imperative as valid. It is not a strange law that demands our obedience, but the "silent voice" of our own nature as man, and as man with an individual character.

But we must go one further step. We can say: to fulfill one's own nature is certainly a moral demand intrinsic in one's being. But why is it an unconditional imperative? Do I not have the right to leave my potentialities unfulfilled, to remain less than a person, to contradict my essential goodness, and thus to destroy myself? As a being that has the freedom of self-contradiction, I should have the right to this possibility, and to waste myself! The moral imperative is unconditional only if I choose to affirm my own essential nature, and *this is* a condition! The answer to this argument is the experience that has been expressed in the doctrine of the infinite value of every human soul in the view of the Eternal. It is not an external prohibition against self-destruction—bodily, psychologically, or morally—that we experience in states of despair, but the silent voice of our own being which denies us the right to self-destruction. It is the awareness of our belonging to a dimension that transcends our own finite freedom and our ability to affirm or to negate ourselves. So I maintain my basic assertion that the unconditional character of the moral imperative is its religious quality. No religious heteronomy, subjection to external commands, is implied if we maintain the immanence of religion in the moral command.

JEAN-PAUL SARTRE

Jean-Paul Sartre (1905–   ) received his philosophical education at the École Normale Supérieure in Paris. He has taught philosophy, chiefly at the Lycée Condorcet, but he left teaching in 1944 to devote himself to writing and editing. He served in the French Army in the Second World War and was both a prisoner of war (1940–1941) and a member of the Resistance (1941–1944).

He began his philosophical career as a phenomenologist and later came to see phenomenology as a method for developing the insights of existentialism. His philosophical reputation rests chiefly on his technical works especially Being and Nothingness, *but he has expressed his views in a variety of other literary forms: criticism, plays, screenplays, short stories, and novels.*

*Existentialism Is a Humanism**

Atheistic existentialism, which I represent, . . . states that if God does not exist, there is at least one being in whom existence precedes essence, a being who exists before he can be defined by any concept, and that this being is man, or, as Heidegger says, human reality. What is meant here by saying that existence precedes essence? It means that, first of all, man exists, turns up, appears on the scene, and, only afterwards, defines himself. If man, as the existentialist conceives him, is indefinable, it is because at first he is nothing. Only afterward will he be something, and he himself will have made what he will be. Thus, there is no human nature, since there is no God to conceive it. Not only is man what he conceives himself to be, but he is also only what he wills himself to be after this thrust toward existence.

Man is nothing else but what he makes of himself. Such is the first principle of existentialism. It is also what is called subjectivity, the name we are labeled with when charges are brought against us. But what do we mean by this, if not that man has a greater dignity than a stone or table? For we mean that man first exists, that is, that man first of all is the being who hurls himself toward a future and who is conscious of imagining himself as being in the future. Man is at the start a plan which

* By permission. From Jean-Paul Sartre, *Existentialism*, trans. by Bernard Frechtman, Philosophical Library, New York, 1947.

is aware of itself, rather than a patch of moss, a piece of garbage, or a cauliflower; nothing exists prior to this plan; there is nothing in heaven; man will be what he will have planned to be. . . . Thus, existentialism's first move is to make every man aware of what he is and to make the full responsibility of his existence rest on him. And when we say that a man is responsible for himself, we do not only mean that he is responsible for his own individuality, but that he is responsible for all men.

The word subjectivism has two meanings, and our opponents play on the two. Subjectivism means, on the one hand, that an individual chooses and makes himself; and, on the other, that it is impossible for man to transcend human subjectivity. The second of these is the essential meaning of existentialism. When we say that man chooses his own self, we mean that every one of us does likewise; but we also mean by that that in making this choice he also chooses all men. In fact, in creating the man that we want to be, there is not a single one of our acts which does not at the same time create an image of man as we think he ought to be. To choose to be this or that is to affirm at the same time the value of what we choose, because we can never choose evil. We always choose the good, and nothing can be good for us without being good for all.

If, on the other hand, existence precedes essence, and if we grant that we exist and fashion our image at one and the same time, the image is valid for everybody and for our whole age. Thus, our responsibility is much greater than we might have supposed, because it involves all mankind. If I am a workingman and choose to join a Christian trade-union rather than be a communist, and if by being a member I want to show that the best thing for man is resignation, that the kingdom of man is not of this world, I am not only involving my own case—I want to be resigned for everyone. As a result, my action has involved all humanity. To take a more individual matter, if I want to marry, to have children; even if this marriage depends solely on my own circumstances or passion or wish, I am involving all humanity in monogamy and not merely myself. Therefore, I am responsible for myself and for everyone else. I am creating a certain image of man of my own choosing. In choosing myself, I choose man.

This helps us understand what the actual content is of such rather grandiloquent words as anguish, forlornness, despair. As you will see, it's all quite simple.

First, what is meant by anguish? The existentialists say at once that man is anguish. What that means is this: the man who involves himself and who realizes that he is not only the person he chooses to be, but also a lawmaker who is, at the same time, choosing all mankind as well as himself, can not help escape the feeling of his total and deep responsibility. . . .

When we speak of forlornness, a term Heidegger was fond of, we mean only that God does not exist and that we have to face all the consequences of this. The existentialist is strongly opposed to a certain kind of secular ethics which would like to abolish God with the least possible expense. About 1880, some French teachers tried to set up a secular ethics which went something like this: God is a useless and costly hypothesis; we are discarding it; but, meanwhile, in order for there to be an ethics, a society, a civilization, it is essential that certain values be taken seriously and that they be considered as having an *a priori* existence. It must be obligatory, *a priori* to be honest, not to lie, not to beat your wife, to have children, etc., etc. So we're going to try a little device which will make it posible to show that values exist all the same, inscribed in a heaven of ideas, though otherwise God does not exist. In other words—and this, I believe, is the tendency of everything called reformism in France—nothing will be changed if God does not exist. We shall find ourselves with the same norms of honesty, progress, and humanism, and we shall have made of God an outdated hypothesis which will peacefully die off by itself.

The existentialist, on the contrary, thinks it very distressing that God does not exist, because all possibility of finding values in a heaven of ideas disappears along with Him; there can no longer be an *a priori* Good, since there is no infinite and perfect consciousness to think it. Nowhere is it written that the Good exists, that we must be honest, that we must not lie; because the fact is we are on a plane where there are only men. Dostoievsky said, "If God didn't exist, everything would be possible." That is the very starting point of existentialism. Indeed, everything is permissible if God does not exist, and as a result man is forlorn, because neither within him nor without does he find anything to cling to. He can't start making excuses for himself.

If existence really does precede essence, there is no explaining things away by reference to a fixed and given human nature. In other words, there is no determinism, man is free, man is freedom. On the other hand, if God does not exist, we find no values or commands to turn to which legitimize our conduct. So, in the bright realm of values, we have no excuse behind us, nor justification before us. We are alone, with no excuses.

That is the idea I shall try to convey when I say that man is condemned to be free. Condemned, because he did not create himself, yet, in other respects is free; because, once thrown into the world, he is responsible for everything he does. The existentialist does not believe in the power of passion. He will never agree that a sweeping passion is a ravaging torrent which fatally leads a man to certain acts and is therefore an excuse. He thinks that man is responsible for his passion.

The existentialist does not think that man is going to help himself by finding in the world some omen by which to orient himself. Because he thinks that man will interpret the omen to suit himself. Therefore, he thinks that man, with no support and no aid, is condemned every moment to invent man. . . .

To give you an example which will enable you to understand forlornness better, I shall cite the case of one of my students who came to see me under the following circumstances: his father was on bad terms with his mother, and, moreover, was inclined to be a collaborationist; his older brother had been killed in the German offensive of 1940, and the young man, with somewhat immature but generous feelings, wanted to avenge him. His mother lived alone with him, very much upset by the half-treason of her husband and the death of her older son; the boy was her only consolation.

The boy was faced with the choice of leaving for England and joining the Free French Forces—that is, leaving his mother behind—or remaining with his mother and helping her to carry on. He was fully aware that the woman lived only for him and that his going off—and perhaps his death—would plunge her into despair. He was also aware that every act that he did for his mother's sake was a sure thing, in the sense that it was helping her to carry on, whereas every effort he made toward going off and fighting was an uncertain move which might run aground and prove completely useless; for example, on his way to England he might, while passing through Spain, be detained indefinitely in a Spanish camp; he might reach England or Algiers and be stuck in an office at a desk job. As a result, he was faced with two very different kinds of action: one, concrete, immediate, but concerning only one individual; the other concerned an incomparably vaster group, a national collectivity, but for that very reason was dubious, and might be interrupted en route. And, at the same time, he was wavering between two kinds of ethics. On the one hand, an ethics of sympathy, of personal devotion; on the other, a broader ethics, but one whose efficacy was more dubious. He had to choose between the two.

Who could help him choose? Christian doctrine? No. Christian doctrine says, "Be charitable, love your neighbor, take the more rugged path, etc., etc." But which is the more rugged path? Whom should he love as a brother? The fighting man or his mother? Which does the greater good, the vague act of fighting in a group, or the concrete one helping a particular human being to go on living? Who can decide *a priori*? Nobody. No book of ethics can tell him. The Kantian ethics says, "Never treat any person as a means, but as an end." Very well, if I stay with my mother, I'll treat her as an end and not as a means; but by virtue of this very fact, I'm running the risk of treating the people around me who are fighting, as means; and, conversely, if I go to join those who are fighting, I'll be treating them as an end, and, by doing that, I run the risk of treating my mother as a means.

If values are vague, and if they are always too broad for the concrete and specific case that we are considering, the only thing left for us is to trust our instincts. That's what this young man tried to do; and when I saw him, he said, "In the end, feeling is what counts. I ought to choose whichever pushes me in one direction. If I feel that I love my mother enough to sacrifice everything else for her —my desire for vengeance, for action, for adventure—then I'll stay with her. If, on the contrary, I feel that my love for my mother isn't enough, I'll leave."

But how is the value of a feeling determined? What gives his feeling for his mother value? Precisely the fact that he remained with her. I may say that I like so-and-so well enough to sacrifice a certain amount of money for him, but I may say so only if I've done it. I may say "I love my mother well enough to remain with her" if I have remained with her. The only way to determine the value of this affection is, precisely, to perform an act which confirms and defines it. But, since I require this affection to justify my act, I find myself caught in a vicious circle. . . .

As for despair, the term has a very simple meaning. It means that we shall confine ourselves to reckoning only with what depends upon our will, or on the ensemble of probabilities which make our action possible. When we want something, we always have to reckon with probabilities. I may be counting on the arrival of a friend. The friend is coming by rail or street-car; this supposes that the train will arrive on schedule, or that the street-car will not jump the track. I am left in the realm of possibility; but possibilities are to be reckoned with only to the point where my action comports with the ensemble of these possibilities, and no further. The moment the possibilities I am considering are not rigorously involved by my action, I ought to disengage myself from them, because no God, no scheme, can adapt the world and its possibilities to my will. . . .

Quietism is the attitude of people who say, "Let others do what I can't do." The doctrine I am presenting is the very opposite of quietism, since it declares, "There is no reality except in action." Moreover, it goes further, since it adds, "Man is nothing else than his plan; he exists only to the extent that he fulfills himself; he is therefore nothing else than the ensemble of his acts, nothing else than his life."

According to this, we can understand why our doctrine horrifies certain people. Because often the only way they can bear their wretchedness is to think, "Circumstances have been against me. What I've been and done doesn't show my true worth. To be sure, I've had no great love, no great friendship, but that's because I haven't met a man or woman who was worthy. The books I've written haven't been very good because I haven't had the proper leisure. I haven't had children to devote myself to because I didn't find a man with whom I could have spent my life. So there remains within me, unused and quite viable, a host of propensities, inclinations, possibilities, that one wouldn't guess from the mere series of things I've done."

Now, for the existentialist there is really no love other than one which manifests itself in a person's being in love. There is no genius other than one which is expressed in works of art; the genius of Proust is the sum of Proust's works; the genius of Racine is his series of tragedies. Outside of that, there is nothing. Why say that Racine could have written another tragedy, when he didn't write it? A man is involved in life, leaves his impress on it, and outside of that there is nothing. To be sure, this may seem a harsh thought to someone whose life hasn't been a success. But, on the other hand, it prompts people to understand that reality alone is what counts, that dreams, expectations, and hopes warrant no more than to define a man as a disappointed dream, as miscarried hopes, as vain expectations. In other words, to define him negatively and not positively. However, when we say, "You are nothing else than your life," that does not imply that the artist will be judged solely on the basis of his works of art; a thousand other things will contribute toward summing him up. What we mean is that a man is nothing else than a series of undertakings, that he is the sum, the organization, the ensemble of the relationships which make up these undertakings. . . .

What art and ethics have in common is that we have creation and invention in both cases. We can not decide *a priori* what there is to be done. I think that I pointed that out quite sufficiently when I mentioned the case of the student who came to see me, and who might have applied to all the ethical systems, Kantian or otherwise, without getting any sort of guidance. He was obliged to devise his law himself. Never let it be said by us that this man—who, taking affection, individual action, and kind-heartedness toward a specific person as his ethical first principle, chooses to remain with his mother, or who, preferring to make a sacrifice, chooses to go to England—has made an arbitrary choice. Man makes himself. He isn't ready made at the start. In choosing his ethics, he makes himself, and force of circumstances is such that he can not abstain from choosing one. We define man only in relationship to involvement. It is therefore absurd to charge us with arbitrariness of choice.

In the second place, it is said that we are unable to pass judgment on others. In a way this is true, and in another way, false. It is true in this sense, that, whenever a man sanely and sincerely involves himself and chooses his configuration, it is impossible for him to prefer another configuration, regardless of what his own may be in other respects. It is true in this sense, that we do not believe in progress. Progress is betterment. Man is always the same. The situation confronting him varies. Choice always remains a choice in a situation. The problem has not changed since the time one could choose between those for and those against slavery, for example, at the time of the Civil War, and the present time, when one can side with the Maquis Resistance Party, or with the Communists.

But, nevertheless, one can still pass judgment, for, as I have said, one makes a choice in relationship to others. First, one can judge (and this is perhaps not a judgment of value, but a logical judgment) that certain choices are based on error and others on truth. If we have defined man's situation as a free choice, with no excuses and no recourse, every man who takes refuge behind the excuse of his passions, every man who sets up a determinism, is a dishonest man.

The objection may be raised, "But why mayn't he choose himself dishonestly?" I reply that I am not obliged to pass moral judgment on him, but that I do define his dishonesty as an error. One can not help considering the truth of the matter. Dishonesty is obviously a falsehood because it belies the complete freedom of involvement. On the same grounds, I maintain that there is also dishonesty if I choose to state that certain values exist prior to me; it is self-contradictory for me to want them and at the same state that they are imposed on me. Suppose someone says to me, "What if I want to be dishonest?" I'll answer, "There's no reason for you not to be, but I'm saying that that's what you are, and that the strictly coherent attitude is that of honesty."

Besides, I can bring moral judgment to bear. When I declare that freedom in every concrete circumstance can have no other aim than to want itself, if man has once become aware that in his forlornness he imposes values, he can no longer want but one thing, and that is freedom, as the basis of all values. That doesn't mean that he wants it in the abstract. It means simply that the ultimate meaning of the acts of honest men is the quest for freedom as such. A man who belongs to a communist or revolutionary union wants concrete goals; these goals imply an abstract desire for freedom; but this freedom is wanted in something concrete. We want freedom for freedom's sake and in every particular circumstance. And in wanting freedom we discover that it depends entirely on the freedom of others, and that the freedom of others depends on ours. Of course, freedom as the definition of man does not depend on others, but as soon as there is involvement, I am obliged to want others to have freedom at the same time that I want my own freedom. I can take freedom as my goal only if I take that of others as a goal as well. Consequently, when, in all honesty, I've recognized that man is a being in whom existence precedes essence, that he is a free being who, in various circumstances, can want only his freedom, I have at the same time recognized that I can want only the freedom of others.

Therefore in the name of this will for freedom, which freedom itself implies, I may pass judgment on those who seek to hide from themselves the complete arbitrariness and the complete freedom of their existence. Those who hide their complete freedom from themselves out of a spirit of seriousness or by means of deterministic excuses, I shall call cowards; those who try to show that their existence was necessary, when it is the very contingency of man's appearance on earth, I shall call stinkers. But cowards or stinkers can be judged only from a strictly unbiased point of view.

Therefore though the content of ethics is variable, a certain form of it is universal. Kant says that freedom desires both itself and the freedom of others. Granted. But he believes that the formal and the universal are enough to constitute an ethics. We, on the other hand, think that principles which are too abstract run aground in trying to decide action. Once again, take the case of the student. In the name of what, in the name of what great moral maxim do you think he could have decided, in perfect peace of mind, to abandon his mother or to stay with her? There is no way of judging. The content is always concrete and thereby unforeseeable; there is always the element of invention. The one thing that counts is knowing whether the inventing that has been done, has been done in the name of freedom.

*Being and Nothingness**

BAD FAITH AND FALSEHOOD

The human being is not only the being by whom *négatités*[1] are disclosed in

* By permission. From Jean-Paul Sartre, *Being and Nothingness*, trans. by Hazel Barnes, Philosophical Library, New York, and Literary Masterworks, Inc., New York, 1956.

[1] Sartre's word for types of human activity which while not obviously involving a negative judgment nevertheless contain negativity as an integral part of their structure; e.g., experiences involving absence, change, interrogation, destruction.

the world; he is also the one who can take negative attitudes with respect to himself. In our Introduction we defined consciousness as "a being such that in its being, its being is in question in so far as this being implies a being other than itself." But now that we have examined the meaning of "the question," we can at present also write the formula thus: "Consciousness is a being, the nature of which is to be conscious of the nothingness of its being." In a prohibition or a veto, for example, the human being denies a future transcendence. But this negation is not explicative. My consciousness is not restricted to *envisioning* a *négatité*. It constitutes itself in its own flesh as the nihilation of a possibility which another human reality projects as *its* possibility. For that reason it must arise in the world as a *Not;* it is as a Not that the slave first apprehends the master, or that the prisoner who is trying to escape sees the guard who is watching him. There are even men (*e.g.*, caretakers, overseers, gaolers) whose social reality is uniquely that of the Not, who will live and die, having forever been only a Not upon the earth. Others so as to make the Not a part of their very subjectivity, establish their human personality as a perpetual negation. This is the meaning and function of what Scheler calls "the man of resentment"—in reality, the Not. But there exist more subtle behaviors, the description of which will lead us further into the inwardness of consciousness. Irony is one of these. In irony a man annihilates what he posits within one and the same act; he leads us to believe in order not to be believed; he affirms to deny and denies to affirm; he creates a positive object but it has no being other than its nothingness. Thus attitudes of negation toward the self permit us to raise a new question: What are we to say is the being of man who has the possibility of denying himself? But it is out of the question to discuss the attitude of "self-negation" in its universality. The kinds of behavior which can be ranked under this heading are too diverse; we risk retaining only the abstract form of them. It is best to choose and to examine one determined attitude which is essential to human reality and which is such that consciousness instead of directing its negation outward turns it toward itself. This attitude, it seems to me, is *bad faith* (*mauvaise foi*).

Frequently this is identified with falsehood. We say indifferently of a person that he shows signs of bad faith or that he lies himself. We shall willingly grant that bad faith is a lie to oneself, on condition that we distinguish the lie to oneself from lying in general. Lying is a negative attitude, we will agree to that. But this negation does not bear on consciousness itself; it aims only at the transcendent. The essence of the lie implies in fact that the liar actually is in complete possession of the truth which he is hiding. A man does not lie about what he is ignorant of; he does not lie when he spreads an error of which he himself is the dupe; he does not lie when he is mistaken. The ideal description of the liar would be a cynical consciousness, affirming truth within himself, denying it in his words, and denying that negation as such. Now this doubly negative attitude rests on the transcendent; the fact expressed is transcendent since it does not exist, and the original negation rests on a *truth;* that is, on a particular type of transcendence. As for the inner negation which I effect correlatively with the affirmation for myself of the truth, this rests on *words;* that is, on an event in the world. Furthermore the inner disposition of the liar is positive; it could be the object of an affirmative judgment. The liar intends to deceive and he does not seek to hide this intention from himself nor to disguise the translucency of consciousness; on the contrary, he has recourse to it when there is a question of deciding secondary behavior. It explicitly exercises a regulatory control over all attitudes. As for his flaunted intention of telling the truth ("I'd never want to deceive you! This is true! I swear it!")—all this, of course, is the object of an inner negation, but also it is not recognized by the liar as *his* intention. It is played, imitated, it is the intention of the character which he plays in the eyes of his questioner, but this character, precisely because he *does not exist,* is a transcendent. Thus the lie does not put into the play the inner structure of present consciousness; all the negations which constitute it bear on objects which by this fact are removed from consciousness. The lie then does not require special ontological foundation, and the explanations which the existence of negation in general requires are valid without change in the case of deceit. Of course we have described the ideal lie; doubtless it happens often enough that the liar is more or less the victim of his lie, that he half persuades himself of it. But these common, popular forms of the lie are also degenerate aspects of it; they represent intermediaries between falsehood and bad faith. The lie is a behavior of transcendence.

The lie is also a normal phenomenon of what Heidegger calls the "*Mit-sein.*"[2] It presupposes my existence, the existence of the *Other,* my experience *for* the Other, and the existence of the Other *for* me. Thus there is no difficulty in holding that the liar must make the project of the lie in entire clarity and that he must possess a complete comprehension of the lie and of the truth which he is altering. It is sufficient that an over-all opacity hide his intentions from the *Other;* it is sufficient that the Other can take the lie for truth. By the lie consciousness affirms that it exists by nature as *hidden from the Other;* it utilizes for its own profit the ontological duality of myself and myself in the eyes of the Other.

The situation can not be the same for bad faith if this, as we have said, is indeed a lie to oneself. To be sure, the one who practices bad faith is hiding a displeasing truth or presenting as truth a pleasing untruth. Bad faith then has in appearance the structure of falsehood. Only what changes everything is the fact that in bad faith it is from myself that I am hiding the truth. Thus the duality of the deceiver and the deceived does not exist here. Bad faith on the contrary implies in essence the unity of a *single* consciousness. This does not mean that it can not be conditioned by the *Mit-sein* like all other phenomena of human reality, but the *Mit-sein* can call forth bad faith only by presenting itself as *a situation* which bad faith permits surpassing; bad faith does not come from outside to human reality. One does not undergo his bad faith; one is not infected with it; it is not a *state.* But consciousness affects itself with bad faith. There must be an original intention and a project of bad faith; this project implies a comprehension of bad faith as such and a pre-reflective apprehension (of) consciousness as affecting itself with bad faith. It follows first that the one to whom the lie is told and the one who lies are one and the same person, which means that I must know in my capacity as deceiver the truth which is hidden from me in my capacity as the one deceived. Better yet I must know the truth very exactly *in order* to conceal it more carefully—and this not at two different moments, which at a pinch would allow us to reestablish a semblance of duality—but in the unitary structure of a single project. How then can the lie subsist if the duality which conditions it is suppressed? . . .

PATTERNS OF BAD FAITH

If we wish to get out of this difficulty, we should examine more closely the patterns of bad faith and attempt a description of them. This description will permit us perhaps to fix more exactly the conditions for the possibility of bad faith; that is, to

[2] A "being-with" others in the world. Tr.

reply to the question we raised at the outset: "What must be the being of man if he is to be capable of bad faith?"

Take the example of a woman who has consented to go out with a particular man for the first time. She knows very well the intentions which the man who is speaking to her cherishes regarding her. She knows also that it will be necessary sooner or later for her to make a decision. But she does not want to realize the urgency; she concerns herself only with what is respectful and discreet in the attitude of her companion. She does not apprehend this conduct as an attempt to achieve what we call "the first approach"; that is, she does not want to see possibilities of temporal development which his conduct presents. She restricts this behavior to what is in the present; she does not wish to read in the phrases which he addresses to her anything other than their explicit meaning. If he says to her, "I find you so attractive!" she disarms this phrase of its sexual background; she attaches to the conversation and to the behavior of the speaker, the immediate meanings, which she imagines as objective qualities. The man who is speaking to her appears to her sincere and respectful as the table is round or square, as the wall coloring is blue or gray. The qualities thus attached to the person she is listening to are in this way fixed in a permanence like that of things, which is no other than the projection of the present of the qualities into the temporal flux. This is because she does not quite know what she wants. She is profoundly aware of the desire which she inspires, but the desire cruel and naked would humiliate and horrify her. Yet she would find no charm in a respect which would be only respect. In order to satisfy her, there must be a feeling which is addressed wholly to her *personality—i.e.,* to her full freedom—and which would be a recognition of her freedom. But at the same time this feeling must be wholly desire; that is, it must address itself to her body as object. This time then she refuses to apprehend the desire for what it is; she does not even give it a name; she recognizes it only to the extent that it transcends itself toward admiration, esteem, respect and that it is wholly absorbed in the more refined forms which it produces, to the extent of no longer figuring anymore as a sort of warmth and density. But then suppose he takes her hand. This act of her companion risks changing the situation by calling for an immediate decision. To leave the hand there is to consent in herself to flirt, to engage herself. To withdraw it is to break the troubled and unstable harmony which gives the hour its charm. The aim is to postpone the moment of decision as long as possible. We know what happens next; the young woman leaves her hand there, but she *does not notice* that she is leaving it. She does not notice because it happens by chance that she is at this moment all intellect. She draws her companion up to the most lofty regions of sentimental speculation; she speaks of Life, of her life, she shows herself in her essential aspect—a personality, a consciousness. And during this time the divorce of the body from the soul is accomplished; the hand rests inert between the warm hands of her companion —neither consenting nor resisting—a thing.

We shall say that this woman is in bad faith. But we see immediately that she uses various procedures in order to maintain herself in this bad faith. She has disarmed the actions of her companion by reducing them to being only what they are; that is, to existing in the mode of the in-itself. But she permits herself to enjoy his desire, to the extent that she will apprehend it as not being what it is, will recognize its transcendence. Finally while sensing profoundly the presence of her own body—to the degree of being disturbed perhaps—she realizes herself as *not being* her own body, and she contemplates it as though from above as a passive object to which events can *happen* but which can neither provoke them nor avoid them because all its possibilities are outside of it. What unity do we find in these various aspects of bad faith? It is a certain art of forming contradictory concepts which unite in themselves both an idea and the negation of that idea. The basic concept which is thus engendered, utilizes the double property of the human being, who is at once a *facticity* and a *transcendence* These two aspects of human reality are and ought to be capable of a valid coordination. But bad faith does not wish either to coordinate them nor to surmount them in a synthesis. Bad faith seeks to affirm their identity while preserving their differences. It must affirm facticity as *being* transcendence and transcendence as *being* facticity, in such a way that at the instant when a person apprehends the one, he can find himself abruptly faced with the other. . . .

But what exactly is necessary in order for these concepts of disintegration to be able to receive even a pretence of existence, in order for them to be able to appear for an instant to consciousness, even in a process of evanescence? A quick examination of the idea of sincerity, the antithesis of bad faith, will be very instructive in this connection. Actually sincerity presents itself as a demand and consequently is not a *state.* Now what is the ideal to be attained in this case? It is necessary that a man be *for himself* only what he *is.* But is this not precisely the definition of the in-itself—or if you prefer—the principle of identity? To posit as an ideal the being of things, is this not to assert by the same stroke that this being does not belong to human reality and that the principle of identity, far from being a universal axiom universally applied, is only a synthetic principle enjoying a merely regional universality? Thus in order that the concepts of bad faith can put us under illusion at least for an instant, in order that the candor of "pure hearts" (*cf.* Gide, Kessel) can have validity for human reality as an ideal, the principle of identity must not represent a constitutive principle of human reality and human reality must not be necessarily what it is but must be able to be what it is not. What does this mean?

If man is what he is, bad faith is for ever impossible and candor ceases to be his ideal and becomes instead his being. But is man what he is? And more generally, how can he *be* what he is when he exists as consciousness of being? If candor or sincerity is a universal value, it is evident that the maxim "one must be what one is" does not serve solely as a regulating principle for judgments and concepts by which I express what I am. It posits not merely an ideal of knowing but an ideal of *being;* it proposes for us an absolute equivalence of being with itself as a prototype of being. In this sense it is necessary that we *make ourselves* what we are. But what *are* we then if we have the constant obligation to make ourselves what we are, if our mode of being is having the obligation to be what we are?

Let us consider a waiter in a café. His movement is quick and forward, a little too precise, a little too rapid. He comes toward the patrons with a step a little too quick. He bends forward a little too eagerly; his voice, his eyes express an interest a little too solicitous for the order of the customer. Finally there he returns, trying to imitate in his walk the inflexible stiffness of some kind of automaton while carrying his tray with the recklessness of a tight-rope-walker by putting it in a perpetually unstable, perpetually broken equilibrium which he perpetually reestablishes by a light movement of the arm and hand. All his behavior seems to us a game. He applies himself to chaining his movements as if they were mechanisms, the one regulating the other; his gestures and even his voice seem to be mechanisms; he gives himself the quickness and pitiless rapidity of things. He is playing, he is amusing himself. But what is he playing? We need not watch long before we can explain it: he is playing *at being* a waiter in a café. There is nothing there to surprise us. The game is a kind of marking out and investigation. The child plays with his body in order to explore it, to take inventory of it; the waiter in the café plays with his condition in order to *realize* it. This obligation is not different from that which is imposed on all tradesmen. Their condition is wholly one of ceremony. The public demands of them that they realize it as a ceremony; there is the dance of the grocer, of the tailor, of the auctioneer, by which they endeavour to persuade their clientele that they are nothing but a grocer, an auctioneer, a tailor. A grocer who dreams is offensive to the buyer, because such a grocer is not wholly a grocer. Society demands that he limit himself to his function as a grocer, just as the soldier at attention makes himself into a soldier-thing with a direct regard which does not see at all, which is no longer meant to see, since it is the rule and not the interest of the moment which determines the point he must fix his eyes on (the sight "fixed at ten paces"). There are indeed many precautions to imprison a man in what he is, as if we lived in perpetual fear that he might escape from it, that he might break away and suddenly elude his condition.

In a parallel situation, from within, the waiter in the café can not be immediately a café waiter in the sense that this inkwell *is* an inkwell, or the glass *is* a glass. It is by no means that he can not form reflective judgments or concepts concerning his condition. He knows well what it "means": the obligation of getting up at five o'clock, of sweeping the floor of the shop before the restaurant opens, of starting the coffee pot going, *etc.* He knows the rights which it allows: the right to the tips, the right to belong to a union, *etc.* But all these concepts, all these judgments refer to the transcendent. It is a matter of abstract possibilities, of rights and duties conferred on a "person possessing rights." And it is precisely this person *who I have to be* (if I am the waiter in question) and who I am not. It is not that I do not wish to be this person or that I want this person to be different. But rather there is no common measure between his being and mine. It is a "representation" for others and for myself, which means that I can be he only in *representation.* But if I represent myself as him, I am not he; I am separated from him as the object from the subject, separated *by nothing,* but this nothing isolates me from him. I can not be he, I can only play *at being* him; that is, imagine to myself that I am he. And thereby I affect him with nothingness. In vain do I fulfill the functions of a café waiter. I can be he only in the neutralized mode, as the act in Hamlet, by mechanically making the *typical gestures* of my state and by aiming at myself as an imaginary café waiter through those gestures taken as an "analogue."[3] What I attempt to realize is a being-in-itself of the café waiter, as if it were not just in my power to confer their value and their urgency upon my duties and the rights of my position, as if it were not my free choice to get up each morning at five o'clock or to remain in bed, even though it meant getting fired. As if from the very fact that I sustain this role in existence I did not transcend it on every side, as if I did not constitute myself as one *beyond* my condition. Yet there is no doubt that I *am* in a sense a café waiter—otherwise could I not just as well call myself a diplomat or a reporter? But if I am one, this can not be in the mode of being-in-itself. I am a waiter in the mode of *being what I am not. . . .*

How then can we blame another for not being sincere or rejoice in our own sincerity since this sincerity appears to us

[3] Cf. *L'Imaginaire.* Conclusion.

at the same time to be impossible? How can we in conversation, in confession, in introspection, even attempt sincerity since the effort will by its very nature be doomed to failure and since at the very time when we announce it we have a prejudicative comprehension of its futility? In introspection I try to determine exactly what I am, to make up my mind to be my true self without delay—even though it means consequently to set about searching for ways to change myself. But what does this mean if not that I am constituting myself as a thing? Shall I determine the ensemble of purposes and motivations which have pushed me to do this or that action? But this is already to postulate a causal determinism which constitutes the flow of my states of consciousness as a succession of physical states. Shall I uncover in myself "drives," even though it be to affirm them in shame? But is this not deliberately to forget that these drives are realized with my consent, that they are not forces of nature but that I lend them their efficacy by a perpetually renewed decision concerning their value? Shall I pass judgment on my character, on my nature? Is this not to veil from myself at that moment what I know only too well, that I thus judge a past to which by definition my present is not subject? The proof of this is that the same man who in sincerity posits that he is what in actuality he was, is indignant at the reproach of another and tries to disarm it by asserting that he can no longer be what he was. We are readily astonished and upset when the penalties of the court affect a man who in his new freedom *is no longer* the guilty person he was. But at the same time we require of this man that he recognize himself as *being* this guilty one. What then is sincerity except precisely a phenomenon of bad faith? Have we not shown indeed that in bad faith human reality is constituted as a being which is what it is not and which is not what it is?

Let us take an example: An homosexual frequently has an intolerable feeling of guilt, and his whole existence is determined in relation to this feeling. One will readily foresee that he is in bad faith. In fact it frequently happens that this man, while recognizing his homosexual inclination, while avowing each and every particular misdeed which he has committed, refuses with all his strength to consider himself *"a paederast."* His case is always "different," peculiar; there enters into it something of a game, of chance, of bad luck; the mistakes are all in the past; they are explained by a certain conception of the beautiful which women can not satisfy; we should see in them the results of a restless search, rather than the manifestations of a deeply rooted tendency, *etc., etc.* Here is assuredly a man in bad faith who borders on the comic since, acknowledging all the facts which are imputed to him, he refuses to draw from them the conclusion which they impose. His friend, who is his most severe critic, becomes irritated with this duplicity. The critic asks only one thing—and perhaps then he will show himself indulgent: that the guilty one recognize himself as guilty, that the homosexual declare frankly—whether humbly or boastfully matters little—"I am a paederast." We ask here: Who is in bad faith? The homosexual or the champion of sincerity?

The homosexual recognizes his faults, but he struggles with all his strength against the crushing view that his mistakes constitute for him a *destiny.* He does not wish to let himself be considered as a thing. He has an obscure but strong feeling that an homosexual is not an homosexual as this table is a table or as this red-haired man is red-haired. It seems to him that he has escaped from each mistake as soon as he has posited it and recognized it; he even feels that the psychic duration by itself cleanses him from each misdeed, constitutes for him an undetermined future, causes him to be born anew. Is he wrong? Does he not recognize in himself the peculiar, irreducible character of human reality? His attitude includes then an undeniable comprehension of truth. But at the same time he needs this perpetual rebirth, this constant escape in order to live; he must constantly put himself beyond reach in order to avoid the terrible judgment of collectivity. Thus he plays on the word *being*. He would be right actually if he understood the phrase, "I am not a paederast" in the sense of "I am not what I am." That is, if he declared to himself, "To the extent that a pattern of conduct is defined as the conduct of a paederast and to the extent that I have adopted this conduct, I am a paederast. But to the extent that human reality can not be finally defined by patterns of conduct, I am not one." But instead he slides surreptitiously towards a different connotation of the word "being." He understands "not being" in the sense of "not-being-in-itself." He lays claim to "not being a paederast" in the sense in which this table *is not* an inkwell. He is in bad faith.

But the champion of sincerity is not ignorant of the transcendence of human reality, and he knows how at need to appeal to it for his own advantage. He makes use of it even and brings it up in the present argument. Does he not wish, first in the name of sincerity, then of freedom, that the homosexual reflect on himself and acknowledge himself as an homosexual? Does he not let the other understand that such a confession will win indulgence for him? What does this mean if not that the man who will acknowledge himself as an homosexual will no longer be *the same* as the homosexual whom he acknowledges being and that he will escape into the region of freedom and of good will? The critic asks the man then to be what he is in order no longer to be what he is. It is the profound meaning of the saying, "A sin confessed is half pardoned." The critic demands of the guilty one that he constitute himself as a thing, precisely in order no longer to treat him as a thing. And this contradiction is constitutive of the demand of sincerity. Who can not see how offensive to the Other and how reassuring for me is a statement such as, "He's just a paederast," which removes a disturbing freedom from a trait and which aims at henceforth constituting all the acts of the Other as consequences following strictly from his essence. That is actually what the critic is demanding of his victim—that he constitute himself as a thing, that he should entrust his freedom to his friend as a fief, in order that the friend should return it to him subsequently—like a suzerain to his vassal. The champion of sincerity is in bad faith to the degree that in order to reassure himself, he pretends to judge, to the extent that he demands that freedom as freedom constitute itself as a thing. We have here only one episode in that battle to the death of consciousnesses which Hegel calls "the relation of the master and the slave." A person appeals to another and demands that in the name of his nature as consciousness he should radically destroy himself as consciousness, but while making this appeal he leads the other to hope for a rebirth beyond this destruction. . . .

But bad faith is not restricted to denying the qualities which I possess, to not seeing the being which I am. It attempts also to constitute myself as being what I am not. It apprehends me positively as courageous when I am not so. And that is possible, once again, only if I am what I am not; that is, if non-being in me does not have being even as non-being. Of course necessarily I *am not* courageous; otherwise bad faith would not be *bad* faith. But in addition my effort in bad faith must include the ontological comprehension that even in my usual being what I *am*, I am not it really and that there is no such difference between the being of "being-sad," for example—which I *am* in the mode of not being what I am—and the "non-being" of not-being-courageous which I wish to hide from myself. Moreover it is particularly requisite that the very negation of being should be itself the object of a perpetual nihilation, that the very meaning of "non-being" be perpetually in question in human reality. If I *were not* courageous in the way in which this inkwell is not a table; that is, if I were isolated in my cowardice, propped firmly against it, incapable of putting it in relation to its opposite, if I were not capable of *determining* myself as cowardly—that is, to deny courage to myself and thereby to escape my cowardice in the very moment that I posit it—if it were not on principle *impossible* for me to coincide with my *not-being-courageous* as well as with my being-courageous—then any project of bad faith would be prohibited me. Thus in order for bad faith to be possible, sincerity itself must be in bad faith. The condition of the possibility for bad faith is that human reality, in its most immediate being, in the intrastructure of the pre-reflective *cogito*, must be what it is not and not be what it is. . . .

FREEDOM AND RESPONSIBILITY

Although the considerations which are about to follow are of interest primarily to the ethicist, it may nevertheless be worthwhile after these descriptions and arguments to return to the freedom of the for-itself and to try to understand what the fact of this freedom represents for human destiny.

The essential consequence of our earlier remarks is that man being condemned to be free carries the weight of the whole world on his shoulders; he is responsible for the world and for himself as a way of being. We are taking the word "responsibility" in its ordinary sense as "consciousness (of) being the incontestable author of an event or of an object." In this sense the responsibility of the for-itself is overwhelming since he is the one by whom it happens that *there is* a world; since he is also the one who makes himself be, then whatever may be the situation in which he finds himself, the for-itself must wholly assume this situation with its peculiar coefficient of adversity, even though it be insupportable. He must assume the situation with the proud consciousness of being the author of it, for the very worst disadvantages or the worst threats which can endanger my person have meaning only in and through my project; and it is on the ground of the engagement which I am that they appear. It is therefore senseless to think of complaining since nothing foreign has decided what we feel, what we live, or what we are.

Furthermore this absolute responsibility is not resignation; it is simply the logical requirement of the consequences of our freedom. What happens to me happens through me, and I can neither affect myself with it nor revolt against it nor resign myself to it. Moreover everything which happens to me is *mine*. By this we must understand first of all that I am always equal to what happens to me *qua* man, for what happens to a man through other men and through himself can be only human. The most terrible situations of war, the worst tortures do not create a non-human state of things; there is no non-human situation. It is only through fear, flight, and recourse to magical types of conduct that I shall decide on the non-human, but this decision is human, and I shall carry the entire responsibility for it. But in addition the situation is *mine* because it is the image of my free choice of myself, and everything which it presents to me is *mine* in that this represents me and symbolizes me. Is it not I who decide the coefficient of adversity in things and even their unpredictability by deciding myself?

Thus there are no *accidents* in a life; a community event which suddenly bursts forth and involves me in it does not come from the outside. If I am mobilized in a war, this war is *my* war; it is in my image and I deserve it. I deserve it first because I could always get out of it by suicide or by desertion; these ultimate possibles are those which must always be present for us when there is a question of envisaging a situation. For lack of getting out of it, I have *chosen* it. This can be due to inertia, to cowardice in the face of public opinion, or because I prefer certain other values to the value of the refusal to join in the war (the good opinion of my relatives, the honor of my family, *etc.*). Anyway you look at it, it is a matter of a choice. This choice will be repeated later on again and again without a break until the end of the war. Therefore we must agree with the statement by J. Romains, "In war there are no innocent victims."[4] If therefore I have preferred war to death or to dishonor, everything takes place as if I bore the entire responsibility for this war. Of course others have declared it, and one might be tempted perhaps to consider me as a simple accomplice. But this notion of complicity has only a juridical sense, and it does not hold here. For it depended on me that for me and by me this war should not exist, and I have decided that it does exist. There was no compulsion here, for the compulsion could have got no hold on a freedom. I did not have any excuse; for as we have said repeatedly in this book, the peculiar character of human-reality is that it is without excuse. Therefore it remains for me only to lay claim to this war.

But in addition the war is *mine* because by the sole fact that it arises in a situation which I cause to be and that I can discover it there only by engaging myself for or against it, I can no longer distinguish at present the choice which I make of myself from the choice which I make of the war. To live this war is to choose myself through it and to choose it through my choice of myself. There can be no question of considering it as "four years of vacation" or as a "reprieve," as a "recess," the essential part of my responsibilities being elsewhere in my married, family, or professional life. In this war which I have chosen I choose myself from day to day, and I make it mine by making myself. If it is going to be four empty years, then it is I who bear the responsibility for this.

Finally, as we pointed out earlier, each person is an absolute choice of self from the standpoint of a world of knowledges and of techniques which this choice both assumes and illumines; each person is an absolute upsurge at an absolute date and is perfectly unthinkable at another date. It is therefore a waste of time to ask what I should have been if this war had not broken out, for I have chosen myself as one of the possible meanings of the epoch which imperceptibly led to war. I am not distinct from this same epoch; I could not be transported to another epoch without contradiction. Thus *I am* this war which restricts and limits and makes comprehensible the period which preceded it. In this sense we may define more precisely the responsibility of the for-itself if to the earlier quoted statement, "There are no innocent victims," we add the words, "We have the war we deserve." Thus, totally free, undistinguishable from the period for which I have chosen to be the meaning, as profoundly responsible for the war as if I had myself declared it, unable to live without integrating it in *my* situation, engaging myself in it wholly and stamping it with my seal, I must be without remorse or regrets as I am without excuse; for from the instant of my upsurge into being, I carry the weight of the world by myself alone without anything or any person being able to lighten it.

Yet this responsibility is of a very particular type. Someone will say, "I did

[4] J. Romains: *Les hommes de bonne volonté;* "Prélude à Verdun."

not ask to be born." This is a naive way of throwing greater emphasis on our facticity. I am responsible for everything, in fact, except for my very responsibility, for I am not the foundation of my being. Therefore everything takes place as if I were compelled to be responsible. I am *abandoned* in the world, not in the sense that I might remain abandoned and passive in a hostile universe like a board floating on the water, but rather in the sense that I find myself suddenly alone and without help, engaged in a world for which I bear the whole responsibility without being able, whatever I do, to tear myself away from this responsibility for an instant. For I am responsible for my very desire of fleeing responsibilities. To make myself passive in the world, to refuse to act upon things and upon Others is still to choose myself, and suicide is one mode among others of being-in-the-world. Yet I find an absolute responsibility for the fact that my facticity (here the fact of my birth) is directly inapprehensible and even inconceivable, for this fact of my birth never appears as a brute fact but always across a projective reconstruction of my for-itself. I am ashamed of being born or I am astonished at it or I rejoice over it, or in attempting to get rid of my life I affirm that I live and I assume this life as bad. Thus in a certain sense I *choose* being born. This choice itself is integrally affected with facticity since I am not able not to choose, but this facticity in turn will appear only in so far as I surpass it toward my ends. Thus facticity is everywhere but inapprehensible; I never encounter anything except my responsibility. That is why I can not ask, "*Why* was I born?" or curse the day of my birth or declare that I did not ask to be born, for these various attitudes toward my birth—*i.e.,* toward the *fact* that I realize a presence in the world—are absolutely nothing else but ways of assuming this birth in full responsibility and of making it *mine*. Here again I encounter only myself and my projects so that finally my abandonment—*i.e.,* my facticity—consists simply in the fact that I am condemned to be wholly responsible for myself. I am the being which *is* in such a way that in its being its being is in question. And this "is" of my being *is* as present and inapprehensible.

Under these conditions since every event in the world can be revealed to me only as an *opportunity* (an opportunity made use of, lacked, neglected, *etc.*), or better yet since everything which happens to us can be considered as a *chance* (*i.e.,* can appear to us only as way of realizing this being which is in question in our being) and since others as transcendences-transcended are themselves only *opportunities* and *chances*, the responsibility of the for-itself extends to the entire world as a peopled-world. It is precisely thus that the for-itself apprehends itself in anguish; that is, as a being which is neither the foundation of its own being nor of the Other's being nor of the in-itselfs which form the world, but a being which is compelled to decide the meaning of being—within it and everywhere outside of it. The one who realizes in anguish his condition as *being* thrown into a responsibility which extends to his very abandonment has no longer either remorse or regret or excuse; he is no longer anything but a freedom which perfectly reveals itself and whose being resides in this very revelation. But as we pointed out at the beginning of this work, most of the time we flee anguish in bad faith. . . .

ETHICAL IMPLICATIONS

Ontology itself can not formulate ethical precepts. It is concerned solely with what is, and we can not possibly derive imperatives from ontology's indicatives. It does, however, allow us to catch a glimpse of what sort of ethics will assume its responsibilities when confronted with a *human reality in situation.* Ontology has revealed to us, in fact, the origin and the nature of value; . . . value is the *lack* in relation to which the for-itself determines its being as *a lack*. . . . [Ontology] must reveal to the moral agent that he is *the being by whom values exist*. It is then that his freedom will become conscious of itself and will reveal itself in anguish as the unique source of value and the nothingness by which the *world* exists. As soon as freedom discovers the quest for being and the appropriation of the in-itself as *its own possibles*, it will apprehend by and in anguish that they are possibles only on the ground of the possibility of other possibles. But hitherto although possibles could be chosen and rejected *ad libitum*, the theme which made the unity of all choices of possibles was the value or the ideal presence of the *ens causa sui*. What will become of freedom if it turns its back upon this value? Will freedom carry this value along with it whatever it does and even in its very turning back upon the in-itself-for-itself? Will freedom be reapprehended from behind by the value which it wishes to contemplate? Or will freedom by the very fact that it apprehends itself as a freedom in relation to itself, be able to put an end to the reign of this value? In particular is it possible for freedom to take itself for a value as the source of all value, or must it necessarily be defined in relation to a transcendent value which haunts it? And in case it could will itself as its own possible and its determining value, what would this mean? A freedom which wills itself freedom is in fact a being-which-is-not-what-it-is and which-is-what-it-is-not, and which chooses as the ideal of being, being-what-it-is-not and not-being-what-it-is.

This freedom chooses then not to *recover* itself but to flee itself, not to coincide with itself but to be always at a distance *from* itself. What are we to understand by this being which wills to hold itself in awe, to be at a distance from itself? Is it a question of bad faith or of another fundamental attitude? And can one *live* this new aspect of being? In particular will freedom by taking itself for an end escape all *situation*? Or on the contrary, will it remain situated? Or will it situate itself so much the more precisely and the more individually as it projects itself further in anguish as a conditioned freedom and accepts more fully its responsibility as an existent by whom the world comes into being. All these questions, which refer us to a pure and not an accessory reflection, can find their reply only on the ethical plane. We shall devote to them a future work.

ALFRED JULES AYER

Alfred Jules Ayer (1910–) was educated at Eaton and Oxford. He became a lecturer at Christ Church, Oxford, in 1933, where he remained until the outbreak of war. He subsequently continued at Oxford until he assumed a professorship in the University of London in 1946; he later returned to Oxford. During his prewar stay at Oxford he was a visiting participant in a remarkable group of philosophers and scientists who met at the University of Vienna, the so-called "Vienna Circle." This group, which included such men as Rudolf Carnap, Herbert Feigl, Philipp Frank, and Kurt Gödel, was the fountainhead of logical positivism. These men wished to bring all knowledge into a single unified system while eliminating all unscientific speculation. The instrument for this latter part of their program was the "verifiability theory of meaning," according to which any statement is judged devoid of reference to facts unless it is possible to find observational evidence either for or against it. In the following selection, Ayer states the verifiability theory and applies it to ethical judgments.

*Language, Truth, and Logic**

THE VERIFIABILITY CRITERION OF MEANING

The criterion which we use to test the genuineness of apparent statements of fact is the criterion of verifiability. We say that a sentence is factually significant to any given person, if, and only if, he knows how to verify the proposition which it purports to express—that is, if he knows what observations would lead him, under certain conditions, to accept the proposition as being true, or reject it as being false. If, on the other hand, the putative proposition is of such a character that the assumption of its truth, or falsehood, is consistent with any assumption whatsoever concerning the nature of his future experience, then, as far as he is concerned, it

* From *Language, Truth, and Logic*, by A. J. Ayer, reprinted through permission by Dover Publications, Inc., New York. The first section heading has been added by the editors.

is, if not a tautology, a mere pseudo-proposition. The sentence expressing it may be emotionally significant to him; but it is not literally significant. And with regard to questions the procedure is the same. We enquire in every case what observations would lead us to answer the question, one way or the other; and, if none can be discovered, we must conclude that the sentence under consideration does not, as far as we are concerned, express a genuine question, however strongly its grammatical appearance may suggest that it does. . . .

In the first place, it is necessary to draw a distinction between practical verifiability, and verifiability in principle. Plainly we all understand, in many cases believe, propositions which we have not in fact taken steps to verify. Many of these are propositions which we could verify if we took enough trouble. But there remain a number of significant propositions, concerning matters of fact, which we could not verify even if we chose; simply because we lack the practical means of placing ourselves in the situation where the relevant observations could be made. A simple and familiar example of such a proposition is the proposition that there are mountains on the farther side of the moon.[1] No rocket has yet been invented which would enable me to go and look at the farther side of the moon, so that I am unable to decide the matter by actual observation. But I do know what observations would decide it for me, if, as is theoretically conceivable, I were once in a position to make them. And therefore I say that the proposition is verifiable in principle, if not in practice, and is accordingly significant. On the other hand, such a metaphysical pseudo-proposition as "the Absolute enters into, but is itself incapable of, evolution and progress,"[2] is not even in principle verifiable. For one cannot conceive of an observation which would enable one to determine whether the Absolute did, or did not, enter into evolution and progress. Of course it is possible that the author of such a remark is using English words in a way in which they are not commonly used by English-speaking people, and that he does, in fact, intend to assert something which could be empirically verified. But until he makes us understand how the proposition that he wishes to express would be verified, he fails to communicate anything to us. And if he admits, as I think the author of the remark in question would have admitted, that his words were not intended to express either a tautology or a proposition which was capable, at least in principle, of being verified, then it follows that he has made an utterance which has no literal significance even for himself.

A further distinction which we must make is the distinction between the "strong" and the "weak" sense of the term "verifiable." A proposition is said to be verifiable, in the strong sense of the term, if, and only if, its truth could be conclusively established in experience. But it is verifiable, in the weak sense, if it is possible for experience to render it probable. In which sense are we using the term when we say that a putative proposition is genuine only if it is verifiable?

It seems to me that if we adopt conclusive verifiability as our criterion of significance, as some positivists have proposed,[3] our argument will prove too much. Consider, for example, the case of general propositions of law—such propositions, namely, as "arsenic is poisonous"; "all men are mortal"; "a body tends to expand when it is heated." It is of the very nature of these propositions that their truth cannot be established with certainty by any finite

[1] This example has been used by Professor Schlick to illustrate the same point.

[2] A remark taken at random from *Appearance and Reality*, by F. H. Bradley.

[3] E.g. M. Schlick, "Postivismus und Realismus," *Erkenntnis*, Vol. I, 1930. F. Waismann, "Logische Analyse des Warscheinlichkeitsbegriffs," *Erkenntnis*, Vol. I, 1930.

series of observations. But if it is recognised that such general propositions of law are designed to cover an infinite number of cases, then it must be admitted that they cannot, even in principle, be verified conclusively. And then, if we adopt conclusive verifiability as our criterion of significance, we are logically obliged to treat these general propositions of law in the same fashion as we treat the statements of the metaphysician.

In face of this difficulty, some positivists[4] have adopted the heroic course of saying that these general propositions are indeed pieces of nonsense, albeit an essentially important type of nonsense. But here the introduction of the term "important" is simply an attempt to hedge. It serves only to mark the authors' recognition that their view is somewhat too paradoxical, without in any way removing the paradox. Besides, the difficulty is not confined to the case of general propositions of law, though it is there revealed most plainly. It is hardly less obvious in the case of propositions about the remote past. For it must surely be admitted that, however strong the evidence in favour of historical statements may be, their truth can never become more than highly probable. And to maintain that they also constituted an important, or unimportant, type of nonsense would be unplausible, to say the very least. Indeed, it will be our contention that no proposition, other than a tautology, can possibly be anything more than a probable hypothesis. And if this is correct, the principle that a sentence can be factually significant only if it expresses what is conclusively verifiable is self-stultifying as a criterion of significance. For it leads to the conclusion that it is impossible to make a significant statement of fact at all.

Nor can we accept the suggestion that a sentence should be allowed to be factually significant if, and only if, it expresses something which is definitely confutable by experience.[5] Those who adopt this course assume that, although no finite series of observations is ever sufficient to establish the truth of a hypothesis beyond all possibility of doubt, there are crucial cases in which a single observation, or series of observations, can definitely confute it. But, as we shall show later on, this assumption is false. A hypothesis cannot be conclusively confuted any more than it can be conclusively verified. For when we take the occurrence of certain observations as proof that a given hypothesis is false, we presuppose the existence of certain conditions. And though, in any given case, it may be extremely improbable that this assumption is false, it is not logically impossible. We shall see that there need be no self-contradiction in holding that some of the relevant circumstances are other than we have taken them to be, and consequently that the hypothesis has not really broken down. And if it is not the case that any hypothesis can be definitely confuted, we cannot hold that the genuineness of a proposition depends on the possibility of its definite confutation.

Accordingly, we fall back on the weaker sense of verification. We say that the question that must be asked about any putative statement of fact is not, Would any observations make its truth or falsehood logically certain? but simply, Would any observations be relevant to the determination of its truth or falsehood? And it is only if a negative answer is given to this second question that we conclude that the statement under consideration is nonsensical. . . .

This criterion seems liberal enough. In contrast to the principle of conclusive verifiability, it clearly does not deny significance to general propositions or to propositions about the past. Let us see what kinds of assertion it rules out.

A good example of the kind of utter-

[4] E.g. M. Schlick, "Die Kausalität in der gegenwärtigen Physik," *Naturwissenschaft*, Vol. 19, 1931.

[5] This has been proposed by Karl Popper in his *Logik der Forschung*.

ance that is condemned by our criterion as being not even false but nonsensical would be the assertion that the world of sense-experience was altogether unreal. It must, of course, be admitted that our senses do sometimes deceive us. We may, as the result of having certain sensations, expect certain other sensations to be obtainable which are, in fact, not obtainable. But, in all such cases, it is further sense-experience that informs us of the mistakes that arise out of sense-experience. We say that the senses sometimes deceive us, just because the expectations to which our sense-experiences give rise do not always accord with what we subsequently experience. That is, we rely on our senses to substantiate or confute the judgements, which are based on our sensations. And therefore the fact that our perceptual judgements are sometimes found to be erroneous has not the slightest tendency to show that the world of sense-experience is unreal. And, indeed, it is plain that no conceivable observation, or series of observations, could have any tendency to show that the world revealed to us by sense-experience was unreal. Consequently, anymore who condemns the sensible world as a world of mere appearance, as opposed to reality, is saying something which, according to our criterion of significance, is literally nonsensical. . . .

CRITIQUE OF ETHICS

There is [an] objection to be met before we can claim to have justified our view that all synthetic propositions are empirical hypotheses. This objection is based on the common supposition that our speculative knowledge is of two distinct kinds—that which relates to questions of empirical fact, and that which relates to questions of value. It will be said that "statements of value" are genuine synthetic propositions, but that they cannot with any show of justice be represented as hypotheses, which are used to predict the course of our sensations; and, accordingly, that the existence of ethics and æsthetics as branches of speculative knowledge presents an insuperable objection to our radical empiricist thesis.

In face of this objection, it is our business to give an account of "judgements of value" which is both satisfactory in itself and consistent with our general empiricist principles. We shall set ourselves to show that in so far as statements of value are significant, they are ordinary "scientific" statements; and that in so far as they are not scientific, they are not in the literal sense significant, but are simply expressions of emotion which can be neither true nor false. In maintaining this view, we may confine ourselves for the present to the case of ethical statements. What is said about them will be found to apply, *mutatis mutandis,* to the case of æsthetic statements also.

The ordinary system of ethics, as elaborated in the works of ethical philosophers, is very far from being a homogeneous whole. Not only is it apt to contain pieces of metaphysics, and analyses of non-ethical concepts: its actual ethical contents are themselves of very different kinds. We may divide them, indeed, into four main classes. There are, first of all, propositions which express definitions of ethical terms, or judgements about the legitimacy or possibility of certain definitions. Secondly, there are propositions describing the phenomena of moral experience, and their causes. Thirdly, there are exhortations to moral virtue. And, lastly, there are actual ethical judgements. It is unfortunately the case that the distinction between these four classes, plain as it is, is commonly ignored by ethical philosophers; with the result that it is often very difficult to tell from their works what it is that they are seeking to discover or prove.

In fact, it is easy to see that only the first of our four classes, namely that which comprises the propositions relating to the definitions of ethical terms, can be said to constitute ethical philosophy. The propositions which describe the phenomena of moral experience, and their causes, must be assigned to the science of psychology, or sociology. The exhortations to moral virtue are not propositions at all, but ejaculations or commands which are designed to provoke the reader to action of a certain sort. Accordingly, they do not belong to any branch of philosophy or science. As for the expressions of ethical judgements, we have not yet determined how they should be classified. But inasmuch as they are certainly neither definitions nor comments upon definitions, nor quotations, we may say decisively that they do not belong to ethical philosophy. A strictly philosophical treatise on ethics should therefore make no ethical pronouncements. But it should, by giving an analysis of ethical terms, show what is the category to which all such pronouncements belong. And this is what we are now about to do.

A question which is often discussed by ethical philosophers is whether it is possible to find definitions which would reduce all ethical terms to one or two fundamental terms. But this question, though it undeniably belongs to ethical philosophy, is not relevant to our present enquiry. We are not now concerned to discover which term, within the sphere of ethical terms, is to be taken as fundamental; whether, for example, "good" can be defined in terms of "right" or "right" in terms of "good," or both in terms of "value." What we are interested in is the possibility of reducing the whole sphere of ethical terms to non-ethical terms. We are enquiring whether statements of ethical value can be translated into statements of empirical fact.

That they can be so translated is the contention of those ethical philosophers who are commonly called subjectivists, and of those who are known as utilitarians. For the utilitarian defines the rightness of actions, and the goodness of ends, in terms of the pleasure, or happiness, or satisfaction, to which they give rise; the subjectivist, in terms of the feelings of approval which a certain person, or group of people, has towards them. Each of these types of definition makes moral judgements into a sub-class of psychological or sociological judgements; and for this reason they are very attractive to us. For, if either was correct, it would follow that ethical assertions were not generically different from the factual assertions which are ordinarily contrasted with them; and the account which we have already given of empirical hypotheses would apply to them also.

Nevertheless we shall not adopt either a subjectivist or a utilitarian analysis of ethical terms. We reject the subjectivist view that to call an action right, or a thing good, is to say that it is generally approved of, because it is not self-contradictory to assert that some actions which are generally approved of are not right, or that some things which are generally approved of are not good. And we reject the alternative subjectivist view that a man who asserts that a certain action is right, or that a certain thing is good, is saying that he himself approves of it, on the ground that a man who confessed that he sometimes approved of what was bad or wrong would not be contradicting himself. And a similar argument is fatal to utilitarianism. We cannot agree that to call an action right is to say that of all the actions possible in the circumstances it would cause, or be likely to cause, the greatest happiness, or the greatest balance of pleasure over pain, or the greatest balance of satisfied over unsatisfied desire, because we find that it is not self-contradictory to say that it is sometimes wrong to perform the action which would actually or probably cause the greatest happiness, or the greatest balance of pleasure over pain, or of satisfied over unsatisfied desire. And since it is not self-contradictory to say that some pleasant things are not good, or that some bad things are desired, it cannot be the case that the sentence "*x* is good" is equivalent to "x is pleasant," or to "x is desired." And to every other variant of utilitarianism with which I am acquainted the same objection can be made. And therefore we should, I think, conclude that the validity of ethical judgements is not determined by the felicific tendencies of actions, any more than by the nature of people's feelings; but that it must be regarded as "absolute" or "intrinsic," and not empirically calculable.

If we say this, we are not, of course, denying that it is possible to invent a language in which all ethical symbols are definable in non-ethical terms, or even that it is desirable to invent such a language and adopt it in place of our own; what we are denying is that the suggested reduction of ethical to non-ethical statements is consistent with the conventions of our actual language. That is, we reject utilitarianism and subjectivism, not as proposals to replace our existing ethical notions by new ones, but as analyses of our existing ethical notions. Our contention is simply that, in our language, sentences which contain normative ethical symbols are not equivalent to sentences which express psychological propositions, or indeed empirical propositions of any kind.

It is advisable here to make it plain that it is only normative ethical symbols, and not descriptive ethical symbols, that are held by us to be indefinable in factual terms. There is a danger of confusing these two types of symbols, because they are commonly constituted by signs of the same sensible form. Thus a complex sign of the form "x is wrong" may constitute a sentence which expresses a moral judgement concerning a certain type of conduct, or it may constitute a sentence which states that a certain type of conduct is repugnant to the moral sense of a particular society. In the latter case, the symbol "wrong" is a descriptive ethical symbol, and the sentence in which it occurs expresses an ordinary sociological proposition; in the former case, the symbol "wrong" is a normative ethical symbol, and the sentence in which it occurs does not, we maintain, express an empirical proposition at all. It is only with normative ethics that we are at present concerned; so that whenever ethical symbols are used in the course of this argument without qualification, they are always to be interpreted as symbols of the normative type.

In admitting that normative ethical concepts are irreducible to empirical concepts, we seem to be leaving the way clear for the "absolutist" view of ethics—that is, the view that statements of value are not controlled by observation, as ordinary empirical propositions are, but only by a mysterious "intellectual intuition." A feature of this theory, which is seldom recognized by its advocates, is that it makes statements of value unverifiable. For it is notorious that what seems intuitively certain to one person may seem doubtful, or even false, to another. So that unless it is possible to provide some criterion by which one may decide between conflicting intuitions, a mere appeal to intuition is worthless as a test of a proposition's validity. But in the case of moral judgements, no such criterion can be given. Some moralists claim to settle the matter by saying that they "know" that their own moral judgements are correct. But such an assertion is of purely psychological interest, and has not the slightest tendency to prove the validity of any moral judgement. For dissentient moralists may equally well "know" that their ethical views are correct. And, as far as subjective certainty goes, there will be nothing to choose between them. When such differences of opinion arise in connection with an ordinary empirical proposition, one may attempt to resolve them by referring to, or actually carrying out, some relevant empirical test. But with regard to ethical statements, there is, on the "absolutist" or "intuitionist" theory, no relevant empirical test. We are therefore justified in saying that on this theory ethical statements are held to be unverifiable. They are, of course, also held to be genuine synthetic propositions.

Considering the use which we have made of the principle that a synthetic proposition is significant only if it is empirically verifiable, it is clear that the acceptance of an "absolutist" theory of ethics would undermine the whole of our main argument. And as we have already rejected the "naturalistic" theories which are commonly supposed to provide the only alternative to "absolutism" in ethics, we seem to have reached a difficult position. We shall meet the difficulty by showing that the correct treatment of ethical statements is afforded by a third theory, which is wholly compatible with our radical empiricism.

We begin by admitting that the fundamental ethical concepts are unanalysable, inasmuch as there is no criterion by which one can test the validity of the judgements in which they occur. So far we are in agreement with the absolutists. But, unlike the absolutists, we are able to give an explanation of this fact about ethical concepts. We say that the reason why they are unanalysable is that they are mere pseudo-concepts. The presence of an ethical symbol in a proposition adds nothing to its factual content. Thus if I say to someone, "You acted wrongly in stealing that money," I am not stating anything more than if I had simply said, "You stole that money." In adding that this action is wrong I am not making any further statement about it. I am simply evincing my moral disapproval of it. It is as if I had said, "You stole that money," in a peculiar tone of horror, or written it with the addition of some special exclamation marks. The tone, or the exclamation marks, adds nothing to the literal meaning of the sentence. It merely serves to show that the expression of it is attended by certain feeling in the speaker.

If now I generalise my previous statement and say, "Stealing money is wrong," I produce a sentence which has no factual meaning—that is, expresses no proposition which can be either true or false. It is as if I had written "Stealing money! !"—where the shape and thickness of the exclamation marks show, by a suitable convention, that a special sort of moral disapproval is the feeling which is being expressed. It is clear that there is nothing said here which can be true or false. Another man may disagree with me about the wrongness of stealing, in the sense that he may not have the same feelings about stealing as I have, and he may quarrel with me on account of my moral sentiments. But he cannot, strictly speaking, contradict me. For in saying that a certain type of action is right or wrong, I am not making any factual statement, not even a statement about my own state of mind. I am merely expressing certain moral sentiments. And the man who is ostensibly contradicting me is merely expressing his moral sentiments. So that there is plainly no sense in asking which of us is in the right. For neither of us is asserting a genuine proposition.

What we have just been saying about the symbol "wrong" applies to all normative ethical symbols. Sometimes they occur in sentences which record ordinary empirical facts besides expressing ethical feeling about those facts: sometimes they occur in sentences which simply express ethical feeling about a certain type of action, or situation, without making any statement of fact. But in every case in which one would commonly be said to be making an ethical judgement, the function of the relevant ethical word is purely "emotive." It is used to express feeling about certain objects, but not to make any assertion about them.

It is worth mentioning that ethical terms do not serve only to express feeling. They are calculated also to arouse feeling, and so to stimulate action. Indeed some of them are used in such a way as to give the sentences in which they occur the effect of commands. Thus the sentence "It is your duty to tell the truth" may be regarded both as the expression of a certain sort of ethical feeling about truthfulness and as the expression of the command "Tell the truth." The sentence "You ought to tell the truth" also involves the command "Tell the truth," but here the tone of the command is less emphatic. In the sentence "It is good to tell the truth" the command has become little more than a suggestion. And thus the "meaning" of the word "good," in its ethical usage, is differentiated from that of the word "duty" or the word "ought." In fact we may define the meaning of the various ethical words in terms both of the different feelings they are ordinarily taken to express, and also the different responses which they are calculated to provoke.

We can now see why it is impossible to find a criterion for determining the validity of ethical judgements. It is not because they have an "absolute" validity which is mysteriously independent of ordinary sense-experience, but because they have no objective validity whatsoever. If a sentence makes no statement at all, there is obviously no sense in asking whether what it says is true or false. And we have seen that sentences which simply express moral judgements do not say anything. They are pure expressions of feeling and as such do not come under the category of truth and falsehood. They are unverifiable for the same reason as a cry of pain or a word of command is unverifiable—because they do not express genuine propositions.

Thus, although our theory of ethics might fairly be said to be radically subjectivist, it differs in a very important respect from the orthodox subjectivist theory. For the orthodox subjectivist does not deny, as we do, that the sentences of a moralizer express genuine propositions. All he denies is that they express propositions of a unique non-empirical character. His own view is that they express propositions about the speaker's feelings. If this were so, ethical judgements clearly would be capable of being true or false. They would be true if the speaker had the relevant feelings, and false if he had not. And this is a matter which is, in principle, empirically verifiable. Furthermore they could be significantly contradicted. For if I say, "Tolerance is a virtue," and someone answers, "You don't approve of it," he would, on the ordinary subjectivist theory, be contradicting me. On our theory, he would not be contradicting me, because, in saying that tolerance was a virtue, I should not be making any statement about my own feelings or about anything else. I should simply be evincing my feelings, which is not at all the same thing as saying that I have them.

The distinction between the expression of feeling and the assertion of feeling is complicated by the fact that the assertion that one has a certain feeling often accompanies the expression of that feeling, and is then, indeed, a factor in the expression of that feeling. Thus I may simultaneously express boredom and say that I am bored, and in that case my utterance of the words, "I am bored," is one of the circumstances which make it true to say that I am expressing or evincing boredom. But I can express boredom without actually saying that I am bored. I can express it by my tone and gestures, while making a statement about something wholly unconnected with it, or by an ejaculation, or without uttering any words at all. So that even if the assertion that one has a certain feeling always involves the expression of that feeling, the expression of a feeling assuredly does not always involve the assertion that one has it. And this is the important point to grasp in considering the distinction between our theory and the ordinary subjectivist theory. For whereas the subjectivist holds that ethical statements actually assert the existence of certain feelings, we hold that ethical statements are expressions and excitants of feeling which do not necessarily involve any assertions.

We have already remarked that the main objection to the ordinary subjectivist theory is that the validity of ethical judgements is not determined by the nature of their author's feelings. And this is an objection which our theory escapes. For it does not imply that the existence of any feelings is a necessary and sufficient condition of the validity of an ethical judgement. It implies, on the contrary, that ethical judgements have no validity.

There is, however, a celebrated argument against subjectivist theories which our theory does not escape. It has been pointed out by Moore that if ethical statements were simply statements about the speaker's feelings, it would be impossible to argue about questions of value.[6] To take a typical example: if a man said that thrift was a virtue, and another replied that it was a vice, they would not, on this theory, be disputing with one another. One would be saying that he approved of thrift, and the other that *he* didn't; and there is no reason why both these statements should not be true. Now Moore held it to be obvious that we do dispute about questions of value, and accordingly concluded that the particular form of subjectivism which he was discussing was false.

It is plain that the conclusion that it is impossible to dispute about questions of value follows from our theory also. For as we hold that such sentences as "Thrift is a virtue" and "Thrift is a vice" do not express propositions at all, we clearly cannot hold that they express incompatible propositions. We must therefore admit that if Moore's argument really refutes the ordinary subjectivist theory, it also refutes ours. But, in fact, we deny that it does refute even the ordinary subjectivist theory. For we hold that one really never does dispute about questions of value.

This may seem, at first sight, to be a very paradoxical assertion. For we certainly do engage in disputes which are ordinarily regarded as disputes about questions of value. But, in all such cases, we find, if we consider the matter closely, that the dispute is not really about a question of value, but about a question of fact. When someone disagrees with us about the moral value of a certain action or type of action, we do admittedly resort to argument in order to win him over to our way of thinking. But we do not attempt to show by our arguments that he has the "wrong" ethical feeling towards a situation whose nature he has correctly apprehended. What we attempt to show is that he is mistaken about the facts of the case. We argue that he has misconceived the agent's motive: or that he has misjudged the effects of the action, or its probable effects in view of the agent's knowledge; or that he has failed to take into account the special circumstances in which the agent was placed. Or else we employ more general arguments about the effects which actions of a certain type tend to produce, or the qualities which are usually manifested in their performance. We do this in the hope that we have only to get our opponent to agree with us about the nature of the empirical facts for him to adopt the same moral attitude towards them as we do. And as the people with whom we argue have generally received the same moral education as ourselves, and live in the same social order, our expectation is usually justified. But if our opponent happens to have undergone a different process of moral "conditioning" from ourselves, so that, even when he acknowledges all the facts, he still disagrees with us about the moral value of the actions under discussion, then we abandon the attempt to convince him by argument. We say that

[6] Cf. *Philosophical Studies*, "The Nature of Moral Philosophy."

it is impossible to argue with him because he has a distorted or undeveloped moral sense; which signifies merely that he employs a different set of values from our own. We feel that our own system of values is superior, and therefore speak in such derogatory terms of his. But we cannot bring forward any arguments to show that our system is superior. For our judgement that it is so is itself a judgement of value, and accordingly outside the scope of argument. It is because argument fails us when we come to deal with pure questions of value, as distinct from questions of fact, that we finally resort to mere abuse.

In short, we find that argument is possible on moral questions only if some system of values is presupposed. If our opponent concurs with us in expressing moral disapproval of all actions of a given type *t*, then we may get him to condemn a particular action A, by bringing forward arguments to show that A is of type *t*. For the question whether A does or does not belong to that type is a plain question of fact. Given that a man has certain moral principles, we argue that he must, in order to be consistent, react morally to certain things in a certain way. What we do not and cannot argue about is the validity of these moral principles. We merely praise or condemn them in the light of our own feelings.

If anyone doubts the accuracy of this account of moral disputes, let him try to construct even an imaginary argument on a question of value which does not reduce itself to an argument about a question of logic or about an empirical matter of fact. I am confident that he will not succeed in producing a single example. And if that is the case, he must allow that its involving the impossibility of purely ethical arguments is not, as Moore thought, a ground of objection to our theory, but rather a point in favour of it.

Having upheld our theory against the only criticism which appeared to threaten it, we may now use it to define the nature of all ethical enquiries. We find that ethical philosophy consists simply in saying that ethical concepts are pseudo-concepts and therefore unanalysable. The further task of describing the different feelings that the different ethical terms are used to express, and the different reactions that they customarily provoke, is a task for the psychologist. There cannot be such a thing as ethical science, if by ethical science one means the elaboration of a "true" system of morals. For we have seen that, as ethical judgements are mere expressions of feeling, there can be no way of determining the validity of any ethical system, and, indeed, no sense in asking whether any such system is true. All that one may legitimately enquire in this connection is, What are the moral habits of a given person or group of people, and what causes them to have precisely those habits and feelings? And this enquiry falls wholly within the scope of the existing social sciences.

It appears, then, that ethics, as a branch of knowledge, is nothing more than a department of psychology and sociology. . . .

CHARLES LESLIE STEVENSON

Charles Leslie Stevenson (1908–) was born in Cincinnati and educated at Yale, Cambridge, and Harvard. He taught philosophy at Yale and is now professor of philosophy at the University of Michigan.

The following selections are from his major work, Ethics and Language, *an extensive and careful study of the functions of moral discourse.*

*Ethics and Language**

ETHICAL DISAGREEMENT

What is the nature of ethical *agreement* and *disagreement*? Is it parallel to that found in the natural sciences, differing only with regard to the relevant subject matter; or is it of some broadly different sort?

If we can answer the question, we shall obtain a general understanding of what constitutes a normative *problem;* and our study of terms and methods, which must explain how this kind of problem becomes articulate and how it is open to argument or inquiry, will be properly oriented. There are certain normative problems, of course, to which the question is not directly relevant—those which arise in personal deliberation, rather than in interpersonal discourse, and which involve not disagreement or agreement but simply uncertainty or growing conviction. But we shall later find that the question is indirectly relevant even to them; and meanwhile there is a convenience in looking chiefly to the interpersonal problems, where the use of terms and methods is most clearly evidenced.

For simplicity let us limit our explicit attention to "disagreement," treating the positive term by implication. And let us begin by distinguishing two broad kinds of disagreement. We can do this in a wholly general way, temporarily suspending any decision about which kind is most typical of normative ethics, and drawing our examples from other fields.

The disagreements that occur in science, history, biography, and their counterparts in everyday life, will require

* By permission. From C. L. Stevenson, *Ethics and Language*, Yale University Press, New Haven, Conn., 1944. Some section headings have been added by the editors.

only brief attention. Questions about the nature of light-transmission, the voyages of Leif Ericsson, and the date on which Jones was last in to tea, are all similar in that they may involve an opposition that is primarily of beliefs. (The term "beliefs" must not, at least for the moment, include reference to ethical convictions; for whether or not the latter are "beliefs" in the present sense is largely the point that is to be discussed.) In such cases one man believes that p is the answer, and another that not-p, or some proposition incompatible with p, is the answer; and in the course of discussion each tries to give some manner of proof for his view, or revise it in the light of further information. Let us call this "disagreement in belief."

There are other cases, differing sharply from these, which may yet be called "disagreements" with equal propriety. They involve an opposition, sometimes tentative and gentle, sometimes strong, which is not of beliefs, but rather of attitudes—that is to say, an opposition of purposes, aspirations, wants, preferences, desires, and so on. Since it is tempting to overintellectualize these situations, giving too much attention to beliefs, it will be helpful to examine them with care.

Suppose that two people have decided to dine together. One suggests a restaurant where there is music; another expresses his disinclination to hear music, and suggests some other restaurant. It may then happen, as we commonly put it, that they "cannot easily agree on which restaurant to choose." The disagreement springs more from divergent preferences than from divergent beliefs, and will end when they both *wish* to go to the same place. It will be a mild, temporary disagreement for this simple case—a disagreement in miniature; yet it will be a "disagreement" in a wholly familiar sense.

Further examples are easily found. Mrs. A has social aspirations, and wants to move with the elite. Mr. A is easy-going, and loyal to his old friends. They accordingly disagree about what guests they will invite to their party. The curator of the museum wants to buy pictures by contemporary artists; some of his advisers prefer the purchase of old masters. They disagree. John's mother is concerned about the dangers of playing football, and doesn't want him to play. John, even though he agrees (in belief) about the dangers, wants to play anyhow. Again, they disagree. These examples, like the previous one, involve an opposition of attitudes, and differ only in that the attitudes in question are a little stronger, and are likely to be defended more seriously. Let us refer to disagreement of this sort as "disagreement in attitude."[1] Two men will be said to disagree in attitude when they have opposed attitudes to the same object—one approving of it, for instance, and the other disapproving of it—and when at least one of them has a motive for altering or calling into question the attitude of the other. Let us be careful to observe, however, that when one man is seeking to alter another's attitudes, he may at the same time be preparing to alter his own attitudes in the light of what the other may say. Disagreement in attitude, like disagreement in belief, need not be an occasion for forensic rivalry; it may be an occasion for an interchange of aims, with a reciprocal influence that both parties find to be beneficial.

The two kinds of disagreement differ mainly in this respect: the former is concerned with how matters are truthfully to be described and explained; the latter is concerned with how they are to be favored or disfavored, and hence with how they are to be shaped by human efforts. . . .

There is a close relationship between

[1] In all of the examples given there may be a *latent* disagreement in belief, in addition to the disagreement in attitude. This is likely to be true of any example that is not painfully artificial; but the present examples are serviceable enough for their introductory purpose.

the sorts of disagreement that have been distinguished. Indeed, in some cases the existence of one may wholly depend on the existence of the other. Suppose that A and B have convergent attitudes toward the *kind* of thing the X *actually* is, but indicate divergent attitudes to X itself simply because A has erroneous beliefs about it, whereas B has not. Discussion or inquiry, correcting A's errors, may resolve the disagreement in belief; and this in turn may be sufficient to resolve the disagreement in attitude. X was an occasion for the latter sort of disagreement *only* because it was an occasion for the former.

In cases of this sort one might be inclined to reject the expression, "Both kinds of disagreement were initially present, the one depending on the other," and say instead, "Only disagreement in belief was initially present, the disagreement in attitude with regard to X being simply apparent." If X was designated without ambiguity, however, so that the same X could be *recognized* by both parties regardless of their divergent beliefs about it, then the latter idiom would be seriously misleading. One man was definitely striving for X, and the other definitely striving to oppose it; and if this involved ignorance, where one of the men was acting to defeat his broader aims, it remains altogether appropriate to say that the initial divergence in attitude, so far as X was concerned, was genuine. It is convenient to restrict the term "apparent" disagreement to cases which involve ambiguity—to cases where the term that seems to designate X for both parties actually designates Y for one of them.

The relationship between the two sorts of disagreement, whenever it occurs, is always factual, never logical. So far as the logical possibilities are concerned, there may be disagreement in belief without disagreement in attitude; for even if an argument must always be motivated, and to that extent involve attitudes, it does not follow that the attitudes which attend opposed beliefs must themselves be opposed. People may share the ideals and aims which guide their scientific theorizing, for instance, and still reach divergent beliefs. Similarly, there may be disagreement in attitude without disagreement in belief. Perhaps every attitude must be accompanied by some belief about its object; but the beliefs which attend opposed attitudes need not be incompatible. A and B may both believe that X has Q, for instance, and have divergent attitudes to X *on that very account,* A approving of objects that have Q and B disapproving of them. Since it may also happen that both sorts of disagreement occur conjointly, or that neither should occur, the logical possibilities are all open. Hence one must appeal to experience to determine which of the possibilities, in any given case or class of cases, is in fact realized. But experience clearly shows, as we shall later see in detail, that the cases which involve *both* sorts of disagreement (or agreement) are extremely numerous. . . .

WORKING MODELS

Any definition which seeks to identify the meaning of ethical terms with that of scientific ones, and which does so without further explanation or qualification, is extremely likely to be misleading. It will suggest that the questions of normative ethics, like those of science, give rise to an agreement or disagreement that is exclusively in *belief.* In this way, ignoring disagreement in attitude, it will lead to only a half-picture, at best, of the situations in which the ethical terms are actually used.

This conclusion must not be pressed insensitively, without regard to the ambiguities and flexibilities of language. It may well be that at *some* times *all* of the effective meaning of ethical terms is scientific, and that at *all* times *some* of it is; but there remain multitudes of familiar cases in which the ethical terms are used in a way that is *not exclusively* scientific, and we must recognize a meaning which suits them to their additional function.

What is the nature of this extrascientific meaning? Let us proceed by analogy, comparing ethical sentences with others that are less perplexing but have a similar use.

Interesting analogues can be found in ordinary imperatives. Is there not a ready passage from "You ought to defend your country" to "Defend your country"? Or more prosaically, is not the expression, "You oughtn't to cry," as said to children, roughly interchangeable with "Stop crying"? There are many differences, unquestionably; but there are likewise these similarities: Both imperative and ethical sentences are used more for encouraging, altering, or redirecting people's aims and conduct than for simply describing them. Both differ in this respect from the sentences of science. And in arguments that involve disagreement in attitude, it is obvious that imperatives, like ethical judgments, have an important place. The example about the restaurant, for instance, by which the conception of disagreement in attitude was first introduced, might begin with the use of imperatives exclusively:

A: Meet me at the Glenwood for dinner at 7.00.
B: Don't let's go to a restaurant with music. Meet me at the Ambassador instead.
A: But do make it the Glenwood . . . etc.

So the argument might begin, disagreement in attitude being indicated either by the ordinary second person form of the imperative, or by the first person plural form that begins with "Let's."

On account of this similar function of imperative and ethical sentences, it will be useful to consider some definitions that *in part* identify them. These definitions will not be adequate to the subtleties of common usage; they will be markedly inaccurate. But they will preserve in rough form much that is essential to ethical analysis, and on that account will be instructive approximations. It is they which will constitute the "working models". . . .

There are many ways in which working models can be devised, but those which follow are perhaps the most serviceable:

1. "This is wrong" means *I disapprove of this; do so as well.*
2. "He ought to do this" means *I disapprove of his leaving this undone; do so as well.*
3. "This is good" means *I approve of this; do so as well.*

It will be noted that the definiens in each case has two parts: first a declarative statement, "I approve" or "I disapprove," which describes the attitudes of the speaker, and secondly an imperative statement, "do so as well," which is addressed to changing or intensifying the attitudes of the hearer. These components, acting together, readily provide for agreement or disagreement in attitude. The following examples will illustrate how this is so:

A: This is good.
B: I fully agree. It is indeed good.

Freely translated in accordance with model (3) above, this becomes,

A: I approve of this; do so as well.
B: I fully concur in approving of it; (continue to) do so as well.

Here the declarative parts of the remarks, testifying to convergent attitudes, are sufficient to imply the agreement. But if taken alone, they hint too much at a bare description of attitudes. They do not evidence the *contagion* of warmly expressed approval—the interaction of attitudes that makes each man's favorable evaluation strengthen and invigorate the other's. This latter effect is highly characteristic of an articulate ethical agreement; and the imperatives in our translated version of the example do something (though in a most imperfect way) to make it evident.

Let us consider an example of disagreement:

A: This is good.
B: No, it is bad.

Translated in accordance with the working models, this becomes,

A: I approve of this; do so as well.
B: No, I disapprove of it; do so as well.

The declarative parts of the remarks show that the men have opposed attitudes, one approving and the other disapproving. The imperative parts show that each man is suggesting that the other redirect his attitudes. Since "disagreement in attitude" has been defined with exclusive reference to an opposition of attitudes and efforts to redirect them or call them into question, it will be clear that a place for this sort of disagreement is retained (though again only in an imperfect way) by the working models that have been suggested.

But if the models are to help us more than they hinder us, they must be used with extreme caution. Although they give a needed emphasis to agreement and disagreement in attitude, they give no emphasis to agreement and disagreement in belief. Hence the *dual* source of ethical problems is not made evident. If traditional theory too often lost sight of attitudes in its concern with beliefs, we must not make the opposite error of losing sight of beliefs in our concern with attitudes. The latter error, which would give ethics the appearance of being cut off from reasoned argument and inquiry, would be even more serious than the former. . . .

The first inadequacy of the models is simply this: The imperative component, included to preserve the hortatory aspects of ethical judgments, and stressed as useful in indicating agreement or disagreement in attitude, is really too blunt an instrument to perform its expected task. If a person is explicitly commanded to have a certain attitude, he becomes so self-conscious that he cannot obey. Command a man's approval and you will elicit only superficial symptoms of it. But the judgment, "This is good," has no trace of this stultifying effect; so the judgment's force in encouraging approval has been poorly approximated.

A further point, somewhat parallel to this, is more serious. Imperatives are often used to exert a unilateral influence. When a man gives direct orders, he may not take kindly to a dissenting reply. Although this is not the only way in which imperatives are used, it is a familiar one; and when imperatives enter bluntly into a context, as they do in the working models, only this usage may be brought to mind. So the models may give a distorted impression of the purposes for which moral influence is exerted. They may suggest that a moralist is obsessed by a desire to make others over into his own pattern—that he wishes only to propagate his preconceived aims, without reconsidering them.

Now if certain moralists have motives of this sort, there can be no doubt that others do not. One who exerts an influence need not thereby cut himself off from all counterinfluence; he may initiate a discussion in which the attitudes of all parties become progressively modified, and directed to objects whose nature is more fully understood. There are many men whose influence looks beyond their own immediate needs, and takes its welcome place in a coöperative moral enterprise. Proceeding with a desire to see all sides of a question, they have no desire for a debater's conquest, and are anxious to submit their moral judgments to the test of other points of view. Although moral judgments are not always advanced in this spirit, we must remember that there is manifestly such a possibility, which in many cases is actualized. There is no excuse for that hardheadedness which can see no more in human nature than the qualities which human nature is ashamed to recognize.

The working models, then, are likely to misrepresent both the manner in which moral influence is exerted and the motives which attend it. How may their inadequacies be avoided? The answer is suggested by current theories about language and meaning—theories which promise to have marked repercussions on philosophy, and which have been emphasized by several contemporary writers on ethics. The effect of ethical terms in directing attitudes, though not wholly dissimilar to that of imperatives, must be explained with reference to a characteristic and subtle kind of *emotive meaning.* The emotive meaning of a word is the power that the word acquires, on account of its history in emotional situations, to evoke or directly express attitudes, as distinct from describing or designating them. In simple forms it is typical of interjections; in more complicated forms it is a contributing factor to poetry; and it has familiar manifestations in the many terms of ordinary discourse that are laudatory or derogatory. In virtue of this kind of meaning, ethical judgments alter attitudes, not by an appeal to self-conscious efforts (as is the case with imperatives), but by the more flexible mechanism of *suggestion.* Emotive terms present the subject of which they are predicated in a bright or dim light, so to speak, and thereby *lead* people, rather than command them, to alter their attitudes. And they readily permit a mutual influence of this sort, as distinct from a unilateral one. The exact nature of emotive meaning, the way in which it functions, and the way in which it coöperates with beliefs, gestures, tones of voice, and so on, are somewhat involved considerations that must be left until later. It need only be remarked, for the present, that emotive meaning need not be taken as usurping the position that rightfully belongs to descriptive meaning. It has many legitimate functions, in ethics and elsewhere, and becomes objectionable only when it is abused.

It is not sufficient, however, to correct only the imperative component of the working models. A further inadequacy attends their declarative component, which for many contexts is much too simple. In order to accentuate agreement and disagreement in attitude, the models reduce descriptive meaning to a bare minimum, suggesting that ethical judgments express beliefs that are solely about the speaker's own attitudes. Now the most obvious objection to this procedure—that it neglects the many other beliefs that are relevant to ethics—is one which we have seen to have no foundation. If the beliefs are stressed, as in the preceding section, in connection with methodology—if they are made evident from the supporting reasons that attend ethical judgments, rather than from the meaning of the judgments themselves—the full nature of ethical issues is properly recognized. . . .

CAN ETHICAL DISPUTES BE SETTLED BY REASON?

Let us examine the methods used in ethical arguments with full attention to details. . . .

Group I. The examples of this group illustrate some of the ways in which ethical methods resemble factual ones. They present *exceptions* to . . . the rule that ethical judgments are supported or attacked by reasons related to them psychologically, rather than logically.

1. A: It would be a good thing to have a dole for the unemployed.
   B: But you have just said that a dole would weaken people's sense of in-

dependence, and you have admitted that *nothing* which has that consequence is good.

Here B attacks A's position by pointing out a formal inconsistency. In general, ethical statements, like all others that have at least *some* descriptive meaning, are amenable to the usual applications of formal logic. Care must be taken, of course, that verbally seeming contradictions are not merely apparent, due to a change in sense of the particularly ambiguous ethical terms; and further care must be taken to avoid emotive repercussions of otherwise innocent tautologies. Otherwise, this aspect of ethical methodology brings with it no special problems.

2. A: It is always wrong to break a promise.

   B: You speak without thinking. There are many cases of that sort which you regard without the least disapproval.

B's reply is an empirical assertion, but note that it contradicts A's judgment . . . and so is logically related to it. A must, in the interest of consistency, either reject B's assertion, or give up his ethical judgment. (He would be very likely to qualify his judgment, saying merely that *most* instances of breaking promises are wrong.)

Even in this simple case, however, we must realize that on occasion B's statement may be more than it seems. He may speak in a tone of incredulity, as if he "simply can't believe" that anyone is *unqualifiedly* opposed to breaking promises, even though he may suspect that A actually is. By so doing, he may lead A to worry for fear his attitude is socially "odd," and thus to come to a state of mind which makes his attitude easier for B to change.

3. A: It is by no means my duty to repay C.

   B: Your moral feelings really torment you for not doing so, as you well know. You say you have no duty as a feeble effort to quiet your conscience, and free the expression of your crude selfishness.

This example is in some respects parallel to the preceding one. If A's statement descriptively means that he has no moral disapproval of his not paying C, and if B's statement is a rough way of saying that A does have such a moral disapproval, then clearly, B's statement is an empirical one which logically contradicts A's, as was the case in (2) above.

It is here more obvious, however, that the logical opposition is subordinate to one of another sort. B supposes that A has conflicting attitudes—that his moral attitudes oppose what his (allegedly) crude selfishness favors. A is trying not to describe his present moral attitudes, but rather to *mis*describe them (perhaps without being aware of it), in order to weaken their force by a kind of autosuggestion. Now B, if we are to assume that he typifies many ordinary people, is opposed to this procedure. So when he mentions the "torment" of A's moral feelings, he is far from having a perfectly calm wish to help A introspect. He is forcibly calling these feelings to A's mind, so that A will be prevented from weakening them. If we should see no more in the example, then, than that A and B are making incompatible statements, "one of which cannot possibly be true," we should ignore the main issue. The *truth about* either party's present attitudes is subordinate to their concern in determining what A's attitudes are *later to be.* The main disagreement is one in attitude, since A wants to weaken his moral feelings, and B does not want him to.

It is very often the case, as this example shows, that when people talk about attitudes (even in language which is not strongly emotive) they are less concerned with describing the existing state of attitudes than with altering them by suggestion. The error of treating language as though its function were always cognitive is almost incredibly naïve; and yet it is an error which is largely responsible for the impracticalities of traditional ethical theory.

4. A: Their friends are all of them shamelessly immoral.
   B: Not knowing them all, you should not generalize so sweepingly.
   A: I know a great number of them, such as C and D and E . . . , and their immorality gives my judgment no little support.

This example is of interest for showing how closely an ethical argument can approximate to ordinary induction. A is arguing from specific judgments, such as "C is immoral," "D is immoral," etc., to the immorality of all members of a class in which C and D, etc., fall. But note that the specific judgments, unlike observation-sentences in science, are open to disagreement in attitude. If they are challenged and are supported by reasons in their turn, the support must ultimately involve arguments unlike (4), and may in fact involve any or all of the other methods that are here being considered. There is no use of induction in ethics that can secure agreement in attitude in the same *direct* way that it can secure agreement in belief.

One may analyze (4), alternatively, as an induction about some unstipulated *factual* characteristics of the people in question, insisting that the ethical element enters only in so far as A "tacitly" makes an adverse judgment about *anyone* having these characteristics. But for logical purposes, "tacit" judgments cannot comfortably be recognized.

Group II. In this group, and those that follow, an ethical judgment is supported or attacked by reasons that are psychologically related to it. Unlike (1) and (2) of Group I, these examples do not call into question the descriptive *truth* of the initial judgment, so long as the judgment describes (in accordance with the first pattern) merely the speaker's present attitudes. They represent efforts to change attitudes, or to strengthen them, by means of altering beliefs. Hence, although the reasons themselves are of an empirical character, and may be rendered probable or improbable by scientific methods, one must not say that they render the ethical judgments "probable" or "improbable" in the same sense. They are simply of a sort that may lead one person or another to have altered attitudes in consequence of altered beliefs, and so, thereafter, to make different ethical judgments.

5. A: The proposed tax bill is on the whole very bad.
   B: I know little about it, but have been inclined to favor it on the ground that higher taxes are preferable to further borrowing.
   A: It provides for a sales-tax on a number of necessities, and reduces income-tax exemption to an incredibly low figure.
   B: I had not realized that. I must study the bill, and perhaps I shall agree with you in opposing it.

A has supported his ethical judgment by pointing out to B the *nature* of that which is judged. Since B is predisposed to oppose anything of that nature, he shows his willingness to change his attitude, unless, perhaps, further study will disclose matters that weigh the balance to the other side. If B were not a person predisposed to disapprove of the provisions mentioned, however, he would find A's reasons unconvincing, and the argument would probably lead to a discussion of whether these provisions are good or bad. This in turn might lend itself to a use of any of the methods that are being exemplified.

In the sense here intended, the "nature" of an object is given by means of factual, contingent statements about the object itself. In another sense, it is given by statements which, though they appear to be about an object, serve actually to *define a term*—a term which does not clearly or unambiguously designate any object until the definition is given. That is to say, the word "nature" often introduces Rudolph Carnap's "quasi-syntactical idiom." Ethical reasons which are in this idiom—those, for instance, which clarify the meaning of a noun which an ethical adjective has been used to modify—do not fall within the present group. They are of particular importance when judgments use such verbal chameleons as "liberalism," "social equality," and the rest. But since the general theory of definitions and their quasi-syntactical equivalents has often been discussed by others, and since the definitions that are of peculiar interest to ethics will be discussed subsequently, the topic need not be developed here.

6. A: The proposed tax bill is on the whole bad.
   B: I know little about it, etc.
   A: It will put a great burden on the poor, and make little difference to the rich.
   B: I had not realized that, etc.

This example is parallel to (5), save that A supports his judgment by pointing out the consequences of that which is judged, rather than its nature. The effect of his reason will depend on B's attitude to these consequences.

The distinction between the nature and consequences of anything is clear enough to merit a separate example for each. It must be remembered, however, that there are many borderline cases where such a distinction is arbitrary; and even in cases where it is readily made, the nature of something is often of interest only because of the consequences it suggests. A's reasons in (5), for instance, would probably not have been accepted by B had they not led him to suppose that the proposed bill would bring with it the consequences explicitly mentioned in (6).

There is no theoretical limit to the number of consequences that may be considered in an ethical argument. Consequences go on without end. In practice, however, they can be known with little certainty when they are remote; and the uncertainty of the remote ones, together with their very remoteness, often makes them have very little effect on present attitudes. Hence many ethical arguments confine attention to the consequence in a not distant future. Some may wish to call these arguments "shortsighted," with condemnation; others may wish to call them "realistic," with praise. The present work must neither condemn nor praise arguments, nor judge the condemnation or praise of others; but it must be remarked that since arguments of the sort in question differ sharply from one another in many ways, any general condemnation or praise is very likely to be too general.

7. A: The government ought to put more severe restrictions on the sale of patent medicines.
   B: That would interfere with freedom of enterprise.
   A: Yes, but it would certainly forward the greatest happiness of the greatest number.

Here consequences are again in question, but consequences of a broader sort.

It is a frequent practice in ethical theory to hold up some very broad kind of consequence as "the" one which determines whether anything ought or ought not to be done. We shall subsequently have reason to question this procedure. But however that may be, all of the familiar "ends" —whether those of the utilitarians, or the evolutionists, or the integrators of attitudes, etc.—have their place in ethical methodology as it is commonly applied; nor are they confused when taken as having a *partial* place. Any person who favors one of these broad consequences, and who comes to believe that a given X will help to bring it about, will thereby be led to favor X—unless some other sort of consequence outweighs this broad one.

Group III. Like the preceding group, this deals with empirical reasons psychologically related to an ethical judgment; but it differs in that the reasons are not limited to the nature and direct consequences of that which is judged. Some of them deal with consequences of another sort, and some have little or nothing to do with consequences.

8. A: C's courtesy to his elder friend is admirable.
   B: Perhaps you would speak with less assurance if you knew how anxious he is to have that elderly friend take him into his business.
   A: Yes, that puts the matter in another light.

In this example B mentions not the nature or actual consequences of C's courtesy, but rather the *motives* that attend it. A's attitude to these motives alters his attitude to C's courteous actions and to C himself, so in effect he withdraws his initial judgment.

Moralists have always paid great attention to motives. One reason for this—though doubtless one among many—is very simple. A person's motives are clues to much else. They are grounds for predicting his subsequent actions, and in turn the results of these. Like the nature of an action, its motivation is usually of interest for the consequences it suggests. To whatever extent moralists have been influenced by such matters, their beliefs about attendant motives have influenced their judgments of specific acts. This point has been so well made by John Dewey that it will here require no further attention.

9. A: It is your duty to vote.
   B: No, my vote will make no difference to the final outcome.
   A: You could scarcely wish that all others should adopt your ways!

A's rejoinder, reminiscent of Kant's categorical imperative, unquestionably has its place in common-sense arguments. How may its relevance be explained? Although it does not name any direct consequence of B's stand, it is fertile in suggesting many indirect ones. B may set a precedent to others which he will not welcome. Or he may nullify his influence in *inducing* others to vote, for people are temperamentally suspicious of those who "do not practice what they preach." Or he may develop habits of noncoöperation, which like the motives discussed in (8) may have effects that extend far beyond the present case. These observations are clearly a part of the explanation of the force of A's reason; and to continue the explanation in this way, rather than in Kant's way, seems only in keeping with the principle of parsimony. . . .

Group IV. In this group B is less concerned with resolving disagreement in attitude than with temporarily evading the force of a disconcerting influence, or altering the means by which it is exerted.

15. A: You are much too[2] hard on your employees.
    B: But you, certainly, are not the one to say so. Your own factory would bear investigation far less easily than mine.

B here makes a counterattack. Finding A's judgment humiliating, and hoping to

[2] Note that "too" is often an ethical term. Here "too hard" has the meaning of "harder than you ought to be."

silence him, he insinuates a still more troublesome judgment in reply. He assumes that A would rather desist from his influence than be subject to one of the same kind. The procedure is recognized by many common sayings, such as "People in glass houses should not throw stones."

There may be other sides to this example. B may be appealing to the weakness of human nature. . . . He may wish to suggest: "You want me to be altruistic in a way that is beyond human attainment, as is shown by the fact that you yourself are incapable of such altruism." Or he may be appealing to A's sense of equality: "Who are you to condemn in me that which you yourself do?" The fact that A may be moved by this latter remark is due to his embarrassment in making an exception of himself—a matter which in turn needs explanation, but which, again in the interest of parsimony, is most plausibly explained not as Kant explained it, but in terms of a purely empirical psychology. Although a complete explanation cannot be attempted here, the following illustration may be of interest: If a monarch extolled the virtues of domestic life, and at the same time kept several mistresses, he might in no way be moved by the charge of making an exception of himself. He might urge, and successfully, that it was the special privilege of his rank. But A, in our example, could not follow a parallel course, because, if for no other reason, he would immediately be made the object of ridicule for his presumption. It is not easy to maintain an attitude to which all others are opposed—not because the others will be led to take forcible steps to prevent it, necessarily, but because their very expression of opposition is psychologically "hard to face."

16. A: You are shamelessly wasting your youth in idleness.
    B: You did the very same thing in your own youth.
    A: I did indeed, and my unfortunate career should be a lesson to you.

Here again B makes a counterattack; but note that it now ceases to be effective. The success of a counterattack depends on whether the opponent is more anxious to escape humiliation than to persist in his influence. . . .

Granted an assumption, one may hope that ethical agreement *can* be obtained by reasons. . . . Let us say that disagreement in attitude is "rooted in" disagreement in belief whenever the former can be reconciled by reconciling the latter. For instance, if A approves of X and B does not, and if they are not content merely to "differ," there will be a disagreement in attitude, regardless of its source. But if this agreement ends when the parties reach similar beliefs about X, then it will be said to be "rooted in" disagreement in belief. The assumption in question can now be stated in this simple way:

> *All disagreement in attitude is rooted in disagreement in belief.*

Strictly speaking, this assumption insures that rational methods will be convincing in ethics only to the extent that they, in turn, are sufficient to bring about agreement in belief; but even so one may hope, granted the assumption, that the growth of empirical knowledge will slowly lead to a world of enlightened moral accord. The assumption itself, however, must be used with caution. Since the days of Hume, who made a somewhat similar assumption, we have learned how problematical any psychological generalization, even when it is less sweeping than this one, must inevitably be.

That there are *some cases* for which the assumption holds is scarcely to be doubted. When people are ignorant of the means to ends vital to them all, their divergent evaluations may easily be rooted in their beliefs. But other cases may be of a different sort. Some ethical disagreements *seem* rooted, rather, in the scarcity of what people want. Several nations may urge that their crowded and suffering populations give them the right to take a disputed territory. Others *seem* rooted in temperamental differences, as when an oversexed, emotionally independent adolescent argues with an undersexed, emotionally dependent one about the desirability of free love. In these cases the growth of science may, for all that we can now know, leave ethical disagreement permanently unresolved.

To be sure, a person can always say that the disagreement is rooted in one in belief, even for these cases; and the complexity of the situations will free him from any immediate refutation. It may always be that when nations dispute a colonial right, all but one would withdraw their claims *if* the full truth were known about consequences, precedents, motives, and so on. That is possible in the sense that it cannot categorically be refuted; but its opposite is also possible. It is even possible that increased knowledge would be hostile to ethical agreement. Plato tacitly assumed so, perhaps, when he urged that the guardians should be taught not the truth about their ancestors, but rather deliberately romanticized untruths. He felt that moral stability could not endure a general dissemination of knowledge, even in a utopian state.

How are we to test the assumption? The ideal procedure would be to experiment in a world where all men had the last word of factual knowledge, and observe whether any disagreement in attitude remained. This being manifestly impossible, one has only indirect procedures, based on the natural laws that seem to govern human beings in their environment. What is now known of these laws is assuredly not enough for any well-founded conclusion. In psychology and the social sciences, particularly, there can be little pretence of knowing the essential facts, and still less pretence of knowing dependable laws. Hence any assurance that may attend the assumption must be tempered by a scientific caution. One may, of course, have occasion tentatively to accept the assumption. There can be no assurance that it will *not* hold in any given case, and its adoption may be beneficial in prolonging the enlightenment of discussion. One may even cling to it in desperation, as the only hope of settling issues that may otherwise lead to serious discord. But that is not to say that it is well confirmed. A victim of a fatal disease may put implicit faith in the belief that medical research will find a cure for it before he dies. We respect the belief as he maintains it, but do not countenance it in a scientific text that deals with the probable developments of medicine.

It must be observed, however, that although the assumption is lacking in confirmation, it is at least free from the fantastic implications that might too easily be ascribed to it. It does not imply, for instance, that all individual differences in temperament are a product of ignorance, and that the growth of science would make men behave with monotonous uniformity. Although individual differences may sometimes prevent ethical agreement, they need not always do so. If the assumption were true, and if all men had unlimited knowledge, it might still be the case that some would be artists, others manufacturers, others athletes, and so on. Men may differ in the way they wish to lead their lives without having attitudes that clash. Both A and B, for instance, may agree in wanting A to be an artist, and agree in wanting B to be a manufacturer. Again, under the above conditions, it might be that different nations would have different forms of government. Nations C and D might agree that a nation like C ought to be democratic, and that a nation like D, facing different problems, ought to be communistic. One must not think, here, that the nations must disagree in attitude simply because each wants for itself a different form of government. When C wants democracy in C, and D wants communism in D, the restricting phrases, "in C" and "in D," keep the objects of attitude distinct, and the attitudes need not necessarily be opposed. Should C want democracy in C, and D want communism *in C*, then the attitudes would indeed be opposed; but that is another matter, and there could be differences among nations without this kind of difference. Hence the assumption we are discussing does not look to a future with drab and fantastic uniformities of conduct, but only to one in which there is a freedom from opposition and discord.

Yet an assumption that is not fantastic may nevertheless be false, nor have we any trustworthy assurance that it is true. Our conclusions about the finality of rational methods in ethics must accordingly be hypothetical:

If any ethical dispute *is* rooted in disagreement in belief, it may be settled by reasoning and inquiry to whatever extent the beliefs may be so settled. But if any ethical dispute is *not* rooted in disagreement in belief, then no *reasoned* solution of any sort is possible.

part 6

RECENT DEVELOPMENTS

When philosophical activity was fully renewed after World War II there was—especially in England and America—a shift in emphasis in the direction of linguistic concerns. Under the influence of Wittgenstein, Ryle, Austin, and others, philosophers turned their attention to the ways in which people actually use language in the concrete activities of everyday life. This emphasis on *ordinary language* exploded several myths about the way in which words can be meaningful. In the first place, Wittgenstein pointed out that language has meaning in endlessly many ways and that confusions and perplexities arise when we attempt to comprehend this multiplicity under a single model. He also attacked the notions that the fundamental use of language is to *describe* the world and that words get their meaning through *standing for* things in the world. Although this traditional view may be adequate for certain aspects of scientific discourse, it misses the point of such diverse linguistic activities as questioning, advising, evaluating, recommending, computing, praying, pledging, greeting, and so on. Thus Wittgenstein recommended that philosophers set aside their preconceptions about the way in which language *must* work and instead turn their attention to the ways in which it *does* function. "Don't think," Wittgenstein said, "look!"

This change in philosophical style—and it was a change in style rather than in doctrine—has had enormous consequences for the development of ethical theory in the last two decades. It encouraged philosophers to employ new models and comparisons for the understanding of the meaning of basic ethical terms. Thus Urmson explores this region using grading labels as a basis for comparison, and Hare constructs an account of the meaning of ethical terms that uses imperatives as the basic model. Interest in ordinary language also led philosophers to take a fresh look at areas closely tied to ethics, e.g., the nature of responsibility and of non-ethical evaluations.

But this commitment to the "way of words" did not displace an interest in traditional ethical problems. In fact, just the reverse took place. In contrast to the assault upon the traditional approaches that is to be found in the ethical relativists, existentialists, voluntarists, and logical positivists, many of the linguistically oriented philosophers of the last two decades return to classical positions and give them a modern restatement. Thus Rawls and Smart defend (competing) versions of utilitarianism; Singer develops an ethical theory that is essentially Kantian in orientation; Firth elaborates an Ideal Observer theory that is reminiscent of Aristotle's conception of the Morally Upright Man, and Searle attempts to ground obligations squarely in fact by challenging the long standing dogma that an *ought* cannot be derived from an *is*. Although these positions differ radically in detail, they share the common assumption that ethics can be pursued as a rational discipline.

J. O. URMSON

*On Grading**,[1]

A. AN OUTLINE OF SOME TYPICAL GRADING SITUATIONS

If you have an apple tree you know very well that all the apples will not be worth eating and that in a normal season there will be more apples on the tree which are fit for eating than you can eat immediately on ripening. Therefore, when you gather your crop, you will probably divide it into three lots—the really good apples, the not-so-good but edible, and the throw-outs. The good ones you will store (or perhaps sell some at a high price), the not-so-good you will use at once (and perhaps sell some at a lower price), the throw-outs you will throw out, or give to your pigs, or sell at a very low price for someone else's pigs. Let us call this process by the name which, in more complicated forms, it bears in the packing sheds of commercial growers—*grading*. Let us call *grading labels* the adjectives which we apply to the different grades as names of those grades—good, bad, indifferent; first-rate, second-rate, third-rate; high quality, medium quality, low quality; and so on.

In the sequel I intend to extend the expressions "grading" and "grading labels" beyond their normal employment to cover operations and words which, from the viewpoint from which I shall discuss them, seem to me to be essentially similar to grading in its narrower sense. There will be no harm in this if we realize that we are doing it and if we make sure that the other operations and words are really essentially similar to the more obvious cases of grading.

First I will make a series of fairly non-controversial remarks about the more obvious and unmysterious cases of grading.

1. Often, instead of carrying out the physical process of grading, which may be futile or impossible, we do something which I shall call mental grading (on the analogy of "mental" arithmetic). For example, a permanent-way inspector examining railway sleepers will presumably grade them mentally in such grades as "in good condition," "in fair condition" and "unserviceable." But though he does not rip the sleepers from the track and put them in piles he is clearly not doing something importantly different from physical grading. Mental grading is obviously more common than physical grading. We shall not often need to distinguish them.

* By permission. *Mind*, Vol. LIX, 1950, pp. 145–159.

J. O. Urmson is a fellow of Christ Church, Oxford University.

[1] Many of my Oxford colleagues will notice unauthorized borrowings, sometimes involving distortions, from their theories. Mr. Hare suffers worst; I have had the benefit of many discussions on this subject with him. Professor Austin suffers next worst, but many others will notice minor peculations.

2. Grading and the application of grading labels are common activities. Inspectors of goods, tea-tasters and the like (and examiners) do it professionally; we all need to do it for the ordinary purposes of life.

3. In the case of physical grading one can learn to carry out the physical processes correctly, in some cases at least, without any previous knowledge of the objects being graded and with absolutely no knowledge of the opinions about and attitude towards the objects being graded of the person from whom one learns to carry out the processes, or, for that matter, of anybody else. Thus, for example, a person who had never seen an apple before, nor tasted one, and who knew nothing of your, or anybody else's, opinions about and attitude towards apples, would, with reasonable intelligence, and after a period of observation, learn to help you to put the apples into the correct piles merely by watching you do it. The greater his intelligence and the longer his apprenticeship, the more nearly infallible he would become; of course, there would be marginal cases in which he would differ from you, but in these you might as easily have differed from yourself. An instructive point should, however, be noticed here. Without further information our intelligent apprentice, although he would have learnt to grade the apples, or sleepers, in the sense in which a parrot can learn to speak English, might realize no more than the parrot that he was grading. He might not guess but that he was playing some rather tedious game, or tidying up, just as if he were sorting out white and black draughts pieces, or assisting in some scientific classification; he need not speculate on what he is doing at all. As we might say that the parrot was not really speaking English, knowing just what we meant to convey by this, so we might say that the apprentice, unlike you, was not really grading. This state of affairs would be particularly likely to occur if you either did not tell him what grading labels you were employing, or else used such words as are not usually used for grading purposes.

Clearly the same possibilities and limitations would occur in the case of mental grading providing that the apprentice heard the grading labels used with reference to the various objects without recognizing them as grading labels.

One moral of this is quite obvious; grading, like speaking English in the sense in which parrots cannot speak English, or lying, or committing murder, is something which you cannot in a full sense do without understanding what you are doing. The other moral, equally obvious, is that grading is quite different from tidying up or scientific classification, but the difference lies in the purpose of the grader, not in its external form.

4. It is perhaps instructive to notice a possible half-way house between your situation as a fully conscious grader and that of your ignorant and inexperienced, but intelligent and observant, apprentice. Suppose that you use the grading labels "good," "indifferent" and "bad" of your piles of apples; then (more on this topic later), since they are adjectives, which are consecrated to use as grading labels, your apprentice, in addition to his former capacity of going through the right motions, will presumably also realize that he is grading. What he will lack which you have will be firstly an understanding of why you grade one pile more highly than another, though he will be able to distinguish the sets and know which you grade more highly, and secondly any conviction whether he would himself choose to grade on your principles if left to himself. Here too, for these reasons, there would be some point, though not as much as in the case imagined in (3) above, in saying that the apprentice is not really grading. Compare with this our tendency to say that the person who merely echoes conventional moral judgments correctly is not really making moral judg-

ments, remembering especially what Plato has to say of those who have only opinion and not knowledge in moral matters.

5. In our examples we have considered cases of grading, mental and physical, where we have dealt with a large number of objects of a certain type, such as apples or railway sleepers. These are perhaps the only cases which can properly be called grading. But we do sometimes apply the same grading labels to single objects without explicit reference to any others, but using the same criteria. I cannot see any important difference in the two situations, and I shall refer to this type of situation as grading as well as the other. This is one of the ways in which, as I admitted, I intend to stretch the word.

6. Finally, it should be clear that, whatever else there may be that is puzzling about grading, in ordinary typical cases, at least, there is no puzzle about or doubt that it is a business done in accordance with principles and which one can learn to do in the way other people do it. There is no doubt that even the most ignorant apprentice can learn how to go through the right motions by watching other people do it. As a spokesman of the Ministry of Agriculture has wisely said, "proficiency in grading to the most rigid standards is easily acquired in practice, although a precise, and at the same time simple, definition of those standards in words or pictures is a matter of difficulty."

B. TYPES OF GRADING LABELS

Before trying to throw any further light on the nature of grading and its difference from other language-using procedures such as scientific classification it would be advisable to examine a little more closely the grading labels which we use in grading.

1. It is clearly possible, and often done, to employ *ad hoc,* without abuse of one's language, a very wide range of words (marks, etc.) as grading labels, including made-up words and words which sometimes are used for purposes other than grading. For example, I might use "red," "white," "blue" in this way, or "class X," "class Y," "class Z," where it would be necessary explicitly to say what order of merit they convey; I could equally well use "red" for the best and "green" for the worst, or vice versa. Still avoiding controversial issues, it might none the less be worth pointing out here one of the advantages of the use of *ad hoc* labels. More professional grading labels naturally tend to become emotionally charged for good or ill, especially extreme ones; using *ad hoc* grading labels in their place is a way of ensuring objective unbiased calm. It is easier to hand back a paper to a pupil marked "D" than marked "stupid and worthless."

2. But there is also a large class of words, called "professional" in the preceding paragraph, which are used almost exclusively, or quite exclusively, as grading labels. Some obvious examples are "first class," "third rate," "good," "indifferent," "bad," "medium quality." These can be used as grading labels without explicit warning; they themselves give warning, if it is not otherwise evident, that the object of the exercise *is* grading. Furthermore, it is easy and natural to choose sets whose order is clearly defined. It would be an abuse of language to use "indifferent" of a higher grade than "good." It is indeed almost a necessary professional qualification of grading words to show their order; not so invariably (nor would we wish it), some show also their absolute position in the hierarchy of grades immediately. Thus "first rate," "second rate," "third rate" show both order and absolute position—therefore they require careful handling as more precise tools do. But, whereas "good," "bad," and "indifferent" show their order, they do not show their absolute position. This has to be determined from time to

time, if precision is required. "Good" for example can be at the top of a hierarchy or quite low down. Many parents have received school reports in which their children's work has been graded in different subjects as V.G., or G., or F., and, at the bottom will appear some such list as

E. = Excellent
V.G. = Very Good
G. = Good
F. = Fair
etc.

One obvious trick of sellers of graded wares is to use "good" very nearly at the bottom and a number of superlatives above it.

3. Some words which are professionally used mainly or exclusively as grading labels can be used in grading many different kinds of objects, persons, activities, etc. This applies, for example to "good," "bad," and "indifferent." Other professional grading words, which, for this and other reasons to be given below, may be called "specialized," are restricted to one or a few types of objects. For example, the terms "Super," "Extra Fancy," and "Domestic" are, so far as I know, used as an ordered series with absolute position only of commercial consignments of apples. No doubt they could be used in a slightly less specialized way of other merchandise. Some, at least, of them could only be used very abnormally and metaphorically for people or activities.

An especially interesting and important set of specialized grading labels must be mentioned here. In calling them grading labels at all I acknowledge my second stretch of the word "grading" and I must defend it. "Rash," "brave," "cowardly," "extravagant," "liberal," "mean," "boorish," "eligible (bachelor)," "arrogant" are examples. Aristotle, in Books III and IV of the *N.E.* and Theophrastus in his *Characters* give numerous examples of such grading labels and seek to set out the criteria for their employment. As Aristotle noticed, we tend to have explicit grading labels only for some positions in some of the implied scales. Similarly "indifferent" is a more sophisticated word than "good" and "bad"; it tends not to be used in popular discourse. They can be recognized as grading labels in that they show order of merit.

If an Army Company Commander were, as a preliminary to choosing a band of men for an important operation, to go through his Company roll marking each man as "rash," "brave," or "cowardly" we would surely not find it abnormal to say he was grading them (from a specialized point of view). If one were merely to say "He is a brave man" one would not normally call it grading; but I cannot see that the stretch of the word so to call it is harmful. One resistance to calling "brave" a grading label arises from the fact that being more specialized than "good" it enables one to predict more accurately, though in a narrower field, the behaviour of a man so graded. This inclines people to think that it is a descriptive word in the way that "ferocious" normally is. But this is just a mistake; the resistance must be overcome. It would be better to regard "brave" as a grading label restricted to human behaviour in tight places, whereas "good" grades in all places, including tight ones.

4. As would be expected, specialized grading labels show absolute position as well as order more explicitly and more frequently than more general ones.

5. In addition to professional and *ad hoc* grading words there are a number of what we might call enthusiastic amateurs —words of which it is difficult to say whether they function as grading labels or in ordinary classification. Sometimes they are obviously being used for the one purpose, sometimes for the other; often we seem to be killing two birds with one stone and grading and classifying at the same

time. Examples of such words would be (*a*) *valuable*; contrast "Her jewels were in bad taste but valuable" with "That was valuable information"; (*b*) nonsensical, especially as it occurs in the works of some Logical Positivists—it is often hard to say whether a Logical Positivist who states that ethical statements are nonsensical wishes thereby to rate them lower than scientific statements, or merely to note a difference of logical type; one often suspects he is doing both. *Normal* is another example..

Conversely, even the most professional grading labels can be used sometimes practically descriptively—almost entirely so in the case of "I walked a good four miles"; and often "He gave him a good hiding" is used more to indicate severity than propriety.

There is nothing surprising or disconcerting in this. It will be convenient in the main, however, to examine typical, unequivocal examples of grading situations. One should be aware of marginal cases, but one should not harp on them.

6. Apart from these marginal cases a further qualification must be made. Sometimes I merely describe an object and do not grade it explicitly when clearly my prime object is to grade. Thus two of the criteria for being a boor which Theophrastus gives us in his *Characters* are singing in one's bath and wearing hobnailed boots. Now I might mention that a man sings in his bath and wears hobnailed boots and not say that he is a boor although my prime object was to grade him as a boor. The reverse, too, can no doubt happen. In the packing sheds an employee might mention that a certain proportion of a batch of apples was Extra Fancy when his prime object was to give the implied descriptive information. Or I might tell you that a man has a good complexion primarily to enable you to recognize him. It seems worth while explicitly to make this point because when made it is clearly not a damaging admission. If I distinguish commands from descriptions it would not be damaging to admit that I might say "The door is open" with the prime intention of getting you to shut it.

7. A further reason for distinguishing specialized from more general grading labels is that the specialized ones tend to have more clear cut and explicit criteria for their employment. This can best be illustrated by an actual example, so I will now quote from a Government publication the directions for the use of the grading labels *Super* and *Extra Fancy*, which were mentioned in (3) and which have been established by regulations made under the Agricultural Produce (Grading and Marketing) Acts of 1928 and 1931.[2] For brevity's sake the criteria for the grades *Fancy* and below are not quoted here. They are similar in principle and are given in full in the original document.

Definitions of Quality

Super Grade (Dessert Apples Only)

Size.—Each apple not less than 2½ in. in diameter. The apples in any tray to be closely uniform in size and not to vary by more than ⅛ in. in diameter.

Ripeness.—Each apple to have reached that stage of maturity which allows the subsequent completion of the ripening process.

Shape.—Each apple to be of good shape.

Blemish (other than russet).—Each apple to be entirely free from all blemishes including mechanical injuries, bruises and apple-scab.

Russeting.—Russeting in which the apple is cracked, and corky russeting, are not permitted on any apple. Solid russeting in the stem cavity and lightly dispersed russeting sprinkled over an aggregate of one-eighth of the surface are permitted.

Colour.—Closely uniform in any tray.

Condition.—The apples in any tray to be closely uniform in stage of maturity.

[2] *Apple Packing*, Bulletin number 84 of the Ministry of Agriculture and Fisheries, Appendix I. Published by H. M. Stationery Office.

Extra Fancy Grade

Size.—Dessert.—Each apple not less than 2¼ in. in diameter. Cooking.—Each apple not less than 2½ in. in diameter.	The apples in any container to be reasonably uniform in size and not to vary more than ¼ in. in diameter.

Ripeness.—Each apple to have reached that stage of maturity which allows the subsequent completion of the ripening process.

Shape.—No apple to be mis-shapen or malformed.

Blemish (other than russet).—Each apple to be free from such blemishes, bruises and other mechanical injuries as may affect keeping quality during the period which normally elapses between the time of packing and retail sale.

Uncracked apple-scab on any one dessert apple not to exceed ⅛ in. square in the aggregate, and no one scab to be larger than 1/16 in. square (a pin head).

Uncracked apple-scab on any one cooking apple not to exceed ⅛ in. square in the aggregate and no one scab to be more than ⅛ in. in diameter.

Other superficial, non-progressive blemishes on any one apple not to exceed ¼ in. square in the aggregate on dessert apples and ⅜ in. square in the aggregate on cooking apples.

Russeting.—Russeting in which the apple is cracked is not permitted. Solid or corky russeting in the stem cavity and eye basin is permitted. Dispersed russeting, together with solid russet spots not exceeding ½ in. in diameter sprinkled over an aggregate of one-third of the surface, is permitted.

Colour.—Dessert apples in any container to be reasonably uniform in colour.

Condition.—Dessert apples in any container to be reasonably uniform in stage of maturity.

8. Many grading labels which have a specialized meaning can also in isolation be used more generally. "Super," in slang usage, is an example. This constitutes a further reason for the use in technical contexts of *ad hoc* grading labels. Since these have no conventional criteria for employment there is no danger of confusing a general with a specialized employment as would be possible in the case of such a statement as "That was a super consignment of apples."

9. In addition to the general philosophical problem of the nature of grading, the more general (less specialized) grading labels raise special problems of their own. It is perhaps partly for this reason that philosophers, who relish difficulties, have concentrated their attention on such general grading labels as "good" and "bad." (There seems to be no good reason why they have neglected "indifferent.") One unfortunate result of concentrating on examples which raise special problems in contexts (ethical ones) which are especially complicated has been that the *general* problem of the nature of grading has been made to appear vastly more difficult than it is.

As a matter of fact "first class" raises practically all the special problems which "good" does, but for convenience I will now mention some of these special problems using "good" as my example.

a. Granted that "good" is a grading label, is it used so generally because the criteria for its employment (corresponding to the technical criteria for the use of Extra Fancy) are very general, or because a different set of criteria is used in each different type of context (one set for apples, one for cabbages, one for guns, one for moral agents, and so on)?

b. Granted that there are criteria for the use of some specialized grading labels which it would be linguistic eccentricity not to accept, is it so obvious that in every situation there are accepted criteria for the use of the label "good," whether general or specially adapted to the context? Certainly if there are any criteria for the employment of the label "good" they will be vague; but are there any, however vague, which are generally accepted? (This will be recognized as the familiar ethical difficulty about moral relativity.)

c. Do there not appear to be many meanings of "good"? Even if it turns out to be a grading label with accepted, though vague, criteria in some contexts (e.g. apple grading) may there not be others where, though not used as a natural description (as in "good hiding"), it is not used as a grading label either?

10. These special difficulties about such very general labels as "good" must be admitted to infect more specialized grading labels in some cases, since many of them conceal a reference to good amongst their criteria. For example, in the show ring some of the criteria for judging animals are such pedestrian questions as whether this bit of the body is in line with that. But nearly always, I suspect, certainly in some cases, points are given for something like "good general appearance" or "good bearing in the ring." See also the example of grading standards given in B(4) above.

C. THE GENERAL NATURE OF GRADING

In B we outlined some of the special problems about "good." Some of the most famous conundrums were missing, but this was partly because they apply to all grading labels. The basic problem *why* I grade higher a truthful man than a liar, or regard a whole apple as better than a pest-infested one, applies equally to the question why the criteria for Super should not be exchanged for the criteria of Extra Fancy. I shall start, therefore, by dealing with some of the general questions about grading, avoiding the special problems raised by "good" and kindred words as long as I conveniently can.

Let us take a symbolic instance where X is a specialized label and A, B and C are the acknowledged natural criteria for its application. Let us further concentrate just on elucidating the question of how logically the use of a sentence "This is X" differs from other uses of sentences, and how much and in what way it resembles some other uses. Thus for the present such questions as *why* A B C are the criteria for X will be disregarded.

The first thing which seems clear is that the question whether this is X is, granted the acknowledged criteria, as definitely decidable as are the empirical questions whether this is A, or B, or C. Of course, if A = "not less than 2 inches in diameter," then the question whether this is X might be disputed in a marginal case because it might be disputed whether it *is* not less than 2 inches in diameter. But this kind of uncertainty obviously need not detain us now. The point is that if this has the empirical characters A, B, C, then it merits the grading label X, and if not, not; and this, in the required sense, is a decidable issue.

The facts noticed in the last paragraph tempt us to say that "This is X" is just an ordinary empirical statement, that X is just an abbreviation for A B C; the relation of "Super" to its criteria will be the same as "Bramleys" to *its* criteria. But this doctrine, which will be recognized as a close relation of the doctrine of ethical naturalism, surely does not survive much reflection. At this stage we may merely note that the puzzle of how our intelligent apprentice was to distinguish apple grading from sorting out black and white draughts pieces is in effect repudiated by this naturalistic doctrine with the answer that there is no real distinction. And this is obviously false.

A second possible theory of the relation of X to A B C is a close relation of the doctrine of ethical intuitionism. Having rejected naturalism, but recognizing the close connection between X and A B C, we shall say, on this view, that X-ness (say, Extra Fanciness) is a non-natural, intuitable, toti-resultant character supervening on situations in which A B C are present, necessarily, but synthetically, connected with A B C. (If X-ness had been goodness and A knowledge this would not have been too much of a parody of intuitionism.) One negative argument for the view is that we have seen that naturalism fails, and that since the question whether this is X is decidable (objective) subjectivism will not do; nor, clearly, is it plausible to regard "This is an Extra Fancy consignment of apples" as a squeal of delight. So in default of other theories Intuitionism stands. More positively we may say that "Extra Fancy" is an adjective used in true or false statements; it must stand for some character; but it is not possible to see, hear, smell, Extra Fanciness, so it must be a non-natural character. Though I clearly do not accept this theory, I shall not attack it; probably even those who support it in the case of "goodness" would not wish to support it in the case of Extra Fanciness or Full Fruit Standardness. The reason for mentioning it as a theoretical possibility is that all the arguments of Moore and Ross can be converted to apply in all cases of grading labels. It is hard to see why it should be true of "goodness" but not of "Extra Fanciness."

I suppose that a case can be made for a Stevensonian[3] analysis in all grading situations. In stressing the close relation between X and A B C, it will be said, we have been concentrating on the second pattern of analysis too closely. Why the equivalence between X and A B C does not hold will become clear if we consider the neglected first pattern of analysis. To call an apple Extra Fancy would perhaps be to express a special type and degree of approval and call for it from others. Grading words will differ from others by the possession of a special emotive charge.

Certainly it cannot be denied that amongst words which are or become highly charged emotively are the more extreme of the more general grading labels ("good" and "bad," but not so much "indifferent," for obvious reasons). But we have already noticed that one extremely valuable use of *ad hoc* grading words is that by using them it is possible to grade without emotional repercussions.[4] It is perfectly intelligible that professional grading words should normally be emotively significant; it is true that we often exploit this emotive significance;[5] but to the true nature of grading these facts appear to be quite peripheral.

But all these three views, naturalism, intuitionism and the emotive theory, have seized on some points of importance (so, we shall see later, have ordinary subjectivism and utilitarianism). Naturalism rightly emphasizes the close connection between the grading label and the set of natural characters which justify its use; intuitionism rightly emphasizes that this close connection is not identity of meaning and insists on the different logical character of grading labels and natural descriptions. Both rightly stress the objective character of grading. The emotive theory, agreeing with intuitionism about the fault of naturalism, rightly stresses that the intuitionist cure of suggesting that grading labels are a special kind of non-natural descriptive adjective will not do.

At some stage we must say firmly (why not now?) that to describe is to describe, to grade is to grade, and to express one's feelings is to express one's feelings, and that none of these is reducible to either of the others; nor can any of them be reduced to, defined in terms of, anything else. We can merely bring out similarities and differences by examples and comparisons. That, too, in the end, would presumably be the only way of bringing out the difference between asking questions and giving orders (here, again, the marginal

[3] C. L. Stevenson, *Ethics and Language.* (Yale University Press, 1944).

[4] See B (1).

[5] See B (2).

case such as "Won't you go now?" must not be overstressed).

We can, for example, tell stories of people sorting out mixed piles of fruit into apples, plums and pears, and of people sorting mixed piles of apples into Blenheims, Bramleys, etc., and notice the difference betwen this activity and that of people who sort piles of mixed fruit into good, bad and indifferent piles, or Super, Extra Fancy, etc., piles. We can tell stories comparing also the distinction between mental classification and grading. Also, since philosophers are wedded to the expectation that indicative sentences will all be used for describing things, it will be as well to remind them of other non-descriptive (and non-emotive) uses of indicative sentences—Austin's performatory sentences, for example.

Or let us go back to the problem of the relation between the natural criteria A B C and the grading label X which they justify. Is the sentence "Anything which is A B C is X" analytic or synthetic? We have already noticed the naturalistic difficulties involved in answering "analytic"; but yet the pointlessness, the impossibility, of maintaining that a thing is X if it is not A B C or denying that it is X if it is A B C makes the answer "synthetic" equally unplausible.[6] But if we see that grading is different from ordinary description we can understand why this dilemma is insoluble; for the question whether the connection between two sets of characteristics is analytic or synthetic is a question which is designed to be asked where the related characters are descriptive. If not pressed too hard, the analogy of the relation between possession of the legal qualifications for a right or privilege and the possession of that right or privilege illuminates better the relation between natural criteria and grade far better than the analogy of expanded descriptive phrases and defined abbreviations. For to assert the possession of the legal qualifications for a certain right (say the vote), e.g. that one is a British subject twenty-one or more years old, not a peer, not mad, etc., is not to assert analytically the possession of the legal right; but to assert the legal right is not to assert the possession of any additional characteristics of a descriptive kind beyond these qualifications. There are, of course, differences too; otherwise, being graded and possessing rights would be indistinguishable.

It may also be helpful to compare and contrast grading and choosing:

a. There is an analogy between examining various objects and then saying "I'll have that one"—which is a choice not a prediction—and mental grading.

b. There is an analogy between examining various objects, and then picking one out to have, and physical grading.

There is a difference also in these cases which can be put by saying that between examining and choosing, one grades and chooses on the basis of one's grading.

Therefore (*c*) we may make up a more artificial example. Two captains picking sides will normally pick them on their estimate of the grade of the candidates for selection. But suppose there were certain rules for picking sides (say, that you have to pick the person who is first in alphabetical order) so that there would be a right and wrong way of picking your side. This example brings out the logical disparity which there can be between a non-descriptive activity like taking as a member of your side and the descriptive criteria for picking, and to that extent should make the relation between a grading label and its criteria less mysterious. It is not surprising that there should be a close con-

[6] This will have to be modified later. See pp. 404–6. But this modification does not detract from the force of the argument in this context, where the acceptance of A B C as criteria is not being questioned.

nection between such an activity as picking something and the rules in accordance with which it is done and yet it be impossible to ask whether this connection is analytic or synthetic; the same thing should not be mysterious in regard to the natural criteria and physical grading. And if we see the unimportance of the difference between choosing something and saying "I will have this" (we cannot ask whether the rule for choosing *entails* "I will have this one"), we might also see how unimportant is the difference between grading and applying a grading label. Of course, choosing in accordance with a rule is very different in many ways from grading; the analogy which I want to stress is between the relation of rule to choice and criteria to grade label.

As a final attempt to bring out the general nature of grading it might be worth considering the word "approve" for a while. It has been used frequently in recent philosophy to elucidate some specific grading situations.

Many philosophers recently[7] have been examining the distinction in English between the present perfect tense (I sit, I run, I play) and the present continuous tense (I am sitting, running, playing). It is obvious that they have very different uses. Some verbs appear to have no present continuous, nor does their use in the present perfect appear similar to the use of other verbs in either the present perfect or present continuous tense (I know, I believe, I regret). "I approve" seems also to be such an anomalous verb. It is, indeed, possible to use its present continuous tense but an example will show how anomalous such a usage is: suppose Smith has to obtain your approval if he wishes to do a certain thing. Then you will signify your approval by writing "I approve" (not "I am approving"). Now supposing someone were to dash into your room and say "What are you doing?" just while you are writing these words, you might possibly answer "Oh, I'm just approving Smith's application." Here "I am approving" describes what I am doing, but the doing which I describe is not asserting, expressing, evincing or having any feeling or emotion or state of mind. I am writing "I approve" and it is this action which I describe when I say "I am approving." To say, or write, "I approve," however, is not to describe anything at all—it can be described but is not itself a case of describing. In the case above it is something like giving your authority for an action.

Our other uses of "approve" differ from this in many ways, but at least resemble it in that they are not descriptive uses.[8] Suppose, for example, someone says "On the whole, I approve of the licensing laws." Clearly this is not so absurd a thing to say as to give his authority for something which does not need his authority. A better suggestion is that he is grading the licensing laws as being on the whole at least satisfactory. He might change this mind and henceforth disapprove, but this kind of change of mind is not the correction of a factual error.

I do not wish to examine further the logic of approval for its own sake. I agree, however, with the subjectivists and emotivists in considering that the analogy between approving and grading is illuminating—but not in the way they think, in that I deny that "I approve" is a description of the subjective events or that "Please approve" is a request to have certain feelings.

That is all I can do in the way of logical description of grading. Before going on to consider such other general problems as how we get the criteria in order to start grading we may first consider some

[7] I have learnt something about this from Professors Ryle and Austin. I do not know who owns the patent.

[8] If I say "I approve—do so as well" there is no descriptive element in my statement.

of the special problems about "good" and other very general grading labels.

D. SOME SPECIAL PROBLEMS ABOUT "GOOD"

We shall start with the assumption (to be argued later) that "good" is a grading label applicable in many different types of contexts, but with different criteria for employment in each. Now first it must be pointed out that such general grading labels have a character equivalent to the vagueness and open texture to which Dr. Waismann has drawn attention[9] in the case of ordinary descriptive words. Take the example of an apple again; what are the criteria for its being good? First no doubt it must have a pleasant taste and straightway we have a case of a vague and open textured criterion. A pleasant taste for whom? it will be asked; and there is no definitely right answer. But we must not exaggerate this vagueness. For if we answer "to a majority of apple eaters" there is nothing seriously wrong with the answer as there would be if we answered "to the Archbishop of Canterbury" or "to squirrels." But can we guarantee that it will be a stable majority? Clearly not; but this should not be philosophically worrying; the simple fact is that but for the contingent fact that there is such a stable majority we should have to give up grading apples altogether or else give up using pleasant taste as one of the criteria for grading apples.[10]

The writings of some philosophers seem to suggest that pleasant taste is the only criterion of goodness in apples,[11] but this is surely false. Other criteria are size, shape, keeping quality, nutritive value, pleasing appearance and, perhaps, feel. Now we have already noticed vagueness and open texture within one criterion. But the list itself has the same properties. No one can give the precise list; some will omit a criterion I have given, add another, vary the emphasis, and none of them need be wrong (though we could produce a list which would be certainly wrong). And it is always possible to think of something else which might be taken as a criterion or which has been implicitly used as such and not been noted. But surely as long as we recognize this it need not worry us any more than the vagueness of the criteria for the use of descriptive adjectives. "Good" is *very* vague—so is "bald," or "middle-aged." So long as there is a general consensus in the employment of criteria all is well. If, as sometimes happens in the case both of vague descriptions and of vague grading labels, this consensus is missing, communication becomes uncertain (democratic, body-line bowling).

In contrast with the apple consider a cabbage (the contrast could be made much greater). Many of the criteria will be quite different from those in the case of apples—firm heart, a bright green or bluish-green colour, few spreading outer leaves, long-standing, etc.

Now, if the grading label "good" were, in each of these and all other cases, merely shorthand for the sum of the criteria (naturalism) we should have the absurd situation that "good" was a homonym with as many punning meanings as the situations it applied to; it could not significantly be used of a theatrical performance

[9] *Proceedings of the Aristotelian Society*, Supplementary Volume for 1945. [Reprinted above, First Series, Ch. VII.—EDITOR.]

[10] As a matter of fact in the technical grading of apples taste is not used as a criterion. This, no doubt, is partly because you cannot both taste and sell whole, partly because the taste of varieties is constant and it is assumed that only varieties will be further graded which have already survived the test of taste.

[11] " 'This is good,' may mean 'This is pleasant' as when we say 'This is good cheese.' " Paton, *Proceedings of the Aristotelian Society*, Supp. Vol. XXII, p. 110.

in the sense in which it is used of an apple. This, granted our present assumptions, constitutes a most graphic refutation of naturalism. On the other hand, to regard the relation between "good" and the criteria for a good apple as synthetic is equally absurd. If someone were to admit that an apple was of 2 inches diameter, regularly shaped, of pleasing taste, high vitamin content and pest-free, nor claimed that it lacked some other essential characteristic but none the less denied that it was a good apple it would not merely be empirically surprising; it would involve a breakdown in communication.

The obvious naturalistic reaction to this, which, though for different reasons, might be shared by other schools of thought, would be to deny any assumption that the criteria are different in each type of situation. "The real criteria," they might say, "for the employment of 'good' are much more general than you have made it appear." The criteria which a show judge might mention for a good Shorthorn cow or a cutler for a good knife are not the real criteria of goodness. The real criterion is easy production of a desired end, approximate or ultimate, in each case. "The so-called criteria," they might say, "of the judge and the cutler are really no more than signs or symptoms that the object in question will satisfy this general criterion." "We must distinguish," they might add, "the various senses of 'good,' provisionally limiting ourselves to the modest distinction of good as a means and good as an end. Then there will be one general criterion of good as a means—already given, and one for good as an end which is perhaps something like 'worth choosing for its own sake.' Perhaps, on reflection," they conclude, "we might wish to distinguish other senses, but we do not require the myriad of punning senses you suggested but only a few which in any case will be paronyms, not homonyms."

No doubt this presentation of their argument could be bettered in many details, but it is not in detail that I wish to attack it, so perhaps it will suffice. Let me first admit that if one examines the kinds of thing which one employs as criteria, then, though this may not be the best way of putting it, one possible division of the criteria employed is into criteria which we choose for themselves and others which we choose for their consequences. Some criteria, too, as Plato pointed out in the *Republic*, we choose both for themselves and their consequences. Let me also admit that some criteria are less central than others, that some *are* used mainly as signs of the presence of criteria more difficult to detect in themselves. But these admissions in no way justify a distinction of two senses of "good"—good as a means and good as an end. Firstly, the criteria which we employ for the grading label "good" in any given case will usually include criteria of both types, and of Plato's dual type; if there are indeed any things for the goodness of which all criteria fall into either class these are limiting cases and not normal types. It would be a great mistake to imagine that farmers, cutlers and fruit growers value their products only as means to ends; and the consumer pays less for an unsightly vegetable because it *is* unsightly and not because of any detrimental effects of unsightliness. If I am asked whether a good apple is good as a means or as an end I should not know how to answer; it is not a real question. But the division of *criteria* which we have admitted would only justify a distinction of two senses of "good" if it were logically impossible to mix the two sets of criteria, if at all.

It might perhaps be replied to this, though even before argument it is not very plausible, that all we have shown is that normally anything which we grade as good we call good in both senses of the word at once—*that* was why I could not answer in which sense of "good" the apple was good. Still I have not established that there really are different sets of criteria for different types of situation. Let us answer that, even if an apple, *per impossibile,* satisfied all the criteria which we require for good as an end and good as a means in the case of cabbages, it would not be a good apple. Though we have agreed that some criteria are less central than others, there still remains a hard core of criteria which have to be satisfied in each different case, which cannot be generalized into any one or two formulae. Why an apple which tasted like a good cabbage would certainly be a very bad apple we have not yet ventured to discuss; but a very bad apple it certainly would be; I cannot see how my imaginary opponents would be able to explain this fact, which seems to require different criteria for goodness in apples and cabbages (and *a fortiori* in men and guns). Omitting consideration of certain cant or slang phrases I see no reason for thinking that there is more than one sense of the word "good." On the other hand, since I deny an analytic identity of meaning between criteria and grading labels I still hold that the criteria are, as the facts seem to require, different in each situation.

I add at this stage two small points which perhaps illuminate and are illuminated by the above discussion.

1. Suppose that I, ignorant of horses, point to a horse in a field and say "That's a good horse." In a way we want to say that I know what I mean—after all I know how to use the various words and understand their syntax. But in a way we might want to say that I do not really know what I mean. For suppose that an expert had said "That's a good horse." Now, looking at it once, and at a distance, he may be mistaken; he needs more facts than he has in order to be confident of the truth of his statement. But the kind of lack of confidence which I ought to feel is quite different; for, unlike the expert, I will not be enabled by further examination of the horse to decide at all whether it is a good horse. And because I have made a statement which I just do not know how to verify or falsify (in the way grading statements are verified and falsified) we tend, as I suggested, to say that I did not really know what I meant.

2. Grading statements being, as I maintain, objectively decidable, they are, for many reasons, more important and impressive than mere indications of personal likes and dislikes. We therefore tend to use them when all we are really entitled to do is to state our likes and dislikes. Thus I might easily say "That's a good horse" being ignorant of the criteria for a good horse and therefore really only entitled to say that I like the look of it. We really know this, as becomes clear when we reflect that only a very conceited person would chance his arm by saying "That's a good horse" unless he knew or believed that his companion was as ignorant of horses as he was. We might say it to a city clerk—but not to a Newmarket trainer. These considerations help, I think, both to bring out the difference between grading and expressing one's likes, and to explain why some people, observing that we naughtily interchange them, tend to confuse them.

So much for the way we use such general grading labels as "good" and how their use differs from that of more specialized grading labels, though the distinction is not a hard and fast one.

E. THE ESTABLISHMENT OF GRADING CRITERIA

So far we have confined our study of grading to cases where it is fairly clear that there are criteria for grading, and without asking whether there must always be accepted criteria, or why the accepted criteria are accepted. We have certainly said nothing whatsoever to deal with such special problems as that raised by the moral reformer, who is often clearly intelligible and yet may almost be defined as the man who does not accept the accepted criteria. I cannot pretend to offer a complete answer to these problems, but there are a few things which are perhaps worth saying about them.

The first point to be made is that the question whether there are any objective and accepted criteria for grading and how they function, which we have just left, is a quite different problem from the problem why we employ and accept these criteria. This, I think, has not always been fully realized; but certain theories could be much more powerfully stated if they took it into account.

Subjectivism, in its traditional varieties as an account of how we use the word "good" in general, for example, is usually stated in a manner which makes it an utterly absurd view. To say that there are no objective criteria, that there is no right or wrong opinion about whether this is good cheese or (to take a case of something which is clearly not good as a means) a good lap-dog, seems quite preposterous. Anyone who knew about cheese or dogs would laugh at you. It is equally preposterous, as Broad points out,[12] to hold that a statement that some cheese is good is a statistical statement about peoples' likes and dislikes, passions and emotions. But if we remodel this latter subjectivist theory and treat it not as a theory about the way we use the word "good" but as a theory about how the criteria for grading cheese or lap-dogs come to be accepted and established, it becomes a much more plausible theory. The theory will now admit our account of how we use the word "good"; its contribution will be as follows: it is a fact that there is a stable majority (we need not now settle among which people the majority will be) who prefer, like, choose, cheese with the characteristics A B C. Then A B C become the charactericties which are accepted even by the minority, for grading cheese. Thus even if one happens to hate all cheese, one will still be able sensibly to distinguish good from bad cheese; *mutatis mutandis* the same applies to lap-dogs or anything else. Before the acceptance of such conventional criteria for good cheese the question whether some sample of cheese is good will have no answer.[13] After their acceptance the question will have a definite answer. This seems to me, thus recast as an answer to a different question, a very formidable theory. In the case of cheese it is just about right.

But few philosophical theories have the monopoly of all truth; any rival which survives long does so because it has got hold of some important point. But most of the prevalent philosophical theories about the meaning of "good" can be recast as theories of how we arrive at criteria of goodness.

Now, *a priori* there is no reason why there should be any one answer to the question why we accept the criteria which we do accept. We might adopt some criteria for certain reasons and some for others. Consider a utilitarian theory of goodness, for example, recast as a theory that we choose the criteria we do choose because things satisfying these criteria in a high degree subserve more easily the ends for which we employ them. As a general theory this is no doubt lamentably inadequate, but as an account of why we employ *some* criteria (e.g. sharpness in the case of a knife) it seems very plausible, and I have no doubt that if it makes this limited claim it is correct.

Or consider social theories of goodness (especially moral goodness) which hold that a man or form of behaviour is good in so far as he or it contributes to social life

[12] See his essay on Hume in *Five Types of Ethical Theory*. I do not necessarily agree that Hume held this preposterous view.

[13] See pp. 405–7 below on this point.

and well-being. Once again, considered as an account of why we accept *some* of the criteria of goodness, I have no doubt that it is of value. No doubt truthfulness as a criterion of a good man is at least in part accepted for this kind of reason. And if anyone wishes to maintain that this is a *rational* ground for accepting the criterion, why not?

I have no doubt that there are other reasons for accepting criteria for grading, but we cannot aim at a complete catalogue; in no circumstance could we have a right to regard any catalogue as complete. No doubt some criteria for some things are retained for all kinds of odd reasons. Perhaps few people nowadays could imagine why a family is better if the names of more of its former members and their interrelationships are recorded.

But what of matters where there is not complete agreement on the criteria for grading something? This is a situation which surely does sometimes arise. If the disagreement is minor it matters no more than minor disagreements about the requirements for baldness. But disagreement is admittedly not always minor; the slayer and eater of aged parents and the moral reformer now rear their (respectively) ugly and reverend heads.

Schematically, the main patterns of moral and other grading disagreements seem to be as follows:

1. We accept roughly or exactly the same criteria of goodness (or of being first class, etc.) but haven't yet examined them all. When one says of some object under discussion that it is good and the other says that it is bad, we will be speculating on partial evidence. We can settle the question by examining the other agreed criteria. This raises no problems, and its frequent occurrence is therefore insufficiently noticed by philosophers.

2. We accept the same criteria but it is a marginal case. Here perhaps we shall never settle our agreement. But this raises no more problems than the unsettleable dispute as to who won a close race. Such disputes quite often occur and naturally last longer and attract more attention than the first type.

3. We have no agreement, or very little, on criteria. Here we just cannot settle our problems for the overwhelmingly good reason that we cannot discuss them. We shall normally assume that we have the same criteria and talk at cross purposes until we find that we cannot settle our dispute. We shall then either recognize what has happened and try to reach some agreed criteria failing which further discussion will be worthless, i.e. we shall stop discussing the undiscussable question whether this O is good and discuss the question how to grade Os. The reasons we shall offer for accepting the criteria we propose will be such as were mentioned in our last discussion. Or if we do not recognize our predicament we shall think each other stupid and/or dishonest and fall back on rhetoric and abuse.

4. We may have important disagreements on criteria and Jones, the reformer, may know it. He may then openly reveal himself as not asking the question whether a thing is good or not by accepted standards, but as advocating new standards, new criteria. In this case it will be clear that we are not arguing whether a thing is good or bad in the ordinary way as in (1) and (2) above but arguing what criteria to use in order to argue that kind of question. More likely, and perhaps not so clearheadedly, he will use the rhetorical device of talking as though his proposed new criteria were the accepted criteria; this is one of the most effective methods of getting new criteria accepted.[14] This trick is commonly employed not merely by moral reformers but also by advertisers—they try to

[14] Stevenson, *Ethics and Language*, Ch. IX "Persuasive Definitions" is very relevant here.

make you accept the characteristics of their wares as criteria of goodness in that class of merchandise by pretending that everyone (or all the best people) knows that these *are* the accepted criteria. If people do not recognize this device for what is it, it may either be successful with enough people to get the standards actually changed or else we shall go through all the trying manœuvres of type (3) above.

It should be added that criteria of grade can change without the impetus of a militant reformer. No doubt "eligible" was a grading word as applied to bachelors in the eighteenth and nineteenth centuries. No doubt also the criteria of eligibility gradually shifted, under the pressure of social evolution, from such things as a baronetcy and land to a good job and railway shares.

If this rough schema of disagreements be accepted (in practice of course the types will be complicated and mixed up with each other) the answer to the problem of disagreement about grading criteria seems to be this: grading words can only be *used* successfully for communication where criteria are accepted. Where they are not there can only be confusion and cross purposes until it is seen that the only discussion possible between such people is what criteria for grading to adopt—grading words must then be discussed, not used.

The need for agreed criteria can perhaps be further illustrated in the following way. There are situations in which we do not naturally use grading words at all and where, therefore, there are no accepted criteria for grading. Consider for example the prime numbers. So far as I know, no one has yet graded the prime numbers as good and bad, or first and second class, and so far as I know there are no criteria for doing so. Unless my inadequate mathematical training misleads me, I suggest that if anyone were to say "17 is an exceptionally bad prime number" there would be a complete failure to communicate—a failure not due to anybody's ignorance or incapacity. Only after criteria were adopted (I cannot imagine what in this case they would possibly be unless superstitious astrological ones) would such a statement be of any use in communication. (Whether it would therefore be previously meaningless may be left to the reader to decide.)

But the extreme vagueness of the criteria in some grading situations undoubtedly makes it appear that there are no criteria to philosophers who like and expect things to be clear cut. Pre-eminently people might think this to be the case with the moral goodness of a person. We cannot hope to deal adequately with this point now but a few observations might be permitted and must suffice.

A good man, without further qualification, obviously must fulfil different criteria in different contexts (for club and church membership, for example). This appears to be so even if we qualify our grading label and write "morally good." In some contexts, one might almost say, the criteria of moral goodness in earlier twentieth-century England can be roughly specified as being conformity to Ross's list of *prima facie* duties. In other contexts what a man does will be less important and why he does what he does more important ("Motive not action makes a man good or bad"). Roughly the way to find out what criteria are being employed is to ask why the man has been graded thus. But however the criteria may vary from context to context they must and can be recognized for effective communication; without it we tend all too often merely to "recite Empedoclean verses."

A further resistance to recognizing the ordinary grading mechanism as operating in morals is set up by the undoubted fact that moral grading is so much more important; we feel so much more strongly about the attainment of high moral grades than others. Being a good cricketer is excellent in its way, but not vital; being a good citizen, a good father, a good man, is very different. This creates the impression that to call someone a good man is logically different from calling him a good cricketer. The one point I shall make about this is that in grading people in non-moral matters and in grading things we are dealing with dispensable qualifications in people and dispensable things. But moral grade affects the whole of one's life and social intercourse—a low grade in this makes other high gradings unimportant. The nearest approach to morals in indispensability is made by manners; and surely it is significant that we feel next most strongly after morals about manners—indeed there is a borderline where it is hard to distinguish which we are dealing with. But when we acknowledge these facts we surely give no reason for expecting a logical difference as well.

F. THE RELATION BETWEEN ALTERNATIVE SETS OF GRADING CRITERIA

Now for the final problem; when there are differences of opinion about what grading criteria to adopt in a given situation is there not a right and wrong about it; can we not say that these are the right, these are the wrong criteria; or are we to say that the distinction, for example, between higher and lower, enlightened and unenlightened, moral codes is chimerical? In some cases we would perhaps be content to admit that there was no right or wrong about it; the differences in criteria arise from different interests, different environments, different needs; each set is adequate to its own sphere. But in others we certainly do not want to say this; the distinction, for example, between higher and lower moral codes cannot be lightly brushed aside. Roughly the question of whether we wish to decide this issue appears to depend largely on whether the simultaneous use of different sets of grading criteria by juxtaposed groups is in departmental, dispensable matters, or in all-embracing matters such as moral codes (more or less enlightened) and manners (more or less polished or cultivated).

This problem is clearly a large one which for adequate treatment would require a book in itself. We can here only sketch a method of dealing with it.

Clearly when we debate which of two moral codes is more enlightened there is no ultimate court of appeal, no umpire, unless some agreed revealed religious code is treated as a *deus ex machina*. Nor will it do to say that "more enlightened" means the same as "the one I advocate." This is shown by the fact that though I cannot admit that the code I advocate is less enlightened than yours, I can admit that it may be; just as I cannot admit that my present belief about anything is mistaken, but can admit that it may be.

The important clue for dealing with this problem is to notice that *enlightened, unenlightened, higher, lower* are grading labels. Of course, we cannot, when debating what criteria to use for moral grading, grade the criteria morally. But we can grade them by enlightenment provided, of course, that the disputants have an agreed set of criteria of enlightenment. We cannot hope now to give a complete and clear list of these criteria; no doubt they are vague; and it is easier to employ criteria than to recognize them. But surely one criterion would be that the reasons for adopting the criteria are not superstitious or magical; that some reasons can be given would seem to be another. Again, the contrast between the health, wealth and happiness of people living under different moral codes cannot prove the superiority of one code over another, but it does seem to be a criterion of enlightenment. The misery of slaves, for example, is surely a potent cause for the rejection of a moral code as unenlightened in which a slave owner or trader is a good man.

If people have not agreed criteria for

enlightenment, I do not know what one can do about it. All co-operative activities, all uses of language, must start from some agreed point. One needs a fixed point to move the world with one's lever.

Finally two postscripts.

1. I am not wedded to the words "grade" and "criterion." I use "grade" rather than "evaluate," for example, largely because "evaluate" tends to be associated with a special kind of theory. Again, in the Government directions for grading apples the word "standard" is used as a synonym for my word "criterion." Possibly it is better in some ways but has the dangerous overtone for philosophers of "moral standard."

2. Nothing has been said in this paper about "right," "wrong," and cognate words. The discussion has ranged widely enough without that. But it might be as well to make it quite clear that I do not regard them as grading labels. They function quite differently, and what I have said does not apply to them.

R. M. HARE

*The Language of Morals**

PRESCRIPTIVE LANGUAGE

If we were to ask of a person "What are his moral principles?" the way in which we could be most sure of a true answer would be by studying what he *did*. He might, to be sure, profess in his conversation all sorts of principles, which in his actions he completely disregarded; but it would be when, knowing all the relevant facts of a situation, he was faced with choices or decisions between alternative courses of action, between alternative answers to the question "What shall I do?," that he would reveal in what principles of conduct he really believed. The reason why actions are in a peculiar way revelatory of moral principles is that the function of moral principles is to guide conduct. The language of morals is one sort of prescriptive language. And this is what makes ethics worth studying: for the question "What shall I do?" is one that we cannot for long evade; the problems of conduct, though sometimes less diverting than crossword puzzles, *have to be solved* in a way that crossword puzzles do not. We cannot wait to see the solution in the next issue, because on the solution of the problems depends what happens in the next issue. Thus, in a world in which the problems of conduct become every day more complex and tormenting, there is a great need for an understanding of the language in which these problems are posed and answered. For confusion about our moral language leads, not merely to theoretical muddles, but to needless practical perplexities.

An old-fashioned, but still useful, way of studying anything is *per genus et differentiam*; if moral language belongs to the genus "prescriptive language," we shall most easily understand its nature if we compare and contrast first of all prescriptive language with other sorts of language, and then moral language with other sorts of prescriptive language. That, in brief, is the plan of this book. I shall proceed from the simple to the more complex. I shall deal first with the simplest form of prescriptive language, the ordinary imperative sentence. The logical behaviour of this type of sentence is of great interest to the student of moral language because, in spite of its comparative simplicity, it raises in an easily discernible form many of the problems which have beset ethical theory. Therefore, although it is no part of my purpose to "reduce" moral language to imperatives, the study of imperatives is by far the best introduction to the study of ethics; and if the reader does not at once

* By permission. *The Language of Morals* (Oxford University Press, Fair Lawn, N.J., 1952).

R. M. Hare is White's Professor of Moral Philosophy, Oxford University.

see the relevance to ethics of the earlier part of the discussion, I must ask him to be patient. Neglect of the principles enunciated in the first part of this book is the source of many of the most insidious confusions in ethics. . . .

The classification of prescriptive language which I propose may be represented as follows:

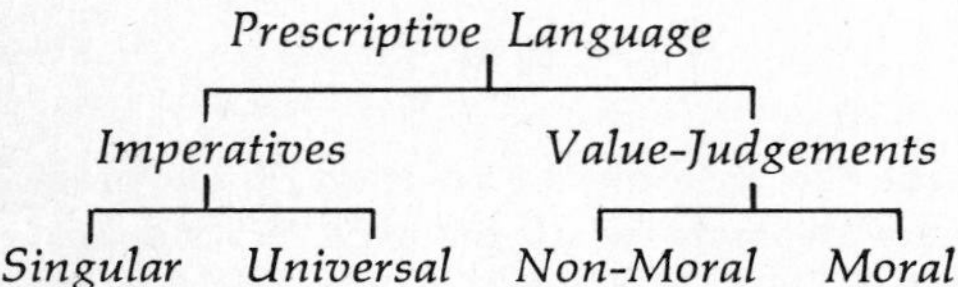

This classification is rough only; it will be made more precise in the course of the book; for example, it will be seen that the so-called "universal imperatives" of ordinary language are not proper universals. Nor do I wish to suggest that the classification is exhaustive; there are, for example, many different kinds of singular imperatives, and of non-moral value-judgements; and there are other kinds of imperatives besides singular and universal. But the classification is good enough to begin with. . . .

IMPERATIVES AND LOGIC

In order to characterize clearly the difference between imperatives and indicatives, it will be helpful so to analyse the two types of sentence, as to make it plain what elements of meaning they have in common, and so isolate the essential difference. . . .

The two sentences "You are going to shut the door" and "Shut the door" are both about the same thing, namely, your shutting the door in the immediate future; but they are used to say different things about it. It is purely an accident of grammar that those parts of the spoken or written sentence which, in either case, refer to this thing that they are about, are not identical. Let us recast the sentences more clearly by writing in both cases an identical phrase for referring to this thing that they are both about. The phrase might be:

> *Your shutting the door in the immediate future.*

We shall then have to add something, different in each case, which supplies the rest of what each sentence conveys. What we have so far tells us quite clearly what the sentences are about. It does not, however, tell us what the speaker is saying about it. We do not know whether he is stating that your shutting the door in the immediate future is what is going to happen or be the case, or whether he is telling us to make it the case, or something else. In order to complete the sentences, therefore, something has to be added to tell us this. We might complete the sentences as a command or a statement respectively, by writing:

> *Your shutting the door in the immediate future, please.*
> *Your shutting the door in the immediate future, yes.*

These two sentences would correspond to the normal English sentences:

> *Shut the door.*
> *You are going to shut the door.*

We shall need technical terms for referring to these different parts of sentences. . . . I shall call the part of the sentence that is common to both moods ("Your shutting the door in the immediate future") the *phrastic*; and the part that is different in the case of commands and statements ("yes" or "please"), the *neustic*. Readers of Liddell and Scott's *Greek Lexicon* will recognize the appropriateness of these terms. "Phrastic" is derived from a Greek word meaning "to point out or indicate," and "neustic" from a word meaning "to nod assent." Both words are used indifferently of imperative and indicative speech. The utterance of a sentence containing phrastic and neustic might be dramatized as follows: (1) The speaker points out or indicates what he is going to state to be the case, or command to be made the case; (2) He nods, as if to say "It *is* the case," or "Do it." He will, however, have to nod in a different way, according as he means one or other of these things.

Now clearly, if we are looking for the essential difference between statements and commands, we have to look in the neustic, not in the phrastic. But, as the use of the single word "neustic" indicates, there is still something in common between indicative and imperative neustics. This is the common notion of, so to speak, "nodding" a sentence. It is something that is done by anyone who uses a sentence in earnest, and does not merely mention it or quote it in inverted commas; something essential to *saying* (and meaning) anything. The absence of inverted commas in written language symbolizes the element of meaning of which I am speaking; to write a sentence without inverted commas is like signing a cheque; to write it within inverted commas is like drawing a cheque without signing it, e.g. to show someone how to draw cheques. We could have a convention that, instead of putting inverted commas round sentences that we were mentioning and not using, we nodded, or made some special mark in writing, when we *were* using a sentence in earnest. The "assertion symbol" in the logical system of Frege and in that of Russell and Whitehead has, among other functions, this one of signifying the use or affirmation of a sentence.[1] It could, in this function, be applied to commands as well as to statements. We may perhaps strain language slightly and use the word "affirm" of both.

Closely allied to such an affirmation sign would be a sign for agreement or assent for use by a hearer. To use such a sign of assent would be tantamount to repeating the sentence with the pronouns, &c., changed where necessary. Thus, if I said "You are going to shut the door," and you answered "Yes," this would be a sign of assent, and would be equivalent to "I am going to shut the door." And if I said "Shut the door," and you answered "Aye, aye sir," this likewise would be a sign of assent; if we wished to express what it is equivalent to, we might say "Let me shut the door" or "I will shut the door" (where "I will" is not a prediction but the expression of a resolve or a promise). Now this should give us a clue to the essential difference between statements and commands; it lies in what is involved in assenting to them; and what is involved in assenting to them is, as I have said, closely allied to what is involved in affirming them in the first place.[2]

If we assent to a statement we are said to be sincere in our assent if and only if we believe that it is true (believe what the speaker has said). If, on the other hand, we assent to a second-person command addressed to ourselves, we are said to be sincere in our assent if and only if we do or resolve to do what the speaker has told us to do; if we do not do it but only resolve to do it later, then if, when the occasion arises for doing it, we do not do it, we are said to have changed our mind; we are no longer sticking to the assent which we previously expressed. It is a tautology to say that we cannot sincerely assent to a second-person command addressed to ourselves, and *at the same time* not perform

[1] See Russell and Whitehead, *Principia Mathematica*, i. 9.

[2] For some interesting remarks about the kindred notions of "admitting" and "confirming,' see P. F. Strawson, "Truth," *Analysis* ix (1948–9), 83, and *Aristotelian Society*, Supplementary vol. xxiv (1950), 129.

it, if now is the occasion for performing it and it is in our (physical and psychological) power to do so. Similarly, it is a tautology to say that we cannot sincerely assent to a statement, and *at the same time* not believe it. Thus we may characterize provisionally the difference between statements and commands by saying that, whereas sincerely assenting to the former involves *believing* something, sincerely assenting to the latter involves (on the appropriate occasion and if it is within our power) *doing* something. . . .

In the case of third-person commands, to assent is to join in affirming. In the case of first-person commands ("Let me do so and so") and resolves ("I will do so and so"), which are closely similar to one another, affirmation and assent are identical. It is logically impossible for a man to dissent from what he himself is affirming (though of course he may not be sincere in affirming it). . . .

There is a malady to which imperatives, like indicatives, are liable, owing to the presence of logical connectives in the phrastics of both of them. This is called, in the case of indicatives, self-contradiction; and the term is equally applicable to imperatives. Commands as well as statements can contradict one another. Even if this were not a normal way of speaking, we might well adopt it; for the feature to which it draws attention in commands is identical with that which is normally called contradiction. Consider the following example, taken from Lord Cunningham's autobiography. The admiral and the captain of a cruiser which is his flagship shout almost simultaneously to the helmsman in order to avoid a collision, one "Hard 'a port" and the other "Hard 'a starboard." Lord Cunningham refers to these two orders as "contrary"; and so they are, in the proper Aristotelian sense. It follows that the two orders contradict one another in the sense that the conjunction of them is self-contradictory; the relation between them is the same as that between the two predictions "You are going to turn hard 'a port" and "You are going to turn hard 'a starboard." Some orders can, of course, be contradictory without being contrary; the simple contradictory of "Shut the door" is "Do not shut the door.". . .

It follows, from the fact that commands may contradict one another, that in order to avoid self-contradiction, a command, like a statement, must observe certain logical rules. These rules are the rules for the use of all the expressions contained in it. In the case of some expressions—the so-called logical words—these rules are what give the expressions all the meaning they have. Thus to know the meaning of the word "all" is to know that one cannot without self-contradiction say certain things, for example "All men are mortal and Socrates is a man but Socrates is not mortal." If the reader will reflect, how he would tell whether someone knew the meaning of the word "all," he will see that the only way he could do it would be by finding out what simpler sentences that person thought were entailed by sentences containing the word "all." "Entailed" is a strong word, and logicians nowadays are not given to using strong words; a full discussion of its meaning, especially in mathematical contexts, would occupy many pages; but for my present purposes it may be defined accurately enough as follows: A sentence P entails a sentence Q if and only if the fact that a person assents to P but dissents from Q is a sufficient criterion for saying that he has misunderstood one or other of the sentences.[3] "Sentence"

[3] More complicated entailments, such as those in mathematics, might be covered by extending this definition as follows: the definition given would be treated as a definition of *direct* entailment, and *indirect* entailment would be defined as holding between two sentences P and R when there is a series of sentences $Q_1\ Q_2 \ldots Q_n$ such that P directly entails Q_1, Q_1 directly entails Q_2, &c., and Q_n directly entails R. But even this may not be sufficiently exact.

here is an abbreviation for "sentence as used by a particular speaker on a particular occasion"; for speakers may on different occasions use words with different meanings, and this means that what is entailed by what they say will also differ. We elicit their meaning by asking them what they regard their remarks as entailing.[4]

Now the word "all" and other logical words are used in commands, as in statements. It follows that there must also be entailment-relations between commands; for otherwise it would be impossible to give any meaning to these words as used in them. If we had to find out whether someone knew the meaning of the word "all" in "Take all the boxes to the station," we should have to find out whether he realized that a person who assented to this command, and also to the statement "This is one of the boxes" and yet refused to assent to the command "Take this to the station" could only do so if he had misunderstood one of these three sentences. If this sort of test were inapplicable the word "all" (in imperatives as in indicatives) would be entirely meaningless. We may therefore say that the existence in our language of universal sentences in the imperative mood is in itself sufficient proof that our language admits of entailments of which at least one term is a command. Whether the word "entail" is to be used for these relations is only a matter of terminological convenience. I propose so to use it. . . .

We shall need, in this inquiry, to consider only the inference from universal imperative sentences, together with indicative minor premises, to singular imperative conclusions. I have already given an example of such an inference, and maintained that, if it were impossible to make inferences of this kind, the word "all" would have no meaning in commands. But this type of inference does raise a further difficulty, because one of the premises is in the indicative, and one in the imperative. The inference is:

Take all the boxes to the station.
This is one of the boxes.

∴ *Take this to the station.*

It might be asked how we are to know, given two premises in different moods, in what mood the conclusion is to be. The problem of the effect upon inferences of the moods of premises and conclusion has been ignored by logicians who have not looked beyond the indicative mood; though there is no reason why they should have ignored it; for how should we set about demonstrating that the conclusion from a set of indicative premises must also be in the indicative? But if, as I do, we regard the entailment-relations of ordinary logic as relations betwen the phrastics of sentences, the problem becomes pressing. Granted that the reason for the validity of the above syllogism is that the phrastics "Your taking all the boxes to the station and this being one of the boxes" and "Your not taking this to the station" are logically inconsistent with one another, because of the logical rules governing the use of the word "all," how are we to know that we cannot add neustics in a different way from the above? We might write, for example:

Take all the boxes to the station.
This is one of the boxes.

∴ *You are going to take this to the station.*

and call this a valid syllogism, which it plainly is not.

Let me first state two of the rules that seem to govern this matter; we may leave till later the question of their justification. The rules are:

1. *No indicative conclusion can be validly*

[4] For an indication of how logical symbols may be defined in terms of the entailment-relations of sentences containing them, see K. R. Popper, "New Foundations for Logic," *Mind*, lvi (1947), 193, and "Logic without Assumptions," *Aristotelian Society*, xlviii (1946–7), 251.

drawn from a set of premises which cannot be validly drawn from the indicatives among them alone.

2. *No imperative conclusion can be validly drawn from a set of premises which does not contain at least one imperative.*

It is only the second rule which will concern us in this inquiry. There is a very important apparent exception to this rule, the so-called "hypothetical imperative," with which I shall deal in the next chapter. For the moment, however, let us take the rule as it stands. It is of the most profound importance for ethics. This will be clear if I give a list of some famous arguments in ethics that seem to me to have been wittingly or inwittingly founded upon it. If we admit, as I shall later maintain, that it must be part of the function of a moral judgement to prescribe or guide choices, that is to say to entail an answer to some question of the form "What shall I do?"—then it is clear, from the second of the rules just stated, that no moral judgement can be a pure statement of fact. . . .

In this logical rule is to be found the basis of Hume's celebrated observation on the impossibility of deducing an "ought"-proposition from a series of "is"-propositions—an observation which, as he rightly says, "would subvert all the vulgar systems of morality," and not only those which had already appeared in his day. . . .

"OUGHT" AND IMPERATIVES

Since a large part of my argument hinges on the assumption, hitherto not fully defended, that value-judgements, if they are action-guiding, must be held to entail imperatives, and since this assumption may very well be questioned, it is time to examine it. It might be held, for example, that I can without contradiction say "You ought to do A, but don't," and that therefore there can be no question of entailment; entailment in any case is a very strong word, and though many might be found to agree that value-judgements are action-guiding in some sense, it might be held that they are action-guiding only in the sense in which even plain judgements of fact may be action-guiding. For example, if I say "The train is just about to depart," this may guide a person who wants to catch the train to take his seat; or, to take a moral case, if I say to a person who is thinking of giving some money to a friend supposedly in distress, "The story he has just told you is quite untrue," this may guide him to make a different moral decision from that which he would otherwise have made. And similarly it might be held that value-judgements are action-guiding in no stronger sense than these statements of fact. It might be urged that, just as the statement that the train is going to depart has no bearing upon the practical problems of someone who does not want to catch the train, and just as, if the man who is thinking of giving money to his friend does not recognize that the truth or otherwise of his friend's story has any bearing on the question, it may not affect his decision, so, if a man has no intention of doing what he ought, to tell him that he ought to do something may not be accepted by him as a reason for doing it. I have put as forcibly as possible this objection, which strikes at the root of my whole argument. The objection alleges, in brief, that "ought"-sentences are not imperatives, neither do they entail imperatives without the addition of an imperative premise. In answer to this, I have to show that "ought"-sentences, at any rate in some of their uses, do entail imperatives. . . .

It is possible for people who have acquired very stable standards of values to come to treat value-judgements more and more as purely descriptive, and to let their evaluative force get weaker. The limit of this process is reached when the value-judgement "gets into inverted commas," and the standard becomes completely "ossified." Thus it is possible to say "You ought to go and call on the So-and-sos" meaning by it no value-judgement at all, but simply the descriptive judgement that such an action is required in order to conform to a standard which people in general, or a certain kind of people not specified but well understood, accept. And certainly, if this is the way in which an "ought"-sentence is being used, it does not entail an imperative; we can certainly say without contradiction "You ought to go and call on the So-and-sos, but don't." I do not wish to claim that all "ought"-sentences entail imperatives, but only that they do so when they are being used evaluatively. It will subsequently become apparent that I am making this true by definition; for I should not say that an "ought"-sentence *was* being used evaluatively, unless imperatives were held to follow from it; but more of that later.

Thus one answer which we can make to the objection is that the cases which appear to support it are not genuine value-judgements. In the example quoted, if a man has no intention of doing what he ought, and if, therefore, telling him what he ought to do is not taken by him as entailing an imperative, that merely shows that, in so far as he accepts that he ought to do so-and-so (and of course *no* premise enables a conclusion to be drawn unless it is accepted), he accepts it only in a non-evaluative, inverted-commas sense, as meaning that so-and-so falls within a class of actions which is generally held (but not by him) to be obligatory in the evaluative, imperative-entailing sense. This is an answer which disposes of some awkward cases, but which will not be accepted as a complete answer unless we extend its scope considerably. For it may be held that there are some genuine value-judgements which do not entail imperatives. . . .

Practical principles, if they are accepted sufficiently long and unquestioningly, come to have the force of intuition. Thus our ultimate moral principles can become so completely accepted by us, that we treat them, not as universal imperatives, but as matters of fact; they have the same obstinate indubitability. And there is indeed a matter of fact to which it is very easy for us to take them as referring, namely, what we call our "sense of obligation." This is a concept that now requires investigation.

It is easy to see how, if we have been brought up from our earliest years in obedience to a principle, the thought of not obeying it becomes abhorrent to us. If we fail to obey it, we suffer remorse; when we do obey it, we feel at ease with ourselves. These feelings are reinforced by all those factors which psychologists have listed;[5] and the total result is what is generally called a feeling of obligation. It is a *fact* that we have this feeling of obligation —different people in different degrees, and with different contents. Judgements that I have a feeling of obligation to do X or Y are statements of empirical fact. This is not the place to argue about their interpretation; it is no doubt possible to dispute whether sentences like "A is suffering from remorse" or "B feels it is his duty to do Y" are reports of private mental events or are to be interpreted behaviouristically; but such controversies do not here concern us. Here it is important to point out a fact which has been singularly ignored by some moralists, that to say of someone that he has a feeling of obligation is not the same as to say that he has an obligation. To say the former is to make a statement of psychological fact; to say the latter is to make a value-judgement. A man who has been brought up in an Army family, but has become affected by pacifism, may well say "I have a strong feeling that I ought to fight for my country, but I wonder whether I really ought." Similarly, a Japanese

[5] Cf. J. C. Flugel, *Man, Morals and Society*, especially ch. iii.

brought up in accordance with Bushido might say "I have a strong feeling that I ought to torture this prisoner in order to extract information which will be to my Emperor's advantage; but ought I really to do so?"

The confusion between psychological statements about a feeling or sense of obligation and value-judgements about obligation itself is not confined to professional philosophers. The ordinary man so very rarely questions the principles in which he has been brought up, that he is usually willing, whenever he has a feeling that he ought to do X, to say on this ground alone that he ought to do X; and therefore he often gives voice to this feeling by saying "I ought to do X." This sentence is not a statement that he has the feeling; it is a value-judgement made as a result of having the feeling. For those, however, who have not studied the logical behaviour of value-judgements, and have not reflected on such examples as those of the pacifist and the Japanese just given, it is easy to take this remark as a statement of fact to the effect that he has the feeling, or to confuse it in meaning with this statement. But anyone, except a professional philosopher maintaining at all costs a moral sense theory, could be got to see that the meaning is not the same, by being asked "Wouldn't it be possible for you to feel just like that, although you really oughtn't to do X?" or "Mightn't you feel like that and be wrong?"

The confusion, however, goes deeper than this. We have seen that there is a conscious inverted-commas use of value-words in which, for example, "I ought to do X" becomes roughly equivalent to "X is required in order to conform to a standard which people in general accept." But it is also possible to use the word "ought" and other value-words, as it were, unconsciously in inverted commas; for the standard which people in general accept may also be the standard which one has been brought up to accept oneself, and therefore not only does one refer to this standard by saying "I ought to do X," but one has feelings of obligation to conform to the standard.

It is then possible to treat "I ought to do X" as a confused mixture of three judgements.

1. "X is required in order to conform to the standard which people generally accept" (statement of sociological fact);
2. "I have a feeling that I ought to do X" (statement of psychological fact);
3. "I ought to do X" (value-judgement).

Even this tripartite division conceals the complexity of the meaning of such sentences; for each of the three elements is itself complex and can be taken in different senses. But even if we confine ourselves to the three elements just given, it is usually impossible for an ordinary person, untrained in logical subtleties, to ask or to answer the question "Which of these three judgements are you making, just (1), or (1) and (2), or all three, or some other combination?" The situation is very similar to that of the scientist who is asked by the logician "Is your statement that phosphorus melts at 44° C. analytic or synthetic; if you found a substance which was in other respects just like phosphorus, but which melted at another temperature, would you say 'It isn't really phosphorus' or would you say 'Then after all some phosphorus melts at other temperatures'?"[6] The scientist might well, as Mr. A. G. N. Flew has pointed out to me, answer "I don't know; I haven't yet come across the case which would make me decide this question; I have got better things to worry about." Similarly, the ordinary person, making moral decisions on the basis of his ac-

[6] See G. H. von Wright, *Logical Problem of Induction*, ch. iii.

cepted principles, very rarely has to ask himself the question that we have just asked. So long as his value-judgements correspond with the accepted standards, and with his own feelings, he does not have to decide which he is saying, because, as we might put it, all three are as yet for him materially equivalent; that is to say, no occasion arises for saying one which is not also an occasion for saying the other two. He therefore does not ask himself "As I am using the word 'ought,' are the sentences 'I ought to do what I feel I ought' and 'I ought to do what everybody would say I ought' analytic or synthetic?" It is the crucial case that makes him answer such a question; and in morals the crucial case comes when we are wondering whether to make a value-decision which is in disagreement with the accepted standards or with our own moral feelings—such cases as I have cited. It is these cases that really reveal the difference in meaning between the three judgements that I have listed.

My answer to the objection then is, that cases which are alleged to be value-judgements not entailing imperatives will always on examination be found to be cases where what is meant is not of type (3) above, but of type (1) or (2) or a mixture of both. This contention is, of course, impossible to prove or even to render plausible, unless we know when we are to count a judgement as of type (3); but I propose to get over this difficulty in the only possible way, by making it a matter of definition. I propose to say that the test, whether someone is using the judgement "I ought to do X" as a value-judgement or not is, "Does he or does he not recognize that if he assents to the judgement, he must also assent to the command 'Let me do X'?" Thus I am not here claiming to prove anything substantial about the way in which we use language; I am merely suggesting a terminology which, if applied to the study of moral language, will, I am satisfied, prove illuminating. The substantial part of what I am trying to show is this, that, in the sense of "value-judgement" just defined, we do make value-judgements, and that they are the class of sentences containing value-words which is of primary interest to the logician who studies moral language. Since what we are discussing is the logic of moral language and not that tangled subject known as moral psychology, I shall not here inquire farther into the fascinating problem, discussed by Aristotle, of *akrasia* or "weakness of will"[7]—the problem presented by the person who thinks, or professes to think, that he ought to do something, but does not do it. The logical distinctions which I have been making shed considerable light on this question: but much more needs to be said, chiefly by way of a more thorough analysis of the phrase "thinks that he ought." For if we interpret my definition strictly, and take it in conjunction with what was said earlier about the criteria for "sincerely assenting to a command," the familiar "Socratic paradox" arises, in that it becomes analytic to say that everyone always[8] does what he thinks he ought to (in the evaluative sense). And this, to put Aristotle's objection in modern dress, is not how we use the word "think." The trouble arises because our criteria, in ordinary speech, for saying "He thinks he ought" are exceedingly elastic. If a person does not do something, but the omission is accompanied by feelings of guilt, &c., we normally say that he has not done what he thinks he ought. It is therefore necessary to qualify the criterion given above for "sincerely assenting to a command," and to admit that there are degrees of sincere assent, not all of which involve actually obeying the command. But the detailed analysis of this problem requires

[7] *Nicomachean Ethics*, VII. 1 ff.

[8] Strictly, "always, if physically and psychologically able"; cf. p. 20.

much more space than I can give it here, and must wait for another occasion.

The best way of establishing the primary logical interest of the evaluative sense of "ought" is to show that, but for the existence of this sense, none of the familiar troubles generated by the word would arise. For of the three possible paraphrases of "I ought to do X" the first two are statements of fact. This is because, if they are expanded, it will be found that the word "ought" in them always occurs in inverted commas or inside a subordinate clause beginning with "that." Thus (1) might be further paraphrased "There is a principle of conduct which people generally accept, which says 'One ought to do X in circumstances of a certain kind'; and I am now in circumstances of that kind." Similarly, (2) might be further paraphrased "The judgement 'I ought to do X' evokes in me a feeling of conviction" or "I find myself unable to doubt the judgement 'I ought to do X'" (though the latter paraphrase is a good deal too strong; for not all feelings are irresistible; there is indeed an infinite gradation from vague uneasy stirrings of conscience to what are often called "moral intuitions"). Now the fact, that when (1) and (2) are expanded the original judgement which they paraphrase occurs within them inside inverted commas, shows that there must be some sense of that original judgement which is not exhausted by (1) and (2); for if there were not, the sentence in the inverted commas would have in its turn to be paraphrased by (1) or (2), and we should be involved in an infinite regress. In the case of (1), I do not know any way of getting over this difficulty; in the case of (2), it can be got over temporarily by substituting for (2) some such paraphrase as "I have a certain recognizable feeling." But the device is only temporary; for if we are asked what this feeling is, or how we recognize it, the reply can only be "It is the feeling called 'a feeling of obligation'; it is the feeling you usually have when you say, and mean, 'I ought to do so-and-so'."

This means that neither (1) nor (2) can give the primary sense of "I ought to do X." Now let us suppose (as is not the case) that (3) generates none of the logical puzzles of the kind that we have been discussing; let us suppose, that is to say, that (3) can be analysed naturalistically. If this were so, then these puzzles would not arise in the cases of (1) or (2) either; for since, besides the expression in inverted commas, there is nothing else in the expansions of (1) and (2) that cannot be analysed naturalistically, it would be possible to effect a completely naturalistic analysis of all uses of "ought," and thus of "good." The fact that this is not possible is entirely due to the intractably evaluative character of (3). It is due ultimately to the impossibility, mentioned earlier, of deriving imperatives from indicatives; for (3), by definition, entails at least one imperative; but if (3) were analysable naturalistically, this would mean that it was equivalent to a series of indicative sentences; and this would constitute a breach of the principle established. Thus it is this fact, that in some of its uses "ought" is used evaluatively (i.e. as entailing at least one imperative) that makes a naturalistic analysis impossible, and hence generates all the difficulties that we have been considering. A logician who neglects these uses will make his task easy, at the cost of missing the essential purpose of moral language. . . .

To guide choices or actions, a moral judgement has to be such that if a person assents to it, he must assent to some imperative sentence derivable from it; in other words, if a person does not assent to some such imperative sentence, that is knockdown evidence that he does not assent to the moral judgement in an evaluative sense —though of course he may assent to it in some other sense (e.g. one of those I have mentioned). This is true by my definition of the word evaluative. But to say this is to say that if he professes to assent to the moral judgement, but does not assent to the imperative, he must have misunderstood the moral judgement (by taking it to be non-evaluative, though the speaker intended it to be evaluative). We are therefore clearly entitled to say that the moral judgement entails the imperative; for to say that one judgement entails another is simply to say that you cannot assent to the first and dissent from the second unless you have misunderstood one or the other; and this "cannot" is a logical "cannot"—if someone assents to the first and not to the second, this is in itself a sufficient criterion for saying that he has misunderstood the meaning of one or the other. Thus to say that moral judgements guide actions, and to say that they entail imperatives, comes to much the same thing. . . .

I am now in a position to answer an objection which may have occurred to some readers. Writers on ethics often condemn "naturalism" or some related fallacy in others, only to commit it themselves in a subtler form. It may be alleged that I have done this. I suggest that the term "naturalist" should be reserved for such ethical theories as are open to refutation on lines similar to those marked out by Professor Moore. We must therefore ask whether any analogous refutation of my own theory can be constructed. Now it is true that I am not suggesting that moral judgements can be deduced from any statements of fact. In particular I am not suggesting the adoption of definitions of value-terms of the sort which Moore mistakenly attributed to Kant. Moore accused Kant of saying that "This ought to be" means "This is commanded."[9] This definition would be naturalistic; for "A is commanded" is a statement of fact; it is expansible into "Someone [it is not disclosed who] has said 'Do A'." The fact that the imperative is in inverted commas prevents it affecting the mood of the complete sentence. Needless to say, I am not suggesting any such equivalence, either for "good" or for "ought" or for any other value-word, except perhaps when they are used in what I have called an "inverted-commas" sense, or in some other purely descriptive way. But it might nevertheless be said that according to my treatment of moral judgements certain sentences would become analytic which in ordinary usage are not analytic—and this would be very like Moore's refutation. For example, consider sentences like the Psalmist's

Eschew evil and do good,[10]

or the line of John Wesley's hymn

In duty's path go on.[11]

On my theory these would, it might be alleged, become analytic; for from "A is evil" is deducible the imperative sentence "Eschew A," and from "Path P is the path of duty" is deducible the imperative sentence "Go on in path P."

Now it must be noticed that such sentences as those quoted are expansible into sentences in which a value-judgement occurs in a subordinate clause. Thus if, instead of the archaic "Eschew evil" we write "Do not do what is evil," this can be expanded into "For all X, if X is evil, do not do X." For this instruction to be applied, it is necessary that we should conjoin it with a minor premise "A is evil," and from the two premises conclude "Do not do A." For this reasoning to be helpful, it is necessary that the minor premise "A is evil" should be a statement of fact; there must be a criterion for telling unambiguously whether it is true or false. The means that in this premise the word

[9] *Principia Ethica*, pp. 127–8.

[10] Ps. xxxiv, v. 14.

[11] *Hymns Ancient and Modern* (1950), no. 310.

"evil" must have a descriptive meaning (whatever further meaning it may have). But if the reasoning is to be valid, the word "evil" in the major premise must have the same meaning as in the minor; there also, therefore, it must have a descriptive meaning. Now it is this descriptive content which prevents the major premise being analytic. Sentences of the sort we are discussing are normally used by people who have firmly established value-standards, and whose value-words have, therefore, a large element of descriptive meaning. In the sentence "Do not do what is evil," the evaluative content of "evil" is for the moment neglected; the speaker, as it were, lets his support of the standard slip for a moment, only in order to ram it back into place with the imperative verb. This is a first-class exercise in the maintenance of our standards, and that is why it is so much in place in hymns and psalms. But it can only be performed by those who are in no doubt as to what the standard is.

Thus my account of the meaning of value-words is not naturalistic; it does not result in sentences becoming analytic which are not so in our ordinary usage. Rather it shows, by doing full justice to both the descriptive and the evaluative elements in the meaning of value-words, how it is that they play in our ordinary usage the role that they do play. A somewhat similar difficulty is presented by Satan's famous paradox "Evil be thou my good." This yields to the same type of analysis, but for reasons of space I am compelled to leave the reader to unravel the problem himself.

It may be asked at this point "Are you not assimilating moral judgements too much to the ordinary universal imperatives that exist in most languages?" It has indeed been objected to all imperative analyses of moral judgements, that they would make a moral judgement like "You ought not to smoke (in this compartment)" the equivalent of the universal imperative "No Smoking." And they are clearly not equivalent, though both, according to the theory which I have been advocating, entail "Do not smoke." It is therefore necessary to state what it is that distinguishes "You ought not to smoke" from "No smoking."

The first thing to notice about "No smoking" is that it is not a proper universal, because it implicitly refers to an individual; it is short for "Do not ever smoke in *this* compartment." The moral judgement "You ought not to smoke in this compartment" also contains references to individuals; for the pronouns "you" and "this" occur in it. But this is not the end of the matter. The moral judgement "You ought not to smoke in this compartment" has to be made with some general moral principle in mind, and its purpose must be either to invoke that general principle or to point to an instance of its application. The principle might be "One ought never to smoke in compartments in which there are young children" or "One ought never to smoke in compartments in which there is a 'No Smoking' notice." It is not always easy to elicit just what the principle is; but it always makes sense to ask what it is. The speaker cannot deny that there is any such principle. The same point might be put another way by saying that if we make a particular moral judgement, we can always be asked to support it by reasons; the reasons consist in the general principles under which the moral judgement is to be subsumed. Thus the particular moral judgement "You ought not to smoke in this compartment" depends on a proper universal, even though it is not itself one. But this is not true of the imperative "Do not ever smoke in this compartment." This invokes no more general principle; it is itself as general as it requires to be, and this is not general enough to make it a proper universal.

The difference in universality between "Do not ever smoke in this compartment" and "You ought not to smoke in this compartment" may be brought out in the following way. Suppose that I say to someone "You ought not to smoke in this compartment," and there are children in the compartment. The person addressed is likely, if he wonders why I have said that he ought not to smoke, to look around, notice the children, and so understand the reason. But suppose that, having ascertained everything that is to be ascertained about the compartment, he then says "All right; I'll go next door; there's another compartment there just as good; in fact it is exactly like this one, and there are children in it too." I should think if he said this that he did not understand the function of the word "ought"; for "ought" always refers to some general principle; and if the next compartment is really exactly like this one, every principle that is applicable to this one must be applicable to the other. I might therefore reply "But look here, if you oughtn't to smoke in this compartment, and the other compartment is just like this one, has the same sort of occupants, the same notices on the windows, &c., then obviously you oughtn't to smoke in that one either." On the other hand, when the Railway Executive is making the momentous decision, on which compartments to put notices saying "No Smoking," nobody says "Look here! You've put a notice on this compartment, so you must put one on the one next to it, because it's exactly like it." This is because "No Smoking" does not refer to a universal principle of which this compartment is an instance.

It is, in fact, almost impossible to frame a proper universal in the imperative mood. Suppose that we try to do this by generalizing the sentence "Do not ever smoke in this compartment." First we eliminate the implicit "you" by writing "No one is ever to smoke in this compartment." We then have to eliminate the "this." A step towards this is taken by writing "No one is ever to smoke in any compartment of British Railways." But we still have left here the proper name "British Railways." We can only achieve a proper universal by excluding all proper names, for example by writing "No one is ever to smoke in any railway compartment anywhere." This is a proper universal; but it is a sentence which no one could ever have occasion to utter. Commands are always addressed to someone or to some individual set (not class) of people. It is not clear what could be meant by the sentence just quoted, unless it were a *moral* injunction or other value-judgement. Suppose that we imagine God issuing such a command. Then it becomes at once like the Ten Commandments in form. Historically speaking "Honour thy father and thy mother" is supposed to have been said, not to everyone in general, but only to members of the chosen people, just as "Render to no man evil for evil" was addressed to Christ's disciples, not to the world at large—though He intended that all men should become His disciples. But suppose that this were not so; suppose that "Render to no man evil for evil" were addressed literally to the unlimited class "every man." Should we not say that it had become equivalent in meaning to the value-judgement "One ought to render to no man evil for evil"? Similarly, a proverbial expression like "Let sleeping dogs lie" may without much of a jolt be paraphrased by the (prudential) value-judgement "One ought to let sleeping dogs lie."

On the other hand, ordinary so-called universal imperatives like "No Smoking" are distinguished from value-judgements by not being properly universal. We are thus able to discriminate between these two kinds of sentence, without in the least abandoning anything that I have said about the relation between value-judgements and imperatives. For both the complete universal and the incomplete entail the singular: "Do not ever smoke in this compartment" entails "Do not (now) smoke in this compartment"; and so does "You ought not to smoke in this compartment," if it is used evaluatively. But the latter also entails, as the former does not, "No one ought to smoke in any compartment exactly like this one," and this in its turn entails "Do not smoke in any compartment exactly like this one."

These considerations alone, however, would not be sufficient to account altogether for the complete difference in "feel" between "You ought not" and "Do not ever." This is reinforced by two other factors. The first has already been alluded to; the complete universality of the moral judgement means that we cannot "get away from it"; and therefore its acceptance is a much more serious matter than the acceptance of an imperative from whose range of application we can escape. This would explain why imperatives such as those laws of a State, which are of very general application, and therefore very difficult to escape from, have a "feel" much more akin to moral judgements than have the regulations of the Railway Executive. But a more important additional factor is that, partly because of their complete universality, moral principles have become so entrenched in our minds—in the ways already described—that they have acquired a quasi-factual character, and are indeed sometimes used non-evaluatively as statements of fact and nothing else, as we have seen. None of this is true of imperatives like "No Smoking," and this in itself would be quite enough to explain the difference in "feel" between the two kinds of sentence. Since, however, I do not wish to deny that there are non-evaluative uses of moral judgements, but only to assert that there are evaluative uses, this difference in "feel" in no way destroys my argument. It would indeed be absurd to pretend that "No Smoking" is in all respects like "You ought not to smoke"; I have been maintaining only that it is like it in one respect, that both entail singular imperatives such as "Do not smoke (now)."

RODERICK FIRTH

*Ethical Absolutism and the Ideal Observer**

. . . There is one kind of analysis of ethical statements which has certainly not been examined with the thoroughness that it deserves—the kind of analysis, namely, which construes ethical statements to be both absolutist and dispositional. . . . And what makes such carelessness especially unfortunate, is the fact that this kind of analysis seems to be capable of satisfying the major demands of certain schools of ethical thought which are ordinarily supposed to be diametrically opposed to one another. It is a kind of analysis, moreover, which may have been proposed and defended by several classical moralists;[1] and this is perhaps one good reason for giving it at least a small share of the attention which is now lavished on positions which are no more plausible.

The following discussion of absolutist dispositional analyses of ethical statements, is divided into two parts. In the first part I have discussed some of the important characteristics which are common to all analyses of this general form. In the second part I have discussed some of the problems which would have to be solved in working out a concrete analysis of this kind, and I have made certain proposals about the manner in which such an analysis can best be formulated.

Part One: Characteristics of the Analysis

1. *It is absolutist.* To explain the precise sense in which a dispositional analysis of ethical statements may be absolutist

* By permission. *Philosophy and Phenomenological Research,* Vol. 12, 1952, pp. 317–45.

Roderick Firth is professor of philosophy at Harvard University.

[1] Adam Smith comes immediately to mind, but Hume can likewise be interpreted as accepting an absolutist dispositional analysis of "right." (*Vide,* e.g., F. C. Sharp, "Hume's Ethical Theory," *Mind,* N.S. Vol. XXX, pp. 53–56. But for a different interpretation of Hume, *vide* Broad, *Five Types of Ethical Theory,* pp. 84–93.) It is even possible to make out a case for including Kant in this list. (*Vide* Part II of this paper on the subject of ethical impartiality.) Sidgwick, although he denied that "right" is analyzable, seems not unwilling to accept an absolutist dispositional analysis of "good." (*Methods of Ethics,* 4th ed., p. 112, last sentence.)

rather than relativist, it is helpful to begin by defining the two terms "relative statement" and "relativist analysis."

Speaking first about statements, we may say that any statement is relative if its meaning cannot be expressed without using a word or other expression which is egocentric. And egocentric expressions may be described as expressions of which the meaning varies systematically with the speaker. They are expressions which are ambiguous in abstraction from their relation to a speaker, but their ambiguity is conventional and systematic. They include the personal pronouns ("I," "you," etc.), the corresponding possessive adjectives ("my," "your," etc.), words which refer directly but relatively to spatial and temporal location ("this," "that," "here," "there," "now," "then," "past," "present," "future"), reflexive expressions such as "the person who is speaking," and the various linguistic devices which are used to indicate the tense of verbs. All of these egocentric expressions can apparently be defined in terms of the word "this."

A moral philosopher is commonly called a relativist, and his analysis of ethical statements is said to be a relativist analysis, if he construes ethical statements to be relative. We may thus say, derivatively, that an analysis of ethical statements is relativist if it includes an egocentric expression, and if it is incompatible with any alternative analysis which does not include an egocentric expression.

It follows, therefore, that relativist analyses, no matter how much they may differ from one another, can always be conveniently and positively identified by direct inspection of their constituent expressions. Thus, to give a few examples, a philosopher is an ethical relativist if he believes that the meaning of ethical statements of the form "Such and such a particular act (x) is right" can be expressed by other statements which have any of the following forms: "*I* like x as much as any alternative to it," "*I* should (in fact) feel ashamed of myself if *I* did not feel approval towards x, and *I* wish that *other people* would too," "Most people *now* living would feel approval towards x if they knew what they really wanted," "If *I* should perceive or think about x and its alternatives, x would seem to *me* to be demanding to be performed," "x is compatible with the mores of the social group to which *the speaker* gives his primary allegiance," and "x will satisfy a maximum of the interests of people *now* living or who *will* live *in the future.*" Each one of these possible analyses contains an egocentric expression (which I have italicized). And it is evident that if any of these analyses were correct, it would be possible for one person to say that a certain act is right, and for another person (provided, in some cases, that he is not a member of the same social group, nor living at the same time) to say that this very same act is not right, without logically contradicting each other. This familiar characteristic of all relativist analyses is not *definitive* of relativism; it is, however, a necessary *consequence* of the fact that relativist analyses contain egocentric expressions.

We may now define an absolutist analysis of ethical statements as one which is not relativist. The kind of analysis which I propose to discuss in this paper, therefore, is one which does not include an egocentric expression. It is a kind of analysis, I suspect, which is closely associated with relativism in the minds of many philosophers, but it is unquestionably absolutist and implies that ethical statements are true or false, and consistent or inconsistent with one another, without special reference to the people who happen to be asserting them.

2. *It is dispositional.* I shall say that a proposed analysis of ethical statements is dispositional if it construes ethical statements to assert that a certain being (or beings), either actual or hypothetical, is (or

are) disposed to react to something in a certain way. To say that a certain being is disposed to react in a certain way is to say that the being in question would react in that way under certain specifiable conditions. Thus a dispositional analysis of an ethical statement may always be formulated as a hypothetical statement of the kind which is commonly called a "contrary-to-fact conditional." A dispositional analysis of statements of the form "x is right," for example, might have the form: "Such and such a being, if it existed, would react to x in such and such a way if such and such conditions were realized."...

A dispositional analysis of ethical statements which was *absolutist*... would construe ethical statements in one of the following three ways: (1) as assertions about the dispositions of all *actual* (past, present, and future) beings of a certain kind; (2) as assertions about the dispositions of all *possible* beings of a certain kind (of which there might in fact exist only one or none at all), or (3) as assertions about the dispositions of a majority (or other fraction) of a number of beings (actual or possible) of a certain kind. It is evident that an analysis of any of these three types would include no egocentric expression, and would therefore construe ethical statements in such a way that they would be true or false, and consistent or inconsistent with one another, without special reference to the people who happen to be asserting them.

It is only the second of these three kinds of analysis which I propose to examine in this paper, for analyses of the other two types, it seems to me, are open to obvious and yet insuperable objections. An analysis of the first type would construe ethical statements to entail that there actually exists a being (perhaps God) whose dispositions are definitive of certain ethical terms. But this would mean that all ethical statements containing these ethical terms are necessarily false if such a being does *not* exist—a consequence which seems to be incompatible with what we intend to assert when we use ethical terms. And in my opinion an analysis of the third type would be even less plausible, because it would imply that ethical statements express judgments which can only be verified or refuted, at least theoretically, by statistical procedures. I shall not amplify these familiar arguments, however, since much of what I shall say about ethical analyses of the second type can be equally well applied to analyses of the other two types, and anyone who so wishes may easily make the necessary translations in reading the second part of this paper.

It will be convenient, throughout the following pages, to use the term "ideal observer" in speaking about a possible being of the kind referred to in an absolutist dispositional analysis. The adjective "ideal" is used here in approximately the same sense in which we speak of a perfect vacuum or a frictionless machine as ideal things; it is not intended to suggest that an ideal observer is necessarily *virtuous,* but merely that he is conceivable and that he has certain characteristics to an extreme degree. Perhaps it would seem more natural to call such a being an ideal *judge,* but this term could be quite misleading if it suggested that the function of an ideal observer is to pass judgment on ethical issues. As an ideal observer, of course, it is sufficient that he be capable of reacting in a manner which will determine by definition whether an ethical judgment is true or false. And it is even conceivable, indeed, that an ideal observer, according to some analyses, should lack some of the characteristics which would make it *possible* for him to pass judgment on ethical issues—which would mean, of course, simply that he would not be able to judge the nature of his own dispositions.

Using the term "ideal observer," then, the kind of analysis which I shall examine in this paper is the kind which would construe statements of the form "x is P," in which P is some particular ethical predicate, to be identical in meaning with statements of the form: "Any ideal observer would react to x in such and such a way under such and such conditions."...

Let us now consider briefly some of the derivative characteristics of an analysis which is both absolutist and dispositional.

3. *It is objectivist.* The adjectives "subjectivist" and "objectivist" are often used in a *logical* sense, and as synonyms, respectively, of the terms "relativist" and "absolutist"; in this sense, as we have seen, an analysis of the kind that we are discussing is objectivist. To avoid duplication of meaning, however, I shall use the terms "subjectivist" and "objectivist" in a traditional *ontological* sense—in the sense in which Berkeley's analysis of all physical statements is subjectivist, and Descartes's analysis of some physical statements is objectivist. We may say, in this sense, that a proposed analysis of ethical statements is subjectivist if it construes ethical statements in such a way that they would all be false by definition if there existed no experiencing subjects (past, present, or future). An analysis may be called "objectivist," on the other hand, if it is not subjectivist. Thus it is evident that in this ontological sense, as well as in the logical sense, an analysis of the kind which we are discussing is objectivist: it construes ethical statements to be assertions about the reactions of an *ideal* observer—an observer who is conceivable but whose existence or non-existence is logically irrelevant to the truth or falsity of ethical statements.

This fact, that a dispositional analysis is objectivist, is obviously a reflection of the fact that ethical statements, according to such an analysis, may always be formulated as conditional statements in the subjunctive mood; they may always be construed, in other words, as asserting that if such and such *were* the case, such and such *would* be the case.... As used in an absolutist dispositional analysis, for example, such statements are not intended to imply *either* that there exists, *nor* that there does not exist, a being who satisfies the description of an ideal observer; they are intended to imply, on the contrary, that the existence or non-existence of such a being is *irrelevant* to the truth of the statement. Since the subjunctive conditional has exactly the same function whether the analysis is absolutist or relativist, it is evident that objectivism and absolutism are logically independent characteristics of an analysis of ethical statements....

4. *It is relational.* An analysis of ethical statements is *relational* if it construes ethical terms in such a way that to apply an ethical term to a particular thing (e.g., an act), is to assert that that thing is related in a certain way to some other thing, either actual or hypothetical. There is no doubt that an absolutist dispositional analysis is relational, since it construes ethical statements as asserting that a lawful relationship exists between certain reactions of an ideal observer and the acts or other things to which an ethical term may correctly be applied. But to avoid misunderstanding, this fact must be interpreted in the light of certain qualifying observations.

It should not be overlooked, in the first place, that if an absolutist dispositional analysis were correct, ethical statements would have the same form that statements about secondary qualities are often supposed to have. Not only phenomenalists and subjectivists, but many epistemological dualists, would agree that to say that a daffodil is yellow is to say something about the way the daffodil would appear to a certain kind of observer under certain conditions; and the analysis of ethical statements which we are considering is exactly analogous to this. Thus the sense in which an absolutist dispositional analysis is relational, is the very sense in which a great many philosophers believe that yellow is a relational property of physical objects; and to say that a statement of the form "x is right" is relational, therefore, is not necessarily to deny that the terms "right" and "yellow" designate equally simple properties.

But the analogy can be carried still further if a distinction is drawn between a relational and a non-relational sense of "yellow." Many philosophers believe that the adjective "yellow" has two meanings; they believe that it designates both a relational property of physical objects and a non-relational property of sense-data—a distinction corresponding roughly to the popular use of the terms "really yellow" and "apparently yellow." And it is quite possible not only that the term "right" is similarly ambiguous, but also that in one of its senses it designates a characteristic of human experience (apparent rightness) which in some important respect is just as simple and unanalyzable as the property of apparent yellowness. And thus we might even decide by analogy with the case of "yellow," that "really right" must be defined in terms of "apparently right"—i.e., that the experiencing of apparent rightness is an essential part of any ethically-significant reaction of an ideal observer.

And finally, it must be remembered that to call an absolutist analysis "relational," is not to imply that it construes the ethical properties of one thing to be dependent by definition on the *existence* of any other thing, either natural or supernatural. Since an ideal observer is a *hypothetical* being, no changes in the relationships of existent things would require us, for logical reasons alone, to attribute new ethical properties to any object, nor to revise any ethical judgment which we have previously made. For this reason an absolutist dispositional analysis is not open to one of the most familiar objections to relational analyses, namely, that such analyses construe the ethical properties of an object to be dependent on facts which seem quite clearly to be *accidental*—on the fact, for example, that certain actual people happen to have a certain attitude toward the object.

5. *It is empirical.* If we define the term "empirical" liberally enough so that the dispositional concepts of the natural sciences may properly be called empirical, there is no doubt that an absolutist dispositional analysis of ethical statements *might* be empirical. Such an analysis would be empirical, for example, if the defining characteristics of an ideal observer were psychological traits, and if the ethically-significant reactions of an ideal observer were feelings of desire, or emotions of approval and disapproval, or some other experiences accessible to psychological observation.

It might be somewhat less evident, however, that an absolutist dispositional analysis *must* be empirical. For most of the philosophers who maintain that ethical properties are non-natural, and that ethical truths are known by rational intuition, have admitted that ethical intuitions may be erroneous under certain unfavorable conditions, or else, if this is regarded as self-contradictory, that under certain conditions we may appear to be intuiting an ethical truth although in fact we are not. And it might seem that to recognize the possibility of error in either of these two ways is to recognize a distinction between the property of apparent rightness and the property of real rightness—a distinction, as we have seen, which is sufficient to permit the formulation of an absolutist dispositional analysis.

On this issue, however, I think we must take the word of the rational intuitionists themselves, and if there is any one fact about which intuitionists agree, it is the fact that some ethical properties are neither introspectable nor analyzable. And from this fact it follows, necessarily, that their ethical theory is epistemologically dualist—i.e., that there is no formula, however complex, by which ethical statements can be translated into statements about experiences which confirm them. Intuitionists must admit, I believe, that they are able to assess the cognitive value of their ostensible intuitions by reference to the conditions under which these intuitions occur, and they must admit that they would not be able to do this unless they had some conception of an ideal observer. Thus Ewing lists four factors which are responsible for false intuitions: (1) lack of experience, (2) intellectual confusions, (3) failure to attend adequately to certain aspects of the situation, (4) psychological causes "such as those with which the psychoanalyst deals." And the very fact that Ewing can compile such a list is proof that he has some conception of an ideal observer whose definition excludes these four factors. But this fact does not make intuitionism any less dualist, of course, for Ewing and other intuitionists will maintain that in formulating these ideal conditions they are merely formulating a *test* for the validity of an ethical statement, and not an analysis of the statement.

Even though we conclude that an absolutist dispositional analysis must be empirical, however, there is still considerable room for disagreement about the precise nature of the ethically-significant reactions of an ideal observer. It seems clear that these reactions, if the analysis is to be at all plausible, must be defined in terms of the kind of moral experience which we take to be evidence, under ideal conditions, for the truth of our ethical judgments. It is important to observe that experiences of this kind—which we may properly call "moral data"—cannot be states of moral *belief*. An absolutist dispositional analysis, like any other analysis which grants cognitive meaning to ethical sentences, would permit us to say that we do have moral beliefs, and even that moral consciousness is *ordinarily* a state of belief. But if the ethically-significant reaction of an ideal observer were the belief (or judgment) that a certain act is right or wrong, it is evident that an absolutist dispositional analysis would be circular: it would contain the very ethical terms which it is intended to define.

In order to define an absolutist dispositional analysis, therefore, it is necessary to maintain that moral data are the moral experiences to which we appeal when *in doubt* about the correct solution of a moral problem, or when attempting to *justify* a moral belief. For the epistemic function of moral data, when defined in this way, will correspond to the function of color sensations in determining or justifying the belief that a certain material object is "really yellow." And in that case moral data could play the same role in the analysis of "right" that color sensations play in the analysis of "really yellow."...

Part Two: The Content of the Analysis

If it is possible to formulate a satisfactory absolutist and dispositional analysis of ethical statements, it must be possible, as we have seen, to express the meaning of statements of the form "x is right" in terms of other statements which have the form: "Any ideal observer would react to x in such and such a way under such and such conditions." Thus even if we are not to discuss the nature of the ethically-significant reactions of an ideal observer in this paper, it might seem that we are nevertheless faced with two distinct questions: (1) What are the defining characteristics of an ideal observer? and (2) Under what conditions do the reactions of an ideal observer determine the truth or falsity of ethical statements? I believe, however, that the second of these questions can be treated as part of the first. . . .

Before attempting to answer this [first] question, however, there are a few remarks which I think should be made about the implications and methodology of any such attempt to define an ideal observer.

It is important, in the first place, to view any attempt of this kind in proper perspective. It would undoubtedly be difficult to arrive at a rational conclusion concerning the plausibility of absolutist dispositional analyses in general, without first experimenting with various concrete formulations. At the present stage in the history of moral philosophy, however, it would be especially unfortunate if the inadequacies of some particular formulation were to prejudice philosophers against absolutist dispositional analyses in general. Any plausible formulation is certain to be very complex, and there is no reason to suppose that philosophers could ever reach complete agreement concerning all the details of an adequate analysis. But this in itself should not prevent philosophers from agreeing that this general *form* of analysis is valid. Nor would it necessarily be irrational for a philosopher to decide that this general form is valid, although he is dissatisfied even with *his own* attempts to formulate a concrete analysis.[2]

Ethical words, moreover, like all other words, are probably used by different people, even in similar contexts, to express somewhat different meanings; and a correct analysis of one particular ethical statement, therefore, may not be a correct analysis of another statement which is symbolized in exactly the same way but asserted by a different person. This kind of ambiguity is a familiar obstacle to all philosophical analysis. . . .

It would be a serious mistake, however, to confuse the kind of ambiguity to which I have just referred with the kind of ambiguity which is definitive of a relativist analysis. The ambiguity which is definitive of relativism, as we have seen, is conventional, systematic, and characteristic only of statements which contain an egocentric expression. The kind of ambiguity which we have just been discussing, on the other hand, is accidental, unsystematic, and characteristic in some degree of all symbols. Thus it is not ordinarily the intention of an ethical absolutist to maintain that the words which we use to express ethical statements have a unique semiotical capacity—the capacity, namely, to express exactly the same meaning no matter who utters them; in fact even those absolutists who believe that ethical words express simple, unanalyzable, concepts, could scarcely maintain that there is any conclusive evidence to show that an ethical word, no matter who employs it, always expresses the *same* unanalyzable concept. The thesis maintained by the absolutist as such, is simply that ethical statements are not *conventionally* ambiguous in a manner which would require them to be analyzed by means of an egocentric expression; and this thesis is quite consistent, of course, with the proposition that ethical statements are *accidentally* ambiguous—perhaps even more ambiguous, indeed, than most other statements.

In the light of this distinction, then, it seems clear that if two philosophers believe that they are in perfect agreement concerning the meaning of ethical statements—i.e., if they believe that their ability to communicate is not limited by accidental ambiguity—they may still be either relativists or absolutists. If they are relativists, and related to one another spatially, temporally, and socially in certain ways, they will believe that neither of them could assert an ethical statement which is logically inconsistent with any ethical statement asserted by the other. If they are absolutists, however, they will believe that they *can* contradict each other in their ethical statements. Thus the absolutist, unlike the

[2] Cf. A. C. Ewing's statement (*The Definition of Good*, p. 43) that he can "see" in advance that nobody will ever be able to produce a satisfactory empirical analysis of ethical statements. Similarly a philosopher might "see" that *only* an empirical analysis which is absolutist and dispositional could be satisfactory.

relativist, believes that nothing stands in the way of the expression of cognitive disagreement about ethical matters except the accidental ambiguity which is characteristic of all symbols. And since the absolutist can consistently admit that this accidental ambiguity may be sufficiently great to prevent philosophers from agreeing on a concrete analysis of ethical statements, the apparent inadequacy of any particular analysis, such as the one which I shall propose, should not be considered as proof that the general form of an absolutist dispositional analysis is unsatisfactory. . . . There cannot be much doubt that the ethically-significant reactions of an ideal observer must be psychological in nature, and that some of the evidence for the occurrence of these reactions could be directly accessible only to an ideal observer himself. It is for this epistemic reason that in practice we are likely to rate moral judges by reference to their similarity to an ideal observer. And it is to be expected, consequently, that any plausible description of an ideal observer will be a partial description of God, if God is conceived to be an infallible moral judge. But of course an ideal observer need not possess such characteristics as the power to create physical objects or even the power to reward and punish, if these characteristics appear to be irrelevant to God's capacities as a moral judge.

Characteristics of an Ideal Observer

1. *He is omniscient with respect to non-ethical facts.* We sometimes disqualify ourselves as judges of a particular ethical question on the ground that we are not sufficiently familiar with the facts of the case, and we regard one person as a better moral judge than another if, other things being equal, the one has a larger amount of relevant factual knowledge than the other. This suggests that an ideal observer must be characterized in part by reference to his knowledge of non-ethical facts. I say "non-ethical" because, as we have seen, the characteristics of an ideal observer must be determined by examining the procedures which we actually take to be the rational ones for deciding ethical questions; and there are many ethical questions (*viz.*, questions about "ultimate ethical principles") which cannot be decided by inference from ethical premises. This does not mean, of course, that an ideal observer (e.g., God) *cannot* have knowledge of ethical facts (facts, that is to say, about his own dispositions); it means merely that such knowledge is not *essential* to an ideal observer.

A difficulty seems to arise from the fact that in practice we evaluate the factual knowledge of a moral judge by reference to some standard of relevance, and regard one judge as better than another if, other things being equal, the one has more complete knowledge of all the facts which are *relevant*. But it is evident that a concept of relevance cannot be employed in *defining* an ideal observer. To say that a certain body of factual knowledge is not relevant to the rightness or wrongness of a given act, is to say, assuming that an absolutist dispositional analysis is correct, that the dispositions of an ideal observer toward the given act would be the same *whether or not* he possessed that particular body of factual knowledge or any part of it. It follows, therefore, that in order to explain what we mean by "relevant knowledge," we should have to employ the very concept of ideal observer which we are attempting to define.

Fortunately, however, we do not seem to think that a person is to any extent disqualified as a moral judge merely because he possesses factual information which we take to be *superfluous*. Our difficulty would be overcome, therefore, if we were simply to stipulate that an ideal observer is *omniscient* with respect to non-ethical facts, and so far as I can see the term "omniscient," when employed in this way, is neither extravagant nor mysterious. We apparently believe not only that the "facts of the case" are relevant to the objective rightness or wrongness of a particular act, but also that there is no point at which we could be logically certain that further information about matters of fact (e.g., further information about the consequences of the act) would be irrelevant. A satisfactory ethical analysis must be so formulated, therefore, that no facts are irrelevant *by definition* to the rightness or wrongness of any particular act. And this is the intent of the term "omniscient," for to say that an ideal observer is omniscient is to insure that no limits are put on the kinds or the quality of factual information which are available to influence his ethically-significant reactions. . . .

2. *He is omnipercipient.* We sometimes disqualify ourselves as judges of certain ethical questions on the ground that we cannot satisfactorily imagine or visualize some of the relevant facts, and in general we regard one person as a better moral judge than another if, other things being equal, the one is better able to imagine or visualize the relevant facts. Practical moralists have often maintained that lack of imagination is responsible for many crimes, and some have suggested that our failure to treat strangers like brothers is in large part a result of our inability to imagine the joys and sorrows of strangers as vividly as those of our siblings. These facts seem to indicate that the ideal observer must be characterized by extraordinary powers of imagination.

The imaginal powers of the ideal observer, to be sure, are very closely related to his omniscience, and the word "omniscience" has sometimes been used to designate an unlimited imagination of perception. But however we may decide to use the word "omniscience," the important point is simply that it is not sufficient for an ideal observer to possess factual knowledge in a manner which will permit him to make true factual judgments. The ideal observer must be able, on the contrary, simultaneously to visualize all actual facts, and the consequences of all possible acts in any given situation, just as vividly as he would if he were actually perceiving them all. It is undoubtedly impossible for us to imagine the experience of a being capable of this kind of universal perception, but in making ethical decisions we sometimes attempt to visualize several alternative acts and their consequences in rapid succession, very much *as though* we wished our decision to be based on a simultaneous perception of the alternatives. And in view of this fact, and the others which I have mentioned, it seems necessary to attribute universal imagination to an ideal observer, thus guaranteeing that his ethical-significant reactions are forcefully and equitably stimulated.

3. *He is disinterested.* We sometimes disqualify ourselves as judges of certain ethical questions on the ground that we cannot make ourselves impartial, and we regard one person as a better moral judge than another if, other things being equal, the one is more impartial than the other. This suggests that one of the defining characteristics of an ideal observer must be complete impartiality. But it is difficult to define the term "impartial" in a manner which will not make our analysis circular or be otherwise inconsistent with our purpose.

It is important, in the first place, not to confuse the impartiality of an ideal observer with the *uniformity* of his ethically-significant reactions. We are likely to think of a judge who is impartial as a judge who arrives at similar decisions in similar cases, and we may be tempted, therefore, to define an ideal observer as an observer whose ethically-significant reactions to two acts would always be the same if the two acts were alike in all ethically-relevant respects. But this will not do. For even if we could find a way to avoid circularity in defining "ethically-relevant respects," the characteristic which we should have analyzed would be more appropriately called "consistency" than "impartiality." And the fact that it is not self-contradictory to say that a person (e.g., a magistrate) is consistently partial, indicates that consistency and impartiality are not identical characteristics. Consistency, as we shall later see, *is* one of the characteristics of an ideal observer. But to say that an ideal observer is consistent is to say something about the uniformity of his ethically-significant reactions, whereas to say that he is impartial is to say something about the factors which *influence* his reactions. . . .

Now it seems to me that a large part of what we mean when we say that an ideal judge is impartial, is that such a judge will not be influenced by interests of the kind which are commonly described as "particular"—interests, that is to say, which are directed toward a particular person or thing but not toward other persons or things of the same kind; and in so far as this is what we mean by "impartiality," we can define the term without falling into either of the errors which we have been considering. For to say that an ideal observer is not influenced by particular interests, is to attribute to him a certain psychological characteristic which does not refer, either explicitly or implicitly, to a moral standard. Nor does it logically entail, on the other hand, either that an ideal observer would react favorably, or that he would react unfavorably, to an act which benefits one person at the expense of a greater benefit to another.

The term "particular interest," to be sure, is a difficult one to define, and raises problems about the nature of particularity which are beyond the scope of this paper; but I think that for present purposes it is not unreasonable to pass over these problems. Since ethical judgments are concerned, directly or indirectly, with acts, let us use "x" to denote the performance of a certain act by a certain agent. Let us first draw a distinction betwen the "essentially general properties" of x and the "essentially particular properties" of x. The properties of x which are essentially particular are those properties which cannot be defined without the use of proper names (which we may understand, for present purposes, to include egocentric particulars such as "I," "here," "now," and "this"); thus one of the essentially particular properties of x might be its tendency to increase the happiness of the citizens of the U.S.A. All other properties are essentially general; thus one of the essentially general properties of x might be its tendency to increase happiness. We may then say that a person has a positive particular interest in x if (1) he desires x, (2) he believes that x has a certain essentially particular property P, and (3) he would not desire x, or would desire it less intensely, if, his other beliefs remaining constant, he did not believe that x had this property P.

It may seem that this definition makes a variety of logical and ontological assumptions, some of which can be questioned. But I think that the intent of the definition is clear enough, and that the distinctions which it requires must be made, in one form or another, by any adequate logic and ontology. The definition is intended to represent the characteristic which we have in mind when we say that a moral judge who lacks impartiality is one who is tempted to "sacrifice principle"—i.e., to judge one act in a manner in which he would not wish to judge other acts which he thought to be of the same kind. And the definition proposes, in effect, that to say in this context that two acts are thought to be "of the same kind," is to say that they are thought to have the same essentially general properties. It is quite likely, of course, that we never actually believe that any two acts *do* have the same essentially general properties; it is for this reason, indeed, that we find it so easy to rationalize and "make exceptions" when judging acts which affect ourselves, our children, or our country. But this fact does not affect the usefulness of the definition, because part (3) is formulated hypothetically in the subjunctive mood: whether or not a person has a particular interest, is something to be decided by inferring, as best we can, how he *would* react *if* his beliefs were altered in certain ways. . . .

Assuming now, that we have found a satisfactory definition of "particular interest," we must still decide how to use this term in our analysis. Shall we say that an ideal observer is completely lacking in particular interests? Or shall we say simply that his ethically-significant reactions are uninfluenced by such interests, leaving open the possibility, so far as our analysis is concerned, that such interests might be present but in some sense "suppressed"? At first thought the latter statement seems to be adequate to represent our concept of an impartial moral judge, for we often admire such a judge precisely because we believe that he does have particular interests but that his desire to be impartial has counteracted their influence. On further reflection it will be discovered, however, that we cannot explain what it means to say a judge is uninfluenced by particular interests, except by reference, directly or indirectly, to the manner in which he *would* react *if* he had no particular interests. And this seems to imply that the first alternative is ultimately unavoidable if our analysis is to be complete. I think we must conclude, therefore, that an ideal observer is entirely lacking in particular interests—that he is, in this sense, *disinterested*.

4. *He is dispassionate.* The concept of impartiality cannot be exhaustively analyzed in terms of interests, for an impartial judge, as ordinarily conceived, is a judge whose decisions are unaffected not only by his interests, but also by his emotions. This suggests that an ideal observer must be defined as a person who is in some sense dispassionate as well as disinterested. It is possible, to be sure, that the supposed effects of an emotion on our ethically-significant reactions, are always the effects of an accompanying or constituent interest; and if this were proved to our satisfaction, our conception of an ideal observer might be somewhat simplified. For our present purpose, however, this is irrelevant so long as it is generally believed that moral near-sightedness or blindness can be caused by the typically passional features of an emotion. We are searching for an analysis of ordinary ethical statements, and it is not to be expected that such an analysis will reflect all those distinctions, or just those distinctions, which would be required for an adequate system of psychology.

It is possible to construct a definition of the term "dispassionate" which will correspond, point by point, with our definition of the term "disinterested." Thus we can define a "particular emotion" as one which is directed toward an object only because the object is thought to have one or more essentially particular properties. And we can say that an ideal observer is dispassionate in the sense that he is incapable of experiencing emotions of this kind—such emotions as jealousy, self-love, personal hatred, and others which are directed towards particular individuals as such. At present this seems to me to be the most satisfactory way of defining the term "dispassionate" as applied to an ideal observer. . . .

5. *He is consistent.* Consistency is ordinarily regarded as one of the characteristics of a good judge, and this fact suggests that an ideal observer must be described in part as a being whose ethically-significant reactions are perfectly consistent with one another. But there are obstacles, as we shall see, to defining the relevant kind of consistency in a manner which avoids circularity and yet makes consistency an in-

dependent characteristic of an ideal observer.

When we say that the ethical decisions of a judge in two different cases are consistent with one another—or, correspondingly, that in two different situations the ethically-significant reactions of an ideal observer are consistent—we are evidently not passing judgment on the logic of any actual process of thought. There is an obvious sense, to be sure, in which a judge might accept consistent or inconsistent *premises* or use consistent or inconsistent *arguments* (either in reaching his decisions or in attempting to justify them); but when we assert that the two decisions of the judge are *themselves* consistent with one another, we intend to say something about a particular relationship between the two ethical statements which express the judge's final conclusions, and nothing, unless perhaps by insinuation, about the judge's processes of thought.

But it is also clear that we do not intend to say merely that these two ethical statements are *logically* consistent with one another. For since the two statements express ethical decisions about two different cases, they necessarily refer to different acts or events, and of course *any* two self-consistent statements are logically consistent with one another if they refer to different acts or events. Thus the kind of consistency which we have in mind must be "stronger" than logical consistency: we must mean to say that it is in some sense *possible* that the two statements are both true, but not merely that it is *logically* possible.

If this is so, however, the consistency or inconsistency of two ethical decisions must depend on the relationship of these decisions to certain general ethical principles which are conceived as restricting the "possible" combinations of ethical statements. And this conclusion is supported, I believe, by examination of the kind of reasoning which actually leads us to conclude that two decisions are consistent or inconsistent with one another. We might assert, for example, that a moral judge is inconsistent because in one case he decided in favor of act x rather than x', whereas in another case he decided in favor of y rather than y'; and if we assert this, an analysis of our reasoning would probably show that we are assuming that it is possible for x to be the right act only if a certain ethical principle (P) is true, whereas it is possible for y to be the right act only if P is false. Our judgment that the two decisions are inconsistent, therefore, is based on the assumption that there is no *other* valid ethical principle (a certain principle Q, for example) which could in some way take precedence over P in one of the two cases. We are not, to be sure, committing ourselves either to the belief that P is true or to the belief that P is false. But we *are* assuming that the facts of the two cases are not different in some respect which is ethically crucial. And to assume even this is to presuppose at least one ethical proposition, namely, that there is no valid ethical principle (e.g., Q) which, together with P, could be used to justify *both* decisions.

I think we must conclude, therefore, that whenever we assert that the decisions of a moral judge in two different cases are consistent with one another, we are presupposing a certain amount of ethical knowledge. And this implies that our analysis would be circular if we made consistency of this kind one of the defining characteristics of an ideal observer.

There is, however, a much more limited kind of consistency which we might wish to attribute to an ideal observer. For if we agree that his ethically-significant reactions are stimulated by his imagination of a possible act, then, since an act may be imagined at any number of different times, there is nothing in our analysis up to this point which would logically require that an ideal observer always react in the same way even when he imagines one *particular* act (i.e., an act occurring at a particular time and place and hence having a certain particular set of alternatives). And if this appears to be a deficiency in our analysis, we could easily correct it by attributing a limited consistency to an ideal observer: we could define him, in part, as a being whose ethically-significant reactions to any particular act would always be exactly similar.

If we decide to do this, however, it is important to notice that consistency, when interpreted in this way, has a status very different from that of omniscience, disinterestedness, and the other defining characteristics of an ideal observer which we have so far considered. For according to the kind of absolutist analysis which we have been examining, ethical statements, as we have previously observed, are statements which depend for their truth or falsity on the existence of certain psychological laws; and if ethical statements are ever true, they are true only because we have defined an ideal observer in such a way that, in virtue of the relevant psychological laws, *any* ideal observer would react in the same way to a particular act. Thus in attributing omniscience, disinterestedness, and other such characteristics to an ideal observer, we are doing something of crucial importance for the kind of analysis which we are considering: we are eliminating from the personality of the ideal observer, so to speak, various factors which actually cause certain people to differ in their ethically-significant reactions from other people—such factors, for example, as selfish desires and ignorance of the facts of the case. And assuming that ethical statements *are* sometimes true, an absolutist dispositional analysis can be adequate only if such facts are completely eliminated from the personality of an ideal observer.

The characteristic of consistency, however, unlike omniscience, disinterestedness, and the others which we have discussed, does not eliminate some particular source of disagreement in ethical reactions. It is, on the contrary, a *consequence* of eliminating such disagreement, since any factor which could cause two different ideal observers to react in different ways to a particular act, could also cause one and the same ideal observer to react in different ways at different times. And this means, to put the matter bluntly, that if it is necessary to attribute consistency to an ideal observer in order to insure that he is psychologically incapable of reacting to the same act in different ways at different times, then we have simply failed to find all the *other* characteristics of an ideal observer which are necessary for the formulation of an adequate analysis. Thus an ideal observer will indeed be consistent if an adequate dispositional analysis can be formulated; but his consistency will be a derivative characteristic—a consequence of his other characteristics together with certain psychological laws.

6. *In other respects he is normal.* An examination of the procedures by which we attempt to decide moral questions, reveals that there are a great many conditions which we recognize, though not always explicitly, to be favorable or unfavorable for making valid moral judgments. Mild bodily exercise such as walking, the presence of other people trying to make similar decisions, and certain kinds of esthetic stimuli, have all been regarded by some people as favorable conditions, whereas mental fatigue, distracting sensory stimuli, and lack of experience, are generally regarded as unfavorable. It seems likely, however, that our analysis will take all these special conditions into account if we attribute such general characteristics as omniscience and disinterestedness to an ideal observer.

It seems fairly clear, on the other hand, that no analysis in terms solely of such general, and highly ideal, characteristics, could be fully adequate to the meaning of ethical statements. For however ideal some of his characteristics may be, an ideal observer is, after all, a *person;* and whatever may be true of the future, our conception of the personality of an ideal observer has not yet undergone the refining processes which have enabled theologians, apparently with clear conscience, to employ the term "person" in exceedingly abstract ways. Most of us, indeed, can be said to have a conception of an ideal observer only in the sense that the characteristics of such a person are implicit in the procedures by which we compare and evaluate moral judges, and it seems doubtful, therefore, that an ideal observer can be said to lack any of the determinable properties of human beings.

The determinate properties of an ideal observer, however, except for the ideal characteristics which we have so far discussed, are apparently not capable of precise definition. We may employ the customary linguistic device, to be sure, and say that the properties of an ideal observer cannot vary beyond the limits of "normality," but there are a number of reasons why it does not seem to be possible to define these limits satisfactorily. It is evident, for example, that normality is a gestalt concept, and that a certain trait which in abstraction might properly be called abnormal, could nevertheless contribute to a total personality which falls within the bounds of normality. And this fact by itself is sufficient to destroy any hope of defining the term "normal" by continuing to add specific characteristics to the ones which we have already attributed to an ideal observer. This difficulty, however, and the others which prevent us from formulating a satisfactory definition of "normal," are practical rather than theoretical, and they do not tend in the slightest degree to disprove the thesis that ethical statements are statements about an ideal observer and his ethically-significant reactions. There are analogous difficulties, moreover, in formulating a dispositional analysis of the statement "This is (really) yellow"; and I have yet to find any convincing reason, indeed, for believing that "yellow" can be defined dispositionally although "right" cannot.

JOHN RAWLS

*Two Concepts of Rules**

In this paper I want to show the importance of the distinction between justifying a practice[1] and justifying a particular action falling under it, and I want to explain the logical basis of this distinction and how it is possible to miss its significance. While the distinction has frequently been made, and is now becoming commonplace, there remains the task of explaining the tendency either to overlook it altogether, or to fail to appreciate its importance.

To show the importance of the distinction I am going to defend ultilitarianism against those objections which have traditionally been made against it in connexion with punishment and the obligation to keep promises. I hope to show that if one uses the distinction in question then one can state utilitarianism in a way which makes it a much better explication of our considered moral judgements than traditional objections would seem to admit.[2] Thus the importance of the distinction is shown by the way it strengthens the utilitarian view regardless of whether that view is completely defensible or not.

To explain how the significance of the distinction may be overlooked, I am going to discuss two conceptions of rules. One of these conceptions conceals the importance of distinguishing betwen the justification of a rule or practice and the justification of a particular action falling under it. The other conception makes it clear why this distinction must be made and what is its logical basis.

I.

The subject of punishment, in the sense of attaching legal penalties to the violation of legal rules, has always been a troubling moral question. The trouble about it has not been that people disagree as to whether or not punishment is justifiable. Most people have held that, freed from certain abuses, it is an acceptable institution. Only a few have rejected punishment entirely, which is rather surprising when one considers all that can be said against it. The difficulty is with the justification of punishment: various arguments for it have been given by moral philosophers, but

* By permission. *Philosophical Review*, Vol. lxiv, 1955.

John Rawls is professor of philosophy at Harvard University.

[1] I use the word "practice" throughout as a sort of technical term meaning any form of activity specified by a system of rules which defines offices, roles, moves, penalties, defences, and so on, and which gives the activity its structure. As examples one may think of games and rituals, trials and parliaments.

[2] On the concept of explication see the author's paper, *Philosophical Review*, Vol. lx (April, 1951).

so far none of them has won any sort of general acceptance; no justification is without those who detest it. I hope to show that the use of the aforementioned distinction enables one to state the utilitarian view in a way which allows for the sound points of its critics.

For our purposes we may say that there are two justifications of punishment. What we may call the retributive view is that punishment is justified on the grounds that wrongdoing merits punishment. It is morally fitting that a person who does wrong should suffer in proportion to his wrongdoing. That a criminal should be punished follows from his guilt, and the severity of the appropriate punishment depends on the depravity of his act. The state of affairs where a wrongdoer suffers punishment is morally better than the state of affairs where he does not; and it is better irrespective of any of the consequences of punishing him.

What we may call the utilitarian view holds that on the principle that bygones are bygones and that only future consequences are material to present decisions, punishment is justifiable only by reference to the probable consequences of maintaining it as one of the devices of the social order. Wrongs committed in the past are, as such, not relevant considerations for deciding what to do. If punishment can be shown to promote effectively the interest of society it is justifiable, otherwise it is not.

I have stated these two competing views very roughly to make one feel the conflict between them: one feels the force of *both* arguments and one wonders how they can be reconciled. From my introductory remarks it is obvious that the resolution which I am going to propose is that in this case one must distinguish between justifying a practice as a system of rules to be applied and enforced, and justifying a particular action which falls under these rules; utilitarian arguments are appropriate with regard to questions about practices, while retributive arguments fit the application of particular rules to particular cases.

We might try to get clear about this distinction by imagining how a father might answer the question of his son. Suppose the son asks, "Why was *J* put in jail yesterday?" The father answers, "Because he robbed the bank at *B*. He was duly tried and found guilty. That's why he was put in jail yesterday." But suppose the son had asked a different question, namely, "Why do people put other people in jail?" Then the father might answer, "To protect good people from bad people" or "To stop people from doing things that would make it uneasy for all of us; for otherwise we wouldn't be able to go to bed at night and sleep in peace." There are two very different questions here. One question emphasizes the proper name: it asks why *J* was punished rather than someone else, or it asks what he was punished for. The other question asks why we have the institution of punishment: why do people punish one another rather than, say, always forgiving one another?

Thus the father says in effect that a particular man is punished, rather than some other man, because he is guilty, and he is guilty because he broke the law (past tense). In his case the law looks back, the judge looks back, the jury looks back, and a penalty is visited upon him for something he did. That a man is to be punished, and what his punishment is to be, is settled by its being shown that he broke the law and that the law assigns that penalty for the violation of it.

On the other hand we have the institution of punishment itself, and recommend and accept various changes in it, because it is thought by the (ideal) legislator and by those to whom the law applies that, as a part of a system of law impartially applied from case to case arising under it, it will have the consequence, in the long run, of furthering the interests of society.

One can say, then, that the judge

and the legislator stand in different positions and look in different directions: one to the past, the other to the future. The justification of what the judge does, *qua* judge, sounds like the retributive view; the justification of what the (ideal) legislator does, *qua* legislator, sounds like the utilitarian view. Thus both views have a point (this is as it should be since intelligent and sensitive persons have been on both sides of the argument); and one's initial confusion disappears once one sees that these views apply to persons holding different offices with different duties, and situated differently with respect to the system of rules that make up the criminal law.[3]

One might say, however, that the utilitarian view is more fundamental since it applies to a more fundamental office, for the judge carries out the legislator's will so far as he can determine it. Once the legislator decides to have laws and to assign penalties for their violation (as things are there must be both the law and the penalty) an institution is set up which involves a retributive conception of particular cases. It is part of the concept of the criminal law as a system of rules that the application and enforcement of these rules in particular cases should be justifiable by arguments of a retributive character. The decision whether or not to use law rather than some other mechanism of social control, and the decision as to what laws to have and what penalties to assign, may be settled by utilitarian arguments; but if one decides to have laws then one has decided on something whose working in particular cases is retributive in form.

The answer, then, to the confusion engendered by the two views of punishment is quite simple: one distinguishes two offices, that of the judge and that of the legislator, and one distinguishes their different stations with respect to the system of rules which make up the law; and then one notes that the different sorts of considerations which would usually be offered as reasons for what is done under the cover of these offices can be paired off with the competing justifications of punishment. One reconciles the two views by the time-honoured device of making them apply to different situations.

But can it really be this simple? Well, this answer allows for the apparent intent of each side. Does a person who advocates the retributive view necessarily advocate, as an *institution*, legal machinery whose essential purpose is to set up and preserve a correspondence between moral turpitude and suffering? Surely not.[4] What retributionists have rightly insisted upon is that no man can be punished unless he is guilty, that is, unless he has broken the law. Their fundamental criticism of the utilitarian account is that, as they interpret it, it sanctions an innocent person's being punished (if one may call it that) for the benefit of society.

On the other hand, utilitarians agree that punishment is to be inflicted only for the violation of law. They regard this much as understood from the concept of punishment itself.[5] The point of the utilitarian ac-

[3] Note the fact that different sorts of arguments are suited to different offices. One way of taking the differences between ethical theories is to regard them as accounts of the reasons expected in different offices.

[4] On this point see Sir David Ross, *The Right and the Good* (Oxford, 1930), pp. 57–60.

[5] See Hobbes's definition of punishment in *Leviathan*, ch. xxviii; and Bentham's definition in *The Principle of Morals and Legislation*, ch. xii, par. 36, ch. xv, par. 28, and in *The Rationale of Punishment* (London, 1830), Bk. I, ch. i. They could agree with Bradley that: "Punishment is punishment only when it is deserved. We pay the penalty, because we owe it, and for no other reason; and if punishment is inflicted for any other reason whatever than because it is merited by wrong, it is a gross immorality, a crying injustice, an abominable crime, and not what it pretends to be." *Ethical Studies* (2nd ed.; Oxford, 1927), pp. 26–27. Certainly by definition it isn't what it pretends

count concerns the institution as a system of rules: utilitarianism seeks to limit its use by declaring it justifiable only if it can be shown to foster effectively the good of society. Historically it is a protest against the indiscriminate and ineffective use of the criminal law.[6] It seeks to dissuade us from assigning to penal institutions the improper, if not sacrilegious, task of matching suffering with moral turpitude. Like others, utilitarians want penal institutions designed so that, as far as humanly possible, only those who break the law run afoul of it. They hold that no official should have discretionary power to inflict penalties whenever he thinks it for the benefit of society; for on utilitarian grounds an institution granting such power could not be justified.[7]

The suggested way of reconciling the retributive and the utilitarian justifications of punishment seems to account for what both sides have wanted to say. There are, however, two further questions which arise, and I shall devote the remainder of this section to them.

First, will not a difference of opinion as to the proper criterion of just law make the proposed reconciliation unacceptable to retributionists? Will they not question whether, if the utilitarian principle is used as the criterion, it follows that those who have broken the law are guilty in a way which satisfies their demand that those punished deserve to be punished? To answer this difficulty, suppose that the rules of the criminal law are justified on utilitarian grounds (it is only for laws that meet his criterion that the utilitarian can be held responsible). Then it follows that the actions which the criminal law specifies as offences are such that, if they were tolerated, terror and alarm would spread in society. Consequently, retributionists can only deny that those who are punished deserve to be punished if they deny that such actions are wrong. This they will not want to do.

The second question is whether utilitarianism doesn't justify too much. One pictures it as an engine of justification which, if consistently adopted, could be used to justify cruel and arbitrary institutions. Retributionists may be supposed to concede that utilitarians *intend* to reform the law and to make it more humane; that utilitarians do not *wish* to justify any such thing as punishment of the innocent; and that utilitarians may appeal to the fact that punishment presupposes guilt in the sense that by punishment one understands an institution attaching penalties to the infraction of legal rules, and therefore that it is logically absurd to suppose that utilitarians in justifying *punishment* might also have justified punishment (if we may call it that) of the innocent. The real question, however, is whether the utilitarian, in justifying punishment, hasn't used arguments which commit him to accepting the infliction of suffer-

---

to be. The innocent can only be punished by mistake; deliberate "punishment" of the innocent necessarily involves fraud.

[6] Cf. Leon Radzinowicz, *A History of English Criminal Law: The Movement for Reform 1750–1833* (London, 1948), esp. ch. xi on Bentham.

[7] Bentham discusses how corresponding to a punitory provision of a criminal law there is another provision which stands to it as an antagonist and which needs a name as much as the punitory. He calls it, as one might expect, the *anaetiosostic*, and of it he says: "The punishment of guilt is the object of the former one: the preservation of innocence that of the latter." In the same connexion he asserts that it is never thought fit to give the judge the option of deciding whether a thief (that is, a person whom he believes to be a thief, for the judge's belief is what the question must always turn upon) should hang or not, and so the law writes the provision: "The judge shall not cause a thief to be hanged unless he have been duly convicted and sentenced in course of law" (*The Limits of Jurisprudence Defined*. ed. C. W. Everett [New York, 1945], pp. 238–239).

ing on innocent persons if it is for the good of society (whether or not one calls this punishment). More generally, isn't the utilitarian committed in principle to accepting many practices which he, as a morally sensitive person, wouldn't want to accept? Retributionists are inclined to hold that there is no way to stop the utilitarian principle from justifying too much except by adding to it a principle which distributes certain rights to individuals. Then the amended criterion is not the greatest benefit of society *simpliciter*, but the greatest benefit of society subject to the constraint that no one's rights may be violated. Now while I think that the classical utilitarians proposed a criterion of this more complicated sort, I do not want to argue that point here.[8] What I want to show is that there is *another* way of preventing the utilitarian principle from justifying too much, or at least of making it much less likely to do so: namely, by stating utilitarianism in a way which accounts for the distinction between the justification of an institution and the justification of a particular action falling under it.

I begin by defining the institution of punishment as follows: a person is said to suffer punishment whenever he is legally deprived of some of the normal rights of a citizen on the ground that he has violated a rule of law, the violation having been established by trial according to the due process of law, provided that the deprivation is carried out by the recognized legal authorities of the state, that the rule of law clearly specifies both the offence and the attached penalty, that the courts construe statutes strictly, and that the statute was on the books prior to the time of the offence.[9] This definition specifies what I shall understand by punishment. The question is whether utilitarian arguments may be found to justify institutions widely different from this and such as one would find cruel and arbitrary.

This question is best answered, I think, by taking up a particular accusation. Consider the following from Carritt:

> *. . . the utilitarian must hold that we are justified in inflicting pain always and only to prevent worse pain or bring about greater happiness. This, then, is all we need to consider in so-called punishment, which must be purely preventive. But if some kind of very cruel crime becomes common, and none of the criminals can be caught, it might be highly expedient, as an example, to hang an innocent man, if a charge against him could be so framed that he were universally thought guilty; indeed this would only fail to be an ideal instance of utilitarian "punishment" because the victim himself would not have been so likely as a real felon to commit such a crime in the future; in all other respects it would be perfectly deterrent and therefore felicific.*[10]

Carritt is trying to show that there are occasions when a utilitarian argument would justify taking an action which would be generally condemned; and thus that utilitarianism justifies too much. But the failure of Carritt's argument lies in the fact that he makes no distinction between the justification of the general system of rules which constitutes penal institutions and the justification of particular applications of these rules to particular cases by the various officials whose job it is to administer them. This becomes perfectly clear when one asks who the "we" are of whom Carritt speaks. Who is this who has a sort of absolute authority on particular occasions to decide that an innocent man shall be "punished" if everyone can be convinced

[8] By the classical utilitarians I understand Hobbes, Hume, Bentham, J. S. Mill, and Sidgwick.

[9] All these features of punishment are mentioned by Hobbes; cf. *Leviathan*, ch. xxviii.

[10] *Ethical and Political Thinking* (Oxford, 1947), p. 65.

that he is guilty? Is this person the legislator, or the judge, or the body of private citizens, or what? It is utterly crucial to know who is to decide such matters, and by what authority, for all of this must be written into the rules of the institution. Until one knows these things one doesn't know what the institution is whose justification is being challenged; and as the utilitarian principle applies to the institution one doesn't know whether it is justifiable on utilitarian grounds or not.

Once this is understood it is clear what the countermove to Carritt's argument is. One must describe more carefully what the *institution* is which his example suggests, and then ask oneself whether or not it is likely that having this institution would be for the benefit of society in the long run. One must not content onself with the vague thought that, when it's a question of *this* case, it would be a good thing if *somebody* did something even if an innocent person were to suffer.

Try to imagine, then, an institution (which we may call "telishment") which is such that the officials set up by it have authority to arrange a trial for the condemnation of an innocent man whenever they are of the opinion that doing so would be in the best interests of society. The discretion of officials is limited, however, by the rule that they may not condemn an innocent man to undergo such an ordeal unless there is, at the time, a wave of offences similar to that with which they charge him and telish him for. We may imagine that the officials having the discretionary authority are the judges of the higher courts in consultation with the chief of police, the minister of justice, and a committee of the legislature.

Once one realizes that one is involved in setting up an *institution,* one sees that the hazards are very great. For example, what check is there on the officials? How is one to tell whether or not their actions are authorized? How is one to limit the risks involved in allowing such systematic deception? How is one to avoid giving anything short of complete discretion to the authorities to telish anyone they like? In addition to these considerations, it is obvious that people will come to have a very different attitude towards their penal system when telishment is adjoined to it. They will be uncertain as to whether a convicted man has been punished or telished. They will wonder whether or not they should feel sorry for him. They will wonder whether the same fate won't at any time fall on them. If one pictures how such an institution would actually work, and the enormous risks involved in it, it seems clear that it would serve no useful purpose. A utilitarian justification for this institution is most unlikely. . . .

If one is careful to apply the utilitarian principle to the institution which is to authorize particular actions, then there is *less* danger of its justifying too much. Carritt's example gains plausibility by its indefiniteness and by its concentration on the particular case. His argument will only hold if it can be shown that there are utilitarian arguments which justify an institution whose publicly ascertainable offices and powers are such as to permit officials to exercise that kind of discretion in particular cases. But the requirement of having to build the arbitrary features of the particular decision into the institutional practice makes the justification much less likely to go through.

II.

I shall now consider the question of promises. The objection to utilitarianism in connexion with promises seems to be this: it is believed that on the utilitarian view when a person makes a promise the only ground upon which he should keep it, if he should keep it, is that by keeping it he will realize the most good on the whole. So that if one asks the question "Why should I keep *my* promise?" the utilitarian answer is understood to be that doing so in *this* case will have the best consequences. And this answer is said, quite rightly, to conflict with the way in which the obligation to keep promises is regarded.

Now of course critics of utilitarianism are not unaware that one defence sometimes attributed to utilitarians is the consideration involving the practice of promise-keeping.[11] In this connexion they are supposed to argue something like this: it must be admitted that we feel strictly about keeping promises, more strictly than it might seem our view can account for. But when we consider the matter carefully it is always necessary to take into account the effect which our action will have on the practice of making promises. The promisor must weigh, not only the effects of breaking his promise on the particular case, but also the effect which his breaking his promise will have on the practice itself. Since the practice is of great utilitarian value, and since breaking one's promise always seriously damages it, one will seldom be justified in breaking one's promise. If we view our individual promises in the wider context of the practice of promising itself we can account for the strictness of the obligation to keep promises. There is always one very strong utilitarian consideration in favour of keeping them, and this will ensure that when the question arises as to whether or not to keep a promise it will usually turn out that one should, even where the facts of the particular case taken by itself would seem to justify one's breaking it. In this way the strictness with which we view the obligation to keep promises is accounted for.

[11] Ross, *The Right and the Good,* pp. 37–39, and *Foundations of Ethics* (Oxford, 1939), pp. 92–94. I know of no utilitarian who has used this argument except W. A. Pickard-Cambridge in "Two Problems about Duty," *Mind,* n.s., xli (April, 1932), 153–157, although the argument goes with G. E. Moore's version of utilitarianism in *Principia Ethica* (Cambridge, 1903). To my knowledge it does not appear in the classical utilitarians; and if one interprets their view correctly this is no accident.

Ross has criticized this defence as follows:[12] however great the value of the practice of promising, on utilitarian grounds, there must be some value which is greater, and one can imagine it to be obtainable by breaking a promise. Therefore there might be a case where the promisor could argue that breaking his promise was justified as leading to a better state of affairs on the whole. And the promisor could argue in this way no matter how slight the advantage won by breaking the promise. If one were to challenge the promisor his defence would be that what he did was best on the whole in view of all the utilitarian considerations, which in this case *include* the importance of the practice. Ross feels that such a defence would be unacceptable. I think he is right insofar as he is protesting against the appeal to consequences in general and without further explanation. Yet it is extremely difficult to weigh the force of Ross's argument. The kind of case imagined seems unrealistic and one feels that it needs to be described. One is inclined to think it would either turn out that such a case came under an exception defined by the practice itself, in which case there would not be an appeal to consequences in general on the particular case, or it would happen that the circumstances were so peculiar that the conditions which the practice presupposes no longer obtained. But certainly Ross is right in thinking that it strikes us as wrong for a person to defend breaking a promise by a general appeal to consequences. For a general utilitarian defence is not open to the promisor: it is not one of the defences allowed by the practice of making promises.

Ross gives two further counterarguments:[13] First, he holds that it overestimates the damage done to the practice of

[12] Ross, *The Right and the Good,* pp. 38–39.

[13] Ross, ibid., p. 39. The case of the non-public promise is discussed again in *Foundations of Ethics,* pp. 95–96, 104–105.

promising by a failure to keep a promise. One who breaks a promise harms his own name certainly, but it isn't clear that a broken promise always damages the practice itself sufficiently to account for the strictness of the obligation. Second, and more important, I think, he raises the question of what one is to say of a promise which isn't known to have been made except to the promisor and the promisee, as in the case of a promise a son makes to his dying father concerning the handling of the estate. In this sort of case the consideration relating to the practice doesn't weigh on the promisor at all, and yet one feels that this sort of promise is as binding as other promises. The question of the effect which breaking it has on the practice seems irrelevant. The only consequence seems to be that one can break the promise without running any risk of being censured; but the obligation itself seems not the least weakened. Hence it is doubtful whether the effect on the practice ever weighs in the particular case; certainly it cannot account for the strictness of the obligation where it fails to obtain. It seems to follow that a utilitarian account of the obligation to keep promises cannot be successfully carried out.

From what I have said in connexion with punishment, one can foresee what I am going to say about these arguments and counterarguments. They fail to make the distinction between the justification of a practice and the justification of a particular action falling under it, and therefore they fall into the mistake of taking it for granted that the promisor, like Carritt's official, is entitled without restriction to bring utilitarian considerations to bear in deciding whether to keep *his* promise. But if one considers what the practice of promising is one will see, I think, that it is such as not to allow this sort of general discretion to the promisor. Indeed, the point of the practice is to abdictate one's title to act in accordance with utilitarian and prudential considerations in order that the future may be tied down and plans coordinated in advance. There are obvious utilitarian advantages in having a practice which denies to the promisor, as a defence, any general appeal to the utilitarian principle in accordance with which the practice itself may be justified. There is nothing contradictory, or surprising, in this: utilitarian (or aesthetic) reasons might properly be given in arguing that the game of chess, or baseball, is satisfactory just as it is, or in arguing that it should be changed in various respects, but a player in a game cannot properly appeal to such considerations as reasons for his making one move rather than another. It is a mistake to think that if the practice is justified on utilitarian grounds then the promisor must have complete liberty to use utilitarian arguments to decide whether or not to keep his promise. The practice forbids this general defence; and it is a purpose of the practice to do this. Therefore what the above arguments presuppose—the idea that if the utilitarian view is accepted then the promisor is bound if, and only if, the application of the utilitarian principle to his own case shows that keeping it is best on the whole—is false. The promisor is bound because he promised: weighing the case on its merits is not open to him.

Is this to say that in particular cases one cannot deliberate whether or not to keep one's promise? Of course not. But to do so is to deliberate whether the various excuses, exceptions and defences, which are understood by, and which constitute an important part of, the practice, apply to one's own case. Various defences for not keeping one's promise are allowed, but among them there isn't the one that, on general utilitarian grounds, the promisor (truly) thought his action best on the whole, even though there may be the defence that the consequences of keeping one's promise would have been *extremely* severe. While there are too many complexities here to consider all the necessary details, one can see that the general defence isn't allowed if one asks the following question: what would one say of someone who, when asked why he broke his promise, replied simply that breaking it was best on the whole? Assuming that his reply is sincere, and that his belief was reasonable (i.e., one need not consider the possibility that he was mistaken), I think that one would question whether or not he knows what it means to say "I promise" (in the appropriate circumstances). It would be said of someone who used this excuse without further explanation that he didn't understand what defences the practice, which defines a promise, allows to him. If a child were to use this excuse one would correct him; for it is part of the way one is taught the concept of a promise to be corrected if one uses this excuse. The point of having the practice would be lost if the practice did allow this excuse.

It is no doubt part of the utilitarian view that every practice should admit the defence that the consequences of abiding by it would have been extremely severe; and utilitarians would be inclined to hold that some reliance on people's good sense and some concession to hard cases is necessary. They would hold that a practice is justified by serving the interests of those who take part in it; and as with any set of rules there is understood a background of circumstances under which it is expected to be applied and which need not—indeed which cannot—be fully stated. Should these circumstances change, then even if there is no rule which provides for the case, it may still be in accordance with the practice that one be released from one's obligation. But this sort of defence allowed by a practice must not be confused with the general option to weigh each particular case on utilitarian grounds which critics of utilitarianism have thought it necessarily to involve.

The concern which utilitarianism raises by its justification of punishment is that it may justify too much. The question in connexion with promises is different: it is how utilitarianism can account for the obligation to keep promises at all. One feels that the recognized obligation to keep one's promise and utilitarianism are incompatible. And to be sure, they are incompatible if one interprets the utilitarian view as necessarily holding that each person has complete liberty to weigh every particular action on general utilitarian grounds. But must one interpret utilitarianism in this way? I hope to show that, in the sorts of cases I have discussed, one cannot interpret it in this way.

III.

So far I have tried to show the importance of the distinction between the justification of a practice and the justification of a particular action falling under it by indicating how this distinction might be used to defend utilitarianism against two long-standing objections. One might be tempted to close the discussion at this point by saying that utilitarian considerations should be understood as applying to practices in the first instance and not to particular actions falling under them except insofar as the practices admit of it. One might say that in this modified form it is a better account of our considered moral opinions and let it go at that. But to stop here would be to neglect the interesting question as to how one can fail to appreciate the significance of this rather obvious distinction and can take it for granted that utilitarianism has the consequence that particular cases may always be decided on general utilitarian grounds.[14] I

[14] So far as I can see it is not until Moore that the doctrine is expressly stated in this way. See, for example, *Principia Ethica*, p. 147, where it is said that the statement "I am morally bound to perform this action" is identical with the statement "*This* action will produce the greatest possible amount of good in the Universe" (my italics).

want to argue that this mistake may be connected with misconceiving the logical status of the rules of practices; and to show this I am going to examine two conceptions of rules, two ways of placing them within the utilitarian theory.

The conception which conceals from us the significance of the distinction I am going to call the summary view. It regards rules in the following way: one supposes that each person decides what he shall do in particular cases by applying the utilitarian principle; one supposes further that different people will decide the same particular case in the same way and that there will be recurrences of cases similar to those previously decided. Thus it will happen that in cases of certain kinds the same decision will be made either by the same person at different times or by different persons at the same time. If a case occurs frequently enough one supposes that a rule is formulated to cover that sort of case. I have called this conception the summary view because rules are pictured as summaries of past decisions arrived at by the *direct* application of the utilitarian principle to particular cases. Rules are regarded as reports that cases of a certain sort have been found on *other* grounds to be properly decided in a certain way (although, of course, they do not *say* this).

There are several things to notice about this way of placing rules within the utilitarian theory.

1. The point of having rules derives from the fact that similar cases tend to recur and that one can decide cases more quickly if one records past decisions in the form of rules. If similar cases didn't recur, one would be required to apply the utilitarian principle directly, case by case, and rules reporting past decisions would be of no use.

2. The decisions made on particular cases are logically prior to rules. Since rules gain their point from the need to apply the utilitarian principle to many similar cases, it follows that a particular case (or several cases similar to it) may exist whether or not there is a rule covering that case. We are pictured as recognizing particular cases prior to their being a rule which covers them, for it is only if we meet with a number of cases of a certain sort that we formulate a rule. Thus we are able to describe a particular case as a particular case of the requisite sort whether there is a rule regarding *that* sort of case or not. Put another way: what the *A*'s and the *B*'s refer to in rules of the form "Whenever *A* do *B*" may be described as *A*'s and *B*'s whether or not there is the rule "Whenever *A* do *B*," or whether or not there is any body of rules which makes up a practice of which that rule is part.

To illustrate this consider a rule, or maxim, which could arise in this way: suppose that a person is trying to decide whether to tell someone who is fatally ill what his illness is when he has been asked to do so. Suppose the person to reflect and then decide, on utilitarian grounds, that he should not answer truthfully; and suppose that on the basis of this and other like occasions he formulates a rule to the effect that when asked by someone fatally ill what his illness is, one should not tell him. The point to notice is that someone's being fatally ill and asking what his illness is, and someone's telling him, are things that can be described as such whether or not there is this rule. The performance of the action to which the rule refers doesn't require the stage-setting of a practice of which this rule is a part. This is what is meant by saying that on the summary view particular cases are logically prior to rules.

3. Each person is in principle always entitled to reconsider the correctness of a rule and to question whether or not it is proper to follow it in a particular case. As rules are guides and aids, one may ask whether in past decisions there might not have been a mistake in applying the utili-

tarian principle to get the rule in question, and wonder whether or not it is best in this case. The reason for rules is that people are not able to apply the utilitarian principle effortlessly and flawlessly; there is need to save time and to post a guide. On this view a society of rational utilitarians would be a society without rules in which each person applied the utilitarian principle directly and smoothly, and without error, case by case. On the other hand, ours is a society in which rules are formulated to serve as aids in reaching these ideally rational decisions on particular cases, guides which have been built up and tested by the experience of generations. If one applies this view to rules, one is interpreting them as maxims, as "rules of thumb"; and it is doubtful that anything to which the summary conception did apply would be called a *rule*. Arguing as if one regarded rules in this way is a mistake one makes while doing philosophy.

4. The concept of a *general* rule takes the following form. One is pictured as estimating on what percentage of the cases likely to arise a given rule may be relied upon to express the correct decision, that is, the decision that would be arrived at if one were to correctly apply the utilitarian principle case by case. If one estimates that by and large the rule will give the correct decision, or if one estimates that the likelihood of making a mistake by applying the utilitarian principle directly on one's own is greater than the likelihood of making a mistake by following the rule, and if these considerations held of persons generally, then one would be justified in urging its adoption as a general rule. In this way *general* rules might be accounted for on the summary view. It will still make sense, however, to speak of applying the utilitarian principle case by case, for it was by trying to foresee the results of doing this that one got the initial estimates upon which acceptance of the rule depends. That one is taking a rule in accordance with the summary conception will show itself in the naturalness with which one speaks of the rule as a guide, or as a maxim, or as a generalization from experience, and as something to be laid aside in extraordinary cases where there is no assurance that the generalization will hold and the case must therefore be treated on its merits. Thus there goes with this conception the notion of a particular exception which renders a rule suspect on a particular occasion.

The other conception of rules I will call the practice conception. On this view rules are pictured as defining a practice. Practices are set up for various reasons, but one of them is that in many areas of conduct each person's deciding what to do on utilitarian grounds case by case leads to confusion, and that the attempt to coordinate behaviour by trying to foresee how others will act is bound to fail. As an alternative one realizes that what is required is the establishment of a practice, the specification of a new form of activity; and from this one sees that a practice necessarily involves the abdication of full liberty to act on utilitarian and prudential grounds. It is the mark of a practice that being taught how to engage in it involves being instructed in the rules which define it, and that appeal is made to those rules to correct the behaviour of those engaged in it. Those engaged in a practice recognize the rules as defining it. The rules cannot be taken as simply describing how those engaged in the practice in fact behave: it is not simply that they act as if they were obeying the rules. Thus it is essential to the notion of a practice that the rules are publicly known and understood as definitive; and it is essential also that the rules of a practice can be taught and can be acted upon to yield a coherent practice. On this conception, then, rules are not generalizations from the decisions of individuals applying the utilitarian principle directly and independently to recurrent particular cases. On the contrary, rules define a practice and are themselves the subject of the utilitarian principle.

To show the important differences between this way of fitting rules into the utilitarian theory and the previous way, I shall consider the differences between the two conceptions on the points previously discussed.

1. In contrast with the summary view, the rules of practices are logically prior to particular cases. This is so because there cannot be a particular case of an action falling under a rule of a practice unless there is the practice. This can be made clearer as follows: in a practice there are rules setting up offices, specifying certain forms of action appropriate to various offices, establishing penalties for the breach of rules, and so on. We may think of the rules of a practice as defining offices, moves, and offences. Now what is meant by saying that the practice is logically prior to particular cases is this: given any rule which specifies a form of action (a move), a particular action which would be taken as falling under this rule given that there is the practice would not be *described as* that sort of action unless there was the practice. In the case of actions specified by practices it is logically impossible to perform them outside the stage-setting provided by those practices, for unless there is the practice, and unless the requisite proprieties are fulfilled, whatever one does, whatever movements one makes, will fail to count as a form of action which the practice specifies. What one does will be described in some *other* way.

One may illustrate this point from the game of baseball. Many of the actions one performs in a game of baseball one can do by oneself or with others whether there is the game or not. For example, one can throw a ball, run, or swing a peculiarly shaped piece of wood. But one cannot steal base, or strike out, or draw a walk, or make an error, or balk; although one can do certain things which appear to resemble these actions such as sliding into a bag, missing a grounder and so on. Striking out, stealing a base, balking, etc., are all actions which can only happen in a game. No matter what a person did, what he did would not be described as stealing a base or striking out or drawing a walk unless he could also be described as playing baseball, and for him to be doing this presupposes the rule-like practice which constitutes the game. The practice is logically prior to particular cases: unless there is the practice the terms referring to actions specified by it lack a sense.

2. The practice view leads to an entirely different conception of the authority which each person has to decide on the propriety of following a rule in particular cases. To engage in a practice, to perform those actions specified by a practice, means to follow the appropriate rules. If one wants to do an action which a certain practice specifies then there is no way to do it except to follow the rules which define it. Therefore, it doesn't make sense for a person to raise the question whether or not a rule of a practice correctly applies to *his* case where the action he contemplates is a form of action defined by a practice. If someone were to raise such a question, he would simply show that he didn't understand the situation in which he was acting. If one wants to perform an action specified by a practice, the only legitimate question concerns the nature of the practice itself ("How do I go about making a will?").

This point is illustrated by the behaviour expected of a player in games. If one wants to play a game, one doesn't treat the rules of the game as guides as to what is best in particular cases. In a game of baseball if a batter were to ask "Can I have four strikes?" it would be assumed that he was asking what the rule was; and if, when told what the rule was, he were to say that he meant that on this occasion he thought it would be best on the whole for him to have four strikes rather than three, this would be most kindly taken as a joke. One might contend that baseball would be a better game if four strikes were allowed instead of three; but one cannot picture the rules as guides to what is best on the whole in particular cases, and question their applicability to particular cases as particular cases.

3 and 4. To complete the four points of comparison with the summary conception, it is clear from what has been said that rules of practices are not guides to help one decide particular cases correctly as judged by some higher ethical principle. And neither the quasi-statistical notion of generality, nor the notion of a particular exception, can apply to the rules of practices. A more or less general rule of a practice must be a rule which according to the structure of the practice applies to more or fewer of the kinds of cases arising under it; or it must be a rule which is more or less basic to the understanding of the practice. Again, a particular case cannot be an exception to a rule of a practice. An exception is rather a qualification or a further specification of the rule.

It follows from what we have said about the practice conception of rules that if a person is engaged in a practice, and if he is asked why *he* does what *he* does, or if he is asked to defend what he does, then his explanation, or defence, lies in referring the questioner to the practice. He cannot say of *his* action, if it is an action specified by a practice, that he does it rather than some other because he thinks it is best on the whole. When a man engaged in a practice is queried about his action he must assume that the questioner either doesn't know that he is engaged in it ("Why are you in a hurry to pay him?" "I promised to pay him today") or doesn't know what the practice is. One doesn't so much justify one's particular action as explain, or show, that it is in accordance with the practice. The reason for this is that it is only against the stage-setting of the practice that one's particular action is described as it is. Only by reference to the practice can one *say* what one is doing. To explain or to defend one's own action, as a particular action, one fits it into the practice which defines it. If this is not accepted it's a sign that a different question is being raised as to whether one is justified in accepting the practice, or in tolerating it. When the challenge is to the practice, citing the rules (saying what the practice is) is naturally to no avail. But when the challenge is to the particular action defined by the practice, there is nothing one can do but refer to the rules. Concerning particular actions there is only a question for one who isn't clear as to what the practice is, or who doesn't know that it is being engaged in. This is to be contrasted with the case of a maxim which may be taken as pointing to the correct decision on the case as decided on *other* grounds, and so giving a challenge on the case a sense by having it question whether these other grounds really support the decision on this case.

If one compares the two conceptions of rules I have discussed, one can see how the summary conception misses the significance of the distinction between justifying a practice and justifying actions falling under it. On this view rules are regarded as guides whose purpose it is to indicate the ideally rational decision on the given particular case which the flawless application of the utilitarian principle would yield. One has, in principle, full option to use the guides or to discard them as the situation warrants without one's moral office being altered in any way: whether one discards the rules or not, one always holds the office of a rational person seeking case by case to realize the best on the whole. But on the practice conception, if one holds an office defined by a practice then questions regarding one's actions in this office are settled by reference to the rules which define the practice. If one seeks to question these rules, then one's office undergoes a fundamental change: one then assumes the office of one empowered to change and criticize the rules, or the office of a reformer, and so on. The summary conception does away with the distinction of offices and the various forms of argument appropriate to each. On that conception there is one office and so no offices at all. It therefore obscures the fact that the utilitarian principle must, in the case of actions and offices defined by a practice, apply to the practice, so that general utilitarian arguments are not available to those who act in offices so defined.

Some qualifications are necessary in what I have said. First, I may have talked of the summary and the practice conceptions of rules as if only one of them could be true of rules, and if true of any rules, then necessarily true of *all* rules. I do not, of course, mean this. (It is the critics of utilitarianism who make this mistake insofar as their arguments against utilitarianism presuppose a summary conception of the rules of practices.) Some rules will fit one conception, some rules the other; and so there are rules of practices (rules in the strict sense), and maxims and "rules of thumb."

Secondly, there are further distinctions that can be made in classifying rules, distinctions which should be made if one were considering other questions. The distinctions which I have drawn are those most relevant for the rather special matter I have discussed, and are not intended to be exhaustive.

Finally, there will be many borderline cases about which it will be difficult, if not impossible, to decide which conception of rules is applicable. One expects border-line cases with any concept, and they are especially likely in connexion with such involved concepts as those of a practice, institution, game, rule, and so on. Wittgenstein has shown how fluid these notions are.[15] What I have done is to emphasize and sharpen two conceptions for the limited purpose of this paper.

IV.

What I have tried to show by distinguishing between two conceptions of rules is that there is a way of regarding rules which allows the option to consider particular cases on general utilitarian grounds; whereas there is another conception which does not admit of such discretion except insofar as the rules themselves authorize it. I want to suggest that the tendency while doing philosophy to picture rules in accordance with the summary conception is what may have blinded moral philosophers to the significance of the distinction between justifying a practice and justifying a particular action falling under it; and it does so by misrepresenting the logical force of the reference to the rules in the case of a challenge to a particular action falling under a practice, and by obscuring the fact that where there is a practice, it is the practice itself that must be the subject of the utilitarian principle.

It is surely no accident that two of the traditional test cases of utilitarianism, punishment and promises, are clear cases of practices. Under the influence of the summary conception it is natural to suppose that the officials of a penal system, and one who has made a promise, may decide what to do in particular cases on utilitarian grounds. One fails to see that a general discretion to decide particular cases on utilitarian grounds is incompatible with

[15] *Philosophical Investigations* (Oxford, 1953), i, pars. 65–71, for example.

the concept of a practice; and that what discretion one does have is itself defined by the practice (e.g., a judge may have discretion to determine the penalty within certain limits). The traditional objections to utilitarianism which I have discussed presuppose the attribution to judges, and to those who have made promises, of a plenitude of moral authority to decide particular cases on utilitarian grounds. But once one fits utilitarianism together with the notion of a practice, and notes that punishment and promising are practices, then one sees that this attribution is logically precluded.

That punishment and promising are practices is beyond question. In the case of promising this is shown by the fact that the form of words "I promise" is a performative utterance which presupposes the stage-setting of the practice and the proprieties defined by it. Saying the words "I promise" will only be promising given the existence of the practice. It would be absurd to interpret the rules about promising in accordance with the summary conception. It is absurd to say, for example, that the rule that promises should be kept could have arisen from its being found in past cases to be best on the whole to keep one's promise; for unless there were already the understanding that one keeps one's promises as part of the practice itself there couldn't have been any cases of promising.

It must, of course, be granted that the rules defining promising are not codified, and that one's conception of what they are necessarily depends on one's moral training. Therefore it is likely that there is considerable variation in the way people understand the practice, and room for argument as to how it is best set up. For example, differences as to how strictly various defences are to be taken, or just what defences are available, are likely to arise amongst persons with different backgrounds. But irrespective of these variations it belongs to the concept of the practice of promising that the general utilitarian defence is not available to the promisor. That this is so accounts for the force of the traditional objection which I have discussed. And the point I wish to make is that when one fits the utilitarian view together with the practice conception of rules, as one must in the appropriate cases, then there is nothing in that view which entails that there must be such a defence, either in the practice of promising, or in any other practice.

Punishment is also a clear case. There are many actions in the sequence of events which constitute someone's being punished which presuppose a practice. One can see this by considering the definition of punishment which I gave when discussing Carritt's criticism of utilitarianism. The definition there stated refers to such things as the normal rights of a citizen, rules of law, due process of law, trials and courts of law, statutes, etc., none of which can exist outside the elaborate stage-setting of a legal system. It is also the case that many of the actions for which people are punished presuppose practices. For example, one is punished for stealing, for trespassing and the like, which presuppose the institution of property. It is impossible to say what punishment is, or to describe a particular instance of it, without referring to offices, actions, and offences specified by practices. Punishment is a move in an elaborate legal game and presupposes the complex of practices which make up the legal order. The same thing is true of the less formal sorts of punishment: a parent or guardian or someone in proper authority may punish a child, but no one else can.

There is one mistaken interpretation of what I have been saying which it is worthwhile to warn against. One might think that the use I am making of the distinction between justifying a practice and justifying the particular actions falling under it involves one in a definite social and political attitude in that it leads to a kind of conservatism. It might seem that I am saying that for each person the social practices of his society provide the standard of justification for his actions; therefore let each person abide by them and his conduct will be justified.

This interpretation is entirely wrong. The point I have been making is rather a logical point. To be sure, it has consequences in matters of ethical theory; but in itself it leads to no particular social or political attitude. It is simply that where a form of action is specified by a practice there is no justification possible of the particular action of a particular person save by reference to the practice. In such cases then action is what it is in virtue of the practice and to explain it is to refer to the practice. There is no inference whatsoever to be drawn with respect to whether or not one should accept the practices of one's society. One can be as radical as one likes but in the case of actions specified by practices the objects of one's radicalism must be the social practices and people's acceptance of them.

I have tried to show that when we fit the utilitarian view together with the practice conception of rules, where this conception is appropriate,[16] we can formulate it in a way which saves it from several traditional objections. I have further tried to show how the logical force of the distinction between justifying a practice and justifying an action falling under it is connected with the practice conception of rules and cannot be understood as long as one regards the rules of practices in accordance with the summary view. Why, when doing philosophy, one may be inclined to so regard them, I have not discussed. The reasons for this are evidently very deep and would require another paper.

[16] As I have already stated, it is not always easy to say where the conception is appropriate. Nor do I care to discuss at this point the general sorts of cases to which it does apply except to say that one should not take it for granted that it applies to many so-called "moral rules." It my feeling that relatively few actions of the moral life are defined by practices and that the practice conception is more relevant to understanding legal and legal-like arguments than it is to the more complex sort of moral arguments. Utilitarianism must be fitted to different conceptions of rules depending on the case, and no doubt the failure to do this has been one source of difficulty in interpreting it correctly.

J. J. SMART

*Extreme and Restricted Utilitarianism**

I.

Utilitarianism is the doctrine that the rightness of actions is to be judged by their consequences. What do we mean by "actions" here? Do we mean particular actions or do we mean classes of actions? According to which way we interpret the word "actions" we get two different theories, both of which merit the appellation "utilitarian."

1. If by "actions" we mean particular individual actions we get the sort of doctrine held by Bentham, Sidgwick, and Moore. According to this doctrine we test individual actions by their consequences, and general rules, like "keep promises," are mere rules of thumb which we use only to avoid the necessity of estimating the probable consequences of our actions at every step. The rightness or wrongness of keeping a promise on a particular occasion depends only on the goodness or badness of the consequences of keeping or of breaking the promise on that particular occasion. Of course part of the consequences of breaking the promise, and a part to which we will normally ascribe decisive importance, will be the weakening of faith in the institution of promising. However, if the goodness of the consequences of breaking the rule is *in toto* greater than the goodness of the consequences of keeping it, then we must break the rule, irrespective of whether the goodness of the consequences of *everybody's* obeying the rule is or is not greater than the consequences of *everybody's* breaking it. To put it shortly, rules do not matter, save *per accidens* as rules of thumb and as *de facto* social institutions with which the utilitarian has to reckon when estimating consequences. I shall call this doctrine "extreme utilitarianism."

2. A more modest form of utilitarianism has recently become fashionable. The doctrine is to be found in Toulmin's book *The Place of Reason in Ethics,* in Nowell-Smith's *Ethics* (though I think Nowell-Smith has qualms), in John Austin's *Lectures on Jurisprudence* (Lecture II), and even in J. S. Mill, if Urmson's interpretation of him is correct (*Philosophical Quarterly,* Vol. 3, pp. 33–39, 1953). Part of its charm is that it appears to resolve the dispute in moral philosophy between intuitionists and utilitarians in a way which is very neat. The above philosophers hold, or seem to hold, that moral rules are more than rules of thumb. In general the rightness of an action is *not* to be tested by evaluating its consequences but only by considering whether or not it falls under a certain rule.

* By permission. *Philosophical Quarterly,* Vol. 6, 1956, pp. 344–54. Several emendations of the author are included.

J. J. C. Smart is professor of philosophy at the University of Adelaide.

Whether the rule is to be considered an acceptable moral rule is, however, to be decided by considering the consequences of adopting the rule. Broadly, then, actions are to be tested by rules and rules by consequences. The only cases in which we must test an individual action directly by its consequences are (*a*) when the action comes under two different rules, one of which enjoins it and one of which forbids it, and (*b*) when there is no rule whatever that governs the given case. I shall call this doctrine "restricted utilitarianism."

It should be noticed that the distinction I am making cuts across, and is quite different from, the distinction commonly made between hedonistic and ideal utilitarianism. Bentham was an extreme hedonistic utilitarian and Moore an extreme ideal utilitarian, and Toulmin (perhaps) could be classified as a restricted ideal utilitarian. A hedonistic utilitarian holds that the goodness of the consequences of an action is a function only of their pleasurableness and an ideal utilitarian, like Moore, holds that pleasurableness is not even a necessary condition of goodness. Mill seems, if we are to take his remarks about higher and lower pleasures seriously, to be neither a pure hedonistic nor a pure ideal utilitarian. He seems to hold that pleasurableness is a necessary condition for goodness, but that goodness is a function of other qualities of mind as well. Perhaps we can call him a quasi-ideal utilitarian. When we say that a state of mind is good I take it that we are expressing some sort of *rational preference*. When we say that it is pleasurable I take it that we are saying that it is enjoyable, and when we say that something is a higher pleasure I take it that we are saying that it is more truly, or more deeply, enjoyable. I am doubtful whether "more deeply enjoyable" does not just mean "more enjoyable, even though not more enjoyable on a first look," and so I am doubtful whether quasi-ideal utilitarianism, and possibly ideal utilitarianism too, would not collapse into hedonistic utilitarianism on a closer scrutiny of the logic of words like "preference," "pleasure," "enjoy," "deeply enjoy," and so on. However, it is beside the point of the present paper to go into these questions. I am here concerned only with the issue between extreme and restricted utilitarianism and am ready to concede that both forms of utilitarianism can be either hedonistic or non-hedonistic.

The issue between extreme and restricted utilitarianism can be illustrated by considering the remark "But suppose everyone did the same." (Cf. A. K. Stout's article in *The Australasian Journal of Philosophy*, Vol. 32, pp. 1–29). Stout distinguishes two forms of the universalization principle, the causal form and the hypothetical form. To say that you ought not to do an action *A* because it would have bad results if everyone (or many people) did action *A* may be merely to point out that while the action *A* would otherwise be the optimific one, nevertheless when you take into account that doing *A* will probably cause other people to do *A* too, you can see that *A* is not, on a broad view, really optimific. If this causal influence could be avoided (as may happen in the case of a secret desert island promise) then we would disregard the universalization principle. This is the causal form of the principle. A person who accepted the universalization principle in its hypothetical form would be one who was concerned only with what would happen *if* everyone did the action *A*: he would be totally unconcerned with the question of whether in fact everyone would do the action *A*. That is, he might say that it would be wrong not to vote because it would have bad results if everyone took this attitude, and he would be totally unmoved by arguments purporting to show that my refusing to vote has no effect whatever on other people's propensity to vote. Making use of Stout's distinction, we can say that an extreme utilitarian would apply the universalization principle in the causal form, while a restricted utilitarian would apply it in the hypothetical form.

How are we to decide the issue between extreme and restricted utilitarianism? I wish to repudiate at the outset that milk and water approach which describes itself sometimes as "investigating what is implicit in the common moral consciousness" and sometimes as "investigating how people ordinarily talk about morality." We have only to read the newspaper correspondence about capital punishment or about what should be done with Formosa to realize that the common moral consciousness is in part made up of superstitious elements, of morally bad elements, and of logically confused elements. I address myself to good hearted and benevolent people and so I hope that if we rid ourselves of the logical confusion the superstitious and morally bad elements will largely fall away. For even among good hearted and benevolent people it is possible to find superstitious and morally bad reasons for moral beliefs. These superstitious and morally bad reasons hide behind the protective screen of logical confusion. With people who are not logically confused but who are openly superstitious or morally bad I can of course do nothing. That is, our ultimate pro-attitudes may be different. Nevertheless I propose to rely on *my own* moral consciousness and to appeal to *your* moral consciousness and to forget about what people ordinarily say. "The obligation to obey a rule," says Nowell-Smith (*Ethics*, p. 239), "does not, *in the opinion of ordinary men*," [my italics], "rest on the beneficial consequences of obeying it in a particular case." What does this prove? Surely it is more than likely that ordinary men are confused here. Philosophers should be able to examine the question more rationally.

II.

For an extreme utilitarian moral rules are rules of thumb. In practice the extreme utilitarian will mostly guide his conduct by appealing to the rules ("do not lie," "do not break promises," etc.) of common sense morality. This is not because there is anything sacrosanct in the rules themselves but because he can argue that probably he will most often act in an extreme utilitarian way if he does not think as a utilitarian. For one thing, actions have frequently to be done in a hurry. Imagine a man seeing a person drowning. He jumps in and rescues him. There is no time to reason the matter out, but usually this will be the course of action which an extreme utilitarian would recommend if he did reason the matter out. If, however, the man drowning had been drowning in a river near Berchtesgaden in 1938, and if he had had the well known black forelock and moustache of Adolf Hitler, an extreme utilitarian would, if he had time, work out the probability of the man's being the villainous dictator, and if the probability were high enough he would, on extreme utilitarian grounds, leave him to drown. The rescuer, however, has not time. He trusts to his instincts and dives in and rescues the man. And this trusting to instincts and to moral rules can be justified on extreme utilitarian grounds. Furthermore, an extreme utilitarian who knew that the drowning man was Hitler would nevertheless praise the rescuer, not condemn him. For by praising the man he is strengthening a courageous and benevolent disposition of mind, and in general this disposition has great positive utility. (Next time, perhaps, it will be Winston Churchill that the man saves!) We must never forget that an extreme utilitarian may praise actions which he knows to be wrong. Saving Hitler was wrong, but it was a member of a class of actions which are generally right, and the motive to do actions of this class is in general an optimific one. In considering questions of praise and blame it is not the expediency of the praised or blamed action that is at issue, but the expediency of the praise. It can be expedient to praise an inexpedient action and inexpedient to praise an expedient one.

Lack of time is not the only reason why an extreme utilitarian may, on extreme utilitarian principles, trust to rules of common sense morality. He knows that in particular cases where his own interests are involved his calculations are likely to be biased in his own favour. Suppose that he is unhappily married and is deciding whether to get divorced. He will in all probability greatly exaggerate his own unhappiness (and possibly his wife's) and greatly underestimate the harm done to his children by the break up of the family. He will probably also underestimate the likely harm done by the weakening of the general faith in marriage vows. So probably he will come to the correct extreme utilitarian conclusion if he does not in this instance think as an extreme utilitarian but trusts to common sense morality.

There are many more and subtle points that could be made in connexion with the relation between extreme utilitarianism and the morality of common sense. All those that I have just made and many more will be found in Book IV Chapters 3–5 of Sidgwick's *Methods of Ethics.* I think that this book is the best book ever written on ethics, and that these chapters are the best chapters of the book. As they occur so near the end of a very long book they are unduly neglected. I refer the reader, then, to Sidgwick for the classical exposition of the relation between (extreme) utilitarianism and the morality of common sense. One further point raised by Sidgwick in this connexion is whether an (extreme) utilitarian ought on (extreme) utilitarian principles to propagate (extreme) utilitarianism among the public. As most people are not very philosophical and not good at empirical calculations, it is probable that they will most often act in an extreme utilitarian way if they do not try to think as extreme utilitarians. We have seen how easy it would be to misapply the extreme utilitarian criterion in the case of divorce. Sidgwick seems to think it quite probable that an extreme utilitarian should not propagate his doctrine too widely. However, the great danger to humanity comes nowadays on the plane of public morality—not private morality. There is a greater danger to humanity from the hydrogen bomb than from an increase of the divorce rate, regrettable though that might be, and there seems no doubt that extreme utilitarianism makes for good sense in international relations. When France walked out of the United Nations because she did not wish Morocco discussed, she said that she was within her rights because Morocco and Algiers are part of her metropolitan territory and nothing to do with U.N. This was clearly a legalistic if not superstitious argument. We should not be concerned with the so-called "rights" of France or any other country but with whether the cause of humanity would best be served by discussing Morocco in U.N. (I am not saying that the answer to this is "Yes." There are good grounds for supposing that more harm than good would come by such a discussion.) I myself have no hesitation in saying that on extreme utilitarian principles we ought to propagate extreme utilitarianism as widely as possible. But Sidgwick had respectable reasons for suspecting the opposite.

The extreme utilitarian, then, regards moral rules as rules of thumb and as sociological facts that have to be taken into account when deciding what to do, just as facts of any other sort have to be taken into account. But in themselves they do not justify any action.

III.

The restricted utilitarian regards moral rules as more than rules of thumb for short-circuiting calculations of consequences. Generally, he argues, consequences are not relevant at all when we are deciding what to do in a particular case. In general, they are relevant only to deciding what rules are good reasons for acting in a certain way in particular cases. This doctrine is possibly a good account of how the modern unreflective twentieth century

Englishman often thinks about morality, but surely it is monstrous as an account of how it is most rational to think about morality. Suppose that there is a rule *R* and that in 99% of cases the best possible results are obtained by acting in accordance with *R*. Then clearly *R* is a useful rule of thumb; if we have not time or are not impartial enough to assess the consequences of an action it is an extremely good bet that the thing to do is to act in accordance with *R*. But is it not monstrous to suppose that if we *have* worked out the consequences and if we have perfect faith in the impartiality of our calculations, and if we *know* that in this instance to break *R* will have better results than to keep it, we should nevertheless obey the rule? Is it not to erect *R* into a sort of idol if we keep it when breaking it will prevent, say, some avoidable misery? Is not this a form of superstitious rule-worship (easily explicable psychologically) and not the rational thought of a philosopher?

The point may be made more clearly if we consider Mill's comparison of moral rules to the tables in the nautical almanack. (*Utilitarianism,* Everyman Edition, pp. 22–23). This comparison of Mill's is adduced by Urmson as evidence that Mill was a restricted utilitarian, but I do not think that it will bear this interpretation at all. (Though I quite agree with Urmson that many other things said by Mill are in harmony with restricted rather than extreme utilitarianism. Probably Mill had never thought very much about the distinction and was arguing for utilitarianism, restricted or extreme, against other and quite non-utilitarian forms of moral argument.) Mill says: "Nobody argues that the art of navigation is not founded on astronomy, because sailors cannot wait to calculate the Nautical Almanack. Being rational creatures, they go out upon the sea of life with their minds made up on the common questions of right and wrong, as well as on many of the far more difficult questions of wise and foolish. . . . Whatever we adopt as the fundamental principle of morality, we require subordinate principles to apply it by." Notice that this is, as it stands, only an argument for subordinate principles as rules of thumb. The example of the nautical almanack is misleading because the information given in the almanack is in all cases the same as the information one would get if one made a long and laborious calculation from the original astronomical data on which the almanack is founded. Suppose, however, the astronomy were different. Suppose that the behaviour of the sun, moon and planets was very nearly as it is now, but that on rare occasions there were peculiar irregularities and discontinuities, so that the almanack gave us rules of the form "in 99% of cases where the observations are such and such you can deduce that your position is so and so." Furthermore, let us suppose that there were methods which enable us, by direct and laborious calculation from the original astronomical data, not using the rough and ready tables of the almanack, to get our correct position in 100% of cases. Seafarers might use the almanack because they never had time for the long calculations and they were content with a 99% chance of success in calculating their positions. Would it not be absurd, however, if they *did* make the direct calculation, and finding that it disagreed with the almanack calculation, nevertheless they ignored it and stuck to the almanack conclusion? Of course the case would be altered if there were a high enough probability of making slips in the direct calculation: then we might stick to the almanack result, liable to error though we knew it to be, simply because the direct calculation would be open to error for a different reason, the fallibility of the computer. This would be analogous to the case of the extreme utilitarian who abides by the conventional rule against the dictates of his utilitarian calculations simply because he thinks that his calculations are probably affected by personal bias. But if the navigator were sure of his direct calculations would he not be foolish to abide by his almanack? I conclude, then, that if we change our suppositions about astronomy and the almanack (to which there are no exceptions) to bring the case into line with that of morality (to whose rules there are exceptions), Mill's example loses its appearance of supporting the restricted form of utilitarianism. Let me say once more that I am not here concerned with how ordinary men think about morality but with how they ought to think. We could quite well imagine a race of sailors who acquired a superstitious reverence for their almanack, even though it was only right in 99% of cases, and who indignantly threw overboard any man who mentioned the possibility of a direct calculation. But would this behaviour of the sailors be rational?

Let us consider a much discussed sort of case in which the extreme utilitarian might go against the conventional moral rule. I have promised to a friend, dying on a desert island from which I am subsequently rescued, that I will see that his fortune (over which I have control) is given to a jockey club. However, when I am rescued I decide that it would be better to give the money to a hospital, which can do more good with it. It may be argued that I am wrong to give the money to the hospital. But why? (*a*) The hospital can do more good with the money than the jockey club can. (*b*) The present case is unlike most cases of promising in that no one except me knows about the promise. In breaking the promise I am doing so with complete secrecy and am doing nothing to weaken the general faith in promises. That is, a factor, which would normally keep the extreme utilitarian from promise breaking even in otherwise unoptimific cases, does not at present operate. (*c*) There is no doubt a slight weakening in my own character as an habitual promise keeper, and moreover psychological tensions will be set up in me every time I am asked what the man made me promise him to do. For clearly I shall have to say that he made me promise to give the money to the hospital, and, since I am an habitual truth teller, this will go very much against the grain with me. Indeed I am pretty sure that in practice I myself would keep the promise. But we are not discussing what my moral habits would probably make me do; we are discussing what I ought to do. Moreover, we must not forget that even if it would be most rational of me to give the money to the hospital it would also be most rational of you to punish or condemn me if you did, most improbably, find out the truth (e.g. by finding a note washed ashore in a bottle). Furthermore, I would agree that though it was most rational of me to give the money to the hospital it would be most rational of you to condemn me for it. We revert again to Sidgwick's distinction between the utility of the action and the utility of the praise of it.

Many such issues are discussed by A. K. Stout in the article to which I have already referred. I do not wish to go over the same ground again, especially as I think that Stout's arguments support my own point of view. It will be useful, however, to consider one other example that he gives. Suppose that during hot weather there is an edict that no water must be used for watering gardens. I have a garden and I reason that most people are sure to obey the edict, and that as the amount of water that I use will be by itself negligible no harm will be done if I use the water secretly. So I do use the water, thus producing some lovely flowers which give happiness to various people. Still, you may say, though the action was perhaps optimific, it was unfair and wrong.

There are several matters to consider. Certainly my action should be condemned. We revert once more to Sidgwick's distinction. A right action may be rationally condemned. Furthermore, this sort of offence is normally found out. If I have a wonderful garden when everybody else's is dry and brown there is only one explanation. So if I water my garden I am weakening my respect for law and order, and as this leads to bad results an extreme utilitarian would agree that I was wrong to water the garden. Suppose now that the case is altered and that I can keep the thing secret: there is a secluded part of the garden where I grow flowers which I give away anonymously to a home for old ladies. Are you still so sure that I did the wrong thing by watering my garden? However, this is still a weaker case than that of the hospital and the jockey club. There will be tensions set up within myself: my secret knowledge that I have broken the rule will make it hard for me to exhort others to keep the rule. These psychological ill effects in myself may be not inconsiderable: directly and indirectly they may lead to harm which is at least of the same order as the happiness that the old ladies get from the flowers. You can see that on an extreme utilitarian view there are two sides to the question.

So far I have been considering the duty of an extreme utilitarian in a predominantly non-utilitarian society. The case is altered if we consider the extreme utilitarian who lives in a society every member, or most members, of which can be expected to reason as he does. Should he water his flowers now? (Granting, what is doubtful, that in the case already considered he would have been right to water his flowers.) . . . As a first approximation, the answer is that he should not do so. For since the situation is a completely symmetrical one, what is rational for him is rational for others. Hence, by a *reductio ad absurdum* argument, it would seem that watering his garden would be rational for none. Nevertheless, a more refined analysis shows that the above argument is not quite correct, though it is correct enough for practical purposes. The argument considers each person as confronted with the choice either of watering his garden or of not watering it. However there is a third possibility, which is that each person should, with the aid of a suitable randomising device, such as throwing dice, give himself a certain probability of watering his garden. This would be to adopt what in the theory of games is called "a mixed strategy." If we could give numerical values to the private benefit of garden watering and to the public harm done 1, 2, 3, etc., persons using the water in this way, we could work out a value of the probability of watering his garden that each extreme utilitarian should give himself. Let a be the value which each extreme utilitarian gets from watering his garden, and let $f(1)$, $f(2)$, $f(3)$, etc., be the public harm done by exactly 1, 2, 3, etc., persons respectively watering their gardens. Suppose that p is the probability that each person gives himself of watering his garden. Then we can easily calculate, as functions of p, the probabilities that exactly 1, 2, 3, etc., persons will water their gardens. Let these probabilities be $p_1, p_2, \ldots p_n$. Then the total net probable benefit can be expressed as

$$V = p_1 (a - f(1)) + p_2 (2a - f(2)) + \ldots p_n (na - f(n))$$

Then if we know the function $f(x)$ we can calculate the value of p for which $dV/dp = 0$. This gives the value of p which it would be rational for each extreme utilitarian to adopt. The present argument does of course depend on a perhaps unjustified assumption that the values in question are measurable, and in a practical case such as that of the garden watering we can doubtless assume that p will be so small that we can take it near enough as equal to zero. However, the argument is of interest for the theoretical underpinning of extreme utilitarianism, since the possibility of a mixed strategy is usually neglected by critics of utilitarianism, who wrongly assume that the only relevant and symmetrical alternatives are of the form "everybody does *X*" and "nobody does *X*"....

I now pass on to a type of case which may be thought to be the trump card of restricted utilitarianism. Consider the rule of the road. It may be said that since all that matters is that everyone should do the same it is indifferent which rule we have, "go on the left hand side" or "go on the right hand side." Hence the only *reason* for going on the left hand side in British countries is that this is the rule. Here the rule does seem to be a reason, in itself, for acting in a certain way. I wish to argue against this. The rule in itself is not a reason for our actions. We would be perfectly justified in going on the right hand side if (*a*) we knew that the rule was to go on the left hand side, and (*b*) we were in a country peopled by super-anarchists who always on principle did the opposite of what they were told. This shows that the rule does not give us a reason for acting so much as an indication of the probable actions of others, which helps us to find out what would be our own most rational course of action. If we are in a country not peopled by anarchists, but by non-anarchist extreme Utilitarians, we expect, other things being equal, that they will keep rules laid down for them. Knowledge of the rules enables us to predict their behaviour and to harmonise our own actions with theirs. The rule "keep to the left hand side," then, is not a logical *reason* for action but an anthropological *datum* for planning actions.

I conclude that in every case if there is a rule *R* the keeping of which is in general optimific, but such that in a special sort of circumstances the optimific behaviour is to break *R*, then in these circumstances we should break *R*. Of course we must consider all the less obvious effects of breaking *R*, such as reducing people's faith in the moral order, before coming to the conclusion that to break *R* is right: in fact we shall rarely come to such a conclusion. Moral rules, on the extreme utilitarian view, are rules of thumb only, but they are not bad rules of thumb. But if we *do* come to the conclusion that we should break the rule and if we have weighed in the balance our own fallibility and liability to personal bias, what good reason remains for keeping the rule? I can understand "it is optimific" as a reason for action, but why should "it is a member of a class of actions which are usually optimific" or "it is a member of a class of actions which as a class are more optimific than any alternative general class" be a good reason? You might as well say that a person ought to be picked to play for Australia just because all his brothers have been, or that the Australian team should be composed entirely of the Harvey family because this would be better than composing it entirely of any other family. The extreme utilitarian does not appeal to artificial feelings, but only to our feelings of benevolence, and what better feelings can there be to appeal to? Admittedly we can have a pro-attitude to anything, even to rules, but such artificially begotten pro-attitudes smack of superstition. Let us get down to realities, human happiness and misery, and make these the objects of our pro-attitudes and anti-attitudes.

The restricted utilitarian might say that he is talking only of *morality*, not of such things as rules of the road. I am not sure how far this objection, if valid, would affect my argument, but in any case I would reply that as a philosopher I conceive of ethics as the study of how it would be *most rational* to act. If my opponent wishes to restrict the word "morality" to a narrower use he can have the word. The fundamental question is the question of rationality of action *in general*. Similarly if the restricted utilitarian were to appeal to ordinary usage and say "it might be most rational to leave Hitler to drown but it would surely not be *wrong* to rescue him," I should again let him have the words "right" and "wrong" and should stick to "rational" and "irrational." We already saw that it would be rational to praise Hitler's rescuer, even though it would have been most rational not to have rescued Hitler. In ordinary language, no doubt, "right" and "wrong" have not only the meaning "most rational to do" and "not most rational to do" but also have the meaning "praiseworthy" and "not praiseworthy." Usually to the utility of an action corresponds utility of praise of it, but as we saw, this is not always so. Moral language could thus do with tidying up, for example by reserving "right" for "most rational" and "good" as an epithet of praise for the motive from which the action sprang. It would be more becoming in a philosopher to try to iron out illogicalities in moral language and to make suggestions for its reform than to use it as a court of appeal whereby to perpetuate confusions.

One last defence of restricted utilitarianism might be as follows. "Act optimifically" might be regarded as itself one of the rules of our system (though it would be odd to say that this rule was justified by its optimificality). According to Toulmin (*The Place of Reason in Ethics*, pp. 146–8) if "keep promises," say, conflicts with another rule we are allowed to argue the case on its merits, as if we were extreme utilitarians. If "act optimifically" is itself one of our rules then there will always be a conflict of rules whenever to keep a rule is not itself optimific. If this is so, restricted utilitarianism collapses into extreme utilitarianism. And no one could read Toulmin's book or Urmson's article on Mill without thinking that Toulmin and Urmson are of the opinion that they have thought of a doctrine which does *not* collapse into extreme utilitarianism, but which is, on the contrary, an improvement on it.

MARCUS G. SINGER

*Generalization in Ethics**

I.

INTRODUCTORY

The question "What would happen if everyone did that?" is one with which we are all familiar. We have heard it asked, and perhaps have asked it ourselves. We have some familiarity with the sort of context in which it would be appropriate to ask it. Thus we understand that it is either elliptical for or a prelude to saying, "If everyone did that, the consequences would be disastrous," and that this is often considered a good reason for concluding that one ought not to do that. The situations in which this sort of consideration might be advanced are of course exceedingly diverse. One who announces his intention of not voting in some election might be met by the question, "What would happen if no one voted?" If no one voted, the government would collapse, or the democratic system would be repudiated, and this is deemed by many to indicate decisively that everyone should vote. Again, one who disapproves of another's attempts to avoid military service might point out "If everyone refused to serve, we would lose the war." The members of a discussion group, which meets to discuss papers presented by members, presumably all realize that each should take a turn in reading a paper, even one who may not want to and prefers to take part in the discussions only, because if everyone refused the club would dissolve, and there would be no discussions. This sort of consideration would not be decisive to one who did not care whether the club dissolved. But it undoubtedly would be decisive to one who enjoys the meetings and wishes them to continue.

Each of these cases provides an example of the use or application of a type of argument which I propose to call *the generalization argument:* "If everyone were to do that, the consequences would be disastrous (or undesirable); therefore, no one ought to do that." Any argument of the form "The consequences of no one's doing that would be undesirable; therefore everyone ought to do that" is also, obviously, an instance of the generalization argument. It is this line of argument, and considerations resembling it, that will be at the very center of this inquiry.

The basic problem about the generalization argument (which can be thought of indifferently as either an argument or a moral principle) is to determine the conditions under which it is a good or valid one, that is to say, the conditions under which the fact that the consequences of

* By permission. *Generalization in Ethics* (New York: Alfred A. Knopf, Inc., 1961)

Marcus G. Singer is a professor of philosophy at the University of Wisconsin.

everyone's acting in a certain way would be undesirable, provides a good reason for concluding that it is wrong for *anyone* to act in that way. For there are conditions under which the generalization argument is obviously not applicable, and it is necessary to determine just what they are. The instances presented above are ones in which the consideration of the consequences of everyone's acting in a certain way seems clearly relevant to a moral judgment about that way of acting. But there are others in which this sort of consideration is just as clearly irrelevant. For instance, while "humanity would probably perish from cold if everyone produced food, and would certainly starve if everyone made clothes or built houses,"[1] it would be absurd to infer from this that no one ought to produce food or to build houses.

It would be thought that this is a counterexample, which proves the generalization argument to be invalid or fallacious generally. To argue that you ought not to do something because of what would happen if *everyone* did, though it is somewhat like arguing that you ought not to do something because of what would happen if *you* do, is also quite different. On the pattern of, "If you were to do that the consequences would be disastrous, therefore you ought not to do that," we can argue, "If everyone were to do that the consequences would be disastrous, therefore not everyone ought to do that." But the transition from "not everyone ought to do that" to "no one ought to do that," from "not everyone has the right" to "no one has the right," seems surely fallacious. It is like saying that no one has red hair because not everyone does. Yet this transition, or something very much like it, is essential to the generalization argument.

But there is actually no fallacy involved in the generalization argument, though there may be in particular applications of it. For it is not always a fallacy to argue from "some" to "all," and the belief that it is always fallacious is merely a prejudice arising out of a preoccupation with certain types of statements. It is a fact of logic that if any one argument of a certain form is invalid then all arguments of that form are invalid, and this is the principle underlying the use of counterexamples. Yet it involves an inference from "some" to "all." It is true that the generalization argument involves an inference from "not everyone has the right" to "no one has the right," from "it would not be right for everyone" to "it would not be right for anyone." This inference, however, is mediated, and therefore qualified, by the principle that *what is right (or wrong) for one person must be right (or wrong) for any similar person in similar circumstances*. For obvious reasons I shall refer to this principle as "the generalization *principle*," even though it has traditionally been known as the principle of fairness or justice or impartiality. . . .

II.

THE GENERALIZATION PRINCIPLE

It is almost axiomatic that "the character of every act depends upon the circumstances in which it is done."[2] As we may otherwise put it: whether an act is right or wrong depends on the circumstances or context in which it is done, or on the conditions or circumstances under which it is done. (Indeed, the actual nature of an act, what the act is, is indeterminate when it is taken apart from its context.) Although such a general statement may raise some doubts this is recognized implicitly in practice, much more extensively than is indicated by such phrases as "extenuating circumstances." It is recognized, for example,

[1] Morris R. Cohen, *The Faith of a Liberal* (New York: Henry Holt and Company, Inc., 1946), p. 86.

[2] J. Holmes, *Schenck v. U.S.*, 249 U.S. (Supreme Court Reports) 47 (1919).

that under certain circumstances one may be justified in breaking a promise, telling a lie, taking a life, or taking something that belongs to another without first obtaining his permission. (Compare the commonplace, "Circumstances alter cases.") Accordingly, the assertion that an act cannot be right for one person unless it is right for everyone would be patently absurd, unless some such qualification as "in the same or similar circumstances" is implicitly understood. If an act can be right in one context and wrong in another, *a fortiori* it can be right for one person and wrong for another, provided they do it in different contexts. However, if an act is right for *A* it *must* be right for *B*, if the circumstances are the same, or sufficiently similar, just as it must be right for *A* on any other occasion if there is no significant difference in the circumstances. The generalization principle could therefore be stated in the form: What is right for one person must be right for anyone in the same or similar circumstances.

The trouble with stating it in this form, however, is that a further necessary qualification is left inexplicit, with the consequence that in this form the principle is ambiguous. It could properly be stated in this form provided it is implicitly understood that the nature, characteristics, relationships, or abilities of the agent who is considered as being in certain circumstances can often make for a significant difference in those circumstances. It would not be a duty of a blind man, or one without legs, to jump into the water to save someone from drowning, while it might be the duty of a good swimmer to do so. If the principle, that what is right or a duty for one person is right or a duty for anyone in similar circumstances, is to be maintained in spite of this, it must be on the ground that one's ability to swim is a factor to be considered, in this context, in determining whether or not something is his duty; and that consequently the circumstances of an act can vary with the characteristics of the agent. The term "circumstances" is to some extent ambiguous. In one sense the circumstances of an act can be determined without any reference to the agent. In another sense they cannot. In this sense in order to specify adequately the circumstances in or under which someone acted, we must take account of *his* characteristics or nature. If the term is used in the first sense then it is false that what is right for one person must be right for anyone in similar circumstances. For what is right for a certain person can depend on his personal characteristics as well as on what might be called his "external circumstances." Stating the generalization principle in the form, "What is right for one person must be right for any *similar person* in similar circumstances," instead of in the form, "What is right for one person must be right for anyone in similar circumstances," is merely a way of making this point explicit.

This qualification, however, merely makes explicit what would ordinarily be understood by the assertion that what is right for one person in certain circumstances would be right for anyone in those circumstances. It is ordinarily recognized that while it may be right for an expert surgeon to undertake a delicate operation under trying circumstances, it might very well be wrong for a medical student or a manifest incompetent, no matter how good his intentions. . . .

There is an obvious resemblance between the generalization principle and what is known as the Golden Rule, which in one of its formulations reads, "Do unto others as you would have them do unto you." The exact nature of this resemblance, however, may not be so obvious. In any of its traditional formulations this rule is not only imprecise, but if taken literally would be an abomination. "One might wish for another's co-operation in sin, and be willing to reciprocate it," as Sidgwick points out.

Understood literally this rule invites, even enjoins, a masochist to become a sadist: one who would have others torture him is enjoined to torture others. Furthermore, as Kant notices, "on this basis the criminal would be able to dispute with the judges who punish him," and "many a man would readily agree that others should not help him if only he could be dispensed from affording help to them."[3] Such literal interpretations of the rule are undoubtedly misinterpretations of what is intended by it. But what this shows is that as it stands the rule is imprecise and needs qualification. It neither says what it means nor means what it says. Stated precisely, the Golden Rule would be an immediate consequence of the generalization principle. Sidgwick remarks that Samuel Clarke's "rule of equity" ("Whatever I judge reasonable or unreasonable that another should do for me; that by the same judgment I declare reasonable or unreasonable that I should *in the like case* do for him") is "the 'Golden Rule' precisely stated." He also claims that the "principle strictly stated must take some such negative form as this: 'it cannot be right for *A* to treat *B* in a manner in which it would be wrong for *B* to treat *A*, merely on the ground that they are two different individuals, and without there being any difference between the natures or circumstances of the two which can be stated as a reasonable ground for difference of treatment.'" and adds that "such a principle manifestly does not give complete guidance—indeed its effect, strictly speaking, is merely to throw a definite *onus probandi* on the man who applies to another a treatment of which he would complain if applied to himself." This last statement can be taken as applying not only to "the Golden Rule precisely stated" but, as I shall point out later on, to the generalization principle itself. . . .

I have said that the generalization principle implies that an act that is right or wrong is right or wrong on "general grounds" and is therefore right or wrong for a class of persons. This class of persons is determined by the reasons in terms of which the act is right or wrong. This may appear to conflict with the fact that there are some acts that would be right for only one person. But there is really no conflict here An act of this sort is still right for a class of persons in the sense that it would be right for anyone who meets certain conditions, even though these conditions may be such that just one person can meet them. The act is still right as an act of a certain kind, or as an instance of a certain class of acts. It may be right for *A* and for no one else to do act *d* in certain circumstances. Yet if *B* were similar to *A* in certain respects then it would be right for *B* to do *d*. (The act may be described in such a way that this last statement may seem absurd. It would amount to saying "if *B* were *A* then. . . ." But this can be met by redescribing the act.) Furthermore, since *d* must be an act of a certain kind (if it were not it could not be described at all), it must be the case that it would be right for everyone similar to *A* to do an act of the same kind (to act in the same way) in similar circumstances.

The following example should make this clear. While it would not be wrong for Mr. Jones to have sexual relations with Mrs. Jones, it would (generally) be wrong for anyone else to do so, and it would certainly be wrong for everyone else to do so. Here we have an act that is right for just one person. But there is no conflict with the generalization principle. This principle does not say that no one ought to do anything that not everyone ought to do. It says that no one ought to do anything that not everyone ought to do, without a reason

[3] Henry Sidgwick, *The Methods of Ethics* (7th ed.; London: Macmillan & Co., Ltd., 1907), p. 380; Immanuel Kant, *Groundwork of the Metaphysic of Morals, in The Moral Law,* transl. by H. J. Paton (London: Hutchinson's University Library, 1948), p. 97 note.

or justification. Mr. Jones is justified in having sexual relations with Mrs. Jones by the fact that he is married to her. If he were not he could (presumably) not be justified in this, and anyone else who was married to Mrs. Jones would be justified in having sexual relations with her. Furthermore, this act is an act of a certain kind, and can be described in a more general way so as to bring this out. Instead of describing Mr. Jones' act as one of "having sexual relations with Mrs. Jones," it can be referred to as "having sexual relations with one's own wife." Everyone is justified in doing an act of this kind in similar circumstances—everyone has the right to have sexual relations with his own wife, though not with anyone else's. (This rule as just stated necessarily does not apply to women. This does not make it unfair or unjust. It can obviously be restated to cover this.) Mr. Jones is justified in having sexual relations with Mrs. Jones because she is his wife. This last statement, it should be evident, is perfectly general. It has no peculiar application to Mr. Jones. It can thus be seen to be a further application of the more general generalization principle.

III.

MORAL JUDGMENTS, MORAL REASONS, AND GENERALITY

What has now been shown about the generalization principle is that it is not vague or useless or inapplicable. What remains to be shown about it is that it is at the heart of moral reasoning. The generalization principle, I shall argue, is involved in or presupposed by every genuine moral judgment, for it is an essential part of the meaning of such distinctively moral terms as "right," "wrong," and "ought," in their distinctively moral senses. It is also an essential feature of moral reasoning, for it is presupposed in every attempt to give a reason for a moral judgment. It thus determines what can count as a moral reason. At the same time, it is the reasons that are given in any particular case that determine the application of the principle, for they determine the scope of the qualification "similar persons in similar circumstances."

It follows from this that there can be no genuine moral judgment apart from reasons, and no moral reasons apart from the generalization principle. This, incidentally, provides all the proof or justification this principle requires, supposing, what is not obvious, that it requires any. If the generalization principle is presupposed in every moral judgment and in all moral reasoning, there is no sense in demanding any further proof of it. For not only is this a demand that cannot possibly be satisfied, it is not even relevant to the subject.

If these contentions are correct, then those theories must be wrong which assert, in any of the variety of ways in which it is asserted, that moral judgments cannot be supported by reasons, or that there is no such thing as a valid moral argument. There is a distinction, which many regard as important, between what have come to be known as emotive and subjective ethical theories. On both these views moral judgments are regarded as having no objective significance. The distinction between them is that while on the subjective theory a moral judgment states that the speaker (or someone else) has a certain attitude, on the emotive theory a moral judgment does not state anything at all, but merely gives expression to an attitude. However, it is not the case that moral judgments are merely vehicles for the expression of emotion, or merely state that someone or other likes or approves or has some other sort of feeling or attitude toward something. An alleged moral judgment that one is unable to support by reasons is not a genuine moral judgment at all, but merely an indication of what someone likes or dislikes, and whether it is taken as a description or as an expression of these feelings or attitudes is of no great import. This will be seen to have some relevance to the ill-defined question whether moral judgments are subjective or objective. . . .

The generalization principle has so far been stated in such a way as to refer more explicitly to actions than to moral judgments. But it can easily be restated so as to make its application to moral judgments more explicit. One of the ways in which Sidgwick stated the principle was this: "Whatever action any of us judges to be right for himself, he *implicitly* judges to be right for all similar persons in similar circumstances." Sidgwick also pointed out that "even when a moral judgment relates primarily to some particular action we commonly regard it as applicable to any other action belonging to a certain definable class; so that the moral truth apprehended is implicitly conceived to be intrinsically universal, though particular in our first apprehension of it."[4] This point may be summarized by the statement that every moral judgment is intrinsically universal, and if not explicitly so, then implicitly. Every moral judgment, in other words, involves a generalization. Moral judgments thus possess what may be called the characteristic of implicit generality.

This point is not really a new one, different from what has been said before. It is just a consequence of the generalization principle itself. For the principle, that what is right for one person must be right for every similar person in similar circumstances, implies that if it is right for *A* to do *x* then it is right for anyone similar to *A* to do *x* (or an act of the same kind as *x*) in similar circumstances. To put it another way, the judgment that *A* ought to do *x* implies that everyone similar to *A* ought to do *x* (or an act of the same kind as *x*) in similar circumstances. Thus the particular judgment that *A* ought to do *x* can be said to imply a general rule, though just what the rule is that it implies cannot be stated with any definiteness apart from the reasons adduced for the claim that *A* ought to do *x*, since apart from these reasons it cannot be determined what persons or circumstances are to be regarded as similar. This is what is meant by saying that moral judgments are governed by the generalization principle. . . .

Apart from this reference to the reasons supporting them, statements like "*x* is right" are indeterminate and merely subjective. Such a statement is merely subjective if the speaker is unable to specify reasons in support of it. (If he is able to, and at the same time refuses to, then from the point of view of the hearer his statement is still merely subjective.) In this case it is merely an indication of what the speaker likes or dislikes, approves of or disapproves of, and it can be taken either as a statement of these attitudes or preferences or as merely an expression of them. "An opinion on a point of conduct, not supported by reasons, can only count as one person's preference; and if the reasons, when given, are a mere appeal to a similar preference felt by other people, it is still only many people's liking instead of one."[5] This point can be extended further: if it can count only as a *preference*, then it cannot count as a *judgment*. Thus a statement of this form, unsupported by reasons, is not really a moral judgment at all. It appears to be one. It has the verbal form of a moral judgment. It is couched in the language in which moral judgments are normally expressed. It contains the term "right," or "wrong," or some synonymous or associated expression. But it is not a statement about what it appears or is supposed to be about. It is

[4] Henry Sidgwick, *The Methods of Ethics* (7th ed.; London: Macmillan & Co., Ltd., 1907), p. 379 (italics added), p. 34.

[5] John Stuart Mill, *On Liberty* (Everyman's Library ed.; New York: E. P. Dutton and Company, 1910), chap. I, par. 6, p. 69.

merely about the emotions or preferences or attitudes of the speaker.

This point, I think, had best be elaborated. What I am maintaining is that one who makes a moral judgment, or a statement having the verbal form of a moral judgment, but is unable to give reasons in support of it, has not really made a *judgment* about the action or whatever it is that is in question. Or, if we choose to call it so, his judgment is merely subjective—it is merely an indication of his attitudes (or desires or feelings). Now, whether it is taken as a statement that one has a certain attitude, or merely as an expression of this attitude, is of no great import, for it is one and the same thing for practical purposes. The judgment is still subjective in a perfectly proper sense: it tells us more about the speaker than about what he was ostensibly talking about, than the action referred to. On the other hand, if one is able to give reasons in support of the judgment then one's judgment is objective. This does not mean that it is necessarily correct or cannot reasonably be disputed. A judgment can be objective without being sound or true. For, even though reasons must be given, they may not be conclusive reasons or even especially good ones. They must be genuine reasons, but there may be better reasons against the judgment. The objectivity of a judgment would thus appear to be a matter of degree, some being more objective than others, and it may thus be better to say that one's judgment is objective to the extent to which one is able to give reasons in support of it. But if a "judgment" is merely subjective, there is a perfectly proper sense in which it is not a genuine moral judgment at all, for it is not about what it appears to be about. It is a spurious moral judgment, a disguised autobiographical statement.

There is a perfectly good reason why a reference to reasons is necessary for objectivity. In giving a reason, my reason, for believing something, I am attempting to give you a reason for believing likewise. A reason necessarily makes a claim to objectivity. *My* reason makes a claim to being *a* reason, that is, a reason independently of the person who so regards it. It is not a reason simply because I regard it as one. It may not in fact be anyone else's reason, but it must be such that it could be, and would be if he were aware of it.[6] To regard something as a reason for arriving at a certain conclusion is to assume that everyone who knows the fact or whatever it is that is regarded as a reason ought to arrive at the same conclusion, and will so far as he is rational. Of course, my reasons for believing something may not be the same as your reasons. There are all sorts of possibilities here. I might be aware of facts that you are not aware of, and vice versa. We might have different reasons for believing the same thing, or our different reasons may lead us to different conclusions. Again, we might weigh the reasons differently. Or something that is given as a reason may be

[6] Cf. Bernard Mayo, "Commitments and Reasons," *Mind*, vol. LXIV (July 1955), pp. 355–8, especially p. 355: "It is in the nature of a moral action or a moral judgment that it can be supported by reasons. But if I advance a reason for my action, then, although it would be correct idiom to speak of 'my' reason for my action, the relation denoted by 'my' is quite different from what it would be if I had spoken of my motives or my inclinations. . . . The difference is this. My having an inclination is logically (though not always causally) independent of other people having similar inclinations; but my having a reason, either for a theoretical conclusion or for a nontheoretical action, is not logically independent of other people having a reason. What counts for me as a reason counts for others, and if I could not regard it as counting for others also, it could not count for me. In other words, it is self-contradictory to say both that I have a reason for doing *X* and that no one else could have that reason for doing *X*."

one only under certain assumptions, which perhaps I do not accept, and so on. It still holds that if I claim that something is a reason I am claiming that anyone who accepts it as true ought also to accept it as a reason, and in the absence of conflicting considerations, as a good reason. Note that to give a reason is not necessarily to give a motive. I am talking here about conviction, not about persuasion. One can be persuaded by all sorts of means, ranging from clubs and social pressure to rhetorical devices and transparently fallacious arguments. Conviction requires rational grounds. I am also not talking about a reason for *doing* something, in the sense in which my reason for sitting in the sun may not be your reason, and may not impel you to do the same; there is no question here of objectivity, or of justification.

In saying that a moral judgment is not objective or genuine if not supported by reasons I do not intend to imply that the speaker must actually give his reasons. If I agree with you in thinking some act to be wrong I will be unlikely to ask for your reasons. Sometimes, indeed in a great many cases, one's reasons are obvious from the context, or simply from the way in which the judgment is formulated, and the fact that they are not actually stated would not make one's judgment subjective or any the less genuine. Yet in cases of doubt or disagreement, in cases where a question arises, then reasons must be given. For in such cases it is not obvious from the context what the reasons are, or, if it is, whether they are sufficient.

Again, in saying that one must be able to give reasons I am not implying that one must be able to *analyze* them. To be able to give an argument in support of one's view is not the same as being able to analyze one's argument. The latter is on a different level of activity. All that I am implying is that one must have a reason—a genuine reason, not "because I am I" or "because I like it that way" or anything of that sort. For if one is unable to give a reason then it may be presumed that he has none.

What I am saying, then, is that someone who says that a certain act is wrong, but is unable to say why it is wrong or what reason there is to believe that it is wrong, has said no more than that he does not approve of the act, or would prefer that it not be done. Note that it is quite possible for someone to approve of an act's being done by one person and to disapprove of its being done by another without being able to specify any relevant difference between the two cases. This should be obvious where one offers as his "reasons" the fact that he likes the one person and does not like the other. It has been said that "I cannot approve of an action of mine without approving of a possible similar action by someone else; likewise I cannot approve of someone else's action unless I am prepared to approve of myself doing it."[7] This is not so. To do this would no doubt involve me in a contradiction, but it is not impossible for me to contradict myself. What is impossible is for it to be right for A to do x and not right

[7] Bernard Mayo, *The Logic of Personality*, p. 152. It is interesting to note that an "emotive theory" of probability can be constructed by analogy to the emotive theory of ethics. "This is probable" can be analyzed as meaning "I have a strong determination to believe this; do so as well." We can also construct on these lines an emotive theory of truth, or epistemology: "This is true" means "I believe this; do so as well." Depending on which statement of the emotive theory, out of the many available, is taken as a model, one can construct analogous extensions to probability and truth. It is thus rather remarkable that the emotive analysis should be thought to apply peculiarly to moral judgments. Cf. H. J. Paton, "The Emotive Theory of Ethics," in *In Defence of Reason* (London: Hutchinson's University Library, 1951), pp. 205–6.

for anyone similar to *A* to do *x* in similar circumstances. But it is not impossible for me to *regard it as right* for *A* to do *x* and as not right for anyone similar in similar circumstances. It is possible for me to believe that *P* is true and also that *P* is false. What is impossible is for *P* to *be* both true and false. This means that my beliefs would be inconsistent, but not that I cannot have them.

It follows that statements like "*x* is right" do not, necessarily or in general, mean "I approve of *x*," or anything along these lines. They do so in case, and only in case, the speaker is unable to provide reasons for his assertion. Of course, from the fact that someone asserts "*x* is right" it can be inferred, if his assertion was honest, that he approves of *x*, that is, that he regards *x* as right. But this holds for any assertion—from the fact that it is made one can infer, on the assumption that it is honestly made, that the speaker believes what he is saying.

It also follows, trivially, that moral judgments can be supported by reasons; a statement having the verbal form of a moral judgment for which one is unable to give reasons does not express a genuine moral judgment at all.[8] It appears that adherents of emotive or subjective ethical theories have not been analyzing genuine moral judgments, but expressions that are parasitic on them.

[8] Essentially this same view has been set forth by Stuart Hampshire in "Fallacies in Moral Philosophy," *Mind*, vol. LVIII (October 1949), p. 471: "If I am not prepared to produce such practical arguments, pointing to what ought to have been done, I shall admit that I am not making a genuine moral judgment, but merely expressing or reporting my own feelings; and I shall admit that it was misleading to use the form of sentence ordinarily associated with moral judgments, and not with expressions of feeling. Doubtless many sentences containing moral terms are ambiguous, and may be normally used both as expressions of practical judgments and as expressions of feeling; but the important point is that, if challenged about our intentions, we are required to *distinguish* between such uses . . ." I am not prepared to go along with Mr. Hampshire's wording of the point, which unduly assumes that people will admit, in the sort of situation he describes, to using a misleading form of words, and seems to imply that this is relevant. It is not.

JOHN R. SEARLE

*How to Derive "Ought" from "Is"**

I.

It is often said that one cannot derive an "ought" from an "is." This thesis, which comes from a famous passage in Hume's *Treatise*, while not as clear as it might be, is at least clear in broad outline: there is a class of statements of fact which is logically distinct from a class of statements of value. No set of statements of fact by themselves entails any statement of value. Put in more contemporary terminology, no set of *descriptive* statements can entail an *evaluative* statement without the addition of at least one evaluative premise. To believe otherwise is to commit what has been called the naturalistic fallacy.

I shall attempt to demonstrate a counterexample to this thesis.[1] It is not of course to be supposed that a single counterexample can refute a philosophical thesis, but in the present instance if we can present a plausible counterexample and can in addition give some account or explanation of how and why it is a counterexample, and if we can further offer a theory to back up our counterexample—a theory which will generate an indefinite number of counterexamples—we may at the very least cast considerable light on the original thesis; and possibly, if we can do all these things, we may even incline ourselves to the view that the scope of that thesis was more restricted than we had originally supposed. A counterexample must proceed by taking a statement or statements which any proponent of the thesis would grant were purely factual or "descriptive" (they need not actually contain the word "is") and show how they are logically related to a statement which a proponent of the thesis would regard as clearly "evaluative." (In the present instance it will contain an "ought".)[2]

Consider the following series of statements:

1. Jones uttered the words "I hereby promise to pay you, Smith, five dollars."
2. Jones promised to pay Smith five dollars.

* By permission. *Philosophical Review*, vol. LXXIII, 1964, pp. 43–58.

John R. Searle is professor of philosophy at the University of California at Berkeley.

[1] In its modern version. I shall not be concerned with Hume's treatment of the problem.

[2] If this enterprise succeeds, we shall have bridged the gap between "evaluative" and "descriptive" and consequently have demonstrated a weakness in this very terminology. At present, however, my strategy is to play along with the terminology, pretending that the notions of evaluative and descriptive are fairly clear. At the end of the paper I shall state in what respects I think they embody a muddle.

3. Jones placed himself under (undertook) an obligation to pay Smith five dollars.

4. Jones is under an obligation to pay Smith five dollars.

5. Jones ought to pay Smith five dollars.

I shall argue concerning this list that the relation between any statement and its successor, while not in every case one of "entailment," is nonetheless not just a contingent relation; and the additional statements necessary to make the relationship one of entailment do not need to involve any evaluative statements, moral principles, or anything of the sort.

Let us begin. How is (1) related to (2)? In certain circumstances, uttering the words in quotation marks in (1) is the act of making a promise. And it is a part of or a consequence of the meaning of the words in (1) that in those circumstances uttering them is promising. "I hereby promise" is a paradigm device in English for performing the act described in (2), promising.

Let us state this fact about English usage in the form of an extra premise:

1*a*. Under certain conditions *C* anyone who utters the words (sentence) "I hereby promise to pay you, Smith, five dollars" promises to pay Smith five dollars.

What sorts of things are involved under the rubric "conditions *C*"? What is involved will be all those conditions, those states of affairs, which are necessary and sufficient conditions for the utterance of the words (sentence) to constitute the successful performance of the act of promising. The conditions will include such things as that the speaker is in the presence of the hearer Smith, they are both conscious, both speakers of English, speaking seriously. The speaker knows what he is doing, is not under the influence of drugs, not hypnotized or acting in a play, not telling a joke or reporting an event, and so forth. This list will no doubt be somewhat indefinite because the boundaries of the concept of a promise, like the boundaries of most concepts in a natural language, are a bit loose.[3] But one thing is clear; however loose the boundaries may be, and however difficult it may be to decide marginal cases, the conditions under which a man who utters "I hereby promise" can correctly be said to have made a promise are straightforwardly empirical conditions.

So let us add as an extra premise the empirical assumption that these conditions obtain.

1*b*. Conditions *C* obtain.

From (1), (1*a*), and (1*b*) we derive (2). The argument is of the form: If *C* then (if *U* then *P*): *C* for conditions, *U* for utterance, *P* for promise. Adding the premises *U* and *C* to this hypothetical we derive (2). And as far as I can see, no moral premises are lurking in the logical woodpile. More needs to be said about the relation of (1) to (2), but I reserve that for later.

What is the relation between (2) and (3)? I take it that promising is, by definition, an act of placing oneself under an obligation. No analysis of the concept of promising will be complete which does not include the feature of the promiser placing himself under or undertaking or accepting or recognizing an obligation to the promisee, to perform some future course of action, normally for the benefit of the promisee. One may be tempted to think that promising can be analyzed in terms of creating expectations in one's hearers, or some such,

[3] In addition the concept of a promise is a member of a class of concepts which suffer from looseness of a peculiar kind, viz. defeasibility. Cf. H. L. A. Hart, "The Ascription of Responsibility and Rights," *Logic and Language*, First Series, ed. by A. Flew (Oxford University Press, Fair Lawn, N.J., 1951).

but a little reflection will show that the crucial distinction between statements of intention on the one hand and promises on the other lies in the nature and degree of commitment or obligation undertaken in promising.

I am therefore inclined to say that (2) entails (3) straight off, but I can have no objection if anyone wishes to add—for the purpose of formal neatness—the tautological premise:

2*a*. All promises are acts of placing oneself under (undertaking) an obligation to do the thing promised.

How is (3) related to (4)? If one has placed oneself under an obligation, then, other things being equal, one is under an obligation. That I take it also is a tautology. Of course it is possible for all sorts of things to happen which will release one from obligations one has undertaken and hence the need for the *ceteris paribus* rider. To get an entailment between (3) and (4) we therefore need a qualifying statement to the effect that:

3*a*. Other things are equal.

Formalists, as in the move from (2) to (3), may wish to add the tautological premise:

3*b*. All those who place themselves under an obligation are, other things being equal, under an obligation.

The move from (3) to (4) is thus of the same form as the move from (1) to (2): If *E* then (if *PUO* then *UO*): *E* for other things are equal, *PUO* for place under obligation and *UO* for under obligation. Adding the two premises *E* and *PUO* we derive *UO*.

Is (3*a*), the *ceteris paribus* clause, a concealed evaluative premise? It certainly looks as if it might be, especially in the formulation I have given it, but I think we can show that, though questions about whether other things are equal frequently involve evaluative considerations, it is not logically necessary that they should in every case. I shall postpone discussion of this until after the next step.

What is the relation between (4) and (5)? Analogous to the tautology which explicates the relation of (3) and (4) there is here the tautology that, other things being equal, one ought to do what one is under an obligation to do. And here, just as in the previous case, we need some premise of the form:

4*a*. Other things are equal.

We need the *ceteris paribus* clause to eliminate the possibility that something extraneous to the relation of "obligation" to "ought" might interfere.[4] Here, as in the previous two steps, we eliminate the appearance of enthymeme by pointing out that the apparently suppressed premise is tautological and hence, though formally neat, it is redundant. If, however, we wish to state it formally, this argument is of the same form as the move from (3) to (4): If *E* then (if *UO* then *O*); *E* for other things are equal, *UO* for under obligation, *O* for ought. Adding the premises *E* and *UO* we derive *O*.

Now a word about the phrase "other things being equal" and how it functions in my attempted derivation. This topic and the closely related topic of defeasibility

[4] The *ceteris paribus* clause in this step excludes somewhat different sorts of cases from those excluded in the previous step. In general we say, "He undertook an obligation, but nonetheless he is not (now) under an obligation" when the obligation has been *removed*, e.g., if the promisee says, "I release you from your obligation." But we say, "He is under an obligation, but nonetheless ought not to fulfill it" in cases where the obligation is *overridden* by some other considerations, e.g., a prior obligation.

are extremely difficult and I shall not try to do more than justify my claim that the satisfaction of the condition does not necessarily involve anything evaluative. The force of the expression "other things being equal" in the present instance is roughly this. Unless we have some reason (that is, unless we are actually prepared to give some reason) for supposing the obligation is void (step 4) or the agent ought not to keep the promise (step 5), then the obligation holds and he ought to keep the promise. It is not part of the force of the phrase "other things being equal" that in order to satisfy it we need to establish a universal negative proposition to the effect that no reason could ever be given by anyone for supposing the agent is not under an obligation or ought not to keep the promise. That would be impossible and would render the phrase useless. It is sufficient to satisfy the condition that no reason to the contrary can in fact be given.

If a reason is given for supposing the obligation is void or that the promiser ought not to keep a promise, then characteristically a situation calling for an evaluation arises. Suppose, for example, we consider a promised act wrong, but we grant that the promiser did undertake an obligation. Ought he to keep the promise? There is no established procedure for objectively deciding such cases in advance, and an evaluation (if that is really the right word) is in order. But unless we have some reason to the contrary, the *ceteris paribus* condition is satisfied, no evaluation is necessary, and the question whether he ought to do it is settled by saying "he promised." It is always an open possibility that we may have to make an evaluation in order to derive "he ought" from "he promised," for we may have to evaluate a counterargument. But an evaluation is not logically necessary in every case, for there may as a matter of fact be no counterarguments. I am therefore inclined to think that there is nothing necessarily evaluative about the *ceteris paribus* condition, even though deciding whether it is satisfied will frequently involve evaluations.

But suppose I am wrong about this: would that salvage the belief in an unbridgeable logical gulf between "is" and "ought"? I think not, for we can always rewrite my steps (4) and (5) so that they include the *ceteris paribus* clause as part of the conclusion. Thus from our premises we would then have derived "Other things being equal Jones ought to pay Smith five dollars," and that would still be sufficient to refute the tradition, for we would still have shown a relation of entailment between descriptive and evaluative statements. It was not the fact that extenuating circumstances can void obligations that drove philosophers to the naturalistic fallacy fallacy; it was rather a theory of language, as we shall see later on.

We have thus derived (in as strict a sense of "derive" as natural languages will admit of) an "ought" from an "is." And the extra premises which were needed to make the derivation work were in no case moral or evaluative in nature. They consisted of empirical assumptions, tautologies, and descriptions of word usage. It must be pointed out also that the "ought" is a "categorical" not a "hypothetical" ought. (5) does not say that Jones ought to pay up if he wants such and such. It says he ought to pay up period. Note also that the steps of the derivation are carried on in the third person. We are not concluding "I ought" from "I said 'I promise,'" but "he ought" from "he said 'I promise.'"

The proof unfolds the connection between the utterance of certain words and the speech act of promising and then in turn unfolds promising into obligation and moves from obligation to "ought." The step from (1) to (2) is radically different from the others and requires special comment. In (1) we construe "I hereby promise . . ." as an English phrase having a certain meaning. It is a consequence of that meaning that the utterance of that phrase under certain conditions is the act of promising.

Thus by presenting the quoted expressions in (1) and by describing their use in (1*a*) we have as it were already invoked the institution of promising. We might have started with an even more ground-floor premise than (1) by saying:

(1*b*) Jones uttered the phonetic sequence: /ai^{+}hirbai^{+}pramis^{+}təpei^{+}yu^{+}smiθ^{+} faiv^{+}dalərz/

We would then have needed extra empirical premises stating that this phonetic sequence was associated in certain ways with certain meaningful units relative to certain dialects.

The moves from (2) to (5) are relatively easy. We rely on definitional connections betwen "promise," "obligate," and "ought," and the only problem which arises is that obligations can be overridden or removed in a variety of ways and we need to take account of that fact. We solve our difficulty by adding further premises to the effect that there are no contrary considerations, that other things are equal.

II.

In this section I intend to discuss three possible objections to the derivation.

FIRST OBJECTION

Since the first premise is descriptive and the conclusion evaluative, there must be a concealed evaluative premise in the description of the conditions in (1*b*).

So far, this argument merely begs the question by assuming the logical gulf between descriptive and evaluative which the derivation is designed to challenge. To make the objection stick, the defender of the distinction would have to show how exactly (1*b*) must contain an evaluative premise and what sort of premise it might be. Uttering certain words in certain conditions just *is* promising and the description of these conditions needs no evaluative element. The essential thing is that in the transition from (1) to (2) we move from the specification of a certain utterance of words to the specification of a certain speech act. The move is achieved because the speech act is a conventional act; and the utterance of the words, according to the conventions, constitutes the performance of just that speech act.

A variant of this first objection is to say: all you have shown is that "promise" is an evaluative, not a descriptive concept. But this objection again begs the question and in the end will prove disastrous to the original distinction between descriptive and evaluative. For that a man uttered certain words and that these words have the meaning they do are surely objective facts. And if the statement of these two objective facts plus a description of the conditions of the utterance is sufficient to entail the statement (2) which the objector alleges to be an evaluative statement (Jones promised to pay Smith five dollars), then an evaluative conclusion is derived from descriptive premises without even going through steps (3), (4), and (5).

SECOND OBJECTION

Ultimately the derivation rests on the principle that one ought to keep one's promises and that is a moral principle, hence evaluative.

I don't know whether "one ought to keep one's promises" is a "moral" principle, but whether or not it is, it is also tautological; for it is nothing more than a derivation from the two tautologies:

> *All promises are (create, are undertakings of, are acceptances of) obligations,*

and

> *One ought to keep (fulfill) one's obligations.*

What needs to be explained is why so many philosophers have failed to see the tautological character of this principle. Three things I think have concealed its character from them.

The first is a failure to distinguish external questions about the institution of promising from internal questions asked within the framework of the institution. The questions "Why do we have such an institution as promising?" and "Ought we to have such institutionalized forms of obligation as promising?" are external questions asked about and not within the institution of promising. And the question "Ought one to keep one's promises?" can be confused with or can be taken as (and I think has often been taken as) an external question roughly expressible as "Ought one to accept the institution of promising?" But taken literally, as an internal question, as a question about promises and not about the institution of promising, the question "Ought one to keep one's promises?" is as empty as the question "Are triangles three-sided?" To recognize something as a promise is to grant that, other things being equal, it ought to be kept.

A second fact which has clouded the issue is this. There are many situations, both real and imaginable, where one ought not to keep a promise, where the obligation to keep a promise is overridden by some further considerations, and it was for this reason that we needed those clumsy *ceteris paribus* clauses in our derivation. But the fact that obligations can be overridden does not show that there were no obligations in the first place. On the contrary. And these original obligations are all that is needed to make the proof work.

Yet a third factor is the following. Many philosophers still fail to realize the full force of saying that "I hereby promise" is a performative expression. In uttering it one performs but does not describe the act of promising. Once promising is seen as a speech act of a kind different from describing, then it is easier to see that one of the features of the act is the undertaking of an obligation. But if one thinks the utterance of "I promise" or "I hereby promise" is a peculiar kind of description—for example, of one's mental state—then the relation between promising and obligation is going to seem very mysterious.

THIRD OBJECTION

The derivation uses only a factual or inverted-commas sense of the evaluative terms employed. For example, an anthropologist observing the behavior and attitudes of the Anglo-Saxons might well go through these derivations, but nothing evaluative would be included. Thus step (2) is equivalent to "He did what they call promising" and step (5) to "According to them he ought to pay Smith five dollars." But since all of the steps (2) to (5) are in *oratio obliqua* and hence disguised statements of fact, the fact-value distinction remains unaffected.

This objection fails to damage the derivation, for what it says is only that the steps *can* be reconstrued as in *oratio obliqua,* that we can construe them as a series of external statements, that we can construct a parallel (or at any rate related) proof about reported speech. But what I am arguing is that, taken quite literally, without any *oratio obliqua* additions or interpretations, the derivation is valid. That one can construct a similar argument which would fail to refute the fact-value distinction does not show that this proof fails to refute it. Indeed it is irrelevant.

III.

So far I have presented a counterexample to the thesis that one cannot derive an "ought" from an "is" and considered three possible objections to it. Even supposing what I have said so far is true, still one feels a certain uneasiness. One feels there must be some trick involved somewhere. We might state our uneasiness thus: How can my granting a mere fact about a man, such as the fact that he uttered certain words or that he made a promise, commit *me* to the view that *he* ought to do something? I now want briefly to discuss what broader philosophic significance my attempted derivation may have, in such a way as to give us the outlines of an answer to this question.

I shall begin by discussing the grounds for supposing that it cannot be answered at all.

The inclination to accept a rigid distinction betwen "is" and "ought," between descriptive and evaluative, rests on a certain picture of the way words relate to the world. It is a very attractive picture, so attractive (to me at least) that it is not entirely clear to what extent the mere presentation of counterexamples can challenge it. What is needed is an explanation of how and why this classical empiricist picture fails to deal with such counterexamples. Briefly, the picture is constructed something like this: first we present examples of so-called descriptive statements ("my car goes eighty miles an hour," "Jones is six feet tall," "Smith has brown hair"), and we contrast them with so-called evaluative statements ("my car is a good car," "Jones ought to pay Smith five dollars," "Smith is a nasty man"). Anyone can see that they are different. We articulate the difference by pointing out that for the descriptive statements the question of truth or falsity is objectively decidable, because to know the meaning of the descriptive expressions is to know under what objectively ascertainable conditions the statements which contain them are true or false. But in the case of evaluative statements the situation is quite different. To know the meaning of the evaluative expressions is not by itself sufficient for knowing under what conditions the statements containing them are true or false, because the meaning of the expressions is such that the statements are not capable of objective or factual truth or falsity at all. Any justification a speaker can give of one of his evaluative statements essentially involves some appeal to attitudes he holds, to criteria of assessment he has adopted, or to moral principles by which he has chosen to live and judge other people. Descriptive statements are thus objective, evaluative statements subjective, and the difference is a consequence of the different sorts of terms employed.

The underlying reason for these differences is that evaluative statements perform a completely different job from descriptive statements. Their job is not to describe any features of the world but to express the speaker's emotions, to express his attitudes, to praise or condemn, to laud or insult, to commend, to recommend, to advise, and so forth. Once we see the different jobs the two perform, we see that there must be a logical gulf between them. Evaluative statements must be different from descriptive statements in order to do their job, for if they were objective they could no longer function to evaluate. Put metaphysically, values cannot lie in the world, for if they did they would cease to be values and would just be another part of the world. Put in the formal mode, one cannot define an evaluative word in terms of descriptive words, for if one did, one would no longer be able to use the evaluative word to commend, but only to describe. Put yet another way, any effort to derive an "ought" from an "is" must be a waste of time, for all it could show even if it succeeded would be that the "is" was not a real "is" but only a disguised "ought" or, alternatively, that the "ought" was not a real "ought" but only a disguised "is."

This summary of the traditional empirical view has been very brief, but I hope it conveys something of the power of this picture. In the hands of certain modern authors, especially Hare and Nowell-Smith, the picture attains considerable subtlety and sophistication.

What is wrong with this picture? No doubt many things are wrong with it. In the end I am going to say that one of the things wrong with it is that it fails to give us any coherent account of such notions as commitment, responsibility, and obligation.

In order to work toward this conclusion I can begin by saying that the picture fails to account for the *different types* of "descriptive" statements. Its paradigms of descriptive statements are such utterances as "my car goes eighty miles an hour," "Jones is six feet tall," "Smith has brown hair," and the like. But it is forced by its own rigidity to construe "Jones got married," "Smith made a promise," "Jackson has five dollars," and "Brown hit a home run" as descriptive statements as well. It is so forced, because whether or not someone got married, made a promise, has five dollars, or hit a home run is as much a matter of objective fact as whether he has red hair or brown eyes. Yet the former kind of statement (statements containing "married," "promise," and so forth) seem to be quite different from the simple empirical paradigms of descriptive statements. How are they different? Though both kinds of statements state matters of objective fact, the statements containing words such as "married," "promise," "home run," and "five dollars" state facts whose existence presupposes certain institutions: a man has five dollars, given the institution of money. Take away the institution and all he has is a rectangular bit of paper with green ink on it. A man hits a home run only given the institution of baseball; without the institution he only hits a sphere with a stick. Similarly, a man gets married or makes a promise only within the institutions of marriage and promising. Without them, all he does is utter words or makes gestures. We might characterize such facts as institutional facts, and contrast them with noninstitutional, or brute, facts: that a man has a bit of paper with green ink on it is a brute fact, that he has five dollars is an institutional fact.[5] The classical picture fails to account for the differences between statements of brute fact and statements of institutional fact.

The word "institution" sounds artificial here, so let us ask: what sorts of institutions are these? In order to answer that question I need to distinguish between two different kinds of rules or conventions. Some rules regulate antecedently existing forms of behavior. For example, the rules of polite table behavior regulate eating, but eating exists independently of these rules. Some rules, on the other hand, do not merely regulate but create or define new forms of behavior: the rules of chess, for example, do not merely regulate an antecedently existing activity called playing chess; they, as it were, create the possibility of or define that activity. The activity of playing chess is constituted by action in accordance with these rules. Chess has no existence apart from these rules. The distinction I am trying to make was foreshadowed by Kant's distinction between regulative and constitutive principles, so let us adopt his terminology and describe our distinction as a distinction between regulative and constitutive rules. Regulative rules regulate activities whose existence is independent of the rules; constitutive rules constitute (and also regulate) forms of activity whose existence is logically dependent on the rules.[6]

Now the institutions that I have been talking about are systems of constitutive rules. The institutions of marriage, money, and promising are like the institutions of baseball or chess in that they are systems of such constitutive rules or conventions. What I have called institutional facts are facts which presuppose such institutions.

Once we recognize the existence of and begin to grasp the nature of such institutional facts, it is but a short step to see that many forms of obligations, commitments, rights, and responsibilities are

[5] For a discussion of this distinction see G. E. M. Anscombe, "Brute Facts," *Analysis* (1958).

[6] For a discussion of a related distinction see J. Rawls, "Two Concepts of Rules," *Philosophical Review*, LXIV (1955).

similarly institutionalized. It is often a matter of fact that one has certain obligations, commitments, rights, and responsibilities, but it is a matter of institutional, not brute, fact. It is one such institutionalized form of obligation, promising, which I invoked above to derive an "ought" from an "is." I started with a brute fact, that a man uttered certain words, and then invoked the institution in such a way as to generate institutional facts by which we arrived at the institutional fact that the man ought to pay another man five dollars. The whole proof rests on an appeal to the constitutive rule that to make a promise is to undertake an obligation.

We are now in a position to see how we can generate an indefinite number of such proofs. Consider the following vastly different example. We are in our half of the seventh inning and I have a big lead off second base. The pitcher whirls, fires to the shortstop covering, and I am tagged out a good ten feet down the line. The umpire shouts, "Out!" I, however, being a positivist, hold my ground. The umpire tells me to return to the dugout. I point out to him that you can't derive an "ought" from an "is." No set of descriptive statements describing matters of fact, I say, will entail any evaluative statements to the effect that I should or ought to leave the field. "You just can't get orders or recommendations from facts alone." What is needed is an evaluative major premise. I therefore return to and stay on second base (until I am carried off the field). I think everyone feels my claims here to be preposterous, and preposterous in the sense of logically absurd. Of course you can derive an "ought" from an "is," and though to actually set out the derivation in this case would be vastly more complicated than in the case of promising, it is in principle no different. By undertaking to play baseball I have committed myself to the observation of certain constitutive rules.

We are now also in a position to see that the tautology that one ought to keep one's promises is only one of a class of similar tautologies concerning institutionalized forms of obligation. For example, "one ought not to steal" can be taken as saying that to recognize something as someone else's property necessarily involves recognizing his right to dispose of it. This is a constitutive rule of the institution of private property.[7] "One ought not to tell lies" can be taken as saying that to make an assertion necessarily involves undertaking an obligation to speak truthfully. Another constitutive rule: "One ought to pay one's debts" can be construed as saying that to recognize something as a debt is necessarily to recognize an obligation to pay it. It is easy to see how all these principles will generate counter-examples to the thesis that you cannot derive an "ought" from an "is."

My tentative conclusions, then, are as follows:

1. The classical picture fails to account for institutional facts.
2. Institutional facts exist within systems of constitutive rules.
3. Some systems of constitutive rules involve obligations, commitments, and responsibilities.

[7] Proudhon said: "Property is theft." If one tries to take this as an internal remark it makes no sense. It was intended as an external remark attacking and rejecting the institution of private property. It gets its air of paradox and its force by using terms which are internal to the institution in order to attack the institution.

Standing on the deck of some institutions one can tinker with constitutive rules and even throw some other institutions overboard. But could one throw all institutions overboard (in order perhaps to avoid ever having to derive an "ought" from an "is")? One could not and still engage in those forms of behavior we consider characteristically human. Suppose Proudhon had added (and tried to live by): "Truth is a lie, marriage is infidelity, language is uncommunicative, law is a crime," and so on with every possible institution.

4. Within those systems we can derive "ought's" from "is's" on the model of the first derivation.

With these conclusions we now return to the question with which I began this section: How can my stating a fact about a man, such as the fact that he made a promise, commit me to a view about what he ought to do? One can begin to answer this question by saying that for me to state such an institutional fact is already to invoke the constitutive rules of the institution. It is those rules that give the word "promise" its meaning. But those rules are such that to commit myself to the view that Jones made a promise involves committing myself to what he ought to do (other things being equal).

If you like, then, we have shown that "promise" is an evaluative word, but since it is also purely descriptive, we have really shown that the whole distinction needs to be re-examined. The alleged distinction between descriptive and evaluative statements is really a conflation of at least two distinctions. On the one hand there is a distinction between different kinds of speech acts, one family of speech acts including evaluations, another family including descriptions. This is a distinction between different kinds of illocutionary force.[8] On the other hand there is a distinction between utterances which involve claims objectively decidable as true or false and those which involve claims not objectively decidable, but which are "matters of personal decision" or "matters of opinion." It has been assumed that the former distinction is (must be) a special case of the latter, that if something has the illocutionary force of an evaluation, it cannot be entailed by factual premises. Part of the point of my argument is to show that this contention is false, that factual premises can entail evaluative conclusions. If I am right, then the alleged distinction between descriptive and evaluative utterances is useful only as a distinction between two kinds of illocutionary force, describing and evaluating, and it is not even very useful there, since if we are to use these terms strictly, they are only two among hundreds of kinds of illocutionary force; and utterances of sentences of the form (5)—"Jones ought to pay Smith five dollars"—would not characteristically fall in either class.

[8] See J. L. Austin, *How to Do Things with Words* (Cambridge, Mass., 1962), for an explanation of this notion.

J. L. AUSTIN

*Three Ways of Spilling Ink**

Most of what I have to say about responsibility in general I have said in another place.[1] But of course the point of what I had to say there was that there isn't much point to discussing it in general terms. I shall repeat it here only in summary. It is a view which I have not so much merely held, but used in practice for some twenty years, and have found it consistently to pay off. Briefly, it is the idea which Aristotle had in a primitive way, without having to fight free of the toils of sophistication that now encumber us: namely, that questions of whether a person was responsible for this or that are prior to questions of freedom. Whatever Aristotle's idea may have been it *worked* this way: to discover whether someone acted freely or not, we must discover whether this, that, or the other plea will pass—for example, duress, or mistake, or accident, and so forth.

We may hope to profit then, in this area of inquiry, from the careful study of what we may call, for the sake of a word, *excuses*—of the different ways, and different words, in which on occasion we may try to get out of things, to show that we didn't act "freely" or were not "responsible." But if we are going to consider this subject and these expressions, we ought to attend as well to what might be called words of *aggravation*—words, that is, that not only don't get us out of things, but may actually make things worse for us, or at any rate may often bring in the very things that excuses, if we had any, would be designed to rule out. I shall concentrate here on a pretty narrow topic, since I don't know enough (or even *think* I know enough) about the whole subject: what follows is a sample only of some contributions that might be of use.

In considering responsibility, few things are considered more important than to establish whether a man *intended* to do *A*, or whether he did *A* intentionally. But there are at least two other familiar words important in this respect. Let us distinguish between acting *intentionally* and acting *deliberately* or *on purpose*, as far as this can be done by attending to what language can teach us.

* By permission. Parts I, II, and III of this essay are based on Austin's handwritten draft; the introductory section is reconstructed from various sources, including seminar notes. The essay in its present form was edited by L. W. Forguson of the State University of New York at Buffalo. It was published in *Philosophical Review*, Vol. LXXV, 1966.

The late J. L. Austin was professor of philosophy at Oxford University.

[1] "A Plea for Excuses" (1956), in *Philosophical Papers*, ed. by J. O. Urmson and G. J. Warnock (Oxford, 1961).

A schoolteacher may ask a child who has spilled the ink in class: "Did you do that intentionally?" or "Did you do that deliberately?" or "Did you do that on purpose (or purposely)?" It appears at first sight to matter little which question is asked. They appear to mean the same or at least to come down to the same in this case. But do they really? There are in fact techniques available for distinguishing between these expressions. I cannot exploit these by any means fully here, but only indicate the resources available. We may consider, for instance, for a start: (i) imagined or actual cases, and (ii) the "grammar," "etymology," and so forth of the words.

I.

First let us consider some cases. Actual cases would of course be excellent: we might observe what words have actually been used by commentators on real incidents, or by narrators of fictitious incidents. However, we do not have the time or space to do that here. We must instead imagine some cases (imagine them carefully and in detail and comprehensively) and try to reach agreement upon what we should in fact say concerning them. If we can reach this agreement, we shall have some *data* ("experimental" data, in fact) which we can then go on to *explain*. Here, the explanation will be an account of the meanings of these expressions, which we shall hope to reach by using such methods as those of "Agreement" and "Difference": what is in fact present in the cases where we do use, say, "deliberately," and what is absent when we don't. Of course, we shall then have arrived at nothing more than an account of certain ordinary "concepts" employed by English speakers: but also at no less a thing. And it is not so little. These concepts will have evolved over a long time: that is, they will have faced the test of practical use, of continual hard cases better than their vanished rivals.

Here, then, are some cases.

1. Suppose I tie a string across a stairhead. A fragile relative, from whom I have expectations, trips over it, falls, and perishes. Should we ask whether I tied the string there intentionally? Well, but it's hard to see how I could have done such a thing unintentionally, or even (what is not the same) not done it intentionally. You don't do that sort of thing—by accident? By mistake? Inadvertently? On the other hand, would I be bound to admit I did it "on purpose" or "purposely"? That has an ugly sound. What could the purpose have been if not to trip at least someone? Maybe I had better claim I was simply passing the time, playing cat's cradle, practicing tying knots.

2. I needed money to play the ponies, so I dipped into the till. Of course, I *intended* (all the time) to put it back as soon as I had collected my winnings. That was my intention: I took it with the intention of putting it back. But was that my *purpose* in taking it? Did I take it for the purpose of, or on purpose to, put it back? Plainly not.

3. As I drive up, I see that there is broken glass on the roadway outside my home; so I throw it onto the sidewalk, and a pedestrian later stumbles over it and is injured. Very likely I did throw the glass onto the sidewalk all right, etc. But did I do it on purpose, purposely? Did I do it deliberately? Conceivably, but in the way we should naturally imagine the incident, certainly not either.

4. The notice says, "Do not feed the penguins." I, however, feed them peanuts. Now peanuts happen to be, and these prove, fatal to these birds. Did I feed them peanuts intentionally? Beyond a doubt: I am no casual peanut shedder. But deliberately? Well, that seems perhaps to raise the question, "Had I read the notice?" Why does it? Or "on purpose"? That seems to insinuate that I knew what fatal results would ensue. Again, why?

We may also consider cases that are stereotypes, the ones evoked by clichés. Here are some.

We say that *A* wounded *B* with the intention of killing him, or of causing him grave bodily injury; or, more formally, with intent to kill him, and so forth. We do not say, "*A* wounded *B* for the purpose of killing him." Why not? Because the killing and the wounding are "not sufficiently separate"—are "too intimately connected"; because there are not "*two things*" that are done? But what does this really mean?

Again, we ask this young man who is paying attentions to our daughter to declare his intentions. What are his intentions? Are his intentions honorable? Here, would it make any difference if we asked him what was the purpose of these attentions, whether he has some purpose in view, whether he is doing these things on purpose or for a purpose? This makes his conduct seem more calculated, frames him as an adventurer or seducer. Instead of asking him to clarify the position, perhaps to himself as well as to us, are we not now asking him to divulge a guilty secret?

Another cliché: we find ourselves fairly often speaking of a "deliberate intention"; "with the deliberate intention of forcing the lock," for example. Just as we may speak of a deliberate choice or a deliberate decision. *But* we do not speak of an intentional deliberation; nor (except in special cases which cannot here be discussed) of an intentional decision or an intentional choice.

Perhaps it would help to think of kinds of case in which a thing is done intentionally but not deliberately, and so forth: cases, that is, where these adverbial expressions are expressly dissociated. The way this happens will commonly reveal some "opposite" of one of the three expressions which is *not* an "opposite" of the other two.

For example, suppose I do a thing impulsively, and possibly even on impulse. Then I shall not be doing it deliberately—and indeed to *say* that I did it impulsively (and perhaps even on impulse) would surely be to rule out the suggestion that I did it deliberately. For example, at a certain juncture in the course of our quarrel, moved perhaps by some turn of emotion or memory, I impulsively stretch out my hand to make things up, and exert all my tact to the same end. Now this is intentional enough: I intend to put out my hand, to bury the hatchet. Actually, I did even stretch out my hand on purpose, purposely. Yet it was not done deliberately: within twenty minutes I may be regretting it. The impulse is strong: I didn't stop to think (but about what?). I act precipitately, so probably not deliberately, but of course I knew what I was doing and meant to do it, even perhaps used my wits in doing it adroitly. (I may have stopped to think about *that*: the impulse may have been merely to make friends, holding out my hand something I thought up to do the trick.) If I acted not even on impulse, but quite *spontaneously* (rather tricky, this), and so even more evidently not deliberately, it is at least plausible to say that I still acted intentionally (cf. Sir Walter Raleigh). Again, a man put into agony of mind and fearful indecision[2] by some crisis may adopt some course such as running back into the blaze. No doubt he runs back into the blaze intentionally enough; he even (*perhaps*) decides to run back—though of course this is not necessary for him to do so "intentionally." But I think it might well be agreed he did not do so deliberately. These examples will suffice to show that what is done intentionally and purposely need not be done deliberately. Moreover, they appear to show some common characteristics: there is something "precipitate" about the act in every case.

[2] Perhaps owing to someone else's fault: but for reasons given below we will *exclude* this possibility, and suppose it an "accidental" crisis, such as a fire.

On the other hand, it is fully possible to act both deliberately and intentionally yet "not on purpose," or at least (*if* this is the same thing—there are distinctions here which we shall have to neglect) for no purpose, without any purpose, purposelessly. So to act may be, typically, to act wantonly. A gang of boys decapitates, seriatim, every one of the line of young trees newly planted along our street: this is deliberate, wanton damage. But they have, we may say, no interest in killing the trees; very likely they haven't given the matter a thought. Do children pull the wings off flies "on purpose"? Yet see them at it, and it is patent that they do it intentionally, and also deliberately.

So far we have shown that a thing done intentionally need not be done deliberately or on purpose, but what about conversely? Can something be done deliberately or purposely but not intentionally? Can we think of a case in which something is done *deliberately* but not intentionally? Certainly this seems more difficult. However, there are cases.

I am summoned to quell a riot in India. Speed is imperative. My mind runs on the action to be taken five miles down the road at the Residency. As I set off down the drive, my cookboy's child's new gocart, the apple of her eye, is right across the road. I realize I could stop, get out, and move it, but to hell with that: I must push on. It's too bad, that's all: I drive right over it and am on my way. In this case, a snap decision is taken on what is essentially an *incidental* matter. I did drive over the gocart deliberately, but not intentionally—nor, of course, unintentionally either. It was never part of my intention to drive over the gocart. At no time did I intend to drive over it. It was incidental to anything I intended to do, which was simply to get to the scene of the riot in order to quell it. However "odd" it may sound, I feel little doubt that we should say here that we did run over the gocart deliberately *and* that we should not care to say we ran over it intentionally. We never intended to run over it.

A similar account should probably be given, too, of some things that will, it can be foreseen, follow as consequences or results of our doing certain actions—namely, that these things are "done" by us deliberately but not intentionally. For example, I realize that by insisting on payment of due debts I am going to "ruin" my debtor—that is, he will be ruined as a consequence of being compelled to pay. I have absolutely no wish to ruin him, even wish not to: but maybe if I don't get payment both I and others are going to suffer severely; and very likely I think he has been faintly improvident. So I demand payment. He is ruined and, if you like, I ruined him. If this is said—I might resist and resent the imputation a bit—I think it must be admitted that I did ruin him deliberately; not, however, that I ruined him intentionally. At no time did I intend to ruin him; it was never any part of my intention. (This, if it be admitted, is an especially interesting case: for plainly I am *not* here responsible for his ruin.)

Finally, can a thing be done on purpose, but yet not intentionally? This seems even more difficult, and may actually be impossible. However, the expression "accidentally on purpose" hints, at least ironically, that something of the sort may be possible; for, if done accidentally, it is not done intentionally. But how ironical is this expression? (Perhaps a case comparable to the debt-collection case could be constructed here.)

II.

We turn now to our second general source of information: grammar and philology. Here we find that "purpose," "intend," and "deliberate" exhibit numerous and striking differences.

1. *Deliberate* and *deliberation*, the

verb and the noun, differ from both *intend/intention* and *purpose/purpose* in some ways in which the latter pair resemble each other. Thus, "I am deliberating" could only be used to describe a process that is going on: but "I am intending" and (if it exists) "I am purposing" could not be used to describe a process. In line with this is the fact that deliberations may be protracted, but intentions and purposes cannot be so.

1*a*. The use of "I intend" (and, so far as it exists, of "I purpose") is quite different from "I deliberate," which if *it* exists could only be a habitual present, describing what I ordinarily do, as in "I deliberate before I act." "I intend to *X*" is, as it were, a sort of "future tense" of the verb "to *X*." It has a vector, committal effect like "I promise to *X*," and, again, like "I promise to *X*," it is one of the possible formulae for making explicit, on occasion, the force of "I shall *X*": (namely, that it was a declaration of intention and not, for example, a forecast or an undertaking). We might feel inclined to say: it is almost an "auxiliary verb." But the fact of the matter is that terms like "future tense" and "auxiliary verb" were not invented with the need to do justice to such a word as "intend" in mind. A complete reclassification of these archaic terms is needed. That reclassification is needed is shown, for example, by the fact that there is some oddity about the combination "I shall intend."

2. If we next consider the adjectival terminations found in "deliber*ate*," "intention*al*," and "purpose*ful*" or "purpos*ive*" (which are also of course incorporated in the corresponding adverbs), it would seem significant that they are different. "Deliber*ate*" is of course formed on the Latin past participle: words of this kind commonly mean that something has happened or been done. We should suspect that the process of deliberation, whatever that may be, has been gone through. So consider*ate* behavior is behavior which shows that there has been consideration (of the feelings of others, as affected by my proposed activities).

The termination -ful, on the other hand, is commonly used in cases where something may be present or may not be present: an accretion or extra. "Thoughtful," "careful," "purposeful" alike refer to things we may (but equally may not) be doing *when* doing *X*: we may be taking thought for the interests and feelings of others, taking care to guard against possible accidents, or pursuing a purpose.

The termination -al, as in "intentional," qualifies, or classifies, as we may say, the act so described much more "directly" and intimately than -ful or -ate. (Incidental note: -ive, as in "purposive," would perform a similar function. But of course it is a term of psychological art, and to my mind requires some justification: because all our ordinary terminology, not merely the adjectival termination, certainly suggests that intention is related to our action in a more intimate way than its purpose, and in quite a different way.)

2*a*. The same lesson is pointed by the negative forms of the adjectives (and adverbs). There is no accepted negative form of "deliberate." "Purpose" takes -less; I may "have no purpose (whatsoever)" in doing something, just as I may take no care. But I don't "have no intention (whatsoever)" in doing something.

Here something of a general justification may be required. Why should we suppose it is significant of anything whatsoever that, for example, these adjectives and their negatives take different forms? Why shouldn't it just be that "thought," for example, is not a Latin word and so can't readily take the Latin -ate termination, whereas "consider" can? Why shouldn't it all be "euphony," or chance, or meaningless luxuriation?

Now we can admit, and indeed positively welcome, all these suggestions, and yet adhere to our superstition that the forms of words and expressions are highly significant for their meaning. Briefly, let us assume, for the sake of argument and because we actually have no right to assume anything else, that "in origin" speech consisted in any person making any noise in any situation to signify anything. Let us also assume, what in a sense is a tautology, that *in the very long run,* the forms of speech which survive will be the *fittest* (most efficient) forms of speech. Now one general criterion of efficiency[3] is simply this, stated loosely: that any unit of speech *U* should sound *tanto quanto* like every other unit of speech that "means" anything like what *U* means, and unlike *tanto quanto* every other unit of speech that means anything unlike what *U* means: or that small variations in meaning should be signified by small concomitant variations in sound. This principle will account, on my view, not merely for the phenomenon of the survival of words in groups where similar-sounding words mean similar things (for example, "fumble," "tumble," "stumble," and the like) but for much of what ought to be included in etymology, and for the whole general evolution of morphology, syntax, and grammar.

In this account of the origin of speech forms on evolutionary lines, it will be seen that *allowance* may be—indeed, to some extent is already fully—made for chance, for luxuriance, for sound preferences (euphony), and for borrowings. *But still,* in the long run, the expressions which survive will be such that their grammatical and morphological characteristics are of the highest significance for their meaning.

3. The prepositions used with "intention," "purpose," and "deliberation" to form adverbial or other expressions likewise point to distinctions between the three words, and associate them with quite distinct families of words. We say *on* purpose (to), *for* the purpose of, but *with* the intention of: (possibly also *with* the purpose of). It seems clear that "on" and "for" (compare "on principle," "on orders," "for the sake of") *dissociate* or *sever* my purpose from my current action in a way that "with" does not do. There are many expressions containing "purpose" ("for the *usual* purposes," "to good purpose," "to some purpose," and so forth) which seem to make purpose as it were *im*personal in a way that is never done with intention.

With "deliberation," perhaps the only, and unexciting, preposition used is "after." "With deliberation" is indeed found, but then the words are used to describe a certain slow style of performance, which makes an impression on the observer. "Deliberately" is used in the same way, as when someone eats his soup deliberately. (Compare the case where he deliberately eats my soup. Here, if he is well advised, he will make haste over it.) Now this sort of secondary sense is fairly common with adverbs of this kind; and "purposefully" is in fact also used in this way. We know the kind of performance it describes: a purposeful air is one of getting the preliminaries, the first stages, each stage *over with,* in order to proceed to the next and get the whole business achieved: it is an air of pressing on. Strikingly enough, however, there is no expression connected with "intentional" which can be used in this manner. The explanation, whatever it is, would seem to lie in the same direction as that of the adjectival terminations referred to above: intention is too intimately associated with ordinary action in general for there to be any *special* style of performance associated with it.

4. Finally, we might consider the trailing etymologies of the three words: for no word ever achieves entire forgetful-

[3] There are others of great importance: brevity, learnability, etc. But of these, some are closely connected with the above in a variety of ways.

ness of its origins. The metaphor in "deliberate" is one from "weighing" or "weighing up," that in "intend" (one which keeps breaking through in many cognate words) is from bending or straining toward (compare "intent of mischief" and "bent on mischief"). In "purpose," the idea is that of setting something up before oneself.

III.

Now let us try to understand the three notions of purpose, intention, and deliberation in the light of our investigations so far. We shan't get so far as defining them though, I fear.

The most subtle of our notions is that of intention. As I go through life, doing, as we suppose, one thing after another, I in general always have an idea—some idea, my idea, or picture, or notion, or conception—of what I'm up to, what I'm engaged in, what I'm about, or in general "what I'm doing." I don't "know what I'm doing" as a result of looking to see or otherwise conducting observations:[4] only in rare and perturbing cases do I *discover* what I've done or *come to realize* what I am or have been doing in this way. It is not in such fashion that *I* know what I'm doing when I strike the match in the vicinity of the haystack. (This is the sense in which in general and obviously I know what I'm doing: *contrast* the sense in which you *suppose*, dubiously, that I know what I'm doing when I strike the match so close to the gasoline.) I must be supposed to have *as it were* a plan, an operation—order or something of the kind on which I'm acting, which I am seeking to put into effect, carry out in action: only of course nothing necessarily or, usually, even faintly, so full blooded as a plan proper. When we draw attention to this aspect of action, we use the words connected with intention.[5]

Now although I say that the "intention" words are connected with this notion of my idea of what I'm doing, it should not be supposed that it will always make sense to stick in "intentionally" after every verb of action in every ordinary sentence with an active personal verb. Only when there is some suggestion that it might have been unintentional does it make non-misleading sense to say, for example, "I ate my dinner intentionally." To this extent, it is true that "intentionally" serves to rule out "unintentionally." What would be wholly untrue is to suggest that "unintentionally" is the word that "wears the trousers"—that is, that until we have grasped certain specific ways of doing things unintentionally, and except as a way of ruling these out, "intentionally" has no positive meaning. There are words of this description: "real," for example, is one. But in the present case, to mention nothing more, there is the verb "intend" to take into account, and it must obviously have a highly "positive" sense; it cannot just be used to rule out "don't (or didn't) intend."

Although we have this notion of my idea of what I'm doing—and indeed we have as a general rule such an idea, as it were a miner's lamp on our forehead which illuminates always just so far ahead as we

[4] I profited when I once heard this remarked by Miss G. E. M. Anscombe.

[5] At this point, the manuscript contains the unfinished sentence, "When we use the great majority of 'active' verbs, e.g., 'kick.' . . ." What Austin probably had in mind was the fact that most "active" verbs include, as part of their sense, some notion or a design or plan to be carried out. Thus, it is generally a mistake to consider them as purely "behavioristic." That I kick someone does not mean merely that my foot moves sharply into contact with his shin. Perhaps this is why, in normal contexts, adding the adverb "intentionally" is somewhat redundant. This point was suggested to me by G. J. Warnock. (L. W. F.)

go along—it is not to be supposed that there are any precise rules about the extent and degree of illumination it sheds. The only general rule is that the illumination is always *limited,* and that in several ways. It will never extend indefinitely far ahead. Of course, all that is to follow, or to be done thereafter, is not what I am intending to do, but perhaps consequences or results or effects thereof. Moreover, it does not illuminate *all* of my surroundings. Whatever I am doing is being done and to be done amidst a background of *circumstances* (including of course activities by other agents). This is what necessitates *care,* to ward off impingements, upsets, accidents. Furthermore, the doing of it will involve *incidentally* all kinds of minutiae of, at the least, bodily movements, and often many other things besides. These will be below the level of any intention, *however* detailed (and it need not of course be detailed at all), that I may have formed.

There is a good deal of freedom in "structuring" the history of someone's activities by means of words like "intention," just as when we consider a whole war we can divide it into campaigns, operations, actions, and the like; but this is fairly arbitrary except in so far as it is based upon the plans of the contestants. So with human activities; we can assess them in terms of intentions, purposes, ultimate objectives, and the like, but there is much that is arbitrary about this unless we take the way the agent himself did actually structure it in his mind before the event. Now the word "intention" has from this point of view a most important *bracketing effect:* when the till-dipper claims that he *intended all along* to put the money back, what he is claiming is that his action—the action that he was engaged upon—is to be judged *as a whole,* not just a part of it carved out of the whole. Nearly always, of course, such a contention as this will carry with it a contention that his action (as a whole) is not to be described by the term chosen to describe (only a part of) it: for example, here, it was not "robbing" the till, because the action taken as a whole would not result in the absence of any money from the till. *Reculer pour mieux sauter* is not to retreat.

Quite distinct is the use of the word "purpose." Certainly, *when* I am doing something for a purpose, this will be known to me, like my intentions, and will guide my conduct. Indeed, like an objective, a purpose will influence the forming of intentions. But my purpose is something to be achieved or effected as a result of what I'm doing, like the death of my aunt, or the sickness of the penguins if I did indeed feed them peanuts on purpose. (Very commonly my purpose is to put myself into a position to be able to go on with the next action, the next operation in the campaign.) I need not, however, have any purpose in acting (even intentionally);[6] just as I need not take care or thought. I act for or on (a) purpose, I achieve it; I act with the intention, I carry it out, realize it.

I act *deliberately* when I have deliberated—which means when I have stopped to ask myself, "Shall I or shan't I?" and then decided to do *X*, which I did. That is to say, I weighed up, in however rudimentary (sometimes almost notional or fictional) a fashion, the pros and cons. And it is understood that there must be some cons, even when what I do deliberately is something unexceptionable, such as paying my taxes. The pros and cons are not confined to *moral* pros and cons, nor need I decide in favor of what I think best or what has the most reasons in favor of it. (Nor, of course, when I have decided to do it, *must* I necessarily carry it out.) Deliberation is not just *any* kind of thinking prior

[6] E.g., feeding starving children: I need have no purpose here.

to action: to act with forethought or with premeditation, or to think about ways and means—all these show that we *took thought*, perhaps over a period of time, but none of these shows that we were acting deliberately, and indeed are quite distinct matters from deliberation. Ways and means are a matter for the planning staff; decision is a matter for the commander. That there should be slowness in moving into action or conducting it (so much relied on by lawyers) is the merest symptom.

I will close by adding a general word of warning: there are overriding considerations, which may be operative in any situation in which I act, which may put all three words out of joint, in spite of the other standard conditions for their use being satisfied. For instance, I may be acting under a threat: however much I weigh up the pros and cons, if I act under the influence of a threat I do not do that act deliberately. This sort of overriding consideration must always be allowed for in any case.[7]

[7] The manuscript contains a few further remarks, but not enough to reconstruct a conclusion that could claim to reflect at all adequately Austin's own intensions for a conclusion. It can be said from these remarks, however, that *one* thing Austin most likely had in mind was this: we should not only compare and contrast these three expressions—"intentionally," "deliberately," "on purpose"—with each other, but each should be compared and contrasted with other expressions as well (e.g., "motive" with both "intention" and "purpose," "premeditation" with "deliberation," and "to mean" with "to intend"). These are Austin's own examples, reproduced also, though inaccurately, in the *Nomos* Appendix. Austin often used in his manuscript notes the marks ") ("—e.g., "*x*) (*y*"—as a way of saying "contrast *x* with *y*," or "*x* as opposed to *y*." In the appendix, these are printed—without explanation and looking most peculiar—simply as reversed parentheses. (L. W. F.)

INDEX

Numbers in italic type indicate main discussion.